The BBI Combinatory Dictionary of English

Your Guide to Collocations and Grammar

Third edition revised by Robert Ilson

Compiled by

Morton Benson
Evelyn Benson
Robert Ilson

John Benjamins Publishing Company

Amsterdam/Philadelphia

™ The paper used in this publication meets the minimum requirements of American National Standard for Information Sciences — Permanence of Paper for Printed Library Materials, ANSI Z39.48-1984.

Dedicated to Morton Benson (1924–1998)

Library of Congress Cataloging-in-Publication Data

Benson, Morton.
  The BBI dictionary of English word combinations / compiled by Morton Benson, Evelyn Benson, Robert Ilson. -- 3rd edition revised by Robert Ilson
    p. cm.
  1. English language--Terms and phrases. I. Benson, Evelyn. II. Ilson, Robert. III. Title.
PE1689.B46   2009
423'.1--dc22   2009012597
ISBN 978 90 272 3260 1 (HB; alk. paper)
ISBN 978 90 272 3261 8 (PB; alk. paper)

John Benjamins Publishing Co. · P.O. Box 36224 · 1020 ME Amsterdam · The Netherlands
John Benjamins North America · P.O. Box 27519 · Philadelphia PA 19118-0519 · USA

Table of contents

Using the BBI: A workbook with exercises is available at:
http://dx.doi.org/10.1075/z.bbi.workbook

Preface to the
BBI Combinatory Dictionary of English:
Your Guide to Collocations and Grammar
Third Edition
Robert Ilson

To use language you must be able to combine words with other words to form phrases and to combine words into grammatical patterns to form clauses and sentences. Traditionally, the combination of words with words has been called collocation and its result has been called phraseology. Traditionally, the combination of words into grammatical patterns has been called colligation or complementation or construction (though in BBI it is called collocation, too) and its result has been called valency. A dictionary that provides both phraseology and valency is a dictionary of word combinations; or, in the terminology of Igor Melchuk, whose work has inspired us, a combinatory or combinatorial dictionary. BBI is a combinatory dictionary.

Consider the sentence ⟨I *badly* **want** *to go* there.⟩. It offers you the phraseological information that the verb **want** can be intensified by the word *badly*. It offers you also the valency information that the verb **want** can take the pattern *to + infinitive*.

BBI offers such information about many types of word. It tells you that **since** collocates with *ever* ⟨I married her and we've been happy *ever* **since**.⟩ and with *long* ⟨a custom *long* **since** abandoned⟩. It tells you that **reveal, revelation**, and **let on** can all take the pattern *that + clause* ⟨Don't ¬**reveal/let on**¬ *that* you know the answer, or your **revelation** *that* you know the answer may disturb everyone.⟩ (where the occasional symbols ¬.../...¬ couple **let on** (two words) with **reveal** (one word) as alternatives). And so on. And so forth.

BBI offers that information by means of Codes (see our Introduction), Exemplification, and Discussion (as in Usage Notes).

In BBI 3, examples may be repeated at more than one word to show a particularly close or memorable relation between the words exemplified. Thus we offer the example ⟨**shock** and **awe**⟩ at both **awe** and **shock**. And the famous phrase ⟨"With **malice** *toward* none; with **charity** *for* all" — Abraham Lincoln, Second Inaugural Address," 1865⟩ appears as an example at both **charity** and **malice**. That shows also how BBI 3 offers examples of real English attributed to their real authors. Such authentic attributed examples help to motivate language-learners — as they would most certainly motivate me !

Moreover, in BBI 3, examples may be transformed to exhibit the relation between the words exemplified. Thus we offer: -

vex *v.* ...It **vexes** me greatly to read such things in the newspapers ...
vexation *n.* ...my great **vexation** to read such things in the newspapers ...
vexed *adj.* ...I'm very **vexed** to read such things in the newspapers ...
vexing *adj.* ...It is very **vexing** to read such things in the newspapers ...

Furthermore, in BBI 3, examples may be combined to create mini-dialogues. Thus at **account II** *v.* we offer ⟨..."how do you **account** *for* the accident?" "it can be partly **accounted** *for* by the bad weather."⟩

The repetition, transformation, and combination of examples help to knit the many entries of BBI together and to enable people to adjust their use of words appropriately to contexts.

The Usage Notes in BBI 3 allow a freer and more discursive explanation of language problems. Thus the Usage Note at **thanks** not only offers the most typical responses to **thanks** and **thank you** but also assesses those responses for their currency (is a response used throughout the English-speaking world or only in a part of it?) and contemporaneity (is a response up to date or old-fashioned?).

For a work to help people to use a cosmopolitan language it is essential to specify where possible the range of acceptability of the items entered in the work. Thus at **thanks** our Usage Note specifies that the response "You're welcome" is nowadays Common English (despite its probable American origin) whereas the response "Don't mention it" is somewhat old-fashioned British English. Similarly, at **omit** we say that though the collocation in the example ⟨she **omitted** his name *from* the list.⟩ is Common English, the colligation in the example ⟨he **omitted** *to explain* why he had been late.⟩ is chiefly British English rather than American English. In fact, the treatment of American-British differences in BBI 3 is one of its most important features.

Whence come the entries in BBI 3? They are several thousand of the items that Morton Benson, Evelyn Benson, and I have found of most value in using our native language, English, and in seeking equivalents for when using other languages.

Whence come the collocations and colligations offered in BBI 3 about those entries? From the authors' intuition, supported by their reading of and listening to contemporary English and by consultation with such valued colleagues as Ms Janet Whitcut and Dr John Kahn. Nowadays, our task is eased not only by the availability of corpuses of contemporary English (such as the British National Corpus) but also by the amazing resource of the Internet itself, which enables us to search in it for a word and find superb examples of that word in context. Nor should it be forgotten that an important source of new information in BBI 3 is, paradoxically, BBI 2, now that the computer allows material from an entry in BBI 2 to be added to other entries in BBI 3 where such material is appropriate.

But the items that occur to us or that we find are passed through the filter of standard lists of complementation patterns in such works as *A Comprehensive Grammar of the English Language* by Randolph Quirk et al. and of collocations (as in the lists of Lexical Functions prepared by Igor Melchuk et al. for use in explanatory and combinatorial dictionaries of various languages). So what users of BBI get is the product of native-speaker intuition *expanded* by our exposure to authentic English and then *refined* through the standard grids for phraseology and valency developed by outstanding scholars.

The result is BBI. It was "highly recommended" by the English-Speaking Union in 1987. We hope that its present incarnation, 20 to 25% larger, will bring it into the 21st Century and provide the sort of information about English that its authors would like to have about the other languages we want to learn!

Preface to the
BBI Dictionary of English Word Combinations
Revised edition of the
BBI Combinatory Dictionary of English

In this revised edition we have expanded and updated the First Edition (1986) and the New Printing (1993) of the BBI, both of which were very favorably received. In selecting new material, we have made use of a variety of sources, such as: (1) critical appraisals from over 50 reviews in numerous journals; (2) additions to the bilingual versions of the BBI, specifically the Maruzen edition (Tokyo, 1993) and the *Longman Dictionary of English Collocations* (Hong Kong, 1995); (3) comments and suggestions of users of the BBI from around the globe, not all of whom can be mentioned here. We would, however, like to acknowledge the contributions of the following three scholars who have made a special effort to send in material: Mrs. Leatrice Lock Fung of Honolulu (Hawaii), Professor Mohamed H. Heliel of Alexandria University (Egypt), and Professor Zai Ming Li of Fuzhou University (People's Republic of China).

The Revised Edition includes items that were missed in the First Edition. Examples of collocations that were added are: *to access data, a blank cassette, a borderline case, a cellular phone, to come on strong, a computer virus, corporate downsizing, a credit note* (in British English), *cultural diversity, a digital clock, to downsize the workforce, to gather speed, a laptop computer, legally binding, to level an accusation at, to nominate a candidate, to overshoot the runway, to program a VCR, to put a spin on something, to remove graffiti, to run a spell check, a security camera, to send a fax, to sound the all clear, twenty-twenty vision, to wave goodbye,* etc.

In addition, a special effort has been made to identify and incorporate collocations that have entered the English language in recent years since the interlinking of computers. Thus, collocations such as *to browse the web, to create a home page, to cruise the World Wide Web, to go online, to send E-Mail, to surf the Internet, to visit a web site, welcome to cyberspace!* etc., have been included. We wish to express our sincere gratitude to Professor John F. Fritz, specialist in computers at the Allegheny University School of Nursing in Philadelphia, who assisted us in gathering these examples.

As in the First Edition, we have adhered to the principle of citing examples in clear, natural, normal English and have excluded collocations that are strictly technical. Once again, we will be grateful for comments and suggestions from users of this *Dictionary*.

M.B., E.B., R.I.

A Practical Guide to the BBI

Background

Learners of English as a foreign or second language, like learners of any language, have traditionally devoted themselves to mastering words — their pronunciation, forms, and meanings. However, if they wish to acquire active mastery of English, that is, if they wish to be able to express themselves fluently and accurately in speech and writing, they must learn to cope with the combination of words into phrases, sentences, and texts.

Students must learn how words combine or 'collocate' with each other. In any language, certain words regularly combine with certain other words or grammatical constructions. These recurrent, semi-fixed combinations, or *collocations,* can be divided into two groups: *grammatical collocations* and *lexical collocations.* Grammatical collocations consist of a dominant word — noun, adjective/participle, verb — and a preposition or a grammatical construction. Lexical collocations, on the other hand, do not have a dominant word; they have structures such as the following: verb + noun, adjective + noun, noun + verb, noun + noun, adverb + adjective, adverb + verb.

The BBI is a specialized dictionary designed to help learners of English find collocations quickly and easily. The BBI consistently pays attention to differences between American English and British English.

How to Find Grammatical Collocations in the BBI

Typical grammatical collocations in English are: (with prepositions) *admiration* (for), *acceptable* (to), *amazed* (at), (by) *accident, to adhere* (to), *eager* (for); (with grammatical constructions) *eager* (to do something), *eagerness* (to do something), *to want* (someone to do something), *to become* (someone or something). In such collocations the noun or the adjective or the verb is the dominant word. The **BBI** lists **grammatical collocations under the dominant word**.

Thus, in order to express in English the collocation *Feindseligkeit gegenüber,* the German speaker must find in the BBI the equivalent of the dominant word, that is, the noun *Feindseligkeit.* Learners of English may already know the dominant word; if not, the word can be found easily in any bilingual dictionary. The user of the BBI would then look up the entry for the noun *hostility* and find corresponding English collocations such as *hostility to* and *hostility towards,* both of which correspond to the German *Feindseligkeit gegenüber.*

The French speaker wishing to express in English the collocation *curieux de* (as in *curieux de quelque chose*) would look up the entry for the adjective *curious* and see that one says in English *curious about* (as in *curious about something*).

Spanish speakers seeking the translation of *los vimos entrar* would find at the entry for the verb *see* that one says in English either *we saw them enter* or *we saw them entering*.

How to Find Lexical Collocations in the BBI

Typical lexical collocations in English are: *to put up resistance, to override a veto, a formidable challenge, a dog barks, a herd of cattle, deeply absorbed, to argue heatedly.*

In order to find lexical collocations in the BBI, follow this step-by-step procedure: **if there is a noun in the collocation, look under the noun; if there are two nouns, look under the second; if there is no noun, look under the adjective; if there is no noun or adjective, look under the verb.**

Consequently, in order to find the English for *poner la mesa* a Spanish speaker would look up the entry for the noun *table* and find that in American English one usually says *to set the table* and that in British English one usually says *to lay the table.* Or, the same speaker would find for *prender fuego a* the corresponding English collocation *to set fire to* in the entry for the noun *fire.* The speaker of Italian who wishes to say in English *sfondare la porta* will find at the entry for *door* the collocations *to break down the door* and *to force the door.*

In order to render *eingefleischter Junggeselle* as *confirmed bachelor* and *der Hund bellt* as *the dog barks,* the German speaker would look up the entries for the nouns *bachelor* and *dog.*

French speakers would find that *un troupeau de moutons* is in English *a flock of sheep* by looking up the entry for the noun *sheep,* and that *un troupeau de bétail* is *a herd of cattle* by looking up the noun *cattle.*

Spanish speakers learn that they can express *bien caliente* in English as *piping hot* by consulting the entry for the adjective *hot.*

Speakers of Russian can find for *krepko spat'* the English equivalent *to sleep soundly* by looking under the entry for the verb *sleep.*

For more detail, see the Introduction to this Dictionary and *Using the BBI: A workbook with exercises* (http://dx.doi.org/10.1075/z.bbi.workbook).

Abbreviations

adj.	adjective		med.	medicine, medical
adv.	adverb		mil.	military
AE	American English		misc.	miscellaneous
Am.	American		mus.	music
anat.	anatomical		*n.*	noun
BE	British English		neg.	negative
Br.	British		obsol.	obsolete
CA	creation and/or activation		occ.	occasionally
CE	Common English		pol.	politics, political
cf.	compare		pred.	predicative
colloq.	colloquial		*prep.*	preposition
comm.	commercial		refl.	reflexive
derog.	derogatory		rel.	religion, religious
EN	eradication and/or nullification		RP	Received Pronunciation
esp.	especially		smb.	somebody
fig.	figurative		smt.	something
GA	General American		subj.	subjunctive
GB	Great Britain		(T)	Trademark
imper.	imperative		tr.	transitive
inf.	infinitive		usu.	usually
intr.	intransitive		US	United States
ling.	linguistics		*v.*	verb
lit.	literary		*	incorrect English
math.	mathematics			

The letters A to S denote the verb patterns, explained in the Introduction, Grammatical Collocations, section G8.

How Entries are Structured in the BBI
A Visual Guide

appointment *n.* ["agreement to meet"] 1. a follow-up;
outpatient ~ 2. to have; keep; give, make, schedule an ~ (with) (the hospital gave me a follow-up
outpatient ~ with their cardiologist) 3. to break;
cancel; miss an ~ 4. by ~ (she sees patients by ~
only) 5. an ~ to + inf. (she had an ~ to see the dean)
["selection"] 6. to confirm; make an ~ 7. to block an
~ 8. an ~ to (we announced her ~ to the committee)
["position"] 9. an ~ as 10. to offer an ~ (we offered
her an ~ as treasurer) 11. to have, hold, receive an
~ 12. an interim; permanent; temporary ~ 13. a political ~ ["designation"] 14. by ~ to Her Majesty

— Definition (of noun in square brackets,
other typeface and double quotation
marks),
referring to 1. – 5.

— Definition, referring to 6. – 8.
— Definition, referring to 9. – 13.
— Definition, referring to 14.

clock I *n.* 1. to regulate, set; wind (up) a ~ 2. to
advance a ~; or: to put, set, turn a ~ ahead/forward
((by) one hour) 3. to put, set, turn a ~ back ((by)
one hour) 4. a digital; cuckoo; electric; grandfather; wall ~ (by/according to my digital ~, it's ten
thirty) 5. a time ~ (to punch a time ~ when starting
or finishing work) 6. a biological ~ (her biological
~ keeps ticking away) 7. a ~ is fast; right; slow
8. a ~ gains time; goes, runs; keeps time; loses
time; runs down; says the time, shows the time,
tells the time (BE), tells time (AE); stops; ticks 9.
a ~ strikes the hour 10. the dial; face; hands of a ~

1. – 10. = Lexical collocations

11. (misc.) to watch the ~ ("to wait impatiently for
the end of the working day"); to work (a)round the
~ ("to work without rest"); to work against the ~
("to strive to meet a deadline"); the ~ ran out ("the
allotted time expired"); to stop the ~ ("to suspend
play in a game so that the clock stops running")
(see also **alarm clock**)

11. = Idioms with paraphrases in double
quotation marks

concerned *adj.* 1. deeply, gravely, greatly; very ~
2. ~ about, for, over; with (~ about safety) 3. (esp.
BE) ~ to + inf. (~ to know your decision) 4. ~ that
+ clause (she is ~ that there is still so much illiteracy; we are ~ that they might have missed the
train) 5. (misc.) as far as I'm ~ USAGE NOTE:

2. – 4. = Grammatical collocations

The phrases *concerned about, concerned over,*
and, less frequently, *concerned for* mean "worried
about" (concerned about your safety). The phrase
concerned with means "interested in" (concerned
with establishing the truth).

USAGE NOTE providing
additional information

Used only in American English

Used only in British English

meat *n.* 1. to barbecue; braise; broil (AE), grill; cook; cure; fry; marinate; roast; sear; stew ~ 2. to carve, cut; slice ~ 3. dark; red; white ~ 4. fatty; lean ~ 5. raw; tender; tough ~ 6. halal; kosher ~ 7. canned (AE), tinned (BE); fresh; frozen ~ 8. boned; chopped (AE), ground (AE), minced (BE); soup ~ 9. ~ goes bad, spoils 10. a cut; joint; piece; slice of ~ (I'd like a couple of slices of your best cut of ~, please) 11. (misc.) ~ off the bone; ~ on the bone

Illustrative phrase

excited *adj.* 1. ~ about, at, by, over (she got ~ about the news that they were coming) 2. ~ to + inf. (she was ~ to learn that they were coming) 3. ~ that + clause (she was ~ that they were coming)

Compound verb

Definition (of verb in parentheses and double quotation marks)

Verb patterns

come out *v.* 1. (d; intr.) to ~ against ("to oppose") (to ~ against a proposal) 2. (d; intr.) to ~ for, in favor of ("to support") (to ~ for a proposal) 3. (d; intr.) to ~ for ("to try out for") (are you ~ing out for the team?) 4. (d; intr.) to ~ with ("to make known; to publish") (to ~ with a new book; to ~ with the truth) 5. (L) it came out that he had cheated 6. (P; intr.) ("to end up, result") to ~ on top ("to be victorious") 7. (s) the pictures came out fine 8. (misc.) to ~ in spots ("to be covered with spots as a result of illness"); they came out from behind the bushes; she meant it as a compliment, but it came out as an insult; she finally came out openly as a liberal

Introduction

General

In English, as in other languages, there are many fixed, identifiable, non-idiomatic phrases and constructions. Such groups of words are called *recurrent combinations, fixed combinations,* or *collocations.* Collocations fall into two major groups: *grammatical collocations* and *lexical collocations.*

Grammatical Collocations

Background

A grammatical collocation is a phrase consisting of a dominant word (noun, adjective, verb) and a preposition or grammatical structure such as an infinitive or clause. For example, Noam Chomsky in his *Aspects of the Theory of Syntax* (page 191) points out that *decide on a boat,* meaning 'choose (to buy) a boat' contains the collocation *decide on* (in his terminology: *close construction*), whereas *decide on a boat,* meaning 'make a decision while on a boat' is a *free combination* (in his terminology: *loose association*). Any native speaker of English feels that the components of *decide on* 'choose' and of other fixed phrases such as *account for, accuse (somebody) of, adapt to, agonize over, aim at,* etc. 'collocate' with each other. The native speaker will reject violations of collocability such as **decide at a boat, *account over a loss, *accuse somebody on a crime, *adapt towards new conditions,* etc.

Free combinations, on the other hand, consist of elements that are joined in accordance with the general rules of English syntax and freely allow substitution. For example, in English a verb may be followed by adverbials (of time, place, and manner). The resultant number of possible combinations is limitless: *they decided — after lunch, at three o'clock, during recess, immediately, in the library, on the boat, quickly, reluctantly, unhesitatingly, with a heavy heart,* etc.

Collocations should be included in dictionaries; free combinations, on the other hand, should generally not be included. (The inclusion of free combinations is sometimes essential to illustrate a sense of a polysemous entry in a general-purpose dictionary.)

We will now describe eight major types of grammatical collocations; all of these are included in this *Dictionary.* The types are designated by G1, G2, etc.

G1

G1 collocations consist of noun + preposition combinations. We do not normally include noun + *of* combinations. A very large number of English nouns can be used with *of*, especially to denote the concepts of 'direct object', 'subject', or 'possession'. Thus, we include the combination *blockade against,* but not *blockade of.* The phrase *the blockade of enemy ports* is a regular transformation of *to blockade enemy ports.* We include *apathy towards,* but not *apathy of.* A phrase such as *the apathy of the electorate* is predictable on the basis of the known functions of the preposition *of.*

We also do not include noun + *by* combinations. The phrase *the blockade of enemy ports by our navy* is a predictable and regular transformation of the sentence: *our navy blockaded the enemy ports.* In addition, as already indicated, we will not include free combinations, such as *apathy among (the members of our party), apathy in (France),* etc.

To save space, we usually do not include such derived prepositions as *concerning, regarding, in regard to, with regard to.* Note that the prepositions just listed are usually synonymous with *about.* Thus, an *argument about* is synonymous with an *argument concerning, an argument regarding,* etc.

G2

G2 collocations consist of nouns followed by *to* + infinitive. There are five syntactic patterns in which this construction is most frequently encountered; these patterns are the following:

1. It was a *pleasure (a problem, a struggle)* to do it.
2. They had the *foresight (instructions,* an *obligation, permission,* the *right)* to do it.
3. They felt a *compulsion* (an *impulse,* a *need)* to do it.
4. They made an *attempt* (an *effort,* a *promise,* a *vow)* to do it.
5. He was a *fool* (a *genius,* an *idiot)* to do it.

Some nouns can also be used with a verb form in -*ing: it's a pleasure to work there* = *it's a pleasure working there* = *working there is a pleasure* (= *to work there is a pleasure).* Such nouns usually occur in the first syntactic pattern listed above. The use of the -*ing* form is shown in the entries.

We do not include nouns if they are followed by infinitives normally associated with the whole sentence rather than with the noun. Such infinitives express purpose; the phrase *in order* may be inserted between the noun and the infinitive with no change of meaning: *they sold their house (in order) to cut down on expenses, he mowed his lawn (in order) to impress his new neighbors, she closed the window (in order) to keep the flies out,* etc.

Nor do we include nouns that occur in phrases such as *a procedure to follow, a book to read, a place to eat, a way to do it,* etc. In such constructions, the infinitive can be replaced by a relative clause: *a procedure that is to be followed, a book that should be read, a place at which one can (should) eat, a way in which one may (should) do it.* The *BBI* does not include colloquial phrases often found in advertisements: *the dictionary to end all dictionaries, a computer to satisfy all needs,* etc.

Lastly, we usually do not include nouns preceded by a descriptive adjective: *an interesting book to read, a difficult person to understand, a clever thing to say,* etc.

Note that in addition to nouns, some adjectives (G6) and some verbs (Pattern E) are followed by *to* + infinitive.

G3

We include here nouns that can be followed by a *that* clause: *we reached an agreement that she would represent us in court; he took an oath that he would do his duty.* The *Dictionary* does not include nouns followed by relative clauses introduced by *that*, i.e., when *that* can be replaced by w*hich: we reached an agreement that would go into effect in a month; he took the same oath that his predecessor had taken.* Nor does it include nouns that can be followed by a clause only when they are objects of a preposition: *it was by chance that we met; it was with (considerable) pride that he presented his findings.*

Some nouns can be followed by a clause with the present subjunctive in formal English: *it was his desire that his estate be divided equally.* See the comments on the use of the subjunctive G8L. The use of the subjunctive is indicated in the entries for such nouns.

G3 nouns expressing emotion *(astonishment, surprise)* may take a 'putative' *should: she expressed surprise that he should be thinking of changing jobs.*

G4

G4 collocations consist of preposition + noun combinations. Examples are: *by accident, in advance, to somebody's advantage, on somebody's advice, under somebody's aegis, in agony, on (the) alert, at anchor,* etc.

G5

G5 collocations are adjective + preposition combinations that occur in the predicate or as set-off attributives (verbless clauses): *they were angry at everyone — angry at everyone, they stayed home — my friends, angry at everyone, stayed home.*

Some adjectives must be followed by a prepositional phrase: *they were fond of children.* One does not normally say: **they were fond.* In the sense 'craving' the adjective *hungry* is always followed by *for* in the predicate: *they were hungry for news.* The sentence *they were hungry* would have a different meaning. In a similar manner the adjective *deaf* in the sense 'unwilling to listen' is always followed by *to: they were deaf to our pleas for help.* Adjectives that are consistently used with a preposition in at least one sense are marked 'cannot stand alone' in the entries.

Derived prepositions such as *concerning, regarding, in regard to, with regard to,* are not included in the entries. Note that the prepositions just listed are usually synonymous with *about.*

In general, we do not include past participles (formed from transitive verbs) followed by the preposition *by*: this construction is regular and predictable. Thus, this *Dictionary* does not give such phrases as *abandoned by, absolved by,* etc.

We include adjective + *of* constructions when the subject of the construction is animate (usually human): *they are afraid (ashamed, confident, critical, demanding, envious,* etc.) *of him.* See G6 for a discussion of adjective + *of* constructions used with a 'dummy' *it* subject.

G6

G6 collocations consist of predicate adjectives and a following *to* + infinitive. Adjectives occur in two basic constructions with infinitives.

1. *it was necessary to work*

In this construction, the *it* is a 'dummy' or 'empty' subject; it has no antecedent. Prepositional phrases with *for* can be inserted into this construction with many adjectives: *it was necessary for him to work.* If the verb is transitive, a direct object is, of course, added: *it was necessary to supervise them closely.* Some adjectives can be used with a prepositional phrase beginning with *of: it was stupid to go — it was stupid of them to go.* (Sometimes, both *of* and *for* are possible: *it was stupid of them to go; it was stupid for them to go.*)

Most adjectives that appear in adjective + *of* constructions (with the 'dummy' *it* subject) followed by *to* + infinitive can also be used in sentences without the infinitive. An example is: *it was stupid of them to go — it was stupid of them* (or: *that was stupid of them*). The possibility of dropping the *to* + infinitive is usually not indicated in the *Dictionary.*

2. *she (the girl) is ready to go; it (the machine) was designed to operate at high altitudes*

In this construction, the subject is 'real' and usually animate. Some adjectives, however, normally occur in this construction with an inanimate subject: *calculated, designed,* etc. (See the example provided above with *designed.*) Several adjectives can occur in this construction with either an animate or an inanimate subject; an example is *bound: she was bound to find out — it ('the accident') was bound to happen.* Other adjectives of this type are *destined, known, liable, likely,* etc.

Several adjectives can be used in both constructions: *it was supposed to rain — she was supposed to work today.* Some adjectives have the same meaning in both constructions: *it was difficult to convince him — he was difficult to convince.* Other adjectives of this type are *easy, hard, impossible,* and *tough.*

It should be noted that a large number of adjectives, when used with adverbs such as *too* and *enough,* can be followed by an infinitive: *he was too absorbed to notice; she was alert enough to see it.* These are not included in the *Dictionary.* The *Dictionary* does not include past participles that can be followed by a *to* + infinitive phrase of purpose: *the text was proofread (in order) to eliminate errors.* Nor does the *Dictionary* include past participles that are used in passive constructions: *she was appointed (chosen, designated, elected,* etc.) *to serve as our delegate.* Such constructions represent, in fact, the passive transformation of verb pattern H. (See below.)

The *Dictionary* does, however, include many other past participles: *he was amazed (amused, annoyed, appalled, astonished,* etc.) *to see the results of our research.*

G6 collocations are normally illustrated in the *Dictionary* by examples. The examples will show in which construction (or constructions) each adjective is used. Note that many adjectives used with *it* and *of* can also be used with *he/she: it was stupid of him/her to go — he/she was stupid to go.*

Some G6 adjectives are normally not used without a following infinitive (or prepositional phrase), especially with an animate subject. We usually do not say **he is destined, *he is easy, *he is likely,* etc., but rather *he is destined to go far, he is easy to get along with, he is not likely to be late,* etc. G6 adjectives of this type are marked 'cannot stand alone' in the entries.

A few G6 adjectives (usually used with the 'dummy' *it*) can also be followed by a verb form in *-ing: it's nice to work here = it's nice working here.* The use of the *-ing* form is shown in the entries.

Note that in addition to adjectives, some nouns (G2) and some verbs (pattern E), are followed by *to* + infinitive.

G7

G7 adjectives (many of which are also in G6) can be followed by a *that* clause: *she was afraid that she would fail the examination; it was nice that he was able to come home for the holidays.* Several adjectives are followed by the present subjunctive in formal English: *it was imperative that I be there at three o'clock; it is necessary that he be replaced immediately.* See the comments on the use of the present subjunctive in G8L.

G8

G8 collocations consist of nineteen English verb patterns, designated by the capital letters A to S. A description of each verb pattern follows.

A. Pattern A verbs allow the *dative movement transformation,* that is, allow the shift of an indirect object (usu. animate) to a position before the direct object, with deletion of *to* when both objects are nouns and when the direct object is a noun: *he sent the book to his brother — he sent his brother the book* and *he sent the book to him — he sent him the book.* However, when both objects are pronouns, this transformation is common only in BE: *he sent it to him — he sent him it* (marginal in AE). BE also allows *he sent it him.*

B. Pattern B verbs are transitive; when they have an indirect object, they do *not* allow the *dative movement transformation,* i.e., the shift of the indirect object (usu. animate) to a position before the direct object with the deletion of *to.* Thus, we have *they described the book to her, they mentioned the book to her, they returned the book to her,* but not **they described her the book,* etc. Compare the A pattern verb *send,* which does allow the transformation: *they sent him the book.* Verbs denoting types of noise fit pattern B: *he screamed something to her.* Other such verbs are: *babble, bark, bellow, growl,* etc.

In a few rare cases, AE and BE usage differs. An example is the verb *recommend*, which in AE belongs to pattern B and in BE to pattern A. Such differences are indicated in the *Dictionary*.

C. In pattern C, transitive verbs used with the preposition *for* allow the *dative movement transformation*, i.e., allow the deletion of *for* and the shift of the indirect object (usu. animate) to a position before the direct object: *she bought a shirt for her husband — she bought her husband a shirt, she bought a shirt for him — she bought him a shirt.*

It must be emphasized that the *Dictionary* gives only those verbs that occur most frequently in the various meanings of *make — create*. For example, in regard to culinary operations, the *Dictionary* includes the verbs *bake, boil, brew, broil, chop, cook, fry, grill, grind, peel, scramble, slice,* and *toast* (as in: *bake me a cake, boil him an egg, brew her some tea, broil us a few steaks,* etc.). However, the *Dictionary* does not include less frequently used verbs that can be used in the same constructions. Examples are: *barbecue, braise, brown, devil, fricassee, oven bake, pan broil, pan fry, parboil, poach, sauté, scallop, shirr, steam, stew,* etc.

D, d. In this pattern, the verb forms a collocation with a specific preposition (+ object). Free combinations such as *to walk in the park* are excluded. In addition, combinations of the type verb + *by* or *with* are excluded when the latter denote 'means' or 'instrument': *they came by train, we cut bread with a knife,* etc.

Collocations consisting of a verb + *as* (+ object) are included in the *Dictionary: to act as, to interpret as, to serve as, to treat as,* etc.

Some D-pattern verbs are normally *not* used without a prepositional phrase. For example, one does not say: **we will adhere, *they based their conclusions, *our committee consists,* etc. Well formed sentences are: *we will adhere to the plan, they based their conclusions on the available facts, our committee consists of six members,* etc. When a verb (or a certain sense of a verb) is normally followed by a prepositional phrase, its pattern is designated by the small letter *d*.

The *Dictionary* does include *compound verbs* followed by prepositions: *break in on, catch up to,* etc. Note that *out of* is treated as a compound preposition.

Transitive D-pattern verbs used with *to* and B-pattern verbs produce identical constructions. We assign to B those verbs that are normally used with an animate indirect object, and to D — verbs normally occurring with inanimate indirect objects. Compare B: *we described the meeting to them* and D: *we invited them to the meeting.*

E. In this pattern, verbs are followed by *to* + infinitive. Examples of this construction are: *they began to speak, she continued to write, he decided to come, we offered to help,* etc. Verbs are not included if they are normally used in phrases of purpose, that is, if *in order* can be inserted with no change of meaning: *they were drilling (in order) to improve their pronunciation, he was running (in order) to catch a train, she stopped (in order) to chat,* etc.

F. This pattern includes the small number of verbs that are followed by an infinitive without *to: we must work.* These verbs, with the exception of *dare, help* (esp. AE), and *need*, are called *modals*. The verbal phrases *had better* and *would rather* also fit this pattern: *he had better (would rather) go.*

G. In this pattern, verbs are followed by a second verb in *-ing*. Typical examples of this construction are: *they enjoy watching television, he kept talking, we miss going to work every day, the house needs painting, she quit smoking, he regrets living so far from his family,* etc.

Note that some pattern G verbs are also in pattern E. Thus, we have approximately synonymous constructions: *he began reading — he began to read, she continued speaking — she continued to speak.*

Several verbs, however, that appear in both G and E have a different meaning in each construction. The sentence *he remembered to tell them* means that 'he intended to tell them and told them'; *he remembered telling them* means that 'he remembered the act of telling them'. In a similar manner, the construction *he forgot to tell them* means that 'he intended to tell them, but forgot to do so'; *he forgot (about) telling them* means that 'he forgot that he (had) told them'.

Note also the difference between the pattern G construction *she stopped chatting* 'she terminated her chat' and *she stopped to chat.* The latter construction contains an infinitive phrase of purpose similar to that in *she dropped in (in order) to chat, she telephoned her friend (in order) to chat,* etc.

H. In this pattern, transitive verbs are followed by an object and *to* + infinitive. Typical examples of this construction are: *she asked me to come; they challenged us to fight; we forced them to leave; he invited me to participate; she permitted the children to watch television.*

Many of the verbs in this pattern can take the infinitive *to be* after the direct object: *we advised them to be careful, she asked us to be punctual, the director authorized us to be in the laboratory,* etc. For verbs that are normally used only with *to be* after the direct object, see pattern M.

Most H-pattern verbs can be passivized: *I was asked to come, we were authorized to use the laboratory,* etc. Some, however, cannot be: *beseech, bring, cable, cause, commit, get, have, intend, like, prefer, telegraph, telephone, thank, trouble, want, wire, wish,* and *write.*

I. In this pattern, transitive verbs are followed by a direct object and an infinitive without *to.* Examples of this construction are: *she heard them leave, we let the children go to the park, they saw her drive up to the house, he watched them unload the car,* etc. Some of these verbs are also used in pattern J.

The use of I-pattern verbs in the passive occurs occasionally: *we felt the earth move — the earth was felt to move; they made us get up — we were made to get up.* Note the appearance of *to* + infinitive in the passive construction. In some instances, the *-ing* form seems more natural when the verb is passivized: *she was seen driving up to the house.* Most I-pattern verbs cannot be passivized: *we had them fix our roof, she helped us move the furniture, they let the children go home, I watched them unload the car,* etc.

J. In this pattern, verbs are followed by an object and a verb form in *-ing*. Typical examples of this construction are: *I caught them stealing apples, we found the children sleeping on the floor, he kept me waiting two hours,* etc. Note that some verbs in this list are also used in pattern I. Thus, we have approximately synonymous constructions: *she heard them leaving — she heard them leave, he felt his heart beating — he felt his heart beat, we watched them dancing — we watched them dance,* etc.

J-pattern verbs can usually be passivized: *they were caught stealing apples, the children were found sleeping on the floor, I was kept waiting two hours,* etc.

K. In this pattern, verbs can be followed by a possessive (pronoun or noun) and a gerund, i.e., a verbal noun. Typical examples of this construction are: *please excuse my waking you so early, this fact justifies Bob's coming late.* Some of these constructions are very close to those in pattern J, which consist of verb + direct object + present participle. Note the following constructions that are virtually synonymous: *I cannot imagine them stealing apples — I cannot imagine their stealing apples; they remembered Bill making that mistake — they remembered Bill's making that mistake,* etc.

The possessive construction is awkward when two objects are joined by a conjunction. Thus, the construction *I can't imagine Bill* (or *Bill's*) *and Mary's doing that* is far less likely to occur than the pattern J construction *I can't imagine Bill and Mary doing that.*

Native speakers of English often have individual preferences for one con-struction and may not find the other construction acceptable. Some speakers tend to avoid the possessive construction, which is considered to be bookish. Thus, instead of *we excused his coming late,* many will say *we excused him for coming late;* instead of *we anticipated his refusing,* they prefer *we anticipated his refusal,* etc. In this *Dictionary* we have attempted to include only the most frequently occurring verbs that can be followed by a possessive.

L. In this pattern, verbs can be followed by a noun clause beginning with the conjunction *that.* Examples are: *they admitted that they were wrong, she believed that her sister would come, he denied that he had taken the money, we hoped that the weather would be nice.* In colloquial English the *that* may be omitted: *they admitted they were wrong, she believed her sister would come,* etc.

Some verbs always take a noun or pronoun object before the *that* clause: *she assured me that she would arrive on time, they convinced us that we should invest our money at once, he informed his students that the examination had been canceled.* Such verbs are marked 'must have an object' in the entries. Other verbs can be used with or without a nominal object: *he bet that it would rain — he bet me that it would rain; we cabled that we would arrive on Tuesday — we cabled them that we would arrive on Tuesday; she promised that she would come — she promised her brother that she would come; we showed that we were good workers — we showed everyone that we were good workers,* etc. Such verbs are marked 'may have an object' in the entries. Most of the objects in the sentences just cited seem to be direct objects, i.e., cannot be preceded by *to.* Note however that the (especially AE) construction *he wrote me that he would come next month* has the CE variant *he wrote to me that he would come next month.* Certain verbs in pattern L (often belonging also to pattern B) may be followed by a prepositional phrase with *to: he swore that he would stop drinking — he swore to us that he would stop drinking.* Such verbs are marked 'to' in the entries.

Some verbs in pattern L allow the insertion of *the fact* with little or no change in meaning: *he acknowledged (admitted, confirmed, forgot, mentioned,* etc.) *that he was guilty* or *the fact that he was guilty.*

Verbs denoting types of noise fit pattern L: *growl, grumble, grunt, mumble,* etc.

Several verbs, in 'correct' or formal English, are followed by a verb in the present subjunctive in the *that* clause. Examples are: *he demanded that I be there tomorrow at ten o'clock, we moved that the resolution be accepted, the officer ordered that the soldier report to his unit immediately, she proposed that our class hold a reunion, they suggested that the firm appoint a new personnel manager.* In BE the modal *should* is normally used (also in AE as a variant): *they suggested that the firm should appoint a new personnel manager.* The verbs used with a following subjunctive in formal English are marked *subj.* in the entries. The variant with *should* is also shown in the entries.

Some L-pattern verbs can be followed by a clause either with the subjunctive or with the indicative; there is a difference in meaning. Compare: *I suggest that she be/ should be there at two o'clock — the facts suggest that she is there.*

A few L-pattern verbs regularly have 'dummy' *it* as their subject: *it appears that they will not come.* Other verbs of this type are: *follow, seem, transpire, turn out,* etc.

M. In this pattern, transitive verbs can be followed by a direct object, the infinitive *to be,* and either an adjective, or a past participle, or a noun/pronoun. In most instances, the same verb can be followed by any of these three forms. Examples of this construction are: *we consider her to be very capable — we consider her to be well trained — we consider her to be a competent engineer; the court declared the law to be unconstitutional — the court declared the law to be superseded by more recent legislation — the court declared the law to be a violation of the Constitution; we found the roads to be excellent — we found the roads to be cleared of snow — we found the roads to be a serious problem for the state treasury.*

Note that this pattern includes verbs that normally take *to be* after the direct object. For verbs that combine freely with infinitives other than *to be,* see pattern H.

N. In this pattern, transitive verbs can be followed by a direct object and an adjective or a past participle or a noun/pronoun. Here are several examples of this construction with an adjective: *she dyed her hair red, we found them interesting, he made his meaning clear, the police set the prisoner free.* Verbs used with adjectives in this construction are marked 'used with an adjective' in the entries.

Examples with a past participle are: *the soldiers found the village destroyed, she had her tonsils removed, we heard the aria sung in Italian.* Verbs used with past participles are marked 'used with a past participle' in the entries.

Examples with a noun/pronoun are: *we appointed (designated, elected, made, named) Bob secretary, her friends call her Becky, they ordained him priest.* Verbs used with nouns/pronouns are marked 'used with a noun' in the entries. Many of these verbs are also used in pattern H (*appoint, designate, elect, name*). Approximately synonymous constructions of the following types can thus be formed: *we appointed (designated, etc.) him secretary;* or: *we appointed him to serve as secretary;* or: *we appointed him to be secretary.*

Some pattern N verbs are also used in pattern M. Note the following synonymous constructions: *we consider her (to be) a competent engineer; the court declared the law (to be) unconstitutional; we found the roads (to be) cleared of snow; we proved him (to be) guilty,* etc.

Finally, it should be noted that some N-pattern verbs are used only with certain adjectives or with a certain adjective. For example, with the verb *paint,* we can say *to paint the walls blue/green/white,* etc. With the verb *shoot,* we can only say *to shoot somebody dead.*

O. In this pattern, transitive verbs can take two objects, neither of which can normally be used in a prepositional phrase with *to* or *for.* Examples of sentences with such double objects are: *the teacher asked the pupil a question, we bet her ten pounds, the police fined him fifty dollars, God will forgive them their sins, she tipped the waiter five dollars,* etc. Note the superficial similarity of the constructions *we bet him ten pounds* and *we sent him ten pounds.* (See pattern A.) Only the second construction allows the transformation *we sent ten pounds to him.*

Pattern O is also very close structurally to pattern N (which has a noun/pronoun following the direct object: *they called him a fool*). The latter construction has one direct object (him), followed by a predicate (object) complement (*a fool*).

Some pattern O verbs can be used with either of their objects alone: *the teacher asked the pupil — the teacher asked a question.* Such verbs are marked 'can be used with one object' in the entries.

Verbs pertaining to gambling such as *bet, lay,* and *wager* are noteworthy in being able to take in effect three objects — a person, an amount, and a clause denoting the point of the bet: *we bet him ten pounds that it would rain. Bet* can be used with any of the three objects alone; *lay* seems to require the first and the second; *wager* can be used with either the second or the third alone.

O-pattern verbs can usually be passivized; in most instances, at least one object can become the subject of the passive construction. Examples are: *no questions were asked, ten pounds were bet, he was fined fifty dollars, they will be forgiven, the waiter was tipped five dollars.*

P. In this pattern, intransitive, reflexive, and transitive verbs must be followed by an adverbial. The adverbial may be an adverb, a prepositional phrase, a noun phrase, or a clause. For example, we cannot normally say in English **he carried himself.* An adverbial is required to form a complete sentence: *he carried himself well;* or: *he carried himself with dignity.* In a similar manner, without adverbials the following sentences are not complete: **Tuesday comes, *we fared, *the meeting will last, *my brother is living* (= 'dwelling'), **a strange man was lurking, *I nosed the car, *she put pressure* (cf.: *she exerted pressure,* which is acceptable), **the boys sneaked, *they tramped, *the trunk weighs,* etc. Acceptable sentences can be formed only if an appropriate adverbial is added: *Tuesday comes after Monday, we fared well, the meeting will last two hours, my brother is living in Utah, a strange man was lurking where we least expected him, I nosed the car (out) into the street, she put pressure on them, the boys sneaked into the auditorium, they tramped through the woods, the trunk weighs thirty pounds.*

Note that some polysemous verbs cited above may have senses that do not require an adverbial: *they are coming, is he still living ? a shot-putter puts the shot,* etc.

Some adverbials of duration may resemble direct objects: *the meeting will last all day, this job took two hours,* etc. In fact, these verbs are intransitive; we can say, for example, *the meeting will last long.* We must also mention here sentences with verbs of measurement, such as *the trunk weighs thirty pounds.* We treat *thirty pounds* as an adverbial complement rather than as a direct object, thus distinguishing this sense of *weigh* (which we consider to be intransitive) from the sense used in the sentence *she weighed the trunk* (which we consider to be transitive).

Some verbs are invariably followed by a particle: *hang around, well up,* etc. Such forms can be considered compound verbs (phrasal verbs) and should be given in dictionaries as separate entries. They are not included in this pattern.

In this *Dictionary* we have attempted to give only the most commonly used verbs and senses that have obligatory adverbials. We have not included all verbs that are followed by a *way*-phrase and an obligatory adverbial: *we elbowed (fought, jostled, made, pushed, worked,* etc.) *our way through the crowd, they bribed their way to success, the Tatar cavalry burned its way through Eastern Europe,* etc. The number of such verbs is very large.

Q. In this pattern, verbs can be followed by an interrogative word: *how, what, when, where, which, who, why;* to these we add *whether* (which often alternates in clauses with *if*). These interrogative forms are often called *wh*-words. Note: verbs that can be followed only by *what* are not included. An example is the verb *want;* we can say *he wants what I want,* but not **he wants how I want.*

The verbs entered in the *Dictionary* can be followed by a *wh*-word and usually by either a *to* + infinitive construction *or* by a clause: *he asked how to do it, she could not decide whether or not to begin, she knew when to keep quiet — he asked how he should do it, she could not decide whether (if) she should begin, she knew when it was best to keep quiet.*

Although most pattern Q verbs do not take a noun/pronoun object before the *wh*-construction, several must have an object: *we told them what to do, they informed us where applications were being accepted,* etc. Such verbs are marked 'must have an object' in the entries. A few verbs can be used with or without an object: *she asked why we had come — she asked us why we had come.* Such verbs are marked 'may have an object' in the entries.

R. In this pattern, transitive verbs (often expressing emotion) are preceded by the dummy *it* and are followed by *to* + infinitive or by *that* + clause or by either. The construction (or constructions) in which each verb usually seems to occur is shown in the entries. Examples are: *it behooves/behoves you to study more; it puzzled me that they never answered the telephone; it surprised me to learn of her decision* and *it surprised me that our offer was rejected.*

S. In this pattern, a small number of intransitive verbs are followed by a predicate noun or by a predicate adjective: *she became an engineer; he was a teacher; he became smug; she was enthusiastic.* The verb *make,* used intransitively, belongs here: *he'll make a good teacher.*

    A somewhat larger group of intransitive verbs can be followed only by a predicate adjective; these verbs are coded with the small letter *s.* Examples are: *she looks fine; the flowers smell nice; the food tastes good.*

Special Note on Transitivity

Verbs are always transitive in the following patterns: A, B, C, H, I, J, K, M, N, O, and R. In four other patterns verbs are consistently intransitive: E, F, G, and S. In the fifteen patterns just listed, verbs are not marked for transitivity. In patterns D, d, and P, verbs of both types occur and are marked as *tr.* or *intr.* In patterns L and Q, verbs can be followed by a clause, and consequently, can be considered to be transitive with a few exceptions such as *appear, emerge, feel, seem.* If another object must be used, the verb is marked 'must have an object'. If another object may be used, the verb is marked 'may have an object'.

Survey of Verb Patterns

In this survey the following special symbols are used: s = subject; v = verb; o = object (direct or indirect); c = complement; a = adverbial (when obligatory); v-ing = verb form in *-ing*.

Pattern Designation			Pattern Designation		
A	=	svo *to* o (or) svoo	K	=	sv possessive v-ing
B	=	svo *to* o	L	=	sv(o) *that*-clause
C	=	svo *for* o (or) svoo	M	=	svo *to be* c
D, d	=	sv prep. o (or) svo prep. o	N	=	svoc
E	=	sv *to* inf.	O	=	svoo
F	=	sv inf.	P	=	sv(o)a
G	=	svv-ing	Q	=	sv(o) wh-word
H	=	svo *to* inf.	R	=	s(*it*)vo *to* inf. (or) s(*it*)vo *that*-clause
I	=	svo inf.	S	=	svc (adjective or noun)
J	=	svov-ing	s	=	svc (adjective)

Note that collocational types G2 and G3 (for nouns) and G6 and G7 (for adjectives) are closely related grammatically to some of the verb patterns given above.

Lexical Collocations

Background

Lexical collocations, in contrast to grammatical collocations, normally do not contain prepositions, infinitives, or clauses. Typical lexical collocations consist of nouns, adjectives, verbs, and adverbs. An example of an adjective + noun collocation is *warmest regards*, as in *I send warmest regards*. Typical violations of lexical collocability are *I send hot regards* and *I send hearty regards*.

Many lexical collocations in English consist of a verb and noun, such as *bring in an acquittal, file an affidavit, put on airs*, etc. The various types of lexical collocations included in the Combinatory *Dictionary* will be described below.

The Combinatory *Dictionary* does not include free lexical combinations. Free lexical combinations are those in which the two elements do not repeatedly co-occur; the elements are not bound specifically to each other; they occur with other lexical items freely. Thus, a construction such as *condemn murder* is a free combination. The verb *condemn* occurs with an unlimited number of nouns: *they condemned — the abduction, abortion, abuse of power, the acquittal*, etc. In a similar manner, *murder* combines freely with hundreds of verbs: *abhor, accept, acclaim, advocate*, etc.

On the other hand, *commit murder* is a collocation. The verb *commit is* limited in use to a small number of nouns, meaning 'crime', 'wrongdoing'; it collocates specifically with *murder.*

We will now describe seven major types of lexical collocations; all of these are included in the *Dictionary*. The types are designated by L1, L2, L3, etc. The *Dictionary* attempts to give only those lexical collocations that are in common use.

L1

L1 collocations consist of a verb (usually transitive) and a noun/pronoun (or prepositional phrase). Most L1 collocations consist of a verb denoting *creation* and/or *activation* and a noun/pronoun. We call such fixed lexical combinations *CA collocations*. Here are examples of collocations with verbs denoting creation: *come to an agreement, make an impression, compose music, set a record, reach a verdict, inflict a wound*. Here are examples of collocations that express the concept of activation: *set an alarm, fly a kite, launch a missile, punch a time clock, spin a top, wind a watch.*

In some instances, the same noun collocates with one verb (or verbs) to denote creation and with another verb (or verbs) to denote activation: *establish a principle* (= creation) — *apply a principle* (= activation); *draw up a will* (= creation) — *execute a will* (= activation).

In many instances the meanings *creation* and *activation* are united in one verb: *call an alert, display bravery, hatch a conspiracy, impose an embargo, produce friction, inflict an injustice, offer opposition, pose a question, lay a smoke screen, put out a tracer, commit treason, issue a warning.*

CA collocations are arbitrary and non-predictable. Non-native speakers cannot cope with them; they must have a guide. They have no way of knowing that one says in English *make an estimate* (but not **make an estimation*), *commit treason* (but not **commit treachery*). In English one says *commit fraud and perpetrate fraud*. However, only the collocation *commit suicide* is possible; one does not say **perpetrate suicide.*

Even the native speaker may need at times to refer to a list of CA collocations. Many may not know which verbs collocate with such nouns as the following: *acquittal, afterburners, authority, barrage, bench warrant, Caesarean section, cartwheel, circuit breaker, cloture, copyright, counsel, coup de grâce, coup d'état*, etc. A native speaker of AE, who says *to take up a collection*, will not know which verb collocates with the colloquial BE synonym of CE *collection*, namely *whip-round (have)*. Speakers of BE prefer *to have a bath;* AE speakers invariably *take a bath*. CE speakers *make a decision;* BE speakers can also *take a decision.*

Many nouns collocate with verbs that refer to the actions of more than one participant. Such nouns will have different CA collocations according to which participant's role is being described. Thus, a copyright office *grants or registers* a copyright, but an author or publisher *holds or secures* one.

CA collocations for polysemous nouns are extremely important. For example, the entry for the noun line has the following collocations: *draw a line* (on paper); *form a line* (= 'line up'); *drop smb. a line* (= 'write smb. a letter'). The entry for *operation* has: *perform an operation* (in a hospital); *carry out (conduct) an operation* (on the battlefield).

As indicated above, the Combinatory *Dictionary* does not include free combinations. Thus, we exclude many combinations with verbs such as *build, cause, cook, grow, make, manufacture, prepare*, etc. even though, strictly speaking, they convey the meanings of 'creation' or 'activation'. Such verbs form an almost limitless number of combinations: *build bridges (houses, roads), cause damage (deafness, a death), cook meat (potatoes, vegetables)*, etc.; such combinations seem to be predictable on the basis of the meaning of their component elements.

On the other hand, we have included in L1 many collocations even if they do not mean 'creation' or 'activation'. Examples are: *do the laundry, decline a noun, take one's seat, carry a story, confirm a suspicion, resist temptation, conjugate a verb*, etc.

L2

L2 collocations consist of a verb meaning essentially *eradication* and/or *nullification* and a noun. Such fixed lexical combinations are called *EN collocations*. Typical examples are the following: *reject an appeal, lift a blockade, break a code, reverse a decision, dispel fear, squander a fortune, demolish (raze, tear down) a house, repeal a law, revoke a license, annul a marriage, suspend martial law, scrub (cancel) a mission, withdraw an offer, countermand an order, renege on a promise, crush (put down) resistance, break up a set* (of china), *rescind a tax, ease tension, quench one's thirst, denounce (abrogate) a treaty, exterminate vermin, override a veto*, etc.

The Combinatory *Dictionary,* does not include predictable free EN combinations. For example, the verb *destroy* can be used with a very large number of nouns denoting physical objects; these have not been entered. Examples are: *to destroy — a barn, bridge, building, city, document, factory, harbor, house, laboratory, port, road, school, village,* etc.

L3

L3 collocations consist of an adjective and a noun. One well known pair of examples is *strong tea* (not **mighty tea*) and *weak tea* (not **feeble tea*). In many instances, more than one adjective (or more than one form of the same adjective) can collocate with the same noun: *warm, warmest* (not **hot*); *kind, kindest; best* (not **good*) *regards.* Other examples of L3 collocations are: *reckless abandon, a chronic alcoholic, a pitched battle, a formidable challenge, a crushing defeat, a rough estimate, an implacable foe, a sweeping generalization,* etc.

As already indicated, the *Dictionary* attempts to give only the most commonly used lexical collocations. Many L3 collocations can be considered to be clichés. The *Dictionary* does not normally give collocations that are used solely in technical language. However, the *Dictionary* does give some technical collocations that will be of interest to students and teachers of English for Special Purposes.

In English, nouns are often used as adjectives. Nouns used attributively may enter into L3 collocations: *house arrest, jet engine, land reform, aptitude test.* These collocations are given at the entry for the second noun. However, if in a 'fused' compound the second noun does not have the same basic meaning as it has when used alone, the compound is not included as an L3 collocation. Examples of such *Multi-Word Lexical Units* (MLUS) are: *bowling alley, sitting duck, long shot, stuffed shirt,* etc. An MLU is listed as a separate headword if it enters into a collocation. For example, the colloquial MLU *double take* ('delayed reaction') is given as a headword since it is part of the collocation *to do a double take.*

In some instances, noun + noun collocations can be found more easily by the user of the *Dictionary* when they are listed at the entry for the first noun rather than at the entry for the second noun. For example, *cabinet reshuffle is* given at **cabinet**, *drug pusher* at **drug**, etc. Such collocations are listed in the entries under *misc.*

L4

L4 collocations consist of a noun and verb; the verb names an action characteristic of the person or thing designated by the noun: *adjectives modify, alarms go off (ring, sound), bees buzz (sting, swarm), blizzards rage, blood circulates (clots, congeals, flows, runs), bombs explode (go off),* etc. The *Dictionary* does not include predictable combinations such as *bakers bake, boxers box, cooks cook, dancers dance, fencers fence,* etc.

L5

L5 collocations indicate the *unit* that is associated with a noun. The structure of an L5 collocation is often *noun₁ of noun₂*. Such collocations may indicate:

a. the larger unit to which a single member belongs: *a colony (swarm) of bees, a herd of buffalo, a pack of dogs, a bouquet of flowers, a pride of lions, a school of whales,* etc.
b. the specific, concrete, small unit of something larger, more general: *a bit (piece, word) of advice, an article of clothing, an act of violence,* etc.

L6

L6 collocations consist of an adverb and an adjective. Examples are: *deeply absorbed, strictly accurate, closely (intimately) acquainted, hopelessly addicted, sound asleep, keenly (very much) aware,* etc.

L7

L7 collocations consist of a verb and an adverb. Examples are: *affect deeply, amuse thoroughly, anchor firmly, apologize humbly, appreciate sincerely, argue heatedly,* etc.

Arrangement of Entries

General

The *Dictionary* provides entries primarily for nouns, adjectives, and verbs. A few entries for adverbs and prepositions are also given. We will now describe the arrangement of each type of entry. Note that the following five principles apply to all entries.

1. Collocational types are indicated by illustrative phrases or sentences rather than by type designations. Verb entries are also coded.

2. Lexical collocations precede grammatical collocations.

3. Words characteristic of one variety of English are marked AE (for American English) or BE (for British English). For details concerning variety labeling, see the Style Guide, Collocational Strings, 9.

4. This *Dictionary* does not normally include idioms, i.e., frozen expressions in which the meaning of the whole does not reflect the meanings of the component parts: *to kill two birds with one stone* 'to achieve two aims with one action'; *to be beside oneself* 'to be in a state of great emotional confusion'. Some phrases, especially those expressing a simile, are transitional between collocations and idioms, that is, the meanings of the component parts are reflected partially in the meaning of the whole. The *Dictionary* does include important phrases of this type. For example, under *misc.,* the entry for

bird has *as free as a bird,* the entry for **feather** has *as light as a feather,* the entry for **sugar** has *as sweet as sugar,* etc.

5. The *Dictionary* does include important fixed phrases that do not fit into any of the types of grammatical and lexical collocations described above. Thus, the entry for **business** gives *to mix business with pleasure,* the entry for **eye** gives *to feast one's eyes on smt.,* etc. Such phrases are normally given under *misc.*

Order of Entries

Headwords, including compounds, are listed in strictly alphabetical order. Thus, the phrasal (compound) verb **go along** follows **goal**. Solid compounds precede those written as two words. For example, **makeup** *n.* precedes **make up** *v.* Homographs, i.e., words with the same spelling, are listed according to the alphabetical order of their part of speech. Their order is, consequently, adjective, adverb, noun, verb. For example, **abandon I** *n.* precedes **abandon II** *v.*

Noun Entries

Collocational types given in noun entries are customarily arranged in the following order: L1, L2, L3, L4, L5, G1, G2, G3, G4. Usually, each collocational type is given in a separate numbered item. However, in order to save space, two collocational types may be shown in the same item. For example, in the entry for **allusion**, we have *to make an allusion to.* This construction shows both L1 and G1.

Adjective Entries

Collocational types are arranged in the following order: L6, G5, G6, G7.

Verb Entries

L7 collocations are given first; they are followed by the verbal patterns of G8, namely A to S. Items showing G8 items are coded, that is, each collocation is marked by a letter designating the appropriate verbal pattern. G8 items are listed in the alphabetical order of their letter codes. When there are several D/d collocations, these are given in the alphabetical order of the collocating prepositions.

Style Guide

The Swung Dash

1. The swung dash (~) usually replaces the headword within the entry. The swung dash is repeated only when necessary.

2. In entries for compound (phrasal) verbs the swung dash represents both the verb and the particle only when they are used in the unseparated infinitive or imperative form and also in the simple present tense, unseparated, with no (third-person singular) ending. The entry for **get away** has an infinitive in the collocation *to ~ from;* the entry for **reach out** has an imperative in the illustrative phrase: *~ your hand to me.* The entry for **run short** has the illustrative phrase *they never ~ of money.* In all other instances, the swung dash represents only the verb; the particle is shown separately. The entry **take down** has the illustrative phrase *to ~ testimony down in shorthand.* (Here the verb and particle are separated in the infinitive form.) The entry **set apart** has the phrase *certain traits ~ them apart from the others.* (Here in the simple present tense the verb and particle are separated.) The entry **run around** has the phrase *he ~s around with a fast crowd.* (Here the verb in the simple present tense has the third-person singular ending.)

3. The headword is used rather than the swung dash when irregular grammatical forms occur. Usually, these are irregular past tense forms of verbs. Occasionally noun plurals must be shown. For example, in the entry for **prisoner of war** we have *to interrogate; repatriate prisoners of war*; in **goose** we have *geese cackle, honk.*

Collocational Strings

1. When a headword collocates with various other words, the *Dictionary* usually lists the resultant collocations in strings. The presentation of collocations in strings not only saves an enormous amount of space, but it also allows the concentration of a great deal of material, facilitating the use of the *Dictionary* by its readers.

2. When collocations are listed in a string, a comma separates synonyms or near synonyms. Members of the collocational string are listed in alphabetical order. The entry for **advice** gives *to give, offer ~.* This string represents the synonymous collocations *to give advice* and *to offer advice.*

3. A semicolon separates non-synonymous collocations that are presented in a string. The entry for **answerable** has *~ for; to.* This string represents the non-synonymous collocations *answerable for* and *answerable to.*

4. Both synonymous and non-synonymous collocations may be listed in one string. The entry for **booth** has *an information; phone, telephone; polling, voting; projection ~.* This string represents the collocation *an information booth,* the synonymous collocations *a phone booth* and *a telephone booth,* the synonymous collocations *a polling booth* and *a voting booth,* and the collocation *a projection booth.* Note that synonymous members of a string are grouped together, even though this upsets the overall alphabetical order. Note also that the article is not repeated in the string.

5. When the same noun collocates with different verbs and with different prepositions, the resultant collocations must be shown in different strings. Thus, under **degree** ('academic title') we have *to award a ~ to; to confer a ~ on.* Note that these collocations are synonymous; the semicolon between them separates different collocational strings

rather than non-synonymous members of the same string. Another example is found in the entry **damage** ('harm'), which gives *to cause, do ~ to; to inflict ~ on*. These two strings represent the three synonymous collocations *to cause damage to, to do damage to, to inflict damage on*.

6. Separate strings are required when differences in the use of articles or of number must be shown. Differences in the use of articles are indicated in **business** 5: *a mail-order ~; show ~; the travel~*. In **atrocity** 2 we see a string of adjectives for the singular: *a dreadful, grisly, gruesome, heinous, horrible, horrid, monstrous, revolting, vile ~*; in **atrocity** 3 we see the allocations normally used in the plural: *death-camp; wartime atrocities*.

7. As indicated above under *Lexical Collocations*, some nouns collocate with verbs that refer to the actions of more than one participant. Only verbs referring to the actions of the same participant may be listed in one string. Thus, the entry for **copyright** has one string for the actions of the copyright office *(to grant, register a ~)* and a different string for the actions of an author or publisher *(to hold; secure a ~)*.

8. The examples given above show that normally each string has one swung dash. The sole exception occurs in strings that include a compound word, i.e., a word consisting of two (or more) roots spelled as one word. The last element of the compound is the same element with which the other members of the string collocate. In such instances, the member of the string preceding the compound must be followed by the swung dash. Under **boat** we have an *assault~; flying ~; gunboat; lifeboat; mosquito ~*.

9. Stylistic and variety labels referring to one member of the string normally follow that member. Under **show** I we have *to catch* (colloq.), *see, take in a ~*. The entry **accountant** has *a certified public* (AE), *chartered* (BE) *~*. Note that the variety label CE is usually not used. Thus, the entry for **different** 2 has *-from, than* (AE), *to* (BE). This means that CE has *different from,* AE has *different than,* and BE has *different to.*

Definitions and Paraphrases

1. Definitions and paraphrases are enclosed in double quotation marks.

2. Definitions of nouns and adjectives in double quotation marks, other typeface, and square brackets refer to items that follow. Note the following example: **accent** *n.* ["pronunciation"] *to affect, assume, imitate, put on; cultivate an ~*, etc. When 'miscellaneous' items are not covered by any previously given definition, they are listed at the end of the entry and are preceded by *misc.* in double quotation marks, other typeface, and square brackets. For an example, see the entry for **account I**.

3. Definitions of senses of verbs and paraphrases of illustrative phrases are given in double quotation marks and parentheses. Such definitions and paraphrases refer to the preceding item. An example of a paraphrase is provided in the entry **aback**. The collocation given is *taken aback;* the illustrative phrase is *I was taken aback,* which is paraphrased as *I was startled.*

4. When verb definitions refer to the headword, they stand immediately after the coding. For example, **go II** 11 has the coding (d; intr.), followed by the definition (*"to pass"*), the collocation *to ~ by,* and the illustrative phrase *to ~ by smb.'s house.* If, however, the meaning of the verb is clear only in combination with the following preposition, the definition follows not the coding, but the collocation. Thus, **go** 12 has the coding (d; intr.), the collocation *to ~ by,* the definition (*"to follow"*), and the illustrative phrase *to ~ by the rules.*

Illustrative Phrases

1. Illustrative phrases follow the collocation that they refer to; they are given in parentheses. The entry **adherence** 2 has the collocation *~ to* followed by the illustrative phrase *strict ~ to a plan.*

2. When synonyms are indicated in an illustrative phrase, they are separated by a slash (/). The entry for **state I** 9 has the illustrative phrase: *affairs/matters of ~.*

3. Note that a collocation may be expanded so as to serve as an illustration. Under **river** 4 we have the L4 collocation *a ~ flows* expanded by the phrase *(into the sea),* enclosed in parentheses. Thus, **river** 4 has: *a ~ flows (into the sea).*

Usage Notes

Usage Notes in the *BBI* provide additional information about the appropriate use of headwords and their collocations. The views of purists concerning correct usage are sometimes given. Usage Notes may also include details about the differences between AE and BE; for additional information about these differences, see the *Lexicographic Description of English.* Note that the swung dash is not used in the Usage Notes.

Pronunciation

In general, the *BBI Dictionary* does not indicate pronunciation. In a few instances, however, phonemic transcription is provided in order to differentiate homographs. Thus, **bow I** is transcribed as /bau/ and **bow III** as /bou/; **use I** is transcribed as /ju:s/ and **use II** as /ju:z/. For details concerning the simplified transcription used in the *BBI,* see the *Lexicographic Description of English* or the comparative table that follows.

It should be noted that in some English homographs the stress of adjectives and nouns on one hand, and that of verbs on the other, may be different. In such instances, the adjective or noun has the stress on the first syllable, and the verb has the stress on the second syllable. Entries given in the *BBI* for such homographs with stress differences include: *absent, abstract, address, ally, annex, compress, conduct, conflict, contract, contrast, convert, defect, discourse, escort, excerpt, extract, impact, implant, increase, intrigue, object, overhaul, permit, present, produce, progress, prospect, protest, rebel, rebound, recall* (in AE), *record, recount, refund, refuse, relay, remit* (in BE), *subject, suspect, transfer, transplant, transport, upset.*

A few nouns have variant stresses, i.e., either on the first or on the second syllable. Examples are: *address* ("place of residence"), *ally, intrigue, recall* (in AE), *remit* (in BE; this noun is not used in AE). Several verbs have variant stresses. Examples are: *ally* (in AE), *annex, transport* (in AE). In the meaning "to summarize", the verb *abstract* is stressed on the first syllable. Note that the noun *upset* is stressed on the first syllable, whereas both the adjective and the verb are stressed on the second syllable; the adjective is, in fact, a past participle form.

Comparative table of Simplified Transcription (ST) and IPA transcription

The ST column (as used in BBI) has GA as its basic variety. The IPA column has RP as its basic variety. Both columns show, whenever necessary, the forms of the other variety.

Vowels				*Consonants*		
as in	*ST*	*IPA*		*as in*	*ST*	*IPA*
beet	/biyt/	/bi:t/		pet	/pet/	/pet/
bit	/bit/	/bɪt/		bet	/bet/	/bet/
bet	/bet/	/bet/		tell	/tel/	/tel/
bat	/baet/	/bæt/		debt	/det/	/det/
balm	/bam/	/ba:m/, /bam/		cat	/kaet/	/kæt/
bob	/bab/; /ò/	/bɒb/, /bab/		get	/get/	/get/
boss	/bos/; /ò/	/bɒs/, /bɔs/		check	/ček/	/tʃek/
bought	/bot/	/bɔ:t/		jet	/džet/	/dʒet/
bull	/bul/	/bʊl/		fat	/faet/	/fæt/
boot	/bu:t/	/bu:t/		vat	/vaet/	/væt/
butt	/bət/	/bʌt/		theft	/theft/	/θeft/
bird	/bə(r)d/	/bɜ:d/, /bɜrd/		then	/th:en/	/ðen/
ago	/ə'gou/	/ə'gəʊ/		self	/self/	/self/
bay	/bey/	/beɪ/		zoo	/zu:/	/zu:/
boat	/bout/	/bəʊt/		shoe	/šu:/	/ʃʊ:/
bite	/bayt/	/baɪt/		vision	/'vižən/	/'viʒən/
bout	/baut/	/baut/		help	/help/	/help/
boy	/boy/	/bɔɪ/		men	/men/	/men/
beer	/biy(r)/	/bɪə/*		net	/net/	/net/
bear	/bey(r)/	/beə/*		ring	/ring/	/riŋ/
boor	/bu:(r)/	/bʊə/*		led	/led/	/led/
				yes	/jes/	/jes/
				wet	/wet/	/wet/

*Some dictionaries indicate that in RP these vowels precede a 'dropped-r' and that in GA they precede an /r/.

A

aback *adv.* taken ~ ("startled") (I was taken ~ at / by his angry words = I was taken ~ when he spoke to me angrily = It took me ~ when he spoke to me angrily)

abacus *n.* 1. to operate, use an ~ 2. with an ~

abandon I *n.* 1. great, reckless, wild ~ 2. with ~ (with reckless ~)

abandon II *v.* (D; tr.) to ~ to (they ~ed us to our fate)

abbreviate *v.* (D; tr.) to ~ to (*Esquire* can be ~d to *Esq.*)

ABC *n.* as easy as ~

abdication *n.* ~ from

abduct *v.* (D; tr.) to ~ from (to ~ a child from its home)

aberration *n.* a mental; sexual; statistical; momentary; temporary ~

abet *v.* (formal) (D; tr.) to ~ in (to ~ smb. in doing smt.; to aid and ~ smb. in doing smt.)

abeyance *n.* in; into ~ (to hold in ~; to fall into ~)

abhor *v.* 1. (D; tr.) to ~ for (she ~s him for smoking) 2. (G) she ~s smoking 3. (K) she ~s his smoking

abhorrence *n.* 1. to show ~ (she showed her ~ of smoking) 2. in, with ~ (of) (she holds smoking in ~ = she regards smoking with ~)

abhorrent *adj.* (formal) 1. to find smt. ~ (she finds smoking ~) 2. ~ to (smoking is ~ to her)

abide *v.* (d; intr.) 1. to ~ by ("to agree to, obey") (we must ~ by her decision) 2. (obsol. and formal) (d; intr.) ("to stay") to ~ with smb. ("In life, in death, O Lord, ~ with me" – H.F. Lyte (1793–1847))

ability *n.* 1. to demonstrate, display, exhibit, show ~ 2. to appreciate, recognize ~ 3. creative; leadership ~ 4. exceptional, great, outstanding, remarkable; limited ~ 5. genuine, innate, natural; latent ~ 6. an ounce of ~ (he doesn't have even an ounce of ~) 7. ~ at, in (to display ~ in mathematics) 8. the ~ to + inf. (the ~ to reason) 9. of ~ (a person of great ~; to the best of one's ~)

ablaze *adj.* 1. ~ with (the city was ~ with lights) 2. to set ~

able *adj.* 1. perfectly ~ 2. ~ to + inf. (I'm perfectly ~ to cope on my own; she tried to reach him but she was not ~ to (reach him)) USAGE NOTE: In passive constructions, *able to* is replaced by *can* – X isn't always able to replace Y = Y can't always be replaced by X.

ablutions *n.* (formal or humorous) to perform one's ~

aboard *adv.* 1. to be; climb, come; go ~ 2. all ~!

abode *n.* 1. (legal) of no fixed ~ 2. (formal or humorous) to take up one's ~; welcome to my humble ~

abortion *n.* 1. to do, perform an ~ on 2. to induce an ~ 3. to get, have an ~ 4. a back-street, criminal,

illegal; induced; spontaneous; therapeutic ~ 5. legalized ~

abound *v.* (formal) (d; intr.) to ~ in, with (this country ~s in / with opportunities = opportunities abound in this country)

about I *adj.* (cannot stand alone) ["ready"] 1. ~ to + inf. (the performance is ~ to begin) ["willing"] (colloq.) (esp. AE) 2. not ~ to + inf. (we are not ~ to stop now; we are not ~ to be taken in by their campaign promises) ["misc."] 3. to set ~ doing smt.

about II *prep.* 1. be quick ~ it ("do it quickly") 2. how / what ~ us? what ~ your promise? how ~ (having) a drink? (see also **what** 1)

about-face *n.* ["sudden change in attitude"] 1. to do an ~ 2. a complete, dramatic; sudden, unexpected ~ 3. a ~ on (the government did a sudden dramatic ~ on foreign policy)

about-turn *n.* (BE) see **about-face**

above *adv.*, *prep.* way; well; up ~

abrasions *n.* multiple ~

abreast *adj.* (usu. does not stand alone) ~ of (to be, keep, stay ~ of the news; to keep smb. ~ of the latest developments)

abroad *adv.* 1. from ~ (he had to return from ~) 2. to go; live; study; travel; work ~

abscond *v.* (D; intr.) to ~ from; with (they ~ed from the country with the funds)

absence *n.* 1. an excused; unexcused ~ 2. a prolonged ~ 3. ~ from (an unexcused ~ from school) 4. during, in smb.'s ~ 5. in the ~ of smt. (in the ~ of concrete evidence, we had to drop the charges) (see also **conspicuous**)

absent I *adj.* ~ from (she was ~ from school)

absent II *v.* (D; refl.) to ~ from (to ~ oneself from a meeting)

absentia *n.* in ~ (to be tried in ~)

absolution *n.* (rel.) 1. to give, grant, pronounce ~ from (to grant ~ from sin) 2. to seek ~

absolve *v.* (D; tr.) to ~ from, of (he was ~d from his promise)

absorb *v.* 1. (D; tr.) to ~ from (to ~ drainage from a wound) 2. (D; tr.) to ~ into (to ~ a small firm into a large cartel)

absorbed *adj.* 1. deeply, completely, thoroughly, totally, utterly ~ 2. ~ by, with; in (she was ~ by / with the problem; the children were ~ in their homework; ~ in thought)

absorbent *adj.* highly, very ~

abstain *v.* (D; intr.) to ~ from (to ~ from alcohol)

abstention *n.* ~ from (~ from alcohol)

abstinence *n.* 1. to practice ~ 2. complete, total ~ 3. ~ from (~ from alcohol)

abstract I *n.* in the ~

abstract II *v.* (technical) (D; tr.) to ~ from (to ~ iron from ore)

absurd *adj.* 1. patently; totally, utterly ~ 2. ~ to + inf. (it was ~ (for us) to leave such a large tip) 3. ~ that + clause (it's ~ that we have to / should have to leave such a large tip)

absurdity *n.* it was the height of ~ (for us) (to leave such a large tip)

abundance *n.* 1. great ~ 2. an ~ of (there was a great ~ of opportunities here) 3. in ~ (we had opportunities in ~) 4. of ~ (a society of ~)

abundant *adj.* (formal) ~ in (~ in opportunities)

abuse *n.* ["insulting language"] 1. to heap, shower ~ on, upon (he showered ~ on her); to hurl, shout ~ at; to shower smb. with ~ (he showered her with ~) 2. to take ~ (she took a lot of ~ from him) 3. verbal ~ 4. a shower, stream, torrent of ~ (she took a torrent of ~ from him) 5. a term of ~ ["rough use"] 6. to take ~ (this car has taken a lot of ~) ["mistreatment"] 7. domestic; emotional; personal; physical; racial; sexual ~ 8. child; elder; spousal ~ 9. human-rights ~s ["improper use, misuse"] 10. alcohol, substance ~ (see also **drug abuse**)

abusive *adj.* ~ to, toward (he became verbally ~ to his guests)

abut *v.* (D; intr.) to ~ against, on, upon

abyss *n.* 1. a gaping, yawning ~ 2. on the brink, edge of an ~

academe *n.* (formal) the groves, halls of ~

academic *adj.* purely ~ (a purely ~ distinction of no practical significance)

academy *n.* 1. a military; naval; police; riding ~ 2. an ~ for (an ~ for boys) 3. at an ~

accede *v.* 1. (D; intr.) ("to agree") to ~ to (they ~d to our demands) 2. (D; intr.) ("to ascend") to ~ to the throne

accelerator *n.* 1. to depress, put one's foot on, step on an ~ 2. to ease up on, let up on; take one's foot off an ~

accent *n.* ["pronunciation"] 1. to affect, assume, imitate, put on; cultivate; have an ~ 2. to speak with; without an ~ 3. to get rid of, lose an ~ 4. a broad; heavy, noticeable, pronounced, strong, thick; slight ~ 5. a foreign; phony; regional ~ 6. (misc.) a hint, trace of an ~ (to speak English without a trace of a foreign ~) ["stress"] 7. to place, put the ~ on (to place the ~ on a syllable) 8. (ling.) an acute; grave; pitch, tonic ~ (see also **stress**)

accept *v.* 1. to ~ blindly; fully; generally, widely; readily; unreservedly, without reservations 2. to ~ gracefully, graciously; gratefully 3. to ~ grudgingly, reluctantly 4. (D; tr.) to ~ as (they ~ed us as their equals) 5. (D; tr.) to ~ for (she was ~ed for admission) 6. (D; tr.) to ~ from (she ~ed an award from a committee) 7. (formal) (BE) (L) people generally ~ that exercise is beneficial

acceptable *adj.* 1. completely, entirely, fully; mutually; socially ~ 2. ~ to (the conditions proved/were ~ to all concerned) 3. ~ to + inf. (is it socially ~ to behave like that?)

acceptance *n.* 1. to gain, win; meet with ~ 2. to seek ~ 3. blind, unquestioning ~ (blind ~ of dogma) 4. general, universal, widespread; growing, increasing; public ~ (the theory met with universal ~) 5. grudging, reluctant ~ 6. a degree of ~ (the theory

gradually met with a certain degree of grudging ~) 7. ~ of (her ~ of an award from a committee)

accepted *adj.* 1. generally, widely ~ 2. ~ that + clause (it is generally/widely ~ that exercise is beneficial)

access I *n.* 1. to gain, get; have ~ 2. to seek ~ 3. to deny, refuse; give, grant ~ 4. direct; easy, free, unlimited, unrestricted; immediate, instant, quick, ready; limited, restricted ~ 5. (computers) random ~ 6. ~ to (we gained/got ~ to the files; ~ to a building by/from/through/via the side entrance; provide wheelchair ~ to the auditorium)

access II *v.* (D; tr.) to ~ from (to ~ information from a computer)

accessary (esp. BE) see **accessory** 1, 2

accessibility *n.* ~ to (the professor's ~ to all students)

accessible *adj.* 1. directly; easily, readily; immediately ~ 2. ~ from; to (the stacks are ~ to the public from the main staircase; the director is friendly and ~ to everyone) 3. wheelchair ~ (we pride ourselves on our wheelchair-accessible auditorium!)

accession *n.* 1. on smb.'s ~ (on his ~ to the throne he inherited vast estates) 2. ~ to (her ~ to power; his ~ to the throne) 3. a new ~ (as in a library)

accessory *n.* ["accomplice"] 1. an ~ to (an ~ to a crime) 2. (legal) an ~ before the fact; an ~ after the fact ["optional equipment"] 3. auto (AE); matching; skiing; smoking ~ries

accident *n.* ["unexpected, typically unpleasant event"] ["catastrophe"] 1. to cause an ~ 2. to have, meet with (they had an ~ during their trip) 3. to survive an ~ 4. to prevent ~s 5. an awful, bad, dreadful, frightful, horrible, horrific, nasty, serious, shocking, terrible, tragic; fatal; freak; unavoidable; unfortunate ~ 6. a minor, slight; near ~ 7. an automobile (AE), road, traffic; hit-and-run; railroad (AE), railway (BE), train ~ 8. a boating; hunting ~ 9. an industrial; nuclear ~ 10. an ~ happens, occurs (a bad ~ happened there) 11. in an ~ (he was involved in a hunting ~) 12. (misc.) (fig.) ~-prone; an ~ waiting to happen (that clumsy waiter is just an ~ waiting to happen!) ["chance"] ["luck"] 13. pure, sheer ~ 14. an ~ that + clause (it was pure ~ that we met; it was no ~ that we met) 15. by ~ (we discovered it by ~; it was by pure ~ that we met; did it happen by ~ or (by) design?, did it happen by ~ or on purpose?)

acclaim I *n.* 1. to earn, receive, win ~ 2. critical ~ (the play opened to critical ~) 3. general, public ~ 4. international, universal, wide, worldwide; national ~ 5. ~ as; for; from; to (the play opened to ~ from the critics for her performance = when the play opened she won ~ from the critics for her performance = when the play opened she won ~ from the critics as a great actress)

acclaim II *v.* 1. (d; tr.) to ~ as (the new medication has been ~ed as a miracle drug) 2. (d; tr.) to ~ for (she was ~ed for her performance) 3. (N; used with a noun) the mob ~ed him emperor

acclamation *n.* by ~ (to elect smb. by ~)

acclimate (AE) see **acclimatize**

acclimatize *v.* (D; intr., refl., tr.) to ~ to (we ~d quickly / ~d ourselves quickly to the jungle; we became ~d quickly to the new surroundings)

accolade *n.* 1. to bestow an ~ on 2. to receive, win an ~ (from) 3. the supreme, ultimate ~

accommodate *v.* (D; intr. (esp. AE), refl., tr.) to ~ to (they ~d themselves easily to the new conditions = (esp. AE) they ~d easily to the new conditions)

accommodation I *n.* ["agreement"] ["adjustment"] 1. to come to, make; reach, work out an ~ 2. to seek an ~ 3. an ~ between; about / on; to; with (to make an ~ to wartime conditions; to reach an ~ with neighboring countries about / on our common borders)

accommodation II (BE) see **accommodations**

accommodations *n.* (AE) ["place to live"] 1. to secure; seek ~ 2. deluxe; first-class ~ 3. hotel; living ~ 4. student, tourist; travel ~ 5. in ~ (live in student ~)

accompaniment *n.* 1. to make an ~ 2. an ~ to (a piano ~ to a song; this dressing makes a good ~ to any salad) 3. to the ~ of (to the ~ of soft piano music)

accompany *v.* 1. (D; tr.) to ~ on (to ~ a singer on the piano) 2. (D; tr.) to ~ to (I will ~ her to the station)

accomplice *n.* 1. an unwitting ~ 2. an ~ in, to (an ~ in crime, an ~ to a criminal)

accomplished *adj.* 1. highly; technically 2. ~ at, in (technically highly accomplished at the piano especially in 19th-Century music)

accomplishment *n.* 1. see **achievement** 1 for adjective + noun collocations 2. no mean ~ 3. an ~ to + inf. (it was a real ~ (for us) to defeat them) 4. of ~ (a man, woman of many ~s)

accord I *n.* 1. to come to, reach sign an ~ 2. an ~ breaks down 3. complete, full ~ 4. a peace ~ 5. an ~ with smb. about / on smt. (we reached an ~ with the neighboring country about our common border but the ~ eventually broke down) 6. an ~ that + clause (they came to an ~ that profits would be shared equally) 7. in ~ (with) (we are in complete ~ (with each other); our information is not entirely in ~ with his report) 8. (formal) of one's own ~ (he participated of his own ~)

accord II *v.* 1. to ~ completely, entirely, fully 2. (A) we ~ed a hero's welcome to him; or: we ~ed him a hero's welcome 3. (d; intr.) to ~ with (our information does not entirely ~ with his report)

accordance *n.* in ~ with (we have acted in ~ with your instructions)

account I *n.* ["description"]["report"] 1. to give, render an ~ 2. an accurate, factual, true; blow-by-blow, detailed, full, graphic; clear; eyewitness; first-hand; running; satisfactory; verbatim ~ (she gave a detailed ~ of the incident) 3. a glowing; lively, vivid ~ 4. a biased, one-sided; unsatisfactory ~ 5. a

brief ~ 6. newspaper, press ~s (according to press ~s) 7. in an ~ (she gave a detailed description of the incident in her ~ of it) 8. by all ~s (by all ~s she is a good pianist) ["explanation"] 9. to call smb. to ~ (for) (he was called to ~ for the missing funds) ["consideration"] 10. to take ~ of smt.; to take smt. into ~ ["arrangement with a bank"] 11. to open an ~ (at, in, with) (I opened an ~ at / with that bank) 12. to close, settle an ~ 13. to have, keep an ~ (I keep an ~ in that bank) 14. to overdraw an ~ 15. to audit; credit; debit an ~ 16. a bank; building-society (BE); checking (AE), current (BE); deposit (BE), savings; money-market; individual retirement (AE) ~ 17. an active; blocked; inactive ~ 18. a joint; numbered ~ 19. an overdrawn ~ 20. in an ~ (the funds were in her ~) ["business arrangement"] ["record of a business arrangement"] 21. to open an ~ (with a store) 22. to close an ~ 23. to have an ~ (with) 24. to charge, debit; credit smb.'s ~ 25. to charge smt. to one's / smb.'s ~ 26. to pay smt. on ~ 27. a charge (AE), credit (BE); expense ~ (see also **expense account**) ["dispute"] 28. to settle an ~ (I have an ~ to settle with him) ["sake"] 29. on smb.'s ~ (do not refuse on my ~) 30. on ~ of (he did it on ~ of me) ["showing"]["performance"] 31. to give a good ~ of oneself ["misc."] 32. on no ~ ("under no circumstances"); of no ~ ("of no importance") (see also **accounts**)

account II *v.* 1. (d; intr.) to ~ for ("to explain") (he could not ~ satisfactorily for the missing funds; "how do you ~ for the accident?" "it can be partly ~ed for by the bad weather") 2. (d; intr.) to ~ for ("to cause the destruction of") (the enemy's guns ~ed for three of our planes) 3. (d; intr.) to ~ (for) to ("to explain") (she has to ~ to her supervisor for time spent in travel) 4. (BE) (N; used with an adjective, noun) ("to consider") we ~ed her guilty; she was ~ed a prodigy

accountable *adj.* 1. directly; strictly ~ 2. ~ for; to (we are ~ to our parents for our actions; she is ~ to her supervisor for time spent in travel) 3. (misc.) to hold smb. ~ for smt.

accountant *n.* a certified public (AE), chartered (BE) ~

accounting *n.* 1. to give, render an ~ 2. a strict ~ 3. cost ~

accounts *n.* ["books, ledgers"] 1. to keep ~ ["record of transactions"] 2. ~ payable; receivable ["disputes"] 3. to settle, square ~ (with)

accredit *v.* (D; tr.) 1. to ~ to (our envoy was ~ed to their new government) 2. (misc.) a fully ~ed university

accreditation *n.* 1. to receive (full) ~ (the university has received full accreditation) 2. to deny ~ (our envoy was denied ~ to their new government)

accrue *v.* 1. (D; intr.) to ~ from 2. (D; intr.) to ~ to (the interest ~d to our account)

accuracy *n.* 1. deadly; historical; pinpoint; reasonable; scientific; strict, total ~ 2. ~ in

accurate adj. 1. completely, deadly; fairly, pretty, reasonably; historically; strictly; ~ 2. ~ in 3. ~ to + inf. (it would be ~ to say that he is lazy)

accusation n. 1. to bring, make an ~ against (he brought an ~ of theft against Smith; more usu. is: he accused Smith of theft) 2. to level an ~ against, at (he leveled an ~ of theft against Smith) 3. to answer; face an ~ (of) (Smith faced an ~ of theft) 4. to drop, retract, withdraw an ~ 5. to deny, reject; refute an ~ 6. a damaging, grave; baseless, false, groundless, scurrilous, unfounded, unjust; sweeping; veiled ~ 7. an ~ against; of (an ~ of theft) 8. an ~ that + clause (Smith denied the ~ that he was guilty of theft)

accuse v. (D; tr.) to ~ of (he ~d Smith of theft)

accused adj. 1. falsely ~ 2. to stand ~ (of) (Smith stood ~d of theft)

accustom v. (d; refl., tr.) to ~ to (we had to ~ ourselves to the warm climate; more usu. is: we had to get ~ed to the warm climate)

accustomed adj. (cannot stand alone) ~ to (~ to hard work; ~ to walking long distances; we got ~ to the warm climate)

ace n. ["a serve that an opponent cannot touch"] (tennis) 1. to score an ~ ["expert combat pilot"] 2. an air, flying ~ ["misc."] 3. within an ~ of ("very close to"); an ~ in the hole ("a concealed advantage, a trump card") (to have an ~ in the hole; to play one's ~ in the hole)

ache I n. 1. a deep; dull; sharp; nagging, steady; slight ~ (he felt a dull ~ in his shoulder) (see **backache, earache, headache, stomachache, toothache**) 2. an ~ gets worse, intensifies; subsides, wears off 3. (misc.) ~s and pains

ache II v. 1. (d; intr.) to ~ for (to ~ for revenge) 2. (E) he is ~ing to get even 3. (misc.) to ~ all over

achievement n. 1. a brilliant, crowning, dazzling, epic, glorious, great, lasting, magnificent, major, memorable, monumental, notable, outstanding, phenomenal, remarkable, signal, staggering, superb, wonderful ~ 2. no mean ~ 3. an ~ in (outstanding ~s in science) 4. an ~ to + inf. (it was no mean ~ (for us) to finish on time!) 5. an ~ that + clause (it was a staggering ~ that we finished on time!)

acid n. 1. corrosive, strong ~ 2. acetic; boric; carbolic; citric; hydrochloric; sulfuric ~ 3. ~ burns (a hole); corrodes 4. (misc.) (slang) to drop/take ~ (LSD) (see also *acid test* at **test I** n.)

acknowledge v. 1. to ~ belatedly; frankly, openly, readily; gratefully; grudgingly; officially, publicly; generally, universally (is it universally ~d that men and women need each other?) 2. (B) the author ~d her debt to her research assistants 3. (D; tr.) to ~ as (she ~d him as her heir) 4. (G) she ~d being indebted to her research assistants 5. (K) she ~d my having been the first to think of it 6. (L; to) she ~d (to us) that she was indebted to her research assistants 7. (rare) (M) they ~d us to be the winners

of the contest 8. (formal and rare) (N; used with a past participle) she ~ed herself indebted to her research assistants

acknowledgment, acknowledgement n. 1. to make an ~ of 2. a belated, frank, open; grateful; public ~ 3. in ~ of

acme n. 1. to attain, reach the ~ of 2. at an ~ (at the ~ of their power)

acquaint v. 1. to ~ thoroughly 2. (d; refl., tr.) to ~ with (the lawyer ~ed herself thoroughly with the facts of the case)

acquaintance n. ["familiarity"] 1. to have an ~ with (he has some ~ with statistics) 2. a slight, superficial ~ 3. on ~ (on closer ~ he proved to be a nice person) 4. an ~ with ["casual friendship"] 5. to make smb.'s ~ 6. to keep up; renew; strike up an ~ with 7. (BE) to scrape ~ with 8. a casual, nodding, passing, slight ~ (to have a nodding ~ with smb.) ["friend"] 9. a casual; intimate; old; personal ~ 10. (misc.) of smb.'s ~ (I introduced her to a lawyer of my ~); friends and ~s

acquaintanceship n. 1. to strike up an ~ with 2. a casual; close, intimate ~ 3. an ~ with

acquainted adj. 1. casually; closely, intimately, thoroughly; personally ~ 2. ~ with (he got/became ~ with the situation; are you ~ with him?; I introduced her to a lawyer I was ~ with)

acquiesce v. (D; intr.) to ~ in, to (they ~d in the decision)

acquiescence n. 1. complete, total ~ 2. ~ in, to (~ in a decision)

acquisition n. 1. to make an ~ 2. (BE) an ~ for/to (he is a valuable ~ for our firm) 3. (misc.) language ~ and language learning

acquit v. 1. (D; tr.) ("to exonerate") to ~ of (the jury ~ted her of all charges) 2. (P; refl.) ("to behave") she ~ted herself well; he ~ted himself like a veteran

acquittal n. (legal) 1. to bring in, return an ~ (the jury brought in an ~) 2. to win an ~ (the lawyer won an ~ for her client)

acrimony n. bitter, sharp ~

acrobatics n. 1. to perform ~ 2. (fig.) mental; verbal; vocal ~

acronym n. 1. to form an ~ 2. an ~ for

across adv. ~ from

act I n. ["action"] 1. to commit; consummate; perform an ~ 2. a barbaric, barbarous; despicable, hostile; terroristic; unfriendly ~ 3. a criminal, illegal, illicit ~ 4. a desperate; foolish, irresponsible, rash; impulsive ~ 5. a courageous; heroic, noble; justified ~ (she performed an heroic ~) 6. a friendly, humane, kind; thoughtful ~ 7. an ~ against (that was an ~ against company policy) 8. an ~ of (an ~ of faith; he committed an ~ of folly) 9. in the ~ (Coleridge was interrupted in the ~ of writing Kubla Khan; criminals caught in the ~) ["performance"] 10. a circus; nightclub; variety (BE), vaudeville (AE) ~ 11. (misc.) to put on an ~ ("to pretend"); to do a balancing ~ ("to maneuver skillfully") ["legislation"] 12. by ~ of (Congress) ["misc."] 13. to get into the ~ ("to participate"); to get one's ~ together ("to begin to work effectively"); to do a disappearing ~ ("to vanish from the scene"); a tough ~ to follow ("smb. or smt. difficult to emulate or to equal") (see also **riot act**)

act II v. 1. to ~ impulsively; irresponsibly, rashly; responsibly 2. (d; intr.) ("to perform") to ~ against (to ~ against one's own client) 3. (d; intr.) ("to serve") to ~ as (she ~ed as our interpreter) 4. (d; intr.) to ~ for ("to replace", and, esp. BE, "to represent as one's lawyer") 5. (d; intr.) ("to behave") to ~ like (the soldier ~ed like a real hero) 6. (D; intr.) ("to take action") to ~ on, upon (to ~ on smb.'s advice; to ~ on a request) 7. (d; intr.) ("to take action") to ~ out of (they ~ed out of fear) 8. (d; intr.) ("to behave") to ~ towards (how did they ~ towards you?) 9. (P; intr.) ("to behave") the soldier ~ed bravely; to ~ guiltily 10. (s) (esp. AE) ("to behave") to ~ guilty 11. (misc.) they ~ed as if they were pleased = (colloq.) (esp. AE) they ~ed like they were pleased; we saw what had to be done and ~ed accordingly

action n. ["activity"] ["act"] 1. to initiate; take ~; to go, swing into ~ (we took immediate ~) 2. to put smt. into ~ (we put our plan into ~) 3. to prod, spur smb. into ~ 4. to do, perform an ~ 5. collective, concerted, united; decisive, firm; direct 6. immediate, prompt, swift ~ (we must take immediate ~) 7. drastic; emergency ~ 8. disciplinary; remedial ~ 9. hasty, rash ~ 10. affirmative ~ ("giving preference to members of minority groups, reverse discrimination, positive discrimination") 11. industrial (BE), (a) job (AE); (a) strike ~ ("a protest by workers") 12. congressional; political ~ 13. (a) reflex ~ ["combat; military or police activity"] 14. to go into ~ 15. to see ~ ("to participate in combat") 16. to break off ~ 17. to take evasive ~ ("to maneuver in order to escape enemy fire") 18. enemy ~; a delaying, holding; police; punitive; rearguard ~ (see also **delaying action**) 19. in ~ (killed/missing in ~) 20. out of ~ (two tanks were put out of ~) ["lawsuit"] 21. to bring, institute, take ~ against smb. for smt. (he brought legal ~ against his neighbor) 22. to dismiss an ~ (the judge dismissed the ~) 23. a civil; class; divorce; legal; libel ~ (see also **civil action**) ["initiative"] ["enterprise"] 24. a man, woman of ~ ["plot of a play, novel"] 25. the ~ drags; picks up; takes place (the ~ picks up in the third act) ["misc."] 26. (colloq.) a piece of the ~ ("participation in an activity"; "a share of the profits"); the time for ~ is now ("this is the moment to act") 27. a course of ~ (follow a course of ~)

active adj. 1. sexually ~ 2. ~ in 3. to keep, stay ~ (try to keep ~ in old age)

activity n. 1. to engage in, participate in, take part in an ~ (all students take part in extracurricular ~ties) 2. to stimulate ~ (to stimulate economic ~) 3. to

resume one's ~ties 4. to break off, terminate an ~ 5. to curb; paralyze ~ (business ~ was paralyzed) 6. ~ picks up; dies down 7. bustling, constant, feverish, frenetic, furious, uninterrupted ~ 8. business, economic; cultural; political; scientific ~ 9. extracurricular; leisure, recreational; social ~ 10. intellectual ~ 11. indoor; outdoor; physical ~ 12. behind-the-scenes; subversive; terrorist; undercover ~ 13. union ~ties 14. to buzz, hum with ~ 15. a burst, flurry, whirl of ~ 16. a beehive, hive of ~

actor, actress n. 1. to audition; cast; work as an ~ 2. an ~ auditions; learns lines, prepares, rehearses; performs; trains 3. a character; ham ~

actuality n. in ~

act up v. (D; intr.) ("to function badly") to ~ on (my leg has been ~ing up on me)

acuity n. mental; visual ~

acumen n. 1. to demonstrate, display, show ~ 2. business, financial; legal; political ~ 3. the ~ to + inf. (she had enough ~ to see through the scheme)

acupuncture n. to do, perform ~ (on)

ad n. (colloq.) 1. to place an ~ 2. to answer an ~ 3. to follow, read the ~s 4. a classified, small (BE); help-wanted (esp. AE); lonely-hearts; want (AE) ~ (see also **advertisement**)

adage n. a familiar; old ~

adamant adj. 1. ~ about; in (~ in his insistence about getting fit) 2. ~ that + clause; may have subj. when the subjects of the clauses are different (he was ~ that he was fit to go; she was ~ that he not/ should not go)

adapt v. 1. (D; tr.) to ~ for; from (to ~ a novel for television; to ~ a television program from a novel) 2. (D; intr., refl., tr.) to ~ to (we ~ed quickly to life in Paris; she had to ~ herself to local conditions; we ~ed our schedule to (meet) their requirements)

adaptation n. 1. to make an ~ 2. an ~ for (an ~ of a novel for television)

add v. 1. to ~ considerably, greatly 2. (D; intr., tr.) to ~ to (we ~ed this amount to the bill; these changes ~ed greatly to the confusion) 3. (L) she ~ed that she would not bring the children

addendum n. an ~ to

addict n. a confirmed; drug ~

addicted adj. 1. chronically, hopelessly ~ 2. ~ to (~ to drugs)

addiction n. 1. chronic, hopeless ~ 2. drug ~ 3. (an) ~ to (~ to drugs)

addictive adj. highly ~

addition n. ["adding of numbers"] 1. to do ~ ["part added"] 2. to make an ~ 3. a welcome ~ 4. an ~ to (an ~ to the family) 5. in ~ (in ~, she brought some fresh fruit) 6. in ~ to (in ~ to his salary, he earns a lot from royalties)

add on v. (D; tr.) to ~ to (to ~ a garage on to/onto a house = to ~ on a garage to a house)

address I n. ["speech"] 1. to deliver, give an ~ (deliver an ~ to the nation) 2. an eloquent, moving, passionate, stirring ~ 3. a commencement;

inaugural; farewell; keynote ~ 4. in an ~ 5. an ~ about, concerning ["place of residence"] ["place for receiving mail"] 6. to change one's ~ 7. a business; E-mail; forwarding; home; mailing; permanent; return; temporary; (BE) term-time; web-site ~ (let me give you my fax number and my E-mail ~) 8. at an ~ (at what ~ does she live?)

address II v. 1. (B) she ~ed her remarks to us; I ~ed the letter to him 2. (d; tr.) to ~ as (you should ~ him as "sir") 3. (d; tr.) to ~ to (~ her mail to this post-office box) 4. (misc.) ~ smb. by name; ~ smb. directly 5. (d; refl.) ("to deal with") to ~ to (the candidates did not ~ themselves to the issues; the book ~es itself to the problem of poverty) USAGE NOTE: While this reflexive form in the meaning of "to deal with" is used as shown in the examples, nowadays the transitive form is more typical – "the candidates did not address the issues" and "the book addresses the problem of poverty".

add up v. (d; intr.) to ~ to (it all ~s up to a hoax; the figures ~ to fifty)

adept adj. ~ at, in (~ at solving crossword puzzles)

adequate adj. 1. barely, hardly ~ 2. ~ for (the food was not ~ for all of us) 3. ~ to (she was not ~ to the task) 4. ~ to + inf. (it would be ~ to list just the basic objections; the supply is not ~ to meet the demand)

adhere v. 1. to ~ closely, doggedly, strictly, stubbornly, tenaciously 2. (d; intr.) to ~ to (to ~ to a plan that must be strictly ~d to)

adherence n. 1. close, strict ~ 2. ~ to (strict ~ to a plan)

adieu n. to bid smb. ~ = to bid ~ to smb.

adjacent adj. 1. immediately ~ 2. ~ to (immediately ~ to our building)

adjective n. 1. to compare an ~ 2. an attributive; demonstrative; descriptive; gradable; non-gradable; possessive; predicate, predicative ~ 3. ~s modify nouns

adjourn v. 1. (D; intr.) ("to stop") to ~ for (to ~ for lunch = to ~ to have lunch) 2. (d; intr.) ("to move") (to ~ to the living room for brandy)

adjudge v. (formal) (M and N; used with an adjective) the court ~d him (to be) guilty; the project was ~d (to be) impractical

adjunct n. an ~ to (an adverb is often an ~ to a verb)

adjure v. (formal) (H) to ~ smb. to tell the truth

adjust v. 1. to ~ downward; upward (our original estimate had to be ~ed upward (to allow) for inflation) 2. (D. intr., refl., tr.) to ~for; to (he had to ~ to the new climate; we ~ed our watches to (show) local time)

adjuster n. a claims, insurance ~

adjustment n. 1. to make an ~ 2. a price; rate ~ 3. an ~ for; in, of (an ~ in/of his salary (to allow) for inflation; an ~ of the brakes) 4. an ~ to (an ~ to a new environment)

adjutant n. see **general II**

administer v. (B) ("to give") to ~ an oath to smb.

administration n. ["management"] 1. business; public ~ ["government"] 2. a centralized; civil; colonial; decentralized; federal ~ ["body of administrators"] 3. a college, university; hospital; school ~ USAGE NOTE: Consider such phrases as the "Clinton Administration" and the "Thatcher Administration" = the government headed by Clinton/Thatcher.

administrator n. a civil; health; hospital; nursing; school; university ~

admiral n. 1. a rear; vice ~; a fleet ~ (US) = an ~ of the fleet (GB) 2. (misc.) the rank of ~

admiration n. 1. to arouse, win; command ~ 2. to express; feel; show ~ 3. (a) blind; deep, great, sincere, strong, undying; grudging; mutual; secret; ungrudging; universal ~ 4. ~ for (he felt great ~ for them/their achievements) 5. in, with ~ (to look at smb. with ~) 6. (misc.) (humorous) a mutual ~ society

admire v. 1. to ~ greatly, very much 2. (D; tr.) to ~ as (we ~d her as a devoted teacher) 3. (D; tr.) to ~ for (we ~ her for her devotion to teaching) 4. (K) they all ~d his behaving in that manner

admirer n. 1. to attract win; have ~s 2. an ardent, devoted, enthusiastic, fervent, great, sincere; secret ~ 3. (misc.) friends and ~s (devoted circles of friends and ~s)

admission n. ["access"] 1. to apply for; gain; seek ~ 2. to deny, refuse; grant ~ 3. free, open; restricted, selective ~; rolling (esp. AE) ~s 4. ~ to (she applied for ~ to the university) ["confession"] 5. to make an ~ of (he made an ~ of guilt) 6. a damaging ~ 7. a grudging ~ 8. an ~ that + clause (his ~ that he had been at the scene of the crime led to his conviction) 9. by, on smb.'s own ~ ["admission charge"] 10. general ~

admit v. 1. to ~ frankly, freely, openly, publicly, readily 2. to ~ grudgingly, privately 3. (B) ("to confess") the accused ~ted his guilt to the police 4. (D; tr.) ("to allow entry") to ~ into, to (the manager ~ted him to the theater; she was ~ted to the university) 5. (formal) (d; intr.) ("to tolerate") to ~ of (the situation ~s of no delay) 6. (formal) (d; intr.) ("to confess") to ~ to (he ~ted to his complicity in the crime; the boy ~ted to stealing the money; he ~ed to having been bored by the opera) 7. (G) ("to confess") the employee ~ted stealing the money; he ~ed having been bored by the opera 8. (L; to) ("to confess") they ~ privately that their plan has failed but deny it publicly; the clerk ~ted (to the police) that he had stolen the money; I must ~ I was bored by the opera 9. (N) children under the age of five are ~ted free

admittance n. 1. to gain ~ to 2. to deny ~ to (he was denied ~ to the concert)

admonish v. (formal) 1. (D; tr.) to ~ for (the teacher ~ed the child for coming late to school) 2. (H) to ~ smb. to do smt.

ado n. 1. to make much ~ about, over 2. without further, much ~

adopt *v.* (D; tr.) to ~ as (they ~ed the child as their heir)

adoption *n.* to give up, put up for ~ (to put a child up for ~)

adore *v.* 1. (D; tr.) to ~ for (we ~ them for their generosity) 2. (G) she ~s visiting museums 3. (misc.) I ~ it when you look at me like that

adorn *v.* (D; tr.) to ~ with (the table was ~ed with flowers = flowers ~ed the table)

adrenaline, adrenalin *n.* the ~ was flowing USAGE NOTE: Adrenalin is a US trademark.

adrift *adj., adv.* 1. to cast, set ~ 2. to cut ~ (from)

adroit *adj.* ~ at, in (~ at staying out of trouble)

adroitness *n.* ~ at, in (~ at staying out of trouble)

adultery *n.* to commit ~ (with)

adulthood *n.* to reach ~

adults *n.* consenting ~

advance I *n.* ["forward movement"] 1. (usu. mil.) to make; press an ~ 2. (usu. mil.) an ~ against, on, to, towards (our troops made an ~ against the enemy) 3. an ~ into (our troops made an ~ into enemy territory) ["progress"] 4. a scientific; technological ~ 5. an ~ in; on (an ~ in science; a significant ~ on earlier methods) ["early payment"] 6. to receive an ~ 7. to pay an ~ 8. an ~ against/on (to receive an ~ on royalties) ["misc."] 9. she paid her rent in ~; in ~ of the main party 10. (used as in auctions to solicit a higher bid) an ~ on ("Any ~ on twenty one pounds the lot?" – British National Corpus) (see also **advances**)

advance II *v.* 1. (A) we ~d a month's salary to him; or: we ~d him a month's salary 2. (D; intr.) to ~ against, beyond, on, to, towards (our troops ~d on the next town and even beyond it) 3. (D; tr.) to ~ to (he was ~d to the rank of corporal)

advanced *adj.* 1. far; technologically ~ 2. ~ in (far ~ in industrial development; an old man far ~ in years)

advancement *n.* 1. to further, speed smb.'s ~ 2. to block smb.'s ~ 3. personal; professional; social ~ 4. rapid; slow ~ 5. ~ in (~ in one's career)

advances *n.* ["effort to become friendly or to enter into negotiations"] 1. to make ~ to (he made ~ to her) 2. to rebuff, reject smb.'s ~ 3. improper ~ (to rebuff smb.'s improper ~)

advantage *n.* 1. to have an ~ of; over (our team had the ~ of experience; her connections gave her an ~ over the others) 2. to gain; press (home) an ~ 3. to take ~ of ("to exploit") (to take full ~ of one's political connections) 4. to outweigh an ~ 5. an added; big, great; clear, decided, definite, distinct, inestimable, obvious; full; mutual; unfair ~ 6. an ~ for, to (his wealth was an obvious ~ to us) 7. an ~ to + inf. (it was an ~ to have that weak team as our opponent in the first round = it was an ~ having that weak team as our opponent in the first round) 8. the ~ that + clause; may be subj. (it was to his ~ that she not/should not participate; it was to our ~ that they did not participate) 9. to smb.'s

~ (many factors worked to our ~) (see also 8) 10. at an ~ (many factors worked to place/put us at a decided ~) 11. (tennis) ~ in; ~ out 12. (misc.) (BE) you have the ~ of me ("you know more than I do"); their political connections were used/turned to good ~

advantageous *adj.* 1. clearly, obviously ~ 2. ~ for; to (his decision was ~ to us) 3. ~ to + inf. (it would be clearly ~ for us to wait)

advent *n.* 1. since the ~ of (life has changed greatly since the ~ of the computer) 2. with the ~ of (life changed greatly with the ~ of the computer)

adventure *n.* 1. to have, meet with an ~ 2. a bold; breathtaking, exciting, real, thrilling; romantic ~; high ~ 3. an ~ to + inf. (it was an ~ to visit that place = it was an ~ visiting that place) 4. (misc.) a sense/spirit of ~

adventurer *n.* a bold, dauntless, intrepid; unprincipled ~

adverb *n.* 1. an interrogative; negative; sentence ~ 2. an ~ modifies; qualifies

adversary *n.* 1. to come up against an ~ 2. a formidable, powerful; political; worthy ~

adverse *adj.* (formal) ~ to (~ to our interests)

adversity *n.* 1. to face (up to); meet with; overcome ~ 2. (misc.) in (the face of) ~

advert I *n.* (BE) see **advertisement**

advert II *v.* (formal) (d; intr.) ("to refer") to ~ to

advertise *v.* 1. (D; tr.) to ~ as (the match was ~d as the event of the decade) 2. (D; intr.) to ~ for (to ~ for a maid) 3. (L) they ~d that a position as maid was open

advertisement *n.* 1. to place, publish, run an ~ for (to run an ~ for a used car in a newspaper) 2. a classified; full-page; magazine; newspaper ~ 3. an ~ for; in 4. in an ~ (what did it say in the ~?)

advertising *n.* classified; outdoor; word-of-mouth ~

advice *n.* 1. to give, offer ~ 2. to act on, follow, heed, take ~ (take my ~ and remain silent!) 3. to ask for, seek, solicit ~ 4. to disregard, ignore, refuse, turn a deaf ear to ~ 5. good, practical, right, sage, sensible, sound, useful, valuable ~ 6. friendly; parting; unsolicited ~ 7. professional; technical ~ 8. conflicting; misleading; useless; wrong ~ 9. a bit, piece, word of ~ 10. ~ about, on 11. ~ to (my ~ to him was that...) 12. ~ to + inf. (we took his ~ to remain silent) 13. ~ that + clause; subj. (my ~ (to you) is that you remain/should remain silent) 14. against smb.'s ~ 15. on, upon smb.'s ~ (on ~ of counsel; I acted on her ~ to remain silent) 16. (misc.) my ~ fell on deaf ears

advisable *adj.* 1. strongly ~ 2. ~ to + inf. (it was not ~ for her to remain silent) 3. ~ that + clause; subj. (it was ~ that she not remain/should not remain/ didn't remain (BE) silent)

advise *v.* 1. to ~ strongly 2. (D; tr.) to ~ about, on 3. (d; intr., tr.) to ~ against (to ~ smb. against a course of action) 4. (formal) (d; tr.) to ~ of (to ~ smb. of the facts) 5. (G) who ~d remaining silent? 6. (H) she ~d us not to say anything 7. (K) who ~d his remaining silent? 8. (L; may take subj.; must have an object in AE) she ~d (us) that we remain/should remain silent 9. (Q; must have an object) he ~d us what to do; they ~d us where to go

advised *adj.* ill; well ~ to + inf. (you would be well ~ to remain silent)

advisement *n.* (often legal) to take smt. under ~

adviser, advisor *n.* 1. an academic; careers (BE); spiritual ~ 2. an economic; financial; foreign-policy; legal; military; political ~ 3. a senior; technical ~ 4. an ~ on; to (an ~ on foreign policy to the president)

advisory *adj.* 1. merely, only, strictly ~ 2. ~ to

advocate I *n.* 1. an aggressive, strong; ardent ~ (of) 2. a client, patient; consumer ~ 3. (the) devil's ~ (to play the devil's ~)

advocate II *v.* 1. to ~ strongly 2. (G) he ~d remaining silent 3. (K) she ~d our remaining silent 4. (formal) (L; subj.) they ~d that we remain/should remain silent

aegis *n.* under smb.'s ~, under the ~ of

aerial *n.* (esp. BE) a television, TV ~ (AE prefers *antenna*)

aerobics *n.* to do, go in for, take up ~

aeroplane (BE) see **airplane**

aether (old-fashioned BE) see **ether**

afar *adv.* from ~

affair *n.* ["romantic liaison"] 1. to carry on, conduct, have an ~ (with) 2. a casual; clandestine, secret; extramarital, illicit; love; passionate, tempestuous, torrid; scandalous ~ (between; with) ["matter"] ["event"]["situation"]["scandal"] 3. to investigate an ~ 4. to cover up, hush up an/the (whole) ~; to wash one's hands of an/the (whole) ~ 5. a delicate; embarrassing; private ~ 6. a sinister, sordid, ugly; sorry ~ 7. an ~ of honor ["social event"] 8. a dull; exciting ~ 9. a formal; gala; informal ~ 10. a catered ~ ["misc."] 11. a long-drawn-out ~ (see also **affairs**)

affairs *n.* 1. to administer, conduct ~ (of state) 2. to arrange; manage, run; settle one's ~ 3. to put one's ~ in order 4. to straighten out one's ~ 5. to wind up one's ~ 6. civil; community; cultural ~ 7. domestic, home (BE), internal; external, foreign; international; national ~ 8. legal; military; political; public; veterans' (AE) ~ 9. current ~ 10. (misc.) to interfere, meddle in smb.'s ~; a state of ~ (see also *affairs of state* at **state I** *n.*)

affect *v.* 1. to ~ adversely; deeply, profoundly, strongly 2. (formal) (esp. BE) (E) he ~ed not to hear

affection *n.* 1. to demonstrate, display, show; return ~ 2. to feel; have ~ 3. to gain, win smb.'s ~ (she won the children's ~) 4. abiding; deep, great, strong, warm; genuine, real; mutual ~ 5. little ~ 6. ~ for (to feel ~ for smb.) 7. with ~ 8. (misc.) a token of smb.'s ~

affectionate *adj.* ~ to, towards, with (~ with children)

affections *n.* 1. to gain, win smb.'s ~ 2. to alienate smb.'s ~ 3. (misc.) the object of smb.'s ~ ("the object of my ~ can change my complexion from white to rosy red" – popular song)

affidavit *n.* (legal) 1. to file, submit; sign an ~ (the lawyer filed an ~ on behalf of her client) 2. a sworn ~

affiliate *v.* (D; intr., refl., tr.) to ~ to, with (to ~ oneself with a national movement; they are ~d with a national movement; to become ~d with)

affiliation *n.* 1. to form, have an ~ 2. business; party, political ~s 3. an ~ to, with

affinity *n.* 1. to demonstrate, show (an) ~ 2. to feel; have (an) ~ 3. (a) close; elective; natural; strong ~ 4. ~ between; for; to; with (he always felt a close ~ with the underdog)

affirm *v.* (L; to) to the ministry ~ed (to us) that the visit had been postponed; he did not swear on the Bible, but said "I do solemnly, sincerely and truly declare and ~ that I shall tell the truth" (– adapted from *Quaker Faith and Practice*)

affirmation *n.* ~ that + clause (I believed the ministry's ~ (to us) that the visit had been postponed)

affirmative *n.* to answer, reply in the ~

affix *v.* (D; tr.) to ~ to (to ~ one's signature to a document)

afflicted *adj.* 1. grievously, severely ~ 2. ~ with (~ with a disease)

affluence *n.* in ~ (to live in ~)

afford *v.* 1. to barely, ill; easily, well ~ 2. (formal) (A) it ~ed great pleasure to him; or: it ~ed him great pleasure 3. (E; preceded by the forms: can – cannot – can't – could – couldn't) we cannot ~ to buy a new house; we can ill ~ to lose this contract = we cannot ~ not to keep this contract 4. (formal) (K; preceded by the forms: can – cannot – can't – could – couldn't) we couldn't ~ his signing up for another course

affront *n.* 1. (formal) to suffer an ~ 2. a personal; shocking ~ 3. an ~ to (it was an ~ to common decency)

afloat *adj.* 1. to keep smt. ~ (to try to keep a company ~ in a recession) 2. to set (a ship) ~ 3. to keep, stay ~

aflutter *adj.* (colloq.) 1. all ~ 2. ~ with (~ with excitement)

afoul *adv.* (AE) to fall, run ~ of (to run ~ of the law) (also **foul I**)

afraid *adj.* 1. deathly (formal), terribly, very, very much ~ 2. ~ for (to be ~ for the future; he was ~ for her/for her safety) 3. ~ of (the child was ~ of the dark even though the dark is nothing to be ~ of; he was ~ of diving off the high board) 4. ~ to + inf. (he was ~ to dive off the high board) 5. ~ that + clause (we were ~ that he would find out) 6. (misc.) is it true? I'm ~ so; is she coming? I'm ~ not; "the answer is 41!" "I'm afraid you're wrong: it's 42." USAGE NOTE: You will often hear such expressions as "? I'm afraid to say you're wrong."

That is an unnecessary blend of "I'm afraid you're wrong" with "I'm sorry to say you're wrong." Do not use it.

after I *adv.* 1. immediately; long; shortly, soon; well ~ 2. the day; morning ~ 3. forever ~

after II *prep.* the police were ~ them

afterburners *n.* to activate, go to ~ (our interceptors had to go to ~)

aftereffects *n.* to feel the ~ (of)

afterglow *n.* to bask in the ~ (of)

aftermath *n.* 1. a grim; immediate ~ 2. an ~ of, (AE) to 3. in the ~ (in the ~ of that incident, he had to leave town) 4. to deal with the ~ of

afternoon *n.* 1. all ~; during the ~; in the ~ (they left early / late in the ~ = they left in the early / late ~); ~s (AE), every ~; the next, the following ~; this ~; that ~; tomorrow ~; yesterday ~; a June ~; a summer ~; on any ~; on/during the ~ of (they left on the ~ of July 26); on Wednesday ~ = Wednesday ~ (AE) 2. an ~ of (after an ~ of conversation, they spent the evening together) 3. from ~ (from ~ to evening) 4. (misc.) the ~ drew to a close; (Good) Afternoon (, everybody)!; to have; spend an ~ (we had a pleasant ~ at a museum; we spent the whole ~ working on the report)

aftershave *n.* to apply, put on; use ~

aftertaste *n.* 1. to leave an ~ 2. a bitter, unpleasant; nice, pleasant ~ (it left a pleasant ~)

afterthought *n.* as an ~ (the most important detail came out almost as an ~)

afterward (AE), **afterwards** see **after I**

agape *adj.* (formal) ["gaping"] ~ with (~ with astonishment)

age *n.* ["stage of life"] 1. to live to, reach an ~ 2. an advanced, great, venerable ~ (she lived to a great ~) (see also **old age**) 3. an early, tender, young; impressionable ~ (at an early ~; at a very young ~) 4. middle ~ 5. college; high-school (AE); preschool; school ~ 6. (a) retirement, retiring (BE); voting ~ 7. (a) legal ~; the ~ of consent 8. at an ~ (at a tender ~; at the ~ of six; she died at the age of eighty); between the ~s of X and Y (teenagers between the ~s of 13 and 19); by an ~ (Mozart was composing music by the tender ~ of six!); from an ~ to an ~; over an ~; under an ~ (children under the ~ of five are admitted free) 9. of an ~ (people of all ~s; of childbearing ~) 10. (misc.) to come of ~ ("to reach adulthood"); to act one's ~ ("to behave maturely"); to look, show one's ~ ("to not have a youthful appearance"); to feel one's ~ ("to feel old"); over ~ ("too old"); under ~ ("too young"); in old ~ ("of advanced years") ["era"]["period"] 11. to usher in an ~ (to usher in the computer ~) 12. a golden; heroic ~ 13. the Dark; Middle ~s (during the Middle ~s) 14. the Bronze; Ice; Iron; Stone ~ 15. the atomic, nuclear; computer; space ~ 16. in an ~ (in the nuclear ~) 17. for ~s (and ~s) 18. through the ~s (true down through the ~s) 19. absolutely, simply ~s (it's been simply ~s since

we did lunch!) USAGE NOTE: In AE you will often hear such phrases as "She died at age 80." Its equivalents in World English are "She died at the age of 80" or "She died at 80 years of age" or "She died aged 80" or just "She died at 80."

agency *n.* 1. an adoption; health-care; home-health (AE); welfare ~ 2. a private; public; voluntary ~ 3. an advertising; detective; employment; escort; ticket; travel ~ 4. an aid; government; intelligence; law-enforcement; regulatory; watchdog ~ 5. a news ~ 6. at, in an ~; through an ~ (she works at a travel ~; she booked her flight through a travel ~)

agenda *n.* 1. to draw up, make up, put together; set an ~ 2. to place, put smt. on the ~ (to put an item on the ~) 3. a hidden ~ ("a secret plan") 4. an item on the ~ 5. (misc.) high on the ~

agent *n.* ["representative"] 1. an estate (BE), real-estate (AE); insurance ~ 2. a literary; press ~ 3. a purchasing; shipping ~ 4. a ticket; travel ~ (she booked her flight through a travel ~) 5. a free ~ 6. an ~ for (an ~ for a large firm) ["smb. engaged in intelligence activities"] 7. a double; enemy; espionage, secret, undercover; special ~ 8. (misc.) an ~ provocateur ["substance"] 9. an asphyxiating; chemical; toxic ~ 10. a cleaning; cleansing ~

aggrandizement *n.* personal; territorial ~

aggregate *n.* in the ~

aggression *n.* ["attack"] 1. to commit ~ (against) 2. to repel ~ 3. armed; brazen, flagrant, naked, outright, stark, unprovoked ~ ["aggressiveness"] 4. to display, express, manifest, show ~ 5. to channel, direct; control, stifle ~ 6. deep-rooted, deep-seated, hidden ~ 7. an act of ~ (to commit an act of ~)

aggrieved *adj.* ~ at, by

aghast *adj.* 1. ~ at (~ at the very thought of going back to work) 2. ~ to + inf. (they were ~ to learn of the bank's failure)

agitate *v.* 1. to ~ strongly 2. (D; intr.) to ~ against; for (they were ~ing for reform)

agitation *n.* 1. political; student; subversive ~ 2. against; for (their ~ for reform) 3. (misc.) in a state of great ~ ("feeling high anxiety")

agitator *n.* a political ~

aglow *adj.* ~ with (~ with happiness)

ago *adv.* 1. ~ that + clause (it was five years ~ that we met) 2. (misc.) ages (and ages) ~; a week ~; a long time ~, long ~; a while ~; many years ~, years (and years) ~

agog *adj.* 1. all ~ 2. ~ over; with (she was all ~ over her new granddaughter) 3. ~ to + inf. (they were all ~ to hear the news)

agonize *v.* (D; intr.) to ~ about, over (to ~ over a decision)

agony *n.* 1. to endure, experience, feel, go through ~ 2. to prolong the ~ 3. acute, deep, great, indescribable, untold; unbearable; mortal ~ 4. in ~ (in great ~)

agree *v.* 1. ("to concur") to ~ completely, entirely,

fully, totally, wholeheartedly; readily 2. (D; intr.) ("to concur") to ~ about; on; to; upon; with (to ~ with smb. about smt.; to ~ on/to a plan) 3. (d; intr.) (of food, climate) to ~ with ("to suit") (the food doesn't ~ with me) 4. (grammar) (D; intr.) ("to correspond") to ~ in; with (Latin adjectives ~ with nouns in gender) 5. (E) ("to consent") they ~d to help 6. (L) ("to concur") we ~d that everyone would receive an equal share 7. (misc.) I could not ~ more USAGE NOTE: In BE, *agree* can be used as a transitive verb – *to agree a plan*. It can mean both 'to agree on a common plan' and 'to agree to smb. else's plan.' In BE, one can say – *Let's all follow the agreed plan*. In World English, that would be – *Let's all follow the agreed-on plan* or *Let's all follow the plan agreed on/agreed to*.

agreeable *adj.* 1. mutually ~ 2. ~ to (they were all ~ to our proposal; is that ~ to you?)

agreement *n.* ["contract, settlement, treaty"] 1. to arrive at, come to, conclude, enter into, negotiate, reach an ~ 2. to draw up, hammer out, make, work out an ~ 3. to seal, sign an ~ 4. to adhere to, be bound by, carry out, honor, live up to, stick to an ~ 5. to break, violate an ~ 6. to cancel, denounce, rescind an ~ 7. a binding; contractual; ironclad; legal; oral, verbal; secret; tacit; tentative; written ~ (we reached a tentative ~) 8. a prenuptial ~ 9. an armistice, ceasefire, peace ~ 10. an arms-control, nonproliferation ~ 11. a sales, trade ~ 12. a bilateral; international; multilateral ~ 13. an ~ about, on; between; with (an ~ was worked out between them on all points) 14. an ~ to + inf. (we reached an ~ with them to cooperate fully at all times) 15. an ~ that + clause (the negotiators came to an ~ that all troops would/should be withdrawn) ["concord, harmony"] 16. to express; reach ~ 17. basic, essential; bipartisan; complete, full, solid, total, unanimous; mutual; tacit ~ (they reached full ~ on all points) 18. ~ about, on, over 19. by ~ (by mutual ~) 20. in ~ (with) (we were in full ~ with them on all points = we were fully in ~ with them on all points; we were in ~ with them that all troops would/should be withdrawn) ["grammatical concord"] 21. grammatical ~ 22. ~ in (~ in case, gender, and number)

aground *adj.*, *adv.* to run ~ (the ship ran ~)

ahead *adj.*, *adv.* 1. comfortably, considerably, far, way, well ~ 2. ~ by (our team was ~ by three points) 3. ~ of (~ of the other competitors; to finish ~ of schedule; to try to reach agreement ~ of the conference) 4. (misc.) dead, straight ~; full speed ~; Danger ~!

aid I *n.* 1. to extend, give, offer, provide, render ~ 2. to come to, go to smb.'s ~ 3. to cut, reduce ~ 4. to cut off, withdraw ~ 5. to increase ~ 6. generous, unstinting ~ 7. audiovisual; teaching; visual ~s (to employ, use visual ~s) 8. first ~ (first ~ to the injured) (see also **first aid**) 9. a hearing ~ 10. economic, financial; emergency; federal (in the US); foreign; government; humanitarian; military;

state (in the US) ~ 11. legal ~ (for the poor) 12. (an) ~ for; from; in; to (an ~ to memorization; economic ~ to developing countries from an unlikely source) 13. with; without the ~ of (to walk with the ~ of crutches) 14. (misc.) to enlist smb.'s; to go to smb.'s ~; (BE; colloq.) what's all this in ~ of? ("what's all this for?")

aid II *v.* 1. (D; tr.) to ~ in, with (we ~ed them in their work; she ~ed me with the translation) 2. (rare) (H) to ~ smb. to do smt. (we ~ed them to do their work; she ~ed us to move the furniture) (see also *aid and abet* at **abet**)

aide *n.* 1. a home health ~ (AE) (BE has *home help*) 2. a military; presidential; senior ~ 3. an ~ to

AIDS *n.* 1. HIV / ~; full-blown ~ 2. to contract, develop, get; have ~ 3. a case of ~

ailment *n.* 1. a chronic; common; minor, slight; physical; serious ~ 2. a back; heart; kidney; skin; stomach ~ (for additional combinations, see **disease, illness**)

aim I *n.* ["purpose"]["goal"] 1. to achieve one's; set oneself an ~ 2. a chief; immediate; long-range, long-term; short-term ~ 3. an avowed; idealistic, lofty, worthy; unrealistic ~ 4. an ~ to + inf. (it was our ~ to complete the work before the end of the month) 5. with an ~ (the project was launched with the ~ of retraining the unemployed) ["aiming of a weapon"] 6. to take ~ at 7. careful; steady ~ (she took careful ~ at the intruder)

aim II *v.* 1. (D; intr., tr.) to ~ at (he ~ed at me; she ~ed the revolver at the intruder) 2. (d; intr.) to ~ for (she ~ed for the heart; he was ~ing for a promotion) 3. (E) we ~ to please 4. (misc.) to ~ high (fig.) ("~ for the highest, expect the least, and you'll never be disappointed" – proverb); Ready, Aim, Fire!

air I *n.* ["atmosphere"] 1. to clear the ~ 2. to breathe (in), inhale; exhale ~ 3. to pollute the ~ 4. balmy, mild; bracing, brisk, crisp, refreshing; clean; compressed; country; dry; foul; fresh; frigid; humid; moist; open; polluted; sea; stale ~ 5. a breath of (fresh) ~; a blast of hot ~; a puff, whiff of ~ 6. in the ~; through the ~ (the decisive battles were fought in the ~; a political demonstration held in the open ~; how fast does sound travel through the ~?) ["transportation by aircraft"] 7. by ~ (to travel by ~) ["medium through which radio signals are transmitted"] 8. on the ~ (to go on (the) ~; our station is on the ~) 9. off the ~ (that station never goes off the ~) ["appearance"] 10. to assume an ~ (to assume an ~ of innocence) 11. a detached; knowing; nonchalant; superior, triumphant ~ ["tune"] 12. a martial ~ (the band struck up a martial ~) ["misc."] 13. in the ~ ("current, imminent"); to walk on ~ ("to be elated"); to give smb. the ~ ("to reject smb."); up in the ~ ("unsettled"); to disappear into thin ~

air II *v.* 1. (B) he is ready to ~ his views to anyone 2. (P) (esp. AE) the program will ~ on Saturday night.

air conditioner *n.* 1. to run; turn on an ~ 2. to turn

off an ~ 3. a central; room ~ 4. the ~ was on, was running

air conditioning *n.* 1. central ~ 2. the ~ was on, was running

air raid *n.* to carry out, conduct an ~ against

aircraft *n.* 1. commercial; enemy; friendly; jet; military; private; unidentified ~ 2. (misc.) to shoot down enemy ~; lowflying ~ strafed enemy lines; to ground all ~ (see also **airplane**)

airing *n.* ["public discussion"] 1. to give smt. an ~ (they gave our proposal a good ~ at the conference) ["ventilation"] 2. to give smt. an ~ (we gave the blankets a good ~)

airlift *v.* (D; tr.) to ~ from; to (the refugees were ~ed to safety from the flooded areas)

airline *n.* 1. a domestic; feeder; international, overseas; local ~ 2. an ~ flies (an ~ that flies mostly between New York and Puerto Rico)

airmail *n.* by ~ (to send a letter by ~)

airplane (AE), **aeroplane** (BE) *n.* 1. to board, get on; take an ~ 2. to get off an ~ 3. to bring down, land; ditch; fly, pilot; navigate an ~ (a pilot flies an ~) 4. to bring down, shoot down; force down; hijack an ~ (enemy fire brought down our ~) 5. a jet; propeller-driven ~ 6. an ~ banks; crashes; cruises; flies; gains altitude; lands, touches down; levels off; loses altitude; reaches an altitude; takes off; taxis along the runway (see also **aircraft**, **plane**)

airport *n.* 1. an international; local; military ~ 2. at an ~

airs *n.* ["affected manners"] 1. to give oneself, put on ~ 2. (misc.) (BE) ~ and graces

air show *n.* to have, hold, put on, stage an ~

air space *n.* to enter; respect; violate a country's ~

air superiority *n.* 1. to establish; gain ~ 2. complete, overwhelming, total ~

aisle *n.* 1. to clear the ~s 2. in the ~ (don't stand in the ~) 3. on the ~ (to sit on the ~) 4. (misc.) to roll in the ~s ("to laugh heartily"); across the ~ (AE) ("so as to co-operate in a bi-partisan way with smb. from another political party") (unlike the other candidates, I've always been willing to reach across the ~ to win support for a good bill)

ajar *adj.* to leave ~ (she left the door ~)

akin *adj.* (formal) (usu. does not stand alone) ~ to (a feeling somewhat ~ to love)

alarm *n.* ["warning device"]["warning"] 1. to activate; give, raise, set off, sound; set; trigger, trip an ~ (she set the ~ to go off at five) 2. to deactivate, turn off an ~ 3. an air-raid; burglar; fire; silent; smoke ~ 4. a false ~ 5. an ~ goes off, rings, sounds ["apprehension, fear"] 6. to express; feel ~ 7. to cause; spread ~ (the incident caused great ~) 8. ~ at, over (to express ~ at the danger of war) 9. ~ that + clause (she expressed ~ that they would miss the train) 10. in, with ~

alarm clock *n.* 1. to set an ~ (she set the ~ to go off at five) 2. an ~ goes off, rings, sounds (the ~ went off at five)

alarmed *adj.* 1. unduly ~ 2. ~ at, by (we were ~ at the news of the earthquake) USAGE NOTE: Currently *alarmed* is also used in the meaning "provided with an alarm" – *this room is alarmed*.

alarming *adj.* 1. ~ to + inf. (it was ~ (for us) to think of the possible danger of war) 2. ~ that + clause (it was ~ (to us) that there was still a possible danger of war)

album *n.* 1. an autograph; family; photograph; stamp; wedding ~ 2. in an ~

alcohol *n.* 1. to distill, make ~ 2. to abstain from; consume, drink ~ 3. to reek of ~ 4. ethyl, grain; methyl, wood; pure, unadulterated; rubbing (AE; BE has *surgical spirit*) ~ 5. a unit; level of ~ (don't consume more than the recommended number of units of ~ a week; the driver's blood contained high levels of ~)

alcoholic *n.* a chronic ~

alcoholism *n.* acute; chronic ~

ale *n.* see **beer**

alert I *adj.* 1. to keep, stay ~ 2. ~ to (~ to danger)

alert II *n.* 1. to call an ~ 2. to place, put (troops) on ~ 3. to call off, cancel an ~ 4. (a) full; high; preliminary; red ~ (the troops were on full ~) 5. on (the) ~ (for) (to be on the ~ for trouble) 6. (misc.) in a state of ~

alert III *v.* (D; tr.) to ~ to (we must ~ the public to the danger)

A-levels *n.* ["Advanced-level secondary-school examinations"] (in the UK except Scotland) 1. to do, sit, take one's; to get, obtain; have ~ 2. in one's ~ (to do well in one's French and German ~) 3. ~ in (to have ~ in French and German)

algebra *n.* to do ~

alias *n.* 1. to adopt, use an ~ 2. an ~ for 3. under an ~

alibi *n.* 1. to give; have; provide an ~ (for) 2. to check out, confirm smb.'s ~ 3. to break, disprove an ~ 4. an airtight, cast-iron, foolproof, unassailable ~ 5. his ~ held up; collapsed

alien I *adj.* (formal) completely, totally, utterly ~ to (such ideas are totally ~ to us)

alien II *n.* 1. to deport; intern an ~ 2. an enemy; illegal; resident ~

alienate *v.* (D; tr.) to ~ from (she was ~d from her family)

alienation *n.* ~ from (~ from one's family)

alight *v.* (formal) (D; intr.) to ~ from; on (to ~ from a vehicle; to ~ on a branch)

align *v.* (D; refl., tr.) to ~ along; with (the wheels must be correctly ~ed with the frame along both sides of the vehicle; he ~ed himself with the left wing of the party)

alignment *n.* in; into; out of ~ (the wheels are out of ~ and must be brought back into ~)

alike *adj.* 1. very, very much ~ 2. ~ in (the sisters are very (much) ~ in all respects; "two households, both ~ in dignity" – Shakespeare, *Romeo and Juliet*) 3. (misc.) as ~ as two peas in a pod

alimony n. (esp. AE) to award, grant; pay ~ (the judge awarded the ex-wife ~) USAGE NOTE: BE now prefers *maintenance*.

alive adj. 1. keenly; very much ~ ("is he still ~?" "yes, indeed: he's (still) very much ~!") 2. (cannot stand alone) ~ to (keenly ~ to the danger of becoming overconfident; ~ to the beauty of nature) 3. ~ with (the campus was ~ with students) 4. (misc.) ~ and kicking, ~ and well ("is he still ~?" "yes, indeed: he's (still) ~ and kicking; in fact, he's ~ and well and living in Argentina!")

all I n. to give one's ~

all II *pronoun, determiner* 1. ~ in ~ (there were about 50 of them ~ in ~ = ~ in ~, there were about 50 ot them) (see also *all together* at **together**; *all told* at **told**) 2. ~ of (we saw ~ of them) USAGE NOTE: The use of the preposition *of* is necessary when a pronoun follows – *the dean saw all of them* ('the dean saw them all'). When a noun follows, three constructions are possible *the dean saw all of the students (on the list)* = *the dean saw all the students (on the list)* = *the dean saw all students (on the list)*.

all clear n. 1. to give, sound the ~ 2. the ~ sounded

allegation n. ["assertion"] 1. to make; substantiate an ~ 2. to drop, retract, withdraw an ~ 3. to deny, reject; rebut, refute an ~ 4. a false; serious; slanderous; unproved, unsubstantiated, unsupported; vague ~ 5. an ~ about; against; of (~s of theft were made against him) 6. an ~ that + clause (their ~ that he had stolen the money proved to be false)

allege v. (L) it has been ~d that he stole the money = they have ~d that he stole the money

alleged adj. ~ to + inf. (he was ~ to have stolen the money)

allegiance n. 1. to give; owe; pledge, swear ~ ("I pledge ~ to the Flag of the United States of America" – U.S. oath) 2. to change, switch one's ~; to change, switch ~s (from; to) 3. to disavow, forsake one's ~ to 4. true, unfailing, unswerving ~ 5. changing, shifting ~s 6. ~ to (~ to a cause)

allergic adj. ~ to (~ to dust)

allergy n. to acquire, develop; have an ~ to

alliance n. 1. to enter into, forge, form; cement an ~ 2. to disband, dissolve an ~ 3. a broad; close; defense, military; political; uneasy; unholy ~ 4. an ~ against; between; of; with (to form an ~ with one's neighbors against the common enemy = to form an ~ of neighbors against a common enemy) 5. an ~ to + inf. (an ~ to defend an area against any invader) 6. in ~ with

allied adj. ~ against; to, with (we were ~ with our neighbors against the common enemy)

allocate v. 1. (B; more rarely – A) the dean ~d the funds to several students 2. (D; tr.) to ~ for (our committee ~d money for the memorial)

allocation n. 1. to make an ~ 2. a budget ~ 3. an ~ for; to

allot v. 1. (A) the city has ~ted space to us; or: the

city has ~ted us space 2. (D; tr.) to ~ for/to (to ~ funds for/to the arts)

allow v. 1. (A; usu. without the preposition *to*) ("to permit") she did not ~ herself time for relaxation 2. (d; intr.) ("to provide") to ~ for (we ~ed for their difference in age; you must ~ for shrinkage) 3. (D; tr.) ("to give") to ~ for (they ~ed an hour for lunch) 4. (formal) (d; intr.) to ~ of ("to permit") (our financial situation ~s of no unnecessary expenditures) 5. (H) ("to permit") we ~ed the children to go to the park 6. (formal) (L) ("to admit") I must ~ that he is capable 7. (O; can be used with one inanimate object) ("to permit") the doctors ~ two meals a day; the doctors ~ him two meals a day; she ~ed herself one glass of wine USAGE NOTE: In some regional varieties of English, the example *I must allow that he is capable* could become *I'll have to allow as how he knows his stuff.*

allowance n. ["taking into account"] 1. to make (an) ~ for (to make ~/~s/an ~ for inexperience; to make ~s for wear and tear) ["sum granted"] 2. to draw; give, grant an ~ 3. to live on an ~ 4. a cost-of-living; depletion; entertainment; housing; mileage; subsistence; trade-in; travel ~ 5. a daily; fixed; weekly ~ 6. an ~ for ["amount allowed"] 7. a baggage; duty-fee ~ USAGE NOTE: Parents may regularly give their children *pocket money*, which in AE is called *an allowance*.

all right adj. (colloq.) ~ to + inf. (it's ~ (for us) to take a break) USAGE NOTE: The spelling *alright* is common but should be avoided. Thus the following example is ambiguous – *the answers are all right*. It can mean either 'the answers are all correct' or 'the answers are OK; i.e., just about acceptable.'

allude v. 1. to ~ vaguely 2. (d; intr.) to ~ to (she didn't ~ to the incident)

allusion n. 1. to make an ~ to (she made no ~ to the incident) 2. to contain an ~ (the statement contains several ~s to the incident) 3. a direct; indirect, oblique; literary; passing; vague, (thinly) veiled ~ (she made a thinly veiled ~ to the incident)

ally I n. 1. a close, faithful, staunch; ~ 2. an ~ against; in (in our friends we felt we had natural ~s in our struggle against the common enemy)

ally II v. (D; intr., refl.) to ~ against; in; to, with (we ~ied ourselves with our friends in our struggle against the common enemy)

alms n. (formal) 1. to dispense, give ~ 2. ~ for; to (~ for the needy)

alone adj. 1. very (much) 2. to leave, let smb./smt. ~ 3. to be, stand ~ 4. ~ against; in (to be ~ in one's grief; to stand ~ in one's struggle ~ against the whole world) 5. (misc.) to live ~; she's all ~ (in the world)

aloof adj. 1. entirely; largely ~ 2. to hold oneself, keep, remain, stand ~ 3. ~ from (he remained entirely ~ from the others)

alphabet n. 1. the Arabic; Cyrillic; Greek; Hebrew; Latin, Roman; Phoenician; Sanskrit ~ 2. a phonetic; runic ~ 3. in an ~ (there are 26 letters in our ~)

altar *n.* 1. at; before; on the ~ (the priest stood at/before the ~ and laid a pinch of incense on it) 2. to lead smb. to the ~ (to marry smb.; typically, to marry a woman)

alteration *n.* 1. to make an ~ 2. a major; minor, slight ~ 3. an ~ in, to

altercation *n.* (formal) 1. to have an ~ 2. an ~ about, over; between; with (to have an ~ with smb. about smt.)

alternate *v.* 1. (D; intr.) to ~ between (they ~ between supporting us and opposing us) 2. (D; intr.) to ~ in (we ~ in doing the household chores) 3. (d; intr., tr.) to ~ with (sunny weather ~d with rain; the coach ~d Jones with/and Wilson)

alternative *n.* 1. to propose an ~ 2. to fall back on an ~ 3. a real, realistic, viable ~ 4. an ~ to 5. no ~ (but, except/(formal) save) ("There Is No Alternative" – attributed to Margaret Thatcher; we have no ~ but/except/save persistence) 6. no ~ but/except/(formal) save to + inf. (we have no ~ but/except/save to persist)

altitude *n.* 1. to gain ~; to reach an ~ of 2. to lose ~ 3. a cruising ~ 4. at an ~ (at high ~s)

altogether *n.* ["nude state"] in the ~

amalgamate *v.* (D; intr., tr.) to ~ with (our firm will be ~d with a Japanese company – unless we ~ (it) with a British one first!)

amateur *n.* 1. a rank ~ 2. an ~ at, in

amaze *v.* (R) it ~d her (to learn) that he had been promoted so quickly

amazed *adj.* 1. ~ at, by (she was ~ at his quick promotion) 2. ~ to + inf. (she was ~ to learn of his quick promotion) 3. ~ that + clause (she was ~ that he had been promoted so quickly)

amazement *n.* 1. complete, sheer, total, utter 2. ~ at (she expressed (her) ~ at his quick promotion) 3. in, with ~ (they stared in ~) 4. to smb.'s ~ (to her utter ~, he was promoted quickly)

amazing *adj.* 1. ~ to + inf. (it was (for her) ~ to learn of his quick promotion) 2. ~ that + clause (it was ~ (to her) that he had been promoted so quickly)

ambassador *n.* 1. to appoint an ~; to exchange ~s 2. to recall an ~ 3. an ~ extraordinary; an ~ plenipotentiary; an ambassador-at-large 4. a goodwill; roving ~ 5. an ~ to (our ~ to Italy)

ambiguity *n.* 1. to clear up, remove an ~; to avoid ~ 2. a certain, a degree of, an element of ~ 3. an ~ about, concerning (a certain ~ about exactly what you want) 4. ~ arises, occurs (a certain ~ can arise in the absence of clarification)

ambition *n.* 1. to achieve, attain, fulfill, realize one's ~; cherish, harbor, have an ~ 2. to spur, stir smb.'s ~ 3. to limit, restrain one's ~ 4. boundless, unbridled; burning, consuming, devouring; driving, overriding ~ 5. frustrated; unrealized ~ 6. personal; political ~ 7. territorial ~s (of an aggressor) 8. an ~ to + inf. (he achieved his ~ to become mayor)

ambitious *adj.* (formal) 1. ~ for (a father ~ for his daughter) 2. (esp. BE) ~ to + inf. (she is ~ to succeed; a father ~ for his daughter to succeed)

ambivalent *adj.* ~ about; toward

amble *v.* (P; intr.) to ~ along the road

ambush *n.* 1. to lay, set an ~ for 2. to draw smb. into an ~ 3. to hide, lie, lurk, wait in ~ (for) 4. to run into, walk into an ~ 5. in; from ~ (to attack from ~; to die in an ~) 6. an ~ takes place (the ~ took place on a deserted country road)

amen *n.* 1. to say ~ 2. (informal) to say ~ to ("to endorse") (I'll say ~ to that any day!)

amenable *adj.* ~ to (~ to compromise)

amendment *n.* 1. to adopt; propose; ratify an ~ 2. a constitutional ~ 3. an ~ to (an ~ to the constitution)

amends *n.* to make ~ (for) (she wanted to make ~ for the damage that she had caused)

amenities *n.* ["comforts"] 1. basic ~ 2. to lack, provide ~ (for) (the house lacks even the most basic ~, such as running water) ["greetings"] (AE) 3. to exchange ~ ["proper manners"] 4. to observe the ~

American *n.* 1. a Native ~ ("an American Indian of the US") 2. General ~ ("the standardized English alleged to be spoken in most of the US")

amiss *adj., adv.* (formal) 1. to take smt. ~ 2. to go ~ (a little courtesy would not go ~)

ammunition *n.* 1. to provide ~ for (also fig.) 2. to issue ~ 3. blank; dummy; live; tracer ~ 4. a round of ~

amnesty *n.* 1. to announce, declare, grant, offer (an) ~ (he was granted ~) 2. a full; general; partial; political ~ 3. an ~ for (the government declared a general ~ for political prisoners)

amok, amuck *adv.* to run ~

amount I *n.* 1. to calculate, figure out an ~ 2. an ample, considerable, enormous, huge, large, tremendous; limited; moderate, modest; negligible, paltry, small ~ 3. the exact; full ~ 4. in ~ (small in ~ but high in quality) 5. (misc.) an equivalent ~ in francs

amount II *v.* (d; intr.) to ~ to (it ~s to fraud; he'll never ~ to anything)

amuse *v.* 1. to ~ greatly, thoroughly, very much 2. (D; refl., tr.) to ~ by, with (she ~d the children with tricks; they ~d themselves by playing games) 3. (R) it ~d us to watch them play; it ~d me that they would never admit to being wrong

amused *adj.* 1. easily; greatly, highly, thoroughly, vastly, very (much) ~ 2. ~ at, by; with (she was ~ at/by that story; children can be easily ~ with tricks) 3. ~ to + inf. (I was ~ to see him playing up to the boss) 4. to keep smb. ~ (he kept the children ~ by reading stories)

amusement *n.* 1. to provide ~ for 2. to find ~ in 3. in, with ~ (to look on in/with ~) 4. to smb.'s ~ (much to my ~, everyone believed her story)

amusing *adj.* 1. highly, very; not in the least ~ 2. ~ to (it was not in the least amusing ~ to anyone)

3. ~ to + inf. (it was (for us) ~ to watch the trained elephants perform)

anaemia (esp. BE) see **anemia**

anaesthesia (esp. BE) see **anesthesia**

anaesthetic (esp. BE) see **anesthetic**

analogous *adj.* 1. roughly ~ 2. ~ to, with

analogy *n.* 1. to draw, make an ~ 2. a close; rough, superficial ~ (there is a close ~ between these two phenomena) 3. an ~ between; to, with 4. by ~ (to reason by ~ with a related phenomenon) 5. on the ~ of (to say *thunk* on the analogy of *sunk*) 6. an ~ holds (good) (upon further analysis the ~ between X and Y just doesn't hold)

analysis *n.* ["examination of component parts"] 1. to carry out, do, make an ~ (of) 2. a careful, detailed, painstaking, thorough, thoroughgoing; critical; in-depth; objective; penetrating; subjective ~ 3. (ling.) discourse ~ 4. (chemistry) qualitative; quantitative ~ 5. (math.) vector ~ (see also *systems analysis* at **system**) 6. on, upon ~ (upon further ~, we concluded that...) 7. in the final, last, ultimate ~ ["psychoanalysis"] 8. to have, undergo (an) ~ (with) (to have (an) ~ with Freud himself!) 9. in ~ (with) (she was in ~ with Freud himself!)

analyst *n.* 1. financial; political ~ (see also *systems analyst* at **system**) ["psychoanalyst"] 2. to see an ~

anarchy *n.* 1. complete, total, utter ~ 2. to descend, slide into 3. ~ reigns

anathema *n.* ~ to (his theories were ~ to his colleagues)

anatomy *n.* comparative; descriptive; human ~

ancestor *n.* a common; remote ~

ancestry *n.* 1. to trace one's ~ (back to) 2. of (a certain) ~ (to be of French ~)

anchor I *n.* 1. to cast, drop ~ 2. to raise, weigh ~ 3. at ~ (to ride at ~)

anchor II *v.* 1. to ~ fast, firmly, securely 2. to ~ to (a boat ~ed securely to a dock)

anecdote *n.* 1. to relate, tell an ~ 2. an amusing, funny, witty; off-color; personal ~ 3. an ~ about

anemia (AE), (esp. BE) **anaemia** *n.* 1. to develop, have ~ 2. pernicious; sickle-cell ~

anesthesia (AE), (esp. BE) **anaesthesia** *n.* 1. to induce, produce ~ 2. to have, undergo ~ 3. general; local ~ 4. the ~ takes effect; wears off 5. under ~

anesthetic (AE), (esp. BE) **anaesthetic** *n.* 1. to administer, give an ~ 2. to have an ~ 3. a general; local ~ 4. to come around, round from an ~ ("The ~ from which none come round" – Philip Larkin, "Aubade" (1977)) 5. an ~ takes effect; wears off 6. under an ~

angel *n.* (lit.) an avenging; fallen; guardian; ministering ~

anger I *n.* 1. to arouse, provoke, stir up ~; to fill smb. with ~ (the new taxes stirred up ~ against the government) 2. to display, express, show; feel ~ 3. to contain, restrain, suppress (one's) ~ 4. to repress, swallow one's ~ 5. to allay, appease, calm, placate; face smb.'s ~ (to face the ~ of one's victims and

try to placate it) 6. to vent one's ~ (on) 7. blind, burning, deep, profound, seething, unbridled; mounting, rising ~ 8. righteous ~ 9. ~ blows over; explodes; subsides; wells up; 10. a blaze, explosion, fit, outburst of ~ 11. ~ about, over; at smt. (he could hardly suppress his ~ about/over the matter; we expressed our deep ~ at his refusal to help) 12. ~ at (AE), towards, with smb. (their ~ at/towards/ with me was ill-concealed) 13. ~ that + clause (our ~ that he had refused to help) 14. in; with ~ (she struck back in ~; *Look Back in Anger* – John Osborne (1956); burning with ~)

anger II *v.* 1. ~ deeply, greatly 2. (R) it ~ed us greatly (to learn) that he had refused to help

angle I *n.* ["space between two straight lines that meet"] 1. an acute; alternate; complementary; exterior; interior; obtuse; right; solid; supplementary ~ 2. an awkward; sharp; slight ~ (at a sharp ~) 3. the side; vertex of an ~ ["deviation from a straight line"] 4. at an ~ (at an ~ of thirty degrees; at a rakish ~; at a right ~) ["viewpoint"]["aspect"] 5. from an ~ (to examine a question from various ~s) ["motive; scheme"] (colloq.) (esp. AE) 6. to have an ~; what's his ~?

angle II *v.* (d; intr.) to ~ for ("to try to obtain") (she was ~ing for an invitation)

angry *adj.* 1. to become, get; grow ~ 2. ~ about, at, over smt. (they were ~ about the changes; we were ~ at his refusal to help; they get ~ over every trifle) 3. ~ at (esp. AE), with smb. (he was ~ at his neighbor; we were ~ with him for refusing to help) 4. ~ to + inf. (we were ~ to learn of his refusal to help) 5. ~ that + clause (we were ~ that he refused to help)

anguish *n.* (formal) 1. to cause ~ 2. acute; bitter; deep; inconsolable; mental ~ 3. ~ at, over 4. in ~ (in ~ over smb.'s death)

animadversion *n.* (formal) to make an ~ on, upon

animadvert *v.* (formal) (D; intr.) to ~ on, upon (to ~ on corruption)

animal *n.* 1. to domesticate an ~; to tame; train a wild ~ 2. to breed, raise, rear ~s (in captivity) 3. to trap an ~ 4. to hunt wild ~s 5. to butcher, slaughter ~s (for food) 6. to skin an ~ 7. to stuff an ~ 8. to neuter an ~ 9. a carnivorous, flesh-eating; meat-eating; herbivorous, plant-eating; omnivorous ~ 10. a dangerous; predatory; wild ~ 11. a domestic; domesticated; pet; tame ~ 12. a circus; draft; farm; herd; pack, social; zoo ~ 13. (misc.) like a caged ~; human beings are social ~s

animation *n.* computer; suspended ~

animosity *n.* 1. to arouse, stir up ~ 2. to feel, harbor ~ 3. bitter, burning, deep, seething ~ 4. personal ~ 5. racial; religious ~ 6. ~ against, to, towards (she felt a burning ~ towards them) 7. ~ between

ankle *n.* 1. to sprain, turn, twist, wrench one's ~ 2. a well-turned ("shapely") ~ 3. around, round smb.'s ~ (wear smt. around one's ~) 4. by the ~ (prisoners fastened by the ~) 5. (misc.) ~-deep in mud

annals *n.* to go down in the ~ (of history as)

annex I (esp. BE) **annexe** *n.* an ~ to (an ~ to the main building; an ~ to a treaty)

annex II *v.* (D; tr.) to ~ to (they ~ed the conquered territory to their country)

annihilation *n.* 1. nuclear ~ 2. threaten with ~ (does global warming threaten us with ~?)

anniversary *n.* 1. to celebrate, commemorate, mark, reach an ~ 2. a wedding ~ 3. a diamond; golden; silver (wedding) ~ 4. on an ~ (on their tenth wedding ~) 5. be, fall (their tenth ~ falls on a Friday this year) 6. (misc.) (I wish you a) happy ~!

annotation *n.* 1. to make an ~ (to make ~s in/on/to a text) 2. copious ~s

announce *v.* 1. (B) they ~d the news of the bonus to the employees = they ~d to the employees the news of the bonus 2. (L; to) they ~d (to the employees) that there would be a bonus

announcement *n.* 1. to issue, make an ~ 2. a birth; wedding ~ 3. a dramatic; formal, official; public ~ 4. a spot ~ 5. an ~ about, of 6. an ~ that + clause (they made a public (to the employees) ~ that there would be a bonus)

announcer *n.* a radio; sports ~

annoy *v.* 1. to ~ greatly, very much 2. (D; tr.) they ~ed me with their continual questions 3. (R) it ~ed me to be kept waiting so long; it ~ed him that his door was unlocked

annoyance *n.* 1. to express; feel; show ~ 2. (a) great; (a) minor ~ 3. ~ at (esp. AE), with smb. 4. ~ at, over smt. 5. ~ that + clause (his ~ that his door was unlocked was evident) 6. to smb.'s ~ (much to his ~, his door was unlocked)

annoyed *adj.* 1. extremely, greatly, very, very much ~ 2. ~ about, at, by smt. (we were ~ at losing the order; we were ~ by the children's rudeness) 3. ~ at (esp. AE), with smb. (he was ~ at/with the children) 4. ~ to + inf. (he was ~ to find his door unlocked) 5. ~ that + clause (he was ~ that his door was unlocked)

annoying *adj.* 1. extremely, highly, most, terribly, very; mildly, slightly ~ 2. ~ to (the delay was ~ to everyone) 3. ~ to + inf. (it was ~ (for him) to find his door unlocked) 4. ~ that + clause (it was ~ (for him) that his door was unlocked)

annulment *n.* 1. to grant an ~ 2. to obtain an ~

anoint *v.* 1. (D; tr.) to ~ with (to ~ smb. with oil) 2. (N; used with a noun) they ~ed him king

anonymous *adj.* to remain ~

another *determiner, pronoun* one way or ~; one after ~; yet ~; ~ two defeats and the war is lost!; he had ~ crazy idea USAGE NOTE: The preposition *of* is used before the plural – *he had another (one) of his crazy ideas.*

answer I *n.* 1. to call forth, elicit an ~ 2. to give, offer, provide an ~ 3. to come up with; have an ~ 4. to guess; know the ~ 5. to get, receive an ~ (from) 6. a clear, definite, straight, straightforward, unequivocal; definitive; direct ~ 7. a civil; diplomatic; wise ~ 8. a favorable; witty ~ 9. an immediate; ready; simple ~ 10. a glib; impertinent; simplistic; stock

~ 11. an equivocal; evasive, vague ~ 12. a blunt, brusque, curt ~ 13. an affirmative, positive ~ 14. a negative ~ 15. a correct, right ~ 16. an incorrect, wrong ~ 17. (BE) a dusty ("unsatisfactory, vague") ~ 18. a written ~ 19. an ~ to 20. in ~ to (in ~ to your question)

answer II *v.* 1. ("to respond") to ~ brusquely, curtly; clearly, unequivocally; immediately, promptly; vaguely 2. (d; intr.) ("to be responsible") to ~ to smb. for smt. (the politicians had to ~ to the voters for their actions) 3. (d; intr.) ("to respond") to ~ to (to ~ to a name; the child ~s only to its nickname) 4. (d; intr.) ("to correspond") to ~ to (she ~s to the description) 5. (D; intr., tr.) ("to respond") to ~ by; with (she ~ed me by nodding = she ~ed me with a nod) 6. (L; may have a personal object) ("to respond") they ~ed (us) that they would come 7. (misc.) if you're so smart why aren't you rich: can you ~ me that? = ~ me that if you can!

answerable *adj.* ~ for; to (politicians are ~ to the voters for their actions)

answer back *v.* (D; intr.) to ~ to (children should not ~ to their parents = children should not answer their parents back)

ant *n.* 1. army; carpenter; fire; harvester; honey; leafcutter; worker ~s 2. white ~s ("termites") 3. a colony of ~s in an ~hill

antagonism *n.* 1. to arouse, stir up ~ 2. to feel (an) ~ 3. bitter, deep, deep-rooted, deep-seated, profound, strong ~ 4. ~ between; to, towards (to feel a strong ~ towards smb.)

antagonist *n.* a formidable ~

antagonistic *adj.* ~ to, towards (he is very ~ to us)

ante *n.* ["stakes"] (colloq.) to up the ~ (also fig.)

antelope *n.* a herd of ~

antenna *n.* 1. a loop; outside; radio; television, TV ~ (BE typically has *aerial*)

anterior *adj.* (formal) ["before, earlier"] ~ to

anthem *n.* a national ~ (the band played/struck up the national ~ and everybody sang it)

anthropology *n.* 1. cultural; physical; social ~ 2. in ~ (a degree in ~)

antibiotic *n.* 1. to prescribe an ~ 2. to take an ~ 3. a broad-spectrum ~ 4. a course of ~s 5. on ~s (she's still on a course of ~s)

anticipate *v.* 1. to ~ eagerly 2. (G) we ~ winning first prize ourselves 3. (K) we ~d his winning first prize 4. (L) we ~d that he would win first prize 5. (Q) could not ~ whether he would win first prize

anticipation *n.* 1. eager, keen ~ 2. in ~ of (an exhibit was scheduled in ~ of his winning first prize) 3. with ~ (to look forward with eager ~ to his winning first prize) 4. that + clause (our eager ~ that he would win first prize)

anticlimax *n.* an ~ after, to (everything was an ~ to his winning first prize)

anticlockwise (BE) see **counterclockwise**

antidepressant *n.* 1. to take an ~ 2. to prescribe an ~ (for) 3. (to be) on ~s 4. to come off ~s

antidote *n.* 1. an effective, powerful; perfect; the best ~ 2. to be, constitute, serve as an ~ 3. to administer, give an ~ 4. to take an ~ 5. an ~ against, for, to (he took an ~ for the poison; the truth is the best ~ to complacency)

antifreeze *n.* to add; drain ~

antipathy *n.* 1. to feel (an) ~ 2. (a) deep, strong; natural ~ 3. ~ against, to, towards (he felt strong/a strong ~ towards smb.)

antique *n.* 1. to collect ~s 2. a genuine; priceless, valuable; rare ~

antithesis *n.* 1. the direct, very ~ 2. an ~ between 3. an ~ of, to (the ~ of/to my theory)

antithetical *adj.* ~ to

antlers *n.* 1. (esp. AE = to lock horns) to lock ~ (over; with) (locked ~s with them over foreign policy) 2. to shed ~ 3. a pair of ~

anxiety *n.* 1. to cause, create, generate; aggravate, heighten, increase ~ 2. to cope with, deal with; feel ~ 3. to allay, alleviate, decrease, dispel, ease, lessen, reduce, relieve; control ~ 4. acute; deep, grave, great, high, mounting; gnawing, unrelieved ~ 5. ~ about, at, over; for (~ for smb.'s safety) 6. ~ to + inf. (in his ~ not to offend them, he agreed to concessions) 7. ~ builds up, grows, increases, mounts, rises 8. ~ decreases, eases, subsides 9. in ~ (see 6) 10. an attack; level of ~ (reduce one's level of ~ by meditation)

anxious *adj.* 1. ~ about (~ about the world situation) 2. ~ for (we were ~ for their safety) 3. ~ to + inf. (she is ~ to help; we were ~ for them to meet you) 4. ~ that + clause; subj. (we were very ~ that they meet/should meet you)

any I *adv.* (used with the comparative form of adjectives and adverbs and with *good*) ~ better (I wonder if they can work ~ better; will it be ~ better living in the country than in the city?); ~ good (I don't think that this wine is ~ good); ~ (the) easier (that doesn't make my job ~ (the) easier); ~ more easily (the door will not shut ~ more easily now than before); ~ more difficult (do not make my job ~ more difficult than it is now); ~ less difficult (you haven't made my job ~ (the) less difficult); ~ worse (will it be ~ worse living in the city than in the country?)

any II *determiner, pronoun* 1. ~ to + inf. (we don't have ~ books to sell; we don't have ~ to sell) 2. ~ of (I did not see ~ of them) USAGE NOTE: The use of the preposition *of* is necessary when a pronoun follows. When a noun follows, the use of *of the* limits the meaning – did you see any students? did you see any of the students whom we had discussed earlier? (see also the Usage Note for **something**)

anybody *pronoun* do you have ~ to talk to? = do you have ~ that you can talk to? (see the Usage Note for **something**)

anyone see **anybody** USAGE NOTE: Note the difference between *anyone can do it* and *any one of you can do it.*

anyplace (AE) see **anywhere**

anything *n., pronoun* 1. do you have ~ to say? 2. ~ else 3. ~ about (do you know ~ about it?) 4. ~ to + inf. (do you have ~ to gain by ignoring the regulations? = is there ~ to be gained by ignoring the regulations?) 5. (misc.) ~ but ("not at all") ("is that enough?" "~ but! I need more!") (see the Usage Note for **something**)

anywhere *adv.* 1. do you have ~ to go? 2. ~ else; ~ near (do you have ~ else to go?; that isn't ~ near enough!) (see the Usage Note for **something**)

apart *adj., adv.* 1. to come, fall; tear ~ 2. to tell ~ 3. far; wide ~ (the two parties are still far ~ on foreign policy) 4. ~ from (~ from everything else) 5. (misc.) to come ~ at the seams (see also *set smt. apart* at **set II** *v.*)

apartment *n.* (esp. AE) 1. to rent an ~ from 2. to rent (out), sublet an ~ to 3. to furnish; redecorate; renovate an ~ 4. a basement; duplex; efficiency; furnished; garden; high-rise; luxury; first-floor; top-floor; one-bedroom; three-bedroom, etc.; one-room; three-room, etc.; penthouse; studio; unfurnished ~ (see also **flat**) USAGE NOTE: When people advertise an en-suite apartment, they mean it has an en-suite bathroom.

apathetic *adj.* ~ about; to, towards (he is ~ about everything)

apathy *n.* 1. growing, increasing 2. to feel; show ~ 3. to cast off, shed, throw off one's ~ 4. ~ about, concerning, towards; ~ among (growing ~ about politics among students)

apes *n.* the anthropoid, great, higher ~

apex *n.* 1. to attain, reach the ~ of 2. at the ~ (at the ~ of their power)

aplomb *n.* 1. the ~ to + inf. (she had the necessary ~ to order the meal in French) 2. with great ~

apologetic *adj.* 1. deeply, profusely; suitably ~ 2. to feel ~ 3. ~ about, for (she was deeply ~ for her blunder) 4. ~ to + inf. (she was deeply ~ to have blundered) 5. ~ that + clause (she was deeply ~ that she had blundered)

apologist *n.* an ~ for

apologize *v.* 1. to ~ humbly; profusely 2. (D; intr.) to ~ for; to (she ~d to us for her blunder) 3. (misc.) to ~ from the bottom of one's heart

apology *n.* 1. to make, offer, present; send an ~; to owe smb. an ~ 2. to demand an ~ 3. to accept an ~ ("I owe you an ~: I'm sorry!" "thank you; ~ accepted!") 4. a full; heartfelt; sincere ~ 5. an official; public; written ~ 6. an abject, humble; belated ~ 7. an ~ for; to (she made an ~ to the teacher for her blunder) 8. by way of ~ (for) (I sent her flowers by way of apology for my misbehavior) 9. (misc.) to make no apologies for (I make no ~ for opposing the government's plans)

apostasy *n.* (formal) 1. guilty of ~ 2. to commit ~ 3. (an) ~ from

apostate *n.* (formal) an ~ from (an ~ from the true faith)

apostle *n.* an ~ to

appall (AE), **appal** *v.* (R) it ~ed me to see such sloppy work; it ~ed us that the murderer had been released on parole

appalled *adj.* 1. absolutely, really, truly ~ 2. ~ at, by (we were ~ at/by the news) 3. ~ to + inf. (I was ~ to see that the murderer had been released on parole) 4. ~ that + clause (everyone was ~ that the murderer had been released on parole)

appalling *adj.* 1. absolutely, really, truly ~ 2. ~ to 3. ~ to + inf. (it was ~ (to us) to see that the murderer had been released on parole) 4. ~ that + clause (it was ~ that the murderer had/should have been released on parole) 5. (misc.) it's ~ how/the way a murderer can be released on parole!

apparel *n.* wearing ~

apparent *adj.* 1. clearly, glaringly; increasingly; painfully ~ 2. ~ to 3. ~ that + clause (it was all too painfully ~ to everyone that he had committed the crime) 4. (misc.) it was clearly ~ to everyone how he'd committed the crime

apparition *n.* 1. a strange ~ 2. an ~ appears; disappears

appeal I *n.* ["request"]["request for review"] 1. to issue; make an ~ 2. (legal) to file, lodge, make; lose; win an ~ 3. (legal) to take an ~ to a higher court 4. (also legal) to deny, dismiss, reject, throw out an ~ 5. (legal) (BE) an ~ lies against the decision ("there is an appeal pending") 6. a broad; desperate, urgent; eloquent, irresistible, moving, ringing, stirring; emotional; final, last; personal ~ 7. an ~ against, from; for; to (to file an ~ against a decision; to make an ~ to the public for donations; there is no ~ from a verdict of the higher court; to make an ~ against a referee's decision; they made an ~ to us to help them) 8. (legal) under ~ (to) (a case currently under ~ to a higher court) ["attraction"] 9. to have ~ 10. esthetic; strong; universal, wide ~ 11. box-office; sales; sex; snob ~ 12. ~ to (just what is his ~ to you anyway?) ["appeal for funds"] 13. to have, hold, organize; launch an ~ (for) (launch an ~ for children in need)

appeal II *v.* 1. (D; intr.) ("to request a review") to ~ against (to ~ against a decision) 2. (D; intr.) ("to request") to ~ for; to (they ~ed to us for help) 3. (d; intr.) ("to request") to ~ to smb. to + inf. (they ~ed to us to help them) 4. (d; intr.) to ~ to ("to resort to") (to ~ to common sense) 5. (d; intr.) to ~ to ("to please") (he doesn't ~ to her) 6. (d; intr.) ("to please") to ~ greatly, very much (he doesn't ~ to her very much) USAGE NOTE: In AE you are now likely to hear – *to appeal a decision.* Its CE equivalent is – *to appeal against a decision.*

appear *v.* 1. (D; intr.) to ~ against; for (she ~ed against him in court; she ~ed for the defense) 2. (D; intr.) to ~ as (to ~ on stage as Hamlet) 3. (d; intr.) to ~ before (she had to ~ before the judge) 4. (D; intr.) to ~ in (to ~ in a leading role) 5. (D; intr.) to ~ on (to ~ on stage) 6. (D; intr.) to ~ to (she ~ed to

him in a dream; how does that ~ to you?) 7. (E) she ~s to be well; she ~ to be a fool 8. (L; to) it ~s (to me) that they will not come 9. (S) to ~ foolish; sad; well (she ~s well/foolish); (esp. BE) to ~ a fool 10. (misc.) to ~ before a committee; to ~ in print; to ~ on the scene; to ~ in person; to ~ live (in concert); to ~ at the door; the story ~ed in the newspaper; suddenly there ~ed a ship on the horizon

appearance *n.* ["appearing"] 1. to make, put in an ~ (the policeman made a timely ~; a lawyer's ~ for the defense) 2. a court; guest; personal; public; stage; TV ~ (the actor made a personal ~ that turned out to be his last stage ~) 3. at smb.'s ~ (the crowd went wild at their first ~ on stage) ["outward impression"] 4. a disheveled; shabby; unkempt, untidy ~ 5. an immaculate, neat ~ 6. general; personal ~ (he was careless in his personal ~) 7. in ~ (neat in ~) 8. at first ~ 9. to give, take on; have an ~ (the marching ants took on the ~ of a great wave moving ever forward) 10. for appearance's sake ("for appearances' sake")

appearances *n.* ["outward looks"] 1. to keep up ~ 2. outward ~ 3. by ~ (to judge by ~) 4. for the sake of ~, for appearances' sake ("for appearance's sake") 5. despite; from, to all ~ (to all ~, the matter is closed) 6. (misc.) ~ can be deceiving (AE)/deceptive (BE)

append *v.* (D; tr.) to ~ to (to ~ a translation to a document)

appendage *n.* an ~ to

appendectomy, (BE) **appendicectomy** *n.* 1. to do, perform an ~ (on) 2. to have an ~

appendix *n.* 1. (anatomical) to have one's ~ out/removed/taken out 2. (anatomical) an inflamed; ruptured ~ 3. (anatomical) an ~ bursts, ruptures ["appended material"] 4. an ~ to (an ~ to a textbook)

appertain *v.* (formal) ["pertain"] (d; intr.) to ~ to (these facts ~ to the case)

appertaining *adj.* (formal) ["pertaining"] (cannot stand alone) ~ to (facts ~ to the case)

appetite *n.* 1. to have; work up an ~ 2. to give smb. an ~ 3. to whet smb.'s ~ 4. to satisfy smb.'s ~ 5. to lose one's ~ 6. to curb; spoil, take away smb.'s ~ 7. a good, healthy, hearty; jaded ~ 8. an enormous, gargantuan, huge, ravenous, voracious; insatiable ~ 9. a poor ~ 10. an ~ for (his latest book has given me an ~ for his earlier ones)

applaud *v.* 1. to ~ heartily, loudly 2. (D; tr.) to ~ as; for (we ~ed them for their courage = we ~ ed them as courageous) 3. (misc.) a decision that deserves to be ~ed

applause *n.* 1. to draw, get, win ~ (from; for) 2. to burst into ~ 3. to hold the ~ 4. enthusiastic, rapturous; heavy, lengthy, prolonged; loud, thunderous, wild ~ 5. light, polite, weak ~ 6. the ~ builds up, increases; dies down, subsides 7. a burst; ripple; round of ~ 8. to (the) ~ (she appeared on stage to the thunderous ~ of her admirers = she appeared on stage to thunderous ~ from her admirers)

apple *n.* 1. to core; grate; peel an ~ 2. cooking; eating ~s 3. a baked; green; sour ~ 4. (misc.) a rotten ~ ("an undesirable person"); the ~ of smb.'s eye ("smb.'s favorite")

apple cart *n.* (colloq.) ["status quo"] to upset the ~

appliances *n.* ["devices"] domestic, household; electrical; kitchen; major; small ~ (see also **electrical appliance**)

applicable *adj.* 1. generally ~ 2. ~ to (~ to a case)

applicant *n.* 1. a successful ~ (the successful ~ will have had at least five years' experience) 2. an ~ for (an ~ for a position)

application *n.* ["request"] 1. to file; fill in (esp. BE), fill out (esp. AE); make, put in, send in, submit an ~ 2. to process; screen ~s 3. to reject, turn down an ~ 4. to withdraw an ~ 5. a fellowship; membership ~ 6. a formal; written ~ 7. an ~ for; to (an ~ for admission to a university) 8. an ~ to + inf. (he filed an ~ to be admitted to the university) 9. by; on ~ (the leaflet is available on ~ (to the appropriate address)) ["putting to use"] 10. ~ to (the ~ of theory to practice) ["placing"] 11. ~ to (the ~ of ointment to a rash)

application form *n.* 1. to fill in (esp. BE), to fill out (esp. AE), fill up (BE, obsol.) an ~ 2. to file, submit an ~

apply *v.* 1. (D; intr.) ("to request") to ~ for; to (we ~lied to the authorities for assistance; the captain ~lied to headquarters for a transfer; she ~lied for a fellowship) 2. (D; intr.) ("to seek admission to") to ~ to (she ~lied to three universities) 3. (D; intr.) ("to be relevant") to ~ in, to (the rule does not ~ to this case and the same ~lies in all other cases) 4. (D; refl.) ("to concentrate one's efforts") to ~ to (she ~lied herself to her new duties with great energy) 5. (D; tr.) ("to put on") to ~ to (to ~ paint to a surface; to ~ ointment to a rash) 6. (D; tr.) ("to put to use") to ~ to (to ~ theory to practice) 7. (d; tr.) ("to channel") to ~ towards (to ~ money towards a purchase) 8. (E) ("to request") he ~lied (to the university) to be admitted (to it)

appoint *v.* 1. (D; tr.) to ~ as (we ~ed her as treasurer) 2. (D; tr.) to ~ to (we ~ed her to the committee) 3. (H) we ~ed her to serve as treasurer 4. (M and N; used with a noun) we ~ed her (to be) treasurer

appointment *n.* ["agreement to meet"] 1. a follow-up; outpatient ~ 2. to have; keep; give, make, schedule an ~ (with) (the hospital gave me a follow-up outpatient ~ with their cardiologist) 3. to break; cancel; miss an ~ 4. by ~ (she sees patients by ~ only) 5. an ~ to + inf. (she had an ~ to see the dean) ["selection"] 6. to confirm; make an ~ 7. to block an ~ 8. an ~ to (we announced her ~ to the committee) ["position"] 9. an ~ as 10. to offer an ~ (we offered her an ~ as treasurer) 11. to have, hold; receive an ~ 12. an interim; permanent; temporary ~ 13. a political ~ ["designation"] 14. by ~ to Her Majesty

apportion *v.* (D; tr.) to ~ among, between (the funds were ~ed among the various departments)

apposition *n.* (grammar) in ~ to (the second noun is in ~ to the first)

appraisal *n.* 1. to carry out, do, give, make a ~ of 2. a down-to-earth; fair; objective; realistic; thoroughgoing ~

appraise *v.* (D; tr.) to ~ at (the house was ~d at seventy thousand dollars)

appreciate *v.* ["to be grateful for smt."] 1. to ~ deeply, greatly, keenly, sincerely, very much 2. (K) we ~ your helping us 3. (misc.) we ~ the fact that you have helped us ["to understand"] 4. to ~ generally, widely; readily 5. (L) is it generally ~d that climate change is a serious problem? ["to increase"] 6. (D; intr.) to ~ by (to ~ by ten percent) 7. (D; intr.) to ~ in (to ~ in value)

appreciation *n.* ["gratitude"] 1. to demonstrate, display, show one's ~ for (let's show him our ~ with a round of applause!) 2. to express; feel ~ 3. deep, great, keen, sincere ~ 4. in ~ of (he did this in ~ of the help that he had received) 5. (misc.) to cultivate an ~ of art and music; as a token of my ~ ["understanding"] 6. general; growing; widespread ~ 7. ~ of (is there growing ~ of just how serious climate change really is?) 8. ~ that + clause (is there growing ~ that climate change is a serious problem?) ["increase"] 9. an ~ of 10. an ~ in (an ~ in value of ten percent)

appreciative *adj.* 1. deeply, greatly, keenly, sincerely, very ~ 2. ~ of (~ of help)

apprehension *n.* ["foreboding"]["fear"] 1. to express; feel; show ~ 2. to allay smb.'s ~(s) 3. grave; growing, increasing ~ 4. ~ about, at; for (we felt ~ for their safety) 5. (misc.) a feeling of ~; a state of ~

apprehensive *adj.* 1. ~ about; for (~ about recent developments; we were ~ for their safety) 2. ~ that + clause (we were ~ that they might be in danger)

apprentice I *n.* an ~ to (he was an ~ to a master craftsman)

apprentice II *v.* (B) at an early age, he was ~d to a master craftsman

apprenticeship *n.* to fill; have, serve an ~ (he served an ~ to a master craftsman)

apprise *v.* (formal) (d; tr.) to ~ of (he was ~d of the decision by his lawyer)

apprised *adj.* to keep smb. ~ of (he was kept ~ of the latest developments by his lawyer)

approach I *n.* 1. to make an ~ 2. to take an ~ (to take a judicious ~ to a problem) 3. a creative, innovative; fresh, new, novel; holistic ~ 4. a careful, cautious; conservative; judicious ~ 5. a direct, forthright; down-to-earth, no-nonsense, pragmatic, realistic, straightforward ~ 6. an objective; rational; scholarly; scientific ~ 7. an easygoing; indirect ~ 8. a simplistic; unrealistic ~ 9. a hard-nosed, inflexible, uncompromising ~ 10. (applied linguistics) the audio-visual; oral-aural ~ 11. at, with the ~ (with the ~ of spring, we began to feel better; the gazelles ran away at the ~ of a lion) 12. an ~ from; to (I like her ~ to the problem; the ~es to a stadium; the pilot began her ~ to the runway)

approach II *v.* 1. (D; tr.) to ~ about (I was afraid to ~ them about this matter; she ~ed us about a loan) 2. (D; tr.) to ~ for (she ~ed us for a loan) 3. (D; intr., tr.) to ~ from (to ~ from the other direction) 4. (d; tr.) to ~ with (to ~ smb. with a request for a loan) 5. (H) she ~ed us to lend her some money = we were ~ed by her to lend her some money

appropriate II *v.* 1. (B) Congress ~d the funds to the states 2. (D; tr.) to ~ for (the committee ~d money for the memorial)

appropriation *n.* 1. to make an ~ for (our government made an ~ for the project) 2. defense; foreign-aid ~s

approval *n.* 1. to give one's ~ for 2. to nod; show; voice one's ~ 3. to gain, get, meet with, receive, win; need, require ~ 4. complete, full, unqualified, wholehearted ~ 5. universal, widespread ~ 6. official; public; tacit ~ 7. limited, qualified ~ 8. final ~ 9. ~ for, of (we received their ~ for/of our research) 10. ~ to + inf. (we received their ~ to continue our research) 11. on ~ (we bought it on ~) 12. (misc.) a roar of ~; to get, receive smb.'s seal, stamp of ~ (see also *approval rating* at **rating**)

approve *v.* 1. to ~ wholeheartedly 2. (D; intr.) to ~ of (we ~d of his decision)

approximate *v.* (BE) (D; intr.) ("to come near") to ~ to (to ~ to the truth) USAGE NOTE: AE would have – *we approximated the truth.*

approximation *n.* to give, make a first, rough ~ (of, to)

apropos *adv.* ~ of (I have a couple of questions ~ of your last comment) USAGE NOTE: **Apropos** can also be a preposition – *I have a couple of questions apropos your last comment.*

apt *adj.* (cannot stand alone) ~ to + inf. (he is ~ to exaggerate)

aptitude *n.* 1. to demonstrate, display, show (an) ~ 2. (a) great, outstanding; inborn, innate, natural; special ~ 3. mechanical; scholastic ~ 4. an ~ for, in (an ~ for painting)

arbitrate *v.* (D; intr.) to ~ among, between (to offer to ~ between the warring parties)

arbitration *n.* 1. to conduct; offer ~ 2. to go to; resort to ~ (the union and management went to ~; the dispute went to ~) 3. to take to ~ 4. binding; voluntary ~ 5. ~ between; of 6. (misc.) the dispute between the union and management was taken to ~ and settled by ~

arbitrator *n.* 1. to appoint an ~ 2. a government ~ 3. an ~ between

arcade *n.* an amusement (BE); penny; video-game ~

arch *n.* 1. a triumphal ~ 2. through, under an ~

architecture *n.* 1. classical; contemporary, modern ~ 2. Baroque; Byzantine; Colonial; Georgian; Gothic; Greek; Modern; Renaissance; Roman; Romanesque; vernacular ~

ardor, ardour *n.* 1. to demonstrate, display ~ 2. to cool, dampen smb.'s ~ 3. fervent, intense; patriotic ~ 4. ~ for

area *n.* ["space"] 1. to close off, rope off, seal off an ~ 2. a metropolitan, urban; rural ~ 3. a built-up; catchment; residential; surface; surrounding ~ 4. a no-smoking; service; storage ~ 5. a disaster; distressed ~ 6. an assembly, staging ~ 7. an impacted (AE) ("crowded with federal employees") ~ 8. (soccer) a penalty ~ 9. (meteorology) a high-pressure; low-pressure ~ 10. (misc.) a gray ("unclear") ~ 11. in; into an ~ (a city expanding into the surrounding ~) ["subject, field"] 12. a growth; controversial, problem ~ (AI is a big growth ~ at present; stem-cell research is a problem ~) 13. (misc.) an ~ of interest (my principal ~ of interest is AI)

arena *n.* 1. a sports ~ 2. the international; political ~ (to enter the political ~)

arguable *adj.* 1. ~ that + clause (it is ~ that some unemployment is necessary) 2. (misc.) it's ~ just how much unemployment is necessary

argue *v.* 1. to ~ bitterly, heatedly, passionately, strenuously, vehemently 2. to ~ calmly, logically, plausibly, sensibly 3. (D; intr.) to ~ about, over; with (we ~d with them about the new law) 4. (d; intr.) to ~ against; for, in favor of (to ~ against the amendment; to ~ for the new policy) 5. (d; tr.) to ~ out of (to ~ smb. out of doing smt.) 6. (L) she ~d logically that the new regulations would harm the poor 7. (misc.) to ~ from a position of strength

argument *n.* ["dispute"] 1. to get into, have; start an ~ 2. to lose; win an ~ 3. to break off, end, terminate an ~ 4. to clinch, settle an ~ 5. an angry, bitter, heated, loud, violent ~ 6. an animated, lively ~ 7. an ~ arises, breaks out 8. an ~ about, over; between; with (I had a bitter ~ with him about politics) ["statement"] 9. to drive home, press (home) an ~ 10. to offer, present, put forward an ~ 11. to confute, rebut, refute; reject an ~ 12. an airtight, balanced, brilliant, cogent, compelling, conclusive, convincing, irrefutable, logical, persuasive, powerful, rational, solid, sound, telling, trenchant, unassailable, valid ~ 13. a circular; convoluted ~ 14. a groundless; tenuous, weak ~ 15. a specious, spurious ~ 16. an ~ about, over; against; between; for (she presented a convincing ~ against the proposal) 17. an ~ that + clause (I cannot accept his ~ that war is inevitable) 18. (misc.) the point, thrust of an ~; (legal) to hear ~s (against; for)

arise *v.* (D; intr.) to ~ from; out of (to ~ from a deep slumber; "I ~ from dreams of thee" – P.B. Shelley (1792–1822); a conflict ~ing from/out of a difference of opinion)

arithmetic *n.* to do ~

arm I *n.* ["upper limb"] 1. to bend; cross; fold; lift, raise; lower; straighten; stretch; swing; wave one's ~s 2. (misc.) to take smb. by the ~; to fling/put/throw one's ~s around smb.; to carry smt. under one's ~; to greet smb. with open/outstretched

~s; to hold smb./smt. in one's ~s; to walk ~ in ~ with; with ~s akimbo; to take smb. in one's ~s (I took her in my ~s and kissed her) 3. on the ~ (she touched him on the ~; the sun shone on her bare ~s) ["power"] 4. the long ~ of the law ["division"] 5. our naval air ~ ["attachment"] 6. a pickup, tone ~ ["misc."] 7. to greet/welcome smb. with open ~s ("to give smb. an enthusiastic welcome"); to keep smb. at ~'s length ("to keep smb. at bay"); to twist smb.'s ~ ("to exert pressure on smb.") (see also **arms**)

arm II *v.* 1. (D; intr., refl., tr.) to ~ against (to ~ against a potential enemy) 2. (D; refl., tr.) to ~ with (they ~ed the peasants with rifles)

armed *adj.* 1. ~ to the teeth 2. (misc.) ~ and dangerous

armistice *n.* 1. to agree on, work out; declare; sign an ~ 2. to violate an ~ 3. to suspend an ~ 4. an ~ between

armor, armour *n.* 1. heavy; light ~ 2. (misc.) to pierce ~

arms *n.* ["weapons"] 1. to bear; take up ~ 2. to call to ~ 3. (mil.) inspection; left shoulder; order; port; present; right shoulder; trail ~! 4. to lay down one's ~ 5. small ~ 6. under ~ ("armed") ["misc."] 7. up in ~ (about, over; against) ("stirred up") (see also **arm**; **coat of arms**)

arms race *n.* 1. to accelerate, step up the ~ 2. to curb the ~ 3. the nuclear ~ 4. the ~ is accelerating, heating up, hotting up

army *n.* 1. to command, lead; drill, train; rally an ~ 2. to mobilize, raise, recruit an ~ 3. to equip, supply an ~ 4. to array, commit, deploy, field; concentrate, mass an ~ 5. to inspect, muster, review an ~ 6. to encircle, envelop, surround; outfight; outflank; outmaneuver; overrun; surprise an ~ 7. to crush, decimate, defeat, rout an ~; to put an ~ to flight 8. to demobilize, disband an ~ 9. a rebel; regular, standing; territorial; volunteer ~ 10. an advancing; conquering; defeated; occupying; retreating; victorious ~ 11. an ~ advances; attacks; conducts war, engages in combat, fights; pulls back, retreats, withdraws 12. (misc.) an ~ of occupation; to join the ~ 13. in the ~ (you're in the ~ now!)

aroma *n.* 1. to give off; have an ~ 2. a delicate, delightful, fragrant, pleasant, pleasing; pungent; faint; tantalizing ~ 3. to smell an ~ 4. an ~ emanates from 5. (misc.) a pleasant ~ wafted in from the kitchen

around *adv.* 1. ~ here 2. to have been ~ ("to have had considerable experience")

arouse *v.* (D; tr.) to ~ from (to ~ smb. from a deep sleep)

aroused *adj.* easily; sexually ~

arraign *v.* (D; tr.) to ~ on (a certain charge)

arraignment *n.* 1. (legal) to hold an ~ for 2. a public ~

arrange *v.* 1. to ~ neatly; tastefully 2. (d; intr., tr.) to ~ for (to ~ for a series of lectures (to be given); we ~d for him to give a series of lectures) 3. (E) we

~d to meet early 4. (L) we ~d that he should give a series of lectures 5. (Q) we ~d where we should meet; we ~d where to meet

arrangement *n.* 1. to come to, make, work out; have an ~ (with) 2. to handle (the) ~s 3. a floral, flower; seating; working ~ 4. an ~ for; with 5. an ~ to + inf. (we made an ~/~s to meet secretly; we made ~s with the university for him to give a series of lectures there) 6. by ~ (by special ~) 7. under an ~ (under a special ~) 8. (misc.) to make the ~s (don't worry: she's already made all the ~s!); an ~ whereby (I have an ~ with them whereby I can cash checks there)

array I *n.* ["order"] 1. in battle ~; drawn up in full ~ ["display"] 2. a bewildering; dazzling, glittering; imposing, impressive; vast ~

array II *v.* (D; tr.) to ~ against (~ed against the enemy)

arrears *n.* in ~ (he is more than a month in ~ with his rent to the tune of $500; he is $500 in ~ with his rent)

arrest I *n.* ["detention"] 1. to make an ~ 2. to resist ~ 3. a citizen's; false ~ 4. an ~ for (to make an ~ for murder) 5. an ~ on a charge/(esp. AE) charges of (to make an ~ on a charge of murder) 6. under ~ (to be under ~; to place/put smb. under ~ (for murder)) (see also **house arrest**) ["stoppage"] 7. (a) cardiac ~

arrest II *v.* 1. (D; tr.) to ~ for (the police ~ed her for murder) 2. (misc.) to ~ on a charge of, on charges of (esp. AE) (she was ~ed on charges of murder)

arrest warrant *n.* (AE) to issue an ~

arrival *n.* 1. an early; late ~ 2. an ~ at, in; from 3. on; with smb.'s ~ (on our ~ in Chicago we were met by friends; with the ~ of our friends all our problems were solved) 4. (misc.) to announce an ~ (as at an airport)

arrive *v.* 1. (D; intr.) to ~ at, in; from (they ~d from Paris) 2. (s) they ~d exhausted; in good spirits; refreshed; safe and sound 3. (misc.) to ~ early; late; on time

arrogance *n.* 1. to demonstrate, display, exhibit ~ 2. insufferable, overpowering, overwhelming, unbelievable ~ 3. ~ towards 4. the ~ to + inf. (he actually had the ~ to ask for more money!)

arrogant *adj.* 1. ~ towards 2. ~ to + inf. (it was ~ for/of him to ask for more money = he was ~ to ask for more money)

arrogate *v.* (formal) (B) to ~ a privilege to oneself

arrow *n.* 1. to aim; shoot an ~ at 2. a poisoned; spent ~ 3. (misc.) as straight as an ~

arson *n.* to commit ~

art *n.* 1. to master; practice an ~ (to practice the occult ~ of the alchemist; to master the ~ of making a good omelet) 2. abstract; classical; contemporary; folk; impressionist; modern; primitive; pop; surrealist(ic) ~ 3. commercial ~ 4. an ~ in, to (there is an ~ to making a good omelet) 5. a work of ~ 6. (misc.) to exhibit, hang; produce works of ~; the fine ~ of (to master the fine ~ of keeping friends) (see also **arts**; *state of the art* at **state I** *n.*)

artefacts (BE) see **artifacts**

artery *n.* ["blood vessel"] 1. a blocked, occluded; ruptured ~ 2. a coronary; main; pulmonary ~ 3. (misc.) hardening of the ~ries ["channel"] 4. a major; traffic ~

arthritis *n.* to develop ~

article I *n.* ["essay"] 1. to submit; write an ~ 2. to accept; commission; feature; publish, run; referee; reject an ~ 3. a journal; leading (BE, old-fashioned = leader, editorial); magazine; newspaper; op-ed ~ 4. in an ~ 5. an ~ about, on (she wrote an ~ about her research) 6. an ~ appears, comes out (in) (the ~ came out in *The New Yorker*) 7. a series of ~s ["section"] 8. according to, under an ~ (according to ~ two of our constitution) ["object"] 9. household; secondhand; toilet ~s 10. (misc.) ~s of clothing; ~s of furniture ["in grammar"] 11. to require, take an ~ (certain nouns always take the definite ~) 12. the definite; indefinite ~

article II *v.* (BE) (d; tr.) ("to apprentice") to ~ to, with (to ~ smb. to a firm of solicitors)

articulate *v.* 1. ("to pronounce") ~ clearly 2. (d; intr.) ("to fit together") to ~ with (these bones ~ with each other)

artifacts, artefacts *n.* ancient; cultural ~

artillery *n.* antiaircraft; coast; field; heavy; light; long-range; medium; self-propelled ~

artist *n.* 1. a gifted, great, talented; struggling; well-known ~ 2. a commercial; folk ~ 3. a graffiti; pavement (BE), sidewalk (AE) ~ 4. a con, flimflam, rip-off, scam; escape; quick-change ~ 5. (misc.) an ~ in residence; an exhibition featuring well-known ~s

artistry *n.* brilliant ~

arts *n.* 1. (the) creative; fine; visual ~ 2. (the) decorative; graphic; plastic ~ 3. (the) applied; industrial ~ 4. the healing ~ 5. (the) liberal ~ 6. (the) martial ~ 7. the performing ~ (the High School for the Performing ~ in New York City) 8. (misc.) ~ and crafts; ~ and sciences

ascend *v.* (D; intr.) to ~ from; to

ascendancy *n.* 1. to attain, gain ~ over 2. (a) clear-cut; overwhelming ~

ascendant *n.* in the ~ (which faction is in the ~?)

ascent *n.* 1. to make an ~ (to make the ~ of a mountain) 2. a gentle, gradual ~ 3. a steep ~ 4. an ~ from; to

ascertain *v.* 1. (L) she ~ed that fraud had been committed 2. (Q) can she ~ when the fraud was committed?

asceticism *n.* to practice ~

ascribe *v.* (d; tr.) to ~ to (we ~ this saying to Shakespeare; they ~d their success to hard work)

ash *n.* volcanic ~ (see also **ashes**)

ashamed *adj.* 1. deeply, thoroughly ~ 2. ~ about, of (she was ~ about her mistake; she was ~ of herself for having made a mistake) 3. ~ to + inf. (she was

~ to admit her mistake) 4. ~ that + clause (she was ~ that she'd made a mistake)

ashes *n.* 1. to rake; scatter, sprinkle, spread ~ (they scattered/sprinkled her ~ in the sea) 2. to reduce to ~ (see also *rise from the ashes* at **rise II** 6)

ashore *adv.* 1. to put, set ~ 2. to come; go ~

aside *adv.* 1. to move; stand; step ~ 2. to brush; draw, take; leave; push, shove; put set, sweep ~ 3. (AE) ~ from ("apart from")

asinine *adj.* ~ to + inf. (it was (of them) ~ to behave like that)

ask *v.* 1. (D; intr., tr.) ("to inquire") to ~ about, after (BE) (they ~ed me about my work; he ~ed about/after her mother) 2. (d; intr., tr.) ("to request") to ~ for (she ~ed me nicely/politely for the book; the guest ~ed for the manager) 3. (D; tr.) ("to request") to ~ smt. of (I have a favor to ~ of you; he is ~ing a great deal of us; working so hard so long is ~ing a lot of us!) 4. (D; tr.) ("to invite") to ~ to (we ~ed them to lunch) 5. (E) ("to request") she ~ed to be excused; we ~ed to see him 6. (H) ("to request") she ~ed us to come to lunch = we were ~ed to come to lunch 7. (L; subj.) ("to request") the family ~ed that the story not be/should not be printed 8. (O; can be used with one object) ("to pose") he ~ed (her) a question (also possible is: he ~ed a question of her) 9. (Q; may have an object) ("to inquire of") he ~ed (his son) point-blank where he was going; she ~ed wistfully how she might help 10. (misc.) to ~ for trouble (wearing those outlandish clothes here is simply ~ing for trouble!); to get ~ed (do beautiful women get ~ed their age a lot?); to mind ~ing (how old are you – if you don't mind me/my ~ing?)

askance *adv.* to look ~ at

asking *n.* (colloq.) for the ~ (it's yours for the ~)

ask out *v.* (D; tr.) to ~ to (to ask smb. out to lunch)

asleep *adj.* 1. to be deeply, fast, sound ~ 2. to fall ~ 3. (misc.) ~ at the switch ("negligent, not alert")

aspect *n.* ["view"] ["side"] 1. a frightening; grim; humorous; serious ~ (the humorous ~ of the situation) 2. to assume, take on an ~ (the situation is starting to take on a distinctly humorous ~) 3. from an ~ (from this ~) 4. in an ~ (in all ~s) ["in grammar"] 5. the imperfective; perfective ~ 6. in an ~ (a verb in the perfective ~)

aspersion *n.* to cast ~s on

aspirant *n.* an ~ for; to (an ~ to the throne)

aspiration *n.* (formal) 1. high, lofty, noble ~s 2. an ~ to (~s to independence) 3. to achieve, realize one's ~; to have ~s 4. ~ to + inf. (she has ~s to study medicine; will she achieve her ~s?)

aspire *v.* (formal) 1. (d; intr.) to ~ to (to ~ to a career in medicine) 2. (E) she ~s to study medicine

aspirin *n.* 1. to take (an) ~ 2. (misc.) an ~ tablet (he took two ~ tablets; or: he took two ~s) 3. a dose of ~ (what's the maximum recommended dose of ~ for a headache?)

ass *n.* ["fool"] 1. a pompous; stupid ~ 2. to make an

~ of oneself ["donkey"] 3. ~es bray, go heehaw, heehaw

assail v. (formal) 1. to ~ bitterly 2. (D; tr.) to ~ with (to ~ smb. with questions)

assassin n. a hired, paid ~

assassination n. 1. to attempt; carry out an ~ 2. character; a political ~

assault n. 1. (often mil.) to carry out, launch, make; lead an ~ (against, on) (the enemy carried out an ~ on our position) 2. to come under ~ (our position came under enemy ~) 3. (legal) to commit (an) ~ (when did the assailant commit the ~?) 4. (usu. legal) aggravated; bodily; criminal; indecent, sexual; violent ~ 5. an all-out; armed; military ~ 6. (usu. mil.) by ~ (the enemy took our position by ~) 7. (misc.) (legal) ~ and battery (to commit ~ and battery) 8. (misc.) a series of ~s; an ~ happens, occurs, takes place (when did the ~ occur?)

assembly n. 1. to elect; convene; dismiss, dissolve an ~ 2. a constituent; constitutional; deliberative; general; legislative; national; public ~ 3. the Northern Ireland; Welsh ~ 4. an ~ meets, sits 5. (misc.) (the) freedom, the right of ~; unlawful ~ 6. (at a school) (we met at/during ~)

assent I n. 1. to give; nod one's; refuse, withhold one's ~ to (she gave her ~ to our plan) 2. by common ~ 3. (BE) (the) royal ~ (the bill has received the royal ~ and will now become law)

assent II v. (formal) (D; intr.) to ~ to (we ~ed to his proposal)

assert v. 1. to ~ boldly (she ~ed her innocence boldly) 2. (L) she ~ed that she was innocent

assertion n. 1. to make an ~ 2. to deny, reject; rebut, refute an ~ 3. a bold; sweeping; unfounded, unsubstantiated ~ 4. an ~ about; of (we do not believe her repeated ~s of innocence) 5. an ~ that + clause (we do not believe her ~ that she is innocent)

assess v. 1. to ~ carefully (she ~ed the situation carefully) 2. (D; tr.) to ~ at (the value of this property was ~ed at one million dollars)

assessment n. 1. to carry out, do, make an ~ (she made a careful ~ of the situation) 2. a careful, critical; preliminary; realistic ~ 3. a risk; tax ~

asset n. 1. an invaluable, valuable ~ 2. an economic natural; political ~ 3. an ~ to (she was an invaluable ~ to our firm)

assets n. 1. to freeze; have; realize; release, unfreeze ~ 2. to mortgage one's ~ 3. to confiscate smb.'s ~ 4. capital; current; financial; fixed; frozen; hidden; intangible; liquid; personal; tangible; toxic ~ 5. ~ amounting to, of (to have ~ amounting to at least one million dollars) 6. (misc.) ~ and liabilities

asseverate v. (formal and rare) 1. to ~ boldly 2. (L) she ~ed that she was innocent

assign v. 1. (A) they ~ed a very difficult mission to us; or: they ~ed us a very difficult mission 2. (D; tr.) to ~ to (headquarters ~ed the soldiers to a different unit; an experienced detective was ~ed

to the case; to ~ a painting to a certain century) 3. (esp. BE) (H) we were ~ed to prepare a meal

assignation n. (formal) 1. to keep, make an ~ 2. an ~ with

assignment n. ["task"]["mission"] 1. to give smb. an ~ 2. to accept, take on; refuse an ~ 3. to carry out, complete an ~ (the ambassador carried out her ~ brilliantly) 4. a dangerous; difficult, rough, tough ~ 5. an easy ~ 6. an overseas ~ 7. a rush; special ~ 8. an ~ to + inf. (an ~ to guard the president) 9. on ~ ("on a mission") (the correspondent was on ~ in the Far East) ["homework"] (esp. AE) 10. to give, hand out an ~ 11. to do; hand in an ~ (the pupils did their ~(s)) 12. a difficult; easy ~ 13. an ~ about, on ["appointment"] (esp. AE) 14. an ~ to (an ~ to a new job)

assimilate v. 1. to ~ completely, fully; easily, readily; rapidly 2. (D; intr., tr.) to ~ into, to (the newcomers tried to ~ into the American way of life; America has ~d millions of immigrants into its way of life) 3. (D; intr.) to ~ with (some newcomers did not ~ with the local population)

assimilation n. ~ into, to (the immigrants' ~ into the American way of life was swift)

assist I n. (colloq.) with an ~ from

assist II v. 1. (D; intr., tr.) to ~ at, in, with (the young nurse was ~ing at his first operation; we ~ed them in their work; she ~ed me with the translation) 2. (formal, rare) (H) to ~ smb. to do smt. (we ~ed them to do their work; she ~ed us to move the furniture)

assistance n. 1. to extend, give, offer, provide, render ~ 2. considerable, great, invaluable ~ 3. clerical; legal; technical ~ 4. economic, financial; material; public ~ 5. (AE) directory ~ (BE has *directory enquiries*) 6. ~ in (they received ~ in launching the project) 7. ~ for; from; to (economic ~ to/for developing countries from an unlikely source) 8. of ~ (he was of considerable ~ to us) 9. with; without (smb.'s) ~ (the project was completed without their ~; my translation was completed with her assistance)

assistant n. 1. a personal ~ (BE; AE has *personal secretary*) 2. a research; teaching ~ 3. a sales, shop ~ (BE) (AE has *salesclerk*) 4. an ~ to (an ~ to the president)

associate I n. 1. a business ~ 2. a close ~ 3. (AE) an Associate in/of Arts

associate II v. 1. to ~ closely; loosely 2. (d; intr., refl., tr.) to ~ with (we ~ with all sorts of people; one usually ~s poverty with misery; I ~ myself with their policies)

association n. ["organization"] 1. to form; disband, dissolve an ~ 2. a bar ~ (AE; BE has *law society*) 3. a building and loan ~/savings and loan ~ (AE; BE has *building society*) 4. a parent-teacher ~ 5. an ~ meets (the ~ meets here every Thursday) ["connection"] 6. a close; loose ~ 7. an ~ between; of; with (an ~ between poverty and misery = an ~ of poverty with misery) 8. in ~ with ["connection in the mind"] 9. to bring up, call up, evoke an ~ 10. free ~

assortment *n.* an odd; rich; wide ~ (of)

assume *v.* 1. to ~ automatically, naturally; erroneously, mistakenly 2. (L) after the accident we naturally ~d (that) he was dead 3. (M) after the accident we naturally ~d him to be dead 4. (misc.) let's ~ (let's ~ – just for the sake of argument – that he's dead)

assumed *adj.* (cannot stand alone) ~ to + inf. (after the accident he was naturally ~ to be dead)

assumption *n.* 1. to make an ~ 2. to base an ~ on 3. an erroneous, false mistaken; questionable ~ 4. an automatic, natural; key; reasonable; safe; valid ~ 5. (an) implicit, unspoken; mere; pure ~ 6. an ~ about; of (to make an ~ of guilt) 7. an ~ that + clause (after the accident we all made the natural ~ that he was dead) 8. on an ~ (after the accident we proceeded on the natural ~ that he was dead) 9. an ~ underlies (to challenge smb.'s underlying ~s)

assurance *n.* 1. to give an ~ that + clause (the contractor gave every ~ that the work would be completed on time) 2. (BE) endowment; life ~ (see the Usage Note for **insurance**) 3. categorical, complete, every, unconditional ~

assurances *n.* 1. to give, provide ~ of (the contractor gave ~s of the work's completion on time) 2. ~ that + clause (the contractor gave ~ that the work would be completed on time)

assure *v.* 1. (d; tr.) to ~ about, of (the contractor assured us of the work's completion on time) 2. (L; must have an object) (the contractor assured us that the work would be completed on time) 3. let me ~ you (despite all rumors to the contrary, let me ~ you that he's not dead)

assured *adj.* 1. to rest ~ of (you can rest ~ of the work's completion on time) 2. to rest ~ that + clause (you can rest ~ that the work will be completed on time)

astonish *v.* 1. to ~ greatly, very much 2. (R) it ~ed us (to learn) that he had escaped

astonished *adj.* 1. greatly, very (much) ~ 2. ~ at, by (we were ~ at/by the news of his escape) 3. ~ + inf. (we were ~ to learn of his escape) 4. ~ that + clause (we were ~ that he had escaped)

astonishing *adj.* 1. simply ~ 2. ~ to 3. ~ to + inf. (it was (to us) ~ to learn that he had escaped) 4. ~ that + clause (it was ~ (to us) that he had/should have escaped)

astonishment *n.* 1. to express ~ 2. ~ at (we could not conceal our ~ at the news that he had escaped) 3. ~ that + clause (we expressed ~ that he had escaped) 4. in ~ (we gaped/gasped in ~) 5. to smb.'s ~ (to our ~, he managed to escape)

astound *v.* (R) it ~ed us (to learn) that he had/should have escaped

astounded *adj.* 1. ~ at, by (we were ~ at/by the news of his escape) 2. ~ + inf. (we were ~ to learn of his escape) 3. ~ that + clause (we were ~ that he had/should have escaped)

astounding *adj.* 1. simply ~ 2. ~ to + inf. (her performance was ~ to watch) 3. ~ that + clause (it was simply ~ that he had/should have escaped)

astray *adv.* 1. to lead smb. ~

astride *prep.* (formal) to sit ~ (to sit ~ smb.'s knee; to sit ~ a horse or ride sidesaddle)

astute *adj.* (formal) 1. very ~ 2. ~ at (~ at conducting negotiations) 3. ~ to + inf. (it was very ~ of you to notice that = you were very ~ to notice that)

asunder *adv.* (formal) to rend, tear ~

asylum *n.* 1. to give, grant, offer, provide ~ to 2. to ask for, request, seek; find, receive ~ 3. to deny, refuse smb. ~ 4. political ~ (they were granted political ~) 5. ~ for 6. ~ from (they requested ~ from the dictatorship for themselves and their children) (see also *asylum-seeker* at **seeker**)

athlete *n.* an all-around (AE), all-round; amateur; born, natural; professional; weekend; world-class ~

athletics *n.* 1. (esp. BE; AE has *track and field*) to go in for ~ 2. (esp. in the USA) intercollegiate ~ 3. in ~ (to win first prize in ~)

atlas *n.* 1. a dialect, linguistic; geographical; world ~ 2. to look smt. up in an ~

atmosphere n 1. to clear, improve the ~ 2. to poison, pollute the ~ 3. a congenial, convivial; cozy; friendly; informal, relaxed; pleasant ~ 4. a carnival; heady ~ 5. a romantic ~ 6. a formal ~ 7. a gloomy; heavy, highly charged; stifling, stultifying; tense; unpleasant ~ 8. a polluted; rarefied ~ 9. the upper ~ 10. (misc.) that restaurant has lots of ~

atom *n.* to split the ~

atone *v.* (D; intr.) to ~ by, with; for (to ~ for one's sins by doing penance)

atonement *n.* 1. to make ~ for (to make ~ for one's sins by doing penance) 2. (misc.) a day of ~

atrocity *n.* 1. to commit an ~ 2. a dreadful, grisly, gruesome, heinous, horrible, horrid, monstrous, revolting, vile ~ 3. death-camp; wartime atrocities 4. an ~ against (to commit atrocities against non-combatants)

attach *v.* 1. to ~ securely (d; refl.) ("to join") to ~ to (she ~ed herself to our group) 2. (D; tr.) ("to fasten") to ~ to (she ~ed an aerial/antenna to the radio; a tag was ~ed to each article) 3. (d; tr.) ("to assign temporarily") to ~ to (the officer was ~ed to headquarters) 4. (d; tr.) ("to ascribe") to ~ to (we ~ed no significance to her statement)

attaché *n.* an air-force; commercial; cultural; military; naval; press ~

attached *adj.* 1. deeply, strongly; very (much) ~ 2. loosely; securely 3. ~ to

attachment *n.* 1. to feel; form an ~ 2. a close; deep; strong ~ 3. a lasting; lifelong ~ 4. a sentimental ~ 5. an E-mail ~ 6. an ~ to (to form a lasting ~ to smb.) 7. (BE) on ~ to ("assigned to")

attack I *n.* ["assault"] (usu. mil.; also fig.) 1. to carry out, make; launch, mount, unleash; lead, spearhead; press an ~ 2. to provoke an ~ 3. to come under ~ 4. to survive, withstand an ~ 5. to blunt, break up, repel, repulse; resist an ~ 6. an all-out, concerted, full-scale; coordinated; major ~ 7. a pre-emptive; retaliatory ~ 8. a mock; sneak, surprise; unprovoked ~ 9. an air; seaborne ~ 10. an enemy; terrorist ~ 11. a flank; frontal ~ 12. a nuclear; torpedo ~ 13. an ~ occurs, takes place; succeeds 14. an ~ fails; fizzles out 15. an ~ against, on (the enemy launched an all-out ~ against our forces) 16. under ~ ["a belligerent action"] (often verbal) 17. to launch; make an ~ 18. a physical; verbal ~ 19. a bitter, blistering, brutal, concerted, savage, scathing, sharp, vehement, vicious, violent; scurrilous; unprovoked; wanton ~ 20. an ~ on (he made a blistering ~ on his opponent) 21. (misc.) the leaked document left us open to ~ ["onset of an ailment"] 22. to have an ~ (she had an ~ of hiccups) 23. an acute; fatal; light, slight; recurrent; sudden ~ 24. (misc.) a series of ~s (see also **heart attack**)

attack II *v.* 1. to ~ brutally, savagely, viciously; physically 2. (D; tr.) to ~ because of, for; with (the burglar attacked me with a knife; he ~ed his opponent because of her failure to oppose the war)

attempt I *n.* 1. to make an ~ 2. to foil, thwart an ~ 3. an all-out, concerted, last-ditch; brave, valiant; deliberate ~ 4. a successful ~ 5. a blatant; bold, brazen, daring ~ 6. a botched; clumsy; crude; feeble, halfhearted, weak; premature ~ 7. an abortive, fruitless, futile, vain; ill-fated, unsuccessful; misguided ~ 8. repeated ~s 9. a rescue; suicide ~ 10. an ~ against, on (an ~ on smb.'s life) 11. an ~ at (an ~ at being funny) 12. an ~ to + inf. (she made an ~ to find a job) 13. in an ~ (in our ~ to finish the job quickly, we ran out of supplies)

attempt II *v.* 1. (E) she ~ed to find a job 2. (rare) (G) he ~ed walking 3. (misc.) to ~ smt. successfully; in vain

attend *v.* 1. (BE) (d; intr.) to ~ on (two nurses ~ed on the patient) 2. (d; intr.) to ~ to (to ~ to one's duties; to ~ to a customer)

attendance *n.* ["people present"] ["number of people present"] 1. to check (the) ~; to take (the) ~ (in school) 2. average; daily ~ 3. decreasing, falling, plummeting; low, poor; increasing, rising ~ 4. perfect; regular ~ 5. ~ has gone up, risen; ~ has dropped, fallen, gone down, plummeted ["presence"] 6. ~ at (~ at a ceremony) 7. in ~ (a nurse was in ~) ["misc."] 8. to dance ~ on smb. ("to fawn over smb.")

attendant I *adj.* (formal) (cannot stand alone) ~ on (the problems ~ on growing up)

attendant II *n.* 1. a flight; wedding ~ 2. an ~ to

attention *n.* ["concentration"] ["notice"] 1. to attract, capture, catch, command, draw, get, grab smb.'s ~ 2. to have, hold, retain smb.'s ~ 3. to call, draw smb.'s ~ to 4. to devote one's ~ to; to concentrate, confine, focus (one's) ~ on; to give one's ~ to; to pay ~ (to); to turn one's ~ to 5. to bring smt. to smb.'s ~ 6. to distract, divert smb.'s ~ 7. to escape

smb.'s ~ 8. close; meticulous; minute; rapt; studious; undivided ~ (this matter will require your undivided ~) 9. ~ to (meticulous ~ to detail) 10. for, to smb.'s ~ (this package was left here for your ~) 11. (misc.) she gave the matter her undivided ~; it came to/did not escape my ~ that she was very ill; they were the center of ~; smb.'s ~ may wander ["position of attention"] (usu. mil.) 12. to call smb. to ~ (the sergeant called his platoon to ~); to come to, snap to ~; to stand at ~; or: to stand at the position of ~; or: (BE) to stand to ~ ["care"] 13. to give ~ to; to lavish ~ on 14. medical ~ (to receive medical ~) 15. individual; personal ~ (the manager gave me her personal ~; I lavished my individual ~ on him)

attentive *adj.* ~ to (~ to our needs)

attest *v.* (formal) (d; intr.) to ~ to (several witnesses can ~ to her good character)

attire *n.* (formal) 1. casual; civilian; formal ~ 2. in ~ (dressed in formal ~)

attitude *n.* 1. to adopt, assume, strike, take; have an ~ 2. to change an ~ 3. a cheerful; conciliatory; constructive; current, prevailing, widespread; flexible; friendly; positive; realistic ~ 4. a respectful; reverent ~ 5. a casual; devil-may-care; frivolous; hands-off; irreverent; nonchalant; wait-and-see ~ 6. a conservative; liberal ~ 7. a cavalier; condescending, patronizing; holier-than-thou ~ 8. a bad, belligerent, defiant, surly; disrespectful; hostile; inflexible, rigid, uncompromising; negative; scornful ~ 9. an ~ about; of; to, towards (to assume an ~ of defiance towards all authority) 10. an ~ that + clause (I didn't like his ~ that he deserves special treatment)

attorney *n.* (esp. AE) 1. to hire, retain an ~ 2. a defense; district (AE; BE has *public prosecutor*); prosecuting ~ 3. an attorney-at-law 4. (CE) an Attorney General (see also **power of attorney**)

attract *v.* 1. to ~ irresistibly, strongly 2. (D; tr.) to ~ to (a crowd was ~ed to the scene of the accident)

attracted *adj.* 1. irresistibly, strongly, very ~ 2. ~ to (he was very ~ to her)

attraction *n.* ["charm"] 1. to feel an ~ to 2. to hold an ~ for 3. a fatal; irresistible, strong; physical, sexual ~ (he felt a strong ~ to her) ["something that attracts"] 4. a box-office; chief, main, major; public; scenic; tourist ~ 5. (misc.) an added ~; the center of ~

attractive *adj.* 1. physically; sexually; very ~ 2. ~ to (the offer is very ~ to us)

attributable *adj.* 1. generally, usually 2. ~ to (their success is ~ to hard work)

attribute *v.* (d; tr.) to ~ to (we ~ this saying to Shakespeare; they ~d their success to hard work)

attrition *n.* 1. a rate of ~ 2. by, through ~ (the staff will be reduced by (natural) ~) 3. (misc.) a war of ~

attune *v.* (D; refl., tr.) to ~ to (you will have to ~ your ears to this type of music)

atypical *adj.* ~ of (such behavior was ~ of him)

auction *n.* 1. to have, hold an ~ 2. an ~ takes place 3. to put smt. up for ~ (items that were put up for ~) 4. a public ~ 5. at (an) ~; by ~ (we bought these items at an ~; they sold those items by ~)

audacious *adj.* ~ to + inf. (it was ~ of him to ask for an increase in salary = he was ~ enough to ask for an increase in salary)

audacity *n.* 1. to demonstrate, display, show ~ (he displayed ~ by asking for an increase in salary) 2. sheer ~ 3. the ~ to + inf. (he had the ~ to ask for an increase in salary)

audible *adj.* 1. barely, hardly, scarcely; perfectly ~ 2. ~ above, over; to (his voice was barely ~ to us above the din)

audience *n.* ["interview"] 1. to give, grant an ~ 2. to have, receive an ~ (with) 3. to seek an ~ with 4. a private ~ (with) 5. at an ~ ["group of spectators or listeners"] 6. to attract, draw an ~ 7. to captivate, electrify, grip, move, stir, sway, turn on an ~ (to electrify an ~ = to turn on an ~ = to turn an ~ on) 8. an appreciative, attentive, enthusiastic, receptive, responsive; friendly; sympathetic ~ 9. a cold, passive, unresponsive; hostile; unsympathetic ~ 10. a capacity; large, wide; mass; standing-room-only ~ 11. a captive; select; target ~ 12. a live; studio ~ 13. an ~ applauds, cheers, claps 14. an ~ boos, hisses, hoots, jeers 15. before, in front of an ~ (a program recorded before a studio ~) 16. (misc.) the speaker was being heckled so she turned on the ~ ("she attacked the audience") USAGE NOTE: In formal BE one can have *an ~ of the Queen*; in AE and ordinary BE one has *an ~ with the Queen*: "I sought an ~ of the King this evening…and tendered to him my resignation…" – Neville Chamberlain (May 10, 1940), quoted in Nicholson Baker, *Human Smoke* (2008, p. 175)

audit *n.* 1. to carry out, conduct an ~ 2. an annual, yearly; external; internal; tax ~

audition I *n.* 1. to give smb. an ~ 2. to have, hold ~s 3. to get, have an ~ 4. an ~ for; with (she had an ~ with the Royal Shakespeare Company for the part / role of Juliet = the RSC gave her an ~ for the part / role of Juliet)

audition II *v.* 1. (D; intr., tr.) to ~ for (she ~ed for the part / role of Juliet; they ~ed her for the part / role of Juliet) 2. (E) she ~ed to play Juliet

auditorium *n.* 1. a main ~ 2. to fill, pack an ~ (a pianist like her can easily pack even the largest ~) 3. to empty an ~ 4. an ~ empties; fills 5. an ~ holds, seats (the ~ seats 700 people = it's a 700-seater ~) 6. in, into an ~ (700 people can fit into the ~)

augur *v.* (P) (formal) to ~ ill; well this success ~s well for the future

aunt *n.* a great ~

aura *n.* 1. to have an ~ about 2. a glittering ~ (of) (a charismatic politician with a glittering ~ of success about her)

auspices *n.* under the ~ of smt. (under the ~ of the mayor's office)

austerity *n.* 1. to practice ~ 2. strict; wartime ~ USAGE NOTE: One can also say, in reference to religious discipline, *to practice austerities.*

authenticate *v.* (D; tr.) to ~ as (the painting was ~ed as genuine)

authenticity *n.* 1. to establish, prove; vouch for the ~ of smt. (tests established the ~ of the painting) 2. to doubt, question the ~ of smt.

author *n.* 1. to read an ~ (Dickens is a much-loved ~ whom nearly everyone claims to have read) 2. an anonymous; beginning; best-selling; classic; contemporary; established, famous, noted, prize-winning, recognized, well-known; much-loved; prolific; rising; talented; young; unpublished ~ 3. an ~ writes (an ~ of children's books who has written several)

authorities *n.* ["officials"] civil, civilian; government; local; military; occupation ~

authority *n.* ["control"] ["power"] 1. to assert, demonstrate, show; assume; establish; delegate; exercise, exert, use, wield; have; invoke ~ 2. to give up, relinquish, yield ~ 3. to challenge, defy; deny, reject; rebel against; undermine; usurp ~ 4. absolute, complete, full, supreme, unquestioned ~ 5. parental ~ 6. ~ for; over (he assumed ~ for overseas operations; a commanding officer has complete ~ over her personnel) 7. in; with; without ~ (who was in ~?) 8. of ~ (a figure, man, woman of ~; there was an air of ~ about her) 9. under smb.'s ~ (these employees are under my ~) ["legal power"] ["authorization"] 10. to abuse, overstep one's ~ 11. legal; ministerial; presidential; reviewing (mil.); royal ~ 12. by, on smb.'s ~ ("by whose ~ were these funds spent?" "she did it on her own ~") 13. the ~ to + inf. (the police had the ~ to conduct a search; a commanding officer with the ~ to send troops into battle) 14. (misc.) a position of ~ (I am in a position of ~ over these employees) ["expert"] ["source"] 15. to cite, invoke an ~ 16. an acknowledged; appropriate, competent, reliable; indisputable, irrefutable, unimpeachable, unquestioned; leading, respected, world ~; the greatest living ~ 17. an ~ on (an outstanding ~ on chess) 18. on ~ (to have smt. on good ~; we have it on the highest ~ that the meeting has been cancelled) ["government office"] 19. health; local authorities; an airport; a port ~; school authorities

authorization *n.* 1. to give, grant ~ 2. to receive ~ 3. to revoke smb.'s ~ 4. official ~ 5. ~ for; from 6. (the) ~ to + inf. (we received ~ from the local authorities to begin demolition) 7. with; without ~

authorize *v.* 1. (H) the director ~d him to enter the vault 2. (K) the director ~d his entering the vault

authorized *adj.* 1. (usu. does not stand alone) ~ to + inf. (he is not ~ to enter the vault)

authorship *n.* to dispute; establish ~ (to establish the ~ of an ancient manuscript)

automate *v.* to ~ fully

automatic *adj.* fully ~

automatic pilot *n.* 1. to engage, switch on; disengage, switch off the ~ 2. on ~

automobile *n.* (AE) to drive, operate; park an ~ (see car 2–11)

autonomy *n.* 1. to grant ~ 2. to enjoy, have ~ 3. to seek ~ 4. full; local ~

autopsy *n.* to do, perform an ~ (on)

autumn *n.* 1. early; last; late; mid-; next ~ 2. during the, in (the) ~ (we met late in the ~ of 1995 = we met in the late ~ of 1995) 3. (misc.) there is a touch of ~ in the air; a harbinger of ~ (see also *autumn equinox, autumnal equinox* at **equinox**)

auxiliary *n.* 1. (grammar) a modal ~ 2. (BE) a nursing ~

avail I *n.* (formal) ["aid"] 1. of little ~ 2. to no ~ (we did what we could but unfortunately it was all to no ~)

avail II *v.* (formal) 1. (d; intr.) ("to help") to ~ against (nothing could ~ against the enemy attack) 2. (d; refl.) ("to make use") to ~ of (she ~ed herself of the offer)

available *adj.* 1. easily, readily ~ 2. to make oneself ~; to make smt. ~ 3. ~ about, on; to 4. ~ for (are you ~ for a meeting tomorrow?) 5. ~ from (information on that subject is readily ~ to anyone from the Internet) 6. ~ to + inf. (is there anyone ~ to replace her?)

avalanche *n.* 1. to set off, trigger an ~ 2. an ~ buries; strikes 3. in an ~ (skiers killed in an ~) 4. (fig.) in, under an ~ of (managers buried under an ~ of memos)

avenge *v.* (D; tr.) to ~ by (she ~d her father's murder by revenging herself on his murderer)

avenue *n.* ["opportunity"] 1. to exhaust, explore, pursue every ~ 2. an ~ to (an ~ to success) ["street"] 3. in (BE), on (AE) an ~

aver *v.* (formal) (L) he ~red that he was innocent

average *n.* 1. to calculate, work out an ~ 2. (misc.) above ~; below ~; on ~/(AE) on the ~ she works seven hours a day; (AE) he finished school with a B ~

average out *v.* (d; intr., tr.) to ~ at, to (snowfall ~s out in this part of the country at/to twenty inches a year)

averse *adj.* (formal) 1. distinctly, markedly, strongly ~; risk-averse (a risk-averse society that won't let children play on their own) 2. ~ to (I wouldn't be ~ to (having) a drink)

aversion *n.* (formal) 1. to develop; feel, have; take an ~ to 2. to overcome an ~ 3. a deep, deep-rooted, distinct, marked, strong; natural; pet ~; risk-aversion 4. an ~ to (to overcome an ~ to animals)

avert *v.* 1. (D; tr.) to ~ from (he ~ed his eyes from the scene of the accident) 2. (misc.) the accident was narrowly ~ed

aviation *n.* civil; military ~

avid *adj.* (formal) (usu. does not stand alone) ~ for (~ for fame)

avoid *v.* 1. to ~ narrowly; studiously 2. (G) to studiously ~ volunteering for anything difficult 3. (misc.) to ~ at all costs; to ~ like the plague (to ~ like the plague volunteering for anything difficult)

avoidance *n.* tax ~ (esp. BE) USAGE NOTE: It is legal to avoid taxes but illegal to evade them; thus tax avoidance is legal but tax evasion is not.

avow *v.* (formal) 1. to ~ openly, publicly 2. to ~ solemnly 3. (L) they ~ed that they had been wrong 4. (M or N; used with a noun) he openly ~ed himself (to be) a socialist = he is an openly ~ed socialist

avowal *n.* 1. to make an ~ 2. an open, public ~ 3. a solemn ~ 4. an ~ to + inf. (his open ~ to be a socialist was soon forgotten) 5. an ~ that + clause (he made an open ~ that he was a socialist!)

await *v.* to ~ eagerly (an eagerly ~ed and long-awaited event)

awake I *adj.* 1. half; fully, wide ~ 2. ~ to (~ to the danger of inflation) 3. (misc.) to lie ~

awake II *v.* 1. (D; intr.) to ~ from, out of (she awoke from a deep sleep) 2. (d; intr.) to ~ to (I awoke to bright sunlight) 3. (E) they awoke to find the house in flames 4. (s) I awoke refreshed

awaken *v.* 1. see **awake II** 2. (d; tr.) to ~ to (to ~ smb. to a sense of duty)

awakening *n.* 1. a rude, sudden ~ 2. a sexual ~ 3. a spiritual ~

award I *n.* 1. to confer, grant, make, present an ~ 2. to accept an ~ 3. to earn, receive, win an ~ 4. a posthumous ~ 5. (BE) a pay ~ 6. the ~ went to the best student 7. an ~ from; for (she won an ~ from the judges for her research)

award II *v.* 1. (A) the judges ~ed the prize to her; or: the judges ~ed her the prize 2. (D; tr.) to ~ for (the judges ~ed her a prize for her research)

aware *adj.* (usu. cannot stand alone) 1. acutely, all too, keenly, only too, painfully, very (much), well ~ 2. dimly, hardly ~ 3. ~ of (they were only too well ~ of the harmfulness of smoking) 4. ~ that + clause (they were only too well ~ that smoking is harmful) USAGE NOTE: The adjective *aware* can be used without a following *of* or *that-clause* when it is preceded by such an adverb as *politically*: a politically aware person who knows what all the candidates stand for.

awareness *n.* 1. growing, heightened ~ 2. public ~ 3. to heighten, increase, raise ~ 4. ~ among 5. ~ that + clause (there is a growing ~ among the general public that smoking is harmful)

awash *adj.* ~ with

away *adv.* 1. far ~ 2. ~ from (he is ~ from home) (see also Usage Notes at **far**)

awe I *n.* 1. to inspire ~ in (he inspired ~ in everyone = he inspired everyone with ~) 2. to hold smb. in ~ 3. deep, great ~ 4. in; with ~ (to contemplate the stars with ~ at their magnificence) 5. ~ at 6. in ~ of (to be/stand in ~ of smb.; to contemplate the stars in ~ of their magnificence) 7. (misc.) shock and ~

awe II *v.* (D; tr.) to ~ into (the stars ~ed me into silence)

awestruck *adj.* 1. ~ at (~ at the sight) 2. ~ to + inf. (they were ~ to see the volcano erupt)

awful *adj.* (colloq.) 1. pretty, really, simply ~ 2. ~ about (I feel ~ about it) 3. ~ for (the situation is ~ for all of us) 4. ~ to + inf. (it was really ~ to work there = it was really ~ working there = working there was really ~; it was ~ of them to do that) 5. ~ that + clause (it's ~ that they ¬were/should have been¬ reprimanded because of my mistake)

awhile *adv.* (see Usage Note at **while**)

awkward *adj.* 1. ~ about, at 2. ~ with (he is ~ with children) 3. (BE) ~ for (Monday is ~ for me) 4. ~ to + inf. (it is ~ to discuss such matters in public = it is ~ discussing such matters in public = discussing such matters in public is awkward)

AWOL *adj.* to be; go ~

awry *adj., adv.* to go ~ (our plans have gone ~)

ax, axe *n.* 1. to swing, wield an ~ 2. with an ~ 3. a blow of an ~ 4. an ~ chops, cuts; falls 5. (misc.) to get the ~ ("to be fired; to lose funding") (when projects get the ~ their employees get the ~, too!); to have an ~ to grind ("to have an ulterior motive")

axiom *n.* 1. to lay down an ~ 2. an ~ that + clause (we accept the ~ that a straight line is the shortest distance between two points)

axiomatic *adj.* ~ that + clause (it is ~ that everyone should pay a fair share of taxes; it's ~ that a straight line is the shortest distance between two points)

axis *n.* 1. a horizontal; vertical ~ 2. along; on an ~ (the Earth rotates on its ~ and revolves around the Sun)

B

babble I *n.* childish; confused; incessant ~

babble II *v.* 1. to ~ ceaselessly, incessantly; incoherently 2. (B) he ~d a few words to her about his problems 3. (D; intr.) to ~ about

babe *n.* 1. a ~ in arms ("a small infant; an inexperienced person") 2. a ~ in the woods ("a naive person")

babel *n.* 1. above the ~ (his voice was heard above the ~) 2. a ~ of tongues; voices

baboon *n.* a band, troop of ~s

baby *n.* 1. (of a woman) to give birth to, have a ~; (of a woman, a man, or both) (colloq.) to make a ~ 2. (of a woman) to carry, expect; lose a ~ (a pregnant woman carries a ~ for nine months; to carry a ~ to term; she lost her stillborn ~) 3. (of a mother) to breast-feed, nurse, suckle a ~ 4. (of a midwife, nurse, doctor) to deliver a ~ 5. (of a clergyman) to baptize a ~ 6. to bath (BE), bathe; change a ~ ("to change the baby's diaper/nappy") 7. to calm, comfort, hush a ~ 8. to lull; put; rock a ~ to sleep 9. to diaper (AE); swaddle a ~ 10. to wean a ~ 11. to bubble (AE), burp a ~ 12. a blue; full-term; newborn; premature; stillborn; test-tube ~ 13. a ~ babbles, coos; bawls; cries; is due (to be born) 14. a ~ burps; drools; teethes; throws up 15. a ~ crawls, creeps; toddles 16. (misc.) a bouncing ~ boy; girl

baby buggy *n.* 1. to push, wheel a ~ 2. in a ~ USAGE NOTE: In AE a baby buggy is a baby carriage. In BE a baby buggy is a push-chair (BE) = a stroller (AE).

baby carriage *n.* (AE) 1. to push, wheel a ~ (BE has *pram*) 2. in a ~

baby-sit *v.* (D; intr.) to ~ for (who ~s for you?)

bachelor *n.* 1. a confirmed; eligible ~ 2. (misc.) a ~ of arts; a ~ of science USAGE NOTE: In some varieties of English, "a confirmed bachelor" can be a euphemism for 'a homosexual man.'

back I *adj., adv.* 1. ~ to (things are ~ to normal) 2. far, way ~ (~ back in the eighteenth century) 3. (misc.) to go ~ on one's promise/word ("to fail to keep one's promise")

back II *n.* ["part of the body opposite to the front"] 1. to turn one's ~ to smb.; (usu. fig.) to turn one's ~ on smb. ("to reject or spurn smb.") 2. to arch one's ~ (the cat arched its ~) 3. a broad ~ 4. on one's, smb.'s ~ (to lie on one's ~; a heavy bag was on his ~) 5. (misc.) the small of the ~; to have a bad ~; to stand ~ to ~; they stood with their ~s to the door; they deceived me when my ~ was turned ["rear part"] 6. at, in; near; towards the ~ (of) (a room at the ~ of the house; we sat in the back of the car) 7. from; (BE) round the ~ (go round the ~ of the house to get into the house from the ~)

["area behind smt."] 8. at the, (AE) in ~ of (BE: a garden at the ~ of the house = AE: a yard in ~ of the house) ["misc."] 9. he did it behind my ~ ("he did it without my knowledge"); at/in the ~ of smb.'s mind ("subconsciously"); to break one's ~ ("to work very hard"); to get one's ~ up ("to balk at smt."); get off my ~ (colloq.) ("leave me alone"); if you scratch my ~, I'll scratch yours (colloq.) ("if you help me, I'll help you"); to have one's ~ to the wall ("to be in a desperate position"); to break the ~ of a job ("to do the hardest part of a job"); to put one's/some (AE) ~ into one's work ("to make a maximum physical effort"); who will sit in ~? (AE); wearing a baseball cap ~ to front (see also *the back of beyond* at **beyond**) USAGE NOTE: Something in back of/behind the house is not in the house itself. Something in the back of the house is. Something at the back of the house can be either in back of/behind the house or in the back part of the house itself. So the expression "at the back of" is ambiguous.

back III *v.* 1. to ~ enthusiastically, wholeheartedly 2. (D; tr.) ("to support") to ~ against (the independents will ~ us against the majority party) 3. (D; tr.) to ~ for (we will ~ her enthusiastically for public office) 4. (d; intr., tr.) ("to move") to ~ into (to ~ into a garage; she ~ed the car into the driveway) 5. (d; intr.) to ~ onto (our building ~s onto the main road) 6. (d; intr., tr.) to ~ out of (he ~ed out of the driveway; to ~ a car out of a garage) 7. (D; intr.) ("to withdraw") to ~ out of (they ~ed out of the deal)

backache *n.* 1. to have ~ (BE)/a ~ (AE) 2. (a) chronic, nagging, persistent ~

back away *v.* (D; intr.) to ~ from

backbone *n.* ["courage"] 1. ~ for 2. the ~ to + inf. (will he have the ~ to tell the truth?)

backchat *n.* (BE) see **backtalk**

backdate *v.* (D; tr.) to ~ to (to ~ an agreement to the beginning of the year)

back door *n.* to get in by, through the ~ (usu. fig.) ("to accomplish smt. by devious means")

back down *v.* 1. (D; intr.) to ~ from (they had to ~ from their demands) 2. (D; intr.) to ~ on, over (they had to ~ over the issue of money)

backdrop *n.* 1. to provide a ~ for 2. a ~ to (the ~ to the hearings was complex) 3. against a ~ of

backer *n.* 1. to secure ~s (for a project) 2. a financial; powerful ~

back formation *n.* (ling.) a ~ from (*to burgle* is a ~ from *burglar*)

background *n.* ["smb.'s experience, past"] 1. to have a ~ (in) (what sort of ~ does she have?) 2. to check smb.'s ~ 3. a broad; narrow; rich, well-rounded; specialized ~ 4. a deprived, disadvantaged; middle-class; privileged; working-class ~ 5. smb.'s academic, educational; cultural; ethnic; political; religious; social ~ 6. a ~ for (to have the right ~ for a job) ["back part of a picture, scene"] 7. against, on a

~ (against a dark ~) ["surroundings"] 8. an appropriate, fitting ~ 9. a ~ to (the music served as a ~ to the recitation of poetry) ["a less important position"] 10. to relegate smb. to the ~ 11. in the ~ (to keep, remain, stay in the ~) 12. into the ~ (to fade into the ~) ["history, past"] 13. an historical ~ 14. a ~ of, to (do you know the ~ to this case?; the ~ to the hearings was complex)

backing *n.* 1. to gain, have, secure, win ~ 2. to lose ~ (the project has the enthusiastic ~ of the government) 3. enthusiastic; financial; powerful; wholehearted ~ 4. ~ for; from; with; without (without financial ~ for our project from the government, we're bound to fail)

backlash *n.* 1. to create, provoke, stir up (a) ~ 2. ~ against; from (let's not provoke a ~ against our project from the voters)

backlog *n.* 1. to accumulate, build up a ~ 2. to clear; reduce a ~

back off *v.* (D; intr.) to ~ from (to ~ from one's demands)

backpack *v.* (P; intr.) to ~ across the continent; to go ~ing through Europe

backseat *n.* to take a ~ to smb. (she will not take a ~ to anyone)

backstroke *n.* to do, swim the ~

backtalk *n.* (AE) (colloq.) don't give me any ~! (BE has *backchat*) (see also **talk back**)

backtrack *v.* (D; intr.) to ~ from

backup *n.* ["substitute; reinforcement"] a ~ for, to

back up *v.* 1. (D; intr.) to ~ to (he ~ed up to the loading platform) 2. (D; tr.) to ~ with (they backed us up with a generous contribution)

backwards *adv.* 1. to go ~; to step ~; to walk ~ 2. to put smt. in ~ (see also *bend over backwards* at **bend II**)

backwater *n.* a cultural; provincial ~

bacon *n.* 1. back (esp. BE) = Canadian (US); crisp; lean; smoked; streaky (BE) ~ 2. a rasher, slice of ~ 3. (misc.) to bring home the ~ ("to succeed"); (BE) to save smb.'s ~ ("to rescue smb. from a difficulty")

bacteria *n.* 1. to grow ~ 2. non-pathogenic; pathogenic; virulent ~ 3. a colony; strain, type of ~

bad I *adj.* 1. ~ for (smoking is ~ for your health) 2. ~ to + inf. (it's ~ to lie; it's ~ for your health to smoke) 3. ~ that + clause (it's too ~ that he was not able to attend the meeting) 4. (misc.) the meat went ~; to feel ~ about smt.; not ~ ("quite good"); not half ~ ("rather good"); that's (just) too ~ ("nothing can be done about that") (see also *bad form* at **form I**) USAGE NOTE: The expression "to feel badly about smt." is an alternative to "to feel ~ about smt."

bad II *n.* 1. (colloq.) to be in ~ with smb. ("to be on bad terms with smb.") 2. to go from ~ to worse

badge *n.* see **button** 8

badger *v.* 1. (D; tr.) to ~ into (they ~ed me into buying a new car) 2. (D; tr.) to ~ with (to ~ smb. with questions) 3. (H) they ~ed me to buy a new car

USAGE NOTE: Note "They kept ~ing me to buy a new car until they finally succeeded in ~ing me into buying one."

badly *adv.* 1. to do ~ (at, in, on) 2. (misc.) are things going ~ for/with you?; to think ~ of (I don't want you to think ~ of me)

baffle *v.* 1. to ~ completely 2. (R) it ~d me that they rejected/should have rejected our offer 3. (misc.) it ~d me why they rejected our offer

bag *n.* ["suitcase"] 1. to pack, unpack one's ~s 2. to check; label one's ~s ["container"]["pouch"] 3. a ~ bursts; contains, holds 4. an air ~ (that inflates within a car on impact) 5. a barracks; duffel; flight; garment; musette (AE); overnight ~ (see also *kit bag* at **kit**) 6. a carrier (BE); clutch; shopping; shoulder ~ 7. a jiffy ("padded bag used for mailing"); mailbag, postbag (BE); paper; plastic ~ 8. a sleeping ~ 9. a body ~ 10. an ice ~ 11. (BE) a sponge ~ ("bag for toilet articles") 12. a doggy ~ ("bag given to a diner in a restaurant to take home leftover parts of a meal") 13. (AE) a grab ~ (BE has *lucky dip*) 14. (misc.) a ~ of (bought a ~ of potatoes) 15. a tea ~ ["leather ball"] 16. (AE) a punching ~ (BE has *punch ball*) ["misc."] 17. (a) diplomatic ~ (the top-secret letter was sent by diplomatic ~) (BE: AE has *diplomatic pouch*) 18. smt. is in the ~ ("smt. is assured of success")

baggage *n.* 1. to check; claim one's ~; (esp. AE) to check one's ~ through (to the final destination) 2. carry-on, hand; excess ~ 3. unclaimed ~ 4. a piece of ~ 5. (misc.) (fig.) emotional; ideological; intellectual ~

bagpipes *n.* 1. to play the ~ 2. ~ skirl, wail

bail I *n.* 1. to grant, set ~ 2. to post, put up, stand ~ for; (colloq.) to go ~ for 3. to make, raise ~ 4. to deny, refuse smb. ~ 5. to forfeit, jump, skip ~ 6. on ~ (to free/release smb. on ~; to be out on ~; to be set free on a thousand dollars' ~)

bail II *v.* 1. (AE) (d; intr.) ("to parachute") to ~ out of (to ~ out of an airplane) 2. (D; tr.) ("to remove") to ~ out of (~ water out of a boat) 3. (d; tr.) ("to help") to ~ out of (to ~ smb. out of trouble)

bailiwick *n.* in one's own ~

bait *n.* (often fig.) 1. to hold out, offer; put out, set out ~ 2. to nibble at; swallow, take the ~ 3. to rise to the ~ 4. tempting ~

bake *v.* (C) he ~d a cake/a potato for us; or: he ~d us a cake/a potato

bakery *n.* at, in a ~ (she works at/in a ~)

balance I *n.* 1. to strike a ~ between 2. to keep, maintain; recover, regain one's ~ 3. to lose one's ~ 4. to disturb, upset the ~; to throw smt./smb. off ~ 5. to shift/tip the ~ in smb.'s favor; to redress/restore the ~ 6. a delicate ~ 7. (bookkeeping) a trial ~ 8. a bank; credit; debit ~ 9. a foreign-trade, trade ~ 10. a favorable; unfavorable ~ (a favorable ~ of trade) 11. the strategic ~ 12. (misc.) to hang in the ~ ("to be uncertain"); on ~ ("all in all"); a work-life ~ (to find a satisfying work-life ~)

balance II v. (d; tr.) to ~ against; with (to ~ one argument against the other)

balanced adj. 1. evenly ~ (between) 2. well-balanced (see also *a balanced diet = a well-balanced diet* at **diet**)

balance of power n. 1. to hold the ~ 2. to change; tip; upset the ~

bale (BE) see **bail II** 1

balk, baulk v. (D; intr.) to ~ at (he ~ed at the price)

Balkans n. in the ~

ball I n. ["game"] 1. (AE) to play ~ 2. (the game of) baseball; basketball; softball ["ball used in a game"] 3. to bat; bounce; bowl; carry; catch; drop; fumble; hit; kick; pass; pitch; throw, toss a ~ 4. a ~ bounces 5. the ~ is dead ("the ball does not bounce") 6. a baseball; basketball; beach; bowling; cricket; cue ~; football; golf; medicine; ping-pong; softball; tennis ~; volleyball (see also **golf ball**) 7. (BE) a punch ~ (AE has *punching bag*) ["rounded mass"] 8. a cannonball; cotton ~ (see also **snowball**) 9. a wrecker's ~ 10. in; into a ~ (to curl/roll up in a ~) ["big glass ball used in fortune telling"] 11. a crystal ~ [(in baseball and softball)] 12. a fly; ground ~ (the batter hit a fly ~ to center field) ["misc."] 13. to get, set, start the ~ rolling ("to begin an activity"); (colloq.) on the ~ ("efficient"); (AE; colloq.) to play ~ (with) ("to cooperate (with)")

ball II n. ["formal dance"] 1. to have, organize a ~ 2. a costume; fancy-dress; inaugural; masked ~ 3. at a ~ (to dance at a ~) 4. (misc.) (colloq.) to have a ~ ("to enjoy oneself")

ballad n. 1. to compose a ~ 2. to perform a ~ 3. a folk; lewd, ribald ~

ballast n. 1. to take on ~ 2. to drop ~

ballet n. 1. to dance, perform (in); choreograph, stage a ~ 2. classical; folk ~; (a) water ~

balloon I n. 1. to fly; launch a ~ 2. to blow up, inflate; deflate; pop a ~ 3. a ~ bursts 4. a ~ comes down, drops; floats; goes up, rises 5. a barrage; captive; hot-air; observation ~ 6. by ~ (to travel by ~) 7. (fig.) a trial ~ (to ¬float/send up¬ a trial ~ to test people's reactions)

balloon II v. (d; intr.) to ~ into (to ~ into a scandal)

ballot n. 1. to cast a ~ 2. to rig; invalidate a ~ 3. an absentee; open; postal; secret; straw; void ~ 4. a ~ against; for 5. by ~ (to vote by secret ~) 6. on a ~ (our candidate's name is on the ~ in every state)

ballot box n. 1. to stuff the ~es 2. at the ~ (the issue will be decided at the ~)

balm n. 1. to apply (a) ~ 2. a healing, soothing ~

bamboozle v. (colloq.) ("to trick") 1. (D; tr.) to ~ into 2. (D; tr.) to ~ out of

ban I n. 1. to impose, place, put a ~ on 2. to lift a ~ from 3. a smoking; (nuclear) test ~ 4. a wartime ~ 5. a ~ on 6. a ~ comes into force, takes effect (the ~ on smoking came into force on Monday)

ban II v. 1. (D; tr.) to ~ from (they were ~ned from attending) 2. (K) the police ~ned their demonstrating in the park

banana n. 1. to peel a ~ 2. a green; ripe; rotten ~ 3. a bunch of ~s

band I n. ["group of musicians"] 1. to conduct, lead; form a ~ 2. a brass; concert; dance; jazz; klezmer; marching; military; ragtime; regimental; rock; school; string ~ 3. a big ~ 4. a ~ member; leader 5. in a ~ 6. a ~ marches; performs, plays 7. (misc.) to strike up the ~; a tribute ~ (they formed a Beatles tribute ~ to perform Beatles songs) ["group"] 8. a predatory; roving ~ 9. an age; income; tax ~ (if you earn more you will fall into a higher tax ~) 10. a ~ of marauders USAGE NOTE: Nowadays "band" can be used colloquially of a symphony orchestra by fans of classical music – under its present conductor the Amsterdam Concertgebouw remains one of the world's greatest ~s.

band II n. ["ring"] 1. a wedding ~ ["range of wavelengths"] 2. a wave ~ 3. a citizens' ~ (or: CB) ["circular strip"] 4. a brake; elastic (BE), rubber; watchband (CE; BE also has *watch strap*) ~

bandage n. 1. to apply, put on; change a ~ 2. to wrap a ~ (around); to roll a ~ 3. to remove a ~ 4. to loosen; tighten a ~

Band-Aid (T) n. (esp. AE; BE has *Elastoplast* (T)) to apply, put on a ~

bandit n. a masked ~

band together v. 1. (D; intr., refl.) to ~ against (the liberals ~ed together against the new legislation) 2. (E) the liberals ~ed together to oppose the new legislation

bandwagon n. ["attractive cause"] to climb aboard/on, jump aboard/on the ~

bandy v. to ~ words with smb. (about smt.)

bang I n. 1. with a ~ (the door slammed shut with a ~) 2. (misc.) (AE) to go over with a ~ ("to be successful"); "This is the way the world ends/Not with a ~ but a whimper." – T.S. Eliot, "The Hollow Men" (1925)

bang II v. 1. (d; intr.) to ~ against, at; into; on (she ~ed on the door; I ~ed into the wall) 2. (D; tr.) to ~ against, on (he ~ed his head on the low ceiling) 3. (N) the door ~ed shut

bang away v. (colloq.) (D; intr.) ("to shoot") to ~ at (the enemy plane kept ~ing away at us)

bang down v. (D; intr., tr.) to ~ on (he ~ed his fist down on the drum; he ~ed down on the table)

banger n. ["firecracker"] (BE) 1. to let off (esp. BE), light, set off a ~ 2. a ~ goes off

banish v. 1. (D; tr.) to ~ for (they were ~ed for supporting a free press) 2. (D; tr.) to ~ from; to (she was ~ed from one country to another)

banister n. to slide down a ~ (BE also has *to slide down the bannisters*)

banjo n. to play; pluck; strum a ~

bank I n. ["financial establishment"] 1. to charter; establish a ~ 2. a central; commercial; credit; export-import; investment; land; national, people's, state; merchant (BE); reserve; savings ~ 3. a drive-in ~ 4. a ~ closes, collapses, fails 5. at, in;

from, out of a ~ (she works at/in a ~; to deposit money in a ~ and withdraw it from a ~) ["fund held in a gambling game"] 6. to break the ~ ["place of storage"] 7. a blood; corneal, eye; data; organ; soil; sperm; tissue ~ 8. a citation ~ (for dictionaries)

bank II v. 1. (d; intr.) to ~ on ("to rely on") (we were ~ing on your support) (see also **bank on**) 2. (D; intr.) to ~ with ("to have a bank account with") ("Who do you ~ with?" "I ~ with my local branch.")

bank III n. ["shore esp. of a river or canal"] 1. a rugged; sloping; steep ~ 2. a river ~ 3. on a ~ 4. (misc.) the ~s were flooded; a cloud ~ USAGE NOTE: the bank(s) of a river or canal; the shore of a lake or sea; the coast (of an ocean).

bank IV n. ["row"]["tier"] an elevator (AE) ~

banker n. an international; investment; merchant (BE) ~

banking n. 1. electronic; international ~ 2. (misc.) where do you do your ~?

bank on v. 1. (d.; intr.) to ~ for (they are ~ing on the government for funds) 2. (E) we were ~ing on you to support us

bankrupt adj. 1. morally ~ 2. to go ~ 3. to declare smb./oneself ~

bankruptcy n. to declare, go into, file for, petition for ~

banner n. 1. to plant; unfurl; wave a ~ 2. a ~ bears a slogan; flutters, waves 3. a regimental ~ 4. (fig.) under a ~ (to do horrible things under the ~ of reform)

banns n. ["declaration of an impending marriage"] to publish, read the ~

banquet n. 1. to arrange, give, have, hold a ~ 2. to cater a ~ 3. an elaborate, lavish, real, sumptuous ~ 4. a farewell; formal; state; wedding ~ 5. a ~ for 6. at a ~

banter n. 1. to exchange ~ with 2. good-natured, light; witty ~

baptism n. 1. to administer ~; to perform a ~ 2. to accept, receive, undergo ~ 3. (misc.) (to undergo) a ~ of fire (my first day in the new job was a real ~ of fire!)

baptize v. (N; used with a noun) they ~d him Joseph

bar I n. ["counter or place where drinks and sometimes food are sold"] 1. to manage, operate, run a ~ 2. to serve behind a; tend (AE) ~ 3. to stop at a ~ (on the way home); to drink at/in a ~; to drop into a ~ 4. a cash; open ("free") (AE) ~ 5. a cocktail; public (BE); saloon (BE) ~ 6. a coffee (BE); salad; snack ~ 7. a gay; singles ~ ["barrier"] 8. a color ~ (to cross the color ~) 9. a ~ to (a ~ to success) ["barrier in a law court"] 10. at the ~ (the prisoner at the ~; to be tried at the ~) 11. before the ~ (of justice) ["the profession of barrister, trial lawyer"] 12. to be admitted, (esp. BE) called to the ~ 13. (esp. BE) to read for the ~ ["metal strip used as a barrier"] 14. behind ~s ("in prison") (he was put behind ~s) ["strip used in gymnastics"]

15. a horizontal ~ 16. parallel ~s 17. on the ~ (to work out on the ~) ["handrail used by ballet dancers"] 18. at the ~ (to warm up at the ~) ["metal strip used in a suspension system"] 19. a torsion ~ ["lever on a typewriter"] 20. a space ~ (to press the space ~) ["oblong piece"] 21. a candy; chocolate ~ ["musical measure"] 22. to hum; play; sing a few ~s ["misc."] 23. a nail ~ (like a beauty parlor for nails)

bar II v. 1. (D; tr.) ("to exclude") to ~ from (he was ~red from the competition) 2. (K) ("to forbid") they ~red his participating in the competition (see also **barred**)

barb n. ["critical remark"] 1. to aim, sling ~s at 2. a ~ stings

barbarism, barbarity n. 1. to demonstrate, display ~ 2. outright, unmitigated, utter ~ 3. an act of ~ (to commit an act of ~)

barbarous adj. ~ to + inf. (it was ~ of them to treat prisoners in that manner)

barbecue I n. ["party at which barbecued meat is served"] 1. to have a ~ 2. at a ~ 3. a backyard ~

barbecue II v. (C) she ~d a steak for me; or: she ~d me a steak

barbed wire, (AE) **barbwire** n. to string ~

barbell n. 1. to clean; lift; press a ~ 2. an adjustable ~

barber n. at the ~'s

barbershop n. (esp. AE) at, in a ~ (he is at/in the ~)

bare I adj. 1. ~ of (the hills were ~ of vegetation) 2. (misc.) to strip smt. ~ (strip the wall bare before painting it) (see also *lay bare* at **lay**)

bare II v. (B) she ~d her soul to us

barefoot adv. to go, walk ~

bargain I n. ["agreement"] 1. to drive; make, strike; seal a ~ 2. to meet one's end of a ~ 3. a Faustian; hard ~ (she drives a hard ~) 4. a ~ between; with (we struck a ~ with them) 5. a ~ to + inf. (they made a ~ not to cut prices) ["advantageously cheap purchase"] 6. to find, get a ~ 7. to hunt for a ~ 8. to shop for ~s 9. a good, real ~ ["misc."] 10. to make the best of a bad ~ ("to do one's best in a difficult situation"); in (AE), into (BE) the ~ ("in addition, along with")

bargain II v. 1. ("to negotiate") to ~ shrewdly 2. (D; intr.) ("to negotiate") to ~ for; over; with (we ~ed with them for the property) 3. (d; intr.) to ~ for, on (AE) ("to count on") (I wasn't ~ing on any trouble; it was more than I had ~ed for)

bargaining n. 1. collective; plea ~ 2. (misc.) a ~ position (don't give in: we're in a very strong ~ position)

barge I n. 1. to drive; float; tow a ~ 2. to load; unload a ~

barge II v. 1. (d; intr.) to ~ into (she ~d into the room) 2. (P; intr., tr.) they ~ed out of the restaurant; he ~d his way past the guard; she ~d through the crowd; she just ~d in without permission

barge in v. (D; intr.) to ~ on (she just ~ed in on our conversation without permission)

baritone *n*. 1. to sing ~ 2. a deep, rich ~ 3. a bass ~

bark I *n*. [" – of a tree"] ~ peels

bark II *n*. ["as of a dog"] 1. to give, let out a ~ 2. a furious; loud, noisy ~

bark III *v*. 1. to ~ furiously 2. (B) the sergeant ~ed an order to his squad 3. (D; intr., tr.) to ~ at (the dog ~ed at the jogger; the general ~ed a command at her staff) 4. (misc.) "Do it!" he ~ed (to his squad)

barn *n*. a car ~ (AE; BE has *waggon shed*)

barnacle *n*. 1. ~s cling (to the bottom of a ship) 2. (misc.) to cling like a ~

barnstorm *v*. 1. (P; intr.) to ~ around the country; to ~ through the whole state 2. (misc.) to go ~ing around the country / through the state

barometer *n*. 1. an aneroid; mercury ~ 2. a ~ is steady; falls; rises

baron *n*. ["magnate"] a cattle; coal; drug; media; oil; press; robber; steel ~

barracks *n*. 1. (AE) to GI the ~ 2. (AE) to police (up) the ~ 3. army; disciplinary; police ~ 4. restricted to ~

barrage *n*. 1. to lay down a ~ 2. to lift a ~ 3. an artillery; rolling ~ 4. an advertising; propaganda ~ 5. (fig.) to face a ~ of questions

barred *adj*. ~ to (esp. AE) (the street was ~ to traffic)

barrel *n*. 1. to tap a ~ 2. a beer ~ 3. (misc.) (colloq.) to have smb. over a ~ ("to have placed smb. in a difficult position")

barricade *n*. 1. to build, erect, place, put up, set up a ~ 2. to storm a ~ 3. to remove, take down a ~ 4. a barbed-wire ~ 5. a ~ across; against

barrier *n*. 1. to erect, place, put up, set up a ~; to form a human ~ 2. to overcome; take a ~ (the horse took the ~ easily) 3. to break down; break through; remove a ~ 4. the sonic, sound ~ (to break the sound ~) 5. a crash (BE); crush (BE), police ~ 6. a cultural; ethnic; language; racial; religious; social ~ (to break a racial ~) 7. a tariff; trade ~ 8. a ~ between 9. a ~ to (old ideas are / constitute / form a ~ to progress and a ~ between peoples) 10. (BE) at a ~ (please show your ticket at the ~ before going on to the platform)

barter I *n*. 1. to engage in ~ (to engage in ~ for furs with the local hunters) 2. ~ between; for; with

barter II *v*. 1. (D; intr., tr.) to ~ for (to ~ tobacco for furs with the local hunters) 2. (D; intr.) to ~ with

base I *n*. ["center of operations"] 1. to establish, set up a ~ 2. to close (down) a ~; live on a ~; return to (a) ~; shop at a ~ 3. an advanced, forward; home; main ~ 4. an air, air-force; army; military; missile; naval ~ 5. an enemy ~ 6. (misc.) a power ~; a ~ of operations ["goal"] (esp. AE) (baseball and softball) 7. to reach; touch (a) ~ 8. to steal a ~ 9. first; second; third ~ (the batter hit a sacrifice that allowed the runner to score from third (base)) 10. (misc.) (colloq.) she couldn't get to first ~ with them ("she couldn't even begin to achieve any success with them"); (esp. AE; colloq.) to touch ~ with ("to

make contact with"); (esp. AE; colloq.) to cover, touch all the ~es ("to discuss everything relevant") (see also *home plate* at **plate** 10) ["collection"] 11. a database ["basic ingredient"] 12. an oil ~ ["foundation"] 13. a firm, solid ~

base II *v*. 1. to ~ largely, mainly; loosely, to some extent 2. (d; tr.) to ~ on, upon (we ~d our conclusions on facts and on certain key assumptions) USAGE NOTE: You will also find such examples as – ? our conclusions are ~ed around certain key assumptions. The construction "? based around" is disliked by many people.

base III *n*. 1. to sing ~ 2. a deep, rich ~

baseball *n*. ["game"] 1. to play ~ 2. night ~ 3. the game of ~ 4. (misc.) a ~ game; player ["ball"] 5. to bat, hit; pitch a ~

basement *n*. 1. (AE) a finished; full ~ 2. a bargain ~ (in a department store) 3. in a ~

bash I *n*. (slang) (BE) ["attempt"] 1. to have a ~ at smt. ["lively party"] 2. to give, have, throw a ~

bash II *v*. (D; tr.) to ~ against (he ~ed his head against the door)

bashful *adj*. ~ about; with

basic *adj*. ~ to

basics *n*. back to (the) ~

basic training *n*. (mil.) to go through, take ~

basin *n*. 1. a river; tidal; yacht ~ 2. a handbasin (BE), washbasin, wash-hand (BE) ~ (see **sink I** *n*.)

basis *n*. 1. to be, form, provide a ~ for 2. a trial ~ 3. a firm, solid, sound; shaky ~; to have no ~ in fact (my theory has a firm ~; yours has no ~ in fact) 4. a first-name ~ 5. a scientific ~ 6. a ~ for, of 7. on a ~ (on a solid ~; she was promoted on the ~ of her accomplishments; to be paid on an hourly ~; to be on a first-name ~ (with)) USAGE NOTE: Remember the alternatives to "on … basis" when discussing repeated action. "To be paid on an hourly basis" is equivalent to "to be paid by the hour"; "to visit smb. on a regular basis" is equivalent to "to visit smb. regularly"; "to visit smb. on a once-a-week basis" is, of course, equivalent to "to visit smb. once a week."

bask *v*. to ~ in (to ~ in the sunshine; to ~ in the adulation of one's followers)

basket *n*. ["receptacle"] 1. to make, weave a ~ 2. a laundry, linen (BE); picnic; sewing; wastebasket (AE), wastepaper ~ 3. a wicker ~ 4. in, into a ~ 5. from, out of a ~ 6. a ~ of (a ~ of fruit) ["goal in basketball"] 7. to make, score, shoot, sink a ~ 8. to shoot at the ~ 9. to miss the ~

basketball *n*. ["game"] 1. to play ~ ["ball used in the game of basketball"] 2. to dribble; pass a ~

bass *n*. 1. to sing ~ 2. a deep, rich ~

bat I *n*. ["club"] 1. to swing a ~ 2. a baseball; cricket; ping-pong, table-tennis ~ ["smb.'s turn batting"] 3. (AE) at ~ (who's at ~?) ["misc."] 4. (colloq.) (BE) at full ~ ("very fast"); (AE) right off the ~ ("immediately"); to go to ~ for ("to act in support of") (he went to ~ for me when I was in a jam)

bat II *n.* ["flying mammal"] 1. ~s fly at night 2. (misc.) as blind as a ~

batch *n.* 1. a fresh ~ (of dough) 2. in ~es

bath *n.* 1. to give (the baby) a ~ 2. to have (BE), take a ~ 3. to draw (esp. AE), run a ~ 4. (BE) a swimming ~ ("an indoor swimming pool") 5. a cold; hot; warm ~ 6. a sitz; steam, Turkish; whirlpool ~ 7. a sunbath 8. a sunken ~ 9. in a ~ 10. (misc.) a blood ~ ("slaughter") USAGE NOTE: In BE, one meaning of *bath* is "bathtub".

bathe *v.* (D; tr.) to ~ in (she ~d her bruises in lukewarm water)

bathed *adj.* ~ in (~ in sunshine)

bather *n.* a sun ~

bathing *n.* sun ~

bathing suit *n.* (esp. AE; old-fashioned in CE) a one-piece; two-piece ~ (see also *bathing suit* at **suit I** *n.*)

bathroom *n.* an en-suite ~ USAGE NOTE: Esp. in AE, "bathroom" can be a euphemism for 'toilet': I need the ~; (I need) to go to, use the ~ (see also the Usage Notes for **apartment**; **room**)

bathtub *n.* (esp. AE; BE prefers *bath*) 1. to fill the ~ (for a bath) 2. to empty the ~ (after a bath) 3. to clean out; scrub (out) a ~

baton *n.* 1. (in a relay race) to pass the ~ 2. (of a drum major or majorette) to twirl a ~ 3. (of an orchestra conductor) to raise a ~ 4. a police ~ 5. (in music) under the ~ of (the Berlin Philharmonic Orchestra under the baton of Wilhelm Furtwängler)

battalion *n.* to command a ~ (a major commands a ~)

batter I *n.* ["mixture for baking"] 1. to mix; pour; stir (a) ~ 2. pancake ~

batter II *v.* 1. (D; intr., tr.) to ~ against, on (the wind ~ed the boat against the rocks) 2. (D; tr.) to ~ into (he ~ed his opponent into submission) 3. (D; tr.) to ~ to (to ~ smt. to pieces)

batter III *n.* ["one whose turn it is to bat"] (baseball) a leadoff ~

battering *n.* to take a ~

battery *n.* ["a group of cells that store and furnish current"] 1. to charge; recharge a ~ 2. to discharge, run down a ~ 3. an alkaline; flashlight (AE), torch (BE); storage ~ 4. a ~ charges (itself) 5. a ~ discharges, runs (itself) down 6. a ~ is dead, flat (BE) ["artillery unit"] 7. to command a ~ (a captain commands a ~) 8. an anti-aircraft; missile ~ (see also *assault and battery* at **assault**)

battle I *n.* 1. to do, give, join ~ 2. to fight; lose; win a ~ 3. to break off, terminate a ~ 4. a bloody; decisive; fierce, pitched, raging; ~ 5. a constant; running ~ 6. a decisive; losing; uphill ~ (engaged in a losing ~) 7. a legal ~ 8. an historic ~ 9. a land; naval ~ 10. a political ~ 11. a ~ royal 12. a ~ takes place; rages 13. a ~ against; among, between; for, over; with (they fought a ~ among themselves for domination of the market; the ~ against inflation; to join ~ with smb.; a ~ between two strong adversaries) 14. a ~ to + inf. (it was a real ~ to win the election; it was a ~ against time to get the patient to the hospital) 15. at a ~ (at the ~ of Gettysburg) 16. in ~ (to be killed in ~) (see also *a battle of wits* at **wits**)

battle II *v.* 1. (D; intr.) to ~ against, with; for, over 2. (misc.) to ~ it out (two teams ~ling it out for the championship); two teams ~ling (in order) to win the championship; only one team can ~ its way to the championship

battlefield *n.* on the ~ (to die on the ~)

battleship *n.* a pocket ~

battle station *n.* to take up one's ~

batty *adj.* (slang) ["crazy, mad"] 1. to drive smb. ~ 2. to go ~ over

baulk (esp. BE) see **balk**

bay I *n.* 1. to hold, keep at ~ 2. to bring to ~

bay II *n.* ["compartment"] a loading ~

bay III *v.* (D; intr.) to ~ at; for (the hounds were ~ing at the fox; the mob was ~ing for blood)

bayonet *n.* 1. to thrust a ~ into (smb.'s body) 2. to fix; unfix ~s

bazaar *n.* 1. a charity; church ~ 2. at a ~

bazooka *n.* to fire; operate a ~

be *v.* 1. (E; usu. in the past) he was never to see his family again; she was to become famous 2. (S) to ~ a teacher; to ~ happy 3. (misc.) you are to appear in court at two o'clock

beach *n.* 1. an isolated; private; public; sandy; shingle ~ 2. across; along; at; on the ~ 3. an expanse, stretch of ~

beachhead *n.* to establish; hold; secure a ~

beacon *n.* 1. a homing; landing; radar; radio; rotating ~ 2. (BE) a Belisha ~ ("a light marking a pedestrian crossing") 3. a ~ to (to serve as a ~ to others)

bead *n.* ["front gunsight"] to draw a ~ on

beads *n.* 1. (rel.) to count, say, tell one's ~ 2. to string; wear ~ 3. (rel.) prayer ~ 4. a string of ~

beam I *n.* ["shaft of light"] 1. to direct, shine a ~ at 2. a high; low ~ (on a car) 3. a ~ from; to ["signal"] 4. a laser; radar; radio ~ 5. (also fig.) off the ~; on the ~ ["piece of wood"] 6. a balance ~ 7. a ~ bears weight, supports smt.

beam II *v.* 1. (B) they ~ed the program to the countries of Central America 2. (AE) (d; tr.) to ~ at (the sales campaign was ~ed at young professionals) 3. (D; intr.) to ~ with (to ~ with joy)

beam down *v.* (D; intr.) to ~ on

bean *n.* 1. broad; French (BE), haricot (BE), kidney; green; lima; navy; pinto; runner (BE), string; soya (AE also has *soybean*); wax ~s 2. coffee ~s 3. baked ~s 4. (misc.) to spill the ~s (slang) ("to reveal a secret"); to use the old ~ (slang) ("to use one's head"); full of ~s (slang) ("mistaken") (AE); ("full of energy") (BE)

bear I *n.* 1. the black; brown; grizzly; koala; Kodiak; polar ~ 2. a teddy ~ 3. ~s growl; hibernate 4. a young ~ is a cub

bear II v. 1. (formal) (A; the omission of *to* is rare) ("to carry") the servants were ~ing food to the guests 2. (A; used without *to*) ("to give birth to") she bore him two children 3. (d; intr.) ("to pertain") to ~ on (these facts ~ on the case) 4. (d; intr.) ("to move") to ~ to (we had to ~ to the right; or we had to ~ right) 5. (d; intr.) ("to have patience") to ~ with (please ~ with me for a few minutes) 6. (E; preceded by: can – cannot – can't – couldn't) ("to stand, tolerate") she can't ~ to watch them suffer 7. (G; often used with: can – cannot – can't – couldn't) ("to stand, tolerate") she can't ~ watching them suffer; her words ~ repeating 8. (K) ("to stand, tolerate"; often used with: can – cannot – can't – couldn't) she can't ~ their suffering so much 9. (O; can be used with one inanimate object) ("to feel") she ~s them a grudge; he ~s (us) no ill will 10. (P; refl.) ("to behave") she bore herself with dignity 11. (misc.) to bring to ~ on (she brought her influence to ~ on the legislators; she can't ~ it when they suffer)

beard n. 1. to grow; have, sport, wear a ~ (you can't get a job wearing a ~ like that!) 2. to shave off; trim one's ~ (you can't get a job unless you shave off your ~!) 3. to stroke one's ~ 4. a bushy, heavy, rough, thick; scraggly, unkempt; tough ~ 5. a light, sparse; neat, trim ~ 6. a ~ grows 7. with a ~ (you can't get a job with a ~ like that!)

bear down v. (d; intr.) to ~ on (the enemy's destroyers bore down on our aircraft carrier; the other car bore down on us without slowing up)

bearing n. ["relation"] 1. to have a ~ on (that fact has no ~ on the case) 2. a direct ~ ["position"] 3. to take a ~ on (we took a ~ on the hill) ["posture"] ["manner"] 4. a dignified; military; proud, regal, royal ~ ["machine part that supports"] 5. to burn out a ~ 6. a ball; roller; wheel ~ ["emblem on a coat of arms"] 7. a heraldic ~

bearings n. ["orientation"] 1. to get one's ~ 2. to lose one's ~

bear up v. (D; intr.) to ~ against, under (to ~ under pressure)

beast n. ["qualities of an animal"] 1. to bring out the ~ in smb. ["animal"] 2. a rare; wild ~ 3. a ~ of burden; a ~ of prey

beat I n. ["a regularly traversed round"] 1. to patrol, pound, walk one's ~ 2. to cover one's ~ 3. a police officer's ~ 4. on one's ~ ["rhythm"] 5. to follow the ~ 6. to miss, skip a ~ 7. on a ~ (to come in on the ~ of three) 8. an irregular; regular, steady ~ 9. to a ~ (to dance to the ~ of the music) ["unit of rhythm"] 10. a ~ to (four ~s to a measure/bar)

beat II v. 1. ("to hit") to ~ brutally, mercilessly, savagely, severely, viciously 2. (sports) ("to defeat") to ~ comfortably; decisively, easily; narrowly; comprehensively, soundly; by ten points 3. (d; intr., tr.) ("to strike") to ~ against (the bird beat its wings against the bars of its cage; the waves ~ against the rocks) 4. (D; tr.) ("to defeat") to ~

at; into (she easily beat me at chess; they beat our team into second place) 5. (D; tr.) ("to strike") to ~ for (to ~ a prisoner for disobedience) 6. (d; tr.) ("to inculcate") to ~ into (to ~ facts into smb.'s head) 7. (d; tr.) ("to hammer") to ~ into (to ~ swords into plowshares) 8. (d; tr.) ("to strike") to ~ into, to (to ~ smb. into submission; to ~ smb. to death) 9. (d; intr.) ("to strike") to ~ on (smb. was ~ing on the door) 10. (d; tr.) ("to extract") to ~ out of (they beat a confession out of him) 11. (colloq.) (D; tr.) ("to arrive ahead of") to ~ to (I'll ~ you to the car!) 12. (N; used with an adjective) ("to strike") they beat him unconscious 13. (colloq.) (R) ("to astound") it ~s me that they turned down the invitation

beat down v. 1. (D; intr.) to ~ on (the sun beat down on us mercilessly) 2. (BE) (D; tr.) ("to persuade to reduce a price") to ~ to (I beat them down to ten pounds)

beating n. 1. to give smb. a ~ 2. to get, take a ~ 3. a bad, brutal, good, merciless, savage, severe, vicious ~ (he got a good ~)

beat out v. (D; tr.) to ~ for (we beat them out for the title by ten points)

beat up v. (AE; slang) (d; intr.) to ~ on ("to beat; beat up") (to ~ on smb.)

beautiful adj. 1. breathtakingly ~ 2. ~ to + inf. (she was ~ to watch)

beauty n. ["a beautiful person or thing"] 1. a dazzling, great, raving, striking ~ 2. a bathing ~ ["good looks"] 3. to enhance ~ 4. dazzling, striking, wholesome ~ ["attractiveness"] 5. natural; scenic ~ 6. of ~ (a work of great ~)

beaver n. 1. a colony of ~s 2. ~s build dams 3. (misc.) an eager ~ ("a zealous person")

beaver away v. (colloq.) (BE) (D; intr.) ("to work hard") to ~ at

because conjunction 1. just ~ (you don't have to drink whiskey just ~ I do! = just ~ I drink whiskey doesn't mean you have to!) 2. (misc.) ~ of (her absence was ~ of illness)

beck n. to be at smb.'s ~ and call

beckon v. 1. (D; intr.) to ~ to (she ~ed to me) 2. (D; intr.) to ~ with (she ~ed me with her finger) 3. (H) she ~ed me to follow her 4. (P; tr.) she ~ed me over 5. (misc.) she ~ed me over with her finger; she ~ed to me with her finger; she ~ed to me to follow her; she ~ed to me for my friends to follow her

become v. 1. (d; intr.) to ~ of (what ever became of her?) 2. (formal) (R) it doesn't ~ you to speak like that 3. (S) she became a teacher; to ~ depressed

becoming adj. ~ to (that tie is not ~ to you)

bed n. ["article of furniture for sleeping"] 1. to make; make up a ~ (I'll make you up a ~ = I'll make a ~ up for you) USAGE NOTE: *to make up a bed* is to put bedclothes on it. *To make a bed* is to re-arrange the bedclothes on it neatly after someone has slept in it. 2. to strip; unmake a ~ 3. to go to ~ with (she went to ~ with a heating pad) USAGE NOTE: *to go to bed with smb.* means "to have sexual intercourse with smb." 4. to be, lie, stay in ~; to lie; sit on a ~; to wet the ~ ("to urinate in it accidentally") 5. to get out of ~ 6. to put smb. to ~ (to put the children to ~) 7. to take to one's ~ ("to remain in bed because of illness") 8. a double; king-size; queen-size; single; twin ~ 9. a bunk; camp (BE); folding; four-poster; hospital; rollaway; sofa; truckle (BE), trundle (AE) ~ 10. a water ~ 11. an unmade ~ 12. a feather ~ ("a feather mattress") (see also *bed and breakfast* at **breakfast**) ["ground at the bottom of a body of water"] 13. a river ~ ["plot of ground"] 14. a flower ~

bedeck *v.* (D; tr.) to ~ with

bedfellow *n.* odd, strange, unlikely ~s (politics make(s) strange ~s)

bedlam *n.* 1. ~ breaks out 2. absolute, complete, sheer, utter ~

bedridden *adj.* ~ with (~ with the flu)

bedroom *n.* a master; spare ~ (the two of you can share the master ~) USAGE NOTE: The size of a home is often measured by its number of bed-rooms: *a three-bedroom apartment.*

bedside *n.* at, by smb.'s ~

bedsore *n.* 1. to develop, get a ~ 2. to prevent a ~

bedtime *n.* it's past my ~

bee I *n.* ["insect"] 1. to keep ~s 2. a bumblebee; honeybee; killer; queen; worker ~; social; solitary ~s 3. ~s buzz, hum; sting; swarm 4. a cluster; colony; hive; swarm of ~s 5. (misc.) as busy as a ~

bee II *n.* (esp. AE) ["meeting to work or compete"] a quilting; sewing; spelling; spinning ~

beef I *n.* 1. to boil; braise; broil (AE), grill; cook; roast; stew ~ 2. chipped; corned; ground (AE), minced (BE); salt (BE) ~ 3. ~ Wellington 4. baby; prime ~ 5. a piece, slice; side of ~ USAGE NOTE: Corned beef in the US is like salt beef in GB and is not the same as corned beef in GB.

beef II *v.* (D; intr.) ("to complain") to ~ about

beef up *v.* (D; tr.) to ~ with (to ~ a proposal with concrete data)

beeline *n.* ["shortest route"] to make a ~ for ("to go directly toward")

beep I *n.* to give a ~

beep II *v.* (D; tr.) to ~ at

beer *n.* 1. to down, drink; guzzle, swig, swill ~ 2. to brew ~ 3. cold; light; strong ~ 4. near ~ 5. (soft drinks) ginger; root ~ 6. draft ~ 7. a barrel; bottle; can; glass; keg; mug, stein of ~ 8. ~ on tap

beet *n.* 1. (a) sugar ~ 2. (misc.) as red as a ~ (AE; BE has: as red as a beetroot)

beetle off *v.* (BE; slang) ("to hurry") (P; intr.) to ~ to London; to ~ home (the variants *beetle, beetle along, beetle away* also occur)

beg *v.* 1. to ~ humbly 2. (D; intr., tr.) to ~ for; from (they ~ged for help/mercy; they ~ged her for help/mercy; they ~ged money from strangers) 3. (formal) (d; tr.) to ~ of (I must ~ a favor of you) 4. (E) they ~ged to be allowed to go; I ~ to differ 5. (H) they ~ged her to help 6. (L; subj.) he ~ged that

his family be/should be spared 7. (misc.) please spare my family, I ~ of you!; to go ~ging ("to be unwanted") (those jobs went ~ging)

begging *n.* to live by ~

begin *v.* 1. (D; intr., tr.) to ~ as (to ~ as a clerk; to ~ a new career as a teacher) 2. (d; intr., tr.) to ~ at (prices ~ at five dollars; they began the bidding at fifty dollars) 3. (D; intr.; tr.) to ~ by, with (they began (the meeting) by saying a prayer; or: they began (the meeting) with a prayer; let's ~ with you) 4. (d; intr.) to ~ on (they began on a new case) 5. (E) she began to work 6. (G) she began working 7. (misc.) to ~ with (to ~ with, let's consider climate change); "To ~ at the beginning" – Dylan Thomas, *Under Milk Wood* (1954)

beginner *n.* an absolute, complete, rank ~

beginning *n.* 1. to make a ~ 2. to mark a ~ 3. an auspicious, promising; fresh, new ~ 4. at, in the ~ ("To begin at the ~" – Dylan Thomas, *Under Milk Wood* (1954); "In the ~ God created the heaven(s) and the earth" – *The Bible*: *Genesis* 1.1) 5. from (the) ~ (from ~ to end; from the very ~)

begrudge *v.* (O; can be used with one inanimate object) he ~s us our success

beguile *v.* (formal) 1. (D; tr.) to ~ into (he ~d me into lending him money) 2. (D; tr.) to ~ out of 3. (D; tr.) to ~ with (to ~ children with stories)

behalf *n.* in (AE), on smb.'s ~ USAGE NOTE: Some purists maintain that in AE *in smb.'s behalf* means "for smb.'s benefit", whereas *on smb.'s behalf* means "as smb.'s representative".

behave *v.* 1. to ~ appropriately; normally; responsibly; well 2. to ~ badly, poorly; inappropriately; irresponsibly; strangely 3. (d; intr.) to ~ like (he ~d like a gentleman) 4. (D; intr.) to ~ towards (how did they ~ towards you?) 5. (misc.) to behave as if, (colloq.) like (to ~ as if an eclipse were an everyday event; how did they ~ when you were around?; if you behave well towards others will they ~ accordingly?)

behavior, behaviour *n.* 1. to change; display, exhibit ~ (to exhibit strange ~) 2. appropriate; diplomatic; disciplined; exemplary; good; model; modest; normal; responsible ~ 3. inappropriate; inconsiderate; inexcusable; obsequious; unacceptable; unbecoming; undignified; undiplomatic; undisciplined; unethical; unruly; unsportsmanlike ~ 4. abnormal; antisocial; asocial; bad; criminal; delinquent; disruptive ~ 5. infantile; irresponsible; willful ~ 6. irrational; neurotic; odd, strange; unorthodox ~ 7. promiscuous; provocative; scandalous ~ 8. sullen; suspicious ~ 9. ~ towards 10. on one's ~ (to be on one's best ~) 11. a code, standard; pattern of ~ 12. (misc.) she got time off for good ~ (in prison) USAGE NOTE: Nowadays *behaviors* is used often, esp. in technical contexts, to mean 'instances, types, or patterns of behavior' – "continuing recourse to addictive substances or behaviours." (British National Corpus)

behest *n.* at smb.'s ~ (at her ~, everyone attended the meeting)

behind *adv., prep.* 1. to fall, lag ~ 2. to remain, stay ~ 3. to leave ~ 4. close ~ 5. ~ by (our team is ~ by two points = our team is two points ~) 6. ~ in, with (he's ~ with his payments) 7. (misc.) to be solidly ~ smb. ("to support smb. wholeheartedly")

beholden *adj.* (cannot stand alone) ~ for; to (we are ~ to nobody for anything)

behoove (AE), **behove** (BE) *v.* (R) (formal) it ~s them to help the needy; it ill ~s you to speak like that

being *n.* 1. to bring into ~; to come into ~ 2. a celestial; divine; extraterrestrial; human; living; mortal; rational; supernatural ~ 3. the Supreme Being

belch I *n.* 1. to emit, give, let out a ~ 2. to stifle, suppress a ~

belch II *v.* (d; intr.) to ~ from (smoke ~ed from the chimney)

belief *n.* 1. to cling to; express; hold a ~ 2. to shake smb.'s ~ 3. to give up, relinquish, renounce one's ~ 4. an ardent, firm, sincere, strong, unshakable; basic; deeply rooted, deep-rooted ~ 5. an erroneous, false, mistaken; fanatical ~ 6. a popular; unpopular ~ 7. a personal; prevalent, widespread ~ 8. political; religious ~s 9. a ~ in (nothing will shake his ~ in ghosts) 10. a ~ that + clause (it is their firm ~ that the earth is flat) 11. beyond ~ 12. in the ~ that... (in the firm but mistaken ~ that the earth is flat) 13. (misc.) against smb.'s ~s; a set of ~s

believe *v.* 1. to ~ firmly, sincerely, strongly; mistakenly 2. (D; intr.) to ~ in (to ~ in ghosts) 3. (D; tr.) to ~ of (I can't ~ it of him!) 4. (L) they ~ firmly but mistakenly that the earth is flat 5. (M) they all ~ the story to be true 6. (misc.) I ~ so = so I ~; I ~ not; it is popularly/widely ~d that...; ~ it or not; you would not ~ how much she has improved!

believer *n.* 1. an ardent, firm, great, sincere, staunch, strong; true ~ 2. a ~ in (he's no ~ in miracles)

bell *n.* 1. to cast a ~ 2. to hear; ring, sound a ~ 3. to answer the ~ (in boxing) 4. a church; door ~ (see also **doorbell**) 5. a diving ~ 6. wedding ~s 7. a ~ chimes, clangs, peals, rings, sounds, tolls 8. (misc.) (boxing) to come out for the ~; to ring a ~ ("to remind smb. of smt.")

bellboy, bellhop *n.* (AE) a hotel ~ (BE has *(hotel) page*)

belligerency *n.* 1. to demonstrate, display, exhibit ~ 2. a state of ~ 3. ~ towards

belligerent *adj.* ~ towards

bellow *v.* 1. (B) he ~ed a command to his platoon 2. (D; intr., tr.) to ~ at (the sergeant was ~ing orders at her squad) 3. (L) he ~ed (to us) that he would fight any man at the bar 4. (misc.) he ~ed to his platoon to charge = "charge!" he ~ed to his platoon

bellows *n.* 1. to operate, use ~ 2. a pair of ~

bellyache *v.* (slang) (D; intr.) ("to complain") to ~ about

belong *v.* 1. (d; intr.) ("to deserve to be") to ~ in (he ~s in jail) 2. (d; intr.) to ~ to ("to be owned by") (the book ~s to her) 3. (d; intr.) to ~ to ("to be a member of") (to ~ to an organization) 4. (d; intr.) ("to be appropriate") to ~ under (this item ~s under a different heading) 5. (d; intr.) to ~ with (these books ~ with the works on history)

belongings *n.* smb.'s earthly; personal ~

below I *adv.* 1. to go ~ 2. down ~ 3. far, way, well ~

below II *prep.* 1. far, way, well ~ 2. ~ in (to be far ~ smb. in rank)

belt I *n.* ["band"] 1. to buckle, do up, fasten one's ~ 2. (also fig.) to tighten one's ~ 3. to loosen; unbuckle, undo, unfasten one's ~ 4. a lap, safety, seat, shoulder; life; trouser ~ 5. a fan ~ 6. a money ~ 7. a cartridge; Sam Browne ~ 8. a garter (AE), suspender (BE) ~ 9. a conveyor; endless ~ 10. (usu. fig.) below the ~ ("unfairly") ["zone"] (AE) 11. the Bible; corn; cotton; green (BE) ~ ["belt worn as a symbol of expertise in a martial art"] 12. a black; brown; white ~ ["misc."] 13. under one's ~ ("experienced, lived through")

belt II *v.* (colloq.) ["hit"] 1. (d. tr.) to ~ in; on (I ~ed him in the face) 2. (O) I ~ed him one 3. (misc.) I ~ed him one in the face

bench *n.* ["judge's seat"] 1. from the ~ (a reprimand from the ~) 2. on the ~ (who will be on the ~ during her trial?) ["places in Parliament"] 3. (from; on) the backbenches; crossbenches; frontbench(es); government ~es; opposition ~es (there was anger on the government ~es and cheers from the opposition ~es) ["place where reserve players sit"] 4. (esp. AE) on the ~ (he spent ten minutes on the ~) ["table"] 5. a carpenter's; work ~ 6. at one's ~ ["long seat"] 7. a park ~ 8. on a ~

bend I *n.* 1. to make a ~ (the river makes a ~) 2. a horseshoe; sharp; slight ~ (in) (a sharp bend in the river) 3. a knee ~ 4. (misc.) (colloq.) (BE) round the ~ ("mentally unsound")

bend II *v.* 1. (D; tr.) to ~ into; out of (she bent the bar into the right shape; the steering wheel is bent out of shape) 2. (D; intr., tr.) to ~ at; to (she bent at the waist to pick up the book; the road ~s to the right; she cannot ~ them to her will) 3. (misc.) to ~ double; she bent down and picked up the book; they bent over backwards to please ("they made every effort to be helpful")

bender *n.* (colloq.) ["drunken spree"] to go on a ~

benediction *n.* 1. to give, offer, pronounce the ~ 2. to pronounce a ~ over

beneficial *adj.* 1. mutually ~ 2. ~ for, to (~ to health) 3. ~ to + inf. (it would be ~ (for you) to keep abreast of developments in Asia)

beneficiary *n.* 1. to name a ~; to name smb. (as) a ~ 2. a chief, main, principal ~

benefit I *n.* 1. to derive, get, reap (a) ~ from 2. to enjoy, have; provide a ~ (she had the ~ of a good education, which provides many ~s in later life) 3.

a death; sickness (BE); supplementary (BE); tax ~ (see also **fringe benefits**) 4. a mutual; tangible ~ 5. to be of ~ to 6. for, to smb.'s ~ (for our mutual ~) 7. (misc.) with the ~ of; without the ~ of (Shakespeare wrote his plays without the ~ of a computer); without ~ of clergy (see also **benefits**; *with the benefit of hindsight* at **hindsight**; *to give smb. the ~ of the doubt* at **doubt I**)

benefit II *v.* (D; intr.; tr.) to ~ by, from (she ~ed from a good education, which ~ed her in many ways in later life; will the rich ~ by/from the new tax laws? = will the new tax laws ~ the rich?)

benefits *n.* 1. to provide ~ 2. to collect; reap ~ 3. to withhold ~ 4. disability; health-care; old-age; retirement; social-security; strike; survivors' (AE); unemployment; veterans'; welfare; workers' ~ (see also **fringe benefits**)

benevolent *adj.* ~ towards

bent I *adj.* ["determined, hell-bent"] 1. ~ on (he was ~ on getting himself hurt; ~ on mischief) ["curved"] 2. ~ double

bent II *n.* ["propensity"] 1. to have; show a ~ for (from an early age she showed a ~ for music) 2. to follow one's (own) ~ 3. an artistic; decided; natural; peculiar ~ 4. with a ~ (a child with a musical ~ = a child with a ~ for music)

bequeath *v.* (formal) (A) she ~ed her fortune to him; or: she ~ed him her fortune

bequest *n.* 1. to leave, make a ~ 2. a ~ from; of; to (the ~ of her fortune from her to him)

berate *v.* (D; tr.) to ~ for

bereavement *n.* 1. to have suffered a recent ~ 2. in one's ~

bereft *adj.* (cannot stand alone) ["stripped"] ~ of (~ of all hope; ~ of one's senses) USAGE NOTE: In the meaning "having recently lost a dear one", the form *bereaved* is used – the bereaved parents.

berry *n.* to pick ~ies

berserk *adj.* to go ~

berth *n.* 1. to make up a ~ 2. a lower; sleeping; upper ~ 3. (misc.) to give smb./smt. a wide ~ ("to avoid smb./smt.")

beseech *v.* (formal) 1. (H) to ~ smb. to show mercy 2. (misc.) have mercy, I ~ you!

beset *adj.* (cannot stand alone) ~ by, with (~ by doubts)

beside *prep.* to be ~ oneself with (he was ~ himself with grief)

besiege *v.* (D; tr.) to ~ with (to ~ smb. with questions)

besotted *adj.* ~ with (~ with drink/love)

best I *adj.* 1. ~ to + inf. (it is ~ not to speak of it in public) 2. ~ that + clause; subj. (it is ~ that she say/should say nothing to the press) USAGE NOTE: In BE the following construction also occurs – *it is best that she says nothing to the press*. 3. (the) ~ at (she's ~ at some things but I'm ~ at others) 4. ~ for (what's ~ for her isn't necessarily (the) ~ for me) (see also **second best**)

best II *adv.* see **better II** *adv.* 1

best III *n.* 1. to do, give; try one's (level/very) ~ 2. to make the ~ (of smt.) 3. to get the ~ (of smb.) 4. to look one's ~ 5. to bring out the ~ in smb. 6. one's level ~ 7. next, second ~ 8. one's ~ to + inf. (she tried her ~ to finish the job on time) 9. at ~ (at ~, our team may win five matches) 10. at one's ~ (she is not at her ~ in the morning) 11. for the ~ (it turned out for the ~; to hope for the ~; it's all for the ~) 12. in the ~ of (he's not in the ~ of health) 13. in one's Sunday ~ 14. to the ~ of (to the ~ of my ability) 15. (misc.) (colloq.) (AE) give my ~ to your family; ~ of all

bestir *v.* (formal) (d; refl.) we must ~ ourselves (in order/if we want) to get there on time

bestow *v.* (formal) (d; tr.) to ~ on, upon (to ~ an honor on smb.)

bestrew *v.* (formal) (d; tr.) to ~ with (the field was bestrewn with bodies)

bet I *n.* 1. to lose; make; win a ~ 2. to have; place a ~ on; with (she placed a ~ with a bookie on her team to win) 3. to accept, take a ~ 4. a good, safe, sure ~ 5. a side ~ 6. a ~ that + clause (she made a ~ that her team would win; it was her ~ that her team would win) 7. as, for, on a ~ (he did it on a ~) 8. (misc.) to hedge one's ~s ("to protect oneself by placing several bets")

bet II *v.* 1. (D; intr., tr.) to ~ on (he bet on that horse; he bet a month's salary on that horse) 2. (L; may have an object) he bet (me) that it would rain 3. (O; can be used with one object, two objects, one object + *that*-clause, or two objects + *that*-clause) we bet ten pounds; we bet him ten pounds; we bet ten pounds that it would rain; we bet him ten pounds that it would rain 4. (misc.) (colloq.) to ~ one's bottom dollar (esp. AE), to ~ one's life ("is it going to rain?" "you ~ your life it will!"); you ~! ("is it going to rain?" "you ~!")

betake *v.* (formal and obsol.) (P; refl.) he betook himself to the fair

betray *v.* (B) the informer ~ed them to the police

betroth *v.* (B) they were ~ed to each other at an early age

betrothal *n.* 1. to announce a ~ 2. a ~ to

better I *adj.* 1. any; far, (very) much; a little; a lot; no; somewhat ~ (is she any ~ today?) 2. ~ at (he is ~ at tennis than (he is) at squash) 3. ~ for (the new job is much ~ for me) 4. ~ to + inf. (it is ~ to give than to receive; it is ~ for us to leave early) 5. ~ that + clause; subj. (it's ~ that she go/should go alone) USAGE NOTE: In BE, the following constructions also occur: *it's better that she goes/went alone*. 6. (misc.) he is no ~ than a common thief

better II *adv.* 1. he had ~ do it; they had ~ come early 2. to be ~ off

better III *n.* 1. to get the ~ of smb. 2. to expect; think ~ of smt. 3. for the ~ (a change for the ~; to take a turn for the ~)

betting *n.* off-track; parimutuel (AE), totalizator (BE) ~

between *adv.* 1. in ~ 2. few and far ~

beverage *n.* 1. an alcoholic; carbonated; intoxicating; non-alcoholic ~ 2. cold; hot ~s

beware *v.* (D; intr.; only in the imper.) ~ of (~ of the dog!)

bewildered *adj.* 1. ~ at, by (she was ~ by their absence) 2. ~ to + inf. (she was ~ to find them gone) 3. ~ that + clause (she was ~ that they were gone)

bewildering *adj.* ~ to + inf. (it was ~ for her to find them gone)

bewilderment *n.* 1. in ~ 2. ~ that + clause (she reacted in ~ that they had gone)

beyond *adv.* 1. far, way, well ~ 2. (misc.) above and ~ the call of duty; the back of ~ (colloq.) ("the middle of nowhere")

bias I *n.* ["prejudice"] 1. to demonstrate, display, exhibit, have, show (a) ~ 2. to root out ~ 3. deep-rooted, strong; personal ~ 4. racial; religious; sexual ~ 5. a ~ against; for, in favor of; towards 6. with; without ~ ["diagonal line"] 7. on the ~ (to cut on the ~)

bias II *v.* (D; tr.) to ~ against; in favor of (their upbringing ~ed them against all foreigners)

biased *adj.* 1. strongly ~ 2. ~ against; in favor of; towards (they were strongly ~ against all foreigners)

Bible *n.* 1. the Holy ~ 2. in the ~

bibliography *n.* 1. to compile, make up, put together a ~ 2. an annotated; comprehensive; exhaustive; select, selective ~

bicentenary *n.* to celebrate, mark, observe a ~

bicentennial (esp. AE) see **bicentenary**

bicker *v.* (D; intr.) 1. to ~ constantly, incessantly 2. to ~ about, over; with

bickering *n.* 1. constant, incessant ~ 2. ~ about, over 3. ~ between; with

bicycle *n.* 1. to pedal, ride a ~ 2. to get on, mount; get off; push, walk, wheel a ~ 3. an exercise, stationary; racing ~ 4. by ~ (to go somewhere by ~)

bid I *n.* ["bidding of an amount"] 1. to enter, file, make, put in, submit a ~ 2. to call for, invite ~s 3. to raise one's ~ 4. to consider, entertain a ~ 5. to accept; reject, turn down a ~ 6. to recall a ~ 7. an opening; sealed ~ 8. a rescue; (hostile) takeover ~ 9. the highest; lowest ~ 10. a ~ for, on (she made a ~ on the painting) ["attempt"] 11. to make a ~ 12. a desperate ~ 13. a ~ for (they made a ~ for control of the company) 14. a ~ to + inf. (they made a ~ to take over the company; a rescue ~ to bail out an ailing company) 15. in a ~ (in a ~ for power; in their ~ to take over the company, they made many enemies; in a desperate ~ for freedom)

bid II *v.* 1. (D; intr.) to ~ against (at the auction, he and she bid against each other for the vase) 2. (D; tr.) to ~ for (she bid twenty pounds for the vase) 3. (D; intr.) to ~ for, on (to ~ on a contract)

bid III *v.* 1. (formal) (A) she bade farewell to them; or: she bade them farewell 2. (obsol.) (H) to ~ smb. to do smt. 3. (obsol.) (I) to ~ smb. do smt. 4. (misc.) "Love bade me welcome; yet my soul drew back" – George Herbert (1593–1633), "Love"

bidder *n.* the highest; lowest ~

bidding *n.* ["offering of bids"] 1. to close; open the ~ 2. competitive; spirited ~ ["request"] 3. to do smb.'s ~ 4. at smb.'s ~

big *adj.* ["kind"] ["good"] (colloq., ironical) 1. ~ of (that's ~ of you) 2. ~ to + inf. (it was ~ of you to do that) ["older"] 3. a ~ boy; brother; girl; sister ["very powerful"] 4. ~ business; government; labor ["misc."] 5. great ~ (I saw a great ~ bear in the woods!)

bigamy *n.* to commit; practice ~

bigot *n.* a fanatical, narrow-minded, vicious; religious ~

bigoted *adj.* 1. strongly ~ 2. ~ against 3. ~ to + inf. (it was ~ to say that)

bigotry *n.* 1. to arouse, stir up ~ 2. to demonstrate, display, show ~ 3. fanatical, ingrained, narrow-minded, vicious; religious ~ 4. ~ against

big time *n.* to get into, reach the ~

bike *n.* 1. to ride a ~ 2. a mountain ~ (see **bicycle**)

bilingual *adj.* 1. completely ~ 2. ~ in (they're completely ~ in Dutch and English)

bilk *v.* (esp. AE) (D; tr.) to ~ out of (they ~ed us out of the money)

bill I *n.* ["proposed law"] 1. to amend; draft; introduce, propose; oppose; pass; support a ~; to sign a ~ into law 2. to move; railroad a ~ through a legislature 3. to quash, reject, vote down; veto a ~ 4. to shelve a ~ 5. an appropriations; revenue, tax ~ ["banknote"] (AE) 6. to break, change; pass a ~ 7. a counterfeit; five-dollar ~ (BE has *note*, as in *a five-pound note*) 8. marked ~s ["statement of money owed"] ["debt"] 9. to run up a ~ 10. to itemize; submit a ~ 11. to foot (colloq.), pay; pick up; settle a ~ 12. a hospital, medical; hotel; telephone; utility (electric; gas; water) ~ 13. a ~ falls due, matures 14. (misc.) to put smt. on smb.'s ~ ["poster"] 15. to post, stick (BE) a ~ (post no ~s!) ["misc."] 16. to fill, fit the ~ ("to meet all requirements") ["restaurant check"] ["bill for a meal"] (BE) 17. (misc.) to ask (the waiter) for the ~ (see also *bill of fare* at **fare**) ["misc."] 18. a double ~ ("a double feature")

bill II *v.* 1. (D; tr.) ("to describe") to ~ as (she was ~ed as a leading expert) 2. (D; tr.) ("to charge") to ~ for (the doctor did not ~ them for the visit) 3. (H) ("to cast"); ("to announce") he was ~ed to appear as Hamlet 4. (O; may be used with one object) the doctor ~ed (them) fifty pounds for the visit

billet I *n.* an officers' ~

billet II *v.* (esp. mil.) (D; tr.) ("to assign to a lodging place") to ~ among; on, upon, with (to ~ troops on the local population)

billiards *n.* 1. to play ~ 2. (BE) bar ~

billing *n.* ["prominence in advertising, promotion"] 1. to get, receive ~ 2. advance; star, top ~ (to get top ~)

bill of health *n.* ["approval"] 1. to give smb. a clean ~ 2. to get, receive; have a clean ~

bill of sale *n.* to make up, prepare a ~

bin *n.* 1. (BE) a dustbin, litter, rubbish; wheelie ~ 2. a storage ~ 3. in; into a ~ 4. (misc.) a ~ liner

("a bag that lines a bin and can be removed from it when full")

bind I *n.* ["trouble"] ["dilemma"] 1. a double ~ 2. in a ~

bind II *v.* 1. (D; tr.) ("to put together") to ~ in (to ~ a book in leather) 2. (D; tr.) ("to tie") to ~ to (they bound him to a post) 3. (D; tr.) ("to require") to ~ to (to ~ smb. to secrecy) 4. (H) ("to require") the contract ~s you to pay interest 5. (misc.) to ~ hand and foot; to ~ together

binder *n.* ["deposit of money"] (esp. AE) 1. to place, put down a ~ on ["holder for sheets of paper"] 2. a loose-leaf; ring ~ ["broad bandage"] (AE) 3. to apply a ~ 4. an abdominal; breast; straight ~

binding I *adj.* 1. legally ~ 2. ~ on, upon (the agreement is ~ on you)

binding II *n.* ["fastening of the sections of a book"] 1. a handsome; leather ~ 2. in a ~ (the book is in a leather ~) ["narrow strip of fabric"] 3. to sew on, tack on a ~

bind over *v.* (legal) 1. (D; tr.) to ~ to (she was bound over to the grand jury) 2. (BE) (H) she was bound over to keep the peace

binge I *n.* (colloq.) ["a drunken spree"] 1. to go on a (weekend) ~ ["unrestrained activity"] 2. a shopping ~

binge II *v.* (d; intr.) to ~ on (to ~ on sweets)

binoculars *n.* 1. to adjust, focus; train ~ on 2. high-powered, powerful ~ 3. a pair of ~ 4. (misc.) to watch smt. through / with ~

biography *n.* an authorized; critical; unauthorized ~

biology *n.* marine; molecular ~

bird *n.* 1. game; land; migratory; tropical; wading; water; woodland ~s 2. ~s of passage; ~s of prey 3. (usu. fig.) a rare ~ 4. ~s chirp, twitter, warble; sing 5. ~s flap their wings; fly; migrate; soar 6. ~s build nests; flock together; molt; peck 7. a covey; flock of ~s 8. (misc.) to ring ~s (for scientific purposes); a ~ in the hand ("smt. already possessed"); ~s of a feather ("people with similar characteristics, tastes, and standards"); as free as a ~ ("absolutely free"); to kill two ~s with one stone ("to accomplish two goals with one action")

bird call *n.* to do, imitate a ~

birdwatching *n.* to go in for, take up ~ (as a hobby)

birth *n.* ["bringing, coming into life"] 1. to give ~ (she gave ~ to twins) 2. to announce; register a ~ 3. a breech; caesarean; live, viable; multiple; normal; premature ~; stillbirth; birthplace = place of ~ 4. at ~ (she weighed seven pounds at ~) ["origin"] 5. by ~ (he's Spanish by ~) 6. of ~ (of noble ~)

birth control *n.* to practise ~

birthday *n.* 1. to attain (formal), have, reach a ~ 2. to celebrate, mark a ~ 3. at, on a ~ (on her tenth ~) 4. happy ~! (to wish smb. a happy ~)

birth pangs *n.* to endure, suffer ~

birthrate *n.* 1. a falling; high; low; rising; stable ~ 2. the crude ~

birthright *n.* a natural ~

biscuit *n.* 1. to bake ~s 2. a sweet ~ (BE; AE has *cookie*) 3. a cream ~ (BE; AE has *sandwich cookie*) 4. baking-powder; soda; tea ~s 5. (misc.) to take the ~ ("to be the best or worst") (BE; CE has *to take the cake*)

bishop *n.* 1. to ordain a ~ 2. an Anglican, Episcopal; Catholic; Orthodox ~ 3. ~ of (the Anglican Bishop of Birmingham)

bison *n.* a herd of ~

bit I *n.* ["share"] 1. to do one's ~ ["small piece, small amount"] 2. a tiny ~ 3. (misc.) every ~ ("all, entirely"); ~ by ~ ("little by little"); he's a ~ of a snob ("he is something of a snob"); she's not the least ~ upset ("she's not at all upset"); wait a ~ ("wait a little"); to blow to ~s ("to destroy completely"); to fall to ~s ("to disintegrate") ["misc."] 4. ~s and bobs (BE), ~s and pieces; two ~s (AE) ("twenty-five cents"); he has a ~ on the side (colloq.) (BE) ("he has a mistress")

bit II *n.* ["mouthpiece on a horse's bridle"] 1. to chafe, champ at the ~ (also fig.) 2. to take the ~ (between one's teeth) (also fig.)

bitch *v.* (slang; vulgar) (D; intr.) to ~ about (they're always ~ing about the food)

bitchy *adj.* (slang; vulgar) ["nasty"] ~ about

bite I *n.* ["act of biting"] ["result of biting"] 1. to have, take a ~ (she took a ~ (out) of the apple) 2. an animal; dog; insect; mosquito; snake ~ ["ability to bite"] 3. a powerful ~ (the large dog has a powerful ~) ["snack"] 4. to grab, have a ~ (to eat) 5. a quick ~ ["request for a loan"] (colloq.) (esp. AE) 6. to put the ~ on smb. ["amount of money deducted"] (colloq.) 7. to take a ~ from, out of (the wage tax takes quite a ~ from his paycheck)

bite II *v.* 1. (D; intr.) to ~ at (also fig.) (to ~ at the bait) 2. (D; intr.) to ~ into, on; through (she bit into the apple)

bitter I *adj.* ~ about, over (he was ~ about his lot)

bitter II *n.* to take the ~ (with the sweet)

bitterness *n.* 1. to feel ~ 2. a touch of ~ 3. ~ about, over; between; towards

bivouac *n.* 1. to go on; set up a ~ 2. to be on ~

bizarre *adj.* 1. ~ to + inf. (it was ~ (for us) to have run into each other in such a remote corner of the world) 2. ~ that + clause (it was ~ that we ran / should have run into each other in such a remote corner of the world)

blab *v.* 1. (B) she ~bed smt. to him 2. (D; intr.) to ~ about

blabber *v.* (D; intr.) to ~ about

black *adj.*, *n.* ["profit"] 1. in the ~ (to operate in the ~) ["sign of mourning"] 2. to dress in, wear ~ ["dark color"] 3. to go, turn ~ 4. coal, jet, pitch ~ 5. (misc.) as ~ as coal; a shade of ~ ["misc."] 6. to put smt. down in ~ and white ("to write smt. down")

blackboard *n.* 1. to clean, wash; erase (esp. AE) a ~ 2. to write on the ~ 3. at; on the ~ (two pupils were at the ~ writing on the ~) 4. (misc.) to send a pupil to the ~

blacklist *n.* on a ~
black magic *n.* to practice ~
blackmail I *n.* 1. to commit ~ 2. emotional ~ (to use emotional ~ (on smb.))
blackmail II *v.* (D; tr.) to ~ into (to ~ smb. into doing smt.)
black market *n.* 1. a ~ in (a ~ in rationed goods) 2. on the ~ (to buy rationed goods on the ~)
black-marketing, black-marketeering *n.* to engage in, to go in for ~
blackout *n.* ["extinguishing or concealment of all lights, as during wartime"] 1. to impose, order a ~ 2. to observe a ~ ["suppression of news"] 3. to impose, order a ~ 4. to lift a ~ 5. to violate a ~ 6. a media; news ~ ["period of unconsciousness"] 7. to have a ~
bladder *n.* 1. to empty one's ~ 2. a full ~
blade *n.* 1. to sharpen a ~ 2. a blunt, dull; sharp ~ 3. a rotary ~ 4. a razor; sword ~
blame I *n.* 1. to ascribe, assign, attribute (the) ~ to smb. 2. to lay, pin, place, put the ~ on smb.; to lay the ~ (fairly and squarely) at smb.'s door 3. to assess; fix the ~ 4. to shift the ~ (on) to smb. (else) 5. to assume, bear, take; get; share the ~ for (she took the ~ for my mistake) 6. to absolve smb. of all ~ for 7. the ~ falls on smb., the ~ lies with smb.
blame II *v.* 1. to ~ unfairly, unjustly 2. (D; tr.) to ~ for (they ~d her for the accident; I don't ~ you for getting angry!) 3. (d; tr.) to ~ on (they ~d the accident on her; they ~d the fire on defective wiring) 4. to be to ~ for (I am not to ~ for the accident)
blanch *v.* 1. (D; intr.) to ~ at (he ~ed at the sight of the mutilated corpse) 2. (D; intr.) to ~ with (to ~ with fear)
blank I *adj.* to go ~ (my mind went completely ~)
blank II *n.* ["empty space"] 1. to fill in the ~s (as on a questionnaire) (see also **entry blank**) 2. (misc.) my mind was a complete ~ ["blank cartridge"] 3. to fire a ~ ["misc."] 4. to draw a ~ ("to achieve no result")
blanket *n.* 1. a bath; electric; receiving; saddle; sheet ~ 2. a security ~ (also fig.) 3. under a ~
blasé *adj.* ~ about (they were very ~ about winning first prize)
blaspheme *v.* (D; intr.) to ~ against (to ~ against God)
blasphemous *adj.* ~ to + inf. (it was ~ for/of them to speak in that manner)
blasphemy *n.* to commit; utter (a) ~ against
blast I *n.* ["explosion"] 1. to set off a ~ ["gust of wind"] 2. an icy ~ ["verbal attack"] 3. to issue a ~ against 4. a vicious, withering ~ ["misc."] 5. (at) full ~ (the work was proceeding at full ~)
blast II *v.* (D; tr.) to ~ through (a tunnel was ~ed through the rock)
blather I *n.* ["nonsense"] 1. sheer, utter ~ 2. ~ about
blather II *v.* (D; intr.) to ~ (on) about
blaze I *n.* 1. to control; fight a ~ 2. to extinguish, put out a ~
blaze II *v.* (D; intr.) to ~ with (her eyes ~d with anger)

blaze away *v.* (D; intr.) to ~ at (to ~ at the enemy)
blazes *n.* go to ~! ("damn you!")
bleach *n.* liquid ~
bleachers *n.* (AE) to sit in the ~ (compare **stands**)
bleed *v.* 1. to ~ profusely, uncontrollably 2. (fig.) (D; intr.) to ~ for (my heart ~s for him) 3. (D; intr.) to ~ from (to ~ from the nose) 4. (N; used with an adjective) to ~ smb. white 5. (misc.) to ~ to death
bleeding *n.* 1. to staunch, stem, stop (the) ~ 2. heavy, profuse, uncontrollable ~ 3. internal; menopausal ~ 4. ~ from (~ from the rectum)
blemish *n.* a minor; ugly ~
blench *v.* (D; intr.) ("to flinch") to ~ at (he ~ed at the sight)
blend *v.* 1. to ~ together (their voices ~ together well) 2. (d; intr., tr.) to ~ into (she ~ed into the crowd) 3. (D; intr., tr.) to ~ with (water does not ~ with oil)
blend in *v.* (D; intr.) to ~ with (she ~ed in with the crowd)
bless *v.* 1. (D; tr.) to ~ for (she ~ed me for my help) 2. (D; tr.) to ~ with (we are ~ed with good health)
blessing *n.* 1. to give, make, pronounce, say a ~ over 2. to chant a ~ 3. to give one's ~ to; to bestow one's ~ on 4. to ask for God's ~ 5. a divine; priestly ~; God's ~ 6. a ~ for, to (it was a ~ for us) 7. a ~ to + inf. (it was a ~ (for us) not to have to make the trip) 8. a ~ that + clause (it was a ~ that we didn't have to make the trip) 9. (misc.) a mixed ~; a ~ in disguise; to count one's ~s; to ask a ~ (before a meal); to have smb.'s ~, with smb.'s ~ (do it with my ~!= do it! you have my ~!)
blight *n.* 1. to cast, put a ~ on, upon 2. a potato ~ 3. urban ~ 4. a ~ on (a ~ on smb.'s honor)
blind I *adj.* ["sightless"] 1. to become, go ~ 2. legally; totally ~ 3. (misc.) as ~ as a bat; ~ in one eye; the ~ and the partially sighted ["blinded"] (cannot stand alone) 4. ~ to (~ to danger) 5. ~ with (~ with rage)
blind II *v.* (D; tr.) to ~ to (his infatuation ~ed him to her faults)
blind III (BE) see **window shade**
blindness *n.* 1. to cause ~ 2. color; congenital; night; snow ~ 3. (misc.) ~ in one eye
blinds *n.* to adjust; draw; lower; raise the ~ (see also **venetian blinds**)
blind spot *n.* to have a ~ when it comes to smt./smb., to have a ~ where smb./smt. is concerned (he has a ~ when it comes to his own faults = he has a ~ where his own faults are concerned)
blink I *n.* (colloq.) to be on the ~ ("to be out of order")
blink II *v.* (D; intr.) to ~ at ("to show surprise") (she didn't even ~ at his outrageous proposal)
bliss *n.* 1. to enjoy ~ 2. complete, pure, sheer, total, utter ~ 3. connubial, domestic, marital, nuptial, wedded ~ 4. ~ to + inf. (it was ~ to be without a telephone = it was ~ being without a telephone; "Bliss was it in that dawn to be alive" – W. Wordsworth (1770–1850), *The Prelude*) 5. a state of ~

blister *n.* 1. to open a ~ 2. a fever ~ (AE; CE has *cold sore*) 3. a ~ bursts; forms

blizzard *n.* 1. a howling, raging; winter ~ 2. a ~ rages; strikes 3. a ~ blows itself out

bloc *n.* 1. (obsolescent) the Communist; Eastern; NATO; Soviet ~ 2. a military; trade, trading; voting ~

block *n.* ["interruption"] ["obstacle"] 1. (Am. football) to throw a ~ at smb. 2. a mental ~ (when it comes to word games, I have a mental ~) 3. (med.) a heart; nerve; saddle ~ 4. a writer's ~ (see also **road block**; **stumbling block**) ["street"] ["city square"] (AE) 5. a city ~ (the building occupies an entire city ~) 6. around the ~; in, on a ~ (they went around the ~; they live in this ~) ["big building"] (BE) 7. a council ~ 8. an office; tower ~ ("a high-rise apartment house") 9. (misc.) a ~ of flats; (CE) a cell ~ (in a prison) ["platform, work surface"] 10. a butcher's; chopping; headsman's ~ ["auctioneer's platform"] 11. the auction ~ 12. on the ~ ("being auctioned") ["group"] ["bloc"] 13. a trade ~ ["rectangular unit used in construction"] 14. a building; cinder; concrete ~ ["support"] ["brace"] 15. a starting ~ (for a runner) ["section of text"] (computers) 16. to copy; delete; end; move a ~ ["misc."] 17. to knock smb.'s ~ off ("to punch smb.") (see also *a chip off the old block* at **chip**)

blockade *n.* 1. to impose; maintain a ~ 2. to break (through); lift; run a ~ 3. an economic; naval ~ 4. a ~ against; of, on

blocks *n.* (esp. AE) to play with ~ (BE has *bricks*)

bloke *n.* (colloq.) (BE) a decent, good, nice ~

blonde *n.* an ash; bottle, peroxide; natural; platinum; strawberry ~

blood *n.* 1. to draw, let ~ 2. to cough (up), spit (up); lose; shed, spill ~ 3. to staunch the flow of ~ 4. to donate, give; type ~ 5. blue; pure; royal ~ 6. whole ~ 7. hot ("fiery") ~ 8. ~ cakes; circulates; clots, coagulates, congeals, curdles; flows, runs; oozes, seeps; spurts (~ spurted from the wound) 9. (fig.) smb.'s ~ boils; freezes; runs cold 10. (fig.) ~ tells 11. by ~ (related by ~) 12. of ~ (of royal ~) 13. (misc.) in a pool of ~; to be, run in the ~ ("to be hereditary"); in cold ~ ("without feeling"); to draw first ~ ("to score the first victory"); fresh, new, (esp. BE) young ~ ("new personnel"); old ~ ("old personnel"); (colloq.) tired ~ ("rundown condition of the body"); there is bad ~ between them ("they are feuding"); ~ is thicker than water ("one's family is more important than anyone else"); to make smb.'s ~ run cold ("to terrify smb."); to make smb.'s ~ boil ("to arouse smb.'s anger"); flesh and ~

blood cell *n.* a red; white ~

blood count *n.* 1. to do a ~ (on) 2. to have a ~ (done)

blood pressure *n.* 1. to monitor; take smb.'s ~ 2. elevated, high; labile; low; normal ~

bloodshed *n.* 1. to cause ~ 2. to avert, prevent ~

blood test *n.* 1. to do a ~ (on) 2. to have a ~ (done)

blood transfusion *n.* 1. to administer, do, give a ~ 2. to get, have a ~

blood vessel *n.* 1. a constricted; occluded ~ 2. a ~ bursts

bloom *n.* 1. to come into ~ 2. full ~ 3. in ~ (the tulips are in full ~)

bloomer (BE) see **blooper**

blooper *n.* (colloq.) (AE) ["blunder"] 1. to commit, make a ~ 2. a prize ~

blossom I *n.* 1. ~s appear, come out 2. in ~ (the trees/tulips are in ~)

blossom II *v.* (D; intr.) to ~ into (their friendship ~ed into true love)

blot *n.* 1. to leave a ~ 2. an ink ~ 3. a ~ on (his actions left a ~ on our name) (see also *a blot on smb.'s escutcheon* at **escutcheon**)

blotter *n.* ["blotting paper"] 1. a ~ absorbs (ink, water) ["record"] 2. a police ~

blouse *n.* a full; peasant; see-through ~

blow I *n.* 1. to deal, deliver, land, strike a ~ (he dealt us a severe ~) 2. to heap, rain ~s on smb. 3. to come to ~s; to exchange ~s 4. to take a ~ (the boxer took several ~s to the head) 5. to cushion, soften; deflect, parry, ward off; dodge a ~ 6. a crippling, crushing, decisive, hammer, hard, heavy, knockout, powerful, resounding, severe, staggering, telling, terrible ~ 7. a bitter, cruel, devastating ~ 8. a fatal, mortal ~ 9. a glancing, light ~ 10. a body ~ 11. indiscriminate ~s (to rain indiscriminate ~s on one's victims) 12. a low ("illegal") ~ (also fig.) 13. an exchange; hail of ~s 14. a ~ against, at (to strike a ~ against poverty) 15. a ~ for (to strike a ~ for freedom) 16. a ~ on, to (a ~ on the head; he took a ~ to the chin; a ~ to smb.'s hopes) 17. a ~ to + inf. (it was a bitter ~ (for us) to learn of their treachery) 18. under ~s (to reel under crushing ~s) 19. a ~ comes (the ~ to his hopes came out of the blue)

blow II *v.* 1. to ~ hard (the wind was ~ing hard) 2. (A; usu. without *to*) she blew him a kiss 3. (d; tr.) to ~ into (the explosion blew him into the water) 4. (D; tr.) to ~ from; off (the wind was ~ing from the west; the wind blew the papers off the table) 5. (D; intr.) to ~ on (~ on the soup: it's too hot) 6. (N; used with an adjective) the wind blew the door shut 7. (misc.) the tank was blown to bits; the ship was blown off course; (slang) he blew ("came") into town

blowout *n.* ["flat tire"] 1. to have a ~ 2. to fix a ~

blow up *v.* ("to enlarge") (D; tr.) to ~ by (to ~ a photograph by twenty percent)

bludgeon *v.* 1. (d; tr.) ("to force by beating") to ~ into (to ~ smb. into doing smt.) (also fig.) 2. (misc.) to ~ smb. to death

blue *adj.*, *n.* ["color"] 1. bright; dark; deep; light; navy; royal ~ 2. to dress in, wear ~ 3. to go, turn ~ 4. a shade of ~ ["something colored blue"] 5. a patch of ~ 6. in ~ (dressed in ~) ["symbol of belonging to a team at Oxford or Cambridge"] (BE) 7. to get, win one's ~ (as in rowing) (AE has *letter*) ["misc."] 8. out of the ~ ("unexpectedly"); a bolt from/out of the ~ ("smt. unexpected")

blueprint *n.* 1. to draw up, make; have a ~ 2. a ~ for; of (fig.: a ~ for peace)

blues *n.* 1. to sing the ~ (usu. fig.: "to complain") 2. to have the ~ ("to be sad") 3. to banish the ~ ("to overcome sadness") (banish the ~ by positive thinking)

bluff I *n.* ["false threat"] 1. to call smb.'s ~ ("to challenge smb. to carry out a false threat") 2. to fall for smb.'s ~ ("to be deceived by a false threat")

bluff II *v.* 1. (D; tr.) to ~ into; out of (they ~ed him into making concessions) 2. to be caught ~ing

blunder I *n.* 1. to commit, make a ~ 2. an awful, colossal, costly, egregious, fatal, glaring, grave, monumental, serious, stupid, terrible ~ 3. a tactical ~ 4. a ~ to + inf. (it was a ~ (for us) to invite them) 5. a series of ~s

blunder II *v.* 1. (d; intr.) to ~ on, upon ("to happen on") 2. (P; intr.) ("to wander clumsily") they ~ed into the wrong room; she ~ed across the road

blurt out *v.* 1. (B) she ~ed out to us the news of her engagement. 2. (L; to) she ~ed out (to us) that she was engaged 3. (Q; to) she ~ed out (to us) where she had gotten engaged

blush I *n.* 1. a deep ~ 2. (misc.) at first ~ ("at first sight"); in the first ~ of youth ("in early youth")

blush II *v.* 1. to ~ deeply; readily 2. (D; intr.) to ~ at (to ~ at the very thought of what I said) 3. (D; intr.) to ~ for, with (I ~ed with shame at what I said) 4. (E) I ~ to think of what I said ("I blush when I think of what I said") 5. (N) to ~ crimson, scarlet

boar *n.* a wild ~

board *n.* ["ship's deck"] ["train"] ["airplane"] 1. to be on ~; to come, go on ~ (fig.) (if we can get her on ~, we're bound to succeed) ["commission"] 2. an advisory; draft (AE); editorial; executive; liquor-control (AE); parole; school; zoning ~ 3. on a ~ (to serve/sit on a ~) 4. (misc.) a ~ of directors; a ~ of education; a ~ of governors; a ~ of management; a ~ of trustees; a seat on a ~ ["footboard"] 5. a running ~ (on a car) ["flat surface"] 6. a baseboard (AE), skirting (BE) ~ 7. a bulletin (AE), notice (BE) ~ 8. a cheese ~ (with several kinds of cheese on it); checkerboard (AE), draughtboard (BE); chessboard; dart ~ 9. a cutting; diving; drawing; ironing ~ USAGE NOTE: The phrase "back to the drawing board" can also mean 'back to square one.' 10. an emery ~ ["misc."] 11. an electronic bulletin ~; a sounding ~; across the ~ ("for everyone") (an across-the-board pay rise); to go by the ~ ("to go to waste or be disregarded")

boarder *n.* ["lodger"] to have, keep (AE), take in ~s

boards *n.* (esp. AE) ["qualifying examination"] 1. to pass; take one's ~ 2. college; state ~

boast I *n.* 1. to make a ~ 2. an empty, idle, vain; proud ~ 3. ~ that + clause (it was their ~ (to the reporters) that they had seen all of the new plays)

boast II *v.* 1. to ~ idly; openly; proudly 2. (D; intr.) to ~ about, of; to (to ~ of one's success) 3. (L; to) they ~ed (to the reporters) that they had seen all of the new plays

boastful *adj.* ~ about, of

boat *n.* 1. to dock, moor; pilot; row; sail; steer a ~ 2. to launch, lower a ~ 3. to board, get into, get on, get onto; take a ~ 4. to disembark from, get off a ~ 5. to capsize, overturn, swamp, upset a ~ 6. an assault ~; gunboat; mosquito, PT (AE; BE has *MTB*); patrol; torpedo ~ (see also **lifeboat**) 7. a fishing ~; rowboat (AE), rowing (BE) ~; sailboat (AE), sailing (BE) ~; steamboat 8. a flying ~ 9. a ~ capsizes, overturns; docks; goes, sails; heaves; leaks; pitches; rolls; sinks 10. a ~ for; from; to 11. by ~ (to cross a river by ~) 12. in; on a ~ (to cross a river in a ~ and sleep on the ~) 13. (misc.) to be in the same ~ ("to be in the same circumstances"); to miss the ~ ("to let an opportunity slip by"); to push the ~ out (BE; colloq.) ("to make a special effort, esp. to celebrate"); to rock the ~ ("to cause a disruption")

bob *v.* to ~ up and down (in the water)

bobsled, bobsleigh *n.* to ride a ~; to race on ~s

bode *v.* (formal) 1. (O) (can be used with one object) this ~s (us) no good 2. (P; intr.) this ~s ill/well for us

body *n.* ["substance"] ["firmness"] 1. to give ~ to ["group"] ["unit"] 2. an advisory; deliberative; elected; governing; legislative; student ~; the ~ politic 3. in a ~ (they presented their petition in a ~) ["physical object"] 4. a foreign ~ (to remove a foreign ~ from one's eye) 5. a gaseous; liquid; solid ~ 6. a celestial, heavenly; the main ~ (a heavenly ~ was found far from the main ~ of the galaxy) ["corpse"] 7. to bury; cremate; embalm; exhume a ~ 8. a bloated; dead; decomposing ~ 9. in; on a ~ (a bullet was found in the ~ and a suicide note was found on the ~) ["physical structure of a person"] 10. to build up, condition, strengthen one's ~ 11. to sell one's ~ (as a prostitute) 12. a healthy; unhealthy ~ 13. (colloq.) the ~ beautiful ["misc."] 14. to keep ~ and soul together ("to have just enough to live on")

bodyguard *n.* a personal ~

bog *n.* a peat ~

bogged down *adj.* to be; get ~ in; with (they got ~ in the swamp; to be ~ with paperwork)

boggle *v.* (d; intr.) to ~ at (the mind ~s at the idea)

boil I *n.* ["state of boiling"] 1. to bring to a (AE)/to the (BE) ~ (bring the milk to a ~) 2. to come to a (AE)/to the (BE) ~ (the water must first come to the ~) 3. to go off the ~ (usu. fig.) (our team went off the ~ in the second half and lost the match)

boil II *v.* 1. to ~ gently; hard; to put a kettle on to ~ 2. (C) he ~ed an egg for her; or: he ~ed her an egg 3. (D; intr.) to ~ with (to be ~ing with rage)

boil III *n.* (med.) ["furuncle"] 1. to lance a ~ 2. a ~ comes to a head, erupts 3. to apply hot compresses to a ~

boil down *v.* 1. (d; intr.) to ~ to (it all ~s down to one simple fact) 2. (D; tr.) to ~ to (she ~ed the whole story down to one paragraph)

boiler *n.* a ~ bursts, ruptures; cracks

boiling-point *n.* to be at; reach (the) ~

boil over *v.* (D; intr.) to ~ into (the situation ~ed over into a real crisis)

bold *adj.* (often used humorously) to be so ~ as to + inf. (may I be so ~ as to ask how old you are?), to make ~ to + inf. (I made ~ to ask her how old she was)

boldface *n.* to print, set in ~

bolshy *adj.* (colloq.) (BE) ["rebellious"] ~ about

bolt I *n.* 1. a lightning ~ 2. (misc.) like a ~ from/out of the blue ("unexpectedly"); to shoot one's ~ ("to make a final effort"); to make a ~ for the door ("to run towards the door")

bolt II *v.* 1. to ~ securely 2. ("to attach") (D; tr.) to ~ to (they ~ed the computer to the floor; they ~ted the X and the Y securely together) 3. ("to run") (P; intr.) she ~ed for the door 4. (misc.) to ~ (down) one's food ("to eat too fast")

bomb *n.* 1. to detonate, explode, set off; fuse a ~ 2. to drop a ~ 3. to plant a ~ 4. to deactivate, defuse a ~ 5. to dispose of an unexploded ~ 6. an atom, atomic, fission, nuclear; cobalt; fusion, hydrogen; neutron ~ 7. a clean; dirty ~ 8. a buzz; cluster; fragmentation; high-explosive; incendiary; nail; napalm; petrol (esp. BE); pipe; plastic; smoke; stink ~ 9. a car; letter; parcel (esp. BE) ~ 10. a time ~ (often fig.) (see also **time bomb**) 11. a smart ("guided") ~ 12. a ticking ~ (usu. fig.) (is global warming a ticking time ~ waiting to go off?) 13. (AE) a cherry ~ ("a type of firecracker") 14. a ~ explodes, goes off; drops, falls 15. (misc.) (colloq.) (BE) to go like a ~ ("to be very successful")

bombard *v.* (D; tr.) to ~ with (we ~ed them with letters of protest)

bombardment *n.* 1. to conduct a ~ 2. aerial, air; artillery; constant; heavy, intensive ~ ("The Fury of Aerial Bombardment" – Richard Eberhart, 1947) 3. under ~ (under constant ~)

bomber *n.* 1. a dive-bomber; fighter; heavy; light; long-range; medium ~ 2. an enemy ~ 3. a suicide ~

bombing *n.* 1. area; around-the-clock; carpet; dive; indiscriminate, random; pin-point, precision; saturation; shuttle; strategic; tactical ~ 2. a terrorist ~ (a wave of terrorist ~s)

bombshell *n.* ["sensation"] to come as; drop a ~ (the news she told us came as a ~ that she hadn't intended to drop)

bomb threat *n.* 1. to get, receive; send a ~ 2. an anonymous ~

bond I *n.* ["certificate"] 1. to issue a ~ 2. to cash (in), redeem a ~ 3. a debenture; development; government; junk; long-term; municipal; negotiable; serial; treasury; war ~ (to invest money in treasury ~s) (see also **savings bond**) ["tie"] ["link"] 4. to create, forge, form; strengthen a ~ (of friendship)

with 5. a close, firm, strong; solemn; spiritual ~ (strong family ~s) 6. a ~ between (to strengthen the ~s of friendship between them) 7. a ~ links (a strong spiritual ~ links the two of us (together)) ["fetters"] 8. to break; cast off one's ~s ["guarantee"] ["obligation"] 9. to set ~ (the judge set ~ for him at two thousand dollars) 10. to furnish, post a ~ 11. to forfeit a ~ ["storage under supervision, as of imported goods"] 12. in ~; out of ~ (to place goods in ~; to take goods out of ~)

bond II *v.* (D; tr.) ("to cause to adhere") to ~ to ("to ~ wood to glass")

bondage *n.* 1. to sell into ~ 2. to hold in ~ 3. to deliver from ~ 4. in ~ to

bond issue *n.* to float a ~

bone *n.* ["part of a skeleton"] 1. to set a (broken) ~ 2. to break, fracture a ~ 3. brittle ~s 4. a (broken) ~ knits 5. to the ~ (chilled/frozen to the ~) ["complaint"] (colloq.) 6. to have a ~ to pick with smb. ["misc."] 7. to make no ~s about smt. ("to be frank about smt."); to feel smt. in one's ~s ("to have a premonition about smt.") (see also **funny bone**)

boner *n.* (slang) (AE) ["blunder"] to commit, pull a ~

bone up *v.* (colloq.) (AE) (D; intr.) to ~ on (she had to ~ on her French before the exam)

bonfire *n.* 1. to build, light, make a ~ 2. to sit (a)round a ~ 3. a blazing, roaring ~

bonkers *adj.* (slang) (BE) ("crazy, insane") 1. ~ to + inf. (she must have been ~ to drive without headlights) 2. to drive smb. ~; to go ~

bonnet (BE) see **hood**

bonus *n.* 1. to give, pay a ~ 2. to get, receive a ~ 3. an annual; Christmas; cost-of-living; special ~ 4. (misc.) as an added ~ you get a free gift

boo *v.* (D; tr.) to ~ off (the actor was ~ed off the stage)

booby trap *n.* 1. to set a ~ 2. to set off, trigger a ~ 3. to deactivate a ~ 4. a ~ explodes, goes off

book I *n.* 1. to author, write; co-author; revise a ~ 2. to edit; proofread a ~ 3. to dedicate, inscribe a ~ 4. to bring out, publish, put out; copyright; have (in stock); reprint; translate a ~ 5. to review a ~ 6. to pirate; plagiarize a ~ 7. to ban; censor a ~ 8. to bind a ~ 9. to set a ~ in type 10. to charge, check a ~ out of a library 11. to renew a ~ (borrowed from a library) 12. to shelve; stack ~s (in a library) 13. a children's; comic ~; cookbook (AE), cookery (BE) ~; phrase; prayer; statute ~ (old laws still on the statute ~s) 14. an address ~; autograph ~; guide ~; handbook; illustrated; logbook; picture; reference ~; schoolbook; phone, telephone ~; textbook 15. a bank; check (AE), cheque (BE); pass; ration ~ 16. a library ~ 17. a rare ~ (our library has a rare ~ collection) 18. (colloq.) the Good Book ("the Bible") 19. a ~ appears, comes out, is published 20. a ~ goes out of print; a ~ is sold out, sells out; a ~ goes through several editions/printings 21. a ~ about, on; by; for (a ~ about computers) 22. in a ~ (to be (entered/listed) in the telephone ~) 23. (misc.) to make ~ ("to make or accept bets"); a closed ~ ("an obscure matter, person"); ("a completed event, condition"); an open ~ ("an accessible subject, person"); (slang) to throw the ~ at smb. ("to punish an accused person severely"); to go by the ~ ("to adhere strictly to regulations"); in my ~ ("in my opinion") (see also **books**)

book II v. (esp. BE) 1. (C) she ~ed a seat for me; or: she ~ed me a seat 2. (D; intr., tr.) to ~ through to; with (can we ~ a ticket through to Berlin with your company?) 3. (misc.) (CE) ~ed solid, fully ~ed

bookcase n. 1. built-in; free-standing ~s 2. from; in a ~

bookends n. a pair of ~

booking n. (esp. BE) see **reservation** 1–7

bookkeeping n. 1. to do the ~ 2. double-entry; single-entry ~

booklet n. a ~ about, on

books n. ["financial records"] 1. to keep (the) ~ 2. to audit, go over, inspect; balance the ~

book up v. to ~ fully, solid (the hotel is ~ed up solid = the hotel is fully ~ed up)

boom n. ["sound"] 1. a sonic ~ (to cause, generate, produce a sonic ~) ["upsurge"] 2. a baby; business, economic; postwar; property, real-estate; wartime ~ 3. during a ~ 4. a ~ in (during the last ~ in property values) ["misc."] 5. to lower the ~ on ("to attack")

boomerang I n. 1. to throw a ~ 2. a ~ always returns

boomerang II v. (D; intr.) to ~ on (the project ~ed on them)

boon n. a ~ to (a ~ to science)

boor n. an insufferable ~

boost n. 1. to give (smb.) a ~ 2. a big; much-needed ~ 3. a ~ in (a ~ in prices) 4. a ~ to (a ~ to their morale)

boot I n. see the Usage Note for **trunk**

boot II n. ["dismissal"] (colloq.) 1. to get the ~ (for) (he got the ~ for sloppy work) 2. to give smb. the ~ (for) (they gave him the ~ for sloppy work)

boot III v. (P; tr.) she ~ed the ball over the fence

booth n. 1. an information; listening; phone, telephone; polling, voting; projection ~ 2. in a ~

boots n. 1. to lace up; put on; take off; unlace (one's) ~ 2. bovver (BE; slang; "heavy boots worn by young rowdies"); hip; leather; riding; rubber; walking ~ 3. a pair of ~ 4. (misc.) to lick smb.'s ~ ("to be overly subservient to smb."); to die with one's ~ on ("to die while still active, to die in harness")

bootstraps n. to pull oneself up by one's (own) ~ ("to emerge from poverty through one's own efforts") (to become a self-made man by pulling oneself up by one's ~)

booty n. 1. to capture, seize, take; divide the ~ 2. war ~

border I n. 1. to draw, establish, fix a ~ 2. to cross; slip across a ~ 3. to guard, patrol a ~ 4. a closed;

common; disputed; fixed; open; recognized; unguarded ~ 5. a ~ between; with 6. across, over a ~ (to smuggle goods across a ~) 7. along; at, on a ~ 8. as far as, up to the ~ (she drove me as far as the ~) 9. (misc.) north of the ~; south of the ~

border II v. 1. (d; intr.) to ~ on (the USA ~s on Mexico) 2. (d; intr.) to ~ on, upon (to ~ on the absurd) 3. (d; tr.) to ~ with (to ~ a dress with lace)

borderline n. 1. a ~ between 2. on the ~ (a joke on the ~ between offensive and funny)

bore I n. 1. a crashing, frightful, insufferable, utter; real ~ 2. a ~ to + inf. (it's a real ~ (for us) to work on this project every day = it's a real ~ working on this project every day)

bore II n. (esp. BE) ["wave"] a tidal ~

bore III v. 1. (D; intr., tr.) ("to dig") to ~ into (her eyes ~d into me; they ~d an opening into the mine shaft) 2. (D; intr., tr.) ("to dig") to ~ through (to ~ a hole through a board) 3. (D; tr.) ("to weary") to ~ to (he ~d us to death/to tears) 4. (N) he ~ed us stiff

bored adj. 1. ~ to (~ to death/to tears) 2. ~ with; BE also has, esp. in children's language: ~ of (~ with life) 3. (misc.) we were ~ doing nothing; we were ~ stiff

boredom n. 1. to relieve (the) ~ 2. complete, sheer, utter; deadly; outright; plain ~ 3. from, out of ~ (he started drinking again out of sheer ~)

boring adj. ~ to + inf. (it was ~ (for us) to sit there without anything to do)

born adj. 1. ~ into (~ into wealth) 2. ~ of (~ of poor parents) 3. ~ to (~ to wealth; ~ to illiterate parents) 4. ~ to + inf. (he was ~ to rule) 5. (misc.) ~ free; ~ lucky; as (if) to the manner ~ ("as if accustomed to smt."); Mark Twain was ~ Samuel Clemens (see also *born to the purple* at **purple III**)

borrow v. 1. to ~ freely, heavily (English has ~ed heavily from many languages) 2. (D; intr., tr.) to ~ from (she ~ed a book from me; they are always ~ing from us) 3. (D; tr.) to ~ from; into (the word was ~ed from German into English)

borrowing n. a ~ from (a ~ from German)

bosom n. 1. an ample, full ~ 2. (formal) in the ~ (in the ~ of one's family) 3. a ~ heaves, rises and falls 4. (misc.) to take smb. into/to one's ~ (see also *clutch to one's bosom* at **clutch**)

boss n. 1. an absolute, undisputed ~, the big ~ 2. a straw ~ ("one who has little authority; an assistant foreman or forewoman") 3. a party, political ~

both determiner, pronoun ~ of (we saw ~ of them) USAGE NOTE: The use of the preposition *of* is necessary when a pronoun follows – we saw both of them ('we saw them both'). When a noun follows, two constructions are possible – we saw both of the students = we saw both (the) students.

bother I n. 1. a ~ to (he was a ~ to everyone but she was no ~ to anyone) 2. a ~ to + inf. (it was no ~ (for us) to take care of them) 3. (BE) a spot of ~ 4. (esp. BE) he had a lot of ~ finding our house because he wanted to save me the ~ of driving to the station and he didn't want to put me to the ~ of picking him up there – and nor did I want to go to the ~ of fetching him!

bother II v. 1. (D; intr., tr.) to ~ about, with (she didn't ~ me about/with the details) 2. (E; usu. in neg. sentences) he didn't ~ to shave; don't ~ to get up 3. (G; usu. in neg. sentences) he didn't ~ getting up 4. (R) it ~ed me (to learn) that she had not been promoted

bothered adj. 1. not (really) ~ (he's not really ~ (about/by) what other people think of him) 2. ~ to + inf. (he couldn't be ~ed to find out what other people thought of him) (see also *all hot and bothered* at **hot**)

bottle n. ["container as for liquids"] 1. to break; cork; empty; fill; open, uncork; rinse a ~ 2. a baby (AE), feeding (BE), nursing (AE); pill ~ 3. a hot-water ~ 4. a Thermos (T) ~ (AE; BE has *Thermos flask*) 5. a disposable, no-deposit, no-return; plastic; returnable, reusable ~ ["alcohol"] 6. to take to the ~ ("to begin to drink to excess") 7. to hit the ~ ("to drink to excess") 8. over a ~ ("while drinking") ["courage"] (slang) (BE) 9. to have a lot of ~ 10. the ~ to + inf. (she hasn't got enough/the ~ to do it)

bottleneck n. 1. to form, produce a ~ 2. to be caught, trapped in a ~; to hit a ~ 3. to eliminate a ~ 4. a ~ in

bottom n. 1. (usu. fig.) to scrape the ~ of the barrel ("to use one's last resources") 2. (fig.) to hit ("reach") ~ 3. to sink to the ~; to touch ~ 4. a double, false ~ 5. a ~ to (there's a false ~ to the suitcase) 6. along, over; at, on the ~ (at the ~ of the well; we never could find out what was at the ~ of the affair; "There are fairies at the ~ of our garden." – Rose Fyleman (1877–1957), "Fairies") 7. (misc.) from top to ~; to get to the ~ of an affair ("to clear up a matter"); ~s up! ("drink up!"); from the ~ of my heart ("very sincerely"); the ~ has dropped out of the market ("prices have fallen dramatically on the stock market"); to hit, reach rock ~ (prices have reached rock ~) (also fig.) ("to sink into complete failure") (his fortunes have hit rock ~)

bottom out v. (D; intr.) to ~ at (their stock ~ed out at fifty dollars a share)

bough n. 1. a slender ~ 2. ~s sway in the breeze

boulevard n. 1. a wide ~ 2. along; down, up; on a ~

bounce I n. 1. a ~ to (there's a ~ to his walk) 2. on the ~ (to catch a ball on the ~; to hit a ball on the first ~)

bounce II v. 1. to ~ high 2. (d; intr.) to ~ against; off; out of (the ball ~ed off the wall; she ~d out of the chair) 3. (d; intr.) to ~ to (he ~d to his feet) 4. (P; intr., tr.) (the ball ~ed across the street; she ~ed the baby on her knee) 5. (misc.) to ~ up and down (she ~d the ball up and down = the ball ~ed up and down)

bounce back v. (D; intr.) to ~ from (our team ~d back from its defeat)

bound I adj. ["headed"] (cannot stand alone) 1. ~ for (~ for London) 2. homeward; outward ~

bound II adj. ["covered"] ~ in (the book was ~ in leather = it was a leather-~ book)

bound III adj. ["sure"] (cannot stand alone) ~ to + inf. (she is ~ to find out)

bound IV adj. ["required"] 1. (in) duty, honor ~ (she is duty ~ to report the incident to the police) (see also **honor bound**) 2. legally; morally (she feels morally ~ by the oath she swore) 3. ~ to + inf. (she is legally ~ to report the incident to the police)

bound V n. ["jump, leap"] in, with a ~ (with one ~ he was out of the room)

bound VI v. ("to border") (formal) (D; tr.) to ~ on, to (Germany ~s France on the east)

bound VII v. ("to jump; to run") (P; intr.) she ~ed out of the room; he ~ed across the field

boundary n. 1. to draw, fix, set; extend; mark; redraw a ~ 2. to form a ~ 3. a common; national ~ 4. a ~ between 5. beyond; on the ~ (to go beyond the ~aries of good taste; a joke on the ~ between wit and offensiveness) 6. (misc.) to overstep the ~aries of good taste; the ~ runs along the river

bounds n. 1. to set the ~ 2. out of ~ (to) (the bar was put off limits to all military personnel and has remained out of ~ to them) 3. beyond, outside the ~ (beyond no ~ of good taste) 4. within ~ 5. (misc.) to know no ~ (her generosity knew no ~)

bound up adj. (cannot stand alone) ["connected"] ~ in; with (~ in one's work; her future is ~ with this firm)

bounty n. 1. to offer; pay a ~ 2. to put a ~ on (smb.'s head) 3. a cash ~ 4. a ~ for

bouquet n. 1. a bridal, wedding ~ 2. a ~ of 3. in a ~ (were there any roses in her ~ of flowers?)

bout n. ["a period of time"] 1. to have a ~ of (depression, drinking, the flu) (see also *drinking bout* at **drinking**) 2. a nasty, severe ~ ["boxing or wrestling match"] 3. a championship; 12-round ~

bow I /bau/ n. ["bending of the head or body"] 1. to give, make; take a ~ (the envoy made a ~ on entering the throne room; the actor took his ~) 2. a courtly; deep, low ~ 3. a ~ to ["debut"] 4. to make one's ~ (he made his ~ as Hamlet) (compare **curtsy**)

bow II v. 1. ("to bend the head or body") to ~ politely 2. (D; intr.) ("to bend the head or body") to ~ before; to (to ~ before an emperor; to ~ politely to one's host; to ~ to the inevitable) 3. (d; intr.) to ~ out of ("to abandon") (to ~ out of politics) 4. (misc.) to ~ and scrape ("to be obsequious") (compare **curtsy**)

bow III /bou/ n. ["device for shooting arrows"] 1. to draw a ~ (in order to shoot an arrow); to release a ~ ["decorative ribbon"] 2. to wear a ~ (in one's hair) ["knot"] 3. to tie a ~; to tie in a ~

bow down /bau/ v. (D; intr.) to ~ before, to

bowels n. 1. to move, (BE) (old-fashioned) open one's ~ 2. loose ~

bowl n. ["dish, vessel"] 1. a begging, cereal; fruit; goldfish; mixing; punch; salad; soup; sugar (AE); toilet; washing-up (BE) ~ 2. a ~ contains, holds (how much can this ~ hold?) ["championship football game"] (AE) 3. the Cotton; Rose; Sugar; Super (T) ~ ["region"] (esp. AE) 4. a dust; rice ~

bowling n. ["(in an alley or on a green)"] 1. (BE) (old-fashioned) tenpin ~ 2. to go in for ~ 3. to go ~ ["(in cricket)"] 4. fast, pace; spin ~

bowling alley n. at a ~ (she works at a ~)

bow out v. (D; intr.) ("to give up") to ~ as (he had to ~ as a contender) (see also **bow II** 3)

bow tie /bou/ n. 1. to tie a ~ 2. to undo, untie a ~

box I n. 1. a cardboard; cigar; collection; jewelry; lunch ~; money ~; shoebox; spice ~; toolbox; window ~ 2. a post-office ~ 3. a safe-deposit, safety-deposit ~ 4. a poor ~ (in a church) 5. a ballot ~ (see also **ballot box**) 6. a suggestion ~ 7. a letter (BE) ~, mailbox (AE), pillar (BE) ~ 8. a call (BE), phone (BE) ~ 9. a signal ~ (BE; AE has *signal tower*) 10. a fire-alarm ~ 11. a black ~ ("electronic recording device") 12. (ice hockey) a penalty ~ 13. a witness ~ (to go into the witness ~) (BE; AE has *witness stand*) 14. a music (esp. AE), musical (BE) ~ 15. a prompt (BE), prompter's (AE) ~ 16. a shooting ~ (BE; CE has *hunting lodge*) 17. a jury; press ~ (for journalists) 18. (BE) a Christmas ~ ("a Christmas gift for a tradesman") 19. in; into; out of a ~ 20. (fig.) to think out of the ~ ("to think laterally") 21. (slang) (BE) on the ~ ("on television") 22. a ~ contains, holds (see also *box office* at **office** 15, *box seat* at **seat** 9) 23. (misc.) a sandbox (for children to play in) (AE; BE has *sandpit*)

box II v. 1. (D; intr.) to ~ against (to ~ against a worthy opponent) 2. (D; intr.; tr.) to ~ for (to ~ for the title; to ~ (against) a worthy opponent for the title = to ~ for the title against a worthy opponent)

boxer n. 1. a clean; dirty ~ 2. ~s box; break; clinch 3. (misc.) to knock out a ~

boxing n. to go in for ~

boy n. 1. an altar; barrow (BE; CE has *street vendor*); chorus; college (esp. AE); delivery; drummer; messenger; office; stock ~ 2. a best ~ ("assistant gaffer on a TV or film set") 3. a ball ~ (who retrieves tennis balls) 4. (AE; southern) a good old (ole) ~ ("a good fellow") 5. a baby; little, small; mere ~ 6. a whipping ~ ("a scapegoat") 7. a blue-eyed (BE), fair-haired (AE) ~ ("a favorite") 8. (BE) a back-room ~ ("a scientist") 9. (esp. AE) a poster ~ (his success made him a poster ~ for early-childhood education) 10. (BE) a rent ~ ("a young male prostitute") 11. a toy ~ ("a younger man dated by an older woman") USAGE NOTE: The meaning "non-white servant", now obsolete, is considered offensive. The AE use of *boy* in the meaning of "black male", now obsolete, is also considered offensive. (See also the Usage Note for **girl**.)

boycott n. 1. to declare; impose a ~ 2. to lift a ~ 3. a consumer; economic, trade; secondary ~ 4. a ~ of, on (they imposed a ~ on all imports; they lifted their ~ of/on imports)

boyfriend n. 1. have a ~ 2. a live-in; steady ~ 3. a series, string of ~s

brace I n. 1. to wear a ~ (on) 2. a back; dental; leg; shoulder ~

brace II v. 1. (D; intr., refl.) to ~ for (to ~ for an attack; she ~d herself for what the doctor would say) 2. (E; refl.) she ~d herself to hear what the doctor would say

bracelet n. 1. to wear a ~ 2. a chain; charm; diamond; gold; silver; watch ~

braces (BE) see **suspenders**

bracket n. ["support"] 1. to put up ~s (on a wall) ["punctuation mark used to enclose"] 2. to enclose (a word) in ~s; to put (a word) in, into ~s 3. to close ~s 4. angle, broken; curly; round; square ~s USAGE NOTE: "Round brackets" are typically called "parentheses" in AE. ["group with similar characteristics"] 5. an age; income; tax; wage ~ (if you earn more you will ¬fall into/be in¬ a higher tax ~)

brag v. 1. (D; intr.) to ~ about, of; to (they ~ged (to us) about how/the way they had outwitted their rivals) 2. (L; to) they ~ged (to us) that they had outwitted their rivals

braid I n. ["threads"] 1. gold; silver ~ ["length of hair"] (esp. AE; CE has *plait*) 2. in a ~ (they wore their hair in ~s)

braid II v. (D; tr.) (esp. AE) to ~ into (to ~ one's hair into pigtails)

brain n. ["mind"] 1. to have a (good) ~ 2. to overtax; tax; use one's ~ 3. to rack one's ~(s) over (she racked her ~ over the problem) 4. to pick smb.'s ~(s) 5. in smb.'s ~; (colloq.) on the ~ (what's going on in that ~ of his?; he has nothing but rock music on the ~)

brains n. 1. to blow one's ~ out ("to shoot oneself through the head") 2. the ~ to + inf. (does he have enough ~ to figure it out?)

brainstorm n. ["sudden bright idea"] (AE) to have a ~ (see the Usage Note for **wave I**)

brake I n. 1. to apply, hit, step on a ~/the ~s; to pump the ~s; to put on the ~s; to jam on/slam on the ~s 2. to ride the ~s ("to use the brakes excessively") 3. (fig.) to put a ~ on (the government put a ~ on plans for expansion) 4. to release, take (one's foot) off a ~/the ~s 5. an air; coaster; disk; electric; emergency; foot; hand; hydraulic; mechanical; power ~ 6. the ~s jammed, locked; faded; failed; held, worked; screeched ["misc."] 7. a shooting ~ (old-fashioned BE; BE now prefers *estate car*; AE has *station wagon*)

brake II v. 1. to ~ gently; hard; suddenly 2. to ~ (in order) to (he ~ed to avoid hitting a child)

branch n. ["division"] 1. the executive; judicial; legislative ~ (of the government) 2. a local ~ ["limb of a tree"] 3. to trim ~es 4. overhanging ~es (see also **olive branch**)

branch off *v.* (D; intr.) to ~ from (the spur ~es off here from the main line)

branch out *v.* 1. (D; intr.) to ~ from; into; to (our firm has ~ed out into various industries) 2. (misc.) to ~ on one's own

brand I *n.* 1. to put a ~ on (an animal) 2. a leading, name, popular ~ (of) 3. (BE) an own ~ (the supermarket's own ~s are cheaper than the name ~s it also stocks)

brand II *v.* 1. (d; tr.) to ~ as (he was ~ed as a traitor) 2. (N; used with a noun) he was ~ed a traitor

brash, (AE) **brassy** *adj.* ~ to + inf. (it was ~ of him to demand a raise)

brass *n.* (colloq.) ["officers"] 1. air-force; army; navy; Pentagon ~ 2. the top ~ ["daring; effrontery"] 3. the ~ to + inf. (he had the ~ to ask for a raise)

brass tacks *n.* to get down to ~ ("to get down to business")

brat *n.* (colloq.) 1. a spoiled ~ 2. an Army ~ ("child of an Army family")

bravado *n.* 1. sheer ~ 2. an act of ~ 3. out of ~ (an act done out of sheer ~)

brave *adj.* ~ to + inf. (it was ~ for/of you to volunteer = you were ~ to volunteer)

bravery *n.* 1. to demonstrate, display, exhibit, show; inspire ~ 2. smb.'s ~ in (your ~ in volunteering was amazing!) 3. for ~ (to get a medal for ~)

brawl *n.* 1. a barroom, drunken; street ~ 2. in a ~ 3. a ~ between; about, over (I found myself caught up in a street ~ between two thugs over a woman)

breach *n.* ["violation"] 1. to commit a ~ (of etiquette, of the peace) 2. to be, constitute a ~ 3. an egregious, flagrant ~ 4. a security ~ (your contact with journalists constitutes a flagrant security ~!) 5. in ~ of (your contact with journalists is in ~ of the agreement you signed with us!) 6. (misc.) (a) ~ of contract ["gap"] 7. to effect, make a ~ (in enemy lines) 8. to close, seal off a ~ 9. to fling oneself, throw oneself into the ~ 10. a ~ in (a ~ in the defenses) 11. (misc.) "Once more unto the ~, dear friends, once more; / Or close the wall up with our English dead!" – Shakespeare, *Henry V* ["break in friendly relations"] 12. to cause a ~ (between) 13. to heal a ~ (between)

bread *n.* ["baked food"] 1. to bake, make ~ 2. to butter; slice; toast ~ 3. to break ~ with ("to eat with") 4. crusty; fresh; moldy; stale ~ 5. black; brown; corn; dark; enriched; leavened; pita, pitta (BE), rye; sliced; unleavened; wheat; white; whole meal (BE), whole wheat (AE) ~ 6. a crust; loaf; hunk; piece, slice of ~ 7. on ~ (I like a little butter on my ~) ["living"] 8. to earn one's daily ~ 9. (misc.) to take the ~ out of smb.'s mouth USAGE NOTE: The phrase "bread and" can mean either (1) bread accompanied by (as in "the prisoner had nothing but *bread and* water") or (2) bread spread with (as in "a big hunk of *bread and* butter/jam").

breadth *n.* (formal) 1. ~ of (enormous ~ of experience and insight) 2. in ~ (ten feet in ~) (see also **hair's breadth**)

break I *n.* ["dash"] 1. to make a ~ (for safety) ["escape"] 2. a mass; prison ~ ["interruption"] 3. to make a ~ 4. a clean ~ (see also **clean break**) 5. a ~ in, with (a ~ in the conversation; to make a ~ with tradition) ["rest"] 6. to have (esp. BE), take a ~ 7. a Christmas, coffee; commercial; Easter; lunch; news; station (AE); tea (esp. BE) ~ 8. during, on; over; without a ~ (what are you doing during/over the Christmas ~?; to work many hours without a ~) ["opportunity, chance"] (colloq.) 9. to give smb. a ~ ["good fortune"] 10. to get a ~ 11. a big; lucky; unexpected ~ 12. a tax ~

break II *v.* 1. (B) ("to communicate") I had to ~ the news to them 2. (D; intr.) ("to curl and fall") to ~ against, on (the waves were ~ing against the rock; "Break, ~, ~ On thy cold grey stones, O Sea!" – Tennyson (1809–82)) 3. (d; intr.) ("to dash") to ~ for (to ~ for cover) 4. (d; intr.) ("to take time") to ~ for (they broke for lunch) 5. (d; intr.) ("to enter forcibly") to ~ into (burglars broke into the house) 6. (d; intr.) ("to begin") to ~ into (to ~ into song) 7. (D; intr., tr.) ("to split") to ~ in half, in two; into (to ~ a chair into pieces) 8. (d; tr.) ("to cure") to ~ of (in time he was broken of his drug habit) 9. (D; intr., tr.) ("to split off") to ~ off (to ~ a branch off a tree) 10. (D; tr.) ("to crack") to ~ on (she broke a tooth on a bone) 11. (d; intr.) ("to escape") to ~ out of (two prisoners broke out of jail; the enemy troops broke out of our encirclement) 12. (d; intr.) ("to penetrate") to ~ through (to ~ through enemy lines) 13. (d; intr.) ("to end relations") to ~ with (I broke with them) 14. (D; tr.) ("to cut off") to ~ with (she broke all ties with her friends) (see also **break free**, **break loose**, *break on the wheel* at **wheel I** 6)

break away *v.* (D; intr.) to ~ from (he broke away from his captors; we broke away from the party to form our own break-away group)

breakdown *n.* 1. to have, suffer a ~ (he had a nervous ~; she is on the verge of a nervous ~) 2. a complete, irretrievable; emotional, mental, nervous ~ (of) (she broke down in tears when she thought of the irretrievable ~ of her marriage) 3. a ~ in (a ~ in communications)

break down *v.* 1. (D; intr., tr.) to ~ into (to ~ a substance into its components) 2. (misc.) to ~ in tears; to ~ irretrievably (she broke down in tears when she realised her marriage had broken down irretrievably)

breaker *n.* (see **circuit breaker**)

break even *v.* (D; intr.) to ~ with

breakfast I *n.* 1. to eat (esp. AE), have ~ 2. to cook; make, prepare; serve ~ 3. a continental; cooked (BE), English (BE), full, Full English (BE), hearty, hot; nutritious, wholesome; substantial; working ~ 4. at ~ (what did you discuss at ~?) 5. for ~ (to eat eggs for ~) 6. (misc.) to have ~ in bed; bed and ~, B&B (as in a tourist home)

breakfast II *v.* (D; intr.) to ~ on (to ~ on scrambled eggs and toast)

break free *v.* (D; intr.) to ~ from

break-in *n.* to commit a ~ (at) (the thieves committed a ~ at the factory from the roof)

break in *v.* 1. (D; intr.) to ~ from; through (the thieves broke in (to the factory) from the roof; we broke in through the door) 2. (D; intr.) to ~ on (she broke in on their conversation) 3. (D; intr.) to ~ with (she broke in (on their conversation) with an inane remark)

breaking *n.* (the crime of) ~ and entering

breaking point *n.* 1. to reach ~ (BE)/the ~ (AE) 2. to push smb. to ~ (BE)/the ~ (AE)

break loose *v.* (D; intr.) to ~ from

break off *v.* (D; intr.) to ~ from (they broke off from the main wing of the party)

breakout *n.* 1. to organize a ~ (from prison) 2. to achieve, effect a ~ (from an enemy encirclement) 3. a prison ~ (to organize a prison ~)

break out *v.* 1. (D; intr.) to ~ in (he broke out ¬in a rash/in spots¬; to ~ in a cold sweat) 2. (misc.) (Am. football) the back broke out in/into the open

breakthrough *n.* 1. to achieve, effect, make, score; be, constitute, represent a ~ 2. a big, dramatic, major, significant ~ 3. a diplomatic; medical; scientific ~ 4. a ~ for; in (with their initiative they scored a major diplomatic ~ for peace in the Middle East = their initiative represented a major ~ for peace in the Middle East)

break through *v.* (D; intr.) to ~ to (they broke through to the encircled unit)

breakup *n.* 1. to lead to a ~ 2. a marital ~

break up *v.* 1. (D; intr., tr.) to ~ into (they broke up the estate into small lots = they broke the estate up into small lots; our party broke up into several splinter groups) 2. (colloq.) (D; intr.) to ~ with (he broke up with his girlfriend) 3. (misc.) ~ it up! ("stop fighting/congregating and separate!")

breast *n.* 1. to beat one's ~ 2. to put a (newborn) infant to (the) ~ 3. (of an infant) to take the ~ 4. a pigeon ~ ("a deformity of the chest") 5. (culinary) chicken; turkey ~(s) 6. (misc.) to make a clean ~ of smt. ("to confess smt.") (see also *clutch to one's breast* at **clutch**) USAGE NOTE: *chicken breast* and *turkey breast* are raw or cooked; *breast of chicken* and *breast of turkey* are cooked.

breaststroke *n.* to do, swim the ~

breath *n.* 1. to draw, take a ~ 2. to catch; hold one's ~; let out a ~ 3. to get one's ~ back 4. to gasp, struggle for ~ 5. to lose one's ~ 6. a deep; long; short ~ (she took a deep ~) 7. out of, short of ~ ("breathless") 8. bad ~ (smokers often have bad ~) 9. (misc.) to spare, save one's ~ ("to avoid a futile conversation"); to waste one's ~ ("to speak in vain"); to take smb.'s ~ away ("to astonish smb."); in the same ~ ("at the same time"); to one's dying/last ~ ("to the end of

one's life"); on smb.'s ~ (I could smell liquor on her ~); under one's ~ ("in a whisper"); with bated ~ ("with the breath held, in suspense") (we waited for the result with bated ~)

breathe *v.* 1. to ~ deeply 2. (d; tr.) to ~ into (she ~d new life into the project) 3. (D; intr.) to ~ through (to ~ through one's nose) 4. (misc.) to ~ in ("to inhale"); to ~ out ("to exhale"); as I live and ~! (colloq.) "well, as I live and ~ if it isn't John! What a surprise!"

breather *n.* ["rest"] to have (BE), take a ~

breathing *n.* 1. deep; heavy, labored, noisy; irregular; regular, steady ~ 2. (ling.) rough; smooth ~

breathtaking *adj.* 1. really, truly ~ 2. ~ to + inf. (it was truly ~ to watch the acrobats perform) 3. (misc.) it was truly ~ watching the acrobats perform

breeches *n.* riding ~

breed *n.* 1. a ~ apart 2. a dying; hardy; new; rare ~ (of)

breeder *n.* a cattle, livestock; horse; poultry; sheep ~

breeding *n.* 1. cattle, livestock; horse; poultry; sheep ~ 2. selective ~ (of) 3. of ~ (a person of good ~)

breeding ground *n.* a ~ for (poverty is an ideal ~ for crime)

breeze I *n.* ["light wind"] 1. a ~ blows, comes up 2. a balmy, fresh, gentle, light, soft; cool; sea ~ 3. in a ~ (leaves trembling in the ~) ["easy task"] (colloq.) 4. a ~ to + inf. (it was a ~ (for us) to get him to agree = it was a ~ getting him to agree) ["misc."] 5. (colloq.) (AE) to bat, shoot the ~ ("to chat")

breeze II *v.* (P; intr.) she ~d through the finals; he ~d into the room; they ~d to an easy victory

brew I *n.* (a) home ~

brew II *v.* (C) she ~ed some tea for us; or: she ~ed us some tea

brew-up *n.* (BE) ["making tea"] to have a ~

bribe I *n.* 1. to give, offer a ~ 2. to accept, take a ~ 3. to refuse, turn down a ~ 4. a ~ of 5. in ~s (they turned down a ~ of $500 but accepted $5000 in ~s later on)

bribe II *v.* 1. (D; tr.) to ~ into (to ~ smb. into collusion) 2. (D; tr.) to ~ with (they ~d him with a free vacation) 3. (H) they ~d him to overlook the violation

brick *n.* (colloq.) (BE) ["blunder, clanger"] to drop a ~

brickbats *n.* ["insults"] to hurl ~ at

bricks *n.* 1. to make ~ 2. to burn, fire ~ 3. to lay ~ (a bricklayer lays ~) 4. to point ~ 5. see **blocks**

bride *n.* 1. to take a; to give away a ~ 2. a ~ takes a husband 3. a beautiful, lovely; blushing ~ 4. a child; war ~ 5. a bride-to-be; a future ~ 6. (misc.) ~ and groom

bridge I *n.* ["structure carrying a roadway over smt."] 1. to build, construct, erect a ~ 2. to throw a ~ across a river 3. to cross a ~ 4. an arch; Bailey; bascule; cantilever; covered ~; drawbridge; footbridge;

pontoon; railroad (AE), railway (BE); suspension; toll; truss ~ (see also **drawbridge**; *the bridge of the nose* at **nose I** *n.*) 5. a jet ~ (at an airport) 6. a ~ collapses; spans (the ~ spanning the harbor collapsed in an earthquake) 7. a ~ across, over; between (a ~ across a river) 8. (misc.) the enemy's planes knocked out our ~ ["partial denture"] 9. to make; put in a ~ ["part of a ship"] 10. on the ~ (the captain was on the ~)

bridge II *n.* ["card game"] 1. to play ~ 2. auction; contract; duplicate ~ 3. (misc.) to win a game; rubber; trick (when playing ~)

bridgehead *n.* 1. to establish a ~ (see also **beach-head**) 2. to develop, enlarge a ~

bridle I *n.* to put on a ~, to put a ~ on

bridle II *v.* (D; intr.) to ~ at (she ~d at her friend's nasty remark)

brief I *n.* ["summary of a legal case"] 1. to draw up; file a ~ ["brevity"] 2. in ~ (in ~, it was a disaster) ["misc."] 3. to hold no ~ for ("not to be in favor of")

brief II *v.* (D; tr.) to ~ smb. about, concerning, on, with regard to (he had to ~ his lawyer on the case)

briefing *n.* 1. a detailed, full ~ 2. to give smb. a ~ 3. to get, receive a ~ 4. a press ~ 5. a ~ about, concerning, on, with regard to (he gave his lawyer a detailed ~ on the case)

brigade *n.* 1. a bucket; fire ~ (BE; AE has *fire department*) 2. (misc.) a brigadier (BE)/brigadier general (AE) commands a ~

brigadier *n.* (BE) 1. (mil.) a ~ commands a brigade 2. to make smb. a ~, to promote smb. to the rank of ~; to have, hold the rank of ~ 3. (misc.) what's your opinion, Brigadier (Smith)?

brigadier general *n.* (AE) see **brigadier**

brilliant *adj.* 1. ~ at, when it comes to (he's ~ when it comes to finding solutions quickly!) 2. ~ + inf. (it was ~ of him to find a solution so quickly! = he was ~ to find a solution so quickly!)

brim I *n.* (up) to the ~ (to fill smt. (up) to the ~)

brim II *v.* (D; intr.) to ~ with (she was ~ming with enthusiasm)

brim over *v.* (D; intr.) to ~ with (she was ~ming over with enthusiasm; her eyes ~med over with tears)

bring *v.* 1. (A) ("to carry") she brought word to them; or: she brought them word 2. (C) ("to carry") he brought a book for me; or: he brought me a book 3. (d; tr.) ("to present") to ~ before (to ~ a proposal before a committee) 4. (d; tr.) ("to summon") to ~ before (he was brought before the court) 5. (d; tr.) ("to carry") to ~ from; into (she brought the chairs into the house from the porch) 6. (d; tr.) ("to move") to ~ into (he brought everything into the open) 7. (d; tr.) ("to cause") (he brought trouble on himself) 8. (d; tr.) ("to move") to ~ through (excellent nursing care brought him through the crisis) 9. (D; tr.) ("to carry") to ~ to (he brought wine to the party) 10. (d; tr.) to ~ to ("to cause to reach") (to ~ water

to a/the boil; her speech brought the crowd to its feet; we must ~ him to his senses; to ~ smb. to life) 11. (d; tr.) to ~ within ("to cause to reach") (another few feet will ~ them within range) 12. (H; no passive) ("to induce") we could not ~ him to share our views; she could not ~ herself to read the letter 13. (J) ("to cause to come") his last-minute appeal brought them rushing to his aid 14. (P; tr.) ("to carry") they brought the sofa down the stairs; we brought the drinks over to the table 15. (misc.) to ~ a child into the world

bring around *v.* (AE) (D; tr.) ("to convince") to ~ to (she brought them around to our point of view)

bring back *v.* 1. (A) she brought the book back to me; or: she brought me back the book 2. (C) bring back a good book for me; or: bring me back a good book 3. (D; tr.) to ~ from (she brought the books back from Europe) 4. (D; tr.) ("to return") to ~ to (to ~ smb. back to life)

bring down *v.* 1. (D; tr.) ("to carry") to ~ from; to (they brought the computer down from the bedroom to the basement) 2. (D; tr.) ("to cause to come down") to ~ on (the enemy's artillery spotter brought down fire on our tanks; his book brought down the wrath of the authorities on his head) 3. (D; tr.) ("to reduce") to ~ to (they finally brought the price down to a reasonable figure)

bring home *v.* (D; tr.) ("to make known") to ~ to (the bombing brought the war home to the civilian population)

bring in *v.* (D; tr.) ("to include") to ~ on (we must ~ them in on our plans)

bring out *v.* 1. (D; intr.) ("to cause, evoke") to ~ in (the crisis brought out the best in her; tension brought her out in spots) 2. (D; tr.) ("to move") to ~ from; into (to ~ everything into the open; she brought out everything from the closet into the bedroom)

bring over *v.* (D; tr.) ("to move") to ~ to (the incident brought them over to our side)

bring round (CE) see **bring around**

bring together *v.* 1. (D; tr.) ("to unite") to ~ for (we brought them together for negotiations) 2. (misc.) (we brought them together (in order) to negotiate)

bring up *v.* 1. (B) I didn't want to ~ the subject to her at that time 2. (d; tr.) to ~ against ("to confront with") (the drought brought us up against serious difficulties) 3. (D; tr.) ("to educate, raise") to ~ as (they were brought up as atheists) (see also **upbringing**) 4. (D; tr.) ("to raise") to ~ for (they brought up a question for discussion = they brought a question up for discussion) 5. (D; tr.) to ~ on, with ("to inculcate with") (they brought the children up on stories about the Old West = they brought up the children on stories about the Old West) 6. (D; tr.) ("to lift") to ~ to (we brought their proficiency up to the required level) 7. (H) ("to educate, rear") our parents brought us up to respect others; they were brought up to be atheists

8. (misc.) her scream brought us up short ("her scream startled us"); to bring children up badly / well; she had a good upbringing because she was brought up well

brink *n.* 1. to bring to, drive to; bring / pull back from the ~ (of ruin) 2. at, on; to the ~ (he teetered on the very ~ of disaster; a country poised at / on the ~ of war; our leaders brought us to the ~ of war)

brinkmanship, brinksmanship *n.* to practice ~

bristle *v.* 1. (D; intr.) to ~ at (he ~d at the remark) 2. (D; intr.) to ~ with (he ~d with anger at the remark)

broach *v.* 1. (B) I would like to ~ the subject to him 2. (D; tr.) to ~ with (I would like to ~ the subject with him)

broadcast I *n.* 1. to carry a ~ 2. to beam a ~ to 3. to record, tape a ~ 4. to jam a ~ 5. a live; local; news; radio ~ (from; to)

broadcast II *v.* 1. to ~ live 2. (B) they ~ the news to the local population every day 3. (N; used with an adjective) they broadcast the interview live from Tirana

broadside *n.* to fire a ~ at

brochure *n.* 1. an advertising; holiday, travel ~ 2. a copy of a ~ (can I please have another copy of your holiday ~ for my wife?)

brogue *n.* 1. to speak (in, with) a ~ 2. a heavy, incomprehensible, thick ~

broil *v.* (AE) (C) he broiled a few steaks for us; or: he broiled us a few steaks (see also **grill II**)

broiled *adj.* (AE) char-, charcoal ~

broke *adj.* (colloq.) ["having no money"] 1. to go ~ 2. flat, stone (AE), stony (BE) ~

broker *n.* 1. to act as a ~ for 2. a commodity; insurance; marriage; real-estate (AE; BE has *estate agent*) ~ 3. (AE) a power ~ 4. an honest ~

bromide *n.* (colloq.) ["platitude"] a (tired, old) ~ about

bronco *n.* 1. to ride a ~ 2. to break a ~ 3. a bucking ~

Bronx cheer *n.* ["raspberry"] (AE) 1. to give, let out a ~ 2. to give smb. a ~

brooch *n.* a gold; silver ~

brood *v.* (D; intr.) to ~ about, on, over

brook *n.* a babbling ~

broth *n.* beef; chicken; clear ~

brother *n.* 1. a big, elder, older; kid (colloq.), little, younger; twin ~ 2. a foster; half ~; stepbrother 3. a brother-in-law 4. a blood; lay; soul ~ 5. a ~ to (he was like a ~ to us) 6. (misc.) Big Brother ("government that exercises complete control") ("Big Brother is watching you." – George Orwell, *Nineteen Eighty-Four* (1949))

brouhaha *n.* ["fuss, kerfuffle"] a ~ over

brow *n.* 1. to knit, wrinkle one's ~ 2. to mop one's ~

browbeat *v.* (D; tr.) to ~ into; out of (they could not ~ him into confessing)

brown *adj., n.* ["color"] 1. dark; deep; golden; light; reddish ~ 2. to dress in, wear ~ 3. to go, turn ~ 4. a shade of ~ ["something colored brown"] 5. a patch of ~ 6. in ~ (dressed in ~)

browse *v.* 1. (D; intr.) ("to feed as cattle do") to ~ on (to ~ on leaves) 2. (D; intr.) ("to examine in a leisurely way") to ~ through (to ~ through books)

browser *n.* a web ~

bruise I *n.* 1. a minor ~ 2. a ~ fades, forms, heals (a minor ~ formed on her face but soon faded and healed completely) 3. (misc.) cuts and ~s

bruise II *v.* to ~ easily

bruised *adj.* badly; easily ~

bruit about, abroad *v.* (formal) 1. (L) it was ~ed about that she had resigned 2. (misc.) the media bruited it about that she had resigned

brunch *n.* 1. to eat (esp. AE), have ~ 2. to cook; make, prepare; serve ~ 3. a late; substantial; working ~ 4. at, over ~ (what did you discuss at / over ~?) 5. for ~ (to eat eggs benedict for ~)

brunt *n.* to bear, take the ~ (our battalion bore the ~ of the enemy's attack)

brush I *n.* 1. to apply a ~ to 2. a bottle; clothes ~; hairbrush; nailbrush; paintbrush; scrub (AE), scrubbing (BE); shaving ~; toothbrush; upholstery ~

brush II *v.* 1. (d; intr.) to ~ against (she ~ed against the table) 2. (d; intr.) to ~ by, past (she ~ed by me) 3. (d; tr.) to ~ from, out of (she ~ed the crumbs out of her handbag) 4. (d; tr.) to ~ off (he ~ed the crumbs off the table) 5. (N; used with an adjective) she ~ed her coat clean

brush III *n.* ["brief unpleasant encounter"] 1. to have a ~ with (to have a ~ with the authorities) 2. a close ~ (a close ~ with the law)

brush-off *n.* ["snub"] to give smb. the ~

brush up *v.* 1. (d; intr.) to ~ against (to ~ against a wall) 2. (D; intr.) to ~ on (she had to ~ on her French before the exam)

brusque *adj.* ~ with

brutal *adj.* ~ to + inf. (it was ~ of him to do that)

brutality *n.* 1. to demonstrate, display, exhibit, show ~ 2. extreme; great; sheer; unprovoked ~ 3. police ~ 4. an act; degree, level; outburst of ~ 5. ~ to, towards, with 6. with ~ (the police behaved with great ~ towards the demonstrators)

bubble I *n.* 1. to blow ~s 2. to prick a ~ 3. to burst a ~ 4. a ~ bursts; forms (on) 5. air; soap ~s

bubble II *v.* (D; intr.) to ~ with (to ~ with enthusiasm)

bubble over *v.* (D; intr.) to ~ with (to ~ with enthusiasm)

bubbling *adj.* ~ with (~ (over) with enthusiasm)

buck I *n.* (colloq.) ["responsibility"] to pass the ~

buck II *v.* (colloq.) (AE) 1. (d; intr.) to ~ against ("to oppose") (to ~ against the system) 2. (D; intr.) ("to make an all-out effort") to ~ for (to ~ for a promotion)

bucket *n.* 1. a coal; fire; ice; water ~ 2. a metal;

wooden ~ 3. an empty; full ~ 4. (misc.) (colloq.) to kick the ~ ("to die"); the rain came down in ~s ("it was raining very hard") (see also *a drop in the bucket* at **drop** I) USAGE NOTE: British children play at the seaside with their buckets and spades; American children play at the seashore with their pails and shovels.

buckle I *n.* 1. to fasten a ~ 2. to undo, unfasten a ~ 3. a belt; brass ~

buckle II *v.* (D; refl., tr.) ("to fasten") to ~ into (she ~ed the baby into the seat)

buckle III *v.* (D; intr.) ("to collapse") to ~ under (to ~ under severe pressure)

buckle down *v.* (colloq.) (D; intr.) to ~ to (to ~ to work)

bud *n.* ["cell embedded in the tongue"] 1. a taste ~ ["early stage"] 2. to come into ~ 3. to nip in the ~ ["the early stage of a flower"] 4. a ~ opens 5. in ~ (the tulips are in ~)

buddy *n.* a bosom, good, great; old ~

budge *v.* 1. (D; intr.) to ~ from (she would not ~ from the spot) 2. (misc.) not to ~ an inch (she would not ~ an inch from her position)

budget I *n.* 1. to draw up a ~ 2. to submit a ~ 3. to balance a ~ 4. to adhere to, stick to; keep, remain, stay within a ~ 5. to exceed, go over; stretch a ~ 6. to cut, reduce, slash a ~ (to slash a ~ by ten percent) 7. an annual; defense; family, household; federal (AE), national; itemized; municipal; state; tight ~ 8. an item in, on a ~ 9. below, within; over (a) ~ (to stay within ~)

budget II *v.* 1. (d; intr.) to ~ for (they ~ed for a new copying machine) 2. (D; tr.) to ~ for (they ~ed a thousand dollars for a new copying machine)

buff *n.* ["the bare skin"] 1. in the ~ 2. (BE) to strip to the ~ ["devotee"] 3. a computer; film, movie; history; jazz; opera, theater ~

buffalo *n.* a herd of ~

buffer *n.* 1. to act as a ~ against; between 2. (misc.) (BE) an old ~ ("an old man") (see also *buffer state* at **state**, *buffer zone* at **zone**)

buffet I *n.* a cold ~

buffet II *v.* to be ~ed from pillar to post ("to be forced to go to many places")

buffoon *n.* to play the ~

bug I *n.* ["listening device"] 1. to install a ~ 2. to remove, tear out a ~ ["illness"] (colloq.) 3. to pick up a ~ 4. a ~ is going around ["defect"] (colloq.) 5. to iron out the ~s

bug II *v.* (colloq.) 1. (D; tr.) ("to annoy") to ~ about (he was ~ging me about the money I owed him) 2. (H) ("to urge") he kept ~ging me to pay him the money I owed him

buggy *n.* (see **baby buggy**)

bugle *n.* 1. to blow, play a ~ 2. a ~ blares, sounds

build I *n.* ["figure"]["physique"] 1. a burly; heavy; medium; powerful; slight; slim; stocky; sturdy ~ 2. the ~ of (he has the ~ of a champion) 3. the (right; wrong) ~ to + inf. (he has the (right) ~ to become

a champion) 4. of a certain ~ (he is of heavy ~ = he is heavy of ~)

build II *v.* 1. (C) they built a new library for us; or: they built us a new library 2. (D; tr.) to ~ around (to ~ a plot around a true story) 3. (D; tr.) to ~ from, of, out of (they built a boat out of wood) 4. (D; tr.) to ~ into (he built cupboards into the walls) 5. (D; intr., tr.) to ~ on (to ~ on earlier success; to ~ a relationship on trust) 6. (D; tr.) to ~ onto (the shed was built onto the garage) 7. (d; intr.) to ~ to (the music was ~ing to a climax)

building *n.* 1. to build, erect, put up; renovate a ~ 2. to demolish, raze, tear down a ~ 3. to gut a ~ (fire gutted the ~) 4. a dilapidated, gutted, ramshackle, tumbledown ~ 5. a low; tall (less frequently: *high*) ~ 6. an adjoining ~ 7. an apartment (AE); government; office; parliament; public; school ~ 8. a listed (BE) ~

buildup *n.* 1. an arms, military; gradual ~ 2. (misc.) during the ~ to the invasion

build up *v.* 1. (D; tr.) to ~ as (they built her up as a contender for the nomination) 2. (D; tr.) to ~ into (they built him up into a huge success) 3. (D; intr.) to ~ to (the music was ~ing up to a climax)

built *adj.* 1. heavily, powerfully, solidly, strongly ~ 2. ~ around (the whole story was ~ around one character) 3. ~ into (quality was ~ into their products) 4. ~ on (her conclusions were ~ on solid data) 5. (misc.) jerry ("cheaply") ~; purpose ~ (BE)

bulb *n.* ["light bulb"] 1. to change, replace; put in, screw in (US) a ~ 2. to take out, unscrew (US) a ~ 3. a ~ blows out; burns out 4. an electric; frosted; incandescent; light; three-way ~ 5. the glare of a ~ ["tuber"] 6. a crocus; tulip ~

bulge *v.* (D; intr.) to ~ with (her suitcase was ~ing with presents)

bulk I *n.* in ~ (to sell smt. in ~)

bulk II *v.* to ~ large (the law case ~ed large in his thoughts)

bull I *n.* ["adult male of a bovine animal"] 1. a ~ charges 2. a ~ bellows; gores ["nonsense"] (colloq.) 3. to shoot the ~ (AE) ["misc."] 4. to take the ~ by the horns ("to confront a problem boldly"); like a ~ in a china shop ("in a rough, crude, or clumsy manner")

bull II *n.* ["letter"] a papal ~

bulldoze *v.* to ~ through (they ~d their way through all obstacles)

bulldozer *n.* to operate a ~

bullet *n.* 1. to shoot a ~ (from; at) 2. a plastic; real; rubber; stray; tracer ~ 3. a ~ flies, whistles, whizzes (through the air) 4. a ~ ricochets 5. a ~ lodges somewhere (the ~ lodged in her shoulder) 6. a hail, volley of ~s 7. (misc.) to bite the ~ ("to perform a very unpleasant task")

bulletin *n.* 1. to issue a ~ about/on 2. an all-points ~ 3. a daily; news ~ 4. the ~ that + clause (we heard the ~ that the dam had burst)

bullfight *n.* to hold, stage a ~

bullion *n.* gold; silver ~

bull's eye *n.* to hit; score a ~

bully I *n.* (colloq.) a big ~

bully II *v.* (D; tr.) to ~ into (they ~ied him into doing it)

bulwark *n.* a ~ against

bum *v.* (colloq.) (AE) (D; tr.) to ~ off (he ~med a cigarette off me)

bump I *n.* to hit a ~ (in the road)

bump II *v.* 1. (d; intr.) to ~ against, into (she ~ed into me) 2. (D; tr.) to ~ against, on (she ~ed her arm against the table) 3. (colloq.) (AE) (D; tr.) ("to remove without warning") to ~ from (he was ~ed from the flight) 4. (d; intr.) to ~ into ("to meet by chance") (when she went to town, she ~ed into an old friend)

bumpkin *n.* a country ~

bump up *v.* (d; intr.) (esp. AE) to ~ against (he ~ed up against me)

bum's rush *n.* (AE) (colloq.) to give smb. the ~ ("to eject smb.")

bum steer *n.* (colloq.) (AE) ["poor guidance"] 1. to give smb. a ~ 2. to get a ~

bun *n.* ["knot of hair that resembles a bun"] 1. in a ~ (she wore her hair in a ~) ["type of pastry"] 2. a cinnamon, sticky; hamburger ~

bundle I *n.* (slang) ["a large amount of money"] to cost; make a ~

bundle II *v.* (d; tr.) to ~ into (they ~d the children into the car and left)

bundle off *v.* (D; tr.) to ~ to (we ~d the children off to school)

bundle up *v.* (D; intr., refl., tr.) to ~ against; in (they ~d up in warm coats against the cold)

bungle *v.* to ~ appallingly, badly, completely (they completely ~d the job; they ~d the job badly)

bunk *n.* (slang) (BE) to do a ~ ("to disappear")

buoy *n.* 1. to anchor a ~ 2. a bell; breeches; life ~

burden I *n.* 1. to bear, carry, shoulder a ~ 2. to impose, place a ~ on smb. 3. to alleviate, ease, lift, lighten, reduce, relieve a ~ 4. to share; shift a ~ 5. to distribute a ~ equitably 6. a crushing, heavy, onerous ~ 7. a financial; tax ~ 8. a ~ on, to (he became a ~ to his family) 9. (misc.) it was a heavy ~ to bear (see also *the burden of proof* at **proof**)

burden II *v.* (D; tr.) to ~ with (he didn't want to ~ his family with his problems)

bureau *n.* a better-business (AE); citizens' advice (BE); credit; farm; information; missing-persons; news; service; speakers'; travel; weather ~ (AE; BE has *the met, meteorological office*)

bureaucracy *n.* a bloated, overgrown, swollen; government ~

burglar *n.* a cat ~

burglar alarm *n.* see **alarm**

burglary *n.* to commit (a) ~

burial *n.* 1. a decent ~ (she didn't even have a decent ~) 2. a ~ takes place (the ~ took place at sea) 3. a ~ in (a ~ in a churchyard)

buried *adj.* 1. ~ underground 2. ~ in, under (~ under a pile of paperwork)

burn I *n.* 1. to get, have, receive a ~ 2. to suffer from a ~ 3. a brush, friction; cigarette ~ 4. a first-degree; second-degree; third-degree ~ 5. a mild, minor, superficial; moderate; severe ~ (see also **slow burn**)

burn II *v.* 1. to ~ brightly; fiercely, furiously 2. (d; refl.) to ~ into (the incident ~ed itself into my memory) 3. (D; intr., tr.) to ~ to (to ~ to the ground; he ~ed the meat to a crisp; the wood ~ed to ashes; she was ~ed to death) 4. (D; intr.) (often fig.) to ~ with (his cheeks ~ed with shame; they were ~ing with curiosity to hear the latest gossip; he was ~ing with passion) 5. (E) I am ~ing to tell you the news 6. (N; used with an adjective) to ~ smb. alive 7. (misc.) to ~ smb. at the stake; she ~ed her hand on the stove; the fire ~ed out of control

burned, burnt *adj.* badly, severely ~

burner *n.* 1. to light, turn on; turn off a ~ 2. a Bunsen; charcoal; gas; oil ~ 3. (misc.) to put smt. on the back ~ ("to postpone action on smt.")

burnout *n.* (colloq.) ["exhaustion"] to experience, suffer ~

burn up *v.* (slang) (AE) (R) it really ~ed me up that she was not promoted

burp *n.* 1. to let out, make a ~ 2. a loud, noisy ~

burrow *v.* (P; intr., tr.) to ~ (a hole) into the ground; to ~ one's way out of a dungeon; to ~ through a wall; to ~ under a building

bursary *n.* (BE) 1. to award a ~ 2. to receive a ~

burst I *n.* 1. ["series of shots"] to fire a ~ at ["outbreak"] 2. a sudden ~ 3. in ~s ["misc."] 4. she finally finished the job in/with a sudden ~ of energy

burst II *v.* 1. (d; intr.) to ~ into (the mob burst into the room; to ~ into flames; to ~ into tears) 2. (d; intr.) to ~ out of (to ~ out of doors) 3. (D; intr.) to ~ with (to ~ with pride; the granaries are ~ing with grain) 4. (E) she was ~ing to tell everyone the news

burst in *v.* (D; intr.) to ~ on, upon (we burst in on them without warning)

burst out *v.* (G) they burst out laughing

burton *n.* (slang) (BE) to go for a ~ ("to be lost; to be broken; to be killed; to fail")

bury *v.* 1. (d; refl., tr.) to ~ in (he ~ied himself in his work) 2. (N; used with an adjective) they ~ied him alive

bus I *n.* 1. to drive a ~ 2. (as a passenger) to board, get on; catch a ~; get off a ~; to come; go, travel by ~; to miss a ~; to ride a ~; to ride in/on a ~; to take a ~ 3. a city; double-decker; local; long-distance (AE; BE has *coach*); school; sightseeing ~ 4. an airbus (for short-haul flights) 5. the ~es are not running today but normally run every half hour and pick people up from this ~ stop 6. a ~ for, to (is this the ~ to the airport?)

bus II *v.* (D; tr.) to ~ to (to ~ children to school)

bush *n.* 1. to prune, trim a ~ 2. a clump of ~es 3. (misc.) to beat about/(AE) around the ~ ("to speak indirectly")

bushel *n.* by the ~ (to sell by the ~)

business *n.* ["commerce"] ["trade"] 1. to conduct, do, transact; drum up ~ (to do ~ with smb.) 2. to lose ~ 3. to go into ~; to go out of ~ 4. big; small ~ 5. a mail-order ~; show ~; the travel ~ 6. retail; wholesale ~ 7. (AE) a land-office ("brisk") ~ (to do a land-office ~ in real estate) 8. ~ drops off; picks up 9. ~ is brisk, booming, flourishing, thriving 10. ~ is bad; slack, slow; ~ is at a standstill 11. in ~ (to be in ~ for oneself; "what (line of) ~ are you in?" "we are in the real-estate ~") 12. on ~ (to travel on ~) ["firm"] 13. to build up; establish, launch, open a ~ 14. to manage, operate, run a ~ 15. to buy into; buy out; take over a ~ ["work"] 16. to get down to ~ 17. to go about one's ~ 18. to talk ~ ["affairs"] 19. to mind one's own ~ 20. bad; dirty; funny; (colloq.) monkey ~ 21. company; personal; unfinished; urgent ~ ["cause"] 22. to have ~ to + inf. (he had no ~ to interfere = he had no ~ interfering) ["misc."] 23. to know one's ~ ("to be competent in one's field"); it was ~ as usual even during the crisis; to state one's ~ ("to explain what one is doing"); to mix ~ with pleasure ("to combine work and recreation"); to mean ~ ("to be serious about achieving one's ends"); to give smb. the ~ (AE) ("to deceive smb."); it's none of your ~ ("the matter doesn't concern you"); the whole ~ strikes me as rather nasty/risky; that's the end of the agenda: (is there) any other ~?

busing *n.* (US) forced; school; voluntary ~

bust *n.* (slang) ["arrest"] 1. to make a ~ 2. a drug, drugs (BE) ~

bustle off *v.* (D; intr., tr.) to ~ to (she ~ed the children off to school)

busy I *adj.* 1. ~ at, with (the children were ~ with their homework) 2. to be ~ doing smt. (she was ~ getting dinner ready) 3. to keep ~; to keep smb. ~ (they keep ~ helping out at the crisis center; we kept the children ~ cutting out pictures) 4. (misc.) I'm sorry: the line/number is ~; as ~ as a bee

busy II *v.* 1. (d; refl.) to ~ by, with (she busied herself by doing various jobs = she busied herself with various jobs) 2. (J; refl.) (she busied herself doing various jobs)

butcher *n.* a family ~ (BE) ("a butcher's business run by a single family"); ("a butcher's business that sells retail rather than wholesale")

butt I *n.* a cigarette; rifle ~

butt II *v.* 1. (d; intr.) to ~ against 2. (colloq.) (d; intr.) to ~ into (to ~ into smb.'s business)

butter *n.* 1. to churn; cream; make ~ 2. to spread ~ (on bread) 3. apple (AE); cocoa; peanut; prune; salted; sweet, unsalted; whipped ~ 4. fresh; rancid ~ 5. a knob (BE), lump (BE); pat; stick of ~ 6. in ~ (to fry in ~) (see also *bread and butter* at **bread**)

butterfly *n.* 1. to collect ~flies 2. a ~ flits from flower to flower 3. (misc.) a social ~ ("one who leads an active but superficial social life"); ~flies and moths

butter up *v.* (colloq.) (d; intr.) to ~ to (he keeps ~ing up to the boss)

butt in *v.* (colloq.) (D; intr.) to ~ on (to ~ on a conversation)

button *n.* ["fastener"] 1. to sew on a ~ 2. to do up; undo one's ~s 3. to lose a ~ 4. to rip off, tear off a ~ 5. a ~ comes off (my ~ came off) ["push button"] 6. to press, push a ~ 7. the panic ~ (colloq.); a push-button ["badge"] (AE) 8. a campaign ~ ["misc."] 9. right on the ~ ("exactly correct")

buy I *n.* (colloq.) ["purchase"] 1. to be; get, have a ~ 2. a good ~ (that book was a very good ~ at only $20!)

buy II *v.* 1. (C) we bought a book for her; or: we bought her a book 2. (D; refl.; tr.) to ~ for (we bought her a book for twenty dollars; she bought (herself) a hat for twenty dollars) 3. (D; tr.) to ~ from (we bought her a book from a local bookshop) 4. (d; intr.) to ~ into (to ~ into a business) (also fig.) (somehow I just don't ~ into that plan of yours!) 5. (misc.) to ~ as is ("to buy with no guarantee of quality"); cheap, cheaply; dear; to ~ retail; to ~ wholesale; to ~ at a reasonable price; to ~ by the dozen; to ~ in bulk

buy back *v.* (D; tr.) to ~ from

buyer *n.* 1. a first-time (house); prospective ~ 2. a ~ for (they found a ~ for the building)

buying *n.* impulse; panic ~

buzz I *n.* (colloq.) ("telephone call") to give smb. a ~

buzz II *v.* 1. (D; intr.) to ~ for (to ~ for one's secretary) 2. (D; intr.) to ~ with (to ~ with activity) 3. (P; intr.) insects were ~ing through the air; photographers were ~ing around the entrance

buzzer *n.* 1. to press, sound a ~ 2. at the ~ (at the ~, stop work immediately!) 3. a ~ goes off, sounds (when the ~ sounds, stop work immediately!)

by (see *by and large* at **large**)

bye *n.* (sports) to draw a ~

by-election see **election**

bygones *n.* to let ~ be ~

bylaws *n.* 1. to draft, draw up ~s 2. to amend, change; approve (the) ~ 3. city, municipal; local; township (esp. AE) ~

bypass *n.* ["operation"] 1. a coronary, heart, multiple ~ ["road"] 2. to take the ~ 3. a part, section of a ~ (get off this section of the ~ at the next exit) 4. on a ~

byplay *n.* ~ between

bystander *n.* an innocent ~

C

cab *n.* 1. a black; yellow (we hailed a black ~ in London and a yellow ~ in New York) 2. to call for; find; flag down; get; hail; hire; take a ~ 3. to get into; get out of a ~ 4. a ~ picks smb. up 5. to drive a ~ (for a living) 6. a radio ~ 7. by ~; in a ~ (to go somewhere by ~) (see also **minicab**)

cabbage *n.* 1. red; savoy; white ~ 2. boiled ~ 3. a head; leaf of ~ 4. (AE) corned beef and ~

cabin *n.* ["compartment"] 1. a first-class; second-class ~ 2. a pressurized ~ (of an airplane) ["small house"] 3. a log ~ (did Abraham Lincoln really rise from a log ~ to the US Presidency?)

cabinet *n.* ["case"] ["cupboard"] 1. a built-in; china; display; kitchen ~ (several bottles of port in the ~) 2. a file (AE), filing ~ ["body of advisers"] 3. the president's; Prime Minister's ~ 4. a coalition; kitchen ("informal") ~ 5. (UK) a shadow ~ ("members of the opposition party who will form the next cabinet") (she joined/entered the shadow ~ several years ago and left it only last year) 6. a ~ meets 7. (misc.) a ~ minister (not US); a ~ reshuffle ["cabinet meeting"] (BE) 8. to hold a ~ 9. in ~ (to take a decision in ~) USAGE NOTE: In the UK cabinet ministers are nowadays typically elected members of the House of Commons. In the USA members of the cabinet are appointed by the President "with the advice and consent of the Senate" (US Constitution) and are typically not elected by the people.

cable I *n.* ["wire"] 1. to lay, string ~ 2. an overhead; submarine; transatlantic; underground ~ 3. an electric, power; telegraph; telephone ~ 4. a ~ carries information/messages; snaps 5. a coil of ~ ["cablegram"] 6. to send a ~ 7. to get, receive a ~ 8. a ~ from; to

cable II *v.* 1. (A) we ~d the message to them; or: we ~d them the message 2. (d; intr., tr.) to ~ for (they ~d for immediate delivery) 3. (H) we ~d them to return home immediately 4. (L; may have an object) she ~d (us) that the manuscript had arrived 5. (Q; may have an object) they ~d (us) where to meet

cablegram *n.* 1. to send a ~ 2. to get, receive a ~ 3. a ~ from; to

cache *n.* an arms ~

cadence *n.* (usu. mil.) 1. to count ~ 2. in ~

cadet *n.* 1. an air-force; military; naval; police ~ 2. (slang) (AE) a space ~ ("an absent-minded person")

cadge *v.* (rare) 1. (D; intr.) to ~ for (to ~ for food) 2. (D; tr.) to ~ from, off (to ~ meals from friends)

caesarean, caesarean section *n.* 1. to do, perform a ~ on 2. to have a ~ 3. (misc.) to be born/delivered by ~

café *n.* a pavement (BE), sidewalk (AE); transport ~

(BE; AE prefers *truck stop* esp. for one that is by a highway and also sells gas)

cafeteria *n.* a school ~

cage *n.* 1. a birdcage 2. a bank teller's (AE) ~

cagey *adj.* (colloq.) ["sly"] ~ about

cahoots *n.* (esp. AE) in ~ with ("in partnership with") (they were in ~ (with each other) to do smt. bad)

cajole *v.* 1. (d; tr.) (with an inanimate object) to ~ from (she ~d some money from him) 2. (d; tr.) (with an animate object) to ~ into (she ~d him into giving her some money)

cake *n.* 1. to bake, make; cut; frost (esp. AE), ice a ~ 2. a birthday; wedding ~ 3. (a) chocolate; Christmas (BE); coffee ~; fruitcake; honey; Madeira (BE), sponge; marble; pound; white (AE) ~ 4. a layer; upside-down ~ 5. a piece, slice of ~ 6. (misc.) a piece of ~ ("smt. very easy to do"); to take the ~ ("to be the best or worst"; BE has also *to take the biscuit*); to go/sell like hot cakes ("to be bought up very quickly")

caked *adj.* ~ in, with (~ with blood)

calamity *n.* 1. to avert; ward off a ~ 2. to survive a ~ 3. a ~ befalls smb. 4. a crushing, dire, grave, great; national ~ 5. a ~ for (the fire was a ~ for everyone)

calculate *v.* 1. (d; intr.) to ~ on (we ~d on a two-day trip) 2. (D; tr.) to ~ as, at (we ~d the length of the trip as two days) 3. (L) we ~d that the trip would take two days 4. (Q) we ~d how long the trip would take

calculated *adj.* 1. ill; well ~ 2. (usu. does not stand alone) ~ to + inf. (his actions were ~ to provoke his opponents)

calculations *n.* 1. to do, make, perform ~ 2. mathematical; precise; rough ~

calculator *n.* 1. to use, operate a ~ 2. an electronic; pocket ~

calculus *n.* ["mathematical method"] 1. differential; integral; vector ~ ["deposit formed in an organ of the body"] 2. a biliary; renal; urinary ~

calendar *n.* ["chart that shows the days and months"] 1. the Chinese; Gregorian; Hindu; Islamic, Muslim; Jewish; Julian; Roman ~ 2. a lunar; solar ~ 3. a perpetual ~ 4. a desk; wall ~ 5. in a ~ (February is the shortest month in the Gregorian ~) ["schedule"] 6. to clear one's ~ 7. a court; school; social ~ 8. a crowded, full ~ 9. on a ~ (what's on your ~ this week?) USAGE NOTE: In BE, a calendar for one's desk or pocket with spaces to write one's appointments in it is called a diary.

calf *n.* 1. a ~ bleats 2. in ~ (the cow was in ~) 3. (misc.) the meat of the ~ is veal

caliber, calibre *n.* ["diameter of the barrel of a weapon"] 1. heavy; light ~ ["quality"] 2. high; low ~ 3. of a certain typically high ~ (there are few workers left of her ~)

calibration *n.* precise ~

calisthenics, callisthenics *n.* 1. to do, perform ~ 2. daily; group, mass ~

call I *n.* ["appeal"] ["summons"] 1. to issue a ~ for (the government issued a ~ to the populace for voluntary contributions) 2. to answer, heed, respond to a ~ (to answer the ~ of duty) 3. a clarion ~ 4. a curtain; last ~ (last ~ for passengers boarding this flight!) (see also **curtain call**) 5. a ~ for (we heard a ~ for help) 6. a ~ to (a ~ to arms) 7. (see also *at smb. 's beck and call* at **beck**) ["visit"] 8. to make, pay a ~ on smb. 9. to make a ~ at a place (the ships made ~s at several ports) 10. a business; courtesy; port; professional ~ 11. a house ~ (my doctor makes house ~s) (esp. AE; BE prefers *home visit*) ["invitation"] 12. to accept, answer a ~ ["telephone call"] 13. to give smb. a ~ 14. to make, place a ~ to smb. 15. to answer; get, receive; return; take; transfer a ~ (who will take her ~?) 16. to put a ~ through (the operator put my ~ right through) 17. a telephone ~ 18. a business; conference; emergency; wake-up ~ 19. a collect (AE), reversed-charge (BE), transferred-charge (BE); dial-direct (AE), direct-dialled (BE); operator-assisted; ordinary (BE), station-to-station (AE); personal (BE, old-fashioned), person-to-person ~ 20. an international; local; long-distance, toll (AE), trunk (BE, old-fashioned); toll-free (AE) ~ 21. an anonymous; crank; nuisance; threatening ~ 22. a ~ from; to ["signal"] 23. a bugle; trumpet ~ ["reading aloud"] 24. a roll ~ ["duty"] 25. on ~ (which nurse is on ~?) ["need"] 26. a ~ for (there is no ~ for such behavior) 27. a ~ to + inf. (there was no ~ to complain) ["formation"] (AE) (usu. mil.) 28. sick ~ (to go on sick ~) ["misc."] 29. a close ~ ("a narrow escape"); a wake-up ~ (also fig.) (was the credit crunch a wake-up ~ to reform the international economic system?) (see also **bird call**)

call II *v.* 1. (C) ("to summon") she ~ed a taxi for me; or: she ~ed me a taxi 2. (d; intr.) ("to visit") to ~ at (the ship will ~ at several ports) 3. (d; intr.) to ~ for ("to fetch") (I'll ~ for you at two o'clock) 4. (d; intr.) to ~ for ("to require") (the position ~s for an experienced engineer; they ~ed for him to resign) 5. (d; intr.) to ~ for ("to seek") (to ~ for help) 6. (d; intr., tr.) ("to order by telephone") to ~ for (they ~ed the pharmacy for aspirin) 7. (d; tr.) ("to summon") to ~ into (she was ~ed into the room) 8. (D; intr.) to ~ on ("to visit") (several friends ~ed on us) 9. (slang) (AE) (d; tr.) to ~ on ("to reprimand") (the boss ~ed me on my sloppy writing) (see also **call on**) 10. (d; tr.) ("to summon") to ~ out of (she was ~ed out of town on business) 11. (D; intr.) ("to shout") to ~ to (she ~ed to me to help her) 12. (d; tr.) ("to summon") to ~ to (to ~ smb. to account; to ~ smt. to mind; the chair ~ed the delegates to order; to be ~ed to the bar) 13. (H) ("to summon") they ~ed her to testify 14. (N; used with a noun or adjective) ("to describe as or name") she ~ed him a stuffed shirt; I would ~ it a disgrace; I ~ that mean; they ~ him Bill; he is ~ed Bill 15. (O) ("to describe as") to ~ smb. a bad name 16. (misc.) (esp. AE) ("to telephone") to ~ collect; long-distance; she ~ed from the office; I always ~ Bill by his first name

call away *v.* 1. (D; tr.) to ~ from (she was ~ed away from her desk) 2. (misc.) they were ~ed away on business

call down *v.* 1. (D; tr.) ("to summon") to ~ on, upon (to ~ the wrath of God on smb.'s head) 2. (D; intr.) ("to shout") to ~ to (he ~ed down to us from the roof)

call in *v.* 1. (D; intr.) ("to visit") to ~ at, on (she ~ed in at our place this morning; the doctor ~ed in on her patient) 2. (D; intr.) ("to telephone") to ~ to; with (he ~ed in to the chat show/talk show; she ~ed in with a comment = she ~ed in (in order) to comment) 3. (s) ("to report by telephone") to ~ sick

call on *v.* 1. (D; tr.) to ~ for (to ~ a pupil for an answer) 2. (H) the mayor ~ed on the people to remain calm = the people were ~ed on by the mayor to remain calm

callous *adj.* 1. ~ to (~ to suffering) 2. ~ to + inf. (it was ~ of him to say that)

call out *v.* 1. (D; intr.) to ~ for (to ~ (to smb.) for help) 2. (D; intr., tr.) ("to shout") to ~ to (he ~ed smt. out to me; he ~ed out to me to help him = "help me!" he ~ed out (to me))

call over *v.* (D; tr.) to ~ to (I ~ed him over to our table)

call up *v.* 1. (D; tr.) to ~ for (they were ~ed up for military service) 2. (D; intr.) ("to shout") to ~ from; to (she ~ed up to us from the basement (to come down)) 3. (D; tr.) to ~ on (to ~ smt. on a computer screen) 4. (D; intr., tr.) to ~ on (to ~ smb. on the telephone) 5. (D; tr.) to ~ to (she was ~ed up to the podium) 6. (H) he was ~ed up to serve in the army

call upon *v.* see **call on**

calm I *adj.* to keep, remain, stay ~

calm II *n.* 1. to shatter the ~ 2. (a) dead, perfect; uneasy ~ (an uneasy ~ descended on the city after the riots) 3. (misc.) the mayor appealed to the people for calm; the ~ before the storm

calories *n.* 1. to count ~ 2. to burn ~ 3. empty ~ (in junk food)

calumny *n.* to heap ~ on

camel *n.* an Arabian, one-humped; Bactrian, two-humped ~

camera *n.* [- "apparatus for taking or transmitting pictures"] 1. to load a ~ 2. an automatic; box; miniature ~ 3. a cine (BE), motion-picture (AE), movie (AE); miniature; television, TV; video ~ 4. a security ~ 5. off ~ ("not being filmed") 6. on ~ ("being filmed") 7. (misc.) to face the ~ (in order to be photographed); the ~s are ready to roll (in a film studio); candid ~ ("taking pictures of people without their knowledge") ["judge's chamber"] 8. in ~ (the trial was held in ~; the case was heard in ~)

cameraman, camerawoman *n.* a motion-picture (AE); television ~

camouflage *n.* 1. to use, utilize ~ 2. natural ~ 3. by ~ (to conceal by ~)

camp *n.* 1. to make, pitch, set up ~ 2. to break, strike ~ 3. an army; base; boot; training ~ 4. a prisoner-of-war, POW, PW (AE) ~ 5. a labor; work ~ 6. a displaced-persons, DP; refugee; repatriation ~ 7. a concentration; detention; internment; transit ~ 8. a day; overnight; summer ~ 9. a trailer ~ (AE; BE has *caravan park, caravan site*) 10. (misc.) the enemy; opposing; rival ~

campaign I *n.* 1. to launch, mount, orchestrate, organize a ~ 2. to carry on, conduct, wage a ~ 3. to intensify, step up; spearhead a ~ 4. an active, aggressive, all-out, hard-fought, relentless, vigorous; whirlwind ~ 5. a feeble, lackadaisical, weak ~ 6. an advertising; membership; publicity, public-relations ~ 7. an election, political; whistle-stop; write-in ~ 8. an anti-smoking; educational ~ 9. a local; national, nationwide ~ 10. a smear; whispering ~ 11. a military ~ 12. the ~ got off to a good start; the ~ fizzled (out) 13. a ~ against; for (during the ~ against smoking; a ~ for equal rights) 14. a ~ to + inf. (they launched a ~ to fight smoking)

campaign II *v.* 1. to ~ actively, aggressively, vigorously 2. (D; intr.) to ~ against; for (they were ~ing actively against teenage smoking) 3. (E) they were ~ing actively to reduce teenage smoking

camp bed (BE) see **cot** 1, 2

camper *n.* 1. (esp. AE) a summer ~ (person) 2. (misc.) (fig.) a happy ~ (no more long faces, guys! We want only happy ~s in this office!)

campus *n.* (esp. AE) 1. a college, university ~ 2. off; on ~ (to live on ~) 3. at a ~ (the university has an uptown ~ at which there are good sports facilities)

can I *n.* 1. (AE) an ash, garbage, trash ~ (BE has *dustbin*) 2. a beer; milk; watering ~ 3. a tin ~

can II *v.* (F) she ~ work (see the Usage Notes for **able**; **must**)

Canadian *n.* a French ~ (a French ~ who speaks Canadian French)

canal *n.* 1. to build, construct, dig a ~ 2. to dredge a ~ 3. an irrigation ~ 4. along; on a ~ 5. (anat.) the alimentary ~ (what's in your alimentary ~?)

canard *n.* 1. to circulate, spread a ~ 2. an absurd, preposterous ~

canary *n.* a ~ sings

cancer *n.* 1. to get, develop; have ~ 2. bowel; brain; breast; cervical; colon, colorectal; lung; rectal; skin; stomach ~ 3. inoperable; metastatic; terminal ~ 4. ~ metastasizes, spreads

candid *adj.* 1. less than (entirely) ~ 2. ~ about 3. ~ with

candidacy, candidature *n.* 1. to announce, file (AE) one's ~ 2. to withdraw one's ~

candidate *n.* 1. to nominate; to put up; run (esp. AE) a ~ (for office) 2. to adopt (BE), choose, select; endorse a ~ 3. (BE) to de-select a ~ ("to decline to re-select or retain a party candidate") 4.

a handpicked; write-in ~ 5. an independent; party; third-party ~ 6. a leading; prospective; strong; successful; victorious ~ (a successful ~ for admission to the university; a victorious ~ for the party's nomination) 7. a defeated; unsuccessful; weak ~ 8. a ~ for (a ~ for the presidency) 9. a ~ runs for, stands for (BE) office 10. (misc.) (esp. AE) a slate of ~s 11. (misc.) the successful ~ for the job will have had at least five years' experience

candle *n.* 1. to dip ~s 2. to light a ~ 3. to blow out, extinguish, snuff out a ~ 4. the ~ was burning; was flickering; was going out; was sputtering 5. a wax ~ 6. a household; votive ~ 7. the flame of a ~ = a ~ flame 8. (misc.) to burn the ~ at both ends ("to dissipate one's energy by doing too many things both by day and at night"); not to hold a ~ to smb. or smt. ("to be far inferior to smb. or smt.")

candlelight *n.* by ~ (to read by ~)

candlestick *n.* 1. brass; silver ~s 2. a pair of ~s

candor, candour *n.* 1. complete; disarming ~ 2. the ~ to + inf. (she had enough ~ to tell them the truth)

candy *n.* (esp. AE) 1. chocolate; cotton; hard ~ (AE; BE has *boiled sweet*) 2. a box; piece of ~ (BE has *sweet*)

cane *n.* ["walking stick"] 1. to carry; twirl a ~ ["plant"] 2. sugar ~ ["stick used for punishment"] (old-fashioned) 3. to get the ~

cannabis *n.* 1. to grow ~ 2. to smoke ~

cannibalism *n.* to engage in, practice ~

cannon *n.* 1. to fire a ~ 2. to aim a ~ at; to train a ~ on 3. to load a ~ 4. a ~ booms, roars; fires 5. a water ~ (the police trained a water ~ on the mob) 6. (misc.) (colloq.) a loose ~ ("a dangerously unpredictable person") (see also *cannon fodder* at **fodder**)

canoe I *n.* 1. to paddle a ~ 2. in a, by ~ (to cross a river by ~)

canoe II *v.* (P; intr.) to ~ along a river bank; to ~ across a lake

canon *n.* ["dogma"] 1. to establish, lay down a ~ ["round"] (mus.) 2. to sing a ~

canter *n.* ["gait of a horse"] at a ~ (to set off at a ~)

cap *n.* ["container holding an explosive charge"] 1. a percussion ~ ["head covering"] 2. to place, put a ~ on one's head 3. a cloth; peaked; skull ~ 4. a bathing; shower ~ 5. a forage (BE), garrison; overseas; service ~ 6. a baseball ~ 7. (BE) a cricket; rugby ~ (showing that the wearer is a member of a national team) 8. (misc.) to wear (a) ~ and gown (at graduation); (fig.) to put on one's thinking ~ (old-fashioned) (to ponder a problem) ["ceiling, upper limit"] 9. to place/put a ~ on (to place a ~ on public spending) ["lid"] 10. to put on, screw on a ~ 11. to screw off, take off, unscrew a ~ ["misc."] 12. the polar ice-cap

capability *n.* 1. to demonstrate, display, show one's ~ties 2. a defense; first-strike; military; nuclear ~ 3. the ~ to + inf. (the ~ to win) 4. beyond; within smb.'s ~ties (doing this job is well within my ~ties!)

capable *adj.* 1. perfectly, truly ~ 2. ~ of (he is ~ of anything)

capacity *n.* ["ability to hold"] 1. to ~ (filled/packed to ~) 2. lung ~ 3. seating; storage ~ 4. a ~ of (a ~ of twenty gallons) ["ability"] 5. intellectual, mental ~ 6. smb.'s earning ~ 7. a ~ for (a ~ for making friends) 8. the ~ to + inf. (she has the ~ to make friends) 9. beyond one's ~; within one's ~ (doing this job is well within my ~!) ["ability to produce"] 10. plant; productive ~ (our country's productive ~) 11. full, peak ~ 12. at ~ (to operate at peak ~) ["function"] 13. an administrative; advisory; professional; supervisory ~ 14. an official; unofficial ~ 15. in a ~ (she acted in an advisory ~; in his ~ as legal adviser, he helped us a great deal)

cape *n.* ["piece of land, headland"] 1. to round a ~ 2. on a ~

caper *n.* 1. to cut a ~ 2. a childish ~

capital *n.* ["wealth"] 1. to borrow; raise ~ 2. to invest, put up; tie up ~ (I hope to get a good return on the ~ I've invested) 3. to sink ~ in, into 4. to withdraw ~ (from) 5. borrowed; circulating, working; fixed, permanent; foreign; idle; venture ~ ["gain"] 6. to make ~ out of smt. 7. political ~ (they made political ~ out of the incident) ["official seat of government"] 8. to establish a ~ 9. a national; provincial; state ~ 10. foreign; world ~s ["main center"] 11. a diamond; fashion; film ~ (where is the film ~ of the world?)

capitalize *v.* (d; intr.) to ~ on (to ~ on smb.'s mistakes)

capital punishment *n.* 1. to impose; introduce ~ 2. to abolish ~

capitulate *v.* (D; intr.) to ~ to (to ~ to the enemy)

capricious *adj.* ~ to + inf. (it was ~ of you to act like that)

capsule *n.* 1. a space; time ~ 2. a seed ~

captain *n.* 1. (AE) a bell ~ 2. a group (BE); ship's; team ~ 3. (AE) a precinct ~ (in the police) 4. (mil.) a ~ commands a company or battery 5. to make smb. a ~, to promote smb. to the rank of ~; to have, hold the rank of ~ 6. (misc.) ~s of industry ("leading industrialists"); what's your opinion, Captain (Smith)?

captive *adj.* to hold smb. ~; to take smb. ~ (they held us ~ for several weeks)

captivity *n.* 1. to hold in ~ 2. to take into ~ 3. to release from ~ 4. (misc.) to breed wild animals in ~

capture *v.* ~ to ~ smt. on film

car *n.* ["automobile, motorcar"] 1. to drive, operate; park; run; start; steer a ~ 2. to bring a ~ to a stop, to stop a ~; to get in, into a ~; to get out of a ~ 3. to back (esp. AE), reverse (esp. BE) a ~ (she backed the ~ into the garage) 4. to ride in a ~ 5. to go, travel by ~ 6. to hire (BE), rent a ~ 7. to break in (AE), run in (BE) a (new) ~ 8. to fix, repair; service; tune up; winterize a ~ 9. to jack up; park; road-test; a ~ 10. to register a ~ 11. to smash up, total, wreck; strip a ~ 12. an antique; veteran (BE); vintage ~

13. an electric ~ 14. a luxury; passenger; sports ~ 15. a racing; stock ~ 16. an armored; command; scout ~ 17. a Panda (BE), patrol, police, prowl (AE), squad; unmarked (police) ~ 18. a getaway ~ 19. an estate ~ (BE; old-fashioned BE also has *shooting brake*; AE has *station wagon*) 20. a new; secondhand, used ~ 21. a company; hire (esp. BE), rental, rented ~ 22. a ~ overtakes, passes; runs; starts 23. a ~ breaks down; stalls 24. (misc.) to take a ~ in for service; to fill a ~ up with gasoline/petrol ["vehicle that moves on rails"] 25. (on a train) (esp. AE; BE also has *carriage, wagon/waggon, van*) a baggage (AE; BE has *luggage van*); box (AE); cattle; club, lounge, parlor; dining, restaurant (BE); first-class (AE; BE has *first-class carriage*); flat; freight (AE; BE has *goods wagon*); mail (BE has *mail van*); railroad (AE; BE has *railway carriage*); sleeping; tank ~ 26. a streetcar (see also **streetcar**); trolley ~ (AE; BE has *tram*) 27. a cable ~ 28. (misc.) to uncouple railroad/railway ~s

carbon *n.* activated; radioactive ~

card *n.* 1. a business, calling (esp. AE), visiting ~ 2. a filing; index (AE), record (BE) ~ 3. a donor, organ-donor; library –; membership; press; ration ~ 4. a time ~ 5. a banker's (BE), cheque (BE); cash (esp. BE), credit (AE) (used at a cash machine); charge (esp. BE), credit (used for making purchases); debit; loyalty; SIM ~ (see also **credit card**; **debit card**) 6. a boarding ~ (for boarding a plane) 7. a report ~ (AE; BE has *school report*) 8. a boxing; race (BE), racing (AE) ~ 9. a flash ~ (used as a teaching aid) 10. a high; low; playing; trump (also fig.); wild (also fig.); winning ~ 11. an anniversary; birthday; Christmas; confirmation; Easter; get-well; graduation; greeting (esp. AE), greetings (BE); Hanukkah; New Year's; sympathy; thank-you ~ 12. a postcard (CE), postal (AE) ~ 13. (misc.) a drawing ~ ("smb. or smt. that attracts large audiences") (see also **trump card**)

cards *n.* 1. to play ~ 2. to have, play a game of ~ 3. to cut; deal; shuffle the ~ 4. playing ~ 5. a deck (esp. AE), pack of ~ 6. (misc.) to stack the ~ ("to prearrange conditions to one's own advantage") (the ~ were stacked and the dice were loaded against us); to hold all the ~ ("to be in a strong negotiating position"); to be in (AE), on (BE) the ~ ("to be destined by fate") (Carmen thought her death was in the ~s); to lay, put one's ~ on the table ("to reveal one's position"); to play one's ~ right ("to negotiate skillfully")

care I *n.* ["caution"] 1. to exercise, take ~ 2. great, meticulous, painstaking, scrupulous, (the) utmost ~ 3. ~ to + inf. (she took ~ to avoid catching cold) 4. ~ that + clause (take ~ that you don't catch cold!) 5. with ~ (to handle smt. with ~) ["solicitude"]["maintenance"]["keep"] 6. to provide ~ for 7. to take ~ of – 8. to entrust smb./smt. to smb.'s ~; to put smb. in smb.'s ~ 9. (tender) loving; parental ~ ("I thank them for their tender loving ~" – Shakespeare,

Henry VI, Part 2, Act 3, Scene 2) 10. child; day; foster ~ (day ~ for children) 11. in smb.'s ~ (the children were left in my ~) ["health maintenance and medical care"] 12. to provide ~ for 13. to get, receive ~ 14. dental; medical; nursing ~ (see also **health care**) 15. antenatal (BE), antepartal (AE), prenatal (AE); coronary; postnatal, postpartum ~ 16. emergency; extended; intensive; long-term; primary (health); special ~ (this patient requires intensive nursing ~) 17. custodial; domiciliary; hospice; respite ~ 18. in-patient; out-patient ~ 19. managed ~ 20. under smb.'s ~ (under a doctor's ~) 21. (misc.) a coronary-care unit; an intensive-care unit; to take into ~ (BE) ("to take a child from its parents under the authority of a court"); driving without due ~ and attention (BE) ["misc."] 22. in ~ of ("at/to smb.'s address")

care II v. 1. (D; intr.) ("to be interested") to ~ about (she doesn't ~ about our opinions) 2. (D; intr.) ("to like") to ~ about, for (he ~s about us; she ~s a lot for you; would you ~ for some more coffee?) 3. (d; intr.) ("to take care of") to ~ for (she ~s for her elderly mother) 4. (E) ("to want") I don't ~ to attend 5. (Q) I don't ~ why she called: I don't want to speak to her!

career n. 1. to carve out, make a ~ (for oneself) 2. to enter on; launch a ~ 3. to abandon, give up one's ~ 4. to cut short smb.'s ~ (the accident cut short her ~) 5. a brilliant, distinguished; checkered (AE), chequered (BE); colorful; promising; successful; turbulent ~ 6. an academic; diplomatic; literary; military; musical; political; professional; public; stage ~ 7. a ~ as (to carve out a ~ as a diplomat) 8. a ~ in (she made a ~ for herself in diplomacy) 9. (misc.) her ~ took off (her ~ really took off when she sang Carmen!)

careful adj. 1. ~ about, of (a good writer is ~ about details) 2. ~ in (to be ~ in negotiating a new trade agreement) 3. ~ with (we must be ~ with dynamite) 4. ~ to + inf. (she was ~ to complete everything on time) 5. ~ that + clause (she was ~ that everything was/would be completed on time) 6. (misc.) be ~ driving home

careless adj. 1. ~ about, in, of, with (~ about one's appearance) 2. ~ to + inf. (it was ~ of you to leave the door unlocked)

carelessness n. ~ about, in, with

caress I n. a gentle, loving ~

caress II v. to ~ gently, lovingly

caretaker n. see **superintendant**

cargo n. 1. to carry, haul (a) ~ 2. to load, take on; stow; transfer ~ 3. to unload ~ 4. contraband; general ~ (see also *cargo plane* at **plane**; *cargo ship* at **ship**)

caricature n. ["an ironic representation"] 1. to draw a ~ (of) 2. a bold, striking ~ ["travesty"] 3. a ~ of the truth (the film is/gives/presents only a grotesque ~ of what actually happened)

carnage n. senseless, terrible ~

carol I n. 1. to sing a ~ 2. a Christmas ~

carol II v. to go ~ing

carp v. (D; intr.) to ~ about; at

carpet n. 1. to beat a ~ 2. to lay; weave a ~ 3. to take up a ~ (the ~ must be taken up and cleaned) 4. to clean; shampoo; vacuum a ~ 5. an oriental; Persian; woven ~ 6. (misc.) to ¬put out/roll out¬ the red ~ for smb. ("to give smb. a warm reception"); a flying, magic ~; to call smb. on the ~ (esp. AE) ("to call people to account for their actions") (see also *to sweep under the carpet* at **sweep**)

carpeting n. ["floor covering"] 1. fitted (BE), wall-to-wall ~ ["severe reprimand"] (BE) 2. to get; give a ~

carriage n. ["vehicle"] 1. see **baby carriage** 2. a railway ~ (BE; AE has *railroad car*) 3. a horse-drawn ~ ["support"] 4. a gun; typewriter ~ ["bearing"] 5. an erect; proud ~

carriageway n. (BE) 1. a dual ~ (BE; AE has *divided highway*) 2. on a ~

carried away adj. ["enthusiastic"] to get ~ (by, with)

carrier n. 1. an aircraft; escort; personnel; troop ~ 2. a letter, mail ~ (AE; CE has *postal worker*) 3. a common, public ~ ("a transport service used by the public") 4. a chronic ~ (of a disease)

carrot n. 1. diced ~s 2. a bunch of ~s

carry v. 1. (B) she ~ied the books to me 2. (d; tr.) to ~ from; to (we ~ied the table from the door to the center of the room) 3. (d; tr.) to ~ into (~ the chairs into the house) 4. (D; tr.) to ~ on (colloq.), with (I never ~ cash on/with me) 5. (d; tr.) to ~ out of (we ~ied the books out of the room) 6. (d; tr.) to ~ through (her cheerful disposition ~ied her through the crisis) 7. (P; refl.) she ~ies herself well 8. (misc.) to ~ to excess, to an extreme ("to go/take too far")

carry about, around v. (D; tr.) to ~ with (I don't want to carry that thing around with me)

carry back v. (B) he ~ied the books back to her; the memory ~ied me back to my youth

carry down v. (D; tr.) to ~ from; to (they ~ied the chair down from the attic to the basement)

carry forward v. (D; tr.) to ~ to (the figures must be ~ied forward to the next page)

carry on v. 1. (D; intr.) ("to complain") to ~ about (he is always ~ing on about his colleagues) 2. (D; intr.) ("to have an affair") to ~ with (the boss is ~ying on with one of the new employees) 3. (BE) ("to continue, keep on") (G) to ~ talking 4. (P; intr.) ("to continue") (~ with your work; ~ as before; down the road)

carry-over n. a ~ from; to (a ~ from the past)

carry over v. 1. (D; tr.) to ~ from; to (~ these figures over to the next page; to ~ a tradition from one generation to another) 2. (D; intr., tr.) to ~ into (she does not let her personal prejudices ~ into her professional life; she does not ~ her personal prejudices into her professional life)

cart n. 1. to draw, pull; load; push; unload a ~ 2. a ~ creaks; lumbers 3. a dustcart (BE: AE has *garbage* *truck*) 4. a shopping ~ (AE; BE has *trolley*) 5. (misc.) to put the ~ before the horse ("to do in the wrong order") (see also **apple cart**)

carte blanche *n.* 1. to give smb. ~ 2. to get, have ~ 3. ~ to + inf. (she gave him ~ to invest her money)

cartel *n.* 1. to form a ~ 2. to break up a ~ 3. a drug (CE), drugs (BE); international, multinational; oil ~

cartilage *n.* (a) torn ~

cart off *v.* (D; tr.) to ~ to (they ~ed him off to jail)

cartoon *n.* 1. to draw a ~ 2. an animated; political ~ 3. a strip ~ (BE; CE has *comic strip*)

cartridge *n.* a blank; practice; ruptured; spent ~

cartwheel *n.* to do, execute, turn a ~

carve *v.* 1. (C) he ~d an ornament for me; or: he ~d me an ornament 2. (D; tr.) to ~ from, out of (to ~ a figure from ivory) 3. (d; intr.) to ~ in (to ~ in wood) 4. (D; tr.) to ~ into (he ~ed the ivory into an ornament for me)

carve out *v.* (D; tr.) to ~ for (she ~d out a new career for herself)

carve up *v.* (D; tr.) to ~ into (they ~d up the region into three areas = they ~d the region up into three areas)

carving *n.* an ivory; wood ~

case I *n.* ["legal action"]["argument"] 1. to hear, try a ~ (the court will not hear this ~) 2. to dismiss, throw out a ~ (the judge dismissed the ~) 3. to take; turn down a ~ (the lawyer agreed to take the ~) 4. to build; prepare a ~ (we can build a strong ~ with the available data) 5. to make (out), present, state a ~ (she made out a convincing ~ for her client; he presented a good ~ for the new legislation) 6. to argue, plead a ~ (the lawyer argued the ~ skillfully) 7. to rest one's ~ ("to cease introducing evidence") (the defense lawyer rested her ~) 8. to lose; win a ~ 9. to decide; settle a ~ (they persuaded their client to settle the ~ out of court) 10. an airtight, ironclad, open-and-shut, watertight; clear, convincing, prima facie; strong ~ 11. a benchmark, landmark ~ 12. a borderline; weak ~ 13. a court ~ 14. a pending; test ~ 15. a civil; divorce ~ 16. a criminal; murder ~ 17. a ~ goes to trial 18. a ~ against (we had an airtight ~ against him) 19. (misc.) to strengthen a ~; to weaken a ~; the president took her ~ to the people; the first recorded ~ under the new law; to have a good ~ ("to have a convincing argument"); is there a ~ for capital punishment? ("can capital punishment be justified?") ["crime, felony"] 20. to break, clear up, crack, solve a ~ (the detective broke the ~) 21. to investigate, work on a ~ (the police worked on the ~ for a year) ["instance, occurrence, example"] 22. to cite a ~ 23. an attested; authenticated; clear; open-and-shut ("easily settled") ~ 24. a borderline; doubtful; hypothetical ~ 25. a celebrated; classic, textbook, typical; similar; special; test ~ 26. an extreme, flagrant; isolated, rare ~ 27. (med.) an acute; advanced; bad; chronic; hopeless; lingering; mild; terminal ~ 28. in a certain ~ (in this ~;

in any ~; in ~ of emergency) 29. (misc.) to be the ~ ("to be so"); a ~ in point ("a pertinent case") ["inflectional form"] 30. to govern, take a ~ (certain Russian verbs take the dative ~) 31. the ablative; accusative; dative; genitive; instrumental; locative; nominative; oblique; prepositional; vocative ~ ["misc."] 32. as the ~ may be; in ~ it rains/should rain; in ~ of (the alarm will go off in ~ of heavy rain); a basket ~ ("smb. without arms or legs or who is in a completely hopeless situation") (fig.) (unless sales rise, your company will be a basket ~!); ~ by ~ (deal with each applicant ~ by ~ = deal with each applicant on a case-by-case basis); to get off smb.'s ~ (slang) ("to stop criticizing smb."); on the ~ (slang) ("in action about smb./smt.") (don't worry, boss: I'm already on the ~!) (see also **caseload**) USAGE NOTE: "In case of" means 'in the event of': *the alarm will go off in case of heavy rain.* "In case + clause" means 'lest': *I took an umbrella in case it rained/should rain; don't lie in case you are/should be found out.* Some Americans may also be able to say *I used to open my umbrella in case it rained,* meaning 'I used to open my umbrella if/when it rained.'

case II *n.* ["container"]["cover"] an attaché; display; jewelry; packing; pillow ~; suitcase; watch ~

case III *n.* ["type of print"] lower; upper ~

case history *n.* 1. to get, take a ~ (on) 2. a detailed ~

caseload *n.* 1. to carry, have a ~ 2. to increase; reduce smb.'s ~ 3. a heavy; light ~ (the social worker carries/has a heavy ~)

cash I *n.* 1. to pay (in) ~ 2. to run out of ~ 3. out of, short of ~ 4. cold, hard; loose; ready; spare ~ 5. petty ~ 6. (misc.) she never carries ~; ~ on the barrel (head) (esp. AE)/on the nail (BE) ("pay now in cash"); ~ on delivery ("pay when the order is delivered")

cash II *v.* (D; tr.) to ~ for (she ~ed the money order for me)

cash in *v.* (colloq.) (d; intr.) to ~ on (to ~ on one's sudden popularity)

casino *n.* a gambling ~

casserole *n.* 1. to do, make a ~ 2. a meat; vegetable ~

cassette *n.* a blank ~

cast I *n.* ["set of performers"] 1. to head a ~ 2. to select a ~ 3. an all-star, star-studded ~ 4. a supporting ~; a ~ of characters; a ~ of thousands ["rigid dressing of gauze"] (med.) 5. to put a ~ on (to put a ~ on a broken leg = the broken leg was put in a ~) 6. a plaster ~

cast II *v.* 1. (D; tr.) ("to assign to a role") to ~ as (he was cast as Hamlet = he was cast in the role of Hamlet) 2. ("to be chosen for a play") to ~ in (he was cast in *Hamlet*) 3. (d; tr.) ("to throw") to ~ on, over (his actions have cast doubts on our entire campaign) 4. (H) ("to assign to a role") he was cast to play Hamlet

cast about, around v. (d; intr.) to ~ for ("to seek") (to ~ for a solution)

caste n. 1. a high; low; warrior ~ 2. (misc.) a ~ system (to belong to a low ~ in a rigid ~ system)

cast in v. to ~ one's lot with smb. ("to join forces with smb.")

casual adj. ~ about (she was very ~ about winning the prize)

casualties n. 1. to cause ~ to; inflict ~ on 2. to incur, suffer, take ~ 3. to report ~ 4. heavy, serious; light ~ (the enemy inflicted heavy ~ on our troops) 5. civilian; military; traffic ~

cat n. 1. to neuter a ~; to spay a (female) ~ 2. an alley; stray ~ 3. an Angora; Burmese; feral; marmalade (BE); Persian; Siamese; tabby ~ 4. ~s arch their backs; meow (AE), miaow (BE); purr; scratch 5. a young ~ is a kitten 6. a male ~ is a tomcat 7. (misc.) ~s have fur or hair and dogs have hair; to let the ~ out of the bag ("to reveal a secret"); to play ~ and mouse with ("to toy with"); to fight like ~ and dog (BE), to fight like ~s and dogs (AE); a fat ~ (derog.) ("a profiteer")

catalog, catalogue n. 1. to compile, make up a ~ 2. an author; card; subject ~ 3. a college, school, university ~ (esp. AE; BE has *prospectus*) 4. a mail-order ~ (it was in the mail-order ~ from which we ordered it) 5. a museum ~

catapult v. (P; intr., tr.) he was ~ed to fame; she ~ed out of obscurity into the limelight

cataract n. (med.) 1. to develop, get, have a ~ 2. to remove a ~

catastrophe n. 1. to face; suffer a ~ 2. to avert, prevent a ~ 3. to survive a ~ 4. an environmental; financial; major, overwhelming ~ 5. a ~ for, to (the fire was a ~ to everyone)

catch I n. ["hook"] 1. to fasten a ~ 2. a safety ~ ["smt. caught"] 3. to bring in, land a ~ (the fishermen landed a good ~) 4. the ~ of the day; the day's ~ ["act of catching"] 5. to make a one-handed; running; two-handed ~ (as in baseball or cricket) ["children's game"] 6. to play ~ ["disadvantage"] 7. a ~ that + clause ("sounds good. What's the ~?" "the ~ is that the pay is low")

catch II v. 1. to ~ red-handed, in the act 2. (C) she caught a small fish for me; or: she caught me a small fish 3. (d; tr.) to ~ by (she caught him by the arm) 4. (D; tr.) to ~ from (she caught a cold from her brother) 5. (D; intr., tr.) to ~ in (the kite caught in a tree) 6. (D; intr., tr.) to ~ on (his shirt caught on a nail = he caught his shirt on a nail) 7. (D; tr.) to ~ with (the police caught them with the stolen goods) 8. (J) we caught him stealing 9. (colloq.) (esp. BE) (O) she caught him one in the eye 10. (misc.) we caught him at a bad time; we caught her unawares

catch on v. 1. (D; intr.) to ~ to ("to comprehend") (he caught on to what I said immediately) 2. (D; intr.) ("to become popular") to ~ with (to ~ with the public)

catch up v. 1. (D; intr.) to ~ on (to ~ on one's

correspondence) 2. (D; intr.) to ~ to (AE), with (I'll ~ with you later; BE also has: I'll ~ you up later) USAGE NOTES: (1) With a non-personal subject, only *catch up with* is used: *his past has finally caught up with him.* (2) Esp. in BE, to *catch up with smb.* can also mean to manage to find someone (such as someone you want to speak to): the presenter said, "Before tonight's concert I *caught up with* the conductor and asked him what he thought of the music to be performed."

catechism n. (rel.) to learn; recite the ~

categorize v. 1. (D; tr.) to ~ according to, by (the books were ~d by language) 2. (D; tr.) to ~ as (she was ~d as a liberal) 3. (D; tr.) to ~ into (the voters were ~d into liberals, conservatives, and undecided)

category n. 1. to establish, set up a ~ 2. to assign to, put into a ~ 3. a main, major ~ 4. to fall into, fit into a ~ 5. a separate; special ~; a ~ of its own (such phenomena belong in a ~ of their own)

cater v. (d; intr.) to ~ for (BE), to (to ~ to all tastes) USAGE NOTE: In BE *cater to* is rare and typically pejorative, meaning 'to pander to.'

cater-cornered, catty-cornered adj., adv. (AE) ~ to

catering n. to do (the) ~ (who is going to do the ~ for our party?)

catheter n. (med.) to change; insert; irrigate; remove a ~

Catholic n. a devout; lapsed; practicing; Roman ~

Catholicism n. Anglo-Catholicism; Roman ~

cattle n. 1. to breed; raise, rear (BE) ~ 2. to drive; graze; herd; round up ~ 3. to brand; rustle ~ 4. beef; dairy; prize ~ 5. ~ graze 6. several head of ~; a herd of ~ 7. young ~ are calves 8. female ~ are cows 9. male ~ are bulls

catty adj. (colloq.) ["malicious"] ~ about

catty-cornered see **cater-cornered**

caucus n. 1. to form; (esp. AE) hold a ~ 2. a party; (BE) trade-union ~

caught adj. to be, get ~ (we were ~ in the rain; the kite got ~ in the tree)

caught up adj. ["involved"] ~ in (~ in radical movements)

cause I n. ["movement"] ["objective"] 1. to advance, champion, fight for, further, help, promote a ~ 2. to serve a ~ 3. to advocate, espouse, plead a ~ 4. to take up a ~ 5. a common; good, just, noble, righteous, worthwhile, worthy ~ (to make common ~ with smb.) 6. a lost ~ ["reason"] 7. to give; show ~ for 8. (legal) probable ~ 9. the biggest (single), chief; a deep-rooted, root, underlying; immediate; leading, major; primary; secondary; ultimate ~ (is smoking the biggest single ~ of cancer or just a major ~?) 10. natural ~s (to die of natural ~s) 11. (a) ~ for (there is no ~ for alarm/complaint) 12. ~ to + inf. (to find ~ to rejoice; there is no ~ to complain; she had good ~ to be disappointed)

cause II v. 1. (C) we ~d them a lot of trouble; or:

we ~d a lot of trouble for them 2. (rare) (H; no passive) the incident ~d me to reflect

caution I *n.* 1. to exercise, use; to advise, recommend ~ 2. due; extreme, great ~ 3. ~ in (you should exercise ~ in/when dealing with them) 4. with ~ (to proceed with ~) 5. (misc.) to fling/hurl/throw ~ to the winds; to sound a note of ~; a word of ~; to err on the side of ~

caution II *v.* 1. (D; tr.) to ~ about, against; (esp. BE) for (she ~ed us against drinking the water; to be ~ed for dangerous driving) 2. (H) she ~ed us not to drink the water 3. (L; must have an object in BE; may have an object in AE) she ~ed (us) that we should not drink the water

cautious *adj.* 1. ~ about, of (he was ~ about committing himself; she was ~ of strangers) 2. ~ in (~ in using firearms) 3. ~ with (she was ~ with strangers)

cavalry *n.* 1. to commit ~ 2. heavy; light ~

cave *n.* 1. to explore a ~ 2. a deep ~

cave in *v.* (D; intr.) to ~ to (they finally ~d in to our demands)

cavil *v.* (formal) (D; intr.) to ~ at

cavity *n.* 1. to fill a ~ (in a tooth) 2. the abdominal; chest; oral ~

CD *n.* 1. to cut, make; release a ~ 2. to play a ~

cease I *n.* without ~

cease II *v.* 1. (E) the old empire has ~d to exist; it never ~d to amaze her (to learn) that he had been promoted so quickly 2. (G) the company has ~d trading 3. (misc.) (esp. legal) to ~ and desist

cease-fire *n.* 1. to broker, mediate, negotiate a ~ 2. to declare; sign; work out a ~ 3. to honor, observe a ~ 4. to break, violate a ~ 5. a temporary ~ 6. the ~ has gone into effect; the ~ is holding

cede *v.* (A) France ~d the territory to them; or: France ceded them the territory

ceiling *n.* ["upper limit"] 1. to place, put, set a ~ (on prices) 2. to lower; raise a ~ 3. to abolish, lift a ~ (on prices) 4. a high; low ~ 5. a price; rent ~ 6. a glass ~ ("invisible ceiling") (is there a corporate glass ~ that keeps women from getting top jobs?) ["top of a room"] 7. a high; low ~ (a beautiful painting on the high ~ of the council chamber) ["misc."] 8. (colloq.) to hit the ~ (AE; CE has *roof*) ("to lose one's temper") (mom will really hit the ~ if we get back late!)

celebrate *v.* 1. to ~ formally; joyously; noisily; officially; privately; publicly; quietly; solemnly 2. (misc.) to ~ in style

celebrated *adj.* 1. ~ as (~ as a painter) 2. ~ for (~ for scientific research; Marie Curie was rightly ~ for her achievements as a scientist)

celebration *n.* 1. to have, hold a ~ 2. a joyous; noisy ~ 3. a private; quiet ~ 4. a centenary (esp. BE), centennial (esp. AE); formal; official; public; religious; solemn ~ 5. in ~ of (a service in ~ of the life of a great scientist)

celebrity *n.* ["famous person"] 1. a film, Hollywood;

international; literary; local; media; national; TV; visiting ~ 2. (misc.) a host of ~ties

celery *n.* 1. crisp ~ 2. a bunch; stalk of ~

celibacy *n.* 1. to practice ~ 2. (misc.) to make/take a vow of ~

cell *n.* ["cubicle, small room"] 1. a jail, prison; monk's; nun's; padded ~ ["small mass of protoplasm"] 2. to form a ~ 3. a cancer; egg; germ; nerve; sperm; stem ~ (see also **blood cell**) ["receptacle containing electrodes and an electrolyte"] 4. a dry; photoelectric; primary; voltaic ~ ["smallest unit of an organization"] 5. to form a ~ 6. a local; party ~

cellar *n.* 1. a cyclone, storm (AE); wine ~ 2. (misc.) a saltcellar (CE; AE also has *saltshaker*)

cello *n.* 1. to play the ~ 2. to string, tune a ~ 3. for; on the ~ (a sonata for unaccompanied ~; a sonata for ~ and piano; to play smt. on the ~) (see also *cello concerto* at **concerto**)

cellophane *n.* to wrap smt. in ~

cement I *n.* 1. to mix; pour ~ 2. Portland ~ 3. ~ sets

cement II *v.* to ~ smt. in, into place; to ~ smt. together

cemetery *n.* 1. a military; national ~ 2. at, in a ~ (she works at/in the ~; to be buried in a ~)

censor I *n.* a government; military ~

censor II *v.* 1. to ~ heavily (the report was heavily ~ed) 2. (D; tr.) ("to remove") (AE) to ~ from (the figures were ~ed from the report)

censorship *n.* 1. to impose, introduce ~ 2. to exercise, practice ~ 3. to abolish, lift ~ 4. rigid, strict ~ 5. film; government(al); military; press ~ 6. ~ of, over

censure I *n.* 1. bitter, strong; public ~ 2. to come under ~ 3. (misc.) a vote of ~

censure II *v.* 1. to ~ bitterly, severely, strongly 2. (D; tr.) to ~ as (they were ~d as traitors) 3. (D; tr.) to ~ for (the senator was ~d for income-tax evasion)

census *n.* 1. to carry out, conduct, take a ~ 2. a national; traffic (BE) ~ 3. at, in a ~ (at the last ~)

cent *n.* (AE) not to have a red ~ (colloq.) ("to have no money at all")

centenary *n.* to celebrate, mark, observe a ~

centennial (esp. AE) see **centenary**

center I centre *n.* ["middle"] 1. dead ~ 2. at, in the ~ (at the ~ of a circle) ["central point"] 3. a storm ~ (also fig.) 4. at, in a ~ (at the ~ of operations; right in the ~ of activity) ["location where an activity takes place; focus of activity"] 5. an amusement; city, town; leisure (BE); sports ~ 6. a community; senior-citizen; social ~ 7. a cultural; literary; music ~ 8. a civic; conference; convention ~ 9. a service; shopping ~ 10. a birthing (AE), childbearing (AE); crisis; day-care; health; medical ~ 11. a research; science ~ 12. a banking; business, commercial; fashion; financial; industrial; manufacturing; trade; wine-producing ~ (London is a major international financial ~ = London is a major international ~ for/of finance) 13. a communications; information ~

14. a job (BE) ~ 15. a remand (BE) ~ 16. (mil.) a separation ~ 17. (fig.) a nerve; storm ~ 18. a national; world ~ ["group of nerve cells"] 19. a nerve ~ ["political position"] 20. to move (away) from the ~; to move to the ~ 21. left of ~; right of ~

center II centre v. (d; intr., tr.) to ~ around, on, round (BE), upon (attention ~ed on their opening statements) USAGE NOTE: Some purists reject *to center around/round* as incorrect or illogical.

center stage n. 1. to occupy, take ~ 2. at ~

central adj. (cannot stand alone) ~ to (such values are ~ to our way of life)

century n. 1. from; to a ~ (from the fifth to the tenth ~/~ries) 2. during, in; throughout a ~ (in the ninth ~; throughout the whole of the ninth ~) 3. over, (down) through the ~ries 4. (misc.) at the beginning of the last/next/past/present ~; at the turn of the ~

cereal n. 1. to cook, make (AE), prepare ~ 2. breakfast; cooked, hot (AE); dry ~ 3. a bowl of ~ (see also **porridge**)

ceremony n. ["formal act"] 1. to conduct, hold, perform a ~ 2. to participate in a ~ 3. to attend a ~ 4. an award(s); flag-raising; graduation; inaugural; initiation; swearing-in; (Japanese) tea ~; welcoming; wreath-laying ~ 5. a civil; funeral; marriage, wedding; religious (to perform a religious ~) 6. a formal; solemn; special ~ 7. a private; public ~ 8. a closing; opening ~ (the opening ~ took place without incident and the closing ~ went off without a hitch) 9. during; at a ~ ["formality"] 10. to stand on ~ 11. appropriate; great ~ 12. with ~ (with appropriate ~) 13. without ~ (they all pitched in without ~)

certain adj. 1. to make ~ 2. absolutely, completely, totally; almost, nearly; quite; very ~ 3. far from ~ 4. for ~ (can you say for ~ where the ceremony will take place?) 5. ~ about, of (we were ~ of his support) 6. ~ to + inf. (she is ~ to agree) 7. ~ that; wh-word + clause (it is ~ that they will sign the contract; make ~ that all doors are locked; are you ~ that you turned the gas off?; are you ~ where the ceremony will be held?; are you ~ who will officiate at the ceremony?; are you ~ how long the ceremony will take?)

certainly adv. 1. almost ~ 2. (misc.) ~ not

certainty n. 1. to express ~ 2. absolute, dead; mathematical; moral; (BE) a racing ~ 3. ~ of (there is no ~ of success) 4. ~ that + clause (there is no ~ that an agreement will be reached) 5. with ~ (to state with ~) 6. (misc.) to know smt. for a ~

certificate n. 1. to issue a ~ 2. to cash (in) a ~ 3. a baptismal; birth; death; marriage; medical ~ 4. a money-market; stock; tax-free; treasury ~ (see also **savings certificate**) 5. a gift ~ 6. a teaching ~ (you cannot teach in this state without a teaching ~) 7. (BE) a school ~ 8. (misc.) a ~ of (to issue a ~ of baptism)

certification n. 1. to grant ~ 2. to receive ~ 3. ~ as

(he was granted ~ as a kindergarten teacher) 4. ~ in (she has her ~ in critical care nursing)

certify v. 1. (D; tr.) to ~ as (he has been ~fied as a critical-care nurse; the psychiatrist ~fied him as insane) 2. (D; tr.) to ~ in (he has been ~fied in critical-care nursing) 3. (L) the psychiatrist ~fied that he was insane 4. (M) did the psychiatrist ~ him to be insane? 5. (N; used with an adjective) he was ~fied insane

certitude n. 1. absolute, complete, utter ~ (my utter ~ in attesting to her good character) 2. ~ that + clause (it is with ~ that I can attest to her good character)

chafe v. (d; intr.) to ~ at, under (to ~ at the delay; to ~ under restrictions)

chaff n. to separate the (wheat from the) ~ (by threshing or winnowing) (also fig.)

chagrin n. 1. to express; feel ~ 2. deep, great, profound ~ 3. ~ at (to feel ~ at being rejected) 4. ~ that + clause (she expressed her ~ that she had been rejected) 5. to smb.'s ~ (to her great ~, she was rejected)

chagrined adj. 1. ~ at (~ at being rejected) 2. ~ to + inf. (she was ~ to have been rejected) 3. ~ that + clause (she was ~ that she had been rejected)

chain I n. ["series of links"] 1. to keep (a dog) on a ~ 2. to put ~s on (the tires of a car) 3. to wear a (gold) ~ (around one's neck) 4. a bicycle; tire ~ 5. a ~ clanks, jangles 6. a link in a ~ ["measuring instrument"] 7. an engineer's; surveyor's ~ ["shackles"] 8. in ~s (the prisoners were in ~s) ["group of associated enterprises"] 9. a department-store; hotel; restaurant ~ ["type of locking device"] 10. to put the ~ on the door ["misc."] 11. to form a human ~; to pull the ~ (BE) ("to flush the toilet"); a mountain ~ = a ~ of mountains; the food ~ ("the hierarchy of living beings in which each one feeds on the one below") (are we human beings really at the top of the food ~?)

chain II v. (D; tr.) to ~ to (to ~ a dog to a fence; to ~ one prisoner to another = to ~ prisoners together)

chair n. ["piece of furniture for sitting"] 1. an armchair; camp (BE), folding; cane; deck; easy; empty, free, unoccupied, high; occasional; reclining; rocking; swivel ~ (he pulled up an empty ~ and sat down in/on it next to us) (see also **push-chair**) USAGE NOTE: You can sit *in* an armchair but are more likely to sit *on* a chair without arms. ["professorship"] 2. to endow; establish a ~ 3. to be appointed to, get, receive a ~ 4. to have, hold, occupy a ~ (to hold a ~ in biology = to hold the ~ of biology) 5. to give up, relinquish a ~ 6. a personal (BE); university ~ ["position of chairperson"] 7. (esp. BE) to occupy; take the ~ 8. a rotating; temporary ~ ["chairperson"] 9. to address one's questions to the ~ [misc.] 10. an electric ~ ("a chair-like device for electrocuting criminals"); stacking ~s (that can be put away by stacking them atop each other) ("I took my place in the semicircle of stacking ~s" – David Lodge, *Deaf Sentence* (2008, p. 290)) (see also **musical chairs**)

chairman *n.* 1. a department(al) ~ 2. ~ of the board
 USAGE NOTE: BE also has *department head,
 head of (the) department* (in an educational institution); in order to promote non-sexist language, the
 terms *chair* or *chairperson* are used more and more
 in place of *chairman* or *chairwoman.*
chairperson see **chairman** 1
chairwoman see **chairman** 1
chalet *n.* a Swiss ~
chalk *n.* 1. to write in, with ~ (on a blackboard) 2. a
 piece, stick (BE) of ~ (see also **long chalk**)
chalkboard *n.* (AE) see **blackboard**
chalk up *v.* 1. (d; tr.) to ~ against (to ~ ten victories
 against two defeats) 2. (D; tr.) to ~ for (to ~ another
 victory for our team) 3. (d; tr.) to ~ to (to ~ smt. up
 to experience/lack of experience)
challenge I *n.* ["dare"] 1. to issue, send a ~ 2. to make,
 mount; pose, present, represent a ~ (for; to) (a fresh
 candidate mounting a formidable ~ to the party
 leader; a fresh candidate mounting a formidable ~
 for the party leadership) 3. to accept, respond to,
 take up a ~ (from) 4. to face, meet a ~; rise to a ~
 5. a direct; formidable, real, serious; leadership ~
 (a fresh candidate mounting a formidable leadership ~) 6. a ~ to (it was a serious ~ to our very
 existence) 7. a ~ to + inf. (it was a real ~ just to
 survive) ["demand for identification"] (usu. mil.) 8. to
 give the ~ (the sentry gave the ~) ["objection to a
 prospective juror"] (legal) 9. a peremptory ~ (to use
 one's peremptory ~)
challenge II *v.* 1. (D; tr.) to ~ for (I ~d her for the
 party leadership) 2. (D; tr.) to ~ on (to ~ the government on its policies) 3. (D; tr.) to ~ to (to ~ smb.
 to a duel) 4. (H) he ~d me to fight
challenger *n.* 1. to take on a ~ 2. a formidable,
 strong; serious ~
chamber *n.* ["hall used by a legislative body or the
 body itself"] 1. the lower; upper ~ 2. an assembly;
 council; parliamentary; senate ~ ["room"]["compartment"] 3. a gas; torture ~ 4. a combustion; decompression ~ ["misc."] 5. to hold a trial in ~s (without
 spectators or the press)
chameleon *n.* ~s change their color
champ *v.* 1. (d; intr.) to ~ at (to ~ at the bit) 2. (E)
 they were ~ing to get home
champagne *n.* 1. to drink; (literary or humorous)
 quaff; sip ~ 2. a bottle; glass of ~
champion *n.* 1. a defending; national; world ~ 2. ~s
 defend their titles against challengers
championship *n.* ["position of a champion"] 1. to
 hold; win a ~ 2. to regain; retain a ~ 3. to give
 up, lose, relinquish a ~ 4. an individual; national;
 team; world ~
championships *n.* ["contest"] 1. to compete in; hold
 ~ 2. (the) national; world ~ 3. ~s take place
chance I *n.* ["opportunity"]["possibility"] 1. to be in
 with, have, stand a ~ of (she has a good ~ of success; "how do you rate his ~s?" "he doesn't have
 a/the ghost of a ~!") 2. to give smb. a ~ 3. to let a

~ slip by; to miss one's ~; to pass up a ~; to spoil
 smb.'s ~s 4. a fighting; good; strong ~; every ~
 (of) (she has every ~ of winning if she doesn't lose
 her nerve) 5. an even, fifty-fifty; fair; sporting ~
 (he has an even ~ of being elected) 6. a faint, fat
 (colloq.), outside, poor, slight, slim, small ~ ("I
 may still win first prize!" "fat ~!") 7. a last; only
 ~ 8. little; no ~ (there is little ~ of that happening) 9. a ~ against (she doesn't stand a ~ against
 such strong competitors) 10. a ~ at, for, of (a ~ for
 success) 11. a ~ to + inf. (she had a ~ to visit her
 family) 12. a ~ that + clause (there is no ~ that she
 will win; I came to see you on the off ~ that you
 might have a screwdriver) ["luck"] 13. to take a ~
 on ("to try one's luck at") 14. to leave smt. to ~ 15.
 pure, sheer ~ 16. a lucky ~ 17. by ~ (it was by pure
 ~ that we met; would you by any ~ happen to have
 a screwdriver?) ["misc."] 18. (the) ~s are [= the odds
 are] that they will not come; I can do it given half
 a ~!; ("I may still win first prize!" "~ would be a
 fine thing!") (BE = fat chance, no chance)
chance II *v.* 1. (d; intr.) to ~ on, upon ("to find by
 chance") (to ~ upon a rare item) 2. (formal) (E) ("to
 happen") I ~d to be there when they arrived
chandelier *n.* a crystal ~
change I *n.* ["alteration"]["transition"] 1. to bring about,
 effect, make a ~ (to make a couple of ~s in/to the
 text; "how's retirement?" "well, it makes a ~ not
 having to go to work every morning = well, it makes
 a ~ not to have to go to work every morning") 2. to
 propose a ~ 3. to undergo (a) ~ 4. an abrupt, quick,
 sudden ~ 5. a complete, dramatic, drastic, great,
 major, marked, momentous, profound, quite a,
 radical, significant, striking, sweeping; irreversible
 ~ 6. a discernible, visible; quantitative; qualitative,
 step ~ 7. a long overdue, (much) needed, welcome
 ~ 8. (a) little, minor, slight ~ (we noticed a slight ~
 in her condition; there was little ~ in his condition)
 9. climate; cultural; economic; political; régime;
 social ~ 10. a ~ occurs, takes place 11. a ~ for (a
 ~ for the better/the worse) 12. a ~ from; into, to
 (the ~ from spring to summer) 13. a ~ in, of (a ~ of
 clothing; a ~ of direction; a ~ of heart; a ~ of pace;
 a ~ in the weather; ~s in personnel; a ~ of diet; the
 ~ of (the) seasons) 14. for a ~ (let's eat out for a
 ~) ["money returned"]["metal coins"] 15. to count out;
 give; make ~ for (can you give me ~ for a pound?)
 16. to count; get one's ~ 17. to keep the ~ (I told
 the driver to keep the ~) 18. loose; small; spare ~
 19. (misc.) could you spare a little ~, sir?; (slang)
 (AE) it cost me $35 and change [= '$35 + a little
 more'] ["change of clothing"] 20. to make a ~ 21. a
 quick ~ (to make a quick ~)
change II *v.* 1. to ~ beyond/out of all recognition;
 to ~ completely, drastically, greatly, radically;
 suddenly 2. (C) ("to exchange") could you ~ a dollar for me? or: could you ~ me a dollar? 3. (D;
 intr.) ("to transfer") to ~ for (we must ~ at the next
 station for Chicago) 4. (D; tr.) ("to exchange") to

~ for (to ~ dollars for pounds) 5. (D; intr.) ("to put on different clothes") to ~ for (to ~ for dinner) 6. (D; intr., tr.) ("to be transformed; to transform") to ~ from; into (the disease ~d him from an athlete into an invalid; to ~ dollars into pounds) 7. (D; intr., tr.) ("to transfer") to ~ from; to (we must ~ from the local to an express; she ~d the appointment to Monday) 8. (D; intr.) ("to put on different clothes") to ~ into (to ~ into smt. less formal) 9. (D; intr., tr.) ("to turn into") to ~ to (the light ~d to green; my mood ~d from despair to hope) 10. (D; tr.) ("to exchange") to ~ with (I would not want to ~ places with her)

change back v. 1. (d; intr.) to ~ from; to (they ~d back to peacetime production) 2. (d; intr.) to ~ into (we ~d back into casual wear)

changeover n. 1. a complete, radical, thorough, total ~ 2. a ~ from; to (a ~ from a peacetime to a war economy)

change over v. (d; intr.) to ~ from; to (the country ~d over to a war economy; to ~ to the decimal system)

changer n. a coin; record ~

channel I n. 1. to change ~s 2. a cable; television, TV ~ (a TV ~ that broadcasts/is on the air 24/7) 3. on a ~ (what's on the other ~s?)

channel II v. 1. (D; tr.) to ~ into (we had to ~ their energy into useful activities) 2. (D; tr.) to ~ towards (we must ~ our efforts towards worthy goals)

channels n. 1. back; diplomatic; military; official; (the) regular, usual ~ 2. through ~ (he sent his request for transfer through (the) regular ~; to go through ~; back-channel negotiations to bypass the official ~s) 3. (misc.) ~ of communication

chaos n. 1. to avert, prevent; cause, create ~ 2. complete, total, utter ~ 3. economic; political; social ~ 4. ~ ensues, results 5. a state of ~ 6. (misc.) on the brink/verge of ~

chap n. (colloq.) a decent, fine, good, nice ~

chapel n. ["place of worship"] 1. (a) hospital; military; prison; ship's ~ 2. interdenominational, nondenominational ~ ["Nonconformist place of worship"] (BE) (used as an adjective) 3. are you church or ~?

chaperon, chaperone I n. to serve as a ~ (to serve as a ~ at a dance)

chaperon, chaperone II v. (D; tr.) to ~ to (we will ~ the students to the theater)

chaplain n. a college, university; hospital; military; prison; school; ship's ~

chapter n. 1. a closing ~ 2. an introductory, opening ~ 3. a ~ about, on 4. (misc.) a closed ~ (in one's life) ("smt. that belongs to the past"); to cite/give/quote ~ and verse ("to cite the exact source or give lots of details") ["period"] 5. to close; open a ~ (the event opened a new ~ in her life)

character n. ["personality"] ["behavior"] 1. to build, form, mold smb.'s ~ 2. smb.'s moral; true ~ 3. an excellent, fine, good; impeccable, irreproachable,

stainless, unblemished; upright ~ 4. a firm, strong ~ 5. a lovable ~ 6. a bad, disreputable, unsavory ~ 7. a weak ~ 8. the national ~ (their recent actions are not in keeping with their national ~) 9. of ~ (a person of good ~) 10. (misc.) defamation of ~ ["person in or as if in a work of fiction"] 11. to play, portray a ~ 12. to create; delineate, depict, draw; develop a ~ 13. to kill off a ~ 14. a cartoon; fictitious; historical ~ 15. a leading, main, major, principal; minor, supporting ~ 16. in ~; out of ~ (his behavior was in ~ with his upbringing; it was completely in ~ for them to answer their correspondence promptly; her actions were out of ~ (for her)) ["person, esp. dubious or eccentric"] 17. a colorful; curious, strange, weird; larger-than-life; reformed; unforgettable ~ 18. a dangerous; disreputable; seedy, shady; suspicious; tough; underworld ~ (he used to be a completely disreputable ~ but now he's a thoroughly reformed ~) ["letter, figure"] 19. to form, trace; write ~s (to write a complete set of Greek ~s) 20. Arabic; Chinese; cuneiform; Cyrillic; Greek; Hebrew; Latin; mathematical; special ~s ["nature, special quality"] 21. to have a ~ of its/one's own 22. an official; political; subversive; unofficial ~ (the statements were of a political ~) 23. (misc.) this is a quaint town with a lot of ~

characteristic I adj. 1. ~ of 2. ~ to + inf. (it was completely/very ~ of them to answer their correspondence promptly)

characteristic II n. 1. a distinctive, marked; distinguishing, identifying; dominant, outstanding; unique ~ 2. a family; individual; national ~ 3. facial; physical ~s

characterize v. (d; tr.) ("to describe") to ~ as (he can be ~d as a fanatic/as fanatical)

charades n. to play ~

charcoal n. 1. to burn ~ 2. activated ~

charge I n. ["accusation"] 1. to bring, file, level, make a ~; to prefer, press ~s 2. to concoct, cook up, fabricate, trump up a ~ (they trumped up various ~s against her) 3. to prove, substantiate a ~ 4. to answer; face a ~ (of) 5. to dismiss, throw out a ~ (the judge dismissed all ~s) 6. to drop, retract, withdraw a ~ 7. to deny; refute; repudiate a ~ 8. a baseless, fabricated, false, trumped-up; frivolous ~ 9. a civil; criminal ~ 10. a ~ against smb. (to bring a ~ of forgery against smb.) 11. a ~ that (he denied the ~ that he had taken bribes) 12. on a ~ of (he was arraigned on a ~ of embezzlement; to be arrested on various ~s) ["attack"] 13. to lead; make a ~ against 14. to sound the ~ 15. to fight off, repel, repulse a ~ 16. a bayonet; baton; cavalry; infantry ~ ["explosive"] 17. to set off a ~ 18. a depth ~ (see also **depth charge**) ["responsibility"] 19. to place, put smb. in ~ of (I was put in sole ~ of the child/department) 20. to take ~ of (I took ~ of the child/department) 21. to be in ~ of (I was in ~ of the child/department) ["custody"] 22. in smb.'s ~ (the child was in my (sole) ~) ["cost"] ["price"] 23. to make; waive a ~ 24.

to reverse, transfer (BE) (the) ~s (when telephoning) 25. an exorbitant, unreasonable; reasonable ~ 26. an admission; carrying; call-out ~ (for going to a customer); cover; minimum; service ~; interest ~s; prescription ~s; shipping ~s 27. a ~ against, to (a ~ to smb.'s account) 28. a ~ for (there will be no ~ for installation) 29. (misc.) free of ~ (the installation is free of ~) ["infusion of stored energy"] 30. to give (a battery) a ~ 31. an electric; quick; slow ~ ["thrill"] (slang) 32. to give smb. a big ~ 33. to get a ~ out of smt. 34. an emotional ~ ["instructions"] 35. to give one's ~ (the judge gave her ~ to the jury) 36. a ~ to (the judge's ~ to the jury)

charge II v. 1. ("to ask in payment") to ~ double 2. (D; intr.) ("to rush") to ~ across (they ~d across the field) 3. (D; intr.) ("to rush") to ~ at, towards (the bull ~d at us) 4. (d; intr.) ("to ask payment") to ~ for (they didn't ~ for it) 5. (D; intr., tr.) to ~ for ("to ask in payment") (they ~d ten dollars for shipping our books; he ~s by the hour for laying a carpet) 6. (d; intr.) ("to rush") to ~ into; out of (to ~ into a room) 7. (D; tr.) to ~ out of ("to borrow from") (to ~ a book out of a library) 8. (D; tr.) ("to impose as an obligation") to ~ to (~ it to my account) 9. (D; tr.) ("to accuse") to ~ with (he was ~d with murder) 10. (D; tr.) ("to suffuse") to ~ with (the air was ~d with tension) 11. (D; tr.) ("to assign") to ~ with (our agency has been ~d with the responsibility of gathering all pertinent information) 12. (L) ("to accuse") they ~d that he had cheated them 13. (O; may be used with one object) ("to ask payment") she ~d (me) fifty dollars for her services; how much did she ~ (for her services)? did she ~ you (for her services)? they ~d me three hundred dollars (in) rent

chargeable adj. ~ to

charge ahead v. (D; intr.) to ~ with (they ~d ahead with the project)

charged adj. 1. emotionally; erotically; highly ~ 2. ~ with (tension/emotion)

charisma n. 1. to have ~ 2. personal ~ 3. of great ~

charitable adj. 1. ~ of 2. ~ towards 3. ~ to + inf. (it was not very ~ of her to say that)

charity n. ["quality"] 1. to dispense, distribute, give ~ to 2. to bestow ~ on, upon 3. to accept; receive ~ 4. to ask for, beg for, plead for ~ 5. an act of ~ 6. ~ for (~ the needy) "With malice toward none; with ~ for all" – Abraham Lincoln, "Second Inaugural Address," 1865) 7. (misc.) (proverb) ~ begins at home ["organization"] 8. to donate, give to ~

charm I n. ["amulet"] 1. to wear a ~ 2. a good-luck, lucky ~ ["attractive quality"] 3. to turn on the/one's, use one's ~ 4. to exude, ooze ~ 5. to have, possess ~ 6. to lend ~ to 7. great, irresistible; natural; particular, special; unfailing ~ 8. the ~ to + inf. (she has enough ~ to win anyone over) (see also *to work like a charm* at **work II**, 13)

charm II v. (D; tr.) to ~ into (she ~ed him into agreeing)

charmed adj. ~ to + inf. (she was ~ed to receive flowers from her grandchildren)

charmer n. 1. (to be) a real ~ 2. a snake ~

charming adj. 1. ~ to (she is ~ to everyone) 2. ~ to + inf. (it was ~ to watch them) USAGE NOTE: "Charming!" is often used ironically: "they left without paying." "(how) charming!"

chart I n. 1. to compile a ~ 2. an aeronautical; bar; clinical; eye; flip; flow; genealogical; pie; statistical; wall ~ (the flow ~ shows how our sales have increased) 3. from; in; on a ~ (from the ~ you can see how our sales have increased)

chart II v. (D; tr.) to ~ for (he has ~ed a difficult course for us)

charter n. 1. to apply for a ~ 2. to take out a ~ 3. to grant a ~ 4. to revoke a ~ 5. a ~ to + inf. (the company was granted a ~ to trade in the occupied territory) USAGE NOTE: "Charter" is sometimes used to mean 'license or permission to do smt. bad': "It turned out to be nothing more than a ~ for busybodies, ..." – British National Corpus.

charter flight n. to organize a ~

chary adj. 1. ~ about (~ about doing smt.) 2. ~ of (~ of strangers)

chase I n. 1. to give ~ to 2. to abandon, give up the ~ 3. a car; police ~ 4. a wild-goose ~ 5. in ~ of (in full ~ of the suspect) 6. (misc.) the thrill of the ~; (AE) to lead smb. a merry ~ (BE has *to lead smb. a merry dance*)

chase II v. 1. (d; intr.) to ~ after (to ~ after fame) 2. (D; tr.) to ~ from, out of (~ the dog out of our yard!) 3. (P; intr., tr.) they ~d the children into the barn; the police ~d the suspect through the park; we ~d across the field into the station

chaser n. 1. a submarine ~ 2. (misc.) (colloq.) an ambulance ~ (esp. AE) ("a lawyer who seeks clients among accident victims"); whiskey with a beer ~ ("whiskey served with a glass of beer")

chasm n. 1. to bridge a ~ 2. a deep; gaping, yawning ~ 3. a ~ between

chat I n. 1. to have a ~ 2. a friendly, nice, pleasant; little ~ 3. a ~ about; with (we had a pleasant ~ with them about our new grandchild) 4. a ~ between

chat II v. (D; intr.) to ~ about; to (BE), with

chatter I n. constant, endless, idle, incessant ~

chatter II v. 1. ("to talk fast") to ~ constantly, endlessly, incessantly 2. (D; intr.) ("to talk fast") to ~ about 3. (D; intr.) ("to click") to ~ from, with (his teeth were ~ing with the cold)

chauvinist n. a male ~

cheap adj. 1. dirt (colloq.), ridiculously ~ 2. to be going; come ~ (rubber gloves are going ~ in that shop; those new cars don't come ~) 3. ~ to + inf. (it's not ~ to live in the city; it is ~er to live there than here) 4. (misc.) to hold life ~ 5. ~ and cheerful; ~ and nasty; on the ~ (you can get rubber gloves on the ~ in that shop)

cheat I n. 1. a downright; notorious ~ 2. a tax ~

cheat II v. 1. (D; intr., tr.) to ~ at (to ~ at cards) 2.

(D; intr.) to ~ on ("to be unfaithful to") (to ~ on one's wife) 3. (D; tr.) to ~ out of (he ~ed us out of our money) 4. (misc.) to ~ on an examination
check I n. ["order to a bank"] (BE has *cheque*) 1. to issue, make out, write (out) a ~ to, make a ~ payable to (write out a ~ for £100 made payable to me) 2. to draw a ~ against one's account; to draw a ~ on a bank 3. to cancel; cash; clear; deposit; honor; present a ~ 4. to cover a ~ (by making a deposit) 5. to endorse; negotiate; sign a ~ 6. to pass a (bad) ~; to kite a ~ ("to write a bad ~"); to raise ("increase fraudulently") a ~ 7. to stop payment of, on a ~ 8. a bad ("not covered"); blank; cashier's; certified; crossed (BE) ~; Eurocheque (obsolescent); negotiable; traveler's ~ 9. a ~ bounces; clears 10. by ~ (to pay by ~) ["verification"]["control"] 11. to carry out, conduct, do, make, run a ~ of, on 12. a background; bed; loyalty; random; safety, security; spot ~ (to run a background ~ on all new employees) (see also **spell check**) ["endangered position of the king"] (chess) 13. to give ~; to put into ~ 14. to discover ~ 15. discovered; perpetual ~ 16. in ~ (your king is in ~) ["bill in a restaurant"] (AE) 17. one ~; separate ~s (give us separate ~s, please, waiter) 18. (misc.) to ask (the waiter) for the ~; to pay the ~, pick up the ~ ["token of ownership, of a right"] (esp. AE) 19. a baggage; claim; hat ~ (see also **rain check**) ["blocking of an opponent"] (ice hockey) 20. a board; body; hook ~ ["restraint"] 21. to hold, keep in ~
check II v. 1. (D; intr.) to ~ into ("to verify") (to ~ into smb.'s story) 2. (d; intr.) to ~ into ("to register at") (to ~ into a hotel) 3. (d; intr.) to ~ on ("to verify") (to ~ on smb.'s story) 4. (d; intr.) to ~ out of ("to announce one's departure from") (to ~ out of a hotel) 5. (d; tr.) to ~ out of ("to borrow from") (she ~ed the book out of the library) 6. (D; intr.) to ~ through ("to look through") (to ~ through the files) 7. (esp. AE) (d; tr.) to ~ through to ("to register as far as") (she ~ed her suitcase through to Chicago) 8. (D; intr.) ("to verify") to ~ with (I'll ~ with the porter) 9. (E) I'll ~ to see whether he's in 10. (L) I'll ~ that he's in 11. (Q) I'll ~ whether he's in; I'll ~ where he is
checkbook n. (AE) (BE has *chequebook*) 1. to balance a ~ 2. to reconcile a ~ with (a bank statement)
checkers n. (AE) (BE has *draughts*) 1. to play ~ 2. Chinese ~ (BE has *Chinese chequers*)
check in v. (D; intr.) to ~ at (to ~ at a hotel)
checking account n. (AE) (BE has *current account*) to balance a ~ (every month)
checklist n. 1. to compile, make up a ~ 2. to go down, go through a ~
check out v. (D; tr.) ("to borrow") to ~ from (she ~ed out a book from the library)
checkpoint n. at; through a ~ (we were stopped at a ~ the army had set up but they let us through (it))
checkup n. 1. to do, give a ~ (the doctor gave me a thorough ~) 2. to go for, have a ~ (I had a ~ at the

hospital yesterday) 3. an annual; periodic ~ 4. a careful; thorough ~ 5. a general; regular ~
check up v. (D; intr.) to ~ on (to ~ on smb.'s story)
cheek n. ["side of the face"] 1. to puff (out) one's ~s 2. burning, flushed; dimpled; chubby, full, rounded; hollow, sunken; pale; rosy, ruddy ~s ["impudence"] (colloq.) 3. the ~ to + inf. (she had the (barefaced) ~ to phone me at home!) ["misc."] 4. to turn the other ~ ("to refuse to respond to an attack or insult"); (with) tongue in ~ ("not seriously, wryly") (a tongue-in-cheek remark that didn't offend anybody)
cheekbones n. high, prominent ~
cheeky adj. (colloq.) ["impudent"] ~ to + inf. (it was ~ of her to phone you at home)
cheer I n. ["rallying cry"]["cry of approval"] 1. to give, shout a ~ (let's give him three ~s: three ~s for him!) 2. to draw a ~ (from) (her performance drew ~s) 3. to acknowledge the ~s (of the crowd) 4. a jubilant; loud, resounding, ringing, rousing ~ (she left amid/to loud ~s from her admirers) 5. (AE) a school ~ (let's give the school ~!) (see also **Bronx cheer**) 6. a ~ rang out; a ~ went up ["good mood"] 7. Christmas; good ~ 8. of ~ (to be of good ~)
cheer II v. 1. to ~ enthusiastically, loudly, wildly 2. (D; intr.) to ~ for (they ~ed loudly for their team) 3. (misc.) they ~ed themselves hoarse
cheerful adj. ~ about (they are ~ about the future)
cheese n. 1. to slice ~ 2. cream; full-fat (BE); grated; grilled (AE), toasted (BE); hard; melted; mild; processed; semi-soft; sharp; smoked; soft ~ 3. a piece, slice of ~ (a piece of ~ on toast) 4. (misc.) (colloq.) say ~! ("smile"!)
chemistry n. ["science that deals with substances"] 1. analytical; inorganic; organic; physical ~ ["chemical characteristics"] 2. the ~ of (the ~ of carbon; the ~ of blood) ["personal feelings"] (colloq.) 3. personal ~; the right; wrong ~ 4. the ~ between
chemist's n. (BE) (see **drugstore**)
cheque (BE) see **check I**, 1–10
chequebook (BE) see **checkbook**
chess n. 1. to play ~ 2. (misc.) a ~ game; match; a ~ master
chest n. ["thorax"] 1. to beat; throw out one's ~ (with pride) 2. a barrel ~ 3. in; on the ~ (he was stabbed in the ~ and was burned on his ~) 4. smb.'s ~ swells with pride ["box"] 5. a hope (AE; BE has *bottom drawer*); ice; medicine; silver; tool; treasure ~ (see also *chest of drawers* at **drawer**)
chestnuts n. 1. to roast ~ 2. (misc.) to pull smb.'s ~ out of the fire ("to extricate smb. from an unpleasant situation")
chew v. 1. (D; intr.) to ~ on (to ~ on bread) 2. (d; intr.) to ~ through (the mouse ~ed through the wall) 3. (D; intr., tr.) to ~ with (she had difficulty ~ing the steak with her new dentures)
chewing gum n. a piece; stick of ~
chic I adj. ["fashionable"] ~ to + inf. (it's very ~ to give up smoking)
chic II n. 1. an indefinable ~ 2. designer; radical ~

chick *n.* 1. to hatch ~s 2. ~s cheep 3. a brood, clutch of ~s

chicken I *n.* 1. a battery; free-range ~ 2. ~s cluck; peck; roost 3. a brood of ~s 4. a young ~ is a chick 5. a female ~ is a hen 6. a young female ~ is a pullet 7. a male ~ is a cock (esp. BE)/rooster (esp. AE) 8. a young male ~ is a cockerel (esp. BE); a male castrated ~ is a capon 9. (as food) baked; barbecued; broiled (AE), grilled; fried; roast; stewed ~ (please have another piece/slice of fried ~) 10. (misc.) to count one's ~s before they are hatched ("to rejoice prematurely")

chicken II *v.* (colloq.) (d; intr.) to ~ out of ("to abandon") (to ~ out of an agreement)

chickenpox *n.* to catch (the) ~, come down with (the) ~, get (the) ~

chide *v.* (D; tr.) to ~ for

chief *n.* 1. an Indian, Native American ~ 2. a fire (AE); police (AE) ~ 3. a tribal ~

chieftain *n.* a clan; tribal ~

child *n.* 1. to adopt; bear, give birth to, have a ~ (she had four children) 2. to carry a ~ (a mother carries a ~ for nine months) 3. to beget; conceive a ~ 4. to bring up, raise, rear a ~ 5. to feed; nurse; wean a ~ 6. to indulge, pamper, spoil a ~ 7. to toilet-train; train a ~ 8. to acknowledge a ~ (as one's own) 9. to marry off one's ~ 10. an adopted; dependent; foster; illegitimate (old-fashioned); only; unwanted ~ 11. a mischievous; problem (old-fashioned) ~ 12. a pampered, spoiled ~ 13. a good, well-behaved ~ 14. a bright, gifted, intelligent ~ 15. a poster (esp AE); precocious; young ~ (his success made him a poster ~ for early-childhood education) (see also *child prodigy* at **prodigy**) 16. a handicapped (old-fashioned); retarded (old-fashioned) ~ 17. a flower ~ (of the 1960s); a latchkey ~ (who has his own house-key because his parents are out at work) 18. a happy; loving; well-cared for ~ 19. an abused, mistreated; disadvantaged; neglected ~ 20. a ~ develops, grows (into adulthood) 21. (misc.) to be with ~ (old-fashioned) ("to be pregnant"); to bus children (to school) (see also **baby**)

childbirth *n.* 1. natural; prepared ~ 2. in ~ (she died in ~)

childhood *n.* 1. to spend one's ~ (somewhere) 2. smb.'s second ~ 3. a happy; repressed; unhappy ~ 4. during; throughout; in smb.'s ~ (in smb.'s early ~) 5. since ~

childish *adj.* ~ to + inf. (it was ~ of him to do that)

child's play *n.* (colloq.) ["easy task"] 1. ~ to (that's ~ to her) 2. ~ to + inf. (it was ~ to solve that riddle)

chill I *n.* 1. (fig.) to cast a ~ on, over 2. to catch; feel a ~ 3. to take the ~ off (take the ~ off the milk) 4. (misc.) there was a (sudden) ~ in our relations; her words sent a ~ through me

chill II *v.* 1. (C) ~ a glass for me; or (rare): ~ me a glass 2. (misc.) ~ed to the bone

chills *n.* 1. to have, get the ~ 2. (misc.) to send ~ up and down smb.'s spine ("to frighten smb.")

chime in *v.* (D; intr.) to ~ with (to ~ with one's opinion)

chimes *n.* 1. to sound ~ 2. organ ~ 3. ~ sound

chimney *n.* 1. smoke goes up a ~ 2. smoke comes out of a ~ 3. ~s belch smoke 4. the ~ draws well 5. a tall ~

chin *n.* 1. a double; receding, weak; smooth ~ 2. a glass ("weak, vulnerable") ~ (of a boxer) 3. on smb.'s/the ~ 4. (misc.) to keep one's ~ up ("not to become discouraged"); to take it on the ~ ("to suffer a misfortune courageously") USAGE NOTE: If you stick your chin out you are perceived to be resolute in the English-speaking world; but in some other places that would be considered a gesture of submission.

china *n.* ["porcelain"] 1. bone; fine ~ 2. a set of ~

chink *n.* a ~ in smb.'s armor ("a weak point")

chip *n.* ["thin slice"] (AE) 1. a potato ~ (BE has *crisp*; BE *chip* = AE *French fry*) USAGE NOTE: In AE, "chip" in its food sense is rarely if ever used on its own. "Potato chip" is standard in AE. ["semiconductor body"] 2. a computer; integrated-circuit; silicon ~ ["misc."] 3. a bargaining ~ ("smt. that can be used to win concessions"); a ~ off the old block ("a child who resembles its parent"); to have a ~ on one's shoulder ("to harbor resentment")

chip away *v.* (d; intr.) to ~ at (to ~ at a rock; the police kept ~ping away at their alibi)

chip in *v.* 1. (D; intr.) to ~ for (they all ~ped in for a present) 2. (D; intr.) to ~ with (we all ~ped in with our suggestions)

chips *n.* ["gambling tokens"] to cash in one's ~ (also fig.) ("to die") (see also *fish and chips* at **fish I**)

chisel *v.* 1. (D; tr.) ("to shape with a chisel") to ~ from, out of (to ~ smt. from wood) 2. (d; tr.) to ~ into (to ~ wood into smt.) 3. (colloq.) (D; tr.) to ~ out of ("to cheat out of") (he ~ed me out of my money)

chiseled, chiselled *adj.* ["shaped"] finely ~ (features)

chitchat *n.* idle ~

chivvy *v.* (colloq.) (BE) ("to nag") 1. (d; tr.) to ~ into (she ~vied me into going) 2. (H) I ~vied them to help

chloroform *n.* to administer, give ~ to

chockablock *adj.* (colloq.) ~ with

chock-full *adj.* (colloq.) ~ of

chocolate *n.* ["candy, sweet food"] 1. bitter; bittersweet; dark (AE), plain (BE); milk; white ~ 2. a bar; piece of ~ ["unit of chocolate"] 3. a box of ~s ["beverage"] 4. drinking; hot ~ 5. a cup; mug of ~

choice *n.* ["act of choosing"] 1. to exercise, make a ~ 2. to have a ~ 3. a good, happy, intelligent, judicious, wise ~ (she made a good ~) 4. first; second ~ (we had first ~) 5. a bad, poor, sorry, unwise, wrong ~ 6. a careful; difficult ~ 7. a wide ~ (you have a wide ~ of colors) 8. (a) free; individual; limited ~ (to exercise individual ~) 9. a ~ among, between; in; of (a ~ between two jobs; did you have any ~ in the matter? a ~ of colors) 10. by; of one's ~ (we did it by ~; the Pilgrims came to America to worship the God of their ~) 11. (misc.) we have a difficult ~ to make; take your ~; freedom of ~; Hobson's ("no") ~; they had no ~ but to agree; we had little ~ in the matter; there are so many possibilities that we're spoilt for ~! ["result of choosing"] 12. an obvious ~ (she was the obvious ~ as their spokesperson = she was the obvious ~ to be their spokesperson)

choir *n.* 1. to form; lead a ~ 2. to sing in a ~ 3. a church; school ~ (compare **chorus**)

choke I *n.* (on a car) 1. to pull out; push in the ~ 2. an automatic; manual ~

choke II *v.* 1. (D; intr.) to ~ on (to ~ on a bone) 2. (d; intr.) to ~ with (to ~ with emotion) 3. (misc.) to ~ to death

choked *adj.* ["blocked"] ~ with (~ with weeds)

choked up *adj.* 1. (all) ~ about (they were all ~ about their friend's loss) 2. (all) ~ with (~ with emotion)

cholera *n.* to contract, get ~

cholesterol *n.* 1. to cut down on ~ 2. high; low in ~

chomp *v.* see **champ**

choose *v.* 1. to ~ carefully, judiciously; to ~ at random 2. (C) ~ a book for me; or: ~ me a book 3. (D; intr.) to ~ among, between, from (to ~ between two jobs) 4. (D; tr.) to ~ as (they chose her as their spokesperson) 5. (D; intr., tr.) to ~ by (to ~ by lot; to ~ by tossing a coin) 6. (D; tr.) to ~ for (~ curtains for a room) 7. (D; tr.) to ~ from (they chose her as their spokesperson from (among) a large number of candidates) 8. (E) she chose to remain at home 9. (H) they chose her to serve as their spokesperson

choosing *n.* of one's own ~

choosy (also **choosey**, AE) *adj.* (colloq.) ~ about

chop I *n.* ["cut of meat"] 1. a chump (BE); lamb; mutton; pork; veal ~ (see also **lamb chops**) ["blow"] 2. a karate ~

chop II *v.* 1. (C) ~ some wood for me; or: ~ me some wood 2. (D; tr.) to ~ into (to ~ smt. into bits) 3. (D; tr.) to ~ off (she ~ped a branch off the tree)

chop off *v.* (D; tr.) to ~ from (she ~ped off a branch from the tree)

chopper *n.* a food; meat ~

chopsticks *n.* to use ~

chop up *v.* 1. (C) ~ some wood for me; or (colloq.): ~ me up some wood 2. (D; tr.) to ~ into (he ~ped the log up into firewood)

chord I *n.* ["combination of three or more musical notes"] 1. to play ~s 2. a dominant; major; minor ~

chord II *n.* ["feeling, emotion"] 1. to strike, touch a ~ 2. a popular; responsive, sensitive, sympathetic ~ (to strike a responsive ~)

chores *n.* 1. to do one's/the ~ 2. daily; domestic, household; routine ~

chortle *v.* 1. (D; intr.) to ~ about, over 2. (D; intr.) to ~ with (to ~ with glee)

chorus *n.* ["group of singers"] 1. a dawn ~ (of birds); female; male; mixed ~ ["simultaneous utterance"] 2. to join in, swell the ~ 3. a ~ of (*A Chorus of Disapproval* – play by Sir Alan Ayckbourn (1984))

chowder *n.* (AE) clam; corn; fish; Manhattan clam ~

christen *v.* (N; used with a noun) they ~ed the child Joseph

christening *n.* 1. to perform a ~ 2. a ~ takes place 3. at a ~

Christian *n.* a born-again; devout; evangelical; fundamentalist; good; practicing ~

Christmas *n.* 1. to celebrate ~ 2. to wish smb. a Merry ~ 3. (a) Happy (BE), Merry ~ (to you)! 4. a white ~ 5. at, for, on, over ~ (we'll get together at ~; where are you going for ~?) 6. on ~ Day; on ~ Eve

Christmas tree *n.* to decorate, trim a ~

chronicle *n.* 1. to keep a ~ 2. a daily; monthly; weekly ~ 3. (misc.) a ~ of events

chuck *v.* (colloq.) 1. (A) ~ the ball to me; or: ~ me the ball 2. (P; tr.) just ~ it away! = (BE) just ~ it!; he ~ed the newspaper into the can 3. (misc.) she ~ed the child under the chin

chuckle I *n.* 1. to give, let out; have a ~ (we had a good ~ about it afterwards) 2. a hearty; throaty ~ 3. a ~ about, over

chuckle II *v.* 1. (D; intr.) to ~ about, at, over (we ~d about it afterwards) 2. (D; intr.) to ~ to (we ~d to ourselves about it afterwards) 3. (D; intr.) to ~ with (to ~ with glee)

chuffed *adj.* (BE) (colloq.) ("happy, pleased") 1. ~ about, at (she was ~ at his prompt arrival) 2. ~ that + clause (she was ~ that he came/arrived on time)

chum *n.* (colloq.) a childhood; old; school ~

chummy *adj.* (colloq.) ["friendly"] ~ with

chum up *v.* (D; intr.) to ~ with

church *n.* 1. to consecrate, dedicate a ~ 2. to attend, go to (a) ~ 3. the Catholic; Christian; (Eastern) Orthodox; Protestant; Uniate ~ 4. the Anglican; Baptist; Christian Science; Congregational; Episcopal; Lutheran; Mennonite; Methodist; Mormon; Presbyterian; Seventh Day Adventist ~ 5. an evangelical; fundamentalist ~ 6. (esp. GB) an established ("official"); free ("Nonconformist") ~ 7. (esp. GB) The Church of England/Ireland; The Church in Wales 8. a parish ~ 9. at, in (a) ~ 10. (misc.) to enter, go into the ~ ("to become a member of the clergy") USAGE NOTES: 1. "A church" is a building, an institution, or a denomination (*there's a big church near here but she goes to a friendly little church around the corner*). "Church" is the religious activity that goes on in a church (*church takes up a lot of her time; she goes to church every Sunday; let's get together after church*). 2. The provinces of the Anglican Communion in the UK and Ireland are the Church of England, the Church of Ireland, the Church in Wales, and the Scottish Episcopal Church. The national Church of Scotland is Presbyterian. The Anglican province in the USA has been the Episcopal Church.

churlish *adj.* ~ to + inf. (it would be ~ (of them) to offer such petty criticism)

cider *n*. hard (AE = 'alcoholic'); sweet (AE = 'non-alcoholic') ~ USAGE NOTE: In GB, cider is typically alcoholic; in the US it is typically non-alcoholic. In both countries non-alcoholic cider is like apple juice.

cigar *n*. 1. to light (up); puff on; smoke a ~ 2. a Havana ~

cigarette *n*. 1. to have; light (up); puff on, smoke a ~ 2. to roll a ~ (he used to roll his own ~s) 3. to extinguish, put out, stub out a ~ 4. a live ~ 5. a filter-tip; king-size; low-tar; mentholated ~ 6. a carton; pack (esp. AE), packet (BE) of ~s

cinch *n*. (colloq.) ["certainty"] 1. (AE) a ~ to + inf. (she's a ~ to win) 2. (esp. AE) ~ that + clause (it's a ~ that she'll win)

cinders *n*. to spread ~ (on a snow-covered road)

cinema *n*. (esp. BE) ["movies"] 1. to go to the ~ 2. at, in the ~ (she was known for her work in the ~) ["movie theater"] 3. to be on at, to be showing at the ~ (what's showing at the local ~ tonight?)

cinematography *n*. slow-motion ~

cipher *n*. ["code"] 1. to break, solve a ~ 2. in ~ (to send a message in ~)

circle *n*. ["circular geometric figure"] 1. to describe, draw a ~ (to draw the ~ that the missile described in flight; to draw concentric or interlocking ~s) 2. to square a ~ (to square a ~ is impossible) 3. the Antarctic; Arctic; polar ~ (at the Arctic ~) 4. the great ~ (on the earth's surface) 5. a traffic ~ (AE; BE has *roundabout*) 6. (sports) the center ~; the winner's ~ (at a racecourse/racetrack) 7. the circumference; diameter; radius of a ~ ["group resembling the figure of a circle"] 8. to form; be in a ~ 9. to join a ~ (she joined the ~ of dancers) ["group"] 10. academic; artistic; literary; professional ~s 11. business, financial; court; diplomatic; official; political; ruling ~s 12. exclusive, select; high ~s (to move in the highest ~s) 13. informed, well-informed ~s 14. a charmed ("exclusive"); close, closed, inner, intimate, narrow; wide ~ (a close ~ of friends that no one wanted to widen) 15. a quilting; sewing ~ 16. a family ~ 17. in a ~ (in our ~ of friends; in informed ~s) ["cycle"] 18. to come full ~ ["misc."] 19. a vicious ~ ("an insoluble, never-ending problem"); to go around in ~s ("to keep coming back to the starting point without finding a solution"); a dress ~ ("the first row of raised seats in a theater")

circuit *n*. ["path of an electric current"] 1. to break; close a ~ 2. a closed; electrical; integrated; printed; short ~ ["route traveled by a judge on tour"] 3. to make a ~ (the judge makes a ~ every year) 4. on ~ (the judge was on ~) ["series of similar events"] 5. the chat-show (BE), talk-show (AE); lecture; rodeo ~

circuit breaker *n*. to trip a ~

circular *n*. 1. to send out a ~ 2. to distribute ~s

circulate *v*. 1. (D; intr., tr.) to ~ among (the host ~d among the guests; to ~ the memo among the staff members) 2. (D; intr., tr.) to ~ through (blood ~s through the body) 3. (D; intr., tr.) (to ~ the memo to all staff members)

circulation *n*. ["distribution"] 1. to put into ~ (to put more money into ~) 2. to take out of ~; to withdraw from ~ (to withdraw old banknotes from ~) 3. (an) enormous, large, wide; general, unrestricted ~ (this magazine has attained a wide ~) 4. (a) national, nationwide ~ 5. (a) limited, restricted, small ~ 6. in; out of ~ (this money is no longer in ~) 7. (misc.) this journal has a ~ of one hundred thousand ["movement"] 8. blood ~; or: ~ of the blood 9. good, healthy, normal ~ 10. abnormal, poor ~

circumcision *n*. 1. to do, perform; reverse a ~ (on) 2. to undergo ~ 3. female ~ ('clitoridectomy')

circumference *n*. in ~ (ten feet in ~)

circumspect *adj*. ~ about; in

circumstance *n*. pomp and ~

circumstances *n*. 1. favorable; unfavorable ~ 2. adverse, difficult, trying; desperate; tragic ~ 3. reduced, straitened ~ 4. extenuating, mitigating ~ 5. compelling; exceptional, special ~ 6. mysterious; suspicious ~ (he was apprehended under the very suspicious ~ surrounding the case) 7. unforeseen ~ 8. a combination of ~ 9. due to ~ (our absence was due to ~ beyond our control) 10. in, under ~ (in certain ~, I would agree; she will not go under any ~ = in no ~ will she go; they lived in difficult ~; in these (present) ~ we can't continue; under the ~, we can't continue)

circus *n*. 1. to present, put on a ~ 2. to go to; join the ~ (she liked the ~ she went to so much she decided to join it) 3. a three-ring; traveling ~ 4. at a ~ 5. (misc.) a three-ring ~ ("hectic activity")

citation *n*. ["attestation"] 1. the earliest ~ (of the use of a word) 2. a ~ from ["summons"] 3. to issue a ~ for 4. a contempt ~ 5. a ~ to + inf. (she received a ~ to appear in court) ["mention of meritorious performance"] (AE) (mil.) 6. to write smb. up for a ~ 7. to receive a ~ (for bravery) (BE has *to be mentioned in dispatches*) 8. a unit ~

cite *v*. 1. (B) she ~d an interesting passage to us 2. (D; tr.) to ~ as (to ~ smt. as an example) 3. (D; tr.) to ~ for (to ~ smb. for bravery) 4. (misc.) to be ~d in divorce proceedings; the example ~d above/below

citizen *n*. 1. a law-abiding; eminent, leading, prominent; respectable, solid, upright, upstanding ~ 2. a senior ~ 3. a private; second-class ~ 4. a native-born (esp. AE); naturalized, new ~

citizenry *n*. an informed ~

citizenship *n*. 1. to grant ~ 2. to apply for ~ 3. to acquire, receive ~ 4. to revoke smb.'s ~ 5. to give up, renounce one's ~ 6. dual ~

city *n*. 1. to govern, manage (AE), run a ~ 2. a big; capital; cosmopolitan; densely populated; garden (BE), planned; great; major; port; provincial ~ 3. twin ~ties 4. (the) central ~ (see also **inner city**) 5. a beleaguered; open ~ (during wartime) 6. in a ~ (to live in the ~) (see the Usage Note for **town**)

civil *adj.* 1. ~ to (he wasn't even ~ to his guests) 2. (formal) ~ to + inf. (it was ~ of them to offer their help) (see also *civil union* at **union**)

civil action *n.* (legal) to bring a ~ (against)

civil disobedience *n.* 1. (to lead) a campaign of ~ 2. an act of ~

civil disorder *n.* 1. to foment, incite, stir up ~ 2. to put down ~

civilian *n.* an innocent; unarmed ~

civilities *n.* to exchange ~

civilization *n.* 1. to introduce; spread ~ 2. to create a ~ 3. to destroy, stamp out (a) ~ 4. an advanced ~ 5. ancient, early; modern ~ 6. (misc.) the cradle of ~; the end of ~ as we know it

civil unrest *n.* see **civil disorder**

clad *adj.* ["clothed"] 1. fully; lightly, scantily; partially ~ 2. smartly ~ 3. ~ in (~ in brown)

cladding *n.* (CE; AE also has *siding*) 1. to install ~ 2. aluminium (BE), aluminum (AE) ~

claim I *n.* 1. to enter, file, lodge, make, put forward, put in, submit a ~ (she filed a ~ against her employer for compensation arising from her accident at work) 2. to authenticate, back up, establish, press, substantiate a ~ 3. to lay ~ to; to stake, stake out a ~ to 4. (esp. AE) to jump ("steal") smb.'s ~ 5. to allow, uphold; challenge, contest, dispute; deny, disallow, dismiss, reject; discredit a ~ 6. to forfeit; give up, relinquish, renounce, waive, withdraw a ~ 7. to adjudicate; settle a ~ (they settled their ~ out of court) 8. a legal; legitimate; moral; rightful; undisputed ~ 9. an excessive, extravagant, unreasonable ~ 10. an outstanding; prior ~ 11. a fraudulent; specious; unsubstantiated, unsupported ~ 12. competing, conflicting, rival ~s 13. a disability; insurance ~; pay ~ (BE) 14. a ~ against; for; on; to (she submitted a ~ for damages against the other driver; there are many ~s on my time; he has no ~ to the estate; a ~ to fame) 15. a ~ that + clause (the ~ that he could reduce taxes proved to be false)

claim II *v.* 1. (E) she ~s to own this property 2. (L) she ~s that she owns this property

claimant *n.* a ~ to (a ~ to the estate)

claim back *v.* (d; intr., tr.) to ~ from (you can ~ some of the money from your insurance = you can claim some of the money back from your insurance)

clam *n.* baked ~s

clamber *v.* (P; intr.) to ~ into/onto a bus

clamor, clamour I *n.* 1. an insistent; loud; public ~ 2. a ~ against; for (a ~ against new taxes)

clamor, clamour II *v.* 1. (d; intr.) to ~ for (to ~ for justice) 2. (E) they were ~ing to have justice

clamp *v.* (d; tr.) to ~ on, upon (to ~ controls on interest rates)

clampdown *n.* a ~ on

clamp down *v.* (D; intr.) to ~ on (to ~ on pickpockets)

clan *n.* a ~ gathers

clang *n.* 1. a metallic ~ 2. to shut with a ~

clang *v.* to ~ shut

clanger *n.* (colloq.) (BE) ("blunder") to drop a ~

clank *v.* to ~ shut

clap I *v.* ("to put") 1. (d; tr.) to ~ in, into (to ~ smb. in jail) 2. (d; tr.) to ~ on; over (to ~ a muzzle on a dog; she ~ped her hand over her mouth) 3. (d; tr.) to ~ to (she ~ped her hand to her mouth)

clap II *v.* ("to applaud") to ~ loudly

clarification *n.* 1. to provide; seek ~ 2. additional, further ~

clash I *n.* 1. an angry; bitter; bloody; violent ~ 2. an armed; border ~ 3. a ~ between (a violent ~ broke out between the two rivals about/over a woman) 4. a ~ with (the rivals ~ed with each other about/over a woman; shot dead in a ~ with the police)

clash II *v.* 1. (D; intr.) ("to argue, struggle") to ~ about/over (the rivals ~ed (with each other) about/over a woman) 2. (D; intr.) ("to struggle") to ~ with (the demonstrators ~ed with the police) 3. (D; intr.) ("not to match") to ~ with (red ~es with green)

clasp I *n.* a tie ~

clasp II *v.* (d; tr.) to ~ to (she ~ed the baby to her bosom)

class I *n.* ["lesson"] 1. to conduct, hold, teach a ~; to give, meet one's ~ (having finished teaching the ~, the teacher said, "the time is up and the ~ is over") 2. to schedule; reschedule a ~ 3. to attend, go to (a) ~; to audit a ~ (AE); come top/bottom of the ~; to sit in on a ~; take a ~ (as student or as teacher) 4. to cut (esp. AE); miss a ~ 5. to call off, cancel; dismiss a ~ (~ dismissed!) 6. an advanced; beginners'; intermediate ~ (to sit in on an advanced English ~) 7. a ~ in modern drama 8. in (a) ~ (she was in ~ when the message came). ["group"] 9. to form a ~ 10. the educated; leisure; lower; middle; privileged; professional (esp. BE); ruling ~; underclass; upper; working ~(es) 11. (BE) the chattering ~es 12. a social ~ 13. (misc.) out of one's ~ ("outclassed"); in a ~ of one's/its own ("unsurpassed"); ~ conflict/struggle/war; world-class (world-class scientific research) ["division of travelers"] 14. business; cabin; economy; first; second; third; tourist ~ (to travel first-class) ["group of pupils, students graduating together"] (AE) 15. the freshman; junior; senior; sophomore ~; the ~ of (the ~ of 1968 included hippies who became yuppies)

class II *v.* see **classify** 1–4

classification *n.* 1. to make a ~ 2. an arbitrary ~

classify *v.* 1. (D; tr.) to ~ according to (the children were ~fied according to age) 2. (D; tr.) to ~ among, under, with 3. (D; tr.) to ~ as (she was ~fied as fit for service; the documents were ~fied as top-secret) 4. (D; tr.) to ~ by (to ~ books by/according to subject) 5. (D; tr.) to ~ into (to ~ the candidates into groups) 6. (N; used with an adjective) to ~ information confidential

clatter *v.* (P; intr.) the cart ~ed over the cobblestones

clause *n.* ["group of words with a subject and predicate"] 1. a conditional; coordinate; dependent, subordinate; independent, main; nominal, noun; nonrestrictive; relative; restrictive; verbless ~ (the main verb in the main ~) ["provision"] ["article"] 2. (esp. AE) a grandfather ~ ("a clause that exempts those already engaged in an activity prohibited by new legislation") 3. an escalator; penalty ~ 4. a most-favored-nation ~

claw I *n.* 1. to get, sink one's ~s into 2. to retract one's ~s (cats retract their ~s) 3. sharp ~s 4. nonretractile; retractile ~s

claw II *v.* 1. (d; intr.) to ~ at (the cat ~ed at my hand) 2. (misc.) to ~ one's way to the top

claw back *v.* (BE) (D; tr.) to ~ from (to ~ some of the payment from the government = to claw some of the payment back from the government)

clay *n.* 1. to knead, model, shape, work ~ 2. to bake; temper ~ 3. modeling; potter's ~ 4. a lump of ~

clean I *adj.*, *adv.* 1. immaculately, spotlessly ~; squeaky-clean (also fig. = 'not corrupt') 2. to keep smt. ~ 3. (misc.) to come ~ ("to confess"); I ~ forgot: we're ~ out of food! ("I completely forgot: we're completely out of food"); ~ of (she scraped the furniture ~ of paint); as ~ as a whistle

clean II *v.* 1. (d; tr.) to ~ from, off (she ~ed the dirt off her shoes) 2. (D; tr.) to ~ out of (the store was ~ed out of cigarettes)

clean break *n.* to make a ~ (with)

cleaner *n.* ["device"] 1. a pipe; vacuum ~ ["person"] 2. a street; window ~

cleaning *n.* 1. to do the ~ 2. dry ~ 3. a spring; thorough ~

cleanliness *n.* personal ~

cleanse *v.* 1. to ~ thoroughly 2. (D; tr.) to ~ of (to ~ one's thoughts of sin)

cleansing *n.* 1. a thorough ~ 2. ethnic ~

clean up *v.* 1. (D; intr.) to ~ after (he had to ~ after the children, who wouldn't ~ after themselves) 2. (colloq.) (AE) (D; intr.) ("to make a profit") to ~ on (to ~ on a deal)

clear I *adj.* 1. abundantly, perfectly; fairly; painfully ~ 2. (cannot stand alone) ~ about (are you ~ about the situation?; let's get ~ about a few things) 3. ~ from (the answer is ~ from these facts) 4. ~ of (the roads were ~ of snow; to keep ~ of trouble) 5. ~ to (the situation is ~ to everyone; it was ~ to everyone that they would not come) 6. ~ that + clause (it was ~ that they would not come; the teacher made it ~ that discipline would be maintained) 7. (misc.) as ~ as crystal = crystal-clear ("perfectly clear"); as clear as mud (colloq.) ("not clear at all"); it is ~ why she came; it is not ~ how he was able to do it; it is not ~ whether they will attend; (as adv.) the ball went ~ over my head (see also *see one's way* (clear) at **way**)

clear II *n.* ["uncoded language"] 1. in the ~ (to send a message in the ~) ["blameless state"] 2. in the ~ (the investigators decided that she was in the ~)

clear III *v.* 1. (D; tr.) ("to authorize"); ("to prepare") to ~ for (to ~ an article for export; our plane was ~ed for takeoff; to ~ the decks for action) 2. (D; tr.) ("to remove") to ~ from (to ~ the snow from the driveway) 3. (D; tr.) ("to free") to ~ of (to ~ a harbor of mines; to ~ smb. of guilt; to ~ land of trees; to ~ the driveway of snow) 4. (d; intr.) to ~ off ("to clean") (~ (off) the table so that we can eat) 5. (d; intr.) to ~ off ("to leave") (~ off my land or I'll call the police!) 6. (colloq.) (d; intr.) to ~ out of ("to leave") (to ~ out of town) 7. (d; tr.) ("to remove") to ~ out of (to ~ things out of a cupboard) 8. (D; tr.) ("to get authorization for") to ~ with (to ~ a shipment with the authorities; ~ your plan with headquarters) 9. (H) ("to authorize") our plane was ~ed to take off

clearance *n.* ["act of clearing away"] 1. slum ~ ["authorization"] 2. to get give; receive ~ for 3. customs ~ 4. ~ to + inf. (the control tower gave our plane ~ to take off) ["space between parts"] 5. valve ~ ["certification of eligibility for access to classified material"] 6. to give; receive ~ 7. (a) security ~

clearinghouse *n.* a ~ for (a ~ for information)

clear off *v.* (D; intr.) ("to leave") to ~ of (AE) (~ of my land or I'll call the police!)

clear up *v.* (D; intr., tr.) to ~ after smb. (he had to ~ after the children, who wouldn't ~ after themselves)

cleavage *n.* ["division"] 1. a sharp ~ between (a sharp ~ developed between the two factions) 2. a gown with a deep ~ = a gown with/that shows a lot of ~

cleave *v.* (formal) (d; intr.) ("to cling") to ~ to (to ~ to old customs)

cleaver *n.* a butcher's ~; meat ~

clemency *n.* 1. to grant; show ~ 2. to beg for, seek ~ 3. to deny ~

clerk I *n.* 1. a booking ~ (BE; AE has *ticket agent*) 2. (AE) (in a hotel) a desk, room ~ 3. a bank (BE); cipher, code; city (AE), town; court; filing; mail, postal ~; salesclerk (AE; BE has *shop assistant*); shipping; stockroom ~ 4. a junior; senior ~

clerk II *v.* (AE) (D; intr.) (legal) to ~ for (the budding lawyer was ~ing for a prominent judge)

clever *adj.* 1. ~ at, in (she is ~ at arranging furniture) 2. ~ with (he is ~ with his hands) 3. ~ to + inf. (it was ~ of her to think of that)

cliché *n.* 1. to mouth, utter a ~ (he's always mouthing ~s) 2. a well-worn ~ 3. (misc.) in ~s (to speak in well-worn ~s)

click *v.* 1. (on a computer) (D; intr.) to ~ on; onto 2. (colloq.) (D; intr.) ("to be successful") to ~ with (the new show ~ed with the public)

client *n.* to serve a ~

clientele *n.* 1. to build up, establish a ~ 2. an exclusive, fashionable, select; international ~

cliff *n.* 1. to climb, scale a ~ 2. a rugged; sheer, steep; towering ~

climate *n.* 1. a friendly, hospitable; hostile, inhospitable; invigorating ~ 2. an arctic, frigid; cold;

continental; damp; dry; equatorial; hot; humid; maritime; Mediterranean; mild, moderate, temperate; severe; subtropical; tropical; warm; wet ~ (see also *climate change* at **change I**) 3. (fig.) an economic; political; social ~ 4. (misc.) a change of ~; to create a friendly ~

climax I *n.* 1. to come to, reach a ~ 2. to bring smt. to a ~; to work up to a ~ 3. to mark a ~ 4. a dramatic, thrilling ~ (in a dramatic ~, the villain is unmasked) 5. a sexual ~ 6. a ~ to (the ~ to our efforts came / was when we won first prize)

climax II *v.* (d; intr.) to ~ in, with (the convention ~ed with the candidate's acceptance speech)

climb I *n.* an arduous, difficult, hard; easy; gradual; rough, rugged; steep; tortuous ~

climb II *v.* 1. (d; intr.) to ~ aboard (to ~ aboard a raft) 2. (d; intr.) to ~ down (to ~ down a hill) 3. (d; intr.) to ~ into (the child ~ed into their bed) 4. (d; intr.) to ~ onto, upon (the child ~ed onto her mother's lap) 5. (d; intr.) to ~ out of (to ~ out of a pit) 6. (d; intr.) to ~ over (to ~ over a fence) 7. (D; intr.) to ~ to (to ~ to the top) 8. (D; intr.) to ~ up (to ~ up a hill) 9. (misc.) the road ~s from the sea to the mountains

climb-down *n.* (BE) ["retreat"] a ~ from (to be forced into a ~ from an untenable position)

climb down *v.* 1. (D; intr.) to ~ from (to ~ from a tree) 2. (BE) (D; intr.) ("to retreat") to ~ from (to ~ from an untenable position)

climber *n.* 1. a mountain ~ 2. a social ~

climb up *v.* (D; intr.) to ~ to (she ~ed up to the top)

clinch *n.* in a ~

cling *v.* 1. to ~ tenaciously 2. (d; intr.) to ~ (on) to (to ~ to one's possessions; to ~ to old customs; they clung to the floating wreckage; he clung to my arm) 3. (misc.) to ~ together

clinic *n.* 1. to hold a ~ 2. an abortion; animal; antenatal, prenatal; dental; diagnostic; family-planning; mental-health; outpatient; postpartum; special; speech; walk-in; well-child (AE); well-woman ~ 3. at, in a ~ (she works at the ~)

clip I *n.* ["device to hold cartridges"] 1. to insert a ~ 2. a cartridge ~ ["device that fastens"] 3. a paper; tie ~ ["excerpt"] 4. a film ~

clip II *n.* (colloq.) ["speed"] at a ~ (to move at a fast ~)

clip III *v.* 1. (esp. AE) (D; tr.) to ~ from (to ~ articles from a newspaper) 2. (d; tr.) to ~ to (to ~ one page to another = to ~ two pages together) 3. (N; used with an adjective) she ~ped his hair short

clipper *n.* 1. a nail ~ 2. a barber's ~s 3. a coupon ~ ("one whose income is derived from stocks and bonds")

clipping *n.* 1. a newspaper; press ~ (from) (AE; BE has *press cutting*) 2. fingernail; toenail ~s

clique *n.* a military; ruling ~

cloak I *n.* ["cover"] under a ~ (under a ~ of secrecy)

cloak II *v.* (d; tr.) to ~ in (~ed in secrecy)

cloakroom see the Usage Note for **room**

clock I *n.* 1. to regulate, set; wind (up) a ~ 2. to advance a ~; or: to put, set, turn a ~ ahead / forward ((by) one hour) 3. to put, set, turn a ~ back ((by) one hour) 4. a digital; cuckoo; electric; grandfather; wall ~ (by / according to my digital ~, it's ten thirty) 5. a time ~ (to punch a time ~ when starting or finishing work) 6. a biological ~ (her biological ~ keeps ticking away) 7. a ~ is fast; right; slow 8. a ~ gains time; goes, runs; keeps time; loses time; runs down; says the time, shows the time, tells the time (BE), tells time (AE); stops; ticks 9. a ~ strikes the hour 10. the dial; face; hands of a ~ 11. (misc.) to watch the ~ ("to wait impatiently for the end of the working day"); to work (a)round the ~ ("to work without rest"); to work against the ~ ("to strive to meet a deadline"); the ~ ran out ("the allotted time expired"); to stop the ~ ("to suspend play in a game so that the clock stops running") (see also **alarm clock**)

clock II *v.* 1. (D; tr.) ("to time") to ~ at (he was ~ed at seventy miles an hour) 2. (J) he was ~ed doing seventy miles an hour

clockwise *adj., adv.* 1. to go ~ 2. to turn (smt.) ~

clockwork *n.* (misc.) to go, work like ~ ("to work perfectly"); as regular as ~ ("completely regular")

clog *v.* (D; tr.) to ~ (up) with (the pipe was ~ged (up) with leaves)

close I *adj., adv.* / klous / ["near"] 1. ~ to (~ to tears; we live ~ to town; ~ to the truth) ["stingy"] (colloq.) 2. ~ with (~ with one's money) ["secretive"] 3. ~ about (~ about one's past) ["on intimate terms"] 4. ~ to, with (~ with one's parents) ["misc."] 5. to see smt. ~ to (BE), up; they were sitting ~ together (see also **near** *adv.*)

close II *n.* / klouz / ["finish"] 1. to bring to a ~ 2. to come to, draw to a ~ ["end of a letter"] 3. the complimentary ~ (of / to a letter) (the complimentary ~ appears at or towards the ~ of a letter)

close III *v.* / klouz / 1. (d; intr.) to ~ about, around, round ("to encircle") (night ~d around us) 2. (D; intr., tr.) to ~ for (to ~ a store for renovations; the store ~d for renovations) 3. (d; intr.) to ~ on ("to get near to") (the police were ~ing on the fugitive) 4. (D; tr.) ("to shut") to ~ on (she ~d the door on him) 5. (D; tr.) ("to shut") to ~ to (they ~d their eyes to the truth) 6. (d; intr.) to ~ with ("to engage") (to ~ with the enemy) ["secretive"] 7. (d; intr., tr.) ("to finish") to ~ with (they ~d the concert with ("by playing") a march) 8. (N; used with an adjective) ("to shut") she ~d the door tight 9. (s) stocks ~d strong; weak

closed *adj.* 1. ~ for (~ for renovations) 2. ~ to (the road was ~ to traffic; the store was ~ to the public for renovations)

close in *v.* / klouz / 1. (D; intr.) to ~ for ("to approach and prepare for") (to ~ for the kill) 2. (D; intr.) to ~ on ("to bring to bay") (the police ~d in on the fugitive)

closer, closest *adj.*, *adv.* ~ to (the park is closer to our hotel than it is to yours; which stop is closest to Times Square?)

closemouthed *adj.* ~ about

closeness *n.* ~ to

close off *v.* (D; tr.) to ~ from, to (they were completely ~d off from the outside world)

closet *n.* ["cupboard"] (esp. AE) 1. a china; clothes; linen; walk-in ~ ["toilet"] (esp. BE) (old-fashioned) 2. a water ~ ["misc."] 3. to come out of the ~ (about smt.) ("to come out into the open about smt.")

closeted *adj.* ~ with (he was ~ with the mayor for an hour)

closure *n.* ["act of closing"] 1. earmarked for ~ (mines earmarked for ~) 2. the ~ of (the ~ of local mines) ["emotional closure"] 3. to achieve ~ (once she knew that he was really dead she could achieve ~ and move on in her life)

clot *n.* 1. to form a ~ 2. to dissolve; remove a ~ 3. a blood ~ 4. a ~ forms

cloth *n.* 1. to dye; weave ~ 2. homespun ~ 3. a drop ~ 4. a loin ~ 5. a bolt; piece; strip of ~

clothe *v.* 1. (D; tr.) to ~ in (~d in wool/black) 2. (misc.) fully; partially ~d

clothes *n.* 1. to change; put on; wear (one's) ~ 2. to take off (one's) ~ 3. to iron; launder, wash; mend ~ 4. baby; maternity; night; summer; swaddling; warm; winter ~ 5. elegant, fashionable; new; plain; old ~ 6. castoff; secondhand, used; shabby ~ 7. civilian; plain ~ 8. in ~ (the soldier was in civilian ~ rather than in uniform; the policeman was in plain ~ rather than in uniform: he was a plain-clothes policeman/officer)

clothesline *n.* to put up, string; take down a ~

clothing *n.* 1. to put on; wear (one's) ~ 2. to take off (one's) ~ 3. heavy; light; outer; protective; warm ~ 4. summer; winter ~ 5. bespoke (BE), custom-made, made-to-measure, tailor-made; off-the peg (BE), ready-to-wear; trendy ~ 6. castoff; secondhand, used; shabby ~ 7. an article, item of ~ 8. (misc.) to model ~

cloture *n.* (AE) to apply, impose, invoke ~

cloud *n.* 1. to disperse ~s (the strong wind dispersed the ~s) 2. cirrus; cumulus; dark; grey; heavy, thick; high; scattered; threatening; white ~s 3. rain, storm ~s (typically fig.); thunderclouds; war ~s 4. a mushroom; radioactive ~ (storm/war ~s were gathering over Europe in the 1930s) 5. ~s disperse; form; gather (the ~s dispersed in the strong wind) 6. ~s scud across the sky 7. (misc.) under a ~ (of suspicion); the gathering ~s of war; in the ~s ("absorbed in one's fantasies"); to seed ~s (to produce rain); to cast a ~ over ("to cause gloom")

cloudburst *n.* a sudden ~

cloudy *adj.* partly ~ (in weather forecasts)

clout *n.* (colloq.) ["influence"] ["power"] 1. to have, wield ~ 2. political ~ (he has a great deal of political ~) 3. the ~ to + inf. (has he got enough ~ to get his plan through Congress?)

clover *n.* ["plant"] 1. a four-leaf ~ ["prosperity"] 2. in ~ ("in luxury")

clown I *n.* 1. to act, play the ~ 2. a circus ~

clown II *v.* (D; intr.) to ~ (around) with

club I *n.* ["association"] 1. to form, organize a ~ 2. to join a ~ 3. to break up, disband a ~ 4. an exclusive; private ~ 5. a book; debating; fan; glee; weight-watchers'; working-men's (BE); youth (esp. BE) ~ (she joined a book ~ to which many members belong and has been in it ever since) 6. an athletic; country; tennis; yachting, yacht ~ 7. a ~ breaks up, disbands 8. a Christmas ~ (esp. AE) ("type of savings account to provide money for the purchase of Christmas presents"); a savings ~ ["implement"] 9. a golf; Indian ~ 10. a set of golf ~s ["misc."] 11. (colloq.) join the ~! ("we are in the same situation!"); (BE) in the ~ ("pregnant") (see the Usage Note for **team**)

club II *v.* ("to beat") to ~ smb. to death

clue *n.* 1. to discover, find, uncover a ~ 2. to follow up a ~ 3. to have a ~ (the police don't have any ~s) 4. to furnish, provide, supply; leave a ~ 5. an important, key, vital ~ 6. a ~ (as) to (the police had no ~ to her identity) 7. (misc.) he doesn't have a ~ ("he's totally ignorant/insensitive")

clue in *v.* (colloq.) (D; tr.) to ~ on ("to inform about")

clumsy *adj.* 1. ~ at (he's ~ at sports) 2. ~ of (spilling the drinks was ~ of you) 3. ~ with (to be ~ with one's hands) 4. ~ to + inf. (it was ~ of you to spill the drinks like that)

cluster I *n.* a consonant ~

cluster II *v.* 1. (d; intr.) to ~ around (the crowd ~ed around the entrance) 2. (P; intr.) they ~ed (together) in small groups

clutch I *n.* ["device for engaging and disengaging a transmission"] 1. to engage, (esp. AE) throw in the ~ ("to release the clutch pedal") 2. to work the ~ 3. to disengage the ~ ("to depress the clutch pedal") 4. to ride the ~ ("to keep the clutch pedal partially depressed") 5. the ~ slips ["crisis"] (AE) 6. in a ~ (to count on smb. in a ~)

clutch II *v.* 1. (d; intr.) to ~ at (to ~ at a branch) 2. (d; tr.) to ~ to (she ~ed her children to her bosom/breast) (see also *to clutch at (any) straws* at **straw** 2)

clutches *n.* ["power"] 1. to fall into smb.'s ~ 2. in smb.'s ~ (in the ~ of the enemy)

cluttered *adj.* ~ (up) with (the room was all ~ (up) with old newspapers)

coach I *n.* ["trainer of an athlete or team"] 1. a basketball; crew; fencing; football; soccer; swimming; tennis; track-and-field; volleyball ~ USAGE NOTE: In AE, a coach can also be the manager of a sports team other than a baseball team. ["trainer of a performer or troupe"] 2. a drama; voice ~ ["personal trainer or counselor"] 3. a life ~ ["long-distance bus"] (esp. BE) 4. to go, travel by ~ ["airplane"] (esp. AE) 5. an air ~

coach II v. 1. (D; tr.) to ~ for (to ~ a team for a championship match) 2. (D; tr.) to ~ in (she ~es us in math) 3. (misc.) she ~ed the team to victory

coal n. 1. to mine, produce ~ 2. to burn, use ~ 3. to shovel ~ (into a furnace) 4. anthracite, hard; bituminous, soft; brown ~ 5. hot, live ~s (to cook meat over hot ~s) 6. ~ burns 7. a chunk, lump, piece of ~; a bed of ~s 8. (misc.) to rake smb. over the ~s ("to criticize smb. harshly")

coalesce v. (D; intr.) to ~ into

coalition n. (pol.) 1. to form a ~ 2. to break up, disband, dissolve a ~ 3. a ~ breaks up, collapses, falls apart 4. a political ~ 5. (esp. AE) a rainbow ~ ("a multiethnic political coalition") 6. a broadly based, umbrella ~ ("a group consisting of many diverse elements") 7. a ~ among, between, of

coast I n. 1. a forbidding, inhospitable; rugged ~ (the rugged ~ stretches from here to there) 2. off a ~ (a ship sank right off the ~) 3. along, on the ~ (there are many fishing towns on the stretch of ~ between here and there) 4. (AE) on the (West) Coast ("on the Pacific Coast of the US") (he moved to the Coast and still lives on the Coast) 5. (misc.) the ~ is clear ("there is no danger in sight"); from ~ to ~ USAGE NOTE: the bank(s) of a river or canal; the shore of a lake or sea; the coast (of an ocean).

coast II v. (P; intr.) ("to move effortlessly") they ~ed down the hill; they ~ed to an easy victory

coastline n. a broken, irregular, jagged; rugged ~

coat n. ["sleeved outer garment"] 1. to have a ~ on, wear a ~ 2. to put on; take off one's ~ 3. an all-weather; fur; fur-lined; mink ~; overcoat; raincoat; sheepskin; spring; trench; winter; zip-lined ~ ["layer of paint, varnish, etc."] 4. to apply, put on a ~ (we had to put on a second ~)

coated adj. ~ in, with

coating n. 1. an outer; protective ~ 2. a thick; thin ~

coat of arms n. a family ~

coattails n. (to hang/ride) on smb.'s ~ ("(to be) totally dependent on smb. else's success for one's own success")

coax v. 1. (H) she ~ed me to go but I didn't 2. (P) she ~ed me into going and I went; the actor tried to ~ some reaction from his audience

cobwebs n. (colloq.) ["confusion"] to blow away, clear, sweep (away) the ~ (from one's brain)

cocaine n. 1. crack ~ 2. to freebase; shoot; smoke; snort; take; use ~ 3. a line of ~

cock n. ["rooster"] (esp. BE) 1. ~s crow, go cock-a-doodle-doo ["valve"] 2. a ball ~

cocktail n. 1. to make, mix, prepare; sip a ~ 2. fruit ~; a prawn (BE), shrimp (AE); seafood ~ 3. a champagne ~

cocoon n. to make, spin a ~

code n. ["cryptographic system"] 1. to design, make up a ~ 2. to break, crack, decipher a ~ 3. a binary; secret ~ 4. (the) Morse ~ (to tap out, use (the) Morse ~ to send (a message) in Morse ~) 5. in ~ (to

send a message in ~) ["body of laws, principles"] 6. to establish, formulate, lay down a ~ 7. a civil; criminal, penal ~; a ~ of justice 8. an ethical, moral ~; a ~ of ethics 9. a building; sanitary ~ 10. a dress ~ ["system of symbols"] 11. an area (AE), dialling (BE) ~ 12. a postal ~ (BE), postcode (BE), zip (AE) ~ 13. a bar ~ ("symbols that are read by a computer") 14. the genetic ~

codicil n. (legal) 1. to draw up a ~ 2. a ~ to (a will)

coequal adj. (formal) ~ with

coerce v. 1. (D; tr.) to ~ into (to ~ smb. into doing smt.) 2. (H) (rare) he was ~d to sign

coercion n. under ~ (to do smt. under ~)

coeval adj. (formal) ["contemporary"] ~ with

coexist v. 1. to ~ peacefully 2. (D; intr.) to ~ with

coexistence n. 1. peaceful ~ 2. ~ with

coffee n. 1. to brew; grind; make; percolate; strain ~ 2. to drink, have ~ 3. to stir ~ (with a spoon) 4. to grow ~ 5. strong; weak ~ 6. black; white (BE) ~, ~ with cream/milk 7. decaffeinated; fresh; hot; iced; instant; Irish; Greek; Turkish ~ 8. a cup of ~; one ~; or: one cup of ~; two ~s; or: two cups of ~ (bring us two cups of ~; or: bring us two ~s) 9. (misc.) the ~ is brewing; I had a ~/a cup of ~; a mug of ~ with milk and sugar in it

coffin n. to lower a ~ into a grave

cogitate v. (formal) (D; intr.) to ~ about, on

cognate adj. ~ to (AE), with (Dutch is ~ with English and German)

cognizance n. (formal) ["notice"] to take ~ of

cognizant adj. (formal) (cannot stand alone) ~ of (~ of the danger)

cohabit v. (D; intr.) to ~ with

coherence n. 1. to lack ~ 2. ~ between

cohesion n. ~ among, between

coil I n. an induction; primary ~

coil II v. 1. (d; intr., refl.) to ~ (a)round (the snake ~ed around its victim) 2. (d; intr., refl.) to ~ (up) into (to ~ (up) into a ball)

coin n. 1. to mint, strike ~s 2. to jingle ~s 3. to drop, put a ~ (into a slot) 4. to spin a ~; or: to flip, throw, toss a ~ (in order to decide an issue) (they tossed a ~ to decide who would go first) 5. to collect ~s 6. antique; copper; counterfeit; fifty-cent; gold; metal; rare; silver; ten-cent; valuable ~s 7. ~s clink, jingle 8. (misc.) common ~ ("smt. that is widely known"); to pay back in the same ~ ("to treat smb. as he or she has treated others")

coincide v. (D; intr.) to ~ in; with (they ~ with each other in their views)

coincidence n. 1. mere, pure, sheer ~ 2. an amazing; happy; interesting; odd, strange; remarkable ~ 3. a ~ that + clause (it was pure ~ that we were seated together) 4. by ~ (it was by pure ~ that we were seated together; we ended up in the same town by sheer ~)

coincidental adj. 1. purely ~ 2. ~ with 3. ~ that + clause (it was purely ~ that we were seated together)

cold I *adj.* ["of a low temperature"] 1. biting, bitter, bitterly, extremely, freezing ~ (it was bitter ~) 2. ~ to (~ to the touch) 3. (misc.) as ~ as ice = ice-cold ["unfriendly"] 4. ~ towards

cold II *n.* ["low temperature"] 1. biting, bitter, extreme, icy, intense, severe ~ (to wrap up warm against the severe ~) 2. the ~ has let up 3. (misc.) to come in out of the ~ ; to go out into the ~ ["illness"] 4. to catch (a) ~ ; to come down with, contract, get, (BE) go down with a ~ 5. to have ; nurse a ~ ; to suffer from a ~ 6. to fight off, shake off, throw off a ~ 7. a bad, heavy, severe ; lingering ; slight ; streaming ~ 8. the common ~ ; a chest ; head ~ ["misc."] 9. to be left out in the ~ ("to be slighted or excluded")

cold feet *n.* (colloq.) ["reluctance"] at the last minute he got ~ and withdrew from the deal

cold light *n.* ["clear view"] in the ~ of reality

cold shoulder *n.* (colloq.) ["snub"] to get the ~ from smb. ; give smb. the ~

cold turkey *n.* (colloq.) ["abrupt cessation of the use of drugs or other harmful substances"] to go ~

collaborate *v.* (D; intr.) to ~ in, on ; with (to ~ on a project with smb. ; Shakespeare may have ~d with John Fletcher on *King Henry VIII* = Shakespeare and John Fletcher may have ~d on *King Henry VIII*)

collaboration *n.* 1. close ~ 2. international ~ 3. between ; in ~ with (Shakespeare may have written *King Henry VIII* in ~ with John Fletcher)

collaborator *n.* 1. in, on ; with (John Fletcher may have been Shakespeare's ~ on *King Henry VIII*) 2. a wartime ~ (with an occupying power) (historical and pejorative)

collapse I *n.* 1. (an) economic ~ 2. an emotional, mental, nervous ~ 3. a complete, total, utter ~ (he was in a state of total ~)

collapse II *v.* 1. (d ; intr.) to ~ from, with (to ~ from exhaustion) 2. (d ; intr.) to ~ under (the weight of smt.) 3. (d ; intr.) to ~ in the face of (our resistance ~d in the face of the enemy's onslaught)

collar *n.* 1. to turn down ; turn up a ~ 2. a button-down ; clerical ; high ; stand-up ; starched ; stiff ; turndown ~ 3. (misc.) hot under the ~ ("very angry")

collate *v.* (D ; tr.) to ~ with (to ~ one edition with another edition)

collateral *n.* 1. to put up ~ for 2. to offer, put up, use smt. as ~ for

collect *v.* 1. (D ; intr.) to ~ around (a crowd ~ed around them) 2. (D ; intr., tr.) to ~ for (to ~ for charity ; to ~ money for a good cause) 3. (D ; tr.) to ~ from (to ~ money from one's colleagues for charity) 4. (D ; intr.) to ~ on (to ~ on one's insurance)

collection *n.* ["of money or things"] 1. to take up a ~ (of money) 2. to amass, assemble ; build up ; break up ; have a ~ (the town has an impressive art ~ that is housed in the municipal museum) 3. an art ; coin ; private ; stamp ~ 4. a priceless ~ ["anthology"] 5. to compile ; edit ; publish a ~

collective *n.* a workers' ~

collector *n.* 1. an art ; coin ; rare-book ; stamp ~ 2. a tax ; ticket ; toll ~ 3. (AE) a garbage, trash ~ (BE has *dustman*) 4. an ardent, avid, keen (BE), serious ~

college *n.* 1. to go to ~ 2. to apply for admission to (a) ~ 3. to enroll, matriculate at (a) ~ ; to enter (a) ~ 4. to finish, graduate from ~ 5. to put smb. through ~ ("to pay for smb.'s college education") 6. to drop out of ; fail out of (AE), flunk out of (AE ; slang) ~ 7. a bible, theological ; business (AE) ; community (AE) ; junior (AE) ; technical (BE) ; a College of Further Education (BE) 8. a war ~ 9. (US) the Electoral College 10. at, in ~ (she's away at ~ ; he made many friends when he was in ~) USAGE NOTE : "A college" is a building or an institution (*there's a big prestigious college in another town but she goes to a college near her home*). "College" is the educational activity that goes on in a college (*college takes up a lot of her time ; she goes to college near her home ; we lost touch with each other after college*). (See also the Usage Notes for **school** ; **university**)

collide *v.* 1. to ~ head-on 2. (D ; intr.) to ~ with (they ~d with another ship ; the ships ~d with each other) 3. (misc.) the ships ~d

collision *n.* 1. to cause a ~ 2. to avoid a ~ 3. a head-on ; midair ~ 4. a near ~ 5. a ~ between ; with (the ~ between the ships was caused by fog = the ~ of the ships (with each other) was caused by fog) 6. (misc.) because of fog, the ships were in collision (with each other)

collocate *v.* (D ; intr.) to ~ with (some verbs ~ with certain nouns = some verbs and certain nouns ~ with each other)

collocation *n.* a grammatical ; lexical ~ USAGE NOTE : In BBI, at *desirous*, "very desirous" is considered a lexical collocation ; "desirous of" and "desirous that + clause" are considered grammatical collocations. Elsewhere, "very desirous" and "desirous of" would both be considered collocations (i.e. combinations of word + word) and "desirous that + clause" would be considered a type of colligation or complementation or construction (i.e. a combination of word + syntactic structure).

colloquy *n.* (formal) a ~ between

collude *v.* 1. (D ; intr.) to ~ in ; with (to ~ with smb. in doing smt.) 2. (E) to ~ with smb. to do smt. = to ~ to do smt.

collusion *n.* 1. ~ between 2. in ~ with (they were in ~ (with each other) to do smt. bad)

colon I *n.* (in punctuation) to place, put in a ~

colon II *n.* (med.) the ascending ; descending ; transverse ~

colonel *n.* 1. a chicken (AE ; slang), full ; lieutenant ~ 2. a ~ commands a regiment 3. to make smb. a ~, to promote smb. to the rank of ~ ; to have, hold the rank of ~ 4. (misc.) what's your opinion, Colonel (Smith) ?

colony *n.* 1. to establish a ~ 2. to disband a ~ 3. a Crown Colony 4. an artists'; leper; nudist; penal ~ 5. an ant ~ (many ants lived in a huge ant ~)

color, colour I *n.* ["hue"] 1. a bright, brilliant; contrasting; dark; dull; garish, gaudy, loud; harsh; light; matching; natural; neutral; pastel; rich; soft; subdued; vivid; warm ~ (I can't remember her hair ~ or her eye ~ but I think they were both a dark ~) 2. (usu. fig.) glowing ~s (to picture smt. in glowing ~s) 3. complementary; primary; secondary ~s 4. ~s clash; fade; match 5. in ~ (in natural ~) 6. a combination of ~s; a riot of ~ 7. (misc.) with illustrations in full ~ ["features"] 8. local ~ ["paint"] 9. oil; water ~s 10. a ~ runs ["vividness"] 11. to add, lend ~ (to a story) ["complexion"] 12. to change, turn ~ ("to become pale; to blush") 13. (misc.) the fresh air brought the ~ back to his cheeks = in the fresh air the ~ came back to his cheeks ["misc."] 14. off ~ ("not proper, bawdy") (AE) 15. off ~ ("poorly") (BE)

color, colour II *v.* 1. (D; intr., tr.) to ~ with (she ~ed the pictures (in) with a yellow crayon) 2. (N; used with an adjective) she ~ed her hair red

coloring, colouring *n.* artificial; natural; protective ~

color line, colour line *n.* ["social boundary between races of different color"] to cross the ~

colors, colours *n.* ["banner, flag"] 1. to display, show the ~ 2. to salute; troop the ~ 3. to dip; haul down, strike the ~ 4. college; regimental; school ~ ["armed forces"] 5. to be called to the ~ ["character"] 6. to reveal, show one's ~ 7. smb.'s true ~ ["misc."] 8. under false ~ ("passing oneself off as another"); to ride under the ~ of a certain stable (see also **flying colors**)

column *n.* ["series of articles"] 1. to write a ~ 2. a fashion; gossip; social, society; sports; syndicated ~ (as in a newspaper) 3. a daily; weekly ~ ["feature of a journal, magazine, or newspaper"] 4. advertising (esp. BE) ~s; correspondence (esp. BE) ~s; a personal ~ ["list of numbers"] 5. to add up a ~ ["shaft"] 6. a steering ~ (on a car) 7. (med.) the spinal, vertebral ~ (the spinal ~ supports the whole body) ["row"] 8. a tank ~ = a ~ of tanks ["misc."] 9. a fifth ~ ("enemy supporters behind one's own lines")

columnist *n.* 1. a sports; syndicated ~ 2. a fifth ~ ("an enemy supporter behind one's own lines")

coma *n.* 1. to fall, go, lapse, slip into a ~ 2. to be in a ~ 3. to come out of a ~ 4. a deep; irreversible ~

comb *n.* 1. a fine-tooth/(BE) fine-toothed ~ (usu. fig.) (we went through the documents with a fine-tooth ~) 2. she ran a ~ through her hair

combat *n.* 1. to engage in, go into ~ 2. to break off ~ 3. close, hand-to-hand; deadly, fierce, mortal ~ 4. ~ against; between; with (the enemies were locked in mortal ~ with each other) 5. in ~ (killed in ~)

combination *n.* 1. an ideal, perfect; rare; strange; winning ~ (strawberries and cream make a perfect ~ on/for a hot summer's day) 2. (ling.) a fixed, recurrent; free ~; word ~s 3. in ~ with

combine *v.* 1. (D; intr., tr.) to ~ against (to ~ forces against a common enemy) 2. (D; intr., tr.) to ~ into (they ~d all the pieces into a whole) 3. (D; intr., tr.) to ~ with (hydrogen ~s with oxygen; to ~ initiative with/and caution; to ~ business with/ and pleasure; should business and pleasure ~ (with each other)?)

combo *n.* (colloq.) a jazz ~

combustion *n.* 1. to produce ~ 2. internal; spontaneous ~

come *v.* 1. (d; intr.) to ~ across ("to meet or find by chance") (I came across an old friend – I came across him working in his garden; I came across a rare coin – I came across it just lying in the street!) 2. (d; intr.) to ~ after ("to follow") (the intermission ~s after the first act) 3. (d; intr.) to ~ after ("to pursue or attack") (the police came after him because he had come after me with a knife) 4. (d; intr.) to ~ around ("to turn") (to ~ around the corner) 5. (d; intr.) to ~ around ("to circle") (to ~ around the mountain) 6. (d; intr.) to ~ as ("to be") (it came as a surprise) 7. (d; intr.) to ~ at ("to attack") (he came at me with a knife) 8. (d; intr.) to ~ before ("to appear") (to ~ before the court) 9. (d; intr.) to ~ between ("to alienate; to separate") (to ~ between two friends) 10. (d; intr.) to ~ by, into ("to acquire") (she came by quite a bit of property; he came into a large inheritance) 11. (d; intr.) to ~ down ("to descend") (to ~ down the stairs) 12. (d; intr.) to ~ for ("to pick up") (she came for her book) 13. (d; intr.) to ~ for ("to participate") (to ~ for lunch; to ~ for a walk) 14. (d; intr.) to ~ from ("to originate") (she ~s from another country; milk ~s from cows) 15. (d; intr.) to ~ into ("to enter") (to ~ into being; to ~ into use; to ~ into focus; to ~ into the open; to ~ into view) 16. (d; intr.) to ~ of ("to result") (this is what ~s of being so careless; no good can ~ of his meddling!) 17. (d; intr.) to ~ off ("to fall off") (the knob came off the door) 18. (d; intr.) to ~ on, upon ("to meet") (to ~ upon a stranger; to ~ upon a shocking scene) 19. (d; intr.) to ~ on ("to begin"); ("to enter") (to ~ on duty; to ~ on the scene) 20. (d; intr.) to ~ out of ("to leave") (he came out of the room) 21. (d; intr.) to ~ over ("to affect") (what has come over you?) 22. (d; intr.) to ~ to ("to amount") (the bill came to twenty dollars) 23. (d; intr.) to ~ to ("to arrive at"); ("to reach") (the incident came to their attention; to ~ to grief; success came to her early; he came to his senses; it came to our knowledge that...; to ~ to terms; to ~ to the point; to ~ to a halt) 24. (D; intr.) to ~ to ("to be due") (he got what was ~ing to him = he had it ~ing to him) 25. (d; intr.) to ~ to ("to happen") (no harm came to them) 26. (d; intr.) to ~ to ("to be remembered by") (her name finally came to me) 27. (d; intr.) to ~ to ("to concern") (when it ~s to politics) 28. (d; intr.) to ~ under ("to fall") (to ~ under the jurisdiction of a court; to ~ under suspicion; to ~ under smb.'s influence; to

~ under fire) 29. (d; intr.) to ~ up ("to ascend") (to ~ up the stairs) 30. (d; intr.) to ~ with ("to be accompanied by") (the car ~s with power brakes) 31. (E) ("to occur") if it came to be known that...; to ~ to pass ("to happen") 32. (E) ("to begin") they finally came to consider me a friend 33. (G) ("to approach") the children came running 34. (P; intr.) ("to occur in a certain order") Tuesday ~s after Monday; Monday ~s before Tuesday 35. (s) to ~ true; everything went wrong at first but came right eventually; the dressing came undone; my horse came third 36. (misc.) what will ~ ("become") of him?; the years to ~; the shape of things to ~; to ~ on strong ("to try to make a very strong impression"); to ~ into a fortune ("to inherit or acquire a fortune"); the case never did ~ before the court; he had it ~ing (to him) ("he deserved his punishment, he got what was coming to him"); (BE) (colloq.) don't ~ the innocent victim with me!

come about v. (L) how did it ~ that you were late?

come across v. 1. (d; intr.) to ~ as ("to appear") (she came across as (being) hostile) 2. (colloq.) (d; intr.) to ~ with ("to make available") (he finally came across with the money)

come along v. (D; intr.) to ~ for (she came along for the ride)

come around v. (D; intr.) ("to come to, wake up"); ("to change") to ~ to (she finally came around to our viewpoint)

come away v. ("to leave") 1. (D; intr.) to ~ from (I came away from the meeting with a favorable impression) 2. (d; intr.) to ~ with (he came away with a favorable impression)

comeback n. ["recovery or return to favor"] 1. to attempt, try; make, stage a ~ 2. a successful; unsuccessful ~ ["retort"] 3. a snappy ~

come back v. 1. (d; intr.) to ~ at ("to react") (to ~ at smb. with a wisecrack) 2. (D; intr.) ("to return") to ~ from (they came back from their honeymoon last week; to ~ from the dead) 3. (D; intr.) ("to return") to ~ to (they came back to their hometown; the details are ~ing back to me)

come by v. (D; intr.) ("to drop in") to ~ for (to ~ for a drink)

come clean v. (D; intr.) ("to admit") to ~ about (he came clean about the bribe)

comedian n. an alternative (BE) ("anti-establishment"); nightclub; radio; stand-up; TV ~

comedown n. a ~ to + inf. (it's a great ~ for us to work for such a low salary)

come down v. 1. (BE) (D; intr.) to ~ from ("to leave") (to ~ from Oxford) 2. (d; intr.) to ~ from ("to originate from") (this statue has come down to us from the fifteenth century) 3. (d; intr.) to ~ on ("to treat") (the teacher came down hard on him for missing class) 4. (d; intr.) to ~ to ("to amount to") (it always ~s down to the same old thing in the end) 5. (d; intr.) to ~ with ("to catch, develop") (to ~ with a cold)

comedy n. alternative (BE); black; gentle; light; musical; romantic; situation; slapstick ~ USAGE NOTE: A romantic comedy can be shortened to a romcom and a situation comedy to a sitcom.

come forth, come forward v. (D; intr.) to ~ with ("to present") (to ~ with new evidence)

come in v. 1. (D; intr.) ("to enter") to ~ by, through (to ~ by the front door) 2. (d; intr.) to ~ for ("to be subjected to") (to ~ for criticism) 3. (D; intr.) to ~ on ("to join") (to ~ on a project) 4. (d; intr.) to ~ on ("to encounter unexpectedly") (he came in on an ugly scene) 5. (s) to ~ handy; my horse came in third

come on v. (colloq.) 1. (d; intr.) to ~ as ("to appear") (he ~s on as a radical) 2. (d; intr.) to ~ to ("to show sexual interest in smb.") (he came on to her at the office party) 3. (see also *come on strong* at **come** 36)

come out v. 1. (d; intr.) to ~ against ("to oppose") (to ~ against a proposal) 2. (d; intr.) to ~ for, in favor of ("to support") (to ~ for a proposal) 3. (d; intr.) to ~ for ("to try out for") (are you ~ing out for the team?) 4. (d; intr.) to ~ with ("to make known; to publish") (to ~ with a new book; to ~ with the truth) 5. (L) it came out that he had cheated 6. (P; intr.) ("to end up, result") to ~ on top ("to be victorious") 7. (s) the pictures came out fine 8. (misc.) to ~ in spots ("to be covered with spots as a result of illness"); they came out from behind the bushes; she meant it as a compliment, but it came out as an insult; she finally came out openly as a liberal

come over v. 1. (D; intr.) ("to come") to ~ as (she came over as a tourist) 2. (D; intr.) ("to come") to ~ from (they came over from Europe) 3. (D; intr.) to ~ to ("to approach, join") (she came over to our table; they came over to our side) 4. (D; intr.) ("to come") to ~ with (their ancestors came over with the Pilgrims) 5. (BE) (s) ("to begin to feel") to ~ (all) faint; (all) nervous

come round see **come around** ("The anaesthetic from which none ~" – Philip Larkin, "Aubade" (1977) = death)

come through v. (D; intr.) to ~ with ("to provide") (he finally came through with the money)

come up v. 1. (d; intr.) to ~ against ("to meet") (to ~ against opposition) 2. (D; intr.) to ~ for ("to be brought up for") (the question finally came up for discussion) 3. (d; intr.) to ~ to ("to reach") (the water came up to our knees; their proposal did not ~ to our standards) 4. (d; intr.) to ~ to ("to approach") ("he came up to me and introduced himself") 5. (d; intr.) to ~ with ("to produce") (she came up with a good idea) 6. (misc.) to ~ to expectations; to ~ in the world; to ~ from/through the ranks; the new project came up as a topic for discussion

comeuppance n. (colloq.) ["well-deserved misfortune"] to get one's ~

comfort n. 1. to bring, give, provide ~ 2. to derive, get ~ from 3. to find, take; seek ~ in (she finds ~ in helping others) 4. to enjoy the ~s (of life) 5. cold, little ~ 6. creature ~s; spiritual ~ 7. a ~ to (they were a great ~ to their parents) 8. a ~ to + inf. (it was a ~ (to us) to know that they were safe) 9. in ~ (to live in ~)

comfortable *adj.* 1. to feel ~ 2. to make smb. ~ 3. ~ with (are you ~ with this decision?) 4. ~ to + inf. (it is ~ to sit here in the shade = it is ~ sitting here in the shade)

comforter *n.* ["duvet"] (AE) a down ~

comforting *adj.* ~ to + inf. (it was ~ to be sure of their support)

coming *n.* 1. the Second Coming 2. with the ~ (of summer)

comma *n.* 1. to place a ~, put in a ~ 2. inverted ~s (BE; CE has *quotation marks*)

command I *n.* ["authority"] ["control"] 1. to assume, take (over) ~ 2. to exercise ~ 3. to give up, relinquish; lose one's ~ 4. firm ~ 5. ~ of, over (he assumed ~ of the regiment) 6. in ~ (of) (he was put in ~ of the task force; who will be placed in ~ (of the division)?) 7. under smb.'s ~ (we were under her ~) 8. the chain of ~ ["headquarters"] 9. the high, supreme ~ 10. a unified ~ ["order"] 11. to carry out, execute; give, issue a ~ 12. a ~ that + clause; subj. (we obeyed their ~ that prisoners be/should be treated properly) 13. at smb.'s ~ (at his ~ we opened fire) ["military unit"] 14. a combat; military ~ ["mastery"] 15. fluent, perfect ~ (fluent ~ of a language)

command II *v.* 1. (H) the captain ~ed the company to fall in 2. (L; subj.) the captain ~ed that the company fall in/should fall in

commandant *n.* (mil.) the ~ of the Marine Corps; the ~ of a military/service school

commander *n.* 1. a lieutenant; naval ~ 2. a battalion; camp; company; division; regimental; supreme ~; Commander-in-Chief 3. a ~ commands a unit

commandment *n.* (rel.) 1. to keep the ~s 2. to violate a ~ 3. the Ten Commandments

commemoration *n.* in ~ of

commence *v.* (formal) 1. (d; intr., tr.) to ~ as (she ~d her career as a dancer) 2. (d; intr., tr.) ("to begin") to ~ at (prices ~ at five dollars; they ~d the bidding at fifty dollars) 3. (D; intr., tr.) to ~ by, with (we'll ~ (the meeting) by reading/with a reading of the minutes of the last meeting) 4. (G) (mil.) ~ firing!

commend *v.* 1. to ~ highly 2. (formal) (B) I ~ him to you 3. (D; tr.) to ~ for (she ~ed him for his bravery) 4. (D; tr.) to ~ on (she ~ed him on his bravery)

commendable *adj.* ~ to + inf. (it is ~ for/of smb. to help others)

commendation *n.* 1. to receive a ~ 2. to present a ~ 3. a ~ for (a ~ for bravery)

commensurable *adj.* ~ with

commensurate *adj.* ~ to, with (a reward ~ with the results achieved)

comment I *n.* ["observation"] ["remark"] 1. to have, make, pass a ~ (on); to have a ~ to make (on); to

invite, solicit, welcome a ~ (on) (the government would welcome ~s on its policies from the public) 2. (an) appropriate, fair, fitting; favorable; incisive; perceptive, shrewd; revealing ~ 3. a casual; passing ~ 4. an ironic, wry ~ 5. a cryptic; inappropriate; off-the-record ~ 6. a caustic, critical, derogatory, sarcastic, scathing, unfavorable; nasty, vicious; provocative; trenchant ~ 7. (a) ~ about, on (there was no ~ about the incident in the press) 8. (a) ~ from (there was no ~ from the other party) 9. a ~ that + clause (her ~ that she was very happy to be a guest in their country was greeted with delight) 10. without further ~; no ~! ["gossip"] ["talk"] 11. to arouse, cause, evoke ~ 12. considerable; critical, scathing; favorable; unfavorable ~ (the incident evoked considerable ~ in the capitals of Europe)

comment II *v.* 1. (D; intr.) to ~ about, on 2. (L) she ~ed that she was very happy to be a guest in their country

commentary *n.* 1. to give a ~ 2. a blow-by-blow, play-by-play, running; political ~ 3. a ~ on 4. (misc.) a sad ~ (as on the world situation) (international terrorism is a sad ~ on the world situation)

commentator *n.* 1. a news; radio; sports; TV ~ 2. a ~ on (a ~ on political affairs)

commerce *n.* 1. to carry on, engage in ~ 2. to develop, expand ~ 3. international; interstate; overseas ~ 4. ~ among; between; with (to carry on ~ with the countries of Central America) 5. (misc.) a Chamber of Commerce

commercial *n.* ["paid spoken advertisement"] a radio; TV ~

commiserate *v.* (d; intr.) to ~ on; with (I ~d with them on their misfortune)

commissar *n.* a political ~

commission I *n.* ["committee"] ["council"] 1. to appoint, establish, set up a ~ 2. to chair a ~ 3. to disband a ~ 4. a fact-finding; investigating; joint; planning; roving ~ 5. (misc.) (GB) a Royal Commission ["certificate conferring rank"] (usu. mil.) 6. to award, confer a ~ 7. to earn, win a (battlefield) ~ 8. to resign one's ~ 9. a battlefield ~ ["fee"] 10. to charge; pay a ~ 11. to get, earn a ~ 12. to deduct; divide a ~ 13. a ~ for, on 14. in; on ~ (to work on ~ and earn a lot in ~) ["operating condition"] 15. to be; go out of ~ 16. to put out of ~ (the storm put all power lines out of ~) ["task"] (formal) 17. to accept, get, receive a ~ 18. to execute a ~ 19. a ~ to + inf. (a ~ to serve)

commission II *v.* 1. (D; tr.) to ~ as (she was ~ed as a captain) 2. (H) she ~ed an artist to paint her portrait 3. (N; used with a noun) she was ~ed a captain

commissioner *n.* 1. a high ~ for (the high ~ for occupied territories) 2. a fire; health; police; water ~ 3. a county; township ~ 4. the Canadian, Ghanaian, etc. High Commissioners in London USAGE NOTE: Commonwealth countries exchange High Commissioners with one another and Ambassadors with other countries.

commit v. 1. (D; refl.) ("to devote") to ~ to (to ~ oneself to a cause) 2. (D; tr.) ("to assign") to ~ to (to ~ funds to a project) 3. (D; tr.) ("to confine") to ~ to (to ~ smb. to a mental hospital; ~ted to prison) 4. (d; tr.) ("to place") (to ~ a child to a relative's care; to ~ a poem to memory; to ~ one's thoughts to paper) 5. (H; usu. refl.; no passive) (AE) ("to pledge") he ~ted himself to support her parents 6. (J; usu. refl.) ("to pledge") he ~ted himself to supporting her parents

commitment n. ["promise"] 1. to have; make a ~ 2. to affirm, honor, meet a ~ 3. a firm; prior ~ 4. a ~ to + inf. (he made a ~ to support her parents) 5. a ~ that + clause (he made a ~ that he would support her parents) ["devotion"] 6. to demonstrate, display, show ~ 7. an all-out, total; deep, passionate ~ 8. (a) ~ to (~ to a cause) (he has always displayed a high level of ~ to his principles)

committed adj. 1. deeply, firmly, totally, whole-heartedly ~ 2. ~ to (~ to his principles) 3. ~ to + inf. (he is ~ to support her parents (AE); or (CE), more usu.: he is ~ to supporting her parents)

committee n. 1. to appoint, establish, form, orga-nize, set up a ~ 2. to chair; sit on a ~ 3. to disband; leave, resign from a ~ 4. an ad-hoc; advisory; budget; congressional; credentials; executive; finance; grievance; legislative; nominating; plan-ning; program; select; special; standing; steering; strike; watchdog; ways-and-means ~; a ~ of the whole 5. a ~ on (a ~ on problems of the elderly) 6. on a ~ (who will be serving on the ~ when it finally meets?) 7. (misc.) to report a bill out of ~

commodity n. 1. to trade in ~ties 2. a basic; farm; marketable; staple ~

common I adj. 1. pretty, quite; very ~ 2. (cannot stand alone after a noun) ~ to (a heritage ~ to both our peoples) 3. ~ to + inf. (it is quite ~ for the trains to be late; it is ~ to read of strikes; it is pretty ~ to find people here who know several languages)

common II n. 1. in ~ with 2. to have in ~ (both our peoples have a lot in ~) 3. (misc.) the (House of) Commons

commonplace I adj. ~ to + inf. (it was ~ for them to travel abroad)

commonplace II n. 1. to state a ~ 2. to exchange ~s (about; with) 3. a ~ to + inf. (it's a ~ to say that people should work hard)

common sense n. 1. to apply, exercise, show, use; have ~ 2. the ~ to + inf. (he had the ~ to remain silent) 3. (misc.) good; plain ~ (just plain good old ~)

commotion n. 1. to cause, create, make, raise a ~ 2. a great ~ 3. a ~ dies down, subsides 4. a ~ about, over (they escaped in the ~ about the news) 5. in a state of ~

commune v. (d; intr.) to ~ with (to ~ with nature)

communicate v. 1. to ~ clearly; officially; unof-ficially 2. to ~ on line 3. (B) she tried to ~ her thoughts to her children 4. (D; intr.) to ~ by, in,

through (to ~ by/in code; to ~ through signals) 5. (D; intr.) to ~ with (to ~ with one's parents)

communication n. ["message"] 1. to address, direct, send (all) ~s (to a certain place) 2. to receive a ~ 3. a direct; official; personal; privileged ("confiden-tial") ~ 4. a ~ from; to ["act, means of communicat-ing"] 5. to establish; improve ~ 6. to cut off ~s 7. mass ~s 8. online; radio; two-way ~ 9. ~ between; with (to establish ~ with the rescue team; to cut off all ~s with the mainland) 10. in ~ (with) (she has been in ~ with her family) 11. (misc.) a means of ~; open lines of ~; a breakdown in ~

communion n. ["sharing"] 1. in ~ (with) ["a Christian sacrament, the Eucharist"] 2. to administer, give ~ 3. to receive; take ~ 4. Holy Communion (how many people were at Holy Communion today?) 5. smb.'s First Communion

communiqué n. 1. to issue a ~ 2. a joint ~ 3. an official ~ 4. a ~ about, on (they issued a ~ on the results of the conference)

communist n. an avowed; card-carrying ~

community n. ["group with common interests"] 1. an (the) academic, college, university; business; eth-nic; gay; intelligence ~; the international ~; a (the) religious; scientific ~ 2. to divide, polarize, split; unite a ~ ["group – who live together"] 3. to establish, found, set up; join a ~ 4. to disband, dissolve; leave a ~ 5. a closed; close-knit ~ 6. a life-care (AE); retirement ~ 7. (AE) a bedroom ~ (BE has *dormitory town*) 8. (misc.) a pillar of the ~

commute I n. (colloq.) ["ride to work"] 1. an easy; long ~ 2. a ~ from; to

commute II v. 1. (D; intr.) ("to travel regularly") to ~ between; from; to (to ~ between two cities; to ~ from the suburbs to the city) 2. (D; tr.) ("to change") to ~ to (the Governor ~d his death sen-tence to life imprisonment)

commuter n. 1. a suburban ~ 2. a ~ between; from; to

compact n. (formal) ["agreement"] 1. to make a ~ with 2. a ~ between; with 3. a ~ to + inf. (we made a ~ not to discuss the matter further)

companion n. 1. smb.'s boon; close, constant, in-separable ~ 2. smb.'s life; traveling ~ 3. a ~ for, to (she worked as a ~ to an elderly woman)

company n. ["military unit consisting of several pla-toons"] 1. to command a ~ (a captain commands a ~) 2. to deploy; form a ~ 3. a cannon; head-quarters; infantry ~ ["companionship"] 4. to keep (smb.) ~; to seek smb.'s ~ 5. to part ~ with 6. good, pleasant ~ 7. (good) ~ for (the children were good ~ for us) ["guests"] 8. to expect; have; invite ~ (for) (we enjoy having ~; ~'s coming tonight!; (on a formal invitation) Professor and Mrs. Jones request the pleasure of your ~ for dinner tonight) ["associ-ates"] ["association"] ["gathering of people"] 9. to keep ~ with 10. mixed ~ (don't use that word in mixed ~!) 11. (colloq.) bad, fast ~ ("reckless, wild associ-ates") (he runs around in/with fast ~) 12. present

~ ("those present") (present ~ excepted) 13. in ~ (to behave appropriately in ~; in ~ with others) ["firm; organization"] 14. to manage, operate, run a ~ 15. to establish, form a ~ 16. a finance; holding; insurance; investment; joint-stock; multinational, transnational; private equity; pharmaceutical; reputable; shipping; transport (esp. BE), transportation (esp. AE) ~ 17. a ballet; dance; opera; repertory (esp. BE), stock (AE); theatrical ~ (how many people are there in the ballet ~?) 18. (BE) a limited; public limited ~ (AE prefers *corporation*) 19. a ~ fails, goes bankrupt ["fire-fighting unit"] (esp. AE) 20. an engine, hose; ladder ~ USAGE NOTE: "ABC Ltd" stands for 'ABC Limited'; "ABC plc" stands for 'ABC public limited company.'

comparable *adj.* ~ to, with

compare I *n.* beyond; without ~

compare II *v.* 1. to ~ advantageously, favorably; unfavorably 2. (d; intr.) to ~ to, with (these roads cannot ~ with ours) 3. (d; tr.) to ~ to, with (how would you ~ this wine with a good French wine?) USAGE NOTE: The construction *to compare x to y* typically means "to claim a similarity between x and y" (to compare New York to a beehive). The construction *to compare x with/and y* typically means "to discuss similarities and differences between x and y" (to compare New York with/and London), as does the construction *x compares/ cannot compare with y* ("And tell me what street compares with Mott Street in July?" – Lorenz Hart (1895–1943), "Manhattan").

comparison *n.* 1. to draw, make a ~ ("on what basis can you make a ~ between them?" "actually, there are several points of ~ between them!") 2. to bear, stand ~ 3. to defy ~ 4. a favorable; invidious; unfavorable ~ 5. a ~ between; to, with (there is no ~ between them; she made a ~ of our literature to/with theirs; I would like to draw a ~ between recent events and those of the 1930s) 6. beyond ~ 7. by ~ (with) (her works suffer by ~ (with those of other writers)) 8. in ~ to (her works suffer in ~ to those of other writers) USAGE NOTE: Note that there can be a difference in prepositions between *a comparison of New York to/and a beehive* and *a comparison of New York with/and London.* See the Usage Note for **compare II**. The preposition *between* can be used with *and* in both meanings – *a comparison between New York and a beehive* and *a comparison between New York and London.*

compartment *n.* 1. a glove ~ 2. a first-class; second-class; sleeping ~ 3. a watertight ~ 4. (in a refrigerator) a freezer; ice ~ 5. in a ~

compartmentalize *v.* (D; tr.) to ~ into

compass *n.* ["device for navigation"] 1. to box the ~ 2. to read a ~ 3. a magnetic; mariner's ~ (see also *the cardinal points of the compass* at **point I** 49) ["limit, range"] 4. beyond; within the ~ (beyond the ~ of the court's jurisdiction)

compassion *n.* 1. to arouse ~ 2. to demonstrate,

display, show; feel, have ~ 3. deep, great, profound, strong ~ 4. ~ for, towards 5. out of, with ~ (to act out of ~)

compassionate *adj.* ~ towards

compatibility *n.* ~ between, with

compatible *adj.* 1. mutually, perfectly ~ 2. ~ with

compel *v.* (H) to ~ smb. to do smt.

compelled *adj.* ~ to + inf. (she felt ~ to offer an apology)

compensate *v.* 1. (d; intr.) ("to make up for") to ~ for (I cannot ~ for my past failings) 2. (D; tr.) ("to reimburse") to ~ for (to ~ smb. for damages)

compensation *n.* 1. to authorize, award, grant; make, pay; offer ~ 2. to deny, refuse ~ 3. to claim; seek ~ 4. to get, obtain, receive ~ 5. adequate, appropriate ~ 6. workmen's (AE) ~ (see also **unemployment compensation**) 7. ~ for (by way of ~ for the damage suffered) 8. as, in ~ for (she received a cash award as/in ~ for the lost suitcase)

compete *v.* 1. (d; intr.) to ~ against, with (that store ~s with us (for customers)) 2. (D; intr.) to ~ for (to ~ for customers) 3. (D; intr.) to ~ in (to ~ in a contest) 4. (misc.) they are ~ting (in order) to attract customers; college chums ~ting (in order) to see who can drink the most beer

competence *n.* ["ability"] 1. to acquire, gain ~ 2. (ling.) communicative; linguistic ~ 3. ~ as (her ~ as an interpreter is well known) 4. ~ for (does she have the necessary ~ for the position?) 5. ~ at, in (~ in English; ~ at/in speaking English) 6. the ~ to + inf. (do they have the ~ to cope with the job of interpreter?) ["jurisdiction"] (legal) 7. beyond, outside; within the ~ (the matter lay within the ~ of the court)

competent *adj.* 1. highly; very ~ 2. ~ as (he is ~ as a teacher) 3. ~ at, in (he is ~ at teaching; he is ~ in English) 4. ~ to + inf. (he is ~ to teach history; ~ to stand trial)

competition *n.* ["rivalry"] ["opposition"] 1. to come up against ~, to face ~ 2. to offer, provide ~ 3. to undercut, undersell the ~ 4. bitter, close, fierce, formidable, heavy, intense, keen, stiff, strong, tough; cutthroat, unfair, unscrupulous ~ 5. fair; free, unfettered; healthy ~ 6. ~ among, between; with (stiff ~ among/between several firms) 7. ~ for (~ for control of the market) 8. ~ to + inf. (there was bitter ~ to control the market) 9. in ~ with ["contest"] ["match"] 10. to hold, stage a ~ 11. to enter; lose; win a ~ 12. a gymnastics; high-diving; speed-skating; violin ~ 13. (an) open ~ 14. a ~ among, between; for (a ~ for the championship) 15. a ~ to + inf. (a ~ between college chums to see who can drink the most beer)

competitive *adj.* 1. fiercely, highly, keenly, very ~ 2. ~ with (to be ~ with the best)

competitor *n.* a formidable, keen, strong; successful; unscrupulous; unsuccessful ~

compilation *n.* 1. to do, make a ~ 2. a ~ from (various sources)

compile *v.* (D; tr.) to ~ from (to ~ a dictionary from various sources)

complacency *n.* ~ about; (AE) towards

complacent *adj.* 1. to become, get, grow ~ 2. ~ about; (AE) towards

complain *v.* 1. to ~ bitterly, loudly, vociferously; constantly 2. (D; intr.) to ~ about, of; to (I ~ed to the manager about the service; she ~ed of indigestion) 3. (L; to) she ~ed (to the manager) that the service was bad

complainer *n.* a chronic ~

complaint *n.* 1. to bring, file, lodge, make, register, swear out a ~ 2. to express, voice; have a ~ 3. to get, receive; accept, act on, respond to a ~ 4. to disregard, ignore; reject a ~ 5. a bitter, loud, vociferous; common, frequent ~ 6. a formal, official; justified; legitimate ~ 7. a frivolous; unjustified ~ 8. a ~ about; with (she filed a ~ about the service with the manager) 9. a ~ against (they lodged a ~ against me) 10. a ~ to (our ~ to the dean was ignored) 11. a ~ that + clause (the manager rejected her ~ that the service was bad) 12. (misc.) grounds for/(a) cause for ~; a flood of ~s

complement *n.* 1. a full; perfect ~ 2. (naval) a ship's ~ ("crew") 3. (grammar) a predicate ~ 4. a ~ to (white wine is/makes a perfect ~ to fish)

complementary *adj.* ~ to

complete I *adj.* ~ with (a turkey dinner ~ with all the trimmings)

complete II *v.* (G) she has just ~d writing her second novel

completion *n.* 1. to approach, near ~ 2. on ~ of (on ~ of this dictionary we will need a rest)

complex *n.* ["bad feelings or repressed desires"] 1. to have, suffer from a ~ (about) 2. to give smb. a ~ (about) 3. an Electra; Oedipus ~ 4. a guilt; persecution ~ 5. an inferiority; superiority ~ ["large system"] 6. the military-industrial ~ 7. an apartment (AE); housing; shopping; sports ~

complexion *n.* ["skin, esp. on smb.'s face"] 1. a clear; dark; fair; flawless; florid, ruddy; good; healthy; light, pale; pasty; sallow; smooth ~ ["aspect"] 2. to put a new and more favorable ~ on smt. that had previously taken on an unfavorable ~ 3. a political ~ (the political ~ of the new administration)

complexity *n.* of (great) ~ (a problem of great ~ = a problem of a high degree of ~)

compliance *n.* 1. ~ with (~ with the law) 2. in ~ with (in ~ with regulations)

complication *n.* 1. to cause ~s 2. to avoid; prevent ~s (to prevent the ~s of pregnancy) 3. ~s arise, occur, (esp. AE) set in

complicity *n.* 1. ~ between; with 2. ~ in (~ between gangsters in a crime)

compliment I *n.* ["praise"] 1. to pay smb. a ~ 2. to lavish, shower ~s on 3. to return a ~ 4. to accept a ~; to take smt. as a ~ 5. to angle for, fish for ~s 6. to bandy ~s 7. a backhanded, dubious, left-handed;

nice, pretty; sincere ~ 8. a ~ on; to (she paid him a nice ~ on his success; her remarks were meant as a ~ to him on his success = (AE) her remarks were meant as a ~ to his success)

compliment II *v.* (D; tr.) to ~ on (I ~ed him on his performance)

complimentary *adj.* 1. highly ~ 2. ~ about

compliments *n.* ["greetings"] 1. to convey, present, send one's/smb.'s ~ 2. (misc.) with the author's ~; with the ~ of the management; my ~ to the chef

comply *v.* (D; intr.) to ~ with (to ~ with the law; to ~ with smb.'s request)

component *n.* a basic, essential, key, main, principal ~

comport *v.* (formal) (P; refl.) to ~ oneself with dignity; to ~ oneself well

compose *v.* 1. (D; tr.) to ~ for (to ~ an ode for an emperor; to ~ a symphony for a special concert) 2. (D; tr.) to ~ an ode to an emperor (= 'to compose an ode in honor of an emperor')

composed *adj.* ["consisting"] (cannot stand alone) ~ of (the team was ~ entirely of seasoned players) (see the Usage Note for **comprised**)

composer *n.* a classical; major; minor; popular ~

composition *n.* ["essay"] 1. to do, write a ~ (on) ["piece of music"] 2. to perform, play a ~ (they performed a ~ by Mozart for violin and piano)

composure *n.* 1. to keep, retain; recover, regain one's ~ (despite the insult he managed to retain his ~ unruffled) 2. to lose one's ~ 3. to ruffle smb.'s ~ 4. with great ~

compound I *n.* ["mixture"] a chemical; organic ~

compound II *n.* ["enclosure"] an embassy; factory; prison ~

comprehend *v.* 1. (K) can you ~ his behaving like that? 2. (L) she did not ~ that he would not return 3. (Q) she could not ~ why he would not return USAGE NOTE: In the meaning 'understand,' *comprehend* is not typically used in simple assertions.

comprehensible *adj.* 1. ~ to 2. (misc.) it is not ~ to me why they refused to come

comprehension *n.* 1. to defy, elude ~ 2. listening; reading ~ 3. beyond ~ 4. (misc.) she gaped at me with (a) dawning ~ but he just stared at me with a total lack of ~.

comprehensives *n.* ["comprehensive examination"] (AE) to take one's ~

compress I *n.* 1. to apply a ~ to 2. a cold; dry; hot; wet ~

compress II *v.* (D; tr.) to ~ into (to ~ a whole paragraph into two sentences)

comprised *adj.* ["consisting"] (cannot stand alone) ~ of USAGE NOTE: Some purists prefer *composed of* to *comprised of.*

compromise I *n.* 1. to agree (BE), agree on, agree to, arrive at, come to, reach, work out a ~ 2. to reject a ~ 3. an acceptable, reasonable ~ 4. a ~ between; on; with (we reached a ~ with them on the payment)

compromise II v. (D; intr.) to ~ on, over; with (they ~d on certain items with us)

comptroller n. the Comptroller General (AE)

compulsion n. 1. to feel a ~ 2. (a) moral ~ 3. a ~ to + inf. (he felt no ~ to do it) 4. under ~ (to give in under ~)

compulsory adj. 1. ~ for 2. ~ to + inf. (it was ~ for voters to register)

compunction n. 1. to feel, have; show ~ 2. ~ about (she felt no ~ about making us wait) 3. without ~ (he violated the law without the slightest ~)

computer n. 1. to boot up; reboot a ~ 2. to operate, use a ~ 3. to switch on, turn on a ~ 4. to switch off, turn off a ~ 5. to program a ~ 6. an analog; desktop; digital; electronic; general-purpose; handheld; home; laptop; mainframe ~; microcomputer; minicomputer; parallel; personal; serial ~ 7. the ~ is down ("the computer is not functioning") 8. the ~ is up ("the computer is functioning") 9. a ~ bombs (AE), crashes; freezes up 10. by ~ (the book was typeset by ~) 11. in a ~ (to store data in a ~) 12. on a ~ (to run a program on a ~)

comrade n. 1. a fallen ~ 2. a ~ in arms 3. an old ~

con v. (colloq.) ("to trick") 1. (D; tr.) to ~ into (to ~ smb. into doing smt.) 2. (D; tr.) to ~ out of (he ~ned me out of my money)

conceal v. 1. (D; tr.) to ~ from 2. (Q) they tried to ~ (from us) how they did it

concede v. 1. (B) he finally ~d the election to his opponent 2. (L; to) she reluctantly ~d (to us) that she had been mistaken

conceded adj. (cannot stand alone) ~ to + inf. (this painting is ~ to be her best work)

conceit n. insufferable, overwhelming ~

conceivable adj. 1. barely, hardly; just (about) ~ 2. ~ that + clause (it is just about ~ that they knew of it beforehand)

conceive v. 1. (d; intr.) to ~ of (can you ~ of such cruelty?) 2. (L) I could not ~ that he would do such a thing 3. (Q) I could not ~ how he could have done that 4. (misc.) to ~ of smb./smt. as smb./smt. else (to ~ of life as a struggle)

concentrate v. 1. to ~ hard 2. (D; intr., tr.) to ~ in (to ~ all the government departments in the capital) 3. (D; intr., tr.) to ~ on (to ~ all our efforts on solving the problem; to ~ hard on solving the problem)

concentration n. 1. to disrupt, disturb smb.'s ~ 2. deep, intense ~ 3. ~ in (the ~ of all government departments in the capital) 4. ~ on 5. in ~ (in deep ~) 6. (misc.) smb.'s powers of ~

concept n. 1. to develop; formulate, frame a ~ 2. to grasp, understand a ~ 3. an abstract ~ 4. the ~ of (the ~ of God) 5. the ~ that + clause (the ~ that trade lessens international tensions is valid)

conception n. ["concept"] 1. to have a ~ (you have no ~ of the problems we must face) 2. a clear; vague ~ 3. the ~ that + clause (the ~ that the superpowers must fight is dangerous) ["becoming pregnant or being conceived"] 4. to prevent ~ 5. at ~ (at the moment of ~)

conceptualize v. (d; tr.) to ~ as (the author ~d the war as a crusade)

concern I n. ["interest"] ["apprehension"] 1. to arouse, cause, give ~ 2. to express, voice; show ~ 3. to feel; share ~ 4. (a) deep, grave, serious; major; paramount; primary ~ (there is grave ~ about the national debt) 5. (a) growing; overriding; widespread ~ 6. (a) common; particular ~ (we have a common ~ over the problems of pollution) 7. (a) national ~ 8. (a) public ~ 9. considerable, utmost ~ (this is a matter of utmost ~ to all of us; they have expressed considerable ~ about the growing crime rate) 10. an object of ~ 11. ~ about, for, over, with (~ about debts; ~ for the children; ~ over the future) 12. ~ to + inf. (~ to know the truth) 13. ~ that + clause (to express ~ that they might fail) 14. ~ of ~ to (the matter was of deep ~ to us; climate change seems of no ~ to him) 15. in one's ~ (in their ~ over the debt) 16. out of ~ (she did it out of ~ for her children) ["firm"] 17. to manage a ~ 18. (misc.) a going ("successful") ~

concern II v. 1. (d; refl.) to ~ oneself about, over, with (she ~ed herself with the problem of illiteracy) 2. (R) it ~s her that there is still so much illiteracy 3. (misc.) to whom it may ~

concerned adj. 1. deeply, gravely, greatly; very ~ 2. ~ about, for, over; with (~ about safety) 3. (esp. BE) ~ to + inf. (~ to know your decision) 4. ~ that + clause (she is ~ that there is still so much illiteracy; we are ~ that they might have missed the train) 5. (misc.) as far as I'm ~ USAGE NOTE: The phrases *concerned about*, *concerned over*, and, less frequently, *concerned for* mean "worried about" (concerned about your safety). The phrase *concerned with* means "interested in" (concerned with establishing the truth).

concert n. ["musical program"] 1. to attend, go to; give, hold, stage a ~ 2. to cancel a ~ 3. a band; benefit, charity; chamber-music; live; orchestral; pop; (BE) prom, promenade; rock; subscription ~ (to hold a series of benefit ~s) (see also *live in concert* at **live I** adv.) 4. a ~ by (to attend a ~ by the Berlin Philharmonic) 5. a ~ of (a ~ of Mozart piano concertos) 6. at a ~ (we met at a ~ to raise money for charity) ["harmony, agreement"] 7. in ~ (with) ("together") (to work in ~; voices raised in ~)

concerto n. 1. to compose, write a ~ 2. to perform, play a ~ 3. a cello; clarinet; piano; violin ~ 4. a ~ for (a ~ for piano and orchestra)

concession n. ["yielding"] 1. to grant, make a ~ 2. a ~ on, to (to make no ~s on foreign policy to the opposition) ["right to conduct business"] 3. to grant; receive a ~ 4. a parking; refreshment ~ 5. a ~ to + inf. (their firm received a ~ to prospect for oil) ["discount"] (BE) 6. a ~ for (are there any ~s for Old-Age Pensioners?)

conclave n. ["meeting"] a party ~

conclude v. 1. (d; intr., tr.) to ~ by, with (she ~d the meeting by asking us to pray, she ~d the meeting with a prayer) 2. (D; tr.) to ~ from (what did they ~ from the evidence?) 3. (L) from the evidence, they ~d that war was inevitable

conclusion *n.* 1. to arrive at, come to, draw, reach a ~ 2. to jump, leap to a ~; point to a ~ 3. to bring to a ~ 4. a correct; logical; reasonable, tenable, valid ~ 5. a foregone; inescapable, inevitable ~ 6. an erroneous, false, invalid, wrong; hasty ~ 7. a ~ that + clause (the evidence pointed to the inescapable ~ that war was inevitable) 8. at the ~ (at the ~ of the meeting she asked us to pray) 9. in ~ (in ~, I repeat that war is wrong)

concoction *n.* (colloq.) to whip up a ~

concomitant *adj.* (formal) ~ with

concord *n.* (formal) in ~ (with)

concordance *n.* ["list of words"] 1. to compile a ~ 2. a ~ to ["harmony"] 3. in ~ with

concordat *n.* (rel.) 1. to conclude, draw up a ~ 2. a ~ between; with

concrete *n.* 1. to pour ~ 2. to set smt. in ~ (also fig.) (don't worry: these rules are not set in ~!) 3. prestressed; ready-mix; reinforced ~ 4. ~ sets 5. a slab of ~

concubine *n.* 1. to have, keep a ~ 2. by one's ~ (he had many children by his ~s)

concur *v.* (formal) ("to agree") 1. to ~ completely, fully, wholeheartedly 2. (D; intr.) to ~ in (to ~ with smb. in supporting a cause) 3. (D; intr.) to ~ with (to ~ with an opinion; to ~ with smb.) 4. (L) we ~ with them/with their opinion that the cause should be supported

concurrence *n.* 1. complete, full, unanimous ~ 2. ~ in 3. in ~ with 4. with the ~ of

concurrent *adj.* ~ with

concussion *n.* 1. to get, have, receive, sustain a ~ 2. a mild; severe; slight ~

condemn *v.* 1. to ~ bitterly, harshly, roundly, strongly; unfairly, unjustly 2. (D; tr.) to ~ as (they were ~ed as traitors) 3. (D; tr.) to ~ for (he was ~ed for stealing a horse) 4. (D; tr.) to ~ to (to ~ smb. to death; ~ed to hard labor) 5. (H) he was ~ed to die

condemnation *n.* 1. to issue a ~ 2. (a) bitter, harsh, scathing, strong; sweeping, universal; unfair, unjust ~ (strong ~ of the measure came from all parties)

condense *v.* (D; tr.) to ~ from; into (you must ~ your paper from a long treatise into a few paragraphs)

condescend *v.* (formal) 1. (d; intr.) to ~ to (don't ~ to your workers: they're people, too!) 2. (E) to ~ to mingle with the workers

condescending *adj.* ~ to, towards (~ to one's employees)

condition I *n.* ["requirement"] 1. to attach, impose, lay down, set (down); state, stipulate a ~ 2. to accept a ~ 3. to fulfill, meet, satisfy; breach a ~ 4. a basic, essential, necessary; sufficient ~ (poverty may be a necessary ~ for crime, but is it a sufficient ~?) 5. a strict ~ 6. a ~ for; on (they imposed strict ~s on the use of the car) 7. on ~ that + clause; subj.

(she will join us on ~ that you also be there = (esp. BE) she will join us on ~ that you are also there; she will join us on one ~: that you also be/(esp. BE) also are there) (see also *terms and conditions* at **terms**) ["state of repair"] 8. (a) bad, poor, terrible ~ 9. (an) excellent, good, mint, peak, perfect, tip-top ~ 10. operating, running ~ 11. in ~ (our house is in good ~; his car is in running ~; the roads are in terrible ~) ["good health"]["fitness"] 12. to get into ~ 13. in ~; out of ~ (he never exercises and is out of ~) ["state of health"] 14. excellent; good ~ 15. fair, satisfactory; stable ~ 16. bad, critical, poor; serious; weakened ~ 17. ~ to + inf. (she is in no ~ to drive) 18. in ~ (the patient was in critical ~) ["ailment"] 19. an acute; chronic; degenerative; disabling; untreatable ~ 20. a heart; lung; skin ~ ["misc."] 21. to endure/ameliorate the human ~ (see also **conditions**)

condition II *v.* 1. (D; refl.) to ~ for 2. (formal) (D; tr.) to ~ on 3. (D; tr.) to ~ to (~ed to life in the jungle) 4. (H) to ~ smb. to do smt.

conditional *adj.* ~ on

conditioned *adj.* ~ to + inf. (the dog was ~ to attack at a certain signal)

conditioner *n.* a hair; skin ~

conditions *n.* ["circumstances"] 1. favorable; normal; optimal; stable ~ 2. abnormal; adverse; appalling; deplorable, pitiful, squalid; difficult; primitive; repressive; unfavorable; unstable ~ 3. driving; housing; living; sanitary; working ~ 4. economic; political; social ~ 5. weather ~ (if weather ~ permit) 6. in ~ (they live in squalid ~) 7. under ~ (to work under difficult ~)

condole *v.* (BE) to ~ with smb. (on smt.) (to ~ with smb. on the death of a parent)

condolences *n.* 1. to convey, extend, express, offer send ~ 2. to accept ~ 3. heartfelt, sincere ~ 4. ~ on (I conveyed our sincere ~ to them on the death of their mother)

condom *n.* to put on; remove, take off; unroll; use, wear a ~

condone *v.* 1. (G) I don't/can't ~ coming late to work 2. (K) I don't/can't ~ his coming late to work

conducive *adj.* (cannot stand alone) ~ to (exercise is ~ to good health)

conduct I *n.* 1. appropriate; chivalrous; ethical; irreproachable; professional; proper ~ 2. disorderly; improper; inappropriate, unbecoming; unethical; unprofessional ~ 3. (mil.) bad; dishonorable (AE) good ~; ~ unbecoming an officer 4. (misc.) a code of ~

conduct II *v.* 1. (d; refl.) to ~ like (he ~ed himself like a good soldier) 2. (P; refl.) to ~ oneself with dignity 3. (formal) (P; tr.) she was ~ed into the conference room; they ~ed us through the museum

conductor *n.* ["smt. that conducts"] 1. a lightning ~ ["person who collects fares"] (BE) 2. a bus ~ ["director"] 3. a guest; orchestra ~

cone n. 1. an ice-cream ~ 2. a fir; pine ~
confederacy n. 1. to enter, join; form a ~ 2. a ~
among, between; with
confederate v. (D; intr.) to ~ with
confederation n. 1. to enter, join; form a ~ 2. a
loose, weak ~ 3. a ~ breaks up, dissolves; forms 4.
a ~ among, between; with 5. in a ~
confer v. 1. (D; intr.) ("to converse") to ~ about;
with (we will ~ with them about this matter) 2. (D;
tr.) ("to bestow") to ~ on (to ~ an award on smb.)
conference n. 1. to give, have, hold; schedule; stage
a ~ 2. to convene, organize a ~ 3. to broadcast;
televise a ~ 4. to attend a ~ (we attended a ~ that
took place in July and met in a big hotel) 5. an annual ~ 6. an international ~ 7. a press; peace; staff
(AE); summit ~ (see also **news conference**) 8. a ~
between 9. a ~ on (to hold a ~ on disarmament) 10.
at a ~ (you'll see her at the press ~) 11. in ~ (he is
in ~ and cannot come to the telephone)
confess v. 1. to ~ frankly, honestly; publicly; vol-
untarily, willingly 2. (B) he ~ed his crime to the
police 3. (D; intr.) to ~ to (to ~ to a crime; to ~ to
the police; he ~ed to cheating on the exam; he ~ed
to having been bored by the opera) 4. (L; to) he
~ed (to the police) that he had committed a crime;
I must ~ I was bored by the opera
confession n. 1. to make; sign a ~ 2. to extort, extract, force a ~ from; to beat a ~ out of (the police
beat a ~ out of him) 3. to repudiate, retract, take
back, withdraw a ~ 4. a deathbed; forced; full;
public; voluntary ~ 5. (rel.) to hear smb.'s ~ 6.
(rel.) to go to ~ 7. a ~ that + clause (he made a ~ to
the police that he had committed a crime) 8. (misc.)
I have a ~ to make: I was bored by the opera!
confetti n. to sprinkle, throw ~
confide v. 1. (B) he ~d his secret to us 2. (d; intr.) to
~ in (she ~s in her sister) 3. (L; to) she ~d (to us)
that she was about to retire
confidence n. ["trust"] ["reliance"] 1. to enjoy, have;
gain, win smb.'s ~ 2. to inspire, instill ~ in smb. 3.
to have; place one's ~ in smb. 4. to take smb. into
one's ~ 5. to shake; undermine smb.'s ~ 6. to betray
smb.'s ~ 7. absolute, complete, every, full, implicit,
perfect, supreme ~ (I have absolute ~ in her ability)
8. public ~ 9. ~ in (my ~ in him was shaken) 10.
(misc.) your ~ in her is misplaced; a vote of ~/of
no ~ ["secrecy"] ["secret"] 11. to exchange ~s 12. to
violate a ~ 13. strict ~ 14. in ~ (she told it to me
in (the) strictest ~) ["belief in one's own ability"] ["firm
belief"] 15. to express; gain; have ~ 16. to exude,
ooze, radiate ~ (he just oozed ~ but his ~ evaporated
in the face of criticism) 17. to bolster, boost smb.'s
~ (she lost ~ in her ability to do the job but got back
the ~ she lacked when a timely compliment boosted
it) 18. to shake; undermine smb.'s ~ 19. buoyant,
unbounded ~ 20. the ~ to + inf. (he doesn't have
enough ~ to proceed on his own) 21. ~ that + clause
(nothing could shake her ~ that she would succeed)
22. (misc.) a crisis of ~ (see also **self-confidence**)

confident adj. 1. supremely, very ~ 2. ~ about, in 3.
~ of (~ of success) 4. ~ that + clause (she was ~ that
she would succeed)
confidential adj. 1. highly, strictly ~ 2. to keep
smt. ~
confidentiality n. 1. to maintain ~ 2. to violate ~
3. strict ~
confine v. 1. (D; refl., tr.) to ~ to (~d to bed; ~ to a
wheelchair; ~d to quarters; the lecturer ~d herself
to one topic; ~ yourself to the facts; please ~ your
comments to the topic under discussion) 2. (misc.)
the difficulty is not ~d to Plan A: it also affects
Plan B
confinement n. ["imprisonment"] ["being confined"] 1.
solitary ~ (they put him in solitary ~) 2. ~ to (~ to
quarters) 3. in ~ (in solitary ~) ["lying-in"] (obsol.) 4.
in ~ (before the birth of a child)
confines n. beyond; within the ~ (impossible within
the ~ of the system)
confirm v. 1. (L) the president ~ed that a summit
conference would take place 2. (Q) the president
did not ~ when the summit conference would take
place 3. (misc.) to ~ in writing
confirmation n. 1. official; unofficial; written ~ 2. ~
that + clause (we have received ~ that the summit
conference will take place) 3. in ~ of
confiscate v. (D; tr.) to ~ from
conflagration n. a major ~
conflict I n. 1. to provoke a ~ 2. to come into ~ with
3. to avert, avoid a ~ 4. to resolve a ~ 5. (an) armed,
military; cultural; direct; ethnic; inter-communal;
internecine; religious ~ 6. (a) bitter ~ 7. (a) ~
about, over; among, between; with (a ~ between
neighboring countries over their common border;
a ~ with one's relatives about the terms of a will)
(see also *conflict of interests* at **interest I** 14) 8. in
(a) ~ with (your version is in ~ with mine)
conflict II v. (D; intr.) to ~ with (your version ~s
with mine)
confluence n. at a ~ (the city lies at the ~ of three
rivers)
conform v. (D; intr.) to ~ to, with (to fail to ~ to
specifications)
conformance n. in ~ with
conformity n. 1. strict ~ 2. ~ to 3. in ~ with
confront v. (D; tr.) to ~ about, over; with (to ~ a
prisoner with a witness)
confrontation n. 1. to have; provoke a ~ 2. to avert,
avoid a ~ 3. an armed, military; direct, head-on ~
4. a bitter ~ 5. a ~ about, over; among, between;
with (a ~ between neighboring countries over their
common border)
confuse v. 1. (d; tr.) to ~ with (I always ~ him with/
and his brother) 2. (R) it ~s me that he and his
brother look so much alike
confused adj. 1. easily; very ~ 2. ~ about, over 3. to
become, get ~ 4. ~ to + inf. (I was ~ to learn of his
latest decision)
confusing adj. 1. ~ for, to (the complicated testimony

was ~ to us = the complicated testimony was ~ for us to listen to) 2. ~ to + inf. (it was ~ (for us) to listen to the testimony) 3. ~ that + clause (it's ~ that he and his brother look so much alike)

confusion *n.* 1. to cause, create; lead to ~ 2. to avoid; clear up ~ 3. ~ arises; reigns 4. to throw into ~ (their unexpected arrival threw our plans into ~) 5. complete, general, mass, total, utter 6. ~ about, over; between (let's try to clear up the ~ between us about who does what) 7. in ~ (to withdraw in utter ~; in the ~ they escaped) 8. a scene; state of ~ (it was a scene of utter ~)

congestion *n.* 1. traffic ~ 2. nasal; lung, pulmonary ~

conglomerate *n.* a financial; industrial; international, multinational, transnational ~

congratulate *v.* 1. to ~ heartily, sincerely, warmly 2. (D; refl., tr.) to ~ on, upon (you are to be ~d on your promotion)

congratulations *n.* 1. to extend, offer ~ on 2. deepest, heartfelt, heartiest, hearty, sincere, warm, warmest ~ 3. ~ on, upon (my warmest ~ on your promotion!) 4. ~ to (~ to you on your promotion)

congress *n.* 1. to convene, hold a ~ 2. an annual; biennial; international; party ~ 3. a ~ meets 4. (misc.) an act of Congress

congruence *n.* (formal or technical) (in) ~ with

congruent *adj.* (formal or technical) ~ to, with

congruity *n.* (formal) ~ with

congruous *adj.* (formal) ~ to, with

conjecture I *n.* (formal) ["guess"] 1. to make a ~ 2. pure ~ 3. a ~ about 4. a ~ that + clause (the press's ~ that a summit conference would take place proved to be true) 5. (misc.) it is a matter for/of ~ whether they can still win = it's open to ~ whether they can still win

conjecture II *v.* (formal) (L) ("to guess") the press ~d that a summit conference would take place

conjugation *n.* ["verb forms"] an irregular; regular ~

conjunction *n.* ["connecting word"] 1. a coordinating; subordinating ~ ["cooperation"] ["coincidence"] 2. in ~ with

connect *v.* 1. to ~ closely, intimately; loosely 2. (d; intr.) to ~ to, with (this bus is supposed to ~ with a train) 3. (D; tr.) to ~ to, with (are you ~ed with this firm? to ~ a TV set to an antenna)

connection, connexion *n.* ["association"] 1. to establish, make a ~ 2. to break, sever a ~ 3. a close, intimate; direct; loose, tenuous ~ 4. a foreign; international ~ 5. a ~ between; to; with (there was no ~ between the two phenomena; to have a ~ with smb.) 6. in a certain ~ (in this ~; in ~ with the other matter) ["acquaintance"] ["tie"] 7. business; professional; social ~s ["transfer during a trip"] 8. to make; miss a ~ ["linking of two telephones"] 9. to get a ~ ["link, linking"] 10. a faulty; loose ~ ["misc."] 11. to have ~s ("to have influential supporters"); to use one's ~s

connect up *v.* (D; tr.) to ~ to, with (to ~ a TV set up to an antenna)

connexion (BE) see **connection**

conniption *n.* ["a strong emotional reaction"] (AE) (colloq.) to have a ~ (mom will have a ~ if we get back late!)

connive *v.* 1. (D; intr.) to ~ at; in; with (to ~ in cheating smb.) 2. (E) they ~d (with each other) to cheat her

conquest *n.* 1. to make a ~ 2. to consolidate; extend one's ~s 3. military; sexual; world ~ 4. by ~ (what the tyrant gained by ~ he lost by his subjects' rebellion)

conscience *n.* 1. to appeal to; arouse, stir smb.'s ~ 2. to have a ~ 3. to have smt. on one's ~ 4. to ease, salve one's ~; to wrestle with one's ~ 5. a clear; guilty ~ (to have a guilty ~) 6. a matter of ~ 7. (misc.) in all ~ (CE), in good ~ (AE), in all good ~ (AE); pangs of ~

conscientious *adj.* ~ about (she is ~ about her work)

conscious *adj.* 1. fully ~ 2. (cannot stand alone) ~ of (~ of danger) 3. ~ that + clause (she became ~ that everyone was staring at her)

consciousness *n.* ["conscious state"] 1. to lose; recover, regain ~ ["awareness"] 2. to raise smb.'s ~ 3. class; political; social ~ ["misc."] 4. (the) stream of ~

conscript *v.* 1. (D; tr.) to ~ for (to ~ troops for national defense) 2. (D; tr.) to ~ into (to ~ youths into the armed forces)

conscription *n.* 1. to introduce ~ 2. to abolish, end ~ 3. military; universal ~

consecrate *v.* 1. (D; tr.) to ~ as (he was ~d as archbishop) 2. (d; tr.) to ~ to (she ~d her life to helping the poor) 3. (N; used with a noun) he was ~d archbishop

consecration *n.* ~ as; to (his ~ as archbishop; the ~ of her life to helping the poor)

consensus *n.* 1. to reach a ~ 2. a general ~ 3. (a) ~ among; on (there is a degree of ~ among the experts on what should be done) 4. a ~ that + clause (there is (a) general ~ among the experts that we should abstain) USAGE NOTE: The phrase "* consensus of opinion" is disliked because "consensus" alone will typically do the trick.

consent I *n.* 1. to give one's ~ to 2. to refuse, withhold one's ~ 3. common; general; informed; mutual; parental; tacit; unanimous ~ 4. by ~ (by mutual ~) 5. (misc.) the age of ~

consent II *v.* 1. (D; intr.) to ~ to (to ~ to a proposal) 2. (E) she ~ed to help

consequence *n.* ["importance"] 1. of ~ (to) (a matter of some/no ~) ["result"] 2. in ~ of

consequences *n.* ["results"] 1. to have ~ for 2. to accept, bear, face, suffer, take the ~ 3. dire, disastrous; grave, serious ~ 4. far-reaching, fateful; inevitable; unforeseeable; unforeseen ~

conservation *n.* 1. energy; forest; soil; water; wildlife ~ 2. (the) ~ of natural resources

conservative I *adj.* 1. deeply, staunchly; politically ~ 2. ~ in (~ in one's views)

conservative II *n.* a diehard, dyed-in-the-wool, staunch, true-blue (BE); political ~

consider *v.* 1. ("to regard") to ~ favorably; seriously 2. (D; tr.) ("to regard"); ("to examine") to ~ as (we ~ed him as a possible candidate) 3. (D; tr.) ("to regard as a candidate") to ~ for (he cannot be ~ed for the job) 4. (G) ("to contemplate") she ~ed resigning 5. (L) ("to take into account") you must ~ that she has been here only one month 6. (M) ("to believe") we ~ed him to be a possible candidate 7. (N; used with an adjective, noun, past participle) ("to believe") we ~ her qualified; we ~ her a genius; we ~ed him a possible candidate 8. (Q) ("to contemplate") we ~ed where to hide the money 9. (misc.) we ~ed it difficult to believe that she had been here only one month USAGE NOTE: Note the contrasts between *consider as* and *consider* in the following text – In her book she considers ("examines") Shakespeare as a playwright and as a poet. She considers ("believes") Shakespeare (to be) both a great playwright and a great poet. However, she considers ("believes") Shakespeare (to be) even greater as a playwright than as a poet.

considerate *adj.* 1. ~ of (he was ~ of everyone) 2. ~ towards 3. ~ to + inf. (it was ~ of her to do that nice thing)

consideration *n.* ["thought"]["concern"] 1. to give ~ to (to give some ~ to a matter) 2. to show ~ for 3. to take smt. into ~ 4. to deserve; require ~ (the matter requires careful ~) 5. careful, detailed; due; serious ~ 6. a major; minor; overriding ~ 7. financial; humanitarian; personal ~s 8. for smb.'s ~ (I submit the enclosed proposal for your ~) 9. in ~ of (in ~ of past services) 10. on careful ~ (of) 11. out of ~ for smb. 12. under ~ (the matter is under ~) 13. with ~ for (with due ~ for your feelings, we must reject your request) ["fee"] 14. for a ~ (for a modest ~, he'll do anything)

consign *v.* 1. (B) they ~ed the shipment to us 2. (d; tr.) to ~ to (the paintings were ~ed to our care)

consignment *n.* ["a sale allowing the dealer to return unsold merchandise"] to sell; ship on ~

consist *v.* 1. (d; intr.) to ~ of ("to be composed of") (our state ~s of thirty counties) 2. (formal) (d; intr.) to ~ in ("to be equivalent to") (freedom ~s in the absence of oppressive laws and in being able to exercise your rights)

consistent *adj.* 1. ~ in (she is not ~ in her support of our party) 2. ~ with (not ~ with our principles)

consistory *n.* (usu. rel.) to convoke, hold a ~

consolation *n.* 1. to afford, offer ~ 2. (of) ~ to (that will be a great ~ to us; that should be of some ~ to you; that is – no/small ~ to me; no one was actually killed – if that's any ~ to you) 3. a ~ to + inf. (it's a ~ to know that they are safe = it's a ~ knowing that they are safe) 4. a ~ that + clause (our only ~ was that no one was actually killed) 5. (misc.) a word of ~

console *v.* 1. (D; tr.) to ~ on (to ~ smb. on the loss of

a loved one) 2. (d; refl.) to ~ with (I ~d myself with the thought that no one was actually killed)

consommé *n.* 1. clear ~ 2. a bowl; cup of ~

consonance *n.* in ~ with

consonant I *adj.* (formal) ~ with

consonant II *n.* 1. to articulate, pronounce a ~ 2. a dental; double, geminate; final; guttural; hard; labial; liquid; palatal; soft; unvoiced, voiceless; velar; voiced ~ (see also *consonant cluster* at **cluster I**; *consonant sound* at **sound II** *n.*)

consort *v.* (formal) (d; intr.) to ~ with

consortium *n.* to form, organize a ~

conspicuous *adj.* 1. ~ for, in 2. (misc.) to be ~ by one's absence

conspiracy *n.* 1. to hatch, organize a ~ 2. to crush; foil; uncover a ~ 3. (a) criminal ~ 4. a ~ against; with 5. a ~ to + inf. (a ~ to overthrow the government) 6. (misc.) a ~ of silence

conspire *v.* 1. (D; intr.) to ~ against; with 2. (E) they ~d to overthrow the government

constable *n.* (BE) ["police officer"] a chief ~

consternation *n.* 1. to cause ~ 2. to express; feel ~ 3. in ~ 4. to smb.'s ~ (to our ~, the current was turned off)

constituency *n.* a core ~

constituent *n.* (ling.) an immediate; ultimate ~

constitute *v.* (S; used with a noun) this ~s a problem

constitution *n.* ["basic law"] 1. to adopt, establish; ratify a ~ 2. to draw up, frame, write a ~ 3. to preserve, safeguard a ~ 4. to abrogate; amend, change a ~ 5. to violate a ~ 6. a written; unwritten ~ ["physical makeup"] 7. a feeble, frail; iron, rugged, strong ~

constitutional *adj.* ~ to + inf. (it is not ~ to censor the press)

constitutionality *n.* to challenge, question, test; establish the ~ (of a law)

constrain *v.* (formal) (H) to ~ smb. to do smt.

constrained *adj.* (formal) (cannot stand alone) ~ to + inf. (we were ~ to act)

constraint *n.* ["restriction"] 1. to impose, place, put a ~ on, upon 2. financial; legal ~s ["compulsion"] 3. under ~ (to act under ~)

construct I *n.* a theoretical ~

construct II *v.* (D; tr.) to ~ of, out of (the house is ~ed of wood)

construction *n.* ["building industry"] 1. in ~ (he is in ~) ["act of building"] 2. shoddy; solid, sturdy ~ 3. commercial; modular; residential ~ 4. of ~ (buildings of shoddy ~) 5. under ~ (the new skyscraper is under ~) ["interpretation"] 6. to put a ~ on (he put the wrong ~ on my statement) ["syntactic phrase"] 7. an absolute; idiomatic ~

construe *v.* 1. (d; tr.) to ~ as (he ~d the statement as a threat) 2. (M) he ~d the statement to be a threat

consul *n.* a ~ general; an honorary ~

consulate *n.* a ~ general

consult *v.* 1. (D; intr.) to ~ about, on; with; without (to ~ with smb. about a problem; they solved the problem without ~ing anyone else) 2. (D; tr.) to ~ about, on (to ~ smb. about a problem)

consultant *n.* 1. a business; legal; medical; nursing; political ~ 2. a ~ for, on; to (a ~ to the president on foreign policy) 3. (med.) a ~ in (a ~ in obstetrics and gynecology)

consultation *n.* 1. to have, hold ~s 2. ~s about, on; with 3. in ~ with (they solved the problem in ~ with several experts) 4. (misc.) was there any sort of public ~ before the government went ahead with its plans?

consulting *n.* online ~

consumed *adj.* ~ with (~ with guilt)

consumption *n.* 1. conspicuous; mass ~ 2. fuel ~ 3. to increase; reduce (increase your ~ of vegetables and reduce your ~ of alcohol) 4. (misc.) unfit for human ~

contact *n.* ["being together"] ["connection"] 1. to come in, into ~; to establish, make ~ 2. to maintain, stay in ~ 3. to bring into ~ 4. to avoid; break off; lose ~ 5. (electrical) to break ~ 6. close, intimate; direct; eye; face-to-face; indirect; physical ~ 7. radar; radio; telephone ~ (the control tower was in radar ~ with the plane) 8. ~ between; with (to establish ~ with one's relatives; to stay in ~ with friends) 9. in ~ (have they been in ~?) 10. on ~ (the bomb exploded on ~ with the ground) 11. a point of ~ ["acquaintance"] ["tie"] 12. to have ~ (with) 13. business; cultural; personal; professional; international; social ~s

contagious *adj.* extremely, highly, very ~

container *n.* a metal; plastic ~ (to store smb. in a metal ~)

contaminate *v.* (D; tr.) to ~ by, with (to ~ smb. with smt.; a wound ~d by bacteria)

contamination *n.* radioactive ~

contemplate *v.* 1. (G) he ~d resigning 2. (misc.) too awful/horrible to ~ (he seriously ~ed resigning – but the thought of resigning was too awful to ~)

contemplation *n.* 1. deep; quiet; silent ~ 2. lost in ~

contemporaneous *adj.* (formal) ~ with

contemporary *adj.* ~ with

contempt *n.* ["scorn"] 1. to betray; demonstrate, display, show; express; feel; have ~ for 2. bitter, deep, profound, total, unmitigated, utter ~ 3. ~ for (his body language betrayed his utter ~ for the dictator; I feel nothing but ~ for such behavior!) 4. beneath ~ 5. in, with ~ (I looked at them with ~) ["disrespect"] (usu. legal) 6. to hold in ~ (to hold smb. in ~ of court) ("to accuse smb. of disrespect for a court") 7. civil; criminal ~ ["misc."] 8. familiarity breeds ~

contemptible *adj.* ~ to + inf. (it was ~ of him to behave like that)

contemptuous *adj.* ~ of (he was ~ of all authority)

contend *v.* (formal) 1. (D; intr.) ("to compete") to ~ for; with (to ~ for a position) 2. (L) ("to claim") he ~ed that he had been cheated

contender *n.* 1. a formidable, leading, main, serious, strong; likely; unlikely ~ 2. a presidential ~ 3. a ~ for (the leading ~ for the heavyweight crown)

content I *adj.* 1. perfectly, very; quite 2. ~ with (they were perfectly ~ with their lot) 3. ~ to + inf. (she was not ~ to remain at home)

content II *n.* to one's heart's ~ ("to one's complete satisfaction")

content III *v.* (formal) (d; refl.) to ~ with (to ~ oneself with a simple life)

contention *n.* ["argument"] 1. to rebut, refute; reject a ~ 2. to substantiate, support a ~ 3. a ~ about 4. a bone of ~ ("something contentious") 5. a ~ that + inf. (it is his ~ that taxes are too low) ["competition"] 6. in ~ (for); (with) (which teams are in ~ for the title?)

contents *n.* 1. to disclose, divulge, reveal the ~ (of a letter) 2. to inspect the ~ (of) 3. a table of ~

contest I *n.* 1. to have, hold, organize, run, stage a ~ 2. to adjudicate, judge a ~ 3. to enter; take part in a ~ 4. to lose; win a ~ (in this ~ only one contestant can win) 5. a bitter, hard-fought; close; one-sided ~ 6. a beauty; public-speaking ~ 7. a ~ among, between; for 8. a ~ to + inf. (a ~ between college chums to see who can drink the most beer)

contest II *v.* to ~ bitterly; successfully; unsuccessfully (the lawyers ~ed the court's decision successfully)

contestant *n.* a ~ for

contested *adj.* bitterly, closely, hotly, vigorously ~

context *n.* 1. a historical; social ~ 2. in; out of ~; within a ~ (to cite a passage out of ~; ideas that must be set within the historical ~ that produced them)

contiguous *adj.* ~ to, with

continent *n.* on a ~

contingency *n.* 1. to provide for every ~ 2. a ~ arises 3. an unforeseen ~

contingent *adj.* (pompous) (cannot stand alone) ~ on, upon (the time of his arrival is ~ on the weather)

continuance *n.* ["adjournment"] (legal) (AE) to grant a ~

continue *v.* 1. to ~ unabated 2. (D; intr.) to ~ as (she will ~ as chairperson) 3. (D; intr.) to ~ by (she ~d by citing more facts) 4. (D; intr.) to ~ with (she ~d with her work) 5. (E) they ~d to write 6. (G) they ~d writing 7. (misc.) to be ~d

continuity *n.* 1. to break the ~ 2. ~ between (there was no ~ between the first and second acts)

continuum *n.* 1. to constitute, form a ~ 2. the health-illness ~ 3. along a ~ 4. a ~ from; to

contorted *adj.* ~ with (her face was ~ with rage)

contraband *n.* 1. to smuggle ~ 2. to seize ~ 3. ~ of war

contraception *n.* 1. to practice, use ~ 2. a method of ~

contraceptive *n.* 1. to use ~s 2. a chemical; oral; vaginal ~

contract I *n.* 1. to conclude, sign; enter into; land (colloq.), secure; negotiate; ratify; tender for a ~ 2. to carry out, execute; honor a ~ 3. to draft, draw up, write (up) a ~ 4. to assign (after bidding), let; award a ~ 5. to abrogate, cancel, repudiate a ~ 6. to breach, break, violate a ~ 7. a binding; exclusive; legal, valid; void ~ 8. an oral, verbal; written ~ 9. (colloq.) (AE) a sweetheart ~ ("an agreement favorable to the employer that was reached without the participation of the union members") 10. (AE) a yellow-dog ~ ("a contract that obligates the workers not to join a union") 11. a marriage ~ 12. a ~ for; with 13. a ~ to + inf. (they landed a ~ to build a bridge) 14. under ~ to, with (that player is under ~ with our team) 15. (misc.) to exchange ~s (with) ("to complete the purchase of a house in England; in Scotland you exchange missives (with)"); to put out a ~ on smb. ("to arrange to have smb. murdered") (see also *(a) breach of contract* at **breach** 6)

contract II *v.* 1. (d; intr.) to ~ for; with (the city ~ed for a new library with their firm) 2. (E) the firm ~ed to construct the bridge

contract III *v.* ("to shorten") (D; intr., tr.) to ~ to (in spoken English, "it is" often ~s/is often ~ed to "it's")

contractions *n.* to time (labor) ~ (in childbirth)

contractor *n.* a building; defense; electrical; general; plumbing ~; a sub-contractor

contract out *v.* 1. (D; intr.) to ~ of (esp. BE) (to ~ of a company pension scheme) 2. (D; tr.) to ~ to (the work was ~ed out to several local firms)

contradict *v.* to ~ flatly

contradiction *n.* 1. an apparent; basic; direct; flat, outright; glaring; inherent ~ 2. a ~ between 3. in ~ to, with (his words and his deeds are in ~ to/with each other = his words are in ~ to/with his deeds) 4. (misc.) a ~ in terms

contradictory *adj.* ~ to

contradistinction *n.* (formal) in ~ to

contrail *n.* to leave a ~ (high-flying aircraft leave ~s)

contralto *n.* 1. to sing ~ 2. a rich ~

contraption *n.* (colloq.) to build, put together, slap together a ~

contrary I *adj.* (cannot stand alone) ~ to (his actions are ~ to the rules)

contrary II *n.* 1. on the ~ ("does your back feel any better?" "on the ~, it feels much worse") 2. to the ~ (I will come next month unless you write to the ~) USAGE NOTE: AE also allows "does your back feel any better?" "to the ~, it feels much worse."

contrast I *n.* 1. to present a ~ 2. a harsh, sharp, stark, startling; marked, striking, vivid ~ 3. a favorable; unfavorable ~ 4. a ~ between, to, with 5. by ~ (with) (their neighbors live opulently; by ~, they live modestly = they live modestly by ~ with their neighbors, who live opulently) 6. in ~ to (in ~ to their neighbors, they live modestly) 7. (misc.) for (the sake of) ~

contrast II *v.* 1. to ~ sharply 2. to ~ favorably; unfavorably 3. (D; intr., tr.) to ~ with (their deeds ~ with their words)

contravention *n.* (formal) in ~ of (to act in ~ of international law)

contribute *v.* 1. (D; tr.) to ~ for (we ~d clothing for the flood victims through a charity) 2. (D; intr., tr.) to ~ to, towards (to ~ generously to charity; we ~d clothing to the flood victims through a direct donation; lack of communication ~d to the breakdown of their marriage)

contribution *n.* ["donation, gift"] 1. to make a ~ (to) 2. to send in a ~ 3. a charitable; in-kind; monetary; voluntary ~ 4. a big, generous, large; small, token ~ (to make a generous ~ to charity) ["accomplishment, presentation"] 5. to make a ~ (to) 6. a brilliant, great, notable, outstanding, remarkable; important; invaluable, key; major, significant, substantial; minor; modest; valuable ~ (she made an outstanding ~ to science) 7. a ~ to, towards

contributor *n.* ["one who gives money"] 1. an anonymous; generous; major; regular ~ 2. a ~ to (a generous ~ to charity) ["one who contributes by writing or drawing"] 3. a prolific; regular ~ 4. a ~ to (a regular ~ to a journal)

contrition *n.* 1. to show ~ 2. to express; feel ~ 3. (often rel.) an act of ~ 4. ~ for

contrive *v.* (E) she somehow ~d to arrange a meeting

control *n.* 1. to establish; exercise, exert, wield; gain, have; retain ~ (over) 2. to assume, take ~ of 3. to bring smt. under ~ (the fire was finally brought under ~) 4. to wrest ~ from 5. to lose; relinquish ~ of (she lost ~ of the car) 6. absolute, complete; close, strict; full ~ (to exert strict ~ over smt.) 7. lax, loose; remote ~ 8. government; parental ~ 9. air-traffic; flight; mission ~ 10. arms; gun ~ 11. communicable-disease; crowd; population; weight ~ (see also **birth control**; **self-control**) 12. cost; quality ~ 13. damage; fire; flood ~ 14. emissions; pest ~ 15. stress; thought ~ 16. price; rent; wage ~ 17. ~ of, over (to establish ~ over prices) 18. in ~ (of) (she was in full ~ of the situation) 19. beyond, out of ~ (the car went out of ~; the fire got out of ~) 20. under ~ (the fire was finally brought under ~; keep them under ~; the area was placed under the ~ of the military) (see also **controls**; *circumstances beyond smb.'s control* at **circumstances** 9)

controlled *adj.* tightly ~

controller *n.* an air-traffic, flight ~

controls *n.* ["restrictions"] 1. to impose, introduce ~ (on) 2. to tighten ~ (on) 3. to lift, remove ~ (from) 4. to relax ~ (on) 5. price; rent; wage ~ ["regulating instruments"] 6. to take over the ~ (the copilot took over the ~) 7. dual ~ 8. at the ~

controversial *adj.* bitterly, extremely, highly, very ~

controversy *n.* 1. to arouse, cause, fuel, generate, spark (off), stir up (a) ~ 2. to settle a ~ 3. a bitter, fierce, furious, heated, lively ~ 4. a ~ dies down; flares up; rages; surrounds smt./smb. 5. a ~ about, over 6. a ~ between, with

convalesce v. (D; intr.) to ~ from

convalescence n. a lengthy, long ~

convenience n. ["comfort"] 1. a ~ to + inf. (it's a great ~ to live in town = it's a great ~ living in town) 2. at smb.'s ~ (answer at your earliest ~) ["device that adds to comfort"] 3. modern ~s (often shortened to "mod cons" esp. in the language of British estate agents) 4. the latest ~s 5. (BE) a public ~ ("a public toilet")

convenient adj. 1. mutually ~ 2. ~ for (will Tuesday be ~ for you?) 3. ~ to + inf. (it is very ~ to have the bus stop so close = it is very ~ having the bus stop so close) 4. ~ that + clause (it's very ~ that the bus stop is so close)

convent n. to enter a ~ ("to become a nun") (she entered a ~ and remained in it for the rest of her life)

convention n. ["assembly"] ["conference"] 1. to have, hold a ~ 2. an annual; national; party; political ~ (the ~ met/took place when all the delegates could be at it) ["agreement"] 3. a copyright ~ ["practice, tradition"] 4. to defy, flout ~ 5. a longstanding ~ 6. ~ dictates (that we eat three meals a day) 7. by ~

conventional adj. 1. ~ in (one's tastes) 2. ~ to + inf. (it is not ~ to go to work in shorts)

converge v. (d; intr.) to ~ on, upon; towards (to ~ on the speaker's platform)

conversant adj. (cannot stand alone) ["familiar"] 1. fully, thoroughly ~ 2. ~ with (~ with procedure)

conversation n. ["talk"] 1. to begin, strike up; carry on, have, hold a ~ 2. to make ~ (we had little in common, and it was difficult to engage him in ~ or make ~ (with him)) 3. to bug, monitor, tap a ~ 4. to hog, monopolize; liven up, stimulate a ~ 5. to break off, end, finish, terminate; interrupt a ~ 6. (an) animated, lively; boring, dull; intimate; light; serious ~ 7. (a) private; telephone ~ 8. (a) ~ lags; picks up 9. fragments, scraps, snatches of (a) ~ (we overheard scraps of their ~ during a lull in our own ~) 10. (a) ~ about; with 11. in ~ (she was in ~ with a friend) ["sexual intercourse"] (legal) 12. criminal ~ ("adultery")

conversations n. ["negotiations"] 1. to hold ~ 2. to break off ~ 3. ~ about; with

converse v. 1. to ~ fluently (to ~ fluently in a foreign language) 2. (D; intr.) to ~ about; with

conversion n. ["change"] 1. condo; loft ~ 2. a ~ from; into, to ["a score made by a kick or pass after a goal has been scored"] (Am. football, rugby) 3. to make a ~ ["adoption of a new religion"] 4. to undergo ~ 5. a religious ~ 6. a ~ from; to

convert I n. 1. to gain a ~ 2. a ~ to (a ~ to Buddhism)

convert II v. 1. (D; intr.) ("to change one's religion") to ~ from; to (they ~ed from Hinduism to Buddhism) 2. (D; intr., tr.) ("to change"); ("to change

---

smb.'s religion") to ~ from; into, to (to ~ smb. to Islam; the plant ~ed to microchip production; they ~ed their money from euros into pounds; to ~ a barn into a garage)

converter n. a catalytic ~

convertible adj. 1. freely ~ 2. ~ into, to (~ into hard currency)

convey v. 1. (B) ("to give") ~ my best wishes to them 2. (D; tr.) ("to transfer") to ~ from; to (the title to the property was ~ed from them to you) 3. (Q) ("to explain") she tried to ~ how she felt

conveyance n. ["vehicle"] a public ~

convict I n. an escaped ~

convict II v. (D; tr.) to ~ of (he was ~ed of murder)

conviction n. ["strong belief"] 1. to carry; lack ~ (his story carries ~; "The best lack all ~" – W.B. Yeats, "The Second Coming" (1921)) 2. a burning, deep, firm, great; strong, unshakeable; lifelong; personal; religious ~ 3. a ~ about 4. a ~ that + clause (she expressed her firm ~, shared by many others, that television was harmful to children) 5. by; with; without ~ (a pacifist by ~ who defended pacifism with great ~) 6. (misc.) to have the courage of one's ~s ["guilty verdict"] 7. to get, win a ~ (the prosecutor got ten ~s last year) 8. to overturn a ~ (the appeals court overturned the ~) 9. a previous ~ 10. a ~ for (a previous ~ for embezzlement)

convince v. 1. (D; tr.) to ~ of (he ~d me of his sincerity) 2. (esp. AE) (H) we ~ed ("persuaded") her to stay home 3. (L; must have an object) we ~d her that she should stay home

convinced adj. 1. absolutely, completely, firmly, thoroughly; not entirely ~ 2. ~ of (they're still not entirely ~ of the feasibility of our project) 3. ~ that + clause (they are not ~ that our project will succeed)

convocation n. ["assembly"] 1. to hold a ~ ["assembly of graduates of a university"] (GB) 2. a member of ~

convoy n. 1. to form a ~ 2. a naval; relief ~ 3. in; under ~ (to travel in ~)

convulsed adj. ~ in, with (~ in/with laughter)

convulsions n. to go into, have ~

cook I n. 1. the chief, head; a good ~ 2. (AE) a short-order ~

cook II v. (C) ~ some vegetables for us; or ~ us some vegetables

cooker n. ["pot"] 1. a pressure ~ (also fig.) ["stove"] (BE) 2. an electric; gas ~

cookie n. AE; BE has *(sweet) biscuit* 1. to bake ~s 2. a chocolate-chip; homemade; sandwich ~ USAGE NOTE: AE sandwich cookie=BE cream (biscuit). 3. (CE) a fortune ~

cooking n. 1. to do the ~ 2. home; home-style ~ 3. (BE) good plain (English) ~

cookout n. (esp. AE; CE has *barbecue*) 1. to have a ~ 2. at a ~

cool I adj. ["calm"] 1. to keep, remain, stay ~ 2. (misc.) (as) ~ as a cucumber ["indifferent"] ["unfriendly"] 3. ~ to, towards (she was ~ to the idea)

cool II *n.* (slang) ["composure"] to blow, lose keep one's ~
cool III *v.* (D; tr.) to ~ to (boil the mixture and then ~ it to room temperature)
coolant *n.* to add ~
coolness *n.* ["indifference"] ~ to, towards
coop *n.* 1. a chicken ~ 2. (misc.) (colloq.) to fly the ~ ("to escape")
cooperate *v.* 1. to ~ closely; fully 2. (D; intr.) to ~ in, on; with (to ~ in/on a project with smb.)
cooperation *n.* 1. close; wholehearted ~ 2. ~ between; in, on; with (~ on a project with another university) 3. in ~ with (their dictionary was published in ~ with the Ministry of Education; the two research teams are working in close ~ (with each other)) 4. with smb.'s ~ 5. (misc.) to enlist smb.'s ~
cooperative, co-op, coop *n.* 1. to form, set up a ~ 2. a consumers'; farmers'; housing; producers'; workers' ~
coop up *v.* (D; tr.) to ~ in; with (we were ~ed up in a small room)
coordinate *v.* 1. to ~ carefully; closely 2. (D; tr.) to ~ with (we must ~ our operations with theirs)
coordination *n.* 1. close ~ 2. ~ among, between; with 3. in ~ (with) (the two research teams are working in close ~ (with each other))
cop *v.* (colloq.) (esp. AE) (D; intr.) to ~ out of ("to renege on") (to ~ out of a responsibility)
cope *v.* (D; intr.) to ~ with (to ~ with difficulties)
cop out *v.* (colloq.) (esp. AE) (D; intr.) ("to renege") to ~ on (to ~ on a responsibility)
copulate *v.* (D; intr.) to ~ with
copy I *n.* ["reproduction"] 1. to make, run off a ~ 2. to Xerox (T) a ~ 3. to print ~pies (the publisher decided to print ten thousand ~pies of the book) 4. to inscribe a ~ (the author inscribed a ~ of her book for him) 5. (a) clean, fair ~; hard ("printed out") ~ (from a computer); a rough; true ~ 6. a backup; blind; carbon; extra; master ~; photocopy; top (BE) ("original"); Xerox (T) ~ ["manuscript"] ["draft of material to be printed"] 7. to edit, (BE) sub-edit, (BE) sub ~ ["issue, publication"] 8. an advance; back; complimentary, presentation ~ ["news"] 9. to make good ~ ("to be newsworthy")
copy II *v.* 1. (D; tr.) ~ for (please ~ the article for me) 2. (D; tr.) to ~ from, out of (she ~ied the paragraph from the encyclopedia)
copybook *n.* (BE) to blot one's ~ ("to ruin one's reputation")
copyright *n.* 1. (for a copyright office) to grant, register a ~ 2. (for an author, publisher) to apply for; claim; have, hold, own; secure a ~ 3. to breach, infringe a ~ 4. an ad-interim; full-term; statutory ~ 5. a ~ expires, runs out 6. a ~ on (a book) 7. in, (AE) under; out of ~
cord *n.* 1. to pull (on) a ~ 2. to tie a ~ (around smt.) 3. a telephone ~ 4. a communication (BE), emergency (AE); electric (AE; BE has *flex*); extension

~ 5. a spinal ~ (see also **umbilical cord**) 6. a length, piece of ~
cordial *adj.* ~ to, towards
cordon *n.* ["protective ring of police, soldiers"] 1. to form a ~ 2. to throw a ~ around (an area)
cords *n.* the vocal ~
core *n.* 1. the hard ~ 2. at the ~ (at the ~ of the problem) 3. (misc.) to get to the ~ of a matter (see also *rotten to the core* at **rotten** 3)
cork *n.* to pop, remove a ~
corn *n.* ["maize"] (esp. AE) 1. to grow, raise; husk, shuck (AE) ~ 2. hybrid; Indian; sweet; young ~ 3. an ear; kernel of ~ 4. (misc.) (CE) ~ on the cob USAGE NOTE: Nowadays BE seems to prefer "sweetcorn" to "maize" as the name for what Americans call "corn." In AE and technical BE, "sweet corn" is a *type* of corn/maize.
corner *n.* 1. to round, turn; take a ~ 2. a blind; tight ~ 3. (also fig.) around the ~ (they live around the ~; to go around the ~; prosperity is just around the ~) 4. at, on a ~ (of a street) 5. in the ~ (as of a room or page) in the upper right-hand ~ 6. (misc.) the four ~s of the earth; I could see her out of the ~ of my eye; (boxing) a neutral ~; to cut ~s ("to do something the easiest and quickest way"); forced into a ~ ("crowded into a difficult position"); to establish a ~ on the market ("to monopolize the market")
cornerstone *n.* to lay a ~
corollary *n.* a ~ to
coronary *n.* 1. to have a ~ 2. a massive ~
coronation *n.* 1. to have, hold a ~ 2. a ~ takes place
corporal *n.* 1. a lance ~ (BE: AE has *private first class*) 2. to make smb. a ~, to promote smb. to the rank of ~; to have, hold the rank of ~ 3. (misc.) what's your opinion, Corporal (Smith)?
corporation *n.* 1. to establish, form, set up a ~ 2. to manage, run a ~ 3. to dissolve a ~ 4. (BE) a public ~ 5. an international, multinational, transnational ~
corps *n.* 1. the diplomatic; officer; press ~ (a post in the diplomatic ~) 2. an army ~ 3. the Air Corps; the Marine Corps; the Signal Corps (AE), the Corps of Signals (BE)
corpse *n.* 1. to bury, inter; lay out a ~ 2. to dig up, exhume a ~ 3. a ~ decays, decomposes, rots
corpus *n.* (ling.) 1. to collect, gather a ~ 2. a closed; spoken; written ~
corpuscle *n.* a red; white ~
correct *adj.* ["true"] 1. ~ in (you are ~ in thinking that he is foolish) 2. ~ to + inf. (it would be ~ to say that we have committed a blunder; you are ~ to think that he is foolish) 3. ~ that + clause (is it ~ that he has resigned?) 4. (misc.) grammatically ~; politically ~ (also PC); substantially ~; ~ in all respects
correction *n.* 1. to make a ~ 2. to mark ~s (in a text)
correctness *n.* political ~ (also PC)
correlate *v.* (d; intr., tr.) to ~ with (to ~ one set of data with another set)

correlation *n.* 1. (a) close, high, strong ~ 2. a ~ between; with

correspond *v.* 1. ("to be similar") to ~ approximately, roughly; closely; exactly 2. (D; intr.) ("to be equal") to ~ to (what German word ~s to *hound*?) 3. (BE) (D; intr.) ("to be in harmony") to ~ with (his actions do not ~ with his words) 4. (D; intr.) ("to write") to ~ about; with (they have been ~ing with each other about this matter for years)

correspondence *n.* ["exchange of letters"] 1. to carry on, conduct; enter into (a) ~ 2. to break off, end (a) ~ 3. business, commercial; personal ~ 4. ~ about; between; from; with 5. in ~ with (to be in ~ with smb. about smt.) ["conformity"] 6. close ~ 7. ~ between (~ between theory and practice)

correspondent *n.* a diplomatic; foreign; special; war ~

corresponding *adj.* ~ to

corridor *n.* 1. an air; long; narrow; winding ~ (a long ~ leads to the living-room) 2. a ~ across; between; through (see also *the corridors of power* at **power** 9)

corruption *n.* 1. to expose ~ 2. moral; political ~ 3. (misc.) bribery and ~; graft and ~ (AE) (there have been many cases of bribery and ~ among top politicians)

corsage *n.* to pin a ~ on

cortex *n.* the cerebral ~

cosigner *n.* a ~ for, of (a ~ for a promissory note)

cosmetics *n.* to apply, put on; use ~

cost I *n.* 1. to bear the ~ 2. to defray the ~ 3. to drive up the ~ 4. to incur; pay ~s 5. to spare no ~ 6. to cut, reduce ~s 7. to estimate; put, set a ~ at (he put the ~ at one hundred dollars) 8. to cover, meet; divide, share, split the ~ 9. advertising; court; direct; fixed; indirect; overhead; production ~s (who will pay the court ~s?) 10. a high ~ (the high ~ of energy) 11. a unit ~ 12. at a certain ~ (at any ~; at all ~s; at the ~ of his health; at a terrible ~; at no ~ to the taxpayer) 13. the ~ in (the ~ in time was considerable) 14. (misc.) the whole community is counting the ~ to it of juvenile delinquency; living ~s; a high ~ of living can mean a low standard of living (see also **cost of living**)

cost II *v.* 1. (D; tr.) to ~ at (they've ~ed the whole project at $50,000) 2. (O; may be used with one inanimate object) "¬how much/what¬ did it cost (you)?" "it cost us ten dollars; it cost ten dollars" 3. (P; with an animate object) his blunder cost us dearly/dear 4. (misc.) it ~s (us) fifty thousand dollars a year to maintain this house

co-star *v.* (D; intr.) to ~ in; with (Vivien Leigh ~ed with Clark Gable in *Gone With The Wind* = Vivien Leigh and Clark Gable ~ed in *Gone With The Wind*)

cost-effective *adj.* ~ to + inf. (it would not be ~ to hire temporary workers)

costly *adj.* ~ to + inf. (it is ~ to run an air conditioner all day)

cost of living *n.* 1. to raise the ~ 2. a high; low ~ 3. a ~ falls, goes down; goes up, rises

costume *n.* 1. an academic; bathing (BE), swimming (BE) ~ 2. (a) folk, national, traditional; Halloween; period ~ (they were all in national ~)

cot *n.* ["folding bed"] (AE; BE has *camp bed*) 1. to open up, unfold a ~ 2. a folding ~ ["child's bed"] (BE) 3. see **crib I**

cottage *n.* a country; summer; thatched; weekend ~

cotton I *n.* 1. to gin; grow; pick; plant ~ 2. (AE) absorbent ~ (CE has *cotton wool*) 3. pure, one hundred percent ~ 4. a bale; reel (BE); wad of ~

cotton II *v.* (colloq.) (d; intr.) ("to take a liking") to ~ to

cotton on *v.* (colloq.) (BE) (D; intr.) ("to understand") to ~ to

cotton up *v.* (colloq.) (esp. AE) (d; intr.) ("to try to ingratiate oneself") to ~ to

couch I *n.* 1. to lie; sit on a ~ (do psychoanalysts still ask patients to lie on a ~?) 2. a studio ~ (see also *couch potato* at **potato** 6)

couch II *v.* (formal) (D; tr.) to ~ in (to ~ a request in tactful language)

cough I *n.* 1. to develop a ~ 2. to give; have a ~ 3. to suppress a ~ 4. a bad, heavy, nasty; chesty; croupy; dry; hacking, persistent; smoker's ~ (see also **whooping cough**)

cough II *v.* to ~ loudly

coughing *n.* a fit of ~

could *v.* (F) he ~ not attend the meeting

council *n.* 1. to convene, convoke a ~ 2. a city (AE), local (BE); county; district; executive; student; township (AE) ~ 3. The Privy Council (GB) USAGE NOTE: In AE a member of a city council is a "councilman" or a "councilwoman." In BE a member of a local council is a "councillor."

counsel I *n.* ["advice"] 1. to give, offer, provide ~ 2. to take ~ (from) 3. sage, wise ~ 4. ~ about, concerning ["lawyer"] 5. (a) legal ~ 6. ~ for (~ for the defense; ~ for the prosecution) ["misc."] 7. to keep one's own ~ ("to keep one's plans secret")

counsel II *v.* 1. (D; tr.) to ~ about, in, on 2. (D; tr.) to ~ against (I ~ed him against going) 3. (H) I ~ed him not to go

counseling, counselling *n.* bereavement; family; guidance; marriage; pastoral; vocational ~ (they sought family ~ for their problems and are getting it every week)

counselor, counsellor *n.* ["adviser"] 1. a bereavement; family; guidance; marriage; pastoral; vocational ~ 2. a ~ to (a ~ to the ambassador)

count I *n.* ["act of counting"] ["total, tally"] 1. to do, have, make, take a ~ 2. to keep ~ of 3. to lose ~ 4. (boxing) to go down for the ~ ("to be counted out"); to take a ~ of ten; to get up at/on the ~ of nine 5. an accurate, correct ~ 6. a final, last ~; the latest ~ 7. a ~ cell; pollen ~ (see also **blood count**; **sperm count**) 8. a body ~ (see also **head**

count) 9. the ~ stands at... 10. at a certain ~ (there were fifty at the latest ~) 11. by smb.'s ~ (by my ~) ["issue"] 12. on a certain ~ (on all ~s) ["charge, accusation"] 13. on a certain ~ (he was guilty on all ~s)

count II v. 1. (d; intr.) ("to be taken into account") to ~ against (your previous convictions will ~ against you) 2. (d; tr.) ("to consider") to ~ among (I always ~ed her among my friends) 3. (d; intr., tr.) ("to be regarded; to regard") to ~ as (the draw ~s as a victory; we ~ed the draw as a victory) 4. (d; intr.) ("to be valued") to ~ for (his opinion ~s for very little) 5. (d; intr.) ("to rely") to ~ for; on, upon (she ~ed on us for help; she ~ed on us to help her) 6. (D; intr.) ("to name numbers") to ~ from; to (to ~ from one to ten) 7. (D; intr.) ("to be taken into account") to ~ towards (do associate members ~ towards a quorum?) 8. (N; refl., tr.; used with an adjective) ("to consider") we must ~ ourselves lucky (to have escaped)

countdown n. 1. a final ~ 2. a ~ from; to (the ~from 10 to zero has begun)

count down v. (D; intr.) to ~ to (to ~ from 10 to zero)

countenance I n. (biblical) a forbidding, stern: radiant, shining ~

countenance II v. 1. (G) they will not ~ cheating on the exam 2. (J) they will not ~ anyone cheating on the exam 3. (K) they will not ~ anyone's cheating on the exam

counter I adj., adv. to act, be, go, run ~ to (that runs ~ to all our traditions)

counter II n. ["surface, table over which business is conducted"] 1. a bargain; notions (AE) ~ 2. a check-in; check-out; ticket ~ 3. a lunch ~ 4. at a ~ ["misc."] 5. over the ~ ("through a broker's office"); ("without a prescription"); under the ~ ("illicitly")

counter III v. 1. (D; intr.) to ~ by (she ~ed by advancing an even stronger argument) 2. (D; intr., tr.) to ~ with (she ~ed with an even stronger argument; she ~ed our argument with an even stronger one of her own) 3. (L) she ~ed that her argument had not been heeded

counter IV n. ["instrument"] 1. to set a ~ 2. a crystal; Geiger ~

counterattack n. 1. to launch, make, mount a ~ 2. a ~ against (see also **attack I**, 1)

counterbalance n. a ~ to

counterblow n. 1. to deal, deliver a ~ 2. a ~ against, to

countercharge n. 1. to bring, file, make a ~ 2. a ~ against (see also **charge I**, 1)

counterclaim n. 1. to bring, enter, make a ~ 2. a ~ against (see also **claim I**, 1–2)

counterclockwise adj., adv. (AE) to go ~; to turn (smt.) ~ (BE has *anticlockwise*)

counterespionage n. 1. to conduct ~ 2. ~ against (see also **espionage**)

counterfeit n. a crude; skillful ~

counterfoil n. (BE) a cheque ~

counterintelligence n. to conduct ~

countermeasures n. 1. to take ~ 2. ~ against

counteroffensive n. 1. to launch, mount, undertake a ~ 2. to go over to the ~ 3. a ~ against 4. on the ~ (the candidate went on the ~ against his opponent)

counteroffer n. to make a ~ (see also **offer I**, 2–3)

counterpart n. 1. a direct, exact ~ 2. to have a ~ in (British diplomats are negotiating with the ~s they have in Russia) 3. a ~ of, to

counterplot n. 1. to hatch a ~ 2. a ~ against (see also **plot I**, 1–6)

counterpoint n. ["accompanying melody"] 1. double; single; triple ~ 2. in ~ to ["contrasting element"] 3. to provide a ~ to; to serve as a ~ to

counterproductive adj. ~ to + inf. (it is ~ to raise so many objections)

counterproposal n. to make, offer a ~ (see also **proposal** 1–3, 8–9)

counterpunch n. to deliver, throw a ~ (see also **punch I**, 1)

counterrevolution n. 1. to foment, stir up a ~ 2. to carry out; organize a ~ 3. a ~ against (see also **revolution** 1–4, 6)

countersign n. to give the ~

countersuit n. (legal) 1. to bring a ~ 2. a ~ against (see also **suit I**, 1–4)

counterweight n. a ~ to (her realism serves as a ~ to his hysteria)

country n. ["nation"] 1. to govern, lead, rule, run a ~ 2. a civilized ~ 3. smb.'s adopted ~; smb.'s mother ~; smb.'s native ~ 4. a host; neighboring ~ 5. a democratic; developing; foreign; free; industrialized; occupied; third-world; underdeveloped ~ ["rural area"] 6. the back ~ 7. open; rough, rugged ~ (in open ~) 8. in the ~ (to live in the ~) ["misc."] 9. (BE) to go to the ~ ("to call a general election")

count up v. (d; intr.) to ~ to (the child could ~ to twenty)

coup n. ["successful action"] 1. to pull off, score a ~ 2. an attempted; bloodless; military ~ (see also **coup d'état**)

coup de grâce n. ["finishing blow"] to administer, deliver, give the ~ (to)

coup d'état n. ["sudden overthrow of a government"] 1. to carry out, mount, stage a ~ 2. an attempted ~ 3. a bloodless; bloody; military ~ (against)

couple I n. 1. a childless; courting; elderly; engaged; loving; married; newlywed; odd; unmarried; young ~ 2. (misc.) at their wedding we toasted the happy ~ by saying "(Here's) To The Happy Couple!"

couple II v. (D; tr.) to ~ to, with (to ~ a dining car to a train)

coupled adj. ~ with (poverty ~ with unemployment can lead to crime)

couplet n. a heroic; rhyming ~

coupon n. 1. to detach; redeem a ~ 2. (misc.) to clip ~s ("to profit from stocks and bonds")

courage *n.* 1. to demonstrate, display, show; have (the) ~ 2. to gather (up), get up, muster, pluck up, screw up, summon up, work up (the) ~ 3. to draw, take ~ (from) 4. to take ~ to + inf. (it takes ~ to tell the truth) 5. dauntless, great, immense, indomitable, sheer; moral; physical ~ 6. an act of ~ 7. the ~ to + inf. (she lacked the ~ to tell the truth) 8. for ~ (to get a medal for ~) 9. of ~ (a person of great ~) 10. (misc.) to have the ~ of one's convictions; take ~ and press on

courageous *adj.* ~ to + inf. (it was ~ of her to tell the truth)

courier *n.* 1. to dispatch a ~ 2. a diplomatic; motorcycle ~ 3. a ~ to 4. by ~ (the message came by ~)

course I *n.* ["organized program of study"] 1. to conduct, do (esp. BE), give, offer, teach a ~ 2. to do (esp. BE), take a ~ 3. to audit (AE), sit in on a ~ 4. to enroll for, join, register for, sign up for a ~ 5. to fail; pass a ~; to take a ~ pass-fail (AE) 6. to complete; drop; drop out of; withdraw from a ~ 7. to introduce; organize, plan a ~ 8. to cancel a ~ 9. a demanding, difficult, rigorous; easy, gut (AE; colloq.) ~ 10. an advanced; beginning, elementary, introductory; intermediate ~ 11. (at a university) a core; crash; elective; graduate, postgraduate (esp. BE); intensive; interdisciplinary; laboratory; lecture; noncredit; pass-fail; remedial; required; survey; undergraduate ~ (see also *coursework* at **work I** *n.*) 12. a correspondence; day-release (BE); extension; makeup; modular; refresher ~ 13. a ~ covers, deals with, treats a subject; lasts, runs (our history ~ covered the nineteenth century and lasted for three terms) 14. a ~ in, on (she took a ~ in mathematics; they offered a ~ on lexicography) ["itinerary"] ["path"] 15. to chart, map out, mark out, plot a ~ 16. to follow, pursue, take a ~ (the law must take its ~) 17. to set ~ for (we set ~ for the nearest port) 18. to alter, change ~ (it's not good to change ~ in midstream) 19. to stay the ~ ("to persist until the end") 20. to run, take its ~ (the disease ran its expected ~; you have to let things take their natural ~) 21. a collision; middle; natural; zigzag ~ (events took their natural ~; to steer a middle ~ between extremes) 22. a ~ of action (to pursue a ~ of action) 23. off ~; on ~ (our ship was right on ~; to be on a collision ~; the plane was off ~; the sailboat was blown off ~) ["playing area"] 24. a golf ~; racecourse (esp. BE) ["training area"] 25. an obstacle ~ ["period"] 26. in the ~ of (in the ~ of an investigation; in the ~ of time; in due ~; in the ordinary ~ of events) ["training area, race"] 27. to do, run a ~ 28. an assault (BE), obstacle; training ~ (the trainees ran the obstacle ~) ["part of a meal"] 29. a first; main ~ ["misc."] 30. of ~ ("naturally") (see the Usage Note for **track**)

course II *v.* (d; intr.) to ~ through (the blood ~d through her veins)

court *n.* ["place where justice is administered"] 1. to adjourn; dismiss (a) ~ 2. to go to ~ (over); take

smb. to ~ (over) 3. to clog the ~s (with frivolous litigation) 4. an appeals (esp. BE), appellate; circuit; city, municipal; county; crown (BE); district (AE); federal (US); high; higher; lower; magistrate's; superior; supreme ~; a law ~ = a ~ of law 5. a criminal; domestic-relations, family; juvenile; orphans'; probate; small-claims; traffic; trial ~ 6. a night; police ~ 7. a kangaroo ("irregular"); moot ~ 8. a ~ of appeal(s); a ~ of common pleas; a ~ of domestic relations; a ~ of law; a ~ of original jurisdiction; a ~ of inquiry (BE) 9. a ~ adjourns; convenes 10. a ~ holds (that), rules (that) 11. before a ~ (when will the case come before the ~?); in ~ (to appear in ~; to testify in ~; in open ~) 12. out of ~ (to settle a case out of ~) ["sovereign's residence"] 13. to hold ~ (now usu. fig.) 14. at ~ (at the ~ of Louis XIV) ["homage"] 15. to pay ~ to smb. ["sports arena"] 16. a badminton; basketball; clay (for tennis); grass (for tennis); handball; indoor; outdoor; squash; tennis; volleyball ~ ["motel"] (obsol.) (AE) 17. a motor, tourist ~

courteous *adj.* 1. ~ to, towards, with (she is ~ to everyone) 2. ~ to + inf. (it was ~ of him to do that) (see also *kind and courteous* at **kind I**, 4)

courtesy *n.* 1. to display, extend, show ~ (they showed us every ~) 2. common; unfailing ~ 3. professional; senatorial (US) ~ 4. an act of ~ 5. ~ to, towards (it was done as a ~ to you) 6. the ~ to + inf. (he didn't have the ~ to answer my letter) 7. by ~ of 8. (misc.) she did me the ~ of remaining silent; a basket of fruit was delivered to our door ~ of the management

courthouse *n.* (esp. AE; CE has *court*) a county; federal; state ~

court martial I *n.* 1. to hold a ~ 2. to try smb. by ~ 3. a drumhead; general; special; summary ~

court-martial II *v.* (D; tr.) to ~ for (he was ~ed for desertion)

courtship *n.* a whirlwind ~

cousin *n.* 1. a distant; first; second ~; a first ~ once removed 2. a ~ of, to (she is a first ~ to the countess) 3. (colloq.) kissing ("friendly") ~s

covenant I *n.* a ~ between

covenant II *v.* (BE) 1. (E) she ~ed to pay the interest 2. (L) she ~ed that she would pay the interest

Coventry *n.* (esp. BE) to send to ~ ("to ostracize")

cover I *n.* ["shelter"] ["concealment"] 1. to run for; seek; take ~ 2. to break ~ 3. (colloq.) to blow smb.'s ~ ("to give smb. away") 4. ~ from (~ from enemy fire) 5. under ~ (under ~ of darkness) ["covering"] 6. cloud ~ (under a thick cloud ~) 7. a dust; mattress; pillow ~ 8. between, under the ~s (the children were huddled under the (bed) ~s) ["defense"] 9. air; protective ~ ["front"] 10. a ~ for (the whole operation was a ~ for foreign agents) ["envelope"] 11. under separate ~ ["binding"] 12. a back; front ~ 13. a book; magazine ~ 14. from ~ to ~ (to read a book from ~ to ~) 15. on the ~ (her picture was on the ~ of the magazine)

cover II v. 1. ("to report on") to ~ live (the event will be ~ed live by/on TV) 2. (D; refl., tr.) ("to protect") to ~ against (this policy will ~ you against flood damage) 3. (d; intr.) to ~ for ("to substitute for; to protect") (to ~ for a friend) 4. (D; tr.) ("to place over") to ~ with (to ~ a child with a blanket)

coverage n. ["insurance"] 1. to provide ~ against, for 2. comprehensive, full ~ ["reporting"] 3. to give; receive ~ 4. complete, extensive, full, wide; front-page ~ (the story received wide ~) 5. live; media; newspaper; television ~

covered adj. ~ in, with (~ in blood)

covering n. a light ~ of (snow)

cover-up n. a ~ by; for

cover up v. 1. (D; intr.) to ~ for ("to protect") (she ~ed up for me when I made that blunder) 2. (D; tr.) to ~ with ("to place over") (she ~ed up the child with a blanket)

covetous adj. ~ of

cow I n. 1. to milk a ~ 2. a beef; dairy, milch (old-fashioned) ~ 3. ~s calve; low, moo 4. a ~ chews its cud 5. a herd of ~s 6. the meat of the ~ is beef 7. a male ~ is a bull 8. a young ~ is a calf; its meat is veal 9. (misc.) (colloq.) holy ~! (AE); silly ~! (BE)

cow II v. (D; tr.) to ~ into (to ~ smb. into making concessions)

coward n. an abject, dirty ~

cowardice n. 1. to display, show ~ 2. abject, rank; moral ~ 3. (misc.) an act of ~; a streak of ~

cowardly adj. ~ to + inf. (it was ~ of them to behave like that)

coy adj. ~ about; with (don't be ~ with me about your past record!)

cozen v. (formal) 1. (d; tr.) to ~ into 2. (d; tr.) to ~ from, out of (to ~ smb. out of his money)

cozy up v. (colloq.) (AE) (D; intr.) to ~ to

CPR (cardiopulmonary resuscitation) n. to do ~ on smb.

crab I n. ["rower's defective stroke"] to catch a ~

crab II v. (colloq.) ("to complain") (D; intr.) to ~ about

crack I n. ["remark"] (colloq.) 1. to make a ~ (about) 2. a dirty, nasty ~ 3. a ~ that (her ~ that you are always late was unjustified) ["moment"] 4. at the ~ of dawn ["attempt"] 5. to have a ~ at (let's have a ~ at it) ["hole"] 6. to peer through a ~ in a fence ["misc."] 7. she opened the window just a ~; the slaves cowered at the ~ of their master's whip

crack II v. 1. (N; used with an adjective) she ~ed it open 2. (P; intr., tr.) she ~ed the eggs into a bowl; to ~ under the strain; his voice ~ed with emotion; she ~ed her head against the wall

crackdown n. 1. to launch a ~ 2. a ~ on (a ~ on drug dealers)

crack down v. (D; intr.) to ~ on (to ~ on drug dealers)

cracked up adj. (colloq.) (cannot stand alone)

["reputed"] ~ to be (this hotel is not all (that)/what it's ~ to be)

cracker n. ["dry biscuit"] 1. (esp. AE) a graham; soda; unsalted ~ 2. (BE) a cream ~

cracking adj. (colloq.) to get ~ (on) ("to start working on smt.")

crackpot n. (colloq.) a ~ to + inf. (he was a ~ to do it)

cradle n. 1. to rock a ~ 2. (misc.) from the ~ to the grave ("during smb.'s whole life")

craft n. ["occupation"] 1. to ply one's, practice a ~ 2. to learn, master a ~ (see also *arts and crafts* at **arts** 8) ["boat"] 3. a landing ~ 4. (in plural) pleasure; small ~

crafted adj. artfully, beautifully; carefully, skillfully ~

craftsman, craftswoman n. a master ~ USAGE NOTE: Note also the term *craftsperson.*

cram v. 1. (D; intr.) ("to study hastily") to ~ for (to ~ for an exam) 2. (d; tr.) ("to jam") to ~ into (to ~ one's things into a suitcase) 3. (D; tr.) to ~ with (the basement was ~med with debris) 4. (misc.) to ~ a suitcase full of clothes

cramp n. 1. to get a ~ (esp. AE)/get ~ (BE) 2. stomach ~(s); writer's ~ 3. (BE) seized with ~

cramped adj. ~ for (space)

cranberry n. to pick ~ries

crane I n. ["machine"] to operate a ~

crane II n. ["bird"] 1. ~s dance (before mating) 2. a flock, kettle of ~s 3. (misc.) a young ~ is a chick or colt

crank n. ["handle"] to turn, use a ~

crap game n. (AE) a floating ~

craps n. (AE) to play, shoot ~

crash I n. ["sudden noise"] 1. a loud, resounding ~ (the plates fell on the floor with a resounding ~) ["violent accident"] 2. a plane ~ (to be killed in a plane ~) ["sudden collapse"] 3. a stockmarket ~ (to lose everything in a stockmarket ~)

crash II v. 1. (d; intr.) to ~ against (waves ~ against the rocks) 2. (d; intr., tr.) to ~ into (the car ~ed into a pole) 3. (d; intr.) to ~ through (the car ~ed through the barrier) 4. (d; intr.) to ~ to (to ~ to the floor) 5. (misc.) the plane ~ed in flames

crass adj. ~ to + inf. (it was ~ of him to ask how much you earn)

crater n. a bomb ~ (to see smb. in a bomb ~)

crave v. 1. to ~ strongly 2. (d; intr.) to ~ for (to ~ for peace and quiet) USAGE NOTE: The phrase *to crave for smt.* is synonymous with *to crave smt.*

craving n. 1. to feel, have; satisfy a ~ 2. an irresistible; powerful, strong ~ 3. a ~ for 4. a ~ to + inf. (a strong ~ to be free)

craw n. ["crop of a bird or insect"] to stick in smb.'s ~ ("to be distasteful to smb.")

crawl I n. ["swimming stroke"] 1. to do, swim the ~ ["act of crawling"] (also fig.) 2. at a ~ (traffic moved at a ~) 3. to a ~ (traffic slowed to a ~)

crawl II v. 1. (d; intr.) to ~ into (to ~ into a hole)

2. (d; intr.) to ~ out of (to ~ out of the ruins) 3. (d; intr.) to ~ with (the city is ~ing with reporters) 4. (P; intr.) to ~ under the bed; she managed to ~ across the floor on her hands and knees; they ~ed from under the ruins

crawl out v. (D; intr.) to ~ from under (they ~ed out from under the ruins)

crayon n. 1. colored; wax ~s (a box of colored ~s) 2. in ~, with a ~ (to draw a picture with a/in ~; to color a picture in with/using a ~)

craze n. 1. the current, latest, newest ~ 2. the ~ swept the country 3. a ~ for

crazed adj. 1. drug-~ 2. ~ with (anger)

crazy adj. (colloq.) ["infatuated"] 1. (cannot stand alone) ~ about (he is ~ about her) ["foolish"] 2. ~ to + inf. (it was ~ of her to drive without headlights = she was ~ to drive without headlights) ["insane"] 3. to drive/make (AE) smb. ~; to go ~

cream n. ["component of milk"] 1. to whip ~ 2. clotted (BE); double (BE), whipping; single (BE); sour, soured (BE); whipped ~ (see also **ice cream**) ["cosmetic"] 3. to apply ~ 4. cleansing; cold; face; hand; moisturizing; shaving; skin; vanishing ~ ["misc."] the ~ of the crop ("the very best")

crease n. 1. to iron out, remove, smooth down the ~s 2. a sharp ~

create v. ("to appoint") (BE) (N; used with a noun) he was ~d duke

creature n. 1. living ~s 2. a ~ of habit

credence n. 1. to attach, give, lend ~ to 2. to gain ~

credentials n. 1. to establish; present one's ~ (as) 2. to evaluate; examine smb.'s ~ 3. excellent, impeccable, sound ~

credibility n. 1. to establish; restore ~ (one's) (as) 2. to lack ~; to lose one's ~ 3. to damage, undermine smb.'s ~ (see also *a credibility gap* at **gap** 5)

credit I n. ["time given for payment; deferred payment"] 1. to allow, give, extend, offer ~ (this store does not give ~) 2. to deny, refuse smb. ~ 3. consumer; interest-free ~ 4. on ~ (to buy smt. on ~) 5. (misc.) a line of ~ = a credit ~ (see also *credit crunch* at **crunch** n = *credit squeeze* at **squeeze** n) ["recognition"] ["honor"] 6. to do ~ to; to reflect ~ on (her work does (great) ~ to her teachers = her work does her teachers (great) ~) 7. to claim (the) ~ for; to get, take (the) ~ for (he took ~ for my work) 8. to deserve ~ (for) 9. to give smb. ~ for (I give her full ~ for being so sensible) 10. a ~ to (they are a ~ to their parents) 11. ~ that + clause (it was to her ~ that she never gave up) 12. to smb.'s ~ (to her ~, she never gave up; she has a dozen publications to her ~) 13. (misc.) (give) ~ where ~ is due (I don't like her but, to give ~ where ~ is due, at least she never gave up!) ["sum allowed, deducted"] 14. an energy (AE); tax ~ ["recognition that a student has completed a course or unit of study"] 15. to earn, get, receive; transfer ~ (for a course) 16. advanced ~

credit II v. 1. (D; tr.) to ~ to (to ~ fifty dollars to smb.'s account) 2. (d; tr.) to ~ with (to ~ smb. with

common sense; she is ~ed with that discovery; to ~ an account with fifty dollars)

credit card n. 1. to accept; issue a ~ 2. a ~ expires (your ~ is no longer valid: it expired last week) 3. by ~ (can I pay by ~?) 4. (misc.) to put a purchase on one's/smb.'s ~

creditor n. to pay off one's ~s

credo n. a ~ that + clause (it is our ~ that everyone is equal)

credulity n. to strain, stretch smb.'s ~ (to the breaking point)

creed n. 1. to adhere to; embrace a ~ 2. a political; religious ~ 3. a ~ that + clause (it is our ~ that everyone is equal) 4. (misc.) all races and ~s

creep v. 1. (d; intr.) to ~ into (to ~ into a hole) 2. (d; intr.) to ~ out of (an insect crept out of the pipe) 3. (P; intr.) to ~ across the floor; the baby crept around the room 4. (misc.) to ~ on all fours; to ~ out from under a bush

creeps n. (colloq.) ["fear"] it gives me the ~

creep up v. (D; intr.) to ~ on (he crept up on me in the dark)

creepy adj. (colloq.) ["weird"] ~ about (there is smt. ~ about him)

crescendo n. 1. to reach a ~, rise to a ~ 2. a deafening; rising ~ USAGE NOTE: Except for "a deafening crescendo," all the other expressions given above are disliked by those who know that a crescendo (as in music) is an increase in loudness, not a peak of loudness. So the following are preferable: to reach a climax; to rise in a crescendo. As for "a rising crescendo," crescendos rise by definition. So "crescendo" will suffice here without "rising."

crest n. ["top"] 1. to ride (on) the ~ of a wave (to ride the ~ of a wave of popularity) 2. at the ~ ["heraldic device"] 3. a family ~

crew n. ["group working together"] 1. a camera; film; ground; gun; road; skeleton; stage; tank; TV; work; wrecking ~ ["ship's personnel"] 2. a ship's ~ 3. a ~ mutinies 4. in a ~ ["rowing team"] (AE) 5. a varsity ~ 6. to go out for ~ [misc.] 7. a motley ~ ("a disparate group")

crib I n. (AE) 1. to assemble, put up a ~ 2. to dismantle a ~ (BE has *cot*)

crib II v. (colloq.) (D; intr., tr.) ("to plagiarize") to ~ from

cricket I n. ["game"] 1. to play ~ 2. the game of ~ 3. (misc.) a ~ game, match ["fair play"] (colloq.) 4. ~ to + inf. (it's not ~ to cheat at cards)

cricket II n. ["insect"] ~s chirp

crier n. a town ~

crime n. 1. to commit, perpetrate a ~ 2. to combat; deter; eradicate, stamp out, wipe out; prevent ~ 3. to prosecute; solve a ~ 4. an atrocious, brutal, heinous, horrendous, horrible, infamous, outrageous, unspeakable, vicious, violent ~ 5. a copycat ~; (a) white-collar ~ 6. (an) economic ~; (a) hate ~ (esp. AE); a victimless ~; a war ~ (see also *war-crimes trial* at **trial**) 7. a daring; major, serious; minor, petty; perfect ~ 8. gun; inner-city; juvenile; knife ~; street ~ (does inner-city ~ often involve drugs?) 9. a ~ of passion 10. organized ~ 11. a ~ against (a ~ against humanity; ~s against the person; ~s against property) 12. a ~ to + inf. (it was a ~ to butcher French like that) 13. a ~ that + clause (it is a ~ that so many people go to bed hungry) 14. (misc.) to investigate a ~; to report a ~ (to the police); many ~s go unreported; it's a ~ how/the way he behaves! (see also *at the scene of the crime* at **scene** 9; *a crime wave* at **wave I**, 5)

criminal I *adj.* 1. ~ to + inf. (it was ~ of him to do that) 2. ~ that + clause (it is ~ that he is/should be allowed to remain in this country)

criminal II *n.* 1. to apprehend, arrest, catch a ~; to bring a ~ to justice; to punish a ~ 2. to pardon; parole; release a ~ 3. to rehabilitate a ~ 4. a born; common; dangerous; desperate; habitual, hardened, inveterate, vicious; infamous, notorious; master; petty; war ~ 5. a band, gang of ~s

crimp *n.* (colloq.) (AE) ["obstacle"] to put a ~ in

cringe *v.* 1. (D; intr.) to ~ at (to ~ at one's mistake) 2. (D; intr.) to ~ before (to ~ before one's superiors) 3. (D; intr.) to ~ with (to ~ with embarrassment)

crisis *n.* 1. to cause, lead to, precipitate, provoke, stir up a ~ 2. to aggravate, worsen a ~ 3. to avert, forestall a ~ 4. to deal with, defuse, overcome, resolve, settle, tackle a ~; to face a ~; to ride out, weather a ~ 5. an acute, grave, serious; impending, looming; mounting ~ 6. a cabinet; constitutional; humanitarian; international; national ~ 7. an economic, financial, fiscal; energy; political ~ 8. a family; food; housing; identity; mid-life; personal ~ 9. a ~ arises; deepens, worsens; looms; eases 10. a ~ over (there was a ~ over the budget deficit) 11. a ~ in (the ~ in health care) 12. in a ~ (see also *a crisis of confidence* at **confidence** 22)

crisp *n.* burned to a ~

criterion *n.* 1. to adopt, establish, lay down; apply a ~ 2. to fulfill, meet, satisfy criteria 3. a reliable, valid ~ 4. a set of criteria 5. a ~ for (of what are the criteria of effectiveness for a new drug to meet?) 6. according to, by a ~ (by which criteria should the effectiveness of a new drug be assessed?)

critic *n.* 1. a harsh, severe, unkind; impartial, unbiased; outspoken ~ (of) 2. an art; drama, theater; film; literary; music; social ~ 3. (misc.) an armchair ~; to be one's own worst/most severe ~

critical *adj.* ["criticizing"] 1. sharply, very ~ 2. ~ of (he was not ~ of my work) ["indispensable"] (AE) 3. ~ for, to (~ to our work) 4. ~ that + clause; subj. (it is ~ that the work ¬be/should be/(BE) is¬ completed on time)

criticism *n.* 1. to arouse, provoke, stir up ~ 2. to come in for; draw ~ 3. to express, offer ~; to level ~ at 4. to accept, take, tolerate ~ 5. to react to, respond to ~ 6. to deflect; reject ~ 7. to temper one's ~ 8. to subject smb./smt. to ~ 9. constructive; fair;

mild; sober; valid ~ 10. nitpicking, petty; unfair ~ 11. adverse, barbed, biting, damaging, devastating, harsh, hostile, scathing, severe, sharp, strong, sweeping, swingeing (BE), telling, unsparing, withering; fresh, new ~ 12. literary; textual ~ 13. (the) higher; lower ~ (of the Bible) 14. a barrage, storm of ~ (by promising reform, the government tried to deflect a storm of fresh ~ of its policies) 15. (misc.) the barbs of ~; beneath ~

criticize *v.* 1. to ~ bitterly, harshly, severely, sharply, strongly; fairly; unfairly; widely 2. (D; tr.) to ~ as (to ~ smb. as a sloppy worker) 3. (D; tr.) to ~ for (to ~ smb. for sloppy work)

critique *n.* to give, present a ~ (of)

crop I *n.* ["produce grown by farmers"] 1. to grow; plant a ~ 2. to gather, harvest, reap a ~ 3. to bear, yield a ~ 4. to rotate ~s 5. to dust, spray ~s 6. a bountiful, bumper, fine, record ~ 7. a poor; subsistence ~ 8. a cash; fodder; staple ~ 9. a ~ fails ["stick"] 10. a riding ~

crop II *v.* (N; used with an adjective) they ~ped the grass short

cropper *n.* (colloq.) ["failure"] to come a ~ ("to fail")

croquet *n.* to play ~

croquettes *n.* chicken; salmon ~s

cross I *adj.* ["irritable"] ~ about, for; at, with (~ at smt.; are you still ~ with me about what happened?)

cross II *n.* ["symbol of the Christian religion"] 1. to die on the ~ (said of Jesus Christ) 2. to make the sign of the ~ 3. (misc.) to bear one's ~ ("to bear a heavy burden") ["the figure + or x"] 4. to make one's ~ (in place of a signature) ["mixture"] 5. a ~ between (a ~ between a peach and a plum)

cross III *v.* 1. (D; intr., tr.) ("to go") to ~ from; to (they ~ed from one bank of the river to the other; we ~ed the valley from one ridge to the other) 2. (d; tr.) to ~ off (to ~ a name off a list) 3. (D; tr.) ("to crossbreed") to ~ with (can you ~ a peach with/and a plum?)

cross-country *adv.* to go, travel ~

cross-examination *n.* 1. to conduct, do a ~ 2. to subject smb. to ~ 3. a rapid-fire ~ 4. during, under ~

cross-examine *v.* 1. to ~ sharply; unmercifully 2. (D; tr.) to ~ about, on

cross-fire *n.* 1. to be caught in a/the ~ 2. to subject to ~ 3. exposed to ~

crossing *n.* 1. to make a ~ 2. a rough; smooth ~ 3. a border ~ 4. a grade (AE), level (BE); pedestrian, pelican (BE), zebra (BE); railroad (AE), railway (esp. BE) ~ 5. a transoceanic ~ 6. at a ~ (at the border ~) 7. on a ~ (hit by a car on a pedestrian ~)

cross over *v.* (D; intr.) to ~ from; into, to (she ~ed over from one lane to the other)

cross-purposes *n.* at ~ (to work at ~)

cross-refer *v.* (D; intr., tr.) to ~ between; from; to

cross-reference *n.* 1. to make a ~ 2. a ~ from; to

crossroads *n.* 1. come to, reach a ~ 2. a ~ in (Britain has reached a ~ in her history) 3. at a ~ (also fig.) (a book called *Britain at the Crossroads*)

crossword (BE) see **crossword puzzle**
crossword puzzle *n.* (esp. AE) to do, work (out) a ~
crow I *n.* 1. ~s caw 2. a flock of ~s 3. (misc.) as the ~ flies ("in a straight line"); (forced) to eat ~ (AE) ("(forced) into a humiliating position, (forced) to eat humble pie")
crow II *v.* (colloq.) ("to exult") (d; intr.) to ~ about, over (to ~ about one's success; to ~ over an enemy's misfortune)
crowd I *n.* ["throng"] 1. to attract, draw, (colloq.) pull; join; stand out from a ~ 2. to control; disperse a ~ (see also *crowd control* at **control**) 3. an angry, hostile, unfriendly; cheering, friendly; enormous, huge, tremendous; lonely; overflow ~ (*The Lonely Crowd* (1950), David Riesman et al.) 4. a ~ collects, gathers; disperses, melts away, thins out; roars 5. a ~ flocks, mills, swarms, throngs (around an entrance); ~s line the streets (~s milled around the entrance and lined the streets nearby) 6. among; in; through a ~ (just one more face in the ~) ["audience"] 7. a capacity ~ ["group"] 8. a bad; fast, wild ~; the wrong ~ (to run around with a fast ~; she got in with the wrong ~)
crowd II *v.* 1. (d; intr.) to ~ around (to ~ around the entrance) 2. (d; intr.) to ~ into, to (to ~ into a small room) 3. (d; tr.) to ~ off, out of (they ~ed me off the road) 4. (d; intr.) to ~ through (they ~ed through the turnstiles) 5. (misc.) to ~ together
crowded *adj.* 1. densely ~ 2. ~ with (the streets were ~ with tourists)
crown I *n.* ["part of a tooth"] 1. to put a ~ on (a tooth) ["monarch's headdress; monarchy"] 2. to offer smb. the ~; succeed to the ~; wear a ~ ["boxing title"] 3. to lose; win the (heavyweight) ~
crown II *v.* 1. (d; tr.) to ~ with (their efforts were ~ed with success) 2. (N; used with a noun) they ~ed him king
crucial *adj.* 1. ~ for, to (these negotiations are ~ for/ to the future of our firm) 2. ~ that + clause; subj. (it is ~ that this matter remain/should remain secret; BE also has *remains secret*)
crude *adj.* ~ to + inf. (it was ~ of him to say that)
cruel *adj.* 1. ~ to, towards (~ to animals) 2. ~ to + inf. (it was ~ of him to say that)
cruelty *n.* 1. to display, show ~; to inflict ~ on 2. consummate, deliberate, wanton ~ 3. mental ~ 4. an act of ~ 5. ~ to, towards (~ to animals)
cruise I *n.* 1. to go on, set off on, take a ~ 2. an extended, long; pleasure; round-the-world, world; shakedown; short ~ 3. a ~ along; around (to take a ~ around the world) 4. a ~ from; to 5. a ~ through 6. on a ~
cruise II *v.* (P; intr.) to ~ along the coast; to ~ around the world; to ~ through the coastal waters
cruiser *n.* 1. a battle; cabin; converted; guided-missile; heavy; light; medium ~ 2. in; on a ~
crumble *v.* (D; intr.) to ~ into
crunch *n.* (colloq.) ["shortage"] 1. a credit; energy;

financial ~ ["showdown"] (colloq.) 2. if/when it comes to the ~
crusade I *n.* 1. to conduct; launch a ~ 2. to embark on; engage in; go on; join a ~ 3. a one-man, one-woman ~ 4. a great; holy; moral ~ 5. a ~ against; for (a ~ against smoking) 6. on a ~ 7. a ~ to + inf. (they launched a ~ to ban smoking)
crusade II *v.* 1. (D; intr.) to ~ against; for (to ~ against smoking) 2. (E) they ~d to ban smoking
USAGE NOTE: Because the medieval crusades were by Christians against Muslims, the word "crusade" is used sparingly nowadays.
crush I *n.* ["infatuation"] (colloq.) 1. a schoolboy; schoolgirl; youthful ~ 2. a ~ on (to develop/have a ~ on smb.)
crush II *v.* 1. (d; intr.) to ~ against (the mob ~ed against the barriers 2. (D; tr.) to get ~ed between two slabs of concrete 3. (D; tr.) to ~ a substance into powder) 4. (misc.) to ~ smb. to death; to ~ smt. underfoot
crust *n.* ["impudence"] (colloq.) the ~ to + inf. (she had the ~ to ask for a raise!)
crutch *n.* 1. to walk on, with ~es 2. a pair of ~es
cry I *n.* 1. to give, raise (formal), utter a ~ 2. an anguished, plaintive; bloodcurdling; great; heartrending; loud, lusty; piercing; rallying; shrill ~ 3. a battle, war ~ 4. a ~ goes up (a ~ went up from the crowd when their leader appeared); a ~ for (a ~ for help) 5. (misc.) a far ~ from ("very far from"); to have a good ~
cry II *v.* 1. to ~ bitterly; loudly 2. (D; intr.) ("to weep") to ~ at (they cried bitterly at the sad news) 3. (d; intr.) ("to appeal") to ~ for (to ~ for justice) 4. (d; intr.) ("to weep") to ~ for, with (to ~ for joy; to ~ with grief) 5. (d; intr.) ("to weep") to ~ over (to ~ over one's bad luck) 6. (d; intr.) to ~ to ("to complain to") (don't come ~ing to me) 7. (L; to) ("to shout") she cried loudly to us) that the house was on fire 8. (misc.) to ~ wolf ("to give a false alarm"); to ~ one's eyes out; to ~ over spilled (AE)/spilt milk ("to complain in vain"); she cried herself to sleep; to ~ on smb.'s shoulder ("to seek sympathy from smb."); to raise a hue and ~
cry out *v.* 1. (d; intr.) ("to appeal") to ~ against; for (to ~ against injustice; to ~ for equal rights) 2. (D; intr.) ("to scream") to ~ in (to ~ in pain) 3. (d; intr., tr.) ("to shout") to ~ to (he cried out to us to stop) 4. (L; to) ("to shout") she cried out (to us) that the rain was coming through the roof
crystal *n.* 1. ~ glitters, sparkles 2. fine ~
crystallize *v.* (D; intr.) to ~ into (their ideas finally ~d into a feasible project)
cube *n.* a bouillon (AE), stock (BE); ice; sugar ~
cube root *n.* to calculate, find, extract the ~
cucumber *n.* 1. to peel; slice a ~ 2. (misc.) (as) cool as a ~
cud *n.* a cow chews its ~
cuddle up *v.* 1. (D; intr.) to ~ to (the twins ~d up to each other) 2. (misc.) to ~ together

cudgels *n.* ["support"] to take up the ~ for
cue *n.* ["signal"] 1. to give the ~ 2. to take one's ~
from smb. 3. to miss the ~ 4. a ~ to + inf. (the
applause was my ~ to enter the room) 5. a ~ for
(the applause was the ~ for me to enter the room)
6. on ~
cuff *n.* 1. a French; trouser (AE) ~ 2. (misc.) (esp.
AE) on the ~ ("on credit")
cull *v.* (D; tr.) to ~ from
culminate *v.* (d; intr.) to ~ in; with (to ~ in victory;
to ~ with an appeal for unity)
cult *n.* 1. to join a ~ 2. a cargo; fertility; religious ~
3. a personality ~ = a ~ of personality (Khrushchev
denounced the cult of ~ surrounding Stalin)
cultivation *n.* under ~
culture *n.* ["pattern of activities, values, and artifacts of a
society"] 1. to develop a ~ 2. (an) ancient; counter-
culture; dependency; enterprise; ethnic; human;
material; modern; pop; primitive; tribal; youth ~
(see also *culture shock* at **shock I**) 3. a ~ arises,
develops; declines 4. in a ~ (different customs in
tribal ~s and modern ~) ["enlightenment"] ["good
taste"] 5. to bring ~ to 6. to disseminate, foster,
spread ~ 7. high ~ ["vocational training"] (AE) 8.
beauty ~ ["cultivation of living material in a media"] 9.
to do, grow a ~ 10. a tissue ~
cunning I *adj.* ~ to + inf. (it was ~ of them to do
that)
cunning II *n.* 1. to show ~ 2. a certain low ~
cup *n.* ["prize"] 1. to lose; win a ~ 2. a challenge ~;
the World Cup (the final round of the challenge ~)
(see also *cup final* at **final**) ["small drinking vessel"] 3.
to drain, empty one's ~ 4. a china; coffee; drinking; paper; plastic ~; teacup 5. a set of (matching)
~s 6. (misc.) to be in one's cups ("to be drunk")
cupboard *n.* 1. an airing (BE); built-in; kitchen ~ 2.
(usu. fig.) a bare ~
cupid *n.* to play ~ (to)
curb *n.* ["restraint"] a ~ on
curd *n.* soybean (AE), soya bean (BE) ~
cure I *n.* 1. to bring about, effect, provide, work a
~ 2. a certain, known, sure; complete; magical;
miraculous; spontaneous ~ 3. a rest; water ~ 4. a ~
for (there is no known ~ for this disease)
cure II *v.* (D; tr.) to ~ of (to ~ smb. of a disease)
curfew *n.* 1. to clamp a ~ on; impose a ~ (they
imposed a ~; the military government clamped a
~ on the town) 2. to lift a ~ 3. to observe a ~ 4. to
violate a ~ 5. a midnight ~ 6. a ~ on 7. under (a) ~
(the town is no longer under ~)
curiosity *n.* 1. to arouse, excite, pique, whet
(smb.'s) ~ 2. to satisfy one's ~ 3. (a) healthy; idle;
insatiable, unquenchable; intellectual; morbid,
unhealthy; natural ~ 4. ~ about 5. out of ~ (he did
it out of ~)
curious *adj.* ["eager to know"] 1. ~ about (~ about
smb.'s past) 2. ~ to + inf. (I would be ~ to know
what really happened) ["odd"] 3. ~ that + clause (it
is ~ that she didn't remember the incident)

curl *v.* (D; intr., tr.) to ~ around (the roots ~ed
around the water pipes; she ~ed her finger around
the doorknob)
curls *n.* 1. natural; tight ~ 2. in ~ (she wears her
hair in ~)
curl up *v.* 1. (D; intr.) to ~ in, into (to ~ into a ball) 2.
(D; intr.) to ~ with (she ~ed up with a good book)
currency *n.* [-"money"] 1. to issue; print ~ 2. to call
in, withdraw ~ 3. to devalue (a) ~ 4. (a) blocked;
convertible, hard; foreign; local; non-convertible,
soft, weak; stable, strong ~ 5. (misc.) they were
paid in local ~ ["general use"] 6. to enjoy, have; gain
~ (to enjoy wide ~)
current *n.* ["flow of electricity"] 1. to switch on, turn
on the ~ 2. to switch off, turn off the ~ 3. alternating; direct; electric; high-tension; low-tension;
oscillating ~ ["flow"] 4. an air; underwater ~ 5. a
powerful, strong; treacherous ~ 6. against; with
the ~
curriculum *n.* 1. to draw up, design a ~ 2. a college,
university; school ~ 3. a basic, core; national (BE)
~ 4. a ~ in (the ~ in engineering) 5. in, on the ~
(which subjects are in/on the ~?)
curry *n.* 1. (a) hot, mild ~ 2. (a) fish; meat;
vegetable ~
curse I *n.* 1. to pronounce, put a ~ on, upon smb. 2.
to utter a ~ 3. to lift a ~ 4. a bitter ~ 5. under a ~
curse II *v.* 1. to ~ bitterly 2. (D; tr.) to ~ for (she ~d
him for his clumsiness) 3. (D; tr.) to ~ with (he has
been ~d with poor health)
cursor *n.* to move a ~ (on a computer)
curt *adj.* ~ with (the hotel clerk was ~ with the
guests)
curtain *n.* 1. to draw; lower; raise a ~ 2. (in the theater) to ring down; ring up the ~ 3. a drop; shower;
stage, theater ~ 4. a billowing; lace; net ~ 5. (fig.)
a bamboo; iron ~ 6. (in the theater) the ~ goes
up, rises; comes down, drops, falls (the ~ rises to
reveal the two main characters) (see also **curtains**)
USAGE NOTES: 1. Remember that to draw a
curtain is either to open it or to close it! 2. What
happened to the Iron Curtain in 1989–91? Some
people say that it came down. But in 1946 Winston
Churchill said "An iron curtain has descended
across the continent": a curtain descends or comes
down or falls to block or separate and rises or goes
up to unblock or remove separation. So it's probably clearer to say simply that in 1989–91 the Iron
Curtain ceased to exist.
curtain call *n.* to get, have; take a ~ (the actor had
five curtain ~s!)
curtains *n.* ["drapes"] 1. to hang, put up ~ 2. to close,
draw; draw, open the ~ 3. window ~ 4. a pair of ~
["ruin"] (colloq.) 5. ~ for (it will be ~ for him if he
loses his job)
curtsy, curtsey I *n.* 1. to bob, give, make a ~ 2. a
deep ~
curtsy, curtsey II *v.* (D; intr.) to ~ to (to ~ to the
Queen)

curve I *n.* ["bend, esp. in a road"] 1. to make a ~ (the road makes a ~ to the right) 2. to take a ~ (in a car) 3. a hairpin, horseshoe; sharp ~ 4. a ~ in (there was a ~ in the road) ["distribution indicated by a line, used in mathematics and statistics"] 5. to plot a ~ ("to locate a curve by plotted points") 6. (teaching) to grade (AE), mark on a ~ 7. a bell, bell-shaped, normal distribution; learning ~ (this new job has been a very steep learning ~ for me) ["misc."] 8. (baseball and fig; AE) to throw smb. a ~ (= (cricket and fig.; BE) *to bowl smb. a googly*: now rare in fig. use)

curve II *v.* 1. to ~ gently; sharply 2. (D; intr.) to ~ to (to ~ to the right) 3. (P; intr.) the missile ~d through the air

cuss *v.* (D; intr.) to ~ at (he ~ed at the other drivers)

custody *n.* ["guardianship"] 1. to award, grant ~ 2. to gain, get, receive, win; have; take ~ (of) 3. to lose ~ (of) 4. joint ~ ["arrest"] 5. to take smb. into ~ 6. remanded in ~ 7. police; protective ~ 8. in ~ ("under arrest") (held in ~)

custom *n.* 1. to establish a ~ 2. to cherish, observe, practice; preserve a ~ 3. to defy ~ 4. (a) local ~ 5. an ancient, old; barbaric; native; pagan; quaint; religious; social; time-honored, traditional; tribal ~ 6. a ~ dies out, disappears; lives on, survives 7. a ~ to + inf. (it is an old ~ for men to tip their hats when greeting smb.) 8. a ~ that + clause (it is an old ~ that men tip their hats when greeting smb.) 9. by ~ 10. (misc.) (BE) old Spanish ~s ("restrictive working practices")

customary *adj.* 1. ~ for 2. ~ to + inf. (is it still ~ for men to tip their hats when greeting smb. ?)

customer *n.* 1. to attract ~s 2. to serve, wait on a ~ 3. an irate; prospective; regular, steady; satisfied ~ 4. a cash ~ 5. (misc.) an odd, tricky ("a strange person"); an ugly ~ ("a violent person") USAGE NOTE: Because passengers are increasingly being called customers, see also **passenger** for relevant phraseology.

customs *n.* 1. to clear, get through, go through, pass through ~ (we got through ~ very quickly) 2. to clear, get smt. through ~ (we got the toys through ~ without difficulty) 3. to declare smt. at ~ 4. to get stopped at ~

cut I *n.* ["wound made by smt. sharp"] 1. to bandage a ~ 2. a clean; deep; nasty; superficial ~ (superficial ~s and bruises that healed quickly) ["reduction"] 3. to make; take a ~ 4. a budget; pay; personnel, staff; spending; tax ~ (we had to take a pay ~) 5. a ~ in (we had to take a ~ in pay) ["haircut"] 6. a crew ~

cut II *v.* 1. ("to gash") to ~ deeply 2. ("to slice") to ~ easily (the meat ~s easily) 3. (C) ("to slice") ~ a piece of cake for me; or: ~ me a piece of cake 4. (d; intr.) ("to go") to ~ across (to ~ across a field) 5. (D; tr.) ("to reduce") to ~ by; from; to (they cut taxes by three percent from eight percent to five percent) 6. (D; tr.) ("to sever") to ~ from, off (to ~ a branch from a tree; he was cut from the team

(AE); she cut a thin slice from the loaf; ~ the crust off the bread) 7. (d; intr.) ("to slice") to ~ into (she cut into the cake) 8. (D; tr.) ("to slice") to ~ into (he cut the meat into small pieces) 9. (D; intr.) ("to break into, interrupt") to ~ into (to ~ into a conversation; work ~s into my leisure time) 10. (D; refl.) ("to gash") to ~ on (she cut herself on a knife) 11. (D; tr.) ("to remove") to ~ out of (she was cut out of the will) 12. (d; intr.) ("to go") to ~ through (they cut through the woods; let's ~ through this building) 13. (D; tr.) to ~ with (to ~ meat with a knife) 14. (N; used with an adjective) ("to trim") she cut her hair short; she cut the bread thin; to ~ smt. open 15. (misc.) to ~ smb. short ("to interrupt smb."); to ~ smb. to the quick ("to insult smb. deeply"); to ~ smt. to pieces; to ~ smt. in half; to ~ and paste

cut ahead, cut in front *v.* (d; intr.) to ~ of ("to cut off") (the other runner cut ahead of her; they cut in front of us)

cut away *v.* (D; tr.) to ~ from

cutback *n.* a ~ in (a ~ in production)

cut back *v.* (D; intr.) to ~ on (to ~ on smoking)

cut down *v.* 1. (D; intr.) to ~ on (to ~ on smoking) 2. (misc.) to ~ smb. down to size ("to deflate smb.'s ego")

cut in *v.* 1. (D; intr.) to ~ on (he cut in on me when I was dancing) 2. (slang) (D; tr.) to ~ on (he cut me in on the deal)

cutlet *n.* a lamb (BE); mutton (BE); veal; vegetarian ~ (a breaded veal ~ or Wiener schnitzel)

cut off *v.* 1. (C) ("to slice") he cut off a slice for me; or: he cut me off a slice 2. (D; tr.) ("to separate") to ~ from (we were cut off from civilization)

cut out I *adj.* ["suited"] 1. ~ for (she wasn't ~ for this job) 2. ~ to + inf. (she wasn't ~ to do this job; she wasn't ~ to be an administrator)

cut out II *v.* 1. (D; tr.) to ~ from, of (to ~ an article out from the newspaper) 2. (G) she had to ~ driving after dark

cutter *n.* 1. a cookie (AE); paper ~ 2. (a pair of) wire ~s

cutting *n.* a newspaper; press ~ (from) (BE; AE has *press clipping*)

cutting edge *n.* ["leading edge"] at the ~ (of)

cut up *v.* 1. (D; tr.) to ~ into (to ~ smt. up into pieces) 2. (misc.) (BE) to ~ rough ("to cause trouble")

cyberspace *n.* 1. in ~ 2. welcome to ~!

cycle *n.* ["repeating pattern"] 1. to complete a (full) ~ 2. to go through, pass through a ~ 3. a boom-and-bust, boom-bust, business; economic; estrous (AE), oestrous (BE); life; menstrual; vicious ~ 4. (as on a washing machine) a delicate; normal; permanent-press; spin ~ 5. in a ~, in ~s (some epidemics occur in ~s) ["bicycle"] (see **bicycle**)

cyclone *n.* 1. a severe, violent; tropical ~ 2. a ~ comes up; hits, strikes; rages (the ~ struck several cities) 3. a ~ blows itself out, blows over, dies down, subsides 4. (in) the eye of a ~

cynical *adj.* ~ about (~ about smb.'s motives)
cynicism *n.* 1. bitter ~ 2. with ~ (she received his
promises with a certain degree of ~)
cypher (esp. BE) see cipher

cyst *n.* to remove a ~
czar *n.* (colloq.) (AE) ["a person with great power"]
a drug; financial; gambling; shipbuilding ~ (BE
spelling is *tsar*; for this meaning BE has *supremo*)

D

dab v. 1. (d; intr.) to ~ at (to ~ at one's eyes with a handkerchief) 2. (d; tr.) to ~ on (she dabbed some lotion on her face)

dabble v. (d; intr.) to ~ at, in, with (to ~ in politics; to ~ at painting)

dagger n. 1. to draw, unsheathe; sheathe a ~ 2. to plunge a ~ into (smb.), to stab (smb.) with a ~ 3. (misc.) to look ~s at ("to look angrily at")

dais n. 1. to get up on, mount the ~ 2. to stand on the ~ 3. from; on the ~

daisy n. 1. to pick ~sies 2. (misc.) as fresh as a ~

dally v. 1. (D; intr.) ("to be slow") to ~ over (to ~ over one's work) 2. (d; intr.) ("to play") to ~ with (to ~ with the idea of studying abroad)

dam n. 1. to build, construct, erect a ~ 2. a hydroelectric; storage ~ 3. a ~ bursts 4. a ~ across (to build a ~ across a river)

damage I n. ["harm"] 1. to cause, do ~ to; to inflict ~ on 2. to suffer, sustain ~ 3. to repair, undo ~ 4. to assess the ~ (trying to assess the extent of) the ~) 5. grave, great, extensive, heavy, incalculable, irreparable, serious, severe; lasting, permanent; widespread ~ 6. light, slight ~ 7. environmental; fire; flood; material; property; structural ~ 8. brain ~ (irreversible brain ~) 9. ~ from (~ from the fire) 10. ~ to (was there much ~ to the car? the ~ done to the house was extensive; to do grave ~ to smb.'s reputation) (see USAGE NOTE at **damage II**)

damage II v. 1. to ~ badly, irreparably, severely 2. easily ~d USAGE NOTE: Typically, inanimate objects (such as cars, houses) or abstractions (such as reputations, credibility) are damaged whereas animate objects (such as people, animals, body parts) are injured (in the accident my car was damaged and I was injured; the accident damaged my reputation as a good driver; his head injury resulted in brain damage). In the last example, the head is regarded as a body part but the brain is used to mean the mind, an abstraction.

damages n. ["compensation"] 1. to award ~ (the court awarded ~) 2. to claim; sue for ~ 3. to pay; receive, recover ~ 4. compensatory; exemplary, punitive; nominal ~ 5. ~ for 6. in ~ (to award one thousand dollars in ~ for injuries sustained in the accident)

damn I n. (colloq.) ["small amount"] it isn't worth a ~; not to give a (tinker's) ~ (CE; BE also has *tinker's curse* or *tinker's cuss*); (I don't give a ~ for their opinions!; "Frankly, my dear, I don't give a ~." – Clark Gable as Rhett Butler, *Gone with the Wind* (1939))

damn II v. (D; tr.) to ~ for (they were ~ed for their sins)

damnation n. eternal ~ (to suffer eternal ~ to hell for one's sins)

damnedest, damndest n. (colloq.) ["utmost"] to do, try one's ~ (to do smt.)

damper n. ["deadening influence"] to put a ~ on

dance I n. 1. to do, perform a ~ (with) 2. to have a ~ with (may I have the next ~?) 3. to sit out a ~ 4. to give, hold a ~ (they held a dinner ~) 5. (the) classical ~; modern ~ 6. a barn; dinner; formal; school ~ 7. a circle, round; country; folk; line; square; sword; tap; tribal; war ~ 8. to go to a ~ 9. at a ~ (they met at a ~) 10. (misc.) (BE) to lead smb. a merry ~ (AE has *to lead smb. a merry chase*)

dance II v. 1. (D; intr.) to ~ to (to ~ to the music of a rock group) 2. (D; intr.) to ~ with 3. (D; intr.) to ~ through (they were ~cing through the park) 4. (P; tr.) he ~d her around the room 5. (misc.) to ~ for, with joy; to ~ to smb.'s tune ("to conform to smb.'s wishes"); to go ~ing (see also *to dance attendance on* at **attendance**)

dancer n. a ballet; ballroom; belly; exotic; folk; lap; pole; tap; taxi ~

dancing n. aerobic; ballet; ballroom, social; belly; break; circle, round; country; folk; line; square; tap ~

dander n. ["temper"] (colloq.) (esp. AE) to get one's / smb.'s ~ up

dandruff n. a flake of ~ (there were a few ~s of dandruff on his collar)

danger n. 1. to constitute, pose, represent; create (a) ~ 2. to expose to ~ 3. to confront; court; face; sense (a) ~ 4. to flirt with ~ 5. to avert (a) ~ 6. (an) acute, deadly, extreme, grave, mortal; immediate, imminent, impending; real ~ (a situation fraught with real ~ to us all) 7. (legal) a clear and present ~ 8. a ~ from; of; to (~ from wild animals; a ~ to national security; there was a real ~ of fire breaking out) 9. a ~ that + clause (there was a real ~ that a fire might break out) 10. in ~ (of) (our lives were in ~; the building is in imminent ~ of collapsing / collapse) 11. out of ~ (the patient is now out of ~)

dangerous adj. 1. extremely ~ 2. ~ for 3. ~ to (it's ~ to your health) 4. ~ to + inf. (it's ~ for children to play in the street) 5. ~ that + clause (it's ~ that so many children play in the street) (see also *armed and dangerous* at **armed**)

dangle v. 1. (d; intr.) to ~ from (his keys ~d from a chain) 2. (d; tr.) to ~ before, in front of (to ~ bait in front of smb.)

dare I n. 1. to take a ~ 2. on a ~ (she did it on a ~)

dare II v. 1. (E) I don't ~ to protest; she didn't ~ to open her mouth 2. (F) I ~ not protest (formal); I don't ~ protest; she didn't ~ open her mouth; how ~ you speak to me like that? 3. (H) he ~d me to sue him 4. (misc.) she was so shy she hardly dared (to) open her mouth! USAGE NOTE: Some purists believe that *I don't dare protest* is an incorrect blend of *I don't dare to protest* and *I dare not protest*.

daring adj. ~ to + inf. (it was ~ (for them) to attempt the climb at night)

dark I *adj.* 1. pitch ("completely"); very ~ 2. to get, grow ~ 3. (misc.) as ~ as night

dark II *n.* ["darkness"] 1. after; before ~ 2. in the ~ (to grope for the door in the ~) 3. (misc.) the child is afraid of the ~ ["ignorance"] 4. to keep smb. in the ~

darkness *n.* 1. complete, pitch, total ~ 2. ~ falls; gathers; lifts 3. in (the) ~ (see also *under cover of darkness* at **cover I**)

darn *n.* (colloq.) ["small amount"] not to give a ~ (I don't give a ~!)

dart I *n.* ["pointed object"] 1. to throw a ~ (at) 2. a poisoned ~ ["rush"] 3. to make a ~ (for) (she made a sudden ~ for the door)

dart II *v.* 1. (d; tr.) to ~ at (to ~ a glance at smb.) 2. (P; intr.) she suddenly ~ed for the door; the hare ~ed along the edge of the clearing

darts *n.* to play ~ USAGE NOTE: A singular verb is used with this noun – *darts is a popular game.*

dash I *n.* ["rush"] 1. to make a ~ for (we made a ~ for cover) 2. a frantic, mad ~ 3. in a ~ (I'm in a ~ to catch the next train)

dash II *v.* 1. (P; intr., tr.) when the rain started, we ~ed for cover 2. (misc.) (informal) sorry, must ~: I'm late for an appointment

data *n.* 1. to access; feed in, input, key in; process; retrieve; store ~ 2. to analyze, evaluate; cite; collect, gather; transfer ~ 3. to plot ~ (on a map or graph) 4. biographical; census; scientific; statistical ~ 5. comparative; concrete; raw; solid ~ USAGE NOTE: Purists insist on *these data are available* and consider *this data is available* to be incorrect.

database *n.* 1. to access; compile, create a ~ 2. to link ~s 3. a central; incomplete; online ~ 4. a ~ contains, holds 5. a ~ of (a ~ of useful information) 6. in, on a ~ (how much information is held on this ~?)

date I *n.* ["time"] 1. to announce; fix, set a ~ (to set a ~ for a wedding = to set a wedding ~) 2. to bring (smb.) up to ~ 3. to bear a ~ (the letter bears no ~) 4. a significant ~ (in history) 5. a closing; cutoff; due; expiration, expiry (BE); opening; sell-by; target ~ 6. at a certain ~ (the meeting will be held at a later ~; at a/some future ~) 7. on a certain ~ (on this ~ in history) 8. to ~ (how many have returned their invitations to ~?) ["rendezvous, meeting"] 9. to have; make a ~ (I made a ~ to see them) 10. to go out on a ~ 11. to break; keep a ~ 12. a blind; double ~ 13. a ~ with (a ~ with a girl; a ~ with destiny) ["misc."] 14. out of ~; to go out of ~; up to ~; to be up to ~ on an issue; to bring smb. up to ~ on smt.; to bring a dictionary up to ~ so as to make it an up-to-date dictionary

date II *v.* (d; intr.) to ~ from (the temple ~s from the tenth century)

date back *v.* (d; intr.) to ~ to (the temple ~s back to the tenth century)

dateline *n.* the international ~ (to cross the international ~)

dating *n.* carbon ~

daub *v.* 1. (d; tr.) to ~ on, onto (to ~ paint on a wall) 2. (D; tr.) to ~ with (to ~ a wall with paint)

daughter *n.* 1. to adopt a ~ 2. to marry off a ~ 3. an older; only; younger ~ 4. an adopted; foster ~; stepdaughter 5. a daughter-in-law 6. a ~ to (she was like a ~ to them)

dauntless *adj.* ~ in (~ in one's resolve)

dawdle *v.* (D; intr.) ("to waste time") to ~ over

dawn I *n.* 1. (formal) ~ breaks 2. at (the crack of); before ~ 3. (misc.) a false ~ (the temporary improvement was a false ~ and we ended up disappointed); from ~ till/to dusk (see also *dawn chorus* at **chorus**)

dawn II *v.* 1. (s) the day ~ed cloudy 2. (misc.) it ~ed on me that the following day would be her birthday; it finally ~ed on us what must be done

day *n.* 1. to spend a ~ (somewhere) 2. a bright, sunny; chilly, cool; clear, fine, nice; cloudy; cold; dreary, gloomy; foggy; hot, stifling; rainy; warm; an eventful, field, memorable, red-letter ~ (we had a field ~ with/criticizing their report) 3. the appointed ~; election (AE), polling (BE); a bad, bad-hair (colloq.); dark; fast; good; holy; opening; visiting; wedding; working ~ (opening ~ of the baseball season) 4. ~ breaks, dawns 5. by ~ (London by ~) 6. by the ~ (to be paid by the ~) 7. during the ~ (the store was open during the ~) 8. for a ~ (we are going to town for the ~) 9. from ~ to ~ (from one ~ to the next) 10. in a ~ (we cannot do the whole job in a ~; back in the old ~s) 11. on a certain ~ (on the following ~; on New Year's Day; on Friday; on our wedding ~) 12. within several ~s (within ten ~s) 13. (misc.) ~ after ~; ~ and night ("all the time"); by ~; all ~ (long); D-day, Day One ("a day on which a significant event is scheduled to begin or take place"); to spend the whole ~ working; to take a ~ off; ~ in, ~ out; to carry, save, win the ~ ("to be victorious"); (just/only) the other ~ ("recently"); his ~s are numbered ("he will die soon"); the dog ~s ("the hot days of July and August"); halcyon ~s; the good old ~s; it was a big ("successful"; "important") ~ for our team; to take one ~ at a time; judgment ~; on the ~ (BE; colloq.) ("when the time comes"); on the ~ of (on the ~ of the concert); it's early ~s yet (BE) ("it is too soon to tell what will develop") 14. (misc.) at the end of the ~ ("when all is said and done"); in this ~ and age ("nowadays"); happy ~s; things were very different in my ~/in my young ~s from how they are these ~s!; as plain as ~ (see also *the day of reckoning* at **reckoning**) USAGE NOTE: The collocation *by day* contrasts with *by night*: London by day is very different from London by night. (See also the Usage Note for **night**.)

daybreak *n.* at ~

daydream I *n.* a ~ about, of

daydream II *v.* 1. (D; intr.) to ~ about 2. (L) she was always ~ing that she would get rich

daylight *n.* 1. in broad ~ 2. before ~

daylights *n.* (colloq.) ["insides"] 1. to beat, knock the (living) ~ out of smb. ["wits"] 2. to scare the (living) ~ out of smb.

daytime *n.* in the ~

daze *n.* in a ~ (he's always in a ~)

dazed *adj.* ~ at, by (~ at the sight of the carnage)

dead I *adj.* ["not alive"] 1. to drop ~ (of a heart attack) 2. brain; clinically; as ~ as a doornail, stone ~ 3. ~ on arrival (also (DOA)) 4. (fig.) ~ and buried (our hopes are now ~ and buried); ~ and gone (our hopes are now ~ and gone) 5. (misc.) ~ or alive (a dangerous criminal wanted ~ or alive); more ~ than alive (she was shivering and seemed more ~ than alive); to not be seen dead in (I wouldn't be seen ~ in such cheap clothes!) (see also *given up for dead* at **give up**; *left for dead* at **leave**; *play dead* at **play**) ["unresponsive"] 6. (cannot stand alone) ~ to (sound asleep and ~ to the world) 7. (misc.) to go ~ (the telephone suddenly went ~; after the injury my arm went ~ and I couldn't move it)

dead II *n.* ["dead people"] 1. to bury the ~ 2. to honor the ~ 3. the war ~ (the war ~ were honored with a monument) 4. the living and the ~ (see also *the quick and the dead* at **quick II**, *rise from the dead* at **rise II**)

dead III *n.* (see *in the dead of (the) night* at **night II**; *in the dead of winter* at **winter II**)

dead end *n.* to arrive at, come to, reach a ~

deadline *n.* 1. to establish, set a ~ 2. to meet a ~ 3. to extend a ~ 4. to miss a ~ 5. to work against/to (BE) a ~ 6. a ~ approaches; passes 7. a tight ~ 8. a ~ for (the ~ for this job is tomorrow)

deadlock *n.* 1. to end in (a) ~, reach a ~ 2. to break, end a ~ 3. a continuing ~ 4. a ~ between; in; over (we tried to break the continuing ~ in the negotiations between them over pay)

deadlocked *adj.* ~ over

deadwood *n.* (also fig.) 1. to cut away, cut out the ~ 2. to get rid of, remove the ~

deaf *adj.* ["unable to hear"] 1. to become, go ~ 2. partially, slightly; profoundly, stone, very ~ 3. (misc.) (as) ~ as a post; ~ in one ear; the ~ and the hard of hearing ["insensitive"] 4. (cannot stand alone) ~ to (they were ~ to all our pleas = our pleas fell on ~ ears)

deafness *n.* 1. to cause ~ 2. congenital ~ 3. partial; profound ~ 4. (misc.) ~ in one ear

deal I *n.* ["transaction"] 1. to close, wrap up (colloq.); to cut (colloq.), do (BE), make (AE), strike a ~ with (we closed the ~ with them yesterday) 2. to accept; offer; reject a ~ 3. a business; done; shady ~ ["treatment"] 4. a fair, square; raw (colloq.), rotten (colloq.), rough (colloq.) ~ (she got a raw ~ from her boss) 5. a ~ goes ahead; falls through 6. a ~ on (I can get you a good ~ on insurance) ["arrangement"] 7. a package ~ ["amount"] 8. a good, great ~ (of) we had a great ~ to talk about; we have a good ~ of work to do; a very great ~ of money

[misc.] 9. (colloq.) a big ~ ("an impressive matter"); it means a good/great/very great ~ to her ("it is very important to her"); it's no big ~ ("it's not so important")

deal II *v.* 1. (A) he dealt a deathblow to the enemy; or: he dealt the enemy a deathblow (formal); she dealt the cards to the other players; or: she dealt the other players their cards 2. (d; intr.) to ~ in (they ~ in furs) 3. (d; intr.) to ~ with (we ~ with many customers; we ~ directly with the wholesalers and bypass the middlemen; to ~ with complaints; I'll ~ with the children later; this chapter ~s with the problem of inflation; they dealt with me as an equal)

dealer *n.* 1. an antique(s); art; book; car; drug; junk ~ 2. a reputable ~ 3. a ~ in (a ~ in rare books)

dealership *n.* an automobile (AE), car ~

dealing *n.* insider ~

dealings *n.* ["business"] 1. business; straight; underhanded ~ 2. ~ with (I have had ~ with them)

deal out *v.* (B) she dealt out the cards to the other players

dear *adj.* ["emotionally important"] 1. (cannot stand alone) ~ to (this project is ~ to my heart) 2. (misc.) to hold (smb.) ~

death *n.* 1. to cause ~ 2. to face ~; to meet one's ~ 3. to feign ~ 4. to cheat, escape ~ 5. to mourn smb.'s ~ 6. to announce; register smb.'s ~ 7. (an) accidental; agonizing; certain, sure; heroic; instant, instantaneous; lingering; living; natural; painful; sudden, unexpected; tragic; untimely; violent; wrongful ~ (to die a natural ~; to meet a violent ~) 8. brain ~ 9. (a) cot (BE), crib (AE) ~ 10. ~ by (~ by drowning; fire; firing squad; hanging; lethal injection) 11. at, upon smb.'s ~ (at her ~ the estate was broken up) 12. to ~ (beaten; bludgeoned; burnt; choked; frozen; put; shot; stabbed; starved; stoned; trampled to ~) 13. (fig.) bored; frightened; sick to ~ 14. (misc.) a fight to the ~; a ~ in the family; (sports) sudden ~ ("an overtime period that ends when the first point or goal is scored"); ~ to tyrants!; in ~ as in life; "till ~ us do part" – from the marriage service in *The (Anglican) Book of Common Prayer* (1662) (see also *life after death* at **life**)

deathbed *n.* on one's ~

deathblow *n.* 1. (formal) to deal a ~ (he dealt a ~ to the enemy; or: he dealt the enemy a ~) 2. a ~ to (the government's decision has proved/dealt a ~ to heavy industry in this country)

death penalty *n.* 1. to impose; introduce the ~ 2. to abolish the ~

deathwatch *n.* to maintain a ~

debar *v.* (formal) (d; tr.) to ~ from (he was ~red from practice)

debatable *adj.* ~ whether + clause (it is ~ whether smoking should be officially banned)

debate I *n.* 1. to chair, moderate; close; conduct, have, hold; open a ~ 2. to encourage; provoke, spark (AE)/spark off (BE); stifle, suppress (a) ~

3. an acrimonious, bitter, heated, sharp, stormy ~
4. a lively, spirited ~ 5. a campaign; national; parliamentary; public ~ 6. (a) formal ~ (informal ~)
7. a ~ about, on, over; between; with 8. in, during a ~; under ~ (the matter is still under ~) 9. (misc.) a matter for ~

debate II *v.* 1. to ~ heatedly, hotly 2. (D; intr.) to ~ about, on (to ~ about disarmament) 3. (D; intr.) to ~ with 4. (G) (esp. BE) Parliament ~d disarming 5. (Q) we ~d (with ourselves) how to do it

debit I *n.* (BE) direct ~ (to pay by direct ~)

debit II *v.* ("to charge") 1. (D; tr.) to ~ against, to (to ~ a purchase against smb.'s account; to ~ an amount to smb.'s account) 2. (D; tr.) to ~ with (~ her account with the entire amount)

debit card *n.* 1. to accept; issue a ~ 2. a ~ expires (your ~ is no longer valid: it expired last week) 3. by ~ (can I pay by ~?) 4. (misc.) to put a purchase on one's/smb.'s ~

debris *n.* to clear ~

debt *n.* 1. to contract, incur, run up; owe a ~; to get into, go into ~ 2. to collect, recover a ~ 3. to discharge, pay (off), settle; wipe out; work off; write off a ~ 4. to cancel; repudiate a ~ 5. a bad; outstanding, unsettled; toxic, unrecoverable ~; mounting ~s (to write off a bad ~) 6. a business; foreign; gambling; personal, private ~ 7. the national ~ 8. in ~ for; to (he is in ~ to me for a large sum, he is deeply in ~ to me; I'm in ~ to my colleagues for their excellent advice) 9. out of ~ (to stay out of ~) 10. (misc.) a ~ of honor; a ~ of gratitude; deep(ly) in ~ (I owe a ~ of gratitude to my colleagues for their excellent advice)

debut *n.* 1. to make one's ~ (to make one's ~ in society) 2. a professional; stage ~ 3. a ~ as (to make one's ~ as an actor)

decadence *n.* 1. to fall into ~ 2. moral ~

decant *v.* 1. (D; tr.) ("to pour") to ~ from; into, to 2. (fig.) (BE) the staff were ~ed from the old building to the new one

decay *n.* 1. to fall into; prevent; stop ~ 2. dental, tooth ~ 3. radioactive ~ 4. environmental; inner-city, urban ~ 5. moral ~

decease *n.* (formal and legal) upon smb.'s ~

deceit *n.* 1. to practice ~ 2. to expose, see through ~ 3. a web of ~ 4. by, through ~ (to obtain smt. by ~)

deceitful *adj.* ~ to + inf. (it was ~ of you to say such things behind her back)

deceive *v.* 1. (D; tr.) to ~ about (she ~d them about her intentions) 2. (D; refl., tr.) to ~ into (to ~ smb. into doing smt.)

decency *n.* 1. common; human ~ 2. the ~ to + inf. (he didn't even have the ~ to call) 3. (misc.) to observe the ~cies; a spark of ~

decent *adj.* ~ to + inf. (it was ~ of her to help us)

deception *n.* 1. to practice ~ 2. to see through (a) ~ 3. (a) cruel; deliberate ~ 4. by, through ~ (to obtain smt. by ~)

decide *v.* 1. to ~ unanimously 2. (d; intr.) ("to make a decision") to ~ against (to ~ against buying a car) 3. (legal) (d; intr.) to ~ against; for, in favor of ("to find for") (the jury ~d for the plaintiff) 4. (D; intr.) ("to choose") to ~ between (it was difficult to ~ between the two of them) 5. (d; intr.) to ~ on ("to choose in favor of") (we have ~d on a new computer) 6. (E) ("to choose") we ~d to stay home 7. (H) (BE) what finally ~d you to stay home? 8. (L) ("to make a decision") she ~d that the children would stay home 9. (Q) ("to make a decision") we could not ~ whether to go out or stay home 10. (misc.) to ~ for oneself (I can't advise you: you'll have to ~ for yourself)

decision *n.* ["act of deciding"] 1. to arrive at, come to, make, reach, take (BE) a ~ 2. (esp. legal) to affirm, uphold; appeal (AE), appeal against; hand down (AE), render a ~ 3. (esp. legal) to overrule, reverse a ~ 4. to defer; reconsider a ~ 5. a big, momentous; crucial; fateful; landmark (esp. legal); weighty ~ 6. a clear-cut; ethical; fair; favorable; good, sensible, wise; popular; just ~ 7. a collective, joint; unanimous ~ 8. a final; firm; irreversible, irrevocable ~ 9. an agonizing, difficult; arbitrary; hasty, rash, snap ~ 10. a bad, poor, unwise; unfair, unjust; unfavorable; unpopular ~ 11. a court; majority; split ("divided") ~ 12. a ~ about, on 13. a ~ to + inf. (the government made the ~ to cut taxes) 14. the ~ that + clause (the government made the ~ that it would cut taxes) 15. (misc.) early ~ (AE; used in the process of admitting students to universities) ["decisiveness"] ["firmness"] 16. to lack ~ 17. of ~ (a man, woman of ~)

deck *n.* ["pack of playing cards"] (AE) 1. to cut; shuffle a ~ 2. to stack a ~ ("to arrange cards dishonestly") (also fig.) ["floor as on a ship"] 3. to swab a ~ 4. an aft, after; flight; lower; main; poop; promenade ~; sundeck; upper ~ 5. below; on ~ (she was on the lower ~; I went up on ~; is standing allowed on the upper ~ of the bus?) 6. (misc.) (usu. fig.) clear the ~s for action! ["device for tape recordings"] 7. a tape ~

deck out *v.* (D; refl., tr.) to ~ in (~ed out in their Sunday best)

declaration *n.* 1. to issue, make a ~ 2. a solemn; unilateral; written ~ 3. a currency; customs ~ 4. a ~ of (a ~ of war; the court's ~ of the law to be unconstitutional) 5. a ~ that + clause (the court's ~ that the law was unconstitutional)

declare *v.* 1. (B) he ~d his love to her 2. (D; tr.) to ~ against, on (to ~ war on another country) 3. (L; to) the court ~d that the law was unconstitutional 4. (M) the court ~d the law to be unconstitutional 5. (N; used with a noun, adjective, past participle) the court ~d the law unconstitutional; the government ~d him persona non grata

declension *n.* an adjective; noun; strong; weak ~

decline I *n.* 1. to go into, sink into, suffer a ~ 2. a gradual, slow; quick, sharp; steady; steep ~ 3. a ~

from; in; to (a ~ in profits of 10%, from $100,000 to $90,000) 4. in (a) ~ (profits are in ~) 5. into (a) ~ (profits fell/went into ~) 6. on the ~ (profits are on the ~) 7. (misc.) *The History of the Decline and Fall of the Roman Empire* (1776–88) – Edward Gibbon

decline II *v.* 1. (D; intr.) to ~ by (profits have ~d by 10%) 2. (grammar) to ~ for (to ~ a noun for case) 3. (D; intr.) to ~ by; from; to (profits have ~d by 10%, from $100,000 to $90,000) 4. (E) she ~d to address the delegates

decorate *v.* 1. (D; tr.) ("to give a medal to") to ~ for (to ~ a soldier for valor) 2. (D; tr.) ("to adorn") to ~ with (to ~ a room with flowers) 3. (D; tr.) ("to paint or paper") (BE) (the room was tastefully ~d in green) 4. (misc.) tastefully ~d

decoration *n.* ["medal"] 1. to award a ~ 2. (AE) to write smb. up for a ~ 3. a ~ for (the soldier was awarded a ~ for valor)

decorations *n.* ["ornaments"] 1. to put up ~ 2. Christmas ~ 3. elaborate; festive; party ~

decorator *n.* 1. an interior ~ 2. (misc.) (BE) a painter and ~

decorum *n.* 1. to display ~ 2. proper; strict ~ 3. (misc.) to behave with ~

decouple *v.* (D; tr.) ("to separate") to ~ from (should the government ~ its tax policy from its inflation policy?)

decoy *v.* (D; tr.) to ~ into (they ~ed us into a corner)

decrease I *n.* 1. a considerable, dramatic, large, sharp, significant, sizable, substantial; gradual; moderate; slight, small; steady ~ 2. a ~ in (a ~ in profits of 10%, from $100,000 to $90,000) 3. on the ~ (profits are on the ~)

decrease II *v.* 1. (D; intr., tr.) to ~ by (profits ~d by 10%) 2. (D; intr., tr.) to ~ from; to (profits ~d from $100,000 to $90,000) 3. (D; intr., tr.) to ~ in (the guards were ~d in number)

decree I *n.* 1. to issue a ~ 2. to rescind, revoke a ~ 3. a consent (legal); divorce; executive; government; royal ~ 4. (GB) a ~ absolute; a ~ nisi 5. a ~ on 6. a ~ that + clause; subj. (we had to obey the ~ that beards be/should be shaved off) 7. by ~ (by royal ~) 8. in a ~ (what was in the royal ~ on beards?)

decree II *v.* (formal) 1. (L; may be subj.) the king ~d that beards be/should be shaved off; the government ~d that it was illegal to traffic in furs 2. (N) the court ~d the law unconstitutional

decry *v.* (formal) 1. (D; tr.) to ~ as (to ~ drunkenness as sinful) 2. (G) to ~ drinking (as sinful) 3. (K) to ~ their drinking (as sinful)

dedicate *v.* 1. (B) the book was ~d to her husband 2. (d; refl., tr.) to ~ to (she ~d her life to science; they ~d themselves to helping the poor)

dedication *n.* 1. to demonstrate, display, show ~ 2. complete, great, total ~ 3. ~ to (~ to the cause of freedom; the book's ~ to the author's husband) 4.

~ to + inf. (they had the ~ to continue their research in spite of the obstacles)

deduce *v.* 1. (D; tr.) to ~ from (what can we ~ from these figures?) 2. (L) on the basis of the evidence we ~d that he was guilty; if all men are mortal and Socrates is a man, then I ~ that Socrates is mortal 3. (Q) the police were able to ~ where the fugitive was hiding

deduct *v.* 1. (D; tr.) (BE) to ~ at source (tax ~ed at source) 2. (D; tr.) to ~ from (to ~ a tax from one's wages)

deductible *adj.* 1. tax-~ 2. ~ from

deduction *n.* ["subtracting"]["deducting"] 1. to make a ~ (from) 2. to make; take a ~ for (income-tax purposes) 3. a ~ for; from (our employer makes a ~ from our salary for the income tax) ["conclusion"] 4. to make a ~ 5. an illogical; logical ~ 6. a ~ about 7. the ~ that + clause (the evidence confirmed our ~ that he was guilty; if all men are mortal and Socrates is a man, then I can make the ~ that Socrates is mortal)

deed I *n.* ["something done"] 1. to do, perform a ~ 2. a dirty (colloq.); evil, foul, wicked ~ 3. in word and ~ ["legal instrument of transfer"] 4. to transfer a ~ 5. a title ~ 6. a ~ to (to hold a ~ to property) 7. by ~ (to transfer property by ~)

deed II *v.* (AE) (B) ("to transfer") he ~ed the property to his daughter

deem *v.* (formal) 1. (M) we ~ed her to be worthy of support 2. (N; used with an adjective, noun) we ~ her worthy of support 3. (misc.) we ~ed it proper that she be/should be supported

deep *adj.* 1. ~ in (~ in thought; ~ in the forest) 2. (misc.) the well was forty feet ~; ~ down she is a good person; I was knee-~ in mud ("I was in mud up to my knees")

deep water *n.* ["trouble"] (colloq.) in ~

deer *n.* 1. a herd of ~ 2. a young ~ is a fawn 3. a female ~ is a doe 4. a male ~ is a buck, stag 5. the meat of a ~ is venison

default I *n.* 1. a ~ on (a ~ on one's mortgage payments) 2. by ~ (to win by ~) 3. in ~ of (anything better) ("in the absence of (anything better)")

default II *v.* (D; intr.) to ~ on (to ~ on one's mortgage payments)

defeat I *n.* 1. to inflict (formal) a ~ on 2. to meet, suffer (a) ~ (at smb.'s hands) 3. to go down in, to ~ 4. to invite ~ 5. to accept, admit, concede ~ 6. a crushing, decisive, disastrous, humiliating, lopsided (AE), overwhelming, resounding, total, utter; ignominious, shameful ~ 7. in ~ (they were resourceful in ~) 8. (misc.) to stare ~ in the face (the former champion is now staring ~ in the face)

defeat II *v.* 1. to ~ decisively, roundly, resoundingly, soundly 2. to ~ narrowly 3. (D; tr.) to ~ by (they were ~ed by three goals to one)

defect I *n.* 1. to correct a ~ 2. a glaring ~ 3. a minor ~ 4. a birth, congenital; character; hearing; mechanical; mental; physical; speech; structural ~ 5. a ~ in (there was a ~ in the transmission)

defect II v. ("to desert") 1. (D; intr.) to ~ from (to ~ from the party) 2. (D; intr.) to ~ to (to ~ to the West)

defection n. 1. a ~ from (a ~ from the party) 2. a ~ to (a ~ to the West)

defective adj. ~ in

defence (BE) see **defense**

defenceless (BE) see **defenseless**

defend v. 1. to ~ staunchly, strongly, vigorously; successfully 2. (D; refl., tr.) to ~ against, from (she ~ed herself against the attack) 3. (G) we cannot ~ drinking on the job 4. (K) I cannot ~ his drinking on the job

defendant n. to acquit, find for; arraign; charge; convict a ~

defender n. 1. a public ~ (US) ("a lawyer who represents poor people at public expense") 2. a staunch ~ (of smt.)

defense, defence n. 1. to conduct, organize, put up a ~ 2. to breach, overwhelm smb.'s ~s 3. an adequate; airtight, impenetrable; heroic; inadequate, weak; strong, vigorous; stubborn ~ 4. civil; national ~ 5. military ~s 6. (sports) a one-on-one; zone ~ 7. a legal ~ 8. a ~ against 9. a ~ that + clause (her ~ that she was provoked was not accepted) 10. in ~ of 11. (misc.) (sports) in (BE), on (AE) ~; (legal) the ~ rests its case, the ~ rests (AE); to spring to smb.'s ~ (see also *defense mechanism* at **mechanism**)

defenseless, defenceless adj. ~ against (~ against any attack)

defense pact, defence pact n. a mutual ~

defensive I adj. ~ about (they were very ~ about their party's record on tax reform)

defensive II n. on the ~ (to put smb. on the ~)

defer v. 1. (D; intr.) to ~ in; to (he ~red to his partner in everything) 2. (D; tr.) to ~ for (the trial was ~red for another month) 3. (D; tr.) to ~ pending (the trial was ~red pending the arrival of the new evidence) 4. (D; tr.) to ~ until (the trial was ~red until the prisoner's recovery) 5. (formal) (G) we ~red going 6. (formal) (K) we ~red our going

deference n. 1. to accord, show ~ to 2. blind; due; great ~ (with due ~) 3. in, out of ~ to 4. with all ~ to (with all ~ to you, I think you are wrong)

deferential adj. ["respectful"] ~ to

defiance n. ["resistance"] 1. to show ~ 2. to glare in ~ 3. ~ against, towards (~ towards all authority) 4. in ~ of (to act in ~ of one's parents) 5. an act of ~

defiant adj. ~ towards

deficiency n. ["defect"] ["inadequacy"] 1. a hearing; hormone; iron; mental; mineral; vitamin ~ 2. a major, serious; minor, slight ~ (he suffers from/ has a slight vitamin ~ that he hopes to remedy by taking supplements) 3. (a) ~ in ["incomplete work"] (as in school) (AE) 4. to make up a ~

deficient adj. ~ in

deficit n. 1. to run, show a ~ 2. to make up; reduce a ~ 3. a budget; operating; trade ~ 4. a ~ in

define v. 1. to ~ clearly 2. (D; tr.) to ~ as (we can ~ *burnout* as *exhaustion*)

defined adj. ["outlined, delineated"] 1. clearly, sharply ~; well-defined 2. ~ against (sharply ~ against a light background)

definite adj. 1. ~ about (she was ~ about it) 2. ~ that + clause (is it ~ that they will sign the contract?)

definition n. 1. to formulate, give, provide, write a ~ 2. a dictionary; formulaic; referential; synonym ~ 3. a clear ~ 4. according to a ~ (according to your ~ of guilt, we are all guilty!) 5. by ~ (isn't murder illegal by ~?)

deflect v. (D; tr.) to ~ from; into; onto

defraud v. (D; tr.) to ~ of (he ~ed them of their money)

deft adj. ~ at (she is ~ at dealing with administrators)

defy v. 1. to ~ openly 2. (H; passive is rare) she ~fied them to prove her guilty

degenerate v. (D; intr.) to ~ from; into (the discussion quickly ~d from a debate into an argument)

degradation n. in ~ (to live in ~)

degrading adj. ~ to + inf. (it was very ~ to work in such conditions)

degree n. ["academic title"] 1. to award a ~ to; to confer a ~ on 2. to do (BE), earn, get, receive, take a ~ 3. an academic; college (AE), university ~ 4. an advanced, graduate, postgraduate (esp. BE); first (BE), undergraduate ~ 5. an earned ("completed and awarded") (AE); honorary ~ 6. an associate; bachelor's; doctoral, doctor's; honours (BE); master's ~ 7. (BE) a good ~ ("a first or upper second at a British university") 8. a ~ from; in (to take a ~ in history; she got her ~ from Cambridge) ["extent"] ["level"] 9. to achieve a ~ (to achieve a high ~ of proficiency) 10. a great, high, large; greater, higher; lesser, lower; low, slight; certain ~ 11. to a ~ (to a greater or lesser ~; to a high ~) ["form of an adjective or adverb"] 12. the comparative; positive; superlative ~ ["of temperature"] 13. to fall to, get as low as; get as high as, reach, soar to a ~ (in the winter the temperature can fall to minus 20 ~s and in the summer it can soar to more than 30 ~s (centigrade) 14. ~s of frost (BE) (see also *degrees of frost* at **frost**) 15. at ~s (at sea level, water freezes at 0 ~s centigrade and boils at 100 ~s centigrade) ["misc."] 16. by ~s ("gradually"); (BE; colloq.) to a ~ ("to a very high degree"); to the nth ~ (carried to the nth ~); with a certain/considerable ~ of (he strove to become famous, with a certain/considerable ~ of success)

deign v. (formal or humorous) (E) she ~ed to mingle with her employees

dejected adj. 1. very ~ 2. ~ to + inf. (he was ~ to learn that he had failed the examination)

dekko n. (slang) (BE) ["look"] to have a ~ at

delay I n. 1. to brook no ~ 2. an agonizing; interminable, long; unavoidable; unexpected, unforeseen ~; minor ~s 3. a ~ occurs 4. a series of ~s (a series of minor ~s of up to 5 minutes) 5. a ~ in (she apologized for the ~ in answering) 6. without ~ (to want a job finished without ~)

delay II *v.* 1. (G) he ~ed calling the police 2. (K) he ~ed my calling the police

delaying action *n.* to fight a ~

delegate I *n.* 1. a party; pledged; super-delegate (US), unpledged ~ 2. a ~ at large 3. a ~ attends (a convention or party congress) 4. a ~ from; to (a ~ from the south to the convention)

delegate II *v.* 1. (B) he ~d his responsibilities to a deputy 2. (H) she was ~d to represent us

delegation *n.* 1. to head a ~ 2. an official; unofficial ~ 3. a member of a ~ 4. a ~ from; to 5. in a ~

delete *v.* (D; tr.) to ~ from (to ~ smt. from a dossier)

deleterious *adj.* ~ to

deletion *n.* 1. to make a ~ 2. a ~ from (she made a ~ from the text)

deliberate I *adj.* ~ in (~ in one's speech)

deliberate II *v.* 1. (D; intr.) to ~ about, on, over (we ~d about where to meet) 2. (rare) (Q) we ~d where to meet

deliberations *n.* ~ about (our ~ about where to meet)

delicacy *n.* 1. extreme, great ~ 2. a matter of extreme ~

delicatessen *n.* 1. a kosher ~ 2. at; in a ~ (to eat in a kosher ~; to buy something at a kosher ~)

delight I *n.* 1. to feel ~; to take ~ in (they took ~ in watching the children play) 2. great, intense, sheer; perverse ~ 3. ~ at (my ~ at hearing such lovely songs) 4. a ~ to + inf. (it was a ~ to hear such lovely songs = such lovely songs were a ~ to hear) 5. ~ that + clause (they expressed their ~ that they had been invited) 6. to smb.'s ~ (to my great ~, I was invited) 7. with ~ (they accepted our invitation with great ~)

delight II *v.* 1. (d; intr.) to ~ in (to ~ in the beauties of nature) 2. (D; tr.) to ~ by; with (they ~ed the children with their funny stories = they ~ed the children by telling them funny stories) 3. (R) it ~ed me (to learn) that you can attend

delighted *adj.* 1. ~ at, by, with 2. ~ to + inf. (we'll be ~ to come) 3. ~ that + clause (I'm ~ that you can attend)

delightful *adj.* ~ to + inf. (it was ~ to swim in the heated pool)

delinquency *n.* 1. juvenile ~ 2. (AE) ~ in

delinquent I *adj.* (AE) ~ in (~ in paying one's rent)

delinquent II *n.* a juvenile ~; tax (AE) ~

delirious *adj.* ~ with

delirium *n.* in a ~ (of)

deliver *v.* 1. (B) they ~ed the merchandise to us 2. (D; tr.) to ~ from; into (they ~ed us into enemy hands; "lead us not into temptation, but ~ us from evil" – "The Lord's Prayer", *The Bible: St. Matthew*) 3. (pompous) (D; refl.) to ~ of (to ~ oneself of an opinion) 4. (D; tr.) to ~ to (they ~ed the

circular to each house; the limousine ~s you to your door) 5. (misc.) to ~ on a promise (esp. AE); to ~ by hand; she was ~ed of a baby girl (formal) ("she gave birth to a baby girl")

deliverance *n.* (formal) ~ from (~ from captivity)

delivery *n.* ["act of delivering"] ["bringing"] 1. to make a ~ (to) 2. to accept, take ~ (of) 3. an emergency ~; (an) overnight; prompt ~ (we guarantee prompt ~) 4. general (AE) ~ (BE has *poste restante*); mail (esp. AE), postal (AE); recorded (BE); rural-free (AE); special ~ 5. a ~ to 6. on ~ (payment on ~) 7. (misc.) door-to-door ~ (they offer door-to-door ~) ["childbirth"] 8. a breech; caesarean; normal ~ ["manner of speaking or throwing"] 9. an effective ~

delude *v.* 1. (D; refl., tr.) to ~ into (don't ~ yourself into thinking that she loves you) 2. (L; refl.) don't ~ yourself that she loves you

deluge *v.* (d; tr.) to ~ with (we were ~d with offers)

delusion *n.* 1. to cherish, cling to a ~ 2. a ~ that + clause (he was under the ~ that she loved him) 3. under a ~ (to labor under a ~) (see also *delusions of grandeur* at **grandeur**)

delve *v.* 1. to ~ deeply 2. (d; intr.) to ~ for (to ~ for information) 3. (d; intr.) to ~ into (to ~ into the background of a case)

demand I *n.* ["urgent request"] 1. to make a ~; to state one's ~s 2. to meet, respond to, satisfy a ~; to give in to, yield to a ~ 3. to ignore; reject a ~ 4. to drop, give up a ~ 5. an excessive, exorbitant, unrealistic; final; moderate, modest, reasonable; nonnegotiable ~ 6. union; wage ~s 7. a ~ for; from; on (a ~ from the victims for compensation; to make ~s on smb.'s time) 8. a ~ that + clause; subj. (they rejected our demand that no one be/should be punished) 9. at, on ~ (payment on ~) ["desire for a commodity"] 10. to create a ~ 11. to meet, satisfy a ~ 12. (a) brisk, enormous, great, heavy, strong; growing, increased, increasing; inelastic ~ 13. (a) limited, little ~ 14. consumer; popular; public ~ 15. ~ drops off, falls off; increases, rises 16. a ~ for (there is a brisk ~ for home computers) 17. by ~ (by popular ~) 18. in ~ (small cars are in great ~) ["misc."] 19. the law of supply and ~

demand II *v.* 1. (D; tr.) to ~ from, of (to ~ an apology from smb.) 2. (E) she ~s to be kept informed of everything 3. (L; subj.) she ~s that she be/should be kept informed of everything

demanding *adj.* 1. emotionally; physically; technically; very ~ (to play a technically very ~ sonata) 2. ~ of (she is very ~ of her employees)

demarcation *n.* a ~ between (lines of ~ between the two zones)

démarche *n.* 1. to make, present a ~ to 2. a diplomatic ~

demean I *v.* (formal) (D; refl.) ("to degrade") to ~ by (I will not ~ myself by cheating on the examination)

demean II *v.* (formal) (d; refl.) ("to behave") (he ~ed himself like a gentleman)

demeaning *adj.* 1. ~ to (is charity ~ to its recipients ?) 2. ~ to + inf. (it is ~ to be kept waiting so long)
demeanor, demeanour *n.* a cheerful, friendly; unfriendly ~
demerit *n.* a ~ for (to get/receive a ~ for being late)
demise *n.* 1. ["death"] on, upon smb.'s ~ 2. (fig.) what has led to the virtual ~ of gloves for women in the west?
demobilization *n.* on, upon ~
democracy *n.* 1. a constitutional; multi-party; parliamentary; representative ~ 2. in a ~ (in a ~ the people vote for their leaders)
Democrat *n.* (US) a registered ~
demon *n.* to exorcise a ~
demonstrable *adj.* clearly ~
demonstrate *v.* 1. to ~ convincingly 2. (B) ("to explain by showing") they ~d the new computer to us 3. (D; intr.) ("to protest by marching") to ~ against (the students ~d against the government) 4. (D; intr.) ("to display support by marching") to ~ for, in favor of (to ~ for lower taxes) 5. (L; to) ("to prove by showing") we ~d (to them) that a new computer would save considerable time 6. (Q; to) ("to explain by showing") she ~d (to him) how the computer works
demonstration *n.* ["explanation"] 1. to attend; give, put on a ~ 2. a practical ~ ["protest"] 3. to go on, join, take part in; mount, organize, stage a ~ 4. to ban; break up, quell; call off a ~ 5. an antinuclear; antiwar, peace; civil-rights; political ~ 6. a disorderly, violent; non-violent, orderly, peaceful ~ 7. a mass; organized; spontaneous; staged ~ 8. a public; student ~ 9. a ~ calls for, demands; takes place 10. a ~ against (we met at/on a student ~ against the wars) ["expression of support"] 11. to mount, organize, stage a ~ 12. a ~ for, in favor of, in support of 13. (misc.) they marched as/in a ~ of support
demote *v.* (D; tr.) to ~ from; to (she was ~d from major to captain)
demur I *n.* (formal) without ~ (they accepted the proposal without ~)
demur II *v.* (formal) (D; intr.) ("to object") to ~ at, to (AE) (to ~ at a proposal)
den *n.* 1. a lion's ~ 2. a gambling; opium ~; a ~ of iniquity; a ~ of thieves
denial *n.* ["refusal, rejection"] 1. to issue a ~ 2. a categorical, emphatic; flat; outright; strenuous, strong, vehement; unqualified ~ 3. a ~ that + clause (they issued a ~ that their firm had been involved) ["a psychological process"] 4. in (a state of) ~ (about) (she was in ~ about the abuse she had suffered as a child)
denomination *n.* ["group"] 1. a religious ~ (to belong to a religious ~) ["unit of money"] 2. large; small ~s (the store did not accept currency in large ~s)
denominator *n.* 1. to find the least (math.)/lowest (math. or fig.) common ~ 2. a common ~

denounce *v.* 1. to ~ angrily, bitterly; openly, publicly; roundly, strongly 2. (B) to ~ smb. to the police 3. (D; tr.) to ~ as (to ~ smb. as a drunkard) 4. (D; tr.) to ~ for (to ~ smb. for drinking too much) 5. (G) she ~d drinking in the strongest possible terms 6. (K) she ~d his drinking
density *n.* 1. population; traffic ~ 2. high; low ~
dent *n.* 1. to make, put a ~ in (he made a ~ in the door; to make a ~ in the backlog of work) 2. to hammer out, remove, straighten out a ~
denture *n.* 1. to put in; remove, take out; wear a ~ 2. a lower; partial; upper ~ 3. complete, full ~s 4. a set of ~s
denude *v.* (D; tr.) to ~ of (the hillside was ~d of trees)
denunciation *n.* 1. to issue, make a ~ 2. an angry, bitter, scathing, strong, vehement; sweeping ~ 3. (misc.) her ~ of him to the police as a drunkard/for being a drunkard
deny *v.* 1. to ~ angrily; categorically, emphatically, fervently, flatly, hotly, strenuously, strongly, vehemently 2. (A; typically used without *to*) he ~ies himself nothing; they were ~ied admittance; to ~ smb. bail; Everton's defence ~ied Liverpool the winning goal; he ~ies nothing to his family; or: he ~ies his family nothing 3. (G) she ~ied knowing anything 4. (L; to) she ~ied that she had been there; there's no ~ing that she must have been there; you can't ~ you were there, so don't even try to! 5. (rare) (M) he ~ied it to be the case
deodorant *n.* 1. to apply, put on (a) ~ 2. to use (a) ~ 3. (a) cream; roll-on; spray; stick; underarm ~
depart *v.* 1. (D; intr.) to ~ for (to ~ for London) 2. (D; intr.) to ~ from (our train is due to ~ in five minutes from platform (BE)/track (AE) seven)
department *n.* ["division of a school, of a university"] 1. to chair (esp. AE), head (esp. BE), run a ~ 2. a strong; weak ~ 3. an accounting; anthropology; astronomy; biology; chemistry; classics; economics; English; French; geology; German; history; Italian; linguistics; mathematics; music; nursing; philosophy; physics; political science; psychology; Slavic, Slavonic; sociology; Spanish ~ 4. the chair (esp. AE), head (esp. BE) of a ~; a member of a ~ USAGE NOTE: You can say both "the English Department" and "the Department of English." ["division of a company or government"] 5. an accounting; finance; fire (AE) (BE has *fire brigade*); health; housing; human-resources, personnel; police; recreation; sanitation; service ~ ["division of a hospital"] 6. an A & E, Accident and Emergency (BE), casualty (BE), emergency (AE) ~ (the victim was taken to the emergency ~ but had to wait to be seen in the ~) ["area, category"] 7. in a certain ~ (he's a bit lacking in the common-sense ~ ("he lacks common sense")) ["smb.'s area of concern or responsibility"] 8. smb.'s ~ (cooking is not my ~: I leave it to the wife)
departure *n.* 1. to be, constitute, mark, represent a ~

from (this marks a ~ from established procedures) 2. a new; sudden ~ 3. a ~ for 4. a ~ from; to 5. (misc.) a point of ~

depend v. 1. to ~ crucially, entirely, heavily, solely; partly; to some extent; in the last analysis, ultimately (on) 2. (d; intr.) to ~ on, upon (she ~s on her parents; the future ~s on what we decide now) 3. (misc.) she ~s on her parents for support = she ~s on her parents to support her; you can ~ on her to do the exact opposite of what you think she will!

dependence n. 1. alcohol; drug; physical; psychological ~ 2. ~ on, upon (his ~ on alcohol; her ~ on her parents for support = her ~ on her parents to support her)

dependency n. 1. a colonial ~ 2. alcohol; drug ~

dependent adj. 1. crucially, entirely, heavily, solely; partly; to some extent; in the last analysis, ultimately ~ 2. for; on, upon (she is ~ on her parents for support = she is ~ on her parents to support her)

depict v. 1. (B) they ~ed the situation to us vividly and in great detail 2. (d; tr.) to ~ as (he was ~ed as a traitor) 3. (J) the artist ~ed him strolling through a garden

deplete v. (D; tr.) to ~ of

deplorable adj. 1. ~ to + inf. (it was ~ to live in such conditions = it was ~ living in such conditions) 2. ~ that + clause (it is ~ that some people live/should live in such conditions)

deplore v. 1. to ~ deeply, strongly, thoroughly 2. (G) we ~ taking drugs 3. (K) we ~ their taking drugs

deploy v. (D; tr.) to ~ from; to (troops were being ~ed from Europe to Asia)

deployment n. 1. large-scale ~ (the large-scale ~ of troops) 2. ~ from; to

deport I v. (formal) ("to behave") 1. (d; refl.) to ~ like (he ~ed himself like a gentleman) 2. (P; refl.) to ~ oneself well

deport II v. (D; tr.) ("to send out of the country") to ~ from; to

deportation n. 1. (a) mass ~ 2. ~ from; to

depose v. (D; tr.) to ~ from

deposit I n. ["money put into a bank account"] 1. to make a ~ 2. a demand; direct; minimum; time ~ 3. on ~ (the money was on ~ in a bank) ["down payment; security payment"] 4. to give, leave a ~; to put a ~ down on 5. to recover, get back one's ~ 6. to forfeit, lose one's ~ 7. a non-refundable; refundable ~

deposit II v. 1. (D; tr.) to ~ in (to ~ money in a bank) 2. (D; tr.) to ~ with (she ~ed the funds with her lawyer)

deposition n. (legal) 1. (of a witness) to make a ~ 2. (of a lawyer) to defend; notice; take a ~ 3. a sworn ~ 4. a ~ that (he made a ~ that he had witnessed the accident)

deposits n. 1. rich ~ 2. coal; mineral; oil; ore ~ (rich ~ of ore)

depot n. an ammunition; arms; bus; freight (AE), goods (BE); fuel; supply ~

depreciate v. 1. (D; intr.) to ~ by (to ~ by ten percent) 2. (D; intr.) to ~ in (to ~ in value)

depress v. (R) it ~ed everyone (to realize) that no progress was made during the negotiations

depressed adj. 1. clinically; deeply, very ~ 2. ~ about, at, over; by (~ at the bad news) 3. ~ to + inf. (everyone was ~ to realize that no progress was made during the negotiations) 4. ~ that + clause (everyone was ~ that no progress was made during the negotiations)

depressing adj. 1. deeply, profoundly, very ~ 2. ~ to + inf. (it is ~ to realize that no progress was made during the negotiations) 3. ~ that + clause (it's ~ that no progress was made during the negotiations)

depression n. ["low economic activity"] 1. to cause; come out of a ~; go into a ~ 2. a major, severe; minor ~ 3. an economic ~ (the country has gone into a major economic ~) 4. (misc.) the Great Depression (of the 1930s) ["dejection"] 5. to cause, lead to; treat ~ 6. to get over; succumb to; suffer from ~ 7. (an) acute; chronic; clinical; deep, severe, total; manic; postnatal, postpartum ~ (he was in a state of total ~) 8. ~ deepens, worsens; lifts 9. an attack, bout, episode; period of ~ (the loss of his job led to the onset of a period of severe ~) 10. in; with ~ (hospitalized with ~)

depressor n. a tongue ~

deprivation n. to suffer ~

deprive v. (d; tr.) to ~ of (to ~ smb. of everything)

depth n. ["distance from top to bottom"]["distance from front to back"] 1. in ~ (the river is thirty feet in ~) ["place at the bottom of a body of water"] 2. at; to a ~ (the water froze to a ~ of two feet; there was ice even at a ~ of two feet!) 3. to reach; sink to a ~ (the divers reached great ~s) ["capability"] 4. beyond, out of one's ~ ["worst part"] 5. in the ~s (in the ~s of the Depression) ["misc."] 6. in ~ ("thoroughly") (to analyze smt. in ~ is to make an in-depth analysis of it); to plumb the ~s of smt. ("to get to the root of smt."); in the ~s of despair; to lack ~ ("to be superficial")

depth charge n. to drop a ~

depute v. (formal) (esp. BE) 1. (B) ("to assign") (he ~d the bookkeeping to me while he was away) 2. (H) ("to appoint as deputy, to delegate") he ~d me to do the bookkeeping while he was away

deputize v. 1. (esp. AE) (D; tr.) ("to appoint") to ~ as (he ~d me as his assistant) 2. (esp. BE) (D; intr.) to ~ for ("to replace") (to ~ for smb. as secretary) 3. (AE) (H) ("to appoint as deputy") he ~d me to do the bookkeeping while he was away

deputy n. 1. to swear in a ~ 2. to act as (a) ~ 3. a special ~ 4. a ~ for

deranged adj. mentally ~

derelict adj. ~ in (~ in one's duty)

derision n. 1. to arouse, provoke ~ 2. an object of ~ 3. ~ for (to show one's ~ for smb. or smt. ridiculous) 4. (misc.) hoots of ~

derivation n. of a certain ~ (words of Latin ~)

derive v. 1. (d; intr.) ("to come") to ~ from (many words ~ from Latin) 2. (D; tr.) ("to trace") to ~ from (to ~ a word from a Latin root) 3. (D; tr.) ("to receive") to ~ from (to ~ pleasure from music)

derogation n. ["permission to bypass typically an EU regulation"] (legal) (BE; AE has *variance*) 1. to grant a ~ 2. to apply for a ~

derogatory adj. ~ of, to, towards

descend v. 1. (d; intr.) to ~ from; to ("to come down from") (do you know from whom you are ~ed?; to ~ from the heights to the depths) 2. (D; intr.) to ~ into ("to go into") (to ~ into a cave) 3. (d; intr.) ("to swoop down") to ~ on, upon (the tourists ~ed on the resort) 4. (d; intr.) ("to stoop") to ~ to (to ~ to a life of petty crime)

descendant n. a direct, lineal ~

descended adj. (cannot stand alone) 1. directly ~ 2. ~ from (~ from a royal family)

descent n. ["origin"] 1. to trace smb.'s/one's ~ 2. direct ~ 3. ~ from 4. of a certain ~ (of mixed ~) ["decline"] 5. a gradual, steep ~ ["visit, influx"] 6. a ~ on, upon (a sudden ~ of tourists on a resort) ["coming down"] 7. to make a ~ from; into; to (to make a ~ into a cave; to make a ~ from the heights to the depths)

describe v. 1. to ~ graphically; minutely; vividly; in detail 2. (B) she ~d the scene to us 3. (D; refl., tr.) to ~ as (he was ~d as (being) very cruel) 4. (G) she ~d living under the occupation 5. (K) she ~d in detail their living under the occupation 6. (Q; to) she ~d (to us) how they lived under the occupation 7. (misc.) words cannot ~ how awful it was to live under the occupation!

description n. 1. to give, provide a ~ 2. to answer to a, fit a ~ (he answers to the ~ of the escaped convict) 3. to beggar, defy ~ 4. an accurate, correct, exact; clear, graphic; matter-of-fact, objective ~ 5. a glowing; lively, picturesque, vivid ~ 6. a blow-by-blow; detailed, full, lengthy, thorough; firsthand ~ 7. a brief, short; superficial ~ 8. a job ~ 9. of a certain ~ (a person of that ~ was seen here yesterday) 10. (misc.) beyond ~

desensitize v. (D; tr.) to ~ to (to ~ smb. to suffering)

desert I n. 1. to cross, traverse; reclaim a ~ 2. a trackless ~ 3. (fig.) a cultural; intellectual ~ 4. across, through; in a ~

desert II v. 1. (D; tr.) to ~ for (to ~ the stage for Hollywood) 2. (D; intr.) to ~ from (he ~ed from his regiment) 3. (D; intr.) to ~ to (to ~ to the enemy)

desertion n. a ~ from (~s from the army have increased)

deserts n. ["reward"] ["punishment"] to get one's just ~

deserve v. 1. to ~ richly 2. (E) she ~d to win; she ~d to be honored (for her work) 3. (G) she ~d being honored (for her work), she ~d honoring (for her work) 4. (misc.) to ~ better (of); to ~ ill of; to ~ well of; I hardly ~ all this bad luck: what have I

done to ~ it?; richly ~d, well ~d (she got a well-deserved award for her work)

deserving adj. 1. richly ~ 2. ~ of (~ of help)

design I n. ["plan"] 1. a creative ~ 2. software ~ 3. intelligent ~ (to defend intelligent ~ against natural selection) 4. a ~ for (a ~ for a new library) 5. in; to ~ (clothes that are simple but elegant in (their) ~; a house built to a ~ by Frank Lloyd Wright) ["intention"] 6. by ~ (did it happen by accident or (by) ~?) (see also **designs**)

design II v. 1. (C) he ~ed a beautiful house for us; or: he ~ed us a beautiful house 2. (d; tr.) to ~ as 3. (d; tr.) to ~ for (~ed for recreational purposes)

designate I adj. (placed after a noun) a minister ~ (the minister ~ met the president elect)

designate II v. 1. (D; tr.) to ~ as (the state was ~d as a disaster area) 2. (H) we ~d him to serve as our delegate 3. (N; used with a noun) the state was ~d a disaster area

designation n. a ~ as

designed adj. (cannot stand alone) 1. ~ for (~ for operation at high altitudes) 2. ~ to + inf. (the machine was ~ to operate at high altitudes)

designer n. an aircraft; dress; fashion; graphic; interior; software ~

designs n. ["evil intentions"] 1. to have, harbor ~ against, on, upon (to have ~ on smb.'s money) 2. sinister ~

desirable adj. 1. highly, very ~ 2. ~ to + inf. (it is ~ (for you) to be there by two o'clock) 3. ~ that + clause; subj. (it is ~ that you ¬be/should be/(BE) are¬ there by two o'clock)

desire I n. 1. to arouse, create, whet (a) ~ 2. to evince, express, voice a ~ 3. to feel, have a ~ 4. to satisfy a ~ 5. to repress, stifle, suppress a ~ 6. (an) ardent, blind, burning, deep, earnest, fervent, insatiable, intense, keen, overwhelming, passionate, strong; sincere; unfulfilled ~ 7. animal; sexual ~s 8. a ~ for 9. a ~ to + inf. (a ~ to excel; her ~ for the estate to be divided equally) 10. a ~ that + clause; subj. (it was her ~ that the estate be/should be/was divided evenly)

desire II v. 1. to deeply, fervently, strongly ~ 2. (E) she ~s to remain neutral in the dispute 3. (formal) (H) she ~d the estate to be divided equally 4. (formal) (L; subj.) she ~d that the estate be/should be/(BE) was divided equally

desirous adj. (formal) (cannot stand alone) 1. very ~ 2. ~ of (~ of fame) 3. ~ that; subj. (she was ~ that the estate be/should be/(BE) was divided equally)

desist v. 1. (formal) (D; intr.) to ~ from (to ~ from further litigation) 2. (misc.) (esp. legal) to cease and ~

desk n. ["counter"] 1. (in a hotel) a front (AE), reception (BE) ~ 2. at the ~ (I'll meet you at the front ~) ["department"] 3. an information ~ 4. (at a newspaper) a city; copy ~ ["table for writing"] 5. to clear; leave one's ~ 6. a cluttered ~ 7. a rolltop;

writing ~ 8. at, behind; in; on a ~ (she was at her ~ at nine, sat behind/at it all day, read the papers on it, found some pens in it, and left it at five) USAGE NOTE: In AE *city desk* means "local news desk" (i.e., news about the city in which a newspaper is published); in BE it means "financial news desk" (perhaps by reference to the City of London, traditionally London's financial district).

desolation *n.* complete, utter ~ (in a state of complete and utter ~)

despair I *n.* 1. to overcome ~ 2. bitter, black, deep, sheer, total, utter ~ 3. the depths of ~ 4. in ~ (in utter ~) 5. out of ~ (to do smt. out of ~) 6. (misc.) to drive smb. to ~ (his untidiness is driving me to ~!)

despair II *v.* 1. to ~ deeply 2. (D; intr.) to ~ of (to ~ of success; he's so untidy sometimes I really ~ of him!)

despatch (BE) see **dispatch I, II**

desperate *adj.* 1. ~ for (~ for help) 2. ~ to + inf. (~ to get help)

desperation *n.* 1. an act of ~ 2. in ~ 3. out of ~ (to do smt. out of sheer ~)

despicable *adj.* 1. utterly ~ 2. ~ to + inf. (it was utterly ~ of him to desert his family!) 3. ~ that + clause (it was utterly ~ that he deserted/should have deserted his family!)

despise *v.* 1. to ~ utterly 2. (D; tr.) to ~ for (I ~d him for his cowardice) 3. (K) I ~ his refusing to accept responsibility 4. (misc.) I hate him, I loathe him, I ~ him!

despoil *v.* (formal) (D; tr.) to ~ of

despondent *adj.* 1. ~ about, over (I grew very despondent about her abandonment of me) 2. ~ to + inf. (I was despondent to hear that she had abandoned me) 3. ~ that + clause (I was despondent that she had abandoned me)

despot *n.* an absolute; benevolent; enlightened ~

destination *n.* 1. to arrive at, reach one's ~ 2. smb.'s final, ultimate ~

destine *v.* 1. (d; tr.) to ~ for (fate ~d her for greatness) 2. (H) fate ~d her to go far in life

destined *adj.* (cannot stand alone) 1. ~ for (the shipment is ~ for New York; she was ~ for greatness) 2. ~ to + inf. (she was ~ by fate to go far in life)

destiny *n.* 1. to achieve, fulfill one's ~ 2. to decide, shape smb.'s ~ 3. (historical) Manifest Destiny 4. ~ to + inf. (it was her ~ to go far in life) 5. ~ that + clause (it was her ~ that she would go far in life)

destitute *adj.* ~ of (~ of feeling)

destitution *n.* in ~ (to die in ~)

destroyer *n.* a tank ~

destruction *n.* 1. to carry out ~ (with a human subject: the soldiers carried out the total ~ of the village) 2. to cause ~ (with any subject: the flood caused great ~) 3. complete, mass, total, utter; wanton; widespread ~ (weapons of mass ~ = WMDs) 4. (misc.) the soldiers left a trail of wanton ~ behind them

destructive *adj.* ~ of

detach *v.* (D; tr.) to ~ from (the officer was ~ed temporarily from her unit)

detail I *n.* ["small part"]["minute treatment"] 1. to bring up, cite; disclose; fill in; furnish, give; go into (the) ~s 2. to go into ~ (you don't need to go into great ~) 3. to work out (the) ~s 4. an essential, important; mere, minor; technical ~ (can you fill in the technical ~s?) 5. (a) gory, graphic, grisly, gruesome, harrowing, lurid, revolting, sordid, unsavory; great, meticulous, microscopic, minute; petty; precise ~ (they went into lurid ~; they brought up petty ~s; the newspapers reported the gruesome ~s; he described the event in graphic ~; only the police knew the sordid ~s of the crime) 6. a wealth of ~ 7. (a) ~ about (the book gives a wealth of ~ about the campaign; they discussed the important ~s about the campaign) 8. for ~s; in ~ (turn to page 26 for further ~s; to treat a topic in minute ~) 9. (misc.) spare me the ~s! (see also **spare** 2); contact ~s (give us your contact ~s if you want to be on our mailing list) ["detachment"] (usu. mil.) 10. to form a ~ 11. a fatigue, work ~

detail II *v.* ("to assign") 1. (D; tr.) to ~ for (to ~ a unit for fatigue duty) 2. (H) they ~ed the unit to do fatigue duty

detain *v.* 1. to ~ forcibly 2. (D; tr.) to ~ for (he was ~ed for questioning) 3. (misc.) the precise details needn't ~ us further

detained *adj.* unavoidably ~

detection *n.* 1. to avoid, escape ~ 2. early ~ (can early ~ of a disease increase its cure rate?)

detective *n.* 1. an amateur; house (obsol.); private ~ 2. a ~ investigates (the ~s assigned to the case are investigating it)

detector *n.* a lie; metal; mine; smoke ~

detention *n.* in ~ (he was kept in ~ for two hours)

deter *v.* (D; tr.) to ~ from

detergent *n.* (a) biodegradable; laundry; liquid; synthetic ~

deterioration *n.* 1. continuing; marked; steady ~ 2. a ~ in (I noted a ~ in her condition)

determination *n.* ["decisiveness"] 1. to show ~ 2. dogged, fierce, firm, great, grim, iron, sheer, strong, unflinching, unyielding ~ ["firm intention"] 3. to express one's ~ 4. to shake smb.'s ~ 5. ~ to + inf. (she expressed her strong ~ to succeed) 6. with ~ (she struggled to succeed with great ~) ["judicial decision"] 7. to come to a ~ (of a case) 8. the final ~ (of a case)

determine *v.* 1. (E) she ~d to succeed (more usu. is: she is ~d to succeed) 2. (L) the police ~d that no crime had been committed 3. (Q) we must ~ where the conference will take place

determined *adj.* 1. very ~ 2. ~ to + inf. (she is ~ to succeed) 3. ~ that + clause (she is ~d that she will succeed)

deterrent *n.* 1. an effective, powerful ~ 2. a nuclear ~; the ultimate ~ 3. a ~ against, to 4. as a ~ (is it true that weapons of mass destruction serve as a ~ to war?)

detest v. 1. to ~ cordially 2. (G) he ~s working 3. (K) we ~ his constantly lying

detestable adj. 1. ~ to + inf. (it is ~ to speak like that; it was ~ of them to do that) 2. ~ that + clause (it was ~ that they did/should have done that!)

detour n. 1. to set up a ~ 2. to follow, make, take a ~ 3. a ~ around

detract v. (d; intr., tr.) to ~ from (the scandal will not ~ from his fame)

detriment n. 1. a ~ to 2. to the ~ of

detrimental adj. ~ to (smoking is ~ to health)

devastation n. 1. to cause ~ 2. complete, total, utter, widespread ~ 3. (misc.) the cyclone left a trail of ~ (behind it)

develop v. 1. to ~ fully; rapidly; slowly 2. (D; intr.) to ~ from; into (to ~ from a child into an adult)

developed adj. highly; well ~

developer n. a property (BE); real-estate (AE) ~

development n. ["advancement, change, maturation"] 1. arrested; economic; historical; intellectual; physical ~ 2. the latest ~s; recent ~s; technological ~s 3. a dramatic, exciting; interesting; new, recent; surprising ~ 4. a ~ in (recent ~s in physics) 5. (misc.) a stage of ~; a stage in the ~ of ["large housing project"] 6. a housing ~ 7. (BE) a ribbon ~ ("line of similar buildings constructed typically along roads leading out of a town")

deviate v. 1. to ~ sharply; slightly 2. (D; intr.) to ~ from

deviation n. 1. a marked, sharp; slight ~ 2. (statistics) a standard ~ 3. a ~ from

device n. 1. a contraceptive; intrauterine (IUD) ~ 2. a laborsaving; timesaving ~ 3. a detonating; explosive; incendiary; thermonuclear ~; an improvised explosive ~ (IED) 4. a literary; mnemonic; rhetorical; stylistic ~ 5. a flotation; listening ~ 6. a ~ for 7. a ~ to + inf. (it was a ~ to mislead the voters) 8. (misc.) left to one's own ~s ("on one's own; unaided; left to one's own resources")

devil n. ["spirit of evil"] 1. go to the ~! ("damn you!") 2. the ~ incarnate ["severe reprimand"] (esp. AE) 3. to catch the ~ ["fellow"] (colloq.) 4. a lucky; poor ~ ["disturbed state"] 5. (in) a ~ of a mess ["misc."] 6. what the ~ is that?! where the ~ did she go?! speak of the ~! there'll be the ~ to pay! he's a little ~!

devoid adj. (cannot stand alone) ~ of (completely ~ of any redeeming features)

devolution n. ~ from; to (the ~ of power from central government to local government)

devolve v. (formal) 1. (d; intr.) ("to be transferred") to ~ on, upon (his duties ~d on his deputy) 2. (D; tr.) ("to transfer") to ~ from (to ~ power from central government) 3. (D; tr.) ("to transfer") to ~ to (to ~ power from central government to local government)

devote v. 1. to ~ oneself completely, entirely 2. (D; refl., tr.) to ~ to (she ~d herself to her work; we must ~ a lot of time to this project)

devoted adj. 1. blindly, completely, deeply,

entirely, thoroughly, utterly, very ~ 2. ~ to (~ to one's family)

devotee n. a ~ of (a ~ of the theater)

devotion n. 1. to demonstrate, display, show ~ 2. to inspire ~ (from) 3. absolute, blind, complete, deep, great, selfless, slavish, thorough, undying, unflagging, unstinting, unswerving, utter ~ 4. religious ~ 5. ~ to (blind ~ to the cause; ~ to one's duty) 6. with ~ (to serve with ~)

devour v. to ~ eagerly, ravenously

dexterity n. 1. to demonstrate, display, show ~ 2. great; intellectual; political; manual ~ 3. ~ in (she showed great political ~ in handling the problem) 4. with ~ (she handled the problem with great political ~)

dexterous, dextrous adj. ~ with (~ with one's hands)

diabetes n. to develop; have ~

diagnose v. (D; tr.) to ~ as (they ~d her illness as diabetes)

diagnosis n. 1. to make a ~ 2. to confirm a ~ (of) (further tests confirmed the initial ~ of diabetes) 3. (med.) (a) differential ~ 4. a ~ that + clause (further tests confirmed the initial ~ that she had diabetes)

diagonal I adj. ~ to

diagonal II n. on the ~ (to cut on the ~)

diagram n. 1. to draw a ~ 2. a ~ shows 3. in, on a ~

dial I n. to turn a ~ (turn the ~ to the correct position and then press the "ON" button)

dial II v. to ~ direct, directly (she ~(l)ed London direct)

dialect n. 1. to speak (in) a ~ 2. a local, regional; non-standard; social; standard ~ 3. in ~ (the stories were written in ~)

dialing, dialling n. direct ~

dialogue n. 1. to enter into a ~ (with); to have a ~ with 2. a constructive, fruitful, meaningful ~ 3. a ~ about, on; between; with

diameter n. in ~ (the circle is ten inches in ~ ("the circle has a ~ of ten inches"))

diamond n. 1. to cut; grind; polish; set a ~ 2. a cut; flawless, perfect; industrial; rare; rough, uncut ~ 3. a ~ sparkles 4. (misc.) a baseball ~; a ~ in the rough (AE), a rough ~ (BE) ("a person who is kinder and/or more intelligent than he/she appears to be")

diaper n. (AE) 1. to change, put on a ~ 2. cloth; disposable ~s (BE has *nappy*)

diaphragm n. ["contraceptive device"] to insert, put in; remove, take out a ~

diarrhea, diarrhoea n. 1. to come down with, get; have ~ 2. severe ~ 3. an attack of ~

diary n. ["personal journal"] 1. to keep a ~ 2. a personal ~ 3. an entry in a ~ ["personal appointments book"] (esp. BE) 4. a desk; pocket ~ 5. in a ~ (put the concert in your ~)

diatribe n. 1. to utter a ~ 2. to launch into a (long) ~ 3. a bitter ~ 4. a ~ against

dice n. 1. to play ~ 2. to roll, throw (the) ~ 3. loaded ~ (the cards were stacked and the ~ were loaded

against us) 4. a roll; throw of the ~ 5. a pair of
~ 6. (misc.) (esp. AE; colloq.) no dice! ("I do
not agree!; nothing doing!; no way!") USAGE
NOTE: In AE one can say "one die, two dice." In
BE one says "one dice, two dice." But the expression "The die is cast (and there's no turning back)"
is CE.

dichotomy n. 1. an absolute; growing ~ 2. a ~
between

dicker v. (esp. AE) to ~ about, over; for; with

dictate v. 1. (D; intr., tr.) to ~ to (she was ~ing to her
secretary; the conqueror ~s terms to the conquered)
2. (L; can be subj.) the financial crisis ~d that he
not begin/should not begin immediately 3. (Q; to)
they ~d (to us) how everything would be done

dictation n. ["dictated material"] 1. to give ~ 2. to take
~ 3. to transcribe ~ ["dictation exercise"] 4. to give a
~ 5. to do, have a ~

dictator n. an absolute; benevolent; brutal; military; ruthless ~

dictatorship n. 1. to establish, set up a ~ 2. to
overthrow a ~ 3. an absolute; benevolent; brutal;
military; ruthless ~ 4. during a ~ 5. (to live) under
a ~

diction n. clear ~

dictionary n. 1. to compile, write a ~ 2. to expand;
revise; update a ~ 3. to consult, look smt. up in,
use a ~ 4. an abridged, desk; bilingual; biographical; college (AE), collegiate (T); combinatorial,
combinatory; concise; dialect; encyclopedic; ety-
mological; general-use, general-purpose; historical; learner's, learners'; medical; monolingual;
multilingual; multivolume; names; orthographic,
spelling; pronouncing; pocket; reverse; technical;
unabridged ~ 5. a ~ of abbreviations; collocations;
foreign words; personal names; place names;
quotations; synonyms 6. an entry in a ~ 7. in a ~ (is
that word (entered/listed) in any ~?)

diddle v. 1. (esp. BE) (colloq.) (D; intr.) ("to cheat")
to ~ out of 2. (AE) (D; intr.) ("to fool around") to
~ with

die I n. the ~ is cast (fig.) (see Usage Note at **dice**)

die II v. 1. to ~ heroically; instantly; suddenly (he
~d heroically at the front) 2. (D; intr.) to ~ by (to ~
by the sword; to ~ by one's own hand) 3. (D; intr.)
to ~ for (to ~ for one's beliefs) 4. (colloq.) (D; intr.)
(only in the progressive) to ~ for ("to want") (she's
dying for a cup of coffee) 5. (D; intr.) to ~ from, of
(he died of tuberculosis; to ~ of natural causes) 6.
(colloq.) (E) (only in the progressive) ("to want")
she's dying to find out 7. (S) she ~d happy; she ~d
young; he ~d a poor man; (legal) to ~ intestate 8.
(misc.) to ~ a horrible death; to ~ in action/battle;
to ~ in one's sleep; (fig.) to ~ laughing; rumors ~
hard; to ~ for (slang) ("to be desired very much")
(she has cheekbones to ~ for!)

diet n. 1. to be on, follow, have, stick to a ~ 2. to
go on a ~ 3. to prescribe a ~; to put smb. on a ~
4. a balanced, healthy, well-balanced; unhealthy

~ 5. a crash; special; starvation; therapeutic ~ 6.
a bland; high-calorie; high-carbohydrate; high-
fiber, high-fibre; high-protein; liquid; low-calorie;
low-carbohydrate; low-cholesterol; low-fat; low-
residue; low-salt, low-sodium; salt-free; soft ~ 7.
a reducing, slimming (esp. BE) ~ 8. a macrobiotic;
vegan; vegetarian ~ 9. in a ~ (there should be more
vegetables in your ~) 10. (misc.) a steady ~ (she
was on a steady ~ of parties)

differ v. 1. to ~ considerably, greatly, markedly,
radically, sharply, widely; slightly 2. (D; intr.) to
~ about, in, on, over 3. (D; intr.) to ~ from (this
arrangement ~s from the one I had in mind) 4. (D;
intr.) to ~ with (I ~ with you on that point) 5. (misc.)
we must agree to ~ (because I can't persuade you
and you can't persuade me); I beg to ~ (because I
disagree with you) (formal; polite)

difference n. 1. to make a ~ ("I took the [road] less
traveled by, And that has made all the ~" – "The
Road Not Taken," Robert Frost (1874–1963))
2. to tell the ~ 3. to have; patch up, reconcile,
resolve, settle, thrash out ~s 4. to set aside ~s 5.
to air ~s 6. to split the ~ ("to take an average") 7.
a considerable, great, huge, marked, striking, vast
~ 8. a basic, essential, fundamental; noticeable,
perceptible, real; significant ~ 9. an irreconcilable;
radical ~ 10. an insignificant, little, minor, slight;
subtle; superficial ~ 11. ~s among; a ~ between;
from 12. a ~ in (a ~ in age) 13. a ~ to (that makes
no ~ to me) 14. (misc.) a world of ~ ("a considerable difference"), with a ~ (for a sport with a ~, try
bungee-jumping)

different adj. 1. basically, completely, entirely,
totally, widely; quite; radically; very ~ 2. ~ in
(they are quite ~ in outlook ("their outlooks are
quite different")) 3. ~ from, than (esp. AE), to
(BE) USAGE NOTE: Some purists consider only
different from to be correct. Note that, as prepositions, *from, than, to* can all introduce full clauses
(different from/than/to what we thought), but only
than can, as a conjunction, become part of a clause
(different than we thought).

differential n. 1. a pay; price ~ 2. a ~ between

differentiate v. 1. to ~ clearly 2. (d; intr.) to ~ between 3. (d; tr.) to ~ from (to ~ right from/and
wrong)

differentiation n. to make a ~ between

differing adj. widely ~

difficult adj. 1. ~ for (typing is ~ for me) 2. ~ to +
inf. (it is ~ to please him = he is ~ to please = he
is a ~ person to please = pleasing him is ~; it is ~
to translate this book = this book is ~ to translate
= this is a ~ book to translate; it is ~ for me to
translate such material = such material is ~ for
me to translate) 3. (misc.) notoriously ~ (weather
conditions are notoriously ~ to predict)

difficulty n. 1. to cause, create, make, present ~ties
(for) 2. to come across, encounter, experience,
face, get into, have, meet, run into ~ties 3. to

clear up, overcome, resolve, surmount a ~ 4. (a) grave, great, insurmountable, serious, severe ~ 5. economic, financial; learning; personal; technical ~ties 6. a ~ arises; lies in 7. ~ in (she has ~ in breathing = she has ~ breathing) 8. ~ties about, over; with (we had ~ties with them about the price) 9. in ~ (he is in serious ~) 10. with; without ~ (he got here only with some ~) 11. (misc.) many ~ties face us

diffident *adj.* ~ about

diffuse *v.* (formal) (D; tr.) to ~ through, throughout (~d through the air)

dig I *n.* (colloq.) ["excavation"] 1. to go on a ~ 2. an archeological ~ ["poke"] 3. to give smb. a ~ in (the ribs) ["critical remark"] 4. (colloq.) to get in, have, take (AE) a ~ at smb.

dig II *v.* 1. (D; intr.) to ~ for ("to search for") (to ~ for gold) 2. (d; intr.) ("to delve, search") to ~ into (to ~ into a report; he dug deep into his own pocket) 3. (d; intr., tr.) ("to jab") to ~ into (his elbow was ~ging into my ribs; he dug his spurs into the sides of the horse) 4. (D; intr., refl., tr.) ("to move earth" and fig.) to ~ into (they dug themselves into a hole) 5. (D; intr., refl., tr.) ("to free, liberate" and fig.) to ~ out of (they dug themselves out of a hole) 6. (D; intr., tr.) ("to move, move earth" and fig.) to ~ through, under (to ~ a tunnel through a mountain; they had to ~ through a lot of red tape; they dug under the street)

dignified *adj.* ~ to + inf. (it was not ~ to behave like that)

dignify *v.* (D; tr.) to ~ by, with (I would not ~ that shack by calling it a hotel; she did not ~ his comment by responding to it; she did not ~ his comment with a response)

dignitary *n.* a local; visiting ~

dignity *n.* 1. to have, possess ~ 2. to maintain one's ~ 3. the ~ to + inf. (does he have enough ~ to cope with a hostile press?) 4. (misc.) to live in ~; to die in/with ~; to behave with ~; beneath smb.'s ~; a person of great ~

digress *v.* 1. (D; intr.) to ~ from 2. (misc.) but I ~ (used esp. in BE to apologize for straying from the main point)

digression *n.* ["act of digressing"] 1. a ~ from ["digressive remarks"] 2. a ~ on (he launched into a ~ on the need for more power plants)

digs *n.* (BE) in ~ (at a university) (do you live in ~ or in hall?)

dilate *v.* (d; intr.) ("to speak or write in detail") (formal) to ~ on, upon (to ~ upon a subject)

dilatory *adj.* (formal) ~ in (they were ~ in acting on your complaint)

dilemma *n.* 1. to confront; face; have a ~ 2. to resolve a ~ 3. an ethical, moral ~ (trying to resolve the ethical ~s posed by stem-cell research) 4. a ~ about, over 5. in a ~ 6. (misc.) on the horns of a ~

diligence *n.* 1. (legal) due ~ 2. the ~ to + inf. (does she have enough ~ to finish the job on time?)

diligent *adj.* ~ about; in (~ in one's work)

dillydally *v.* (D; intr.) to ~ over; with

dilute *v.* (D; tr.) to ~ with (to ~ the punch with water)

dimension *n.* ["importance"] 1. to add, introduce; assume, take on a ~ (the issue assumed serious ~s and the invasion added a whole new ~ to the problem) 2. (misc.) a problem of international ~s ["measurement"] (can be fig.) 3. a third ~ 4. in a ~ (in two ~s) 5. (misc.) time has been referred to as the fourth ~

diminish *v.* 1. (D; intr.) to ~ by (to ~ by ten percent) 2. (D; intr.) to ~ in (to ~ in value)

din *n.* ["noise"] 1. to make a ~ 2. an infernal ~ 3. above, over the ~

dine *v.* 1. (D; intr.) to ~ on ("to eat") (to ~ on steak) 2. (D; intr.) to ~ with 3. (misc.) to ~ at home, to ~ in; to ~ out

dining *n.* congregate ~ (AE)

dinner *n.* 1. to eat (esp. AE), have ~ 2. to cook, make, prepare; serve ~ 3. to give a ~ 4. a cold; formal; hot; light; nutritious, wholesome; substantial; TV ~ 5. at, during; over ~ (they were all at ~; what did you discuss at/during/over ~?) 6. for ~ (what are we having for ~?) 7. (misc.) to give smb. ~ (esp. BE); to take smb. to ~

dint *n.* by ~ of (by ~ of hard work)

dioxide *n.* carbon ~

dip I *n.* ["short swim"] 1. to have (BE), take (esp. AE) a ~ ["a soft food"] 2. a cheese ~ ["drop"] 3. to make a ~ (the road makes a ~) 4. a sharp ~ 5. (misc.) there is a sharp ~ in the road up ahead; a ~ in share prices

dip II *v.* 1. ("to drop") to ~ sharply (the road ~s sharply; the news made share prices ~ sharply) 2. (d; intr.) ("to drop, fall") to ~ below (the sun ~ped (down) below the horizon) 3. (d; tr.) ("to lower") to ~ in, into (she ~ped her pen into the ink) 4. (d; intr.) to ~ into ("to withdraw from") (to ~ into one's savings)

diphtheria *n.* to come down with, contract, get; have; prevent ~

diploma *n.* 1. to award, confer, present a ~ 2. to earn; receive a ~ 3. a college; high-school (AE) ~ 4. a ~ in (a ~ in Applied Linguistics)

diplomacy *n.* 1. to rely on, resort to ~ 2. dollar; gunboat; high-level; media; public; quiet; shuttle ~ 3. (misc.) with tact and ~ (to resolve a problem with tact and ~)

diplomat *n.* a career, professional; foreign ~

diplomatic *adj.* ~ to + inf. (it was not ~ to make such demands)

diplomatic immunity *n.* 1. to grant ~ 2. to claim; have ~ 3. to withdraw ~

direct *v.* 1. to ~ mainly, principally; specifically 2. (d; tr.) ("to point") to ~ against, at (the enemy ~ed their attacks mainly against our seaports) 3. (d; tr.) ("to address") to ~ at, to (the remark was ~ed specifically at you) 4. (D; tr.) ("to guide") to ~ to (can you ~ me to the palace?) 5. (d; tr.) ("to aim") to ~ to, towards (our efforts were ~ed towards the elimination of poverty and away from lesser problems) 6. (H) ("to order") the government ~ed us to send supplies to the flooded areas 7. (L; subj.) ("to order") the government ~ed that supplies be / should be / were (BE) sent to the flooded areas

direction n. ["course"] 1. to change ~ 2. the general; opposite; right; same; wrong ~ 3. an anticlockwise (BE), counterclockwise (AE); clockwise ~ 4. from; in a ~ (from the opposite ~; in my ~; in the general ~ of London; in a clockwise ~; a step in the right ~) 5. a sense of ~ ["supervision"] 6. under smb.'s ~ ["guidance"] 7. to give ~ to (beginners need ~ from someone qualified to give ~ to them)

directions n. ["instructions"] 1. to ask for; give, issue ~ 2. to follow; read (the) ~ 3. clear; explicit, precise, specific; stage ~ 4. ~ for; to (~ for using the printer; they gave us ~ to the palace) 5. ~ that + clause; subj. (she gave ~ that her estate be given / should be given to charity) ["courses"] 6. all; both (shots came from both ~ and people were running in all ~)

directive n. 1. to issue a ~ 2. a ~ requires smt.; takes effect 3. a ~ about, on; against (the latest EU ~ requiring stricter standards takes effect from next Monday) 4. a ~ that + clause; may be used with the subj. (the government issued a ~ that all firearms be / must be / should be handed in) 5. in accordance with, under the terms of a ~ (under the terms of the latest EU ~, stricter standards will be required) 6. an advance ~ (a living will giving smb.'s wishes in case of terminal illness)

director n. 1. an acting; deputy; managing ~ 2. an athletic (AE); funeral; music; program ~ 3. a casting; film, movie (esp. AE) ~ 4. a board of ~s; the post / position of ~

directorate n. interlocking ~s

directory n. 1. to consult, look smt. up in, use a ~ 2. a business; city; classified; telephone ~ 3. in a ~ (is that name (entered / listed) in the ~?)

dirge n. a funeral; mournful ~

dirt n. 1. in the ~ (to play in the ~) 2. a speck of ~ 3. (misc.) to hit the ~ ("to fall to the ground") (AE); to dig up ~ about smb. ("to seek and find negative information about smb."); to dish the ~ about smb. (BE) ("to say or write bad things about smb.") (see also **pay dirt**)

dirty linen n. to wash one's ~ in public ("to air one's problems in public")

disability n. 1. to have a ~ 2. a learning; mild; moderate; physical; serious, severe ~ (children with learning ~ties)

disabled adj., n. learning; physically ~ (learning-disabled children; help for the learning ~)

disabuse v. (D; tr.) to ~ of

disadvantage n. 1. to have, suffer a ~ 2. to offset, outweigh a ~ 3. an added; clear, decided, definite, distinct, obvious ~ 4. a ~ for, to (his poverty was an obvious ~ to him) 5. a ~ to + inf. (it was a ~ not to have a car available = it was a ~ not having a car

available) 6. at a ~ (many factors worked to place / put us at a decided ~) 7. to smb.'s ~ (many factors worked to our ~)

disadvantaged adj. culturally; economically; educationally; physically ~

disadvantageous adj. 1. clearly, obviously ~ 2. ~ for; to (his decision was ~ to us) 3. ~ to + inf. (it would be clearly ~ for us to delay)

disagree v. 1. to ~ bitterly, profoundly, sharply; completely, entirely, totally, utterly 2. (D; intr.) to ~ about, on, over; with (to ~ with smb. about smt.; to ~ on a plan) 3. (of food) to ~ with (the sauce ~d with me) 4. (misc.) I could not ~ more

disagreeable adj. ~ to

disagreement n. 1. to express (a) ~ 2. to have a ~ (with) 3. to resolve, settle a ~ 4. a bitter, marked, serious, sharp; slight; total ~ 5. a ~ among, between, with 6. a ~ about, on, over 7. in ~ (with) (we were in bitter ~ with them on all points = we were bitterly in ~ with them on all points) 8. (misc.) both sides are (locked) in total ~ over the terms of a settlement

disappear v. 1. to ~ completely 2. (D; intr.) to ~ from (to ~ from view; the story has ~ed completely from the media) 3. (D; intr.) to ~ in, into (they ~ed into the darkness)

disappearance n. 1. a mysterious; sudden ~ 2. a ~ from (the story's mysterious ~ from the media)

disappoint v. 1. to ~ bitterly, deeply 2. (R) it ~ed everyone (to learn) that she had failed the course

disappointed adj. bitterly, deeply, greatly, very; obviously, visibly ~ 2. ~ about, at, in, with (~ at / with the results; I was deeply ~ in / with him) 3. ~ to + inf. (she was ~ to learn that she had failed the course) 4. ~ that + clause (everyone was ~ that she had failed the course)

disappointing adj. 1. deeply, very ~ 2. ~ to + inf. (it is ~ to analyze the results) 3. ~ that + inf. (it was ~ that she had failed the course)

disappointment n. 1. to express; feel ~ 2. (a) bitter, cruel, deep, great, keen, profound, terrible ~ 3. ~ about, at, over (she felt deep ~ at having failed the course) 4. a ~ for, to (her failure was a bitter ~ to everyone) 5. ~ that + clause (everyone expressed keen ~ that she had failed the course) 6. to smb.'s ~ (to everyone's great ~, she failed the course)

disapproval n. 1. to express; indicate, show, voice (one's) ~ 2. complete, total; public; strong ~ 3. in; of; with ~ (she reacted to his plan with ~ and sneered in ~ of it) 4. (misc.) a chorus of ~; a note of ~; a show of ~

disapprove v. 1. to ~ completely, strongly, thoroughly, utterly 2. (D; intr.) to ~ of (we ~d strongly of his decision)

disarmament n. general, universal; multilateral; nuclear; phased; unilateral ~

disarray n. 1. complete, sheer, total, utter ~ 2. in ~ (to break up in total ~) 3. (misc.) a state of ~; to throw a meeting into ~

disassociate, dissociate v. (D; refl.) to ~ from
USAGE NOTE: Some purists prefer *dissociate*,
which is also the prevailing variant.

disaster n. 1. to bring ~ in its wake; cause (a); to
invite ~ 2. to experience, face, meet, suffer (a) ~ 3.
to court, risk ~ 4. to spell ~ (for) 5. to cope with;
recover from (a) ~ 6. to avert, prevent (a) ~ 7. a
major, terrible, tragic, unmitigated, unqualified ~ 8.
a near ~ 9. an ecological; environmental; impending; national; natural ~ 10. (a) ~ looms, strikes

disastrous adj. 1. ~ for, to 2. ~ to + inf. (it would be
~ for us not to wait)

disbar v. (D; tr.) to ~ from (to ~ from practice)

disbelief n. 1. complete, total, utter; mock ~ 2. in (~
in astrology) 3. in ~ (to shake one's head in ~)

disburse v. (B) to ~ funds to the states

disc n. ["tag"] (BE) (mil.) 1. an identification; tax ~
["recording"] 2. to cut a ~ (see **disk**) 3. a compact ~
(also CD); laser ~ (see also **disk**)

discern v. (formal) 1. (L) they soon ~ed that he was
lying 2. (Q) they could not ~ who was telling the
truth

discharge I n. 1. a dishonorable; general; honorable; medical; undesirable ~ (from the armed
forces) 2. a ~ from (a ~ from a hospital)

discharge II v. 1. (D; tr.) to ~ for (to ~ an employe
for stealing) 2. (D; refl., tr.) to ~ from (to ~ smb.
from hospital/from a hospital) 3. (D; tr.) to ~ into
(to ~ waste into a river)

disciple n. an ardent, devoted; fanatical ~

discipline I n. ["control; training"] 1. to enforce, keep;
establish; maintain ~ 2. to crack down on violations of ~ 3. to ease up on, relax ~ 4. to undermine
~ 5. to violate ~ 6. firm, harsh, iron, rigid, severe,
stern, strict ~ 7. lax, loose, slack ~ 8. military;
party ~ 9. ~ breaks down 10. the ~ to + inf. (they
didn't have enough ~ to cope with the job) (see
also **self-discipline**) ["branch of learning"] 11. an
academic ~ 12. across ~s (similar problems can be
found across a whole range of academic ~s)

discipline II v. 1. (D; tr.) to ~ for 2. (H; usu. refl.)
(she ~d herself to exercise every day)

disciplined adj. highly, very ~

disclaimer n. 1. to bear a ~ 2. to issue, publish a ~
3. a ~ about

disclose v. 1. (B) the authorities finally ~d the facts
to the press 2. (L; to) the authorities finally ~d (to
the press) that she had served time in prison

disclosure n. 1. to make a ~ (to) 2. a financial; full;
public; sensational, startling ~ 3. a ~ that + clause
(the ~ that she had served time in prison ruined her
chances for public office)

discomfort n. 1. to cause ~ 2. to bear; experience;
put up with ~ 3. to alleviate ~ 4. acute; physical ~
5. an amount, degree; level of ~ 6. in ~ (patients
may experience a certain degree of ~ but should
not be left in ~ too long)

disconcert v. (formal) (R) it ~ed us (to learn) that
they had refused our offer

disconcerting adj. 1. highly, profoundly, very ~ 2.
~ to + inf. (it was ~ (for us) to learn that they had
refused our offer) 3. ~ that + clause (it was ~ (to us)
that they had refused our offer)

disconnect v. (D; tr.) to ~ from

disconsolate adj. ~ about, at, over

discontent n. 1. to cause, fuel, stir up ~ 2. deep;
outspoken; public; simmering; widespread ~ 3. ~
about, at, over, with; ~ among 4. (misc.) to fan the
flames of ~; murmurs of ~; rumblings of ~ (the
government's announcement fanned the flames of
~ among consumers over price increases)

discontinue v. (G) she ~d paying rent

discord n. 1. to arouse, foment, generate, stir up;
spread ~ 2. domestic, family, marital ~ 3. bitter;
widespread ~ 4. ~ among, between 5. ~ in (~ in
smb.'s family relationships) 6. (misc.) a note of ~

discount n. 1. to give a ~ 2. a cash ~ 3. a ~ of; on (to
give a ~ of 10% on all purchases over £30) 4. at a
~ (she sold it at a ~)

discourage v. 1. to ~ actively; strongly 2. to ~
greatly, no end, very much 3. (D.; tr.) to ~ from
(she strongly ~d me from loving her) 4. (P.; intr.)
("to get discouraged") (I don't ~ easily!) 5. (R) it
~d us no end (to learn) that so many had/should
have failed 6. (misc.) it ~s us no end when so many
have failed

discouraged adj. 1. deeply, very ~ 2. ~ about, at,
over (we were deeply ~ at the failure of so many)
3. ~ to + inf. (we were very ~ to learn that so many
had/should have failed) 4. ~ that + clause (we were
very ~ that so many had/should have failed)

discouragement n. 1. deep ~ 2. ~ at, on, upon (our
deep discouragement upon learning that so many
had/should have failed) 3. ~ to + inf. (our deep
discouragement to learn that so many had/should
have failed) 4. ~ that + clause (our deep discouragement that so many had/should have failed)

discouraging adj. 1. deeply, very ~ 2. ~ for; ~ to 3.
~ to + inf. (it's deeply ~ (for/to us) to learn that so
many had/should have failed) 4. ~ that + clause
(it's deeply ~ (for/to us) that so many had/should
have failed)

discourse I n. ["connected speech"] 1. (grammar) direct; indirect ~ ["speech, talk"] (formal) 2. to deliver
a ~ (on, upon)

discourse II v. (formal) (D; intr.) to ~ on, upon

discourteous adj. 1. ~ to 2. ~ to + inf. (it was ~ of
him to say that)

discourtesy n. 1. to show ~ 2. (a) grave ~

discover v. 1. (J) we ~ed him cooking in our kitchen
2. (L) we ~ed that he could cook 3. (rare) (M) we
were surprised to ~ him to be a good cook 4. (Q) I
never have ~ed how to cook

discovery n. ["finding"] 1. to make a ~ 2. a dramatic;
exciting, startling, surprising, world-shaking 3. a
scientific ~ 4. a ~ that + clause (we made the surprising ~ that he was a really good cook) ["pretrial
disclosure of facts"] (legal) 5. to conduct ~

discredit *n.* 1. to bring ~ on, to 2. a ~ to (they are a ~ to our family) 3. to smb.'s ~

discreet *adj.* 1. ~ in 2. ~ to + inf. (it was not ~ of her to say that)

discrepancy *n.* 1. a glaring, striking, wide ~ 2. a ~ between; in

discretion *n.* 1. to exercise, show, use ~ in (remember to exercise in this matter all the ~ it requires) 2. complete, full, wide ~ 3. parental; viewer ~ 4. ~ to + inf. (she has full ~ to make decisions) 5. at one's ~ (to act at one's own ~) 6. with; without ~ (to proceed with ~) 7. (misc.) the soul of ~

discriminate *v.* 1. (D; intr.) to ~ against; in favor of (to ~ against minorities on specious grounds) 2. (d; intr.) to ~ among, between (to ~ between right and wrong) 3. (d; tr.) to ~ from (to ~ right from wrong)

discrimination *n.* 1. to practice ~ 2. to subject smb. to ~ (I was subjected to the worst ~ I have ever experienced) 3. age; racial; religious; reverse; sex ~ 4. blatant; outright ~ 5. ~ occurs 6. instances; levels of ~ 7. ~ against; in favor of (instances of blatant ~ against minorities have been known to occur) 8. ~ among, between (~ between right and wrong)

discus *n.* to throw the ~

discuss *v.* 1. (D; tr.) to ~ with (to refuse to ~ smt. with smb.) 2. (Q) we ~ed how we would do it

discussion *n.* 1. to arouse, provoke, stir up (a) ~ 2. to conduct; have; hold; lead; moderate a ~ 3. to be up for; bring smt. up for ~; to come up for ~ 4. an animated, brisk, heated, lively, spirited; brief; candid, frank, open; lengthy, long; quiet, peaceful; serious; wide-ranging ~ 5. a group; panel; round-table ~ (to lead a panel ~) 6. a ~ about, of 7. open for, open to ~ 8. under ~ (their case is now under ~) 9. (misc.) the point of a ~

discussions *n.* 1. to have, hold; schedule ~ 2. to curtail, end, terminate ~ 3. high-level; preliminary ~ 4. ~ among, between; with 5. ~ about

disdain I *n.* 1. to have; show ~ 2. ~ for (to have the greatest ~ for smt.) 3. with ~

disdain II *v.* (esp. BE) (formal) 1. (E) she ~ed to speak to them 2. (G) they ~ed watching TV

disdainful *adj.* ~ of; towards

disease *n.* 1. to come down with, contract, get, (BE colloq.) go down with; have a ~ 2. to carry; spread, transmit (a) ~ 3. to cure; prevent (a) ~ 4. to combat, fight; conquer, eradicate, stamp out, wipe out (a) ~; to bring a ~ under control 5. a common; rare ~ 6. a mild; serious ~ 7. a deadly; debilitating, wasting; degenerative; fatal; incurable, untreatable ~ 8. an acute; chronic ~ 9. an acquired; congenital; hereditary ~ 10. a childhood; communicable, contagious, infectious; sexually transmitted, social, venereal; tropical ~ 11. caisson; (a) deficiency; heart; (an) industrial, occupational; kidney; (a) skin ~ 12. Addison's; Alzheimer's; Hodgkin's; Legionnaire's ~ 13. foot-and-mouth, hoof-and-

mouth ~ 14. a ~ spreads 15. the outbreak of a ~ (for additional combinations, see **ailment, illness**)

disembark *v.* (D; intr.) to ~ from

disengage *v.* (D; refl., intr., tr.) to ~ from

disentangle *v.* (D; refl., tr.) to ~ from

disfavor, disfavour *n.* 1. to fall into ~ with 2. in ~ 3. (misc.) to look with ~ on

disfigured *adj.* badly ~

disgorge *v.* (D; tr.) to ~ into (the sewer ~d waste material into the river)

disgrace I *n.* 1. to bring; suffer ~ (their whole family has suffered the ~ they brought on it!) 2. (a) deep; public ~ 3. a ~ to (they are a ~ to their family) 4. a ~ to + inf. (it was a ~ to behave like that = it was a ~ behaving like that) 5. a ~ that + clause (it's a ~ that they behaved like that) 6. in ~ (he quit in ~ over the bribe)

disgrace II *v.* (D; refl., tr.) to ~ by (he ~d himself by accepting a bribe)

disgraceful *adj.* 1. ~ to + inf. (it was absolutely ~ to behave like that = it was ~ behaving like that) 2. ~ that + clause (it was utterly ~ that he accepted/should have accepted a bribe)

disgruntled *adj.* 1. ~ at, over, with ("~ at being dragged out of his dream" – British National Corpus; "more than 330,000 East Germans ~ with Communism" – British National Corpus) 2. ~ that + clause ("at first she seemed ~ that she had been proved wrong" – British National Corpus)

disguise I *n.* 1. to adopt, assume a ~ 2. to shed, throw off a ~ 3. a clever ~ (when she saw through the clever ~ he had assumed, he shed it at once) 4. in ~

disguise II *v.* 1. heavily; thinly ~d 2. (D; refl., tr.) to ~ as (he was ~d as a waiter) 3. (D; tr.) to ~ from (you can't ~ your plans from us!)

disgust I *n.* 1. to express; feel ~ 2. complete, deep, great, utter; obvious ~ (he expressed the utter ~ her behavior inspired in him) 3. ~ at, with (he expressed his utter ~ at her behavior) 4. in ~ (he left in great ~) 5. to smb.'s ~ (to my ~ I discovered that...)

disgust II *v.* 1. to ~ completely, thoroughly 2. (R) it ~ed everyone (to learn) that they had taken bribes

disgusted *adj.* 1. completely, thoroughly, totally, utterly, very ~ 2. ~ at, with 3. ~ to + inf. (she was ~ to learn that they had taken bribes) 4. ~ that + clause (she was ~ that they had taken bribes)

disgusting *adj.* 1. ~ to + inf. (it was ~ to watch him = he was ~ to watch = he was a ~ person to watch = watching him was ~) 2. ~ that + clause (it's ~ that they took/should have taken bribes)

dish *n.* ["food served in a dish"] 1. a favorite; main; side ~ ("I've made/cooked/prepared your favorite ~!) 2. in a ~ ["container typically for food"] 3. to do, wash; dry the ~es 4. a chafing; serving ~ 5. in a ~ (see also **dishes**; Usage Note at **wash up**) ["antenna"] 6. a satellite ~

disharmony *n.* 1. to stir up ~ 2. ethnic; racial; religious ~

dishearten v. (formal) 1. to ~ greatly, no end, very much 2. (R) it ~d us no end (to learn) that so many had/should have failed 3. (misc.) it ~s us no end when so many have failed

disheartened adj. (formal) 1. deeply, very ~ 2. ~ about, at, over (we were deeply ~ at the failure of so many) 3. ~ to + inf. (we were very ~ to learn that so many had/should have failed) 4. ~ that + clause (we were very ~ that so many had/should have failed)

disheartening adj. (formal) 1. deeply, very ~ 2. ~ for; ~ to 3. ~ to + inf. (it's deeply ~ (for/to us) to learn that so many had/should have failed) 4. ~ that + clause (it's deeply ~ (for/to us) that so many had/should have failed)

dishes n. ["dirty containers, cutlery, and utensils left after a meal"] 1. to do, wash; dry; rinse; stack the ~ 2. dirty ~ ["containers for holding food"] 3. plastic ~ 4. a set of ~ USAGE NOTE: BE uses *to wash up* more typically than *to do, wash the dishes.*

dishonest adj. 1. intellectually; morally ~ 2. ~ in (~ about; in; with) (don't be ~ about this matter with us!; to be ~ in one's dealings) 3. ~ to + inf. (it is ~ to lie about one's age)

dishonor, dishonour n. 1. to bring ~ on, to 2. a ~ to (they are a ~ to their country)

dishonorable, dishonourable adj. ~ to + inf. (it is ~ to deceive them with false promises)

dish out v. (B) he was ~ing out food and advice to the women

dish up v. (B) he was ~ing up food to the women

dishwasher n. (CE; colloq. BE also has *washing-up machine*) 1. to run, use a ~ 2. to load, stack; empty, unload a ~ 3. an automatic ~

disillusioned adj. ~ about, at; with

disinclined adj. (cannot stand alone) ~ to + inf. (he seems ~ to put up resistance)

disk n. ["structure in a spinal column"] 1. to slip ("dislocate") a ~ 2. a slipped ~ ["flat plate for computer storage"] 3. to back up; format; insert a ~; to copy onto a ~; to save on/to (a) ~ 4. a back-up; fixed, hard; floppy; magnetic; optical ~ USAGE NOTE: BE prefers the spelling *disc* for 1 and 2. See **disc**

diskette n. see disk 3

dislike I n. 1. to take a ~ to 2. to have; show a ~ for, of 3. an active, cordial, deep, hearty, strong, violent; instant; instinctive; mutual ~ 4. (misc.) smb.'s likes and ~s

dislike II v. 1. to ~ deeply, very much 2. (G) he ~s reading 3. (K) we ~ his hanging around with that crowd; I ~ your frowning USAGE NOTE: The verb *dislike* can be used with *it* + clause – I dislike it when you frown.

dislodge v. (D; tr.) to ~ from (the doctor ~d the bone from her throat)

disloyal adj. 1. ~ to 2. ~ to + inf. (it's ~ not to help a friend in need)

disloyalty n. to demonstrate, show ~ to

dismay I n. 1. to express; feel ~ 2. ~ at, over, (AE) with 3. in, with ~ (to moan in ~ over what had happened) 4. to smb.'s ~ (to my great ~, she was absent again = much to my dismay, she was absent again)

dismay II v. (formal) (R) it ~ed him (to learn) that the project had been canceled

dismayed adj. 1. ~ at, over, (AE) with 2. ~ to + inf. (he was ~ to learn that the project had been canceled) 3. ~ that + clause (he was ~ that the project had been canceled)

dismaying adj. ~ to + inf. (it was ~ to learn that the project had been canceled)

dismiss v. 1. to ~ curtly, summarily; lightly; out of hand 2. (D; tr.) to ~ as (he was ~ed as incompetent) 3. (D; tr.) to ~ for (I was ~ed for being late) 4. (D; tr.) to ~ from (she was ~ed from her job) 5. (misc.) (BE; cricket) the bowler ~ed the next batsman for six runs

dismissal n. 1. an abrupt, curt; constructive (BE), summary ~ 2. a ~ from

dismount v. (D; intr.) to ~ from

disobedience n. 1. blatant; willful ~ 2. civil ~ (see also **civil disobedience**) 3. ~ to (~ to orders)

disobedient adj. ~ to

disorder n. ["lack of order"] 1. to throw into ~ 2. in ~ (to retreat in ~) ["riot"] 3. violent ~s 4. ~s break out (the army put down the violent ~s that had broken out) 5. civil; public ~ (an outbreak of public ~) (see also **civil disorder**) ["illness"] 6. a brain; circulatory; digestive; eating; emotional; mental; minor; nervous; personality; post-traumatic stress ~ (PTSD); respiratory; stomach ~ (doctors treating the respiratory ~s that principally affect the young)

disoriented, disorientated adj. ~ about, as to (~ as to time and place)

disparity n. 1. a considerable, great, wide; growing ~ 2. a ~ between, in (a considerable ~ in wealth is opening up between different parts of the country)

dispatch I n. ["news item"]["message"] 1. to file; send a ~ 2. to dateline a ~ 3. a ~ from; to 4. a ~ that + clause (we read her ~ that war had been declared) 5. (misc.) (BE; mil.) to be mentioned in ~es (for bravery in combat) (AE has *to receive a citation*) ["promptness"] 6. with great ~

dispatch II v. 1. (D; tr.) to ~ from; to (the message was ~ed from battalion headquarters to each company) 2. (rare) (H) he was ~ed to carry the message

dispensation n. 1. to give, grant (a) ~ 2. to obtain; request (a) ~ (from) 3. (a) papal; royal; special ~ 4. a ~ to + inf. (they obtained a ~ to travel abroad)

dispense v. 1. (B) to ~ charity to the needy; to ~ equal justice to all 2. (D; intr.) to ~ with (to ~ with the formalities)

dispenser n. a cash; coffee; drinks (BE); soap ~

dispersed adj. widely ~

displace v. (D; tr.) to ~ as (she was ~d as champion)

display I *n.* 1. to make, put on a ~ (to make a vulgar ~ of one's wealth; to make a public ~ of one's ignorance to everyone) 2. to put smt. on ~ 3. a dazzling, imposing, impressive; lavish, ostentatious, spectacular; modest; public; vulgar ~ (to make a public ~ of grief; to put on a dazzling ~ of one's skill) 4. a firework (BE), fireworks (AE) ~ 5. a graphic ~ (of a computer) 6. on ~ (the new models were on ~)

display II *v.* (B) he ~ed his ignorance to everyone

displeased *adj.* 1. greatly, highly, very ~ 2. ~ about, at, by, with 3. ~ to + inf. (we are ~ not to have been there) 4. ~ that + clause (she was ~ that the proposal had not been accepted)

displeasure *n.* 1. to incur smb.'s ~ 2. to feel; show; voice one's ~ with 3. to smb.'s ~ (much to her ~, the proposal was not accepted)

disposal *n.* ["availability"] 1. to have at one's ~ (I had a huge car at my ~) 2. to place, put smt. at smb.'s ~ 3. at smb.'s ~ (if I can be of help in any way, remember that I'm always at your ~) ["elimination"] 4. bomb; garbage; garbage (esp. AE), rubbish (esp. BE); sewage; waste ~ ["device used to grind up garbage"] (esp. AE) 5. a garbage ~; or: a garbage-disposal unit

dispose *v.* 1. (d; intr.) to ~ of ("to deal with") (to ~ of the opposition) 2. (d; intr.) to ~ of ("to get rid of") (to ~ of the rubbish) 3. (formal) (H) ("to incline") what ~d him to do it?

disposed *adj.* (formal) ["inclined"] (cannot stand alone) 1. ~ to, towards (he seems favorably / well ~ towards us) 2. ~ to + inf. (she is ~ to accept our offer)

disposition *n.* ["inclination"] 1. a ~ to + inf. (a ~ to argue) ["personality"] 2. a bland; buoyant, cheerful, genial, happy, lively, pleasant, sunny; mild; nervous; sour, unpleasant ~ (people of a nervous ~ should not watch this program)

dispossess *v.* (D; tr.) to ~ of (they were ~ed of their wealth)

disproportionate *adj.* ~ to (the punishment was ~ to the crime)

dispute I *n.* 1. to stir up a ~ about 2. to adjudicate; arbitrate; resolve, settle a ~ (to settle a ~ out of court) 3. an acrimonious, bitter, heated, sharp ~ 4. a public ~ 5. a border; demarcation; industrial, labor; international; jurisdictional; legal; pay; territorial ~ (a long-simmering territorial ~ between two countries that finally erupted into open warfare) 6. a ~ about, over; with 7. in ~ (this point is in ~; labor is in ~ with management) 8. in a ~ (he is in a ~ with his insurance company)

dispute II *v.* 1. to ~ fiercely, hotly (a fiercely ~d point) 2. (D; intr.) (esp. BE) to ~ about, over; with (they are always ~ting with each other over politics) 3. (L) I do not ~ that he was there: no one can!

disqualification *n.* 1. to lead to, result in ~ 2. ~ for (the incident led to her ~ for cheating) 3. ~ from (it resulted in his ~ from the contest)

disqualify *v.* 1. (D; tr.) to ~ for (the athlete was ~fied for taking drugs) 2. (D; tr.) to ~ from (the athlete was ~fied from the competition for taking drugs)

disregard I *n.* 1. to show ~ 2. (a) blatant, callous, complete, flagrant, total; reckless; willful ~ 3. ~ for, of, 4. in ~ of (in total ~ of the regulations)

disregard II *v.* 1. to ~ completely 2. (K) we cannot ~ his coming late to work so often

disrepair *n.* 1. a state of ~ 2. in ~ (the building is in ~) 3. to fall into ~

disrepute *n.* 1. to fall into ~ 2. to bring smt. into ~ 3. to hold smb. in ~

disrespect *n.* 1. to show ~ 2. to intend, mean no ~ 3. deep, profound; healthy ~ 4. ~ for (I meant no ~ for your traditions; to show a healthy ~ for bureaucracy)

disrespectful *adj.* 1. ~ of, to (~ of / to one's elders) 2. ~ to + inf. (it was ~ of them to say that)

disruption *n.* 1. to cause (a) ~ 2. (a) complete, total; widespread ~ 3. ~ in, of, to (some ~ to services is likely to occur)

dissatisfaction *n.* 1. to express, voice; feel ~ 2. deep, keen, profound; growing; widespread ~ 3. ~ about, at, over, with (they expressed deep ~ with working conditions) 4. ~ among (~ among the workers) 5. rumblings of ~

dissatisfied *adj.* ~ with (we are ~ with the poor results)

dissension *n.* 1. to cause, sow, stir up; introduce 2. (a) deep; growing; widespread ~ 3. ~ among, between 4. rumblings of ~

dissent I *n.* 1. to express ~ 2. to brook (formal), tolerate no ~ 3. to squash, stifle ~ 4. political; strong ~ 5. ~ from 6. (misc.) rumblings of ~; voices of ~

dissent II *v.* (D; intr.) to ~ from

dissertation *n.* 1. to defend; do, write a ~ (to write a ~ under smb.'s supervision) 2. to supervise a ~ 3. (esp. AE) a doctoral ~ 4. a ~ about, on USAGE NOTE: AE prefers a *doctoral dissertation, master's thesis*; BE prefers a *doctoral thesis, master's dissertation / master's essay*.

disservice *n.* 1. to do smb. a ~ 2. a ~ to (you're doing a great ~ to your employers by saying their products are no good)

dissident *n.* a political ~

dissimilar *adj.* 1. ~ in (~ in outlook) 2. ~ to

dissimilarity *n.* 1. a ~ between; in (there is a marked ~ between them in outlook)

dissociate *v.* (D; refl., tr.) to ~ from (we ~d ourselves from his views) (see the Usage Note for **disassociate**)

dissolve *v.* 1. (D; intr., tr.) to ~ in (to ~ sugar in water) 2. (misc.) to ~ in / into laughter

dissonance *n.* cognitive ~ ("the holding of incompatible beliefs simultaneously")

dissuade *v.* (D; tr.) to ~ from

distance I *n.* 1. to cover; run; travel; walk a ~ 2. to keep a ~ (to keep a safe ~ between cars) 3. to close the ~ between 4. a discreet; good, great, long, vast; safe; short ~ (we traveled a short ~) 5. commuting; driving; hailing; shouting; striking; walking ~ (it's within easy walking ~ (of here); targets within striking ~ of our missiles) 6. (a) braking, stopping ~ 7. a ~ between; from; to (the ~ between New York and London is about three thousand miles; the ~ from Philadelphia to Chicago is less than eight hundred miles) 8. at a ~ (at a discreet ~; we spotted them at a ~ of two hundred yards) 9. from a ~ (I spotted her from a ~) 10. in the ~ (the city was visible in the ~) 11. (misc.) to keep one's ~ ("to not allow familiarity"); a short ~ away; quite a ~; some ~ (they are still some ~ apart); the middle ~ (disappeared into the middle ~)

distance II v. (D; refl.) to ~ from

distant adj. ~ from

distaste n. 1. to develop; express; feel; show (a) ~ 2. (a) strong ~ 3. (a) ~ for 4. with ~

distasteful adj. 1. ~ to (his behavior was ~ to everyone) 2. ~ to + inf. (it was ~ for me to have to enforce discipline)

distil, distill v. (D; tr.) to ~ from (to ~ whiskey from grain)

distinct adj. ~ from (man is ~ from the apes and, as ~ from the apes, can create language)

distinction n. ["differentiation"] 1. to draw, make a ~ 2. to blur a ~ 3. a clear-cut; essential, fundamental; fine; obvious; subtle; valid ~ 4. a class ~ (class ~s lie at the heart of many social problems) 5. a ~ between (we must treat all classes alike, without any ~ between them) ["eminence"] ["superiority"] 6. to enjoy, have, hold a ~ (he holds the dubious ~ of being the first person to break the new speed limit) 7. an academic, doubtful, dubious ~ 8. of ~ (an artist of ~) 9. with ~ (to serve with ~)

distinctive adj. ~ of

distinguish v. 1. (d; intr.) to ~ among, between (the twins are so much alike I can't ~ between them; to ~ between good and evil) 2. (d; refl.) to ~ as (she ~ed herself as a painter) 3. (d; refl.) to ~ by (he ~ed himself by running five marathons) 4. (D; tr.) to ~ from (to ~ good from/and evil) 5. (d; refl.) to ~ in (they ~ed themselves in the fine arts)

distinguishable adj. 1. clearly, easily, plainly; barely, hardly ~ 2. ~ from

distinguished adj. ~ for

distortion n. a crude, gross, grotesque; deliberate; malicious; willful ~

distract v. (D; tr.) to ~ from (the music ~ed them/ their attention from their studies)

distraction n. 1. to drive smb. to ~ 2. a ~ from (the music was a ~ from their studies)

distraught adj. ~ about, at, over; with (~ with grief at her death)

distress I n. 1. to cause ~ 2. to feel; suffer ~ 3. to alleviate, ease ~ 4. deep, great, profound ~ 5. economic, financial ~ 6. emotional, mental, psychological; physical ~ 7. ~ at, over, with 8. in ~

(they were in deep ~ over their loss) 9. to smb.'s ~ (to our ~, her condition did not improve)

distress II v. 1. to ~ deeply 2. (R) it ~ed me (to read) that a new epidemic had broken out

distressed adj. 1. deeply ~ 2. ~ about, at, by, over, with (~ at the news) 3. ~ to + inf. ; ~ that + clause (I was deeply ~ (to read) that a new epidemic had broken out)

distressing adj. 1. deeply, very ~ 2. ~ for, to 3. ~ to + inf. ; ~ that + clause (it was ~ to me (to read) that a new epidemic had broken out)

distribute v. 1. to ~ equitably, fairly; evenly; inequitably, unfairly; unevenly; widely 2. (B) the instructor ~d the test papers to the students; to ~ food free of charge to the poor 3. (D; tr.) to ~ among (to ~ food free of charge among the poor)

distribution n. 1. (an) equitable, fair; even; inequitable, unfair; uneven; wide ~ 2. (math.) normal ~ 3. (ling.) complementary ~ 4. ~ among; to (the ~ of surplus food free of charge among/to the poor)

district n. 1. the business (esp. AE); financial; red-light; tenderloin (AE); theater ~ 2. a congressional; health; postal; school; voting ~ (a postal ~ whose boundaries extend a long way and in/within which many people live)

distrustful adj. ~ of

disturb v. (R) it ~ed me (to read) that a new epidemic had broken out

disturbance n. 1. to cause, create, make a ~ 2. to quell, put down a ~ 3. a minor ~ (a minor ~ of the peace involving only a few people)

disturbed adj. 1. emotionally, mentally, psychologically ~ 2. seriously, severely ~ 3. ~ about, at, by, over 4. ~ to + inf. ; ~ that + clause (I was ~ (to read) that a new epidemic had broken out)

disturbing adj. ~ to + inf. ; ~ that + clause (it was deeply ~ to me (to read) that a new epidemic had broken out)

disuse n. to fall into ~

ditch n. 1. to dig a ~ 2. a deep; shallow ~ 3. an anti-tank; drainage ~ (to fall into a deep drainage ~)

dither I n. in a ~ (about, over)

dither II v. (D; intr.) to ~ about, over

ditty n. 1. to sing a ~ 2. a popular ~

dive I n. 1. to make a ~ (at) 2. to go into a ~ (the plane went into a ~) 3. a swallow (BE), swan (AE) ~ 4. a back; headfirst; high ~ 5. a crash ~ (of a submarine) 6. a power ~ (of a plane) (see also **nose dive**) 7. a ~ for (they made a ~ for the ditch) 8. a ~ from; into 9. (misc.) (colloq.) to take a ~ ("to lose a boxing match deliberately")

dive II v. 1. to ~ headfirst 2. (D; intr.) to ~ for (to ~ for pearls; to ~ for cover) 3. (D; intr.) to ~ from; into (she ~d into the pool from the high diving board) 4. (D; intr.) to ~ off (he ~d off the boat) 5. (P; intr.) he ~d under the bed; she ~d to a depth of thirty feet; they ~d over the side of the boat

diverge v. 1. to ~ markedly, sharply, widely 2. (D; intr.) to ~ from

divergence *n.* 1. (a) marked, sharp, wide ~ 2. a ~ between (there was a sharp ~ between their views) 3. a ~ from (they found a wide ~ from the norm)

diversion *n.* ["amusement"] 1. a favorite; popular ~ ["turning"] 2. a ~ from; to (a ~ of traffic from the damaged bridge to an alternative route; the sign said "Bridge Damaged: Buses on Diversion" (BE)) ["distraction"] 3. to create a ~ 4. a welcome ~

diversity *n.* 1. cultural; ethnic; multicultural; religious ~ 2. (misc.) the USA's motto "E Pluribus Unum" expresses its commitment to unity in or from ~

divert *v.* (D; tr.) to ~ from; to

divest *v.* (formal) (d; refl., tr.) to ~ of (they ~ed themselves of all stocks and bonds)

divide I *n.* 1. a continental ~; (in North America) the Great Divide 2. (fig.) the great ~ ("death") (to cross the great ~) 3. a ~ between

divide II *v.* 1. to ~ equally, evenly 2. (D; tr.) to ~ among, between; with (to ~ profits among the partners) 3. (D; tr.) to ~ by (to ~ six by three and get two) 4. (D; tr.) to ~ from (the channel ~s the island from the mainland) 5. (D; intr., refl., tr.) to ~ into (they ~d the loot into equal shares; to ~ three into six and get two) 6. (misc.) to ~ in half; to ~ in two

divided *adj.* 1. deeply, sharply; hopelessly ~ 2. ~ on, over (they are sharply ~ over the choice of a new chairperson)

dividend *n.* ["sum divided among stockholders"] 1. to declare a ~ 2. (also fig.) to pay a ~ (healthy living pays ~s!) 3. a share, stock (esp. AE) ~ 4. a handsome, large ~

divide off *v.* (D; tr.) to ~ into (the room was ~d off into three alcoves by a partition)

divide up *v.* (D; tr.) to ~ among, between; into (they ~d up the profits into equal shares)

dividing line *n.* 1. to draw a ~ between 2. to cross the ~ 3. a thin ~ (how thin is the ~ between genius and madness?)

divisible *adj.* ~ by; into

division *n.* ["mathematical operation of dividing"] 1. to do ~ 2. long; short ~ ["major military unit"] 3. an airborne; armored; infantry; motorized ~ ["classification"] 4. to make a ~ 5. an arbitrary ~ 6. (BE; sports) first ~; premier; second ~; etc. (our club is in the second ~ of the league) ["dividing"] 7. a deep; equal; equitable; sharp; unequal ~ 8. cell ~ 9. ~ among; between; within (deep ~s within the party as well as between the parties) ["type of voting, vote"] (BE) 10. to force a ~

divisor *n.* a common ~

divorce *n.* 1. to file for, sue for ~ 2. to get, receive a ~ 3. to grant a ~ 4. a messy ~; (a) no-fault ~; an uncontested ~; (a) ~ by mutual consent 5. a ~ comes through (when did your ~ finally come through?) (see also *divorce settlement* at **settlement**)

divorced *adj.* ~ from (he got/was ~d from his wife)

divulge *v.* 1. (B) to ~ information to the press 2. (L; to) they ~d (to us) that the stock had already been sold 3. (Q; to) they did not ~ (to us) when the stock was sold

dizzy *adj.* 1. ~ from (~ from the rays of the sun) 2. ~ with (~ with success)

do *v.* 1. (C) ("to perform") she did a favor for me; or: she did me a favor 2. (d; tr.) to ~ about ("to help improve") (what can we ~ about his schoolwork?) 3. (d; tr.) to ~ about, with ("to deal with, treat") (what should we ~ about/with students who fail?) 4. (d; intr.) to ~ by ("to treat") (the firm did very well by her when she retired) 5. (colloq.) (BE) (d; intr.) to ~ for ("to act as housekeeper for") (she does for me twice a week) 6. (colloq.) (BE) (d; intr.) to ~ for ("to ruin") (that long hike nearly did for me!) 7. (d; tr.) to ~ for ("to make arrangements for") (what did you ~ for light when the electricity was turned off?) 8. (D; tr.) to ~ for ("to help") (what can I ~ for you?) 9. (d; tr.) to ~ out of ("to cheat out of") (they did him out of his inheritance) 10. (d; tr.) to ~ to ("to inflict on") (what did they ~ to her?) 11. (d; tr.) to ~ to, with ("to change") (what have they done to the center of the city? what have you done with your hair?) 12. (d; tr.) to ~ with ("to use for") (what should we ~ with this old typewriter?) 13. (d; tr.) to ~ with ("to concern") (their suggestion has/is nothing to ~ with the problem) 14. (d; intr.) to ~ without ("to manage without") (we had to ~ without fresh fruit) 15. (G; only in the perfect) he is (AE)/has (CE) done talking 16. (P; intr.) ("to fare") she is ~ing very well; he is ~ing nicely; our business is ~ing very well financially 17. (misc.) you did well to tell me; she could ~ with a long vacation (see also **doing, done**) USAGE NOTE: In the meaning "to fare", the verb *do* can have a medical meaning – the patient is doing well after the operation; mother and child are doing well after a difficult delivery.

do away *v.* (d; intr.) to ~ with ("to eliminate") (they did away with that department several years ago)

dock I *n.* ["basin for ships"] 1. to go into ~ 2. a dry, floating ~ 3. at, on a ~; in (a) ~ (there was labor trouble down at the ~s; the ship was in ~) ["wharf; jetty"] (AE) 4. at, on a ~ (there was labor trouble down at/on the ~s)

dock II *v.* 1. (D; intr.) to ~ at (the ship ~ed at Portsmouth) 2. (D; intr.) to ~ with (the spaceship ~ed with the satellite)

dock III *n.* ["place for the accused in a court"] to put smb. in the ~

dock IV *v.* (D; tr.) ("to deduct, take") to ~ by; for; from (they ~ed ten dollars from her wages for being late = they ~ed her wages by ten dollars for being late)

docket *n.* ["agenda"] on the ~

doctor *n.* 1. a family; NHS; private ~ (you should register with an NHS ~ if you move to a new area) 2. a witch ~ 3. a barefoot ~ ("an auxiliary medical worker in a rural area, esp. in China") 4. ~s prescribe medication 5. ~s examine; see; treat (their) patients 6. (misc.) to see ("consult") a ~; a spin ~ ("one who puts a special interpretation on events")

doctorate *n.* 1. to award, grant a ~ 2. to earn; get, obtain, receive; have, hold a ~ 3. an earned (AE = "completed and awarded"); honorary ~ 4. a ~ from; in (a ~ in physics from Cambridge)

doctrine *n.* 1. to apply; preach a ~ 2. to establish a ~ 3. to disprove a ~ 4. (a) sound ~ 5. a basic; defense; religious ~ 6. a point of; body of ~ (there are only a few disputed points of ~ in that whole vast body of ~) 7. a ~ that + clause (it was their basic ~ that nothing was better than free trade)

document *n.* ["general sense"] 1. to draw up; issue; sign a ~ 2. to file; store ~s 3. (esp. AE) to notarize a ~ 4. to classify; declassify a ~ 5. to falsify; forge a ~ 6. to shred ~s 7. a classified; confidential; historic; legal; official; restricted; secret; top-secret ~ 8. an authentic ~ 9. a ~ about, concerning ["computers"] 10. to create; display; edit; retrieve a ~

documentary *n.* 1. to film; make a ~ 2. to show a ~ 3. a ~ about, on 4. in a ~ (there were real revelations in the fly-on-the-wall ~ she made about the organization)

documentation *n.* 1. to provide ~ for 2. adequate, appropriate, proper; inadequate, insufficient, weak; strong ~

dodge I *n.* a tax ~

dodge II *v.* 1. (D; intr.) to ~ behind (to ~ behind a door) 2. (rare) (G) he ~d serving in the armed forces

dodger *n.* ["evader"] a draft; tax ~

dog *n.* 1. to breed; keep; train ~s 2. to walk a ~ (on a leash) 3. to muzzle a ~ 4. (AE) to curb one's ~ 5. a mad, rabid; stray; vicious; wild ~ 6. a bird (AE), gun (BE); Eskimo; guard (BE), watchdog; guide, seeing-eye (AE); hunting ~; lapdog (also fig.); pet; police; sheep; sniffer (esp. BE); toy ~; working ~ 7. ~s bark; bite; growl; howl; salivate; snap; snarl; wag their tails; whine; yelp 8. a pack of (wild) ~s 9. a young ~ is a pup(py) 10. a female ~ is a bitch 11. (misc.) ~s have hair and cats have hair or fur; a lucky ~ ("a lucky person"); a running ~ ("a lackey"); a ~'s life ("a wretched existence"); to fight like cat and ~ (BE), to fight like cats and ~s (AE); to work like a ~ ("to work very hard") USAGE NOTES: 1. In CE a *police dog* is one used by the police; in AE it can also mean a breed of dog called a *German shepherd* in AE and an *Alsatian* in BE. 2. You can praise a dog by saying "Good dog!" and scold it by saying "Bad dog!"

dogfight *n.* ["aerial combat"] (also fig.) to engage in a ~

doghouse *n.* (AE) ["disfavor"] (colloq.) in the ~

dogma *n.* (an) economic; political; religious ~ (are people beginning to question or even to reject the economic ~s of the past?)

dogmatic *adj.* ~ about

doily *n.* a lace; linen; paper ~

doing *n.* 1. that took some ~! ("that required great effort") 2. that's none/not of my ~!

doldrums *n.* (colloq.) ["stagnation"] in the ~

dole *n.* (colloq.) (BE) ["unemployment insurance"] off; on the ~ (to be on the ~; to go on/sign on the ~ until you find paid employment and can come off the ~)

dole out *v.* (B) she ~d out some food to the children = she ~d some food out to the children

doll *n.* 1. a baby, Barbie (T); china; Kewpie (T); paper; rag ~ 2. (misc.) a dollhouse (AE), doll's ~ (BE) (to play with ~s in a dollhouse)

dollar *n.* 1. a half; silver ~ 2. a falling; rising; strong; weak ~ (the international markets experienced difficulties with the falling ~) 3. (misc.) the ~ was strong against the euro

doll up *v.* (colloq.) (D; refl., tr.) to ~ for (she ~ed herself up for the party)

dolphin *n.* 1. a school of ~s 2. a young ~ is a calf 3. a female ~ is a cow 4. a male ~ is a bull

domain *n.* ["sector"] the public ~ (in the public ~)

dominance *n.* 1. ~ in 2. ~ over (their ~ over everyone else in the arts and sciences)

domination *n.* 1. world ~ 2. ~ over 3. under smb.'s ~

dominion *n.* ~ over ("we hold Dominion over palm and pine" – "Recessional," Rudyard Kipling (1865–1936))

donate *v.* 1. (D; tr.) to ~ for (to ~ money for a charity) 2. (D; tr.) to ~ to, towards (to ~ money to a charity towards the funding of a helpline)

donation *n.* 1. to make a ~ 2. to send in a ~ 3. a charitable; voluntary ~ 4. a big, generous, large, sizable; small ~ 5. a ~ to (to make a ~ to a charity) 6. in ~s (to receive vast sums in ~s)

done *adj.* 1. ~ with (we're ~ with the chores) 2. (BE) to have ~ with (we've ~ with the plates) 3. (misc.) after that hike, I'm ~ for ("I'm completely exhausted")

donkey *n.* 1. to ride (on) a ~ 2. ~s bray, go heehaw, heehaw

donor *n.* 1. an anonymous; generous ~ 2. a blood; organ ~

doom I *n.* 1. to seal smb.'s ~ 2. to go to, meet one's ~ 3. impending ~ 4. (misc.) the crack of ~; a sense of ~ hung over us

doom II *v.* (D; tr.) to ~ to (that will ~ him to oblivion)

doomed *adj.* 1. ~ to (~ to disappointment; ~ to failure) 2. ~ to + inf. (she is ~ to eke out a miserable existence)

door *n.* 1. to hang a ~ 2. to bar, bolt; close, shut; lock; open; slam; unlock a ~ 3. to break down, force a ~ 4. to knock at, on a ~ 5. to answer the ~ 6. the ~ is ajar; bolted; closed; locked; open; unlocked 7. a back; double; French (AE; BE has *French window*); front, main; revolving; screen; side; sliding; stage; storm (esp. AE) ~ (see also **back door**) 8. a ~ closes, shuts; creaks, squeaks; jams; opens; slams shut 9. a ~ to (the ~ to this room is never locked) 10. at the ~ (who is at the ~?) 11. (misc.) behind closed ~s ("in secret"); they live next ~ to us; to sell from ~ to ~; to close the ~ on any compromise ("to rule out the possibility of any compromise"); at death's ~ ("almost dead"); to show smb. the ~ ("to ask smb. to leave") (see also *show smb. to the door* at **show II**)

doorbell *n.* 1. to ring a ~ 2. to answer a ~ 3. a ~ rings

doornail *n.* (misc.) as dead as a ~

doorstep *n.* at, on smb.'s ~ ("very close")

doorway *n.* 1. (fig.) the ~ to (the ~ to freedom) 2. in; through the ~ (she stood in the ~ and then stepped through it)

dope *n.* ["drugs"] (colloq.) to take ~

doped up *adj.* (colloq.) 1. ~ on (~ on pills) 2. ~ with (~ with medication)

dormancy *n.* (in) a state of ~

dormant *adj.* to lie, remain, stay ~

dose *n.* 1. to administer, give a ~ 2. to measure out a ~ 3. to receive; take a ~ 4. a fatal, lethal ~ (see also **overdose**) 5. a heavy, massive, strong ~ 6. a light, small, weak ~ 7. (misc.) she received a massive ~ of radiation; in small ~s (also fig.) (your brother-in-law is all right – in small ~s!)

dosed up *adj.* ~ with (she was ~ with cough medicine)

dossier *n.* to have; keep a ~ on smb.

dot *n.* 1. a tiny ~ 2. (misc.) on the ~ ("precisely") (see also *from the year dot* at **year**)

dotage *n.* to be in one's ~

dote *v.* (d; intr.) to ~ on, upon (she ~s on her grandchildren)

dotted *adj.* ~ with

dotted line *n.* to sign on the ~ ("to agree to smt. by signing a document")

double I *n.* ["accelerated pace"] 1. at, on (esp. AE) the ~ ["betting"] 2. the daily ~ ["misc."] 3. more than ~ (here it costs more than ~ its price abroad!)

double II *v.* 1. (D; intr.) ("to do smt. additional") to ~ as (the gardener ~d as the chauffeur) 2. to more than ~ (its price has more than ~d in only a few short years!)

double back *v.* (P; intr.) she ~d back towards the park

double-date *v.* (colloq.; esp. AE) (D; intr.) to ~ with

double fault *n.* (tennis) to commit a ~

double figures *n.* in ~ (inflation was in ~)

doubles *n.* (tennis) 1. to play ~ but not singles 2. ladies' (BE), women's; men's; mixed ~ 3. (misc.) to play in the ~ but not in the singles

double up *v.* 1. (D; intr.) ("to share living accommodations") to ~ with 2. (misc.) to ~ in pain

doubt I *n.* 1. to plant; raise (a) ~ (her proposal raised serious ~s in my mind) 2. to cast ~ on 3. to feel ~; to entertain, harbor, have ~s about 4. to express, voice (a) ~ 5. to allay, clear up, dispel, resolve a ~ 6. (a) deep, serious, strong; gnawing; lingering;

reasonable; slight ~ 7. ~s appear, arise; exist; persist 8. a ~ about, of 9. (a) ~ that + clause (he expressed serious ~ that he could finish the job on time) 10. beyond (a shadow of) (a) ~; without a ~ 11. in- (the result was never in serious ~) 12. (misc.) to give smb. the benefit of the ~; (colloq.) there is no ~ about it: she's the best; you say she's the best – but I have my ~s (about that) USAGE NOTE: Some purists recommend that *whether* or the more informal *if* be used with the noun *doubt*, especially in the meaning "uncertainty" – she expressed doubt (about/as to) whether they would finish on time ("she was not certain whether they would finish on time"). In the meaning of "disbelief", the conjunction *that* is common – she expressed doubt that they would finish on time ("she did not believe that they would finish on time"). Note that in interrogative sentences the use of *that* prevails – is there any doubt that they will finish on time? In negative sentences the conjunction *that* must be used – there is no doubt that they will finish on time.

doubt II *v.* 1. to ~ strongly, very much 2. (L, Q) I ~ that/if/whether she will want to participate USAGE NOTE: See the Usage Note for **doubt I**. Thus, to express "uncertainty", one can say – she doubted whether they would finish on time. To express "disbelief", one can say – she doubted that they would finish on time. In negative sentences, only *that* is used – she doesn't doubt that they will finish on time.

doubtful *adj.* 1. ~ about, of 2. ~ that/if/whether + clause (it's ~ that she will be present) USAGE NOTE: See the Usage Note for **doubt I**. Thus, to express "uncertainty", one can say – it is/I am doubtful whether they will finish on time. To express "disbelief", one can say – it is/I am doubtful that they will finish on time.

dough *n.* 1. to knead, mix, roll (out), work ~ 2. flaky; firm; stiff ~ 3. ~ rises 4. a lump, piece of ~

doughnuts, donuts *n.* 1. to make ~ 2. glazed; jelly ~

dove *n.* 1. a gentle ~ 2. ~s coo

dovetail *v.* (D; tr., intr.) ("to fit") to ~ into, with

down I *adj.* (colloq.) ["angry"] ~ on (he's ~ on us)

down II *adv.* 1. ~ against (the dollar was ~ against the yen) ["dependent"] (BE) 2. ~ to (the fault is ~ to you; the decision is ~ to you; it's ~ to you to decide; it's ~ to you whether we go) ["misc."] 3. ~ on one's luck; we were ~ to our last five dollars; ~ with tyranny!; inflation is ~ by ten percent; that topic was ~ for discussion (see also **upside down**)

downfall *n.* 1. to bring about smb.'s ~; to hasten smb.'s ~; to lead to smb.'s ~ 2. to head for a ~

downgrade *v.* (D; tr.) to ~ to (our embassy was ~d to a legation)

downhill *adv.* to go ~ (also fig.)

download *v.* (D; tr.) to ~ to (to ~ a program to a computer)

down payment *n.* 1. to make a ~ 2. a ~ on

downpour *n.* 1. a brief; steady; sudden; torrential
~ 2. caught in a ~
downsizing *n.* corporate ~
downstairs *adv.* to come; go; run; walk ~
downturn *n.* 1. a modest, slight ~ 2. a sharp ~ 3. a
~ in (there was a sharp ~ in the economy = there
was a sharp economic ~) 4. (misc.) the economy
took a slight ~
dowry *n.* to provide a ~ for
dozen *n.* 1. a baker's; a half ~, half a ~; a round ~ 2.
by the ~ (they're cheaper by the ~)
draft I *n.* ["rough copy"] 1. to make, prepare a ~ 2. a
final, polished; first, preliminary, rough; working
~ ["conscription"] (AE) 3. to abolish, end; introduce
the ~ 4. to avoid; dodge, evade; resist the ~ ["current of air"] 5. to feel; sit in a ~ (I felt a cold ~ of
air blowing on my neck) ["order for payment"] 6. to
honor a ~ 7. a bank ~ 8. a ~ for; on (a ~ on the
Paris branch of our bank for one thousand pounds)
["drawing of liquid"] 9. on ~ (beer on ~) USAGE
NOTE: BE prefers the spelling *draught* in senses
5 and 9.
draft II *v.* 1. (D; tr.) ("to conscript") (AE) to ~ into
(to ~ young people into the army) 2. (H) they ~ed
her to serve as their delegate
draft in *v.* (BE) (H) they ~ed her in to serve as their
delegate (see **draft II,** 2)
drag I *n.* ["puff"] 1. to have, take a ~ (at/on a cigarette)
["obstacle"] (colloq.) 2. a ~ on (a ~ on the economy)
["street"] (colloq.) 3. the main ~ ["women's clothing
worn by a male transvestite"] (slang) 4. in ~ (see also
drag queen at **queen**)
drag II *v.* 1. (d; intr.) ("to search at the bottom of a
lake, river, sea") to ~ for (to ~ for a body) 2. (D;
tr.) ("to search") to ~ for (they ~ged the lake for
the body) 3. (d; intr.) ("to draw deeply") to ~ on
(to ~ on a pipe) 4. (P; tr.) ("to pull, tug") they ~ged
the tables into the garden; to be ~ged into a war;
we ~ged the old sofa out of the house; they ~ged
the logs through the forest; they ~ged him (over)
to the door
drag down *v.* (usu. fig.) 1. (D; tr.) to ~ into (to ~
smb. down into the gutter) 2. (D; tr.) to ~ with (If
you ruin my life I'll ~ you down with me!)
dragnet *n.* 1. to cast a ~ (to apprehend a criminal)
2. a police ~
dragoon *v.* (d; intr.) ("to coerce") to ~ into
drain I *n.* 1. to clean out, clear, unblock, unclog a ~
2. to block, clog a ~ 3. (misc.) a brain ~; supporting
them is a ~ on our resources; to go down the ~
("to be lost")
drain II *v.* 1. (d; intr.) to ~ from (the blood ~ed from
his face when he heard the news) 2. (D; tr.) to ~ of
(~ the tank of all water) 3. (N; used with an adjective) they ~ed the swamps dry 4. (P; intr., tr.) they
~ed all the water from/out of the tank; they ~ed the
liquid into the basin; they ~ed the water out of the
basement; the liquid ~ed through a porous layer 5.
(s) the swamp eventually ~ed dry

drama *n.* 1. a courtroom ~; docudrama; epic; historical; television ~ 2. high ~ 3. a ~ unfolds 4. a ~
about 5. in a ~ (see also *drama queen* at **queen**)
dramatics *n.* 1. to study ~ 2. amateur ~
drape *v.* 1. (D; intr., tr.) to ~ around, over (she ~d
her scarf around her shoulders) 2. (D; tr.) to ~ in,
with (he was ~d in a sheet)
drapes *n.* (AE; CE has *curtains*) 1. to hang, put up
~ 2. to close, draw; draw, open the ~ 3. window ~
4. a pair of ~
draught (BE) see **draft I** 5, 9
draughts *n.* (BE) see **checkers**
draw I *n.* ["act of drawing a weapon"] 1. on the ~
(quick on the ~) (also fig.) 2. (misc.) to beat smb.
to the ~ ["lottery"] (esp. BE) 3. to hold a ~ (AE has
drawing) 4. a prize ~ ["misc."] 5. the luck of the ~
("pure chance") ["tied game"] 6. to end in a ~ 7. a ~
against, with (the match against Liverpool ended
in a goalless ~)
draw II *v.* 1. (C) ("to sketch") ~ a picture for me;
or: ~ me a picture 2. (misc.) to ~ freehand 3. (D;
tr.) to ~ against, on ("to take from") (to ~ a check/
cheque against an account) 4. (D; intr.) ("to pick
a number at random") to ~ for (to ~ for a prize)
5. (D; tr.) ("to remove") to ~ from, out of (to ~
money from an account; to ~ water from a well) 6.
(D; tr.) ("to elicit") to ~ from (to ~ applause from
an audience) 7. (d; tr.) ("to bring") to ~ into (they
were drawn into the family quarrel) 8. (d; intr.)
("to move") to ~ into (the train was ~ing into the
station) 9. (d; intr.) ("to puff") to ~ on (to ~ on a
pipe) 10. (d; intr.) to ~ on, upon ("to take from")
(to ~ on one's reserves; to ~ on an account) 11. (D;
tr.) ("to attract") to ~ to (to ~ smb.'s attention to
smt.; what drew you to her in the first place?) 12.
(d; intr., tr.) ("to move, to pull") to ~ to, towards
(to ~ to a close; she drew me towards her) 13. (D;
intr., tr.) ("to tie") to ~ with (our team drew (3–3,
3-all) with the visitors) 14. (J) ("to sketch") the artist drew them looking out at the sea 15. (N; used
with an adjective) ("to pull") ~ the rope tight 16.
(misc.) he drew a gun on his opponent
draw ahead *v.* (D; intr.) to ~ of (she drew ahead of
the other runners)
draw alongside *v.* (D; intr.) to ~ of (he drew
alongside of our car) (esp. AE: CE has *he drew
alongside our car*)
draw away *v.* (D; intr.) to ~ from ("to increase the
distance from") (the leader drew away from the
pack)
drawback *n.* 1. a major ~ 2. a ~ to
draw back *v.* (D; intr.) to ~ from (she drew back
from the edge of the cliff; she drew back from
resigning from the government)
drawbridge *n.* to lower; raise a ~
drawer *n.* 1. to close, push in a ~ 2. to open, pull
out a ~ 3. a bottom; top ~ (he pulled out the top ~
and took out of it what was in it) (see also *bottom
drawer* at **chest**) 4. (misc.) a chest of ~s

draw up v. 1. (D; intr.) to ~ to (he drew up to the entrance) 2. (misc.) he drew himself up to his full height; she drew up even with us

drawing n. ["picture"] 1. to do, make a ~ (can you do me a ~ with an animal in it? = can you do me a ~ that includes/shows an animal?) 2. a rough ~ ["representation by lines"] 3. mechanical ~ 4. (a) freehand; line ~ ["lottery"] (esp. AE) 5. to hold a ~ (BE has *draw*)

drawing board n. ["planning stage"] 1. on the ~ 2. (misc.) back to the ~ (see also *drawing board* at **board**)

drawl n. 1. a Southern; upper-class ~ 2. (to speak) in, with a ~

drawn adj. pale and ~

draw off v. (D; tr.) to ~ from (they drew off some coolant from the radiator = they drew some coolant off from the radiator)

dread I n. 1. to have a ~ of smt. 2. to fill smb. with ~; to strike ~ into smb. 3. to live in ~ of smt.

dread II v. 1. (rare) (E) I ~ to think what lies ahead!; she ~s to go to the dentist 2. (G) she ~s going to the dentist

dreadful adj. 1. ~ to + inf. (it is ~ to contemplate the possibility that there may be another war) 2. ~ that + clause (it's ~ that there may be another war)

dream I n. ["images seen while sleeping"] 1. to have a ~ 2. to interpret ~s 3. a bad; odd; recurring; wet; wild ~ 4. a ~ about, of ["hope"]["goal"] 5. to achieve, realize one's ~s 6. a childhood; visionary; wild ~ 7. a ~ comes true (getting that job was like a ~ come true!) 8. a ~ of 9. a ~ to + inf. (it was his ~ to become a teacher) 10. a ~ that + clause (it was only a ~ that she might be elected) 11. beyond smb.'s wildest ~s 12. (misc.) never in my wildest ~s did I imagine becoming President!; now I've got the job of my ~s!; "I want to become President!" "in your ~s, mate: you haven't a hope!"

dream II v. 1. (D; intr.) to ~ about, of 2. (L) she never ~ed that she would some day write dictionaries; "What made us ~ that he could comb grey hair?" – "In Memory of Major Robert Gregory" (1919), W.B. Yeats 3. (misc.) "I want to become President!" "dream on, mate: you haven't a hope!"

dreary adj. it was very ~ to do the same job every day = it was very ~ doing the same job every day

dredge v. (D; intr., tr.) to ~ for (to ~ a river for a missing swimmer)

dregs n. the ~ of society

drenched adj. 1. thoroughly ~ 2. ~ in, with (they were ~ in sweat) 3. ~ to (we were ~ed to the skin)

dress I n. ["attire"] 1. casual, informal; evening, formal; fancy (esp. BE); national, traditional ~ 2. improper; proper ~ 3. in ~ (in informal ~) ["woman's frock"] 4. a casual; cocktail; evening (esp. BE = esp. AE *evening gown*); low-cut; maternity; party; summer ~ 5. a ~ is long; short; tight 6. a ~ fits (well) 7. in a ~ (she was in a summer ~)

["women's garment for sleeping"] (BE) 8. a nightdress (= esp. AE *nightgown*)

dress II v. 1. to ~ casually, informally; conservatively; elegantly, smartly; lightly; neatly; warmly 2. (d; intr., tr.) to ~ as (he was ~ed as a sailor) 3. (d; intr.) to ~ for (to ~ for dinner) 4. (d; intr., tr.) to ~ in (to ~ in black) 5. (D; tr.) to ~ with (to ~ a salad with oil and vinegar) 6. (misc.) to get ~ed; fully ~ed; poorly ~ed; provocatively, scantily ~ed; well ~ed; (mil.) ~ right!; ~ed to kill (in one's best and showiest frock)

dressing n. ["bandage"] 1. to apply, put on a ~ (to apply a ~ to a wound) 2. to change, replace; remove a ~ 3. a sterile ~ 4. a ~ comes off ["sauce"] 5. (a) salad ~ (who will make the salad ~?; this will make an excellent salad ~) 6. a ~ for (this will make an excellent ~ for any salad) 7. a ~ of (to make an excellent salad ~ of oil and vinegar) 8. in, with (salad in/with an oil-and-vinegar ~) ["misc."] 9. window ~ ("smt. presented to show only the favorable aspects") 10. power ~ (as when a female executive wears tailored suits and big shoulder pads)

dressing down n. ["scolding"] 1. to give smb. a ~ 2. to get, receive a ~

dress up v. 1. (D; intr., tr.) to ~ as (he ~ed up as a sailor; they ~ed her up as a ballerina) 2. (D; intr.) to ~ for (she got ~ed up for the party)

dribble I n. (basketball) a double ~

dribble II v. (P; intr., tr.) she ~d the ball across the court; the milk ~d down my shirt

drier see **dryer**

drift I n. ["pile"] 1. a deep ~; a snowdrift ["movement"] 2. a ~ to, towards (a ~ to the right) ["meaning"] (colloq.) 3. to catch, get; lose the ~

drift II v. 1. (d; intr.) to ~ into (to ~ into a life of crime) 2. (D; intr.) to ~ with (to ~ with the current) 3. (P; intr.) the boat ~ed down the river; we ~ed from town to town; to ~ out to sea; to ~ towards shore 4. (misc.) to ~ apart; to ~ aimlessly

drift away v. (D; intr.) to ~ from (to ~ from shore)

drift back v. (D; intr.) to ~ to (the strikers gradually ~ed back to work)

drill I n. ["boring tool"] 1. to operate, use a ~ 2. a dentist's; electric, power; hand; pneumatic; rotary ~ ["exercise"] 3. to conduct a ~ 4. (mil.) close-order; rifle ~ 5. an air-raid; civil-defense; evacuation; ~ (see also **fire drill**) ["procedure"] (BE) 6. (misc.) what's the ~? I don't know the ~

drill II v. 1. (D; intr.) ("to prospect") to ~ for (to ~ for oil) 2. (D; tr.) ("to train") to ~ in (to ~ students in pronunciation) 3. (d; tr.) ("to instill") to ~ into (to ~ discipline into cadets)

drink I n. 1. to fix (esp. AE), make, mix a ~ 2. to pour a ~ 3. to down; have, knock back (colloq.), take; nurse a ~ 4. a cold, cool; fizzy (BE) ("sparkling"); hot; potent, stiff, strong; quick; still (BE) ("not sparkling"); warm; weak ~ 5. a mixed; soft ~ 6. over a ~ (we had a nice chat over a ~) 7. (misc.) to drown one's sorrows in ~; to buy a round of

~s; he took to ~ in his old age; a ~ of milk/water; food and ~

drink II *v.* 1. (d; intr.) to ~ from, out of (I always ~ tea from a glass) 2. (d; intr.) to ~ to (let's ~ to his success) 3. (D; tr.) to ~ to (to ~ a toast to his success) 4. (misc.) to drink heavily; to ~ one's whiskey neat/straight; to ~ oneself to death; to ~ smb. under the table; don't ~ and drive

drinker *n.* a binge, hard, heavy; light, moderate; social ~

drinking *n.* 1. excessive; binge, hard, heavy; social ~ 2. (misc.) a ~ bout

drip I *n.* 1. a steady ~ 2. an intravenous; saline ~ 3. on a ~ (they put her on a saline ~ but took her off it the next day)

drip II *v.* 1. (D; intr.) to ~ from (the water was ~ping from the tap) 2. (D; intr.) to ~ with (fig.) (she was literally ~ping with diamonds!) 3. (P; intr., tr.) water ~ped over me; oil ~ped onto the road; she was ~ping the juice all over the floor

drive I *n.* ["trip in a vehicle"] 1. to go for, go on, take (AE) a ~ 2. an easy ~ (it's an easy half-hour ~ (over) to their place: their place is an easy half-hour drive ¬away/from here¬; they live within half-an-hour's drive (from here)) 3. a test ~ ["campaign"] 4. to initiate, launch a ~ (for) (to launch a ~ for flood relief = to launch a flood-relief ~) 5. a charity; economy; fund-raising; membership; recruiting ~ 6. a ~ to + inf. (they launched a ~ to raise funds for flood relief) ["energy"] 7. the ~ to + inf. (does she have enough ~ to finish the job?) ["impulse"] 8. a basic; sex ~ ["type of propulsion"] 9. a chain; disk; fluid; four-wheel; front-wheel; rear-wheel ~ (see also **driveway**) [(in baseball)] 10. a line ~ (the batter hit a line ~ to center field)

drive II *v.* 1. to ~ fast; slow 2. (d; intr.; used with *-ing* forms) to ~ at ("to suggest") (what is she ~ving at?) 3. (d; tr.) to ~ from, out of ("to force") (to ~ an invader out of a country; they drove her out of office; the noise drove me out of my mind) 4. (d; tr.) ("to direct") to ~ through; with (to ~ a nail through a wall with a hammer) 5. (d; tr.) to ~ to ("to bring to") (to ~ smb. to despair/drink/distraction) 6. (H) ("to force") he was driven by necessity to steal 7. (N; used with an adjective) ("to make") he drove me crazy 8. (P; intr., tr.) ("to go; transport") I drove across town; she drove me past the station; who ~s the children to school? we drove through the park 9. (misc.) don't drink and ~

drive away *v.* (D; intr., tr.) to ~ from (we drove away from their house)

drive down *v.* (D; intr.) to ~ to (we drove down to their house)

drive home *v.* 1. (B) to ~ a point home to smb. 2. (L; to) we could not ~ (to her) that we couldn't afford a new car 3. (Q; to) we must ~ (to her) how much a new car costs

drive over *v.* (d; intr., tr.) to ~ to (we drove over to their house)

driver *n.* 1. a bus; cab, taxi; limousine; lorry (BE); truck; mule; tractor ~ 2. (BE) an engine ~ (AE has *engineer*) 3. a learner (BE), student (AE) ~ 4. a drunk, drunken; hit-and-run; reckless ~ 5. a careful, cautious, defensive, safe; designated ~ 6. a backseat ~

driver's license *n.* (AE) 1. to issue; revoke; suspend a ~ 2. to apply for; get, obtain; lose a ~ (BE has *driving licence*)

driveway *n.* (esp. AE; BE prefers *drive*) 1. to pave, surface a ~ 2. to share a ~ 3. a ~ between (a ~ between two houses)

driving *n.* 1. to do; share the ~ 2. careful, defensive, safe; careless, reckless ~ 3. city; highway (AE), motorway (BE); turnpike (AE) ~ 4. rush-hour; stop-and-go ~ 5. drink-driving (BE), drunk (esp. AE), drunken (esp. AE) ~ 6. (misc.) ~ under the influence (also DUI); (BE) he was fined for driving without due care and attention

driving licence *n.* (BE) (see **driver's license**)

drool *v.* (colloq.) (D; intr.) ("to show pleasure") to ~ over (they were ~ing over their new grandchild)

drop I *n.* ["fall"] 1. an abrupt, sudden; sharp; sheer ~ 2. a ~ in (a sharp ~ in the interest rate) ["depository"] 3. a mail ~ ["an insignificant amount"] 4. a ~ in the bucket (AE) = a ~ in the ocean (BE) (see also **drops**; *teardrop* at **tear I** *n.*)

drop II *v.* 1. (A; used without *to*) ("to communicate") ~ me a line when you get there; I ~ped her a hint 2. (d; intr.) ("to lag") to ~ behind (he ~ped behind the other runners) 3. (D; intr., tr.) ("to fall; to let fall") to ~ from (the book ~ped from her hand; his name was ~ped from the list) 4. (d; intr., tr.) ("to fall; to let fall") to ~ into (the stone ~ped into the water; I ~ped a coin in(to) the slot) 5. (D; tr.) ("to let fall") to ~ on (she ~ped a book on the floor) 6. (d; intr.) to ~ out of ("to abandon") (to ~ out of school) 7. (d; intr.) to ~ out of ("to disappear") (to ~ out of sight) 8. (D; intr.) ("to fall") to ~ to (prices ~ped to the lowest point in a year; everyone ~ped to the ground) 9. (misc.) prices ~ped by 15% from their level last year to their level this year; prices ~ped below last year's levels; to ~ dead

drop behind *v.* (D; intr.) to ~ in (to ~ in one's work)

drop by *v.* (D; intr.) to ~ for (to ~ for a drink)

drop down *v.* 1. (D; intr., tr.) to ~ from (the apples ~ped down from the tree; she ~ped the apples down from the tree) 2. (D; tr.) to ~ to (I'll ~ this down to you)

drop in *v.* 1. (D; intr.) to ~ for (I'll ~ for a visit) 2. (D; intr.) to ~ on (~ on me at any time)

drop off *v.* 1. (D; tr.) ("to leave") to ~ at (could you ~ the books at the library? = could you drop the books off at the library?; could you ~ me off at the station?) 2. (misc.) to ~ to (to sleep)

droppings *n.* animal ~

drops *n.* (med.) 1. to instill (technical), put in ~ 2. cough; ear; eye; knockout; nose ~ (see also **raindrops**)

drought *n.* 1. to experience (a) ~ 2. a prolonged; severe ~ 3. during, in a ~

droves *n.* in ~ (the tourists came in ~)

drown *v.* 1. ("to drench") (D; tr.) to ~ in, with (to ~ the meat in ketchup) 2. (misc.) to ~ one's sorrows in drink

drowsiness *n.* to induce ~

drubbing *n.* ["beating"] 1. to give smb. a ~ 2. to get, take a ~ (our team took a ~) 3. a severe ~

drudgery *n.* sheer ~

drug *n.* 1. to administer, give; discontinue; inject; prescribe a ~ 2. to take a ~ (for) 3. to ban; test a ~ 4. a dangerous, toxic; mild; potent, powerful, strong; weak ~ 5. an addictive; habit-forming; hallucinogenic; non-addictive ~ 6. an ethical, prescription; generic; nonprescription, over-the-counter; proprietary ~ 7. an anti-inflammatory; miracle, wonder; sulfa (AE), sulpha (BE) ~ 8. a ~ wears off 9. (misc.) a ~ addict; a ~ dealer/peddler/pusher (see also **drugs**; *a drug on the market* at **market**)

drug abuse *n.* to combat ~

drugs *n.* 1. to do (colloq.), take, use ~ 2. to deal, peddle, push, sell, traffic in (illicit) ~ 3. hard; soft ~ 4. illegal, illicit ~ 5. on ~ (to be on ~)

drugstore *n.* (esp. AE; BE has *chemist's*) at, in a ~ (he works at/in a ~)

drum I *n.* ["percussion instrument"] 1. to beat (also fig.), play a ~ 2. a bass ~; kettledrum; side; snare ~ 3. muffled ~s 4. the ~s roll ["cylinder"] 5. a brake ~ ["container"] 6. an oil ~

drum II *v.* 1. (d; tr.) to ~ into (to ~ smt. into smb.'s head) 2. (P; intr.; tr.) the rain was ~ming against the windows; she was ~ming on the table with her fingers = she was ~ming her fingers on the table

drumfire *n.* ["barrage"] to keep up an incessant ~

drum up *v.* (D; tr.) to ~ for (he ~med up some business for us)

drunk I *adj.* 1. blind, dead, roaring, stinking ~ 2. to get ~ on (he got ~ on cheap wine) 3. ~ with (~ with power)

drunk II *n.* to roll ("rob") a ~ (colloq.)

drunkard *n.* a habitual ~

dry I *adj.* 1. bone ~, as ~ as a bone 2. to go, run ~ (the well ran ~)

dry II *v.* (D; refl., tr.) to ~ with (he dried himself and his children with a towel)

dryer *n.* 1. to turn on a ~ 2. to turn off a ~ 3. to load; unload a ~ 4. a clothes; spin (esp. BE); tumble (BE) ~ 5. a hair ~ 6. (misc.) is the ~ running? the ~ is off/on

dry off *v.* (D; refl., tr.) to ~ with (he dried himself and his children off with a towel)

dub I *v.* (N; used with a noun) ("to name") they ~bed him *Bud*

dub II *v.* (D; tr.) ("to provide with a new soundtrack") to ~ into (to ~ a film into English)

dubious *adj.* 1. ~ about, of (AE) 2. ~ if (esp. AE), that (esp. AE), whether + clause (it's ~ if they'll come)

duck I *n.* 1. ~s quack; waddle 2. a young ~ is a duckling 3. a male ~ is a drake 4. (misc.) to take to smt. like a ~ (takes) to water ("to adapt to smt. quickly and easily") (see also **sitting duck**)

duck II *v.* 1. (d; intr.) to ~ out of ("to evade") (to ~ out of an obligation) 2. (P; intr.) ("to move") we ~ed into the nearest building; she ~ed behind the partition; the children ~ed under the table

ducking *n.* 1. to give smb. a ~ 2. to get a ~

dudgeon *n.* ["indignation"] in high ~

due I *adj.* 1. (cannot stand alone) ~ for (~ for a promotion) 2. (cannot stand alone) ~ to (her absence was ~ to illness) 3. to come, fall ~ (the note has fallen ~) 4. ~ to + inf. (the train is ~ to arrive at ten o'clock) USAGE NOTE: Purists prefer to use *due to* as an adjectival predicate phrase modifying the subject – her absence was due to illness. Otherwise, *because of* or *owing to* is preferred – she was absent because of illness; owing to illness she was absent

due II *n.* ["recognition, due credit"] to give people their ~ (I don't like her but, to give her her ~, at least she never gave up!)

duel I *n.* 1. to have, fight a ~ (over) 2. to challenge smb. to a ~ 3. a ~ between; with (I fought a ~ with him over her = he and I fought a ~ over her) 4. a ~ to the death

duel II *v.* 1. (D; intr.) to ~ over 2. (D; intr.) to ~ with (I ~ed with him over her = he and I ~ed over her)

due process *n.* (legal) 1. to deprive of; observe ~ (she was deprived of due ~) 2. (misc.) by; without ~ of law

dues *n.* 1. to pay ~ 2. annual; membership ~ (CE also has *membership fees*)

duet *n.* 1. to play; perform; sing a ~ 2. a piano ~

dukes *n.* (colloq.) ["fists"] to put up one's ~

dumb *adj.* ["stupid"] (colloq.) (esp. AE) 1. to play ~ 2. ~ to + inf. (it was ~ of you to say that) ["mute"] 3. to strike smb. ~

dumbfounded *adj.* 1. completely ~ 2. ~ at, by (~ at the news) 3. ~ to + inf. (he was ~ to learn that his wife had left him) 4. ~ that + clause (he was ~ that his wife had left him)

dumbstruck see **dumbfounded**

dummy *n.* (BE) see **pacifier**

dump I *n.* ["place for dumping"] (esp. AE) 1. a garbage, trash ~; the town ~ (BE prefers *refuse tip*) ["dilapidated place"] (colloq.) 2. a real ~ (this town is a real ~) ["storage area"] 3. an ammunition; supply ~ (see also **dumps**)

dump II *v.* 1. (slang) (esp. AE) to ~ on ("to project bad experiences or feelings on") (I have enough troubles of my own – don't ~ on me!) 2. (P; tr.) they ~ed their bags unceremoniously (down) on the floor; the company was ~ing waste products in/into the river

dumping ground *n.* a ~ for

dumps *n.* down in the ~ ("dejected")

dun *v.* (D; tr.) to ~ for (to ~ smb. for payment)

dune *n.* a sand ~

dungarees *n.* a pair of ~

dunk *v.* (D; tr.) to ~ in (to ~ doughnuts in coffee)

dupe I *n.* an innocent ~

dupe II *v.* (D; tr.) to ~ into (he was ~d into signing)

duplicate *n.* 1. to make a ~ 2. in ~ (to prepare all documents in ~)

duplicity *n.* ~ in

duration *n.* 1. (a) long; moderate; short ~ 2. of a certain ~ (of short ~) 3. for the ~ (of the war)

duress *n.* under ~ (to sign a confession under ~)

dusk *n.* 1. at; before ~ 2. (misc.); from dawn till / to ~

dust I *n.* 1. to collect, gather; raise ~ 2. fine, powdery ~ 3. chalk; coal; cosmic; gold; radioactive; volcanic ~ 4. a cloud; layer; particle, speck of ~ 5. ~ collects; lies; settles (a thick layer of ~ had settled on the furniture) 6. (misc.) from ~ to ~

dust II *v.* 1. (D; tr.) to ~ for (to ~ smt. for fingerprints) 2. (D; tr.) to ~ with (to ~ smt. with insecticide)

dustbin *n.* (BE) (see **can I**, 1)

duster *n.* (see the Usage Note for **eraser**)

dusting *n.* a light ~ (of snow)

duty *n.* ["obligation"] ["service"] 1. to assume, take on a; report for ~ 2. to carry out, discharge, do, perform one's ~ 3. to relieve people of their ~ties; to suspend people from their ~ties 4. to shirk one's ~ 5. an ethical, moral; legal; professional ~ 6. a painful, unpleasant; pleasant ~ 7. a ceremonial; civic; official; patriotic; public ~ 8. supervisory ~ties 9. (esp. mil.) active; combat; detached; fatigue; guard; light; noncombatant; overseas; sea;

special; temporary ~ (to see active ~) 10. a ~ to (a ~ to one's country) 11. a ~ to + inf. (physicians have a ~ to report such cases) 12. on ~; off ~ (who was on ~ yesterday? when do you get / go off ~? she was never on active ~) 13. (misc.) (a) dereliction of ~; a sense of ~; in (the) line of ~; ~ calls; (BE) a ~ of care to (to have a ~ of care to those in one's charge); smb.'s bounden ~ (formal) (it's her bounden ~ to report the incident to the police) (see also *(in) duty bound* at **bound IV** adj.; **tour of duty**) ["tariff"] ["tax"] 14. to impose a ~ on 15. to pay (a) ~ on 16. to lift a ~ from 17. to exempt smt. from ~ 18. customs; excise ~ties 19. (BE) (obsol.) (a) death ~ (CE has *inheritance tax*)

dwell *v.* (d; intr.) to ~ on (to ~ on a question; to ~ on one's personal problems; don't ~ on the past)

dweller *n.* a cave-; city-; cliff-; country-; lake-; town-~

dwindle *v.* (D; intr.) to ~ (away) to (to ~ to nothing)

dye I *n.* 1. to apply ~ to 2. natural; synthetic; vegetable ~s 3. (a) ~ fades; takes

dye II *v.* (N; used with an adjective, noun) she ~d the dress (a lovely shade of) blue

dynamite *n.* 1. ~ explodes 2. a stick of ~ (the stick of ~ she detonated exploded) 3. (misc.) (fig.) political ~

dynasty *n.* 1. to establish, found a ~ 2. to overthrow a ~ 3. a ~ begins; ends; lasts; rules

dysentery *n.* 1. to come down, go down (BE) with, get ~; have ~ 2. an attack; epidemic; outbreak of ~ 3. amebic ~

E

each *determiner, pronoun* ~ of (~ of them) USAGE NOTE: The use of the preposition *of* is necessary when a pronoun follows. When a noun follows, two constructions are possible – we saw each student; we saw each of the students

eager *adj.* 1. ~ for (~ for success) 2. ~ to + inf. (she's ~ to help) 3. (formal; esp. BE) ~ that + clause (we were ~ that she should help)

eagerness *n.* 1. ~ to + inf. (we appreciate her ~ to help) 2. (misc.) in their ~ to please, they went too far

eagle *n.* 1. a bald; golden ~ 2. ~s scream; soar 3. a young ~ is an eaglet (see also *eagle eye* at **eye**)

ear *n.* 1. to perk up (AE), prick up; wiggle one's ~s 2. to pierce smb.'s ~s 3. a musical ~ 4. the inner; middle; outer ~ 5. smb.'s ~s perk up (AE), prick up; pop; ring 6. an ~ for (to have an ~ for music) 7. by; in; on ~ (to play music by ~; wear earrings in your ~s; wear a hearing-aid in your ~; I hit him on the ~) 8. (misc.) to be all ~s ("to listen attentively"); to lend an ~ to ("to pay attention to") ("Friends, Romans, countrymen, lend me your ~s" – Shakespeare, *Julius Caesar*); to turn a deaf ~ to ("to pay no attention to"); to fall on deaf ~s ("to be disregarded") (our pleas fell on deaf ears = they were deaf to all our pleas); a cauliflower ~ ("an ear deformed by repeated blows"); to have smb.'s ~ ("to have access to smb. who is superior in rank"); to box smb.'s ~s ("to strike smb. on the ears"); the loud music grated on our ~s; up to one's ~s in debt ("heavily in debt"); to play it by ~ ("to improvise"); her ~s were burning ("she felt that others were talking about her"); to have a word in smb.'s ~

earache *n.* to have an ~ (esp. AE), to have ~ (BE)

eardrum *n.* a perforated ~

earful *n.* 1. to give smb. an ~ 2. to get an ~ (from)

earliest *n.* at the ~ (they will not arrive before tomorrow at the ~) (see also *at your earliest convenience* at **convenience**)

early *adj.* the train was five minutes ~

earmark *v.* 1. (d; tr.) to ~ for (money has been ~ed for the new library) 2. (H) money has been ~ed to go to the new library

earmarks *n.* ["characteristics"] to have all the ~ of

earmuffs *n.* 1. to put on; take off; wear ~ 2. a pair of ~

earn *v.* 1. (C) his accomplishments ~ed respect for him; or: his accomplishments ~ed him respect 2. (misc.) well ~d (he got a lot of well-earned respect for his accomplishments and then took a well-earned vacation)

earnest I *adj.* ~ about

earnest II *n.* 1. in (deadly) ~ 2. in ~ about

earnings *n.* 1. annual, yearly; average; export, overseas; gross, pre-tax; invisible; net, take-home ~ 2. ~ from (average ~ from overtime rose significantly) 3. (misc.) earnings-related (an earnings-related pension)

earphones *n.* 1. to put on; take off; wear ~ 2. to plug in; unplug ~ 3. a pair, set of ~

earplug *n.* 1. to insert, put in an ~ 2. to remove, take out an ~ 3. a pair of ~s

earrings *n.* 1. to wear ~ 2. to put on; take off ~ 3. a pair of ~

earshot *n.* in, within; out of ~

earth *n.* ["our planet"] 1. to circle; orbit the ~ 2. the ~ revolves around the sun; rotates on its axis 3. above the (surface of the) ~; on (the) ~ (is there more land or more water on ~?) 4. (misc.) down to ~ ("practical"); who on ~ would ever do that?; what on ~ is that? (see also *the four corners of the earth* at **corner**) ["soil"] 5. a clod, clump, lump of ~ 6. above the; in the; under the ~ (to dig for gold under the ~)

earthquake *n.* 1. to record an ~ 2. a devastating, destructive; light; strong, severe ~ 3. an ~ strikes (a severe ~ struck the area) 4. the magnitude of an ~ 5. an ~ measures six on the Richter scale 6. in an ~

earwax *n.* to remove ~

ease I *n.* 1. at ~ (to put smb. at ~) (see also *ill at ease* at **ill**) 2. at ~ with (she feels at ~ with us) 3. (formal) for ~ in; for ~ of (for (greater) ~ in sleeping; for (greater) ~ of use) 4. with ~ (he can lift a hundred pounds with great ~; "O, he flies through the air with the greatest of ~, This daring young man on the flying trapeze." – George Leybourne (died 1884), "The Man on the Flying Trapeze" (song)) 5. (misc.) (mil.) (to stand) at ~

ease II *v.* 1. (N; used with an adj.) they ~d the door shut/open 2. (P; refl., tr.) they ~d the piano through the window; they ~d their way toward the exit; he ~ed himself into an armchair

easement *n.* ["right of way"] (legal) to grant an ~

ease up *v.* 1. (D; intr.) to ~ on (you should ~ on your workers: you've been pushing them too hard)

east I *adj., adv.* 1. directly, due, straight ~ 2. ~ of (~ of the city) 3. (misc.) to face; go, head ~; northeast by ~; southeast by ~

east II *n.* 1. from the ~; in the ~; to the ~ 2. (AE) back ~ ("in the eastern part of the US") 3. (BE) out ~ ("in, to Asia") 4. the Far East; the Middle East, the Mideast (esp. AE); the Near East USAGE NOTE: The *Far East* refers to the countries of eastern Asia. The *Middle East* = (esp. AE) the *Mideast* refers to the countries of the eastern Mediterranean. The *Near East* is now generally an old-fashioned synonym of the preceding term; formerly it referred to the Balkans and the Ottoman Empire.

Easter *n.* at; for ~ (all the children came home for ~)

easy *adj.* ["not difficult"] 1. fairly; very ~ 2. ~ for (that job was ~ for her) ["lenient"] 3. (cannot stand alone) ~ on (you are too ~ on the children; go ~ on him: he's been sick) ["showing moderation"] 4. (cannot stand alone) ~ on (go ~ on the hot peppers) ["not difficult"] 5. (cannot stand alone) ~ to + inf. (this book is ~ to translate = it is ~ to translate this book = this is an ~ book to translate; Bob is ~ to please = it is ~ to please Bob = Bob is an ~ person to please; it is not ~ to be a parent = it is not ~ being a parent; it is ~ for you to say that) 6. (misc.) as ~ as ABC, as ~ as falling off a log, as ~ as pie (there's nothing to it: it's as ~ as falling off a log!) ["misc."] 7. (colloq.) ~-peasy (there's nothing to it: it's ~-peasy!), (colloq.) (BE) ~-peasy Japaneesee; free and ~; "shall we eat in or out tonight?" "I'm ~." (colloq.) (BE); rest ~ – everything will be all right!

easy street *n.* on ~ (to be on ~) ("to be well off")

eat *v.* 1. to ~ heartily, like a horse, voraciously 2. (d; intr.) to ~ into, through (acid ~s into metal) 3. (d; intr., tr.) to ~ out of (our cat ~s out of its own dish) 4. (d; intr., tr.) to ~ with (to ~ with one's fingers) 5. (misc.) let's ~ in/out this evening; to ~ (up) everything on one's plate

eat away *v.* (d; intr.) to ~ at (the waves ate away at the shore)

eater *n.* a big, heavy; compulsive; fussy, picky; light ~

eavesdrop *v.* (D; intr.) to ~ on (to ~ on a conversation)

ebb *n.* 1. at a low ~ 2. on the ~ (the tide is on the ~) 3. (misc.) ~ and flow

eccentric *adj.* 1. ~ in (~ in one's habits) 2. ~ to + inf. (she thought it was ~ to go swimming at night) 3. (misc.) he was ~ enough to go swimming at night

echelon *n.* 1. (mil.) the forward; rear ~ 2. the higher, top, upper; lower ~s of society

echo I *n.* 1. to produce an ~ 2. to find; hear an ~ (her campaign for equal rights found an ~ in many hearts) 3. an ~ dies away; sounds (the faint distant ~ gradually died away)

echo II *v.* (P; intr.) the news ~ed around the world; the park ~ed to the sounds of the children; the courtroom ~ed with the shouts of the spectators; their screams ~ed through the corridors

eclipse *n.* ["obscuring of the moon or sun"] 1. a full, total; lunar; partial; solar ~ ["dimming of smb.'s influence"] 2. to go into ~ 3. in ~

ecology *n.* deep; human, social ~

economical *adj.* ["inexpensive"] ~ to + inf. (it's more ~ to go by bus = it's more ~ going by bus)

economics *n.* micro-economics; supply-side; trickle-down ~

economize *v.* (D; intr.) to ~ on (to ~ on fuel)

economy *n.* ["frugality"] 1. to practice ~ 2. strict ~ ["economic structure"] 3. a capitalist, free-market, market; command; mixed; national; peacetime; planned; socialist; wartime ~ 4. the real ~ ("the production of goods and services by contrast with

the financial and banking sectors") (has the credit crunch begun to affect the real ~ yet?) 5. an ailing, shaky, weak; sluggish; sound, stable, strong ~ ["the science of economics"] 6. political ~

ecstasy *n.* 1. pure, sheer; religious ~ 2. in ~ about, at, over 3. (misc.) a look of ~; they went into ~sies over the new furniture/at the thought of getting new furniture

ecstatic *adj.* ~ about, at, over (~ at being selected)

edge I *n.* ["margin, border"] (also fig.) 1. a cutting; jagged, ragged; sharp ~ (see also **cutting edge**) 2. at, by, near, on an ~ (she stood at the very ~ of the crater) ["advantage"] (colloq.) 3. to have, hold an ~ on, over 4. an ~ on (to gain a competitive ~ on smb.; what gives us an ~ on the competition?) ["misc."] 5. to take the ~ off smb.'s appetite ("to satisfy smb.'s appetite partially"); to be on ~ ("to be tense")

edge II *v.* 1. (d; tr.) to ~ out of (to ~ smb. out of a job) 2. (P; intr., tr.) to ~ one's way through a crowd; she ~d towards the door; to ~ gingerly along a narrow path

edge up *v.* ~ (D; intr.) to ~ to (she ~d up to the door)

edgy *adj.* (colloq.) ["nervous"] ~ about

edict *n.* 1. to issue an ~ 2. to recall, rescind, withdraw an ~ 3. a royal; solemn ~ 4. an ~ that + clause; subj. (the government issued an ~ that all prisoners ¬be/should be¬ released)

edification *n.* for smb.'s ~ (I said that for your ~)

edition *n.* 1. to bring out, publish an ~ (to bring out a new ~) 2. (of a book, dictionary) an abridged; annotated; corrected; critical; deluxe; enlarged, expanded; first; hardback; limited; paperback; revised; thumb-indexed; unabridged; unexpurgated; variorum ~ 3. (of a newspaper) a city, home; evening; final; morning; special ~ 4. (misc.) (BE) an omnibus ~ ("the rebroadcast of all the week's episodes of a soap opera or of a series"); the ~ went through three printings

editor *n.* 1. a city ~ 2. a copy (esp. AE) ~ (AE also has *copy reader*), subeditor (esp. BE); fashion; managing; news; political; senior; society; technical ~; editor-in-chief USAGE NOTE: In AE, *city editor* means "local news editor"; in BE it means "London financial editor". (See also the Usage Note at **desk**)

editorial *n.* 1. to write an ~ 2. to carry, publish, run an ~ 3. an ~ about, on (the paper ran a hard-hitting ~ on juvenile knife crime) (old-fashioned BE has *leader, leading article*)

editorship *n.* under the ~ of

educate *v.* 1. (D; tr.) to ~ about, in, on; for, to (~d to one's responsibilities) 2. (H) to ~ smb. to do smt.

educated *adj.* highly, well; poorly; privately ~

education *n.* 1. to give, provide an ~ 2. to get, obtain, receive an ~ 3. to complete one's ~ 4. compulsory; formal; free ~ 5. private; public (AE), state (BE) ~ (private ~ is costly; funds for public ~ are scarce)

6. (BE) a public-school ~ 7. elementary (esp. AE), primary; higher, tertiary (BE); secondary ~; a college (AE), university ~ 8. adult (AE), continuing, further (BE) ~ 9. health; physical; religious; sex ~ 10. in-service; pre-professional; professional; vocational ~ 11. remedial; special ~ 12. a broad, general; classical; liberal ~; (a) progressive ~ 13. the ~ to + inf. (does she have enough ~ to cope with the job?)

eel n. 1. a conger; electric ~ 2. (misc.) as slippery as an ~

effect n. ["result"] ["influence"] 1. to have, produce an ~ on 2. to heighten an ~ 3. to take ~ (the drug took ~) 4. to feel an ~ (I feel the ~ of the narcotic) 5. to mar; negate, nullify; sleep off the ~ (of smt.) 6. a beneficial, good, salutary; desired ~ (her calm manner had a salutary ~ on the children) 7. a dramatic; exhilarating; hypnotic ~ 8. a calculated; cumulative; deterrent; far-reaching; full; long-term; net, overall; practical; profound ~ 9. a limited, marginal; minimal; short-term ~ 10. an adverse, bad, deleterious, harmful; chilling; crippling, damaging, deadening, disastrous ~ 11. a domino; retroactive; ripple ("gradually spreading") ~ 12. an environmental; greenhouse ("warming of the earth's surface") ~ 13. a halo ("overly favorable judgment based on irrelevant factors"); knock-on (BE) ("additional") ~ 14. a placebo; side ~ 15. an ~ lasts; wears off 16. to good; little; no; some ~ ["operation"] 17. to put into ~ (to put new regulations into ~) 18. to come into, go into, take ~ (when does the new law take ~?) 19. in ~; with ~ (from) (the ordinance is still in ~; with ~ from tomorrow, the ordinance must be obeyed; the ordinance bans smoking with immediate ~) ["desired impression"] 20. for ~ (she said that purely for ~) ["meaning"] 21. to the ~ (he said smt. to the ~ that he might be late; words to that ~) ["reality"] ["practice"] 22. in ~ (the ordinance is still, in ~, a denial of freedom of speech; their claim is, in ~, that they have been mistreated) (see also **effects**)

effective adj. 1. ~ against (~ against the common cold) 2. ~ in (~ in fighting forest fires) 3. ~ to + inf. (it would be more ~ (for you) not to respond to the charges)

effects n. ["belongings"] 1. household; personal ~ ["impressions"] 2. sound; special ~ ["results"] 3. to counteract the ~ (of) 4. ill; side ~ (they experienced no ill ~)

efficiency n. 1. to improve, increase, promote ~ 2. to impair ~ 3. fighting; maximum, peak ~ 4. ~ in (~ in combating absenteeism) 5. with ~ (to work with improved ~) 6. (misc.) (at peak ~)

efficient adj. 1. ~ at, in (she was very ~ at getting things done; they were very ~ in reducing waste) 2. ~ to + inf. (it is not ~ to set up two offices)

effigy n. to burn; hang smb. in ~

effort n. 1. to make, put forth an ~; to put ~ into 2. to concentrate; intensify; redouble one's ~s 3. to

devote one's ~s to 4. to spare no ~; to make every ~ 5. to foil, stymie, thwart smb.'s ~s 6. an all-out, bold, concerted, conscious, furious, gallant, great, Herculean, heroic, massive, maximum, painstaking, sincere, strenuous, studious, superhuman, valiant ~ 7. a collaborative, joint, united ~ 8. an abortive; desperate; frantic; minimal; useless, vain ~ 9. best, ceaseless, unceasing; unsparing, untiring; wasted ~s (despite our best ~s, they failed to thrive) 10. a team ~; the war ~ 11. an ~ to + inf. (they made an all-out ~ to finish the work on time: the amount of ~ they put into finishing the work was unbelievable!; they made every ~ to finish on time) 12. with a certain ~ (it was only with great ~ that we could do the job)

effrontery n. the ~ to + inf. (he had the ~ to demand more money)

egg n. 1. to fertilize; hatch; incubate; lay ~s 2. to beat, whisk (BE); boil; crack; fry; poach an ~ 3. to candle ~s 4. an addled, bad, rotten ~; free-range; fresh ~ 5. a boiled; coddled; deviled; fried; hard-boiled; poached; raw; Scotch (BE); shirred (AE); medium-boiled; soft-boiled ~s 6. scrambled ~s, scrambled ~ (esp. BE) 7. a box; clutch of ~s 8. the white of an ~; the yolk of an ~ (see also **egg whites**) 9. (misc.) a bad/rotten ~ ("a bad person"); a good ~ ("a good person"); to have ~ on one's face ("to be in an embarrassing position"); (BE) to teach one's grandmother to suck ~s ("to try to tell smb. smt. that they already know") (see also **nest egg**)

egg on v. (H) to ~ smb. on to do smt. = to egg on smb. to do smt.

egg whites n. to beat, whip, whisk ~

ego n. 1. to bolster, boost, flatter smb.'s ~ 2. to bruise, deflate smb.'s ~ 3. an enormous, inflated, overbearing 4. an alter ~

either determiner, pronoun ~ of (~ of the two; ~ of them) USAGE NOTE: The use of the preposition of is necessary when two or a pronoun follows. When a noun follows, the following constructions are used – either student will know the answer; either of the students will know the answer.

eject v. (D; intr., tr.) to ~ from (to ~ from a disabled plane; they were ~ed from the room for disorderly conduct)

eke out v. 1. (d; tr.) ("to supplement or make last longer") to ~ by, with (he ~d out his meager pension (by) doing odd jobs) 2. (d; tr.) ("to get or earn with difficulty") (he ~d out his meager livelihood (by) doing odd jobs)

elaborate v. (D; intr.) to ~ on

Elastoplast (T) n. (BE) see **Band-Aid**

elated adj. 1. ~ about, at, over (~ at the good news) 2. ~ to + inf. (they were ~ to hear the good news)

elbow I n. 1. tennis ~ ("an elbow that hurts because of excessive exercise") 2. above; below; by the ~ (to take smb. by the ~; to amputate an arm below the ~) 3. at smb.'s ~ ("close to smb.") 4. (misc.) to

rub ~s with smb. ("to have contact with smb.");
(BE, colloq.) to give smb. the ~ ("to end a relationship with smb.")

elbow II *v.* (P; tr.) they ~ed me out of the way;
he ~ed his way up to the front; she ~ed her way
through the crowd

elbow grease *n.* ["great effort"] 1. to use ~ 2. to put
~ into smt.

elbowroom *n.* 1. to give smb. ~ 2. to have ~ 3. ~
for

elders *n.* 1. to respect one's ~ 2. the church;
village ~

elect I *adj.* (placed after a noun) the president ~ (the
minister designate met the president ~)

elect II *v.* 1. to ~ unanimously 2. (D; tr.) to ~ as (she
was ~ed as vice-president) 3. (D; tr.) to ~ to (she
was ~ed to the vice-presidency) 4. (formal) (E) he
~ed to become a physician 5. (H) she was ~ed to
represent us 6. (M) the nation ~ed her to be vice-
president 7. (N; used with a noun) the nation ~ed
her vice-president

elected *adj.* democratically; popularly;
unanimously ~

election *n.* 1. to hold, schedule an ~ 2. to call for ~s
3. to carry, win an ~ 4. to run for (esp. AE), seek,
stand for (BE); win ~ 5. to decide, swing an ~ (her
last speech swung the ~ in her favor) 6. to concede;
lose an ~ 7. to fix, rig an ~ 8. a close, hotly contested; rigged ~ 9. a free (and fair); general; local;
national; primary; runoff ~ 10. smb.'s ~ to (her ~
to the senate was welcome news) 11. at, in an ~
(she was defeated in the last ~) 12. (misc.) ~ fever
("excitement before an election"); (BE) the runup
to an ~ ("the pre-election period") (there was a lot
of excitement in/during the runup to the ~)

electrical appliance *n.* 1. to plug in an ~ 2. to unplug an ~

electrician *n.* to call (in) an ~

electricity *n.* 1. to generate; induce ~ 2. to conduct ~
3. to hook up, turn on the ~ 4. to cut off, disconnect,
turn off the ~ 5. mains (BE); static ~ 6. ~ flows 7.
(misc.) the ~ is off; the ~ is on; the ~ went off; the
~ came on/went on

electrocardiogram *n.* 1. to do; have an ~ 2. to
interpret, read an ~

elegance *n.* 1. faded; sheer ~ 2. sartorial ~

element *n.* ["component"] 1. a basic, essential, key,
vital ~ ["group"] 2. a foreign ~ 3. diverse; extremist;
radical ~s 4. criminal; rowdy, unruly; subversive;
undesirable ~s ["substance"] 5. ~s combine 6.
chemical ~s ["natural environment"] 7. in one's ~;
out of one's ~ ["factor"] 8. the human ~ ["misc."] 9. to
brave the ~s ("to go out in bad weather")

elephant *n.* 1. a rogue ("wild") ~ 2. ~s trumpet 3.
a herd of ~s 4. a young ~ is a calf 5. a female ~ is
a cow 6. a male ~ is a bull 7. ~s have trunks and
may have tusks

elevate *v.* (formal) (D; tr.) to ~ to (to ~ smb. to the
peerage)

elevation *n.* ["height"] 1. at a certain ~ (at an ~ of two
thousand meters) ["raising"] 2. smb.'s ~ to (her ~ to
the vice-presidency)

elevator *n.* ["device for raising and lowering people
and freight"] (AE for 1–6; BE has *lift*) 1. to operate
an ~ (an ~ operator operates an ~) 2. to call; take
an ~ (we took the ~ to the tenth floor) 3. a down;
express; self-service; up ~ 4. a freight (AE) ~ 5.
a service ~ 6. a bank of ~s ["storage building"] 7.
a grain ~

elicit *v.* (D; tr.) to ~ from

eligibility *n.* 1. ~ for 2. ~ to + inf. (~ to vote)

eligible *adj.* 1. ~ for (~ for promotion) 2. ~ to + inf.
(she is ~ to vote)

eliminate *v.* (D; tr.) to ~ from

elimination *n.* 1. ~ from 2. (misc.) by the process
of ~

elite *n.* a cultural; intellectual; party; power;
social ~

elixir *n.* the ~ of life; the ~ of youth

elk *n.* 1. a herd of ~ 2. a female ~ is a cow 3. a male
~ is a bull USAGE NOTE: The European *elk* is
the North American *moose* – though *moose* is now
coming into use as an alternative name for the European *elk*, too. The North American *elk*, or *wapiti*,
resembles the European *red deer*, but is larger.

elope *v.* (D; intr.) to ~ with (she ~d with her childhood sweetheart)

eloquence *n.* 1. flowery ~ 2. ~ about

eloquent *adj.* 1. to wax ~ 2. ~ about

E-mail, e-mail I *n.* 1. to send (an) ~ (to) 2. to get,
receive; delete; print out (an) ~ (from) 3. by ~ (to
send a message by ~) 4. to be on ~, to have ~

E-mail, e-mail II *v.* (A) they ~ed a message to me;
or: they ~ed me a message (see also **fax II**)

emanate *v.* (d; intr.) to ~ from

emancipate *v.* (D; tr.) to ~ from (to ~ serfs from
bondage)

emancipation *n.* 1. political ~ 2. ~ from

embankment *n.* 1. a high, steep ~ 2. a railroad,
railway ~

embargo *n.* 1. to enforce; impose an ~ 2. to place,
put an ~ on 3. to lift, remove an ~ from 4. an arms;
trade ~ 5. an ~ against, on 6. under ~

embark *v.* 1. (D; intr.) to ~ for (to ~ for France) 2.
(d; intr.) to ~ on, upon (to ~ on a new career)

embarrass *v.* 1. to ~ deeply 2. (R) it ~ed him to be
caught cheating

embarrassed *adj.* 1. deeply, very ~ 2. financially ~
3. ~ about, at, over 4. ~ to + inf. (he was ~ to be
caught cheating) 5. ~ that + clause (he was ~ that
he was caught cheating)

embarrassing *adj.* 1. ~ to + inf. (it was ~ for him to
be caught cheating) 2. ~ that + clause (it was ~ for
him that he was caught cheating)

embarrassment *n.* 1. to cause ~ 2. to feel ~ 3. acute;
deep ~ 4. ~ about, at, over (we felt ~ about the
disclosure; his ~ at having been caught cheating)
5. an ~ to (his outburst was an ~ to his family) 6.

~ that + clause (his ~ that he was caught cheating) 7. to smb.'s ~ ((much) to his ~, he was caught cheating)

embassy *n.* 1. a foreign ~ 2. at, in an ~ (she works at/in the ~)

embed *v.* 1. to ~ deeply; firmly 2. (D; refl., tr.) to ~ in 3. (D; tr.) to ~ with (journalists ~ded with the invading troops)

embellish *v.* (D; tr.) to ~ with (she ~ed her story with a few lurid details)

embers *n.* 1. burning; hot; live ~ 2. dying ~ 3. the glow of (burning) ~

embezzle *v.* (D; intr., tr.) to ~ from

embezzlement *n.* 1. to commit (an act of) ~ 2. ~ from

emblazoned *adj.* 1. ~ across, on 2. ~ with

emblem *n.* a national ~

emblematic *adj.* ~ of

embodiment *n.* a living ~ (of an ideal)

embody *v.* (D; tr.) to ~ in

embolden *v.* (formal) (H) what ~ed him to make the attempt?

embolism *n.* an air; cerebral; coronary; pulmonary ~

emboss *v.* 1. (D; tr.) to ~ on (to ~ designs on wall paper) 2. to ~ with (to ~ wall paper with designs)

embrace I *n.* 1. a loving, tender, warm; passionate; tight ~ 2. in an ~ (clasped in a tight ~)

embrace II *v.* 1. to ~ passionately; tenderly, warmly 2. to ~ wholeheartedly (our party has ~d reform wholeheartedly = our party has wholeheartedly ~d reform)

embroider *v.* 1. (D; tr.) to ~ for (she ~ed a towel for me) 2. (D; tr.) to ~ on; with (she ~ed designs on the towel; she ~ed the towel with designs)

embroil *v.* (D; refl., tr.) to ~ in

embroiled *adj.* ~ in; with

embryo *n.* 1. to implant an ~ 2. a human ~ 3. an ~ develops

emerge *v.* 1. (d; intr.) to ~ as (he ~d as the leading contender) 2. (D; intr.) to ~ from; out of (the sun ~d from behind the clouds; to ~ from the shadows) 3. (L) it ~d that she was an heiress 4. (s) they ~d unscathed

emergency *n.* 1. to cause, create; declare an ~ 2. a grave, serious; life-and-death; life-threatening; national ~ 3. a state of ~ 4. in case of an ~ (esp. AE); in (the event of) an ~

emigrate *v.* (D; intr.) to ~ from; to

eminence *n.* 1. to achieve, win ~ 2. ~ as (she achieved ~ as a painter) 3. ~ in (their ~ in the arts and sciences) 4. of ~ (a person of great ~)

eminent *adj.* 1. ~ as (she was ~ as a painter) 2. ~ in

emissary *n.* 1. a peace; personal ~ 2. an ~ to

emission *n.* 1. to control; reduce; test ~s (to try to reduce the level of harmful ~s) 2. sulfur (AE), sulphur ~s 3. a nocturnal ~ 4. the sun's ~s

emit *v.* (D; tr.) to ~ into (to ~ smoke into the air)

emotion *n.* 1. to stir up, whip up ~(s) 2. to display,

show; express ~ 3. to contain, control, curb, suppress ~ 4. bottled-up, pent-up, repressed; deep, sincere; strong ~(s) 5. conflicting, mixed ~s 6. a flood of ~; a wide range of ~s 7. with ~ (to speak with deep ~) 8. (misc.) her voice broke with ~

empathize *v.* (D; intr.) to ~ with

empathy *n.* 1. to feel; show ~ 2. ~ with

emphasis *n.* 1. to lay, place, put ~ on 2. great, particular, special ~

emphasize *v.* 1. (B) she ~d its importance to me 2. (L) she ~d to me that it was very important that everyone should come on time

emphatic *adj.* ~ about, in

empire *n.* 1. to govern, rule an ~ 2. to build, build up; consolidate an ~ 3. to break up an ~ 4. a business; colonial; commercial; industrial; publishing ~ 5. (misc.) *The History of the Decline and Fall of the Roman Empire* (1776–88) – Edward Gibbon; "[Britain] has lost an ~ but has not found a role." – Dean Acheson (1893–1971)

emplacement *n.* an antiaircraft; concealed; gun ~

employ I *n.* (to be) in smb.'s ~

employ II *v.* 1. to ~ gainfully 2. (D; tr.) to ~ as; (she was ~ed as a programmer in an IT company) 3. (H) to ~ smb. to solve a problem 4. (misc.) you'd be better ~ed looking after your children than chasing other women!

employee *n.* 1. to engage (esp. BE), hire (esp. AE), take on an ~ 2. to dismiss, fire, lay off, sack (colloq.) an ~; (BE) to make an ~ redundant 3. a government; white-collar ~ 4. a full-time; part-time ~ 5. a fellow ~

employer *n.* an equal-opportunities (BE), equal-opportunity (AE) ~

employment *n.* 1. to give, provide ~ 2. to find; look for, seek ~ 3. casual (BE); full; full-time; paid; part-time; seasonal; steady ~ (falling levels of ~ led to government policies aimed at restoring full ~) 4. ~ falls; peaks; rises 5. ~ is down; up (~ is way down over last year) 6. ~ as (to find ~ as a mechanic)

empower *v.* (H) to ~ smb. to do smt.

empty I *adj.* 1. half ~ (optimists say that the glass is half full; pessimists, that it's half ~) 2. ~ of (~ of meaning)

empty II *v.* 1. (D; tr.) ("to remove from") to ~ from, out of (she ~tied the grain from the sacks) 2. (d; intr.) ("to flow") to ~ into (the Danube ~ties into the Black Sea) 3. (D; tr.) ("to make empty") to ~ of (she ~tied the briefcase of its contents) 4. (P; tr.) ("to put") she ~tied the cakes onto the plate; I ~tied all the toys into the bin

enable *v.* (H) to ~ smb. to do smt.

enamored, enamoured *adj.* 1. deeply ~ 2. ~ of, with (AE)

encase *v.* (D; tr.) to ~ in

enclose *v.* (D; tr.) to ~ in; with (to ~ a check in an envelope; to ~ a check with a letter; please find ~d with this letter a check for $25)

encore *n.* 1. to do; play; sing an ~ 2. an ~ to 3. as, for (as an ~ he played a short piano piece; that was great – but what will you do for an ~?)

encounter *n.* 1. to have an ~ (with) 2. a brief, fleeting; casual; chance; close ~ 3. an ~ between; with

encourage *v.* 1. ~ actively; strongly; warmly 2. to ~ greatly, no end, very much 3. (D.; tr.) to ~ in (she actively ~d us in our work) 4. (H) she actively ~d us to work harder 5. (K) she strongly ~d our working harder 6. (R) it ~d us greatly (to learn) that so many had/should have succeeded 7. (misc.) it ~s us no end when so many have succeeded

encouraged *adj.* 1. actively; strongly ~ 2. to ~ greatly, very 3. ~ at, by (we were very ~ at/by the success of so many) 4. ~ to + inf. (we were very ~ to learn that so many had/should have succeeded) 5. ~ that + clause (we were greatly ~ that so many had/should have succeeded)

encouragement *n.* 1. to give, offer, provide ~ 2. to find ~ in 3. warm ~ 4. ~ to

encouraging *adj.* 1. very; warmly ~ (warmly ~ remarks) 2. ~ for; ~ to 3. ~ to + inf. (it's very ~ (for/to us) to learn that so many had/should have succeeded) 4. ~ that + clause (it's very ~ (for/to us) that so many had/should have succeeded)

encroach *v.* (d; intr.) to ~ on, upon (to ~ on smb.'s territory)

encrusted *adj.* ~ in, with

encumber *v.* (D; tr.) to ~ with

encyclopedia, encyclopaedia *n.* 1. to compile, write an ~ 2. to expand; revise; update an ~ 3. to consult, look smt. up in, use an ~ 4. (humorous) a walking ~ 5. an article, entry in an ~ 6. in an ~ (is that name/subject (entered) in any ~?)

end I *n.* ["finish"] 1. to bring smt. to an ~; to come to the ~ of smt.; put an ~ to smt.; to reach the ~ of (a story) (we all want an ~ to violence – but how do we put an ~ to it?) 2. a violent ~ (she met (with) a violent ~) 3. at an ~ (her career was at an ~) 4. at the ~ (at the ~ of the word) 5. by the ~ (by the ~ of the year) 6. to the ~ (to the bitter ~) 7. (misc.) he met his ~ in a shootout with the police ["side"] 8. the deep; shallow ~ (of a pool) 9. the far, opposite; other ~ 10. from ~ to ~; from (the) beginning to (the) ~; on (its) end (to stand a box on its ~) ["purpose"] 11. to accomplish, achieve one's ~s 12. (misc.) an ~ in itself (should money be an ~ in itself or only a means to an ~?); to what ~? ["misc."] 13. to be on the receiving ~ (of) ("to be a recipient"); to make ~s meet ("to manage to get along on one's income"); to change ~s; to the ~s of the earth ("to the most remote parts of the earth"); in the ~ ("finally"); for hours on ~ ("for long periods of time") (see also *at the end of the day* at **day**; **dead end**; **loose end**; **fag end**; **loose ends**; **means** 5; *the end of the road* at **road**; *both ends of the spectrum* at **spectrum**; **tag end**; **tail end**; *the wrong end of a telescope* at **telescope I** *n.*)

end II *v.* 1. (d; intr., tr.) to ~ by (he ~ed his remarks by quoting Lincoln) 2. (d; intr.) to ~ in (the word ~s in a consonant; to ~ in a draw; to ~ badly/in disaster/in tears) 3. (D; intr., tr.) to ~ with (he ~ed his remarks with a quotation from Lincoln)

endear *v.* (D; refl., tr.) to ~ to (she ~ed herself to everyone by singing a song; his snide remarks didn't exactly ~ him to anyone)

endeavor, endeavour *v.* (formal) (E) he ~ed to remain calm

endemic *adj.* ~ among, in, to

ending *n.* 1. a happy; perfect; sad; storybook; surprise ~ (to have a happy ~; our dinner together was the perfect ~ to a wonderful week-end) 2. (grammar) a case; feminine; grammatical; inflectional; masculine; neuter; plural ~

endorsement *n.* ["approval"] 1. to give one's ~ 2. to get, receive smb.'s ~ 3. to seek smb.'s ~ 4. to withdraw; withhold one's ~ 5. a full; official; strong; qualified; ringing; unqualified; wholehearted ~ (there was wholehearted ~ for/of the plan from both ends of the political spectrum)

endow *v.* 1. to ~ richly 2. (d; tr.) to ~ with ("all men … are ~ed by their Creator with certain unalienable rights …" – the U.S. Declaration of Independence (signed July 4th, 1776))

endowment *n.* to provide an ~ for

end up *v.* 1. (d; intr.) to ~ as (she ~ed up as governor of the state) 2. (d; intr.) to ~ by (she ~ed up by becoming governor of the state) 3. (d; intr.) to ~ in (to ~ in a draw; to ~ in a free-for-all) 4. (d; intr.) to ~ with (I ~ed up with the estate) 5. (G) she ~ed up becoming governor of the state 6. (S) she ~ed up governor of the state; to start off/out poor and ~ rich

endurance *n.* 1. to test smb.'s ~ 2. physical ~ (astounding feats of physical ~) 3. the ~ to + inf. (does she have enough ~ to run the entire distance?) 4. beyond ~ 5. (misc.) smb.'s powers of ~

endure *v.* 1. (E) "he would not ~ to be defeated" – British National Corpus 2. (G) he couldn't ~ being defeated 3. (K) I cannot ~ his constant complaining! 4. (misc.) to ~ to the bitter end

enema *n.* 1. to administer, give an ~ 2. to get, have an ~

enemy *n.* 1. to conquer, overcome, rout an ~ 2. to confront, engage, face an ~ 3. to have an ~; to make an ~ (of) 4. an arch, avowed, bitter, deadly, implacable, insidious, irreconcilable, mortal, relentless, sworn, vicious; formidable, powerful ~ 5. a common, mutual; natural; political; secret ~ (are dogs and cats natural ~mies?) 6. a public ~ (public ~ number one) 7. (misc.) to be one's own worst ~

energy *n.* ["capacity"] 1. to apply one's ~ (to); to expend one's ~ (on) 2. to devote one's ~ to 3. to direct (one's) ~ to, towards; redirect one's ~ (to, towards) 4. to dissipate; sap smb.'s ~ 5. boundless, limitless, unflagging; latent; misguided ~ 6. an amount; burst; level of ~ 7. the ~ to + inf. (does she

have the ~ to get all of these jobs done?) ["usable power"] 8. to provide ~ for 9. to consume; waste ~ 10. to conserve ~ 11. to harness ~ (to harness solar ~) 12. atomic, nuclear; electric; geothermal; hydroelectric; kinetic; renewable; solar ~ 13. sources of ~ (see also *energy crisis* at **crisis**)
enforce *v.* to ~ rigidly, strictly, stringently
enforcement *n.* 1. rigid, strict, stringent ~ 2. law ~
engage *v.* 1. (D; tr.) to ~ as (to ~ smb. as a guide) 2. (d; intr., tr.) to ~ in (to ~ in sports; to ~ smb. in conversation) 3. (d; intr.) to ~ with (the first gear ~s with the second) 4. (esp. BE) (H) we ~d him to drive us round the city
engaged *adj.* ["busy"] 1. actively; directly; otherwise ~ (he couldn't come because he was otherwise ~) 2. ~ in, on (esp. BE) (we are ~ in conversation; we are ~ in/on (the project of) compiling a dictionary) USAGE NOTE: Consider the use of *engaged in* and *engaged on* in the following examples: two of the guests were *engaged* in (making) small talk/ conversation.; he is *engaged* in writing a dictionary. = (*Brit*) he is *engaged* on a dictionary (project). = he is working on a dictionary (project).; he is *engaged* in/(*Brit*) on research. = he is *engaged* in (esp. AE)/(BE) on a research project. BE prefers *engaged on* before a noun or noun phrase, especially one that is countable (such as *dictionary* or *project*) rather than typically not countable (such as *research* or *small talk*). ["betrothed"] 3. to get ~ 4. ~ to (Bill is ~ to Betty) ["hired"] 5. (esp. BE) ~ to + inf. (he was ~ to drive us round the city)
engagement *n.* ["betrothal"] 1. to announce an ~ 2. to break (off) an ~ 3. an ~ to (her ~ to him was announced in the local paper) ["appointment"] ["obligation"] 4. to cancel an ~ 5. a luncheon; previous, prior; social; speaking ~ (he couldn't come because he had a previous ~) ["battle"] 6. to break off an ~ 7. a naval ~
engine *n.* ["motor"] 1. to crank, start; gun, race; jump-start; operate, run; rev up an ~ 2. to lubricate; repair; service; tune (up) an ~ 3. to cut, kill, switch off, turn off; start (up), switch on; warm up an ~ 4. an air-cooled; aircraft; diesel; donkey; electric; internal-combustion; jet; radial; reciprocating; rocket; rotary; (computer) search; steam; two-hundred horsepower; turbojet; V-8; valve-in-head ~ 5. a cold ~ (don't drive fast on a cold ~) 6. an ~ functions, runs, works; idles; starts; warms up 7. an ~ backfires; breaks down; dies, fails, stalls; floods; gets overheated; knocks, pinks (BE), sputters (the ~ died because there was no gas in it) 8. an ~ burns gasoline (AE), petrol (BE) 9. an ~ runs on gas (AE), gasoline (AE), petrol (BE), electric power; solar energy ["vehicle"] 10. a fire ~
engineer *n.* ["skilled specialist in a branch of engineering"] 1. a chemical; civil; electrical; flight; graduate; highway; marine; mechanical; metallurgical; mining; operating; sanitary; systems; transportation (esp. AE) ~ ["driver"] 2. a locomotive ~ (AE;

BE has *engine driver*) ["technician"] 3. an operating; radio; sound ~
engineered *adj.* (cannot stand alone) ~ to + inf. (~ to last for a century)
engineering *n.* aeronautical; chemical; civil; electrical; genetic; highway; human; hydraulic; light; marine; mechanical; metallurgical; sanitary; systems; traffic; transportation (esp. AE) ~
English *n.* 1. American; Australian; Basic; Black; British; Canadian; Common, World; Indian; Irish; Malaysian; Middle; Modern; New Zealand; North American; Old; Scottish; South African; Singaporean; Welsh; West Indian, etc., etc. ~ 2. BBC; colloquial; current; idiomatic; the King's, the Queen's; Shakespearean; standard ~ 3. spoken; written ~ 4. broken, fractured; nonstandard; pidgin; substandard ~ 5. in fluent; good; plain ~
engrave *v.* 1. (d; refl., tr.) to ~ on (the events ~d themselves on my memory; a design was ~d on the dishes) 2. (D; tr.) to ~ with (the dishes were ~d with a design)
engrossed *adj.* 1. deeply, very ~ 2. ~ in, with (AE) (~ in one's work)
engulf *v.* (D; tr.) to ~ in
enigma *n.* an ~ to
enjoin *v.* (formal) 1. (d; tr.) ("to forbid") to ~ from 2. (d; tr.) ("to order") to ~ on (to ~ a duty on smb.) 3. (H) ("to order") to ~ smb. to obey the law
enjoy *v.* 1. to ~ enormously, greatly, immensely, very much 2. (G) she ~s singing and swimming 3. (K) they ~ her singing 4. (misc.) to ~ oneself
enjoyable *adj.* 1. highly, very ~ 2. ~ to + inf. (it is ~ to swim in the ocean)
enjoyment *n.* 1. to give, provide ~ 2. to derive, get ~ from 3. full, great; sheer ~ 4. for ~ (she's an amateur who sings purely for the sheer ~ of it)
enlarge *v.* 1. (D; tr.) ("to make larger") to ~ by (to ~ a photograph by ten percent) 2. (D; tr.) ("to make larger") to ~ into, to (to enlarge an office into a conference room) 3. (d; intr.) to ~ on, upon ("to discuss in more detail")
enlargement *n.* to make an ~ (of a photograph)
enlighten *v.* (D; tr.) to ~ about, on (can you ~ me on this subject?)
enlightening *adj.* 1. thoroughly, very ~ 2. ~ to + inf. (it was ~ to read the old newspaper accounts of the incident)
enlist *v.* 1. (D; intr.) to ~ for (to ~ for three years) 2. (D; intr.) to ~ in (to ~ in the army) 3. (H) we ~ed them to help
enlistment *n.* 1. to extend one's ~ 2. ~ in (~ in the Peace Corps)
enmeshed *adj.* (cannot stand alone) ~ in, with (esp. AE) (~ in legal details)
enmity *n.* 1. to arouse, stir up ~ 2. to feel ~ 3. to incur smb.'s ~ 4. (a) bitter; deep; longstanding; seething ~ 5. ~ against (AE), towards; among, between (she felt (a) deep ~ towards them; there was (a) deep ~ between her and them)

enough *adj., determiner, pronoun* 1. ~ for (that's ~ for me) 2. ~ to + inf. (it's ~ to know that they are safe; we've had ~ excitement to last a lifetime) 3. ~ of (~ of them) 4. (misc.) ~ and to spare = more than ~ USAGE NOTE: 1. The use of the preposition *of* is necessary when a pronoun follows. When a noun follows, the use of *of the* limits the meaning – we have seen enough documentaries; we have seen enough of the documentaries/documentary that we discussed earlier. 2. *Enough money* is more common than *money enough* – he has enough money to retire = he has enough money (so) that he can retire.

enquire (BE) see **inquire**

enquiries *n.* (BE) (to assist in finding telephone numbers) 1. directory ~ (AE has *directory assistance* or *information*) 2. international ~ (AE has *international information*)

enquiry (BE) see **inquiry**

enrage *v.* (R) it ~ed us (to learn) that he had refused to help

enraged *adj.* 1. ~ at, by, over (we were ~ at his refusal to help) 2. ~ to + inf. (we were ~ to learn that he had refused to help) 3. ~ that + clause (we were ~ that he had refused to help)

enroll, enrol *v.* 1. (D; intr., tr.) to ~ as (she ~ed as a special student) 2. (D; intr., refl., tr.) to ~ for, in (to ~ for a course; to ~ students in a course)

enrollment, enrolment *n.* 1. (a) heavy, large; light, small ~ 2. open ("unrestricted") ~ 3. ~ for, in (the ~ in several courses went up)

en route *adv.* ~ from; to (they are ~ from Edinburgh to London)

ensconced *adj.* (cannot stand alone) 1. comfortably; firmly; safely; snugly ~ 2. ~ in (snugly ~ in an easy chair)

ensemble *n.* a brass; string; woodwind ~

enshrined *adj.* ~ in (these rights are ~ in the constitution)

ensnare *v.* (D; tr.) to ~ in (~d in red tape)

ensue *v.* (D; intr.) to ~ from

ensure *v.* (formal) 1. (A; usu. used without *to*) the present contract cannot ~ you a job 2. (K) I cannot ~ your getting a job 3. (L) no one can ~ that you'll get a job

entail *v.* 1. (G) this job ~s moving to another city 2. (K) this job would ~ your moving to another city

entangle *v.* (D; tr.) to ~ in, with

entanglement *n.* 1. a barbed-wire ~ 2. ~ in, with

enter *v.* 1. (D; intr.) ("to come in") to ~ by (to ~ by the rear door) 2. (D; intr., tr.) ("to enroll") to ~ for (BE), in (to ~ smb. for/in a contest; they ~ed their horse for/in the race; I've ~ed for/in the mile run) 3. (d; intr.) to ~ into ("to participate in") (to ~ into negotiations) 4. (D; tr.) ("to put into") to ~ in; into; on (to ~ data into/in a computer; to enter data in/on a database) 5. (D; intr.) to ~ on, upon ("to begin") (to ~ on a new career)

enterprise *n.* ["ownership"] 1. free; private ~ ["undertaking"] 2. to embark on, start an ~ 3. a joint ~ 4. a

commercial ~ 5. in an ~ (who is the most important person in this ~?) ["initiative"] 6. of ~ (a person of great ~ who shows ~ in everything she does)

entertain *v.* (D; tr.) to ~ by, with (to ~ children by telling them funny stories; to ~ children with funny stories)

entertaining I *adj.* ~ to + inf. (it's ~ (for us) to watch people dancing)

entertaining II *n.* ["acting as a host"] to do ~ (they do very little ~)

entertainment *n.* 1. to provide ~ 2. adult; family; live; private; public ~ 3. ~ to + inf. (it was pure ~ to watch them dance) 4. to smb.'s ~ (to everyone's ~, she showed up in a clown's costume) 5. ~ for 6. for smb.'s ~

enthralling *adj.* ~ to + inf. (it was ~ to watch them dance)

enthuse *v.* (colloq.) (D; intr.) to ~ about, over

enthusiasm *n.* 1. to arouse, drum up, kindle, stir up, whip up ~ 2. to demonstrate, display, show; radiate ~ 3. to blunt, dampen smb.'s ~ 4. to feel ~ 5. to lose ~ 6. boundless, contagious, great, infectious, unbounded, unbridled, unflagging, wild ~ 7. ~ grows, mounts, rises 8. ~ wanes 9. a burst of ~ 10. ~ for 11. the ~ to + inf. (they had enough ~ to continue the campaign in spite of the difficulties)

enthusiastic *adj.* 1. very, wildly; less than ~ 2. ~ about, at, over (she was less than ~ about my plan)

entice *v.* 1. (D; tr.) to ~ into (to ~ smb. into a life of crime) 2. (D; tr.) to ~ with (they ~d the children with candy) 3. (H) the display ~d them to enter the shop

entice away *v.* (D; tr.) we could not ~ the children away from the cakes

entirety *n.* in its ~

entitle *v.* 1. (d; tr.) to ~ to (your years of service ~ you to a pension) 2. (H) your years of service ~ you to receive a pension 3. (N) ("to call, name") they ~d their dictionary *The BBI* = their dictionary is ~d *The BBI*

entitled *adj.* (cannot stand alone) ["having the right"] 1. ~ to (you are fully ~ to a pension) 2. ~ to + inf. (you are fully ~ to receive a pension)

entrance *n.* 1. to gain ~ (to) (they gained ~ to his apartment) 2. to make an/one's ~ 3. a back, rear; front, main; service; side ~ 4. a dramatic, grand, triumphal ~ (to make a grand ~) 5. an ~ from; into, to (the ~ to this building) 6. at; through an ~ (go through the front ~ and wait for me at the rear ~) 7. (misc.) we were refused ~ into the country; she always makes a late ~; the police sealed off the ~ to the building

entranced *adj.* ~ at, by, over, with

entrap *v.* (D; tr.) to ~ in, into

entreat *v.* (formal) (H) to ~ smb. to do smt.

entree *n.* ["access"] to gain; have ~ into, to

entrenched *adj.* 1. deeply, firmly ~ 2. ~ in

entrepreneur *n.* an independent; private ~

entrust *v.* 1. (B) he ~ed his money to me 2. (d; tr.) to ~ with (he ~ed me with his money)

entrusted *adj.* (cannot stand alone) 1. ~ with (I was ~with his money) 2. ~ to + inf (can he be ~ to be alone with little children?)

entry *n.* ["headword and definition"] (in a dictionary) 1. to give, include an ~ 2. a main; run-on ~; subentry 3. at, in, under an ~ ["act of entering"] 4. to make an ~ (to make a triumphal ~; to make an ~ in a diary) 5. to gain ~ to (they gained ~ to his apartment) 6. to allow, grant; refuse ~ (they refused us ~ into the country) 7. forced, illegal ~ (of a burglar) 8. an ~ into (she announced her ~ into the presidential race; our ~ into the war) ["bookkeeping procedure"] 9. to make an ~ for 10. double; single ~ ["participation in a contest"] 11. to submit an ~ (to) 12. a winning ~

entry blank, entry form *n.* 1. to fill in, fill out (esp. AE) an ~ 2. to send in, submit an ~ for

entwine *v.* (D; refl., tr.) to ~ around (the vines ~d themselves around the tree)

enumerate *v.* (B) to ~ the facts to smb.

enunciate *v.* 1. to ~ clearly 2. (B) she ~d her theory to her colleagues

envelop *v.* (D; intr.) to ~ in

envelope *n.* 1. to address; open; seal an ~ 2. a pay ~ (AE; BE has *pay packet*) 3. an air-mail; manila; self-addressed; stamped; window ~ (the manila ~ contained an official document) USAGE NOTE: AE has *stamped self-addressed envelope*; BE has *stamped addressed envelope (SAE)*.

envious *adj.* ~ of

environment *n.* 1. to clean up the ~ 2. to preserve, protect the ~ 3. to pollute the ~ 4. a clean, healthy ~ 5. a polluted, unhealthy ~ 6. a friendly, pleasant ~ 7. a hostile, unfriendly ~ 8. a social; working ~ 9. in an ~ (we try to create a friendly working ~ in which our staff can feel at home)

envisage *v.* 1. (d; tr.) to ~ as (we ~ this dictionary as a handbook for serious students) 2. (G) she had not ~d marrying him 3. (J) we could not ~ them getting married 4. (K) we hadn't ~d her marrying him 5. (L) she had not ~d that she would marry him 6. (Q) we could not ~ why on earth she married him!

envision *v.* (AE) see **envisage**

envious *adj.* 1. very ~ 2. ~ of

envoy *n.* 1. to dispatch, send an ~ 2. a peace; personal; special ~ 3. an ~ to (our ~ to Paris)

envy I *n.* 1. to arouse, cause; stir up ~ (of) 2. to feel ~ 3. to show ~ 4. out of ~ (she did it out of ~) 5. ~ at, of, towards 6. (misc.) an object of ~; consumed/green with ~

envy II *v.* (O) they ~ us our new house

epic *n.* 1. a folk; historical; Hollywood ~ 2. an ~ about

epicenter, epicentre *n.* at the ~ (of)

epidemic *n.* 1. to touch off, trigger an ~ 2. to contain, control an ~ 3. an ~ breaks out, strikes; rages; spreads 4. an AIDS; cholera; flu; measles; typhoid; typhus ~ 5. during, in an ~ (how many people died in the last flu ~?)

epigram *n.* to compose; deliver an ~

epilepsy *n.* to have ~

epilogue *n.* an ~ to

episode *n.* 1. a dramatic; funny, humorous; thrilling; touching; tragic ~ 2. during, in an ~

epitaph *n.* 1. a fitting, perfect ~ 2. an ~ for; on (lines that make a fitting ~ for a national hero)

epithet *n.* 1. to hurl ~s at 2. a harsh, offensive, vicious, vile ~

epoch *n.* 1. to mark; usher in an ~ 2. a glacial; revolutionary ~ 3. during, in an ~

equal I *adj.* 1. ~ in (~ in price) 2. ~ to, with (one kilometer is ~ to five eighths of a mile; ~ to the occasion; she felt fully – indeed more than – ~ to the task) 3. (misc.) all other things being ~ ("ceteris paribus") (all other things being ~, we might as well get the cheapest of the three)

equal II *n.* an ~ in (to have no ~ in political cunning)

equal III *v.* 1. (D; tr.) to ~ as (no one could ~ her as a dancer) 2. (D; tr.) to ~ in (no one could ~ her in dancing)

equality *n.* 1. to achieve, attain ~ 2. racial; religious; sexual; social; total ~ 3. ~ among, between; with (~ between the sexes) 4. ~ in (~ in pay) 5. ~ of (~ of opportunity)

equanimity *n.* 1. to maintain; regain one's ~ 2. to disturb, upset smb.'s ~ 3. with ~ (to react with ~ to upsetting news)

equate *v.* (D; intr., tr.) to ~ to, with (one should not ~ wealth with happiness; your likely royalties ~ to an annual salary of $5,000)

equation *n.* 1. to formulate, state an ~ 2. to reduce; solve, work (esp. AE), work out an ~ 3. a differential; first-degree; identical; integral; linear; quadratic; simple ~; an ~ in one unknown; an ~ in two unknowns 4. (misc.) the human ~

equator *n.* above; at, on; below the ~

equidistant *adj.* ~ between; from (the Equator is ~ from the North Pole and the South Pole, which means that it's ~ between the Poles)

equilibrium *n.* 1. to establish; maintain; regain; restore smb.'s ~ 2. to lose one's ~ 3. to disrupt, disturb, upset the ~ 4. in (a state of) ~

equinox *n.* the autumn, autumnal; spring, vernal ~

equip *v.* 1. (d; tr.) to ~ for; with (her training ~ped her with the skills needed for her new job) 2. (H) her training ~ped her to cope with her new job

equipment *n.* 1. to install, set up; operate; test ~ 2. to maintain; repair ~ 3. audiovisual; camping; electronic; firefighting; military; office; sports ~ 4. heavy; light ~ 5. (the) ~ for (~ for road construction) 6. the ~ to + inf. (do you have enough ~ to do the job?)

equipped *adj.* 1. badly, ill; well ~ 2. ~ for; with 3. ~ to + inf. (our hospital is ~ to handle emergency cases) 4. (misc.) to come ~ with (the flashlight comes ~ with batteries)

equity *n.* ["supplementary system of justice"] 1. in ~ (a

suit in ~) ["value net of debts"] 2. negative ~ (the fall in house prices means some mortgage-holders are faced with negative ~) ["misc."] 3. private ~ (an old firm bought by a private-equity company)
equivalent I *adj.* ~ in; to (your likely royalties are ~ in real terms to an annual salary of $5,000)
equivalent II *n.* an approximate; exact ~
equivocal *adj.* ~ about
era *n.* 1. to introduce, usher in an ~ 2. the Christian, Common; Roman ~ 3. a bygone ~; the horse-and-buggy ~ 4. an ~ in (the automobile ushered in a whole new ~ in transportation) 5. in an ~ (in the Roman ~; in the ~ of the horse and buggy) 6. (misc.) the beginning of a new ~; the end of an ~ (her farewell performance marked the end of an ~) USAGE NOTE: The abbreviation CE (*Common Era*) is used by some non-Christians instead of AD. Thus, 1920 CE equals 1920 AD or AD 1920, and 100 BCE equals 100 BC. Likewise, the fourth century CE equals the fourth century AD and the fourth century BCE equals the fourth century BC.
erase *v.* (D; tr.) to ~ from
eraser *n.* a blackboard; ink ~ USAGE NOTE: In BE an *eraser* is usu. called a *rubber*; a *blackboard eraser* may be called a *duster*.
erect *adj.* to hold oneself ~; to stand ~
erosion *n.* 1. gradual, slow; severe ~ 2. beach; glacial; soil; wind ~
errand *n.* 1. to do, run an ~; to go on an ~ 2. personal ~s 3. a fool's ("useless") ~ 4. an ~ for (could you run an ~ for me?) 5. on an ~ 6. (misc.) an ~ of mercy
erroneous *adj.* ~ to + inf. (it's ~ to assume that the press always prints the truth)
error *n.* 1. to commit, make an ~ 2. to compound an ~ 3. to correct, rectify an ~ 4. to admit to (making) an ~ 5. a cardinal, costly, egregious, flagrant, glaring, grievous, gross, major, serious; tragic ~ 6. a fatal; foolish; minor, slight ~ 7. a clerical; grammatical; printer's, typographical; programming; textual; typing ~ 8. a human; tactical ~ 9. (statistics) (a) random ~ 10. ~s abound; occur (~s abound on every page) 11. an ~ in (an ~ in judgment) 12. an ~ to + inf. (it was an ~ to appoint her = it was an ~ appointing her) 13. by, through ~ (her name was omitted by ~) 14. in ~ (her name was omitted in ~; she was in ~ in saying that) 15. (misc.) a margin of ~; by trial and ~
erudition *n.* 1. to display; flaunt one's ~ 2. great ~
erupt *v.* (D; intr.) to ~ in, into (to ~ in a frenzied demonstration that ~ed into violence)
eruption *n.* 1. a volcanic ~ 2. a skin ~
escalate *v.* (D; intr.) to ~ into (the local war threatened to ~ into a major conflict)
escalator *n.* 1. to take an ~ 2. an ~ down; up ~ 3. an ~ carries its passengers
escapade *n.* a childish, schoolboy; wild ~
escape I *n.* ["act of escaping"] 1. to organize, plan, plot an ~ 2. to make an ~; to make good one's ~

3. to foil, thwart an ~ 4. a daring, dramatic; hair-breadth, narrow ~ 5. an ~ from (an ~ from prison) 6. (misc.) they had a narrow ~ ["misc."] 7. a fire ~ ("an emergency staircase")
escape II *v.* 1. (D; intr.) to ~ from; to (to ~ from the police) 2. (G) a famous actor cannot ~ being recognized 3. (s) to ~ unhurt USAGE NOTE: *To escape from the police* means "to escape from police custody". *To escape the police* means "to elude the police without being caught".
escort I *n.* 1. to provide an ~ for 2. an armed; fighter; motorcycle; police ~ 3. an ~ for 4. under ~
escort II *v.* 1. (D; tr.) to ~ from; to 2. (P; tr.) the president was ~ed through the city; they were ~ed out of the building
escrow *n.* 1. to place, put in ~ 2. to hold, keep in ~
escutcheon *n.* 1. an armorial ~ 2. (misc.) (humorous) a blot on smb.'s ~
espionage *n.* 1. to conduct, engage in ~ 2. industrial; military ~
esprit de corps *n.* 1. to develop (an) ~ 2. (a) strong ~
essay *n.* 1. to write an ~ about, on 2. a critical; literary ~ 3. a collection of ~s 4. in an ~ (see the Usage Note for **dissertation**)
essence *n.* 1. the very ~ of smt. 2. in ~ (their claim is, in ~, that they have been mistreated) 3. of the ~ (time is of the ~)
essential *adj.* 1. ~ for; to 2. ~ to + inf. (it is not ~ for all students to be present) 3. ~ that + clause; subj. (it is not ~ that all students ¬be/should be/ are (BE)¬ present)
essentials *n.* the bare, basic ~
establish *v.* 1. (d; refl., tr.) to ~ as (the press ~ed him as the leading contender) 2. (L) the police ~ed conclusively that she was innocent of the crime 3. (Q) the police ~ed how the crime was committed
establishment *n.* 1. an educational; financial; political; research ~ 2. (misc.) to fight the Establishment ("to struggle against the established order")
estate *n.* 1. to administer, manage an ~ 2. a country ~ 3. (BE) a council, housing ~ 4. (BE) an industrial ~ 5. on an ~ 6. (misc.) to come into an ~ ("to inherit smt.")
esteem I *n.* 1. to hold smb. in high ~ 2. to fall; rise in smb.'s ~ 3. high ~ 4. self-esteem
esteem II *v.* to ~ greatly, highly
estimate I *n.* 1. to give, make; submit an ~ (the contractors had to submit ~s for the work/of the cost of the work) 2. (colloq.) (esp. AE) a ballpark ("approximate, rough") ~ 3. an approximate, rough; conservative; long-range; preliminary; realistic; short-range; written ~ 4. an ~ that + clause (it's my ~ that the interest rate will drop by two percent) 5. at an ~ (at a rough ~, the interest rate will drop by two percent) 6. by smb.'s ~ (by my ~, the interest rate will drop by two percent)
estimate II *v.* 1. (d; tr.) to ~ at (we ~d the cost at five hundred dollars) 2. (BE) (d; intr.) to ~ for (to ~ for

the repairs) 3. (L) we ~ that the cost will be $500 4. (M) we ~ the cost to be $500 5. (Q) we could not ~ how much the repairs would cost
estimation *n.* 1. to fall; rise in smb.'s ~ 2. in smb.'s ~ (in my ~ the situation is not critical)
estranged *adj.* ~ from (he was ~ from his wife)
estrangement *n.* (an) ~ between; from
etch *v.* 1. to ~ sharply 2. (D; tr.) to ~ in, into, on, onto (sharply ~ed into/in my memory; his name was ~ed into/on the glass) 3. (D; tr.) to ~ with (the glass was ~ed with his name)
ether *n.* under ~
ethic *n.* the (Protestant) work ~
ethical *adj.* ~ to + inf. (it is not ~ to plagiarize)
ethics *n.* 1. business; medical; professional ~ 2. a code of ~
etiquette *n.* 1. to prescribe ~ 2. courtroom; diplomatic; legal; medical; military; professional; social ~ 3. the rules of ~ 4. (misc.) a breach of ~
etymology *n.* 1. to ascertain, determine, trace an ~ 2. (a) folk ~ (the professor explained the origin of the word as a/by folk ~)
Eucharist *n.* to celebrate; give; receive, take the ~
eulogy *n.* 1. to deliver a ~ (for) 2. a touching ~
euphemism *n.* a ~ for
euphoria *n.* a feeling; state; wave of ~ (about, at, over)
euro *n.* 1. a falling; rising; strong; weak ~ (the international markets experienced difficulties with the falling ~) 2. (misc.) the dollar was strong against the ~
evacuate *v.* (D; tr.) to ~ from; to (the civilians were ~d from the city to the country) USAGE NOTE: Nowadays one can also have "the city was evacuated."
evacuation *n.* 1. to carry out an ~ (to carry out the ~ of civilians/of a city) 2. a mass ~ 3. an ~ from; to (the mass ~ of civilians from the city to the country)
evade *v.* (G) they ~ paying taxes by subterfuge
evaluate *v.* (D; tr.) to ~ as (he was ~d as unfit for military service)
evaluation *n.* 1. to make an ~ 2. a critical; fair, objective; realistic ~
evasion *n.* draft (AE); tax ~ (see also Usage Note at **avoidance**)
eve *n.* 1. Christmas Eve; New Year's Eve (on New Year's Eve) 2. on the ~ (on the ~ of the revolution) USAGE NOTE: In AE *Christmas Eve* means "the night before Christmas"; in BE it can also mean "the entire day before Christmas".
even *adj.* 1. to get ~ (with smb.) ("to avenge oneself by taking revenge on smb.") (don't get mad, get ~!) 2. (misc.) to break ~ (when betting)
evening *n.* 1. all ~; during the ~; in the ~ (they left early/late in the ~; they left in the early ~); ~s (AE), every ~; the next, the following ~; this ~; that ~; tomorrow ~; yesterday ~; a June ~; a summer ~; on any ~; on/during the ~ of (they left

on the ~ of July 26); on Wednesday ~ = Wednesday ~ (AE) 2. an ~ of (after an ~ of conversation, they went home for the night) 3. from ~ (from ~ to night) 4. (misc.) the ~ drew to a close; (Good) Evening (, everybody)!; to have; spend an ~ (we had a pleasant ~ at the theater; we spent the whole ~ working on the report!)
event *n.* 1. an auspicious; major; outstanding; significant ~ (a ceremony to celebrate/commemorate/mark such a major ~) 2. a dramatic; earth-shaking, earth-shattering; sensational; spectacular; world-shaking ~ 3. a disastrous; tragic ~ 4. a historical; literary ~ 5. a gala; social; solemn ~ 6. a sporting ~ 7. a media ~ (to stage a media ~) 8. a blesséd ~ ("a birth") (old-fashioned) 9. the main ~ 10. current ~s 11. (sports) athletics, track-and-field (esp. AE) ~s 12. an ~ occurs, takes place 13. in the ~ that + clause (in the ~ that he comes/should come) 14. in an ~ (in the ~ of fire; in any ~) 15. (misc.) the media sometimes manipulate ~s; a chain of ~s, a sequence of ~s; a turn of ~s (a dramatic and unexpected turn of ~s); in the normal course of ~s; in either ~; at/in (AE) all ~s; in the ~ ("as it turns out") (I thought I'd win, but in the ~ I lost)
ever *adv.* 1. ~ so (much/many) (I feel ~ so much better now!; I saw ~ so many elephants!; Thank you ~ so much! = (BE) (colloq.) Ta, ~ so!) 2. hardly ~; if ~; rarely/seldom if ~ ("What, *never?*" "Hardly ~! He's hardly ~ sick at sea!" – *H.M.S. Pinafore* (1878), Gilbert & Sullivan) 3. (misc.) who ~ would do smt. like that?; what ~ is that?; why ~ not?
evict *v.* (D; tr.) to ~ from
eviction *n.* 1. to face ~ 2. (an) ~ from
evidence *n.* 1. to furnish, give, introduce, produce, provide ~ 2. to collect, gather ~ 3. to dig up, find, turn up, unearth ~ 4. to piece together ~ 5. to fabricate, falsify, trump up ~ 6. to plant ~ (on smb.) 7. to tamper with ~ 8. to conceal; destroy; suppress; withhold ~ 9. to corroborate (the) ~ 10. to turn King's (BE), Queen's (BE), state's (AE) ~ 11. ample, overwhelming, strong, substantial; clear, cogent, compelling, convincing; conclusive; concrete, hard; incontestable, indisputable, irrefutable, undeniable, unquestionable; reliable, trustworthy; satisfactory ~ 12. direct; documentary; fresh, new; material; prima facie; statistical ~ 13. admissible; anecdotal; circumstantial; forensic; hearsay; inadmissible; scientific ~ 14. conflicting; damaging; inconclusive; telltale ~ 15. (the) ~ indicates, points to, suggests 16. a body of ~ 17. a piece; scrap, shred of ~ 18. ~ against; for, in favor of 19. ~ that + clause (the defendant's lawyer produced conclusive ~ that the accused could not have been at the scene of the crime) 20. as, in ~ (they were very much in ~ throughout the proceedings) 21. on the ~ of (on the ~ of this music, your son Wolfgang will become a fine composer!) 22. (misc.) the bulk of the ~
evident *adj.* 1. ~ from; to 2. ~ that + clause (from the vote so far, it is ~ to us all that she will be elected)

evil I *adj.* ~ to + inf. (it is ~ to kill)

evil II *n.* 1. to do ~ 2. to root out ~ 3. an unmitigated ~ 4. a necessary ~ 5. (misc.) the lesser of two ~s; ~ incarnate

evocative *adj.* (formal) (cannot stand alone) ~ of

evolution *n.* 1. a gradual; historical ~ 2. an ~ from; into, to

evolve *v.* (d; intr.) to ~ from, out of; into

exact I *adj.* ~ in; with

exact II *v.* (formal) (D; tr.) to ~ from (to ~ tribute from the population)

exaggerate *v.* to ~ greatly, grossly

exaggerated *adj.* greatly, grossly, highly ~

exaggeration *n.* 1. a gross ~ 2. ~ to + inf. (it is an ~ to claim that inflation has been controlled)

exam *n.* ["test"] 1. see **examination** 2. (colloq.) (AE) to ace an ~

examination *n.* ["test"]["set of questions"] 1. to administer, conduct, give an ~ 2. to draw up, make up, prepare, set (BE) an ~ 3. to invigilate (BE), monitor, proctor (AE), supervise an ~ 4. to do (BE), sit (BE), take an ~ 5. to fail, flunk (AE; colloq.); pass an ~ 6. a difficult, stiff; easy ~ 7. a bar; civil-service; state-board (AE) ~ 8. a comprehensive; doctoral; master's ~ 9. an end-of-term (BE); final; makeup ~ 10. an essay; multiple-choice; open-book; pass-fail; true-false ~ 11. an oral; written ~ 12. a competitive; entrance; external (BE); placement; qualifying ~ 13. an ~ in, on (an ~ in physics; an ~ on irregular verbs) ["inspection"]["scrutiny"] 14. to do, give, make an ~ 15. to fail; get, have, undergo; pass a (physical) ~ 16. a careful, close, complete, in-depth, thorough; cursory, perfunctory, superficial ~ 17. a physical ~ (the doctor did a thorough physical ~ of/on the patient, which revealed no signs of disease) 18. an ~ in, of, on (an ~ in mathematics; an ~ on new material) 19. on ~ (on closer ~ of the facts, she discovered that…) 20. under ~

examine *v.* 1. to ~ carefully, closely, thoroughly 2. (D; tr.) to ~ for (to ~ a car for defects) 3. (D; tr.) to ~ in, on (to ~ students in physics = to ~ students on their knowledge of physics; I was ~d on irregular verbs)

examiner *n.* 1. a bank; medical ~ 2. an external; internal ~

example *n.* 1. to cite, give, provide an ~ 2. to be, serve as, set an ~ (for) 3. to make an ~ of 4. to follow smb.'s ~ 5. a classic; concrete; extreme; glaring, striking; illustrative; impressive; inspiring; perfect; prime, shining; textbook; typical ~ 6. an ~ for, to 7. for ~ 8. (misc.) to lead by (personal) ~

exasperate *v.* (R) it ~d her that they never kept their promises

exasperated *adj.* 1. ~ about, at, by, over, with 2. ~ to + inf. (she was ~ to find that they never kept their promises) 3. ~ that + clause (she was ~ that they never kept their promises)

exasperating *adj.* 1. ~ to 2. ~ to + inf. (it was ~ for/to her to find that they never kept their promises) 3.

~ that + clause (it was ~ for/to her that they never kept their promises)

exasperation *n.* 1. ~ at (~ at bureaucrats) 2. in ~ (in her ~, she slammed the door)

ex cathedra *adv.* to speak ~

excavations *n.* to carry out archeological ~ (that reveal a lot about the past)

exceed *v.* (D; tr.) to ~ in (to ~ smb. in productivity by at least 10%)

excel *v.* (D; intr.) to ~ at, in (to ~ at sports)

excellence *n.* 1. a center of ~ 2. ~ at, in (we intend to make this new school a center of ~ in medical research!)

exception *n.* ["exclusion"] 1. to make an ~ for 2. to grant an ~ 3. an ~ to (an ~ to the rule) 4. with an ~ (everything is fine with the notable ~ of one major item; with few ~s) 5. (misc.) without ~ ["objection"] 6. to take ~ to (she took strong ~ to what he said)

excerpt I *n.* 1. to play, quote, show, use an ~ 2. an ~ from

excerpt II *v.* (D; tr.) to ~ from (to ~ a passage from a work)

excess *n.* 1. in ~ of 2. to ~ (to drink to ~)

exchange I *n.* ["act of exchanging"] 1. to agree to; make an ~ 2. a cultural ~; an ~ of ideas/views 3. a hostage; prisoner-of-war ~ 4. in ~ (for) 5. an ~ between ["place where items are bought or sold"] 6. a commodity; corn (BE), grain (AE); farmers'; post (AE); stock ~ (see also **stock market**) ["central office"] 7. an employment (BE), labour (BE); telephone ~ ["argument"] 8. to have an ~ (about) 9. an angry, heated ~ (of words) (they had an angry ~ with the other party about the new proposal) ["currency"] 10. foreign ~ 11. a rate of ~ (see also **exchange rate**) USAGE NOTE: The BE terms *employment exchange* and *labour exchange* have been largely superseded by *employment office* and *Job Centre/Jobcentre*.

exchange II *v.* 1. (D; tr.) to ~ for (I ~d the defective tire for a good one; I bought this hat here: will you ~ it for me?) 2. (D; tr.) to ~ with (to ~ places with smb.)

exchange rate *n.* 1. to set an ~ 2. to apply an ~ 3. a fixed; floating ~ 4. (misc.) what's the current ~ of the dollar against the euro?

excited *adj.* 1. ~ about, at, by, over (she got ~ about the news that they were coming) 2. ~ to + inf. (she was ~ to learn that they were coming) 3. ~ that + clause (she was ~ that they were coming)

excitement *n.* 1. to arouse, cause, create, stir up ~ 2. to feel ~ 3. to buzz, throb with ~ 4. considerable, great, intense; mounting ~ (the news has caused considerable ~ among members of the public) 5. ~ builds (to a climax); dies down; mounts, rises 6. ~ about, at, over 7. in ~ 8. (misc.) a tingle, tremor of ~

exciting *adj.* 1. ~ to + inf. (it was ~ for her to learn that they were coming) 2. ~ that + clause (it was ~ for her that they were coming)

exclaim v. (formal) 1. (BE) (D; intr.) to ~ at; in (she ~ed in amazement at his appearance in shorts) 2. (L) he ~ed that he was innocent

exclude v. (D; tr.) to ~ from (do certain members of the public feel ~d from real political power?)

exclusion n. 1. ~ from 2. to the ~ of (they watched her to the ~ of everyone else)

exclusive adj. 1. mutually ~ 2. ~ of (the price is ~ of sales tax)

excommunication n. to decree, order, pronounce (an) ~

exculpate v. (formal) (D; tr.) to ~ from

excursion n. 1. to go on, make an ~ 2. an ~ to

excursus n. (formal) 1. to make an ~ 2. an ~ into

excuse I n. 1. to find; have; make; make up an ~ for 2. to accept an ~ 3. to reject an ~ 4. an acceptable, good, satisfactory, valid; convincing; perfect; plausible ~ 5. a feeble, flimsy, lame, poor, unacceptable, unsatisfactory, weak ~ 6. a convenient; glib; ready-made ~ 7. an ~ for (an ~ for being late) 8. an ~ to + inf. (it was just an ~ (for him) to leave early) 9. an ~ that + clause (they accepted the ~ that I had been ill) 10. (misc.) the slightest ~ (he'll stay home from work at the slightest ~); a poor ~ for smt. (what you've got there is a pretty poor ~ for a dictionary, if you ask me!); to make one's ~s (he made his ~s and left)

excuse II v. 1. (D; tr.) to ~ as (he was ~d as physically unfit for duty) 2. (D; tr.) to ~ for (to ~ smb. for coming late) 3. (D; tr.) to ~ from (he was ~d from drill; BE also has: he was ~d drill) 4. (G) we will never ~ taking innocent hostages 5. (K) please ~ my arriving late

ex-directory adj. (BE) to go ~ ("to have one's number removed from the telephone book so as to have an unlisted number")

execute v. 1. (D; tr.) to ~ as (he was ~d as a deserter) 2. (D; tr.) to ~ for (he was ~d for desertion)

execution n. 1. to carry out an ~ (the ~ that was going to take place was about to be carried out when there was a last-minute stay of ~) 2. a mass; public; summary ~ 3. ~ by (~ by firing squad) (see also *stay of execution* at **stay I** n.)

executive n. a business; chief; corporate; junior; senior ~

exempt I adj. ~ from (~ from the draft)

exempt II v. (D; tr.) to ~ from (to ~ smb. from the draft)

exemption n. 1. to claim an ~ 2. to grant an ~ 3. a draft (AE); tax ~ 4. an ~ for (he received the ~ for his elderly parents which they had claimed and to which they were entitled) 5. (an) ~ from (to grant smb. an ~ from the draft)

exercise I n. ["bodily exertion"] 1. to engage in, go in for ~; to take (BE) ~ 2. to get ~ (she gets plenty of ~ at her job) 3. to do ~s 4. (a) hard, strenuous, vigorous; regular ~ 5. (an) aerobic; body-building; flexibility; isometric; relaxation; remedial; setting-up; warming-up ~ 6. physical ~ 7. a form of ~

(brisk walking is an excellent form of aerobic ~, during which you will feel better) ["practice drill"] 8. oral; written ~s (as in a language textbook) ["effort to achieve smt."] 9. to conduct an ~ 10. a marketing; public-relations ~ (the government has conducted a cynical public-relations ~ to justify its policies) 11. what is the object/purpose of the ~? ["misc."] 12. an ~ in futility ("an unsuccessful attempt") (see also **exercises**)

exercise II v. to ~ hard, strenuously, vigorously; regularly

exercised adj. ["upset"] 1. very ~ 2. to be; get ~ 3. ~ about, over (they got very ~ over the plan to close their local post-office)

exercises n. ["ceremony"] (esp. AE) 1. to attend; hold ~ 2. commencement, graduation ~

exertion n. physical; strenuous ~

exhausted adj. completely, totally; very ~ (from)

exhaustion n. 1. heat; nervous; total ~ 2. a state of ~

exhibit I n. ["exhibition"] (AE) 1. to have, hold, mount, organize, put on an ~ 2. to close; open an ~ 3. an art; photo; traveling ~ 4. on ~ ["piece of evidence shown in court"] (legal) 5. ~ A

exhibit II v. (B) she ~ed her paintings to the public

exhibition n. 1. to have, hold, mount, organize, put on an ~ 2. to close; launch, open an ~ 3. an art; international; photo; trade; traveling ~ (the ~ of contemporary art will run from June to October) 4. (esp. BE) on ~ 5. (misc.) to make an ~ of oneself (by behaving badly)

exhilarating adj. ~ to + inf. (it's ~ to climb mountains)

exhort v. 1. (D; tr.) to ~ to (to ~ smb. to action) 2. (H) to ~ students to work harder

exile I n. ["forced absence"] 1. to send smb. into ~ 2. to go into ~ 3. ~ from (her ~ from her homeland lasted many years) 4. from ~ (they have returned from ~) 5. in ~ (to live in ~) ["person forced to leave"] 6. a political; tax ~

exile II v. (D; tr.) to ~ from; to

exist v. (D; intr.) to ~ on (to ~ on bread and water)

existence n. 1. to have, lead a certain ~ (to lead a drab ~) 2. to eke out a (miserable) ~ 3. a drab, miserable; hand-to-mouth, precarious ~ 4. in; into; out of ~ (a way of life that came into ~ long ago but is rapidly going out of ~ now)

exit I n. 1. to make an/one's ~ (she made a hasty ~) 2. (in a plane) an emergency; tail; window; wing ~ 3. an emergency; fire ~ 4. an ~ from; to 5. at an ~ (she waited for me at the ~) 6. (misc.) the police sealed off the ~; no ~! USAGE NOTE: *Exit* is CE; however, BE often uses the notice *Way Out* to indicate the way to the exit.

exit II v. (D; intr.) to ~ from; to (to ~ (from) the system on a computer)

exodus n. 1. a mass ~ (there is a mass ~ from Paris every August) 2. an ~ from; to

exonerate v. (D; tr.) to ~ from

exorcise v. (D; tr.) to ~ from

expand v. 1. (D; tr.) ("to make larger") to ~ by (they ~ed the dictionary by twenty percent) 2. (D; intr., tr.) ("to become larger") ("to make larger") to ~ into (to ~ an idea from an article into a book) 3. (d; intr.) to ~ on, upon ("to explain in detail") (to ~ on a topic)

expanse n. a broad, vast, wide; open ~ (of) (a broad ~ of grassland stretched into the distance)

expatiate v. (formal) (d; intr.) to ~ on, upon ("to discuss in detail")

expatriate v. (formal) (D; tr.) to ~ from; to

expect v. 1. (D; tr.) to ~ from, of (we ~ed more from him) 2. (E) "does every man ~ to do his duty?" "yes, every man ~s to" 3. (H) England ~s every man to do his duty 4. (L) "England ~s every man will do his duty." – Lord Nelson at Trafalgar (1805) 5. (misc.) I ~ not; I ~ so; behavior that was only to be ~ed in the circumstances; such things happen when you least ~ them to

expectancy n. life ~

expectation n. 1. in ~ of 2. an ~ that + clause (it was our ~ that they would come early)

expectations n. 1. to come up to, live up to, meet ~ 2. to exceed, surpass ~ 3. to fall short of ~ 4. great, high ~ 5. ~ for (they had great ~ for their daughter) 6. beyond ~ (to succeed beyond all ~) 7. (misc.) contrary to ~ (contrary to all ~, she did not come); a revolution of rising ~

expedient adj. ~ to + inf. (sometimes it is ~ to make concessions)

expedition n. 1. to launch, mount, organize; lead; send an ~ 2. to go on an ~ 3. an archeological; scientific ~ 4. a hunting; mountain-climbing ~ 5. a military; punitive ~ 6. an ~ into, to (to lead an ~ to the Amazon) 7. (misc.) a fishing ~ ("an attempt to obtain information")

expel v. (D; tr.) to ~ from, for (to ~ a child from school for misbehavior)

expend v. (D; tr.) to ~ for, on (to ~ considerable funds on a new skating rink)

expenditure n. 1. to curb, curtail, cut down (on), reduce ~s 2. a capital ~ 3. public ~s 4. an item; level of ~ 5. an ~ for, on

expense n. 1. to incur, run up an ~ 2. to go to great ~; to put smb. to great ~ 3. to curb, curtail, cut down (on), reduce ~s 4. to spare no ~ (we spared no ~ to make the event a success) 5. to cover, defray ~s 6. to reimburse ~s 7. to share ~s 8. (a) business; entertainment; funeral; household; incidental; legal; living; operating; out-of-pocket; overhead; personal; tax-deductible; traveling ~(s) 9. at smb.'s ~ (at my ~; at government ~; at great ~, they sent their children to college) 10. (misc.) please take part in our conference – all ~s paid!

expense account n. 1. to be on, have an ~ 2. to pad an ~

expensive adj. ~ to + inf. (is it more ~ to live in the city than in the country?)

experience n. ["practice"] ["participation"] 1. to acquire, gain, gather, get ~ (from) 2. to have ~ (in) 3. broad, extensive, wide; direct, firsthand; hands-on; past, previous; practical; relevant ~ 4. an educational, learning ~ 5. the ~ to + inf. (they don't have enough ~ to do the job) 6. by, from ~ (to know from previous ~) ["adventure"] ["event"] 7. to have; share an ~ (I had quite an ~!) 8. a bitter, painful, terrible, traumatic, unpleasant ~ 9. a frightening, hair-raising, harrowing, terrifying, unnerving ~ 10. an enlightening, ennobling, rewarding; interesting; memorable, unforgettable; pleasant ~ 11. a common ~

experienced adj. 1. very ~ 2. ~ at, in

experiment I n. 1. to carry out, conduct, do, perform, run; replicate an ~ (on) 2. a control; controlled ~ 3. a chemistry; laboratory; physics; thought ~ 4. an ~ fails; succeeds; works 5. an ~ in (an ~ in communal living) 6. during; in an ~ 7. (misc.) The Story of my Experiments with Truth (1927) – M. K. Gandhi

experiment II v. (D; intr.) to ~ on, upon, with

expert I adj. ~ at, in

expert II n. 1. to call in, consult an ~ 2. an acknowledged, recognized ~ 3. a demolition; efficiency; foreign-policy; legal; self-styled; technical ~ 4. an ~ at, in, on (an ~ at troubleshooting; an ~ in computer science)

expertise n. 1. to display ~ 2. technical ~ 3. ~ in 4. the ~ to + inf. (does she have the ~ to do the job?)

expiration n. at, on the ~ (what will she do at the ~ of her term in office?)

explain v. 1. to ~ briefly; clearly; fully; satisfactorily 2. (B) she ~ed the problem to me 3. (L; to) he ~ed (to us) that the examination would take place later 4. (Q; to) he ~ed (to us) why the examination would take place later 5. (misc.) I can ~ (everything)!; let me ~

explanation n. 1. to give, offer, provide an ~ 2. to accept an ~ 3. to demand an ~ 4. to owe smb. an ~ 5. a brief, concise, simple, succinct; clear, lucid; convincing; rational; satisfactory; unsatisfactory ~ 6. an ~ for; of 7. an ~ that + clause (they accepted her ~ that she had been unavoidably detained) 8. (misc.) inconsistencies in your story that are in need of an ~

expletive n. ~ deleted

explicit adj. 1. sexually ~ 2. ~ about

explode v. (D; intr.) to ~ in, into; with (to ~ with rage)

exploit I n. 1. to perform an ~ 2. a daring; fantastic; heroic ~

exploit II v. to ~ ruthlessly

exploitation n. 1. commercial ~ 2. ruthless ~

exploration n. space; underwater ~ (we continued to carry out the underwater ~s that had been taking place here for several years)

explore v. 1. to ~ carefully, gingerly (they had to ~ this possibility very gingerly) 2. (D; intr., tr.)

to ~ for (we're ~ing this whole area for natural resources)

explorer *n.* a brave; intrepid ~

explosion *n.* 1. to set off, touch off, trigger an ~ 2. a deafening, loud; powerful; tremendous ~ 3. a nuclear ~ 4. a population ~ 5. an ~ ripped through the laboratory

explosive *n.* 1. to detonate; set off an ~ 2. to plant an ~ 3. to sniff out ~s 4. (a) high; plastic ~

exponent *n.* ["champion"] a leading ~ (a leading ~ of reform)

export I *n.* 1. a chief, leading, major ~ 2. an ~ from, to

export II *v.* (D; intr., tr.) to ~ from; to (we ~ to many countries; they ~ tractors from the West Coast to several Asian countries)

expose *v.* 1. (B) she ~d the plot to journalists 2. (D; tr.) to ~ as (she was ~d as an impostor) 3. (D; refl., tr.) to ~ to (to ~ smb. to danger; ~d to the elements)

exposition *n.* 1. to hold an ~ 2. an international, world ~

expostulate *v.* (formal) (D; intr.) ("to argue, expound") to ~ about, on; with

exposure *n.* ["being exposed"] 1. ~ to (~ to the elements) 2. of ~ (to die of ~) ["time during which film is exposed"] 3. a double; time ~ ["baring one's private parts"] 4. indecent ~ ["location in relation to the sun"] 5. a southern ~ (a house with a southern ~) ["publicity"] 6. media; wide ~

expound *v.* (formal) 1. (B) she ~ed her theory to her colleagues 2. (d; intr.) to ~ on (to ~ on one's favorite subject (to one's colleagues))

express I *n.* ["fast train"] 1. see **train I**, 3 ["special postal service"] (BE) 2. by ~ (to send a letter by ~)

express II *v.* 1. to ~ clearly; forcefully 2. (B) he ~ed his sympathy to the bereaved family 3. (BE) (D; tr.) ("to squeeze") (formal) to ~ from, out of (to ~ juice from an orange) 4. (D; refl., tr.) to ~ in (to ~ oneself in good English) 5. (Q) I/words cannot ~ (to you) how grateful I am!

expression *n.* ["making known"]["showing"] 1. to give ~ to (she tried to give ~ to her feelings) 2. to find ~ in (he finds ~ in his painting) ["phrase"] 3. a colloquial; common; elliptical; figurative; fixed; hackneyed, trite; idiomatic; old-fashioned; technical ~ ["look"] 4. an amused; happy; pleasant ~ 5. a blank; bored; deadpan ~ 6. a silly, vacuous ~ 7. a puzzled, quizzical ~ 8. a grim; grave, serious; intense ~ 9. an angry; pained ~ (she had a pained ~ on her face)

expressive *adj.* ~ of

expropriate *v.* (D; tr.) to ~ from (to ~ land from the absentee owners)

expulsion *n.* ~ for; from (he faces ~ from college for cheating)

expunge *v.* (D; tr.) to ~ from

expurgate *v.* (D; tr.) to ~ from

extend *v.* 1. (A) ("to convey") they ~ed a warm welcome to us; or: (esp. AE) they ~ed us a warm

welcome 2. (d; intr.) ("to reach") to ~ beyond (the forest ~s beyond the border) 3. (d; intr.) ("to reach") to ~ from; to (the border ~s to the river) 4. (D; tr.) ("to prolong") to ~ from; to (we ~ed the fence to the edge of our property) 5. (d; intr.) ("to continue") to ~ into (the cold wave ~ed into March) 6. (d; intr., tr.) ("to spread") to ~ over (their power ~s over the whole country) 7. (d; tr.) (she ~ed her hand to us in friendship) 8. (P; intr.) ("to stretch") (the plateau ~s (for) many miles

extension *n.* ["increase in time allowed"] 1. to grant an ~ 2. to ask for, request; get, receive an ~ ["branch"] (AE) 3. a university ~ ["misc."] 4. by ~ ("consequently")

extent *n.* 1. the full ~ (the full ~ of the damage) 2. to a certain ~ (to a greater or lesser ~; when did the Roman Empire reach its greatest ~?; they were emaciated to such an ~ that they required special treatment)

exterior *n.* a calm; forbidding, stern ~ (a soft heart under a stern ~)

extermination *n.* complete, total ~

external *adj.* ~ to (formal)

extinction *n.* to threaten with ~ (is the red squirrel threatened with ~?)

extinguisher *n.* (see **fire extinguisher**)

extol, extoll *v.* 1. to ~ to the skies 2. (D; tr.) to ~ as (they were ~ed as heroes)

extort *v.* (D; tr.) to ~ from (to ~ money from merchants)

extortion *n.* 1. to commit; practice ~ 2. to pay ~

extract I *n.* ["substance extracted"] 1. almond; lemon; vanilla ~ ["excerpt"] 2. an ~ from (an ~ from a book)

extract II *v.* (D; tr.) to ~ from (to ~ information from smb.)

extraction *n.* ["origin"] of a certain ~ (a family of Irish ~)

extradite *v.* (D; tr.) to ~ from; to

extradition *n.* 1. to ask for, request, seek (smb.'s) ~ (from; to) 2. to grant (smb.'s) ~ 3. to deny (smb.'s) ~ 4. to contest, fight, oppose ~ 5. to waive ~ ("to agree to be extradited")

extraneous *adj.* ~ to

extraordinary *adj.* ~ that + clause (it was ~ that no one reported the incident to the police)

extrapolate *v.* (D; intr., tr.) to ~ from, on the basis of

extravagance *n.* ~ in

extravagant *adj.* ~ in, with (~ in spending their father's money)

extreme *n.* 1. to go to an ~ (to go from one ~ to the other) 2. at an ~ (at the other/opposite ~) 3. in the ~ ("extremely") ("perplexed in the ~" – *Othello*, Shakespeare) 4. (misc.) to carry to an ~

extremist *n.* a political; religious ~

extremities *n.* ["limbs"] the lower; upper ~

extricate *v.* (D; refl., tr.) to ~ from (she ~d herself from a difficult situation)

extrinsic *adj.* (formal) ~ to

exuberance *n.* 1. sheer ~ 2. in; out of; with ~

exude *v.* (d; intr.) to ~ from

exult *v.* (D; intr.) to ~ at, in, over

exultation *n.* ~ at, in, over

eye *n.* ["organ of sight"] 1. to blink; close, shut; open; roll; squint one's ~s 2. to avert; drop, lower; lift, raise one's ~s 3. to rest; strain one's ~s 4. to clap (BE; colloq.), lay, set one's ~s on smt. ("to see smt.") 5. to keep one's ~s open, peeled, skinned (BE) ("to be watchful") 6. the naked ~ (the meteor could be seen with the naked ~ because it was visible to the naked ~) 7. bloodshot; bulging; glassy; sunken ~s 8. bright, clear ~s 9. ~s blaze; blink; dilate, widen; shine, sparkle; tear, water; twinkle 10. a pair of ~s 11. in smb.'s ~s (tears were in his ~s; fear could be seen in their ~s) ["vision, sight"] 12. good, strong; weak ~s 13. an eagle ~ ("keen sight") ["area around the eyes"] 14. (also fig.) a black ~ (to give smb. a black ~) ["look, glance"] 15. to cast an ~ on smt. ("Cast a cold ~ On life, on death." – W. B. Yeats, "Under Ben Bulben", 1938); to run one's ~ over smt.; to fix one's ~ on smt. 16. to take one's ~s off (they could not take their ~s off Hannah) 17. an anxious; critical; sharp, watchful, weather; suspicious ~ 18. a jaundiced ~ ("an envious, hostile look") 19. (of one who flirts) bedroom ("seductive") ~s; a roving, wandering ~ (he has a roving ~) 20. curious, prying; piercing ~s ["attention"] ["interest"] ["observation"] 21. to catch smb.'s ~ (we couldn't catch the waiter's ~ to order our meal) 22. to open smb.'s ~s (to the truth) 23. to close, shut one's ~s (to the truth); to turn a blind ~ to smt. ("to let smt. pass as if unnoticed") (the police turned a blind ~ to illegal gambling) 24. to have, keep an ~ on smt./smb. ("to keep smt./smb. under observation") 25. to have, keep an ~ out for smt. ("to watch for smt./smb. attentively") 26. the public ~ (to be constantly in the public ~) 27. with an ~ to (with an ~ to public opinion) ["judgment"] ["viewpoint"] 28. a good, keen ~ 29. an ~ for (she

has a good ~ for distances) 30. to the trained/untrained ~ 31. in smb.'s ~s (in the ~s of the law, she is innocent until proved guilty) ["perception"] ["appreciation"] 32. to open smb.'s ~s to smt. 33. an ~ for (an ~ for beauty; to have an ~ for a good bargain) ["device that detects"] 34. an electric ~ ["detective"] (colloq.) 35. a private ~ ["prosthesis for an eye"] 36. an artificial, glass ~ ["misc."] 37. an ~ for an ~ ("an equivalent retaliation"); to feast one's ~s on smt. ("to look at smt. with great pleasure"); to give smb. the ~ ("to flirt with smb.") or ("to give smb. a visual signal"); to make ~s at smb. ("to look lovingly at smb."); to see ~ to ~ with ("to agree with"); in one's mind's ~ ("in one's imagination or memory"); the evil ~ ("a look intended to inflict harm"); his ~ fell on a bargain ("he discovered a bargain"); under the teacher's watchful ~; easy on the ~s ("pretty"); more than meets the ~ ("more than is seen"); to look someone in the ~ ("to look at someone directly"); before one's very ~s; through smb. else's ~s; with one's own ~s (you have to believe me: I saw it with my own ~s!); without batting an ~ (AE) ("while remaining calm") (see also **eyelash, eyelid**; *as far as the eye can see* at **far**; *(in) the eye of a storm* at **storm I** *n.*)

eyebrow *n.* 1. to pluck, tweeze one's ~s 2. bushy, thick ~s 3. (misc.) to lift, raise an ~ ("to express one's surprise")

eyeglasses *n.* (AE: CE has *glasses*) a pair of ~

eyelash *n.* 1. to flutter one's ~s ("to flirt") 2. the lower; upper ~es 3. (misc.) without batting an ~ (AE) ("while remaining calm") (see **eye, eyelid** 3)

eyelid *n.* 1. drooping ~s 2. the lower; upper ~ 3. (misc.) without batting an ~ (esp. BE) ("while remaining calm") (see **eye, eyelash** 3)

eye shadow *n.* to apply, put on ~

eyesight *n.* deteriorating, failing, poor, weak; keen; perfect ~

eyeteeth *n.* to cut one's ~ on smt. ("to learn about smt. when young")

eyewitness *n.* an ~ to (there was an ~ to the crime)

F

fable *n.* a ~ about

fabric *n.* ["material"] 1. to weave a ~ 2. a cotton; rayon; silk; synthetic; woolen; wrinkle-free ~ 3. a length, piece, strip of ~ ["structure"] 4. a basic; social ~ (the basic ~ of the country)

fabrication *n.* a complete, outright, total ~; (a) pure ~

face I *n.* ["grimace"] 1. to make, pull (BE) a ~ (at) ["prestige"] 2. to save ~ 3. to lose ~ ["front part of the head"] 4. to press one's ~ (against a window) 5. (fig.) to show one's ~ (he didn't dare to show his ~) 6. to powder one's ~ 7. a beautiful, lovely, pretty; handsome; ruddy; ugly ~ 8. a hatchet; oval; round ~ 9. a familiar; strange ~ 10. (misc.) with a smile on one's ~; to come/meet ~ to ~; to bring ~ to ~; to look smb. in the ~; I would never say that to her ~; to laugh in smb.'s ~; ~ down ["expression"] 11. an angry; long; sad; serious ~ 12. a happy; funny ~ (to make a funny ~; to make, pull (BE) a long ~) 13. a poker, straight ~ (to keep a straight ~) 14. a ~ lights up (her face lit up) ["makeup"] (colloq.) 15. to put one's ~ on ["character"] 16. the changing ~ of the contemporary world ["misc."] 17. in the ~ of serious difficulties ("facing serious difficulties"); on the ~ of it ("judging by appearances"); to disappear from/off the ~ of the earth; to fly in the ~ of smt. ("to disregard, contradict"); to fall flat on one's ~ (usu. fig.); as plain as the nose on your ~ (see also *to stare smb. in the face* at **stare II** *v.*)

face II *v.* 1. to ~ squarely 2. (d; tr.) to ~ with (to ~ smb. with irrefutable evidence) 3. (G) I could not ~ going there alone 4. (P; intr.) to ~ east; to ~ towards the back of the room

face up *v.* (d; intr.) to ~ to (to ~ to reality)

facial *n.* 1. to do a ~ 2. to get, have a ~

facilitate *v.* (formal) 1. to ~ greatly 2. (K) their help will ~ our finishing the job on time

facilities *n.* ["installations"] 1. to provide ~ for 2. ample; excellent; modern; support ~ 3. outmoded; poor; run-down ~ 4. airport; port; public; storage; transportation (esp. AE), transport (esp. BE) ~ (our city has excellent port ~) 5. dining, eating; hotel; recreational ~ 6. daycare; educational; medical; public health; research ~ 7. ~ for

facility *n.* ["skill"] 1. a ~ for, in, with (to have a ~ for languages) ["installation"] 2. to operate a ~ 3. (AE) a correctional ~ ("a prison")

facsimile *n.* in ~

fact *n.* ["something that is true"] 1. to ascertain, establish a ~ 2. to check, confirm, verify a ~ 3. to cite, present; collect, gather, get, marshal (the) ~s 4. to classify; evaluate, explain, interpret (the) ~s 5. to face (the) ~s 6. to get one's ~s right/wrong; stick to the ~s 7. to distort, twist; embellish, embroider,

put a spin on (the) ~s 8. to ignore a ~ 9. an accepted, demonstrable, established; cold, dry, hard, incontestable, incontrovertible, indisputable, irrefutable, proven, undeniable, unquestionable; inconvenient, uncomfortable ~ 10. a basic, essential, pertinent; historical; little-known; statistical; (well-)known ~ 11. the bare ~s 12. a ~ that + clause ("the mere ~ that some officials are corrupt doesn't mean they all are!" "nevertheless, the ~ remains that some officials ARE corrupt!"; you have to face the ~ that he isn't coming) ["reality"] 13. to distinguish ~ from fiction 14. in ~, in actual ~, in point of ~ ["misc."] 15. a question of ~; the ~s of the case; the ~s of life; as a matter of ~; oh wow, is that a ~?!! USAGE NOTES: 1. "The fact (that)" is often used between a preposition and a clause: "Besides the fact that they had been lovers, what else connects the defendant with the victim?" "Despite the fact that they'd been lovers, there had been no contact between them for several years." "She's interested in the fact that he writes poetry." 2. "The fact that" is also used before a that-clause after a verb (such as *to face*) that doesn't occur in our pattern L: you have to face the fact that he isn't coming. 3. "In the fact that" is often heard nowadays where "in that" ("because") could be used: "*I'm lucky in the fact that I have a good job." That construction is wrong. The right construction is: "I'm lucky in that I have a good job."

faction *n.* a contending; extremist; opposing; rebel ~; warring ~s (within the country/party)

factor I *n.* 1. a contributing; critical, crucial, deciding, determining, essential, important, key, major; risk ~ (we must take account of several essential ~s) 2. (math. and fig.) a common ~ 3. (meteorology) a wind-chill ~ 4. a safety ~ (see also **safety factor**) 5. a genetic ~ 6. a ~ in

factor II *v.* (d; tr.) to ~ into (they ~ed the effects of taxation into their policy recommendations)

factory *n.* 1. to manage, operate, run a ~ 2. to open a ~ 3. to close, shut down a ~ 4. an automobile (AE) car; clothing; munitions; shoe; textile ~ 5. at, in a ~ (she works at/in a ~)

faculties *n.* ["capacities"] 1. smb.'s mental ~ 2. her ~ were failing 3. (misc.) in (full) possession of one's ~

faculty *n.* ["division of a university"] (esp. BE; CE has *school*) 1. a ~ of arts and sciences; education; law; medicine; science ["teaching staff"] (esp. AE; BE prefers *staff*) 2. on the ~ (she is on the ~) 3. a college, university; school ~ 4. the standing (AE), tenured ("permanent") ~ ["ability"] 5. a ~ for (a ~ for learning languages)

fad *n.* 1. the latest, newest ~ 2. a passing ~ 3. a ~ in

faddism *n.* food ~

fade *v.* 1. (d; intr.) (usu. fig.) to ~ from, out of (to ~ from the picture) 2. (d; intr.) to ~ into (to ~ into obscurity) 3. (misc.) (AE) to ~ in the stretch ("to drop out of contention near the end of a contest")

fag end *n.* (BE) (colloq.) ["tag end, tail end"] at the ~ (of smt.)

fail I *n.* without ~

fail II *v.* 1. to ~ completely; dismally, miserably 2. (D; intr.) to ~ in (to ~ in business) 3. (D; tr.) to ~ in, on (to ~ a student in/on an examination) 4. (E) she ~ed to comprehend the seriousness of the situation that the rest of us couldn't ~ to notice

failing *n.* 1. to have a ~ 2. a common ~ 3. smb.'s worst ~

failure *n.* 1. to experience ~ 2. an abject, complete, dismal, hopeless, ignominious, miserable, outright ~ 3. a box-office; business; crop ~ 4. kidney; respiratory ~ (see also **heart failure**) 5. an engine; mechanical; power ~ 6. a ~ to + inf. (her ~ to comprehend the seriousness of the situation; the ~ of the patient to respond to treatment was discouraging) 7. (misc.) doomed to ~; to end in ~

faint I *adj.* to feel ~ from (she felt ~ from lack of air)

faint II *n.* 1. to fall into a ~ 2. a dead ~ (to fall into a dead ~)

faint III *v.* (D; intr.) to ~ from (to ~ from loss of blood)

fair I *adj.* ["just"] 1. perfectly, scrupulously ~ 2. ~ to, with (he's ~ to his employees) 3. ~ to + inf. (it's ~ to say that she deserved the promotion; it was not ~ to take advantage of the situation) 4. ~ that + clause (it's only ~ that she got the promotion; it's not ~ that she has to work so hard) ["of medium quality"] 5. ~ at, in (she's ~ at mathematics) 6. (misc.) ~ to middling ("not too bad"); to be ~ (to be ~ (to her), we should give her another chance)

fair II *n.* 1. to hold, host; organize; stage a ~ 2. an annual; book; county ~; funfair (BE); health; livestock; state (US); trade; world's ~ (the annual ~ takes place in July) (see also **funfair**)

fairness *n.* 1. ~ in (we expect ~ in their judgment to be guaranteed) 2. in ~ to (in (all) ~ to her, we should give her another chance)

faith *n.* ["firm belief, trust"] 1. to have ~ (in); to place, put one's ~ in 2. to lose ~ (in) 3. to shake; test smb.'s ~ (in) 4. (an) abiding, enduring, steadfast; blind; deep, strong, unshakable; implicit; saving; simple ~ 5. on ~ (to accept on ~) ["fidelity to one's promises"] 6. to break; keep ~ with 7. to demonstrate, show good ~ 8. in good ~; in bad ~ (she acted in good ~) ["religion"] 9. to adhere to, practice a ~ 10. to abjure, recant, renounce one's ~ 11. the true ~ (brought up in the true ~) 12. by ~ (she is a Buddhist by ~) 13. (misc.) an article of ~; a leap of ~ (it's an article of ~ for her that if you are nice to people they'll be nice to you – but for me that belief would require a leap of ~)

faithful I *adj.* ~ in; to ("I have been ~ to thee, Cynara! in my fashion" – Ernest Dowson (1867–1900), "Non Sum Qualis Eram ...")

faithful II *n.* (plural) the party ~

faithfulness *n.* ~ to

fake *v.* (esp. AE) (usu. sports) (d; tr.) to ~ out of (to ~ an opposing player out of position)

fall I *n.* ["dropping, coming down"] 1. to have, take a ~ 2. to break a ~ 3. a bad, nasty ~ (she had a bad ~ and broke her ankle) 4. a free ~ (of a parachutist) 5. a sharp, steep; sudden ~ 6. a ~ from (a ~ from a horse; a ~ from grace) 7. a ~ in, of (a sudden ~ in prices; a sudden ~ of snow = a sudden snowfall) 8. (misc.) *The History of the Decline and Fall of the Roman Empire* (1776–88) – Edward Gibbon ["autumn"] (AE) 9. early; last; late; next ~ 10. during the, in (the) ~ (we met late in the ~ of 1995 = we met in the late ~ of 1995) 11. (misc.) there is a touch of ~ in the air; a harbinger of ~

fall II *v.* 1. ("to drop") to ~ flat, headlong; short 2. (d; intr.) to ~ behind ("to lag") (to ~ behind the others) 3. (D; intr.) ("to drop") to ~ down (to ~ down the stairs) 4. (d; intr.) to ~ for ("to be tricked") (we fell for their sales pitch) 5. (colloq.) (d; intr.) to ~ for ("to become infatuated with") (he fell for her) 6. (D; intr.) ("to drop") to ~ from (to ~ from a tree; to ~ from grace) 7. (d; intr.) ("to come"); ("to drop") to ~ into (to ~ into disfavor; to ~ into disrepute; to ~ into place; to ~ into a trap) 8. (d; intr.) ("to be divided") to ~ into (to ~ into three categories) 9. (D; intr.) ("to drop") to ~ off (to ~ off a table) 10. (D; intr.) ("to drop") to ~ on (to ~ on one's back; the stress ~s on the last syllable) (also fig,) (formal) (the responsibility fell on us; it fell on me to break the news) 11. (d; intr.) ("to come") to ~ on (the holiday fell on a Monday) 12. (d; intr.) to ~ on ("to attack") (the soldiers fell on the refugees and killed them) 13. (d; intr.) ("to drop") to ~ out of (to ~ out of bed; to ~ out of favor) 14. (d; intr.) ("to drop") to ~ over (she fell over the side of the ship) 15. (D; intr.) ("to drop") to ~ through (to ~ through a hole in the ice) 16. (formal) (d; intr.) ("to devolve") to ~ to (the responsibility fell to us; it fell to me to break the news) 17. (D; intr.) ("to drop") to ~ to (he fell to his knees; the book fell to the floor; her voice fell to a whisper) (also fig.) (formal) (he fell to brooding) 18. (D; intr.) ("to be defeated") to ~ to (the city fell to the enemy) 19. (d; intr.) ("to drop") ("to come") to ~ under (to ~ under a train; to ~ under smb.'s influence; facts that ~ under three categories) 20. (S) to ~ due; to ~ silent; she fell ill; she fell pregnant (BE); we fell victim to their sales pitch 21. (misc.) to ~ afoul (AE)/foul of the law; to ~ apart; to ~ asleep; to ~ below (temperatures that can ~ below zero); to ~ in love with smb.; to ~ in battle; to ~ on hard times; to ~ outside (matters that ~ outside (of) our jurisdiction); to ~ to pieces; to ~ into step; to ~ through the cracks ("to be neglected through error or omission") (see also *fall on deaf ears* at **deaf** and at **ear**)

fallacious *adj.* (formal) ~ to + inf. (it's ~ to assume that all politicians are corrupt)

fallacy *n.* 1. a ~ to + inf. (it's a ~ to assume that all politicians are corrupt) 2. a ~ that (it's a ~ that all politicians are corrupt)

fall back *v.* 1. (D; intr.) to ~ into (to ~ into an easy chair) 2. (D; intr.) to ~ on, to (the troops fell back to their defensive positions; when challenged, he fell back on the same old excuses)

fall behind *v.* (D; intr.) to ~ in, with (to ~ with the rent)

fall down *v.* to ~ on the job

fall in *v.* 1. (d; intr.) to ~ with ("to join") (to ~ with the wrong crowd) 2. (d; intr.) to ~ with ("to agree") (she fell in with their suggestion)

falling out *n.* (colloq.) ["quarrel"] to have a ~ with

fallout *n.* 1. radioactive ~ 2. ~ from (also fig.)

fall out *v.* 1. (D; intr.) ("to quarrel") to ~ with (to ~ with smb.) 2. (misc.) the platoon fell out on the company street

fallow *adj.* ["uncultivated"] to lie ~ (the field lay ~)

false *adj.* 1. to ring ~ 2. a ~ to + inf. (it's ~ to assume that all politicians are corrupt) 3. a ~ that (it's just plain ~ that all politicians are corrupt!)

false front *n.* ["deceptive manner"] to put up a ~

falsehood *n.* 1. to tell, utter a ~ 2. an absolute, downright, utter ~

falsetto *n.* to sing ~

falter *v.* (D; intr.) to ~ in (to ~ in one's determination)

fame *n.* 1. to achieve, attain, win; enjoy ~ 2. to seek ~ 3. international; national; undying ~ (Shakespeare's undying ~ rests on his plays) 4. (misc.) a claim to ~; at the height of one's ~; ~ and fortune

familiar *adj.* ["known"] 1. ~ to (is this area ~ to you?) 2. (misc.) all too; eerily; strangely ~ (the area seemed strangely ~ to me even though I'd never been there before) ["acquainted"] 3. thoroughly ~ 4. ~ with (are you ~ with this area?; are you ~ with the details?)

familiarity *n.* 1. to demonstrate, display, show ~ (with) 2. thorough ~ 3. ~ to; with (the area's ~ to me = my ~ with the area) 4. (misc.) ~ breeds contempt

familiarize *v.* (d; refl., tr.) to ~ with (she had to ~ herself with the facts of the case)

family *n.* ["social unit traditionally consisting of parents and children"] 1. to start a ~ 2. to bring up, raise, rear; clothe; feed; support a ~ 3. the close, immediate; extended; nuclear ~ 4. a good ("respected") ~ (she comes from a good ~) 5. a blended; dysfunctional; single-parent; two-income ~ 6. the royal ~ 7. the head of a ~; a member of a ~ 8. in the ~ (poor vision runs in the ~) 9. (misc.) ~ planning ("birth control"); (old-fashioned) in the ~ way ("pregnant") ["group of related languages"] 10. a language ~

family style *adv.* (esp. AE) to serve (a meal) ~

famine *n.* 1. widespread ~ 2. ~ strikes (~ struck several provinces) 3. (misc.) a potato ~

famous *adj.* 1. ~ as (he is ~ internationally as an actor) 2. ~ for (the city is world ~ for its museums) 3. (misc.) some celebrities are ~ just for being ~; gossip about the rich and ~

fan I *n.* ["electrical device for cooling"] 1. to turn on; turn off a ~ 2. a ceiling; electric; exhaust (AE), extractor (BE) ~ ["paper or cloth fan"] 3. to wave a ~

fan II *n.* ["admirer"] ["supporter"] 1. an ardent, avid ~ 2. (AE) a ~ roots (for a team) USAGE NOTE: In CE one can be a *fan* of a certain sport – a football fan. In CE one can also be a fan of a certain team – a Dodger fan, Manchester United fan. In BE, however, one would typically be called a *supporter* of a club and would be more likely to *support* one's favourite club than *root for* it.

fanatic *n.* 1. a dangerous; real ~ 2. a fitness, keep-fit; religious; sports ~ 3. (misc.) he had to be a ~ (in order) to do that!

fancy I *n.* 1. to take a ~ to 2. to catch, strike, take (BE), tickle smb.'s ~ 3. a passing ~ 4. a flight of ~

fancy II *v.* 1. (d; tr.) ("to like") to ~ as (I don't ~ him as an actor) 2. (G) ("to like") I don't ~ going there 3. (G) ("to imagine") just ~ winning first prize! 4. (L) ("to imagine") she ~cied that she heard footsteps 5. (N) (BE) ("to imagine") when she was young she ~cied herself a great actress

fanfare *n.* 1. to sound a ~ 2. with great ~

fangs *n.* an animal bares its ~

fan out *v.* to ~ in all directions

fantasize *v.* 1. (D; intr.) to ~ about (when young she would ~ about becoming a great actress) 2. (L) when young she would ~ that some day she would become a great actress

fantastic *adj.* ["very good"] (colloq.) ~ to + inf. (it's ~ to work with them = it's ~ working with them = they're absolutely the most ~ people to work with!)

fantasy *n.* 1. to act out a ~ 2. to indulge in a ~ 3. a childhood; sexual ~ 4. a ~ about (when young she had/harbored a ~ about becoming a great actress) 5. a ~ that + clause (when young she had/harbored the ~ that some day she would become a great actress) 6. (misc.) (to live in) a world of ~/a ~ world

far *adj., adv.* 1. ~ from (~ from the city; the problem is ~ from being solved) 2. by ~, ~ and away (she is by ~ the better player) 3. (misc.) as ~ as the eye can see; ~ away; ~ beyond; ~ into (the future); ~ and wide; so ~ so good; to go ~ on one's connections; ~ be it from me to criticize, but… USAGE NOTES: 1. The phrases *by far* and *far and away* mean "very much" – she is by far/far and away the better player. In nonstandard BE the two phrases can be blended to produce *by far and away* – ??she is by far and away the better player. 2. *By far* can go either before or after the phrase it modifies – she is by far the better player = she is the better player by far. *Far and away* and the BE nonstandard ??*by far and away* can go only before the phrase they modify – she is far and away the better player.

farce *n.* 1. a ~ about 2. a ~ to + inf. (it was a complete ~ to conduct a trial in such conditions! = it was a complete ~ conducting a trial in such conditions!)

farcical *adj.* ~ to + inf. (it was completely ~ to

conduct a trial in such conditions! = it was completely ~ conducting a trial in such conditions!)

fare I *n.* ["payment for transportation"] 1. to charge; pay a ~ 2. a full; half; reduced ~ 3. (AE) carfare (she gambled away most of her money and was left with just the/her ~ home) 4. at a ~ (at a reduced ~) ["food"] 5. simple, wholesome ~ 6. a bill of ~ ("a menu")

fare II *v.* (formal) (P; intr.) she ~d well in the big city

farewell *n.* 1. to make one's ~s 2. an emotional; fond; sad; tearful ~ 3. a ~ to (she blew them a kiss in ~; to say/wave ~ to one's friends and neighbors) (see also *to bid smb. farewell* at **bid III**) USAGE NOTE: As a formula of leave-taking, *Farewell* has been more or less replaced by *Goodbye*.

farm *n.* 1. to manage, operate, run, work a ~ 2. a chicken, dairy; fish; poultry; sheep; stock; stud; truck (AE) ~ (BE has *market garden* where AE has *truck farm*) 3. a city; collective; cooperative; private; working ~ 4. on a ~ (to work on a ~) 5. (misc.) "How you gonna keep them down on the ~, after they've seen Paree [?]" – song by Young, Lewis, & Donaldson

farmer *n.* a dirt (AE); gentleman; tenant ~

farming *n.* 1. to be engaged in, to be in; to work in ~ 2. chicken; dairy; fish; poultry; sheep; stock ~; truck ~ (AE; BE has *market gardening*) 3. collective; cooperative ~ 4. subsistence ~

farmland *n.* to cultivate, work ~

farm out *v.* (D; tr.) to ~ to (the work was ~ed out to several sub-contractors)

farsighted *adj.* ~ to + inf. (it was ~ of them to provide for their old age)

farsightedness *n.* the ~ to + inf. (they had enough ~ to provide for their old age)

fascinated *adj.* 1. ~ at, by, with (~ at the spectacle of a rocket launching; ~ by the work they do) 2. ~ to + inf. (I was ~ to learn of their work)

fascinating *adj.* 1. endlessly ~ 2. ~ to + inf. (it's ~ to work with them = it's ~ working with them = they're absolutely the most ~ people to work with!) 3. ~ that + clause (it's ~ (to me) that migratory birds never get lost)

fascination *n.* 1. to have, hold a ~ for (the Himalayas have/hold a special ~ for climbers) 2. a morbid; special ~ 3. ~ at, over, with (climbers have a special ~ with the Himalayas)

fashion I *n.* ["vogue"] 1. to set a ~ 2. to come into ~; to go out of ~ (big hats have gone out of ~) 3. contemporary, current ~(s); the height of ~; the latest ~(s) (big hats are no longer the height of ~) 4. high ~ 5. a ~ in (~s in hats change constantly) 6. in ~ (big hats are no longer in ~) 7. out of ~ 8. a (dedicated) follower of, a slave of ~ ["manner"] 9. after a ~ ("in a way, up to a point") (though they'd quarreled they stayed friends after a ~ – but were no longer close friends) 10. in a ~ (she behaved in a strange ~; "I have been faithful to thee, Cynara! in

my ~" – Ernest Dowson (1867–1900), "Non Sum Qualis Eram ...")

fashion II *v.* 1. (D; tr.) to ~ from, out of (to ~ a pipe out of clay) 2. (d; tr.) to ~ into (to ~ clay into a pipe)

fashionable *adj.* 1. among, with (is recycling now very ~ among the young?) 2. ~ to + inf. (is it now very ~ (for young people) to recycle?)

fast I *adv., adj.* 1. to hold ~ to (they held ~ to their beliefs) 2. to stand ~

fast II *n.* 1. to go on; keep, observe a ~ 2. to break a ~

fasten *v.* 1. to ~ loosely; securely; tightly; together (to ~ two signs together securely) 2. (N; used with an adjective) to ~ a box shut; to ~ smt. tight 3. (P) to ~ a sign on/onto/to a wall with tape/by taping it there; to ~ a corsage to a lapel; to ~ one's hair (with a clip)

fastidious *adj.* ~ about, when it comes to (~ about one's appearance)

fast one *n.* (colloq.) ["trick"] to pull a ~ (on)

fast-talk *v.* (colloq.) (D; intr. tr.) to ~ into; out of (to ~ smb. into doing smt.; to ~ one's way oit of trouble)

fat I *adj.* (misc.) as ~ as a pig

fat II *n.* 1. to skim off; trim (away) the ~ 2. animal; vegetable ~ 3. polyunsaturated; saturated ~ 4. deep; excess ~ (to fry in deep ~) 5. subcutaneous ~ 6. (misc.) (colloq.) to live off the ~ of the land ("to live very well"); to chew the ~ ("to chat")

fatal *adj.* 1. ~ for, to (that hesitation was ~ to his career) 2. ~ to + inf. (it proved ~ for him to hesitate)

fatalities *n.* 1. to cause ~ 2. highway (AE), motorway (BE), traffic ~

fate *n.* 1. to decide, seal smb.'s ~ 2. to tempt ~ 3. to meet; share, suffer a ~ (they both shared/suffered a similar ~) 4. (a) bitter, cruel ~ (abandoned to a cruel ~) 5. blind, inexorable ~ 6. a quirk, stroke, twist of ~ 7. ~ to + inf. (it was our ~ never to meet again) 8. (misc.) ~ decreed that we would win the lottery; a cruel ~ befell them; would it be a ~ worse than death not to wear the latest fashions?

fated *adj.* (formal) 1. ~ to + inf. (they were ~ never to meet) 2. ~ that + clause (it was ~ that they should/would never meet again)

father *n.* 1. an expectant (AE); proud ~ 2. an adoptive; biological; foster; grandfather; lone (BE), single ~; stepfather 3. a father-in-law 4. a ~ to (he was like a ~ to them) 5. (misc.) the city ~s; a founding ~; the Founding Fathers; the Pilgrim Fathers (see also *father figure* at **figure**)

fatigue *n.* 1. to feel ~ 2. battle, combat; mental ~ 3. metal ~ 4. ~ dissipates, lifts; sets in 5. a state of ~ (she was in a state of complete ~)

faucet *n.* (AE) 1. to turn on a ~ 2. to turn off a ~ 3. a ~ drips, leaks 4. a leaky ~ 5. a cold-water; hot-water ~ (CE has *tap*)

fault I *n.* 1. to find ~ with 2. to correct a ~ (to correct a ~ in the system) 3. to overlook smb.'s ~s 4.

a grievous; human ~ (see also **double fault**; **foot fault**) 5. a ~ that + clause (it was not my ~ that he was late; don't blame me: it was your own ~ that you failed) 6. at ~ (we were all at ~) 7. through smb.'s ~ (let us help those who through no ~ of their own cannot help themselves) 8. to a ~ (she is fastidious to a ~) 9. (misc.) for, with all smb.'s ~s ("With all your ~s, I love you still" – "It Had To Be You" (1924), song by Jones & Kahn)

fault II v. (D; tr.) ("to blame") to ~ for

fauna n. flora and ~ ("plants and animals")

faux pas n. 1. to commit, make a ~ 2. a grave, serious ~

favor II favour n. ["friendly act, service"] 1. to do, grant (smb.) a ~ 2. to perform a ~ (for smb.) 3. to owe; return a ~ 4. a special ~ ["approval"] ["liking"] 5. to win smb.'s ~ 6. to curry ~ with 7. to vie for smb.'s ~ 8. to find, gain ~ with; to find ~ in smb.'s eyes 9. to lose ~ 10. universal ~ 11. in ~ with 12. out of ~ (with) (to fall out of ~) 13. to look with ~ on smt. ["support"] 14. to come out in ~ of 15. in ~ of (these facts speak in ~ of his acquittal; he is strongly in ~ of raising taxes) 16. in smb.'s ~ (the odds are in her ~) (see also **favors**)

favor II favour v. 1. (D; tr.) to ~ smb. over smb. else 2. (formal) (D; tr.) to ~ with (she will now ~ us with a song) 3. (G) he strongly ~s raising taxes

favorable, favourable adj. ~ for, to

favored, favoured adj. heavily ~ 2. ~ to + inf. (our team is heavily ~ to win)

favorite, favourite n. 1. a heavy, hot, strong; odds-on ~ 2. a ~ with 3. to play ~s

favoritism, favouritism n. 1. to show ~ 2. strong ~

favors, favours n. ["small gifts"] 1. party ~ ["sexual privileges"] 2. to grant one's ~ to smb.; to bestow one's ~s on

fawn v. (d; intr.) to ~ on, over

fax I n. 1. to send a ~ (to) 2. to get, receive a ~ (from) 3. by ~ (to send a document by ~)

fax II v. 1. (A) they ~ed the document to us; or: they ~ed us the document 2. (D; tr.) to ~ about (they ~ed us about the meeting) 3. (d; intr., tr.) to ~ for (we ~ed for immediate delivery) 4. (H) we ~ed them to return home immediately 5. (L; may have an object) she ~ed (us) that the manuscript had been received 6. (Q; may have an object) they ~ed (us) where to meet

faze v. (L; must have an object) it did not ~ me at all that she declined the offer

fear I n. 1. to arouse, instill, kindle ~ 2. to express; feel; show ~ (she felt ~ for their safety) 3. to confirm smb.'s (worst) ~s 4. to allay, calm, dispel ~ 5. to overcome ~ (he finally overcame his ~ of snakes) 6. (a) grave, mortal, strong; groundless; growing, increasing, mounting; idle; inarticulate; lingering; morbid; sudden; well-founded ~ (he was paralysed with groundless ~s; the news came amid mounting ~s that the pound was weakening against the euro) 7. ~ that + clause (there are ~s that

no compromise can be worked out) 8. for ~ of (he lied for ~ of being punished) 9. in ~ of (he is in ~ of his life) 10. out of ~ (he did it out of ~) 11. (misc.) to strike ~ into smb.'s heart; ~ and loathing (the very idea of work fills him with ~ and loathing); ~ and trepidation (the very idea of work fills him with ~ and trepidation); a cry of ~

fear II v. 1. to ~ greatly, very much; rightly 2. (d; intr.) to ~ for (she ~ed for their safety) 3. (E) I ~ to think what may happen 4. (K) he ~s my getting involved 5. (L) we ~ that we will not be able to attend

fearful adj. 1. ~ of 2. ~ that + clause (they were ~ that the river would flood)

feasibility n. 1. commercial, financial; technical ~ 2. the ~ of (we're looking into the technical ~ of building a bridge at that point)

feasible adj. ~ to + inf. (it was not technically ~ to build a bridge at that point)

feast I n. 1. to give; have a ~ 2. a royal, sumptuous; wedding ~

feast II v. (formal) (D; intr., tr.) to ~ on, upon (to ~ on steak and potatoes; to ~ one's eyes on beautiful scenery)

feat n. 1. to accomplish, perform, pull off (colloq.) a ~ 2. a brave, heroic; brilliant, notable, noteworthy, outstanding, remarkable ~ (to perform a remarkable ~) 3. no mean, no small ~ (it was no mean ~ to get him to agree = it was no mean ~ getting him to agree)

feather n. 1. to pluck ~s (from a chicken) 2. (misc.) as light as a ~ ("very light"); a ~ in smb.'s cap ("a symbol of accomplishment"); to smooth smb.'s ruffled ~s ("to calm smb.") (see also **white feather**)

feature I n. ["quality"] 1. a characteristic, distinctive, distinguishing; notable; noteworthy, salient; special; typical ~ 2. a redeeming ~ ["contour"] ["line"] 3. aquiline; coarse; facial; physical; prominent; sharp; striking ~s 4. delicate, fine; regular; soft ~s ["main film"] 5. a double ~ ("a program consisting of two films in a movie theater") ["special item"] 6. an optional ~ (we chose several optional ~s for our new car)

feature II v. (D; tr.) to ~ as (she was ~d as a dancer)

federation v. (D; intr., tr.) to ~ into; with

federation n. 1. to enter, join; form a ~ 2. a loose, weak ~ 3. a ~ breaks up, dissolves; forms 4. a ~ among, between; with 5. in a ~

fed up adj. ~ about, of (BE), with

fee n. 1. to charge a ~ 2. to accept; offer; pay; receive a ~ 3. to split ~s (as of lawyers, doctors) 4. to waive one's ~ 5. a fat, large; flat; nominal ~ 6. an administrative; admission, entrance; contingency; laboratory; membership; registration ~ 7. a ~ for (a ~ for service) 8. for a ~ (for a nominal ~) 9. (misc.) fee-paying (esp. BE) (go to a private ~ school rather than a state school)

feed *v.* 1. (A) they fed erroneous information to us; or: they fed us erroneous information 2. (d; tr.) to ~ into, to (to ~ data into a computer) 3. (D; intr., tr.) to ~ on (horses ~ on oats and hay; farmers ~ horses on oats and hay) 4. (d; tr.) to ~ with (they fed us with erroneous information)

feedback *n.* 1. to give, provide ~ 2. to get, receive ~ 3. ~ from (we welcome ~ from our customers) 4. negative; positive ~ 5. ~ concerning, on

feeding   *n.*   breast;   communal;   forced; intravenous ~

feel I *n.* 1. (colloq.) to have a (good) ~ for (she has a good ~ for sincerity in other people) 2. to have a ~ of (just have a ~ of this fabric!) 3. to get the ~ of (the new car) 4. I like the ~ of (this fabric)

feel II *v.* 1. ("to believe") ("to experience") to ~ deeply, keenly, strongly 2. (D; intr.) ("to have an opinion") to ~ about (how do you ~ about this problem?) 3. (d; intr.) ("to grope") to ~ (around) for (he felt around in his pockets for his keys) 4. (colloq.) (d; intr.) to ~ for ("to sympathize with") (I really ~ for them) 5. (D; tr.) ("to experience") to ~ for (to ~ pity for smb.) 6. (I) ("to sense") he could ~ his heart beat = his heart could be felt to beat 7. (J) ("to sense") he could ~ his heart beating = his heart could be felt beating 8. (L) ("to believe") we ~ that you should return home 9. (Q) I could not ~ where the swelling was 10. (s) to ~ comfortable; I ~ cheated; I ~ foolish; to ~ sorry about smt.; to ~ good ("happy"); to ~ fine/well ("healthy"); to ~ happy; to ~ bad ("unwell") or ("sad"); to ~ unhappy 11. (BE) (S) I ~ such a fool 12. (misc.) it ~s good to be on vacation; it felt nice to swim in the heated pool; she felt proud of her children; to ~ bad/badly ("sad") or ("guilty") about smt.; (esp. BE) I ~ rather poorly today; to ~ up to ("to feel capable of") (do you ~ up to a drive to town?) (see also **feel like**)

feeler *n.* ["probe"] to put out, throw out a ~ (to)

feeling *n.* ["emotional reaction"] 1. to arouse, inspire, stir up ~ (he aroused deep ~s in his audience when he played the music with such great ~) ["appreciation"] 2. to develop; have a ~ for (to develop a ~ for classical music) ["sentiment"] ["sensation"] 3. to express; show; vent one's ~s 4. to experience, have a ~ (some music gives me a ~ of peace that I experience every time I hear it) 5. to harbor, have ~s (to harbor warm ~s of friendship towards smb.; although they've split up, he still has ~s for her) 6. to bottle up, repress, suppress; conceal, hide, mask one's ~s 7. to lose ~ (he lost all ~ in his foot) 8. a deep, strong; eery, strange; friendly, tender, warm; gloomy, sad; hostile; indescribable; intangible; intense; gnawing; pleasant; queasy; satisfied; sick; sinking; sneaking; uneasy; unpleasant ~ (I had an unpleasant ~ in my foot) 9. (colloq.) a gut ("instinctive") ~ 10. smb.'s innermost, intimate; pent-up ~s 11. bad, hard, ill ~s ("feelings of anger or resentment") (we have no hard ~s towards you

about it: there are no hard ~s between us) (see also **ill feeling**) 12. a ~ that + clause (I had an eery ~ that I had been there before) ["attitude"] ["opinion"] 13. definite; strong ~s (we have strong ~s about this matter) 14. popular ~ (popular ~ was running high against the president) 15. ~s about, on (to have definite ~s on a subject) ["sensitivity"] 16. to hurt; spare smb.'s ~s 17. delicate, sensitive ~s ["premonition"] 18. a ~ that + clause (I had an eery ~ that I would be there again)

feel like *v.* 1. (G) she ~s like resting 2. (S; used only with nouns) to ~ a fool; it ~s like satin; it ~s like rain 3. (misc.) (esp. AE) it ~s like it's going to rain (= it feels as if/as though it's going to rain); we ~ like you should return home

feint *n.* 1. to make a ~ 2. a ~ to (the right)

fellow *n.* ["scholar"] ["fellowship holder"] 1. an honorary; research; senior; teaching ~ ["man"] 2. a fine, good; honest; nice, regular (AE); young ~

fellowship *n.* ["stipend; support for studies"] 1. to award, grant; establish a ~ 2. to apply for; to receive, win a ~ 3. a graduate, postgraduate (esp. BE); postdoctoral ~ ["community of interest"] 4. to foster, promote (good) ~ 5. to enjoy good ~ 6. close, strong, warm ~ 7. ~ with 8. a sense of ~

felony *n.* 1. to commit, perpetrate a ~ 2. to compound a ~ ("to waive prosecution in return for compensation")

feminist *n.* an ardent, dedicated; militant; moderate; radical ~

fence I *n.* 1. to build, erect, put up a ~ 2. a high; low ~ 3. a barbed-wire; chain-link; picket; rail; snow; wooden; wrought-iron ~ (we spoke over/across the picket ~ between our properties) (see also **political fences**) 4. a ~ around; between 5. (misc.) to mend ~s ("to set things right"); on the ~ ("uncommitted"); to straddle the ~ ("to be uncommitted")

fence II *v.* (d; intr.) ("to vie") to ~ for (the drivers were ~cing (with each other) for position)

fence off *v.* (D; tr.) to ~ from (the yard was ~d off from the street)

fend *v.* to ~ for oneself (when she walked out he was left to ~ for himself)

fender *n.* (AE) a dented ~ (BE has *wing*)

ferment *n.* 1. intellectual; political; social ~ 2. in ~ (the country was in (a state of) ~)

ferry I *n.* 1. to board; take a ~ 2. by ~ (to cross a river by ~)

ferry II *v.* 1. (d; tr.) to ~ across (to ~ troops across a river) 2. (P; tr.) we have to ~ the children to and from school

fertilization *n.* in-vitro ~

fertilizer *n.* 1. to spread ~ 2. artificial; chemical; natural ~

fervor, fervour *n.* 1. great ~ 2. evangelical; messianic; patriotic; religious ~ 3. for; with ~ (she spoke with the great ~ for the cause that she always showed)

festival *n.* 1. to hold a ~ 2. a dance; drama; film; folk; harvest; music; religious ~ (we met at/during the music ~ that takes place every summer)

festoon *v.* (D; tr.) to ~ with (the hall was ~ed with lights)

fetch *v.* (C) please ~ my pipe for me; or: please ~ me my pipe

fete *n.* (esp. BE) 1. to hold a ~ 2. a church; village ~ (we met at/during the village ~ that takes place every summer)

fetish *n.* 1. to make a ~ of smt. (they made a ~ of good grooming) 2. (esp. BE) to have a ~ about (smt.)

fettle *n.* they were in fine ~

fetus, foetus *n.* 1. to abort a ~ 2. a human; viable ~ 3. a ~ develops

feud I *n.* 1. to stir up a ~ 2. a bitter, deadly, internecine ~ 3. a blood; family; personal ~ 4. a ~ between, with 5. a ~ about, over

feud II *v.* (D; intr.) to ~ about, over; with (the Montagues and the Capulets finally agreed to settle their ~ with each other)

fever *n.* ["elevated temperature of the body"] 1. to catch, contract, come down with, develop, get; go down with (BE) a ~ (he's in bed with a bout of the recurrent ~ he developed some time ago) 2. to have, run a ~ 3. a burning; constant; high; intermittent; mild, slight; recurrent; remittent, remitting ~ 4. a ~ breaks, subsides ["disease or condition"] 5. glandular (CE also has *mononucleosis*); hay; relapsing; rheumatic; Rocky Mountain spotted; trench; typhoid; undulant; yellow ~ (see also **scarlet fever**)

few I *determiner, pronoun* 1. comparatively, relatively ~ (we saw relatively ~ of them) 2. ~ in number 3. a ~, a fair ~ (BE), a good ~, quite a ~ of (we saw a ~ of them) 4. (misc.) ~ if any of (many people came of whom we knew ~ if any) USAGE NOTE: The use of the preposition *of* is necessary when a pronoun follows: we saw few of them – and the ~ (of them) that we saw we didn't recognize! As for nouns, compare the following constructions – we saw very few (of the) students ("we didn't see many students"); we saw (only) a few ("several") (of the) students; we saw quite a few students; we saw quite a few of the students.

few II *n.* 1. (a) precious, very ~ 2. a fair ~ (BE), a good ~, quite a ~ 3. (misc.) to have a ~ too many ("to drink too much"); ~ and far between ("rare"); just a ~, only a ~; ~ if any (many people came: we knew ~ if any)

fewer I *determiner, pronoun* 1. ~ in number 2. ~ of (we saw ~ of them than we expected to)

fewer II *n., adv.* no ~ than (we saw no ~ than 80% of them)

fiasco *n.* 1. to end in a ~ 2. a complete, total, utter ~

fib *n.* to tell a ~

fiber, fibre *n.* 1. artificial, synthetic; coarse; cotton; dietary; rayon; wool ~ 2. optical ~ (for the electronic transmission of information) 3. nerve ~ (see also **moral fiber**)

fiction *n.* 1. pure ~ (her story was pure ~) 2. light; popular; romantic; science ~ 3. a work of ~ (a novel is a work of ~) 4. (misc.) to distinguish fact from ~

fiddle I *n.* 1. to play the ~ 2. (AE; colloq.) a bass ~ (CE has *double bass*) 3. (BE; colloq.) on the ~ ("cheating") 4. (misc.) as fit as a ~ ("very healthy") (see also **second fiddle**)

fiddle II *v.* (d; intr.) ("to fool around") to ~ with (he kept ~ling with his computer)

fiddle around *v.* (D; intr.) ("to fool around") to ~ with (he kept ~ling around with his computer)

fidelity *n.* ["loyalty"] 1. to pledge, swear ~ 2. ~ to ["quality of electronic reproduction"] 3. high ~

fidget *v.* (D; intr.) to ~ with (he kept ~ing with his computer)

field *n.* ["cultivated area"] 1. to cultivate; plow; till, work a ~ 2. a corn; rice; wheat ~ = a ~ of corn; rice; wheat 3. in a ~ (farmers were working in the ~s) ["area used for athletic events"] 4. to take the ~ 5. a baseball; cricket; football, soccer; hockey; rugby ~ (BE often has *pitch*); playing ~ 6. off; on the ~ (how many players were on the football ~ and how many were sent off it?) ["area used as a landing strip"] 7. a flying, landing ~ 8. on the ~ ["area used for practical work"] 9. to work (out) in the ~ (to work (out) in the ~ doing fieldwork) ["unbroken expanse"] ["space"] 10. an open ~ 11. a battlefield 12. a visual ~ = a ~ of vision ["area producing a natural resource"] 13. a coal; gold; oil ~ ["space in which electric lines of force are present"] (physics) 14. an electromagnetic, magnetic; gravitational ~ ["area of activity"] 15. in a ~ (in the ~ of science) 16. in smb.'s ~; outside (of) smb.'s ~ (her works are outside of my ~ (of interest)) ["group of competitors"] 17. to lead the ~ (our dictionary leads a strong ~ of rivals) ["baseball or softball playing area"] 18. center ~; infield; left ~; outfield; right ~ (hit a line drive to center ~) ["misc."] 19. on the ~ of honor; (esp. AE) to play the ~ ("to avoid committing oneself, esp. romantically")

fieldwork *n.* to conduct, do ~ (to work (out) in the field doing ~ with the local population; to do ~ on the local flora and fauna)

fiend *n.* a coke; dope; sex ~

Fifth *n.* (colloq.) (US) ["the Fifth Amendment to the U.S. Constitution, protecting witnesses against self-incrimination"] to invoke, plead, take the ~ (also fig.) ("are you dating smb. else?" "I'm afraid I'll have to take the ~ on that")

fight I *n.* ["struggle"] 1. to pick, provoke, start a ~ (he picked a ~ with me) 2. to put up, wage a ~ (to wage a ~ against corruption) 3. to get into; have a ~ (to get into a ~ with a neighbor about the property line) 4. to lose; win a ~ 5. to break up, stop a ~ 6. a bitter, desperate, fierce, hard, stubborn; last-ditch ~ (to put up a last-ditch ~; to put up a stubborn ~ against terminal illness) 7. a clean, fair; dirty, unfair ~ 8.

a ~ to the death; a ~ to the finish 9. a fist; gun-fight; knife fight; snowball ~ (see also **bullfight**; **dogfight**) 10. a ~ breaks out, starts; rages 11. a ~ about, over; against; among, between; for; with (a ~ for justice; a ~ between local politicians) 12. a ~ to + inf. (we joined the ~ to reduce waste) ["boxing match"] 13. to hold, stage; promote a ~ 14. to fix a ~ ("to influence the results of a ~ illegally") 15. a clean; dirty; grudge ~ 16. a championship, title ~ 17. (misc.) the big ~ (everyone was talking about the big ~)

fight II v. 1. to ~ bravely, heroically; clean; desper-ately, hard, stubbornly; dirty, unfairly; fair, fairly 2. (D; intr., tr.) to ~ about, over; against; among; for; with (he was always ~ing with his neighbors about the noise; Great Britain fought with Turkey against Russia; they are always ~ing among themselves; the United States fought (a war) with Mexico over their common border; the war was fought for a just cause; the dogs were ~ing over a bone) 3. (D; intr.) to ~ like (they fought like heroes) 4. (E) they fought to remain alive 5. (misc.) to ~ (in order) to win; to ~ like cat and dog (BE), to ~ like cats and dogs (AE); to ~ to the finish; to ~ with one's fists; to ~ tooth and nail; to ~ it out (two teams ~ing it out for the championship); two teams ~ing (in order) to win the championship; only one team can ~ its way to the championship USAGE NOTE: "X fought with Y" is possible if and only if it is also possible to say "X and Y fought": *he often fought with his wife until their divorce = he and his wife often fought (with each other) until their divorce; Flatland fought with Ruritania over oil = Flatland and Ruritania fought (with each other) over oil.* In those examples "fight with" means 'fight against.' But *fight with* can also mean 'fight on the same side as' when another opponent is specified: *Flatland fought with Ruritania against Nastiland = Flatland and Ruritania fought (together) against Nastiland.* Otherwise, use *fight against* or *fight: let's all fight (against) poverty.*

fight back v. 1. (D; intr.) to ~ against, at (AE) (to ~ at terrorism) 2. (misc.) to ~ in self-defense USAGE NOTE: To *fight back at terrorism* seems to be an AE blend of *fight back against terrorism* + *strike back at terrorism.*

fighter n. ["pugilist"] 1. a clean; dirty ~ 2. a street ~ ["fighting aircraft"] 3. a long-range; medium-range ~ ["misc."] 4. a firefighter

fighting n. 1. to step up the ~ 2. bitter, fierce, hard, heavy; hand-to-hand ~ 3. clean; dirty ~ 4. street ~ 5. (the) ~ breaks out; escalates; rages 6. (the) ~ dies down 7. ~ about, over; among, between

fight on v. to ~ to the bitter/very end

figure I n. ["impression"] ["appearance"] 1. to cut a (fine) ~ ("to make a strong impression") 2. a conspicuous, dashing, fine, handsome, imposing, striking, trim ~ (to cut a dashing ~; she has a curvaceous; full; slim ~) 3. a ridiculous, sorry ~

["person"] ["personage"] 4. a familiar; key, leading; national; prominent, well-known; public ~ 5. a political; religious; underworld ~ 6. an authority; father; mother; parental ~ ["number"] 7. to bandy ~s 8. to round down (esp. BE); to round off (esp. AE); to round up (esp. BE) ~s 9. approximate, ball-park (esp. AE; colloq.), round; available; census; exact; government; official; reliable ~s 10. in ~s (in round ~s) 11. (misc.) she earns a six-figure salary (between 100,000 and 1,000,000) (see also **double figures**) ["form"] 12. a symmetrical ~ 13. (misc.) to do a ~ eight/a ~ of eight (BE) (as in ice skating)

figure II v. 1. (d; intr.) ("to play a role") to ~ in (she ~d prominently (among the most important people) in history) 2. (colloq.) (esp. AE) ("to estimate") (L) we ~d that we would stay a few days 3. (col-loq.) (esp. AE) (M) ("to estimate") I ~d him to be worth a few hundred thousand 4. (misc.) (esp. AE) (slang) "How could she betray me like that?" "Go ~! (= Search me!)"

figure on v. (colloq.) (esp. AE) (G) ("to intend") we ~d on staying a few days

figure out v. (colloq.) 1. (L) he ~d out that we could not possibly get there on time 2. (Q) she could not ~ how to do it

filch v. (D; tr.) (colloq.) ("to steal") to ~ from

file I n. ["dossier"] ["folder"] 1. to make up, open, start a ~ 2. to keep a ~ 3. to close a ~ 4. official ~s 5. a circular (esp. AE) (colloq.); confidential ~ (if it's not important, it goes in the circular ~ (= the wastebasket)) 6. a vertical ~ 7. a ~ on (to keep a ~ on smb.) 8. on ~ (these documents are kept on ~ (with/by the police)) ["collection of data in a computer"] 9. to access; copy; create, open; delete, erase; download; edit; print; save a ~ 10. a batch; data; text ~

file II v. 1. (D; intr.) ("to apply") to ~ for (to ~ for divorce) 2. (D; tr.) ("to classify") to ~ under (mate-rial about the weather is filed under W) 3. (D; tr.) ("to submit") to ~ with (she ~d an application with several employment agencies)

file III n. ["row"] 1. single ~ 2. in single ~ 3. (misc.) to form a single ~ and then walk in single ~

file IV v. ("to move in a line") 1. (d; intr.) to ~ by, past (to ~ past a coffin) 2. (d; intr.) to ~ into; out of (to ~ into an auditorium; the jury ~d out of the courtroom) 3. (P) to ~ across; along; through

file V n. ["tool for smoothing surfaces"] a nail ~

file VI v. ("to smooth or shape") (N) she ~d her nails smooth

filibuster I n. to carry on, conduct, engage in a ~ (against)

filibuster II v. (D; intr.) to ~ against

filing n. ["storage of data"] to do typing and ~

fill I n. ["what is necessary to satisfy"] to drink; eat; have one's ~ (to have one's ~ of trouble)

fill II v. 1. (D; tr.) to ~ to (the auditorium was ~ed to capacity; to ~ to overflowing; to ~ to the brim/

top) 2. (D; intr., tr.) to ~ with (the lecture hall ~ed with people; to ~ a hole with sand; her eyes ~ed with tears)

fill-in *n.* ["replacement or substitute"] a ~ for (she is a ~ today for the regular announcer)

fill in *v.* 1. (D; intr.) to ~ for ("to replace") (to ~ for a friend) 2. (D; tr.) to ~ on ("to inform") (to ~ smb. in on the details) 3. (D; tr.) ("to make full") to ~ with (to ~ a hole with dirt = to ~ a hole in with dirt)

filling *n.* (dental) 1. to have; need; put in; replace a ~ 2. to cement a ~ 3. to lose a ~ 4. a broken, cracked ~ 5. a permanent; temporary ~ 6. a ~ breaks, cracks; chips; falls out; lasts

fill up *v.* ("to make full") (D; tr.) to ~ with (to ~ the car with gas/petrol = to ~ the car up with gas/petrol)

film *n.* ["cinema picture, motion picture"] 1. to cut, edit; direct; make, produce, shoot a ~ (the ~ of the book was shot on location) 2. to distribute; promote; release; show a ~ 3. to ban; censor a ~ 4. to rate; review a ~ 5. to see, take in, watch a ~ 6. an action; gangster; travel ~ 7. a documentary; educational; instructional; propaganda; training ~ 8. a children's ~ 9. an adult, blue (BE), erotic, pornographic, X-rated ~ 10. a black-and-white; color; colorized ~ (there's one color scene in this black-and-white ~) 11. a feature; silent; sound; made-for-television, television, TV ~ 12. (misc.) (BE) to work in ~s ("to work in the film industry"); to act in a ~ USAGE NOTE: In a theater, one *sees a film*; on a home TV, one *watches a film* or *sees a film*. ["roll of material used to take photographs"] 13. to insert, load; remove; rewind; wind ~ 14. to develop; expose ~ 15. to splice ~ 16. black-and-white; color; fast ~ 17. 8-millimeter; 16-millimeter; 35-millimeter ~ 18. a roll of ~ 19. (misc.) to capture smt. on ~; ~ footage

filter I *n.* 1. to pass smt. through a ~ 2. a cloth; dust; oil; sand ~

filter II *v.* 1. (d; intr.) to ~ into (foreign influence began to ~ into the country) 2. (d; intr.) to ~ out of (they slowly ~ed out of the room) 3. (d; intr.) to ~ through (sunlight ~ed through the drapes)

filter down *v.* (D; intr.) to ~ to (news slowly ~ed down to us)

filter through *v.* (D; intr.) to ~ to (reports have started to ~ to headquarters)

filth *n.* in ~ (to live in ~)

fin *n.* a caudal; dorsal; pectoral; pelvic ~

final *n.* a cup ~ (two sides that clashed in an exciting cup ~) (see also **finals**)

finale *n.* the grand ~

finals *n.* ["final examinations"] 1. to sit (BE), take one's ~ ["last competition"] 2. to get/go through to the; get into, get to, reach the ~

finance *n.* high; public ~

financing *n.* deficit; private; public ~

find I *n.* 1. an archeological ~ 2. an important; lucky; rare ~ (we made an important archeological

~ in/on a site that had already produced/yielded several others)

find II *v.* 1. (C) ~ an interesting book for me; or: ~ me an interesting book 2. (legal) (d; intr.) ("to decide") to ~ against; for (to ~ for the plaintiff) 3. (D; tr.) ("to discover") to ~ for (have you found a suitable candidate for the job?) 4. (J) ("to discover") we found him working on his book 5. (L) ("to discover") we found that he was working on his book 6. (M) ("to discover") we found London and Paris to be fascinating cities 7. (N; used with an adjective, noun, past participle) we found London and Paris fascinating cities; to ~ smb. wanting; the soldiers found the village destroyed; she was found guilty by the jury 8. (Q) we could not ~ where the money was hidden 9. (misc.) we found it difficult to believe

finding *n.* 1. a preliminary ~ (a preliminary ~ about/on drug use for one small group cannot be generalized across the whole population) 2. a ~ against; for (the court's ~ for the plaintiff) 3. (a) ~ that + clause (it was the court's ~ that no crime had been committed) 4. (misc.) to rubber-stamp a committee's ~s; research ~s

find out *v.* 1. (D; intr.) to ~ about (we found out about the concert only yesterday) 2. (D; intr.) to ~ for (she found out about the concert for me) 3. (D; intr., tr.) to ~ from (we found it out from a reporter) 4. (L) we found out (from the timetable) that the train would be late 5. (Q) I finally found out how to operate the new computer

fine I *adj.* 1. ~ for (that restaurant is ~ for a special occasion but too expensive to eat at all the time) 2. ~ to + inf. (it's ~ for the government to reduce taxes, but the deficit will be increased) 3. ~ that + clause (it's ~ that the government is to reduce taxes, but the deficit will be increased)

fine II *n.* 1. to impose, issue, levy a ~ on smb. 2. (colloq.) to slap a ~ on smb. 3. to draw, receive; pay a ~ 4. a big, heavy, hefty, stiff ~ 5. a small ~ 6. a mandatory ~ 7. a ~ for (I got a ~ for illegal parking, which I had to pay; to owe a lot of money in unpaid ~s for illegal parking)

fine III *v.* 1. (D; tr.) to ~ for (to ~ smb. for illegal parking; to get ~d heavily for smoking) 2. (O; can be used with one animate object) the police ~d him twenty dollars (for illegal parking); the police ~d him (for illegal parking)

finery *n.* ["showy clothing"] in all one's ~ (dressed up in all their ~)

finger I *n.* 1. to drum, tap one's ~s 2. to point a ~ at 3. (usu. fig.) to snap one's ~s (I jump when she snaps her ~s) ("I obey her commands without question") 4. an accusing; warning ~ (to point an accusing ~ at smb.) 5. a forefinger, index ~; little ~ (AE and Scottish also have *pinkie*); middle; ring; trigger ~ 6. (misc.) to eat with one's ~s; to eat chicken ~s ("chicken ~s were another meal they never argued about" – Michael Crichton, *Prey*, London, Harper,

2006 [2002], p. 101); to eat fish ~s (esp. BE =
AE *fish sticks*); she ran her ~s through her hair;
to get one's ~s burned ("to bear unpleasant consequences"); to prick a ~; she jammed her ~ in the
door; to lay a ~ on smb. ("to harm smb."); I can't
quite lay (esp. AE)/put my ~ on what is wrong ("I
cannot discover what is wrong"); to count on one's
~s (I can do simple calculations by counting on my
~s; I can count on the ~s of one hand the people I
really respect); to keep one's ~s crossed ("to hope
for smt."); to not lift a ~ ("to make no effort")
(she didn't lift a ~ to help us!); to have one's ~ in
smt. ("to be involved in smt."); the ~ of suspicion
points at/to you ("you are under suspicion"); to
have smb. wrapped around one's little ~ ("to have
smb.'s complete devotion")

finger II *v.* (colloq.) (D; tr.) ("to identify") to ~ as
(he was ~ed as one of the escaped convicts)

fingernails *n.* 1. to cut, trim; file; manicure smb.'s ~
2. to bite, chew one's ~

fingerprints *n.* 1. to leave ~ 2. to take smb.'s ~ 3.
telltale ~ 4. a set of ~ (the police got a clean set of
~) 5. (misc.) to dust for ~; the ~ had been carefully
wiped off

fingertips *n.* 1. at one's ~ (to have information at
one's ~) 2. to one's ~ (he's a gentleman to his ~!)

finicky *adj.* ~ about

finish I *n.* ["end"] 1. a close; photo ~ (there was a
very close ~ to the race) 2. at the ~ 3. to the ~ (to
fight to the ~) 4. (misc.) from start to ~ ["polish"] 5.
a dull; glazed; glossy; matte ~

finish II *v.* 1. (D; intr., tr.) to ~ by, with (they ~ed
their performance by singing a song/with a song;
are/have you ~ed with your work?) 2. (G) they
~ed working at four o'clock; she has just ~d writing her second novel 3. (s) to ~ last

finish line, (BE) **finishing line** *n.* to cross; reach
the ~

finish up *v.* 1. (D; intr., tr.) to ~ by, with (we ~ed up
the year with no profit; they ~ed up by scrubbing
the floor) 2. (G) she ~ed up buying two suits instead
of one 3. (s) to start off/out poor and ~ rich

fire I *n.* ["destructive burning"] 1. to set (AE), start a
~ 2. to set ~ to (they set ~ to the barn = they set the
barn on ~) 3. to catch ~ (the barn caught ~) 4. to
contain; douse, extinguish, put out; fight; stamp
out a ~ 5. to bring a ~ under control 6. a raging,
roaring ~ 7. a brush; chemical; electrical; forest
~ 8. a ~ breaks out; burns; rages (out of control);
smoulders; spreads (the ~ burned out of control for
two hours) 9. a ~ goes out 10. on ~ (the house was
on ~) ["burning, combustion"] 11. to build, kindle a
~, lay the (BE) ~; light, make a ~ 12. to add fuel
to, fuel; poke, stir; stoke a ~ 13. to bank; douse,
extinguish, put out a ~ 14. a ~ burns; goes out;
smoulders 15. (misc.) the ~ is out; the glow of a ~;
cook it over a low or an open ~ ["shooting"] 16. to
commence, open ~ (the enemy opened ~ on us) 17.
to exchange ~ (with the enemy) 18. to call down

~ on 19. to attract, draw ~ 20. to return ~ 21. to
cease ~ (cease ~!) 22. to hold one's ~ 23. concentrated, fierce, heavy, murderous; rapid ~ 24. cross;
friendly; harassing; hostile; incoming; interdic-
tory ~ 25. artillery; automatic; machine-gun; rifle;
semiautomatic; small-arms ~ 26. under ~ (we came
under heavy enemy ~ as we tried to advance) (also
fig.) (the Prime Minister is coming under heavy
media ~) 27. (misc.) (directly) in the line of ~; a
baptism of ~ ["misc."] 28. to play with ~ ("to take a
risk"); to fight ~ with ~ ("to use extreme measures
as countermeasures"); to set the Thames (BE)/the
world on ~ ("to be very successful") ["heater"] (BE)
29. to switch/turn on a ~ 30. to switch/turn off a ~
31. an electric; gas ~

fire II *v.* 1. to ~ point-blank 2. (B) the quarterback
~d a pass to an end 3. (D; intr., tr.) to ~ at (he ~d
at me; he ~d his pistol at me) 4. (D; intr., tr.) to ~
into (he ~ed his pistol into the air; the troops ~d
into the crowd) 5. (D; intr.) to ~ on (the troops ~d
on the crowd) (D; tr.) to ~ with (they ~d me with
enthusiasm) 6. Ready, Aim, Fire!

firearms *n.* to carry ~s (in Britain the police don't
usually carry ~)

fire away *v.* (D; intr.) to ~ at (to ~ at the enemy)

fire back *v.* (D; intr.) to ~ at (to ~ at the enemy)

firecracker *n.* (esp. AE = BE often prefers *banger*)
1. to let off (esp. BE), light, set off a ~ 2. (esp. AE)
to shoot off ~s 3. a ~ goes off

fire drill *n.* 1. to conduct, hold a ~ 2. at a ~

fire extinguisher *n.* 1. to train a ~ (on a fire) 2. to
operate a ~ 3. to recharge a ~

fired up *adj.* ["excited"] (all) ~ about, with

fireside *n.* by the ~ (to sit by the ~)

fireworks *n.* 1. to let off (esp. BE), set off, shoot
off (esp. AE) ~ 2. a spectacular display of ~ = a
spectacular ~ display

firing line *n.* ["line from which soldiers fire their weapons"] in (BE), on (AE) the ~ (also fig.) USAGE
NOTE: The *firing line* can also be called *the line of
fire*, esp. when used literally.

firing squad *n.* to face, stand before a ~ for one's
crimes

firm I *adj.* ["competitive, strong"] 1. ~ against (the
pound was ~ against the dollar) ["strict"] 2. ~ with
(~ with the children)

firm II *n.* ["company"] 1. to establish; manage, operate, run a ~ 2. an advertising; business; law, legal;
manufacturing; shipping ~ 3. a reputable ~ 4. in a
~ (she works in a reputable ~)

first *adj., adv., n.* 1. to come (in), finish ~ (in a race)
2. the ~ to + inf. (she was the ~ to arrive and the last
to leave) 3. among the ~ (she was among the ~ to
arrive and among the last to leave) 4. at ~ (see also
put first things first at **thing**) ["first gear"] 5. to put (a
vehicle) into ~ 6. in ~ (the car's in ~) ["undergraduate first-class honours degree at a British university"] 7.
to get a ~ 8. a double; starred ~ 9. a ~ in (to get a
~ in English)

first aid *n.* 1. to administer, give ~ (to give ~ to the injured) 2. to get, receive ~

first-class *adv.* to travel ~

fish I *n.* 1. to catch (a) ~; to farm ~ (farmed or wild ~) 2. baked; broiled (AE), grilled; dried; filleted; fresh; freshwater; fried; frozen; saltwater; smoked ~ 3. tropical ~ 4. ~ bite at bait; breathe through gills; hatch; swim 5. a school, shoal of ~ 6. (misc.) to drink like a ~ ("to drink excessive amounts of alcohol"); an odd, queer ~ ("a strange person"); a cold ~ ("an unfriendly person"); fish and chips, fish'n'chips (fish and chips is my favorite dish) USAGE NOTE: Although "chips" 'French fries' is generally BE, the expression above is CE.

fish II *v.* (D; intr.) to ~ for (to ~ for trout; to ~ for compliments) (see also **fishing**)

fish around *v.* (D; intr.) to ~ for (to ~ for information; to ~ in one's pockets for one's keys)

fish fry *n.* to have a ~

fishing *n.* 1. to go ~ 2. to go in for ~ 3. to do some ~ 4. deep-sea ~ USAGE NOTES: 1. to go trout-fishing = to go fishing for trout. 2. Compare *to go in for fishing* with *to go fishing*: "I like going fishing." "Me, I don't go in for fishing much: I hardly ever do it. I'd rather go hunting."

fishy *adj.* (colloq.) ~ about (there is smt. (very) ~ about them)

fission *n.* binary; nuclear ~

fist *n.* 1. to clench; raise; shake one's ~ 3. a tight ~ 4. (misc.) an iron ~ ("a harsh policy"); a mailed ~ ("a threat of armed force")

fisticuffs *n.* (formal) to engage in ~

fit I *n.* ["strong emotional reaction"] 1. to have, throw a ~ (colloq.) (mom will throw a ~ if we get back late!) 2. during, in a ~ (she threw things at him in a ~ of rage; the comedian had them rolling in the aisles in ~s of laughter) ["misc."] 3. by ~s and starts ("in irregular bursts of activity")

fit II *adj.* ["qualified"] ["physically capable"] 1. physically ~ 2. ~ for (~ for duty; ~ for human consumption; ~ for purpose (BE)) 3. ~ to + inf. (he is not ~ to work) 4. to keep ~ 5. (misc.) as ~ as a fiddle/flea (BE) ("very fit and healthy"); ~ and well ["suitable"] 6. to see, think ~ to + inf. (they saw ~ to employ smb. else) 7. (misc.) ~ for a king/queen (see also *survival of the fittest* at **survival**)

fit III *n.* ["manner of fitting"] 1. a good; loose; perfect; snug, tight ~ 2. goodness of ~ (is there goodness of ~ between our theory and the data?)

fit IV *v.* 1. to ~ together 2. (D; tr.) to ~ for (to ~ a customer for a new suit; to ~ smb. for glasses) 3. (D; intr.) to ~ in, into (everything fit into the suitcase) 4. (d; tr.) to ~ in, into (she was able to ~ all the books into one carton) USAGE NOTE: In BE the past and past participle of *fit* are usu. *fitted*. AE usu. has *fit* when the verb cannot be used in the passive form – the tailor fitted the customer carefully (CE); the suit was fitted carefully by the tailor

(CE); the suit fit me a year ago (AE) = (BE) the suit fitted me a year ago.

fit in *v.* (D; intr.) to ~ with ("to blend in") (she fit (AE) = fitted (BE) right in with our crowd)

fitness *n.* 1. physical ~ 2. a certain level of ~ 3. ~ for

fit out *v.* 1. (d; tr.) to ~ as (the ship was ~ted out as a tender) 2. (d; tr.) to ~ for (the expedition was ~ted out for a long trip) 3. (d; tr.) to ~ with (the bus was ~ted out with new air conditioning)

fitting I *adj.* 1. ~ to + inf. (it is ~ to pay tribute to the early pioneers) 2. ~ that + clause; may take subj. (it is ~ that she be/should be honored; it is ~ that she was honored; "It is altogether ~ and proper that we should do this." – Abraham Lincoln, The Gettysburg Address (Nov. 19, 1863))

fitting II *n.* ["small part"] 1. an electrical; female; gas; male ~ ["trying on of a garment"] 2. to go for a ~ 3. (misc.) a ~ room ["misc."] (BE) 4. fixtures and ~s (when we moved in, we had to pay extra for the ~s and fittings)

fix I *n.* (colloq.) ["difficult situation"] 1. to be in a ~ 2. a fine, nice, pretty ~ ["injection of a narcotic"] (slang) 3. to get; need a ~ ["solution"] 4. a quick ~ (there's no quick ~ for/to such a complex problem)

fix II *v.* 1. (AE) (C) ("to prepare") ~ a drink for me; or: ~ me a drink 2. (d; tr.) to ~ on (she ~ed her gaze on him) 3. (colloq.) (esp. AE) (E: used only as *fixing*) ("to be getting ready") they're ~ing to eat

fixation *n.* ["obsession"] a ~ about, on, with (to have a ~ on smt.)

fixing *n.* 1. price ~

fixings *n.* ["trimmings"] (esp. AE) (colloq.) (roast turkey with all the ~)

fixture *n.* 1. a lighting; plumbing; shop (esp. BE), store (esp. AE) ~ 2. (misc.) (BE) ~s and fittings (when we moved in, we had to pay extra for the ~s and fittings)

fix up *v.* (D; tr.) (colloq.) to ~ with ("to match with") (to ~ smb. up with a good job; my friends ~ed me up with her)

flag *n.* 1. to display, fly, show; hang out; hoist, raise, run up, unfurl; wave a ~ 2. to dip, lower a ~; to strike the ~ 3. a garrison; national ~ 4. the black; red; white ~ ("symbol of surrender") 5. a ~ flaps, flies, flutters, waves (the ~ was flying at half-mast) 6. under a ~ (the ship sailed under the Panamanian ~) 7. (misc.) to show/wave the ~ ("to demonstrate one's patriotism"); (under) a ~ of truce; to register a ship under a ~ of convenience

flair *n.* 1. to develop; have; show a ~ for 2. a distinctive ~ (a pianist with a distinctive ~ for the music of Chopin)

flak *n.* ["criticism"] (colloq.) to catch; come in for, run into; take ~ (he took a lot of ~ for that one!)

flake *n.* a ~ of dandruff; a ~ of snow = a snowflake; a ~ of soap = a soapflake (a few ~s of snow began to fall)

flammable *adj.* (esp. AE) highly, very ~

flame *n.* 1. (also fig.) to douse, extinguish, put out, snuff out; kindle a ~ 2. (fig.) to fan, stir, stoke the ~s (of racism) 3. to burst into ~(s) 4. a clear; open ~ 5. a ~ burns; goes out; shoots out/up; smoulders 6. in ~s (to go up in ~s; the house was in ~s) 7. (misc.) an (the) eternal ~; the Olympic ~; an old ~ ("an old love"); a wall of ~

flank *n.* 1. to turn ("go around") a ~ (to turn the enemy's ~) 2. on a ~ (on the left ~) (see also *flank attack* at **attack I**)

flap *n.* (slang) ["commotion"] 1. a political ~ 2. be/get in a ~ about, over

flare I *n.* 1. to light; shoot up a ~ 2. to set out, set up a ~ (they set up ~s along the runway) 3. a parachute ~

flare II *v.* (d; intr.) to ~ into (to ~ into violence)

flare up *v.* 1. (D; intr.) to ~ at (to ~ at the slightest provocation) 2. (D; intr.) to ~ in (to ~ in anger)

flash I *n.* 1. a blinding ~ 2. an electronic ~ (for a camera) 3. a hot ~ (AE; BE has *hot flush*) 4. a news ~ (about; from) 5. in a ~; as quick as a ~ ("very quick")

flash II *v.* 1. (usu. B; rarely A) ("to convey by light") they ~ed a signal to the crew 2. (d; intr.) ("to pass") to ~ across, through (an old memory ~ed across my mind; a thought ~ed through my mind) 3. (D; tr.) ("to shine") to ~ at (the driver ~ed his lights at us) 4. (d; intr.) ("to come suddenly") to ~ into (a brilliant idea ~ed into her mind) 5. (D; intr.) ("to glow") to ~ with (her eyes ~ed with anger)

flashback *n.* 1. to experience, have a ~ 2. a ~ to (a ~ to smb.'s childhood)

flashlight *n.* (AE; BE has *torch*) 1. to turn on a ~ 2. to shine, train a ~ on 3. to turn off a ~

flask *n.* 1. a Thermos (T) (BE), vacuum (BE) ~; AE has *Thermos* (T) *bottle* 2. a hip ~ 3. a ~ of

flat I *adj.* ["flavorless, stale"] 1. to go ~ (the beer has gone ~) ["extended at full length"] 2. (also fig.) to fall ~ (as an actor he fell ~) 3. (also fig.) she fell ~ on her face 4. (misc.) to lie ~; as ~ as a pancake

flat II *adv.* ["exactly": used after an expression of lengthy of time] 1. she ran a mile in seven minutes ~ 2. (misc.) in nothing ~ ("very quickly") (don't worry: I can do it in nothing ~!)

flat II *n.* ["deflated tire"] (esp. AE; BE prefers *flat tyre* or *puncture*) 1. to get; have a ~ 2. to change; fix, repair a ~ ["apartment"] (esp. BE) 3. to rent a ~ from 4. to let, rent out; sublet a ~ 5. to furnish; redecorate; renovate a ~ 6. a basement; council; furnished; garden; high-rise; penthouse; service; studio; unfurnished ~ (AE has *apartment*) 7. converted; purpose-built ~s 8. a block of ~s (AE has *apartment building/apartment house*) 9. (misc.) a ground-floor; top-floor, etc.; one-bedroom; two-bedroom, etc.; one-room; two-room, etc. ~

flatter *v.* 1. (D; refl.) to ~ on (to ~ oneself on one's knowledge of history) 2. (D; tr.) to ~ smb. about, on

flattered *adj.* 1. ~ at, by (she was ~ at the invitation)

2. ~ to + inf. (she was ~ to have been invited) 3. ~ that + clause (she was ~ that she had been invited)

flattering *adj.* 1. ~ to + inf. (it was ~ for her to have been invited) 2. ~ that + clause (it was ~ for her that she'd been invited)

flattery *n.* 1. to resort to, use ~ 2. to see through ~ 3. to succumb to ~

flaunt *v.* 1. to ~ openly, shamelessly (she ~ed her power openly by publicly flouting the rules) 2. (d; tr.) to ~ in front of, to (she shamelessly ~ed her wealth in front of all the guests!) 3. (misc.) "if you've got it, ~ it!" (saying)

flavor, flavour I *n.* ["characteristic quality"] 1. to give, impart a ~ to 2. a colloquial; foreign; old-world ~ ["taste"] 3. to bring out, enhance a ~ 4. a bitter; delicate; pleasant; strong; tart ~ 5. an artificial; natural ~ 6. (misc.) (the) ~ of the month (also fig.) (misery memoirs seem to be ~ of the month just now)

flavor, flavour II *v.* (D; tr.) to ~ with (to ~ the punch with orange syrup)

flavoring, flavouring *n.* 1. artificial; natural ~ (we use no artificial ~s or colorings in our home-made jam!) 2. a drop; spoonful of ~

flaw *n.* 1. a fatal; fundamental ~ 2. a ~ in (there's a fatal ~ in your reasoning)

flea *n.* 1. to get; have ~s 2. ~s bite; jump

flee *v.* (D; intr.) to ~ from; to

fleece *v.* (D; tr.) to ~ of

fleet I *adj.* ~ of foot

fleet II *n.* ["group of vehicles, typically ships"] 1. a fishing ~ 2. a ~ sails 3. (misc.) a ~ calls at a port; the ~ is in

flesh *n.* 1. to mortify the ~ 2. proud ~ 3. in the ~ ("live, in person") (we've seen her on TV – now here she is in the ~!) 4. (misc.) ~ tones (a painter renowned for his ~ tones); ~ and blood; that dreadful story is enough to make your ~ crawl/creep!; to go the way of all ~ ("to be mortal")

flesh out *v.* (D; tr.) to ~ with (to ~ a report with greater detail)

flexibility *n.* 1. to demonstrate, show ~ 2. ~ in; towards 3. the ~ to + inf. (she has enough ~ to cope with the job)

flexible *adj.* 1. very ~ 2. ~ about, as regards, when it comes to 3. ~ in; towards, with 4. (misc.) she is ~ enough to cope with the job

flick I *n.* at; with a ~ (at the ~ of a switch, the whole room was flooded with light; with a ~ of his wrist he sent the ball over the net)

flick II *v.* (d; intr.) to ~ through ("to go through quickly, to flip through") (to ~ quickly through a report)

flier *n.* see **flyer**

flies (BE) see **fly III**

flight I *n.* ["flying"]["airplane"] 1. to catch, take; miss a ~ 2. to cancel; delay; overbook a ~ 3. a chartered; coast-to-coast; connecting; cross-country; direct; domestic; international; long-haul; maiden; manned; nonstop; reconnaissance; round-the-world; scheduled; shakedown; short-haul; solo; suborbital; supersonic; unmanned ~ (see also **charter flight**; **space flight**; **test flight**) 4. a bumpy, rough; smooth ~ 5. a ~ from; to (~ number 10 from Philadelphia to Frankfurt is now boarding at/from gate 33, will take off in about 15 minutes, and is due to arrive/land this evening) 6. a ~ over (a ~ over the South Pole) 7. in ~ (at that moment the plane was in ~ over the Mediterranean) 8. during; on a ~ (she was on a ~ to Chicago during which she experienced air turbulence) 9. (misc.) the ~ out/there; the ~ back = the return ~ (see also *flight attendant* at **attendant**)

flight II *n.* ["fleeing"] 1. to take ~ 2. to put to ~ (their army was put to ~) 3. full, headlong ~ (we were in full ~ from the enemy to what we hoped would be safety)

flinch *v.* (D; intr.) to ~ at; from (sensitive people may ~ from blood/at the sight of blood)

fling I *n.* (colloq.) ["attempt"] 1. to have a ~ at smt. ["period of self-indulgence"] 2. to have a last ~

fling II *v.* 1. (d; tr.) to ~ at (to ~ a stone at smb.) 2. (d; tr.) to ~ to (they flung their rifles to the ground) 3. (N; used with an adjective) we flung the doors open 4. (P; tr.) they flung their hats into the air; she flung her coat across the room (see also *fling/hurl/throw caution to the winds* at **caution**)

flip *v.* 1. (slang) (D; intr.) ("to lose one's mind") to ~ over (he ~ped over her) 2. (d; intr.) to ~ through ("to go through quickly, to flick through") (to ~ quickly through a report)

flirt I *n.* an incorrigible; terrible ~

flirt II *v.* (D; intr.) to ~ with

flirtation *n.* to carry on, engage in, have a ~ with

flit *v.* (P; intr.) bees ~ from flower to flower; the idea ~ted into her brain (see also **moonlight flit**)

float *v.* (P; intr., tr.) they ~ed the logs downstream; we ~ed across the lake; she ~ed to the surface

flock I *n.* to tend a ~ (of sheep)

flock II *v.* (P; intr.) the crowd ~ed around the speaker; customers ~ed into the store; to ~ together ("birds of a feather ~ together" – proverb)

floe *n.* an ice ~

flood I *n.* 1. a flash; raging ~ 2. the ~ inundated; struck (several cities) 3. a ~ subsides 4. (misc.) she collapsed in ~s of tears

flood II *v.* 1. (d; intr.) to ~ into (refugees ~ed into the city) 2. (D; tr.) to ~ with (to ~ the market with cheap goods)

flood level *n.* to reach, rise to ~

floodlight *n.* to focus; shine a ~ on

floor *n.* ["story"] 1. the bottom; first; ground; lower; main; second; top; upper ~ (see also **ground floor**) 2. on a ~ (on the second ~) ["lower surface of a room"] 3. to mop; scrub; sweep; wash; wipe a ~ 4. to buff; polish; wax a ~ 5. a dirt (AE), earth (BE); inlaid; parquet; tile; wooden ~ (old wooden ~s sometimes creak) 6. all over; on a ~ (he was sleeping on the ~; there were papers on the ~; in

fact, they were all over the ~!) ["right to speak"] 7. to ask for; get, take the ~ 8. to give smb. the ~ 9. (AE) to yield the ~ ["place where members sit"] 10. to clear the ~ 11. on; from the ~ (a motion was made from the ~ which was then debated on the ~) ["misc."] 12. the ocean ~ USAGE NOTE: In AE the *first floor* and the *ground floor* are usually the same. In BE, the *first floor* is the floor above the *ground floor*.

flop I *n.* 1. a commercial; complete, total ~ 2. a ~ as (she was a complete ~ as a stage actress)

flop II *v.* 1. (D; intr.) to ~ as (she ~ped completely as a stage actress) 2. (P; intr.) his head ~ped to the side

flora *n.* 1. intestinal ~ 2. (misc.) ~ and fauna ("plants and animals")

floss *n.* 1. dental ~ 2. candy ~ (BE; AE has *cotton candy*)

flour *n.* 1. to mix ~ with 2. to sift ~ 3. bleached; cake; enriched; self-rising (AE), self-raising (BE); unbleached; white ~ 4. (BE) corn ~ (AE has *cornstarch*) 5. a bag, sack of ~

flout *v.* to ~ openly, publicly; shamelessly (she flaunted her power openly by publicly ~ing the rules)

flow I *n.* 1. to regulate a ~ 2. to cut off; staunch, stem, stop the ~ (of blood) 3. a smooth; steady ~ 4. a cash ~ 5. a lava ~ 6. a ~ from; through; to (the rate of) ~ of traffic from the country through the suburbs to/into the city) 7. (misc.) ebb and ~

flow II *v.* 1. (D; intr.) to ~ from, out of (water ~ed from the pipe) 2. (D; intr.) to ~ from; to (the river ~s from east to west) 3. (D; intr.) to ~ into, to (rivers ~ into the sea) 4. (P; intr.) traffic ~ed across town; traffic ~ed from the country through the suburbs to/into the city; blood ~s through the body; tears ~ed down her cheeks; the river ~s east

flower *n.* ["plant"] 1. to grow; plant ~s 2. to pick, pluck; water ~s 3. to arrange ~s 4. a fragrant ~ 5. artificial; cut; dried; pressed ~s 6. (US) a state ~ 7. ~s bloom; fade, wither, wilt; grow 8. in; into ~ (the tulips have come into ~ and are in full ~ now) 9. (misc.) a bouquet; bunch; spray of ~s

flu *n.* 1. to catch, come down with, get, go down with (BE) (the) ~; have (the) ~ 2. Asian; avian, bird; gastric, stomach; intestinal; swine ~ 3. a strain of ~ (virus) 4. an attack, bout; outbreak; touch of (the) ~

fluctuate *v.* 1. to ~ widely; wildly 2. (D; intr.) to ~ between 3. (D; intr.) to ~ with (his mood ~s with the weather)

fluctuation *n.* 1. wide; wild ~s 2. ~ of, in (the daily ~ of/in commodity prices) 3. ~ according to (the ~ of/in his mood according to the weather)

fluency *n.* 1. to acquire ~ 2. to demonstrate, display ~ 3. ~ in (~ in a foreign language) 4. ~ to + inf. (she has enough ~ to order a meal in English)

fluent *adj.* ~ in (~ in English)

fluids *n.* 1. (med.) to force, push; measure; restrict; withhold ~ 2. to drink, take ~ 3. to replace; retain ~ 4. body; clear; cold; hot ~

fluke *n.* (colloq.) ["stroke of luck"] 1. a pure ~ 2. by a ~ (he won by a ~ (of luck))

flunk *v.* (colloq.) (esp. AE) (D; intr.) to ~ out of (he ~d out of school, went back, and ~ed out again!)

flurry *n.* 1. a brief; sudden ~ 2. a snow ~ = a ~ of snow 3. a ~ of activity

flush I *adj.* ["even"] 1. ~ with (~ with the ground) ["rich in"] 2. ~ with (~ with cash)

flush II *n.* ["a rush of blood"] 1. a hot ~ (BE; AE has *hot flash*) ["excitement"] 2. the first ~ (of success)

flush III *v.* (D; intr.) ("to become red, blush") to ~ with (to ~ with pride)

flush IV *v.* 1. (d; tr.) ("to get rid of") to ~ down (she ~ed the poison down the toilet) 2. (d; tr.) ("to chase") to ~ from, out of (they were ~ed from their hiding place) 3. (d; tr.) ("to remove") to ~ out of (to ~ the waste products out of one's body)

flute *n.* to play the ~

flutter *n.* ["confused state"] in a ~

flux *n.* ["constant change"] 1. in ~ 2. a state of ~ (the market is in a state of ~)

fly I *n.* 1. to shoo away the flies 2. to swat a ~ 3. a fruit; tsetse ~ 4. flies buzz; fly; land, settle (see also *a fly in the ointment* at **ointment**)

fly II *v.* 1. (D; intr.) to ~ across, over (to ~ across the ocean) 2. (d; intr.) to ~ at ("to attack") 3. (D; intr., tr.) ("to travel by plane") ("to pilot") to ~ from; to (she flew from New York to London; he flew his private plane to Florida) 4. (d; intr.) to ~ into ("to arrive by plane") (to ~ into Chicago) 5. (d; intr.) to ~ into ("to go into") (to ~ into a rage) 6. (d; intr.) to ~ out of ("to depart by plane") (to ~ out of Chicago) 7. (P; intr., tr.) to ~ south; they flew the equipment over to Tokyo; to ~ high/low over the ground 8. (misc.) to ~ blind ("to ~ a plane solely with the help of instruments"); to ~ high ("to be elated or successful"); to ~ nonstop; to ~ in the face of tradition ("to defy tradition"); to ~ off the handle ("to become angry"); (misc.) (informal) sorry, must ~: I'm late for an appointment

fly III *n.* (esp. AE; BE has *flies*) ["opening on trousers"] 1. to button (up), close, do up (BE), zip (up) one's ~ 2. to open, unbutton, undo, unzip one's ~ ["fly ball in baseball and softball"] 3. a sacrifice ~ (the batter hit a sacrifice ~ that allowed the runner to score from third (base))

fly down *v.* (D; intr.) to ~ to the islands

flyer *n.* ["small advertising circular"] to distribute ~s (in the neighborhood) (also *flier*)

fly in *v.* (D; intr.) to ~ from (they flew in from London)

flying *n.* blind; formation; instrument; stunt ~

flying colors, flying colours *n.* ["success"] to come through with ~

flying saucer *n.* ["unidentified flying object, UFO"] 1. to sight a ~ 2. (misc.) a ~ abduction; sighting

fly out *v.* (in baseball and softball) (D; intr.) to ~ to (the batter flied out to center field)

flyover (BE) see **overpass**

foam *v.* to ~ at the mouth

fob off *v.* (colloq.) 1. (D; tr.) ("to get rid of by deceit") to ~ as (he ~ed off the copy as an original = he ~ed the copy off as an original) 2. (D; tr.) ("to get rid of by deceit") to ~ on (to ~ inferior merchandise on customers = to ~ inferior merchandise off on customers) 3. (BE) (D; tr.) ("to deceive") to ~ with (to ~ customers with inferior merchandise = to ~ customers off with inferior merchandise)

focus I *n.* 1. to bring smt. into ~ (we must bring two other major problems into sharper ~) 2. a ~ shifts (the ~ of our attention must shift to two other major problems) 3. in ~; out of ~

focus II *v.* (D; intr., tr.) to ~ on (we must ~ (our attention) on two other major problems)

fodder *n.* 1. cannon ~ 2. ~ for

foe *n.* 1. a bitter, implacable; formidable ~ 2. a political ~ 3. (misc.) to vanquish a ~; friend and/or ~

foetus (esp. BE) see **fetus**

fog *n.* (a) dense, heavy, thick; light; patchy ~ 2. a ground ~ 3. a ~ burns off, clears, dissipates, lifts; shrouds smt. 4. a blanket of ~; a patch of ~ = a ~ patch 5. (misc.) in a ~ ("bewildered")

foible *n.* 1. have a ~ 2. a human ~

foil I *n.* ["thin metallic covering"] aluminium (BE), aluminum (AE); gold; silver ~; tinfoil

foil II *n.* ["comparison"] to act as a ~ for, to

foist *v.* (d; tr.) to ~ on (they ~ed their problems on us; to ~ inferior merchandise on customers)

foist off *v.* (D; tr.) to ~ on (to ~ inferior merchandise on customers = to ~ inferior merchandise off on customers)

fold I *n.* ["group"] 1. in the ~ (they are all back in the ~ now) 2. to return to the ~ 3. to welcome smb. back into the ~

fold II *v.* 1. to ~ double, in half 2. to ~ neatly 3. (D; tr.) to ~ into (she ~ed the newspaper into a hat) 4. (N; used with adj.) to ~ a map flat 5. (s) this map can ~ flat

folder *n.* a manila ~

fold up *v.* 1. to ~ neatly 2. (D; intr., tr.) to ~ into (the bed ~s up into the wall) 3. (N; used with adj.) to ~ a map up flat 4. (s) this map can ~ flat

foliage *n.* 1. dense ~ 2. autumn ~

follow *v.* 1. to ~ blindly; faithfully 2. to ~ close behind, closely 3. (d; intr.) to ~ in (to ~ in smb.'s footsteps) 4. (L) it ~s necessarily from what has been said that he cannot be considered for the job 5. (P; tr.) she ~ed me out of the room; they ~ed us through town

follower *n.* 1. to attract a ~ 2. a devoted, faithful ~ 3. a band, group of ~s

following *n.* ["followers"] 1. to attract a ~ 2. a devoted, faithful, loyal; large ~

follow through *v.* (D; intr.) ("to continue") to ~ with

follow-up *n.* 1. to do a ~ on (the reporter did a ~ on her first story) 2. a ~ to (this letter is a ~ to our telephone conversation)

follow up *v.* 1. (D; intr.) to ~ on (the reporter ~ed up on her first story) 2. (D; intr., tr.) to ~ with (we should ~ our telephone conversation with a letter)

folly *n.* 1. sheer ~ 2. ~ to + inf. (it was sheer ~ for him even to try; "where ignorance is bliss, 'Tis ~ to be wise" – Thomas Gray (1716–71), "Ode on... Eton College")

fond *adj.* (cannot stand alone) ~ of (she is very ~ of him)

fondness *n.* 1. to display, show (a) ~ for 2. (a) great ~ 3. (a) ~ for (her great ~ for him)

font *n.* ["bowl"] a baptismal ~

food *n.* 1. to cook, prepare; heat; reheat ~ 2. to bolt, gulp (down); chew; digest; eat; swallow; taste ~ 3. appetizing, delicious, tasty; exotic; gourmet; plain; spicy ~ 4. nourishing, nutritious, wholesome ~ 5. coarse; fine; heavy; light; rich; simple ~ 6. canned (AE), tinned (BE); catfood; dogfood; frozen ~ 7. halal; kosher; soul (AE) ~ 8. comfort; health; junk ~ 9. ~ keeps; goes bad, goes off, spoils 10. morsels; scraps of ~ 11. (misc.) ~ for thought; ~ and drink

fool I *n.* 1. to play the ~ 2. to make a ~ of smb./ oneself 3. a big; complete; doddering (old); poor; silly; stupid; utter; young ~ 4. a ~ to + inf. (he was a ~ even to try)

fool II *v.* 1. (D; tr.) to ~ into (she ~ed them into investing their money) 2. (D; intr.) to ~ with

fool about (BE) see **fool around**

fool around *v.* (D; intr.) to ~ with (don't ~ with fire)

foolhardy *adj.* ~ to + inf. (it was ~ of him even to try = he was ~ even to try)

foolish *adj.* ~ to + inf. (it was ~ to take the test without preparation; it was ~ of him even to try = he was ~ even to try)

foolishness *n.* ~ to + inf. (it was ~ for him even to try)

fool's paradise *n.* to live in a ~

foot *n.* ["lower extremity of a leg"] 1. to stamp; tap one's (left; right) ~ 2. to shuffle one's feet 3. to get to, rise to one's feet; to pull oneself to one's feet 4. to set ~ on (she has never set ~ on foreign soil) 5. bare feet; flat feet 6. in one's stocking feet 7. at smb.'s feet (the dog lay at their feet) 8. on ~ (they came on ~) 9. (misc.) to drag one's feet ("to move very slowly") or ("to refuse to act"); fast/light/quick on one's feet; to put one's best ~ forward ("to attempt to make a good impression"); to put one's ~ down ("to say 'no' firmly"); to get a ~ in the door ("to make an initial step"); underfoot ("beneath one's feet"); to put one's ~ in one's mouth ("to make an inappropriate statement"); she always lands on her feet ("she always manages to get out of difficulty"); to stand on one's own two feet ("to show independence"); to have a ~ in both camps (by being on good terms with both sides); the ball of one's ~; the sole of one's ~; from head to ~; feet first ["bottom, end"] 10. at the ~ of (at the

~ of the bed) ["unit of measurement equaling twelve inches"] 11. a cubic; square ~ 12. by the ~ (to sell carpeting by the square ~)

football *n.* 1. to play ~ 2. association ~ ("soccer") 3. the game of ~ 4. a political ~ ("an issue debated by politicians") 5. (misc.) a ~ field (AE), pitch (BE); a ~ game (esp. AE), match (BE); player (esp. AE; BE has *footballer*)

foot fault *n.* (tennis) to commit a ~

foothold *n.* 1. to establish, gain, get, secure, win a ~ 2. a firm; precarious ~

footing *n.* 1. to keep one's ~ 2. to lose one's ~ 3. an equal; firm, secure, solid, sure; unequal ~ 4. a friendly; war ~ 5. on a certain ~ (to be on a friendly ~ with smb.; to place a country on a war ~)

footnote *n.* a ~ to (the ~s to a chapter)

footprint *n.* to leave a ~ (in the snow, "leave behind us Footprints on the sands of time" – H.W. Longfellow (1807–82), "A Psalm of Life")

footrace *n.* to run a ~

footsie *n.* (slang) ["collusion" (AE)] ["footplay"] to play ~ with

footstep *n.* 1. to dog smb.'s ~s 2. to follow in smb.'s ~s 3. heavy; light ~s

footwork *n.* fancy ~ (as of a boxer)

forage *v.* (D; intr.) to ~ for (to ~ for food)

foray *n.* 1. to make a ~ 2. a bold ~ 3. a ~ into

forbear *v.* (formal, rare) 1. (d; intr.) to ~ from (she forbore ~ from (making) any predictions) 2. (E) she forbore to make any predictions

forbid *v.* 1. to ~ categorically, expressly, outright 2. (D; tr.) to ~ from (she has forbidden him from smoking in her presence) 3. (H) she has forbidden him to smoke in her presence; I ~ you to take the car! 4. (misc.) God ~!, heaven ~! (God ~ anyone should commit such a horrible crime!)

force I *n.* ["compulsion"] ["violence"] 1. to apply, resort to, use ~ 2. to renounce (the use of) ~ 3. armed; brute; deadly; lethal; physical ~ 4. moral; spiritual ~ 5. by ~ ["military power"] 6. to marshal, muster, rally one's ~s 7. to join ~s against; with 8. allied, friendly ~s 9. enemy, hostile ~s 10. armed, military; ground; naval; nuclear; security ~s (the enemy's strong naval ~s began to shell our positions) 11. an air ~ 12. an expeditionary; guerrilla; occupation; peacekeeping ~ (a U.N. peacekeeping ~) (see also **task force**) 13. a show of ~ ["organized body, group"] 14. a labor; police; sales; task ~ (see also **workforce**) 15. in full ~ (the police were out in full ~) ["energy"] ["power"] 16. to spend its/one's ~ (the storm has spent its ~) 17. centrifugal; centripetal ~ 18. a driving; explosive; irresistible; magnetic; motivating ~ (what happens when an irresistible ~ meets an immovable object?) 19. the vital ~ ("basic force") 20. a ~ for (can self-interest ever be a ~ for good?) ["effect"] 21. in ~ (the regulation is still in ~) ["misc."] 22. ~ of circumstance (we were compelled to leave by/through ~ of circumstance = we had to leave through ~ of circumstance); gale-force winds; market ~s (market ~s drive prices up and down) (see also *force of nature* at **nature**)

force II *v.* 1. (d; tr.) to ~ into (they ~d their way into the building and then out of it again) 2. (d; tr.) to ~ off (we were ~d off the road) 3. (d; refl., tr.) to ~ on (she tried to ~ her views on us) 4. (d; tr.) to ~ through (to ~ one's way through a crowd) 5. (H) they ~d her to sign 6. (N; used with an adjective) he ~d the door open

foreboding *n.* 1. to have a ~ 2. a gloomy ~ 3. a ~ that + clause (she had a (feeling/sense of) ~ that an accident would happen)

forecast I *n.* 1. to do, give, make a ~ 2. an economic; long-range; political; short-range; weather ~ (to give the weather ~)

forecast II *v.* (L) she forecast that an earthquake would occur

foreclose *v.* (D; intr.) to ~ on (they will ~ on us) ("they will foreclose our mortgage")

foredoomed *adj.* ~ to (~ to failure)

forefront *n.* in the ~

foreground *n.* at/in the ~

forehead *n.* a high; low ~

foreign *adj.* ~ to

forerunner *n.* ["precursor"] a ~ of, to

foresee *v.* 1. (K) nobody could have ~n his running away 2. (L) nobody could have ~n that he would run away 3. (Q) who can ~ how the elections will turn out?

foresight *n.* the ~ to + inf. (he had the ~ to provide for the education of his children)

forest *n.* 1. to clear, cut down; denude a ~ 2. a dense, thick; impenetrable; luxuriant; primeval; virgin ~ 3. a broadleaf; coniferous; deciduous; evergreen; (tropical) rain ~ 4. a national; state (US) ~ 5. the huge expanse of ~ stretches for miles

foretell *v.* 1. (L) nobody could have foretold that he would run away 2. (Q) who can ~ how the elections will turn out?

forethought *n.* the ~ to + inf. (he had enough ~ to provide for the education of his children)

forewarn *v.* 1. (D; tr.) to ~ about, of 2. (L) we were ~ed that there would be a hurricane 3. "~ed is forearmed" – proverb

foreword *n.* a ~ to (a ~ to a book)

forfeit *v.* (B) he ~ed the game to his opponent

forge *v.* (d; intr.) ("to move ahead") to ~ into the lead

forge ahead *v.* (D; intr.) to ~ with (they were ~ing ahead with their grandiose plans)

forgery *n.* 1. to commit a ~ 2. a clever; crude; skillful ~ 3. the crime of ~

forget *v.* 1. to clean (colloq.), completely, quite (esp. BE); conveniently ~ 2. (D; intr.) to ~ about (she forgot about the concert) 3. (E) I forgot to call 4. (G; usu. in neg. and interrogative constructions) the children will never ~ visiting this park 5. (K) the audience will not ~ your singing this role 6. (L) don't ~ that we are going out this evening!

7. (Q) a person never ~s how to swim 8. (misc.) I'll ~ you said that! ("I'll pretend I didn't hear what you've just said"); ~ about it! ("don't even think about it!") (AE) (slang) "You want to date the boss's daughter? Forget about it!"; forgive and ~ USAGE NOTE: The sentence *she forgot to buy a newspaper* means that she did not buy a newspaper. The sentence *she forgot about buying a newspaper* may mean either that she did not buy a newspaper or that she bought a newspaper but does not remember buying it.

forgetful *adj.* ~ of (he has become ~ of things)

forgive *v.* 1. (D; tr.) to ~ for (to ~ smb. for a mistake; ~ me for saying this, but I think you're completely wrong!) 2. (biblical) (O; may be used with one object) ~ us our sins 3. (misc.) ~ and forget

forgiveness *n.* 1. to ask for, beg, seek smb.'s ~ 2. ~ for

fork *n.* ["pronged device"] 1. a tuning ~ ["division into branches"] 2. at a ~ in the road ["implement for eating"] 3. a carving; dinner; salad; toasting ~ 4. (misc.) a knife and ~ (some people prefer chopsticks to a knife and ~)

fork over *v.* (colloq.) (B) we had to ~ our savings to our creditors = we had to ~ our savings over to our creditors

form I *n.* ["printed document"] 1. to fill in (esp. BE), fill out (esp. AE), fill up (obsol. BE) a ~ 2. to file, hand in, submit a ~ 3. an application; booking (esp. BE); entry; order; requisition; tax ~ (see also **application form, entry blank, entry form**) ["shape"]["manner"] 4. to assume, take (on) a ~ (to assume human ~) 5. an abridged, condensed; comprehensive; concise; convenient, handy; revised ~ (sometimes it's hard to find a convenient concise ~ of words) 6. in a ~ (the book came out in abridged ~; we reject fraud in any (shape or) ~; a fiend in human ~) ["grammatical element"] 7. a bound; colloquial; combining; diminutive; free; inflectional; negative; obsolete; plural; positive; singular; surface; underlying; verbal ~ ["behavior"] 8. bad; good, proper ~ (it's bad ~ for guests to come late to a formal reception) ["condition"] 9. bad; excellent, good, superb ~ 10. in (certain) ~ (she was in superb ~ today – she didn't lose a single game) ["good condition"] 11. in (AE), on (BE) ~ (I'm not in ~ today) 12. off ~ ["table giving information"] 13. a racing ~ ["secondary school class"] (BE) 14. in a ~ (in the fourth ~) 15. (misc.) an art ~ (is cinema/jazz now considered an art ~?); a life ~ (a carbon-based life ~ like those on Earth); a verse ~ (a sonnet is a verse ~)

form II *v.* 1. (D; tr.) to ~ from, out of (they ~ed patties out of chopped beef) 2. (d; tr.) to ~ into (they ~ed chopped beef into patties)

formal *adj.* ~ with (he is always ~ with his colleagues)

formalities *n.* 1. to complete, go through the ~ 2. bureaucratic; legal ~ 3. the usual ~

format *n.* 1. a set; suitable ~ 2. in a ~

formation *n.* ["arrangement of troops, ships, aircraft"] 1. to break ~ 2. close; tight ~ 3. battle ~ (drawn up in battle ~) 4. in ~ (to fly in close ~) ["structure"] ["grouping"] 5. a cloud; rock ~ (see also **back formation**)

formula *n.* ["milk mixture for infant feeding"] (AE) 1. to make up, prepare ~ ["symbolic representation"] ["method"] 2. to come up with, devise, hit on a ~ 3. a chemical; mathematical; scientific; winning ~ 4. a ~ for (to come up with a ~ for settling the strike) 5. a ~ to + inf. (to come up with a ~ to settle the strike)

form up *v.* (D; intr.) to ~ in (to ~ in three ranks)

fort *n.* 1. a strong ~ 2. a ~ falls; holds out 3. (misc.) to hold, hold down (AE) the ~ ("to bear responsibility in the absence of others")

fortify *v.* 1. (D; tr.) to ~ against 2. (D; refl., tr.) to ~ by, with (he ~ied himself with/by having a shot of whiskey)

fortitude *n.* 1. to demonstrate, display, show ~ 2. (humorous) intestinal ~ ("great courage, guts") 3. moral ~ 4. the ~ to + inf. (they had enough ~ to finish the job) 5. with ~ (they underwent their ordeal with great ~)

fortnight *n.* (BE) 1. to spend a ~ (somewhere) 2. (the) last, past, the previous; next; an/the entire, whole ~ 3. for a ~ (they came here for a ~) 4. in a ~, in a ~'s time (they'll be here in a ~) 5. (misc.) a ~ ago; every ~; once/twice a ~; a ~'s holiday; a whole ~ has gone by and we've still heard nothing!

fortress *n.* 1. to besiege; storm, take a ~ 2. an impenetrable, impregnable; strong ~ 3. a ~ falls, surrenders; holds out

fortunate *adj.* 1. ~ for 2. ~ in (we consider ourselves ~ in having such a nice house) 3. ~ to + inf. (we consider ourselves ~ to have such a nice house) 4. ~ that + clause (we are ~ that we have such a nice house = it is fortunate (for us) that we have such a nice house)

fortune *n.* ["wealth"] 1. to accumulate, amass, make a ~ (to make a ~ from/out of property speculation and amass a ~ in property) 2. to come into, inherit a ~ 3. to seek one's ~ 4. to dissipate, run through, spend, squander; lose a ~ 5. an enormous, large, vast ~ 6. a family ~ 7. (misc.) it cost me a small ~ to repair our car; fame and ~ ["luck"] 8. to try one's ~ 9. the (good) ~ to + inf. (we had the good ~ to get there at the right time) 10. (good) ~ that + clause (it was our good ~ that we got there at the right time) 11. ~ smiled on us 12. a stroke of good ~ (see also *a reversal of fortune* at *reversal*) ["fate"] 13. to improve the ~s of (is it too late to improve the ~s of the party?) 14. to tell smb.'s ~

forum *n.* 1. to conduct, hold a ~ 2. to provide, serve as a ~ for (discussions that served as a ~ for debate on many issues) 3. an open, public ~ 4. a ~ about, on

forward *v.* 1. (usu. B; occasionally A) they always ~ my mail to me 2. (D; tr.) to ~ from; to (to ~ letters to a new address; the books were ~ed from Amsterdam to Tokyo)

foul I *adv.* 1. see **afoul** 2. to fall ~ of (to fall ~ of the law)

foul II *n.* 1. to commit a ~ 2. an intentional, professional (BE); personal; team; technical ~ 3. a ~ against, on (BE) (she committed a ~ against the other guard)

foul III *v.* (esp. basketball) (D; intr.) to ~ out of (to ~ out of a game)

foul out *v.* (esp. basketball) (D; intr.) to ~ on (he ~ed out on five personals)

foul play *n.* ["violence"] 1. to meet with ~ 2. to rule out; suspect ~

found *v.* (D; tr.) to ~ on (our country was ~ed on certain principles)

foundation *n.* ["underlying base"] 1. to lay; shore up a ~ 2. to shake, subvert, undermine a ~ (revelations that shook our society to its ~s) 3. a firm, secure, solid, sound, strong ~ (hopes built on a firm ~) 4. a shaky; weak ~ 5. the ~ (of a building) settles 6. without ~ (rumors completely without ~) ["an endowed institution"] 7. a charitable, philanthropic; educational ~ 8. a ~ for (a ~ for cancer research) 9. a ~ to + inf. (a ~ to conduct cancer research)

fountain *n.* 1. a drinking, water ~ 2. (esp. AE) a soda ~

fours *n.* ["two hands and two feet"] on all ~

fox *n.* 1. an arctic, white; desert; red; silver; city, urban ~ 2. a ~ barks; yelps 3. a young ~ is a cub, pup 4. a female ~ is a vixen 5. ~es live in dens or lairs 6. (misc.) (esp. AE) as sly/wily as a ~; a wily ~ (usu. fig.)

foyer *n.* 1. a hotel; theater ~ 2. in the ~ (let's meet in the ~)

fraction *n.* 1. to reduce a ~ 2. a common; complex, compound; decimal; improper; irreducible; partial; proper; simple, vulgar ~ (to express a decimal as a ~)

fracture *n.* 1. to get, sustain; have a ~ 2. to reduce, set a ~ 3. a compound; compression; greenstick; hairline; simple; stress ~ 4. multiple ~s

frailty *n.* human ~

frame I *n.* a bicycle; mirror; picture; window ~

frame II *v.* (D; tr.) ("to incriminate wrongly") to ~ for (she was ~d for murder)

framework *n.* 1. a conceptual; theoretical ~ (does their theory provide a valid conceptual ~ for the discussion of social problems?) 2. within a ~

franchise *n.* ["the right to vote"] 1. a restricted; universal ~ 2. to exercise one's ~ (should women exercise the ~ that has been extended to them?) ["the license to sell a product or services in a certain area"] 3. to grant a ~ 4. to get; have, hold a ~ 5. to withdraw a ~ (from)

frank *adj.* 1. brutally, perfectly ~ (let's be perfectly ~, to be perfectly ~; to be ~ with you, I don't think your plan will work) 2. ~ about; with (she was ~ with us about everything)

frankness *n.* 1. disarming ~ 2. ~ about; with

frantic *adj.* ~ about, over; with (~ with worry over the child's whereabouts)

fraternity *n.* (US) 1. to pledge a ~ ("to agree to join a fraternity") 2. a college ~ (see also **sorority**)

fraternize *v.* (D; intr.) to ~ with

fratricide *n.* to commit ~

fraud *n.* 1. to commit ~; to perpetrate (a) ~ 2. to expose (a) ~ 3. computer; mail; vote ~

fraudulent *adj.* ~ to + inf. (it was ~ (for/of them) to claim an exemption of that type)

fraught *adj.* (cannot stand alone in AE) ~ with (the situation was ~ with danger)

fray *n.* to enter, join the ~

frayed *adj.* ~ at the edges

frazzle *n.* burnt to a ~ ("completely burnt"); worn to a ~ ("completely worn out or exhausted")

freak *n.* a ~ of nature

freak out *v.* (slang) (D; intr., tr.) to ~ on (to ~ on drugs)

free I *adj.* 1. ~ from, of (~ from pain; ~ of charge; ~ of debt) 2. ~ for (are you ~ for dinner?) 3. ~ with (~ with advice) 4. ~ to + inf. (are you ~ to come to dinner with me?) 5. (misc.) as ~ as a bird; as ~ as the wind; to set smb. ~; I got it for ~! = I got it ~ of charge; ~ and easy; "can I have some more cake?" "feel ~ (to)!"

free II *v.* 1. (D; tr.) to ~ for; from, of (the new schedule ~d me from many burdens and so ~d me for new activities) 2. (H) the new schedule ~d me to undertake new activities

freedom *n.* 1. to gain, secure, win ~ 2. to give, grant ~ (to) 3. to abridge, curtail; deny (a) ~ 4. academic; individual, personal; political; press; religious ~ (they moved to a place where they could enjoy religious ~) 5. ~ of action; of assembly; of information; of inquiry; of movement; of choice; of the press; of religion, worship; of speech 6. an amount, degree, level of ~ (a country that enjoys a considerable degree of political ~) 7. ~ from (~ from want; does ~ of the press imply ~ from censorship?) 8. the ~ to + inf. (the new schedule gave me the ~ to undertake new activities)

free-for-all *n.* to join in a ~

free hand *n.* ["freedom of action, carte blanche"] 1. to give smb. a ~ 2. to get; have a ~ 3. a ~ to + inf. (she had a ~ to do whatever she wanted)

free throw *n.* (basketball) to get, be awarded, be given; make a ~

free will *n.* 1. to exercise one's ~ 2. of one's own ~

freeze I *n.* ["frost"] ["freezing"] 1. a deep, hard ~ ["freezer"] (BE) 2. a deep ~ ["fixing at a certain level"] 3. to impose; lift a ~ 4. a nuclear; price; wage ~ 5. a ~ on (to impose a ~ on wages)

freeze II *v.* 1. to ~ hard, solid (it froze hard last night) 2. (D; tr.) to ~ out of (to ~ smb. out of a conversation) 3. (D; intr.) to ~ to (his exposed skin froze to the metal; to ~ to death)

freezer *n.* 1. to defrost a ~ 2. a home ~ (see also *freezer compartment* at **compartment**)

freezing-point *n.* to be at; reach (the) ~

freight *n.* ["goods, cargo"] 1. to carry; handle; load; ship ~ ["freight train"] (colloq.) (AE) 2. to hop, jump ("board") a ~

French *n.* Canadian ~ (natives of Quebec speak Canadian ~; a French Canadian who speaks Canadian ~)

frenzy *n.* 1. a wild ~ 2. in a ~ (in a ~ of despair) 3. (misc.) to work oneself (up) into a ~

frequency *n.* ["number of repetitions"] 1. alarming; decreasing; great, high; increasing; low ~ 2. with ~ (with alarming ~) ["number of periodic waves per unit of time"] (physics) 3. high; low; medium; ultrahigh ~ 4. a radio ~ 5. a band, range of ~cies 6. on a ~

fresco *n.* to paint a ~

fresh I *adj.* ["recent"] ["new"] 1. ~ from, out of (~ out of school) 2. (misc.) (as) ~ as a daisy/(BE) as paint

fresh II *adj.* (colloq.) (AE) ["bold"] ["impudent"] ~ with (don't get ~ with me!)

freshener *n.* an air, room ~

freshman *n.* 1. (AE) a college; high-school ~ 2. a university ~

fret *v.* 1. (D; intr.) to ~ about, over 2. (misc.) to ~ and fume = to fume and ~

friction *n.* 1. to create, generate, produce; ease; eliminate; reduce ~ 2. ~ among, between; with (there has been some ~ between the union and management)

friend *n.* 1. to be; make a ~ 2. to be; make ~s (with smb.) (he and I are ~s = he's ~s with me and I'm ~s with him) 3. a bosom, close, good, intimate, old; faithful, fast, loyal, staunch, strong, true; lifelong ~ 4. a mutual; personal; special ~ 5. a fair-weather; false ~ 6. inseparable ~s 7. a pen ~ (BE; CE has *pen pal*) 8. a ~ to (she was a good ~ to us) 9. (misc.) my good ~; ~ and/or foe; smb.'s best ~ (she's my best ~ and I'm her best ~ = she and I are best ~s = she's best ~s with me and I'm best ~s with her)

friendliness *n.* 1. to show ~ 2. ~ to, towards, with

friendly *adj.* 1. ~ of (that was ~ of you) 2. ~ to, towards, with 3. ~ to + inf. (it was not very ~ of you to refuse to help) 4. (misc.) user-friendly

friendship *n.* 1. to cement, develop, form, make, strike up a ~ 2. to cherish, cultivate a ~ 3. to promote (international) ~ 4. to break up, destroy a ~ 5. a close, firm, intimate, lasting, strong, warm; lifelong; long; special ~ 6. the bonds of; the hand of ~ 7. (a) ~ among, between; with (a lasting ~ developed between them)

fright *n.* 1. to get; have; give smb. a ~ 2. (esp. BE) to take ~ at smt. 3. a nasty; sudden ~ 4. in, with ~ (to scream with ~) (see also **stagefright**)

frighten *v.* 1. (D; tr.) to ~ into (to ~ smb. into doing smt.) 2. (D; tr.) to ~ out of (to ~ smb. out of doing smt.) 3. (R) it ~d us that no one answered the doorbell 4. (misc.) to ~ smb. (half) to death = to ~ the life out of smb.

frightened *adj.* 1. ~ about, at, by, of (~ at the very thought; ~ of the dark; they are ~ed of saying anything) 2. ~ to + inf. (they are ~ to say anything) 3. ~ that + clause (we were ~ that the roof would collapse) 4. (misc.) to be ~ (half) out of one's wits; to be ~ (half) to death

frighteners *n.* (slang) (BE) to put the ~ on smb. ("to intimidate smb.") (if he won't pay up I'll put the ~ on him!)

frightening *adj.* 1. ~ to + inf. (it's ~ to contemplate that possibility = that possibility is ~ to contemplate = it's a ~ possibility to contemplate) 2. ~ that + clause (it's ~ that a war could break out at any time)

frightful *adj.* see **frightening**

fringe *n.* 1. the lunatic ~ 2. on the ~s (of society)

fringe benefits *n.* to get; provide ~

fritter away *v.* 1. (D; tr.) to ~ on (to ~ one's time away on unimportant things = to ~ one's time on unimportant things) 2. (misc.) to ~ one's time doing unimportant things

frivolous *adj.* ~ to + inf. (it was ~ of him to make such a silly accusation)

frog *n.* 1. a bullfrog; grass; green; wood ~ 2. ~s croak; hop, jump 3. an immature ~ is a tadpole 4. (misc.) to have a ~ in one's throat ("to be hoarse"); ~s and toads

front I *adv.* to face ~

front II *n.* ["front line"] (mil.) 1. at, on the ~ (the war correspondents spent two days at the ~; there has been no activity on this ~) ["area of activity"] 2. the home; political ~ 3. on a ~ (on a broad ~; on the home ~) ["advanced part"] 4. at the ~ of; in ~ of; wearing a baseball cap back to ~ ["movement"] ["campaign"] 5. a popular; united ~ (to present a united ~) ["boundary"] (meteorology) 6. a cold; occluded; stationary; warm ~ (a warm ~ is forming and will probably soon approach) ["walk, road along a body of water"] (BE) 7. a river; sea ~ 8. along a ~ (to walk along the sea ~) 9. on a ~ (is there a hotel on the sea ~?) ["behavior"] 10. to put on, put up a ~ 11. a bold, brave, brazen ~ (to put on a bold ~) (see also **false front**) ["facade"] 12. a ~ for (the store was a ~ for illegal drug sales) ["misc."] 13. up ~ (colloq.) ("in advance") (I want € 5 000 up ~ before I do a stroke of work!); ("frank, candid") (to be absolutely up ~ with you, I think you're completely wrong!) USAGE NOTE: Something in front of the house is not in the house itself. Something in the front of the house is. Something at the front of the house can be either in front of the house or in the front part of the house itself. So the expression "at the front of" is ambiguous.

front III *v.* 1. (d; intr.) to ~ for (to ~ for the mob) 2. (d; intr.) to ~ on, onto (our building ~s on the main road)

frontage *n.* 1. lake; ocean; river ~ 2. ~ on

frontier *n.* 1. to advance, extend, push back, roll back a ~ (to extend/roll back the ~s of knowledge) 2. to cross a ~ 3. the final ~ (Space: the final ~!) 4. a ~ between 5. across, over a ~ (to smuggle goods across a ~) 6. along; at, on a ~

front line *n.* at, in, on the ~

frost *n.* 1. a bitter, hard, heavy, severe; ground; light, slight ~ 2. eternal ~, permafrost 3. ~ forms, sets in 4. a touch of ~ 5. degrees of ~ (BE) ("degrees below zero") (five degrees of ~ were reported last night)

froth *v.* to ~ at the mouth

frown I *n.* 1. to wear a ~ (to wear a ~ when answering) 2. an angry; perpetual ~ 3. with a ~ (to answer with a ~ on one's face)

frown II *v.* 1. (D; intr.) to ~ at ("to look with displeasure at") (the teacher ~ed at the noisy children) 2. (d; intr.) to ~ on, upon ("to disapprove of") (they ~ on all forms of affection in public) 3. (misc.) to ~ with displeasure/dissatisfaction

frozen *adj.* ~ hard, solid, stiff

frugal *adj.* (formal) 1. ~ of (esp. BE) (old-fashioned), with (~ with one's money) 2. ~ in ("Both were ~ in their use of energy and time." – British National Corpus)

frugality *n.* (formal) to practice ~ (to practice ~ with one's money)

fruit *n.* 1. to grow ~ 2. (also fig.) to bear ~ (not all trees bear ~) 3. to pick, pluck ~ (off a tree) 4. ripe; unripe ~ 5. fresh; luscious; young ~ 6. citrus; tropical ~ (our country exports citrus ~) 7. (fig.) forbidden ~ 8. candied; glazed; canned (AE), tinned (BE); dried; fresh; frozen ~ 9. a piece of ~ 10. (misc.) (fig.) the ~s of one's labor; the first ~s of the government's recovery program should become apparent very soon

fruitcake *n.* (misc.) (colloq.) as nutty as a ~ ("completely insane")

fruition *n.* 1. to bring smt. to ~ 2. to come to, reach ~

fruitless *adj.* ~ to + inf. (it is ~ even to try)

frustrated *adj.* 1. ~ about, at, by, with; in (he was ~ in his attempts to find support among his friends) 2. ~ to + inf. (he was ~ to find no support among his friends) 3. ~ that + clause (he was ~ that he found no support among his friends)

frustrating *adj.* 1. ~ to + inf. (it was ~ for him to find no support among his friends) 2. ~ that + clause (it was ~ for him ~ that he found no support among his friends)

frustration *n.* 1. to express one's ~ 2. to vent one's ~ on 3. deep, great; growing, mounting ~ 4. ~ builds up, mounts 5. ~ about, at, over, with (his ~ at finding no support among his friends) 6. ~ that + clause (his ~ that he found no support among his friends)

fry *v.* (C) ~ an egg for me; or: ~ me an egg

fry-up *n.* (colloq.) (BE) ["frying of foods"] 1. to do, have a ~ ["dish of fried foods"] 2. to do, make, prepare a ~

fudge *v.* (D; intr.) ("to hedge") to ~ on (to ~ (on) an issue)

fuel *n.* 1. to take on ~ 2. to run out of ~ 3. to conserve, save ~ 4. aviation; high-octane; jet; leaded; liquid; nuclear; solid; unleaded ~ 5. fossil; synthetic ~s (do all cars run on fossil ~s like gasoline?) 6. (misc.) (usu. fig.) to add ~ to the fire

fugitive *n.* 1. to track down a ~ 2. a ~ from (a ~ from justice)

fulfillment, fulfilment *n.* 1. to find; seek ~ (in) 2. personal; wish ~ (a sense of personal ~; a theory based on nothing more than wish ~) 3. partial ~ (of the requirements for a doctoral degree)

full *adj.* 1. half ~ 2. ~ of (the tank was ~ of water) 3. ~ to the brim; ~ to overflowing (the tank was ~ to the brim with water = the tank was ~ of water to the brim)

fulminate *v.* (D; intr.) to ~ against

fumble I *n.* to make a ~

fumble II *v.* 1. to ~ blindly 2. (d; intr.) ("to grope") to ~ for (he was ~ling in his pocket for the key) 3. (d; intr.) to ~ with ("to handle clumsily") (she was ~ling with the lock)

fumble about, fumble around *v.* (D; intr.) to ~ for (he was ~ling around in his pocket for the key)

fume *v.* 1. (D; intr.) to ~ about, at, over (to ~ at the delay) 2. (D; intr.) to ~ with (she was ~ming with annoyance) 3. (misc.) to fret and ~ = to ~ and fret

fumes *n.* 1. to emit, give off ~ 2. to inhale, be overcome by ~ 3. cigar; cigarette; gas ~ 4. noxious, toxic ~ 5. clouds of ~

fun *n.* 1. to have ~ (we had a lot of ~) 2. to make ~ of smb., to poke ~ at smb. 3. to spoil the ~ 4. clean, good, great, harmless ~ 5. a bit of ~ 6. ~ to + inf. (it was ~ to go on the roller coaster = it was ~ going on the roller coaster) 7. for, in ~ (to play for ~) 8. (misc.) let's go just for the ~ of it; it was so much ~/such ~!; no ~ (it's no ~ to get up early! = it's no ~ getting up early!) (see also *poke fun at smb.* at **poke II** *v.*)

function I *n.* ["characteristic action"] 1. to fulfill, perform a ~ 2. a grammatical ~ 3. the bodily ~s ["mathematical correspondence"] 4. an exponential; inverse; linear; trigonometric ~ ["social event"] 5. to attend a ~ 6. an annual; official; public; social ~

function II *v.* 1. to ~ properly 2. (d; intr.) to ~ as (this valve ~s as a safety device)

fund *n.* 1. to establish, set up a ~ 2. to administer, manage a ~ 3. an inexhaustible ~ 4. a consolidated (BE); contingency, emergency; hedge; investment; pension; relief; secret; sinking; sovereign wealth (SWF); slush (colloq.); strike; trust ~ 5. a mutual ~ (AE; BE has *unit trust*) 6. a ~ for (to set up a trust ~ for a child) 7. a ~ to + inf. (to set up a trust ~ to pay for a child's education) (see also **funds**)

fundamental *adj.* ~ to

funded *adj.* federally; government-; locally; poorly; privately; publicly; state -; well-~

funding *n.* 1. to approve ~ 2. to cut off, terminate,

withdraw ~ 3. federal; government; local; private; public; state ~ 4. the ~ to + inf. (we have the ~ to complete the work)

funds *n.* 1. to allocate, allot ~ 2. to disburse, pay out ~ 3. to raise ~ 4. federal; government; local; public; state ~ 5. matching ~ 6. private ~ 7. limited; unlimited ~ 8. (stamped on a check) insufficient ~ (AE; BE has *refer to drawer*) 9. ~ dry up, run out 10. the ~ to + inf. (we have the ~ to complete the work) (see also **fund**)

funeral *n.* 1. to conduct; hold a ~ 2. to attend a ~ 3. a military; state ~ 4. a ~ takes place 5. at a ~

funfair *n.* (BE) at a ~

funk *n.* ["depressed state"] (colloq.) a blue ~ (in a blue ~)

funnel I *n.* to pour smt. through a ~

funnel II *v.* (B) to ~ arms to the partisans

funny *adj.* (colloq.) ["strange"] ["interesting"] 1. ~ about (there's smt. ~ about that affair) 2. ~ to + inf. (it's ~ to watch how people order in a restaurant = it's ~ watching how people order in a restaurant) 3. ~ that + clause (it's ~ that people keep changing their orders in restaurants) 4. (misc.) it's ~ how/ the way people keep changing their orders in restaurants

funny bone *n.* to tickle smb.'s ~

fur *n.* 1. to wear (a) ~ 2. artificial, fake; genuine, real ~ 3. (misc.) the ~ started to fly ("a violent discussion began")

furious *adj.* 1. ~ about, at, over smt. (he was ~ about the loss of his pay check) 2. ~ at (esp. AE), with smb. 3. ~ to + inf. (he was ~ to learn that his pay check had been lost) 4. ~ that + clause (he was ~ that his pay check had been lost)

furlough *n.* (esp. AE) on ~

furnace *n.* 1. to stoke a ~ 2. a blast; coal; coke; gas; hot-air; oil; open-hearth ~ 3. a glowing; roaring ~

furnish *v.* 1. to ~ elegantly; luxuriously; plainly, sparsely; tastefully 2. (B) to ~ supplies to the refugees 3. (D; tr.) ("to provide") to ~ for (to ~ supplies for the refugees) 4. (D; tr.) ("to provide") to ~ with (can you ~ the refugees with the necessary supplies?) 5. (D; tr.) ("to supply with furniture") to ~ with (they ~ed the room with very expensive tables, chairs, and drapes)

furniture *n.* 1. to arrange ~ 2. to upholster ~ 3. antique; colonial; modern; period ~ 4. garden, lawn, outdoor, patio; office; street (BE) ~ 5. secondhand, used; unfinished (esp. AE) ~ 6. an article, piece, stick (colloq.) of ~

furor, furore *n.* 1. to create a ~ 2. a ~ over (the ~ created by/over his statement has begun to die down)

furrow *n.* 1. to make, turn a ~ 2. an even, straight ~

further *adv.* ~ to (~ to your letter of last week, enclosed please find the goods you requested)

furtherance *n.* in ~ of (in ~ of one's aims)

fury *n.* 1. to turn, vent one's ~ on, upon 2. to fly into a ~ 3. to fill smb. with ~; to provoke smb.'s ~ 4. to contain, restrain, suppress (one's) ~ 5. to allay, appease, calm smb.'s ~ 6. blind; elemental; pent-up; mounting, rising; savage, unbridled ~ 7. ~ explodes; wells up; blows over; subsides 8. a blaze, explosion, fit, outburst of ~ 9. ~ about, over; at smt. (he could hardly suppress his ~ about/over the matter) 10. ~ that + clause (our ~ that he had refused to help) 11. in; with ~ (she struck back in ~; burning with ~)

fuse I *n.* ["safety device"] 1. to blow, blow out (esp. AE) a ~ 2. to change a ~ 3. a safety ~ 4. a ~ blows, blows out (esp. AE) 5. (misc.) to blow a ~ ("to get very angry")

fuse II *n.* ["tube, wick used to set off an explosive charge"] 1. to light a ~ 2. a slow ~ (also fig.)

fuse III *n.* (AE) ["detonating device"] 1. to arm, set a ~ 2. a contact; delayed; percussion; proximity; time ~ (AE also has **fuze**)

fuse IV *v.* (D; intr.) to ~ with (to ~ X with Y = to ~ X and Y (together))

fusion *n.* nuclear ~

fuss I *n.* 1. to kick up, make, put up, raise a ~ 2. a ~ blows over, dies down, subsides 3. a ~ about, over (the ~ they kicked up over the new plan soon blew over) 4. (misc.) (BE) to make a ~ of smb.

fuss II *v.* 1. (D; intr.) to ~ about, over 2. (D; intr.) to ~ with

fussy *adj.* ~ about

futile *adj.* 1. completely, utterly ~ 2. ~ to + inf. (it's ~ to speculate about what might have been = it's ~ speculating about what might have been)

futility *n.* 1. complete, utter 2. an exercise in ~

future *n.* ["future time"] 1. to foretell, predict the ~ 2. to plan (out) the ~ 3. to face the ~; to look forward to the ~; to look into the ~ 4. a bleak; dismal; uncertain ~ 5. a bright, glorious, promising, rosy ~ 6. the distant; unforeseeable ~ 7. the foreseeable; immediate, near ~ 8. a ~ for (there is no ~ for them here) 9. for; in the ~ (in the near ~) 10. (BE) in ~ ("from now/then on") (be more careful in ~) 11. (misc.) what does the ~ hold?; what will the ~ bring? ["future form of a verb"] 12. in the ~

fuze (AE) see **fuse III**

G

gadfly *n.* ["annoying person"] a ~ to (the reporter was a constant ~ to the government)

gadget *n.* 1. a ~ for (they have a ~ for cleaning windows) 2. a ~ to + inf. (a ~ to clean windows)

gaff *n.* (slang) (BE) to blow the ~ ("to reveal a secret")

gaffe *n.* ["blunder"] to commit, make a ~

gag I *n.* (colloq.) ["joke"] as, for a ~ (she did it as/ for a ~)

gag II *v.* (D; intr.) to ~ on (to ~ on food)

gaga *adv.* (colloq.) ["enthusiastic"] to go ~ over smt./ smb.

gage see **gauge**

gain I *n.* 1. to make ~s (in recent years minority groups have made considerable political ~s) 2. to consolidate one's ~s (from successful trading) 3. to nullify a ~ 4. a considerable, enormous, notable, substantial, tremendous ~ 5. a personal; tangible ~ 6. (an) economic, financial; electoral, political; weight ~ 7. ill-gotten ~s 8. (economics) capital ~s

gain II *v.* 1. (D; tr.) to ~ by; from (to ~ independence from a colonial power; she stood to ~ a great deal from/by going to college; what do you hope to ~ by betraying me?) 2. (D; intr.) to ~ in ("to acquire") (to ~ in experience) 3. (D; intr.) to ~ on ("to move faster than and get closer to") (the police were ~ing on the fugitive; to ~ on one's prey)

gait *n.* 1. a shambling; steady; unsteady ~ 2. at/with a certain ~ (at/with a steady ~)

gale *n.* 1. a heavy, raging, severe, strong ~ 2. a sudden ~ (we got caught in a sudden heavy ~) 3. a ~ blows itself out, blows over; blows up; dies down, subsides; rages

gall I *n.* (colloq.) ["impudence"] 1. unmitigated ~ 2. the ~ to + inf. (he had the ~ to sue for damages when he was at fault!)

gall II *v.* (R) it ~ed them (to learn) that they were not invited

gallant *adj.* ~ to + inf. (it was ~ of him to say that)

gallantry *n.* 1. to display, show ~ 2. outstanding ~ 3. for ~ (to receive a medal for displaying outstanding ~ in battle)

gallery *n.* 1. an art; fresco ~ 2. a press; public; visitors' ~ 3. a shooting ~ (for target practice or, in slang, for addicts to inject drugs) 4. at, in a ~ 5. (misc.) to play to the ~ ("to attempt to attract public attention")

galling *adj.* 1. ~ to 2. ~ to + inf. it was ~ (to them) to learn that they were not invited

gallon *n.* 1. an imperial ~ 2. by the ~ (to sell fuel by the ~)

gallop *n.* 1. to break into a ~ 2. at a ~ (at full ~)

gallows *n.* to be sent to the ~

galoshes *n.* ["rubber overshoes"] 1. to put on; wear ~ 2. a pair of ~

galvanize *v.* (d; tr.) to ~ into (to ~ smb. into action)

gambit *n.* (chess) 1. to play a ~ 2. to accept; decline a ~ 3. an opening ~

gamble *v.* 1. (D; intr.) to ~ at (to ~ at cards) 2. (D; intr.) ("to risk") to ~ on (to ~ on smb.'s cooperation/cooperating) 3. (D; intr.) to ~ with (to ~ with smb.'s future) 4. (L) to ~ that smb. will cooperate

gambler *n.* a compulsive, inveterate; professional ~

gambling *n.* 1. to ban; legalize ~ 2. compulsive; illegal; legal; offshore; organized ~

game I *adj.* ["ready, willing"] 1. ~ for (are you ~ for a swim?) 2. ~ to + inf. (are you ~ to go for a swim?)

game II *n.* ["contest, match"] 1. to have, play a ~ 2. to draw; lose; win a ~ 3. (AE) to call ("cancel") a (baseball) ~ 4. to throw ("purposely lose") a ~ 5. a close; crucial; fair ~ 6. a bowl (Am. football); championship; home; practice; wild-card (Am. professional football) ~ ["form of recreation"] 7. to play a ~ (to play a ~ of chess with the chess champion) 8. a ball; board; card; chess; children's; computer; numbers; parlor; party; team; video; word ~ 9. a ~ of cards; a ~ of chance; a ~ of chess; a ~ of skill (see also **crap game**; **games**) ["deception"] 10. to see through smb.'s (little) ~ 11. a con, confidence ~ (AE; BE has con trick, *confidence trick*) ["tactic, strategy"] 12. a long (esp. BE); waiting ~ (to play a waiting ~ and not say Yes too quickly) 13. a cat-and-mouse ~ (to play a cat-and-mouse-game with people and leave them in suspense) ["hunted animals"] 14. to bag; hunt; stalk ~ 15. big; small ~ 16. (fig.) fair ~ ("a legitimate object of attack") (to be fair ~ for smb.) 17. (misc.) a ~ preserve, refuge ["prostitution"] (colloq.) (BE) 18. on the ~ ["misc."] 19. the mating ~; to raise one's ~ (under pressure, true champions can raise their ~ to meet the challenge) (see the Usage Note for **match**)

games *n.* ["competition"] ["maneuvers"] 1. to hold, host, organize, stage; participate in, take part in ~ 2. war ~ 3. the Commonwealth; Olympic; summer; winter ~

gamut *n.* 1. to run the ~ from; to 2. the whole ~ (her performances ran the whole ~ from outstanding to terrible)

gander *n.* (colloq.) ["look"] to have, take (esp. AE) a ~ at

gang *n.* 1. to form a ~ 2. to join a ~ 3. to break up, bust (up) a ~ 4. a chain; section; street; work ~ 5. an inner-city; juvenile ~

gangrene *n.* ~ sets in

gangster *n.* a big-time, notorious ~

gang up *v.* 1. (d; intr.) to ~ against, on 2. (d; intr.) to ~ with

gaol (BE) see **jail I, II**

gap *n.* 1. to leave a ~ 2. to bridge, close, fill, narrow a ~ 3. to widen a ~ 4. an unbridgeable, wide, yawning ~ 5. a communications; credibility; culture; generation; gender; trade ~ 6. a ~ between 7. a ~ in 8. (BE) a ~ year ("a year off between secondary school and university")

gape *v.* (D; intr.) to ~ at

garage *n.* 1. a parking ~ (AE; BE has *multi-storey car park*) 2. (misc.) to park a car in a ~

garage sale *n.* (AE) to have, hold a ~

garb I *n.* 1. ceremonial; everyday; formal, official ~ 2. in (formal) ~

garb II *v.* (formal) (d; refl.) to ~ in (they ~ed themselves in colorful costumes)

garbage *n.* (esp. AE) 1. to collect, pick up the ~ 2. to dispose of; dump ~ (BE prefers *rubbish*) (see also **refuse, trash**)

garden *n.* 1. to lay out; plant a ~ 2. to maintain a ~ 3. to water; weed a ~ 4. a botanical; formal; herb; market garden (BE; AE has *truck farm*); rock; rose; sunken; terraced; vegetable; zoological ~ (see the Usage Note for **yard I**) ["misc."] 5. I never promised you a rose ~! ("I never said things would be easy or ideal!")

gardening *n.* 1. to do, go in for ~ 2. landscape ~; market ~ (BE; AE has *truck farming*)

garlic *n.* 1. to crush; peel; sprinkle ~ 2. to smell of ~ 3. a clove of ~ 4. a whiff of ~

garment *n.* a foundation ~

garnish *v.* (D; tr.) to ~ with (to ~ a salad with parsley)

gas *n.* ["accelerator"] 1. to step on the ~ ["combustible gaseous mixture"] 2. to connect; cook with; light, turn on the ~ 3. to cut off, disconnect; turn off the ~ 4. butane; Calor (T) (BE); coal; greenhouse; natural ~ ["substance dispersed through the air to disable the enemy"] 5. mustard; nerve; toxic ~ (see also **poison gas**; **tear gas**) ["misc."] 6. laughing ~ ("nitrous oxide") (see also **gasoline**)

gash *n.* 1. to get; have; make a ~ 2. a deep, nasty; long ~ 3. a ~ on (to have a nasty ~ on one's leg)

gasket *n.* to blow a ~ (colloq.) ("to lose one's temper")

gasoline *n.* (AE) high-octane; leaded; lead-free, unleaded; premium; regular ~ (BE has *petrol*)

gasp I *n.* 1. to emit, give, let out a ~ 2. an audible ~ 3. a ~ for (a ~ for breath) 4. (misc.) the last ~ ("the last effort")

gasp II *v.* 1. (d; intr.) to ~ at, in, with ("to express surprise at") (they ~ed at our offer; she ~ed in amazement) 2. (D; intr.) ("to breathe with difficulty") to ~ for (to ~ for breath)

gas range *n.* 1. to light, turn on a ~ 2. to turn off a ~

gate *n.* 1. to close, shut; open a ~ 2. the back; front; main ~ 3. a ~ closes, shuts; opens 4. a starting ~ (at a racetrack) 5. at; through a ~ 6. (misc.) passengers for flight ten proceed to (departure) ~ five; (AE) (colloq.) to give smb. the ~ ("to reject smb."); (AE) (colloq.) to get the ~ ("to be dismissed")

gateway *n.* a ~ to (the ~ to the west)

gather *v.* 1. (d; intr.) ("to assemble") to ~ around (they ~ed around the speaker) 2. (d; tr.) ("to conclude") to ~ from (I ~ed as much from the expression on your face) 3. (L) ("to conclude") I ~ (from the expression on your face) that you don't like him 4. (misc.) so I ~ ("she seems not to like him." "so I ~")

gathering *n.* 1. to attend a ~ 2. a family; public; social ~

gauge *n.* ["measuring device"] 1. a fuel; oil; pressure; rain; tire-pressure; water; wind ~ ["distance between rails"] 2. broad, wide; narrow; standard ~

gauntlet I *n.* ["challenge"] 1. to throw down the ~ 2. to pick up, take up the ~

gauntlet II *n.* ["ordeal"] to run a ~ (to run the ~ of reporters)

gavel I *n.* 1. to rap a ~ 2. a rap of the ~

gavel II *v.* (d; tr.) to ~ into (he ~ed the protesters into silence)

gawk *v.* (colloq.) (D; intr.) to ~ at

gawp *v.* (BE) (D; intr.) to ~ at

gaze I *n.* 1. to avert; fix; lower one's ~ 2. an admiring; intense, rapt, steady, unblinking; lingering; penetrating, piercing; wistful ~ 3. under smb.'s ~ (he wilted under her penetrating ~)

gaze II *v.* 1. to ~ intently 2. (d; intr.) to ~ at 3. (d; intr.) to ~ into (to ~ into the distance; she ~d into my eyes)

GCSEs n ["General Certificates of Secondary Education"] (GB) 1. to do, sit, take 'one's' ~ 2. in one's ~ (to do well in one's French and German ~) 3. ~ in (to have ~ in French and German)

gear I *n.* ["toothed wheel as part of a transmission"] 1. to change (BE), shift ~(s) 2. to reverse ~s 3. to strip ~s 4. bottom (BE), low; high (AE), top (BE); reverse ~ 5. a worm ~ 6. ~s clash, grind; jam, lock, stick; mesh 7. in ~; out of ~ ["equipment"] 8. fishing; hunting; riot; skiing ~ (see also **landing gear**) ["clothing"] (colloq.) (esp. BE) 9. trendy ~ (kids in / wearing trendy ~)

gear II *v.* (d; tr.) to ~ to (the whole economy is ~ed to the tourist trade)

gear up *v.* (d; intr., tr.) to ~ for (the whole economy is ~ing up for the tourist trade)

gem *n.* (colloq., fig.) 1. an absolute ~ ("smb. or smt. extraordinary") 2. a ~ of an idea ("an excellent idea")

gender *n.* 1. grammatical ~ 2. (the) feminine; masculine; neuter ~ (many languages have no neuter ~) 3. (misc.) ~ neutral (to use gender-neutral terms in advertising a job vacancy)

gene *n.* 1. to carry; transfer, transplant ~s 2. to cut; splice ~s 3. a defective; dominant; recessive ~ 4. a ~ for (a ~ for a trait)

general I *adj.* in ~ ("generally")

general II *n.* 1. an adjutant; brigadier general (US / UK has *brigadier*); commanding; four-star; lieutenant; major ~ 2. (US) a five-star ~ = a ~ of the

Army 3. to make smb. a ~, to promote smb. to the rank of ~; to have, hold the rank of ~ 4. (misc.) what's your opinion, General (Smith)?

generality *n.* 1. a broad, sweeping; vague ~ 2. (to speak) in ~ties

generalization *n.* 1. to make a ~ 2. a broad, sweeping; valid ~ 3. a ~ about 4. a ~ that + clause (it is a valid ~ that exercise promotes good health)

generalize *v.* 1. (D; intr.) to ~ about 2. (D; intr.) to ~ from (to ~ from several specific cases)

general quarters *n.* to sound ~

generation *n.* 1. the baby boom/baby boomer; coming, future, next; new; older; present; younger ~ 2. future; past ~s 3. the greatest; a lost ~ 4. for ~s; in a ~ (the result won't be known in this ~ and perhaps not for several ~s to come) 5. (misc.) from ~ to ~ (see also *generation gap* at **gap**)

generosity *n.* 1. to demonstrate, display, show ~ 2. great, lavish, magnanimous, unstinting ~ 3. ~ in; to, towards; with (~ with money) 4. (misc.) to abuse, take advantage of smb.'s ~

generous *adj.* 1. ~ in; to, towards; with (~ with money) 2. ~ to + inf. (it was ~ of her to contribute such a large sum)

genial *adj.* ~ towards

genitalia *n.* (plural) female; male ~

genius *n.* ["great mental capacity, ability"] 1. to demonstrate, show ~ 2. an inventive; rare ~ (she is a mathematician an of rare ~) 3. a flash, spark, stroke; work of ~ ["ability"] 4. a ~ for (he has a ~ for getting into trouble) ["person of great mental capacity, ability"] 5. an artistic; budding; inventive; mathematical; mechanical; military; musical ~ 6. a rare; real ~ 7. a ~ at (she is a ~ at mathematics) 8. a ~ to + inf. (she was a ~ to have thought of that!)

genocide *n.* to commit, perpetrate ~

gentle *adj.* 1. ~ on; with (be ~ with yourself by using a soap that's ~ on your skin!) 2. (misc.) as ~ as a lamb

gentleman *n.* 1. a complete, perfect, real, true ~ 2. a country ~ 3. (misc.) every inch a ~; a ~ of the old school; (my lords,) ladies and gentlemen....

gentry *n.* the landed; local ~

gen up *v.* (slang) (BE) (D; intr., refl., tr.) ("to inform") to ~ about, on (they ~ned me up on the situation)

geography *n.* biogeography; dialect, linguistic; economic; physical; political ~

geometry *n.* analytic (AE), analytical; descriptive; Euclidean; non-Euclidean; plane; projective; solid ~

germ *n.* ["microorganism"] 1. ~s multiply 2. (some) ~s cause disease

germane *adj.* ~ to (~ to the discussion)

gestation *n.* 1. (a) period of ~ = a ~ period 2. in ~

gesticulate *v.* 1. to ~ angrily, frantically, wildly 2. (D; intr.) to ~ with (to ~ with one's hands at a taxi (in order) to attract the driver's attention)

gesture I *n.* 1. to make a ~ 2. to use ~s to

communicate = to communicate by using ~s = to communicate with ~s 3. an angry; derogatory; obscene; rude ~ 4. an empty, meaningless; frantic; habitual; symbolic; token ~ 5. a bold; defiant ~ 6. a haughty, imperious ~ 7. a conciliatory; friendly; humane, kind ~ 8. a glorious, grand, grandiose, magnificent, noble ~ (in a magnificent ~ of renunciation, the Emperor Charles V abdicated and entered a monastery) 9. (misc.) to eke out one's meaning with ~s

gesture II *v.* 1. (D; intr.) to ~ at; to (the teacher ~d at/to the pupil to stop talking) 2. (D; intr.) to ~ with (to ~ with one's hand) 3. (misc.) the teacher ~d for the pupil to stop talking

get *v.* 1. (B) ("to deliver") I have to ~ a message to her 2. (C) ("to obtain") she got a newspaper for me (for $1); or: she got me a newspaper (for $1); is $1 really enough to ~ you a newspaper these days? 3. (d; intr., tr.) to ~ across, over ("to cross"); ("to cause to cross") (to ~ across a bridge; the general finally got his troops across the river) 4. (d; intr.) to ~ after ("to exert pressure on") (you'll have to ~ after them if they keep making noise) 5. (d; intr.) to ~ around ("to evade") (we cannot ~ around the regulations) 6. (d; intr.) to ~ at ("to suggest") (what are you ~ting at?) 7. (d; intr.) to ~ at ("to reach") (I hope that the children cannot ~ at the medicine; you're safe here: your enemies cannot ~ at you; to ~ at the truth) 8. (esp. AE) (d; intr.) to ~ behind ("to support") (we must ~ behind her campaign) 9. (d; intr.) to ~ between ("to try to separate") (never ~ between fighting dogs) 10. (D; tr.) ("to receive") to ~ for (what did you ~ for your birthday? she got one hundred dollars for her sewing machine; he got five years for larceny) 11. (d; intr.) ("to obtain, receive") to ~ from, out of (is $1 really enough to ~ you a newspaper from a shop these days?; she got the truth out of him; he ~s pleasure from smoking) 12. (d; intr., refl., tr.) to ~ in, into ("to enter"); ("to cause to enter") (to ~ into trouble; to ~ oneself into trouble; to ~ smb. into trouble; to ~ into a car; to ~ into a fight) 13. (d; intr.) to ~ into ("to affect") (what got into him?) 14. (d; intr., refl., tr.) to ~ off ("to leave"); ("to cause to leave") (to ~ off a train) (to ~ smt./smb. off a train) 15. (d; intr.) to ~ on ("to enter") (to ~ on a train) 16. (d; intr.) to ~ on ("to affect") (to ~ on smb.'s nerves) 17. (d; tr.) to ~ on ("to cause to enter") (he finally got the whole group on the train) 18. (d; intr.) to ~ onto ("to enter") (she could not ~ onto the train) 19. (d; intr.) to ~ onto ("to take up for discussion") (we got onto a very interesting topic) 20. (colloq.) (esp. AE) (d; intr.) to ~ onto ("to become aware of") (we finally got onto her schemes) 21. (d; intr., refl., tr.) to ~ out of ("to leave"); ("to extricate"); ("to extricate oneself from") (to ~ out of a car; I got him out of trouble; to ~ (oneself) out of trouble; when did he ~ out of prison?) 22. (d; intr.) to ~ over ("to overcome") (you'll have to ~ over your fear of speaking in public) 23. (d; intr.) to ~ over ("to recover from") (has she got/gotten over the shock?) 24. (d; intr., tr.) to ~ past ("to slip by") (we got past the guard; we got it past the guard) 25. (d; intr.) ("to be unnoticed") to ~ past (the error got past him) 26. (d; intr., tr.) ("to pass") ("to cause to pass") to ~ through (to ~ through a door; we could not ~ the piano through the window) 27. (d; intr.) to ~ to ("to reach") (to ~ to a telephone; to ~ to the point; we got to the theater late) 28. (colloq.) (d; intr.) to ~ to ("to affect") (her pleas got to me) 29. (colloq.) (d; intr.) to ~ to ("to bribe") (they got to the mayor himself) 30. (d; tr.) ("to deliver") to ~ to (to ~ smb. to a hospital) 31. (d; intr.) to ~ within ("to come") (don't ~ within range of the enemy artillery) 32. (E) ("to succeed in") if you can ~ to see her, you may receive some help; if you ~ to know her, you'll like her 33. (colloq.) (E; used in the perfect tenses) ("to be obliged to, to have to") she's got to finish the work by tomorrow; (BE) I'd got to finish the work by yesterday! 34. (G) ("to begin") he finally got going 35. (H; no passive) ("to bring about") she finally got the television to work; I got a gardener to cut the grass 36. (J; more usu. is H) ("to bring about") she finally got the television working 37. (N; used with an adjective, past participle) ("to make") we got our tools ready; he got us involved; try to ~ them interested 38. (P; intr.) ("to arrive") he finally got home 39. (s) ("to become") to ~ angry; to ~ drunk; to ~ loose; to ~ rid of; to ~ even with smb. 40. (S) (BE) you are ~ting a big girl now! 41. (misc.) to ~ clear of (to ~ clear of all obstacles); to ~ cracking ("to start moving"); to ~ in touch with smb.; to ~ nowhere ("to be unsuccessful"); to ~ somewhere ("to score a success") (see also *get-up-and-go* at **go I**; *don't get me wrong* at **wrong I** *adj.*) USAGE NOTE: In AE, the past participle of *to get* is usu. *gotten* – they'd gotten everything ready. In BE, it is *got* – they'd got everything ready. (Note that *ill-gotten gains* is CE.) However, CE does use *have got*: *he's got work*; *I've got to go*. Only BE uses *had got* to form the past tense of this construction – *I'd got to do it yesterday* "I had to do it yesterday". BE also has *he'd got work* "he had work".

get across *v.* (B) ("to make clear") she tried to ~ her ideas across to us

get after *v.* (H) ("to induce") you'll have to ~ him to trim the bushes

get ahead *v.* (d; intr.) to ~ of ("to occupy a position in front of") (try to ~ of him)

get along *v.* 1. (D; intr.) ("to manage") to ~ on (we cannot ~ on his salary) 2. (D; intr.) ("to relate") to ~ with (how does she ~ with her brother?)

get around *v.* 1. (d; intr.) ("to find time") to ~ to (we finally got around to answering our correspondence) 2. (L) it got around that she was resigning

getaway *n.* 1. to make (good) one's ~ 2. a quick ~

get away *v.* 1. (D; intr.) ("to escape") to ~ from (to

~ from one's pursuers) 2. (D; intr.) ("to escape") to ~ with (the thieves got away with the loot) 3. (d; intr.) to ~ with ("to succeed in") (they didn't ~ with their scheme)

get back *v.* 1. (d; intr.) ("to get revenge") to ~ at; for (we got back at him for his insult) 2. (D; intr.) ("to return") to ~ from (we got back from our trip early) 3. (D; tr.) ("to receive") to ~ from (we got the money back from him; they got back a lot of money from their investment = they got a lot of money back from their investment) 4. (D; intr.) ("to come back, return") to ~ to (I got back to New York yesterday; I'll ~ to you) 5. (d; intr.) to ~ to ("to resume") to ~ to work)

get behind *v.* (D; intr.) ("to be late") to ~ in, with (to ~ with one's payments)

get by *v.* 1. (D; intr.) ("to manage") to ~ on (to ~ on very little) 2. (D; intr.) ("to manage") to ~ with (we'll have to ~ with one car)

get down *v.* 1. (D; intr.) ("to dismount") to ~ from (to ~ from a horse) 2. (D; tr.) ("to bring down") to ~ from (she got the book down from the shelf) 3. (d; intr.) to ~ to ("to begin"); ("to take up") (to ~ to work; to ~ to details) USAGE NOTE: In BE children may ask to get down (from the table) when they have finished their meal and want to leave.

get in *v.* ("to join") 1. (d; intr.) to ~ on (to ~ on the act) ("to participate in"); (to ~ on the ground floor) ("to join at the very beginning") 2. (d; intr.) to ~ with (to ~ with the wrong crowd) 3. (misc.) to ~ out of the rain; to ~ a word in edgeways/(esp. AE) edgewise

get off *v.* 1. to ~ lightly 2. (B) we got a letter off to them yesterday 3. (d; intr.) to ~ to ("to begin with") (to ~ to a good start) 4. (D; intr.) ("to escape") to ~ with (he got off with a light sentence; to ~ with a few scratches)

get on *v.* 1. (d; intr.) ("to fare") to ~ at (she is ~ting on well at her job) 2. (d; intr.) ("to advance") to ~ in (to be ~ting on in years) 3. (d; intr.) ("to continue") to ~ with (to ~ with one's work) 4. (esp. BE) (d; intr.) ("to get along") to ~ with (how does she ~ with her brother?)

get out of *v.* (G) I couldn't ~ doing it

get over *v.* (D; intr.) ("to pass") to ~ to (to ~ to the other side)

get round (BE) see **get around**

get through *v.* 1. (B) ("to deliver") (she finally got the message through to them) 2. (D; intr.) ("to reach") to ~ to (we could not ~ to her) 3. (D; intr.) ("to finish") (esp. AE) to ~ with (we must ~ with our work)

get-together *n.* to have a ~

get together *v.* 1. (d; intr.) to ~ on ("to agree on") (we finally got together on a compromise) 2. (D; intr.) ("to meet") to ~ with (we got together with some friends last night)

get-up *n.* ["outfit"] an elaborate ~

get up *v.* 1. (colloq.) (BE) (d; refl., tr.) ("to dress up") to ~ as, like (she got herself up as a ballerina for the party) 2. (D; intr.) ("to rise") to ~ from (to ~ from the table)

ghastly adj. ~ to + inf. (it was ~ of him to say that)

ghetto n. a golden; inner-city, urban ~ (a golden ~ where only rich people lived)

ghost n. ["apparition"] 1. to see a ~ 2. to exorcise a ~ 3. a ~ appears; haunts (the ~ of Hamlet's father haunted Elsinore) 4. to believe in ~s 5. (misc.) as pale/white as a ~; to look as if one has seen a ~

gibe I n. 1. make a ~ 2. a ~ about; at

gibe II v. (D; intr.) to ~ at

gift n. ["present"] 1. to give, present a ~ to; to make smb. a ~ of smt. 2. to bear ~s for, to 3. to heap, lavish, rain ~s on 4. to exchange ~s with 5. an extravagant, lavish; generous; outright ~ (for) 6. a farewell; graduation; shower (AE); wedding ~ 7. to unwrap; wrap a ~ ["talent"] 8. to have a ~ for 9. a ~ for (a ~ for languages)

gifted adj. 1. academically; highly, very; intellectually; musically; physically ~ 2. ~ at; in; with

giggle I n. 1. to get, have the ~s 2. an infectious; nervous; silly ~ 3. an attack of the ~s 4. a ~ about (the girls had quite a ~ about what had happened) 5. (misc.) (colloq.) (BE) as/for a ~ ("as a prank")

giggle II v. (D; intr.) to ~ about, at (the girls ~d about what had happened)

gimmick n. an advertising, promotional; election; sales ~ (the latest promotional ~)

girder n. a steel ~

girdle n. 1. a tight ~ 2. a panty ~

girl n. 1. a career; chorus; college (esp. AE); dancing; flower; office; pinup; stock; working ~ 2. a ball ~ (who retrieves tennis balls) 3. a call ~ ("prostitute who can be summoned by telephone") 4. a baby; little, small; mere ~; a slip of a ~ 5. (esp. AE) a poster ~ (her success made her a poster ~ for early-childhood education) USAGE NOTE: It can be offensive to call a woman a *girl*. Thus, *career woman* and *working woman* are considered by many to be more acceptable than *career girl* and *working girl*. (See the Usage Note for **woman**.) Besides, in some circles *working girl* can be a euphemism for *prostitute*. In addition, the former use of *girl* in the meaning of "black female" is considered offensive. (See also the Usage Note for **boy**.)

girlfriend n. 1. have a ~ 2. a live-in; long-suffering; steady ~ 3. a series, string of ~s

giro n. ["system of transferring money"] (BE) by ~ (to transfer money by ~)

girth n. to measure the ~ of

gist n. (colloq.) ["main meaning"] to get; give the ~ of

give v. 1. (A) she gave the book to me; or: she gave me the book 2. (D; tr.) to ~ for (she gave money for a new health center) 3. (misc.) they gave generously of their time (see also *give smb. to understand* at **understand**)

giveaway n. (colloq.) ["unintentional revelation"] a dead ~ (of)

give away v. 1. (B) ("to donate") she gave all her money away to the poor = she gave away all her money to the poor 2. (D; tr.) ("to betray") to ~ to (they gave him away to the police) 3. (Q) ("to betray") they did not ~ where the money was hidden

give back v. (usu. B; sometimes A) she gave the money back to us = she gave back the money to us = (sometimes) she gave us back the money

give in v. (D; intr.) ("to yield") to ~ to (we had to ~ to their demands)

given adj. (cannot stand alone) 1. ~ to (~ to exaggeration) 2. ~ that + clause (given that he exaggerates, can we trust him?) 3. ~ + wh-word + clause (given how often he exaggerates, can we trust him?)

give out v. (B) we gave the food out to those who needed it = we gave out the food to those who needed it

give over v. 1. (D; refl.) ("to abandon oneself") to ~ to (to ~ oneself over to grief) 2. (esp. BE) (D; tr.) ("to turn over") to ~ to (the building was given over to the youth club) 3. (colloq.) (BE) (used in the imper.) (G) ("to stop") ~ hitting the child

give up v. 1. (B) ("to yield") he gave up his seat to a man on crutches 2. (D; intr.) ("to lose hope") to ~ on (we have given up on her) 3. (D; refl., tr.) ("to turn over") to ~ to (the murderer gave himself up to the police) 4. (G) ("to stop") she gave up attempting to influence them 5. (misc.) they were given up for dead

give way v. 1. (d; intr.) ("to yield") to ~ to (reason gave way to hysteria) 2. (d; intr.) ("to collapse") to ~ under (the table gave way under the sheer ~ of the food)

glad adj. 1. only too; very ~ 2. ~ about, of 3. for (we are very ~ for them both) 4. ~ to + inf. (I'm very ~ to have been invited to the meeting) 5. ~ that + clause (I'm very ~ that I've been invited to the meeting)

glance I n. 1. to cast, dart, shoot; have; sneak, steal a ~ at 2. to exchange ~s 3. an admiring; amused; imploring; shy; wistful ~ 4. a casual, cursory, fleeting, passing ~ 5. a knowing; meaningful, significant; penetrating, probing, searching ~ 6. a backward; conspiratorial; furtive; quizzical; sidelong; stolen, surreptitious; suspicious ~ 7. a disapproving, indignant; hostile; withering ~ 8. at a ~ (I recognized her at a ~; I could see at a ~ that she was glad/how glad she was)

glance II v. 1. ("to look") to ~ admiringly; casually; furtively, surreptitiously; imploringly; indignantly; knowingly; meaningfully; quizzically; shyly; suspiciously 2. (d; intr.) ("to look") to ~ at 3. (d; intr.) ("to look") to ~ down (she ~d down the list) 4. (d; intr.) ("to ricochet") to ~ off (the rock ~d off the window)

gland n. 1. the pituitary; prostate; thyroid ~ 2. the adrenal; ductless, endocrine; eccrine, sweat; lachrymal; lymph; mammary; salivary ~s (endocrine ~s secrete hormones) 3. swollen ~s

glare I *n*. 1. in the ~ (in the ~ of publicity) 2. the ~ of headlights = the ~ from the headlights

glare II *v*. 1. (D; intr.) ("to stare angrily") to ~ at 2. (d; intr.) ("to shine") to ~ into (the sun ~d into my eyes)

glass *n*. ["transparent substance"] 1. to blow, make; break, shatter ~ 2. clear, translucent; colored; cut; ground; plate; safety; sheet; stained ~ 3. a pane, sheet; piece, sliver, splinter of ~ ["tumbler"] ["container"] 4. to drink a ~ (of water) 5. to drain; fill a ~ 6. to raise one's ~ (to give a toast) (to) 7. to clink, touch ~es (when giving a toast) 8. a champagne; cocktail; drinking; shot; water; wine ~ 9. a measuring ~ ["optical instrument"] 10. a magnifying ~

glasses *n*. ["spectacles"] 1. to need; put on; take off; wear ~ 2. to be fitted for ~ 3. dark, sun; horn-rimmed; reading ~ 4. a pair of ~ ["binoculars"] 5. to focus, train ~ on 6. field; opera ~ ["misc."] 7. to see life through rose-colored, rose-tinted (BE) ~ ("to see only the good in life")

gleam I *n*. 1. a faint ~ 2. a wild ~ (there was a wild ~ in his eyes)

gleam II *v*. 1. (D; intr.) to ~ with 2. (s) the coin ~ed gold in the sunlight

glean *v*. (D; tr.) to ~ from (I ~ed from the government statement that nothing would change)

glee *n*. 1. to express ~ 2. with ~ (to dance with ~)

glide *v*. (P; intr.) to ~ across enemy lines; to ~ through the air

glider *n*. 1. to fly a ~ 2. to launch; tow a ~ 3. a ~ flies; glides; soars

glimmer I *n*. a faint, pale, slight, tiny, weak ~ (there remained just the faintest ~ of hope)

glimmer II *v*. (D; intr.) to ~ with (the heavens ~ed with stars)

glimpse *n*. 1. to catch a ~ of 2. a brief, fleeting; tantalizing ~ 3. a ~ into (a book that gives you a ~ into the life of a coal miner)

glint *v*. (D; intr.) to ~ with

glisten *v*. (D; intr.) to ~ with

glitch *n*. (slang) ["mishap"] an unexpected ~ (in)

glitter *v*. 1. (D; intr.) to ~ in (to ~ in the sunlight) 2. (D; intr.) to ~ with

gloat *v*. (D; intr.) to ~ over

globe *n*. 1. to circle, girdle; span the ~ 2. all over; (all) around the ~ (people came to the event from all over the ~!)

gloom *n*. 1. to express ~ 2. (an) all-pervading, deep, deepening, unrelieved ~ 3. a pall of ~ 4. ~ about, over (to express ~ over the situation; the earlier statistics cast a pall of deep ~ over everyone, which lifted when the later statistics were released)

gloomy *adj*. ~ about, over

glorious *adj*. ~ to + inf. (it would be ~ to live in a peaceful world)

glory I *n*. 1. to achieve, win ~ 2. to bring ~ to 3. to reflect ~ on 4. crowning; eternal, everlasting; reflected ~ 5. military ~ 6. a blaze of ~ 7. ~ to (eternal ~ to our heroes!) 8. in (one's/smb.'s) ~ (to bask in

smb.'s ~; to be in one's ~) 9. (misc.) to restore smt. to its former ~; covered in, with ~

glory II *v*. (d; intr.) to ~ in (to ~ in one's triumph)

gloss I *n*. ["luster"] 1. to give smt. a ~ 2. a high ~

gloss II *v*. (d; intr.) to ~ over ("to cover up") (to ~ over one's mistakes and then ~ over them again = to ~ over one's mistakes and then ~ them over again)

glove *n*. 1. boxing; lace; leather; rubber; suede; work ~s (see also **kid gloves**) 2. an oven ~ (esp. BE; AE has *oven mitt, pot holder*) 3. a pair of ~s 4. (misc.) to fit like a ~ ("to fit perfectly")

glow I *n*. 1. to cast, emit a ~ 2. an eerie ~ 3. a bright; dim; soft; warm ~ 4. (misc.) the award brought a warm ~ of pride to her cheeks

glow II *v*. 1. to ~ brightly; dimly 2. (D; intr.) to ~ with (the award made her positively ~ with pride!) 3. (s) the sun ~ed red as it set

glower *v*. (D; intr.) to ~ at

glued *adj*. (cannot stand alone) ~ to (he was ~ to his TV set; her eyes were ~ to the door)

glum *adj*. ~ about

glut I *n*. a ~ on the market

glut II *v*. (D; refl., tr.) to ~ with (to ~ the market with cheap goods)

glutton *n*. a ~ for punishment

gnaw *v*. 1. (d; intr.) to ~ (away) at 2. (D; intr.) to ~ through (the rodents ~ed through the wood)

go I *n*. (colloq.) ["attempt"] 1. a ~ at (let's have a ~ at it) ["misc."] 2. to make a ~ of it ("to make it succeed"); always on the ~; it's all ~ here from morning till night!; get-up-and-go ("energy and initiative") (have you got the get-up-and-go to make a success of this shop?)

go II *v*. 1. to ~ badly; fast, quickly; slow; slowly; well 2. (d; intr.) ("to proceed") to ~ about (to ~ about one's business) 3. (d; intr.) to ~ across ("to cross") (to ~ across a river) 4. (d; intr.) to ~ after ("to follow") (this piece of the puzzle ~es after that one) 5. (d; intr.) to ~ after, at ("to seek to reach") (the dog went after/at the intruder; she went after the job and then went at it energetically) 6. (d; intr.) to ~ against ("to be opposed to"); ("to be unfavorable to") (this ~es against my principles; to ~ against the grain; the war began to ~ against them) 7. (d; intr.) to ~ around ("to circle") (they went around the block) 8. (d; intr.) to ~ before ("to precede") (this piece of the puzzle ~es before that one) 9. (d; intr.) to ~ beyond ("to exceed") (to ~ (above and) beyond the call of duty) 10. (d; intr.) to ~ by ("to travel") (to ~ by car) 11. (d; intr.) ("to pass") to ~ by (to ~ by smb.'s house) 12. (d; intr.) to ~ by ("to follow") (to ~ by the rules) 13. (d; intr.) ("to be known") to ~ by (he used to ~ by another name) 14. (d; intr.) to ~ down ("to descend") (to ~ down a hill) 15. (d; intr.) ("to leave") to ~ for (to ~ for a drive; to ~ for a walk; to ~ for the doctor) 16. (d; intr.) ("to be spent") to ~ for (half our money ~es for food) (see also 27) 17. (d; intr.) ("to be sold") to ~ for (the painting went for a hundred dollars) 18. (d; intr.) to ~ for ("to attack") (he went straight for me; to ~ for the jugular) 19. (d; intr.) ("to try") to ~ for (she went for first prize) 20. (d; intr.) to ~ for ("to concern") (what he said ~es for you too) 21. (colloq.) (d; intr.) to ~ for ("to like") (I could ~ for her; we could really ~ for a drink!) 22. (d; intr.) ("to move") to ~ from; to (to ~ from the sublime to the ridiculous) 23. (d; intr.) to ~ into ("to enter") (to ~ into town; to ~ into the army; to ~ into detail; five ~es into ten twice = five ~es twice into ten) 24. (d; intr.) to ~ off ("to leave") (to ~ off duty; the train went off the tracks; to ~ off the air) 25. (d; intr.) to ~ on ("to leave") (to ~ on a trip) 26. (colloq.) (d; intr.) to ~ on ("to judge by"); ("to rely on") (we must ~ on the assumption that he'll agree; we don't have much to ~ on) 27. (esp. BE) (d; intr.) to ~ on ("to be spent for") (half our money ~es on food) (see also 16) 28. (d; intr.) to ~ out of ("to leave") (to ~ out of the house; to ~ out of business) 29. (d; intr.) to ~ over ("to examine") (to ~ over the books) 30. (d; intr.) to ~ over ("to cross") (they went over the mountain) 31. (d; intr.) to ~ through ("to be sold out in") (the dictionary went through three printings) 32. (d; intr.) ("to pass") to ~ through (to ~ through a red light; to ~ through a door; to ~ through channels) 33. (d; intr.) to ~ through ("to endure") (she went through a lot) 34. (d; intr.) to ~ through ("to spend, squander") (he went through his inheritance in six months) 35. (d; intr.) to ~ through ("to repeat") (to ~ through the main points again) 36. (d; intr.) to ~ through ("to conduct") (to ~ through a ceremony) 37. (d; intr.) to ~ through ("to examine") (to ~ through the books) 38. (d; intr.) ("to travel") to ~ to (we went to Alaska) 39. (d; intr.) ("to move") to ~ to (she went to the door) 40. (d; intr.) to ~ to ("to attend") (to ~ to school; to ~ to college) 41. (d; intr.) to ~ to ("to be received by") (the estate went to her; first prize went to my cousin) 42. (d; intr.) to ~ to ("to reach") (this road ~es to town; the railway ~es to the border) 43. (d; intr.) ("to move") to ~ towards (she went towards the exit) 44. (d; intr.) to ~ towards ("to be designated for") (our contributions went towards setting up a shelter for the homeless) 45. (d; intr.) to ~ up ("to ascend") (to ~ up a hill) 46. (d; intr.) to ~ with ("to date"); ("to be a companion to") (Jim ~es with Nancy) 47. (d; intr.) ("to combine") ("to match") to ~ with (which verb ~es with that noun? "does this blouse ~ (together) with that skirt?" "the blouse ~s well with the skirt: the blouse and the skirt ~ well together") 48. (d; intr.) to ~ without ("to get along without") (to ~ without water) 49. (E) ("to serve") that just ~es to show you that I'm right; (usu. in progressive tenses to show subsequent time) we are ~ing to see them tomorrow but we had been ~ing to see them yesterday 50. (F) she told me to go (and) see who was at the door, so ¬I went and saw/I went to see¬ who was

there 51. (G) to ~ shopping 52. (s) to ~ unnoticed; everything went wrong at first but came right eventually 53. (misc.) to ~ abroad; to ~ the bad ("to be corrupted"); ("to turn sour"); to ~ bankrupt; to ~ to bed; to ~ begging ("to be in little demand"); to ~ broke ("to run out of money"); (BE) to ~ to the country ("to call a general election"); to ~ easy on smb. ("to treat smb. leniently"); to ~ to great expense ("to spend a great deal") (they went to great expense to make things nice); to ~ to extremes; to ~ out of one's mind; to ~ native ("to behave like the natives"); to ~ overboard ("to exaggerate"); to ~ to pieces ("to disintegrate"); to ~ to press ("to be printed as a periodical"); to ~ to sea ("to become a sailor"); to ~ steady (with) (esp. AE) ("to be a boyfriend or girlfriend of"); to ~ to trial (the case went to trial); to ~ to waste ("to be wasted"); to ~ wrong ("to be corrupted"); to ~ from bad to worse ("to become much worse"); she has a lot ~ing for her ("she has many advantages"); cows ~ "moo"; (slang) so I went "well, I never!"

go about v. (G) they went about seeking new customers

goad v. 1. (D; tr.) to ~ into (to ~ smb. into doing smt.) 2. (D; tr.) to ~ with (she kept ~ing him with insults) 3. (H) he kept ~ing me to fight

go-ahead n. 1. to give smb. the ~ 2. to get the ~ 3. the ~ to + inf. (we got the ~ to proceed with the investigation)

go ahead v. 1. (D; intr.) to ~ of (she went ahead of me) 2. (D; intr.) ("to proceed") to ~ with (to ~ with one's plans)

goal n. 1. to set a ~ 2. to achieve, attain, reach, realize a ~ 3. (sports) to allow, concede (esp. BE); deny (esp. BE); kick, make, score a ~ 4. (sports) to nullify a ~ 5. a clear; immediate; realistic; ultimate ~ 6. a long-range, long-term ~ (we have the immediate ~ of making things better and the ultimate ~ of changing society) 7. a short-range, short-term ~ 8. (sports) a disputed; field; winning ~ 9. (BE) (soccer) an own ~ ("a goal scored by a player against his own team") (also fig.) 10. (soccer) in ~ (who's (playing) in ~ for Spurs?)

goal line n. to cross; reach the ~

go along v. 1. (D; intr.) to ~ for ("to participate") (to ~ for the ride) 2. (D; intr.) to ~ with ("to agree to") (to ~ with a compromise)

go around v. 1. (d; intr.) ("to keep company") to ~ with (they were ~ing around with undesirable characters) 2. (G) they went around seeking new customers

goat n. 1. to keep (BE), raise (esp. AE) ~s 2. a mountain ~ 3. ~s bleat 4. a flock, herd of ~s 5. a young ~ is a kid 6. a female ~ is a doe or nanny goat 7. a male ~ is a buck or billy goat 8. (misc.) to get smb.'s ~ ("to irritate smb.")

go away v. (D; intr.) to ~ for (to ~ for a rest)

go back v. 1. (d; intr.) ("to renege") to ~ on (to ~ on one's promise) 2. (D; intr.) ("to return") to ~ to (he went back to his home) 3. (d; intr.) ("to date back") to ~ to (this painting ~es back to the seventeenth century)

God *n.* 1. to bless; praise; pray to; worship ~ 2. to believe in ~ 3. (misc.) in praise of ~; thank ~!; ~ forbid!; for ~'s sake! = (AE) for God sakes!; almighty ~/~ almighty; good ~!; the god of war; to believe that ~ exists = to believe that there is a ~

go down *v.* 1. (d; intr.) ("to become known") to ~ as; in (to ~ in history as a great ruler) 2. (D; intr.) ("to descend") to ~ into (to ~ into a mine) 3. (d; intr.) ("to descend") to ~ to (to ~ to the river) 4. (BE) (d; intr.) ~ with ("to catch, develop, come down with") (to ~ with a cold) 5. (misc.) to ~ to defeat; they went down with their ship; (BE) last year he went down from Cambridge ("he left Cambridge last year"); (esp. BE) her speech went down well/ badly with them

godsend *n.* 1. a real ~ 2. a ~ to

godspeed *n.* (old-fashioned) to bid, wish smb. ~

go forward *v.* (d; intr.) ("to proceed") to ~ with (to ~ with one's plans)

goggle *v.* (D; intr.) to ~ at

goggles *n.* 1. to put on; take off; wear ~ 2. a pair of ~

go in *v.* 1. (d; intr.) ("to occupy oneself") to ~ for (to ~ for gardening) 2. (d; intr.) to ~ with ("to join") (he agreed to ~ with them)

going *n.* ["progress"] rough, slow ~ (to face rough ~)

going-over *n.* ["beating"]["inspection"] 1. to give smb./ smt. a ~ 2. to get a ~ 3. a good ~ (to get a good ~)

gold *n.* 1. to mine; pan, pan for; prospect for ~ 2. to strike ~ (also fig.) ("to discover smt. valuable") 3. pure, solid ~ 4. a (rich) vein of ~ 5. a bar of ~ 6. (misc.) as good as ~

golf *n.* 1. to play ~ 2. clock (BE); miniature ~ 3. a round of ~ (to play a round of ~)

golf ball *n.* to drive; putt a ~

gong *n.* to sound a ~

gonorrhea *n.* 1. to catch, contract, get; have ~ 2. a case of ~

good I *adj.* 1. any; no; very ~ ("is he any ~ at chess?" "I'm afraid he's no ~ at chess at all!"; it's no ~ (you/ your) protesting your innocence: no one believes you!) 2. ~ at, in (she is ~ at/in mathematics) 3. ~ for (exercise is ~ for you; this ticket is ~ for a month) 4. ~ to (he is ~ to his parents) 5. ~ with (he is ~ with his hands) 6. ~ to + inf. (it's no ~ (for you) to protest your innocence: no one believes you!; it's ~ to be home again; it was ~ of you to come) 7. ~ that + clause (it's ~ that we're home again; it was that you came) 8. (misc.) ~ for ("for ever"); she is ~ about baby-sitting ("she doesn't mind baby-sitting"); they made ~ their escape ("they succeeded in escaping"); so far so ~; as ~ as gold ("very good and esp. very obedient") (the baby's been as ~ as gold!); would you be ~ enough to help us? = would you be so ~ as to help us?; she said she'd help us and she was as ~ as her word ("...and she kept her word")

good II *n.* ["something useful"] 1. to do ~ 2. the common; highest ~ ["positive qualities"] 3. to bring out the ~ in smb. ["favor"] 4. in ~ with smb. ["favorable result"] 5. to come to no ~ ["restitution"] 6. to make ~ (for) ["benefit, help"] 7. to do smb. ~ (a vacation will do you a/the world of ~/a power of ~; it will do you ~ to take a vacation) ["misc."] 8. to be up to no ~ ("to be plotting mischief"); for smb.'s own ~ (I'm punishing you – but it's for your own ~!); the greatest ~ for the greatest number

goodbye *n.* to say; wave ~ (to)

goods *n.* 1. to order ~ 2. to send, ship ~ 3. to sell; stock ~ 4. capital; consumer; dry (esp. AE), soft (esp. BE); durable; manufactured; piece, yard (AE) ~ 5. damaged; shoddy; stolen ~ 6. (misc.) to have the ~ on (colloq.) ("to have evidence against"); smb.'s worldly ~; to deliver the ~ ("to keep one's word"); ~s and services

goodwill *n.* 1. to display, show ~ 2. to promote ~ 3. international ~ 4. a gesture, sign, token of ~ 5. ~ to, towards

go off *v.* (D; intr.) ("to leave") to ~ with (she went off with my pen)

go on *v.* 1. (d; intr.) ("to continue") to ~ about (to ~ (and on endlessly) about one's own problems) 2. (d; intr.) ("to continue") to ~ as (he went on as chairman) 3. (D; intr.) ("to perform") to ~ as (he went on as Hamlet) 4. (d; intr.) to ~ at ("to nag") (stop ~ing on at me all the time about my mistakes!) 5. (d; intr.) ("to advance") to ~ to (she went on to fame and fortune) 6. (D; intr.) ("to continue") to ~ with (they went on with their work) 7. (E) ("to advance") she went on to become rich and famous 8. (G) ("to continue") he went right on typing

goose *n.* 1. geese cackle, honk; waddle 2. a flock of geese, a gaggle of geese (on the ground) (literary), a skein of geese (in flight) (literary) 3. a young ~ is a gosling 4. a male ~ is a gander

goose bumps, gooseflesh, goose pimples *n.* 1. to give (smb.) ~ 2. to get; have ~

go out *v.* 1. (D; intr.) ("to leave") to ~ for (to ~ for a walk) 2. (esp. AE) (D; intr.) ("to try out") to ~ for (to ~ for a team) 3. (BE) (d; intr.) to ~ to ("to emigrate") (she went out to New Zealand) 4. (D; intr.) ("to go steady") to ~ with (Olga has been ~ing out with Joe) 5. (G) they went out drinking every night 6. (misc.) our hearts ~ to the bereaved ("we have deep sympathy for the bereaved"); to ~ into the world ("to become independent")

go over *v.* 1. (d; intr.) ("to pass") to ~ from; to (let's ~ from this side of the room to the other side of the room = let's ~ from this side of the room over to the other side of the room; to ~ to the attack) 2. (d; intr.) to ~ to ("to desert to") (to ~ to the enemy) 3. (misc.) her speech went over well/badly (with the audience) ("her speech was a success/failure")

gorge *v.* (D; refl.) to ~ on, with (to ~ oneself on sweets)

gorilla *n.* a band, troop of ~s

gospel, Gospel *n.* 1. to preach, proclaim; spread the ~ 2. to believe in the ~ (see also *the gospel truth* at **truth**)

gossip I *n.* 1. to spread ~ 2. (BE) to have a ~ (with) 3. common; idle; juicy; malicious, vicious; silly ~ 4. a bit, piece, tidbit (AE), titbit (BE) of ~ 5. ~ about (have you heard the ~ about his intention to resign?) 6. ~ that + clause (have you heard the ~ that he intends to resign?)

gossip II *v.* (D; intr.) to ~ about; with

go through *v.* (d; intr.) ("to proceed") to ~ with (to ~ with one's plans)

goulash *n.* Hungarian ~

go up *v.* 1. (d; intr.) to ~ against ("to oppose") (to ~ against a formidable foe) 2. (D; intr.) ("to rise") to ~ by (prices went up (by) ten percent) 3. (d; intr.) to ~ to ("to approach") (she went up to him and introduced herself) 4. (D; intr.) ("to ascend") to ~ to (to ~ to the top) 5. (BE) to ~ to (to ~ to London; to ~ to university) 6. (misc.) to ~ north

governess *n.* a ~ for, to (she served as a ~ to three small children)

government *n.* 1. to form a ~ 2. to head; operate, run a ~ 3. to recognize a (new) ~ 4. to bring down, overthrow, topple; destabilize, subvert; dissolve; seize a ~ 5. (a) clean; corrupt; stable; strong; unstable; weak ~ 6. a caretaker; civil; coalition; interim; military; provisional; puppet; shadow ~ 7. an authoritarian, autocratic; communist; conservative; democratic; dictatorial, totalitarian; liberal; parliamentary; reactionary; socialist ~ 8. (a) central; federal; local; municipal; national; provincial ~ 9. a student ~ 10. a ~ comes to power, takes office; falls; resigns 11. a member of a ~ (a back-bencher who became a member of the ~) 12. in; under a ~ (which people are in the ~?; which party is in ~?; to live under a democratic ~) 13. (misc.) (BE) ~ and opposition; the ~ benches; a ~ of national unity USAGE NOTE: In BE, the noun *government* may be used with either a singular or a plural verb. In AE, this noun is always used with a singular verb.

governor *n.* 1. to appoint; elect smb. ~ 2. a deputy, lieutenant; military; prison (BE); school (BE) ~ 3. a ~ general 4. a board of ~s

gown *n.* an academic; dressing; evening (AE), ball; formal; hospital ~; nightgown (esp. AE); wedding ~ USAGE NOTES: (1) Both *dressing gown* and *bathrobe* are CE. But BE uses *dressing gown* for any such garment not made of toweling, whereas AE can use *bathrobe* for all but the most luxurious *dressing gowns.* (2) BE prefers *evening dress* and *night dress* to *evening gown* and *nightgown.*

GP *n.* 1. a family; local; NHS; private ~ (you should register with an NHS ~ if you move to a new area) 2. ~s prescribe medication 3. ~s examine; see; treat (their) patients 4. ~s refer (their) patients to consultants/hospitals/specialists 5. (misc.) to see ("consult") a ~

grab *v.* 1. (C) ~ a few for me (from the table); or: ~

me a few (from the table) 2. (d; intr.) to ~ at (she ~bed at my arm) 3. (d; tr.) to ~ by (he ~bed me by the shoulder) 4. (d; intr.) to ~ for (she ~bed for his pistol)

grabs *n.* (colloq.) up for ~ ("readily available to anyone")

grace I *n.* ["short prayer"] 1. to say ~ ["sense"] ["decency"] 2. the ~ to + inf. (she had the good ~ to concede defeat) ["favor"] 3. divine ~ 4. to fall from ~ 5. by the ~ of God 6. in smb.'s good ~s 7. (rel.) a state of ~ ["willingness"] 8. with (a) bad; good ~ ["attractiveness or movement"] 9. effortless ~ (she moves with effortless ~) ["feature"] 10. a saving ~ (her saving ~ is her sense of humor)

grace II *v.* (d; tr.) to ~ with (she ~d us with her presence)

graceful *adj.* as ~ as a swan

gracious *adj.* 1. ~ to, towards (she is ~ to all) 2. ~ to + inf. (it was ~ of him to make the offer)

gradation *n.* 1. (ling.) vowel ~ 2. a ~ in

grade I *n.* ["mark, rating"] (esp. AE) 1. to make out ~s; to give a ~ 2. to get, receive a ~ 3. an excellent, high; failing; fair, mediocre; low; final; passing ~ 4. (a student's) average; top ~s (she got top ~s in all her exams) ["standard"] 5. to make the ~ 6. a high; low; medium; prime ~ 7. at, on a certain ~ (people on the highest ~s need to set an example for others) ["degree of descent, rise, gradient, slope"] 8. a gentle, gradual; slight; steep ~ ["school year"] (AE) 9. to fail; skip a ~ (the worst students failed Fourth Grade but the best students skipped it and went on to Fifth Grade)

grade II *v.* 1. to ~ high; low 2. to ~ on a curve

gradient *n.* a gentle, gradual; slight; steep ~

graduate I *n.* 1. a college (esp. AE), university; high-school (AE) ~ 2. a ~ in (a ~ in medicine) 3. a ~ of (a ~ of Harvard = a Harvard ~)

graduate II *v.* 1. (D; intr., tr.) to ~ from (to ~ from Harvard) 2. (D; intr.) to ~ in (to ~ in medicine) 3. (misc.) to ~ with honors, cum laude USAGE NOTE: CE has *to graduate from Harvard* or, formally, *to be graduated from Harvard.* AE has also *to graduate Harvard/college/high school.*

graduate work *n.* to do ~

graduation *n.* 1. a college; university; high-school (AE) ~ 2. ~ from (~ from college/Harvard)

graduation ceremonies, graduation exercises *n.* to attend; hold ~

graffiti *n.* 1. to daub/deface walls with ~ = to daub ~ on walls 2. to remove ~ 3. a piece of ~

graft I *n.* ["act of grafting, inserting"] 1. to do a ~ 2. a bone; skin ~ 3. a (skin) ~ takes (the first skin ~ was rejected but the second one took) ["bribes"] (AE) 4. ~ and corruption ["work"] (colloq.) (BE) 5. hard ~

graft II *v.* (D; tr.) to ~ on to, onto

grain *n.* ["food plants"] 1. to grow ~ 2. to store ~ ["texture"] 3. a fine; rough; smooth ~ 4. (to go) against the ~; with the ~ ["misc."] 5. to take smt. with a ~ of salt ("to regard smt. with skepticism")

grammar *n.* 1. comparative; descriptive; functional; generative; historical; normative; prescriptive; structuralist; systemic; transformational ~ 2. a rule of ~ (to learn the ~s of English grammar) 3. (misc.) it's bad ~ to say *ain't*

grand *adj.* see **great**

grandeur *n.* delusions of ~

grant I *n.* 1. to award, give; refuse a ~ 2. to apply for a ~ 3. to get, receive; have a ~ (from) 4. a block; cash; categorical (AE); federal (AE); government; matching; research ~ 5. a ~ for (a ~ from a government body for research on folklore) 6. a ~ to + inf. (we received a ~ to attend the conference)

grant II *v.* 1. (A) the government ~ed a pension to her; or: the government ~ed her a pension 2. (L; may have an object) I ~ (you) that this is true 3. (formal) (M) I ~ this to be true 4. (misc.) (even) ~ing (that) it's true, so what?

granted *adj.* 1. to take smb. for ~ ("to assume that smb. will agree, cooperate") 2. to take smt. for ~ ("to assume that smt. is certain to happen") 3. (misc.) (even) ~ (that) it's true, so what?

grapefruit *n.* 1. pink; seedless; white ~ 2. (misc.) half a ~; a ~ section

grapes *n.* 1. to pick ~ 2. to press ~ 3. seedless; sweet ~ 4. a bunch of ~ 5. (usu. fig.) sour ~

grapevine *n.* ["circulation of rumors, gossip"] by, on, through the ~ (to hear news through the ~)

graph *n.* 1. to draw a ~ 2. a bar ~ 3. in, on a ~ (to draw a ~ showing useful information on it)

graphics *n.* computer; media ~

grapple *v.* 1. (d; intr.) to ~ for (they ~d for the key) 2. (d; intr.) to ~ with (to ~ with a problem; they ~d with each other for the key)

grasp I *n.* ["comprehension"] 1. to have a good ~ (of a subject) 2. a firm; thorough ~ 3. an intuitive ~ ["reach"] 4. to slip from smb.'s ~ 5. beyond smb.'s ~ 6. within smb.'s ~

grasp II *v.* 1. (d; intr.) to ~ at, for 2. (D; tr.) to ~ by (to ~ smb. by the arm) 3. (L) they finally ~ed that it was true 4. (Q) they could never quite ~ how to do it

grass I *n.* 1. to cut, mow; water the ~ 2. high, tall; short ~ 3. a blade; clump, tuft of ~ 4. across; through; in; on the ~ (to run across/through the ~; to find a coin in the tall ~; to spread a blanket on the short ~) 5. (misc.) keep off the ~!; to put smb. out to ~ (usu. fig.)

grass II *v.* (slang) (BE) ("to inform against smb.") 1. (d; intr.) to ~ on (the criminal ~ed on his accomplices (to the police)) 2. (d; intr.) to ~ to (the criminal ~ed (on his accomplices) to the police)

grasshopper *n.* 1. ~s jump, leap 2. ~s chirp

grass up *v.* (slang) (BE) (D; tr.) ("to grass on smb.") to ~ to (he ~ed his accomplices up to the police = he ~ed up his accomplices to the police)

grate *v.* (D; intr.) to ~ on (the noise ~s on my ears)

grateful *adj.* 1. deeply, profoundly; everlastingly; very ~ 2. ~ for; to (I am ~ to you for your help) 3.

~ to + inf. (we were ~ to be alive) 4. ~ that + clause (I'm ~ that you can help)

gratification *n.* 1. to express ~ 2. deep, profound ~ 3. instant ~ 4. smb.'s ~ at (we expressed our profound ~ at the acceptance of our proposal) 5. ~ that + clause (we expressed our profound ~ that our proposal had been accepted)

gratified *adj.* 1. ~ at, by, over, with (~ at the outcome) 2. ~ to + inf. (we were very ~ to learn that our proposal had been accepted) 3. ~ that + clause (we were very ~ that our proposal had been accepted)

gratifying *adj.* 1. ~ to + inf. (it was profoundly/very ~ (for us) to learn that our proposal had been accepted) 2. ~ that + clause (it was ~ profoundly/very (for us) that our proposal had been accepted)

gratitude *n.* 1. to express; feel; show ~ 2. deep, profound, sincere, undying; eternal, everlasting ~ 3. ~ at; for (we expressed our profound ~ at/for the acceptance of our proposal) 4. ~ to (we expressed our profound ~ to him for the acceptance of our proposal) 5. ~ that + clause (we expressed (to him) our profound ~ that our proposal had been accepted) 6. in, with ~ to (we are making this contribution in ~ to all of you)

grave *n.* 1. to dig a ~ 2. to desecrate a ~ 3. a common, mass; pauper's; unmarked; watery ~ 4. at; in; on a ~ (to pray at and put a wreath on a ~ while thinking of the person (lying) in it) 5. beyond the ~ (is there anything beyond the ~?) 6. (misc.) a gravedigger; from (the) cradle to (the) ~

graveside *n.* at a ~ (to pray at a ~) (see also *graveside service* at **service**)

gravitate *v.* (d; intr.) to ~ to, towards

gravity *n.* ["seriousness"] 1. to grasp the extreme/great ~ (of a situation) ["weight"] 2. to defy ~ 3. specific; zero ~ 4. the center; force of ~ (the dancer's leaps seemed to defy the force of ~!)

gravy *n.* 1. to make; pass; pour; serve ~ 2. thick; watery ~ (to pour more thick ~ on the meat)

gray (AE) see **grey**

graze *v.* (d; intr.) to ~ against (he ~d against the table)

grease *n.* 1. to cut, dissolve ~ 2. axle ~ 3. a smear; spot of ~ (see also **elbow grease**)

great *adj.* (colloq.) 1. ~ at (she's ~ at improvising) 2. ~ to + inf. (it was ~ of you to help; it was ~ to see everyone again = it was ~ seeing everyone again) 3. ~ that + clause (it was ~ that we could see everyone again) 4. (misc.) huge ~ (BE) (I saw a huge ~ bear in the woods!); "I think continually of those who were truly ~" – Sir Stephen Spender (1909–95)

great guns *n.* (colloq.) to go ~ ("to have great energy")

greatness *n.* to achieve ~

great one *n.* (colloq.) ["enthusiast"] a ~ for (he's a ~ for telling fibs)

greed *n.* 1. to demonstrate, display ~ 2. insatiable ~ 3. ~ for 4. consumed with ~

greedy adj. 1. ~ for 2. ~ to + inf. (it was ~ of them to eat up all the candy)

Greek n. (colloq.) it was (all) ~ to me ("it was incomprehensible to me")

green I adj. 1. (of a traffic light) to go, turn ~ 2. (cannot stand alone) to be; go, turn ~ with (envy) 3. as ~ as grass

green II n. ["color"] 1. (a) bright; dark; light; pale ~ 2. to dress in, wear ~ 3. to go, turn ~ 4. a shade of ~ ["something green"] 5. a patch of ~ 6. in ~ (dressed in ~) ["green light"] 7. on ~ (turn on ~ only)

green light n. ["permission to continue"] 1. to give smb. the ~ 2. to get the ~ 3. the ~ to + inf. (we got the ~ to proceed with the investigation)

greet v. 1. to ~ warmly 2. (D; tr.) to ~ with (they were ~ed with cheers; the news was ~ed with alarm) 3. (misc.) to ~ with open arms ("to welcome warmly")

greeting n. 1. to extend a ~ 2. to respond to a ~ 3. a cordial, friendly, sincere, warm; enthusiastic ~ 4. an official ~

greetings n. 1. to exchange ~ 2. to extend, send ~ 3. to receive ~ 4. to return ~ 5. cordial, friendly, sincere, warm, warmest; enthusiastic ~ 6. official ~ 7. holiday, season's ~ (see also **regards**)

grenade n. 1. to launch; lob, throw a ~ 2. a hand; percussion; rifle ~ 3. (misc.) to pull the pin on a ~

grey n. 1. to go, turn ~ ('he's/his hair is' starting to go a bit ~ at the temples) 2. dark; light; pale ~

gridlock n. (esp. AE) 1. to cause ~ 2. (misc.) ~ paralyzed the western end of the city

gridlocked adj. (AE) hopelessly ~ (traffic was hopelessly ~)

grief n. 1. to cause ~ 2. to express; feel, suffer ~ (at, for, over) 3. to come to ~ 4. to ease smb.'s ~ 5. (slang) (BE) to give smb. ~ ("to criticize or make trouble for smb.") (don't give me any more ~ about it!) 6. bitter, deep, inconsolable, overwhelming, profound ~ 7. ~ at, over 8. of ~ (to die of ~) 9. (misc.) good ~! ("exclamation expressing mild dismay")

grievance n. 1. to air, vent a ~ 2. to file, submit a (formal/official) ~ 3. to hear a ~ (the committee heard the ~) 4. to harbor, nurse a ~ 5. to redress; settle a ~ 6. a genuine, justified, legitimate, valid; unjustified ~ 7. a ~ against

grieve v. 1. to ~ deeply 2. (D; intr.) to ~ at, for, over 3. (R) it ~d me (to learn) that she had been severely injured

grill I n. 1. a charcoal ~ 2. (a) mixed ~

grill II v. ("to broil") (C) ~ a hamburger for me; or: ~ me a hamburger

grill III v. ("to question") 1. to ~ mercilessly, relentlessly 2. (D; tr.) to ~ about (he was ~ed about his role in the swindle)

grimace I n. to give, make a ~ (he gave a ~ of disgust at the thought of eating it)

grimace II v. (D; intr.) to ~ in, with (to ~ with pain) (he ~d in/with disgust at the thought of eating it)

grime n. a layer of ~

grin I n. 1. to break into, give, flash a ~ 2. a broad; contagious, infectious; foolish, silly; sardonic; sheepish ~ 3. (misc.) wipe that silly ~ off your face!

grin II v. 1. to ~ broadly 2. (D; intr.) to ~ at 3. (D; intr.) to ~ with (to ~ with pleasure) 4. to ~ from ear to ear

grind I n. ["boring activity"] the daily ~

grind II v. 1. (C) ~ a pound of coffee for me; or: ~ me a pound of coffee 2. (D; tr.) to ~ into (to ~ wheat into flour) 3. (D; tr.) to ~ from, out of (to ~ flour from wheat) 4. (N: used with an adjective) I ground the coffee very fine 5. (misc.) to ~ to a halt; she ground her heel into the dirt

grind away v. (colloq.) (D; intr.) ("to work hard") (esp. AE) to ~ at (to ~ at one's studies)

grinder n. 1. a coffee ~ 2. (AE) a meat ~ (to pass meat through a meat ~) (BE has *mincing machine, mincer*)

grip n. ["grasp"]["hold"] 1. to get a ~ on; to strengthen one's ~ on 2. to lose one's ~ 3. to loosen, relax, release; tighten one's ~ (he had a firm grip that he refused to loosen) 4. a firm, iron, strong, tight, vise-like; loose, weak ~ ["control"] 5. to get a ~ on oneself 6. to lose one's ~ 7. in the ~ of (in the ~ of a general strike; do you remember when young people were in the ~ of Beatlemania?) ["device that grips"] 8. a hair ~ (BE; AE has *bobby pin*) ["stagehand"] 9. a first, key ~ (see also **grips**)

gripe I n. (colloq.) ["complaint"] 1. a legitimate ~ (she has a legitimate ~) 2. a ~ about (she has a ~ about not being treated fairly) 3. a ~ that + clause (her ~ is that she is not treated fairly)

gripe II v. (colloq.) 1. (D; intr.) ("to complain") to ~ about, at (she kept ~ping to everyone about not being treated fairly) 2. (L; to) (she kept ~ping to everyone that she was not being treated fairly)

grips n. to come to, get to (esp. BE) ~ with smt. ("to confront, deal with")

grist n. ~ for (AE), to (BE) smb.'s mill ("smt. used to good advantage")

grit n. ["courage, perseverance"] (colloq.) 1. to display, show ~ 2. true ~ 3. the ~ to + inf. (they had enough ~ to hold out in the face of real hardship)

groan I n. 1. to emit, give, heave, let out, utter a ~ 2. a loud; muffled ~

groan II v. 1. (D; intr.) to ~ about, over (to ~ over new taxes) 2. (D; intr.) to ~ in, with (to ~ with frustration) 3. (d; intr.) to ~ under (the table ~ed under the weight of the food) 4. (L) he ~ed (to us) that he had been shot = "I've been shot!" he ~ed (to us) 5. (misc.) to ~ under the weight of oppression; to grunt and ~; to moan and ~

groom v. 1. (d; tr.) to ~ as (she was ~ed as our next candidate) 2. (d; tr.) to ~ for (to ~ smb. for the presidency) 3. (H) they were ~ing her to assume the presidency

grooming n. good; immaculate ~

groove *n.* 1. (stuck) in a ~ 2. to fit into a ~ 3. to slide along a ~ 4. a ~ in (to cut a ~ in a piece of wood)

grope *v.* 1. to ~ blindly 2. (D; intr.) to ~ for (to ~ for one's keys) 3. (P; intr.) to ~ around (in the dark); they ~d their way along the corridor

grotesque *adj.* ~ to + inf. (it was ~ of/for him to come dressed like that)

ground *n.* ["contested area"] 1. to gain ~ on 2. to hold, stand one's ~ 3. to give ~ 4. to lose, yield ~ ["soil"] ["terrain"] 5. firm, hard, solid; frozen; high; soft; swampy ~ (a patch/piece of solid ~) 6. hallowed, holy ~ 7. on the ~ ["interest"] 8. common ~ (to find common ~ with smb.) ["area used for a specific purpose"] 9. a burial; camping; dumping ~; fairground; hunting; parade; picnic ~; playground; recreation (BE) ~ (what did you do at the fairground?) (see also **breeding ground**; **dumping ground**; **proving ground**) ["area of knowledge"] 10. to cover, go over ~ (we covered the same ~ yesterday) ["misc."] 11. to break ~ ("to begin building"); to break new ~ ("to explore smt. new"); from the ~ up ("from the very beginning"); on delicate ~ ("in a situation that demands great tact"); to get off the ~ ("to get started"); on dangerous ~ ("exposed to danger"); on safe ~ ("in safety"); on shaky ~ ("without a firm basis"); smb.'s favorite stamping ~ ("smb.'s favorite spot"); (to occupy) the center, middle ~ in politics; (to occupy) the moral high ~ ["basis, foundation"] 12. on ~ (on what ~ do you base your charge?) (see also **grounds**; **middle ground**)

grounded *adj.* (usu. does not stand alone) ~ in (she is well ~ in grammar)

ground floor *n.* to be in on/get in on the ~ ("to be part of an undertaking from the beginning")

ground rules *n.* to establish, lay down the ~

ground zero *n.* at ~ (a camp was set up at ~)

grounding *n.* ["training"] 1. to get, receive a (good) ~ (in) 2. a ~ in (she got a good ~ in grammar)

grounds *n.* ["basis, foundation"] 1. to give smb. ~ 2. ample; solid ~ 3. moral ~ 4. ~ for (~ for denying bail) 5. ~ to + inf. (we had sufficient ~ to sue; there were no ~ to deny bail) 6. on ~ (on what ~ do you base your charge?) ["sediment"] 7. coffee ~ ["area used for a specific purpose"] 8. hospital ~ 9. in, on (AE) the (hospital) ~

groundwork *n.* to do, lay the ~ (basic) for

group I *n.* 1. an affinity; age; family; social ~ 2. an ethnic, minority; special-interest; splinter ~ 3. a peer; pressure ~ 4. a control; discussion; encounter; focus; self-help; therapy; working ~ 5. (music) a pop; rock ~ 6. (BE) a ginger ~ ("a group of activists") 7. (medical) a blood ~ 8. a member of a ~ = a ~ member

group II *v.* 1. (d; intr.) to ~ around (the scouts ~ed around their leader) 2. (d; tr.) to ~ by (the children were ~ed by age) 3. (d; tr.) to ~ into (the teams were ~ed into two leagues) 4. (d; tr.) to ~ under (to ~ several types under one heading)

grouse I *n.* (colloq.) ["complaint"] 1. a ~ about (she

has a ~ about not being treated fairly) 2. a ~ that + clause (her ~ is that she is not treated fairly)

grouse II *v.* (colloq.) 1. (D; intr.) ("to complain") to ~ about, at (she kept ~sing to everyone about not being treated fairly) 2. (L; to) (she kept ~sing to everyone that she was not being treated fairly)

grove *n.* a lemon; olive; orange ~ (compare **orchard**)

grovel *v.* 1. (D; intr.) to ~ to (she will not ~ to anyone) 2. (misc.) to ~ at smb.'s feet; to ~ in the dirt

grow *v.* 1. (D; intr.) to ~ by (the city grew (by) ten percent) 2. (d; intr.) ("to develop") to ~ from (oaks ~ from acorns) 3. (d; intr.) ("to develop") to ~ into (acorns ~ into oaks) 4. (colloq.) (d; intr.) to ~ on ("to become likable") (the strange new sculpture just ~s on you) 5. (d; intr.) to ~ out of ("to become too large for, outgrow") (the children grew out of their clothes) 6. (d; intr.) ("to develop") to ~ out of (the city grew out of a small village) 7. (d; intr.) ("to develop") to ~ to (to ~ to adulthood; to ~ to one's full height) 8. (E) ("to begin") we grew to love them 9. (s) ("to become") to ~ longer; old; older; taller (in the autumn/fall the days ~ longer) USAGE NOTE: The verb *grow* "to become" often suggests a gradual process rather than a sudden change. Compare *it grew cold* (gradually) and *it turned cold* (suddenly).

growl *v.* 1. (B) he ~ed a few words to us 2. (D; intr., tr.) to ~ at (the dog ~ed at the jogger; he ~ed a few words at us) 3. (L; to) he ~ed (at/to us) that he would be late = "I'm going to be late!" he ~ed (at/to) us 4. (misc.) he ~ed at/for/to us to wait for him

growth *n.* 1. to foster, promote, stimulate ~ 2. to arrest, inhibit, retard, stifle, stunt ~ 3. rapid; untrammeled; zero ~ 4. economic; population ~ (zero population ~) 5. (med.) a benign, non-cancerous, non-malignant; cancerous, malignant; inoperable ~ (to remove a malignant ~) 6. (biology) cell ~ 7. ~ in 8. (misc.) a scraggly ~ (of beard)

grow up *v.* (E) she grew up to be an able politician

grub I *n.* (colloq.) pub ~ (BE) ("pub food")

grub II *v.* (d; intr.) ("to rummage") to ~ for (to ~ in the garbage for food)

grudge I *n.* 1. to bear, harbor, have, hold, nurse a ~ 2. a bitter; deep-seated ~ 3. a ~ against

grudge II *v.* (O) he ~s us our success

grumble I *n.* 1. to have a ~ 2. a ~ about, at, over; to (to have a ~ to us about the new taxes)

grumble II *v.* 1. to ~ constantly 2. (D; intr.) to ~ about, at, over; to (to ~ at the new taxes) 3. (L; to) they ~ed (to us) that the new taxes were too high

grumbler *n.* a chronic, constant ~

grumbling *n.* chronic, constant ~

grumpy *adj.* (colloq.) ~ about

grunt I *n.* 1. to give, let out, utter a ~ (of) 2. with a ~ (he lifted the box with a loud ~ of effort)

grunt II *v.* 1. (B) she ~ed a few words to them 2. (L; to) he ~ed (to her) that he would get up later 3. (misc.) to ~ and groan

guarantee I *n.* ["assurance of quality"] ["warranty"] 1. to give, offer, provide a ~ 2. a cast-iron; lifetime, money-back; written ~ 3. a ~ expires, runs out; lasts 4. a ~ against; on (a ~ against mechanical defects; a two-year ~ on a new car) 5. under ~ (the new car is still under ~) ["assurance, pledge"] 6. to give a ~ 7. a cast-iron, firm ~ (we gave a firm ~ of our willingness to abide by the rules) 8. a ~ that + clause (we have a firm ~ that the work will be finished on time)
guarantee II *v.* 1. to ~ fully 2. (A; usu. without *to*) we cannot ~ you regular hours 3. (D; tr.) to ~ against (to ~ a new car against mechanical defects) 4. (D; tr.) to ~ for (to ~ a new car for one year) 5. (H) it's ~d to last five years 6. (L) we can ~ (to you) that the work will be finished on time 7. (formal) (M) the owner ~d the coins to be genuine 8. (misc.) satisfaction ~d or your money back!
guard I *n.* ["group of sentries"] ["sentry"] 1. to call out the ~ 2. to mount, post the ~ 3. to change, relieve the ~ 4. an advance; armed; color; honor ~ = ~ of honor; palace; police; rear; security ~ (they slipped past the palace ~) 5. under ~ ["guard duty"] 6. to stand ~ over 7. on ~ (to go on ~) ["militia"] 8. a home ~ ["police officer"] ["auxiliary police officer"] 9. a crossing ~ (AE); a school-crossing ~ (BE) 10. a prison ~ (AE; BE has *warder, wardress*) (see also **National Guard** and the Usage Note for **warden**) ["alertness"] ["readiness to fight"] 11. off ~; on ~ (to be caught off ~) 12. to put smb. on their ~ 13. to keep one's ~ up 14. to let one's ~ down ["protective article of clothing"] 15. a knee; nose; shin ~
guard II *v.* 1. to ~ closely (the player was ~ed closely by her opponent) 2. (d; intr.) to ~ against (to ~ against catching cold) 3. (D; tr.) to ~ against (to ~ an embassy against intruders) 4. (D; tr.) to ~ from (to ~ smb. from harm)
guardian *n.* 1. to appoint smb. ~ 2. (often fig.) a self-appointed ~ 3. a legal ~
guerrilla *n.* 1. an armed; urban ~ 2. (misc.) a ~ band = a band of ~s
guess I *n.* 1. to have (esp. BE), hazard, make, take (AE), venture a ~ 2. an educated, informed, shrewd; inspired; lucky; random, wild; rough ~ 3. a ~ that + clause (it is only a ~ that she will be appointed) 4. at a ~ (at a ~, I'd say she'll be appointed)
guess II *v.* 1. to ~ shrewdly; wildly 2. (D; intr.) to ~ at (to ~ at smb.'s age from their appearance) 3. (L) "I could never have ~ed that she would be late" "but knowing her, you might have ~ed she'd be late!" 4. (Q) ~ where the money is 5. (misc.) to keep smb. ~ing; (AE) I ~ she's late; I ~ not; I ~ so
guesswork *n.* (I got the answer by pure ~
guest *n.* 1. to greet, welcome; introduce a ~ 2. to have ~s (for dinner) 3. a dinner; wedding; weekend ~ 4. an invited; welcome ~ 5. an unexpected; uninvited; unwelcome ~ 6. a paying; regular ~ (at

a hotel) 7. (misc.) "can I have some more cake?" "be my ~!" (see also *guest of honor* at **honor**)
guff *n.* (colloq.) ["back talk"] to take ~ (I will not take any of your ~!)
guffaw *n.* 1. to emit, give, let out a ~ 2. a loud ~
guidance *n.* 1. to offer ~ to; to provide ~ for 2. to seek ~ (about) 3. friendly; parental; spiritual; vocational ~ 4. under smb.'s ~
guide I *n.* ["guidebook"] 1. a handy; pocket ~ 2. a ~ to (this handbook is a good ~ to London) ["person who guides"] 3. a tour ~
guide II *v.* (P; tr.) to ~ smb. around a city; she ~ed us out of the congested area
guidelines *n.* 1. to draw up, establish ~ for 2. to adhere to, follow ~ 3. to ignore; violate ~ 4. clear; flexible; rigid ~ 5. a set of ~ (a set of clear ~s from the EU about standards of hygiene)
guilt *n.* 1. to establish, prove smb.'s ~ 2. to bear (the) ~ for 3. to admit; expiate one's ~ 4. collective ~ 5. a pang, twinge of ~ (I felt a twinge of ~ about / for what I'd done) 6. (misc.) ~ by association; the burden of ~
guiltless *adj.* ~ of
guilt trip *n.* (slang) to lay a ~ on smb.
guilty *adj.* 1. to find; pronounce ~ of (the jury found him ~ of murder) 2. to feel ~ about smt. 3. ~ of 4. (misc.) to plead ~; to plead not ~; ~ as charged
guinea pig *n.* to serve as a ~; to be used as a ~
guise *n.* in, under the ~ of (under the ~ of friendship)
guitar *n.* 1. to play a / the ~; to play ~ (esp. AE) 2. to pluck, strum a ~ 3. an acoustic; electric, steel; Hawaiian ~
gulf *n.* 1. a wide, yawning ~ 2. a ~ between (a wide ~ between generations)
gull *v.* (old-fashioned) ("to trick") 1. (D; tr.) to ~ into 2. (D; tr.) to ~ out of
gulp *n.* 1. to take a ~ 2. at, in a ~ (she swallowed the whole spoonful at one ~) 3. (misc.) she gave a ~ of surprise when she heard the news = she heard the news with a ~ of surprise
gum *n.* 1. to chew ~ 2. bubble ~ (see also **chewing gum**) 3. a stick, wad of ~
gumption *n.* (colloq.) ["courage"] 1. to show ~ 2. the ~ to + inf. (will she have enough ~ to refuse?)
gun I *n.* 1. to aim; fire; point a ~ at 2. to turn a ~ on smb. 3. to draw a ~ (on) 4. to hold a ~ on smb. 5. to hold a ~ to smb.'s head 6. to load; unload a ~ 7. (artillery) to lay ("adjust") a ~ 8. to carry, pack (AE, colloq.) a ~ 9. to silence an enemy ~ 10. to spike ("make unusable") a ~ 11. an antiaircraft; antitank; BB; burp (colloq.), submachine, Tommy (colloq.); field; heavy; ray; riot ~; shotgun; starter's; stun; toy; zip (AE) ~ (see also **machine gun**) 12. a grease; spray ~ 13. a ~ fires, goes off; jams; misfires 14. (misc.) to jump the ~ ("to start too early"); to stick to one's ~s ("to defend one's position staunchly"); a smoking ~ ("dramatic

proof") (see also **great guns**; *at gunpoint* at **point I** *n.*)

gun II *v.* (d; intr.) to ~ for ("to search for with a gun") (also fig.) (the media are ~ning for the Prime Minister)

gunfire *n.* 1. concentrated, fierce, heavy, murderous ~ 2. a burst of ~ 3. under ~ (we came under heavy enemy ~ as we tried to advance)

gung ho *adj.* (slang) ["enthusiastic"] ~ about

gunpoint *n.* to hold smb. at ~

gunpowder *n.* 1. smokeless ~ 2. a grain of ~

gurgle *v.* (B) the baby ~d a few sounds to us

gush *v.* 1. (d; intr.) to ~ from (a column of oil ~ed from the ground) 2. (d; intr.) to ~ over (they were ~ing over their new grandchild)

gusher *n.* ["oil well from which oil gushes"] to hit a ~

gush forth *v.* (D; intr.) to ~ from (a column of oil ~ed forth from the ground)

gust *n.* 1. fitful; strong ~s (the wind was blowing in fitful ~s) 2. a ~ of wind

gusto *n.* with ~ (with great ~)

gutless *adj.* (colloq.) ~ to + inf. (it was ~ of him to lie)

guts *n.* (colloq.) 1. the ~ to + inf. (he doesn't have the ~ to do it) 2. (misc.) to hate smb.'s ~ ("to hate smb. very much")

gutter *n.* (fig.) 1. to get down into the ~ 2. to drag smb. down into the ~

guy *n.* (colloq.) 1. a great, nice, regular (AE); an ordinary ~ 2. a bad; good ~ USAGE NOTE: In AE *you guys* (colloq.) can now be used in speaking not only to a group of men, but also to a group of men and women, and even to a group of women only (it's time for *you guys* to get ready); *guys* (colloq.) can be used vocatively to the same groups (it's time to get ready, *guys*!).

gymnastics *n.* 1. to do ~ 2. at; for; in ~ (she's very good at ~ and has won several prizes for/in it)

gyp *v.* (slang) (D; tr.) to ~ out of (he ~ped me out of my share)

gyrate *v.* 1. ~ wildly 2. (D; intr.) to ~ to (the young people were ~ting wildly to the music)

H

habeas corpus *n.* (to obtain; seek) a writ of ~

habit *n.* ["custom"] ["usual manner"] 1. to acquire, develop, form, pick up; have a ~ 2. to make a ~ of smt. (she makes a ~ of getting up early) 3. to fall into, get into a ~ (she got into the ~ of getting up late) 4. to break, shake a ~; to get out of a ~; (slang) to kick the ~ (she broke the ~ of a lifetime when she started getting up early) 5. to break smb. of a ~ 6. an annoying; bad; deplorable; strange ~ 7. an entrenched, fixed, ingrained; incurable ~ 8. a filthy; nasty; repulsive ~ 9. a good ~ 10. irregular; regular ~s 11. a ~ of (he has a bad ~ of interrupting people) 12. by force of ~ 13. in the ~ of (she is in the ~ of getting up early) 14. out of ~ (I did it out of ~) (see also *a creature of habit* at **creature** 2; **habits**) ["costume"] 15. a monk's; nun's; riding ~

habitat *n.* 1. to provide a ~ for 2. a natural ~ (these marshes provide a ~ for many creatures whose natural ~ is threatened elsewhere)

habits *n.* ["customs"] drinking; eating; sleeping; work ~

habituated *adj.* ~ to (they became ~ to drugs early in life)

hack I *n.* ["hireling"] a party ~

hack II *v.* 1. ("to chop") (d; intr.) to ~ at (to ~ at the dense undergrowth) 2. (computers) (d; intr.) ("to penetrate") to ~ into (to ~ into secret files) 3. (misc.) they ~ed their way through the forest; to ~ (a body) to pieces

hack away *v.* (D; intr.) ("to chop away, reduce") to ~ at (to ~ at the dense undergrowth; to ~ at the work force)

hacking *n.* computer ~

hackles *n.* ["anger"] to raise smb.'s ~

haemorrhage (BE) see **hemorrhage**

haggle *v.* (D; intr.) to ~ about, over; with

hail I *n.* 1. to have ~ (we had ~ yesterday) 2. ~ falls; melts 3. in the ~ (to get caught in the ~) 4. through the ~ (to run through the ~)

hail II *v.* 1. (C) ("to summon") ~ a taxi for me; or: ~ me a taxi 2. (esp. AE) (d; intr.) to ~ from ("to be from") (where do you ~ from?) 3. (D; tr.) ("to proclaim") to ~ as (she was ~ed as a heroine) 4. (rare) (N; used with a noun) ("to name") to ~ smb. emperor

hailstones *n.* ~ fall

hair *n.* 1. to brush; comb; curl ~ 2. to backcomb (BE), tease (AE); braid, plait; do; set; style ~ 3. to cut; trim ~ 4. to blowdry, dry; shampoo, wash ~ 5. to color, dye, tint ~ 6. to part one's ~ (he parts his ~ in the middle, and I part mine on the side) 7. to stroke smb.'s ~ 8. to lose, shed one's ~ (people lose their ~; animals shed their ~) 9. braided, plaited; curly; dry; kinky; normal; oily; straight; wavy ~

10. bobbed, short; long; thick; thinning ~ 11. unmanageable, unruly ~ 12. dark; light ~ 13. black; blond; brown; dark; grey; light; red; silver (literary), white ~ 14. body; facial; pubic ~ 15. ~ falls out; grows 16. a single ~ 17. a curl, lock; strand; wisp of ~ 18. a head; shock of ~ (he has a thick head of ~) 19. (misc.) how does she wear her ~? to tear one's ~ out ("to become extremely agitated"); to split ~s ("to nitpick"); to get in smb.'s ~ ("to annoy smb."); to let one's ~ down ("to lose one's inhibitions"); by a ~ ("by a small margin")

haircut *n.* 1. to get; have a ~ 2. to give smb. a ~ 3. a short ~

hairline *n.* a receding ~

hair's breadth *n.* 1. (to miss) by a ~ 2. (to come) within a ~ (of)

half *determiner, pronoun* 1. (in telling time) ~ past the hour (it's ~ past four) 2. ~ of (~ of them) 3. (misc.) it's not ~ bad ("it's fairly good"); to go halves (on smt.) ("to divide smt. evenly, esp. a bill"); you have a lot and I have only ~ as much; you have very little and I have ~ again as much/ ~ as much again (AE)! USAGE NOTE: The use of the preposition *of* is necessary when a pronoun follows. When a noun follows, the *of* may be omitted – half (of) the students; half (of) the audience. However, compare – she spent half (of) the money; she spent her half of the money. Note the constructions – a half hour, half an hour.

half-mast *n.* at ~ (the flags were flying at ~)

half price *n.* at ~ (to admit children at ~)

halftime *n.* at ~ (the band performed at ~)

halfway *adj., adv.* 1. ~ between; through 2. (misc.) to meet smb. ~ ("to compromise with smb.")

hall *n.* 1. a city, town, village; concert; dance; entrance; lecture; mess; music; pool; study ~ 2. (esp. BE) a ~ of residence 3. (BE) in ~ (at a university) (to dine; live in ~)

hallmarks *n.* ["characteristics"] to have all the ~ of

hallucination *n.* 1. to have ~s 2. a drug-induced ~

halo *n.* a ~ (a)round (the sun, moon)

halt *n.* 1. to call a ~ (to smt.) 2. to bring smt. to a ~ 3. to come; grind, screech to a ~ 4. an abrupt; complete; grinding, screeching ~

halter *n.* to put a ~ on an animal

ham *n.* 1. baked; cured; honey-roast (BE), sugar-cured (AE); smoked ~ 2. a piece; slice of ~ 3. (misc.) ~ on the bone

hamburger *n.* to grill a ~

hammer I *n.* 1. to swing a ~ 2. (sports) to throw the ~ 3. a drop ~ 4. to come under the (auctioneer's) ~ ("to be sold at auction") 5. with a ~ (to hit a nail with a ~)

hammer II *v.* 1. (d; intr.) to ~ at (the enemy ~ed at our positions) 2. (D; tr.) to ~ into (to ~ a nail into a wall; to ~ an idea into smb.'s head) 3. (N) to ~ smt. shut

hammer and tongs *adv.* to go at smb.; smt.; it ~ ("to go at with great energy")

hammer away v. (d; intr.) to ~ at (to ~ at a compromise; the enemy ~ed away at our positions)

hamper v. (D; tr.) to ~ in

hand I n. ["part of the arm below the wrist"] 1. to shake smb.'s ~; to shake ~s (with smb.) 2. to clasp, grab, grasp; press; pump; seize, take smb.'s ~ 3. to hold; join ~s 4. to lay one's ~s on 5. to cup; fold one's ~s 6. to clap one's ~s 7. to wring one's ~s 8. to lower; raise one's ~ 9. bare; delicate; dishpan (esp. AE); gentle ~s (he grasped the hot metal with his bare ~s); a free ~ (he waved to me with his free ~; if you wear a rucksack you can keep your ~s free) 10. a pair of ~s 11. by ~ (to do smt. by ~); in smb.'s ~ (to hold smt. in one's ~); on smb.'s ~ (he has a tattoo on his left ~) 12. by the ~ (to lead smb. by the ~; to grab, grasp, seize, take smb. by the ~) 13. ~s off; ~s up ["help"]["active participation"] 14. to give, lend smb. a ~ 15. to lift a ~ (he would not lift a ~ to help) 16. to have a ~ in 17. a guiding ~ (see also **helping hand**) 18. a ~ at, in, with (give me a ~ with the dishes) ["worker"] 19. a factory, mill (BE); hired; ranch ~ ["smb. experienced"] 20. an old ~ (at smt.) ["pointer on a clock"] 21. an hour; minute; second, sweep-second ~ ["ability"] 22. to try one's ~ at smt. ["control"] 23. to get out of ~ 24. to take smb. in ~ 25. a firm; iron ~ (see also **upper hand**) ["pledge of betrothal"] (formal) 26. to ask for smb.'s ~ ["cards held by a player"] (also fig.) 27. to show, tip one's ~ 28. to have, hold a ~ 29. a good, strong; losing; weak; winning ~ (she held a strong ~) ["possession"]["ownership"] 30. to fall into smb.'s ~s 31. to change ~s 32. enemy; private; safe ~s (the documents fell into enemy ~s; the files were in safe ~s) ["source"] 33. at first ~ ("directly") 34. at second ~ ("indirectly") ["viewpoint"] 35. on one (AE), on the one ~ ("from one viewpoint"); on the other ~ ("from the other viewpoint") ["closeness"] 36. at, on ~ (near at ~) ["applause"] 37. to give smb. a ~ 38. to get, receive a ~ 39. a big ~ (they got a big ~ after their performance) ["misc."] 40. do you have a free ~? ("are you free to help?") ("can you function without restrictions?"); she is good with her ~s ("she has great manual dexterity"); a show of ~s ("a vote taken by raising hands"); to lay a ~ on smb. ("to harm smb.") (I never laid a ~ on her, officer!); from ~ to mouth ("barely existing"); to have one's ~s full ("to be very busy"); to eat out of smb.'s ~ ("to be subservient to smb."); to force smb.'s ~ ("to compel smb. to act"); to throw up one's ~s ("to give up"); to wash one's ~s of smt. ("to shed all responsibility for smt."); with a heavy ~ ("crudely"); to suffer at smb.'s ~s; with clean ~s ("innocent"); to go ~ in ~ ("to go together"); to dismiss/reject out of ~ ("to dismiss/reject unreservedly"); to win ~s down ("to win easily"); all ~s on deck! ("all sailors on deck"); to have time on one's ~s ("to have free time"); to have worthless property on one's ~s ("to be burdened by worthless property"); ~ in glove with ("conspiring with"); a

dab ~ at doing smt. (BE) (colloq.); a safe pair of ~s ("smb. reliable") (see also **free hand**; **old hand**; **second hand**; **whip hand**)

hand II v. 1. (A) ~ the salt to me; or: ~ me the salt 2. (misc.) you have to ~ it to her! ("you must give her credit!")

hand back v. (usu. B; occ. A) she ~ed the documents back to me = she ~ed back the documents to me = she ~ed me back the documents

handball n. 1. to play ~ 2. team ~

handbook n. a ~ for (a ~ for beginners)

handcuff v. 1. (D; tr.) to ~ to (the prisoner was ~ed to the bars; the prisoner was ~ed to another prisoner = the prisoners were ~ed to each other) 2. (misc.) the prisoners were ~ed together

handcuffs n. 1. to put (the) ~ on smb. 2. to remove ~ 3. a pair of ~ 4. in ~ (the prisoner was led away in ~)

hand down v. 1. (D; tr.) to ~ from; to (to ~ a tradition to the next generation = to ~ a tradition down to the next generation; to ~ old clothes from one child to the next = to ~ old clothes down from one child to the next) 2. (misc.) she ~ed it down to me from the shelf

handicap n. ["assigned advantage or disadvantage, as in golf"] 1. to assign, give; have a ~ ["hindrance"] 2. to overcome a ~ 3. a mental, physical ~ 4. a ~ to (lack of experience can prove a serious ~ to the beginner) 5. under a ~

hand in v. (B) to ~ homework to the teacher = to ~ homework in to the teacher

handle I n. ["part grasped by the hand"] 1. to turn a ~ 2. (BE) a starting ~ 3. (to pick up smt.) by the ~ ["misc."] (colloq.) 4. to fly off the ~ ("to lose one's temper"); to get a ~ on smt. ("to comprehend smt.")

handle II v. to ~ carefully; to ~ with care

handler n. a baggage; food ~

handling n. 1. delicate; gentle; sensitive; tactful ~ (the matter requires delicate ~) 2. careless, inept; rough ~ 3. special ~ (by the post office)

hand on v. (D; tr.) to ~ to (to ~ a tradition to the next generation = to ~ a tradition on to the next generation)

hand organ n. to grind, play a ~

handout n. (colloq.) ["alms"]["leaflet"] 1. to give smb. a ~ 2. to ask for a ~

hand out v. (B) to ~ food to the needy = to ~ food out to the needy

hand over v. (B) to ~ a criminal to the police = to ~ a criminal over to the police

handpicked adj. 1. ~ for (she was ~ for the job) 2. ~ to + inf. (she was ~ to do the job)

handrail n. 1. to grasp a ~ 2. to hold on to a ~

handshake n. 1. to give smb. a ~ 2. a cordial, hearty; warm; firm; limp ~ 3. (misc.) a golden ~ ("a gift presented to smb. who is retiring or leaving a firm")

handspring n. to do, execute, perform, turn a ~

handstand *n.* to do, execute, perform a ~
handwriting *n.* 1. to decipher smb.'s ~ 2. clear, legible; illegible ~ 3. in smb.'s ~ (the letter was in her own clear ~) 4. (misc.) (AE) to see the ~ on the wall (for CE, see **writing** *n.* 5) ("to foresee impending doom") (we saw the ~ on the wall for the international monetary system = the ~ was on the wall for the international monetary system)
handy *adj.* 1. to have, keep smt. ~ 2. ~ at; with (she's ~ at using tools = she's ~ with tools) 3. ~ for (this tool is ~ for (doing) various jobs; this house is ~ for the local pharmacy) 4. ~ to + inf. (it's ~ to have a pharmacy so close = it's ~ having a pharmacy so close) 5. (misc.) to come in ~ (this tool may come in ~ for (doing) various jobs)
hang I *n.* (colloq.) ["knack"] to get the ~ of smt.
hang II *v.* 1. ("to be suspended") to ~ limp; loose, loosely 2. (colloq.) (d; intr.) to ~ around ("to frequent") (to ~ around a bar) 3. (D; intr.) ("to be suspended") to ~ by (to ~ by a thread; to ~ by a rope (from a spike)) (see also 16) 4. (D; tr.) ("to execute by hanging") to ~ for (he was ~ed for murder) 5. (d; intr.; tr.) ("to be suspended; to suspend") to ~ from (flags hung from the windows; to ~ a flag from a window; to ~ (by a rope) from a spike) 6. (d; intr.) ("to cling") to ~ on (to ~ on smb.'s arm) 7. (d; intr.) to ~ on, upon ("to listen closely to") (to ~ on smb.'s every word) 8. (d; intr.) to ~ on ("to depend on") (the outcome ~s on the results of the election) 9. (d; intr.) to ~ on ("to be oppressive") (time ~s (heavy) on their hands) 10. (d; intr., tr.) ("to be suspended"); ("to suspend") to ~ on (she hung the picture on the wall) 11. (d; intr.) ("to cling") to ~ onto (he hung onto my arm) 12. (colloq.) (d; intr.) to ~ onto ("to keep, retain") (we intend to ~ onto this property; they hung onto their privileges) 13. (d; intr.) ("to lean") to ~ out of (to ~ out of a window) 14. (d; intr.) ("to be suspended") to ~ over (the coat was ~ing over the chair; the threat of war hung over the country) 15. (d; tr.) ("to drape, suspend") to ~ over (she hung the wet towel over the tub) 16. (misc.) her paintings were ~ing in the museum; to ~ by a thread ("to be in a critical situation"); to ~ in the balance ("to be undecided") (see also *hang loose* at **loose I** *adj.*; *hang tough* at **tough**) USAGE NOTE: The past and past participle of *hang* are *hung* or *hanged*. The form *hanged* is more usual in the sense "killed by hanging". In other senses the form *hung* is usual.
hang around *v.* (colloq.) ("to spend time") 1. (D; intr.) to ~ at (they ~ at the senior citizens' club) 2. (d; intr.) to ~ with (he likes to ~ with the boys down at the bar)
hang back *v.* (D; intr.) to ~ from (to ~ from giving information)
hang down *v.* (D; intr.) to ~ from; to (to ~ from a branch)
hanger *n.* a coat ~
hang on *v.* 1. (D; intr.) to ~ to ("to grasp") (to ~ to

the rail; he hung on to my arm) 2. (D; intr.) to ~ to ("to keep") (we intend to ~ on to this property; they hung on to their privileges) 3. (misc.) to ~ for dear life; (BE) to ~ like grim death
hangout *n.* (colloq.) ["gathering place to hang out in"] a ~ for (a ~ for me and my friends)
hang out *v.* (slang) (D; intr.) ("to spend time") to ~ with (to ~ with one's friends)
hangover *n.* 1. to have a ~ 2. to sleep off a ~
hang-up *n.* (colloq.) ["worry"] to have a ~ about
hang up *v.* (D; intr.) to ~ on (she hung up on me) ("she broke off her telephone conversation with me")
hanker *v.* (colloq.) 1. (d; intr.) to ~ after, for ("to want") (to ~ for a good steak) 2. (E) ("to want") she ~ed to have a good steak
hankering *n.* (colloq.) 1. a ~ after, for (a ~ for a good steak) 2. a ~ to + inf. (a ~ to have a good steak)
happen *v.* 1. (d; intr.) to ~ on, upon ("to find by chance") (to ~ upon a rare item) 2. (D; intr.) to ~ to (what ~ed to you?) 3. (D; intr.) to ~ with (what's ~ing with your new project?) 4. (E) I ~ed to be there when they arrived 5. (L) it (so) ~ed that I was there when they arrived
happiness *n.* 1. to bring ~ (to) 2. to find; seek ~ 3. to wish smb. ~ 4. personal ~ 5. a feeling, glow of ~
happy *adj.* 1. blissfully, deliriously, perfectly; very ~; as ~ as a lark; not entirely ~ 2. ~ about; at; in; with (she was ~ about/at the good news; he was ~ in his interesting work; they were ~ with the good results) 3. ~ for (we are ~ for them both) 4. ~ to + inf. (we felt ~ to be together; I'm ~ to have been invited to the meeting; she'll be ~ to work here) 5. ~ that + clause (we felt ~ that we were together; I'm very ~ that I've been invited to the meeting) 6. (misc.) she'll be ~ working here
harakiri *n.* to commit, perform ~
harangue I *n.* to deliver, launch into a ~
harangue II *v.* (D; tr.) to ~ about (she always ~s the children about their untidy rooms)
harassment *n.* 1. to engage in ~ 2. to subject to ~ 3. police; sexual ~
harbor, harbour *n.* 1. to clear; dredge a ~ 2. to blockade; mine a ~ 3. an artificial; natural ~ 4. a safe ~ (also fig.)
hard I *adj.* ["demanding"] 1. (cannot stand alone) ~ on (she's very ~ on herself) ["difficult"] 2. ~ to + inf. (this book is ~ to translate = it is ~ to translate this book = it is a ~ book to translate; she is ~ to understand = it is ~ to understand her; it is ~ to get them to participate = it is ~ getting them to participate) 3. ~ for (this job will be ~ for me; it is ~ for us to concentrate) ["misc."] 4. to play ~ to get ("to pretend to be uninterested in an invitation or proposal"); ~ of hearing; as ~ as a rock; as ~ as nails (see also *the hard way* at **way**)
hard II *adv.* 1. ~ at (~ at work) 2. (misc.) they've been ~ at it all day long!

hardback *n.* in ~ (the book came out in ~)
hardened *adj.* (cannot stand alone) ~ to (~ to suffering)
hard-pressed *adj.* 1. ~ for (~ for time; ~ for money) 2. ~ to + inf. (she was ~ to find the money to pay her rent)
hard put *adj.* ["facing difficulties"] 1. ~ to + inf. (she was ~ to pay her rent) 2. (misc.) she was ~ (to it) to pay her rent
hardship *n.* 1. to bear, endure, face, suffer, undergo ~ 2. to overcome (a) ~ 3. severe, unrelieved ~ (to live in unrelieved ~) 4. a ~ to + inf. (it was a real ~ for her to pay her rent)
hard time *n.* (colloq.) 1. to give smb. a ~ ("to make things difficult for smb.") 2. (misc.) she had a hard ~ paying her rent; to fall on ~s; "A hard ~ we had of it." – T.S. Eliot (1888–1965), "Journey of the Magi"
hard up *adj.* (colloq.) ("in need of") ~ for (she's ~ for money to pay her rent)
hardware *n.* 1. computer ~ 2. military ~
hark back *v.* (d; intr.) ("to revert") to ~ to (to ~ to the old days)
harm *n.* 1. to cause, do ~ 2. to undo ~ 3. to come to ~ 4. considerable, grave, great, immeasurable, irreparable, severe ~ 5. actual (BE) bodily; bodily; grievous bodily ~ 6. ~ in; to (there is no ~ (in) doing that; was any ~ done to the children?) 7. ~ to + inf. (it will not do you any ~ to try again) 8. (misc.) to come to ~ (I don't want them to come to (any) ~ = I don't want any harm to come to them); to mean no ~ (I'm sorry: I meant (you) no harm!); out of ~'s way; (esp. AE) in/into ~'s way
harmful *adj.* 1. ~ to (smoking is ~ to one's health) 2. ~ to + inf. (it's ~ (to your health) to smoke)
harmless *adj.* 1. ~ to 2. ~ to + inf. (it's ~ to daydream)
harmonica *n.* to play a/the ~
harmonize *v.* (D; intr.) to ~ with
harmony *n.* ["concord, agreement"] 1. to achieve; maintain ~ 2. close; perfect ~ 3. ethnic; marital; racial; religious ~ 4. in ~ (with) ["congruity"] (ling.) 5. vowel ~
harness I *n.* in ~ ("at work")
harness II *v.* (D; tr.) to ~ to (to ~ horses to a coach)
harp I *n.* to play the ~
harp II *v.* (D; intr.) to ~ on (about) (to keep ~ing on the same old theme)
harpoon *n.* to hurl, throw; shoot a ~
harsh *adj.* ~ to, with (he's too ~ with the children)
harvest *n.* 1. to bring in, reap a ~ 2. an abundant, bountiful, bumper, rich; poor ~ 3. (fig.) a bitter ~ (a bitter ~ of resentment)
hash I *n.* ["failure, mess"] to make a ~ of smt.
hash II *v.* (colloq.) (AE) (d; intr.) to ~ over ("to discuss") (we ~ed over the problem and then we ~ed over it again = we ~ed over the problem and then we ~ed it over again)

hassle I *n.* ["struggle"] a ~ to + inf. (it was a real ~ to get a visa! = it was a real ~ getting a visa!)
hassle II *v.* (D; tr.) to ~ about, over; with
haste *n.* 1. to make ~ ("to hurry") 2. with great, excessive, indecent, unseemly ~ 3. in ~ (they acted in great ~) 4. (misc.) in their ~ to leave, they forgot their keys
hasten *v.* (E) he ~ed to apologize
hat *n.* 1. to don, put on a ~; to place, put a ~ on one's head 2. to doff, take off; tip a ~ 3. to have a ~ on, to wear a ~ 4. a bowler, derby (AE); cowboy, stetson, ten-gallon; top ~ 5. a broad-brimmed; fur; panama; straw ~ 6. a cardinal's ~ 7. (misc.) to pass the ~ ("to collect money"); to hang up one's ~ ("to retire"); to take one's ~ off to smb. ("to congratulate smb.; to feel respect for smb."); to talk through one's ~ ("to say foolish things"); to throw one's ~ in/into (esp. AE) the ring ("to enter a political campaign"); to keep smt. under one's ~ ("to keep smt. confidential"); at the drop of a ~ ("without hesitation") (see also *hat trick* at **trick I** *n.*)
hatch *n.* 1. to batten down the ~es 2. an escape ~ 3. (misc.) down the ~! (colloq.) (used when about to raise a drink to one's mouth)
hatchet *n.* to bury the ~ ("to make peace")
hate I see **hatred**
hate II *v.* 1. to ~ bitterly, deeply, intensely, passionately, profoundly, utterly, very much 2. (E) he ~s to work 3. (G) he ~s working 4. (J) he ~s them watching when he works 5. (K) he ~s their watching when he works 6. (misc.) (colloq.) I'd really ~ you/for you (AE) to think that my mistake was intentional = what I'd really ~ is for you to think that my mistake was intentional; he ~s it when/if they watch when he works
hateful *adj.* 1. ~ to 2. ~ to + inf. (it was ~ of him to say that)
hatred *n.* 1. to arouse, incite, stir up ~ 2. to instill ~ 3. to incur ~ 4. to develop; express; feel; show ~ 5. abiding, bitter, blind, deep, deep-rooted, great, implacable, intense, profound, violent, virulent ~ 6. ~ for, of, towards 7. out of ~ 8. consumed with, filled with ~
haul I *n.* ["distance"] a long; short ~ (also fig.) (see also **longhaul**; **shorthaul**)
haul II *v.* (D; tr.) to ~ from; to (to ~ coal from the mines to the city)
haul off *v.* 1. (D; tr.) to ~ to (they were all ~ed off to jail) 2. (misc.) (colloq.) she ~ed off and hit him
haul up *v.* (D; tr.) to ~ before (to ~ smb. up before a magistrate)
haunt *n.* a favorite; old; quiet ~ (to revisit one's old ~s)
have *v.* 1. (d; tr.) ("to keep") to ~ about (BE), around (it's dangerous to ~ a gun around the house) 2. (d; tr.) to ~ against ("to consider as grounds for rejection, dislike") (I ~ nothing against him) 3. (D; tr.) to ~ for ("to consume") (what are we ~ing for

dinner?) 4. (colloq.) (d; tr.) to ~ on ("to possess evidence against") (you ~ nothing on me) 5. (E) ("to be obligated") we ~ to leave 6. (H) I ~ a great deal/nothing/something to say to her; I ~ nothing to wear; we ~ smt. to tell you; I ~ a job to do 7. (esp. AE) (I) ("to cause") he had a gardener cut the grass (CE also has: he got a gardener to cut the grass); she had her research assistant look up the information; (CE) what would you have me do? 8. (J) we soon had them all laughing 9. (N; used with an adjective; past participle) ("to consume"); ("to cause") he had the grass cut by a gardener; she had the information looked up by her research assistant; we had a meal sent up to our room; they had the building torn down; she had her tonsils removed; I'll have my martini dry; I ~ my coffee black 10. (misc.) he had two children by his first wife; to ~ one's tonsils out; to ~ it in for smb. ("to have a grudge against smb."); she had a strange thing happen to her ("a strange thing happened to her"); he had it coming (to him) ("he deserved it"); I had it out with them ("we had a very frank discussion"); she had her handbag stolen ("her handbag was stolen"); she had a hat on (her head); "do you ~ anything on (for) tonight?" "no, I'm free" USAGE NOTE: *Have got* can be used except in 3, 7, and 9 above. As for 10, the following are possible: *he'd got two children by his first wife; to have got it in for smb.; he'd got it coming to him; she'd got a hat on her head; have you got anything on for tonight?* Bear in mind that whereas *have got* is CE, *had got* is esp. BE.

haven *n.* 1. a safe; tax ~ 2. a ~ for (the woods are a ~ of peace for wildlife)

havoc *n.* 1. to play, raise, wreak ~ with 2. to cause, create ~ for

hay *n.* 1. to make ~ 2. to bundle, gather, stack ~ 3. a haystack 4. a bale of ~; a wisp of ~ 5. (misc.) (AE; colloq.) to hit the ~ ("to go to sleep")

haymaker *n.* (colloq.) ["punch"] to throw a ~

hayride *n.* to go on a ~

haywire *adj.* (colloq.) to go ~ ("to be ruined") ("to go crazy")

hazard *n.* 1. a health; fire; moral; occupational; safety ~ 2. a ~ to (a ~ to health)

hazardous *adj.* 1. ~ to (~ to one's health) 2. ~ to + inf. (it is ~ to work at that height = it is ~ working at that height)

haze *n.* 1. a light ~ 2. the ~ lifts 3. in; through a ~

hazy *adj.* ~ about (she's ~ about the details)

head I *n.* ["upper part of the body"] 1. to nod; shake one's ~ (he nodded his ~ Yes; she shook her ~ No) 2. to bare; bow; drop, duck, hang, lower; lift, raise; move; poke, stick; scratch; toss; turn one's ~ (to scratch one's ~ in amazement; to poke one's ~ around the corner) 3. to hold one's ~ high ("to be proud") 4. from ~ to foot/toe ["length of a horse's head"] 5. by a ~ (our horse won by a ~) ["poise"] 6. to keep; lose one's ~ ("If you can keep your ~

when all about you Are losing theirs and blaming it on you ..." – Rudyard Kipling (1865–1936), "If") 7. a cool, level ~ (to keep a level ~) ["person"] 8. to count ~s 9. per ~ (to charge two dollars per/a ~) ["brain"] 10. to use one's ~ 11. to cram, fill, stuff smb.'s ~ (with nonsense) 12. a clear ~ 13. to have a ~ for (figures) 14. (misc.) it never entered my ~ that they would not support the proposal! ["climax"] 15. to bring smt. to a ~ 16. to come to a ~ (the boil came to a ~; when will the crisis come to a ~?) ["front part"] 17. at the ~ (of a column) ["leader"] 18. a titular ~ 19. (misc.) crowned ~s (of state) (see also *head of state* at **state I** *n.*) ["chairperson"] (esp. BE) 20. (the) department ~, (the) ~ of (the) department (AE usu. has *chair, chairman, chairperson*) ["misc."] 21. a thick ~ of hair; success went to his ~ ("his success made him conceited"); ~ first; ~ over heels ("completely") (they're ~ over heels in love); ~s up! ("watch out!"); to get smt. through one's ~ ("to finally comprehend smt."); to hang one's ~ in shame ("to be greatly embarrassed"); to be ~ and shoulders above smb. ("to be greatly superior to smb."); to keep one's ~ above water ("to manage to survive"); over smb.'s ~ ("incomprehensible"); out of one's ~ ("delirious"); ~s or tails?; to make ~ or tail of ("to comprehend") (I can't make ~ or tail of these equations!); to put ~s together ("to collaborate") (they put their ~s together and came up with a solution"); prejudice reared its ugly ~ ("prejudice appeared"); he took it into his ~ to leave ("he suddenly decided to leave"); success turned her ~ ("she was spoiled by success"); to bury one's ~ in the sand ("to isolate oneself from reality"); to have a swelled, swollen (BE) ~ ("to be conceited"); to bang/beat/knock one's ~ against a stone wall ("to be cruelly frustrated") (see also *head and shoulders above* at **shoulder I** *n.*; *head of steam* at **steam I** *n.*)

head II *v.* 1. (d; intr.) ("to go") to ~ for (to ~ for the city; to ~ for a downfall) 2. (P; intr., tr.) they ~ed (their boat) east; to ~ out of town; to ~ for the west coast; they were ~ing towards the city

headache *n.* 1. to get; have a ~ 2. a bad, racking, severe, splitting; migraine; sick; slight; tension ~ 3. the noise gave her a ~

head back *v.* 1. (D; intr.) to ~ from (to ~ from the theater) 2. (D; intr.) to ~ to, towards (to ~ towards home)

head count *n.* to do, have, make, take a ~

heading *n.* 1. a chapter ~ 2. under a ~ (which heading does this topic come under?)

headlights *n.* 1. to turn on the ~ 2. to turn off the ~ 3. to dim, dip (BE) the ~ 4. (misc.) (in) the glare of the ~

headline *n.* 1. to carry a ~ 2. banner; front-page; screaming ~s 3. the ~s say ... 4. in (banner) ~s 5. the story made the ~s

headlock *n.* ["wrestling hold"] to get, put; have a ~ on smb.

headquarters *n.* 1. to set up ~ 2. supreme ~ 3. an army; corps; military; police ~ 4. at ~

headstand *n.* to do, execute, perform a ~

headstart *n.* to have a ~ on, over

headway *n.* to gain, make ~ against; with

heal *v.* (D; tr.) to ~ of (she was ~ed of her illness)

healer *n.* a faith ~

healing *n.* faith ~

health *n.* ["condition of the body and mind"] 1. to enjoy good ~ 2. to look after, maintain; promote (good) ~ 3. to recover, regain one's ~ 4. to risk; ruin, undermine smb.'s ~ 5. bad, broken, delicate, deteriorating, failing, feeble, fragile, frail, ill, poor ~ 6. (rude) good; robust; excellent ~ 7. holistic; mental; physical ~ 8. for one's ~ (she swims for her ~; smoking is bad for one's ~) 9. in a certain ~ (they are in (rude) good ~ = they are in the best of ~) 10. (misc.) the state of smb.'s ~ ["science of protecting the health of the community"] 11. community, public; occupational ~ ["misc."] 12. (here's) to your (good) ~!

health care *n.* 1. to deliver, provide ~ 2. holistic ~

health insurance *n.* 1. to have ~ 2. national ~ 3. compulsory; voluntary ~

healthy *adj.* ["promoting health"] 1. ~ for (smoking is not ~ for you) ["safe"] (colloq.) 2. ~ to + inf. (it's not ~ for you to smoke; it's not ~ to walk there at night = it's not ~ walking there at night)

heap I *n.* 1. a compost; dump; scrap ~ 2. in; on a ~ (everything was piled up in a ~ on which more things were thrown constantly)

heap II *v.* 1. (d; tr.) to ~ on, on to, onto, upon (she ~ed food on my plate) 2. (D; tr.) to ~ with (she ~ed my plate with food) 3. (misc.) a ~ed spoonful (BE) = a ~ing spoonful (AE)

hear *v.* 1. (d; intr.) ("to learn") to ~ about, of (we have heard of her; have you heard about the earthquake?) 2. (d; intr.) ("to receive word") to ~ from (I have not heard from him about this matter) 3. (I) ("to perceive by ear") I heard them go out = they were heard to go out 4. (J) ("to perceive by ear") I heard them going out = they were heard going out; we heard the aria being sung in Italian = the aria was heard being sung in Italian 5. (L) ("to learn") we have heard that he is in town 6. (N; used with a past participle) ("to listen to") we heard the aria sung in Italian 7. (Q) ("to learn") we heard why she left

hearing *n.* ["perception of sounds"] 1. acute, good, keen ~ 2. bad, defective, impaired ~ 3. hard of ~ (help for the hard of ~) 4. hearing-impaired (help for the hearing-impaired) ["session of a committee, court"] 5. to conduct, hold a ~ 6. a fair, impartial; open ~ (he got a fair ~) 7. Congressional ~s 8. an administrative; court; judicial; pre-trial; public ~ 9. at a ~ (to testify at a ~)

heart *n.* ["organ that circulates the blood"] 1. to transplant a ~ 2. a bad, weak; good, healthy, strong ~ 3. an artificial ~ 4. a ~ beats; fails, stops; palpitates,

throbs; pounds, thumps; pumps blood ["the heart as the center of emotion"] 5. to gladden; harden smb.'s ~ 6. to break; steal, win smb.'s ~ 7. my ~ aches, bleeds (for her); my ~ goes out to the homeless; my ~ is broken; my ~ leaps up ("My ~ leaps up when I behold A rainbow in the sky" – W Wordsworth (1770–1850), "My Heart Leaps Up"); my ~ skips a beat 8. from the ~ (to speak from the ~) (see also *from the bottom of my heart* at **bottom**) 9. in one's ~ (of ~s) (in my ~ (of ~s) I know that she is right) ["disposition"] 10. a cold, cruel, hard; good, kind, soft, tender, warm; stout ~ (she has a kind ~); a ~ of gold/stone ["liking"] 11. to have no ~ for (she has no ~ for this type of work) 12. after smb.'s own ~ (he's a man after my own ~) ["sympathy"] 13. to have a ~ (have a ~ and lend me some money) ["essence"] 14. to get to the ~ of smt. 15. at ~ (he's not bad at ~; to be young at ~) ["feeling"] 16. to have a change of ~ 17. a heavy; light ~ 18. with a (heavy) ~ ["courage"] 19. to take ~ from (he took ~ from her example) 20. to lose ~ 21. a brave; faint ~ ("Faint ~ never won fair lady!" – Sir W.S. Gilbert (1836–1911), *Iolanthe*) 22. my ~ sank 23. the ~ to + inf. (I didn't have the ~ to tell her) ["memory"] 24. by ~ (to know a poem by ~) ["resolve"] 25. to set one's ~ (on doing smt.) 26. a change of ~ ["misc."] 27. a bleeding ~ ("one who always supports the underdog"); to eat one's ~ out ("to brood"); to lose one's ~ to ("to fall in love with"); to have one's ~ in the right place ("to have good intentions"); to do smb.'s ~ good ("to make smb. happy"); with all one's ~ ("wholeheartedly"); to take smt. to ~ ("to take smt. seriously"); the way to smb.'s ~ ("how to please smb."); my ~ was not in it ("I did not really want to do it"); I gave her everything her ~ could want!; ~ to ~ ("intimately") (we finally began to speak ~ to ~); could you put your hand on your ~ and swear she's the culprit?; we must strive to win the ~s and minds of the people!; ~ and soul (I'll support you ~ and soul!); she poured out her ~ to me and told me everything

heart attack *n.* 1. to have a ~ 2. a fatal; massive; mild; severe; sudden ~

heartbroken *adj.* 1. ~ about, at, over (~ over a friend's death) 2. ~ to + inf. (I'm ~ to hear that he cannot come) 3. ~ that + clause (I'm ~ that he cannot come)

heart failure *n.* 1. to experience, have, suffer ~ 2. congestive; massive ~

heartless *adj.* ~ to + inf. (it was ~ of her to say that)

heartstrings *n.* ["deep feelings"] to tug at smb.'s ~ (the sentimental song really tugged at my heartstrings!)

heat I *n.* ["warmth"] 1. to conduct; generate, produce; radiate ~ 2. to absorb (the) ~ 3. to alleviate the ~ 4. blistering, extreme, great, intense, oppressive, scorching, stifling, sweltering, unbearable ~ 5. dry; latent (technical); penetrating; radiant; red; white ~ 6. animal; body ~ 7. ~ builds up, increases;

dissipates; emanates from (an oven) 8. (misc.) the body loses ~ ["excitement"] 9. in the ~ (of battle; of the moment) ["estrus, sexual excitement"] 10. in (AE), on (BE) ~ (the bitch was in ~) ["heating system"] 11. to raise, turn up; turn on the ~ 12. to lower, turn down; turn off the ~ 13. electric; gas; steam ~ ["preliminary race, race"] 14. to end in, run a dead ~ 15. a qualifying ~ ["pressure"] (colloq.) 16. to put the ~ on (the police were putting the ~ on him)

heat II v. 1. (C) ~ some water for me; or: ~ me some water 2. (D; tr.) to ~ to (she ~ed the oven to two hundred degrees; to gas mark 4 (BE))

heater n. 1. to turn on; turn up the ~ 2. to turn down; turn off the ~ 3. an electric; gas; hot-water, immersion (BE); kerosene (AE), paraffin (BE); oil; radiant; space; storage (BE) ~

heating n. 1. to turn on; turn up the ~ 2. to turn down; turn off the ~ 3. central; forced-air; space ~

heave I n. to give a ~

heave II v. 1. (P; tr.) ("to throw") they ~d the trash into the pit 2. (misc.) as we were ready to leave, our friends hove into view USAGE NOTE: As the past of heave, hove is nowadays virtually limited to the expression above.

heave-ho n. (colloq.) ["ejection"] to give smb. the (old) ~

heaven n. 1. to go to ~ 2. in ~ 3. (misc.) in seventh ~ ("in a state of bliss"); to move ~ and earth ("to make a maximum effort") (we moved ~ and earth to help them!); for ~'s sake; smb.'s idea of ~; can we create the kingdom of ~ here on earth?

hedge n. ["row of shrubs"] 1. to crop, trim a ~ ["protection against loss"] 2. a ~ against (a ~ against inflation)

hedged adj. (esp. BE) ~ about / round with (the project was ~ round with many restrictions)

heed n. to pay ~ to; to take ~ of

heedful adj. (cannot stand alone) ~ of (~ of advice)

heedless adj. (cannot stand alone) ~ of (~ of danger)

heel n. ["tyrannical oppression"] 1. under the (iron) ~ (under the ~ of the occupier) ["misc."] 2. to turn on one's ~ ("to turn away abruptly"); smb.'s Achilles' ~ ("smb.'s vulnerable point"); down at ~, down at the ~ (AE) ("shabby") (see also **heels**)

heels n. 1. to click one's ~ 2. built-up; high, stiletto; low ~ 3. to be at / on smb.'s ~ ("to follow smb. closely") 4. (misc.) to cool / kick (BE) one's ~ ("to be kept waiting"); to dig in one's ~ ("to be stubborn; to resist"); (esp. AE) down at the ~ ("shabby"); to drag one's ~ ("to move slowly"); to kick up one's ~ ("to be very lively"); to show one's ~ ("to flee"); to take to one's ~ ("to flee"); hard / hot on smb.'s ~ ("close to smb.") (also fig.) (another disaster came hot on the ~ of the first one!)

hegemony n. 1. to have ~ over 2. under smb.'s ~

height n. 1. to attain, reach a ~; to rise to a ~ 2. to clear; scale a ~ 3. a dizzy, precipitous, vertiginous ~ 4. dizzying ~s 5. one's full ~ (she rose to her full

~) 6. a ~ above; below (to fly at a ~ of ten thousand feet above sea level) 7. at; to a ~ (at the ~ of one's success; to fly at a ~ of ten thousand feet; to rise to a ~ of 10,000 feet) 8. in ~ (ten feet in ~) 9. (misc.) to adjust the ~ of a table; to achieve new ~s

heir n. 1. to fall ~ (they fell ~ to a large estate) 2. an ~ apparent; an ~ presumptive 3. an immediate; rightful ~ 4. ~ to USAGE NOTE: The form heiress is used in some combinations as, for example, in heiress to a large fortune (she fell heir to a large fortune and so became heiress to a large fortune).

heirloom n. a family; priceless ~

helicopter n. 1. to fly, pilot a ~ 2. an attack ~ = a ~ gunship (see also **airplane**)

hell n. (colloq.) ["the netherworld"] 1. go to ~! 2. to be in ~ ["scolding"] 3. to catch, get ~ 4. to give smb. ~ ["great suffering"] 5. to go through ~ 6. sheer, unmitigated, unspeakable ~ 7. ~ to + inf. (it was ~ to work there = it was ~ working there) ["misc."] 8. to beat (the) ~ out of smb. ("to give smb. a good thrashing"); to raise ~ ("to make trouble") (he's going to raise ~ if we're late!); to wait till ~ freezes over ("to wait for ever"); living there was ~ on earth ("it was terrible to live there"); a / one ~ of a team ("an excellent team"); for the ~ of it ("for no real reason"); to be ~ on ("to be harmful to"); bloody ~! (BE; slang); what the / in ~ is that?!; where the / in ~ did she go?!; why the / in ~ not?; from ~ (colloq.) (it was the vacation from ~: it rained all the time and the food was awful!)

hell-bent adj. (cannot stand alone) ["determined"] 1. ~ for, on (~ on balancing the budget) 2. ~ to + inf. (~ to balance the budget)

hello n. 1. to say ~ (to) 2. a big ~ (they gave me a big ~)

helm n. 1. to take (over) the ~ 2. at the ~

helmet n. 1. to put on; take off; wear a ~ 2. to have a ~ on 3. a crash, safety; football; pith, sun ~ 4. a steel ~

help I n. 1. to extend, give, offer, provide ~ 2. to call for, seek ~ 3. to cry for, plead for ~ 4. a big ~ (to) (they were a big ~ to us) 5. (a) great, invaluable, tremendous; little ~ 6. of ~ (to) (she was of great ~ to us; they were of little ~ to me) 7. (misc.) ~ wanted (as in a newspaper advertisement); domestic ~; (BE) a home ~ (AE has home health aide); will the new legislation be a ~ or a hindrance to us?

help II v. 1. (D; tr.) ("to assist") to ~ across (we ~ed them across the street) 2. (D; tr.) ("to assist") to ~ in, with (we ~ed them in their work; she ~ed me with the translation) 3. (D; tr.) ("to assist in moving") to ~ into; off; out of (~ them into the house; ~ her off the train; ~ him out of the car) 4. (D; tr.) ("to assist") to ~ through (they ~ed us through the crisis) 5. (D; refl.) ("to serve oneself") to ~ to (she ~ed herself to the cake) 6. (D; tr.) ("to serve") to ~ to (can I ~ you to some cake?) 7. (E) they ~ed to cook the meal 8. (F) ("to assist") they ~ed cook the meal 9. (G; often used with: cannot

– can't – couldn't) ("to keep from") we couldn't ~ laughing 10. (H) they ~ed us to cook the meal = we were ~ed to cook the meal 11. (I) they ~ed us cook the meal = we were ~ed to cook the meal 12. (misc.) I couldn't ~ but laugh; "can I have some more cake?" "(please) ~ yourself!"; will the new legislation ~ or hinder us?

helpful adj. 1. ~ in; to (she's been very ~ to us) 2. ~ of (that was very ~ of you) 3. ~ to + inf. (it's always ~ to be well-informed; it was ~ of you to do that)

helping n. a generous; second ~ (of)

helping hand n. to give, lend (smb.) a ~

helpless adj. 1. to leave, render smb. ~ (the stroke left him ~) 2. ~ against (we were ~ against the invasion) 3. ~ to + inf. (we were ~ to resist the invasion)

helplessness n. 1. complete, utter ~ 2. learned ~ (to overcome learned ~ by changing one's behavior)

help off v. (d; tr.) to ~ with (he ~ed me off with my coat)

help on v. (d; tr.) to ~ with (he ~ed me on with my coat)

help out v. 1. (D; intr., tr.) to ~ by (she ~ed me out by giving me some good advice) 2. (D; intr., tr.) to ~ with (she ~ed me out with some good advice) 3. (misc.) she ~s them out in her own way

helter-skelter adv. to flee ~

hem n. 1. to let down, let out, lower a ~ 2. to raise, take up a ~ 3. to pin up a ~ 4. to straighten a ~

hemisphere n. 1. the eastern; northern; southern; western ~ 2. the left; right ~ (of the brain)

hemline n. to lower; raise a ~

hemmed in adj. ~ on all sides

hemorrhage n. 1. a brain, cerebral; internal ~ 2. a massive ~

hen n. 1. ~s cackle, cluck 2. ~s lay eggs

hepatitis n. infectious; serum ~

herbs n. 1. dried; fresh; medicinal ~ (to garnish food with fresh ~) 2. a bunch of ~

herd I n. 1. to drive; round up a ~ 2. to tend a ~ 3. a dairy ~ 4. (misc.) to ride ~ on ("to control"); to follow the ~ ("to go along with the crowd"); the common ~ ("the great mass of people")

herd II v. (P; tr.) the prisoners were ~ed into the compound; the children were ~ed out of the classroom; the tourists were ~ed through the exhibition

here adv. 1. from; (up) to ~ 2. down; over; up ~ 3. from ~ on 4. (misc.) I've had it up to ~ with your constant complaining! ("I've had more than enough of your constant complaining")

hereafter n. in the ~

heresy n. 1. to be guilty of ~; to commit ~ 2. to preach ~ 3. ~ to + inf. (it was ~ to talk like that)

heritage n. 1. to cherish one's ~ 2. to repudiate one's ~ 3. a priceless, proud, rich ~ (we must preserve and protect our priceless ~ of art and culture!) 4. a cultural; family; national; religious ~

hernia n. a hiatal; hiatus; inguinal ~

hero n. 1. a conquering; folk; local; military; war;

national; popular; unsung ~ 2. a ~ to (when she returned, she was a ~ to her followers)

heroic adj. ~ to + inf. (it was ~ of them to oppose the invader)

heroin n. 1. to do (colloq.), inject, shoot (colloq.), shoot up (with) (colloq.), smoke ~ 2. a shot of ~

heroine n. see **hero**

heroism n. to demonstrate, display ~

herpes n. 1. to come down with, contract, get ~ 2. genital ~

hesitancy n. 1. to show ~ 2. ~ about, in (I have no ~ about throwing him out)

hesitant adj. 1. ~ about (they are ~ about signing a contract) 2. ~ to + inf. (they were ~ to sign the contract)

hesitate v. 1. (D; intr.) to ~ over (to ~ over a choice) 2. (E) they ~ed to sign the contract; do not ~ to call me

hesitation n. 1. to show ~ 2. (a) momentary, slight ~ 3. ~ about, in (I have no ~ about throwing him out)

het up adj. (slang) ["excited"] to get (all) ~ about, over

hew v. (d; intr.) ("to adhere") (AE) to ~ to (to ~ to the party line)

hex n. (AE) to put a ~ on smb.

heyday n. ["most successful period"] 1. to have one's ~ 2. in smb.'s ~

hiatus n. a brief ~

hiccup n. 1. to give, let out a ~ 2. to get; have the ~s 3. to get rid of the ~s 4. an attack of (the) ~s

hide I n. 1. to tan a ~ 2. (misc.) to save smb.'s ~ ("to rescue smb."); to tan smb.'s ~ ("to spank smb.")

hide II v. 1. (D; intr.) to ~ behind (to ~ behind a legal technicality) 2. (D; intr., tr.) to ~ from

hide-and-seek n. to play ~

hideaway n. a secret ~

hideous adj. ~ to + inf. (it was ~ to watch the massacre = the massacre was ~ to watch = it was a ~ massacre to watch = it was ~ watching the massacre = watching the massacre was ~)

hideout n. a secret ~

hide out v. to ~ from (to ~ from the police)

hiding I n. ["concealment"] 1. to go into ~ 2. to come out of ~ 3. in ~

hiding II n. (colloq.) ["a beating"] 1. to give smb. a ~ 2. to get a ~ (he got a good ~ for his misbehavior) 3. a good, sound ~ 4. (misc.) to deserve a good ~

hierarchy n. 1. to rise in the ~ 2. an academic; church; corporate; military; ruling ~

high I adj. 1. ~ in (~ in iron) 2. (misc.) ~ up; (colloq.) to get ~ on (a drug); as ~ as the sky = sky-high; the building is 200 feet ~ = it is a 200-foot-high building; shoulder-high; waist-high

high II n. ["acme"] 1. to reach a ~ 2. an all-time ~ ["state of euphoria"] (slang) 3. to reach a ~ 4. to be on a (perpetual) ~

highball n. ["type of drink"] to make, mix a ~

highhanded adj. ~ to + inf. (it was ~ of him to remove the equipment without permission)

high horse *n.* (colloq.) ["arrogance"] to get on one's ~ ("to start to show arrogance")

highness *n.* (her, his, your) royal ~ ; their royal ~es

high-pressure *v.* (AE) 1. (D; tr.) to ~ into (she was ~d into signing) 2. (H) she was ~d to sign

high road *n.* ["direct route"] 1. to take the ~ (to) 2. (misc.) (fig.) the ~ to success

high sign *n.* (esp. AE) ["signal"] 1. to give smb. the ~ 2. to get the ~

highway *n.* 1. (AE) a divided ~ (BE has *dual carriageway*) 2. a limited-access ~ (BE prefers *motorway*) 3. (to drive) on the ~ 4. the ~ to 5. (misc.) the Information Highway; the public ~ (BE)

hijack *v.* (D; tr.) to ~ to (they were ~ed to an unknown country)

hijacking *n.* 1. to carry out, commit a ~ 2. to foil, thwart a ~

hike I *n.* 1. to go on; organize a ~ 2. a long; short ~ (they went on a long ~ from one place to another) 3. an overnight ~ (as of Boy Scouts)

hike II *v.* (P; intr.) they ~d to town on foot; we ~d around the village; the scouts ~d over the mountain; they ~d from one place to another

hike III *n.* (colloq.) 1. a pay; tax ~ 2. an across-the-board; annual (pay) ~

hill *n.* 1. to climb up, go up; come down a ~ 2. rolling ~s; a steep ~ 3. in the ~s (to live in the ~s) 4. on a ~ (the house stood on a ~) 5. (lit.) the brow of a ~ 6. the bottom, foot of a ~ 7. the top of a ~ 8. a ~ rises 9. a chain, group of ~s 10. down; over; up a ~ 11. (misc.) the height of a ~ ; (colloq.) to take to the ~s ("to take refuge in or escape to the hills")

hilt *n.* ["limit"] to the ~ (he plunged the dagger in up to the ~ ; we were mortgaged (up) to the ~ and couldn't afford any more)

hinder *v.* 1. (D; tr.) to ~ from 2. (D; tr.) to ~ in 3. (misc.) will the new legislation help or ~ us?

hindrance *n.* a ~ to (will the new legislation be a help or a ~ to us?)

hindsight *n.* with (the benefit/wisdom of) ~ (with the benefit of ~, we could see that the plan was doomed from the start!)

hinge *v.* (d; intr.) ("to depend") to ~ on, upon (the future ~s on what we decide now)

hint I *n.* 1. to drop, give a ~ 2. to take a ~ 3. a broad, heavy, obvious; delicate, gentle, subtle; helpful ~ 4. the merest, slightest ~ 5. a ~ about, on; of (a ~ about the answer; a ~ of suspicion; a book that gives helpful ~s on child care) (also fig.) (there's just a ~ of garlic in the sauce) 6. a ~ that + clause (she dropped a ~ that she would retire soon) 7. at a ~ (they fled at the first ~ of trouble)

hint II *v.* 1. (d. intr.) to ~ at 2. (L; she) she ~ed (to us) that she would retire soon

hip *n.* 1. to shake, sway, wiggle one's ~s 2. (misc.) they stood with their hands on their ~s

hire I *n.* for ~

hire II *v.* 1. (D; tr.) to ~ as (to ~ smb. as a guide) 2. (esp. BE) (D; tr.) to ~ from (to ~ a car from an

agency) (AE usu. uses *to rent*) 3. (H) we ~d her to mow our lawn

hired *adj.* ~ to + inf. (she was ~ to mow our lawn)

hire out *v.* (D; refl., tr.) to ~ as ; to (he ~d himself out as a mercenary to the highest bidder)

hire purchase *n.* (BE) on ~ (to buy smt. on ~) (AE has *the installment plan*)

hiss *v.* 1. (D; intr.) to ~ at (the crowd ~ed at the delay) 2. (D; tr.) to ~ off (the actor was ~ed off the stage) 3. (misc.) "be quiet!" she ~ed (at us)

history *n.* 1. to make ~ 2. to record, take down; trace the ~ of smt./smb. 3. to distort; revise, rewrite ~ 4. to go down in ~ as (he went down in ~ as a tyrant) 5. ancient; art; medieval; modern; past; recorded ~ 6. cultural; military; natural ~ 7. a case; family; life; medical; personal; social ~ (I recorded his personal ~) (see also **case history**) 8. (an) oral ~ 9. a ~ of (she had a long ~ of drug abuse/ violence) 10. in, throughout ~ (people have struggled for freedom throughout recorded ~) 11. (misc.) ~ repeats itself; ~ shows that ..., ~ tells us that ... ; a page in ~ ; the nurse did/got/took the patient's ~; she was a mere extra – but that's all past ~ now because she finally got a chance to replace the star – and the rest is ~ !

hit I *n.* ["blow that strikes the target"] 1. to score a ~ 2. to take a ~ (our ship took several direct ~s) 3. a direct ~ ["success"] (colloq.) 4. to make a ~ with (she made quite a ~ with the audience) 5. a big, smash ~

hit II *v.* 1. ("to strike") to ~ hard 2. (d; tr.) ("to strike") to ~ against, on (he hit his head on the ceiling) 3. (d; intr.) to ~ at ("to attack") (the press hit hard at government corruption) 4. (slang) (AE) (d; tr.) to ~ for ("to request") (he hit me for twenty dollars) 5. (D; tr.) ("to strike") to ~ in, on, over (to ~ smb. in the face; she hit me on the hand) 6. (slang) (AE) ("to make sexual overtures to") to ~ on smb. 7. (d; intr.) to ~ on, upon ("to discover") (they finally hit on an acceptable compromise) 8. (BE) (O; can be used with one animate object) ("to strike") he hit me a hard blow 9. (P; tr.) she hit the ball over the net; the batter hit the ball into the bleachers

hit back *v.* (D; intr.) to ~ at (President Hits Back At Critics – headline)

hitch I *n.* (colloq.) ["obstacle"]["stoppage"] 1. a slight; technical ~ 2. a ~ in (there's been a slight ~ in our plans) 3. without a ~ (it went off without a ~) ["period of military service"] (esp. AE) 4. to do a ~ 5. to sign up for another ~

hitch II *v.* (d; tr.) to ~ to (to ~ horses to a cart)

hitch up *v.* (D; tr.) to ~ to (to ~ horses to a cart)

hit off *v.* to ~ it off with smb. ("to get along well with smb.")

hit out *v.* (D; intr.) to ~ against, at (they ~ against their political rivals)

hitter *n.* (esp. AE; baseball and fig.) 1. a designated ~ 2. a leadoff; pinch ~

hit up *v.* (slang) (AE) (d; tr.) ("to request") to ~ for (he hit me up for a loan)

hoax *n.* 1. to perpetrate a ~ 2. to play a ~ on smb. 3. a literary ~

hobble *v.* (P; intr.) she ~d across the street; they ~d into the room

hobby *n.* to have, pursue; take up a ~

hobnob *v.* (d; intr.) to ~ with

hock *n.* (colloq.) (esp. AE) 1. in ~ ("pawned"); out of ~ (my watch is in ~ but I'll soon get it out of ~ again) 2. in ~ to ("in debt to") (I'm in ~ to a loan shark to the tune of $30,000!)

hockey *n.* 1. to play ~ 2. field (AE); ice ~

hoist *v.* (d; tr.) to ~ onto, to (the workers were ~ed onto the roof)

hold I *n.* ["grip"] 1. to catch, get, grab, lay, seize, take ~ of 2. to keep ~ of 3. to loosen, relax; lose, relinquish one's ~ (of) 4. to tighten one's ~ 5. a firm, strong, tight ~ 6. a ~ on ["type of wrestling grip"] 7. to break a ~; to get smb. in a ~ ["control, domination"] 8. to consolidate; have; maintain; tighten a ~ 9. to loosen; relinquish one's ~ 10. a firm, strong, tight ~ 11. a ~ on, over (they refused to relinquish their ~ over this area; they thought they had a ~ on us) ["waiting"] 12. on ~ (the plan is on ~ until next year; when I called him, he put me on ~; I cannot leave the phone because I'm still on ~)

hold II *v.* 1. ("to keep") to ~ high (to ~ one's head high; also fig.) 2. ("to keep, support") to ~ tight, tightly (~ tight and don't fall off!) 3. (d; tr.) to ~ against ("to take into account") (we will not ~ your past blunders against you; they held his criminal record against him) 4. (D; tr.) to ~ by ("to keep, support") (to ~ smb. by the hand) 5. (d; tr.) to ~ in ("to regard") (to ~ smb. in contempt; to ~ smb. in high esteem) 6. (d; intr.) to ~ onto ("to seize and cling to") (~ onto my arm) 7. (d; intr.) ("to adhere") to ~ to (to ~ to the terms of a contract) 8. (d; tr.) ("to make smb. comply") to ~ to (they held us to the terms of the contract) 9. (d; tr.) ("to restrict") to ~ to (we held the visiting team to a tie) 10. (d; intr.) ("to agree") to ~ with (I don't ~ with his ideas) 11. (L) (formal) ("to assert") we ~ that these truths are self-evident 12. (M) ("to consider") we ~ him to be responsible; "We ~ these truths to be self-evident" – U.S. Declaration of Independence, July 4, 1776 13. (N; used with an adjective) ("to consider"); ("to keep") to ~ smb. responsible; she held the ladder steady; they ~ life cheap; we ~ these truths self-evident

hold III *n.* ["interior of a ship below decks"] in the ~

hold back *v.* 1. (D; tr.) ("to keep") to ~ from (lack of education held him back from promotion) 2. (d; intr.) to ~ with (to ~ with one's reserves)

holder *n.* 1. a candle; cigarette; napkin ~ 2. a lease-holder; license-holder, permit-holder; office-holder; passport-holder; policy-holder; record-holder 3. (AE) a pot ~ (AE also has *oven mitt*; BE has *oven glove*)

hold forth *v.* (D; intr.) ("to give an opinion") to ~ about, on (to ~ about various matters)

holdings *n.* ["investments"] 1. to diversify one's ~ 2. far-flung ~

hold off *v.* (G) to ~ making a decision

hold on *v.* to ~ tight, tightly (~ tight and don't fall off!)

hold out *v.* 1. (B) ("to offer") they didn't ~ much hope to us; to ~ a helping hand to smb. = to ~ a helping hand out to smb.; she held her hand out to us in friendship = she ~ed out her hand to us in friendship 2. (D; intr.) to ~ against ("to resist") (they held out against the enemy for a month) 3. (D; intr.) to ~ for ("to demand") (they held out for better terms) 4. (d; intr.) to ~ on ("to keep information from") (don't ~ on me) 5. (D; intr.) ("to persevere") to ~ to (to ~ to the end)

holdover *n.* a ~ from (a ~ from the old days)

hold up *v.* 1. (d; tr.) to ~ as (to ~ as an example) 2. (esp. AE) (D; intr.) to ~ on (they had to ~ on their travel plans) 3. (d; tr.) to ~ to (to ~ smt. up to ridicule)

hole *n.* 1. to bore; burrow; dig; drill; make a ~ 2. to fill (in), plug a ~ 3. a deep; gaping, yawning ~ 4. a plug (esp. BE); rabbit; watering ~ (pull the plug out of the plug ~ and let the water out) 5. a bullet ~ 6. (misc.) to pick ~s in smt. ("to find flaws in smt."); to poke a ~ in smb.'s argument; (golf) to shoot a ~ in one; we're five hundred dollars in the ~ ("we owe five hundred dollars that we cannot pay")

holed up *adj.* (colloq.) ~ in (they were ~ in an old farmhouse)

hole up *v.* (colloq.) (d; intr.) to ~ in (they ~d up in an old farmhouse)

holiday *n.* ["day set aside for the suspension of business, labor"] 1. to celebrate, observe a ~ 2. a bank (BE), legal (AE), public; national; religious ~ ["period of rest"] (esp. BE; AE prefers *vacation*) 3. to have, take a ~ 4. to be on; go on ~ 5. a summer ~ 6. a ~ from 7. on ~ (she was away on ~) ["misc."] 8. a busman's ~ ("a holiday spent in doing one's usual work") (see the Usage Note at **vacation**)

holler *v.* (colloq.) (esp. AE) 1. (B) she ~ed a few words to him 2. (D; intr., tr.) to ~ at (they ~ed at the children) 3. (misc.) "Be careful!" she ~ed; they ~ed at the children to stop shouting; they ~ed to the children to be careful

hollow *v.* (d; tr.) to ~ out of (to ~ a canoe out of a log)

holocaust *n.* a nuclear ~

holster *n.* a shoulder ~

holy orders *n.* ["ordination"] to receive, take ~

homage *n.* 1. to pay ~ to 2. in ~ to

home *n.* ["establishment providing care or service"] 1. to manage, operate, run a ~ 2. a convalescent; funeral (AE); nursing; remand (BE); rest; retirement ~ ["residence"] 3. to build; establish a ~ 4. to provide a ~ for 5. to make one's ~ at, in 6. an ancestral;

childhood; country; mobile; summer; winter ~
7. (a) ~ for, to (San Francisco was ~ to them for
years) 8. at ~ (make yourself at ~; she is never at ~;
AE also has: she is never ~) ["family"] 9. a broken;
foster; good; happy ~ [misc.] 10. to romp ~ ("to
score an easy victory"); she is at ~ in/with Greek
literature; to go ~; a ~ away from ~ (AE) = (BE) a
~ from ~ USAGE NOTE: In many instances *home*
is used as an adverb – to go home, to get home
from work, etc.

home in v. (D; intr.) to ~ on (to ~ on a target)
USAGE NOTE: The incorrect variant **hone in on*
is sometimes encountered.

home page n. (computers) to create; view; visit a ~

home run n. (AE; baseball and fig.) ["hit that allows
the batter to score a run"] to hit a ~

homesick adj. 1. to get ~ 2. ~ for

home straight (BE), **homestretch** n. to come into
the ~

homework n. 1. to do, prepare ~ 2. to assign, set
(BE) ~ 3. to hand in ~ 4. to correct; grade, mark ~
(a teacher corrects ~)

homicide n. 1. to commit ~ 2. justifiable ~

homily n. 1. to deliver a ~ 2. a ~ about, on

hone v. 1. (D; tr.) to ~ to (to ~ smt. to a point) 2.
(misc.) finely ~d

honest adj. 1. ~ about; in; with (be ~ about this matter with us; to be ~ in one's dealings; to be ~ with
you, I don't think your plan will work) 2. ~ to + inf.
(it's not ~ to lie about one's age)

honesty n. 1. to impugn smb.'s ~ 2. ~ about; in;
with 3. in all ~ (in all ~, do you believe him?) 4.
the ~ to + inf. (she had the ~ to report the bribe)

honey n. 1. to gather ~ 2. (BE) runny ~ 3. (misc.)
as sweet as ~

honeycombed adj. (cannot stand alone) ~ with

honeymoon n. 1. to go for/on one's ~ (they went
to Hawaii on/for their ~) 2. to spend one's ~ (they
spent their ~ in Hawaii) 3. a second ~ 4. (misc.) the
~ is over (usu. fig.)

honk v. (D; intr.) to ~ at

honor I honour n. ["respect"] ["credit"] 1. to bring,
do ~ to (she brought ~ to her family) 2. an ~ to
(they are an ~ to their country) 3. in smb.'s ~; in
~ of (to give a reception in smb.'s ~) ["distinction"]
["recognition"] 4. to win (an) ~ 5. to bestow, confer
an ~ on 6. a dubious; great, high, signal ~ 7. an ~
that + clause (it was a great ~ that we were chosen)
8. (to graduate) with ~s 9. (misc.) she did us the ~
of attending our party ["privilege"] 10. to have the ~
(may I have the ~ of your company?) 11. an ~ to +
inf. (it was an ~ to serve with you; it was a great ~
for us to have been chosen) ["integrity"] ["reputation"]
12. to stake one's ~ on smt. 13. one's word of ~;
an affair of ~ 14. on one's (word of) ~ ["rite"] 15. to
do the ~s ("to serve as host") 16. military ~s (to be
buried with full military ~s) ["misc."] 17. a (military)
guard of ~; the guest of ~

honor II honour v. 1. (D; tr.) to ~ as, for (she was

~ed as a community leader = she was ~ed for being
a community leader) 2. (D; tr.) to ~ by; with (he
was ~ed by being invited)

honor bound, honour bound adj. 1. ~ to + inf. (we
were ~ to get the job done on time) 2. (formal) in ~
(we were in ~ to get the job done on time)

honorable, honourable adj. ~ to + inf. (it is not ~ to
deceive them with false promises)

honorarium n. to accept; offer; pay; receive an ~

honored, honoured adj. 1. deeply, greatly, highly,
very 2. ~ to + inf. (he was ~ to be invited) 3. ~ that
+ clause (he was ~ that you invited him)

hood n. (AE) ["cover over a front car engine"] to check
under the ~ (of a car) (BE has *bonnet*)

hoodwink v. 1. (D; tr.) to ~ into 2. (D; tr.) to ~ out
of

hoof n. 1. a cloven ~ 2. hoofs/hooves clatter 3. on
the ~ (to buy cattle on the ~)

hook n. ["curved implement"] 1. a crochet; meat;
pruning ~ 2. (misc.) to hang a coat on a ~; to leave
the phone off the ~ ["blow delivered with bent arm"]
3. to deliver a ~ (he delivered a right ~ to his opponent's jaw) ["implement used to catch fish"] 4. to
bait a ~ ["misc."] (slang) 5. off the ~ ("relieved of
responsibility")

hooked adj. (slang) ["addicted"] ~ on (~ on drugs)

hookey, hooky n. (colloq.) (AE) to play ~ ("to play
truant")

hooks and eyes n. ["type of fastening"] 1. to fasten;
unfasten ~ 2. to sew on ~

hookup n. 1. a satellite ~ 2. a ~ with

hook up v. 1. (D; tr.) to ~ to (to ~ a telephone up
to the cable = to ~ a telephone to the cable) 2. (D;
intr.) to ~ with ("to join")

hoop n. to roll a ~

hoopla n. (slang) (AE) ["bustle, noise, fuss"] the ~
subsides

hoot I n. (colloq.) ["slightest care"] not to give a ~ (see
also *hoots of derision* at **derision**)

hoot II v. 1. (D; intr.) ("to shout") to ~ at (they ~ed
at me to get moving) 2. (misc.) the actor was ~ed
off the stage

hop I n. ["short flight"] 1. a short ~ 2. a ~ from; to (it's
a short ~ from Detroit to Cleveland)

hop II v. 1. (d; intr.) to ~ into (the children ~ped into
their nice warm beds) 2. (d; intr.) to ~ out of (to ~
out of a chair) 3. (P; intr.) the children ~ped across
the puddle; to ~ (onto) a bus

hope I n. 1. to arouse, inspire, stir up ~ 2. to build up,
raise smb.'s ~s 3. to get smb.'s ~s up 4. to express,
voice a ~ 5. to cherish, entertain, nurse a ~ 6. to
cling to a ~ 7. to pin, place, put one's ~s on 8. to
crush, dash, deflate, shatter; thwart smb.'s ~s 9.
to abandon, give up, lose ~ 10. an ardent, fervent,
fond; devout; pious; sincere ~ 11. a real; realistic,
reasonable ~ 12. a dim, faint, slender, slight; false,
idle, illusory, vain; unrealistic, unreasonable ~
13. high ~s 14. ~s are fulfilled, are realized, come
to fruition 15. ~s crumble, are dashed, fade 16. a

flicker, glimmer, ray, spark of ~ 17. ~ for; in; of (~ for better times; we had high ~s for her) 18. a ~ that + clause (it was our ~ that they would settle near us; there was little ~ that she would be elected) 19. in, with the ~ (we returned to the park in the ~ of finding her wallet) 20. beyond, past (all) ~ 21. (misc.) they are our best ~ for a medal in/at the games; "We shall nobly save, or meanly lose, the last best ~ of earth." – Abraham Lincoln (December 1, 1862)
hope II v. 1. to ~ fervently, sincerely, very much 2. (D; intr.) to ~ for (to ~ for an improvement) 3. (E) she ~s to see them soon 4. (L) she ~s that she will see them soon 5. (misc.) I ~ so; I ~ not; here's ~ing!; we ~ and pray that she will be forgiven
hopeful I adj. 1. ~ of 2. ~ that + clause (she's ~ that she will see them soon)
hopeful II n. a presidential; young ~
hopeless adj. 1. ~ at, with (he's ~ with figures; he's ~ at balancing his checkbook) 2. ~ to + inf. (it's ~ to expect her to help)
hopper n. (AE) ["container for bills that are being considered"] 1. a legislative ~ 2. in a ~
hopscotch n. to play ~
horizon n. 1. (fig.) to broaden, expand one's ~s 2. above; below; beyond the ~ 3. on the ~ (to appear on the ~)
hormone n. a female; growth; male; sex ~
horn n. ["device on a car"] 1. to blow, honk, sound, toot a ~ 2. ~s blare, blow 3. a ~ gets stuck ["musical instrument"] 4. to play a ~ 5. an English (esp. AE; BE prefers cor anglais); French ~ ["misc."] 6. on the ~s of a dilemma ("in a dilemma"); to lock ~s ("to come into conflict") ~ (over; with) (locked ~s with them over foreign policy); to take the bull by the ~s ("to confront a problem boldly"); (AE) to blow/toot one's own ~ ("to boast") (BE has to blow one's own trumpet)
hornet n. ~s sting
hornets' nest n. ["angry reaction"] to stir up a ~
horn in v. (colloq.) (D; intr.) to ~ on ("to interrupt") (to ~ on smb. else's conversation)
Horn of Africa n. in, (esp. AE) on the ~
horoscope n. 1. to read smb.'s ~ 2. smb.'s ~ says
horrible adj. 1. ~ to (she was ~ to her workers) 2. ~ to + inf. (it is ~ to work there = it is ~ working there) 3. ~ that + clause (it's ~ that he has to work there)
horrid adj. 1. ~ to (she was simply ~ to her children!) 2. ~ to + inf. (it was ~ of her to tease her children like that = she was ~ to tease her children like that)
horrified adj. 1. ~ at, by (we were ~ at/by the news that their house had burned down) 2. ~ to + inf. (we were ~ to learn that their house had burned down) 3. ~ that + clause (we were ~ that their house had burned down)
horrify v. (R) it ~fied us (to learn) that their house had burned down

horrifying adj. ~ to + inf.; that + clause (it was ~ (to learn) that their house had burned down!)
horror n. 1. to express; feel ~ 2. to have a ~ of 3. indescribable, unspeakable, sheer ~ 4. ~ at (we expressed our ~ at the news that their house had burned down) 5. in ~ (to scream in ~) (see also to recoil in horror at **recoil**) 6. to smb.'s ~ (to our ~, their house burned down!) 7. (misc.) a scream, shriek of ~
horror-stricken, horror-struck adj. 1. ~ at 2. ~ + inf. (we were ~ to learn that their house had burned down)
horse n. ["animal"] 1. to mount; ride; spur (on); walk a ~ 2. to lead a ~ by the bridle 3. to dismount, get off a ~ 4. to bridle; curry; groom; harness; hobble; saddle; shoe a ~ 5. to break (in) a ~ 6. to breed, raise; train a ~ 7. a cart (BE), draft (AE), dray; race; saddle; thoroughbred; wild ~; a workhorse (usu. fig.) 8. ~s bolt; canter; gallop; rear; shy; trot; walk 9. ~s neigh; nicker (BE), snicker (AE), whicker; whinny 10. an unbroken ~ bucks (the ~ bucked and threw its rider) 11. a herd of (wild) ~s; a pair; team of ~s 12. a young ~ is a foal 13. a female ~ is a mare 14. a male ~ is a stallion; a castrated male ~ is a gelding 15. a young female ~ is a filly 16. a young male ~ is a colt ["padded block"] (gymnastics) 17. a pommel, side (AE); vaulting ~ ["misc."] 18. to back the wrong ~ ("to support the losing side"); to beat/flog a dead ~ ("to discuss an issue that has already been settled"); from the ~'s mouth ("from an original or authoritative source"); to hold one's ~s ("to behave more carefully"); a ~ of a different color ("an entirely different matter"); to eat like a ~ ("to eat a great deal"); to work like a ~ ("to work very hard"); to play the ~s ("to bet on horse races"); to look a gift ~ in the mouth ("to be very critical of a gift") (see also **high horse**; **pony**)
horse around v. (colloq.) (D; intr.) to ~ with
horseback n. 1. to ride ~ 2. on ~
hose n. ["flexible tube"] 1. to play, train a ~ on 2. a fire; garden; rubber; water ~ ["stockings"] 3. mesh ~; stretch; support ~ (see also **pantyhose**)
hosiery n. support ~
hospitable adj. 1. ~ to, towards (~ to strangers) 2. ~ to + inf. (it is not ~ to turn a stranger away)
hospital n. 1. to establish, found a ~ 2. to manage, run a ~ 3. to be admitted to ~ (BE)/to be admitted to the/a ~ (AE), to enter ~ (BE)/to enter the/a ~ (AE), to go into, to ~ (BE)/to go into, to the/a ~ (AE) 4. to be discharged from ~ (BE), to leave ~ (BE)/to be discharged from the/a ~ (AE), to leave the/a ~ (AE) 5. a base; evacuation; field; military; station; veterans' ~ 6. a children's; general; mental ~ 7. a city, municipal; community, non-profit; cottage (BE); private, proprietary (AE); state; teaching ~ 8. at, in a ~ (she works at/in a ~) 9. in ~ (BE)/in the/a ~ (AE) (she's ill and has been in/in the ~ for a week) USAGE NOTE: In BE, the phrases to go to hospital, to be in hospital mean

"to be hospitalized"; in AE one says *to go to the/ a hospital, to be in the/a hospital*. But: *she went to the hospital to visit her mother* is CE.

hospitality *n*. 1. to extend, offer, show ~ 2. to enjoy; repay smb.'s ~ 3. to abuse smb.'s ~ 4. cordial, warm; lavish ~

host *n*. 1. to play ~ to (who will play ~ to our foreign guests?) 2. to act as ~ 3. a congenial, gracious, perfect ~ (he was a perfect ~ to all his guests) 4. a chat-show (BE), talk-show (AE); game-show ~ 5. ~ to (which city will be ~ to the next Olympics?)

hostage *n*. 1. to take smb. ~ 2. to seize, take ~s 3. to hold smb. (as a) ~ (they were held ~) 4. to exchange ~s 5. to free, liberate ~s

hostel *n*. a youth ~

hostess *n*. 1. see **host** (1, 2, 3, and sometimes 4) (at home she ia always a perfect hostess; at work, she is a well-known game-show host/hostess) 2. an air (BE), airline (AE) ~ 3. a dance-hall; nightclub ~ USAGE NOTE: In AE, the phrase *flight attendant* has almost completely replaced *airline hostess*.

hostile *adj*. 1. openly ~ 2. ~ to, towards

hostilities *n*. ["war"] 1. to begin, open ~ 2. to end; suspend ~ 3. impending ~ 4. ~ begin, break out, erupt; cease, end 5. an outbreak of ~ 6. ~ between

hostility *n*. 1. to arouse, stir up ~ 2. to display, show ~ 3. to express; feel ~ 4. (a) bitter, deep, profound; open; veiled ~ 5. ~ against, to, towards 6. ~ between

hot *adj*. 1. boiling, burning, piping, red-hot, scalding, steaming; unbearably; uncomfortably ~, white-hot 2. (misc.) ~ on smb.'s heels/trail ("close behind smb. being pursued"); all ~ and bothered ("disturbed or excited") (see also *hot under the collar* at **collar** 3)

hotel *n*. 1. to manage, operate, run a ~ 2. a deluxe, five-star, luxury; first-class; four-star; posh, swanky (colloq.); three-star ~ 3. a run-down, seedy ~ 4. at, in a ~ (she works at/in a ~) 5. (misc.) to check in at, check into, register at a ~; to check out of a ~; to go to a ~; to stay at a ~

hound I *n*. ["hunting dog"] 1. a pack of ~s 2. (esp. BE) to ride to ~s, to follow the ~s, to hunt with ~s ("to hunt on horseback with dogs") 3. ~s bay ["enthusiast"] 4. autograph ~s

hound II *v*. 1. (d; tr.) to ~ from, out of (they ~ed her out of office) 2. (d; tr.) to ~ into (they finally ~ed me into getting a haircut) 3. (H) they kept ~ing me to get a haircut

hour *n*. 1. to show, tell the ~ (my watch shows the minute and ~) 2. a solid ("full") ~ (the police grilled him for three solid ~s) 3. an ungodly ("very early"); ("very late") ~ (she called at an ungodly ~) 4. the decisive ~; or: the ~ of decision 5. the cocktail ~ 6. business, peak; unsocial (BE); visiting ~s (during peak ~s more trains run; to get extra pay for working unsocial ~s) (see also **office hours**; **working hours**) 7. flexible; irregular; regular ~s (she keeps regular ~s) 8. the rush ~ (traffic is very

heavy during the rush ~) 9. at a certain ~ (at the appointed ~; we had to get up at an ungodly ~) 10. by the ~ (to pay workers by the ~) 11. during, in, on a certain ~ (during the lunch ~; in smb.'s ~ of need) 12. in, inside, within an ~ (she'll be here in an ~; or BE: in an ~'s time) 13. on the ~ ("hourly") (coaches for Birmingham leave (every ~) on the ~; coaches for Bradford leave (every ~) on the half-hour; coaches for Bolton leave (every ~) at 20 minutes past the ~) 14. (BE) out of ~s (I cannot see you out of (normal working) ~s, which are between (the ~s of) nine and five) 15. (misc.) they spent many happy ~s playing cards; to keep late ~s ("to go to bed late"); smb.'s darkest/finest ~ ("the worst/noblest period in smb.'s life or history"); in the wee ~s of the morning ("late at night"); after ~s ("after work"); (a) happy ~ ("period in which a bar sells alcoholic drinks at a reduced price"); H-hour/zero hour ("time at which a significant event is scheduled to begin")

house *n*. ["building"]["home"] 1. to build, put up a ~ 2. to redecorate, refurbish, remodel, renovate a ~ 3. to demolish, raze, tear down a ~ 4. to rent a ~ from smb. 5. to let (BE), rent (out) a ~ to smb. 6. (BE) to move ~ (AE has: *to move*) 7. a dilapidated, ramshackle 8. an apartment (AE); council (BE) ~ 9. a detached; one-family, single; ranch (AE); row (AE), terrace (BE), terraced (BE); semidetached; town; tract (AE) ~ 10. a country; doll's house (esp. BE), dollhouse (AE); manor (esp. BE); summer; tree; Wendy (BE) ~ 11. a brick; clapboard (AE), weatherboard; frame; prefabricated ~ 12. a lodging (esp. BE), rooming (AE) ~ 13. a haunted ~ 14. (AE) a fraternity; sorority ~ ["housekeeping"] 15. to clean ~ 16. to keep ~ for smb. ["theater"] 17. to bring the ~ down ("to win thunderous applause") 18. an empty; full, packed ~ (to play to a packed ~) 19. an opera ~ ["chamber of a legislative body"] 20. a lower; upper ~; both ~s of Congress (see also *the House of Commons* at **common**; *the House of Lords* at **lord**; *a house of worship* at **worship I** *n*.) ["firm"] 21. a banking; clearing ~ (see also **clearinghouse**) 22. a discount; mail-order; pharmaceutical; publishing ~ 23. a gambling ~ 24. a slaughterhouse (literal or fig.) (BE prefers *abattoir* in literal sense) ["place providing a public service"] 25. a boarding; halfway; safe; settlement ~ ["bar"] (BE) 26. a free; public; tied ~ ["shelter"] 27. a reptile ~ (at a zoo) ["misc."] 28. a ~ of correction/detention ("a prison"); a disorderly ~ ("a brothel"); (AE) a station ~ ("a police station"); drinks are on the ~ ("drinks are served free") (see also *(the) drinks are on me* at **on**); an open ~ (AE)/ show ~ (BE) ("a residence being sold or rented out that is open for inspection") (see also **open house**)

house arrest *n*. to place, put smb. under ~

household *n*. 1. to establish, set up a ~ 2. to run a ~ 3. (the) head of (a) ~

housekeeping *n*. 1. to set up ~ 2. to do ~ 3. light ~

housewarming *n*. to have a ~

housework *n.* 1. to do ~ 2. light ~

housing *n.* affordable, low-cost, low-income, social (BE); council (BE); public (AE); fair (AE), open (AE); off-campus; rent-controlled; student; subsidized; substandard ~

hovel *n.* a miserable, wretched ~

hover *v.* 1. (d; intr.) to ~ around (we ~ed around our guide) 2. (d; intr.) to ~ between (to ~ between life and death) 3. (d; intr.) to ~ over (the fear of a new war ~ed over us)

how *determiner, adv.* 1. ~ about (~ about them?) 2. (used in exclamatory sentences) ~ wonderful! 3. (misc.) ~ ¬on earth/ever¬ can she do it?; ~ else?; ~much/many/often?

howl I *n.* to give, let out a ~ (of)

howl II *v.* 1. (D; intr.) to ~ at 2. (D; intr.) to ~ in, with (to ~ with pain)

howler *n.* ["blunder"] to make a ~

Hoyle *n.* according to ~ ("according to the rules")

hub *n.* ["focal point"] at the ~ (at the ~ of activity)

huddle I *n.* 1. to go into a ~ 2. in a ~

huddle II *v.* (P; intr.) to ~ around a fire; to ~ together

hue *n.* to raise a ~ and cry

huff *n.* (to leave) in a ~

hug I *n.* 1. to give smb. a ~ 2. an affectionate, loving; bear; big; tight ~ (she gave him a big bear ~) 3. a ~ and a kiss

hug II *v.* 1. to ~ tightly 2. (misc.) to ~ smb. to one (he hugged her tightly to him)

hum *v.* 1. (usu. B; occ. A) ~ the tune to me 2. (D; tr.) to ~ for (to ~ a tune for smb.) 3. (D; intr.) to ~ with (the town was ~ming with activity)

human *adj.* ~ to + inf. (it's only ~ to seek a better life)

humane *adj.* ~ to + inf. (it's not ~ to treat people like that)

humanism *n.* secular ~

humanity *n.* ["quality of being humane"] 1. to display ~ 2. common ~ ["the human race"] 3. a crime against ~

humble *v.* (D; refl.) to ~ before (to ~ oneself before God)

humble pie *n.* (forced) to eat ~ ("(forced) into a humiliating position, (forced) to eat crow")

humiliate *v.* to ~ deeply

humiliating *adj.* 1. ~ to + inf. (it is ~ (for us) to take orders from him) 2. ~ that + clause (it's ~ that we have to take orders from him)

humiliation *n.* 1. to suffer ~ 2. abject; bitter; deep; public ~

humility *n.* 1. to demonstrate, display, show ~ 2. in, with ~ (she recognized her responsibility with deep ~)

humor, humour *n.* ["something funny"] 1. bitter, caustic; black; gallows; gentle ~ 2. deadpan, dry, straight; sly, wry; subtle ~ 3. earthy; infectious; irrepressible; slapstick ~ 4. a sense of ~ (see also **sense of humor**) 5. a dash, trace, vein of ~ ["mood"]

6. (a) bad, ill (esp. BE); good ~ (she's in good ~ today) 7. a ~ to + inf. (he's in no ~ to be fooled with!) 8. in a certain ~ (in bad ~)

hump *n.* ["fit of depression"] (colloq.) (BE) 1. it gives me the ~ ("it depresses me") 2. I got; had the ~ ["worst part"] (colloq.) 3. over the ~

hunch *n.* (colloq.) ["feeling"]["suspicion"] 1. to back, play a ~ ("to act on the basis of a hunch") 2. a ~ that +clause (I have a ~ that she will not come) 3. on a ~ (she did it on a ~)

hundred *n.* by the ~s, in the ~, in their (BE) ~s (the crowd streamed into the studio by the ~s)

hunger I *n.* 1. (formal) to allay, alleviate, appease one's ~; to experience ~; more usu. is: to be hungry 2. to satisfy smb.'s ~; to gratify one's ~ (fig.) 3. (a) gnawing, ravenous ~ 4. (to have) a ~ for (~ for knowledge) 5. of ~ (to die of ~)

hunger II *v.* 1. (d; intr.) to ~ after (formal), for (to ~ for the truth; "Blessed are they which do ~ and thirst after righteousness" – "The Sermon on the Mount," *The Bible: St. Matthew*) 2. (E) (formal) to ~ to know the truth

hungry *adj.* 1. ravenously ~ 2. (cannot stand alone) ~ for (~ for the truth) 3. to be, feel; get; go ~

hunker down *v.* (D; intr.) ("to settle down") to ~ for (to ~ for the night)

hunt I *n.* 1. to organize, stage a ~ 2. to go on a ~ 3. a ~ for (a ~ for big game; the ~ for a new director) (see also **witch-hunt**)

hunt II *v.* 1. (D; intr.) to ~ for (to ~ for big game; to ~ for a new director) 2. (misc.) to ~ high and low (for smt. lost)

hunter *n.* a bargain; big-game; bounty; fortune; head; souvenir ~

hurdle *n.* 1. to clear, overcome, take a ~ 2. to hit, knock down a ~ 3. (the) high; low ~s 4. (misc.) to fall at the last ~ (usu. fig.) ("to fail at the last minute")

hurl *v.* 1. (d; refl., tr.) to ~ at (the enemy troops ~ed themselves at us; to ~ insults at smb.) 2. (misc.) to ~ oneself into the fray

hurrah *n.* the last ~ ("a last attempt")

hurricane *n.* 1. a severe, violent ~ 2. a ~ comes up; hits, strikes; rages (the ~ struck several cities) 3. a ~ blows itself out, blows over, dies down, subsides 4. (in) the eye of a ~

hurry I *n.* 1. in a ~ (in their ~ to leave, they forgot their keys) 2. a ~ to + inf. (we were in a ~ to finish; they were in no ~ to leave the party)

hurry II *v.* 1. (E) we ~ried to finish 2. (P; intr.) to ~ across the road; to ~ towards the school; to ~ to the scene

hurry back *v.* (D; intr.) to ~ to (she ~ried back from her lunch break to her desk)

hurt I *adj.* ["insulted"] 1. deeply, very ~ ["injured"] 2. badly, seriously; slightly ~

hurt II *v.* 1. to ~ badly, seriously; deeply; slightly 2. (R) it ~s (me) to cough = it ~s when I cough; it ~s me to see her ruin her life

hurtful *adj.* 1. very ~ 2. (formal) ~ to

hurtle *v.* (d; intr.) to ~ through the air (a large rock came ~ling through the air)

husband *n.* 1. to beat; desert, leave; divorce one's ~ 2. a common-law; cuckolded; estranged ~; ex-husband, former; faithful; future; henpecked; jealous; late; philandering, unfaithful ~ 3. (misc.) she had two children by her first ~; ~ and wife

husbandry *n.* animal ~

hush *n.* 1. a ~ fell (over/on the crowd) 2. a breathless, deathly ~ ("There's a breathless ~ in the Close to-night" – Sir Henry Newbolt (1862–1938), "Vitaï Lampada")

hustings *n.* ["route of an election campaign"] to go out on the ~

hustle I *n.* (slang) ["quick movement"] to get a ~ on (AE)

hustle II *v.* (P; tr.) the police ~d the prisoner into a cell

hut *n.* 1. a bamboo; thatched ~ 2. a Nissen (BE), Quonset (AE) ~

hutch *n.* a rabbit ~

hydrant *n.* 1. to open, turn on a ~ 2. to turn off a ~ 3. a fire ~

hyena *n.* 1. a brown; laughing; spotted; striped ~ 2. a ~ howls 3. a clan, pack of ~s

hygiene *n.* 1. to practice (good) ~ 2. dental, oral; feminine; field; industrial; mental; personal; sexual; social ~

hygienist *n.* a dental, oral ~

hymen *n.* 1. to rupture a ~ 2. an intact ~

hymn *n.* 1. to chant, sing a ~ 2. a rousing; solemn ~ 3. a ~ to (a ~ to freedom)

hype *n.* 1. to fall for; see through ~ 2. media ~ 3. ~ surrounds (the media ~ surrounding their romance) 4. ~ about (I hope you haven't fallen for all the media ~ about their romance!)

hypersensitive *adj.* 1. ~ about (~ about charges of corruption) 2. ~ to (~ to criticism)

hypertension *n.* essential; malignant; mild; severe ~

hypnosis *n.* 1. to induce, produce ~ 2. to put smb. under ~ 3. to experience, have, undergo ~ 4. during, under ~

hypnotism *n.* to practice ~

hypocrisy *n.* 1. to display ~ 2. sheer ~ 3. ~ about (her ~ about the other political party's tax policy) 4. ~ to + inf. (it was sheer ~ to criticize the other political party for its tax policy)

hypocritical *adj.* 1. ~ about (she was being ~ about the other political party's tax policy) 2. ~ to + inf. (it was ~ of her to criticize the other political party for its tax policy)

hypothesis *n.* 1. to advance, formulate, propose, put forth/forward a ~ 2. to confirm, vindicate; disconfirm; support; test a ~ 3. to accept; refute; reject a ~ 4. a null; working ~ 5. a ~ about, on (her working ~ about the role of rodents in spreading the disease) 6. that + clause (she advanced the ~ that the disease was spread by rodents) 7. on the ~ (on the ~ that the disease is spread by rodents, we should acquire some cats)

hypothesize *v.* 1. (D; intr.) to ~ about (she ~d about the role of rodents in spreading the disease) 2. (L) she ~d that the disease was spread by rodents

hysterectomy *n.* 1. to do, perform a ~ (on) 2. to have, undergo a ~

hysteria *n.* 1. to produce ~ 2. mass ~ 3. an attack, fit; note of ~ 4. ~ about, over (~ about imaginary threats)

hysterical *adj.* ~ about, over (~ about imaginary threats)

hysterics *n.* 1. to have ~ 2. a fit of ~ (to have a fit of ~) 3. in ~ (about, over) (her jokes had us in ~)

I

ice *n.* 1. to form, make, produce ~ 2. to melt ~ 3. hard; thick ~ 4. cracked; crushed; ~ 5. dry ~ 6. black; pack ~ 7. ~ forms; melts 8. a block; patch; sheet of ~ 9. on the ~ (to slip on the ~) 10. (misc.) to break the ~ ("to create a more relaxed atmosphere"); to cut no ~ (with) ("to have no effect 'on'"); on thin ~ ("in a dangerous situation"); on ~ ("in reserve"); (a) water ~
iceberg *n.* 1. to hit, strike an ~ (the ship struck an ~) 2. (misc.) (fig.) the tip of the ~
icebox *n.* (colloq.) (AE) to raid the ~ ("to eat heartily esp. during the night")
ice cream *n.* 1. to make ~ 2. hand-dipped ~ 3. chocolate; French (AE); Italian (esp. BE); strawberry; vanilla ~ 4. a portion; scoop; tub (esp. BE) of ~
icicle *n.* an ~ forms; hangs down
icon *n.* ["religious"] 1. to paint an ~ ["computers"] 2. to click on an ~ ["celebrity"] 3. a cultural ~
I. D. see **identification** 4
idea *n.* 1. to come up with, conceive, get, hit upon; develop; have an ~ 2. to consider, explore, entertain, toy with an ~ 3. to communicate, disseminate ~s 4. to market, package an ~ 5. to implement an ~ 6. to endorse, espouse, favor an ~ 7. to dismiss, drop, reject an ~ 8. a bright, brilliant, clever, good, great, ingenious; logical ~ 9. a fresh, new, novel ~ 10. a clear; fixed; general; main ~ 11. a daring; grandiose ~ (the glimmering of a daring new ~ came into my head – and then another one occurred to me!) 12. an approximate, rough; vague ~ 13. any, no; the faintest, foggiest, slightest ~ (she didn't have any ~ (of) what I meant, she had no ~ what I meant, she didn't have the faintest ~ of what I meant) 14. an old, outmoded, stale, warmed-over (AE) ~ 15. an absurd, bad, crackpot, crazy, fantastic, far-fetched, foolish, wild; desperate; silly, simplistic, stupid; strange ~ (such a foolish ~ will never catch on!) 16. an ~ about, of; behind (what's your ~ of a good night out?; *The Idea of a University* (1852, 1858)– John Henry, Cardinal Newman; the ~ behind our advertising campaign is to appeal to young people) 17. an ~ to + inf. (it was her ~ to attend the meeting; was it really such a good ~ for her to attend the meeting?) 18. the ~ that + clause (I had no ~ that she would attend the meeting) 19. (misc.) "have you any ~ why she attended the meeting?" "No, I have absolutely no ~ why!"; he didn't get the ~ ("he did not understand"); an association of ~s; what's the big ~?
ideal I *adj.* 1. ~ for 2. (misc.) less than ~ (lots of stress is less than ~ for mental health)
ideal II *n.* 1. to attain; realize an ~ 2. a lofty, noble ~; high ~s
idealistic *adj.* ~ about

identical *adj.* ~ to, with (his hat is ~ to mine)
identification *n.* ["process of identifying"] 1. to make an ~ 2. (a) positive ~ 3. a means of ~ ["document"] 4. to carry; show ~ (see also *identification parade* at **parade**)
identify *v.* 1. to ~ positively 2. (B) she ~fied the intruder to the police 3. (D; refl., tr.) to ~ as; to (he ~fied himself as an old friend of the family; she ~fied him to the police as the intruder) 4. (D; tr.) to ~ by (the police ~fied her by her fingerprints) 5. (d.; intr., refl., tr.) to ~ with (she always ~fies (herself) with the underdog; he didn't want to be ~fied with the liberals)
identity *n.* 1. to establish smb.'s ~ 2. to conceal; reveal one's ~ 3. to assume smb.'s ~ 4. mistaken ~ (it was a case of mistaken ~) (see also *identity parade* at **parade**)
ideology *n.* 1. to embrace; espouse; reject an ~ 2. the dominant, prevailing ~ (to reject the prevailing ~)
idiocy *n.* 1. congenital ~ 2. ~ to + inf. (it was sheer ~ for him to arrive late!)
idiot *n.* 1. a blithering, blooming, blundering, confounded, driveling, gibbering; prize, proper (BE); real, right (BE) ~ 2. the local, village ~ 3. an ~ to + inf. (he was a real ~ to have arrived late!)
idiotic *adj.* ~ to + inf. (it was ~ for/of him to arrive late = he was ~ to arrive late! = to arrive late was an ~ thing for him to do!)
idle *adj.* 1. to lie, remain, stand ~ (the machinery stood ~ for a month) 2. to be left ~ 3. bone ~ (don't ask her to help: she's bone ~!)
idol *n.* 1. to worship an ~ 2. (fig.) a fallen; matinee; national; pop; popular ~; an ~ with feet of clay
idolize *v.* (D; tr.) to ~ as (she was ~d as a movie star)
ignition *n.* (in a car) 1. to switch on, turn on the ~ 2. to switch off, turn off the ~ 3. in the ~ (the key is already in the ~)
ignorance *n.* 1. to betray, demonstrate, display, show ~ 2. blissful ~ 3. abysmal, appalling, blatant, complete, crass, profound, total ~ 4. ~ about; of (I had to admit my complete ~ of the facts) 5. in ~ (of) (I was in complete ~ of the facts; in my ~, I believed that there were tigers in Africa)
ignorant *adj.* 1. blissfully ~ 2. abysmally, appallingly, blatantly, completely, crassly, profoundly, totally ~ 3. ~ in; of (~ of the facts)
ignore *v.* 1. to ~ completely, totally; conveniently (they conveniently ~d some uncomfortable facts) 2. (K) you'll have to ~ their talking so loud 3. (misc.) to ~ at one's peril (we ~ these inconvenient facts at our peril!)
ilk *n.* ["kind"] of a certain ~ (people of that/his ~ are not to be trusted!)
ill *adj.* 1. to be taken ~ 2. to become, fall, get; feel ~ 3. chronically; critically; dangerously; desperately; gravely, seriously; incurably, terminally ~ 4. emotionally; mentally; physically ~ 5. ~ with

(she is ~ with a tropical disease) 6. (misc.) ~ at ease ("uncomfortable"); the situation bodes ~ for the future; it makes me ~ to smell that sewage; it ~ becomes/behoves (BE)/behooves (AE) you to say such things

ill-advised *adj.* ~ to + inf. (you would be ~ to come late)

ill-disposed *adj.* (formal) (cannot stand alone) ~ to, towards (they are ~ towards me)

illegal *adj.* 1. ~ for (smoking is ~ for minors) 2. ~ to + inf. (it is ~ to for minors to smoke)

illegitimate *adj.* ~ to + inf. (is it really ~ to pose such questions?)

ill feeling *n.* 1. to foment, stir up ~ 2. to bear, harbor ~ 3. ~ against 4. ~ over (there was a great deal of ~ stirred up over the appointment)

ill-informed *adj.* ~ about, on

illiteracy *n.* 1. to eliminate, stamp out ~ 2. adult; computer; functional; widespread ~ 3. ~ in (~ even in one's native language)

illiterate *adj.* 1. completely; functionally ~ 2. computationally, computer ~ 3. ~ in (~ even in one's native language)

illness *n.* 1. to get over an ~ 2. to come down with, go down with (BE), develop an ~ 3. to die of an; succumb to an ~ 4. (an) acute; sudden ~ 5. (a) chronic; lingering 6. (a) minor; slight ~ 7. (a) catastrophic; grave, major, serious ~ 8. (a) fatal; incurable, untreatable; terminal ~ 9. mental; organic; psychosomatic ~ 10. (misc.) the management; treatment of an ~ (for additional combinations, see **ailment, disease**)

illogical *adj.* 1. ~ of 2. ~ to + inf. (it's ~ of/for us to assume that they won't attend)

ills *n.* economic; social ~

illuminating *adj.* ~ to + inf. (it was ~ to read the candidate's earlier speeches)

illusion *n.* 1. to create, give, produce an ~ 2. to cherish, harbor, have an ~ 3. to dispel, shatter an ~ 4. an optical ~ 5. an ~ about 6. an ~ to + inf. (it's an ~ for him to think that she really loves him) 7. an ~ that + clause (he has no ~s that she really loves him) 8. under an ~ (he's under no ~s that she really loves him)

illustrate *v.* 1. (D; tr.) to ~ by, with (she ~d her lectures by showing slides/with slides) 2. (L) their report ~d that we had gone wrong 3. (Q; to) the incident ~d (to us) where we had gone wrong

illustration *n.* ["example"] 1. to give, offer, provide an ~ 2. a powerful; verbal ~ 3. by way of ~ ["picture"] 4. to draw an ~ 5. a graphic ~ 6. an ~ reveals, shows (the ~ showed exactly where we'd gone wrong)

illustrative *adj.* ~ of (~ of smb.'s views)

ill will *n.* 1. to stir up ~ 2. to bear, feel, harbor ~ towards smb. (despite everything, I bear no ~ towards him = despite everything, I bear him no ~) 3. ~ about, over; between (there's no ~ between us about what happened)

image *n.* ["position, standing"] 1. to conjure up;

project an ~ 2. to bolster, improve; change smb.'s ~ 3. a corporate; cultural; negative; positive; public; tarnished ~ (~ consultants will help us to change our somewhat negative corporate ~ and project a more positive one) ["picture"] 4. (computers) to digitize an ~ 5. a clear ~ 6. a mental ~ (I have a clear mental ~ of that place, conjured up by my memories of it and reinforced by photographs) 7. a mirror ~ ["misc."] 8. a spitting ~ (he's the spitting ~ of George Washington!); to be created in the ~ of God; a graven ~; a virtual ~ (computers)

imagery *n.* poetic; vivid ~

imagination *n.* 1. to capture, excite, fire smb.'s ~ 2. to have (an) ~ 3. to show, use one's ~ 4. to lack ~ 5. to defy, stagger, stir smb.'s ~ 6. an active, fertile, lively, vivid; creative ~ 7. a feeble; wild ~ 8. a figment of smb.'s ~ 9. the ~ to + inf. (does she have the ~ to figure out what happened?) 10. in smb.'s ~ 11. (misc.) by no stretch of the ~ (by no stretch of the ~ can he be called a genius!); it is pure ~ on your part; to leave nothing to the ~

imagine *v.* 1. (d; tr.) to ~ as (can you ~ him as an actor?) 2. (G) he can't ~ becoming an actor without strong motivation 3. (J) can you ~him becoming an actor? 4. (K) it is difficult to ~ his becoming an actor 5. (L) I don't ~ that he will become an actor 6. (N; used with an adjective, noun, past participle) can you ~ him an actor? 7. (Q) can you ~ how thrilled he must have been to become an actor?! 8. (misc.) has he really become an actor – or am I just ~ning things?

imbalance *n.* 1. to correct, redress an ~ 2. a trade ~ 3. an ~ between, in (a trade ~ in imports and exports between two countries)

imbecile *n.* an ~ to + inf. (he was a real ~ to have arrived late!)

imbecilic *adj.* ~ to + inf. (it was ~ for/of him to arrive late = he was ~ to arrive late! = to arrive late was an ~ thing for him to do!)

imbed see **embed**

imbued *adj.* (cannot stand alone) 1. deeply, profoundly, thoroughly ~ 2. ~ with (~ with fighting spirit)

imitation *n.* 1. to do, give an ~ of 2. a pale ~ 3. in ~ of

imitative *adj.* (formal) ~ of

immaterial *adj.* 1. wholly ~ 2. ~ to 3. (misc.) it is ~ whether she attends or not; it is ~ how or when they get here

immature *adj.* 1. emotionally; mentally; physically ~ 2. ~ for (she is ~ for her age) 3. to + inf. (it was ~ of her to do that)

immaturity *n.* to display ~

immerse *v.* 1. to ~ deeply 2. (D; refl., tr.) to ~ in (she ~d herself in the water; ~d in one's work)

immersion *n.* 1. total ~ 2. ~ in (total ~ in one's work)

immigrant *n.* 1. an illegal; legal ~ 2. an ~ from; to (~s to Canada)

immigrate *v.* (D; intr.) to ~ from; into, to (to ~ into a country)

immigration *n.* 1. illegal; legal ~ 2. a flood; wave of ~ 3. ~ from; into, to

immodest *adj.* 1. ~ about (she was ~ about her achievements) 2. ~ in (she was ~ in boasting about her achievements) 3. ~ to + inf. (it was ~ of her to boast about her achievements)

immoral *adj.* ~ to + inf. (it's ~ to steal)

immune *adj.* ["exempt"] 1. ~ from (~ from prosecution; her prestige made her ~ from criticism) ["unaffected"] 2. ~ to (~ to a disease; her self-confidence made her ~ to criticism)

immunity *n.* ["resistance to disease"] 1. to acquire, develop; have ~ 2. to confer, give ~ (this shot will give you ~ for about twelve months; that vaccine will confer lifelong ~) 3. acquired; natural ~ 4. active; passive ~ 5. ~ against ["exemption; special status"] 6. to grant ~ to 7. to have ~ 8. ~ from, to (~ from prosecution; ~ to a disease) (see also **diplomatic immunity**)

immunization *n.* 1. to carry out a (mass) ~ against 2. active; passive ~

immunize *v.* (D; tr.) to ~ against (the children have been ~d against polio)

impact I *n.* 1. to have, make an ~ on, upon 2. to lessen, soften; sustain, take, withstand the ~ 3. (a) considerable, strong; cumulative; great; lasting; profound ~ 4. (a) dramatic; emotional; favorable ~ 5. (an) environmental ~ 6. on ~ (the pole collapses on ~)

impact II *v.* (d; intr.) to ~ on, upon (global warming ~ing on the environment) USAGE NOTE: Those who use *impact* as a verb can also use it as a transitive verb: *global warming ~ing the environment*.

impaired *adj.* hearing-impaired; visually ~

impairment *n.* (a) hearing; memory; mental; physical; speech; visual ~

impale *v.* (D; tr.) to ~ on, upon (the driver was thrown from the car and ~d on a fence)

impart *v.* (B) to ~ knowledge to students

impartiality *n.* 1. to demonstrate, display, show ~ 2. ~ in

impasse *n.* 1. to reach an ~ 2. to break an ~ 3. at an ~ (negotiations were at an ~)

impatience *n.* 1. to display, show ~ 2. ~ at; with (we noted their ~ at the delay and their ~ with the organizers of the conference) 3. ~ to + inf. (we noted their ~ for the conference to start)

impatient *adj.* 1. ~ at, with (~ at the delay; ~ with the organizers of the conference) 2. ~ for (I was ~ for the conference to start) 3. ~ to + inf. (I was ~ to start)

impeach *v.* (D; tr.) to ~ for (to ~ smb. for taking bribes)

impediment *n.* 1. a speech ~ 2. an ~ to (an ~ to progress)

impel *v.* (formal) 1. (d; tr.) to ~ into, to 2. (H) her conscience ~led her to intervene

impelled *adj.* (cannot stand alone) ~ to + inf. (she felt ~ to intervene)

imperative I *adj.* 1. ~ to + inf. (it is ~ to act now) 2. ~ that + clause; subj. (it is ~ that you be/should be/ are (esp. BE) present)

imperative II *n.* 1. a moral ~ 2. an ~ that + clause; subj. (it is a moral ~ that you be/should be/are (esp. BE) present)

imperceptible *adj.* ~ to (~ to the touch)

imperfect *n.* (grammar) the future; past; present ~

imperfection *n.* a slight ~ (in)

impersonation *n.* to do, give an ~

impertinence *n.* the ~ to + inf. (he had the ~ to demand a raise!)

impertinent *adj.* 1. ~ to 2. ~ to + inf. (it was ~ of him to demand a raise = he was ~ to demand a raise)

impervious *adj.* ~ to (~ to criticism)

impetuous *adj.* ~ to + inf. (it was ~ of her to do that)

impetus *n.* 1. to give, provide an ~ 2. to gain ~ 3. an extra added; fresh ~ 4. a powerful, strong ~ 5. an ~ to (there was no ~ to hard work) 6. an ~ to + inf. (there was no ~ to work harder)

impinge *v.* (formal) (d; intr.) to ~ on, upon (to ~ on smb.'s rights)

impingement *n.* an ~ on, upon

implant I *n.* a breast; dental; heart; kidney ~

implant II *v.* 1. to ~ deeply 2. (d; tr.) to ~ in (to ~ respect for democracy in the younger generation)

implicate *v.* (D; tr.) to ~ in (to ~ smb. in a scandal)

implication *n.* 1. to have an ~ 2. a derogatory, negative; serious; significant; subtle ~ 3. an ~ for 4. an ~ that + clause (I resent your ~ that my work is unsatisfactory!) 5. by ~ (he attacked our organization and, by ~, the whole concept behind our work!) 6. (misc.) to realize the full ~s of smt.

implicit *adj.* 1. ~ in (~ in the contract) 2. ~ that + clause (it is ~ in the contract that she will be a partner)

implore *v.* (formal) (H) they ~d her to help

imply *v.* (L; to) she ~lied (to us) that she knew more than she had told the reporters

impolite *adj.* 1. ~ to (interrupting people who are speaking is ~ to them) 2. ~ to + inf. (it is ~ to interrupt someone who is speaking; it was ~ of them not to respond)

impoliteness *n.* 1. ~ to

impolitic *adj.* ["inexpedient"] ~ to + inf. (it would be ~ to get involved in their affairs)

import I *n.* 1. a chief, leading, major ~ 2. an ~ from; into, to (~s from abroad)

import II *v.* (D; intr., tr.) to ~ from; into (we ~ from abroad)

importance *n.* 1. to acquire, assume ~ 2. to attach, attribute ~ to 3. (a) considerable, great, overriding, paramount, primary, prime, utmost, vital ~ (the matter assumed paramount ~) 4. minor, secondary ~ 5. ~ arises from; lies in, resides in (it was a question whose great ~ to us arose from its possible consequences) 6. ~ for, to 7. of ~ (it was a question of great ~ to us)

important *adj.* 1. vitally ~ 2. ~ for (irrigation is ~ for farming) 3. ~ to (attending the meeting was very ~ to her) 4. ~ to + inf. (it is ~for everyone to attend) 5. ~ that + clause; subj. (it is ~ that everyone attend/should attend/attends (BE))

importune *v.* (formal) 1. (D; tr.) to ~ for (he ~d us for help) 2. (H) he ~d us to help him

impose *v.* 1. (D; intr., refl.) to ~ on, upon ("to take advantage of") (to ~ on smb.'s good nature; don't ~ yourself on them) 2. (D; tr.) ("to levy") to ~ on (to ~ a new tax on cigarettes)

imposition *n.* an ~ on

impossible I *adj.* 1. almost, next to, practically, quite, virtually, well-nigh ~ 2. physically ~ 3. ~ for (nothing is ~ for them) 4. ~ to + inf. (it is ~ for them to predict the future; that child is ~ to control = it is ~ to control that child = he's an ~ child to control) 5. ~ that + clause (it is ~ that we will be able to attend)

impossible II *n.* 1. to attempt the ~ 2. to do the ~

impracticable *adj.* ~ to + inf. (it was ~ to put up a new building there)

impractical *adj.* ~ to + inf. (it's ~ to live in one city and work in another)

imprecation *n.* (formal) 1. to hurl, utter an ~ 2. an ~ against

impregnate *v.* (d; tr.) to ~ with

impress *v.* 1. to ~ deeply; favorably 2. (D; tr.) to ~ as (she ~ed me as a scholar) 3. (d; tr.) to ~ on, upon (he tried to ~ on them the importance of being punctual) 4. (D; tr.) to ~ with (she ~ed me with her grasp of the subject) 5. (R) it ~ed me (to learn) that they had cooperated so willingly

impressed *adj.* 1. easily ~ 2. deeply, favorably, greatly, highly, strongly, very; none too; unfavorably ~ 3. ~ by, with (I was ~ by/with their willingness to cooperate) 4. ~ to + inf. (I was ~ to learn that they had cooperated so willingly) 5. ~ that + clause (I was ~ that they had cooperated so willingly)

impression *n.* ["effect"] 1. to convey, create, give an ~ 2. to make an ~ on, upon 3. a deep, indelible, lasting, profound, strong, vivid ~ (they made a lasting ~ on the visitors) 4. an excellent, favorable, good ~ 5. an erroneous, false, inaccurate, wrong ~ (they created an erroneous ~ of their capabilities) 6. a bad, unfavorable ~ 7. a first ~ 8. an ~ that + clause (she conveyed the false ~ that her family was wealthy) ["opinion"] 9. to form, get, gain, have an ~ 10. an accurate; fleeting; general; personal ~ (I got only a fleeting ~ of her performance) 11. an excellent, favorable, good ~ 12. an erroneous, false, inaccurate, wrong ~ (we formed an erroneous ~ of their abilities) 13. a bad, unfavorable ~ 14. a first ~ 15. an ~ that + clause (we had the false ~ that her family was wealthy) 16. under an ~ (we were under the ~ that her family

was wealthy) ["mark"] 17. to make, take an ~ of a key ["imitation"] 18. to do an ~ (the comedian does humorous ~s)

imprimatur *n.* 1. to get, receive an ~ 2. the official ~

imprint I *n.* 1. to bear an ~ (to bear the ~ of genius) 2. to leave one's ~ on 3. an indelible ~ 4. (misc.) published under the ~ of a vanity press

imprint II *v.* (d; refl., tr.) to ~ in, on, upon (the scene ~ed itself on their minds)

imprison *v.* (D; tr.) to ~ for (to ~ smb. for fraud; to be ~ed for life)

imprisonment *n.* life ~

improbable *adj.* 1. equally; highly, very ~ 2. ~ that + clause (it's highly ~ that she will show up)

improper *adj.* 1. ~ for (their attire is ~ for this occasion) 2. ~ to + inf. (it is ~ to enter that restaurant without a jacket) 3. ~ that + clause; subj. (it is ~ that she state/should state/states (BE) her own opinion)

impropriety *n.* 1. crass ~ 2. the ~ of (we condemned the crass ~ of passing off smb. else's work as one's own) 3. with ~ (to behave with crass ~)

improve *v.* 1. to ~ beyond all recognition, dramatically, greatly, noticeably, significantly, very much; gradually, slowly; rapidly 2. (D; intr.) to ~ in (she has ~d in English) 3. (d; intr.) to ~ on, upon (I cannot ~ on her performance) 4. (misc.) to ~ with age; your work is much ~d!

improvement *n.* 1. to bring about an ~ 2. to show (an) ~ 3. a considerable, decided, definite, distinct, dramatic, great, marked, noticeable, significant, substantial; gradual, slow; minor, slight; rapid ~ 4. an ~ in, of (an ~ in her work; an ~ of service) 5. an ~ on, over, upon (this edition is an ~ over the previous one)

improvisation *n.* to do an ~

improvise *v.* (D; intr., tr.) to ~ on (to ~ on a given theme)

imprudent *adj.* ~ to + inf. (it was ~ of you to sell that property so soon = you were ~ to sell that property so soon)

impudence *n.* 1. brazen ~ 2. the ~ to + inf. (she had the ~ to answer back like that!)

impudent *adj.* ~ to + inf. (it was ~ of her to answer back like that! = she was ~ to answer back like that!)

impulse *n.* ["driving force"] 1. to feel an ~ 2. to curb, repress, resist an ~ 3. an irresistible; sudden ~ 4. an ~ to + inf. (she felt an irresistible ~ to intervene) 5. the ~ behind (what was the ~ behind her intervention?) 6. on, under (an) ~ (to act on ~) ["stimulus"] 7. to convey, transmit an ~ 8. an electrical; nerve ~

impunity *n.* with ~ (to act with ~)

impute *v.* (formal) (d; tr.) to ~ to (to ~ base motives to smb.)

in I *adv.* (colloq.) 1. ~ for ("facing") (they are ~ for trouble) 2. ~ with ("on intimate terms with") (they are ~ with highly influential people)

in II *n.* (colloq.) ["influence"] to have an ~ with smb.

in III *prep.* 1. ~ smb. to + inf. (it's not ~ me to lie; she doesn't have it ~ her to break her word) 2. ~ that + clause (I'm lucky ~ that I have a good job) (see also Usage Note 3 at **fact**)

inability *n.* 1. to demonstrate, display, exhibit, show ~ 2. ~ at, in (to display ~ in mathematics) 3. ~ to + inf. (her ~ to pay caused trouble)

inaccessible *adj.* ~ to ~ from; to (unfortunately, the stacks are ~ to the public from the main staircase; the director is remote and ~ to anyone!)

inaccuracy *n.* 1. (a) glaring; total ~ 2. ~ in

inaccurate *adj.* 1. completely; somewhat; strictly, totally ~ 2. ~ in 3. ~ to + inf. (it would be ~ to say that he is lazy)

inadequate *adj.* 1. completely, grossly, totally, woefully ~ 2. ~ for; to (the food was ~ for all of us) 3. ~ to (she was ~ to the task; ~ to the occasion) 4. ~ to + inf. (the supply is ~ to meet the demand)

inadvisable *adj.* 1. ~ to + inf. (it was ~ for her to remain silent) 2. ~ that + clause; subj. (it was ~ that she remain/should remain/remained (BE) silent)

inapplicable *adj.* ~ to (~ to this particular case)

inappropriate I *adj.* 1. entirely, highly, wholly ~ 2. ~ for; to (~ for us; ~ to the occasion) 3. ~ to + inf. (it is ~ (for passengers) to tip a bus driver) 4. ~ that + clause; may be subj. (it is wholly ~ that passengers tip/should tip a bus driver; it is entirely ~ that he is/should be present)

inattention *n.* ~ to (~ to our needs; ~ to detail)

inattentive *adj.* ~ to (~ to our needs; ~ to detail)

inaudible *adj.* 1. almost, completely, nearly ~ 2. ~ above, over; to (his voice was almost completely ~ to us above the din)

inaugurate *v.* (D; tr.) to ~ as (to be ~d as president)

inauguration *n.* 1. to have, hold an ~ (for) 2. the presidential ~ 3. ~ as (his ~ as president)

incantation *n.* to chant, intone, utter an ~

incapable *adj.* (cannot stand alone) ~ of (she is ~ of cheating)

incarnation *n.* (in) a previous ~

incense *n.* 1. to burn ~ 2. a stick of ~ (the smell of a stick of burning ~)

incensed *adj.* 1. greatly, highly, very ~ 2. ~ about, at, over (she was very ~ over their failure to invite her) 3. ~ to + inf. (she was greatly ~ to learn that they had failed to invite her) 4. ~ that + clause (she was highly ~ that they had failed to invite her)

incentive *n.* 1. to give, offer, provide an ~ 2. to have an ~ 3. a powerful, strong ~ 4. a tax ~ 5. an ~ for 6. an ~ to (an ~ to harder work) 7. an ~ to + inf. (they have no ~ to work harder)

inception *n.* at; from; since smt.'s ~

incest *n.* 1. to commit ~ (with) 2. the crime of ~ 3. ~ between

inch I *n.* 1. to contest, fight for every ~ of one's land 2. a cubic; square ~ 3. every ~ ("to the utmost degree") ("every ~ a king" – Shakespeare, *King Lear*) 4. (to) within an ~ ("almost") (he was beaten (to)

within an ~ of his life) 5. (misc.) ~ by ~; to miss smt. by ~es

inch II *v.* (P; intr.) to ~ forward slowly; to ~ towards the goal; to ~ along a corridor

incidence *n.* a high; low ~ (a high ~ of crime in the population, especially among young people)

incident I *adj.* (formal) (cannot stand alone) ~ to (the problems ~ to growing up)

incident II *n.* 1. to cause, give rise to, provoke an ~ 2. to cover up, suppress an ~ 3. an amusing, funny, humorous; curious; nasty, painful, ugly, unpleasant; pleasant; strange; touching ~ 4. a border; diplomatic; international ~ 5. an ~ occurs, takes place 6. without ~ (the ceremony went off without ~)

incidental *adj.* ~ to (the problems ~ to growing up)

incision *n.* 1. to make an ~ 2. a deep ~ 3. an ~ into

incisors *n.* central; lateral ~

incite *v.* 1. (D; tr.) to ~ to (to ~ workers to rebellion) 2. (H) to ~ workers to rebel

incitement *n.* ~ to (~ to riot/rebellion)

inclination *n.* 1. to feel an ~ 2. a natural; strong ~ 3. an ~ for, to, towards 4. an ~ to + inf. (the carburetor has an ~ to flood)

incline *v.* (esp. BE) 1. (d; intr.) to ~ to, towards (he ~s to laziness; I ~ to the belief that she is innocent) 2. (d; tr.) to ~ to (the evidence ~s me to the belief that she is innocent) 3. (E) I ~ to believe that she is innocent 4. (H) the evidence ~s me to believe that she is innocent

inclined *adj.* (cannot stand alone) 1. academically; artistically; intellectually; mechanically; musically; romantically; favorably; strongly; very ~ 2. ~ to; towards (I am favorably ~ towards them; I am ~ to the belief that she is innocent) 3. ~ to + inf. (I am ~ to agree; I am ~ to believe that she is innocent) 4. (misc.) I never suspected that he liked dancing: who would have thought he was that way ~?

include *v.* (D; tr.) to ~ among, in (to ~ smb. in a list of candidates; who was ~d among the guests?)

inclusive *adj.* ~ of (is the price ~ of sales tax?)

incognito *adj., adv.* to go, travel; remain ~

incognizant *adj.* (formal) ~ of (~ of the risks involved)

income *n.* 1. to earn an ~ 2. to have an ~ 3. to generate (an) ~ 4. an annual, yearly; monthly; weekly ~ 5. a gross; net; taxable ~ 6. an earned; unearned ~ 7. a fixed; independent ~ 8. a good, high, sizeable ~ 9. a limited, low ~ 10. (an) ~ from (~ from investments) 11. per capita ~ 12. beyond one's ~ (they live beyond their ~) 13. on a certain ~ (to live on a fixed ~) 14. within one's ~ (they live within their ~) 15. (misc.) a source of ~ (what is your principal source of ~?)

incommensurable *adj.* ~ with

incommensurate *adj.* ~ to, with (a reward ~ with the results achieved)

incommunicado *adv.* to hold smb. ~

incompatibility *n.* ~ between, with

incompatible *adj.* 1. mutually ~ 2. ~ with

incompetence *n.* 1. ~ as (her ~ as an interpreter is well known) 2. ~ at, in (~ in English; ~ at/in speaking English)

incompetent *adj.* 1. grossly, hopelessly, totally; very ~ 2. as ~ (he is hopelessly ~ as a teacher) 3. ~ at, in (he is hopelessly ~ at teaching) 4. ~ to + inf. (he is ~ to judge)

incomplete *n.* ["academic deficiency"] (esp. AE) to make up an ~ (the student had to make up three ~s)

incomprehensible *adj.* 1. ~ to 2. ~ that + clause (it is ~ that they refused to come) 3. (misc.) it is ~ to me why they refused to come

inconceivable *adj.* 1. ~ to 2. ~ that + clause (it is ~ that she could be considered for the job)

incongruous *adj.* 1. ~ with 2. ~ that + clause (it was ~ that those two bitter rivals should be playing on the same team)

inconsiderate *adj.* 1. ~ of (he's ~ of anyone's feelings) 2. towards ~ 3. ~ to + inf. (it was ~ of her to do that nasty thing)

inconsistency *n.* ~ in

inconsistent *adj.* 1. ~ in (she is ~ in her support of our party) 2. ~ with (~ with our principles)

inconvenience I *n.* 1. to cause ~ 2. to put up with (an) ~ 3. (a) considerable, great; minor, slight; temporary ~ 4. an ~ for 5. an ~ to + inf. (it's an ~ to have to shop so far from home)

inconvenience II *v.* (H) I hope that it will not ~ you to stop by tomorrow

inconvenient *adj.* 1. ~ for (will Tuesday be ~ for you?) 2. ~ to + inf. (it is very ~ to have the bus stop so far away = it is very ~ having the bus stop so far away) 3. ~ that + clause (it's very ~ that the bus stop is so far away)

incorporate *v.* (D; tr.) to ~ into

incorrect *adj.* 1. ~ in (you are ~ in thinking that he is wise) 2. ~ to + inf. (it's ~ to say that she is a good administrator; you are ~ to think that he is wise) 3. (misc.) grammatically ~; politically ~; completely ~ in all respects

increase I *n.* 1. a considerable, dramatic, large, sharp, significant, sizable, substantial; gradual; moderate; slight, small; steady ~ 2. a cost-of-living; pay; rate ~ 3. an ~ in (to get a cost-of-living ~ in one's salary; an ~ in coal consumption) 4. on the ~

increase II *v.* 1. (D; intr., tr.) to ~ by (production ~d by ten percent) 2. (D; intr., tr.) to ~ from; to (the physician ~d the dosage from one to four) 3. (D; intr., tr.) to ~ in (the guards were ~d in number)

incredible *adj.* 1. absolutely ~ 2. ~ to 3. ~ that + clause (it was absolutely ~ to me that nobody ¬paid/should have paid¬ attention to the new invention = I find it absolutely ~ that nobody ¬paid/should have paid¬ attention to the new invention)

increment *n.* an ~ in (an ~ in salary)

incriminate *v.* (D; tr.) to ~ in

inculcate *v.* 1. (D; tr.) to ~ in, into (to ~ ideas in (the

minds of) young people) 2. (d; tr.) to ~ with (to ~ (the minds of) young people with ideas)

incumbent I *adj.* (cannot stand alone) ~ on, upon + to + inf. (it's ~ on you to warn them = warning them is ~ on you)

incumbent II *n.* to unseat an ~

incursion *n.* 1. to make an ~ 2. an armed ~ 3. an ~ into (to make an armed ~ into neutral territory)

indebted *adj.* 1. deeply, heavily; (very) much ~ 2. (cannot stand alone) ~ for; to (we are ~ to her for her help)

indecent *adj.* ~ to + inf. (it was ~ of her to refuse to help us!)

indecision *n.* ~ about, over

indecisive *adj.* ~ about

indefinite *adj.* ~ about

indelicate *adj.* 1. highly, very ~ 2. ~ to + inf. (it was highly ~ of her to raise that matter in public)

indemnification *n.* ["compensation, damages"] 1. to award ~ (the court awarded ~) 2. to claim; sue for ~ 3. to pay; receive ~ 4. ~ for 5. in ~ (to award one thousand dollars in ~ for injuries sustained in the accident)

indemnify *v.* (D; tr.) to ~ for (to ~ smb. for injuries sustained in an accident)

indemnity *n.* 1. to pay an ~ 2. double ~ 3. an ~ against, for, from

indent *v.* (d; intr.) ("to request officially") (BE) to ~ for; on (we had to ~ on the company for new computers)

indentation *n.* to make an ~

independence *n.* 1. to achieve, gain, win ~ from (when did the state gain its ~ from the church in your country?) 2. to assert, declare one's ~ from, of (the state's ~ of the church) 3. to grant ~ 4. to lose one's ~ 5. financial; political ~

independent *adj.* 1. fiercely, very ~ 2. financially ~ 3. ~ from, of (when did you become financially ~ of/from your parents?; in our country church and state are ~ of each other)

independently *adv.* ~ of (scientists working ~ of one another)

index *n.* ["alphabetical list"] 1. to compile, do, make an ~ 2. an author; card; cumulative; subject ~ 3. an ~ to (an ~ to a book) ["indicator"] 4. a consumer-price, cost-of-living; price; retail-price ~ 5. an ~ to (an ~ to economic progress) ["ratio of one dimension to another"] 6. a cephalic; cranial; facial ~

indexed *adj.* ~ to (pensions ~ to the cost-of-living index are index-linked pensions)

Indian *n.* an American ~ USAGE NOTE: To somebody from Canada or the United States, a primary meaning of *Indian* is "American Indian". To somebody from other English-speaking countries, the primary meaning is "somebody from India." Note that a *West Indian* is always somebody from the West Indies. In contemporary usage, *American Indian* is being replaced by *Native American* in the USA and by *First-Nation person* in Canada.

indicate *v.* 1. to ~ clearly 2. (B) she ~d her reasons to us 3. (L; to) they ~d (to us) that they would sign the contract 4. (Q; to) they ~d (to us) why they would sign

indication *n.* 1. to give an ~ 2. a clear ~ 3. every; no ~ 4. an ~ that + clause (there is every ~ that she will recover)

indicative I *adj.* ~ of

indicative II *n.* (grammar) in the ~ (the verb was in the ~)

indict *v.* (D; tr.) to ~ for (to ~ smb. for murder)

indictment *n.* (usu. legal) 1. to hand up (AE), issue, present, return an ~ 2. to waive (the) ~ 3. to quash an ~ 4. (fig.) a damning, stinging, swingeing (BE); sweeping ~ (of) (a book that is a damning ~ of modern materialism) 5. an ~ against 6. an ~ for (there was an ~ against him for a crime) 7. on ~ (to try a case on ~)

indifference *n.* 1. to affect, feign ~ 2. to display, show ~ 3. complete; marked; studied ~ 4. ~ about, concerning 5. ~ to, towards 6. with ~ 7. (misc.) it's a matter of complete ~ to me whether or not she comes

indifferent *adj.* 1. to remain ~ 2. ~ about, concerning 3. ~ to, towards

indigenous *adj.* ~ to

indigestion *n.* 1. to cause ~ 2. to give smb. ~ (pickles give me ~) 3. to get; have; suffer from ~ 4. acute, severe; chronic ~ 5. an attack; touch of ~

indignant *adj.* 1. ~ about, at, over 2. ~ that + clause (we were ~ that the performance was canceled) 3. (misc.) to wax ~ (over smt.)

indignation *n.* 1. to arouse ~ (in smb.); to fill smb. with ~ 2. to express; feel, show ~ 3. burning; deep; growing, rising; helpless; public; righteous ~ 4. ~ about, at, over (to feel ~ at gross injustice) 5. to smb.'s ~ (to our ~, the performance was canceled) 6. ~ that + clause (our ~ that the performance was canceled)

indignity *n.* 1. to inflict an ~ on 2. to suffer ~ties

indiscreet *adj.* 1. ~ in 2. ~ to + inf. (it was ~ of her to say that)

indiscretion *n.* 1. to commit an ~ 2. a youthful ~

indiscriminate *adj.* ~ in

indispensable *adj.* ~ for, to (~ to life)

indisposed *adj.* (formal) ~ to + inf. (she appears ~ to go)

indisputable *adj.* ~ that + clause (it is ~ that the evidence was tampered with)

indistinguishable *adj.* ~ from

individualism *n.* rugged ~

individuality *n.* to express one's ~

indoctrinate *v.* 1. (D; tr.) to ~ against; in; with 2. (H) their leaders ~d them to believe that their culture was superior

indoctrinated *adj.* ~ to + inf. (they were ~ to believe that their culture was superior)

indoctrination *n.* ~ against; in; with

indoors *adv.* to be; come; go; stay ~

induce *v.* (H) she could not ~ us to work harder

inducement *n.* 1. to give, offer, provide; have an ~ 2. a powerful, strong ~ 3. a financial, monetary ~ 4. an ~ to (money can be a powerful ~ to harder work) 5. an ~ to + inf. (we had no ~ to work harder)

induct *v.* (D; tr.) to ~ into (to ~ smb. into an official position); (esp. AE: to ~ smb. into the armed forces)

induction *n.* ~ into

indulge *v.* (d; intr., refl., tr.) to ~ in (to ~ in the luxury of a nice warm bath; he ~s her in everything)

indulgence *n.* 1. to grant an ~ 2. to ask for smb.'s ~ 3. ~ to, towards

indulgent *adj.* ~ to, towards

industry *n.* 1. to build up, develop (an) ~ 2. (an) ~ springs up 3. a basic, key; fledgling ~ 4. a cottage; defense; service; high-tech ~ 5. heavy; light; manufacturing ~ 6. the aerospace; aircraft; automobile (esp. AE), car, motor-manufacturing (BE); building, construction; coal; computer; cosmetics; dairy; film; food; leisure; machinetool; meat-packing; music; pharmaceutical; shipbuilding; steel; textile; tourist, travel; trucking (esp. AE) ~ 7. a smokestack ("old, obsolete") ~ 8. (misc.) government often regulates ~; a branch of ~ USAGE NOTE: Such phrases as "the Shakespeare industry" or "the race-relations industry" describe and denigrate activity in a named area whose practitioners seem more interested in the quantity of their work than in its quality and may even do more harm than good: "another mediocre production of *Hamlet* from the Shakespeare ~."

ineffective *adj.* 1. ~ against (~ against the common cold) 2. ~ in (~ in fighting crime) 3. ~ to + inf. (it would be ~ (for you) to respond to the charges)

inefficiency *n.* 1. gross ~ 2. ~ in (gross ~ in fighting crime)

inefficient *adj.* 1. grossly, hopelessly, very ~ 2. ~ at, in (she was very ~ at getting things done; they were very ~ in reducing waste) 3. ~ to + inf. (it's ~ to set up two offices)

inelegant *adj.* ~ to + inf. (it was ~ to phrase the request in that manner)

ineligibility *n.* 1. ~ for 2. ~ to + inf. (~ to vote)

ineligible *adj.* 1. ~ for 2. ~ to + inf. (she is still ~ to vote)

inept *adj.* ~ at, in

ineptitude *n.* 1. to demonstrate, display ~ 2. ~ at, in

inequality *n.* 1. to increase; maintain; reduce ~ 2. gross; racial; religious; sexual; social ~ 3. ~ among, between (~ between the sexes) 4. ~ in (~ in pay) 5. ~ of (~ of opportunity)

inertia *n.* 1. sheer ~ 2. through ~

inessential *adj.* 1. ~ for; to 2. ~ to + inf. (it is ~ for all students to be present) 3. ~ that + clause; subj. (it is ~ that all students ¬be/should be/are (BE)¬ present)

inevitable *adj.* ~ that + clause (it was ~ that she would find out)

inexcusable *adj.* 1. ~ to + inf. (it was ~ of him to blurt it out) 2. ~ that + clause (it was ~ that he blurted it out)
inexperienced *adj.* 1. very ~ 2. ~ at, in, with (very ~ at using computers = very ~ with computers)
infallibility *n.* 1. papal ~ 2. ~ in
infallible *adj.* ~ in
infancy *n.* ["first stage"] in one's/its ~ (the industry was still in its ~)
infant *n.* 1. to breast-feed, nurse, suckle an ~ 2. to bubble (esp. AE), burp an ~ 3. to wean an ~ 4. a newborn; premature ~ (see also **baby** 7–9, 13–15, *infant mortality* at **mortality**)
infanticide *n.* to commit ~
infantile *adj.* ~ to + inf. (it was ~ of/for you to behave like that = you were ~ to behave like that)
infantry *n.* light; motorized; mountain ~
infatuated *adj.* ~ with
infatuation *n.* ~ with
infect *v.* (D; tr.) to ~ with (they were ~ed with an unidentified virus)
infection *n.* 1. to cause; pass on, spread, transmit (an) ~ 2. to prevent (an) ~ 3. to treat an ~ 4. ~ an acute; chronic; deep; latent; localized; minor, slight, superficial; primary; secondary; serious, severe; systemic ~ 5. (an) ~ sets in; spreads
infer *v.* 1. (D; tr.) to ~ from (to ~ a conclusion from the facts) 2. (L) I ~ that my proposal has been accepted 3. (Q) we had to ~ why she had done it
inference *n.* 1. to draw, make an ~ from 2. an invalid; valid ~ 3. an ~ that + clause (I drew the ~ that my proposal had been accepted) 4. by ~
inferior *adj.* 1. clearly, decidedly, definitely, far, (very) much, vastly ~ 2. ~ in (~ in numbers; ~ in rank) 3. ~ to (he felt ~ to all the other competitors)
inferiority *n.* 1. intellectual; social ~ 2. a feeling of ~ 3. ~ in; to (a feeling of ~ in skill to the other competitors)
inferno *n.* a blazing, raging, roaring ~
infested *adj.* ~ with (their clothing was ~ed with lice)
infidelity *n.* 1. conjugal, marital ~ 2. ~ to (~ to one's ideals)
infighting *n.* 1. political ~ 2. ~ among, between
infiltrate *v.* (D; intr., refl., trans.) to ~ into
infiltration *n.* ~ into; through (enemy ~ into our lines)
infinitive *n.* 1. to split an ~ 2. a split ~
infinity *n.* to ~
inflamed *adj.* ~ with (they were ~d with enthusiasm for their cause)
inflammable *adj.* highly, very ~
inflammation *n.* 1. to cause; reduce (an) ~ 2. a mild; severe ~ 3. (an) ~ subsides 4. (an) ~ in (an ~ in the throat)
inflation *n.* 1. to cause; fuel, increase ~ 2. to bring down, control, curb, reduce ~ 3. creeping; double-digit ("10% or more"); galloping, high, rampant, runaway, uncontrolled; single-digit ("less than 10%") ~ 4. the rate of ~ (the rate of ~ stands at three percent)
inflection, inflexion *n.* a falling; rising ~
inflexibility *n.* 1. to demonstrate, show ~ 2. ~ in; towards 3. the ~ to + inf. (she has too much ~ to cope with the job)
inflexible *adj.* 1. very ~ 2. ~ about, as regards, when it comes to 3. ~ in; towards, with 4. (misc.) (she is too ~ to cope with the job)
inflict *v.* (D; tr.) to ~ on, upon (the enemy ~ed heavy losses on us)
influence I *n.* 1. to exert, have ~ on; to exercise ~ over 2. to use one's ~ 3. to wield ~ 4. to bring ~ to bear 5. to flaunt one's ~ 6. (colloq.) to peddle ~ 7. to consolidate, strengthen one's ~ 8. to counteract, curb, neutralize smb.'s ~ 9. (a) bad, baneful, negative; pernicious; undue; unwholesome ~ 10. (a) beneficial, good, positive, salutary; calming; civilizing; leavening; moderating ~ 11. (a) considerable; far-reaching; lasting; major; powerful, profound, strong ~ 12. (a) direct; indirect ~ 13. (a) cultural; moral ~ 14. an ~ for (an ~ for good) 15. ~ on; with 16. the ~ to + inf. (they have enough ~ to get the bill passed) 17. under smb.'s ~; under the ~ of (to come under smb.'s ~; to drive under the ~ (of alcohol)) 18. (misc.) outside ~s = ~s from outside; a sphere of ~; an ~ peddler (AE), pedlar
influence II *v.* 1. to ~ deeply, profoundly, strongly 2. (D; tr.) to ~ in (who ~d her in her decision to do that?) 3. (H) who ~d her to do that?
influential *adj.* ~ in
influx *n.* an ~ from; into
inform *v.* 1. (D; tr.) to ~ about, of (we ~ed them of the incident) 2. (d; intr.) to ~ against, on (the criminal ~ed on his accomplices (to the police)) 3. (L; must have an object) she ~ed them that she would come = "I'll come," she ~ed them. 4. (Q; must have an object) the thief ~ed the police where the money was hidden
informal *adj.* ~ with (she's ~ with everyone)
informant *n.* a native ~
information *n.* 1. to disseminate, furnish, give, offer, provide ~ 2. to collect, dig up, find, gather; extract ~ 3. to classify ~ 4. to disclose, divulge, leak ~ 5. to declassify ~ 6. to feed ~ (into a computer) 7. to access; retrieve ~ (from a computer) 8. to save; store ~ (in a computer) 9. to cover up, suppress, withhold ~ 10. classified, confidential; detailed; firsthand; inside; misleading; reliable; secondhand; secret; useful ~ 11. (AE) long-distance ~ (BE has *long-distance enquiries, trunk enquiries*) 12. ~ relates to (we have ~ relating to her return to this country) 13. an item, piece of ~ 14. ~ about, on (statistics that provide reliable ~ about poverty) 15. ~ that + clause (we have ~ (to the effect) that she has returned to this country) 16. for smb.'s ~ (for your ~, she has already returned to this country!) USAGE NOTE: *For Your Information* can be abbreviated to *FYI*.

informative *adj.* 1. ~ about (the statistics were very ~ about poverty) 2. ~ to + inf. (it was ~ to read the latest statistics about poverty)

informed *adj.* 1. officially; reliably; unofficially 2. to keep smb. ~ 3. ~ about, of (we were reliably ~ of her return to this country) 4. ~ that + clause (we were reliably ~ that she had returned to this country)

informer *n.* 1. to turn ("become") ~ 2. a police ~

infraction *n.* 1. to commit an ~ 2. a major; minor ~ (to commit a minor ~ of the law)

infringe *v.* (d; intr.) to ~ on, upon (to ~ on smb.'s rights)

infringement *n.* an ~ of, on (does wire-tapping constitute an ~ of people's rights?)

infuriate *v.* (R) it ~d me (to read) that he had been indicted

infuriated *adj.* 1. ~ about, at, over; with (I was ~ at the news of his indictment = I was ~ about his indictment) 2. ~ to + inf. (I was ~ to read that he had been indicted) 3. ~ that + clause (I was ~ that he had been indicted)

infuriating *adj.* 1. ~ to + inf. (it was ~ to read that he had been indicted) 2. ~ that + clause (it was ~ that he had been indicted)

infuse *v.* 1. (d; tr.) to ~ into (to ~ new life into the troops) 2. (d; intr.) to ~ with (to ~ the troops with new life)

infusion *n.* 1. an herbal ~ 2. an intravenous ~ 3. an ~ into (an ~ of new resources into a project; an ~ of new life into the troops)

ingenious *adj.* ~ to + inf. (it was ~ of her to solve the problem so quickly)

ingenuity *n.* 1. to exercise; show ~ 2. human ~ 3. the ~ to + inf. (she had the ~ to solve the problem quickly when everyone else had failed)

ingot *n.* a gold ~

ingrained *adj.* 1. deeply ~ 2. ~ in

ingratiate *v.* (D; refl.) to ~ with (she ~d herself with the boss)

ingratitude *n.* 1. to demonstrate, display, show ~ 2. base, rank ~ 3. ~ to, towards

ingredients *n.* 1. to combine ~ (in baking) 2. basic, essential; principal ~ 3. the ~ for, of, 4. (misc.) the book has all the ~ of a best-seller = the book has all the ~ to become a best-seller

inhale *v.* to ~ deeply

inhere *v.* (formal) to ~ in

inherent *adj.* ~ in, to

inherit *v.* (D; tr.) to ~ from (she stands to ~ a fortune from an uncle of hers)

inheritance *n.* 1. to claim one's ~ 2. to come into an ~ (she claimed the ~ from her uncle that she had come into when her uncle died)

inhibit *v.* (D; tr.) to ~ from (shyness ~ed him from talking to women)

inhibited *adj.* ~ about, from, in (he felt ~ from/ in talking to women = he felt ~ about talking to women)

inhibitions *n.* 1. to have ~ (about) (some men seem to have no ~ about talking to women) 2. to lose one's ~ (he lost his ~ after a few drinks)

inhospitable *adj.* 1. ~ to, towards (~ to strangers) 2. ~ to + inf. (it is ~ to turn a stranger away)

inhumanity *n.* 1. to display, show ~ 2. (misc.) man's ~ to man

inimical *adj.* (formal) ~ to (actions ~ to the maintenance of friendly relations between our countries)

iniquity *n.* a den of ~

initiate *v.* (d; tr.) to ~ into (to ~ students into the mysteries of linguistics)

initiation *n.* 1. to conduct, hold; offer, provide an ~ 2. an ~ into (conduct an ~ into a fraternity; provide an ~ into the mysteries of linguistics)

initiative *n.* ["decisiveness"] 1. to demonstrate, display, exercise, show ~ 2. to take the ~ (in) 3. to stifle ~ 4. to lose the ~ 5. private ~ 6. the ~ to + inf. (does she have enough ~ to get this job done?) 7. on one's (own) ~ (she made the decision on her own ~) ["plan of action"] 8. to undertake an ~ 9. a fresh, new ~ 10. a series of ~s 11. an ~ against 12. an ~ to + inf. (the government decided to undertake a series of new ~s to prevent further bloodshed)

inject *v.* 1. (D; tr.) to ~ into (to ~ a note of humor into the proceedings; to ~ new money into a business) 2. (D; tr.) to ~ with (they were ~ed with a new drug)

injection *n.* 1. to administer, give an ~ 2. to get, have an ~ 3. a lethal ~ 4. a hypodermic; intradermal; intramuscular; intravenous; subcutaneous ~ 5. an ~ against, for 6. by ~ (to take a drug by ~) 7. (misc.) an ~ of new money into a business from rich investors

injudicious *adj.* (formal) ~ to + inf. (it was ~ of you to speak to the press)

injunction *n.* 1. to grant, hand down (AE), issue an ~ 2. to deliver an ~ 3. to get; seek an ~ 4. an ~ against (an ~ against picketing) 5. a permanent; temporary ~ 6. an ~ to + inf. (an ~ to prevent picketing) 7. an ~ that + clause; subj. (the court issued an ~ that picketing not take/should not take place)

injure *v.* to ~ badly, critically, seriously, severely; slightly (see USAGE NOTE at **damage II**)

injurious *adj.* ~ to

injury *n.* 1. to inflict (an) ~ on 2. to receive, suffer, sustain an ~ 3. to escape ~ 4. a fatal; minor, slight; serious, severe ~ 5. bodily ~; an internal ~; multiple ~ries 6. an ~ to (an ~ to the head) 7. (misc.) to add insult to ~ (see USAGE NOTE at **damage II**)

injustice *n.* 1. to do smb. an ~ 2. to commit; perpetrate an ~ 3. to redress, remedy an ~ 4. (a) blatant, festering, gross, monstrous, rank ~ 5. an ~ to

ink *n.* 1. indelible; India (AE), Indian (BE); invisible; marking; permanent; printer's; secret; washable ~ 2. ~ smudges 3. a blob, blot, drop, spot of ~ 4. (misc.) pen and ~

inkling *n.* 1. to give smb. an ~ 2. to have an ~ 3. the faintest, slightest; first ~ 4. an ~ about, of 5. an ~

that + clause (I didn't have the slightest ~ that he was ill: the first ~ I had (of it) was when he didn't answer the phone)

inlaid *adj.* ~ with (~ with silver)

inland *adv.* to go, travel ~

inmate *n.* a prison ~

inn *n.* a country; roadside, wayside ~

innate *adj.* ~ in

inner city *n.* to redevelop, revitalize the ~

innocence *n.* 1. to establish, prove, show smb.'s ~ 2. to assert, declare; maintain, protest one's ~ 3. (misc.) an air of (injured) ~; (in) wide-eyed ~; in one's ~ (in their ~ they really believed I would sell them Brooklyn Bridge!)

innocent *adj.* ~ of

innovation *n.* 1. a daring; major; radical ~ 2. to come up with, make; encourage; stifle ~ 3. an ~ happens, occurs 4. an ~ in (radical ~s in science and technology occurred in the 19th Century)

innuendo *n.* 1. to cast, make an ~ 2. a snide; veiled ~ 3. an ~ about 4. an ~ that + clause (she made an ~ that he had a prison record)

inoculate *v.* (D; tr.) 1. to ~ against (to ~ a dog against rabies) 2. (D; tr.) to ~ with (they were ~d with a vaccine)

inoculation *n.* 1. to give an ~ 2. to get, have, receive an ~ 3. an ~ against (an ~ against tetanus)

input I *n.* 1. ~ into, to 2. (misc.) the ~ of our customers is welcome

input II *v.* (D; tr.) to ~ into (we ~ted data into our computer)

inquest *n.* 1. to conduct, hold an ~ 2. a coroner's; formal, official ~ 3. the findings of an ~ 4. an ~ into

inquire *v.* 1. (D; intr.) to ~ about, after; into 2. (formal) (D; intr.) to ~ of (may I ~ of you where the meeting is?) 3. (Q) he ~d where we were to meet = "where are we to meet?" he ~d USAGE NOTE: In BE, the spelling *enquire* is also used – we enquired about her health.

inquiry *n.* 1. to conduct, hold, make; launch an ~ 2. a discreet; exhaustive, thorough; official; private; public ~ 3. an ~ about (to make ~ries about a matter) 4. an ~ about, into (an official ~ into the incident was launched, which found that no one was to blame) USAGE NOTE: The noun *inquiry* can mean "question" or "investigation". In BE, the spelling *enquiry* has been recommended for the meaning "question" – an enquiry about her health. Compare – an official inquiry into the incident.

inquisition *n.* 1. to carry out, conduct an ~ 2. a cruel, senseless ~

inquisitive *adj.* 1. very ~ 2. ~ about

inroads *n.* 1. to make ~ 2. deep ~ 3. ~ in, into, on, upon (to make ~ on the freedom of the press)

insane *adj.* 1. criminally ~ 2. to go ~ 3. ~ to + inf. (it was ~ of him to risk everything)

insanity *n.* 1. (legal) to plead ~ 2. outright, pure, sheer ~ 3. (legal) temporary ~ 4. ~ to + inf. (it was sheer ~ on his part to risk everything!)

inscribe *v.* 1. (D; tr.) to ~ for (to ~ a book for smb.) 2. (D; tr.) to ~ in; on (to ~ one's name in a book on the very first page) 3. (D; tr.) to ~ with (to ~ a book with one's name)

inscription *n.* 1. to bear, have an ~ 2. to decipher an ~ 3. an ~ in; on

insecticide *n.* to spray, spread, use an ~

insects *n.* 1. ~ bite; crawl, creep; fly 2. a swarm of (flying) ~

insecure *adj.* ~ about; in

insecurity *n.* 1. growing, increasing, mounting ~ 2. financial; job ~ 3. a feeling, sense of ~ (a sense of mounting financial ~)

insemination *n.* artificial ~

insensibility *n.* 1. to display, show ~ 2. ~ to (to display ~ to pain)

insensible *adj.* 1. (formal) (BE) ~ of (they seemed totally ~ of the danger that they faced) 2. ~ to (~ to pain)

insensitive *adj.* 1. highly, very ~ 2. ~ to (~ to criticism; ~ to the feelings of others) 3. ~ to + inf. (it was ~ of/for her to bring that up = bringing that up was an ~ thing for her to do)

insensitivity *n.* 1. to display, show ~ 2. complete, total ~ 3. ~ to (to display total ~ to criticism)

inseparable *adj.* ~ from

insert *v.* (D; tr.) to ~ between; in, into (to ~ a new paragraph between two others; to ~ a new sentence into a paragraph; to ~ a key into a lock)

inside I *adv.* ~ out ("with the inner surface facing out"); ("thoroughly") (to know a subject ~ out) USAGE NOTE: The compound preposition *inside of* can refer to time or space. Referring to time, it is colloq. CE – to finish a job inside (of) an hour; referring to space, it is colloq. AE – inside (of) a building.

inside II *n.* (colloq.) ["confidential information"] (AE) 1. to have the ~ on ["position of trust"] 2. to be on the ~

insight *n.* 1. to gain; have (an) ~ into 2. to give, offer, provide (an) ~ 3. a deep, profound; new; sudden ~ 4. a flash of ~ 5. the ~ to + inf. (she had the ~ to predict what would happen) 6. the ~ that + clause (she had the sudden ~ that something bad was about to happen) 7. (misc.) a person of great ~

insignia *n.* military; royal ~

insignificance *n.* to fade, pale into ~

insinuate *v.* 1. (d; refl.) ("to ingratiate") to ~ into (to ~ oneself into smb.'s good graces) 2. (L; to) ("to suggest") she ~ (to us) that her partner had embezzled funds

insinuation *n.* 1. to make an ~ (to) 2. an ~ about 3. an ~ that + clause (we didn't like her ~ (to us) that her partner had embezzled funds)

insist *v.* 1. to ~ absolutely, definitely, positively; strongly; stubbornly 2. (D; intr.) to ~ on (they ~ on more money; she ~ed on coming with us; she ~ed on everyone('s) attending the meeting) 3. (L;

can be used with the subj.) she ~ed that everyone attend/should attend/(esp. BE) attended the meeting, and after the meeting she ~ed that everyone had actually attended it
insistence *n.* 1. dogged, firm, stubborn ~ 2. ~ on (her ~ on everyone('s) attending the meeting) 3. ~ that + clause ; can be subj. (we resented her ~ that everyone attend/should attend/(BE) attended the meeting, though we understood her ~ afterward that everyone had actually attended it) 4. at smb.'s ~ (at her ~, everyone actually attended the meeting)
insistent *adj.* 1. ~ on, upon (she was ~ on everyone('s) attending the meeting) 2. ~ that + clause ; can be subj. (she was ~ that everyone attend/should attend/(esp. BE) attended the meeting, and after the meeting she was ~ that everyone had actually attended it)
insolence *n.* 1. to display, show ~ 2. gross ~ 3. the ~ to + inf. (they had the ~ to demand special treatment)
insolent *adj.* 1. ~ in (~ in their manner) 2. ~ to, towards 3. ~ to + inf. (it was ~ of them to demand special treatment)
insoluble *adj.* ~ in (water) = water-insoluble
insolvency *n.* to force into ~
insomnia *n.* to suffer from ~
inspect *v.* to ~ carefully, closely, thoroughly ; perfunctorily ; visually (we ~ed the pipes closely for leaks)
inspection *n.* 1. to carry out, conduct, make an ~ 2. a careful, close, thorough ; cursory, perfunctory, superficial ; on-site ; visual ~ (we carried out a close ~ of the pipes for any leaks) 3. a technical ~ 4. on ~ (on closer ~ the money turned out to be counterfeit) 5. (misc.) the troops were getting ready for ~
inspector *n.* 1. a customs ; fire ; health ; mine ; police ; safety ~ 2. the ~ general
inspiration *n.* 1. a great ~ 2. to give, offer, provide ~ 3. to derive, draw ~ from 4. to find ~ in 5. divine ~ 6. ~ comes (from many sources) 7. a flash, spark ; source of ~ 8. an ~ for (what provided the ~ for the statue ?) 9. an ~ to (their lives were an ~ to young people) 10. the ~ to + inf. (what gave him the ~ to do it ?)
inspire *v.* 1. (D ; tr.) to ~ in ; with (the latest consumer reports do not ~ confidence in that product ; her recent speeches ~d hope in her followers = her recent speeches ~d her followers with hope) 2. (D ; tr.) to ~ to (the leaders set out to ~ the rank and file to greater productivity) 3. (H) the leaders set out to ~ the rank and file to produce more 4. (misc.) divinely ~d (our leader is wonderful – but she isn't divinely ~ by any means !)
inspiring *adj.* ~ to + inf. (it was ~ to hear her recent speeches = it was ~ hearing her recent speeches = her recent speeches were ~ to hear)
instability *n.* economic ; emotional ; political ~
install *v.* 1. (d ; tr.) to ~ as (to ~ smb. as president) 2. (P ; refl.) they ~ed themselves in front of the TV ; the protesters ~ed themselves at the entrance

installations *n.* military ; naval ; port ~
installment, instalment *n.* 1. to pay an ~ 2. monthly ; quarterly ~s 3. in ~s (the book came out in ~s ; to pay in ~s)
installment plan *n.* (AE) on the ~ (to buy smt. on the ~) (BE has *hire purchase*)
instance *n.* ["example"] 1. to cite, give an ~ 2. an isolated, rare ~ 3. for ~ 4. in an ~ (in rare ~s ; in a few isolated ~s)
instant *n.* 1. at a certain ~ (at that ~ I realized who had planned the whole scheme) 2. (misc.) for an ~ ; in an ~
instigate *v.* (H) (esp. BE) to ~ smb. to do smt.
instigation *n.* at smb.'s ~ (at her ~, everyone who attended the meeting heckled the speakers)
instill, instil *v.* 1. to ~ deeply, firmly 2. (D ; tr.) to ~ in, into (to ~ respect for the law in the younger generation)
instinct *n.* 1. to arouse an ~ 2. to follow one's (own) ~s 3. a basic, gut ; destructive ; herd ; human ; killer ; maternal ; natural ~ 4. animal ; predatory ~s 5. an unerring ~ 6. an ~ for (he has an unerring ~ for saying just the wrong thing !) 7. the ~ to + inf. (nothing can destroy the ~ to survive) 8. by, on ~
institute *n.* 1. a research ~ 2. an ~ for (an ~ for theoretical research) 3. at, in an ~ (to work at/in an ~)
institution *n.* 1. to endow ; support an ~ 2. a charitable ; educational ; financial ; penal ; philanthropic ; political ; private ; social ; state-supported ~ 3. a heavily endowed ~ 4. (misc.) an ~ of higher learning ; the ~ of marriage ; visiting your parents at Thanksgiving is a national ~ in the USA
instruct *v.* 1. (D ; tr.) ("to teach") to ~ in (to ~ soldiers in field hygiene) 2. (H) ("to order") she ~ed us to begin work at once 3. (L ; must have an object) ("to inform") we have been ~ed that the matter has been settled by our lawyers 4. (Q ; must have an object) ("to order") we were ~ed where to meet
instruction *n.* 1. to conduct, give, provide ~ 2. to take ~ (before converting to a religion) 3. advanced ; beginning, elementary ; bilingual ; intermediate ; remedial ~ 4. computer-assisted ~ 5. ~ in (to provide advanced ~ in mathematics)
instructions *n.* 1. to give, issue ~ 2. to leave ~ (for smb.) 3. to get, receive ; have ~ 4. to carry out, follow ~ (to the letter) 5. to await (further) ~ 6. oral ; verbal ; written ~ 7. clear, explicit, precise ~ 8. specific ~ 9. a list, set of ~ 10. ~ for 11. ~ to + inf. (we had ~ to report to her) 12. ~ that + clause ; subj. (she left ~ that her estate be/should be divided evenly) 13. according to, in accordance with, on ~ (we acted on your ~)
instructive *adj.* ~ to + inf. (it will be ~ to analyze the results)
instructor *n.* an ~ in, of (an ~ in physics)
instrument *n.* ["implement"] 1. a blunt ; delicate ; sharp ~ 2. surgical ~s 3. ~s of torture 4. an ~ for (an ~ for good) ["musical instrument"] 5. to tune, tune up an ~ 6. to play an ~ 7. a brass ; keyboard ; musical ;

percussion; stringed; wind; woodwind ~ ["misc."]
8. pilots study their ~s before taking off
instrumental *adj.* (cannot stand alone) ~ in (her help was ~ in tracking down the criminal)
insubordinate *adj.* ~ to
insubordination *n.* 1. gross, rank ~ 2. ~ to (~ to authority)
insufficient *adj.* 1. ~ for; in 2. ~ to + inf. (it's ~ to cite only one example)
insulate *v.* (D; refl., tr.) to ~ against, from
insulation *n.* ~ against, from
insult *n.* 1. to fling, hurl, shout an ~ at 2. to swallow, take an ~ 3. to avenge an ~ 4. a gratuitous; imaginary; nasty, vicious ~ 5. an ~ to (an ~ to smb.'s intelligence) 6. (misc.) to trade ~s; a stream of ~s; to add ~ to injury
insulted *adj.* 1. deeply ~ 2. ~ to + inf. (I was deeply ~ to have been overlooked)
insurance *n.* 1. to provide ~ for 2. to sell, write ~ 3. to underwrite ~ 4. to carry; take out ~ (our firm carries fire ~ ; to take out life ~ on a relative) 5. to cancel; renew ~ 6. accident; automobile (AE), motor (BE), motor-car (BE); collision; flight; marine; travel ~ 7. disability; hospitalization; life, whole life (esp. AE); major-medical (AE); medical ~ (see also **health insurance**) 8. fire; flood; hurricane; terrorism ~ 9. homeowner's; property; title ~ 10. group; liability (AE), third-party (BE); no-fault; term (esp. AE) ~ 11. comprehensive; compulsory; voluntary ~ 12. (GB) National Insurance 13. social ~ (see also **unemployment insurance**) 14. ~ against; for, on (~ against loss from flood; ~ on one's personal effects) (see also *insurance policy* at **policy II**; *insurance premium* at **premium**) USAGE NOTE: BE has traditionally distinguished between *insurance* (to provide compensation for what may happen) and *assurance* (to provide compensation for what will happen); thus – *fire insurance* and *life assurance*. However, nowadays, *life insurance* is also used in BE.
insure *v.* 1. (D; refl., tr.) to ~ against; for (to ~ one's home against loss from fire; to ~ one's life for fifty thousand dollars) 2. (L) ("to ensure") (esp. AE) their support ~d that the project would receive financial backing; no one can ~ that you'll get a job USAGE NOTE: In AE, the verb *insure* may be used as a synonym of *ensure*.
insured *adj.* 1. fully; heavily ~ 2. against; for (my home is fully ~ against loss from fire and my life is ~ for $50,000)
insurrection *n.* 1. to foment, stir up an ~ 2. to crush, put down, quell, suppress an ~
insusceptible *adj.* ~ to
integrate *v.* (D; intr., tr.) to ~ into; with
integration *n.* 1. economic; racial; school; token ~ 2. ~ into
integrity *n.* 1. to display, show; have ~ 2. great ~ 3. territorial ~ 4. the ~ to + inf. (he had the ~ not to

accept bribes) 5. (misc.) a person of ~ who always behaves with ~
intellect *n.* 1. to appeal to the ~ 2. (a) keen, sharp, superior ~ 3. of ~ (a person of keen ~ who exercises her intellect by solving puzzles)
intelligence *n.* ["ability to comprehend, learn"] 1. to demonstrate, exhibit, show; have, possess ~ 2. acute, great, high, keen; limited; low; normal; outstanding, remarkable ~ 3. native, natural ~ 4. (computers) artificial ~ 5. the ~ to + inf. (she had the ~ to see through their scheme) 6. of a certain ~ (she is a person of considerable ~, so don't insult her ~ by talking down to her!) (see also **IQ**; *intelligence quotient (IQ)* at **quotient**; *intelligence test* at **test I**) ["information"] 7. to collect, gather ~ 8. classified; combat, military; industrial; (top) secret ~ 9. ~ that + clause (we have ~ (to the effect) that there will be an attack soon)
intelligent *adj.* ~ to + inf. (it would not be ~ to provoke her) (see also *intelligent design* at **design I**)
intelligible *adj.* ~ to
intend *v.* 1. (d; tr.) ("to design") to ~ as (it was ~ed as a joke) 2. (d; tr.) ("to design") to ~ for (we've ~ed this dictionary for serious students) 3. (E) ("to plan") she ~s to file suit; she left the office yesterday fully ~ing to resign 4. (G) ("to plan") what do you ~ doing? 5. (H) ("to want") we never ~ed her to get involved 6. (L; subj.) ("to want") we never ~ed that she get/should get involved
intended *adj.* (cannot stand alone) ~ for (this dictionary is ~ for serious students)
intent I *adj.* (cannot stand alone) ~ on, upon (she is ~ on getting the job done quickly)
intent II *n.* 1. criminal ~ 2. ~ to + inf. (with ~ to kill) 3. by ~ 4. (misc.) for (esp. AE), to all ~s and purposes ("practically, for all practical purposes"); (legal) loitering with ~ (to ~ to commit a crime)
intention *n.* 1. to announce, declare, state one's ~ 2. to make one's ~s clear/known 3. every; no ~ (she has every ~ of accepting the invitation; she has no ~ of resigning) 4. bad, evil; good; honorable ~s 5. the ~ to + inf. (have you heard of her ~ to resign?) 6. with the ~ of (she left the office yesterday with the ~ of resigning)
interact *v.* (d; intr.) to ~ with
interaction *n.* ~ among, between; with
interactive *adj.* ~ with
interbreed *v.* (D; intr.) to ~ with
intercede *v.* 1. (D; intr.) to ~ for; with (to ~ with the authorities for smb.) 2. (misc.) to ~ on smb.'s behalf (to ~ (with the authorities) on smb.'s behalf)
interchangeable *adj.* 1. freely ~ 2. ~ with
intercom *n.* on, over, through, via the ~
interconnect *v.* 1. to ~ closely; inextricably 2. (D; tr.) to ~ with (these events are inextricably ~ed with each other)
intercourse *n.* 1. to have ~ with 2. anal; oral; sexual ~ 3. social ~ 4. ~ occurs, takes place 5. ~ among, between; with

interest I *n.* ["concern"] ["curiosity"] 1. to arouse, drum up, excite, generate, kindle, pique, spark, stimulate, stir up; maintain, sustain; revive ~ (in) 2. to hold smb.'s ~ 3. to demonstrate, display, evince, exhibit, express, have, manifest, show ~ 4. to pursue an ~ (he pursued his ~ in historical research) 5. to take an ~ in (she took a keen ~ in the project) 6. to lose ~ (in) (they lost all ~ in sports) 7. an academic; active; lifelong; passing; vested ~ 8. a burning, consuming, deep, great, intense, keen, lively, profound, serious, strong ~ 9. broad, wide; common, mutual; general; narrow; universal, widespread ~s 10. human ~ (this story has a lot of human ~) 11. personal; popular ~ 12. the national; (the) public ~ 13. ~ drops off, flags, wanes; grows, increases; peaks; picks up 14. a conflict of ~(s) 15. ~ in (to show no ~ in financial matters) 16. ~ to + inf. (it's in/to our ~ to have stable prices) 17. in smb.'s ~ (to act in one's own best ~; whose ~ is this new policy in anyway?) 18. in a certain ~ (in the national ~; in the public ~; this new policy is not in the ~ of small businesses!) 19. in the ~(s) of (in the ~s of safety; in the ~s of our organization) 20. of ~ (to) (this story will be of ~ to us; these new developments are of local ~ only) 21. to smb.'s ~ (see 16) ["money paid for the use of money"] 22. to bear, earn, pay, yield ~ 23. to draw; receive ~ 24. to lose ~ 25. to add; calculate; charge; compound ~ 26. compound; simple ~ 27. ~ accrues (to an account) 28. ~ on (~ on a loan; six percent ~ is paid on all accounts) 29. at a certain (rate of) ~ (at six percent ~) 30. (misc.) to return a high rate of ~ ["share"] 31. to own a controlling ~ (in a business) 32. a half ~ (see also **interests**)

interest II *v.* 1. to ~ greatly, very much 2. (D; tr.) to ~ in (could I ~ you in this project?)

interested *adj.* 1. deeply, greatly, highly, keenly, very (much) ~ 2. ~ in (we are not very ~ in politics; would you be ~ in this project?; will you be ~ in knowing when an agreement has been reached?) 3. ~ to + inf. (you will be ~ to know that an agreement has been reached)

interesting *adj.* 1. highly, very ~ 2. ~ for; to 3. ~ to + inf. (he's ~ to watch = it's ~ to watch him = he's an ~ person to watch) 4. ~ that + clause (it's ~ that the incident was not reported in the newspapers)

interests *n.* ["stakes, investments"] 1. to have ~ (to have ~ throughout the world) 2. to advance, further, promote smb.'s ~ 3. to defend, guard, look after, protect smb.'s ~ 4. to serve smb.'s ~ (it serves their ~ to have stability in the area) 5. far-flung; international; worldwide ~ 6. ~ clash; coincide ["groups having a common concern"] 7. banking; business, commercial; shipping ~ 8. competing; controlling; special; vested ~

interface I *n.* 1. an ~ between; with 2. at an ~

interface II *v.* (D; intr., tr.) to ~ with (to ~ a machine with a computer)

interfere *v.* (D; intr.) to ~ between (BE); with; in

USAGE NOTE: In BE, *to interfere with smb.* often means "to molest smb. sexually".

interference *n.* 1. to brook, stand for, tolerate no ~ 2. unwarranted ~ 3. military; outside ~ 4. ~ in, with 5. (misc.) (esp. Am. football) to run ~ for

interim *n.* in the ~

interior *n.* in the ~ (the situation in the ~ of the country was critical)

interject *v.* (D; tr.) to ~ into (to ~ new issues into a campaign)

interjection *n.* an ~ into (the ~ of new issues into a campaign)

interlace *v.* (d; tr.) to ~ with

interlard *v.* (formal) (d; tr.) to ~ with (to ~ a speech with Biblical references)

interlink *v.* 1. to ~ closely; inextricably 2. to ~ electronically 3. (D; tr.) to ~ with (these events are inextricably ~ed with each other)

interlude *n.* 1. a romantic ~ 2. a musical ~ 3. a brief ~

intermarriage *n.* ~ between, with

intermarry *v.* (D; intr.) to ~ with (to ~ with the local population)

intermediary *n.* 1. an ~ between (an ~ between the warring groups) 2. through an ~

intermingle *v.* (d; intr.) to ~ with (to ~ with the crowd)

intermission *n.* an ~ between USAGE NOTE: In AE, *intermission* has the meaning "pause between parts of a theatrical performance". In BE, *interval* is used in this meaning.

Internet *n.* 1. to browse; cruise; surf the ~ 2. to join the ~ 3. on the ~ (to find smt. on the ~)

internship *n.* (AE) to serve one's ~

interplay *n.* ~ among, between

interpolate *v.* (D; tr.) to ~ into (to ~ Biblical references into a speech)

interpose *v.* (D; refl., tr.) to ~ among, between

interpret *v.* 1. (B) I had to ~ the passage to them 2. (d; tr.) to ~ as (they ~ed his response as an admission of guilt) 3. (D; intr., tr.) to ~ for (to ~ for foreign visitors) 4. (H) they ~ed his response to be an admission of guilt

interpretation *n.* 1. to make an ~ 2. to put a certain ~ on (they put a completely different ~ on his behavior) 3. a broad, free, liberal, loose; strict ~ (of the law)

interpreter *n.* 1. to serve (smb.) as an ~ 2. to communicate, speak through an ~ 3. a conference; court; simultaneous ~

interpreting *n.* conference; simultaneous ~

interrelate *v.* 1. to ~ closely; inextricably 2. (D; tr.) to ~ with (these events are inextricably ~ed with each other)

interrogation *n.* 1. to conduct an ~ 2. a police ~ 3. under ~

interrogator *n.* 1. to serve as an ~ 2. a prisoner-of-war ~

interrogatory *n.* (legal) to file; serve an ~

intersect *v.* (d; intr.) to ~ with (this street ~s with the main road)

intersection *n.* 1. a busy; dangerous ~ 2. at an ~

intersperse *v.* (P; tr.) to ~ Biblical references throughout a speech

intertwine *v.* (D; intr.) to ~ with

interval *n.* ["space of time between events"] 1. a brief, short; irregular; regular ~ 2. a lucid ~ 3. at a certain ~ (at regular ~s) ["distance"]["gap"] 4. to maintain an ~ (the proper ~ should be maintained between vehicles) 5. an ~ between (see the Usage Note for **intermission**)

intervene *v.* 1. (D; intr.) to ~ between 2. (D; intr.) to ~ in; with (to ~ in smb.'s affairs; to ~ with the authorities on behalf of a political prisoner)

intervention *n.* 1. armed, military; government ~ 2. medical; nursing; surgical ~ 3. divine ~ 4. ~ from, on the part of

interview I *n.* 1. to conduct an ~ (a reporter conducted an ~ with the celebrity) 2. to give, grant an ~ (the celebrity gave an ~ to a reporter) 3. to have, hold an ~ (a reporter had an ~ with the celebrity = the celebrity had an ~ with a reporter; the dean of admissions had/held ~s with prospective students; the prospective students had ~s with the dean of admissions after they toured the campus) 4. an exclusive; job; personal; taped; telephone; television, TV ~ 5. an ~ for; with (to have an ~ with the personnel director for a job)

interview II *v.* (D; tr.) to ~ about; for (a reporter ~ed the celebrity about his love-life; to ~ smb. for a job)

interwoven *adj.* ~ with

intestate *adj.* to die ~

intestine *n.* the large; small ~

intimacy *n.* ~ between; with

intimate I *adj.* ~ with

intimate II *v.* 1. (B) (formal) she ~d her wishes to us 2. (L; to) they ~d (to us) that an agreement would be worked out soon = "an agreement will be worked out soon," they ~d (to us) 3. (Q; to) they would not ~ (to us) how the agreement would be worked out

intimation *n.* 1. to give an ~ 2. ~ that + clause (there was no ~ that she would retire; they gave us absolutely no ~ that an agreement would be worked out soon) 3. (misc.) "Ode: Intimations of Immortality from Recollections of Early Childhood" – William Wordsworth (1770–1850)

intimidate *v.* (D; tr.) to ~ into (to ~ smb. into doing smt.)

into *prep.* (colloq.) ["interested in; involved in"] she is ~ classical music; when did you get ~ relaxation?

intolerable *adj.* 1. ~ to 2. ~ to + inf. (it's ~ to allow hardened criminals to roam our streets) 3. ~ that + clause (it is ~ that hardened criminals are allowed to roam our streets)

intolerance *n.* ["lack of tolerance"] 1. to display, show ~ 2. to stir up ~ against 3. racial; religious ~ ["sensitivity"] 4. ~ to (drugs)

intolerant *adj.* ~ of

intonation *n.* a falling; rising ~

intoxication *n.* a state of ~

intransigence *n.* ~ about

intransigent *adj.* ~ about

intricacy *n.* labyrinthine ~

intrigue I *n.* 1. to carry on, engage in (an) ~ 2. petty; political ~ 3. a hotbed; web of ~ 4. an ~ against

intrigue II *v.* 1. (d; intr.) to ~ against; with (to ~ against the government) 2. (R) it ~d me (to learn) that she had resigned

intrigued *adj.* ~ to + inf. (I was very ~ to learn that she had resigned)

intriguing *adj.* ~ to + inf. (it was very ~ to learn that she had resigned)

intrinsic *adj.* ~ in, to

introduce *v.* 1. (B) she ~d me to her friends as her husband = she ~d me to her friends by saying, "May I ~ you all to my husband John?" = she ~d me to her friends by saying, "I'd like you all to meet my husband John" 2. (D; tr.) to ~ into (to ~ new methods into an industry) 3. (d; tr.) to ~ to (to ~ students to the elements of computer science)

introduction *n.* 1. to make an ~ 2. to serve as an ~ 3. a formal ~ 4. an ~ into, to (an ~ to a book) 5. (misc.) a letter of ~

introductory *adj.* (formal) ~ to

intrude *v.* 1. (D; intr.) to ~ into 2. (D; intr.) to ~ on, upon (to ~ on smb.'s privacy)

intrusion *n.* 1. to make an ~ 2. an unwarranted; unwelcome ~ 3. an ~ into (to make an ~ into enemy territory) 4. an ~ on, upon (an ~ on my time) 5. (misc.) pardon my ~

intuit *v.* (esp. BE) (L) she ~ed that something was wrong

intuition *n.* 1. an ~ that + clause (she had an ~ that something was wrong) 2. by ~ (by ~, she sensed that something was wrong)

inundate *v.* (D; intr.) to ~ with (we were ~d with requests)

inure *v.* (formal) (d; tr.) to ~ to (to ~ smb. to hardship; ~d to danger)

invalid *v.* (BE) 1. (d; tr.) to ~ home 2. (d; tr.) to ~ out of (to be ~ed out of the army)

invaluable *adj.* ~ for, to

invasion *n.* 1. to carry out; launch, mount an ~ 2. to repel, repulse an ~ 3. an enemy ~

invective *n.* 1. to hurl ~ (CE)/~s (AE) at 2. bitter; coarse, vulgar ~ 3. a stream, torrent of ~ (CE)/~s (AE) 4. ~ against (to hurl a stream of ~ against the government)

inveigh *v.* (formal) (d; intr.) to ~ against (to ~ against the government)

inveigle *v.* (d; tr.) to ~ into; out of (to ~ smb. into doing smt.)

invention *n.* 1. to come up with, make an ~ 2. to patent, register an ~ 3. to market, promote an ~ 4. a brilliant, ingenious ~

inventory *n.* 1. to make an ~ (of); to take (an) ~ (of)

2. (AE) to reduce (an) ~ (by having a sale) 3. an annual ~ 4. closed for ~ 5. in, on an ~

invest v. 1. ("to place money or resources") to ~ heavily 2. (D; intr., tr.) ("to place money or resources") to ~ in (to ~ heavily in municipal bonds; to ~ surplus funds in stocks) 3. (formal) (d; tr.) ("to entrust") to ~ with (to ~ smb. with authority)

invested adj. (formal) (cannot stand alone) ~ with (~ with authority)

investigation n. 1. to carry out, conduct, make; launch an ~ 2. a cursory, perfunctory; full, painstaking, thorough; impartial; ongoing; pending ~ 3. a criminal; internal; police ~ 4. an ~ discovers, reveals (the ~ revealed the cause of the fire) 5. an ~ into, of (to launch an ~ into the cause of the fire) 6. on, upon ~ (on closer ~ we discovered the cause of the fire) 7. under ~ (the cause of the fire is under ~)

investigator n. a government; private ~

investment n. 1. to make an ~; to diversity one's ~s 2. a good, lucrative, profitable; safe; solid, sound ~ 3. a bad, poor; risky ~ 4. capital; heavy; inward; long-term; overseas ~s 5. an ~ in (~s in oil stocks) (see also *investment portfolio* at **portfolio**)

investor n. a heavy; large; small; speculative ~

invidious adj. (formal) ~ to + inf. (it is ~ to deprive workers of health insurance) (see also *invidious comparison* at **comparison**)

invigorating adj. ~ to + inf. (it's ~ to swim in the sea = swimming in the sea is ~)

invisible adj. 1. ~ from (the house was ~ from the road) 2. to (~ to the naked eye)

invitation n. 1. to extend, issue, send an ~ 2. to send out ~s 3. to get, receive an ~ 4. to accept an ~ 5. to decline, refuse, spurn, turn down an ~ 6. a cordial, kind; formal; informal; open, standing; personal ~ (thank you for your kind ~, which we must unfortunately decline because of a previous engagement) 7. an ~ from; to (an ~ to a party from some friends) 8. an ~ to + inf. (she has received an ~ from friends to attend the party) 9. at smb.'s ~ (they came at my ~) 10. by ~ (participation is by ~ only) 11. (misc.) in that dormitory an unlocked drawer is an open ~ to theft

invite v. 1. to ~ cordially (everyone is cordially ~d) 2. (D; tr.) to ~ to (we ~d them to our party) 3. (H) we ~d them to come to our party

invite out v. (D; tr.) to ~ for, to (they ~d us out (to a restaurant) for dinner)

invite over v. (D; tr.) to ~ for; to (we ~d them over to our place for a drink)

invocation n. to offer, pronounce the / an ~

invoice I n. 1. to issue; make out; pay; process; send, submit an ~ 2. a duplicate; original ~ 3. a final ~ 4. an ~ for (we sent them an ~ for the full amount)

invoice II v. (D; tr.) to ~ for (we ~d them for the full amount)

involve v. 1. (D; tr.) to ~ in; with (to ~ smb. in a

project; we were ~d with the technical details) 2. (G) that job would ~ traveling a great deal 3. (K) that job would ~ my traveling a great deal

involved adj. 1. deeply; directly; emotionally ~ (with) 2. ~ in; with (I got her ~ in the project; to become (emotionally) ~ with smb.)

involvement n. 1. an emotional ~ 2. (a) direct ~ 3. ~ in; with

invulnerable adj. ~ to

inward adv. ~ bound

IQ n. 1. to test smb.'s ~ 2. to have a certain ~ (she has an ~ of 130) 3. an average, normal; high; low ~ 4. an ~ of (an ~ of one hundred; the ~ of a genius) (see also *IQ test* at **test I**)

irate adj. ~ about

ire n. 1. to arouse, draw, incur, provoke, raise, rouse smb.'s ~ 2. (formal) to visit one's ~ upon smb.

irk v. (R) it ~s her to have to get up so early; it ~s her that she has to get up so early

irksome adj. (formal) 1. ~ to + inf. (it is ~ for her to have to get up so early) 2. ~ that + clause (she finds it ~ that she has to get up so early)

iron n. ["type of metal"] 1. to mine; smelt ~ 2. cast; corrugated; crude; pig; scrap; wrought ~ ["device for pressing clothes"] 3. to plug in an ~ 4. to unplug an ~ 5. to pass, run an ~ over a shirt 6. a cool; hot ~ 7. an electric; steam ~ ["rodlike device used for branding"] 8. a branding ~ ["tool used to apply solder"] 9. a soldering ~ ["instrument used to curl hair"] 10. a curling ~ ["hook"] 11. a climbing; grappling ~ ["utensil for making waffles"] 12. a waffle ~ ["misc."] 13. to have several ~s in the fire ("to be involved in several activities at the same time"); to strike while the ~ is hot ("to act at the proper moment") (see also **irons**)

ironic, ironical adj. ~ that + clause (it's ~ that the weakest student in mathematics was / should have been elected class treasurer)

ironing n. 1. to do the ~ 2. a heap, pile of ~ (see also *ironing board* at **board**)

irons n. ["shackles"] 1. to clap, put smb. into ~ 2. in ~

irony n. 1. bitter ~ 2. dramatic; tragic ~ 3. a touch of ~ 4. an ~ that + clause (it was a tragic ~ that he was killed in a traffic accident after the war) 5. (misc.) the ~ (of it) was that he was killed in a traffic accident after surviving the war!

irrational adj. ~ to + inf. (it was ~ to expect miracles)

irreconcilable adj. ~ with

irregular adj. grossly, highly, very ~

irregularity n. 1. a gross ~ 2. voting ~ties 3. ~ in (an ~ in the accounts; ~ties in voting)

irrelevant adj. 1. ~ to (the evidence is ~ to the case) 2. ~ to + inf. (it's ~ to cite such outdated evidence) 3. ~ that + clause (it's ~ that she was out of town) 4. (misc.) is it ~ whether she was present at the scene of the crime?

irrespective adj. ~ of

irresponsibility *n.* 1. the height of ~ 2. ~ to + inf. (it was the height of ~ for him to speak to reporters that way!)
irresponsible *adj.* 1. highly, very ~ 2. ~ to + inf. (it was highly ~ for/of him to speak to reporters that way!)
irreverent *adj.* 1. ~ of 2. ~ to + inf. (it would be ~ to whistle during a religious ceremony)
irritant *n.* an ~ to
irritate *v.* 1. to ~ greatly, very much 2. (R) it ~d me (to learn) that she had been promoted behind my back
irritated *adj.* 1. ~ at (~ at being awakened so early) 2. ~ to + inf. (I was ~ to learn that she had been promoted behind my back) 3. ~ that + clause (I was ~ that she had been/should have been promoted behind my back)
irritating *adj.* 1. ~ to + inf. (it was ~ to learn that she had been promoted behind my back) 2. ~ that + (it was ~ that she had been/should have been promoted behind my back)
irritation *n.* ["anger"] 1. to express, show; feel ~ 2. to conceal, hide one's ~ 3. ~ at, with 4. ~ that + clause (I could not hide my ~ that she had been/should have been promoted behind my back) ["sore"] 5. to exacerbate, worsen an ~ 6. to relieve, soothe an ~
irrupt *v.* 1. (D; intr.) to ~ into ("to enter suddenly") (the demonstrators ~ed into the palace) 2. (D; intr.) ("to erupt") (AE) to ~ in; into (to ~ in a frenzied demonstration that ~ed into violence)
irruption *n.* ["act of entering suddenly"] 1. an ~ into (the ~ of the demonstrators into the palace) ["eruption"] (AE) 2. an ~ in; into (the students' ~ in a frenzied demonstration and its ~ into violence)
island *n.* 1. a desert, deserted, uninhabited; tropical ~ 2. a safety (AE), traffic ~ 3. a chain, group of ~s 4. on an ~
isolate *v.* (D; refl., tr.) to ~ from
isolated *adj.* ~ from
isolation *n.* in ~ (from) (to live in ~ (from))
isotope *n.* a radioactive ~
issue I *n.* ["number of a journal"] 1. to bring out, publish an ~ 2. a back; current; special; thematic ~ 3. an ~ comes out, is published (your poem is in the next ~, which will come out on Thursday) ["question"]["problem"] 4. to bring up, raise an ~ 5. to address; confront; deal with, face; debate; discuss; explore; straddle an ~ 6. to settle an ~ 7. to avoid,

evade, sidestep; skirt an ~ 8. a basic; collateral, side ~ 9. a burning, important; dead; hot-button (colloq.); sensitive; substantive ~; the real ~ 10. a contentious, controversial, debatable, thorny; divisive ~ 11. a complex, complicated, involved, knotty, perplexing, thorny ~ 12. a delicate, ticklish ~ 13. a minor, petty ~ 14. an environmental; moral; political; social ~ 15. a global; local; national ~ (there are a number of important ~s about climate change that have arisen in our discussions) 16. an ~ arises, comes up 17. at ~ (the point at ~) 18. (misc.) to confuse the ~; to force the ~; to make an ~ of smt.; to take ~ with smb. on smt. ("to disagree with smb. about smt."); to have ~s about/with ("to have problems with/about") (colloq.) (we're having meat for dinner – do you have an ~ about/with that?) ["children"] (formal) 19. without ~ (to die without ~) (see also **bond issue**)
issue II *v.* 1. (B) ("to distribute") the school ~d new textbooks to the pupils 2. (formal) (d; intr.) ("to come") to ~ from (blood ~d from the wound; smoke ~d from the chimneys) 3. (BE) (d; tr.) to ~ with (the pupils were ~d with new textbooks)
it *pronoun* of ~ (they made a mess of ~; to have had a hard time of ~)
italics *n.* to put smt. into ~ and keep smt. in ~
itch *n.* ["itchy feeling"] 1. to relieve; scratch an ~ 2. ["wish, yen"] (colloq.) an ~ to + inf. (she had an ~ to go bowling)
itching I *adj.* (colloq.) (cannot stand alone) 1. ~ for (he's ~ for a fight) 2. ~ to + inf. (he's ~ to start fighting)
itching II *n.* 1. to cause ~ 2. to alleviate, relieve (the) ~
itchy *adj.* to feel ~ all over
item *n.* 1. a luxury ~ 2. a budget ~ 3. a collector's ~ (BE also *collector's piece*) 4. a news ~ 5. a vocabulary ~ 6. ~ by ~ (she answered all their objections ~ by ~) 7. (misc.) an ~ of clothing/food/furniture/vocabulary ...; an ~ of considerable importance/interest; an ~ on an agenda (what's the next ~ on the agenda?)
itinerary *n.* 1. to plan (out), prepare an ~ 2. a tentative ~ (we followed the tentative ~ she had prepared, which included various items of interest) 3. according to an ~
ivy *n.* 1. ~ climbs 2. (misc.) the ivy-covered walls of an ancient university; (US) poison ~

J

jab I *n.* ["short punch"] 1. to throw a ~ 2. a left; right ~ 3. a ~ to (a left ~ to the head) ["injection"] (BE) 4. to give smb. a ~ 5. to get; have a ~ 6. a booster; flu ~

jab II *v.* 1. (D; intr.) to ~ at (he ~bed at the other boxer with his left) 2. (D; tr.) to ~ in (she ~bed me in the ribs) 3. (d; tr.) to ~ into (she ~bed a knife into the roast) 4. (D; tr.) to ~ with (she ~bed the roast with a knife)

jabber *v.* (D; intr.) to ~ about

jack *n.* ["human being"] (esp. BE) (colloq.) every man ~ (see also *jack-of-all-trades* at **trade I** *n.*)

jackal *n.* a pack of ~s

jackass *n.* a damned; stupid ~

jacket *n.* ["garment for the upper body"] 1. a battle (AE); bulletproof (BE); dinner; donkey (BE); field; flak; pea; smoking; sport (AE), sports ~ (see also **life jacket**) ["cover"] 2. (AE) a record ~ 3. a dust ~ ("cover for a book") ["potato skin"] 4. to bake potatoes in their ~s

jackpot *n.* 1. to win the ~ 2. to hit the ~ (also fig.)

jacks *n.* to play (a game of) ~

jag *n.* (colloq.) (esp. AE) ["state of intoxication"] 1. to have a ~ on ["spell"] 2. a crying ~

jail I *n.* 1. to go to, be sent to ~ (he went to ~ for his crime; she was sent to ~ for shoplifting) 2. to keep smb. in ~ 3. to serve/spend time in ~ 4. to release smb. from ~ 5. to be released from ~ 6. to break ~; to break out of, escape from ~

jail II *v.* (D; tr.) to ~ for (to be ~ed for fraud; to be ~ed for life)

jailbreak *n.* 1. to attempt; make a ~ 2. a daring; mass ~

jam I *n.* ["food made by boiling fruit with sugar"] 1. to spread ~ (on bread) = to spread (bread) with ~ 2. apricot; blackberry, blueberry; cherry; gooseberry; grape; peach; plum; quince; (red) raspberry; strawberry ~

jam II *n.* ["blockage"] 1. a log; traffic ~ ["difficult situation"] 2. (to be/get) in a ~

jam III *v.* 1. to ~ solidly; tightly 2. (D; tr.) to ~ in (she ~med her fingers in the door; or: she got her fingers ~med in the door) 3. (d; intr., tr.) to ~ into (they all tried to ~ (themselves) into the small room; he ~med everything into one suitcase) 4. (d; tr.) to ~ on (he ~med a hat on his head) 5. (D; tr.) to ~ with (the street was ~med with traffic) 6. (N; used with an adjective) to ~ smt. full; solid; tight

jamboree *n.* a boy scout; girl scout ~

jam-packed *adj.* ~ with (the street was ~ with traffic)

jangle *v.* (D; intr.) to ~ on ("to irritate") (to ~ on smb.'s nerves)

janitor *n.* see **superintendant**

jar I *n.* ["jolt"] 1. to feel a ~ 2. a slight ~

jar II *v.* 1. (d; intr.) to ~ against ("to strike") (I ~red against the table) 2. (d; intr.) to ~ on ("to irritate") (the noise ~red on my nerves) 3. (d; intr.) ("to clash") to ~ with 4. (N; used with an adjective) to ~ a tooth loose

jar III *n.* ["container"] 1. a biscuit (BE), cookie (AE) ~ 2. an earthenware; glass; Mason (esp. AE); plastic; stone ~

jargon *n.* 1. to speak in, use ~ 2. computer; legal; medical; military; professional, technical, trade ~ 3. a piece of ~ (to use a piece of ~ that no one else can understand)

jaunt *n.* ["pleasure trip"] 1. to go on a ~ 2. a ~ through; to

javelin *n.* to hurl, throw the ~

jaw I *n.* 1. to move one's ~ (his ~ was broken and he could not move it) 2. to set one's ~ (she set her ~ in determination) 3. to dislocate one's ~ 4. the lower; upper ~ 5. (misc.) to snatch victory from the ~s of defeat

jaw II *v.* (colloq.) 1. (AE) (D; intr.) ("to speak angrily") to ~ about; at 2. (BE) (D; intr.) ("to chat") to ~ about

jealous *adj.* 1. bitterly, blindly, violently ~ 2. ~ of

jealousy *n.* 1. to arouse, cause, stir up ~ (of) 2. to feel ~ 3. to show ~ 4. bitter, blind; fierce; groundless, unfounded; petty; pure, sheer ~ 5. professional ~ 6. a fit of ~ 7. out of ~ 8. ~ at, of, towards (she did it out of sheer ~ of his success)

jeans *n.* 1. to have ~ on, to wear ~ 2. to put on ~ 3. to take off ~ 4. to button up; unbutton; unzip; zip up one's ~ 5. baggy; blue (AE); cut-off; designer; long; skinny; tight ~ 6. a pair of ~

jeer *v.* (D; intr.) to ~ at

jelly *n.* ["food made with boiled fruit juice"] apple; blackberry; cherry; red-currant; grape; mint; peach; plum; quince; (red) raspberry; strawberry ~

jeopardy *n.* 1. to place, put (smb.) in ~ 2. (legal) double ~ 3. in ~ (our lives were in ~)

jerk *n.* ["sudden movement"] with a ~ (the train started with a ~)

jest I *n.* (formal) 1. an idle ~ 2. in ~ (that was said in ~)

jest II *v.* (formal) (D; intr.) to ~ about; with

jester *n.* a court ~

jet I *n.* to fly, pilot a ~ 2. to travel by ~ 3. a jumbo ~ (see also **airplane** 1, 2)

jet II *v.* (P; intr.) ("to fly by jet") to ~ around the world; to ~ across the country; to ~ from New York to London

jewel *n.* 1. to mount a ~ 2. crown; precious; priceless ~s

jewelry, jewellery *n.* 1. antique; costume; imitation; junk ~ 2. a piece of ~

jibe I *n.* see **gibe I**

jibe II *v.* see **gibe II**

jibe III *v.* (colloq.) (esp. AE) (D; intr.) ("to agree") to ~ with (her story doesn't ~ with yours)

jiffy *n.* (colloq.) ["short time"] in a ~

jig *n.* to dance, do; play a ~

jigsaw (BE) see **jigsaw puzzle**

jigsaw puzzle *n.* (AE) to do, put together a ~

jingle *n.* 1. to compose, make up a ~ 2. to hum a ~ 3. an advertising; rhyming ~

jinx *n.* (colloq.) (esp. AE) to put a ~ on smb.

jitters *n.* (colloq.) ["panic"] 1. to get; have the ~ 2. to give smb. the ~ 3. a case of the ~ (she had a bad case of the ~)

job *n.* ["task"] 1. to do; finish a ~ 2. to take on a ~ 3. a backbreaking; difficult, hard; dirty; time-consuming ~ 4. odd ~s (he does odd ~s) 5. a ~ to + inf. (it was quite a ~ to find him = it was quite a ~ finding him) ["employment"] 6. to create; find, get, land, take; have a ~ (she got a ~ addressing envelopes; I have a ~ as a receptionist) 7. to apply for a ~ 8. to hunt for, look for a ~ 9. to fill; hold, hold down a ~ (she holds a responsible ~ as an executive secretary in/with a law firm) 10. to give up, quit; resign from a ~ 11. to lose; shed (esp. BE) a ~ (the company is shedding hundreds of ~s!) 12. a cushy, easy, soft; desk ~ 13. a demanding ~ 14. a dead-end; menial ~ 15. a full-time; part-time; permanent; proper (esp. BE); responsible; steady; summer; temporary ~ 16. a ~ as; in; with (he took a ~ in construction; he got a ~ as an announcer with a radio station) 17. at ~ (she was working at two ~s) 18. on the ~ (he is always on the ~) (also fig.) 19. (misc.) to be between ~s; my ~ pays well; right now she is out of a ~; they all walked off the ~ in protest ["criminal act"] (colloq.) 20. to do, pull a ~ 21. an inside ~ ["misc."] 22. the job of ~ (does the ~ of radio announcer require a deep voice?) ["misc."] 23. a snow ~ (AE) ("deceit") (to do a snow ~ on smb. = to give smb. a snow ~); to do a hatchet ~ on smb. ("to criticize smb. harshly"); a put-up ~ ("a prearranged deceitful scheme"); he really did a ~ on his opponent (colloq.) (esp. AE) ("he inflicted a crushing defeat on his opponent") (see also *a job of work* at **work I** *n.*) USAGE NOTE: In colloq. BE, *on the job* can also mean "having sex."

jockey I *n.* a disc (BE), disk (AE) ~

jockey II *v.* 1. (D; intr.) to ~ for (to ~ for position) 2. (d; refl., tr.) to ~ into (to ~ smb. into position)

jog *v.* (P; intr.) to ~ across the park; we ~ged around the track

jogging *n.* 1. to go in for ~ 2. (misc.) to go ~

join *v.* 1. (D; tr.) to ~ for (would you ~ us for a drink?) 2. (d; intr.) to ~ in (they all ~ed in singing the national anthem) 3. (D; tr.) to ~ in (to ~ smb. in a drink; they all ~ed us in singing the national anthem) 4. (D; tr.) to ~ to, with (to ~ one wire to another; they all ~ed hands with one another; to ~ forces with one's allies) 5. (D; intr.) to ~ with (we must ~ with them in fighting tyranny) 6. (misc.) to ~ together (to ~ two wires together) (see also **join together**)

join in *v.* 1. (D; intr.) to ~ as (she ~ed in as a

volunteer) 2. (D; intr.) to ~ with (they all ~ed in with us in singing the national anthem)

joint *n.* 1. (med.) to dislocate a ~ 2. (anatomical) an elbow; hip; knee; shoulder ~ (I tripped and dislocated my shoulder ~) 3. (med.) an arthritic; painful ~ 4. (technical) a ball-and-socket; mortise; riveted; toggle; universal; welded ~ 5. (misc.) (slang) to case a ~ ("to inspect a place before robbing it") (also fig.); to put smt. out of ~ (I tripped and put my shoulder out of ~)

join together *v.* (D; intr.) ~ in; with (to ~ in worship)

join up *v.* (D; intr.) to ~ with (we'll ~ with you in the next town)

joke I *n.* 1. to crack, make, tell a ~ (about) 2. to ad-lib a ~ 3. to play a ~ on 4. to carry a ~ too far 5. to take a ~ (he can't take a ~) 6. to make a ~ of smt. 7. to get ("understand") a ~ 8. a clean; funny; harmless ~ 9. an old, stale; private; standing ~ 10. a practical; sick ~ 11. a blue (BE), coarse, crude, dirty; obscene, off-color, smutty ~ 12. a ~ comes off; falls flat 13. the butt, object of a ~ 14. the point of a ~ 15. a ~ about (she ~d about a woman needing a man like a fish needs a bicycle) 16. (colloq.) no ~ to + inf. (it's no ~ to oppose smb. like her = it's no ~ opposing smb. like her) 17. (misc.) as a ~; to turn smt. into a ~; the ~ was on me

joke II *v.* 1. (D; intr.) to ~ about; with (I was ~king with her about her latest escapade) 2. (L) she ~d that a woman needs a man like a fish needs a bicycle = "a woman needs a man like a fish needs a bicycle," she ~d 3. (misc.) "that can't be true – you must be ~king! = that can't be true – you've got to be ~king!" "you're right – I was only/just ~king."

joker *n.* 1. a practical ~ 2. (cards) ~s wild; a ~ in the pack (also fig.)

joking *n.* 1. ~ apart, aside 2. (misc.) "you've just won the Nobel Prize!" "no ~?!"

jolt I *n.* ["shock"] 1. to give smb. a ~ 2. to get, receive a ~ 3. to feel a ~ 4. a severe ~ 5. a ~ to (it was quite a ~ to her pride) 6. with a ~ (I woke up with a ~)

jolt II *v.* 1. (D; tr.) to ~ into (they were ~ed into action by the shocking news) 2. (D; tr.) to ~ out of (she was finally ~ed out of her depression)

josh *v.* (colloq.) (D; tr.) to ~ about (I was ~ing her about her latest escapade)

jostle *v.* 1. (d; intr.) to ~ for (to ~ for position) 2. (d; intr.) to ~ with (the children were ~ling with each other)

journal *n.* ["diary"] 1. to keep a ~ ["magazine"] 2. to publish, put out a ~ 3. to edit a ~ 4. to subscribe to, take (old-fashioned; esp. BE) a ~ 5. a learned, professional, scholarly; trade ~ 6. a ~ appears, comes out, is published (the ~ comes out quarterly)

journalism *n.* 1. broadcast; print ~ 2. advocacy; check-book; gutter, yellow; investigative, muckraking ~ 3. a piece of ~ (the article was nothing but a piece of cheap gutter ~!)

journey I *n.* 1. to begin, embark on, go on, set

off on, start on a ~ 2. to make, undertake a ~ 3. to break, interrupt a ~ (we broke our ~ to Nairobi at Cairo) 4. an arduous; long; perilous; pleasant; safe; sentimental; short; tiring ~ (we had a pleasant ~) 5. a round-the-world ~ 6. a leg, stretch of a ~ 7. a ~ across; around; from; into; through; to 8. during; throughout a ~ 9. on a ~ (they were on a ~ to Europe) 10. (misc.) the ~ out; the ~ back/home; (have a) safe ~! ("bon voyage!")

journey II *v.* (P; intr.) to ~ across the desert; to ~ around the world

joust *v.* (D; intr.) ("to compete") 1. to ~ for (to ~ for position) 2. to ~ with

jowls *n.* heavy ~

joy *n.* 1. to express; feel ~ 2. to find, take ~ 3. to be bursting with; radiate ~ 4. boundless, deep, great, indescribable, ineffable, overwhelming, pure, sheer, unbounded ~ 5. ~ at, in (they found ~ in helping others) 6. a ~ to (such children are a ~ to their parents) 7. a ~ to + inf. (such children are a ~ to behold = it's a ~ to behold such children) 8. (a) ~ that + clause (she could not hide her ~ that everyone was safe) 9. for, with ~ (to dance with ~; to jump for ~ at such good news) 10. to smb.'s ~ (to our great ~, our friends will be able to come)

joyful *adj.* ~ about, over

joyride *n.* to go for, on a ~

jubilant *adj.* ~ about, at, over (they were ~ over their victory)

jubilation *n.* 1. to express; feel ~ 2. ~ about, at, over (~ over a victory)

jubilee *n.* 1. to celebrate a ~ 2. a diamond; golden; silver ~

Judaism *n.* Ashkenazi; Conservative; Hasidic; Liberal (BE), Progressive (BE); Orthodox; Reform; Sephardic ~ USAGE NOTE: *Liberal Judaism* and *Progressive Judaism* in Great Britain are approximately equivalent to *Reform Judaism* in North America. *Reform Judaism* in Great Britain is approximately equivalent to *Conservative Judaism* in North America.

judge I *n.* 1. a fair, impartial; harsh, severe; lenient ~ 2. a hanging ("severe") ~ 3. a circuit; district; itinerant; trial ~ 4. (sports) a field ~ (the field judges' decision is final!) 5. (mil.) a ~ advocate; a ~ advocate general 6. a panel of ~s 7. (misc.) the ~ directed the jury to find for the defendant; a good ~ of character

judge II *v.* 1. to ~ fairly, impartially; harshly, severely, sternly; leniently 2. (d; intr.) to ~ by, from (~ging by appearances; to ~ from the facts) 3. (colloq.) (L) I ~ed that the project was impractical 4. (M) I ~ed the project to be impractical 5. (N; used with an adj.) the project was ~d impractical 6. (Q) I cannot ~ whether the project is practical or impractical

judgment, judgement *n.* 1. to display, exercise, show ~ (she always exercises good ~) 2. to form, make a ~ 3. to hand down (AE), pass, pronounce,

render ~ on 4. to sit in ~ on (how dare you sit in ~ on me!) 5. to defer, reserve, suspend ~ 6. bad, poor; good, sound; impaired; sober ~ (to display poor ~) 7. a moral; snap; value ~ 8. a ~ against; for 9. a ~ that + clause (I repeat my ~ that the project is impractical) 10. in smb.'s ~ (in my ~, the project is impractical) 11. (misc.) an error of ~; use your own ~; I agreed against my better ~ (see also *rush to judgment* at **rush I**)

judiciary *n.* the federal (US) ~

judicious *adj.* (formal) ~ to + inf. (it was hardly ~ of you to speak to the press like that!)

juggle *v.* (D; intr.) to ~ with (they shouldn't be ~ling with the figures)

jugular *n.* ["jugular vein"] to go for the ~ (colloq.) ("to attempt to finish off")

juice *n.* 1. digestive, gastric ~s 2. apple; fruit; grape; grapefruit; lemon; orange; pineapple; tomato; vegetable ~

jump I *n.* 1. to clear, take a ~ (on horseback) 2. to make a ~ (with a parachute), to make a parachute ~ 3. (sports) the broad (AE), long; high; ski; triple ~ 4. (sports) a water ~ 5. a delayed (parachute) ~ 6. (basketball) the center ~ 7. a quantum ~ 8. a ~ from; to 9. a ~ in (a ~ in profits) 10. (misc.) to get the ~ on smb. ("to anticipate smb."); to give a ~ (the sound of the bell made me give a ~); with a ~ (I woke up with a ~)

jump II *v.* 1. (d; intr.) to ~ across (to ~ across a stream) 2. (d; intr.) to ~ at ("to be eager for") (to ~ at an opportunity) 3. (d; intr.) to ~ for, with (to ~ for joy) 4. (d; intr.) to ~ from, off (she ~ed from her chair; he ~ed off the roof) 5. (d; intr.) to ~ from; to (to ~ from one topic to another) 6. (d; intr.) ("to leap") to ~ into; onto (the child ~ed into bed; the dog ~ed onto the sofa) 7. (d; intr.) to ~ on ("to attack") (he ~ed on his opponent) 8. (d; intr.) to ~ out of (to ~ out of a window) 9. (d; intr.) to ~ over (to ~ over a fence) 10. (d; intr.) to ~ to (to ~ to one's feet) 11. (d; intr.) ("to rush") to ~ to (to ~ to conclusions; to ~ to smb.'s defense) 12. (misc.) to ~ down smb.'s throat ("to berate smb."); to ~ up and down (for joy); to ~ clear of the wreckage; she ~ed out of her chair

jump down *v.* (D; intr.) to ~ from, off; to (he ~ed down from/off the roof to the ground)

jump off *v.* (d; intr.) to ~ from; to (he ~ed off from the roof to the ground; she ~ed off to a good start)

jump up *v.* 1. (D; intr.) to ~ from (she ~ed up from her chair) 2. (D; intr.) to ~ on, onto, to (to ~ onto the table; he ~ed up from the ground onto/to the roof) 3. (D; intr.) to ~ out of (she ~ed up out of her chair)

jumpy *adj.* (colloq.) ["nervous"] ~ about

junction *n.* at a ~

juncture *n.* ["transition"] 1. (ling.) close; open; terminal ~ ["situation"] 2. a critical ~ (we had reached a critical ~) 3. at a certain ~ (we were at a critical ~)

jungle *n.* ["tropical forest"] ["rain forest"] 1. a dense;

teeming; tropical ~ 2. in a ~ ["dangerous place"] 3. an asphalt, concrete; blackboard ~ 4. in a ~

junior I *adj.* 1. ~ in (~ in rank) 2. ~ to (he is ~ to me by three years; "'Dockery was ~ to you, Wasn't he?' said the Dean." – Philip Larkin, "Dockery and Son," 1963)

junior II *n.* 1. ~ by (he is my ~ by three years) 2. (AE) a college; high-school ~

junket *n.* (esp. AE) ["pleasure trip"] 1. to go on a ~ 2. a fact-finding ~ 3. a ~ to (the legislators went on a ~ to Hawaii)

junta *n.* 1. a military; revolutionary; ruling ~ 2. a member of a ~ 3. by ~ (government by ~)

jurisdiction *n.* 1. to claim; exercise; have; obtain ~ 2. local ~ 3. original; primary ~ (a court of original ~) 4. ~ over (to have ~ over a case) 5. outside; under, within a ~ (that case is under the ~ of this court) 6. (misc.) to fall within the ~ of a court; to accept (or reject) the ~ of a court

jurisprudence *n.* analytical; medical ~

juror *n.* 1. to challenge; dismiss a (prospective) ~ 2. to suborn a ~ 3. an alternate (AE); prospective ~

jury *n.* 1. to convene, empanel, swear in a ~ 2. to charge, instruct; sequester a ~ (the judge charged the ~) 3. to dismiss a ~ 4. to fix ("corrupt"), tamper with a ~ 5. to serve on a ~ 6. a hung ("deadlocked") ~ 7. a grand (US); petit; trial ~ 8. a blue-ribbon (AE) ("special") ~ 9. a ~ deliberates 10. a ~ arrives at, comes to, reaches a verdict 11. (misc.) the ~ is still out ("the jury is still deliberating"); the ~ is still out on him ("a final decision has still not been reached concerning him"); (a) trial by ~; a ~ of one's peers

just *adj.* 1. ~ of 2. ~ to, towards 3. ~ to + inf. (was it ~ of/for you to accuse me without proof?) 4. ~

that + clause (was it ~ that I was/should be accused without proof?)

justice *n.* ["rules of law"] ["administration of law"] 1. to administer, dispense, mete out, render ~ 2. to obstruct ~ 3. to deny; pervert (the course of) ~ 4. to temper ~ with mercy 5. divine; poetic ~ 6. frontier (AE); rough; summary ~ 7. ~ prevails 8. a miscarriage; parody, travesty of ~ 9. to bring (a criminal) to ~ 10. (misc.) the scales of ~; ~ is blind (fig.) ["recognition, appreciation"] 11. to do ~ to (her portrait does not do ~ to her/her portrait does not do her ~; she's strict – but, to do her ~, she's fair) 12. in ~ to (she's strict – but, in ~ to her, she's fair) ["judge"] 13. an associate (esp. US); chief (esp. US) ~; Lord Chief Justice (GB); Supreme Court ~ (esp. US) ["magistrate"] 14. a traffic-court ~; a ~ of the peace USAGE NOTE: The plural of *Lord Chief Justice* is *Lords Chief Justice.*

justification *n.* 1. to find ~ for 2. in ~ of

justified *adj.* 1. completely, fully, totally ~ 2. ~ in (are we ~ in assuming that she will attend?)

justify *v.* 1. (B) can you ~ your actions to me? 2. (G) nothing ~fies cheating on an exam 3. (K) what ~fied his being late?; desperation can hardly ~ his cheating on the exam!

jut out *v.* 1. (D; intr.) to ~ from; over (the balcony ~s out from the hotel over the swimming pool) 2. (D; intr.) to ~ into (the cliff ~s out into the sea)

juxtapose *v.* (D; tr.) to ~ with (to ~ one idea with another = to ~ two ideas (with each other))

juxtaposed *adj.* ~ with (one idea ~ with another = two ideas ~ (with each other))

juxtaposition *n.* in ~ with (one idea in ~ with another = two ideas in ~ (with each other))

K

kangaroo *n.* 1. ~s hop, jump, leap 2. (Australian) a mob of ~s 3. a young ~ is a joey
kayak *n.* to paddle a ~
keel *n.* on an even ~ ("well-balanced")
keel over *v.* (D; intr.) to ~ from (to ~ from the heat)
keen *adj.* ["very interested"] (esp. BE) 1. ~ on (he's ~ on her; she's ~ on music; she's ~ on passing the examination) ["eager"] (BE) 2. ~ to + inf. (she is ~ to pass the examination) 3. (misc.) as ~ as mustard (BE); mad ~ = very ~ (she's mad ~ on passing the examination = she's mad ~ to pass the examination)
keep I *n.* ["maintenance"] to earn one's ~
keep II *v.* 1. (D; tr.) ("to have") to ~ about (esp. BE), around (do you ~ a screwdriver around the house?) 2. (d; intr.) to ~ after ("to keep persuading") (~ after the children to clean up after themselves; they kept after me to buy a new car) 3. (d; tr.) to ~ at ("to hold") (she kept them at their studies) 4. (d; tr.) ("to hold") to ~ for (the librarian will ~ the book for you) 5. (d; intr.) to ~ from ("to refrain") (she could not ~ from talking) 6. (d; tr.) ("to conceal") to ~ from (to ~ a secret from smb.) 7. (d; refl., tr.) ("to hold back"); ("to prevent") to ~ from (the rain kept us from going; don't ~ her from her work; you cannot ~ Romeo and Juliet from getting married; she could not ~ herself from talking) 8. (d; tr.) ("to hold") to ~ in (to ~ smb. in ignorance; to ~ a car in a garage) 9. (d; intr.) ("to remain") to ~ off (~ off the grass) 10. (d; tr.) ("to hold") to ~ off (~ the children off the street) 11. (d; intr.) ("to remain") to ~ out of (~ out of my way; I kept out of their quarrel) 12. (d; tr.) ("to hold") to ~ out of (~ the guests out of the house) 13. (d; intr.) ("to be confined") to ~ to (she kept to her room) 14. (d; intr.) ("to continue") to ~ to (to ~ to the right) 15. (D; tr.) ("to reserve") to ~ to (to ~ a secret to oneself) 16. (G) ("to continue") she kept reading; she kept repeating the same thing 17. (J) ("to cause") he kept us waiting 18. (N; used with an adjective, noun, past participle) ("to maintain"); ("to hold") she kept us busy; they kept us prisoner; the fire kept us warm; we kept ourselves warm by the fire; she kept the children amused with her stories 19. (s) ("to remain") to ~ quiet; we kept warm by the fire (see also *to keep kosher* at **kosher**) 20. ("misc.") to ~ (to the) right; does butter ~ well in a refrigerator?
keep abreast *v.* 1. (d; intr.) ("to be informed") to ~ of (she kept abreast of the news) 2. (D; refl., tr.) ("to inform") to ~ of (she kept herself abreast of the news)
keep ahead *v.* (D; intr.) ("to remain in front") to ~ of (he kept (well) ahead of his rivals)

keep aloof *v.* (D; intr.) to ~ from ("to remain at a distance from") (she kept aloof from the others)
keep away *v.* (D; intr., tr.) to ~ from (he kept away from us; she kept the dogs (well) away from the children)
keep back *v.* (D; tr.) to ~ from (they kept her back from the crowd)
keep clear *v.* (D; intr., tr.) to ~ of (to ~ (well) clear of him; they kept the roads clear of snow)
keeping *n.* ["care"] 1. in ~ (in safe ~; to leave smt. in smb.'s ~) ["conformity"] 2. in ~ with (in ~ with regulations) 3. out of ~ with
keep on *v.* (G) ("to continue") she kept on reading; she kept on repeating the same thing
keep up *v.* 1. (D; intr.) to ~ with ("to remain on the same level with") (I ran to ~ with the others; she worked hard to ~ with the other students) 2. (misc.) to ~ with the Joneses ("to strive to have as much and be as successful as other people")
keg *n.* a powder ~
kelter (BE) see **kilter**
ken *n.* ["understanding"] beyond; within smb.'s ~
kettle *n.* 1. to put a ~ up to boil 2. (esp. BE) to put a ~ on ("to prepare tea or coffee") 3. a teakettle 4. a ~ boils; whistles 5. (misc.) (colloq.) a fine ~ of fish ("a mess"); a different ~ of fish ("smb. very different")
kettledrum *n.* to play a ~
key I *n.* ["device for turning the bolt of a door"] 1. to duplicate; make a ~ 2. to insert, put in a ~ 3. to turn a ~ (in a lock) 4. to fit, match a ~ 5. a duplicate; master; passkey; skeleton ~ 6. ~s dangle (on a chain); fit (into locks); open (doors) 7. a bunch of ~s 8. a ~ to (a ~ to a door) (see also *under lock and key* at **lock I** *n.*) ["solution"] 9. a ~ to (to hold the ~ to a mystery; a ~ to the exercises in a textbook; the ~ to the diagram explains everything in it; is hard work the ~ to success?) ["system of notes"] (mus.) 10. a high; low; major; minor ~ 11. in a (certain) ~ (played in the ~ of C) 12. off ~ (to sing off ~) ["button on a keyboard"] 13. to press, strike a ~ 14. to jam a ~ 15. (on a typewriter) a backspace; dead; shift ~ 16. (on a computer) a control; escape; function, soft; return ~ ["device for turning on the ignition in a car"] 17. an ignition ~
key II *v.* see **keyed**
keyboard *n.* 1. a computer; typewriter ~ 2. a piano ~ 3. a standard ~
keyed *adj.* (esp. BE) (cannot stand alone) ~ to (~ to the needs of our armed forces; our plants are ~ to producing civilian aircraft)
keyed up *adj.* ["psychologically ready"] ["tense"] ~ about; for, over ((all) ~ for the big game)
keyhole *n.* to look through, peep through a ~
keypunch *n.* to operate a ~
keystone *n.* a ~ of, to (AE) (is hard work the ~ of success?)
kibosh *n.* (colloq.) ["end"] to put the ~ on smt.
kick I *n.* ["blow delivered with the foot"] 1. to give

smb. a ~ 2. a nasty, vicious ~ 3. a ~ in (a ~ in the groin) 4. (football, rugby) a drop ~ 5. (soccer) a free; penalty ~ ["thrill"] (slang) 6. to get a ~ out of smt. ["strong effect"] (slang) 7. to have a ~ (this vodka has a ~ to it)

kick II v. 1. (colloq.) (d; tr.) to ~ out of ("to expel") (he was ~ed out of school) 2. (P; tr.) they ~ed sand in my face; she ~ed the ball over the fence

kick off v. (slang) (d; intr.) to ~ by; with ("to begin") (they ~ed off the conference with a cocktail party = they ~ed off the conference by having a cocktail party)

kick out v. (d; intr.) to ~ at (the mule ~ed out at the farmer)

kicks n. (colloq.) ["thrill"] (just) for ~ (they did it for ~)

kid v. (colloq.) (D; tr.) ("to tease good-naturedly") to ~ about (they ~ded him about his paunch)

kid around v. (colloq.) (D; intr.) ("to fool") to ~ with

kid gloves n. to treat smb. with ~ ("to treat smb. with great deference or mildness")

kidney n. ["organ"] 1. to transplant a ~ 2. an artificial; floating ~ ["sort"] (formal) 3. of a certain ~ (people of that/his ~ are not to be trusted!)

kill I n. 1. to make a ~ (the lion made the ~) 2. at the ~ (to be in at the ~) 3. (misc.) to close in/go in/move in for the ~

kill II v. 1. to ~ (smb.) outright 2. (usu. mil.) ~ed in action 3. (colloq.) (R) it just ~s me to think about the money we lost (see also *to kill smb. with kindness* at **kindness**)

killer n. ["murderer"] 1. a copycat; multiple, serial; psychopathic ~ 2. a ~ strikes 3. (misc.) a giant-killer ("one that defeats a more powerful opponent, as David killed Goliath")

killing n. ["putting to death"] 1. (a) mercy ~ ["large profit"] (colloq.) 2. to make a ~

kilter n. ["order"] out of ~

kin n. 1. next of ~ (to notify the next of ~) 2. (misc.) kith and ~ ("friends and relations")

kind I adj. 1. ~ of (that was very/most ~ of you) 2. ~ to (~ to animals) 3. ~ + inf. (it was ~ of you to help us) 4. (misc.) ~ and courteous; would you be ~ enough to help us? = would you be so ~ as to help us?

kind II n. ["sort"] 1. of a ~ (of all ~s; of several ~s; two of a ~; a person of that ~ = that ~ of person) 2. (misc.) ~ of thing (always going on about his enemies, his problems – that ~ of thing); to like all ~s of music; "was it satisfactory?" "it was nothing of the ~ – it was awful!" ["same manner"] 3. in ~ (to be paid (back) in ~; to respond in ~) ["goods"] 4. in ~ (to pay smb. back in ~ rather than in cash)

kindergarten n. to attend, go to (a) ~

kind of adv. (colloq.) ["more or less, rather"] I ~ expected it (to happen); it was ~ nice, actually

kindly adv. ["readily"] not to take ~ to ("not to accept readily") (I don't take ~ to being called a fool!)

kindness n. ["quality of being good, kind"] 1. to display, show ~ 2. elementary; human ~ 3. ~ to, towards 4. out of ~ (she did it out of elementary human ~) 5. an act of ~ 6. (misc.) the milk of human ~; to kill smb. with ~ ["good, kind act"] 7. to do smb. a ~ 8. to repay, return a ~

king n. 1. to crown a ~ 2. to crown; proclaim smb. ~ 3. to depose, dethrone a ~ 4. (chess) to checkmate a ~ 5. a despotic; popular; strong; weak ~ 6. a ~ ascends, mounts, succeeds to the throne 7. a ~ reigns; rules 8. a ~ abdicates 9. (misc.) to toast the ~; how was life under the old ~?

kingdom n. the animal; mineral; plant, vegetable ~

king's evidence n. (BE) to turn ~ (see also **queen's evidence**, **state's evidence**)

kink n. ["imperfection"] to iron out the ~s

kinship n. 1. to feel (a) ~ with smb. 2. (a) ~ between, with

kiosk n. a telephone ~ (BE; CE has *telephone booth*)

kiss I n. 1. to blow, throw; give (smb.) a ~ 2. to steal a ~ 3. an affectionate; fervent, passionate; French; goodnight; loving, tender ~ 4. a ~ on (to plant a ~ on smb.'s cheek) 5. (misc.) the ~ of death; (BE) the ~ of life ("mouth-to-mouth resuscitation") (AE has *cardiopulmonary resuscitation* or *CPR*); to give smb. a hug and a ~

kiss II v. 1. to ~ passionately; tenderly 2. (D; tr.) to ~ on (she ~ed the baby on the cheek) 3. (O; can be used with one object) (she ~ed him goodnight; they ~ed goodnight)

kit n. ["equipment"] 1. a drum; first-aid; instruction; mess; sewing; shaving; survival; tool ~ ["clothing and equipment"] (BE) 2. camping; travelling ~ 3. (misc.) (mil.) (BE) a ~ bag

kitchen n. a communal; field; fitted (BE); soup ~

kite n. 1. to fly a ~ 2. (misc.) (AE; colloq.) go fly a ~! ("go away")

kith n. ~ and kin ("friends and relations")

kitty n. ["fund, pool"] in the ~ (how much is in the ~?)

knack n. ["skill"] 1. to get; have; lose the ~ of smt. 2. an uncanny ~ 3. a ~ for, of (she has a ~ for getting into trouble; she has the ~ of getting what she wants) 4. a ~ to (there's a ~ to baking a good cake)

knee I n. 1. to bend one's ~s 2. to dislocate; wrench one's ~ 3. a trick ("defective") ~ 4. ~s buckle 5. (fig.) at smb.'s ~ (she learned the language at her mother's ~) 6. (usu. fig.) on bended ~ (s) (I beg you for mercy on bended ~!) 7. (misc.) to drop/fall to one's ~s; to get down on one's ~s; to get down on one ~ (as when proposing marriage); will the credit crunch bring the economy to its ~s?; I go all weak at the ~s whenever she smiles at me

knee II v. (D; tr.) to ~ in (she ~d her attacker in the groin)

kneel *v.* 1. (D; intr.) to ~ before 2. (misc.) to ~ in prayer

knell *n.* 1. to sound, toll the ~ 2. the death ~ (for, of) (the government's decision has sounded the death ~ for heavy industry in this country)

knife *n.* ["instrument for cutting"] 1. to draw, pull a ~ (on smb.) 2. to brandish, wield a ~ 3. to plunge a ~ into smb. 4. to put a ~ to smb.'s throat 5. to stab smb. with a ~ 6. to sharpen, whet a ~ 7. a blunt, dull; sharp ~ 8. a bowie; boy-scout; clasp; hunting ~; penknife, pocketknife; Swiss Army (T) ~ 9. a bread; butcher (esp. AE), butcher's (esp. BE); butter; carving; electric; fish; kitchen; paring; steak; table ~ 10. a flick (BE; AE has *switchblade*); sheath; trench ~ 11. a paper ~ (BE; AE has *letter opener*) 12. (misc.) a ~ and fork (some people prefer chopsticks to a ~ and fork); to go through smt. like a ~ through butter ("very easily and quickly, without meeting resistance") (see also *knife crime* at **crime**) ["surgery"] (old-fashioned) 13. under the ~ (she went under the ~ yesterday and was under the ~ for two hours)

knight *n.* 1. to dub, make smb. a ~ 2. a ~ errant; a ~ in shining armor (fig.) 3. a ~'s wife is a lady

knighthood *n.* to bestow, confer a ~ on, upon

knit *v.* (C) ~ a scarf for me; or: ~ me a scarf

knitting *n.* ["action of knitting"] 1. to do ~ 2. a piece of ~ ["one's own business"] (colloq.) (esp. AE) 3. to mind, stick to, tend to one's (own) ~

knob *n.* 1. to turn, twist a ~ 2. a control ~

knock I *n.* ["thumping noise"] 1. engine ~ 2. a gentle; loud ~ 3. a ~ at, on (a ~ at/on the door) ["blow"] (colloq.) 4. hard ~s (she has taken some hard ~s in her life)

knock II *v.* 1. ("to rap") to ~ gently; loudly 2. (colloq.) (d; intr.) ("to wander") to ~ about, around (he ~ed around the western part of the state for a few months) 3. (d; intr., tr.) ("to strike") to ~ against (she ~ed her head against the ceiling; she ~ed a stick against the ceiling) 4. (D; intr.) ("to rap") to ~ at, on (to ~ at/on the door) 5. (d; tr.) ("to pound") to ~ into (to ~ some sense into smb.'s head) 6. (d; tr.) ("to fell") to ~ off (he ~ed me off my feet) 7. (d; tr.) ("to remove") to ~ out of (the impact ~ed two teeth out of his mouth) 8. (d; tr.) to ~ to (she ~ed him to the ground) 9. (N; used with an adjective) ("to render by striking") to ~ smb. cold/unconscious 10. (P; tr.) ("to render by striking") she ~ed me down; she ~ed me out; she accidentally ~ed the vase off the table 11. (misc.) ~ it off! (slang) ("stop!")

knock down *v.* (colloq.) (BE) (D; tr.) ("to persuade to reduce a price or to get a reduced price") to ~ by; from; to (I ~ed him/his price down from £20 to £10 – so the price was ~ed down by £10!)

knockout *n.* 1. to score a ~ 2. a technical ~

knot *n.* 1. to tie; tighten a ~ 2. to loosen; undo, untie a ~ 3. the Gordian ~ (to cut the Gordian ~) 4. a

loose; tight ~ 5. a bowline; granny; reef, square ~ 6. (misc.) (all) tied up in ~s

know I *n.* in the ~ (about)

know *v.* 1. (D; intr.) to ~ about, of (we knew about the incident) 2. (D; tr.) to ~ as (I knew her as a colleague) 3. (d; tr.) to ~ by (to ~ smb. by name; I knew her by sight only) 4. (d; tr.) to ~ from ("to be able to differentiate") (the little child doesn't ~ a dog from a cat) 5. (E) (esp. AE) does he ~ to call you if he gets lost? 6. (H; only in the past and perfect) I've never known him to lose his temper 7. (BE) (I; only in the past and perfect) I've never known him lose his temper 8. (L) we ~ that they will come; she employed him even ~ing full well that he had spent time in prison!; does he ~ that he should call you if he gets lost? 9. (formal) (M) I ~ him to be a fool 10. (Q) she ~s how to drive 11. (misc.) to ~ smt. for a fact ("to know smt. to be true"); to ~ smt. by heart; to ~ smt. inside out, to ~ smt. backwards and forwards; to ~ smt. like the back of one's hand; you should ~ enough not to have stayed out late; you should ~ better; you should have ~n better than to stay out late; she always ~s best; to ~ for certain/for sure; "how well do you ~him?" "I ~ him intimately but she hardly ~s him at all." (see also **known**)

know-how *n.* 1. the necessary ~ (he doesn't have the necessary ~ for the job) 2. technical ~ 3. the ~ to + inf. (he doesn't have the necessary ~ to do the job)

knowing *n.* there's no ~ (what they'll do)

knowledge *n.* 1. to acquire, accumulate, gain ~ 2. to absorb, assimilate, soak up ~ 3. to have ~ (of a subject) 4. to broaden, deepen one's ~ 5. to brush up (on) one's ~ (of a subject) 6. to demonstrate, display, show ~ 7. to communicate, disseminate; impart ~ 8. to flaunt, parade one's ~ (of a subject) 9. to deny (all) ~ (of smt.) 10. detailed; extensive; profound, thorough ~ 11. rudimentary; slight, superficial ~ 12. direct; inside, intimate; intuitive; practical ~ 13. (a) fluent; reading; speaking; working ~ (to have fluent/a fluent ~ of English; to have reading/a reading ~ of several languages) 14. common ~ 15. (formal) carnal ~ (to have carnal ~ of) 16. ~ about, of 17. the ~ to + inf. (she has enough ~ about the subject to write a good book) 18. the ~ that + clause (it is common ~ that he has spent time in prison; she employed him (even) in the ~ that he had spent time in prison!) 19. to smb.'s ~ (to my ~, she has never been here) 20. to come to smb.'s ~ (it came to our ~ that she had left town) 21. (misc.) to the best of smb.'s ~ (to the best of my ~, she has never been here); a person of great ~

knowledgeable *adj.* ~ about

known *adj.* 1. internationally; nationally; well; widely ~ 2. ~ as (she is ~ as a patron of the arts) 3. ~ for (~ for being witty) 4. ~ to (~ to everyone) 5. (cannot stand alone) ~ to + inf. (she is ~ to frequent that bar; she is ~ to be a patron of the arts; he is ~ to have spent time in prison) 6. ~ that + clause (it is well ~ (to everyone) that he has spent time

in prison) 7. (misc.) better/otherwise ~ as (Samuel
Clemens, better ~ as Mark Twain)

knuckle *n.* 1. to rap smb. on, over the ~s ("to reprimand") (he was rapped over the ~s for being late)
2. to bruise; scrape one's ~ 3. to crack one's ~s 4.
brass ~s (AE; CE has *knuckle duster*)

knuckle down *v.* (D; intr.) to ~ to (to ~ to work)

knuckle under *v.* (D; intr.) ("to submit") to ~ to (to
~ to an aggressor)

kosher *adj.* to keep ~ (they keep ~ in their
household)

kowtow *v.* (d; intr.) to ~ to ("to fawn over") (to ~
to the boss)

kudos *n.* (colloq.) ["praise"] (AE) 1. to earn, win ~
2. ~ to smb. for smt. (~ to our mayor for reducing
taxes!) ["glory, prestige"] (esp. BE) 3. to get ~ for (to
get (a lot of) ~ for reducing taxes) 4. (misc.) the ~
'of/attached to' being Poet Laureate

L

label I *n.* ["sticker"] 1. to affix, attach, put on, stick on; sew on a ~ 2. to bear, carry, have a ~ 3. to remove, take off a ~ 4. an adhesive, gummed ~ 5. a brand; designer; manufacturers'; union ~ (on a garment) ["descriptive phrase in a dictionary entry"] 6. to apply, use a ~ 7. a field; regional; stylistic; temporal; usage ~ ["recording company"] 8. for, on, under a ~ (on which ~ was the song recorded?) ["misc."] 9. to pin a ~ on smb. ("to assign smb. to a category"); a warning ~; a product that does just what it says on the ~ (and does not mislead users)

label II *v.* 1. (d; tr.) to ~ as (he was ~ed as a delinquent) 2. (D; tr.) to ~ with (all items should be ~ed with a price) 3. (N; used with an adjective, noun) her story was ~ed false/a hoax; he was ~ed a delinquent

labeled, labelled *adj.* clearly, correctly ~

labor I labour *n.* ["work"] 1. to do, perform; withdraw ~ (the workers who perform the ~ are threatening to withdraw their ~ and go on strike.) 2. backbreaking; manual, physical; menial; painstaking; productive; sweated (BE), sweatshop; skilled; unskilled ~ 3. a division of ~ 4. (misc.) a ~ of love ["servitude"] 5. forced; hard; slave ~ (he got ten years at hard ~ = he got ten years' hard ~; democratic countries forbid forced ~; slave ~ has been outlawed) ["work force"] 6. casual (BE); child; migrant; organized; seasonal; skilled; unskilled ~ ["giving birth"] 7. to induce ~ 8. to go into ~ 9. a difficult, prolonged, protracted; easy; false ~ 10. in ~ (she was in ~ for five hours)

labor II labour *v.* 1. (d; intr.) to ~ as (to ~ as a migrant worker) 2. (d; intr.) to ~ under (to ~ under a misapprehension/ misconception) 3. (misc.) "we must ~ to be beautiful" – W.B. Yeats (1865–1939), "Adam's Curse"

laboratory *n.* 1. a chemistry; crime; experimental; language; physics; research ~ 2. at, in a ~

laborer, labourer *n.* 1. a common; day; immigrant; itinerant; skilled; unskilled ~ 2. (BE) an agricultural labourer (CE has *farm worker*) 3. (BE) a casual labourer (AE has *transient worker*)

lace I *n.* delicate; exquisite; fine ~ (see also **shoelace**)

lace II *v.* 1. (d; intr.) to ~ into ("to attack verbally") (they ~d into her for being late) 2. (D; tr.) to ~ with ("to add to") (they ~d the punch with rum)

laceration *n.* 1. a deep; minor, superficial; severe 2. multiple ~s 3. to sustain a ~ 4. a ~ to (he sustained multiple ~s to his left arm)

lack I *n.* 1. for ~ of (for ~ of fuel, their planes were grounded) 2. (misc.) no ~ of (there's never any ~ of reasons to be/for being idle!)

lack II *v.* (D; intr.) to ~ for (formal) (we don't ~ for anything)

lacking *adj.* 1. badly, completely, sadly, totally, utterly ~ 2. ~ in (~ in common sense)

lacquer *n.* to apply ~

lad *n.* 1. a young ~ 2. a bunch, group of ~s (a group of ~s and lasses) 3. (BE) a bit of a ~, a bit of a Jack the Lad (who gets into trouble from time to time)

ladder *n.* ["framework with rungs for climbing"] 1. to put up a ~ 2. to steady a ~ 3. to lean a ~ (against a wall) 4. to climb, go up, mount a ~ (he mounted his ~ and is still up/on it) 5. to come down, descend a ~ 6. an aerial; extension; rope ~ 7. an accommodation ~ (over the side of a ship) ["unraveled stitches in a stocking"] (BE; CE has *run*) 8. to get, have a ~ (in) ["path"] 9. the ~ to success ["hierarchy"] 10. a career ~; the social ~ (climbing the career ~)

laden *adj.* 1. fully, heavily ~ 2. ~ with

lady *n.* 1. a leading; young ~ 2. the first ~ ("wife of the President or of a state governor") 3. a bag ~ ("a destitute woman living on the streets") 4. a cleaning; a dinner (BE) ~ (in a school) 5. (misc.) the first ~ of the American theater; (my lords,) ladies and gentlemen...; smb.'s good ~ ("smb.'s wife") (BE) (considered somewhat condescending to women) (and how's your good ~?) (see also *smb.'s lady wife* at **wife**)

lag I *n.* 1. a cultural; time ~ 2. jet ~

lag II *v.* 1. to ~ badly 2. (D; intr.) to ~ behind; in (she ~ged far behind the others in the race) 3. (D; intr.) to ~ by (their party was ~ging by ten points in the polls)

lag behind *v.* 1. (D; intr.) to ~ by (their party was ~ging behind by ten points in the polls = their party was ~ging ten points behind in the polls) 2. (D; intr.) to ~ in (to ~ in one's work)

laid up *adj.* ~ with (~ with the flu)

lake *n.* 1. a deep; dry ~ 2. an artificial ~ 3. the shore of a ~ = a lake ~ 4. across; at, on a ~ (they have a summer bungalow at/on a ~)

lam I *n.* (slang) (esp. AE) ["flight"] on the ~ (she took it on the ~ and was on the ~ for several years) ("she fled and remained in flight")

lam II *v.* (slang) (d; intr.) to ~ into ("to attack physically or verbally")

lamb *n.* ["animal"] 1. a sacrificial ~ 2. ~s bleat 3. (misc.) as gentle as a ~; like a ~ to (the) slaughter ["meat"] 4. to roast; stew ~ 5. roast; stewed ~ (see also *lamb stew* at **stew**) 6. a leg; piece, slice; rack; shoulder of ~ 7. (misc.) a ~ shank

lamb chops *n.* 1. to broil (AE), grill ~ 2. a rack of ~

lame *adj.* 1. ~ in (~ in one leg) 2. to go ~

lament I *n.* 1. a bitter ~ 2. a ~ for

lament II *v.* 1. to ~ bitterly, deeply 2. (D; intr.) to ~ over

lamented *adj.* the late ~ (smb.) (to mourn the passing of the late ~ (John Smith))

lamp *n.* 1. to plug in a ~ 2. to turn on a ~ 3. to light a ~ 4. to unplug a ~ 5. to turn off a ~ 6. an Anglepoise

(T) (BE), arc; bedside; floor (AE), standard (BE); gooseneck; table; wall ~ 7. a blowlamp (BE; CE has *blowtorch*); reading; safety ~; sunlamp; ultraviolet ~ 8. an electric; fluorescent; halogen; incandescent; neon ~ 9. a kerosene (AE), paraffin (BE); oil; spirit ~

lance *n.* to throw a ~

land I *n.* ["soil"]["ground"] 1. to clear ~ (to clear ~ of trees and brush) 2. to cultivate (the), work the ~; irrigate; reclaim (the) ~ 3. to redistribute (the) ~ 4. arable; barren; fertile; grazing, pasture; marginal ~ 5. private; public ~ 6. a plot of ~ ["solid surface of the earth"] 7. to raise, sight ~ (from a ship) 8. to reach ~ 9. dry ~ 10. a body of ~ 11. by ~ (to travel by ~) 12. on (the) ~ ["rural area"] 13. to go back to the ~ ["country"]["domain"] 14. smb.'s native ~ ("This is my own, my native ~!" – Sir Walter Scott (1771–1832)) 15. a promised ~ (we were in the promised ~) ["area"] 16. no man's ~ (in no man's ~; shot while crossing no man's ~) ["misc."] 17. Cloud-Cuckoo Land, Never-Never Land; the Holy Land; the lay (AE)/lie (BE) of the ~

land II *v.* 1. (d; intr., tr.) ("to arrive by air; to cause to land") to ~ at (when do we ~ at Heathrow?) 2. (d; intr., tr.) to ~ in ("to get involved in"; "to involve in") (he ~ed in trouble; such behavior ~ed her in trouble) 3. (d; intr., tr.) to ~ on ("to fall on") (she tripped and ~ed on her back) 4. (colloq.) (O) ("to punch") she ~ed him one in the eye

landfill *n.* a sanitary ~

landing *n.* ["coming down to earth"] 1. to make a ~ 2. a belly; blind; bumpy; crash; emergency; forced; hard; instrument; pancake; three-point ~ 3. a safe; smooth; soft ~ 4. a parachute ~ 5. (misc.) (fig.) after years of boom, is the economy due for a hard uncomfortable ~ or a soft easy one? ["level part of a staircase"] 6. off; on a ~

landing gear *n.* 1. to raise, retract a/the ~ 2. to let down, lower a/the ~ 3. (a) retractable ~

landlord *n.* 1. an absentee; slum ~ 2. (BE) a pub ~

landowner *n.* a big, large ~

landscape *n.* 1. a beautiful, magnificent, picturesque ~ 2. a bleak, gloomy ~ 3. a desert; lunar ~ 4. to dominate the ~ (a nuclear-power station dominated the ~) 5. (misc.) the political ~ (Winston Churchill dominated the British political ~ during World War II)

land up *v.* 1. (d; intr.) to ~ in (he ~ed up in Moscow; he ~ed up in trouble) 2. (s) they ~ed up penniless; she ~ed up drifting from job to job

lane *n.* 1. to change, shift ~s 2. to cross over into, get over into the other ~ 3. the fast (also fig.); inside; outside; overtaking (esp. BE), passing; slow (also fig.) ~ 4. a bicycle, cycle; bus ~ 5. a four-lane highway (AE)/motorway (BE) 6. (BE) the nearside ("left"); offside ("right") ~ 7. an air; sea; shipping ~ 8. in a ~ (you youngsters like life in the fast ~; we oldsters prefer life in the slow ~!)

language *n.* ["linguistic system of communication"] 1.

to use a ~ 2. to plan; standardize a ~ 3. to acquire, master; learn, study a ~ 4. to speak (in) a ~ 5. to butcher, murder a ~ 6. to enrich; purify a ~ 7. (the) spoken; written ~ 8. smb.'s first, native; second ~ 9. a cognate; foreign; international, world; national; official; universal; vehicular; vernacular ~ 10. colloquial, informal; formal; idiomatic; (a) literary, (a) standard; (a) nonstandard; nontechnical; substandard; technical ~ 11. an ancient; artificial; classical; creolized; dead, extinct; living; modern; natural; trade ~ 12. an agglutinative; inflecting; isolating; synthetic; tone ~ 13. an object, target; source; working ~ 14. sign ~ (to communicate in sign ~) ["style of speaking or writing"] 15. to use (a) ~ 16. biblical; elegant; flowery; rich ~ 17. everyday, plain, simple, vernacular; polite ~ 18. abusive; bad, coarse, crude, dirty, foul, nasty, obscene, offensive, street, unprintable, vile, vulgar; blunt, explicit; rough, strong, vituperative ~ 19. children's; diplomatic; men's; PC, politically correct; nonsexist; sexist; women's ~ ["system of signs, symbols used by a computer"] 20. an assembly; computer, machine, programming; high-level ~ ["misc."] 21. ~ acquisition; ~ learning; ~ maintenance; ~ teaching; body ~; to reduce a ~ to writing

languish *v.* (D; intr.) to ~ in (to ~ in prison)

lantern *n.* 1. to light; put out a ~ 2. to shine a ~ on 3. a battery-operated; kerosene (AE), paraffin (BE); propane ~ 4. a ~ flashes; gleams; shines

lap I *n.* ["complete circuit around a track"] 1. to complete, do, finish; drive; run a ~ (they are running the last ~ of the race) 2. on a ~ (they are on the last ~) 3. (misc.) a (BE) ~ of honour/(AE) victory ~; how many ~s do they have to go? ["part of the body from the knees to the waist of a sitting person"] 4. in, on smb.'s ~ (the little girl sat in her mother's ~) 5. (misc.) in the ~ of the gods ("with an uncertain future") (see also *in the lap of luxury* at **luxury**)

lap II *v.* 1. to ~ gently 2. (P) the waves ~ped against the sides of the boat and around and over the people in it

lapse I *n.* 1. a momentary, temporary; occasional ~ (of memory) 2. a linguistic ~ 3. a ~ in, of (a ~ in judgment; we met again after a ~ of several months)

lapse II *v.* (d; intr.) to ~ into (to ~ into a coma)

larceny *n.* 1. to commit ~ 2. aggravated; grand; petty; simple ~

lard I *n.* to render ~

lard II *v.* (formal) (d; tr.) to ~ with (to ~ a speech with biblical references)

larder *n.* a full, well-stocked ~

large *n.* 1. at ~ ("uncaptured") (the prisoner was still at ~) 2. an assemblywoman at ~ ("an assemblywoman who represents several or all districts") 3. by and ~ ("in general")

lark I *n.* ["prank"] 1. as a ~ 2. for a ~ (he did it just for a ~)

lark II *n.* ["type of bird"] 1. ~s sing, warble 2. a bevy of ~s 3. (misc.) as happy as a ~

lash v. 1. (d; intr.) to ~ against (the rain ~ed against the roof) 2. (d; intr.) to ~ at, into (the speakers ~ed into the government) 3. (d; tr.) to ~ into (to ~ a crowd into a fury) 4. (d; tr.) to ~ to (to ~ the cargo to the deck)

lash back v. (D; intr.) to ~ against, at (to ~ at one's critics after their last attacks)

lash out v. (D; intr.) to ~ against, at (to ~ at one's critics before their next attacks)

lass n. 1. a young ~ 2. a bunch, group of ~s (a group of lads and ~es)

lasso n. 1. to throw a ~ 2. to catch with a ~

last I adj., adv. 1. to come (in) ~ (in a race) 2. the ~ to + inf. (she was the first to arrive and the ~ to leave) 3. among the ~ (she was among the first to arrive and among the ~ to leave) 4. at ~; at long ~

last II n. 1. to breathe one's ~ 2. (misc.) to see the ~ of smb.

last III v. 1. (d; intr.) to ~ from; to, till, until (the meeting ~ed from one to three) 2. (P; intr.) the examination ~ed (for) two hours; the food will ~ (us) (for) a week; the meeting ~ed (for) an hour

last post n. ["bugle call"] (BE) the last ~ (see **taps**)

last rites n. 1. to administer, give, perform (the) ~ 2. to receive (the) ~

last word n. 1. to get in, have the ~ (she had the ~ in the argument) 2. to be the ~ (this car is the ~ in speed and style!)

latch v. (colloq.) (d; intr.) to ~ onto (since he didn't know anyone else, he ~ed onto us)

late adj. 1. ~ for (she was ~ for class) 2. ~ in (we were ~ in filing our tax return; I was ~ in getting up) 3. ~ with (they are ~ with the rent) 4. of ~ ("recently") 5. (misc.) the train was five minutes ~

later adv. ~ on

latest n. 1. the ~ about (have you heard the ~ about the elections?) 2. at the ~ (they will arrive tomorrow at the very ~)

lathe n. 1. to operate a ~ 2. a turret; vertical ~

lather n. ["sweating"] 1. to work oneself into a ~ ["foam"] 2. to work up a ~

latitude n. ["freedom of action"] 1. to allow smb. ~ in (we are allowed quite a bit of ~ in selecting our subjects) ["distance measured in degrees north or south of the equator"] 2. high; low ~s 3. at a ~ (at a ~ of ten degrees north)

laudable adj. (formal) ~ to + inf. (it was ~ of you to help them)

laugh I n. 1. to get, raise a ~ (the joke got a big ~) 2. to stifle, suppress a ~ 3. a belly; derisive; forced; hearty, loud; infectious; sardonic; scornful; subdued ~ 4. (misc.) to have the last ~ on smb.; to do smt. for a (bit of a) ~, to do smt. for ~s

laugh II v. 1. to ~ aloud, out loud; hard; loud; uproariously 2. (D; intr.) to ~ about ("to show one's amusement by laughing") (everyone ~ed about the incident) 3. (D; intr.) to ~ at ("to respond to smt. funny by laughter") (to ~ at a joke) 4. (D; intr.) to ~ at ("to show one's derision for") (they ~ed at our

efforts; she ~ed at us and our warnings) 5. (d; tr.) to ~ out of ("to drive out by laughter") (he was ~ed out of court) 6. (D; intr.) to ~ with ("to join with smb. else in laughter") (I'm not ~ing at you – I'm ~ing with you!) 7. (D; intr.) to ~ with (a certain feeling) ("to laugh because of a certain feeling") (I ~ed with relief when I realized I was safe.) 8. (N; used with an adjective) he ~ed himself hoarse 9. (misc.) to ~ up one's sleeve ("to laugh secretly"); to burst out ~ing; sometimes the world seems so absurd you (just) have to ~!; sometimes the world seems so absurd you have to ~ to keep (yourself) from crying! (see also no laughing matter at **matter I**)

laughingstock n. 1. to make a ~ of smb. 2. to be; become a ~

laughter n. 1. to cause, provoke ~ 2. to burst into; dissolve into ~ 3. contagious, infectious; convulsive; derisive; forced; hearty, loud, raucous, uproarious; hysterical; sardonic; scornful; subdued ~ 4. a burst, fit, gale, roar; ripple of ~; peals of ~ 5. (misc.) to double up with ~; to roar with ~; canned ~

launch v. 1. (D; tr.) ("to fire") to ~ against, at (the missiles were ~ed against enemy targets) 2. (d; intr.) to ~ into ("to begin") (to ~ into a tirade)

launcher n. a missile; rocket ~

laundry n. ["clothes, linens that are to be washed or have been washed"] 1. to do (the) ~ 2. to dry; fold; iron; sprinkle the ~ 3. clean; dirty ~ (see also **wash I** n. 1–3) ["establishment for washing clothes, linens"] 4. a self-service ~ 5. at, in a ~ (they work at a ~)

laurels n. 1. to gain, reap, win ~ 2. to rest on one's ~

lava n. 1. to spew ~ (volcanoes spew ~) 2. molten ~ 3. ~ flows

lavatory n. (BE) 1. to go to, need, use the ~ 2. to flush a ~ 3. a gents'; ladies'; public ~ 4. down the ~ (to flush smt. down the ~)

lavish I adj. ~ in, with (~ with donations and praise; ~ in donating money to charity)

lavish II v. (d; tr.) to ~ on (to ~ praise and gifts on smb.)

law n. ["statute, regulation"] 1. to administer, apply, enforce, uphold a ~ 2. to adopt, enact, pass; draft; introduce; promulgate a ~ 3. to obey, observe a ~ 4. to interpret a ~ (courts interpret ~s) 5. to block; veto; vote down a ~ 6. to abrogate, repeal; rescind ~ 7. to annul, repeal, revoke a ~; to declare a ~ unconstitutional (US) 8. to break, flout, violate a ~ 9. to challenge, test; cite; strike down a ~ (in the courts) 10. a fair, just; stringent; unfair ~ 11. a blue (US); ex-post-facto; federal (US); lemon (US); shield (US); state (US); sunset (US); sunshine (US); sus (GB); unwritten; zoning ~; the licensing ~s (GB) 12. a ~ allows; decrees, says; comes into effect, takes effect; forbids, prohibits; requires (the new ~ takes effect next week) 13. ~ about, on; against; for (there is no ~ against fishing) 14. ~ to

+ inf. (they introduced a ~ to rescind the new tax) 15. ~ that + clause (they introduced a ~ that would rescind the new tax; there is a ~ that (says that) all income must be reported) 16. according to, under a ~ (they introduced a ~ under which the new tax would be rescinded; there is a ~ under which all income must be reported) 17. (misc.) dietary ~s; Congress makes ~s ["body of statutes, regulations"] 18. to administer, apply, enforce, uphold the ~ 19. to obey the ~ 20. to interpret the ~ (courts interpret the ~) 21. to break; flout the ~ 22. case; common; constitutional; parliamentary; statutory ~ 23. civil; criminal; military ~ (see also **martial law**) 24. administrative; antitrust; business, commercial; contract; corporate ~ 25. copyright; environmental; family, marriage; immigration; international; labor; maritime; patent; tax ~ 26. canon; Islamic, Sharia; Mosaic; Roman ~ (does canon ~ require it, allow it, or forbid it?) 27. the supreme ~ (of the land) 28. according to the ~ 29. against; outside; within the ~ (it is against the ~ to smoke in an elevator) 30. as the ~ stands, by ~ (by ~ you are not allowed to smoke in an elevator) ["jurisprudence"] ["lawyer's profession"] 31. to practice ~ 32. to study ~ ["principle"] 33. Mendel's; Newton's; Parkinson's; the periodic; Sod's (colloq.) (BE) ~ 34. the ~ of diminishing returns; the ~ of gravity; the ~s of motion; the ~ of supply and demand; the ~ of the jungle (also fig.) ["misc."] 35. to take the ~ into one's own hands; to lay down the ~; (BE) to go to ~; in the eyes of the ~; (AE) an attorney at ~; everyone is equal under the ~; the letter of the ~; the spirit of the ~; a higher ("divine") ~; natural ~; above the ~ (bureaucrats who think they are above the ~ and unaccountable for their actions to anybody)

law and order n. 1. to establish; keep, maintain; restore ~ 2. a breakdown in/of ~

lawful adj. 1. ~ for (is smoking ~ for minors?) 2. ~ to + inf. (is it ~ for minors to smoke?)

lawn n. 1. to mow, trim a ~ 2. to sprinkle, water a ~

lawn mower n. to operate, work a ~

lawsuit n. 1. to bring, file, institute; lose; settle; win a ~ (to settle a ~ out of court) 2. to dismiss a ~ 3. a civil; class-action; frivolous; libel; malpractice; pending ~ 4. a ~ against; over (to bring a class-action ~ against the government over civil liberties)

lawyer n. 1. to hire, retain a ~ 2. a practicing ~ 3. a civil-rights; corporation; criminal; defense ~; divorce; (esp. AE) trial ~ (BE prefers *barrister*) 4. (AE) a Philadelphia ("shrewd") ~ 5. (humorous; often mil.) a barrack-room (esp. BE), guardhouse (esp. AE) ~ ("a soldier who claims to know all about military law"); a jailhouse ~ (AE)

lax adj. 1. ~ about (they are very ~ about their appearance; the police were ~ about law-enforcement) 2. ~ in (the police were ~ in enforcing the law)

laxative n. 1. to take a ~ 2. to prescribe a ~ 3. an effective; mild; strong ~ 4. a ~ works

lay v. 1. (N; used with an adjective) ("to render");

("to place") she laid her soul bare; they laid the boards flat (see also *lay waste* at **waste I** n.) 2. (colloq.) (O; can be used with two objects + *that*-clause) ("to bet") he laid me ten dollars that it would not rain; he laid me (odds of) two to one that it would not rain 3. (P; tr.) ("to place") we laid the books on the table 4. (misc.) to ~ oneself open to criticism/ridicule; the system ~s itself open to abuse; to ~ ten dollars on a horse to win

layer n. 1. the bottom; outer; top ~ 2. an even; thick; thin; uneven ~ 3. a protective ~ 4. the ozone ~ 5. in ~s (to dress in ~s)

lay off v. 1. (D; tr.) to ~ from (she was laid off from her job at the factory) 2. (G) he laid off smoking

layout n. ["design"] 1. an artist's; typographer's ~ 2. page ~

layover n. a ~ between (a ~ between planes)

leach out v. (D; tr.) ("to separate") to ~ from

lead I /liyd/ n. ["position in front"] ["leading position"] 1. to assume, take a/the ~ in; to go into the ~ 2. to build up, increase one's ~ 3. to hold, maintain a/ the ~ 4. to follow smb.'s ~ 5. to give up, lose, relinquish the ~ 6. a comfortable, commanding; overall ~ 7. a ~ over (she built up a commanding ~ over her closest rivals) 8. in the ~ ["principal role"] 9. to play the ~ (in a play) 10. the female; male ~ ["clue"] 11. to run down, track down a ~ 12. the police have no ~s on/to/as to who is guilty 13. a good, promising ~ ["leash"] (BE) 14. see **leash** 1, 2 ["cord"] (BE) 15. an extension; television ~

lead II /liyd/ v. 1. (D; tr.) ("to guide") to ~ against (to ~ troops against the enemy) 2. (D; tr.) ("to guide") to ~ by (to ~ smb. by the hand; to ~ a horse by the bridle; to ~ by example) 3. (d; intr.) ("to go") to ~ from; to (the path ~s from the house to the river; all roads ~ to Rome) 4. (d; tr.) ("to guide") to ~ from; to (she led the group from the bus to the auditorium) 5. (D; tr.) to ~ in (to ~ the students in a cheer) 6. (d; intr.) ("to guide") to ~ into (the prisoners were led into the courtroom) 7. (d; tr.) ("to guide") to ~ off; onto (she led the team onto the field and then off the field) 8. (d; tr.) ("to guide") to ~ out of (the fire fighters led them out of the burning building) 9. (d; tr.) ("to guide") to ~ through (to ~ smb. through the fog) 10. (d; intr.) to ~ to ("to result in") (the infection led directly to gangrene; these evening courses will ~ eventually to an academic degree; can you describe the events that led to your decision?) 11. (d; intr.) ("to begin") to ~ with (the boxer led with a left jab) 12. (H) ("to induce") what led her to resign?; I was led to believe that she would accept our offer 13. (P; intr., tr.) ("to go") ("to guide") the road ~s nowhere; she led them over the mountain across the border 14. (misc.) to ~ smb. a merry chase (AE) = to ~ smb. a merry/pretty dance (BE)

lead back v. (D; intr., tr.) ("to return") to ~ from; to (the road ~s back to town; she led us back from the road to the starting point)

lead down *v.* 1. (d ; intr.) ("to go") to ~ from ; to (the path ~s down from the top of the hill to the beach) 2. (d ; tr.) ("to guide") to ~ from ; to (she led us down from the top of the hill to the beach)
leader *n.* 1. a born, natural ; decisive, strong ; undisputed ; weak ~ 2. (in a legislature) a floor ; majority ; minority ; opposition ; party ~ 3. a cheerleader ; labor ; military ; political ; troop ; world ~ (a summit of world ~s in Cairo) 4. a squadron ~ 5. a ~ in 6. (misc.) (BE) the Leader of the Opposition
leadership *n.* 1. to assume, take on, take over the ~ 2. to exercise, provide ~ 3. to relinquish, surrender ~ 4. firm, strong ~ (the party won several elections with firm ~ from her) 5. collective ; party ; political ~ 6. ~ in 7. under ~ (the party won several elections under her ~)
lead off *v.* (D ; intr.) ("to begin") to ~ by ; with (she led off by singing a lively song = she led off with a lively song)
lead up *v.* 1. (d ; intr.) ("to go up") to ~ from ; to (the path ~s up from the beach to the top of the hill) 2. (d ; intr.) to ~ to ("to precede and cause") (can you describe the events that led up to your decision?) 3. (D ; tr.) ("to guide") to ~ from ; to (she led us up from the beach to the top of the hill)
leaf I *n.* 1. a bay ; lettuce ; tea ~ 2. gold ~ 3. autumn ; deciduous leaves 4. leaves fall ; rustle ; turn (the leaves were turning yellow) 5. (misc.) to turn over a new ~ ("to make a fresh start") ; to take a ~ from / out of smb.'s book ("to follow smb.'s example")
leaf II *v.* (d ; intr.) to ~ through ("to look through superficially") (to ~ through a book)
leaflet *n.* propaganda ~s (to drop propaganda ~s over enemy lines)
league *n.* ["alliance"] 1. to form a ~ 2. in ~ with ["group of teams"] 3. to form a ~ 4. (esp. Am. baseball) a big, major ; bush (colloq.), minor ~ ; (soccer) the premier ~ ["level"] 5. in the same ~ ; out of one's / smb.'s ~ (I'm out of my ~ trying to argue with an expert like you! ; don't even think of dating her – she's way out of your ~ !)
leak I *n.* 1. to spring a ~ 2. to plug, stop a ~ 3. a ~ from ; in (to stop a ~ from a hole in a pipe) 4. (misc.) a security ~ (there appears to have been a security ~ from headquarters, Sir!)
leak II *v.* 1. (B) ("to divulge") they ~ed the news to the press 2. (d ; intr.) ("to enter by flowing") to ~ into (water ~ed into the basement) 3. (D ; intr.) ("to escape by flowing") to ~ out of (the oil ~ed out of the tank) 4. (D ; intr.) ("to be divulged") to ~ to (the news ~ed to the press)
leak out *v.* 1. (D ; intr.) to ~ to (the news ~ed out to the press) 2. (L ; to) it ~ed out (to the press) that the president's trip had been canceled
lean *v.* 1. (d ; intr.) to ~ across, over (to ~ across a table) 2. (d ; intr., tr.) to ~ against, on (to ~ against a wall ; to ~ on a desk) 3. (d ; intr.) to ~ on ("to rely on") (they had to ~ on their friends for help) 4. (colloq.) (d ; intr.) to ~ on ("to exert pressure on")

in the end we had to ~ on them ("we finally had to exert pressure on them") ; we had to ~ them to pay 5. (d ; intr.) to ~ out of (to ~ out of a window) 6. (d ; intr.) to ~ to (to ~ to one side) 7. (d ; intr.) ("to tend") to ~ to, towards (they are now ~ing to our position) 8. (misc.) to ~ over backwards to help smb. ("to make a maximum effort to help smb.")
leaning *n.* 1. a strong ~ 2. a ~ towards (to have a strong ~ towards political conservatism)
leap I *n.* 1. to give, make, take a ~ 2. a giant, great ; quantum ~ 3. a ~ ahead, forward (to make a great ~ forward) 4. a ~ from ; to 5. (misc.) by ~s and bounds
leap II *v.* 1. (d ; intr.) to ~ at ("to be eager for") (to ~ at an opportunity) 2. (d ; intr.) to ~ to ("to rush to") (to ~ to conclusions ; to ~ to smb.'s defense) 3. (P ; intr.) ("to jump") to ~ across a barrier ; to ~ over a fence ; to ~ into the bus ; to ~ to one's feet
leap down *v.* (D ; intr.) to ~ from, off ; to (he ~ed down from / off the roof to the ground)
leapfrog I *n.* to play ~
leapfrog II *v.* (d ; intr.) to ~ from ; to (American forces ~ged from one island to another)
leap up *v.* 1. (D ; intr.) to ~ from (she ~ed up from her chair) 2. (D ; intr.) to ~ on, onto, to (to ~ onto the table ; he ~ed up from the ground onto / to the roof) 3. (D ; intr.) to ~ out of (she ~ed up out of her chair)
learn *v.* 1. (d ; intr.) to ~ about, of 2. (d ; intr.) to ~ by, through (to ~ by experience) 3. (D ; intr., tr.) to ~ from (to ~ from experience ; she ~ed everything from me) 4. (E) she is ~ing to drive 5. (L) we have ~ed from them that he has found a job 6. (Q) she is ~ing how to drive 7. (misc.) to ~ by heart ; to ~ by rote
learning *n.* 1. book (colloq.) ; cognitive ; distance ; higher ; language ; programmed ; rote ~ 2. (misc.) a seat of ~
lease I *n.* 1. to hold a ~ (on) 2. to take (out) a ~ (on) 3. to extend ; lose ; renew a ~ 4. to cancel a ~ 5. mining ; (off-shore) oil ~s 6. a long ; short ~ 7. a ~ expires, runs out ; is due for renewal 8. a clause in a ~ ; the terms of a ~ 9. a ~ on 10. by ~, on, under (a) ~ (to hold land under (the terms of) a ~) 11. (misc.) a new ~ of (BE), on (AE) life ("a new chance to lead a happy life")
lease II *v.* 1. (usu. B ; occ. A) to ~ property to smb. 2. (D ; tr.) to ~ as (they ~d the building as a warehouse) 3. (D ; tr.) to ~ from (to ~ property from smb.)
lease out *v.* (B) to ~ property to smb. = to ~ property out to smb.
leash *n.* ["strap"] 1. to slip ("get free of") a ~ 2. on a ~ (to walk a dog on a ~) ["control"] ["restraint"] 3. to hold in ~ 4. to strain at the ~ ("to attempt to cast off controls")
least *n.* 1. the ~ of (that's the ~ of my worries !) 2. by far the, far and away the, much the ~ (it was much the ~ interesting film I've seen lately : I hated it !) 3. at ; at the ; at the very ; in the ; not in the ~

leather *n.* composition; genuine; imitation; patent; saddle ~

leave I *n.* ["period of absence from duty, work"] 1. to give, grant a ~ 2. to extend smb.'s ~ 3. to go on ~; to take a ~ 4. to overstay one's ~ 5. to cancel smb.'s ~ 6. (an) annual; compassionate; maternity; paternity; research; sabbatical; shore; sick; terminal ~ 7. (a) ~ of absence 8. on ~ (she was on maternity ~) (see the Usage Note for **vacation**) ["permission"] (formal) 9. to ask, beg (literary) ~ (to do smt.) 10. to give ~ (to do smt.) (he was given ~ to appeal against the verdict) 11. by smb.'s ~ 12. without so much as a by-your-leave ("without asking permission") (he took my coat without so much as a by-you-leave!) ["departure"] (formal) 13. to take (one's) ~ of ["misc."] 14. to take ~ of one's senses ("to act irrationally")

leave II *v.* 1. (A) ("to bequeath") he left his estate to her; or: he left her his estate 2. (C) ("to entrust") she left the report for me; or: she left me the report 3. (D; intr.) ("to depart") to ~ for (they have left for London) 4. (D; tr.) ("to abandon") to ~ for (she left her comfortable home for a rugged life in the desert; he left his wife for another woman; he was left for dead on the battlefield; to ~ Paris for London) 5. (D; intr.) ("to depart") to ~ from (they left from the main station) 6. (d; tr.) ("to omit") to ~ out of (we had to ~ this paragraph out of the text) 7. (d; tr.) ("to abandon") to ~ to (I ~ the decision to your judgment; to ~ nothing to the imagination) (see also *left to one's own devices* at **device**) 8. (d; tr.) ("to cause to remain") to ~ with (they left the children with her mother; she left her books with us) 9. (H) ("to take leave of") we left them to muddle through on their own; they were left to fend for themselves 10. (J) ("to abandon") I left him working in the garden 11. (N; used with an adjective, past participle, noun) ("to cause to be in a certain state or condition") they left the fields fallow; the film left me cold; the flood left them homeless; ~ me alone!; the enemy left the countryside devastated; the war left her an orphan 12. (P; tr.) ("to forget") I left my books at home 13. (misc.) it ~s nothing to be desired; we left this decision up to her (see also *leave smb. in the lurch* at **lurch III** *n.*)

lectern *n.* at; on a ~ (to stand at a ~; a book on a ~)

lecture I *n.* ["formal talk"] 1. to deliver, give a ~ 2. to attend; follow ("understand") a ~ 3. a public ~ 4. a series of ~s 5. a ~ about, on; to (to deliver a ~ about climate change in German to a large audience) 6. at; during; in a ~ (there was a lot of applause during the ~ and there were a lot of good points in it) ["reprimand"] 7. to give smb. a ~ (about smt.)

lecture II *v.* 1. (D; intr.) ("to discuss formally") to ~ about, on; in (to ~ on climate change in German to a large audience) 2. (D; tr.) ("to reprimand") to ~ for (she ~d the boys for being late) 3. (d; intr.) ("to discuss formally") to ~ to (to ~ to advanced students)

lecturer *n.* 1. a senior ~ (BE) 2. a ~ in, on (a ~ in English) (see the Usage Note for **professor**)

lectureship *n.* a ~ in

leech *n.* to apply ~es to

leer *v.* (D; intr.) to ~ at

leery *adj.* ~ about, of

leeway *n.* to allow, give, provide ~ (they gave him more ~)

left I *adv.* to bear, go, turn ~

left II *n.* ["left side"] 1. to keep to the ~ 2. on the ~; to the ~ ["radical, leftist groups"] 3. the extreme, far, radical ~; left-leaning (a left-leaning think tank) ["punch delivered with the left hand"] 4. to deliver, throw a ~ 5. a hard, stiff ~ 6. a ~ to (a ~ to the head) ["turn to the left"] (colloq.) 7. to hang (slang), make, take a ~ 8. to make a sharp ~

leftovers *n.* 1. to eat up; use up ~ 2. to warm up, warm over (AE) ~

left-winger *n.* an extreme ~

leg I *n.* ["lower limb"] 1. to bend; cross; kick; lift, raise; lower; spread; straighten; stretch one's ~s 2. a game, gammy (BE) ("lame") ~ 3. an artificial, wooden ~ 4. (an animal's) front; hind ~s 5. (misc.) he doesn't have a ~ to stand on ("he has no defense"); to pull smb.'s ~ ("to deceive smb. playfully"); on one's last ~s ("near collapse"); to get a ~ up on smt. (AE; slang) ("to be in command of a situation"); to stretch one's ~s ("to exercise one's legs") ["part"] 6. the last ~ (of a race)

leg II *v.* (colloq.) to ~ it ("to run") (when the police arrived we ~ged it out of there pretty fast, I can tell you!)

legacy *n.* 1. to bequeath, leave; hand down a ~ 2. an enduring, lasting; rich ~ 3. a ~ from; to (the enduring ~ of freedom handed down from the Founding Fathers to us)

legal *adj.* 1. ~ for (is smoking ~ for minors?) 2. ~ to + inf. (is it ~ for minors to smoke?)

legend *n.* ["inscription"] ["wording"] 1. to bear a ~ ["myth, story"] 2. to pass into ~ (Babe Ruth's batting exploits have passed into ~) 3. a ~ arises; endures, lives on 4. a living; local; popular ~ 5. ~ has it (~ has it that George Washington couldn't tell a lie) 6. the stuff of ~ (Babe Ruth's batting exploits have become the stuff of ~) 7. a ~ to (her exploits were a ~ to millions) 8. a ~ that + clause (the ~ that George Washington couldn't tell a lie) 9. (misc.) myths and ~s ["notable person"] 10. to be, become a ~ (in one's own lifetime)

legislation *n.* ["statutes, laws"] 1. to administer, apply, enforce, uphold; to adopt, enact, pass; draft; introduce ~ 2. to block; veto; vote down ~ 3. to abrogate, repeal; rescind ~ 4. current, existing; emergency; enabling; progressive; remedial; social ~ 5. ~ comes into effect, takes effect (the emergency ~ takes effect next week) 6. a piece of ~ 7. ~ about, on; against; for (they introduced a piece of ~ against the new tax) 8. ~ to + inf. (they introduced a piece of ~ to rescind the new tax) 9.

~ that + clause (they introduced a piece of ~ that would rescind the new tax) 10. under ~ (they introduced a piece of ~ under which the new tax would be rescinded; under current/existing ~, you cannot smoke in an elevator)

legislature *n.* 1. to convene a ~ 2. to disband, dismiss, dissolve a ~ 3. a bicameral ~ 4. a state ~ (US) 5. a ~ debates; votes 6. before a ~ (new proposals coming before the ~)

legitimacy *n.* 1. to confirm; establish the ~ (of smt.) 2. to challenge, question the ~ (of smt.)

legitimate *adj.* ~ to + inf. (is it ~ to pose such questions?)

legwork *n.* (colloq.) to do the ~

leisure *n.* at (one's) ~

lemon *n.* 1. to slice, squeeze a ~ 2. a slice of ~

lend *v.* 1. (A) she lent the money to him; or: she lent him the money 2. (d; refl.) to ~ to ("to be suitable for") (it ~s itself to satire) (see the Usage Note for **loan II**)

length *n.* 1. full ~ 2. at ~ (she described each event at great – indeed inordinate – ~) 3. in ~ (snakes that can grow to be ten feet in ~) 4. (misc.) to keep smb. at arm's ~ ("to keep smb. at a certain distance"); to go to any/great ~s to do smt. ("to make a great effort to do smt."); the horse won by two ~s; to travel the ~ and breadth of the country

lengthen *v.* 1. (D; tr.) to ~ by (to ~ trousers (by) two inches) 2. (D; tr.) to ~ to (to ~ a short manuscript to book size)

leniency *n.* 1. to show ~ 2. ~ to, towards, with

lenient *adj.* ~ to, towards, with

lens *n.* 1. to grind a ~ 2. a concave; convex; crystalline; telephoto, telescopic; wide-angle; zoom ~ 3. contact; corrective ~es 4. plastic ~es; thick ~es

leopard *n.* 1. a snow ~ 2. a young ~ is a cub 3. a female ~ is a leopardess

leprosy *n.* 1. to develop, get ~ 2. to have, suffer from ~

lesion *n.* an open ~

less I *determiner, pronoun* 1. ~ to + inf. (we have ~ to do) 2. ~ of (we see ~ of them than we used to; I wanted to read it all but I read ~ of it than I wanted to) USAGE NOTE: The use of the preposition *of* is necessary when a pronoun follows – less of them/ it. When a noun follows, the use of *of the* limits the meaning – we drank less wine; we drank less of the wine that you brought yesterday.

less II *adv., n.* 1. a bit, little ~ 2. no ~ than (we drank no ~ than 80% of it) 3. much ~ (we drank much ~ of it than they did) 4. much, still ~ (we don't even like them – much ~ love them!)

lesson *n.* ["instruction"] 1. to give ~s 2. to have, take ~s (to take ~s in English from a native speaker; I have three ~s a week with Professor Brown, during which I learn a lot) 3. to study one's ~s ["something that should be known"] 4. to learn a ~ (she learned a ~ from that experience) 5. to teach smb. a ~ 6. a moral; object; valuable ~ 7. a ~ about, in (to teach

smb. a ~ in good manners) 8. a ~ to (let that be a ~ to you, young man!)

let *v.* 1. (esp. BE; CE has *to rent out*) (B) ("to give the use of in return for payment") to ~ rooms to students 2. (I) ("to allow") we cannot ~ them go without a struggle = they cannot be ~ go without a struggle 3. (misc.) to ~ smb. alone; ~ us continue for a while; to ~ smb. off a bus; to ~ smb. on a bus; I was let on (the bus) when I signaled the bus to stop and ~ me on and I was let off (it) where I wanted to get off (it); to ~ the air out of a tire; I don't have five dollars, ~ alone ten dollars!; to ~ oneself go ("to relax"; "to neglect oneself"); she let drop her plan to retire = she let drop that she planned to retire

lethargy *n.* (in) a state of ~

let in *v.* 1. (D; refl., tr.) to ~ for ("to cause") (you'll be ~ting yourself in for a lot of trouble if you take her in as a partner) 2. (d; tr.) to ~ on ("to share") (to smb. in on a secret)

let off *v.* 1. to ~ lightly 2. (D; tr.) ("to release") to ~ with (he was let off with a small fine)

let on *v.* (colloq.) 1. (D; intr.) to ~ about ("to reveal") (she did not ~ about her promotion; he didn't ~ about the fact that/the way that/how the judge could be bribed) 2. (L) ("to pretend, make out") (AE) she let on that she was more surprised than she really was 3. (L; to) ("to indicate") he let on (to the accused) that the judge could be bribed 4. (Q; to) ("to indicate") he let on (to the accused) how to bribe the judge

let out *v.* (esp. BE) (B) to ~ rooms to students = to ~ rooms out to students (see also **let I 1; rent II; rent out**)

let's (verbal form) (F) ~ continue; ~ go; ~ see ("~ go to the movies, shall we?" "yes, ~!; no, ~ not.") USAGE NOTE: The emphatic form *do let's* may be used more by women than by men. The negatives of *let's* are *let's not* (CE), *don't let's* (esp. BE), and *let's don't* (esp. AE) (sometimes considered non-standard).

letter *n.* ["written message"] 1. to compose, write; type a ~ 2. to mail, post (BE), send; seal a ~ 3. to get, receive; open, unseal a ~ (I received a ~ enclosing/containing a check) 4. to acknowledge; answer, reply to, respond to a ~ 5. to drop, put a ~ in a mailbox (AE), letter box (BE) 6. to certify; register; trace a ~ 7. to take (down), transcribe a ~ 8. to dictate a ~ 9. to address; deliver; forward a ~ 10. a brief; detailed; long; rambling ~ 11. an anonymous; bread-and-butter, thank-you; business; chain; cover; fan; follow-up; form; friendly; hand-written; love; open; pastoral; personal; poison-pen; threatening; typed ~ 12. an airmail; certified; dead; express; registered; special-delivery ~ 13. the ~s crossed in the mail (esp. AE), post (BE) 14. a ~ about 15. a ~ from; to (we received a ~ from her about the incident; the newspaper publishes lots of ~s to the editor)

16. in a ~ ["unit of an alphabet"] 17. a block; capital, large, upper-case; lower-case, small ~ (to write in capital ~s) ["first letter of the name of a school, college denoting membership in a sports team"] (AE) 18. to earn, win one's ~ (as for rowing) (BE has *blue*) 19. a school ~ ["misc."] 20. to follow instructions to the ~; to follow the ~ of the law

lettuce *n.* 1. to shred ~ 2. crisp; limp ~ 3. bib; cos (BE), romaine (AE); iceberg; leaf ~ 4. a head; leaf of ~

letup *n.* a ~ in (there was no ~ in the bickering)

let up *v.* (D; intr.) ("to ease up") to ~ on (she should ~ on the children)

leukemia, leukaemia *n.* 1. to develop, get ~ 2. to have ~ 3. to suffer from ~ 4. acute ~

level I *adj.* ~ with (~ with the street; I drew ~ with him; he and I were ~ with each other)

level II *n.* ["height"] ["plane"] ["degree"] 1. to achieve, attain; exceed; reach a ~ 2. a high; low; record ~ 3. (a) crime; energy; population; poverty; subsistence ~ (are crime ~s rising or falling?) 4. eye; floor; ground; sea; water ~ (see also **flood level**) 5. the federal (US), national; international; local; state (US) ~ 6. above; at, on; below a ~ (at sea ~; at the highest ~s; on the international ~) 7. (misc.) all vehicles leave from Level Six ["instrument for determining a horizontal plane"] 8. a spirit ~

level III *v.* 1. (d; tr.) to ~ against (to ~ charges against smb.) 2. (D; tr.) to ~ to (the village was ~ed to the ground) 3. (colloq.) (d; intr.) to ~ with ("to tell the truth to") (she ~ed with me)

lever *n.* 1. to depress; pull; push; use a ~ 2. a gear ~ (BE; AE has *gearshift*)

leverage *n.* 1. to apply; wield; have ~ 2. political ~ (they have no political ~) 3. the ~ to + inf. (has he got enough ~ to get his plan through Congress?)

levy I *n.* to impose a ~ (to impose a ~ on rum)

levy II *v.* (D; tr.) to ~ on (to ~ a tax on rum)

lexicon *n.* to compile a ~

liability *n.* 1. to accept, acknowledge, assume, incur, take on a ~ 2. to exempt smb. from ~ 3. full; limited ~ 4. a ~ for (we assumed full ~ for our children's debts) 5. (misc.) assets and ~ties USAGE NOTE: The *Ltd* in the name of a firm (such as *Smith and Jones Ltd*) stands for "Limited."

liable *adj.* ["legally obligated"] 1. fully ~ 2. ~ for; to (we are fully ~ to them for our children's debts) ["likely"] 3. (cannot stand alone) ~ to + inf. (she is ~ to show up at any time)

liaise *v.* (BE) (D; intr.) ("to keep in touch") to ~ between; with (government departments sometimes fail to ~ closely with each other)

liaison *n.* ["communication"] 1. to establish; maintain ~ 2. a ~ between; with (government departments sometimes fail to maintain a close ~ with each other) ["love affair"] 3. to enter into a ~ with 4. to have a ~ with

liar *n.* an abject, compulsive, congenital, incorrigible, inveterate, outright, pathological;

accomplished, consummate, convincing, good; bad, poor, unconvincing ~

lib *n.* (colloq.) gay; women's ~ (see **liberation** 1)

libel *n.* 1. to commit ~ 2. (a) ~ against, on

liberal I *adj.* 1. politically; staunchly ~ 2. ~ in; with (~ in one's views; ~ with one's donations to charity)

liberal II *n.* a bleeding-heart; knee-jerk; political; staunch ~

liberate *v.* (D; tr.) to ~ from

liberation *n.* 1. animal; gay; women's ~ 2. ~ from

liberties *n.* ["undue familiarity"] to take ~ with

liberty *n.* ["freedom"] 1. to gain ~ 2. individual, personal; political; religious ~ 3. civil rights and civil ~ties ["permission"] 4. to take the ~ (of doing smt.) (may I take the ~ of reminding you of your promise?; I took the ~ of opening your package) ["authorized absence"] (AE) (naval) 5. on ~ [misc.] 6. are you at ~ to give us any information?; unfortunately, I'm not at ~ to say any more

library *n.* 1. to accumulate, build up a ~ 2. to computerize a ~ 3. a children's; circulating, lending; free, municipal, public; law; mobile; music; reference; rental; research; school; university ~ 4. at, in (she works at/in the ~) 5. to borrow smt. from a ~ and then return it

license I licence *n.* 1. to grant, issue a ~ 2. to apply for; receive; renew a ~ 3. to revoke; suspend a ~ 4. a driver's (AE), driving (BE); dog; export; gun; hunting; liquor (esp. AE); marriage; state (esp. US) ~ 5. poetic ~ 6. a ~ to + inf. (we had a ~ to sell beer) 7. under ~ (the product is made under foreign ~)

license II licence *v.* (H) she is ~d to practice nursing

lick *v.* 1. (d; intr.) to ~ against, at (the flames ~ed at the roof of the next house) 2. (N; used with an adjective) she ~ed the plate clean

licking *n.* ["a beating"] (colloq.) 1. to give smb. a ~ 2. to get a ~ 3. a good ~

lid *n.* ["cover"] 1. to cover smt. with a ~ 2. to keep; put a ~ on smb. 3. to take off a ~ ["curb"] 4. to clamp, clap, put a ~ on smt. ["eyelid"] 5. drooping ~s 6. the lower; upper ~

lie I *n.* ["falsehood"] 1. to tell a ~ 2. to give the ~ to ("to prove to be false") 3. a bald-faced, barefaced, blatant, brazen, deliberate, downright, monstrous, outright, transparent, whopping; obvious, unconvincing ~ 4. a white ~ 5. a pack, tissue, web of ~s 6. (misc.) to live a ~ ("to conceal the truth about oneself")

lie II *v.* ("to tell a lie") 1. to ~ flatly, outright 2. to be obviously lying 3. (D; intr.) to ~ about; to (he lied to the judge about the accident)

lie III *v.* 1. ("to be") to ~ ahead 2. (d; intr.) ("to be") to ~ with (responsibility lies with the president) 3. (P; intr.) ("to be located") to ~ in bed; Mexico ~s to the south 4. (s) ("to be in a reclining position") to ~ flat; still 5. (s) ("to remain") to ~ fallow (the field lay fallow) 6. (misc.) to ~ on one's back/side/ stomach (in bed); to ~ low (see also *lie in ambush* at **ambush**; *lie awake* at **awake**; *lie in wait for* at **wait I**)

lie-detector test *n.* 1. to administer, give a ~ 2. to subject smb. to a ~ 3. to take, undergo a ~ 4. to fail; pass a ~

lie down *v.* (misc.) to take smt. lying down ("to accept smt. without protest"); to ~ on the job ("to work very little")

lien *n.* ["legal claim"] 1. to put, slap (esp. AE; colloq.) a ~ on smt. 2. to have a ~ on smt.

lieutenant *n.* 1. a first; flight (GB); second ~ 2. a ~ junior grade (US)

life *n.* 1. to have, lead, live a ~ (to lead a busy ~, not a ~ of idleness) 2. to prolong; save; spare a ~ 3. to dedicate/devote one's (entire/whole) ~ (to smt.) 4. to go through, live, spend one's ~ (doing smt.) 5. to give, lay down, sacrifice; lose; risk one's ~ 6. to claim, cost, snuff out, take a ~ (she took her own ~; the accident claimed many lives) 7. to ruin smb.'s ~ 8. to bring; restore smb. to ~ 9. to come to; to take on ~ (the statue took on ~ in the sculptor's skilled hands) 10. an active; busy, hectic; exciting ~ 11. a charmed; full; good; happy; idyllic ~ 12. an easy; peaceful, quiet, serene; sheltered; simple ~ 13. an ascetic, austere; cloistered; monastic ~ 14. a difficult, hard, miserable, tough; dull; lonely, solitary; unhappy ~ 15. a dissipated, dissolute; stormy, turbulent ~ 16. a long; short ~ 17. daily, everyday; modern; real ~ 18. campus (esp. AE), college, university; city; country, rural; suburban; village ~ 19. army; civilian; political; public ~ (in civilian ~ the sergeant was a teacher) 20. (a) nomadic ~ (the hunters led a nomadic ~) 21. smb.'s family; home; love; married; personal; private; sex; social ~ (to lead a hectic social ~; married ~ seemed to agree with them; in private ~ she was very easygoing) 22. animal; bird; human; intelligent; marine; plant ~ (has there ever been plant ~ on Mars?) 23. (in) adult; early; later ~ (in early ~ he was happy but in later ~ he was sad) 24. the shelf ~ (of smt. being sold in a store) 25. in ~ (early in ~ he was happy but later (on) in ~ he was sad; the actor played villains but in real ~ he was a nice guy; is there a new woman in his ~?) 26. (misc.) in the prime of ~; the facts of ~; the accused got ~ ("the accused was sentenced to life imprisonment"); to show signs of ~; (to hang on) for dear ~ ("with all one's energy"); not on your ~! ("not for anything in the world"); to start a new ~; to make a new ~ for oneself; to breathe/infuse (new) ~ into smt.; to bring back to ~; to stake one's ~ on smt.; a mode, style, way of ~; to pester the ~ out of smb.; a matter of ~ and death; a ~ of ease; a ~ of luxury; full of ~; (slang) get a ~! ("don't be so obsessive!"); ("do smt. new, useful, constructive!"); the bright, sunny; seamy side of ~; the idea seemed to take on a ~ of its own; I've never seen the like in all my

~!; do you believe in ~ after death? (see also *life form* at **form I**; *the (great) love of smb.'s life* at **love I**; *the quality of life* at **quality**; *the right to life* at **right III**; *within an inch of one's life* at **inch**; *a slice of life* at **slice I** *n.*)

lifeboat *n.* 1. to launch, lower a ~ 2. to swamp a ~ (the ~ was swamped in the surf) 3. (misc.) to take to the ~s

life jacket *n.* 1. to inflate a ~ 2. to put on a ~

lifeline *n.* ["rope used to save a life"] 1. to throw smb. a ~ ["vital route"] 2. to hold out, offer, throw a ~ (to hold a ~ out to a company in financial trouble) 3. to cut a ~ 4. a ~ to

lifestyle *n.* 1. to have, lead a certain ~ 2. an alternate (AE), alternative; luxurious; ostentatious; sedentary; simple ~ 3. (misc.) you should change your ~ because a change of/in ~ would benefit you. USAGE NOTE: The collocation *live a lifestyle* is found but considered non-standard by some.

life support *n.* on ~ (the patient was put on ~ but eventually taken off (it) when his condition became hopeless) (see also *life-support system* at **system**)

lifetime *n.* 1. to dedicate, devote a ~ (to smt.) (one can dedicate an entire/a whole ~ to promoting peace) 2. during, in one's ~ 3. (misc.) to last a ~; it seems a ~ ago now!; once in a ~ (seize a once-in-a-lifetime opportunity); the chance, opportunity of a ~; a (single) ~ wouldn't be long enough to tell you everything! (see also *a legend in one's own lifetime* at **legend**)

lift I *n.* ["device for raising and lowering people and freight"] (BE; AE has *elevator*) 1. to operate a ~ (a liftboy or liftman operates a ~) 2. to take a ~ (we took the ~ to the tenth floor) 3. a freight; service ~ (see also **elevator** 1–6) ["conveyor suspended from a cable"] 4. a chair, ski ~ ["ride"] (colloq.) 5. to bum (AE); get a ~ (from smb.) 6. to give smb. a ~ ["boost, inspiration"] (colloq.) 7. to get a ~ (from smb. or smt.) 8. to give smb. a ~ (your words of encouragement gave us a real ~)

lift II *v.* 1. (D; tr.) ("to raise") to ~ from (she did not ~ her eyes from the TV set) 2. (d; tr.) ("to steal") to ~ from (the material was ~ed from smb.'s dissertation) 3. (D; tr.) ("to raise") to ~ out of (they ~ed the crates out of the hold) 4. (misc.) the jet ~ed off the runway

lift down *v.* (D; tr.) to ~ from; to (they ~ed the trunk down from the shelf to the floor)

lift up *v.* (D; tr.) to ~ from; to (they ~ed the trunk up from the floor to the shelf)

ligament *n.* to strain; tear a ~

light I *adj.* 1. to make ~ of ("to attach little importance to") 2. ~ of foot, light on one's feet, light-footed 3. (misc.) as ~ as a feather = feather-light ("very light")

light II *n.* ["illumination"] ["source of brightness"] 1. to put on, switch on, turn on a ~ 2. to shine, throw a ~ on smt. 3. to cast, shed ~ on smt. (can you shed any ~ on this mystery?) 4. to dim; extinguish, switch off, turn off, turn out a ~ 5. to dim the ~s, turn the ~s down; to turn the ~s up 6. a blinding; bright, strong; harsh ~ (we brought the strange object into the bright ~ of an open bulb – the ~ from the bulb helped us to identify the object) 7. a dim, dull, faint; soft ~ 8. moonlight; sunlight (see also **daylight**; **daylights**) 9. an electric; firelight; klieg; landing; neon; night; overhead; pilot; strobe; torchlight; traffic; warning ~ (see also *torchlight parade* at **parade**) 10. (on a car) a backup (AE), reversing (BE); brake; dome; instrument; parking ~; taillight 11. a ~ flashes; flickers; gleams; glimmers; glows, shines; goes on; the ~s are on (the gold ring caught the gleaming ~ of our lamp and in the ~ we could see it clearly) 12. a ~ goes off; goes out; the ~s are off; out 13. ~ travels (very fast) (~ travels at the speed of ~) 14. (BE) the ~s have fused ("a fuse has blown") 15. by the ~ of (to read by the ~ of a candle) ["traffic light"] 16. to go through a (red) ~ 17. the ~ changes, switches (to green/red) (esp. AE), the ~s change, switch (to green/red) 18. against a ~ (to cross against the ~ (esp. AE), to cross against the ~s) 19. at a ~ (to stop at a ~ (esp. AE), to stop at the ~s) (see also Usage Note at **traffic light**) ["flame used to light a cigarette"] 20. to give smb. a ~ ["flame used to light a stove, fire"] (AE) 21. a low ~ (cook it on/over a low ~) ["misc."] 22. in ~ of (esp. AE), in the ~ of ("in view of"); in the harsh ~ of reality; a guiding ~ ("one who sets an example"); to see the ~ ("to comprehend the truth"); to bring smt. to ~ ("to make smt. known"); to come to ~, to see the ~ of day ("to become known"); she wanted to see her name in ~s ("she wanted to succeed on the stage and become famous"); the northern ~s; the southern ~s (see also **cold light**; **green light**; *light at the end of the tunnel* at **tunnel I** *n.*)

light III *v.* 1. (d; intr.) to ~ into ("to attack") (he really lit into his opponent) 2. (C) he ~ed/lit a cigarette for me; or: he ~ed/lit me a cigarette 3. (D; intr.) to ~ on, upon ("to come across") (he ~ed on a rare dictionary) 4. (misc.) a brightly; dimly ~ed/lit street

light bulb see **bulb** 1–5

lighter *n.* a cigarette ~

light out *v.* (colloq.) (esp. AE) (D; intr.) to ~ for ("to leave for") USAGE NOTE: The past and past participle of this verb are usu. *lit out* – she lit out for home.

light up *v.* (D; intr.) to ~ with (her face ~ed/lit up with pleasure)

lighting *n.* 1. dim; good; poor; soft ~ 2. artificial; electric; fluorescent ~ 3. diffused; direct; indirect ~

lightning *n.* 1. ball; forked; heat, sheet ~ 2. ~ flashes; strikes 3. a bolt, flash, streak, stroke of ~ 4. thunder and ~

like I *prep.* (colloq.) ~ smt. to + inf. (it was not ~ them to be late)

like II *v.* 1. to ~ a great deal, a lot, very much 2. (E)

he ~s to read 3. (G) he doesn't ~ reading 4. (H; no passive) (often with the conditional); I ~ people to tell me the truth; I'd ~ you to go; AE also has, slightly colloq.: I'd ~ for you to go; CE has: what I'd ~ is for you to go 5. (M) we ~ our friends to be honest 6. (N; used with an adjective) I ~ my steak rare 7. (misc.) do what/whatever you ~: I don't care!; leave if you ~: I don't care USAGE NOTE: The verb *like* can be used with *it* + clause – I like it when you smile; I'd like it if you smiled.

likelihood *n.* 1. every; great; little ~ (there is every ~ of her coming) 2. a good, strong ~ 3. ~ that + inf. (there is every ~ that she'll come) 4. in all ~ (in all ~ she'll come)

likely *adj.* 1. equally; hardly; highly, very ~ 2. (cannot stand alone) ~ to + inf. (she is not ~ to show up; she's hardly ~ to show up after being insulted last time!; it is not ~ to snow) 3. ~ that + clause (it is not ~ that she will show up; it is not ~ that it will snow)

liken *v.* (d; tr.) ("to compare") to ~ to (her estate could be ~ed to a fortress)

likeness *n.* 1. to catch a ~ (the artist caught the sitter's ~) 2. to bear a ~ 3. a living; striking, uncanny; strong; true ~ 4. a family ~ 5. a ~ between; to

likewise *adv.* to do ~ (go and do ~)

liking *n.* 1. to take a ~ to 2. to develop; have a ~ for 3. to smb.'s ~ (that is not to my ~)

limb *n.* 1. a lower; upper ~ 2. to stretch one's ~s 3. an artificial ~ (he got an artificial ~ when one of his ~s had to be amputated) 4. (misc.) out on a ~ ("in a precarious position")

limbo *n.* in ~ (in political ~)

limelight *n.* 1. to get, have, hold the ~ 2. to grab; hog the ~ 3. to be in the ~ ("to have high public visibility") (he was thrust into the ~ after the scandal, stayed in the ~ for a while, and then dropped out of the ~)

limit I *n.* 1. to impose, place, put, set a ~ on 2. to disregard, exceed a ~ 3. to reach a ~ (she reached the ~ of her endurance) 4. an age; credit; term; time; weight ~ (see also **speed limit**) 5. a ~ for; on; to 6. above, over; below; beyond a ~ 7. within ~s 8. (misc.) to push smb. to the ~ (I'll have to push myself to the very ~ to finish on time!); over the ~ ("having drunk too much alcohol") (he was fined for driving while over the ~) (see also **limits**)

limit II *v.* (D; refl., tr.) to ~ to (she had to ~ herself to twenty minutes)

limitations *n.* 1. to put ~ on 2. budgetary, financial ~ 3. within certain ~ (see also **statute of limitations**)

limited *adj.* 1. (very) strictly ~ 2. ~ in (~ in resources) 3. ~ to

limits *n.* 1. (AE) city ~ 2. (AE) (esp. mil.) off ~ (to); on ~ (to) (the bar was put off ~ to all military personnel and has remained out of bounds to them) 3. beyond; within (reasonable) ~

limo *n.* ["limousine"] (colloq.) a stretch ~

limousine *n.* 1. to hire; take a ~ 2. an airport; bulletproof; chauffeur-driven ~

limp *n.* 1. to have a ~ 2. a decided, marked, pronounced; slight ~ 3. with a ~

line I *n.* ["long thin mark"] 1. to draw a ~ 2. a broken; solid, unbroken ~ (see also **dotted line**) 3. a contour; crooked; curved; diagonal; straight; wavy; zigzag ~ 4. a fine, thin; heavy, thick ~ 5. a horizontal; parallel; perpendicular; vertical ~ ["row of people waiting; queue"] 6. to form a ~ 7. (AE) to buck ("push into") a ~ (BE has *jump a queue*) 8. to get in; into ~; to stand, wait in ~ 9. a bread; check-in; checkout; chow ~ (see also **poverty line**) 10. a ~ forms ["row"] 11. to form a ~ 12. a police; receiving ~ (see also **picket line**) ["row of characters"] 13. to indent; insert a ~ 14. (fig.) to read between the ~s ["unit of text"] 15. to deliver a ~ (as an actor) 16. to go over, rehearse; memorize one's ~s (the actors had to rehearse their ~s several times) 17. to fluff one's ~s 18. a dull; witty ~ (there isn't a dull ~ in the whole play) ["route"] 19. to change from/ to; introduce a (new); to take, use a ~ 20. to discontinue a ~ 21. a branch; feeder; main ~ 22. (on) a bus; commuter; high-speed; steamship; streetcar (AE), tram (BE); subway (AE), underground (BE) ~ (took the Northern ~ to Euston and changed to the Victoria ~ there = changed at Euston from the Northern ~ to the Victoria ~; Euston is on both the Northern ~ and the Victoria ~) 23. supply ~s (to cut enemy supply ~s) ["path"] 24. to follow a ~ (to follow a ~ of reasoning; to follow the ~ of least resistance; a tree is blocking my ~ of sight) ["telephone connection"] 25. to get a ~; to give smb. a ~ 26. the ~ is busy (esp. AE), engaged (BE), tied up (esp. AE) 27. the ~ is free, open 28. the ~ goes dead 29. an outside; party ("shared"); private ~ 30. a helpline, hot ~ (a helpline for desperate people; a hot ~ for missing children; to establish/set up a hot ~ between Washington and Moscow to link heads of state) 31. on the ~ (to stay on the ~) ["note"] 32. to drop smb. a ~ ["information"] 33. to get a ~ on smb. ["type of merchandise"] 34. to carry; handle; introduce a ~ 35. to discontinue, drop a ~ 36. a complete, full ~ ["policy"] 37. to adopt, take; adhere to, follow, hew to (AE), pursue a ~ (on) 38. a firm, hard, tough; official ~ (to hew to the official ~; take a tough ~ on terrorism) (see also **party line**) ["flattering talk"] (colloq.) 39. to feed, give, hand smb. a ~ ["wire"] ["pipe"] ["conduit"] 40. a fuel; oil; sewage; steam; telegraph; telephone ~ 41. high-voltage; power ~s (the power ~s are down; several power ~s were downed during the storm) (see also **supply lines**) ["boundary"] 42. (AE) a city; county; state; township ~ 43. a boundary; snow; squall; tree ~ (see also **dividing line**) 44. (sports) a base; end; foul; goal; service ~; sideline 45. at, on a ~ (at the goal ~; on the base ~; on the sidelines) ["established position along a front"] ["boundary"] (mil.) 46. to hold a ~ 47. a battle; cease-fire; ~ (see also **firing line**;

front line) 48. (the) enemy ~s (behind enemy ~s) 49. at, on a ~ (on the cease-fire ~) ["conveyor belt"] 50. an assembly, production ~ (to work on an assembly ~; to automate a production ~) ["occupation"] ["field of interest"] 51. what ~ are you in? ["contour"] 52. the ~s of a ship ["limit"] 53. to hold the ~ (on prices) 54. to draw the ~ ("to set a limit") ["turn"] ["order"] 55. in ~ for (she is next in ~ for promotion; who is third in the ~ of succession to the throne?) ["alignment"] 56. in ~; out of ~ (the wheels are out of ~) ["conformity"] 57. to toe the ~ 58. to bring smb. into ~; to keep smb. in ~ 59. to get into ~; to get out of ~ 60. in ~ with (in ~ with your stated policy) ["cord, device for catching fish"] 61. to cast a ~ 62. to reel in; reel out a ~ 63. a fishing ~ ["rope"] 64. to throw a ~ to smb. (who is in the water) 65. a plumb ~ ["division"] 66. to cross a ~ 67. a color ~ (see also **color line**; **poverty line**) ["tendency"] 68. along, on certain ~s (along modern ~s) ["dynasty"] 69. to establish, found a ~ 70. an unbroken ~ (of succession) ["distinction"] 71. a fine, nebulous, thin ~ between (is there really only a fine ~ between genius and madness?) ["misc."] 72. the bottom ~ ("the final result"); to be on the firing ~ ("to be at the center of activity"); a plot, story ~ (they're working on the story ~s of the series for the next six months); to walk a straight ~; to put smt. on the ~ ("to risk smt."); to lay it on the ~ ("to speak candidly"); in the ~ of duty; top of the ~ ("best quality"); on ~ ("in operation"); is this the end of the ~ for typewriters?; to go online ("to become linked to a computer network"; see also **online**) (see also *a line of credit* = *a credit line* at **credit I** *n.*)

line II *v.* (D; tr.) to ~ with (she ~d the shelf with paper)

lineage *n.* 1. to trace smb.'s ~ (she could trace her ~ back to the Pilgrim Fathers!) 2. an ancient; royal ~

lined up *adj.* 1. ~ for (~ for roll call) 2. ~ in (~ in three columns; ~ in a row) 3. ~ with (~ with each other = ~ together)

linen *n.* 1. to change the (bed) ~ 2. fresh ~ 3. bed; fine; pure; table ~ (see also **dirty linen**)

line out *v.* (in baseball and softball) (D; intr.) to ~ to (the batter ~d out to center field)

liner I *n.* ["steamship"] a cruise; luxury; ocean; passenger; transatlantic ~ (a job on a luxury cruise ~)

liner II *n.* ["lining"] a helmet ~

lineup *n.* 1. a police ~ (AE: BE has *identity parade, identification parade*) (she picked out the criminal in the police ~) 2. (AE) to be in a ~ (as a suspect) 3. (sports) a starting ~

line up *v.* 1. (D; intr.) to ~ behind (to ~ behind the table) 2. (D; intr., tr.) to ~ for (the teacher ~d the pupils up for roll call = the teacher ~d up the pupils for roll call) 3. (D; intr., tr.) to ~ in (to ~ in three columns; to ~ in a row) 4. (D; intr., tr.) to ~ with (to ~ one thing up with another = to ~ one thing with another = to ~ two things up together)

linger v. (d; intr.) to ~ over ("to take one's time with") (don't ~ over your coffee)

lingo n. (colloq.) ["language, dialect"] 1. to speak the ~ 2. to understand the ~ 3. the local ~

linguistics n. applied; comparative; computational; contrastive; descriptive; general; generative; historical ~; psycholinguistics; sociolinguistics; structural; transformational ~

liniment n. to apply, rub in, rub on ~

lining n. 1. a brake; coat ~ 2. a zip-in ~ 3. (misc.) a silver ~ ("the bright side of a problem") (don't despair – every cloud has a silver ~!)

link I n. 1. to establish, forge, form a ~ 2. to sever a ~ 3. a causal; direct ~ (there may well be a ~ between the two phenomena – but is it a direct causal ~?) 4. a close; strong; weak ~; the weakest ~ (as in a chain) 5. a connecting; rail; road ~ 6. the missing ~ (the missing ~ between apes and man) 7. a cuff ~ 8. a ~ between; to, with (he has ~s to the underworld)

link II v. 1. to ~ causally; closely; directly; inextricably 2. to ~ electronically 3. (D; tr.) to ~ to, with (these events are inextricably ~ed with each other = this event and that event are inextricably linked (together/with each other))

linkage n. (a) ~ between, to, with (there may well be a ~ between the two phenomena – but is it a direct causal ~?)

links n. ["golf course"] (out) on the ~

link-up n. a ~ between; to; with (there was a ~ between our forces and theirs on the Danube = there was a ~ of our forces with/and theirs on the Danube)

link up v. (D; intr.) to ~ to, with (we ~ed up with their forces on the Danube = our forces and theirs ~ed up on the Danube)

linoleum n. inlaid ~

lion n. 1. a mountain ~ 2. ~s prowl; roar 3. a group, pride of ~s 4. a young ~ is a cub 5. a female ~ is a lioness 6. a male lion has a mane 7. the lion's color is tawny 8. (misc.) the ~ is the king of beasts (see also **sea lion**)

lip n. 1. to curl; lick; move; part; pucker (up); purse; round one's ~s 2. to press one's ~ to (she pressed her ~s to the baby's forehead) 3. chapped; dry; moist ~s 4. thick; thin ~s (his thick ~s quivered/trembled in anticipation) 5. the lower; upper ~ 6. from smb.'s (own) ~s (I heard it from her own ~s) 7. on one's ~s (she died with a prayer on her ~s) 8. on everyone's ~s (her name was on everyone's ~s) 9. (misc.) to bite one's ~ ("to restrain oneself"); to moisten one's ~s; to lick/smack one's ~s ("to anticipate or remember with pleasure"); to keep a stiff upper ~ ("to refuse to become discouraged"); don't give me any of your ~! ("don't be impudent with me"); to seal smb.'s ~s ("to induce smb. to remain silent") (don't worry – your secret is safe with me – my ~s are sealed!); to read ~s and be a lip-reader;

"Will you raise taxes?" "Read my ~s: I said No New Taxes!"

lip service n. ["meaningless promise"] to pay ~ to

lipstick n. 1. to apply, put on; remove, wipe off ~ 2. to have ~ on = to wear ~ 3. ~ smudges

liquid n. 1. (a) clear; cloudy; thick ~ 2. (a) dishwashing (AE), washing-up (BE) ~ 3. ~ evaporates; coagulates 4. a drop; pool of ~ 5. (misc.) in ~ or in solid form

liquor n. ["alcoholic drinks, esp. spirits"] (esp. AE) 1. to ply smb. with ~ 2. to hold one's ~ 3. hard, strong; intoxicating ~ 4. malt ~

list I n. ["catalog, roll"] 1. to compile, draw up, make (up), put smb./smt. on a ~ 2. to head a ~ 3. to go down, read down a ~ 4. the dean's ~ (AE); a reading ~ 5. an alphabetical ~; checklist; shopping ~ (to go down a checklist) 6. a cast; guest; mailing; waiting ~ (a cast ~ for tonight's performance) 7. the honours ~ (GB) (she hoped that her name would be in the honours ~) 8. a long; short ~ (of candidates) 9. a casualty ~ (a daily casualty ~ was posted) 10. a danger ~ (esp. BE) (she rang the hospital to find out if her mother was still on the danger ~) 11. a hit; wish ~ (we were asked to draw up a wish ~ for the new project and a hit ~ of those opposed to it) 12. a wine ~ (asked the waiter to bring the wine ~) 13. in, on a ~ (she was third on the ~; high on the ~ of priorities) 14. (misc.) at the bottom of a ~; at the top of a ~ (see also **voting lists**)

list II v. ("to include") 1. (d; intr.) to ~ among (to be ~ed among the casualties) 2. (d; refl., tr.) to ~ as (she ~ed herself as an independent voter; he was ~ed as missing) 3. (d; tr.) to ~ under (the new journals are ~ed under acquisitions)

list III n. ["tilt"] a ~ to (the ship has developed a ~ to starboard)

list IV v. (D; intr.) ("to tilt") to ~ to (the ship ~s to starboard)

listen v. 1. to ~ attentively, carefully, closely, intently 2. (d; intr.) to ~ for (to ~ for a signal) 3. (D; intr.) to ~ to (to ~ to their advice; to ~ to their singing; to ~ to them singing; to ~ to them sing (esp. AE)) 4. (misc.) "I kept telling her not to do it – but would she ~ (to me)? No way!"

listener n. 1. a good, sympathetic ~ (a sympathetic ~ to your problems) 2. a regular ~ (regular ~s to the station will note some changes) 3. younger ~s (a radio program unsuitable for younger ~s)

listen in v. (D; intr.) to ~ on, to (to ~ on smb.'s conversation)

listen out v. (D; intr.) to ~ for (to ~ for a signal)

listing n. an exclusive ~ (of a property being sold)

lists n. ["combat arena"] (also fig.) to enter the ~ (decided to enter the (political) ~ by running for election)

lit adj. brightly; dimly ~ (a dimly ~ street = a dimly lighted street)

litany n. 1. a boring; long ~ 2. (misc.) a ~ of complaints (we had to listen to their long boring ~ of complaints)

literacy n. 1. to promote; spread ~ 2. adult; computer; functional; widespread ~ 3. ~ in (~in more than one language)

literate adj. 1. completely; fully; functionally; highly ~ 2. computationally, computer ~ 3. ~ in (~ in more than one language)

literature n. 1. to produce (a) ~ 2. (an) extensive, voluminous ~ 3. belletristic; classical; contemporary; great; modern; professional; promotional; pulp ~ 4. comparative ~ 5. a piece, work; body of ~ (a considerable body of ~) 6. ~ about, on (there was (an) extensive ~ on the topic) 7. (misc.) to keep abreast of the ~ (in one's field); to review the ~ (when beginning a research project)

litigation n. 1. to initiate, start ~ 2. ~ against; over; with 3. in ~ (the case was in ~)

litter n. 1. to drop, leave; strew ~ 2. to clear up, pick up ~ (see also *litter bin* at **bin** n; *litter lout* at **lout** n)

littered adj. ~ with (the streets were ~ with old newspapers)

little I determiner, pronoun 1. ~ to + inf. (we have ~ to do) 2. ~ of (we see ~ of them nowadays; I wanted to read it all but I read comparatively ~ of it) USAGE NOTE: The use of the preposition *of* is necessary when a pronoun follows – little of them / it. When a noun follows, the use of *of the* limits the meaning – we drank very little wine; we drank very little of the wine that you brought yesterday.

little II n., adv. 1. precious ~ 2. ~ by ~ ("gradually") 3. (misc.) a ~ bit; a ~ closer; a ~ further; a ~ longer; a ~ shorter

liturgy n. to chant; offer; recite the ~

live I / layv / adv. ["directly"] to come ~ (this telecast is coming to you ~ from Wimbledon; you can catch her ~ in concert this evening) (also fig.) (colloq.) (the government's tax reforms will go ~ this fall)

live II / liv/ v. 1. to ~ comfortably; dangerously; high; simply 2. to ~ long; as long as I ~ I'll never forget the end of the war! 3. (d; intr.) to ~ by ("to adhere to") (to ~ by certain principles) 4. (d; intr.) ("to exist") to ~ for (they ~ only for their children) 5. (d; intr.) to ~ in (to ~ in fear; to ~ in luxury; to ~ in poverty) 6. (d; intr.) ("to subsist") to ~ off, on (they ~ on her salary; you cannot ~ on love alone; to ~ off one's parents) 7. (D; intr.) ("to survive") to ~ to (she ~d to ninety; she lived to a great age) 8. (d; intr.) ("to cohabit or live under the same roof") to ~ with (John and Mary ~ with each other; he's 30 but he still ~s with his parents) 9. (colloq.) (d; intr.) to ~ with ("to tolerate") (can you ~ with this arrangement?; we can't cure your pain: you'll just have to learn to ~ with it!) 10. (E) she ~d to regret her decision; she ~d to be ninety; she ~d to be very old; I thought I'd never ~ to see the day when people stood on the Moon! 11. (P; intr.) ("to reside") to ~ in the country 12. (misc.) they ~ beyond their means ("they spend more than they earn"); to ~ from hand to mouth ("to eke out a bare

living"); to ~ from day to day ("to be concerned only with the present"); John and Mary are ~ving together ("to cohabit"); long ~ the King/Queen!; to have ~d through almost the whole of the 20th Century (see also *as I live and breathe* at **breathe**; *live a life* at **life**)

livelihood n. 1. to earn, eke out a/one's ~ (to eke out a precarious ~ (by) doing odd jobs) 2. to lose one's ~ 3. a source of ~ 4. (misc.) to depend on smt. for one's ~

live up v. 1. (d; intr.) to ~ to ("to satisfy") (to ~ to expectations) 2. (misc.) (colloq.) to ~ it up ("to enjoy oneself ostentatiously")

livestock n. to graze; keep ~

livid adj. ~ with (~ with rage)

living n. ["livelihood"] 1. to earn, get (BE), make a ~ (she makes a good ~ by selling cars) 2. to eke out, scrape (esp. BE) a ~ (to eke out a precarious ~ (by) doing odd jobs) 3. a comfortable, decent, good; honest ~ (to earn a comfortable ~) 4. (misc.) what do you do for a ~? ["manner of existence"] 5. communal; gracious; high; suburban ~ 6. a cost; standard of ~ (a high cost of ~ can mean a low standard of ~)

living room n. a sunken ~

load I n. 1. to bear, carry, transport a ~ 2. to lessen, lighten a ~ (also fig.) 3. to dump, shed; shift a ~ 4. a heavy; light ~ (the central beam must bear a very heavy ~) 5. a capacity, full, maximum, peak ~ 6. a teaching ~; workload (have/carry a heavy workload) (see also **caseload**) 7. under a ~ (the table collapsed under its heavy ~ of food) 8. (misc.) to take a (great) ~ off smb.'s mind ("to ease or relieve one's mind"); it was a (great) ~ off my mind ("I felt relieved") (see also **loads**)

load II v. 1. (D; tr.) to ~ into, onto (to ~ cargo into/ onto/on a ship) 2. (d; tr.) to ~ to (to ~ a ship to full capacity) 3. (D; tr.) to ~ with (to ~ a ship with cargo)

load down v. (D; tr.) to ~ with (the poor mule was ~ed down with heavy bales)

loads n. ["lots, a great deal"] we had ~ to talk about; we have ~ of work to do; ~ of money

load up v. (D; tr.) to ~ with (they ~ed up the ship with cargo = they ~ed the ship up with cargo)

loaf n. 1. a fish; meat; sliced ~ 2. a ~ of bread 3. (misc.) (slang) (BE) use your ~! ("use your head/ brains!") USAGE NOTE: Note the plurals in "They baked two *loaves* of bread and two meat *loaves/loafs*."

loan I n. 1. to float, negotiate, raise a ~ 2. to give, make; offer a ~ 3. to apply for, ask for; get, receive, take out a ~ 4. to secure; underwrite a ~ 5. to pay off, repay a ~ 6. to call in a ~ 7. a bank; bridge (AE), bridging (BE); interest-free; long-term; low-interest; short-term ~ 8. interlibrary ~ (she got the book on/through interlibrary ~ – could have borrowed it on/through interlibrary ~?) 9. a ~ to 10. on ~ from; to (the painting was on ~ to the National Gallery from the Louvre) 11. (misc.) could I have the ~ of a few dollars till payday?

loan II *v.* (A) she ~ed the money to me; or: she ~ed me the money USAGE NOTE: When *to loan* means "to lend officially", it is CE – the Louvre has loaned a painting to the National Gallery. When it means "to lend", it is esp. AE – she loaned me the money.

loanword *n.* 1. to adopt a ~ 2. a ~ from (a ~ from German)

loath, loth *adj.* (pompous or lit.) (cannot stand alone) ~ to + inf. (we are ~ to summon the authorities)

loathe *v.* 1. to ~ deeply, intensely 2. (G) he ~s working

loathing *n.* 1. deep, intense ~ (the very idea of work fills him with deep ~) 2. ~ for, of (he has a deep ~ of work) 3. with ~ (he regards work with deep ~) 4. fear and ~ (the very idea of work fills him with fear and ~)

lob *v.* 1. (D; tr.) to ~ at, to (to ~ a ball at smt.) 2. (D; tr.) to ~ over (she ~bed the ball over the net)

lobby I *n.* ["pressure group"] 1. an education; environmental; farm; labor; oil ~ (a powerful farm ~ has been organized) ["large hall"] 2. a hotel; theater ~ 3. in the ~ (let's meet in the ~)

lobby II *v.* 1. to ~ actively; hard 2. (D; intr.) to ~ against; for, on behalf of (to ~ against higher taxes; to ~ for a bill; to ~ on behalf of farmers) 3. (H) we ~bied our delegate to support the proposal

locate *v.* 1. (P; tr.) ("to place") we ~d our firm in Florida 2. (P; intr.) (esp. AE) ("to move") our firm is going to ~ in Florida

location *n.* 1. to find; give, pinpoint, show a ~ 2. a central; exact ~ 3. at a ~ (at an undisclosed ~) 4. on ~ (to shoot a film on ~ rather than in a studio)

lock I *n.* 1. to force; pick a ~ 2. a combination; deadbolt; double; mortise; safety; secure; time ~ 3. a Chubb (T); Yale (T) ~ 4. under ~ and key ("locked up securely")

lock II *v.* 1. (d; intr.) to ~ on, onto ("to sight and track") (to ~ onto a target) 2. (d; tr.) to ~ out of (they were ~ed out of their room and couldn't get in) 3. (d; tr.) to ~ in (they were ~ed in their room and couldn't get out) (see also *lock antlers* at **antler**; *lock horns* at **horn**)

locked *adj.* ["bound"] (cannot stand alone) ~ in (~ in mortal combat; they were ~ in a fierce struggle with the government over pension rights)

locket *n.* a gold; silver ~

lockjaw *n.* to develop ~

locomotive *n.* 1. to drive a ~ 2. a diesel; electric; steam ~

locusts *n.* 1. ~ swarm 2. a swarm of ~

lodge I *n.* ["house"] 1. a hunting; ski ~ ["organization, society"] 2. a fraternal; Masonic ~ ["motel"] (AE) 3. a motor ~

lodge II *v.* 1. (D; tr.) to ~ against; with (to ~ a complaint against a neighbor with the police) 2. (d; intr.) to ~ in (the bullet ~d in his shoulder)

lodger *n.* to have, keep (AE), take in ~s

lodgings *n.* to find; look for, seek ~

log I *n.* ["record"]["diary"] 1. to keep a ~ 2. a captain's; ship's ~ (see also *logbook* at **book I** *n.*) ["piece of timber"] 3. to float ~s (down a river) 4. to put a ~ on a fire; to split a ~; to saw a ~ in two 5. a ~ burns (in a fire) ["misc."] 6. to sleep like a ~ ("to sleep very soundly")

log II *v.* (d. intr.) to ~ into, onto (to ~ onto a computer system)

logarithm *n.* a common; natural ~

loggerheads *n.* at ~ with ("in disagreement with") (we were at ~ with each other about/over which course to take)

logic *n.* 1. to apply, use ~ 2. clear; cold; incontrovertible; irrefutable; simple ~ 3. false, specious, spurious ~ 4. deductive; formal; inductive; symbolic ~ 5. ~ suggests (~ suggests that we should all go in one car) 6. ~ behind, in, to (there is no ~ in their policy)

logical *adj.* 1. only; perfectly, very 2. ~ to + inf. (it is only ~ for us all to go in one car) 3. ~ that + clause (it's only ~ that we should go in one car)

logjam *n.* 1. to break (up), clear a ~ 2. (fig.) (esp. AE) a legislative ~

logo *n.* 1. a characteristic; distinctive; identifying; well-known, well-recognized ~ 2. a company, corporate ~ 3. to display; feature a ~ (the company's ad displays the distinctive company ~)

loins *n.* ["power"] to gird one's ~ ("to prepare oneself for conflict or a difficult task") (to ~ one's loins for a struggle)

lollipop *n.* to lick, suck a ~

lolly *n.* ("frozen desert on a stick") (BE) 1. to lick, suck a ~ 2. an ice, iced ~

lonely *adj.* 1. very ~ 2. ~ for

lonesome *adj.* (AE) 1. very ~ 2. ~ for

long I *adj.* (colloq.) ["strong"] ~ on (~ on common sense)

long II *adv.* 1. ~ after; ago 2. ~ before

long III *n.* 1. before ~ (our guests will arrive before ~) 2. for ~ (they will not be here for ~)

long IV *v.* 1. (d; intr.) to ~ for (to ~ for the return of peace) 2. (E) she ~ed to return home; I ~ed for peace to return

long chalk (BE) see **long shot**

long-distance *adv.* to call, telephone ~

long haul (esp. AE) see **long run** (see also *long-haul flight* at **flight I**)

longing *n.* 1. to express; feel, have a ~ ("I have Immortal ~s in me." – Shakespeare, *Antony and Cleopatra*) 2. a secret; strong ~ 3. a ~ for (I had a ~ for the return of peace) 4. a ~ to + inf. (I had a ~ for peace to return; she has a ~ to visit the village where she was born)

longitude *n.* at a ~ (at a ~ of ten degrees west)

long run *n.* ["long-range outlook"] in, over the ~ ("In the ~, we are all dead." – John Maynard, Lord Keynes (1923))

long shot *n.* ["slight chance"] not by a ~ (AE) ("absolutely not")

long term see **long run**

long way *n.* 1. we took the ~ home 2. a ~ from; to (it's a ~ from our house to the station; "It's a long, long way to Tipperary" -- H. Williams & J. Judge, song, 1907-8)

loo *n.* (colloq.) (BE) 1. to go to, need, use the ~ 2. to flush a ~ 3. a gents'; ladies'; public 4. down the ~ (to flush smt. down the ~)

look I *n.* ["glance"] ["expression"] 1. to get, have, take a ~ (at) (we got a good ~ at their new car) 2. to dart, shoot, throw a ~ (at) 3. to sneak, steal a ~ (at) 4. to give smb. a ~ 5. to get, receive a ~ (from) 6. an adoring, loving, tender ~ (she got an adoring ~ from her mother) 7. an admiring; close, hard, long hard; curious, inquiring, searching; cursory, perfunctory; eloquent, meaningful; initial; knowing; penetrating; pensive, thoughtful; piercing; rapt; significant; steady; ~ (we must take a closer ~ at their proposal even though we have already had a cursory initial ~ through it) 8. a come-hither, inviting; provocative ~ 9. a blank, distant, faraway, vacant; strange ~ (she had a faraway ~ in her eyes) 10. an anxious, worried; pleading ~ (he shot a pleading ~ at the teacher) 11. a bemused, puzzled, quizzical; bewildered; skeptical; troubled ~ (she gave the instructor a bewildered ~) 12. a disapproving, stern; grim; icy; scathing; sharp; withering ~ 13. an angry; baleful; belligerent; dirty, nasty, vicious; furtive, shifty, sinister; hostile; resentful; sour; sullen; suspicious ~ (she gave us a dirty ~) 14. a second ~ (to take a second ~ at smt.) ["appearance"] 15. a tailored ~ 16. a haggard; hungry; lean ~ 17. a curious, strange; different; new ~ 18. a guilty; innocent ~ ["misc."] 19. by, from the ~(s) of it, the situation is serious

look II *v.* 1. (d; intr.) to ~ after ("to watch") ("to take care of") (to ~ after the children) 2. (D; intr.) to ~ around ("to watch") (to ~ around the corner; I ~ed around me for something to eat) 3. (D; intr.) to ~at ("to examine") (to ~ carefully but admiringly at a painting; to ~ at a child tenderly and lovingly; to ~ at one's enemies hostilely or at least icily; we must ~ more closely at their proposal even though we have already looked through it cursorily; just ~ at him jump, will you! (AE) = just ~ at him jumping, will you!) 4. (D; intr.) to ~ for ("to seek") (to ~ for a job) 5. (d; intr.) to ~ into ("to investigate") (to ~ into a complaint) 6. (d; intr.) to ~ like ("to resemble") (this horse ~s like a winner; BE also has: this horse ~s a winner) 7. (d; intr.) ("to appear") to ~ like (it ~s like being another fine day!; it ~s like rain = it ~s like it's going to rain (esp. AE) = it ~s as if/as though it will rain) 8. (D; intr.) ("to watch") to ~ out (AE), out of (to ~ out of a window) 9. (d; intr.) to ~ over ("to watch") (to ~ over a wall) 10. (d; intr.) to ~ through ("to direct one's gaze through") (to ~ through a telescope) 11. (d; intr.) to ~ through ("to examine") (to ~ through one's files) 12. (d; intr.) to ~ to ("to turn to") (to ~ to one's

parents for help) 13. (d; intr.) to ~ to ("to appear") (how does this ~ to you?) 14. (S) she ~s terrible; this horse ~s a winner (BE) 15. (misc.) to ~ smb. squarely in the eye; to ~ from one to the other; to ~ one's age; to ~ everywhere; to ~ all over; to ~ high and low (for smt.) = to ~ everywhere (for smt.) = to ~ all over (for smt.); to ~ under the bed (see also **looks**) USAGE NOTE: When *look over* and *look through* are used literally, they are construed as *v* + *prep*: I looked over the wall and then I looked over it again; I looked through the telescope and then I looked through it again. When *look over* and *look through* mean 'examine,' they can also be construed as *v* + *prep* (I looked over/through their proposal and then I looked over/through it again). However, *look over* can also be construed as *v* + *adv* (I looked their proposal over and then I looked it/the proposal over again), and in this meaning *look through* can be construed as *v* + *adv* with a short pronoun (I looked through their proposal and then I looked it through again).

look about (BE) see **look around**

look ahead *v.* (D; intr.) to ~ to (to ~ to a bright future)

look around *v.* (d; intr.) to ~ for ("to seek") (to ~ for something to eat)

look away *v.* (D; intr.) to ~ from (I ~ed away from the stage)

look back *v.* 1. (D; intr.) to ~ at, on (to ~ at the past year) 2. (misc.) *Look Back in Anger* – play by John Osborne (1956)

look down *v.* 1. (d; intr.) to ~ at; from ("to direct one's gaze down at") (to ~ at the beach from the balcony of the hotel) 2. (d; intr.) to ~ on ("to despise") (to ~ on all forms of corruption; to ~ on the working class) 3. (misc.) to ~ one's nose at ("to look down on smb.") (to ~ one's nose at the working class) (see also **look up**)

look forward *v.* (d; intr.) to ~ to (to ~ to spring; to ~ to a meeting with eager anticipation; I ~ to going)

look in *v.* (D; intr.) to ~ on (to ~ on the children)

look on *v.* 1. (d; intr.) to ~ favorably; unfavorably (they ~ed on the new project favorably = they ~ed favorably on the new project) 2. (D; tr.) to ~ as (we ~ her as a friend) 3. (D; intr., tr.) to ~ with (they ~ed on the new project with favor)

lookout *n.* 1. to post a ~ 2. to keep a (sharp) ~ for (to keep a sharp ~ for burglars) 3. to be on the ~ for burglars)

look out *v.* 1. (d; intr.) to ~ for ("to watch for") (the police were ~ing out for burglars) 2. (d; intr.) to ~ for ("to protect") (to ~ for one's own interests) 3. (d; intr.) to ~ on, onto, over ("to face") (our windows ~ onto the square)

look round (BE) see **look around**

looks *n.* ["appearance"] 1. to lose one's ~ (a former movie star who'd lost her ~) 2. boyish; good ~ (an unemployed actor who'd lost his boyish good ~)

look up *v.* 1. (d; intr.) ("to stare") to ~ at (we ~ed up

at the skyscraper) 2. (d; intr.) to ~ to ("to respect") (children ~ to their parents) (see also **look down**)
look upon see **look on**
loom I n. 1. to weave with a ~ 2. a hand; power ~
loom II v. 1. (P; intr.) a ship ~ed (up) out of the fog 2. (misc.) to ~ large (the law case ~ed large in his thoughts)
loop n. 1. to make a ~ 2. to loop the ~ (in an airplane) 3. (misc.) to throw smb. for a ~ ("to shock smb.")
loophole n. 1. to find a ~ 2. to close, plug a ~ 3. a legal; tax ~ 4. a ~ in
loose I adj. 1. to cut (smb.) ~ 2. to let, set, turn (smb.) ~ 3. to break; come; get; hang; work ~
loose II n. on the ~
loose end n. (BE) at a ~ (let's get together if you're at a ~) (see **loose ends** 2)
loose ends n. 1. to clear up the ~ 2. (AE) at ~ ("with no definite obligations")
looting n. 1. to engage in ~ 2. widespread ~ 3. an outbreak of ~
lope v. (P; intr.) she ~d through the park
lord I n. 1. to worship the Lord 2. a feudal ~; a warlord 3. (misc.) a Law Lord (GB); Good Lord!; (my ~s,) ladies and gentlemen....; the (House of) Lords
lord II v. to ~ it over smb. ("to flaunt one's superiority over smb.")
lorry n. (BE) 1. to drive, operate; steer a ~ (CE has *truck*) 2. to load; unload a ~ 3. an articulated ~ (AE has *semi, semi-trailer, tractor-trailer, trailer truck*) 4. a breakdown ~ (AE has *tow truck*) 5. a tipper ~ (AE has *dump truck*) 6. a dustbin ~ (AE has *garbage truck*) 7. a ~ jackknifes
lose v. 1. (D; intr., tr.) to ~ to (our team lost to them by three points; we lost the match to them) 2. (O) his errors lost him the match 3. (misc.) to ~ by a mile; to ~ by three points; to ~ (by) 5-2
lose out v. 1. (D; intr.) to ~ on (to ~ on a deal) 2. (D; intr.) to ~ to (she lost out to her rival)
loser n. 1. a bad, poor, sore; born; good ~ 2. the real ~ (the poor will be the real ~s under the government's tax policy)
loss n. 1. to inflict ~es on (the enemy inflicted heavy ~es on our forces) 2. (sports) to hand smb. a ~ (they handed our team its first ~ of the season) 3. to incur, suffer, sustain, take ~es (our forces sustained heavy ~es at the hands of the enemy) 4. to cut; make up, offset, recoup, replace a ~ (to recoup one's gambling ~es; retreat and cut your ~es) 5. to make good a ~ 6. to report a ~ (to the police) 7. heavy; light ~es 8. a great; irredeemable, irreparable, irreplaceable, irretrievable; sad; total ~ (we are here to mourn the sad ~ of our best friend) 9. a hearing; heat; memory; weight ~ 10. a net ~ 11. a ~ in, of; on (a ~ in weight; to make a ~ on a deal) 12. a ~ to (an irreplaceable ~ to our nation) 13. at a ~ (to be at a ~ for words; to operate a business at a ~) 14. (misc.) ~es in dead and wounded; it was no great ~ to the nation that such a fool was not

elected; ~s increase, rise; maximize your profits and minimize your ~es
lost adj. 1. irretrievably; totally ~ 2. to get ~ (the small child got ~) 3. ~ to (~ to the world) 4. (misc.) (slang) get ~! ("go away!"); ~ at sea; ~ in thought
lot n. ["one's fate, destiny"] 1. to cast, throw in one's ~ with 2. a happy; hard, sorry, unhappy ~ 3. smb.'s ~ to + inf. (it fell to her ~ to break the sad news) ["object used in deciding by chance"] 4. by ~ (to choose by ~) (see also **lots**) ["plot of ground"] (esp. AE) 5. an empty, vacant ~ 6. a parking ~ (AE; BE has *car park*) 7. a used-car ~ ["large amount"] 8. an awful, whole ~ (of) 9. (misc.) we had a ~ to talk about; we have a ~ of work to do and we're going to have a ~ more!; a ~ of money; a fat ~ (derog.) (colloq.) (a fat ~ of good you've done!; (a) fat ~ you care!)
loth adj. see **loth**
lotion n. 1. to apply, rub in, rub on (a) ~ 2. an aftershave; body; hand; skin; suntan ~
lots n. 1. to cast, draw ~ (to see who wins) ["a lot, a great deal, loads"] 2. we had ~ to talk about; we have ~ of work to do and we're going to have ~ more!; ~ of money, ~ and ~ of money
lottery n. 1. to hold a ~ 2. to win a ~ 3. a daily; weekly ~ 4. a national; state ~ 5. a ~ raises money (a ~ that raises lots of money for good causes) 6. in, on a ~
loud adv. to count out ~
loudspeaker n. (to speak) over, through a ~
lounge I n. 1. a cocktail ~ 2. a sun ~ (BE; AE has *sun parlor, sun porch*) 3. a departure; transit ~ (at an airport) 4. a VIP ~ (at an airport) 5. in a ~ USAGE NOTE: In BE, *lounge* can also mean 'living room.' But this meaning of *lounge* is disliked by many.
lounge II v. (P; intr.) she enjoys ~ging around the pool; she enjoys just ~ging around doing nothing
lour see **lower I**
louse n. a plant; wood ~
lousy adj. (slang) ~ to + inf. (it's ~ to be without work = it's ~ being without work)
lout n. (derog.) 1. a drunken; stupid ~ 2. (BE) (colloq.) a lager; litter ~
love I n. ["deep affection"] 1. to inspire ~ for 2. to declare, express one's ~ for smb. 3. blind; brotherly; calf (esp. BE), puppy; cupboard (BE); deep, profound, sincere, true; platonic; romantic; undying; unrequited ~ 4. ~ of (~ for/of one's country; smb.'s ~ of music; to have no ~ for smb.) 5. for, out of ~ (to do smt. for ~) 6. to be in ~ (with smb.) (to be head over heels in ~ with smb.; deeply/hopelessly/madly in ~) 7. to fall in; out of ~ (with smb.) 8. ~ between (the undying ~ between us) 9. ~ from (the letter ended "With) Love from mom and dad") 10. (misc.) ~ at first sight; she's the (great) ~ of his life ["expression of deep affection"] 11. to give; send one's ~ (give them our ~; the letter ended "With all my ~, John") ["sexual activity"] 12. to make ~ (to, with) ("to have intercourse") 13. free ~ ["misc."] 14. I wouldn't do it for ~ or money!

love II v. 1. to ~ blindly; dearly; deeply; madly; passionately; really, very much (I would dearly ~ to see them again) 2. (E) she ~s to swim 3. (G) she ~s swimming 4. (N; used with an adjective) she ~s her steak rare 5. (misc.) (colloq.) I ~ it when you smile; I'd ~ you/for you (AE) to come over and see our new TV = what I'd ~ is for you to come over and see our new TV

lovely adj. (colloq.) 1. ~ to + inf. (it was ~ of you to arrange this party; it was ~ to see you again = it was ~ seeing you again) 2. ~ that + clause (it was ~ that we could see each other again)

lover n. 1. (for a woman) to take a ~ 2. to jilt, reject a ~ 3. to become ~s 4. a great; live-in (colloq.); lousy (colloq.) ~ 5. (misc.) an art; music; nature ~

low I adj. ["lacking"] (cannot stand alone) ~ in, on (she is ~ in funds; they were ~ on ammunition; food ~ in salt = low-salt food) (see also *to lie low* at **lie III**)

low II n. 1. to hit, reach an all-time ~ 2. an all-time; new ~

lowdown n. to get; have the ~ on smb.

lower I /lau-/ v. (D; intr.) ("to frown") to ~ at

lower II /lou-/ v. 1. (D; tr.) to ~ by (he ~ed the bar (by) ten inches) 2. (D; tr.) to ~ from; to (they ~ed supplies from the surface to the stranded miners; she ~ed her voice from a shout to a whisper; they ~ed the flag to half-mast) 3. (d; refl., tr.) to ~ into; onto (she gently ~ed herself into the armchair; she ~ed the baby onto the mat)

loyal adj. 1. steadfastly ~ 2. ~ to

loyalty n. 1. to command, inspire ~ 2. to demonstrate, show ~ 3. to pledge, swear ~ 4. blind; deeprooted, steadfast, strong, unquestioned, unshakable, unswerving ~ 5. party ~ 6. divided; shifting ~ties 7. ~ to (to show unswerving ~ to one's friends)

lozenge n. a cough; fruit; throat ~

luck n. ["success"] ["good fortune"] 1. to bring ~ 2. to try one's ~ (at smt.) 3. to press, push one's ~ 4. pure, sheer ~ 5. to wish smb. ~ 6. beginner's; dumb ~ 7. smb.'s ~ holds; improves, turns; runs out 8. a bit, stroke of ~ 9. ~ at, in, with (~ at gambling) 10. the ~ to + inf. (she had the good ~ to hold the winning ticket; it was pure ~ to find him = it was pure ~ finding him; we had the good ~ to find him at home) 11. ~ that + clause (it was sheer ~ that we found him) 12. in; with ~ (we were in ~ to have found him at home) 13. down on one's ~; out of ~ ["fate"] ["chance"] 14. to trust to ~ 15. bad, hard, tough ~ 16. good; pure, sheer ~ (we had bad ~) 17. the ~ to + inf. (we had the bad ~ not to find him at home) 18. ~ that + clause (it was bad ~ that he wasn't at home when we tried to find him) 19. (misc.) she has had a run of bad ~

lucky adj. 1. ~ at, in, with (~ at cards; ~ in love; they were ~ with their new car) 2. ~ for (that was ~ for you) 3. ~ to + inf. (you are ~ to be alive!; we were ~ to have gotten here early) 4. ~ that + clause (it's ~ that we got here early = we were ~ that we

got here early; you are ~ that you didn't die in the accident!)

ludicrous adj. 1. ~ to + inf. (it's ~ to have to show our pass each time we come here!) 2. ~ that + clause (it's ~ that we have to show our pass each time we come here!)

lug v. (P; tr.) she ~ged the boxes into the other room; we will have to ~ the equipment upstairs

luggage n. 1. to check, register (esp. BE) one's ~ 2. (esp. AE) to check one's ~ through (to the final destination) 3. to claim one's ~ 4. carry-on, hand ~ 5. personalized ~ 6. unclaimed ~ 7. a piece of ~

lukewarm adj. ["halfhearted"] 1. ~ about, to (~ about a proposal; ~ to an idea) ["tepid"] 2. ~ to (~ to the touch)

lull I n. 1. a momentary, temporary ~ 2. a ~ in 3. during a ~ (we escaped during a momentary ~ in the fighting)

lull II v. 1. (d; tr.) to ~ into (to ~ smb. into a false sense of security) 2. (d; tr.) to ~ to (to ~ a child to sleep)

lullaby n. to hum; sing a ~ to

lumbar puncture n. to do, perform a ~ (on)

lumber I n. (AE) 1. to float, raft ~ (down a river) 2. green, unseasoned; seasoned ~ (CE has *timber*)

lumber II v. (P; intr.) the bear ~ed through the forest

lumber III v. (colloq.) (BE) (D; tr.) ("to burden") to ~ with (I've been ~ed with all their problems)

lump n. 1. to bring a ~ to smb.'s throat ("to cause to be overcome with emotion"); to have a ~ in one's throat ("to be overcome with emotion") 2. the doctor discovered a ~ in her breast that had probably formed some time ago

lumps n. (colloq.) ["punishment"] to take one's ~

lump together v. (D; tr.) to ~ with (they ~ed all of the workers together with the managers)

lunacy n. 1. sheer ~ 2. ~ to + inf. (it was ~ to climb that mountain)

lunatic n. 1. a raving ~ 2. a ~ to + inf. (he was a ~ to try that)

lunch I n. 1. to eat (esp. AE), have ~ 2. to cook; make, prepare; serve ~ 3. a cold; hot; light; nutritious, wholesome; substantial ~ 4. a brown-bag (AE); business, working; expense-account; liquid ("alcoholic"), three-martini; school; set (esp. BE) ~ 5. a box; picnic ~ 6. at, during; over ~ (they were all at ~; what did you discuss at/over ~?) 7. for ~ (we had a salad for ~) 8. (misc.) to give smb. ~ (esp. BE); to take smb. to ~

lunch II v. 1. (D; intr.) to ~ on ("to eat") (to ~ on a sandwich) 2. (D; intr.) to ~ with 3. (misc.) to ~ at home; to ~ out

lunchtime n. at ~ (we'll meet at ~)

lung n. 1. an iron ~ 2. congested ~s 3. a collapsed ~ 4. in, into smb.'s ~s 5. on one's ~ (a spot on one's ~) 6. (misc.) they were screaming at the top of their ~s

lunge I n. 1. to make a ~ 2. a ~ at, for, towards (he made a ~ at me with a knife) lunge II v. (D; intr.) to ~ at, for, towards (he ~d at me with a knife)

lurch I n. ["sudden movement"] to give a ~ (the stricken ship gave a ~)

lurch II v. (P; intr.) he ~ed towards me; the stricken ship ~ed to starboard

lurch III n. ["vulnerable position"] in the ~ (to leave smb. in the ~)

lure v. (P; tr.) to ~ smb. into a trap; he was ~d to his death

lure away v. (D; tr.) to ~ from; to (she was ~d away from her comfortable rural home to the big city)

lurk v. (P; intr.) to ~ in the shadows

lust I n. 1. to arouse, rouse ~ 2. to feel, have ~ 3. to gratify, satisfy one's ~ 4. blood; insatiable, unquenchable; pure; unbridled ~ 5. ~ for (a ~ for power; an insatiable ~ for life) 6. (humorous) in ~ with; out of ~ with (he's not in love with her but he certainly seems to have fallen in ~ with her!)

lust II v. (d; intr.) to ~ after, for (to ~ for power)

luster, lustre n. ["glory"] 1. to add ~ to (his success added ~ to his home town) 2. to take on a new ~, to take on (an) added ~ (because of, from) (his home town took on an added ~ because of his success)

luxuriate v. (D; intr.) to ~ in (to ~ in newly acquired wealth)

luxury n. 1. to enjoy (a) ~ (to enjoy the ~ of a hot bath) 2. to afford a ~ (can we afford the ~ of a second car?) 3. pure, sheer; unaccustomed ~ 4. ~ to + inf. (it was sheer ~ to relax on the beach = it was sheer ~ relaxing on the beach) 5. in ~ (they lived in ~; to wallow in the ~ of a hot bath) 6. (misc.) in the lap of ~; what is a ~ for some is a necessity for others (see also a life of luxury at life)

lyre n. to play the ~

lyrical adj. ~ about, over (to wax ~ about the scenery)

lyrics n. 1. ~ by (a song with music by Richard Rodgers and ~ by Oscar Hammerstein) 2. ~ for (Richard Rodgers wrote the music for the song and Oscar Hammerstein wrote the ~ (for it))

M

mace *n.* ["staff used as a symbol of authority"] a ceremonial ~ = the ~ of office

machete *n.* to brandish, wield a ~

machine *n.* 1. to operate, run, use, work a ~ 2. to shut down a ~ 3. an adding, calculating ~ 4. an answering; video-game ~ 5. a cash, money-access (AE); cigarette; slot (BE), vending ~ 6. a composing, linotype, typesetting; copy, copying, duplicating; fax ~ 7. a heart-lung; X-ray ~ 8. an earth-moving; milking; milling; sanding; sewing; threshing ~ (see also **washing machine**; **washing-up machine**) 9. a voting ~ 10. a mincing ~ (BE; AE has *meat grinder*) 11. a fruit (BE), slot (AE); pinball ~ (to play a pinball ~) (BE also has *pintable*) 12. a party; political ~ (I felt I was just a small cog in a well-oiled political ~) 13. a ~ functions, runs; breaks down (see also *machine tool* at **tool**)

machine gun *n.* 1. to fire, operate a ~ 2. a heavy; light; medium ~ 3. an air-cooled; water-cooled ~ 4. a ~ jams

machine-gun nest *n.* to clean out, wipe out a ~

machinery *n.* ["machines"] 1. to install; operate, run ~ 2. to maintain; repair ~ 3. farm; heavy ~ 4. a piece of ~ ["apparatus"] 5. administrative; law-enforcement; propaganda ~ 6. ~ for (~ for negotiations)

mad *adj.* ["infatuated"] (colloq.) 1. (cannot stand alone) ~ about (they are ~ about each other) ["angry"] (colloq.) 2. hopping ~ 3. to get ~ 4. ~ at (she's ~ at him; to get ~ at smb.) ["insane"] 5. stark raving ~ 6. to go ~ 7. to drive smb. ~ 8. ~ with (~ with pain) 9. ~ to + inf. (she was ~ to drive without headlights)

maddening *adj.* 1. ~ to + inf. (it's ~ to have to wait here) 2. ~ that + clause (it's ~ that we have to wait here)

made *adj.* (cannot stand alone) ~ from, of, out of; with USAGE NOTE: Compare these examples, which illustrate general tendencies – 1. *a stew can be made with vegetables* (vegetables are not the only ingredient). 2. *a stew can be made of/out of vegetables; a chair can be made of/out of wood; shoes are usually made of/out of leather* (only one major substance or ingredient is used). 3. *synthetic rubber can be made from petroleum; paper can be made from wood* (the basic substance has been greatly changed). (see **make II**)

made-to-order *adj.* ~ for (they were ~ for each other!)

madness *n.* 1. sheer, utter ~ 2. ~ to + inf. (it was sheer ~ for her to drive without headlights) (see also *there's method in smb.'s madness* at **method**)

magazine *n.* ["supply depot"] 1. a powder ~ ["journal, periodical"] 2. to publish, put out a ~ 3. to subscribe

to, take (BE) a ~ 4. an alumni (esp. AE); fashion; glossy (esp. BE), slick (AE); illustrated; men's; women's; popular ~ 5. a copy; issue of a ~

maggots *n.* crawling with ~

magic *n.* 1. to perform; work ~ (on) 2. black; white ~ 3. pure, sheer ~ 4. by ~ (the medicine worked as if by ~)

magistrate *n.* a police (esp. AE); stipendiary (BE) ~

magnanimity *n.* 1. to display, show ~ towards 2. great ~

magnanimous *adj.* 1. ~ towards 2. ~ to + inf. (it was ~ of you to make the offer = you were ~ to make the offer)

magnate *n.* a coal; industrial; shipping; steel; tobacco ~

magnet *n.* a ~ attracts iron

magnetism *n.* animal; personal; physical; sheer ~

magnitude *n.* 1. considerable, great ~ 2. of a certain ~ (of considerable ~)

magpie *n.* ~s chatter

maid *n.* ["female servant"] a chambermaid; housemaid; kitchen ~; lady's ~; parlormaid (who waits at table)

mail I *n.* (esp. AE; BE usu. has *post* for 1–5, 8–10) ["letters"] ["postal system"] 1. to address; send out (the) ~ 2. to collect; deliver; redirect ~ 3. to forward; get, receive; open; sort (the) ~ 4. incoming; internal; outgoing; return ~ 5. airmail; certified; domestic; express; first-class; foreign; franked; registered; second-class; special-delivery; surface; third-class ~ 6. fan; hate; junk ~ 7. an item, piece (esp. AE) of ~ 8. the ~ comes (has the ~ come yet?) 9. by return ~ (BE has *by return of post*) 10. in the ~ (our letters crossed in the ~) 11. (misc.) electronic ~, E-mail; voice ~

mail II *v.* (esp. AE; BE usu. has *post*) 1. (A) she ~ed the package to me; or: she ~ed me the package 2. (D; tr.) to ~ from; to (the letter was ~ed from Oregon to Pennsylvania) (see also *mailing list* at **list**; for BE see **post II**)

mail III *n.* ["armor"] chain ~

main *n.* ["main pipe, duct"] 1. an electric; gas; sewer; water ~ 2. the water ~ burst

mainland *n.* 1. from; to the ~ 2. on the ~

mains *n.* (BE) to turn smt. off at the ~ (stop the leak by turning the water off at the ~)

mainstream *n.* 1. in the ~ (of politics) 2. outside the ~

maintain *v.* (L) she ~s that the accusation is groundless

maintenance *n.* 1. preventive; routine ~ 2. building; child; health; road ~ (the children's mother was entitled to child ~ from their absent father)

majesty *n.* ["sovereign"] 1. Her; His; Your Majesty; Their Majesties ["grandeur"] 2. in all its ~

major I *n.* ["academic specialization"] (AE) 1. to give, offer a ~ (our department gives an English ~) 2. a ~ in (our department offers a ~ in English) ["student who is specializing"] (AE) 3. a ~ in (she is a ~ in English; or: she is an English ~) ["officer"] 4. a ~ commands a battalion; your battalion is ready, Major (Smith)! 5. to make smb. a ~, to promote smb. to the rank of ~; to have, hold the rank of ~ **major II** v. (AE) (d; intr.) ("to specialize") to ~ in (to ~ in English) (BE has *to read English*)

majority n. ["number of votes greater than half or greater than anyone else gets"] (CE); ["greater number of votes"] (BE) 1. to get, receive a ~ 2. to have, hold a ~ (the Democrats have a slim ~ in the House) 3. a clear; great, large; overwhelming, vast ~ 4. a bare, narrow, slender, slim, small ~ 5. an absolute ~ (BE; AE has *majority*) 6. a (relative) ~ (BE; AE has *plurality*) 7. a simple; two-thirds; working ~ 8. by a ~ (to win the election by an overwhelming ~) 9. (misc.) the silent ~ (i.e., those who have moderate or conservative views but do not voice them); in a ~ (we were in the ~; in the ~ of cases) ["full legal age"] 10. to attain, reach one's ~ USAGE NOTE: Compare the verbs in the following constructions – the majority of the (two hundred) votes *were* for peace; a majority of two hundred votes *was* enough to win.

make I n. (colloq.) ["search for gain or sexual favors"] 1. on the ~ (he's always on the ~) ["brand"] 2. a ~ of (my favorite ~ of car = a car of my favorite ~)

make II v. 1. (A) ("to propose") she made an offer to us; or: she made us an offer 2. (C) ("to prepare") ~ an omelet for me; or: ~ me an omelet 3. (d; intr.) to ~ for ("to head for") (she made for the exit; the ship made for the open sea) 4. (d; intr.) to ~ for ("to lead to") (willingness to compromise ~s for success in negotiations) 5. (D; tr.) ("to provide") to ~ for (to ~ room for smb.) 6. (D; tr.) ("to create") to ~ from, of, out of, with (to ~ butter from cream; to ~ a film out of a novel; she made a table out of wood; tires can be made from/of/out of synthetic rubber; to ~ a stew with vegetables) 7. (d; tr.) ("to transform") to ~ into (to ~ cream into butter; to ~ a novel into a film; she took the wood and made it into a table; the experience made her into a skeptic; she made him into a good husband) 8. (slang) (AE) (d; intr.) to ~ like ("to imitate") (to ~ like a clown) 9. (d; tr.) to ~ of ("to interpret") (what do you ~ of their offer?) 10. (d; tr.) ("to create") to ~ of, out of (to ~ a fool of smb.; the army made a man out of him; she made a good husband out of him) 11. (D; tr.) ("to create") to ~ with (you ~ a stew with meat and vegetables) 12. (I) ("to cause"); ("to force") she made the children clean their room = the children were made to clean their room; we made them wait = they were made to wait; the police could not ~ him talk = he could not be made to talk by the police; your problems ~ mine seem unimportant = my problems are made to seem unimportant by comparison with yours 13. (N; used with an adjective, noun, past participle) ("to cause to become") the news made us happy; the rough sea made them seasick; we made our position clear; he

made me his deputy; she could not ~ herself understood; she made him a good husband 14. (S; used with nouns) ("to prove to be") she made a good deputy 15. (misc.) (AE; colloq.) he finally made colonel ("he was finally promoted to the rank of colonel"); the story made all the papers; we made the station just in time; we made it to the party on time; the ship barely made it to port; she made it to the top; to ~ good one's escape; smt. made to last; he made (as if) to leave USAGE NOTES: (1) When pattern I is put into the passive, *to* is inserted – we were made *to* wait. (2) Note that it is possible to have both "She made him a good wife" [= 'she made a good wife for him'] and "She made him a good husband" [= 'she made him into a good husband']. (See also Usage Note at **made**)

make away see **make off** (the thieves made away with the silverware)

make believe v. (L) let's ~ that we are on a space ship

make do v. (D; intr.) to ~ with ("to manage with") (we'll have to ~ with this stove; we'll have to ~ with this old car)

make off v. (d; intr.) to ~ with ("to steal and take away") (the thieves made off with the silverware)

make out v. 1. (colloq.) ("to have success") (D; intr.) to ~ with (how did you ~ with the new boss?) 2. (colloq.) (esp. AE) ("to have sexual success") (D; intr.) to ~ with (he's tried to ~ with every woman who works here!) 3. (misc.) he ~s himself out to be very important; she is not so bad as she is made out to be

makeover n. 1. to get; have a ~ (she had a complete ~ from a health-and-beauty consultant) 2. to give smb. a ~ (a health-and-beauty consultant gave her a complete ~)

make over v. 1. (B) ("to transfer legally") she made the bonds over to me 2. (D; tr.) ("to create") to ~ from; into (she made the boy's jacket over from her father's coat = she took her father's coat and made it over into the boy's jacket; a health-and-beauty consultant made her over completely)

maker n. 1. an auto ~ (esp. AE); filmmaker; marketmaker; policymaker 2. (misc.) to meet one's ~ ("to die and go to heaven")

makeup n. ["cosmetics"] 1. to apply, put on; use ~ 2. to remove ~

make up v. 1. (D; refl., tr.) ("to change one's appearance") to ~ as (he made himself up as an old man) 2. (D; tr.) ("to create") to ~ into (she took her father's coat and made it up into the boy's jacket) 3. (d; intr.) to ~ for ("to recoup") (to ~ for lost time) 4. (colloq.) (d; intr.) to ~ to ("to gain favor with") (you should try to ~ to your boss) 5. (D; intr.) ("to become reconciled") to ~ with (she made up with her sister) 6. (H) he made himself up to look like an old man 7. (misc.) I couldn't take the children for a treat today, but I promised to ~ it up to them next week

making *n.* ["evolution"] 1. in the ~ (a revolution in the ~) ["creation"] 2. not of smb.'s ~ (the problem is not of my ~)

makings *n.* ["potential"] to have the ~ of (she has all the ~ of a good orator)

maladjustment *n.* an emotional ~

malady *n.* (lit.) a fatal; serious; strange ~

malaise *n.* a general; spiritual ~

malaria *n.* 1. to catch, get, come down with, go diwn with (BE), develop ~ 2. to eradicate, stamp out; treat ~

malarkey *n.* (slang) ["nonsense"] (just) plain; pure, sheer ~

malevolence *n.* 1. pure, sheer ~ 2. out of ~ (he did it out of sheer ~)

malformation *n.* a congenital ~ (of) (suffers from a congenital ~ of the spine)

malice *n.* 1. to bear ~ towards 2. (legal) with ~ aforethought 3. (misc.) "With ~ toward none; with charity for all" – Abraham Lincoln, "Second Inaugural Address" (1865)

malicious *adj.* ~ towards

mall *n.* 1. a pedestrian; shopping ~ 2. at a ~ (she works at a shopping ~)

malpractice *n.* legal; medical; professional ~

mammals *n.* 1. the higher; lower ~ 2. among ~ (sexual rivalry among ~)

man *n.* 1. an attractive; average; fat; grown; handsome; mere; middle-aged; old; short; tall; thin; ugly; wise; young ~ 2. Cro-Magnon; Heidelberg; Java; Neanderthal; Peking; Piltdown ~; primitive ~ 3. a divorced; family; married; single ~ 4. a betting, gambling; con, confidence; fancy (esp. BE); hatchet; hit (esp. AE); ideas; ladies'; marked; organization; party (pol.); professional; Renaissance; right-hand; self-made; straight; straw ~ (AE; BE has *man of straw*); yes-man 5. an anchorman; businessman; leading ~; liftman (BE); maintenance ~; newspaperman; rewrite; stunt ~; weatherman 6. a moving (AE), removal (BE) ~ 7. a second-story ~ (AE; CE has *cat burglar*) 8. (pol.) (AE) an advance ~ 9. enlisted men (AE; BE has *other ranks*) 10. a university ~ (BE; AE has *college graduate*) 11. a lollipop ~ (BE; CE has *crossing guard*) 12. a best ~ (at a wedding) 13. the common ~, the ~ in the street, the ~ on the Clapham ominibus (BE) 14. a ~ on horseback ("a potential dictator") 15. in ~ (pregnancy lasts typically nine months in ~) 16. to a ~ ("everyone") (they stood up and applauded him to a ~) 17. (misc.) as one ~ (they stood up and applauded him as one ~); he's a ~ of his word; ~ is mortal; a dirty old ~ (pejor.) ("an immoral old man"); a medicine ~; the ~ of the year; a ~ of letters; a ~ of action; a ~ of the world; a ~ Friday (see also *every man jack* at **jack**; *men's magazine* at **magazine**)

manacle *v.* 1. (D; tr.) to ~ to (the prisoner was ~d to the bars; the prisoner was ~d to another prisoner = the prisoners were ~d to each other) 2. (misc.) the prisoners were ~d together

manacles *n.* to cast off, throw off one's ~

manage *v.* 1. (D; intr.) ("to cope") to ~ on (we cannot ~ on our present income) 2. (colloq.) (D; intr.) ("to cope") to ~ with (we cannot ~ with our present income) 3. (D; intr.) ("to cope") to ~ without (we cannot ~ without a car) 4. (E) ("to succeed") she somehow ~d to see him 5. (misc.) we simply cannot ~ on our own any longer!

management *n.* 1. efficient; poor ~ 2. middle; senior, top ~ 3. anger, stress ~ 4. under ~ (under new ~)

manager *n.* 1. an assistant; bank; area, branch; business; campaign; city; credit; general; hotel; office; sales; service; stage ~ 2. a baseball ~ USAGE NOTE: For other sports *coach* is used.

mandate I *n.* ["order"] 1. to seek; win a ~ 2. to have a ~ 3. to carry out a ~ 4. a clear ~ 5. a ~ to + inf. (we had a clear ~ to eliminate illiteracy) 6. under a ~ (to do smt.) 7. with; without a ~ (we were elected with a clear ~ to eliminate illiteracy) ["assignment to administer an area"] 8. a ~ over 9. under (a) ~

mandate II *v.* (formal) 1. (H) the president is ~d to carry out the laws 2. (esp. AE) (L; subj.) the constitution ~s that the president carry out the laws

mandated *adj.* federally ~ (US)

mandatory *adj.* 1. ~ for 2. ~ to + inf. (in certain countries it is ~ for all citizens to vote)

mane *n.* a horse's; lion's ~

maneuver I manoeuvre *n.* 1. to carry out, conduct, execute a ~ 2. (mil.) to conduct, hold ~s 3. a brilliant, clever; military; political; tactical ~ 4. on ~s (they were on ~s for two weeks)

maneuver II manoeuvre *v.* 1. (d; intr.) to ~ for (the players ~ed for position) 2. (d; tr.) to ~ into (we ~ed the players into position) 3. (d; tr.) to ~ out of (the players were ~ed out of position)

mangle *v.* to ~ beyond recognition

manhole *n.* an open ~

manhood *n.* to reach ~

manhunt *n.* 1. to carry out, conduct; launch, organize a ~ 2. a ~ for

mania *n.* 1. to have a ~ 2. a ~ for (do you remember when young people had a ~ for the Beatles?) USAGE NOTE: One can also use *-mania* to form words: *do you remember when young people were in the grip of Beatlemania?*

maniac *n.* a homicidal; raving ~

manicure *n.* 1. to give smb. a ~ 2. to get a ~

manifest *n.* 1. a plane's; ship's ~ 2. on a ~

manifestation *n.* a clear ~ (the protests were a clear ~ of the workers' discontent = the protests were a clear ~ that the workers were discontented)

manifesto *n.* 1. to draft, draw up; issue a ~ 2. to adopt a ~ 3. an election (BE); party (esp. BE); political ~ 4. an item in a ~ (see also **platform**)

manner *n.* 1. a charming; cheerful, lively; friendly; gentle, mild; gracious ~ 2. a courteous, polite; debonair; elegant, grand, polished, suave ~ 3. a casual, hit-or-miss, offhand, relaxed; intriguing

~ 4. a businesslike; dignified; forthcoming; matter-of-fact; professional; statesmanlike ~ 5. a stern, unsmiling ~ 6. an awkward; sheepish ~ 7. a cursory; flippant; slipshod, sloppy; supercilious ~ 8. an affected; cloying; ingratiating, servile, unctuous; pretentious; prim ~ 9. an abrupt, brusque; aggressive; arrogant, cavalier, imperious, overbearing; hostile ~ 10. a boorish; coarse, crude, rude, uncouth; obnoxious; rude; sullen, surly; taciturn ~ 11. bad; good ~s (it's bad ~s for a host to keep his guests waiting!) 12. table ~s 13. (a doctor's) bedside ~ 14. in a certain ~ (they behaved in a statesmanlike ~ = they were statesmanlike in their ~; in the grand ~; in an awkward ~; everything was done in a well-organized ~) 15. (misc.) to the ~ born ("as if so from birth"); in a ~ of speaking ("as it were"); to mind one's ~s ("to behave properly")

manoeuvre (BE) see **maneuver**

mansion n. (US) a governor's ~

manslaughter n. 1. to commit ~ 2. involuntary; voluntary ~

mantle n. ["symbol of authority"] to assume; inherit; wear the ~ (of authority)

manual n. 1. an instruction(al); laboratory; owner's; teacher's ~ 2. a ~ (a ~ for beginners = a beginners' ~)

manufacturer n. an aircraft; automobile (AE), car, motorcar (BE); clothing; computer; drug; furniture; radio; shoe; television ~

manure n. 1. to spread ~ 2. a heap, pile of ~

manuscript n. 1. to edit; proofread; revise a ~ 2. to submit a ~ (for publication) 3. to accept; reject a ~ 4. an authentic; unpublished ~ 5. an illuminated ~ 6. (misc.) the original ~ dates back / goes back to the fifteenth century

many determiner, pronoun 1. a good, great ~ 2. ~ to + inf. (we have ~ to sell; we have ~ books to sell) 3. ~ of (~ of them) USAGE NOTE: The use of the preposition of is necessary when a pronoun follows. When a noun follows, the use of of the limits the meaning – we saw many students; we saw many of the students whom we had met earlier.

map n. 1. to draw; trace a ~ 2. to consult; read a ~ 3. a large-scale; small-scale ~ 4. a contour; dialect; military; Ordnance-Survey (GB); relief; road; street; strip; weather ~ 5. off; on a ~ (to find a village on a ~) 6. (misc.) to put a place on the ~ ("to make a place well known"); to wipe smt. off the ~ ("to destroy smt.")

map out v. (d; tr.) to ~ for (to ~ a future for one's children)

marathon n. 1. to organize, stage a ~ 2. to run a ~ 3. a dance ~

marauder n. a band of ~s

marble n. a block; slab of ~

marbles n. 1. to play ~ 2. a game of ~ 3. (misc.) (colloq.) to lose one's ~ ("to lose one's mind")

march I n. ["procession"] 1. to go on, join, take part in; lead; organize a ~ 2. to ban; break up; call off

a ~ 3. a death; forced; hunger ~ 4. an antinuclear; antiwar, peace; civil-rights; political ~ protest; a ~ past (BE) (the Queen reviewed the ~ past of the troops) 5. a ~ against; for, in favor of, in support of; from; into; on; to (a ~ for peace and against war; the 1963 March On Washington) 6. on the ~ (science is on the ~) ["music that accompanies marching"] 7. to compose; play; strike up a ~ 8. a funeral; military; wedding ~ 9. a lively, rousing, stirring ~ ["misc."] 10. to steal a ~ on smb. ("to do smt. before smb. else")

march II v. 1. (d; intr.) to ~ against; for, in favor of, in support of (to ~ for peace and against war; to ~ against the enemy) 2. (D; intr., tr.) to ~ from; into; on; to; towards (the battalion ~ed from the barracks to the parade ground) 3. (d; intr., tr.) to ~ into (the troops ~ed into town) 4. (d; intr., tr.) to ~ on (the troops ~ed on the next town; to ~ on Washington to demand civil rights) 5. (P; intr., tr.) to ~ along the road; ~ing through Georgia; the teacher ~ed the students out of the room; the students ~ed out of the room

march down v. (d; intr., tr.) to ~ to (the teacher said that if we didn't behave, she would ~ us down to the principal's office)

marching orders n. ["notice of dismissal"] (colloq.) (BE) to give people their ~ (also fig.) (she gave her lover his ~ when he cheated on her) (AE has walking papers)

march off v. (D; intr., tr.) to ~ to (they were ~ed off to prison)

march on v. (D; intr.) to ~ to (the troops ~ed on to the next town)

mare n. a brood, stock ~

margarine n. 1. to spread ~ 2. soft; vegetable ~ 3. a pat; tub of ~ 4. in ~ (to fry in ~)

margin n. 1. to adjust; set a ~ (when typing) 2. to justify a ~ (in setting type, in word processing) 3. a close, narrow, slender, slim, small ~ 4. a comfortable, decisive, handsome, large, wide; safe ~ 5. by a ~ (they won by a slim ~ over the opposition) 6. in, on a ~ (to make notes in the ~s) 7. (misc.) a ~ of error; a ~ of safety; a ~ of victory; a profit ~; on the ~s (of society)

marihuana, marijuana n. 1. to grow ~ 2. to smoke ~

marina n. a municipal, public ~

marine n. a mercantile (BE), merchant (AE) ~ (see also **navy**)

marionette n. to manipulate, move, pull the strings of a ~

mark I n. ["sign, symbol"] 1. to make one's ~ ("to make a cross in place of a signature") 2. an accent, stress; diacritical; exclamation (BE; AE has exclamation point); question; quotation, quote ~ (see also **punctuation mark**; **question mark**; a mark of respect at **respect**) 3. a hash ~ 4. a laundry ~ ["impression, imprint"] 5. to get; have a ~; leave, make one's ~ (you've got a black ~ on your collar;

they have made their ~ in politics and they will leave their ~ on history) 6. a distinguishing; highwater; indelible ~; a check ~ (AE; BE has *tick*) (to make/put a check ~ beside/by the right answer) ["target"] 7. to find, hit the ~ (the bullet found its ~) 8. to miss; overshoot the ~ 9. to fall short of the ~ 10. off the ~, wide of the ~ ["skin blemish"] 11. a birthmark, strawberry (esp. BE) ~ ["victim"] 12. an easy ~ ["starting line of a race"] 13. on your ~s! ["misc."] 14. to toe the ~ ("to adhere to the rules"); to bear the ~ of Cain; the actress won high ~s for her performance; she managed to get a pass ~ in French at A-level (BE) (see also **grade I** 1–4; **marks**)

mark II *v.* 1. (D; tr.) to ~ as (these items were ~ed as acceptable) 2. (d; tr.) to ~ for (~ed for death) 3. (K) this birthday ~s his coming of age 4. (N; used with an adjective) these items were ~ed acceptable (see also **grade II**)

mark down *v.* (D; tr.) to ~ by; from; to (the instructor ~ed her down from A to B; these items have been ~ed down from $12 to $11.95 – and these others by 50%!)

marker *n.* ["IOU"] (colloq.) (AE) to call in a ~

market *n.* ["store, shop"] ["group of shops or stalls"] 1. a fish; food ~; hypermarket (BE); meat ~; supermarket 2. a farmers'; flea; open-air ~ 3. at, in a ~ (to shop at the ~) ["place where trade is conducted"] 4. to open a new ~ 5. a commodity; money; stock ~ 6. a free, open; overseas; spot ~ 7. on; onto a ~ (to buy oil on the spot ~; to put a new product on the ~; a new computer has just come (out) on the ~) ["stock market"] 8. to gamble on, play, speculate on the ~ ("to speculate") 9. to depress the ~ 10. a bear ("falling"); bull ("rising") ~ 11. the ~ is active; volatile; sluggish 12. the ~ is firm, steady; rising; up 13. the ~ is depressed; down; falling 14. the ~ rallies; slumps 15. the ~ closes strong; weak 16. the ~ opens strong; weak (see also **stock market**) ["supply of goods, services"] 17. to capture, corner, monopolize a ~ 18. to flood, glut a ~ 19. the housing; labor ~ 20. a buyer's; seller's; niche, specialized; social ~ ["demand"] 21. to create a ~ 22. to study the ~ 23. to depress a ~ 24. a ~ for (there is no ~ for large cars – except perhaps at the upper end of the ~) 25. in the ~ for (we're in the ~ for a new house) 26. a drug on the ~ ("smt. for which there is little demand") ["trade"] 27. the bond; commodities; second-hand-car, used-car; securities; wheat ~ (see also *market economy* at **economy**; *market forces* at **force**)

marketplace *n.* in the ~

marks *n.* (esp. BE) 1. to get; give ~ 2. full, top ~ 3. ~ out of (the teacher gave me 10 out of 10 ~s on the English exam and my parents were delighted that I'd got full ~ in English!) 4. (fig.) full ~ (full ~ to Sherlock Holmes for catching the villain!)

marksman, markswoman *n.* a crack, expert, skilled ~

markup *n.* a ~ on (their ~ on merchandise was small)

marmalade *n.* orange ~

marriage *n.* 1. to enter into a ~ 2. to announce a ~ 3. to consummate a ~ 4. to arrange a ~ 5. to solemnize a ~ 6. to propose ~ 7. to annul a ~ 8. to break up, dissolve a ~ 9. a good, happy, stable ~ 10. a bad, unhappy; broken ~ 11. an arranged; civil; common-law; communal; first; group; morganatic; open; previous; proxy; secret; trial ~ (she has several children from a previous ~) 12. an interfaith; interracial; mixed ~ 13. a ~ breaks up, collapses, dissolves 14. a ~ of convenience 15. a ~ into (a family) 16. a ~ to (smb.) 17. by ~ (we're related by ~) 18. (misc.) to give (one's child) in ~ (Brabantio was reluctant to give Desdemona in ~ to Othello)

married *adj.* 1. happily ~ 2. to get ~ (to) (Othello and Desdemona got ~ (to each other))

marrow *n.* 1. bone ~ 2. vegetable ~ (BE; AE has *squash*)

marry *v.* 1. (D; intr.) to ~ for (to ~ for love) (Othello married Desdemona for love) 2. (d; intr.) to ~ into (to ~ into a good family) 3. (D; tr.) to ~ (to) ("to perform a marriage ceremony for") (Friar Laurence married Romeo and Juliet to each other) = Friar Laurence married Romeo to Juliet)

marry off *v.* (D; tr.) to ~ to (Brabantio was reluctant to ~ off Desdemona to Othello = Brabantio was reluctant to ~ Desdemona off to Othello)

marshal *n.* an air; field ~

marshmallow *n.* to roast, toast ~s

martial law *n.* 1. to declare, impose, invoke ~ 2. to lift, rescind; suspend ~ 3. under ~ (the area was placed under ~)

martini *n.* ("type of cocktail") 1. to fix (esp. AE), make, mix a ~ 2. a dry ~

martyr *n.* 1. to make a ~ (of smb.) 2. a ~ to (a ~ to tyranny) 3. (misc.) to burn a ~ at the stake; to play the ~

martyrdom *n.* to face; suffer, undergo ~ (to suffer ~ for one's beliefs)

marvel I *n.* 1. to achieve, do, work ~s 2. a ~ to 3. a ~ that + clause (it's a ~ to me that we didn't get lost)

marvel II *v.* 1. (d; intr.) to ~ at (to ~ at smb.'s skill) 2. (L) (esp. BE) I can but ~ that we didn't get lost!

marvelous, marvellous *adj.* 1. absolutely, quite (esp. BE) ~ 2. ~ to + inf. (it's ~ to have a day off = it's ~ having a day off; it was ~ of you to help) 3. ~ that + clause (it's ~ that we had the day off; it was ~ that you decided to help!)

mascara *n.* 1. to apply, put on ~ 2. to remove, wipe off ~ 3. ~ runs

mask *n.* 1. to put on; wear a ~ 2. to take off a ~ 3. a death; gas; oxygen; ski; stocking; surgical ~

masochism *n.* to display ~

masonry *n.* 1. crumbling, falling ~ 2. ~ comes off, falls off

masquerade *v.* (D; intr.) to ~ as (to ~ as a policeman)

mass I *n.* ["body of matter"] 1. a shapeless; sticky; tangled ~ (a tangled ~ of hair) 2. a land ~ 3. a critical ~ 4. a dense ~ (of smoke) 5. (med.) a fixed; hard; irregular; movable; nodular; palpable ~
mass II *n.* ["religious celebration of the Eucharist"] 1. to celebrate, offer, say (a, the) ~ 2. to attend, go to, hear ~ 3. (a) high; low; nuptial; pontifical; requiem; solemn; votive ~ 4. a ~ for (a requiem ~ is a ~ for the dead)
massacre *n.* 1. to carry out, perpetrate a ~ 2. a brutal ~ 3. a ~ happens, takes place
massage *n.* 1. to give (smb.) a ~ 2. to get a ~ 3. a back; body; facial; therapeutic ~
mast *n.* 1. a tall ~ 2. (to fly) at half ~ 3. (misc.) (lit.) before the ~ ("at sea as a sailor")
master I *n.* 1. to find, meet one's ~ ("to find one who is superior") 2. a question ~ (BE; AE has *quizmaster*) 3. (chess) a chess; grand ~ 4. a past ~ 5. a ~ at, of (a past ~ of deceit)
master II *v.* to ~ completely, thoroughly (a scoundrel who has thoroughly ~ed the art of deceit)
masterpiece *n.* 1. to create a ~ 2. an enduring ~ 3. a literary ~
mastery *n.* 1. to demonstrate, display, show ~ 2. to achieve, acquire ~ 3. (a) complete; thorough ~ 4. ~ of; over (~ of one's subject; ~ over other people; a scoundrel who has achieved thorough ~ of the art of deceit)
mat *n.* 1. to weave a ~ 2. a bath; beer; exercise; place; prayer; ~ (see also **welcome mat**)
match I *n.* ["that catches fire when struck"] 1. to blow out, extinguish; light, strike a ~ 2. to light, put, set a ~ to 3. a safety ~ 4. a book; box of ~es 5. (misc.) children should not play with ~es
match II *n.* ["marriage"] ["marriage partner"] 1. to make a ~ 2. a good ~ 3. a ~ for ["contest"] 4. to promote, stage a ~ 5. a championship; crucial; play-off; return; test (BE) ("international cricket or rugby") ~ 6. a football ~ (esp. BE; AE has *football game*) 7. a boxing; chess; cricket; fencing; golf; hockey; polo; tennis; wrestling ~ 8. a ~ between; with (a wrestling ~ between two strong competitors took place last week, during which one was injured) ["equal competitor"] 9. to meet one's ~ 10. no ~ for (she proved to be no ~ for me; I was no ~ for her) 11. smb.'s ~ in (she was more than my ~ in ability = she was more than a ~ for me in ability; no one is his ~ in speed and agility) ["pair"] 12. a good; perfect ~ 13. a ~ for USAGE NOTE: When two teams compete before spectators, BE typically has *match* (a football match); AE typically has *game* (a football game). However, when the team game is of North American origin, BE often uses *game* too (a basketball game). Moreover, *game* is starting to become more frequent in BE generally. A *chess match* is CE.
match III *v.* 1. (D; tr.) to ~ against, with ("to pit against") (she was ~ed against/with a formidable opponent) 2. (D; tr.) ("to equal") to ~ for, in (no

one can ~ him in speed and agility) 3. (D; tr.) to ~ with ("to find the equivalent of") (she wants to ~ this candlestick with a similar one)
matched *adj.* evenly; ideally ~
matchmaker *n.* a professional ~
match up *v.* (D; intr.) to ~ to, with (he doesn't ~ to his opponent)
mate I *n.* ["petty officer"] (naval) 1. a boatswain's; first; machinist's ~ ["junior partner"] 2. (BE) a plumber's ~ 3. (US; pol.) smb.'s running ~
mate II *v.* (D; intr., tr.) to ~ with (cats and dogs can't ~ (with each other); zebras don't ~ with donkeys; to ~ a donkey with a mare)
material I *adj.* ~ to (this evidence is ~ to our case)
material II *n.* ["data"] 1. to collect, gather ~ 2. source ~ 3. ~ about, on (to gather ~ about the case) 4. ~ for (to gather ~ for a dictionary) ["matter"] 5. building ~ 6. radioactive; raw; synthetic ~ 7. promotional; reading; reference ~ 8. writing ~s 9. packing ~ ["cloth"] 10. a piece, swatch of ~
materialism *n.* dialectical; historical ~
materialize *v.* (d; intr.) to ~ out of (the apparition we expected failed to ~ out of the shadows)
mathematics *n.* applied; elementary; higher; pure ~
matrimony *n.* 1. holy ~ (they were joined/united in holy ~) 2. the state of ~
matron *n.* 1. a dignified ~ 2. a ~ of honor (at a wedding)
matter I *n.* ["affair"] 1. to deal with, pursue, take up a ~ 2. to bring up, broach, raise; discuss, go into a ~ 3. to arrange a ~ 4. to clear up, settle, straighten out a ~ 5. to complicate; simplify a ~ 6. to give a ~ (attention, thought) (we have given this ~ considerable thought) 7. to not mince ~s ("to express oneself candidly") 8. to drop a ~, to let a ~ drop 9. a business; personal, private ~ 10. a complex, complicated; delicate ~ 11. an important, pressing, serious, weighty ~ 12. a petty, trifling, trivial; simple ~ 13. no easy, no laughing ~ (it's no easy ~ to find a house in this city = it's no easy ~ finding a house in this city; being accused of assault is no laughing ~) 14. ~s came to a head (when he tendered his resignation) 15. a ~ for (a ~ for conjecture; a ~ for speculation) 16. a ~ of (a ~ of grave importance) 17. in ~s of (in ~s of finance) 18. (misc.) as a ~ of fact ("really"); to take ~s into one's own hands; the fact of the ~ is that...; a ~ of record (legal); for that ~ ("concerning that"); a ~ of a few minutes; a ~ of (personal) opinion/taste; a ~ of some urgency; a ~ of life and death; the crux/heart of the ~; no ~ how she tries, she gets no credit; you look so sad – what's the ~? you haven't done this properly – what's the ~ with you? ["material"] ["substance"] 19. printed; reading ~ (see also **subject matter**) 20. gaseous; inorganic; liquid; organic; solid; vegetable ~ 21. gray ~ ("brains") 22. the back; front ~ (of a book) USAGE NOTE: The expression *what's the matter?* can express

sympathy; *what's the matter with you/him etc?* is often critical.

matter II *v.* 1. (D; intr.) to ~ to (her financial status hardly ~s to us – but it ~s a great deal to her!) 2. (R; to) it doesn't ~ (to us) that we are not rich 3. (misc.) it doesn't ~ (to us) whether or not we are rich = what does it ~ (to us) whether or not we are rich?

mattress *n.* 1. a firm; lumpy; orthopedic; soft ~ 2. a double, full; king-size; queen-size; single, twin ~ 3. an air ~ 4. on; under a ~

mature *adj.* 1. emotionally; mentally; physically; sexually ~ 2. ~ for (she is ~ for her age)

maturity *n.* 1. to reach ~ 2. full ~ 3. emotional; mental; physical; sexual ~

maxim *n.* a ~ that + clause (is it a valid ~ that competition increases productivity?)

maximum *n.* 1. to fall below; reach; set a ~ 2. at a ~ (excitement was at its ~)

may *v.* 1. (F) she ~ (well) still show up 2. (misc.) we ~ as well give in; they ~ or ~ not have been here earlier; ~ we wish you a Happy New Year! (see also **might II**) USAGE NOTE: In today's English and esp. BE, *may* is often used wrongly for *might.* It is correct to say "the ambulance arrived so quickly that the victim may/might have survived – we don't know yet" but incorrect to say "if the ambulance had arrived in time, the victim **may* [= might] have survived – but unfortunately didn't."

mayhem *n.* to commit ~

meadow *n.* in a ~

meal I *n.* ["repast"] 1. to cook, fix (esp. AE; colloq.), prepare a ~ 2. to put together, slap together, whip together a ~ 3. to eat, have; enjoy a ~ 4. to make a ~ of (to make a ~ of soup) 5. to order; serve a ~ 6. to skip a ~ 7. a big, heavy; decent, hearty, solid, square; hot; slap-up (BE colloq.), sumptuous ~ (to have a square ~) 8. a light, small; simple; skimpy ~ 9. an evening (BE); main; mid-day; set (esp. BE) ~ (the main ~ of the day) ["misc."] 10. (BE; colloq.) to make a ~ of smt. ("to behave as if smt. easy were difficult") USAGE NOTE: Because of the confusion in BE about *dinner, supper,* and *tea,* BE tends increasingly to use *evening meal* to avoid ambiguity. That is particularly true in official notices: "we offer tourists bed, breakfast and an evening meal." BE also to some extent uses *mid-day meal* to avoid the potential ambiguity of *lunch* and *dinner.*

meal II *n.* ["ground seeds"] Indian ~ (BE; CE has *cornmeal*)

mean I *adj.* 1. ~ about (he was very ~ about the loan) 2. ~ with (esp. BE) 3. ~ to (he's ~ to everyone) 4. ~ to + inf. (it was ~ of her to say that) USAGE NOTE: *Mean* can be both 'stingy' (esp. BE) and 'nasty' (esp. AE). Real ambiguity is possible but sometimes prevented in context: In *mean with, mean* is probably 'stingy'; in *mean to,* probably 'nasty.'

mean II *n.* ["mathematical value"] 1. to find a ~ 2.

an arithmetic; harmonic ~ ["middle point"] 3. a golden ~

mean III *v.* 1. (A; usu. used without *to*) she meant them no harm 2. (d; tr.) to ~ as (her remark was meant as a compliment) 3. (d; tr.) to ~ for (his remark was meant for you) 4. (D; tr.) to ~ to (her words meant nothing to me) 5. (E) I meant to write; she never meant to harm them 6. (H) we never meant you to go without us; she meant her remark to be a compliment = her remark was meant to be a compliment 7. (L) though she said, "it's getting late," she really meant that she wanted us to leave 8. (S) *Hund* ~s "dog"; waiting longer ~s driving after dark 9. (misc.) they never knew what it meant to be hungry; she ~s what she says, but I'm not sure she always says what she really ~s

meander *v.* (P; intr.) the brook ~s through the valley

meaning *n.* 1. to acquire, take on; distort, twist; have; misconstrue a ~ 2. an accepted; basic; clear; connotative; double, equivocal; figurative; hidden, obscure; literal 3. grammatical; lexical; referential ~ 4. a shade of ~ 5. in a ~ (in the accepted ~ of the word)

meaningful *adj.* ~ to (the ceremony was very ~ to all those who came)

meaningless *adj.* ~ to (the lecture was ~ to all those who did not understand the language)

meanness *n.* 1. ~ to 2. out of ~ (she did it out of ~) (see also Usage Note at **mean I** *adj.*)

means *n.* ["method"] 1. fair; foul ~ (by fair ~ or foul) 2. an effective ~ 3. by any ~ (by any ~ necessary) 4. by ~ of (the roof is held in place by ~ of steel cables) 5. (misc.) the end does not justify the ~; a ~ to an end ["resources"] ["wealth"] 6. independent, private; moderate ~ 7. the ~ to + inf. (do they have the ~ to buy such a large house?) 8. according to, within one's ~ (to live within one's ~) 9. beyond one's ~ (to live beyond one's ~) 10. of ~ (a person of moderate ~) ["misc."] 11. by all ~ ("yes, of course"); by no ~ ("in no way"); ways and ~; a vagrant with no visible ~ of support

meant *adj.* (cannot stand alone) ["destined"] 1. ~ for (they were ~ for each other) ["intended"] 2. ~ as (her remark was ~ as a compliment) 3. ~ to + inf. (her remark was ~ to be a compliment) ["supposed"] (colloq.) (BE) 4. ~ to + inf. (Brighton is ~ to be lovely in summer)

meantime, meanwhile *n.* in the ~

measles *n.* 1. to catch, come down with, get, go down with (BE) (the) ~ 2. German ~ ("rubella") 3. an epidemic; outbreak of ~ 4. a case of ~

measure I *n.* 1. (a) cubic; dry; liquid; metric; square ~ 2. a tape ~ 3. in a certain ~ (in large ~ = in no small ~; "that cause for which they here gave the last full ~ of devotion" – A. Lincoln, "The Gettysburg Address," 1863) 4. (misc.) for good ~ ("as smt. extra"); made to ~ ("custom-made"); to take smb.'s ~ ("to evaluate smb."); it's early days yet to get the full ~ of the man (see also **measures**)

measure II *v.* 1. (d; tr.) to ~ against (to ~ one's accomplishments against smb. else's) 2. (D; tr.) to ~ for (to ~ smb. for new shoes) 3. (P; intr.) the room ~s twenty feet by ten

measurement *n.* 1. to take a ~; to take smb.'s ~s 2. exact ~s 3. a metric ~ 4. a scientific ~ 5. bust, chest; hip; inside leg; waist ~s 6. a system; unit of ~

measures *n.* 1. to carry out, take ~ 2. farsighted; interim; stopgap, temporary ~ 3. corrective; precautionary, preventive, prophylactic; safety, security ~ 4. emergency; extraordinary ~ 5. austerity, draconian; drastic, harsh, stern, stringent, tough; extreme, radical ~ 6. coercive; compulsory; punitive ~ 7. ~ to + inf. (we took ~ (in order) to ensure their safety) 8. ~ against (to take ~ against smuggling)

measure up *v.* (D; intr.) to ~ to (how did he ~ to his opponent?)

meat *n.* 1. to barbecue; braise; broil (AE), grill; cook; cure; fry; marinate; roast; sear; stew ~ 2. to carve, cut; slice ~ 3. dark; red; white ~ 4. fatty; lean ~ 5. raw; tender; tough ~ 6. halal; kosher ~ 7. canned (AE), tinned (BE); fresh; frozen ~ 8. boned; chopped (AE), ground (AE), minced (BE); soup ~ 9. ~ goes bad, spoils 10. a cut; joint; piece; slice of ~ (I'd like a couple of slices of your best cut of ~, please) 11. (misc.) ~ off the bone; ~ on the bone

mecca *n.* 1. a tourist ~ 2. a ~ for (the mall was a ~ for shoppers)

mechanic *n.* an automobile (AE), car, motorcar (BE); master ~

mechanics *n.* celestial; fluid; quantum ~

mechanism *n.* 1. to activate, actuate, set off, trigger a ~ 2. a defense; escape; fail-safe; survival ~

medal *n.* 1. to award, give a ~ 2. to earn, get, win a ~ 3. to strike ("make") a ~ 4. a bronze; gold; silver ~ (as a prize) 5. a ~ for (to earn a ~ for bravery)

meddle *v.* (D; intr.) to ~ in; with (don't ~ in their affairs)

media *n.* 1. the electronic; local; mass; national; news; print ~ 2. in the ~ (the elections were covered in the local ~) USAGE NOTE: Purists insist on *are the media reliable?* and consider *is the media reliable?* to be incorrect.

mediate *v.* (D; intr.) to ~ among, between (to offer to ~ between the warring parties)

mediation *n.* 1. to conduct; offer ~ 2. to go to ~ (the dispute went to ~) 3. ~ among, between (to offer ~ between the warring parties)

mediator *n.* 1. to appoint a ~ 2. a government ~ 3. a ~ between

Medicaid *n.* (US) on ~ (is that treatment available on ~?)

Medicare *n.* (US) on ~ (we will be on ~ next year)

medication *n.* 1. to take (a) ~ (for) 2. to administer, dispense, give (a) ~ 3. to order; prescribe (a) ~ 4. to put smb. on ~ 5. to discontinue (a) ~ 6. to take smb. off ~ 7. (an) effective; mild; potent, strong ~ 8. a

nonprescription, over-the-counter; proprietary ~ 9. (an) intramuscular; intravenous; oral; parenteral; topical ~ 10. to be on ~ for (she is now on ~ for high blood pressure)

medicine *n.* ["method, science of treating disease"] 1. to practice ~ 2. to study ~ 3. aerospace, space; aviation; military; sports; tropical ~ 4. community, social; industrial, occupational; preventive ~ 5. family; internal; physical ~ 6. clinical; forensic, legal ~ 7. molecular; nuclear ~ 8. allopathic; ayurvedic; holistic; homeopathic; osteopathic ~ 9. alternative, complementary (BE), fringe (BE); folk; traditional ~ 10. defensive ~ 11. socialized (esp. AE) ~ 12. veterinary ~ ["remedy"] 13. to take (a) ~ (to take ~ for a cold) 14. to prescribe (a) ~ 15. a cough; nonprescription, over-the-counter; patent; proprietary ~ 16. strong ~ (also fig.) 17. a dose; course of ~ 18. ~ for ["punishment"] (colloq.) 19. to take one's ~ ("to accept one's punishment")

meditate *v.* 1. to ~ deeply 2. (D; intr.) to ~ on, upon (to ~ deeply on impermanence)

meditation *n.* 1. to do, go in for, practice ~ 2. insight; transcendental ~ 3. deep, profound ~ (on, upon) 4. (deep) in ~ (to be deep in ~ on impermanence)

medium *n.* ["middle degree"] 1. a happy ~ 2. a ~ between (a ~ between two extremes) ["system"] 3. a ~ of instruction ["means"] 4. by, through a ~ (to be transmitted through the ~ of air; to be broadcast through the ~ of radio)

meet I *n.* (esp. AE) (sports) 1. to hold, organize a ~ 2. a dual; swim, swimming; track; track-and-field ~

meet II *v.* 1. (D; intr., tr.) to ~ for (we met them for dinner) 2. (d; intr.) to ~ with ("to encounter") (to ~ with approval; they met with an accident) 3. (esp. AE) (d; intr.) to ~ with ("to have a meeting with") (our negotiators will ~ with them tomorrow) 4. (misc.) to ~ smb. halfway ("to compromise with smb."); to ~ face to face; to ~ head-on; smt. strange is going on – there's more to this than ~s the eye!; "Mr. Smith, this is Mr. Jones." "Pleased to ~ you, Mr. Jones!"

meeting *n.* 1. to call, convene; open a ~ 2. to attend a ~ 3. to arrange, organize, schedule a ~ 4. to have, hold a ~ 5. to chair, conduct, preside over a ~ 6. to adjourn; break up; close a ~ (they close their ~s with a prayer) 7. to call off, cancel; postpone; reschedule a ~ 8. to disrupt a ~ (the protesters disrupted the ~ by shouting slogans) 9. a clandestine, secret; closed; emergency; mass; open; private; protest; public ~ 10. a board; business; cabinet; committee; departmental; faculty (esp. AE); prayer; revival; staff; town (US) ~ 11. an athletics ~ (BE; AE has *track meet*) 12. a race (BE; AE has *racing card*) 13. a series of ~s (they held a series of ~s to resolve their differences) 14. a ~ between, of; about 15. at; in a ~ (I saw her at the ~; she's in a ~ and cannot be disturbed) 16. (misc.) to call a ~ to order; a chance ~; at the Annual General

Meeting (at the AGM) of an association (esp. BE); a ~ of minds (after our discussions we seemed to have reached a ~ of minds that made co-operation possible between us)

meet up v. (AE) (D; intr.) to ~ with (our negotiators will ~ with them tomorrow)

megaphone n. (to speak) through a ~

melody n. 1. to hum; play; sing; whistle; write a ~ 2. a catchy; haunting; lilting ~

melon n. 1. a juicy; ripe; tasty ~ 2. a honeydew ~; watermelon 3. a slice of ~

melt v. (d; intr.) to ~ into (to ~ into the crowd)

melting-point n. to be at; reach (the) ~

member n. 1. to recruit new ~s 2. an active; associate; card-carrying; charter (AE), founder (BE); full; honorary; individual; institutional; life; paid-up; ranking; staff; sustaining ~ 3. a corresponding; overseas ~ (of an academy) 4. a board; group ~ 5. (misc.) to admit new ~s into an organization 6. a ~ of

membership n. 1. to apply for ~ 2. to renew one's ~ 3. to grant ~ 4. to deny, refuse ~ (to smb.) 5. to drop, resign one's ~ 6. closed; open ~ 7. (an) agency, institutional; associate; full; honorary; individual; life; permanent; temporary ~ 8. a ~ lapses 9. ~ in (AE), of (BE) (~ in/of an organization)

membrane n. 1. a mucous ~ 2. ~s rupture (her ~s ruptured too early in labor)

memo n. 1. to write out, write up a ~ 2. an interoffice; office ~ 3. a ~ from; to (see also **memorandum**)

memoirs n. 1. to publish; write one's ~ 2. misery ~ (about people's unhappy lives)

memorandum n. 1. to draw up, prepare a ~ 2. to send around a ~ (in an office) 3. to initial a ~ 4. a confidential, secret; diplomatic; interoffice; official; private ~ 5. a ~ about, on 6. a ~ from; to

memorial n. 1. to build, erect, put up a ~ 2. to unveil a ~ 3. a war ~ 4. a ~ to

memory n. ["power of recalling"] 1. to jog, refresh smb.'s ~ 2. to commit smt. to ~ 3. to slip smb.'s ~ (the date has slipped my ~) 4. to lose one's ~ 5. a bad, poor; good; infallible; long; photographic; powerful; retentive; short ~ 6. (med.) long-term; short-term; visual ~ 7. a ~ for (a good ~ for names) 8. (to speak) from ~ 9. (misc.) a lapse of ~; a ~ like a sieve (my cousin has a very poor ~; in fact, he has a ~ like a sieve!); if ~ serves (we met in 1966, if ~ serves) ["something recalled, recollection"] 10. to bring back, call up, conjure up, dredge up, evoke, revive, stir up a ~ (the incident evoked painful ~ies that came back after they'd started to fade) 11. to blot out, bury, suppress a ~ (I have no ~ of meeting him in 1966 even though he has a very clear ~ of it: I must have suppressed the ~ of our meeting!) 12. bitter; bittersweet; dim, vague; enduring; fond, happy, pleasant; haunting, poignant; painful, sad, unpleasant ~ries ["collective remembrance"] 13. to honor, perpetuate, revere, venerate smb.'s ~ 14. a blessed, sacred ~ 15. in ~ of (to erect a monument

in smb.'s ~) 16. in living ~ (nothing like it had happened in/within living ~!) 17. of blessed, sacred ~ 18. (misc.) dedicated to smb.'s ~ ["capacity for storing information in a computer"] 19. (a) random-access; read-only; virtual ~

menace I n. 1. to be, constitute, pose, represent a ~ 2. a ~ to

menace II v. (D; tr.) to ~ with (to ~ smb. with reprisals)

mend n. on the ~ ("improving")

mending n. invisible ~

menopause n. 1. to go through (AE), go through the ~ 2. the male ~ (is there really such a thing as a/ the male ~?)

mentality n. a bunker, siege ~

mention I n. 1. to make ~ of 2. to deserve ~ 3. honorable ~ (conferred in a contest for an accomplishment of merit that does not win a prize) 4. special ~ (her work deserves special ~ at this time) 5. at the ~ (at the very ~ of his name I shuddered)

mention II v. 1. (B) he ~ed my lateness to her 2. (D; tr.) to ~ as (she was ~ed as a possible candidate) 3. (K) he failed to ~ (to her) my being late twice last week 4. (L; to) he ~ed (to her) that I had been late twice last week 5. (Q; tr.) he forgot to ~ (to her) how often I had been late last week 6. (misc.) to ~ smb. by name; not to ~ (I was late twice last week – not to ~ all the times I'd been late previously!); now you come to ~ it (Oh, now you come to ~ it, I suppose you HAVE been late quite often recently); "Thank you!" "Don't ~ it!" (esp. BE) (see also *mentioned in dispatches* at **dispatch**)

mentor n. a ~ to (who is the ~ to the young prince?)

menu n. ["bill of fare"] 1. to bring a ~ (the waiter brought the ~) 2. a certain ~ (besides its regular ~ the restaurant has/offers a special children's ~ and a vegetarian ~, too, so that all the family can choose/order what they like from the ~!) 3. on a ~ (what's on the ~?) ["list of commands for a computer program"] 4. an edit; main; print ~

mercenary n. a foreign ~

merchandise n. 1. to buy, purchase; order ~ 2. to flog (BE, colloq.), hawk, sell ~ 3. to ship ~ 4. to carry (a line of) ~ 5. first-class, high-quality ~ 6. assorted; general ~ 7. defective, inferior, shoddy ~ 8. a line; piece; range of ~ (the American Flag should never be treated as just a piece of ~!)

merciful adj. 1. ~ to, towards 2. ~ to + inf. (it was ~ of her to offer help)

merciless adj. ~ to, towards

mercy n. 1. to have ~ on 2. to show ~ to, towards 3. to beg for, implore (smb.'s) ~ 4. to throw oneself on smb.'s ~ 5. divine; infinite ~; smb.'s tender ~cies (ironic) (we turned him over to the tender ~cies of the student court) 6. at smb.'s ~ 7. (misc.) and may God have ~ on your soul!; well, ~ me! (used esp. by women as an expression of mild surprise); "we missed the train but at least it's stopped raining" "well, let's be thankful/grateful for small mercies!"

merely adv. see **only** adv., adj.

merge v. 1. to ~ gradually; imperceptibly 2. (D; intr., tr.) to ~ into (to ~ several small companies into one large one) 3. (D; intr., tr.) to ~ with (several small companies ~d with theirs to form one large one)

merger n. 1. to carry out, effect a ~ 2. a ~ between, of; into; with (to carry out the ~ of several small companies into one large one) 3. a ~ is approved, goes through; is blocked, is opposed

merit n. 1. intrinsic ~ 2. relative ~s 3. according to, on (the basis of) ~ (to decide a case on its ~s) 4. of ~ (their case is of dubious ~)

merry adj. to make ~ (lit.)

merry-go-round n. 1. to ride (on) a ~ 2. to get on a ~ 3. to get off a ~ (CE; BE has *roundabout*)

mesh v. (D; intr.) to ~ with (the gears ~ with each other)

mess I n. ["untidy condition"] (may be fig.) 1. to make a ~ (they made a ~ of the project; the dog's made a ~ on the carpet) 2. to leave a ~ 3. to clean away, clean up, clear away, clear up, straighten out, straighten up, sweep out, sweep up; deal with, sort out (esp. BE) a ~ 4. a complete, terrible, unsightly, utter ~ 5. in a ~ (to leave things in an utter ~) ["dining hall"] (mil.) 6. an enlisted (AE); officers' ~ 7. at, in a ~ (they always eat at the company ~)

mess II v. (colloq.) 1. (d; intr.) to ~ in (esp. AE) (don't ~ in their affairs) 2. to ~ with (don't ~ with him)

mess about (BE) 1. ~ in ("simply ~sing about in boats" – Kenneth Grahame (1859–1932), *The Wind in the Willows*) 2. see **mess around** USAGE NOTE: BE can also use *mess smb. about* to mean 'make trouble for smb., confuse smb.': *stop ~ing me about!*

message n. 1. to convey; relay; send, transmit a ~ 2. to deliver; leave a ~ 3. to get, receive a ~ 4. to intercept a ~ 5. to garble; scramble; unscramble a ~ 6. a clear; coded; cryptic, secret; garbled; urgent ~ 7. an E-mail ~ (she sent me an E-mail ~) 8. (on a computer) an error ~ 9. a ~ from; to (they received an urgent ~ from their partner) 10. a ~ to + inf. (we got a ~ to meet them at the restaurant) 11. a ~ that + clause (we got a ~ that we were to meet them at the restaurant) 12. in a ~ 13. (misc.) to get the ~ ("to grasp the situation, to get the point"); to send mixed ~s ("to be ambiguous or vague about one's intentions"); a divine ~ (from God)

mess around v. (colloq.) (AE) (D; intr.) to ~ with (don't ~ with him)

messenger n. to dispatch a ~

Messiah n. to await, wait for the ~

metabolism n. 1. to disturb, upset smb.'s ~ 2. basal ~

metal n. 1. to pour ~ 2. scrap ~ (to recycle scrap ~) 3. (a) base; ferrous; heavy; nonferrous; precious ~ (to transmute base ~ into gold) 4. molten; sheet ~ 5. ~ may conduct electricity; corrodes, rusts 6. a bar; lump; piece of ~ 7. in ~ (a design worked in ~)

metamorphose v. (D; intr., tr.) to ~ from; into (the creature ~d from a frog into a handsome prince)

metamorphosis n. 1. to undergo ~ 2. a complete, radical, total ~ 3. a ~ from; into (the creature underwent a complete ~ from a frog into a handsome prince)

metaphor n. 1. a dead; mixed ~ 2. a ~ for ("Just how good is the Internet as a ~ for God?" – Charles Henderson, *Cross Currents*, Spring/Summer 2000, Vol. 50, Issues 1/2.)

mete out v. (B) to ~ justice to everyone = to ~ justice out to everyone

meter I metre n. ["verse rhythm"] ["arrangement of syllables"] 1. anapaestic, anapestic; dactylic; heroic; iambic; trochaic ~ ["unit of length"] 2. a cubic; square ~ 3. by the ~ (to sell carpeting by the square ~)

meter II n. ["instrument for measuring"] 1. to read a ~ (she came to read the gas ~) 2. an electric; exposure; gas; parking; postage; water ~ (she parked her car at a parking ~)

method n. 1. to apply, employ, use a ~ 2. to adopt; devise a ~ 3. to give up, scrap a ~ 4. an antiquated, obsolete; crude; devious; infallible, sure; modern, up-to-date; orthodox, traditional; refined, sophisticated; sound; unorthodox ~ 5. the case; deductive; empirical; inductive; scientific; Socratic ~ 6. unscrupulous (business) ~s 7. the audiovisual; direct, oral; grammar-translation ~ (of foreign language instruction); the tutorial ~ (of instruction) 8. teaching ~s 9. the rhythm ~ (of contraception) 10. a ~ for; in, to (a ~ for learning languages; they devised a ~ for extracting the ore; there is a definite ~ in her manner of interrogation; her plan's unusual, but there's ~ in her madness: she knows what she's doing) 11. a ~ to + inf. (esp. AE) (they devised a ~ to extract the ore)

methodical adj. ~ in (~ in one's work)

methodology n. (a) teaching ~

meticulous adj. ~ about, in (she is ~ in her dress)

mettle n. 1. to prove, show one's ~ 2. to put people on their ~

mezzanine n. (AE) ["first rows of a balcony in a theater"] in the ~

mickey, Mickey Finn n. (slang) ["a drink to which a strong drug or narcotic has been added"] to slip smb. a ~

microcosm n. in ~ (is New York City the whole USA in ~?)

microphone n. 1. to hook up, set up a ~ 2. to speak into, through a ~ 3. a concealed, hidden; throat ~ 4. a ~ picks up sound

microscope n. 1. a compound; electron; optical ~ 2. under a ~ (they examined the tissue under the ~) (also fig.) (our panel of experts will put/examine the EU under the ~; in tonight's panel discussion the EU will come under the ~)

midair *n.* in ~ (the planes collided in ~ = the planes had a ~ collision)

midday *n.* 1. at ~ 2. from ~ (to midnight)

middle *n.* 1. in the ~ (in the ~ of the last century; in the ~ of the room) 2. (misc.) to split smt. down the ~ (into two equal parts) (see also *middle of the road* at **road**)

middle ground *n.* 1. to find (a) ~ 2. (a) ~ between (they could find no ~ between the opposing sides)

midmorning *n.* 1. at ~ 2. from ~ (to early evening)

midnight *n.* 1. at ~ 2. from ~ (to early morning)

midpoint *n.* 1. to reach a ~ 2. at (the) ~

midriff *n.* 1. to expose one's ~ 2. a bare ~

midsemester *n.* (AE) at ~

midst *n.* in the ~ of

midstream *n.* 1. to reach ~ 2. in ~ (also fig.)

midway *adj.*, *adv.* ~ between; through

midyear *n.* at ~

mien *n.* (lit.) an impassive; proud ~

miffed *adj.* (colloq.) 1. ~ about, at (she was ~ at his late arrival) 2. ~ that + clause (she was ~ that he came/arrived so late)

might I *n.* 1. armed, military ~ 2. with all one's ~ 3. (misc.) ~ is right (BE) = ~ makes right (AE) ("you can't fight City Hall")

might II *v.* 1. (F) she ~ (well) still show up 2. (misc.) we ~ as well go; they ~ or ~ not have been here earlier (see also **may**)

migraine *n.* 1. a severe ~ 2. an attack of ~

migrate *v.* 1. (d; intr.) to ~ between 2. (D; intr.) to ~ from; to

migration *n.* 1. internal; mass ~ 2. annual ~ (the annual ~ of birds) 3. ~ from; to

mildew *n.* ~ forms

mile *n.* 1. a land, statute; nautical, sea ~ 2. (misc.) to miss by a ~ ("to miss by a great deal")

mileage *n.* 1. to get ~ (I get good ~ with this small car; to get good ~ out of tires) 2. (misc.) the press got a lot of ~ out of the scandal

mileometer (BE) see **odometer**

milestone *n.* 1. to reach a ~ (usu. fig.) 2. (misc.) a ~ in human history

military *n.* 1. to call in the ~ 2. to serve in the ~

military service *n.* compulsory, universal; voluntary ~

militate *v.* (d; intr.) to ~ against (see also **mitigate**)

militia *n.* 1. to call out, mobilize the ~ 2. to serve in the ~ 3. a citizen ~

milk I *n.* 1. to boil; drink ~ 2. to express (breast) ~ 3. curdled, sour; fresh ~ 4. attested (BE), certified; chocolate; condensed; evaporated; fermented; fortified; fresh; homogenized; long-life (BE); low-fat; non-fat; pasteurized; powdered; raw; reconstituted; skim (AE), skimmed (esp. BE); UHT (BE); whole ~ 5. breast; cow's; ewe's, sheep's; goat's ~ 6. coconut ~ 7. ~ curdles, turns sour 8. a gallon; half-gallon; half-pint; pint; quart of ~ 9. a

bottle; carton; cup; glass of ~ (see also *the milk of human kindness* at **kindness**)

milk II *v.* 1. (D; tr.) to ~ from, of, out of (to ~ information from smb. = to ~ smb. of information; to ~ a company of thousands of dollars = to ~ thousands of dollars from a company) 2. (N; used with an adjective) to ~ smt. dry

mill I *n.* ["machine for grinding"] 1. a coffee; pepper ~ ["factory"] 2. a flour; lumber; paper; rolling; steel; textile ~ ["place where results are achieved in a quick, routine way"] 3. a diploma; divorce; marriage; propaganda; rumor ~ ["misc."] 4. to go through the ~ ("to acquire experience under difficult conditions")

mill II *v.* (d; intr.) to ~ about, (a)round (to ~ around the entrance)

million *n.* by the ~s, in the ~s, in their (BE) ~s (some dictionaries sell in the ~s)

millstone *n.* ["heavy burden"] to have a ~ around one's neck

mime *n.* 1. to act a play in ~ 2. (misc.) the art of ~

mincemeat *n.* to make ~ of ("to defeat decisively")

mincer *n.* (BE) AE has *meat grinder*

mind I *n.* 1. to make up one's ~ 2. to make up one's ~ to do smt. 3. to broaden, cultivate, develop one's ~ 4. to speak one's ~ 5. to change one's ~ 6. to bear, have, keep (smt.) in ~ (please bear this request in ~; they had (it) in ~ to leave before dawn; keep in ~ that you have to leave early in the morning; bear in ~ that the deadline is tomorrow) 7. to bring, call smt. to ~ 8. to keep one's ~ on smt. 9. to put, set one's ~ to smt. (I set my ~ to finish/finishing my assignment quickly) 10. to ease one's ~, to set one's ~ at ease 11. to take one's ~ off smt. 12. to cross, enter one's ~ (it never crossed my ~ to telephone; it crossed my ~ that the store would be closed at five o'clock; that possibility never (even) entered my ~) 13. to come, spring to ~ (some names come readily to ~) 14. to know one's own ~ 15. to slip one's ~ (it slipped my ~ that I had an appointment) 16. to lose one's ~ 17. an analytical, brilliant, disciplined, keen, logical, nimble, quick, sharp ~ 18. a clear, sound, uncluttered ~ 19. an inquiring, inquisitive, open, scientific ~ (to keep an open ~; to have an inquiring ~) 20. a closed, narrow, one-track ~ 21. a deranged, dirty, sick, twisted, unbalanced, unsound, warped ~ 22. in one's ~ (in one's right ~; in one's subconscious ~) 23. on smb.'s ~ (what's on your ~?) 24. out of one's ~ (to go out of one's ~) 25. (misc.) I have half a ~ to vote for smb. else ("I may well vote for smb. else"); to give smb. a piece of one's ~ ("to state one's own views to smb. very bluntly"); we were all of the same ~, we were all of one ~ ("we all had the same opinion"); a state of ~; it was a load off my ~ ("I felt relieved"); to be of sound ~; the noise drove me out of my ~; at the back of smb.'s ~; smb.'s ~ is wandering (see also *at/in the back of smb.'s mind* at **back II**; *a meeting of minds* at **meeting**; **presence of mind**)

mind II *v.* 1. (G) I don't ~ waiting; would you ~

opening the window?; I don't ~ admitting that
the noise really scared me! 2. (J) would you ~
me opening the window? 3. (K) he didn't ~ their
smoking; would you ~ my opening the window? 4.
(L) do you ~ (it) that he is late? 5. (Q) would you ~
(it) if I opened the window?; ~ how you go! (esp.
BE) 6. (misc.) never ~ about that – I don't ~ about
it in the slightest!; "shall we eat in or out tonight?"
"I don't ~ (either way)."

minded *adj.* (BE) ~ to + inf. (the Prime Minister is
~ to ask for a vote of confidence)

mindful *adj.* (cannot stand alone) ~ of (~ of one's
responsibilities)

mindless *adj.* ~ of (~ of any danger)

mine I *n.* ["excavation from which minerals are taken"]
1. to open (up); operate, run, work a ~ 2. to close
down a ~ 3. a coal; copper; diamond; gold; iron;
lead; salt; silver; tin; zinc ~ 4. an abandoned;
open-cast (BE), open-pit (AE), strip (AE) ~ 5.
(misc.) the ~ was worked out ["explosive charge"] 6.
to arm; lay a ~ 7. to hit, strike a ~ 8. to detonate, set
off a ~ 9. to clear, remove, sweep ~s 10. to defuse;
detect; disarm a ~ 11. a ~ blows up, explodes 12.
an antipersonnel; antitank; contact; drifting, floating; land; magnetic; pressure; submarine ~

mine II *v.* (D; intr.) to ~ for (to ~ for coal)

minerals *n.* metallic; nonmetallic; rock ~ (see also
mineral deficiency at **deficiency**)

mingle *v.* (D; intr.) to ~ with (to ~ with the crowd)

mini-cab *n.* (in the UK) 1. to call for, telephone for;
get; take a ~ 2. to get into; get out of a ~ 3. a ~
picks smb. up; takes smb. somewhere (I phoned
for a ~ to pick me up in the morning and take me to
the airport) 4. to drive a ~ (for a living) 5. by ~; in
a ~ (to go somewhere by ~)

miniature *n.* in ~

minimal pair *n.* (ling.) to be, constitute, represent;
produce a ~

minimum *n.* 1. to exceed; set a ~ 2. a bare; irreducible ~ 3. at a ~ (sales were at a ~)

mining *n.* open-cast (BE), open-pit (AE), strip
(AE); shaft ~

minister I *n.* 1. to accredit a ~ 2. a ~ plenipotentiary;
a ~ without portfolio 3. a cabinet; chief; deputy
prime; first; foreign; junior; prime ~ (the Prime
Minister of the UK; the Chief Minister of Singapore; the First Minister of Scotland) 4. a ~ from;
to 5. (misc.) (formal) a ~ of religion

minister II *v.* (d; intr.) to ~ to (to ~ to smb.'s needs)

ministry *n.* ["organized religion"] 1. to enter the ~ 2.
a lay ~ ["a government department"] (UK) 3. a defence; foreign; health ~, etc. (or: a ~ of defence;
foreign affairs; health, etc.)

minor I *n.* 1. to serve ~s (this bar does not serve ~s)
2. an emancipated ~

minor II *v.* (AE) (d; intr.) to ~ in (to ~ in French)
("to have French as a secondary subject")

minority *n.* 1. an ethnic; religious ~ 2. in a ~ (we
were in the ~; in a ~ of cases)

minuet *n.* to dance; play a ~

minus see **plus** 2

minute *n.* ["sixtieth part of an hour"] 1. in a ~ (she'll
be here in a ~) ["instant"] 2. the last ~ (at the last ~)
["present time"] 3. this ~ 4. (esp. BE) at the ~ (she's
not here at the ~) 5. up to the ~ (see also *minute
hand* at **hand**)

minutes *n.* ["official record"] 1. to keep, take ~ 2. to accept, approve; correct; read the ~ 3. to reject the ~

miracle *n.* 1. to accomplish, perform, work a ~ 2. a ~
to + inf. (it will take a ~ to save them) 3. a ~ that +
clause (it's a ~ that she survived) 4. by a ~ (she survived by a/some ~) 5. (misc.) a miracle- worker

miraculous *adj.* ~ that + clause (it's ~ that she sur-
vived/should have survived)

mirage *n.* 1. to see a ~ 2. a ~ appears; disappears

mire *n.* (to be stuck) in the ~

mired *adj.* to get ~ (in the mud)

mired down (esp. AE) to get ~ (in the mud)

mirror *n.* 1. to hang; look at one's reflection in;
look in a ~ 2. a full-length; hand; pocket; rear-
view; sideview (AE), wing (BE); two-way ~

mirth *n.* 1. to provoke ~ 2. general ~

misapprehension *n.* 1. (to labor) under a ~ 2. a ~
that + clause (we were laboring under the ~ that we
would receive help)

miscalculate *v.* to ~ badly

miscalculation *n.* 1. to make a ~ 2. to correct a ~ 3. a
bad, glaring, grave, serious ~ 4. a ~ about

miscarriage *n.* ["abortion"] 1. to have a ~ ["failure"] 2.
a gross ~ (of justice)

mischief *n.* 1. to cause, do, make; mean; plot, stir up
~ 2. to be up to, get into ~ 3. malicious ~ 4. out of
~ (to stay out of ~; to keep children out of ~) 5. full
of ~ 6. up to ~ 7. (misc.) there was ~ brewing

misconception *n.* 1. a common; general, popular ~
2. a ~ that + clause (it's a common ~ that one can
lose weight by exercise alone)

misconduct *n.* gross; professional; serious; sexual ~

miscount *n.* to make a ~

misdeed *n.* 1. to commit a ~ 2. to rectify a ~ 3. a
glaring ~

misdemeanor, misdemeanour *n.* to commit a ~

miserable *adj.* 1. ~ about, over (I feel ~ about working there) 2. ~ to + inf. (it is ~ to work there = it is
~ working there)

misery *n.* 1. to cause; prolong ~ (working there
causes me ~!) 2. to alleviate, relieve ~ 3. abject,
acute, deep; sheer, untold ~ 4. ~ to + inf. (it is sheer
~ to work there = it is sheer ~ working there) 5. in
~ (to live in ~)

misfit *n.* a social ~

misfortune *n.* 1. to have, suffer (a); be dogged by ~
2. ~ strikes (~ can strike just when you least expect
it to) 3. the ~ to + inf. (she had the ~ to get there at
the wrong moment)

misgivings *n.* 1. to harbor, have ~ about (we had ~
about his backing out of the agreement) 2. to express one's ~ 3. to allay smb.'s ~ 4. initial; serious,

strong ~ 5. ~ arise; persist 6. ~ about (he tried to allay the ~ that had arisen about whether he would back out of the agreement) 7. ~ that + clause (he tried to allay our ~ that he would back out of the agreement)

mishap *n.* (formal) 1. to have a ~ 2. a ~ befell us 3. without ~ (we completed the project without ~)

misinformation *n.* 1. to give, peddle, plant, spread ~ 2. to correct ~ 3. ~ about

misinformed *adj.* 1. badly, grossly ~ 2. ~ about

misinterpret *v.* 1. (B) the teacher ~ed the passage to the students 2. (d; tr.) to ~ as (they ~ed his response as an admission of guilt) 3. (H) they ~ed his response to be an admission of guilt

misjudge *v.* to ~ badly, completely

mislead *v.* 1. (D; tr.) to ~ about (we were seriously misled about this matter) 2. (D; tr.) to ~ into (he was misled into a life of crime)

misleading *adj.* 1. grossly, seriously, very ~ 2. ~ to + inf. (it is ~ to cite only certain sources)

mismanagement *n.* gross ~

misnomer *n.* a ~ to + inf. (it's a ~ to call this village a city)

mispronounced *adj.* commonly, frequently ~

misread *v.* (D; tr.) to ~ as (they misread me as a liberal)

misrepresent *v.* (D; tr.) to ~ as (the press ~ed them as revolutionaries)

misrepresentation *n.* gross ~

miss I *n.* 1. a clean; near ~ 2. (colloq.) (BE) to give smt. a ~ ("not to do smt.") (the play doesn't sound very interesting – I think I'll give it a ~)

miss II *v.* 1. to ~ terribly, very much (she ~es her family very much) 2. to ~ narrowly (he narrowly ~ed being hit by a car) 3. (D; tr.) to ~ about (what do you ~ most about home?) 4. (G) I ~ walking in the park; we ~ going to church every week 5. (misc.) to ~ by a mile ("to miss by a great deal")

missed *adj.* deeply, sorely ~

missile *n.* 1. to fire, launch; guide a ~ 2. to intercept a ~ 3. an air-to-air; air-to-ground, air-to-surface; antiaircraft, ground-to-air, surface-to-air; antimissile; ballistic; cruise; ground-to-ground, surface-to-surface; guided; intercontinental ballistic; intermediate-range, medium-range; long-range, strategic; nuclear; short-range, tactical; submarine-launched ~

missing *adj.* 1. to go ~ (esp. BE) (they went ~ for three whole days!) 2. ~ from (~ from a group) 3. (misc.) ~ in action (mil.); to turn up ~

mission *n.* ["task"] 1. to accomplish, carry out, perform a ~ 2. to undertake a ~ 3. (mil.) to fly a ~ 4. (usu. mil.) to abort, cancel, scratch, scrub a ~ 5. a bombing; combat; dangerous; military; reconnaissance; search-and-destroy; space; suicide ~ 6. a rescue ~ 7. a training ~ 8. a diplomatic; fact-finding; goodwill; pioneering; trade ~ 9. on a ~ (they went on a goodwill ~ to Asia; to go on a manned space ~ to Mars) 10. a ~ to + inf. (our

~ was to work out a trade agreement) 11. (misc.) ~ impossible (often humorous) (see also *mission statement* at **statement**) ["group sent to perform a task"] 12. a diplomatic; military; trade ~ 13. a ~ from; to (a trade ~ to Africa)

missionary *n.* 1. a foreign; medical ~ 2. a ~ from; to

miss out *v.* (D; intr.) to ~ on (to ~ on a profitable deal)

misstatement *n.* 1. to make a ~ (to make a ~ of fact) 2. a ~ about (to make a ~ about the facts)

mist *n.* 1. (a) dense, heavy, thick ~ 2. (a) fine, thin ~ 3. (a) ~ clears, dissipates, lets up, lifts, rises 4. a covering, curtain, layer, veil of ~ (nothing was visible through the thick curtain of ~)

mistake I *n.* 1. to make a ~ 2. to correct, rectify a ~ 3. to excuse, forgive a ~ 4. to admit; learn from one's ~ (s) 5. a bad, big, costly, dreadful, ghastly, glaring, serious, terrible, tragic ~ 6. a fatal; foolish; honest; minor, slight ~ 7. ~s happen, occur 8. ~s abound (on every page) 9. a ~ about; in (we made a ~ about that; she made a ~ in counting on their help) 10. a ~ to + inf. (it was a ~ to count on their help = it was a ~ counting on their help) 11. by ~ (to do smt. by ~)

mistake II *v.* 1. (d; tr.) to ~ as (they mistook his response as an admission of guilt) 2. (d; tr.) to ~ for (he mistook me for my brother) 3. (H) they mistook his response to be an admission of guilt 4. (misc.) there's no ~ me for my brother – we're completely different!; there was no ~ the love for him in her eyes

mistaken *adj.* 1. gravely; (very) much; profoundly; sadly; very ~ 2. ~ about; in (they were very ~ in interpreting his response as an admission of guilt) 3. ~ for (I was ~ for my brother)

mistletoe *n.* ["Christmas decoration"] 1. to hang the ~ 2. to stand under the ~ (in order to indicate one's willingness to be kissed, during the Christmas season) 3. a sprig of ~

mistress *n.* 1. to have; take a ~ 2. a string of ~es (King Charles II had a string of royal ~es)

mistrial *n.* (legal) to declare a ~

mistrust *n.* 1. to arouse, cause, create, evoke, give rise to, sow, stir up ~ 2. to harbor ~ 3. to allay, dispel ~ 4. groundless, unfounded ~ 5. deep, profound; slight, vague; well-founded ~ 6. ~ between; of; towards (there was some ~ of her motives)

mistrustful *adj.* ~ of

misunderstanding *n.* 1. to cause, give rise to, lead to a ~ 2. to have a ~ (with) 3. to clear up, resolve a ~ 4. a complete, fundamental, total; simple, slight ~ 5. a ~ arises 6. a ~ about, over; between (a slight ~ had arisen between us that was easy to clear up)

mitigate *v.* (d; intr.) (substandard) to ~ against ("to militate against")

mitt *n.* ["glove"] 1. an oven ~ (AE; AE also has *pot holder;* BE has *oven glove*) 2. (baseball) a catcher's; first-baseman's ~

mix I *n.* ["mixture"] 1. a cake; cement; pancake; soup ~ 2. a curious, strange; fascinating ~ (of) (a curious ~ of people at the party)

mix II *v.* 1. (C) ~ a nice drink for me; or: ~ me a nice drink 2. (D; intr., tr.) to ~ with (he doesn't ~ with people like that; she ~ed the brandy with wine = she ~ed the brandy and the wine together)

mixed up *adj.* 1. ~ in (~ in a scandal) 2. ~ with (she got herself ~ with criminals)

mixer *n.* ["informal dance, party"] (AE) 1. to give, hold a ~ ["device for mixing"] 2. a cement, concrete; electric ~ ["person who mixes socially"] 3. a good; poor ~

mixture *n.* 1. a cake ~ 2. a curious, strange; fascinating ~ (of) (a curious ~ of people at the party) 3. with a ~ of X and Y (he viewed me with a curious ~ of envy and disdain)

mix-up *n.* 1. to cause a ~ 2. a ~ about, in, over

mix up *v.* (D; tr.) to ~ with (I always ~ him up with his brother = I always ~ him and his brother up)

moan I *n.* 1. to emit, give, let out; have a ~ 2. a barely audible, feeble, weak; loud ~ (to let out a loud ~ of ecstasy) 3. a ~ about, over; at, to (they had a bit of a ~ to us about the new taxes) 4. with a ~ (of)

moan II *v.* 1. to ~ constantly; feebly; loudly 2. (D: intr.) to ~ about, over; to (to ~ over the new taxes) 3. (D; intr.) to ~ in, with (to ~ with pain/ecstasy) 4. (L; to) they ~ed (to us) that the new taxes were too high 5. to ~ and groan (they're constantly ~ing and groaning to us about the new taxes)

mob I *n.* 1. to inflame, stir up a ~ 2. to control, subdue a ~ 3. to disperse a ~ 4. an angry; undisciplined, unruly, wild ~ 5. a ~ disperses; gathers; runs amok, runs wild

mob II *v.* (D; tr.) to ~ for (fans were ~bing her for her autograph)

mobile *adj.* highly; very; socially; upwardly ~

mobility *n.* social; upward ~

mobilization *n.* 1. to order (a) ~ 2. to carry out ~ 3. full, general; partial ~

mobilize *v.* 1. (D; intr., tr.) to ~ for (we are ~zing our party for the campaign) 2. (H) we are ~zing our party to participate in the campaign

mobster *n.* a big-time, notorious ~

mockery *n.* 1. to make a ~ of (to make a mere ~ of justice) 2. a mere; shocking ~

mock-up *n.* ["model"] to do, prepare a ~ (of)

mode *n.* ["fashion"] 1. the latest ~ ["the setting of equipment"] 2. (a tape recorder) in play-back; recording ~ 3. (a space craft) in re-entry ~ 4. an access; insert ~ (on a computer)

model I *n.* 1. to take as a ~ 2. to pose; serve as a ~ 3. a role ~ 4. an artist's; fashion; male; photographer's ~ 5. a full-scale; scale; working ~ (not just a toy but a full-scale working ~) 6. (of a car) a deluxe; economy; late ~ 7. a ~ for (she can serve as a role ~ for us all!)

model II *v.* 1. (d; refl., tr.) to ~ after, on (the academy

was ~ed after a British public school) 2. (d; intr., tr.) to ~ in (to ~ in clay) 3. (d; tr.) to ~ into; out of (the children ~ed toys out of clay) USAGE NOTE: Some people can also say *the children ~ed clay into toys.* Other people can't.

moderate *adj.* ~ in (they were ~ in their consumption of alcohol)

moderation *n.* 1. to display, show ~ 2. ~ in (~ in the consumption of alcohol) 3. in ~ (to drink in ~)

modest *adj.* 1. ~ about (she was ~ about her achievements) 2. ~ in (she was ~ in not boasting about her achievements) 3. ~ to + inf. (it was ~ of her not to boast about her achievements)

modesty *n.* 1. to affect; display, show ~ 2. false ~ (without false ~, I think I am entitled to at least *some* of the credit!) 3. ~ forbids (~ forbids me to speak of my part in the achievement) 4. ~ about; in (her ~ in not boasting about her achievements) 5. in all ~ (in all ~, I think I am entitled to at least *some* of the credit!)

modification *n.* 1. to make a ~ in 2. to undergo ~s 3. extensive; slight ~s 4. behavior ~ 5. a ~ in, to (there will be several ~s to the plan before it goes into effect)

modifier *n.* a dangling (esp. AE), misrelated; noun ~

modulation *n.* frequency ~ (FM)

module *n.* 1. a command; lunar; service ~ 2. a ~ counts (each of the four ~s into which the course is divided counts 25% towards the final grade)

modus operandi *n.* to establish, work out a ~

modus vivendi *n.* to establish, reach, work out a ~

mogul *n.* a media; movie; television ~

moisture *n.* 1. to absorb, soak up ~ 2. a drop of ~

molar *n.* 1. to cut a ~ 2. an impacted ~ 3. a first; second ~; third ~ ("wisdom tooth")

mold I mould *n.* ["furry growth"] 1. to gather ~ 2. ~ forms, gathers

mold II mould *n.* 1. a jello (AE), jelly (BE); plaster ~ 2. in a ~ (to be cast in a ~) 3. (misc.) to break out of a ~ = to break a ~ USAGE NOTE: The phrase *break the mold* has two different but related meanings, as in "After the gods made you, darling, they broke the mold" (i.e. 'You, darling, are unique') and "Our new party seeks to break the out-of-date mold of traditional politics!" (i.e. 'our party wants to do smt. new'). Both meanings stress newness and originality. Nowadays the second meaning is by far the more likely.

mold III mould *v.* 1. (D; tr.) to ~ from, in, out of (she ~ed a figure in/out of clay) 2. (D; tr.) to ~ into (she ~ed clay into a figure)

mole *n.* ["burrowing animal"] 1. ~s burrow, dig, tunnel their way ["spy"] 2. to plant a ~ ["on skin"] 3. to remove a ~ 4. a hairy ~

molestation *n.* child; sexual ~

mom *n.* (AE) a hockey; soccer ~ USAGE NOTE: Both hockey moms and soccer moms are so interested in their children as to take the time to attend their sons' sports matches. Indeed, it is possible that the two phrases are synonymous. However, the phrase *hockey mom*, probably of Canadian origin but popularized by Sarah Palin, Governor of Alaska and Republican Vice-Presidential candidate in 2008, may well suggest a tough working-class mom rather than an upper-middle-class soccer mom. The latter, but not the former, may also shepherd her daughter to ballet classes. If so, the difference is attributable in large measure to the difference in connotation for North Americans between (ice) hockey (a game of North American origin and therefore manly) and soccer (a game of British origin considered less manly than North American football).

moment *n.* 1. to choose, pick; savor the ~ 2. an appropriate, suitable; auspicious, opportune; critical, crucial; embarrassing, inappropriate, inopportune; propitious; solemn ~ 3. a rash, unguarded ~ (in a rash ~) 4. the psychological, right ~ ("the most favorable time") (you've got to know how to pick the right ~ to say or do smt.) 5. a ~ for (this is a ~ for action) 6. a ~ to + inf. (this is the ~ to act) 7. at a ~ (at that (very) ~) ("then"); (at the/this (very) ~) ("now") 8. for the ~ (for the ~ let us drop this subject) 9. in a ~ (she'll be here in a ~; in a crucial ~ of smb.'s life) 10. (misc.) there's never a dull ~; is this a good ~ to have a word with you?; a ~ or two more – and it would have been impossible!; from that ~ on, we knew we'd win!; at this ~ in time (considered a cliché) (see also *at a moment's notice* at **notice I** *n.*)

momentum *n.* 1. to gain, gather ~ 2. to lose ~ 3. ~ decreases; increases (the increasing ~ of social change)

monarch *n.* an absolute; constitutional ~

monarchy *n.* 1. to establish, set up a ~ 2. to overthrow a ~ 3. an absolute; constitutional; hereditary; limited ~

money *n.* 1. to coin; make, produce; print ~ 2. to counterfeit ~ 3. to circulate ~ 4. to earn, make ~ 5. to bank; change; deposit; draw, withdraw ~ (to deposit ~ in a bank; to withdraw ~ from a bank) 6. to contribute, donate; put up ~ (to donate ~ to a worthy cause) 7. to collect, raise; refund, return ~ 8. to owe; save; spend; tie up ~ 9. to lose; squander, throw away, waste ~ (they threw away their ~ on worthless investments) 10. to borrow; lend, (esp. AE) loan ~ 11. to invest ~ in; to put ~ into (they invested their ~ in stocks and bonds; she put her ~ into municipal bonds) 12. (colloq.) to sink (a lot of) ~ into (a venture) 13. to launder (illegally acquired) ~ 14. counterfeit; earnest; easy; hush; marked; paper; pin, pocket, spending; prize; seed; tight ~ 15. blood; danger; conscience ~ 16. tax ~ (politicians should not waste tax ~) 17. (esp. AE) mad ~ ("a small amount of money carried formerly for emergency use or now for impulse buying") 18. ~ for (I have the ~ for the rent) 19. for ~ (to do

smt. for the ~) 20. out of ~ (we have run out of ~ and are now out of ~) 21. (misc.) to have ~ to burn ("to have a great deal of money"); that was ~ well spent!; I wouldn't do it for love or ~!

monitor I *n.* 1. an electronic; heart ~ 2. a video ~ (for a computer) 3. on a ~

monitor II *v.* to ~ closely

monkey *n.* 1. a howler; rhesus; ring-tailed; spider ~ 2. a band, horde, troop of ~s 3. (misc.) (colloq.) to make a ~ (out) of smb. ("to make a fool of smb.")

monkey about (BE) see **monkey around**

monkey around *v.* (colloq.) (AE) (D; intr.) to ~ with

monkey wrench *n.* ["disruption"] (colloq.) (esp. AE) to throw a ~ into smt. ("to disrupt smt.")

monogamy *n.* to practice ~

monologue, monolog *n.* to recite a ~

mononucleosis *n.* infectious ~ (CE also has *glandular fever*)

monopoly *n.* 1. to establish, gain a ~ 2. to enjoy, exercise; have, hold a ~ 3. to break (up) a ~ 4. a government, state; virtual ~ 5. a ~ of, on, over 6. (misc.) to play Monopoly (T)

monotone *n.* in a ~

monotonous *adj.* ~ to + inf. (it is ~ to watch television every day = it is ~ watching television every day)

monotony *n.* to break, relieve the ~

monoxide *n.* carbon ~

monstrous *adj.* 1. ~ to + inf. (it is ~ to preach hatred) 2. ~ that + clause (it's ~ that some people (should) still preach hatred)

month *n.* 1. to spend a ~ (somewhere) 2. a calendar; lunar ~ 3. every; last; next; this ~ 4. the coming; current; past ~ 5. future; past; recent ~s 6. a ~ from (Tuesday) 7. by the ~ (she is paid by the ~) 8. by ("before or in") a ~ (by next ~, prices may have doubled) 9. during the ~ 10. for a ~ (he'll be here for a ~) 11. for, in (esp. AE) ~s (they have not been here for/in ~s) 12. in a ~ (we can't finish the whole job in just one ~; they will get here in a ~, (esp. BE) they will get here in a ~'s time) 13. in a certain ~ (in the ~ month of May; in past ~s) 14. in, to (colloq.) a ~ (there are four weeks in a ~) 15. (misc.) a ~ ago; once a ~; ~ after ~; ~ by ~; ~ in, ~ out; from ~ to ~; to take a ~ off; all ~ (long); the first time in (esp. AE), for (BE) a ~; she is five ~s old; up to last ~

monument *n.* 1. to build, erect, put up; unveil a ~ 2. an ancient; historic; historical; literary; national ~ 3. a ~ to

mooch *v.* (slang) (AE) 1. (D; tr.) ("to beg for") to ~ from, off (he ~ed a cigarette from me) 2. (d; intr.) ("to sponge") to ~ off of, on (to ~ on one's friends)

mood I *n.* ["state of mind"] 1. a cheerful; ebullient; festive, holiday; genial, good, happy, jovial, joyful ~ 2. a mellow; nostalgic; pensive; tranquil ~ 3. a melancholy; solemn, somber ~ 4. an angry; bad, foul; bellicose; bilious; defiant; resentful; sullen ~ 5. in a ~ (in a good ~) 6. a ~ changes 7. a ~ for (I'm not in the ~ for TV; he's in no ~ for fooling with!) 8. a ~ to + inf. (I'm not in a ~ to read; he's in no ~ to be fooled with!) USAGE NOTE: CE has "in a good ~; in an ebullient ~; in a defiant ~; in a confrontational ~; in an unrepentant ~." BE has also "in defiant ~; in confrontational ~; in unrepentant ~." When can BE drop *a/an*? Perhaps when *mood* is related in meaning to *mode*, and implies readiness to act. But when *mood* is related in meaning to *moodiness*, and implies a state of feeling merely, BE retains *a/an*.

mood II *n.* ["verb form"] the conditional; imperative; indicative; subjunctive ~

moon I *n.* 1. the ~ revolves around the earth 2. a crescent; full; gibbous; half; harvest; new; quarter ~ 3. the ~ wanes; waxes 4. the ~ climbs (higher in the sky); comes out; rises; goes down; goes in (behind a cloud); shines 5. an eclipse of the ~ = a lunar eclipse 6. the light; rays of the ~ (= moonlight; the moon's rays) 7. on the ~ (astronauts have walked on (the surface of) the ~)

moon II *v.* (D; intr.) to ~ over

moonlight *n.* 1. by ~ 2. in the ~

moonlight flit *n.* (colloq.) (BE) ["a move without paying one's rent, debts"] to do a ~

moor *v.* (D; tr.) to ~ to (to ~ a boat to a pier)

moose *n.* 1. a band, herd of ~ 2. a young ~ is a calf 3. a female ~ is a cow 4. a male ~ is a bull (see the Usage Note for **elk**)

mooted *adj.* 1. ~ as (she has been ~ as his successor) 2. ~ that + clause (it has been ~ (about) that she will be his successor)

mop I *n.* a dry, dust, wet ~

mop II *v.* 1. (D; tr.) to ~ from, off (to ~ the sweat from one's brow; to mop the dirt off the floor) 2. to ~ with (to ~ a floor with a cloth) 3. (N; used with an adjective) we ~ped the floor clean (of dirt)

moped *n.* to ride a ~

moral *n.* a ~ to; the ~ of (there's a ~ to the story; what's the ~ of the story?)

morale *n.* 1. to boost, lift, raise ~ 2. to keep up ~ 3. to destroy, undermine ~ 4. high; low ~ 5. ~ rises; sinks

moral fiber, moral fibre *n.* the ~ to + inf. (does she have the ~ to adhere to principle?)

morality *n.* private; public; sexual ~

moralize *v.* (D; intr.) to ~ about, on, over, upon

morals *n.* 1. to protect, safeguard (public) ~ 2. to corrupt smb.'s ~ 3. lax, loose; strict ~ 4. public ~

morass *n.* to get bogged down in a ~

moratorium *n.* 1. to declare a ~ 2. to lift a ~ 3. a ~ on

morbid *adj.* ~ about (don't be ~ about the future)

more I *determiner, pronoun* 1. ~ to + inf. (we have ~ to do) 2. ~ of (~ of them) USAGE NOTE: The use of the preposition *of* is necessary when a pronoun follows. When a noun follows, the use of *of the*

limits the meaning – we drank more wine; we drank more of the wine that you brought yesterday.

more II *n., adv.* 1. a bit, little ~ 2. no ~ than 3. many; much, plenty ~

mores *n.* cultural; sexual; social ~

morgue *n.* 1. a city (esp. AE); newspaper ~ 2. at, in a ~ (to work in a ~)

morning *n.* 1. all ~; during the ~; in the ~ (they left early/late in the ~ = they left in the early/late ~; she works in the ~); ~s (AE) (she works ~s), every ~; the next, the following ~; this ~; that ~; tomorrow ~; yesterday ~; a June ~; a summer ~; on any ~; on/during the ~ of (they left on the ~ of July 26); on Wednesday ~ = Wednesday ~ (AE) 2. a ~ of (after a ~ of conversation, they spent the afternoon and evening together) 3. from ~ (from ~ to night) 4. (misc.) the ~ drew to a close; (Good) Morning (, everybody)!; to have; spend a ~ (we had a pleasant ~ at a museum; we spent the whole ~ working on the report)

moron *n.* (colloq.) 1. an utter ~ 2. a ~ to + inf. (he must have been an utter ~ to have arrived late!)

moronic *adj.* ~ to + inf. (it was ~ for/of him to arrive late = he was ~ to arrive late! = to arrive late was a ~ thing for him to do!)

morsel *n.* a choice, juicy, tasty ~ (of)

mortal *n.* a mere, ordinary ~

mortality *n.* 1. infant; maternal ~ 2. the incidence, rate of ~ 3. ~ from (the incidence of infant ~ from pneumonia)

mortar *n.* ["type of cannon"] 1. a trench ~ ["bowl"] 2. a ~ and pestle

mortgage *n.* 1. to give; hold a ~ (the local bank gave us a twenty-year ~; the bank holds our ~) 2. to get, receive; take out a ~ on (we got a twenty-year ~ from the bank) 3. to pay off a ~ 4. to finance; foreclose; refinance a ~ 5. a chattel; conventional; endowment (esp. BE); first; second; sub-prime ~ 6. a ~ on (do you have a ~ on your house?)

mortgaged *adj.* ~ to the hilt ("to the limit") (we were ~ (up) to the hilt and couldn't afford any more)

mortification *n.* 1. deep, everlasting ~ 2. to smb.'s ~ (to my everlasting ~, I got the answer wrong!)

mortified *adj.* ["embarrassed"] 1. deeply ~ 2. ~ to + inf. (we were ~ to learn that our manuscript had been rejected) 3. ~ that + clause (we were ~ that our manuscript had been rejected)

mortuary *n.* at, in a ~ (to work in a ~)

Moses *n.* holy ~! (esp. AE; colloq.)

Moslem see **Muslim**

mosquito *n.* 1. ~s bite; fly; hum 2. ~s carry, spread disease 3. a swarm of ~es

most *determiner, n., pronoun* 1. ~ to + inf. (we have ~ to do when our clients call after lunch) 2. to get the ~ (out of life) 3. to make the ~ (of one's opportunities) 4. by far the, far and away the, much the ~ (it was much the ~ interesting film I've seen lately: I loved it!) 5. ~ of (~ of them) 6. at, at the; at the very ~ USAGE NOTE: The use of the preposition *of* is necessary when a pronoun follows. When a noun follows, the following constructions are used – most American wine comes from California; most of the wines that we import come from Europe; we like most students; we like most of the students who study in this department.

motel *n.* 1. to manage, operate, run a ~ 2. at, in a ~ (she works at/in a ~) 3. (misc.) to check in at, check into, register at a ~; to check out of a ~; to go to a ~; to stay at a ~

mothballs *n.* ["protective storage"] 1. to put into ~ (to put ships into ~) 2. to take out of ~

mother *n.* 1. an expectant; nursing 2. a lone (BE); single; unwed; welfare; working ~ 3. an adoptive; biological, birth, natural; foster ~; grandmother; stepmother; surrogate ~ 4. a mother-in-law 5. a ~ to (she was like a ~ to them) 6. (misc.) a den ~; a ~ superior

motif *n.* 1. a guiding, leading ~ 2. a ~ runs through a work

motion I *n.* ["proposal"] 1. to make a ~ 2. to second a ~ 3. to accept; adopt, carry, pass a ~ 4. to defeat, reject, vote down a ~ 5. to consider, entertain, vote on a ~ 6. (AE) to table a ~ ("to postpone voting on a motion") 7. (BE) to table a ~ ("to call for a vote on a motion") 8. to withdraw a ~ 9. the ~ carried, passed, was carried, was passed; was defeated, was lost, was rejected 10. a ~ to + inf. (she made a ~ to stop debate) 11. a ~ that + clause; subj. (she made a ~ that debate be/should be stopped) 12. on a ~ (on my ~ they debated admitting new members) ["movement"] 13. to make a ~; set smt. in ~ 14. harmonic; perpetual ~ (see also **slow motion**) ["misc."] 15. to go through the ~s ("to pretend to do smt.")

motion II *v.* 1. (d; tr.) to ~ into; out of (she ~ed us into the room) 2. (D; intr.) to ~ to (she ~ed to us) 3. (H) she ~ed (to/for) us to come into the room

motivate *v.* (H) what ~d her to master English?

motivated *adj.* highly, strongly ~ (she is strongly ~ to master English)

motivation *n.* 1. strong ~ 2. the ~ to + inf. (she has a strong ~ to master English)

motive *n.* 1. to establish, find a ~ 2. to doubt, question, suspect smb.'s ~s 3. altruistic; honorable; noble ~s; the highest ~s (to have nothing but the highest ~s) 4. base, dishonorable, sinister; selfish; ulterior ~s 5. the profit ~ 6. an underlying ~ 7. a ~ behind, for; in (the police could not find a ~ for the murder; what was her ~ in committing the crime?; she had no ~ for committing the crime) 8. a ~ to + inf. (she had no ~ to commit the crime)

motor I *n.* 1. to start a ~ 2. to turn off a ~ 3. an outboard ~ 4. a ~ runs, works; stalls (see also **engine** 1–9)

motor II *v.* (d; intr.) to ~ to (they ~ed to town)

motorbike *n.* 1. to get off; get on; ride a ~ 2. to ride on a ~ (as a passenger)

motorcar *n.* (BE) to drive; park a ~ (see **car** 1–12)

motorcycle *n.* 1. to drive, ride; get off; get on a ~ 2. to ride on a ~ (as a passenger)

motor scooter *n.* to drive, ride a ~

motorway (BE) see **highway**

motto *n.* 1. to coin, devise a ~ 2. a school; state ~

mound *n.* 1. a burial; pitcher's ~ 2. (baseball) (AE) to take the (pitcher's) ~

mount *n.* an engine ~

mountain *n.* 1. to climb, go up, scale a ~ 2. to come down, go down a ~ 3. high; rugged; snow-capped, snow-clad, snow-covered ~s 4. block; folded; volcanic ~s 5. a ~ rises 6. a chain, range of ~s 7. down; over; up a ~ 8. on a ~ (the flag was planted on a ~) 9. (misc.) the elevation, height of a ~; to make a ~ out of a molehill ("to exaggerate"); the peak, top of a ~; what shall we do with our ~ of surplus food?

mounted *adj.* ["astride"] 1. ~ on (~ on a fine horse) ["fixed"] 2. ~ on (the specimens were ~ed on a poster)

mourn *v.* (D; intr.) to ~ for, over

mourning *n.* ["for smb.'s death"] 1. to declare, proclaim (a period of) ~ 2. to go into ~ 3. deep ~ 4. national ~ 5. in ~ for 6. a sign of ~ ["clothes for mourning"] 7. to wear ~ 8. (to be dressed) in ~

mouse I *n.* ["a small rodent"] 1. to catch mice 2. a field; house; meadow; white ~ 3. mice gnaw; scamper; squeak 4. (misc.) as quiet as a ~

mouse II *n.* ["a device on a computer"] to click; move; use a ~

moustache, mustache *n.* 1. to grow a ~ 2. to shave off; trim a ~ 3. to finger, twist one's ~ 4. a drooping; handlebar; walrus ~

mouth *n.* 1. to close, shut; open one's ~ 2. to cram, stuff one's ~ (with food) 3. to rinse one's ~ (out); wipe one's ~ 4. a ~ opens 5. the back; front; roof; side of the ~ 6. at the ~ (of a cave; river) 7. in smb.'s ~ (don't talk with food in your ~! = don't talk with your ~ full!) 8. (misc.) (colloq.) a big ~ ("a gossip"); to shoot off one's ~ ("to talk too much"); to make smb.'s ~ water ("to create a desire or appetite in smb."); to keep one's ~ shut ("to remain silent"); by word of ~ ("orally")

mouthful *n.* (colloq.) ["something true"] 1. to say a ~ ["enough food to fill a mouth"] 2. to swallow a ~

mouth off *v.* (colloq.) (D; intr.) to ~ about; at; to (he kept ~ing off (at/to me) about his troubles)

mouth organ *n.* to play a/the ~

mouthpiece *n.* ["spokesperson"] (derog.) 1. to act, serve as a ~ for 2. smb.'s official ~

move I *n.* ["act"] 1. to back, support; make; oppose a ~ (who will make the first ~?) 2. a false ~ (one false ~ would be costly; (make) one false ~ and I'll shoot!) 3. a bold; brilliant, clever, good; shrewd, smart, wise; decisive; bad ~ 4. a ~ to + inf. (they made a ~ to settle the dispute and their ~ to settle it was backed by nearly everyone) ["moving of a piece as in chess, checkers"] 5. to make; take back a ~ 6. a brilliant; stupid, wrong ~ 7. an opening ~ (he tried to take back his stupid opening ~) (also fig.) 8. a ~ in (the opening ~ in a courtship) ["act of moving"] 9. a ~ from; to (our firm's ~ from here to the Coast) 10. (misc.) (colloq.) to get a ~ on ("to go faster"); to make a ~ on smb. ("to approach smb. sexually") (colloq.) (he made a ~ on her at the office Christmas party); on the ~; a ~ in the right direction

move II v. 1. ("to stir") to ~ deeply, profoundly 2. ("to change the position of") to ~ bodily 3. (d; intr.) ("to request") to ~ for (to ~ for a new trial) 4. (D; intr., tr.) ("to change or cause to change one's position, place of residence, place of work") to ~ from; into, to; out of (let's ~ from this table to that one; they ~d from the city to the suburbs; our firm's moving from here to the Coast; let's ~ the chair from/out of this room to that one; he ~d his family from/out of an old house into a new apartment; we are ~ving our main office from/out of the city to a small town) 5. (D; intr.) ("to act") to ~ on (to ~ on a matter) 6. (D; tr.) ("to stir") to ~ to (she was ~d to tears) 7. (d; intr.) ("to change one's position") to ~ towards (to ~ towards the exit) 8. (E) ("to propose") the committee ~d to block her nomination 9. (H) ("to induce") what ~d the committee to block her nomination? 10. (L; subj.) ("to propose") the committee ~d that her nomination not be/should not be approved 11. (P; intr.) ("to circulate") she ~s in the best society; to ~ among the elite; to ~ near the very top of power

move ahead v. (D; intr.) to ~ of (to ~ of the pack)

move away v. (D; intr.) to ~ from; to (to ~ from the city to the country)

move down v. 1. (D; intr.) to ~ into, to (he has ~d down to the position of office boy from the position of general manager) 2. (D; intr.) to ~ through (to ~ through the ranks from general to private)

move in v. 1. (d; intr.) ("to close in") to ~ for (to ~ for the kill) 2. (D; intr.) to ~ on ("to close in on") (the police ~d in on the fugitives) 3. (D; intr.) to ~ on ("to establish control of") (organized crime was moving in on the industry) 4. (D; intr.) to ~ on (AE), with ("to take up residence with") (her lover wanted to ~ with her, so they decided to ~ together)

movement n. ["organized effort to attain a goal"] 1. to launch a ~ 2. to support a ~ 3. to ban; oppose; suppress a ~ 4. a civil-rights; consumer; feminist, women's; labor; mass; peace; political; radical, revolutionary; resistance; social ~ 5. a ~ against; for; towards (the ~ for equal pay) ["division of a musical composition"] 6. to perform; play a ~ (there is a fugue in the ~ that they have just played) ["military maneuver"] 7. a pincer, pincers (AE) ~ ["move"] 8. a downward; upward ~ 9. deft, dext(e)rous; graceful; rhythmic ~ 10. awkward; erratic; jerky; uncoordinated ~s 11. a ~ towards ["evacuation"] 12. a bowel ~ (to have a bowel ~)

move on v. (D; intr.) to ~ to (to ~ to the next town)

move up v. 1. (D; intr.) to ~ into, to (he has ~d up from office boy to general manager) 2. (D; intr.)

to ~ through (to ~ through the ranks from private to general)

movie n. (esp. AE) ["film"] 1. to make, produce a ~ 2. to direct a ~ 3. to see, watch a ~ 4. (CE) a home ~ USAGE NOTE: In a theater, one *sees a movie*; on a home TV, one *watches a movie* or *sees a movie*. See also **film** 1–12

movies n. (AE) ["cinema"] 1. to go to the; to work in the ~ 2. silent ~ 3. at the ~ (what's on at the ~ this week?)

mower n. 1. to operate, work a ~ 2. a hand; power ~ (see also **lawn mower**)

much I determiner, n., pronoun 1. to make ~ of smt./smb. 2. ~ of (we did not believe ~ of what we heard; he isn't ~ of an artist) 3. ~ to + inf. (she has ~ to say; we have ~ to learn) 4. (misc.) ~ as we want to help, we are unable to USAGE NOTE: The use of the preposition *of* is necessary when a pronoun follows – we did not believe much of what [= that which] we heard. When a noun follows, the use of *of the* limits the meaning – much sorrow is caused by drug abuse; much of the sorrow that is caused by drug abuse could be avoided.

much II adv. 1. ~ closer; ~ further; ~ longer; ~ shorter; ~ less interesting; ~ more interesting 2. ~ the best; ~ the worst; ~ the least interesting; ~ the most interesting (it was ~ the most interesting movie I'd seen for ages!)

muck n. ["mess"] (colloq.) (BE) to make a ~ of smt.

muck about v. (colloq.) (BE) to ~ with ("to mess around with")

mucus n. 1. to cough up 2. to discharge; secrete ~ 3. nasal ~

mud n. ["wet earth"] 1. to spatter ~ 2. ~ cakes; dries; oozes, squishes 3. a layer of ~ 4. (misc.) to spatter smb. with ~; to wallow in the ~ ["malicious charges"] 5. to sling, throw ~ at smb. (see also **sling II** 3)

muddle n. ["confusion"] 1. to make a ~ of smt. 2. in a ~

mufti n. ["civilian clothes"] in ~

mug n. a beer; shaving ~

mulct v. (D; tr.) ("to defraud") to ~ of (to ~ people of their money)

mule n. 1. to drive; ride a ~ 2. ~s bray 3. a team of ~s 4. (misc.) as stubborn as a ~

mull over v. (Q) we ~ed over whether to accept the proposal

multiplication n. to do ~

multiply v. (D; tr.) to ~ by (to ~ six by three and get 18 = to ~ three by six and get 18)

mum adj. 1. to keep, remain ~ 2. ~ about 3. (misc.) ~'s the word

mumble v. 1. (B) she ~d smt. to me 2. (D; intr., tr.) to ~ about (she ~d smt. (to me) about her job) 3. (L; to) she ~d (to us) that she had a new job

mumps n. to catch, come down with, get, go down with (BE) (the) ~

munch v. (D; intr.) to ~ on (they were ~ing on their sandwiches)

munch away *v.* (D; intr.) to ~ at (they were ~ing away at their sandwiches)

murder *n.* ["homicide"] 1. to commit ~ 2. a brutal, cold-blooded, grisly, heinous, savage, vicious, wanton ~ 3. an attempted; premeditated; ritual ~ 4. (AE) (a) first-degree; second-degree ~ 5. mass ~ 6. multiple, serial ~s 7. a ~ takes place ["ruinous influence"] (colloq.) 8. ~ on (the rainy weather has been ~ on business) ["great hardship"] 9. it was ~ standing out in the cold ["misc."] 10. to get away with ~ (typically fig.) (he ruins everything and gets away with it – people really let him get away with ~!)

murderer *n.* a cold-blooded, vicious; mass ~

murmur I *n.* ["complaint"] 1. to let out a ~ (she didn't let out a ~) 2. without a ~ (of protest) ["abnormal sound"] (med.) 3. a heart ~ ["low noise"] 4. a gentle, low, soft ~ 5. in; with a ~ (to speak in a low ~)

murmur II *v.* 1. to ~ gently; softly 2. (D; intr., tr.) to ~ to (he ~ed a few words to her and kept on ~ing to her) 3. (d; intr.) to ~ about (what were they ~ing about?) 4. (d; intr., tr.) to ~ into (he ~ed a few words into her ear) 5. (E) he ~ed to her to stay with him 6. (L; to) he ~ed (to her) that he wanted her to stay with him = "Please stay with me," he ~ed (to her)

muscle *n.* 1. to contract; flex, tense; move; pull, strain; relax; wrench a ~ (to flex the ~s in/of one's arm) 2. to develop one's ~s 3. bulging ~s 4. involuntary; smooth; striated; voluntary ~s 5. ~s ache; contract

muscle in *v.* (colloq.) (D; intr.) to ~ on (to ~ on smb.'s territory)

muse *v.* (D; intr.) to ~ about, over, upon

museum *n.* 1. to go to, visit a ~ 2. an art (esp. AE; BE prefers *art gallery*); children's; ethnographic; public; science; wax ~ 3. a ~ contains, houses; displays, shows 4. at, in a ~ (to work at a ~)

mushroom I *n.* 1. to pick ~s 2. an edible ~

mushroom II *v.* (D; intr.) to ~ from; into, to

music *n.* 1. to compose, write ~ 2. to arrange ~ (for) (to arrange organ ~ for (the) piano) 3. to perform, play ~ 4. to put, set smt. to ~ 5. to read ~ 6. background; canned, piped; incidental; light; recorded; soft, sweet ~ 7. bluegrass; country, hillbilly; folk; western; world ~ 8. ballet; band; chamber; classical; dance; instrumental; klezmer; orchestral; organ ~ 9. funky; gospel; march, martial; modern; pop; popular; rock; sacred; serious; soul ~ 10. choral; vocal ~ 11. sheet ~ 12. a note; piece of ~ 13. (fig.) ~ to (what she said was ~ to my ears) 14. to ~ (to dance (in time) to the ~ of a big band) 15. (misc.) to face the ~ ("to accept one's punishment")

musical *n.* 1. to produce, stage a ~ 2. a Broadway ~

musical chairs *n.* to play ~

musician *n.* 1. an accomplished; natural; strolling ~ 2. a ~ performs; practices; rehearses

Muslim *n.* a Black; Shiite; Sunni ~

muslin *n.* bleached; unbleached ~

must *v.* 1. (F) we ~ go 2. (misc.) I really ~ go; you surely ~ know; they ~ have left USAGE NOTE: AE has "their coats are still here so they ~ not have left yet." BE prefers "their coats are still here so they can't have left yet."

mustache see **moustache**

mustard *n.* 1. Dijon; French; English; hot ~ 2. (misc.) (colloq.) BE as keen as ~

muster I *n.* to pass ~

muster II *v.* 1. (d; tr.) to ~ into (to ~ smb. into the army) 2. (d; tr.) to ~ out of ("to discharge from") (to be ~ed out of the army)

mutation *n.* 1. to induce a ~ 2. a gene, genetic; random ~

mute *adj.* to stand ~ ("to remain silent during an arraignment")

mutiny I *n.* 1. to foment, incite, stir up; organize a ~ 2. to crush, put down, quell a ~ 3. a ~ breaks out 4. a ~ against (Fletcher Christian incited the mutiny that broke out against Captain Bligh of HMS Bounty)

mutiny II *v.* (D; intr.) to ~ against (the crew of HMS Bounty ~nied against Captain Bligh)

mutter *v.* 1. (B) she ~ed smt. to me 2. (D; intr., tr.) to ~ about (she ~ed smt. (to me) about her job) 3. (L; to) she ~ed (to me) that she might get a new job

mysterious *adj.* ~ about (~ about one's past)

mystery *n.* 1. to be, pose a ~ (her disappearance poses a real ~) 2. to clear up; solve, unravel a ~ 3. an unsolved ~ 4. a murder ~ 5. a ~ deepens (the ever-deepening mystery of/surrounding her disappearance) 6. a ~ to (it was a ~ to me) 7. (misc.) an air of ~; cloaked, shrouded, wrapped in ~; a veil of ~

mystified *adj.* 1. ~ to + inf. (she was ~ to find that her watch was gone) 2. ~ that + clause (she was ~ that her watch was gone)

mystifying *adj.* 1. ~ to 2. ~ to + inf. (it was ~ (to her) to find that her watch was gone) 3. ~ that + clause (it was ~ (to her) that her watch was gone)

myth *n.* 1. to create; perpetuate a ~ 2. to debunk, dispel; explode a ~ 3. a popular ~ 4. a ~ about (we dispelled the ~ about the invincibility of their army) 5. a ~ that + clause (we dispelled the ~ that their army was invincible) 6. (misc.) ~s and legends

N

nadir *n.* 1. to fall to, reach a ~ 2. at a ~ (at the ~ of their power)

nag *v.* 1. (D; intr.) to ~ at (he kept ~ging at her (to buy a new car)) 2. (D; tr.) to ~ into (he ~ged her into buying a new car) 3. (H) he kept ~ging her to buy a new car

nail I *n.* ["to be hammered into smt."] 1. to drive, hammer a ~ (he drove a ~ into the board) 2. to remove a ~ 3. a loose ~ 4. (misc.) as hard/tough as ~s; to hit the ~ on the head ("to describe smt. succinctly and correctly") ["of fingers and toes"] 5. to cut, pare, trim; do; file; manicure; paint, polish one's ~s 6. to break, split a ~ 7. to bite; chew one's ~s 8. a fingernail; toenail ["misc."] 9. to fight tooth and ~

nail II *v.* 1. (D; tr.) to ~ to (she ~ed the plaque to the wall) 2. (P; tr.) she ~ed the boards together

naive *adj.* 1. ~ of (that was ~ of you) 2. ~ to + inf. (it's ~ (of you) to trust everyone; you are ~ to trust everyone)

naked *adj.* 1. stark ~ 2. (misc.) to walk around ~

name I *n.* ["appellation"] 1. to adopt, assume, take; bear, have; go by, go under; change; use a ~ 2. to give smb. a ~ 3. to call smb. a (bad) ~; to call smb. ~s 4. to immortalize smb.'s ~ 5. to invoke God's ~ 6. to sign one's ~ 7. an assumed; code; double-barrelled (BE); legal; pen-name; personal; professional; proper; stage ~ (she took a stage ~ when she began her acting career; I asked Peregrine Chimp-Gibbon about his double-barrelled ~; Samuel Clemens adopted the pen-name (of) Mark Twain) 8. a Christian (esp. BE), first, given (AE); family; last; maiden; married; middle ~ (she still uses her middle ~; Virginia Woolf's maiden ~ was Virginia Stephen; please call me by my first ~) (see also **surname**) 9. a bad, dirty; fancy; pet ~ 10. a geographic(al) ~ 11. a brand, proprietary, trade ~ 12. a file ~ 13. a common, vernacular ("not technical") ~ 14. a ~ for (there is no ~ for such conduct!) 15. by ~ (to know smb. by ~ only) 16. in ~ (she is the chairperson in ~ only: smb. else is really in charge) 17. in smb.'s ~ (the book was charged out in your ~) 18. under a ~ (under an assumed ~; Samuel Clemens wrote under the pen-name (of) Mark Twain) ["reputation"] 19. to make a ~ (for oneself) 20. to clear one's ~ 21. to besmirch, smear smb.'s (good) ~ 22. to give smb. a bad ~ 23. a bad; big; good; great ~ (she is a big ~ in fashion and one of the greatest ~s in fashion now) ["misc."] 24. to drop ~s ("to boast of one's connections or acquaintances"); to name ~s; in the ~ of the law; who in God's ~ would do smt. like that?; what in God's ~ is that?; why not, in God's ~?; to lend one's ~ to (a good cause)

name II *v.* 1. (d; tr.) to ~ after, for (AE) (Hannah

was ~d after her great-grandmother) 2. (d; tr.) to ~ as (she was ~d as the winner of the contest) 3. (H) (esp. AE) they ~d me to head the commission 4. (N) she was ~d (the) winner of the contest; the file that had been ~d "urgent" has now been renamed "miscellaneous"

name-calling *n.* to engage in, go in for, resort to ~

nameless *adj.* to remain ~

nanny *n.* (esp. BE) a ~ for, to (she served as a ~ to three small children)

nap *n.* 1. to have, take a ~ 2. an afternoon; morning ~

napkin *n.* 1. to fold a ~ 2. to tuck a ~ (under one's chin) 3. a cocktail; dinner; linen; paper ~ 4. a sanitary ~ (AE; BE has *sanitary towel*; CE has *sanitary pad*)

nappy (BE) see **diaper**

narcosis *n.* 1. to produce (a state of) ~ 2. (a) ~ wears off 3. under ~

narcotics *n.* to smuggle ~ (into a country)

narrate *v.* (B) she ~d her story to us

narration *n.* 1. a graphic; gripping ~ 2. (misc.) the ~ of her story to us

narrow down *v.* (D; tr.) to ~ to (the choice was ~ed down to a few candidates = they ~ed the choice down to a few candidates = they ~ed down the choice to a few candidates)

narrow-minded *adj.* ~ to + inf. (it was ~ of her to say that)

nasty *adj.* 1. ~ about (they were very ~ (to everyone) about the whole incident) 2. ~ to (they were ~ to everyone) 3. ~ to + inf. (it was ~ of them to go on about the whole incident)

nation *n.* 1. to build, create; establish a ~ 2. a civilized; developing; friendly; independent; industrial; peace-loving; sovereign ~ 3. belligerent, warring ~s 4. across the ~ (there were strikes across the ~) 5. (misc.) a member ~ (of the UN) (see also *nation state* at **state**; Usage Note at **tribe**)

national *n.* ["citizen"] a foreign ~

National Guard *n.* (US) to call out; federalize the ~

nationalism *n.* 1. to foster ~ 2. extreme; rampant ~

nationhood *n.* to achieve ~

native *adj.* 1. ~ to (this flower is ~ to our state) 2. (misc.) to go ~ ("to behave like the local population when in a foreign country")

natter *v.* (colloq.) (BE) (D; intr.) ("to chatter") to ~ about; to (to ~ (on) to smb. about smt.)

natural I *adj.* 1. (AE) ~ to (that comes ~ to me) 2. ~ to + inf. (it's only ~ for children to love ice cream) 3. ~ that + clause (it's perfectly ~ that children love/should love ice cream)

natural II *n.* (colloq. esp. AE) ["person who seems to be destined for success"] 1. a ~ for (she is a ~ for this kind of job) 2. a ~ to + inf. (she's a ~ to win the election)

nature *n.* ["character, quality"] 1. an impetuous; placid ~ 2. human ~ (it's only human ~ to want to live well) 3. second ~ (that is almost second ~ to me; it was second ~ for her to help) 4. smb.'s true ~ 5. by ~ (she is friendly by ~) 6. in (smb.'s) ~ (it was not in her ~ to complain; behavior that is friendly in ~) 7. of a certain ~ (wounds of a serious ~) ["physical universe"] 8. to harness (the forces of) ~ 9. (misc.) mother ~; a freak of ~; back to ~; let ~ take its course; to appeal to smb.'s better ~; don't stand in her way – she's like a force of ~!

naught *n.* (lit.) 1. to come to ~ 2. all for ~

naughty *adj.* 1. ~ of 2. ~ to + inf. (it was (of them) ~ to do that = they were ~ to have done that = it was a ~ thing for them to do)

nausea *n.* 1. to bring on, cause ~ 2. to experience ~ (he experiences ~ when he rides in a car) 3. a wave of ~ (she felt a wave of ~ come over her; a wave of ~ came over her)

nauseated *adj.* 1. to become, feel ~ (he feels ~ when he rides in a car) 2. to make smb. ~

nauseating *adj.* 1. ~ to 2. ~ to + inf. (it was ~ (to/for us) to watch them)

nauseous *adj.* 1. to become, feel ~ 2. to make smb. ~ USAGE NOTE: Some purists still claim that *nauseous* means only "nauseating". In fact, most speakers now use it as a synonym of *nauseated*.

navigate *v.* (d; intr.) to ~ by (to ~ by the stars)

navigation *n.* celestial; electronic ~

navy *n.* 1. a merchant ~ (BE; AE has *merchant marine*) 2. the Royal Navy; the US Navy 3. in the ~ (to serve in the ~)

near *adv.* ~ to (~ to tears; we live ~ to town; ~ to the truth; she came ~ to winning the title) USAGE NOTE: When *near* is a preposition, it is not used in the collocation **near to*. Compare *close to*: the golf links are close to/near the station.

nearer, nearest *adj., adv.; prep.* ~ to (the park is nearer to our hotel than it is to yours; which stop is nearest (to) Times Square?)

nearness *n.* ~ to

neat *adj.* ~ in (~ in one's habits)

necessary *adj.* 1. absolutely ~ 2. ~ for; to 3. ~ to + inf. (it is ~ (for us) to sleep) 4. ~ that + clause; subj. (it is ~ that we all get/should get enough sleep)

necessitate *v.* 1. (G) the promotion would ~ living abroad 2. (K) the promotion would ~ his living abroad

necessity *n.* 1. to obviate a ~ 2. an absolute, dire; military ~ 3. the bare; daily ~ties 4. a ~ arises 5. a ~ for 6. a ~ to + inf. (there is no ~ (for us) to leave so early) 7. of ~ (you will of ~ remain silent) 8. (misc.) the (bare) ~ties of life; what is a luxury for some is a ~ for others

neck I *n.* ["of body"] 1. to crane; crick one's ~ 2. to twist, wring smb.'s ~ 3. (to have) a stiff ~ 4. the back, nape of smb.'s ~ 5. (misc.) to save one's ~; it's a pain in the ~ (to go/going there); what are you doing in this ~ of the woods?; the two leading competitors are ~ and ~ ("even"); to risk one's ~ ("to risk one's life"); to break one's ~ trying to

do smt. ("to make a maximum effort to get smt. done"); to stick one's ~ out ("to expose oneself to danger"); by a ~ ("by a close margin"); up to one's ~ in work ("swamped with work")

neck II *v.* (colloq.) (D; intr.) ("to hug and kiss") to ~ with

neckline *n.* a high; low, plunging; sweetheart ~

necktie *n.* (AE) 1. to knot, tie; put on; wear; loosen; tighten a ~ 2. a garish, loud ~ (CE has *tie*) (see also **bow tie**)

need I *n.* 1. to create a ~ 2. to feel, have a ~ 3. to fill, meet; obviate a ~ 4. to satisfy a ~ 5. to minister, tend to smb.'s ~s 6. an acute, compulsive, crying, desperate, dire, great, overriding, pressing, urgent; growing; special ~ 7. a basic, fundamental; personal; unfulfilled, unmet; universal ~ 8. a biological; emotional, psychological; physical; physiological; spiritual ~ 9. bodily; emergency; material ~s 10. a ~ arises; exists 11. a ~ for (a crying ~ for food for the refugees; there is no ~ for violence) 12. a ~ to + inf. (there was a pressing ~ to act immediately; there was no ~ for you to be violent) 13. in ~ (to live in dire ~; badly in ~) 14. in ~ of (the refugees are badly in ~ of food = the refugees are in urgent ~ of food)

need II *v.* 1. to ~ badly, desperately, sorely, urgently 2. (D; tr.) to ~ for (we ~ you for this job) 3. (E) we all ~ to work; my coat badly ~s to be mended 4. (F; in neg. and occ. in interrogative sentences) she ~ not work; or: she doesn't ~ to work; ~ she go? or: does she ~ to go? 5. (G) my coat ~s mending badly 6. (H) I badly need smb. to mend my coat 7. (N; used with a past participle) I badly ~ my coat mended 8. (s; used with a past participle) (BE) (nonstandard) my coat badly ~s mended USAGE NOTE: The sentence *she needn't have gone* implies that she did go (though there was no need for her to go). The sentence *she didn't need to go* does not indicate if she went or not.

needed *adj.* badly, much ~ (to take a much-needed vacation)

needle I *n.* 1. to thread a ~ 2. a darning; hooked; knitting; sewing ~ 3. a gramophone (BE), phonograph (AE) ~ 4. an acupuncture; hypodermic ~ 5. a pine ~ 6. the eye; point; prick of a ~ 7. (misc.) a ~ in a haystack ("smt. that is impossible to find"); to mend your coat you need ~ and thread; a sensation of pins and ~s; on pins and ~s ("extremely anxious")

needle II *v.* 1. (D; tr.) to ~ about (she was ~ling him about his blunder) 2. (D; tr.) to ~ into (~d me into losing my temper)

needlepoint *n.* to do ~

needless *adj.* ~ to + inf. (it is ~ (for you) to worry) (see also *needless to say* at **say II** *v.*)

needlework *n.* to do ~

negative *n.* ["exposed film"] 1. to develop; make a ~ ["phrase that rejects"] 2. in the ~ (to answer/reply in the ~) (see also *test negative* at **test II** *v.*) ["expression that contains negation"] 3. a double ~

neglect I *n.* 1. benign; complete, gross, total; willful ~ 2. child, parental ~ 3. a state of ~ 4. to the ~ of (he concentrated on his work to the neglect of his family)

neglect II *v.* 1. to ~ completely, totally; willfully 2. (E) she ~ed to pay the fine

neglectful *adj.* 1. completely, totally ~ 2. ~ of (he concentrated on his work and became ~ of his family)

negligence *n.* 1. contributory; criminal; gross; rank; willful ~ 2. (legal) gross; ordinary; slight ~ 3. ~ in; towards 4. through ~ (he did harm through ~ in looking after his family)

negligent *adj.* 1. grossly ~ 2. ~ about; in (he did harm through being ~ in looking after his family)

negotiate *v.* 1. (D; intr.) to ~ about, over 2. (D; intr.) to ~ for 3. (D; intr.) to ~ with (we ~d with them for (the) release of the hostages; to ~ with smb. about a common border) 4. (E) we ~d with them to release the hostages 5. (misc.) to ~ from a position of strength

negotiation *n.* under ~ (the release of the hostages is still under ~)

negotiations *n.* 1. to conduct, hold; enter into, open ~ 2. to renew, resume ~ 3. to break off ~ 4. delicate; direct; exploratory, preliminary; formal; high-level, top-level; informal; marathon; round-the-clock; private, secret ~ 5. arms-control, arms-limitation; contract; diplomatic; peace ~ 6. successful ~ 7. fruitless, unsuccessful ~ 8. ~ succeed 9. ~ break down, collapse 10. ~ between, with 11. ~ for (we've opened ~ with the rebels for the release of the hostages) 12. ~ to + inf. (we've opened ~ with the rebels to release the hostages) 13. (misc.) ~ to release the hostages are deadlocked over several points; the next round of ~ will be held in the summer

negotiator *n.* a management; union ~

neighbor I neighbour *n.* 1. a next-door ~ 2. a ~ to (she was a good ~ to us) 3. (misc.) we have lots of friends and ~s here

neighbor II neighbour *v.* (esp. BE) (D; intr.) to ~ on (the USA ~s on Mexico)

neighborhood, neighbourhood *n.* 1. a friendly; good, nice, pleasant ~ 2. a changing ~ 3. a bad, rough, tough ~ 4. an ethnic; residential ~ 5. the immediate ~ (all of our friends live in the immediate ~) 6. in a ~ (we live in a nice ~) 7. in the ~ of (to earn (something/somewhere) in the ~ of $50,000 a year)

neighborly, neighbourly *adj.* ~ to + inf. (it was ~ of you to do that)

neither *determiner, pronoun* ~ of (~ of the two; ~ of them) USAGE NOTE: The use of the preposition *of* is necessary when *two* or a pronoun follows. When a noun follows, two constructions are possible – neither student knew the answer; neither of the students knew the answer.

nelson *n.* ["type of wrestling hold"] a full; half ~

nemesis *n.* to meet one's ~

neologism *n.* to coin a ~

nerve *n.* ["assurance"] ["gall"] (colloq.) 1. to display, have ~ 2. the ~ to + inf. (she had the ~ to ask for another day off) ["self-confidence"] 3. to lose one's ~ ["sensitivity"] 4. a raw ~ (his remark hit a raw ~) ["band of nervous tissue"] 5. the cranial ~s

nerves *n.* ["nervousness"] 1. an attack; bundle of ~ ["mental state"] 2. to fray, frazzle smb.'s ~; to get on smb.'s ~ 3. to calm, settle, steady one's ~ 4. frayed, frazzled, jangled; steady; strong; taut; weak ~ ["misc."] 5. to have ~ of steel ("to be very strong emotionally"); my ~ are shot; a war of ~

nervous *adj.* 1. to make smb. ~ 2. ~ about, of (BE) (we were ~ about the recent reports of local violence)

nest *n.* 1. to build, make a ~ 2. (misc.) to feather one's ~ ("to enrich oneself") (see also **machine-gun nest**; **hornets' nest**)

nest egg *n.* ["money set aside as a reserve"] to accumulate; set aside a (little) ~

nestle *v.* 1. (d; intr., tr.) to ~ against, next to (the children ~d against their mother) 2. (P; intr.) the small village ~d in the green hills

nestle up *v.* (d; intr.) to ~ against, next to, up (the children ~d up against/to their mother)

net *n.* 1. to weave a ~ 2. to cast, spread a ~ (we try to spread our ~ as wide(ly) as possible to attract a wide range of customers) 3. (computers) to surf the ~ (see also **Internet**) 4. a butterfly; fishing; mosquito ~ 5. a life (AE), safety (also fig.) ~ 6. in, with a ~ (to catch fish in a ~)

netting *n.* mosquito; wire ~

nettles *n.* ~ sting

network I *n.* 1. an old-boy; old-girl ~ 2. a communications; computer; road; support ~ (after a bereavement it's important to have a support ~ of close friends) 3. (computers) a local area ~ (LAN) 4. a national ~ (of radio, TV stations) 5. over a ~ (over a national ~)

network II *v.* (D; intr., tr.) to ~ with (the computers were ~ed with each other; to ~ with the right people)

neurosis *n.* mild; severe ~

neurotic *adj.* 1. mildly; severely, very ~ 2. ~ about

neutral I *adj.* ~ in (~ in a dispute)

neutral II *n.* ["position of disengaged gears"] in ~ (to run an engine while in ~)

neutrality *n.* 1. to maintain, observe ~ 2. to declare one's ~ 3. armed; strict ~

new *adj.* 1. brand ~ 2. ~ at; in (I'm ~ at this) 3. ~ to (this procedure is ~ to us)

newcomer *n.* a ~ to

news *n.* ["new information"] 1. to announce, give, report; break, spring; cover the ~ 2. to spread (the) ~ 3. to censor; control; cover up, suppress (the) ~ 4. to color, distort, twist (the) ~ 5. good, welcome, wonderful; interesting ~ (at the good ~ of her victory, everyone cheered) 6. unexpected

~ 7. earthshaking, earth-shattering, headline, sensational, shocking, startling, worldshaking ~ 8. bad, devastating, grim ~ 9. international; local; national; political ~ 10. the latest ~ (have you heard the latest ~?) 11. ~ spreads, travels 12. a bit, item, piece of ~; a ~ item 13. ~ about, of; from (~ about the earthquake; is there any news of them?; have you heard the ~ about the closure of the border?; *News from Nowhere* – William Morris, 1890) 14. the ~ that + clause (have you heard (the ~) that the border has been closed?) ["newscast"] 15. to hear, listen to; turn on; watch the ~ 16. the late; morning; nightly ~ (on TV) 17. on the ~ (we heard that item on the late ~) 18. (misc.) to make (the) ~ ("to be newsworthy")

news conference *n.* to broadcast; hold; schedule; televise a ~

newspaper *n.* 1. to edit; get out, publish, put out; print a ~ 2. to deliver ~s 3. to subscribe to a ~ 4. a local; national (esp. BE) 5. a daily; evening; morning; Sunday; weekly ~ 6. a school ~ 7. a ~ comes out, is published 8. (misc.) to make the ~s ("to be printed in the newspapers"); a ~ proprietor (BE), publisher (AE)

New Year *n.* 1. to greet, ring in, usher in the ~ 2. to wish smb. a Happy New Year by saying "Happy New Year!"

next *adj., adv.* 1. (cannot stand alone) ~ to (there's a newsstand ~ to the hotel) 2. (misc.) ~ of kin; ~ in line

nibble *v.* (D; intr.) to ~ at, on (the children were ~ling at pretzels; to ~ on cheese)

nibble away *v.* (D; intr.) to ~ at, on (the children were ~ling away at pretzels)

nice *adj.* 1. ~ about; to, with (she's very ~ to the children about their mistakes) 2. ~ to + inf. (it's ~ just to sit and relax = it's ~ just sitting and relaxing; she is ~ to work with = it is ~ to work with her = it is ~ working with her = she is a ~ person to work with; it was ~ of you to come) 3. ~ that + clause (it's ~ that you could come) 4. (misc.) it's ~ and hot; we have a ~ little house in the country

niche *n.* ["position"] 1. to carve out a ~ (she has carved out a ~ for herself in her field) 2. to occupy a ~ (she occupies a special ~ in her field)

nick *n.* (misc.) (just) in the ~ of time ("precisely when needed but almost too late")

nickname *v.* (N; used with a noun) he was ~d *Butch*

niggardly *adj.* (lit.) ~ in; with (a miser who's ~ with his money and ~ in tipping waiters)

niggle *v.* (D; intr.) to ~ about, over (to ~ over every sentence)

nigh *adv.* ["near"] 1. well-nigh (it was well-nigh midnight before we left!) 2. (old-fashioned) ~ on, onto, unto (we hadn't seen each other for/in ~ onto ten years!)

night *n.* 1. to have; spend a ~ (we had a restless ~ waiting for news; we spent the whole ~ working

on the report) 2. a clear; moonlit; starlit ~ 3. a dark, murky; moonless; overcast; stormy ~ 4. a restless, sleepless ~ 5. an early; late ~ 6. a first, opening ~ (of a play) 7. a wedding ~ 8. all ~ (long) (to work all ~ long); during the ~; in the ~ (they left late in the ~); every ~; last ~; the next, the following ~; that ~; tomorrow ~; tonight; a June ~; a summer ~; on any ~; on/during the ~ of (they left on the ~ of July 26; on that ~ they were ready to leave!); on Wednesday ~ = Wednesday ~ (AE) 9. ~ falls 10. a ~ of (after a day of work, they were looking forward to a ~ of revelry!) 11. at ~ (to work at ~; late at ~) 12. by ~ (London by ~) 13. for a ~ (to put smb. up for the ~) 14. from ~ to (from ~ to ~); after ~; a ~ in; a ~ off; a ~ out; ~ and day 15. all through, throughout the ~ (to work all through the ~) 16. (misc.) to bid, wish smb. good ~; to say good ~ to smb.; (Good) Night (, everybody)!; (AE) to work ~s (to work ~s and sleep days); in the dead of (the) ~; on the ~ (BE; colloq.) ("when the time comes") (don't worry – it'll be all right on the ~!) USAGE NOTE: The collocation *at night* is typically used with verbs (she works at night) and contrasts with *during the day*. The collocation *by night* is typically used with nouns (London by night) and contrasts with *by day*. However, *at night* can also contrast with *by day*: "London at night was more obviously changed than London by day." – Pat Barker, *Life Class*, London, Hamish Hamilton, 2007, *Part One, Chap. Sixteen*, p. 123 (see also the Usage Note for **day**)

nightcap *n.* ["last drink of the night"] 1. to have a ~ 2. (misc.) to invite smb. in for a ~; to join smb. in a ~

nightclub *n.* at, in a ~ (to work at/in a ~)

nightfall *n.* at ~

nightingale *n.* ~s sing, warble

nightlight *n.* a ~ glows dimly

nightmare *n.* 1. to have a ~ 2. a horrible, terrible ~ 3. a ~ about

nightshift *n.* 1. to work the ~ 2. (to work) on the ~

nighttime *n.* in the ~

nip I *n.* ["stinging cold"] (there is) a ~ in the air

nip II *v.* (colloq.) (BE) (P; intr.) ("to move quickly") she ~ped out and bought some bread

nipples *n.* cracked; sore, tender ~

nitpick *v.* (colloq.) (D; intr.) to ~ at

nitty-gritty *n.* (colloq.) ["essence"] to get down to the ~

no *n.* ["negative response"] 1. they would not take ~ for an answer 2. to answer; say; vote No 3. a definite, emphatic, resounding ~ 4. (a) ~ to (a request) 5. (misc.) all I want is a simple Yes or No; to say No but (really) mean Yes (see also *a No vote* at **vote I** *n.*; *no way* at **way**)

noble *adj.* ~ to + inf. (it was ~ of him to make the sacrifice)

nobody *pronoun* we had ~ to talk to = we had ~ that we could talk to

nod I *n.* ["movement of the head"] 1. to give a ~ 2. an affirmative, approving ~ 3. a ~ to (she passed on to her own work with the merest ~ to her predecessors' contributions!) 4. (misc.) a ~ of approval; (BE) the proposal was approved/passed on the ~ (without the need for a vote) ["awarding of a decision"] (usu. sports) 5. to get the ~

nod II v. 1. (D; intr., tr.) to ~ at, to (when she entered the room, she ~ded (a greeting) to us) 2. (misc.) to ~ in agreement

node n. a lymph ~

noise n. 1. to make, produce (a) ~ 2. to cut (AE; colloq.), cut down (on), reduce the ~ 3. (a) background; extraneous ~ 4. (a) constant, persistent; deafening; loud; shrill; strange ~ 5. a ~ abates, dies down; increases 6. the ~ from, of 7. above, over the ~ (we could barely make ourselves heard over the ~ from/of the sound system!)

noise about, noise abroad v. (L) it was ~d about that she had resigned

noises n. ["signs, indications"] (colloq.) to make all the right ~ and send all the right signals

nominate v. 1. (D; tr.) to ~ as (she was ~d as our candidate) 2. (D; tr.) to ~ for (she was ~d for the presidency) 3. (H) (she was ~d to run for the presidency)

nomination n. 1. to place, put smb. (smb.'s name) in ~ 2. to get, win a ~ (she got our party's ~ as our candidate to run for the presidency) 3. to accept; reject a ~ 4. a ~ for; to (she got our party's ~ for the presidency; a ~ to a committee)

nominative n. (grammar) the ~ absolute

nonconformity n. ~ in; to; with

none determiner, n., pronoun ~ of (~ of them) (see also none the worse at **worse**) USAGE NOTES: (1) The use of the preposition of is necessary when a pronoun follows. When a noun follows, the use of of the limits the meaning; no replaces none when the meaning is not limited – we saw none of the students whom we had discussed earlier; we drank none of the wine that you brought; we saw no students; we drank no wine. (2) Everyone says "none of the wine is good." But some people prefer "none of the students is good"; others (perhaps the majority) prefer "none of the students are good."

nonexistent adj. virtually ~

nonsense n. 1. to speak, talk ~ 2. to brook, put up with, tolerate no ~ 3. (colloq.) (AE) to cut (out) the ~ 4. arrant (lit.), complete, outright, perfect, pure, sheer, total, utter ~ 5. a load, lot of ~ 6. ~ to + inf. (it was sheer ~ to trust them) 7. (misc.) (BE) to make ~ (a) of ("to spoil") (the recession made a ~ of our plans for expansion)

nonsensical adj. ~ to + inf. (it was ~ to trust them)

nook n. 1. a cozy ~ 2. a breakfast ~ 3. (misc.) every ~ and cranny

noon n. 1. high ~ 2. at ~ 3. from ~ (to evening)

no one pronoun we had ~ to talk to = we had ~ that we could talk to USAGE NOTE: Note the

difference between no one can do it and no one of you can do it.

noose n. 1. to tighten a ~ around (they tightened the ~ around his neck) 2. a hangman's ~ 3. a ~ tightens (the ~ tightened around his neck) 4. (misc.) to put one's head into the ~ (also fig.)

noplace (AE) see **nowhere**

norm n. ["standard"] 1. to establish, set a ~ 2. to deviate from the ~ (his behavior deviated from the very ~ he had helped to establish!) ["average"] 3. above; below the ~

normal adj. 1. above; below ~ 2. ~ to + inf. (it's only ~ to expect equal pay for equal work) 3. ~ that + clause (it's only ~ that we should expect equal pay for equal work) 4. (misc.) back to ~

north I adj., adv. 1. directly, due, straight ~ 2. ~ of (~ of the city) 3. up ~ 4. (misc.) to face; go, head ~; northeast by ~; northwest by ~

north II n. 1. magnetic; true ~ 2. from the ~; in the ~; to the ~

northeast I adj., adv. 1. ~ of (to be ~ of the city) 2. (misc.) to go, head ~; north by ~

northeast II n. from; in; to the ~

North Pole n. at the ~

northwest I adj., adv. 1. ~ of (to be ~ of the city) 2. (misc.) to go, head ~; north by ~

northwest II n. from; in; to the ~

nose I n. 1. to blow; powder; wipe one's ~ 2. to pick one's ~ 3. an aquiline, Roman; bulbous; pug, snub, turned-up ~ 4. a blocked-up, stuffed-up; bloody; running, runny ~ (the child has a runny ~) 5. through the ~ (to breathe through the ~) 6. a ~ bleeds; points down; points up; runs; twitches 7. (misc.) the bridge of the ~; the traffic was ~ to tail! (BE) ("bumper to bumper"); to bury one's ~ in a book ("to become absorbed in a book"); to count ~s ("to count those present"); to cut off one's ~ to spite one's face ("to harm one's own interests"); to lead smb. by the ~ ("to order smb. around"); to pay through the ~ ("to pay an exorbitant price"); to keep one's ~ out of smb. else's business; to poke, stick one's ~ into smb. else's business; to thumb one's ~ at smb./smt. ("to defy smb./smt."); to keep one's ~ to the grindstone ("to work long and hard"); under smb.'s (very) ~ ("in smb.'s plain sight"); to turn up one's ~ at ("to sneer at"); on the ~ (AE; colloq.) ("exactly"); a ~ for scandal ("an ability to ferret out scandal"); by a ~ ("by a small margin"); to follow one's ~ ("to go straight forward"); to tweak ("pinch") smb.'s ~; to keep one's ~ clean ("to stay out of trouble"); to follow one's ~ ("to go straight ahead"); as plain as the ~ on your face (see also look down one's nose at at **look down**)

nose II v. 1. (colloq.) (D: intr.) to ~ into (to ~ into smb.'s affairs) 2. (P; intr., tr.) she ~d the car into the street

nosebleed n. 1. to get; have a ~ 2. to stop a ~ 3. a light; severe ~

nose dive n. 1. (also fig.) to go into, take a ~ (stocks took a ~) 2. to come out of, pull out of a ~

nostalgia n. 1. to evoke; feel ~ 2. a wave of ~ 3. ~ for (the taste of the cake evoked a wave of ~ for the past that I could not but feel)

nostrils n. flaring, wide ~

nosy, nosey adj. (colloq.) ~ about

notable adj. ~ for

notch n. ["cut"] 1. to make a ~ 2. a ~ in

notch up v. (esp. BE) (d; tr.) ("to score") to ~ against (our team has ~ed up seven victories against them)

note I n. ["memorandum"] ["record"] 1. to make a ~ of (she made a ~ of the exact time) 2. to take ~ of 3. (BE) a credit ~ (for returned merchandise; AE has *credit slip*) 4. a mental ~ (she made a mental ~ of the exact time) ["short letter"] ["official letter"] 5. to compose, write; type a ~ 6. to address; deliver a ~ 7. to drop, send smb. a ~; to get, receive; open a ~; to acknowledge; answer, reply to, respond to a ~ 8. a diplomatic; protest ~ 9. a suicide; thank-you ~ (did the deceased leave a suicide ~?) 10. a ~ from; to (what was in the ~ you got from him yesterday?) ["musical tone"] 11. to hit, strike; hold a ~ (she hit the high ~ beautifully) 12. a false ~ (also fig.) 13. a high; low ~ 14. (AE) an eighth; half; quarter; whole ~ ["characteristic feature"] 15. to strike a ~ (to strike a sour ~) 16. a festive; fresh; lighter; optimistic; positive; triumphant ~ 17. a personal ~ 18. a discordant; false; jarring; negative; pessimistic; sour; warning ~ (on a ~ (the meeting ended on an optimistic ~; on a lighter ~, here's a joke I've just heard) ["comment"] 20. a usage ~ (as in a dictionary) ["document relating to a debt"] 21. to discount a ~ 22. to hold a ~ 23. to call in a ~ 24. a demand; promissory; treasury ~ 25. a ~ matures ["paper money"] 26. a banknote; five-pound ~ (esp. BE: AE prefers *bill*, as in a *five-dollar bill*) ["importance"] 27. of ~ (several people of ~ were present; nothing of ~; worthy of ~) (see also **notes**)

note II v. 1. (L) we ~d that she was late again; please ~ that the example is on page 3 2. (Q) ~ how it is done 3. (misc.) please ~ the example on page 3

notebook n. a loose-leaf ~ (AE)

noted adj. 1. duly ~ 2. (cannot stand alone) ~ for (our city is ~ for its fine restaurants)

notes n. ["condensed record"] 1. to make, take ~ (on) (our students always take copious ~ on the lectures they hear) 2. (usu. fig.) to compare ~ 3. copious, detailed ~

nothing n., pronoun 1. to ask (for) ~ (to ask ~ in return) 2. to gain ~ by (we will gain ~ by ignoring the regulations) 3. ~ about (we know ~ about it) 4. ~ to (they are ~ to us) 5. ~ to + inf. (we have ~ to lose) 6. (misc.) to leave ~ to chance; to make ~ of being awarded an honor; we expect ~ of him; you can expect ~ from them; good for ~; ~ doing ("definitely not"); we have ~ that we can discuss; there is ~ between them; it cost next to ~; I got it

for next to ~; ~ else but that blouse will do!; lovers whispering sweet ~s into each other's ears

notice I n. ["heed"] ["attention"] 1. to take ~ of 2. to attract; to come to ~ 3. to escape ~ 4. scant ~ (to attract scant ~) 5. ~ that + clause (it came to our ~ that she would be retiring) ["sign"] 6. to place, post, put up a ~ ["announcement"] ["notification"] 7. to bring smt. to smb.'s ~ 8. to serve ~ on 9. advance, warning ~ 10. a ~ that + clause (we read the ~ (saying) that the water would be turned off for two hours) 11. at, on (AE) a moment's, short ~ (she can be ready at a moment's ~!) 12. until further ~ ["warning of one's intention to end an agreement"] 13. to give ~ 14. to put smb. on ~ 15. a month's; week's ~ 16. (colloq.) ~ to + inf. (the landlady gave him ~ to move) 17. subject to ~ ["review"] 18. to get, have, receive; give rave ~s (the play got rave ~s from the critics = the critics gave the play rave ~s) ["mention"] 19. a brief ~ 20. a book ~

notice II v. 1. (esp. AE) (I) we ~d him leave the house 2. (J) we ~d him leaving the house 3. (L) we ~d that he was leaving the house 4. (Q) did you ~ where he went after leaving the house?

noticeable adj. 1. barely, hardly; very ~ (a hardly ~ blemish) 2. ~ to 3. ~ that + clause (it was ~ to the neighbours that he had left the house)

notification n. 1. to send ~ 2. to get, receive ~ 3. ~ that + clause (we read the ~ that our building had been sold) 4. pending (further) ~

notify v. 1. (BE) (B) to ~ a crime to the police 2. (D; tr.) to ~ about, of (we ~fied the police of the crime; she ~fied us of her acceptance of the job; we will ~ her about/of when the job begins) 3. (BE) (H) we'll ~ her to draw up a contract 4. (L; must have an object) she ~fied us that she would accept the job 5. (formal) (Q) we will ~ her when the job begins

notion n. 1. to entertain, have a ~ 2. to dispel a ~ 3. an abstract, concrete, foggy, hazy, vague; ludicrous; odd, strange; preconceived; widespread ~ 4. a ~ about, of (she didn't have the foggiest/slightest ~ of what I meant) 5. a ~ that + clause (we tried to dispel the ~ that benefits would be curtailed)

notoriety n. 1. to achieve, gain ~ 2. ~ for (~ for being corrupt) 3. ~ surrounding (the ~ surrounding the published accounts of corruption in high places)

notorious adj. 1. ~ as (he was ~ as an outlaw) 2. ~ for (~ for being corrupt)

nought n. (esp. BE) see **naught**

noun n. 1. to decline, inflect a ~ 2. an abstract; attributive; collective; common; compound; count; mass, uncountable; plural; predicate; proper; singular; verbal ~ 3. a feminine; masculine; neuter ~ 4. a ~ may decline; inflect

nourishment n. 1. to get, take ~ 2. to give ~ 3. adequate; inadequate ~ 4. ~ for

novel n. 1. to publish; write a ~ 2. an autobiographical; best-selling; detective, mystery; historical; prize-winning; romantic; science-fiction ~ 3.

a ~ is set; takes place 4. a ~ about (she wrote a prize-winning autobiographical ~ about coming of age that was set in the Welsh valleys) 5. (misc.) to make a ~ into a film

novelty *n.* 1. to outgrow smt.'s ~ (it soon outgrew its ~) 2. a ~ wears off (its ~ soon wore off) 3. a ~ for, to 4. a ~ to + inf. (it was a ~ (for us) to sleep so late)

novice *n.* 1. a rank ~ 2. a ~ at, in

now *adv.*, *n.* 1. just; right ~ 2. before; by ~ 3. for ~ (good-bye for ~ = good-bye just ~ (Scottish)) 4. from ~ on 5. until, up to ~

nowhere *adv.* 1. to get, go; lead ~ (with) ("to fail to produce a result") 2. ~ to + inf. (we had ~ to go) 3. ~ else; ~ near (we had ~ else to go; that's ~ near enough!) 4. (misc.) from, out of ~ (she came from/out of ~ to win the race); the middle of ~ ("the back of beyond")

nuance *n.* a delicate, fine, slight, subtle ~

nuclear weapons *n.* to ban; dismantle, scrap ~

nucleus *n.* ["core"] to form a ~

nude *n.* in the ~ (to pose in the ~)

nudge I *n.* 1. to give smb. a ~ 2. a little ~ 3. (misc.) a ~ in the ribs

nudge II *v.* 1. (d; tr.) to ~ into, towards (they ~d us into a compromise) 2. (H) she ~d me to finish quickly 3. (misc.) to ~ smb. in the ribs

nugget *n.* a gold ~

nuisance *n.* 1. to cause, create a ~ 2. to make a ~ of oneself (those noisy children can make a confounded ~ of themselves when I want to work!) 3. a confounded, damned, dreadful ~ (those noisy children can be a confounded ~ when you want to work!) 4. a public ~ 5. a ~ to 6. a ~ to + inf. (it was quite a ~ to move during the semester = it was quite a ~ moving during the semester) 7. a ~ that + clause (it was a real ~ that we had to move during the semester)

null *adj.* (misc.) ~ and void

numb *adj.* 1. to go ~ (my arm went completely ~) 2. ~ from; with (my arm went completely ~ from the cold/with cold)

number I *n.* ["symbol indicating quantity"] 1. to round down (esp. BE); to round off (esp. AE); to round up (esp. BE) ~s 2. to square a ~ = to raise a ~ to the second power 3. an even; odd ~ 4. a high; low ~ 5. an algebraic; binary; cardinal; complex; compound; decimal; imaginary; infinite; irrational; mass; mixed; natural; negative; ordinal; positive; prime; quantum; random; round; whole ~ ["symbol serving to identify smt."] 6. the daily; lucky; winning ~ (of a lottery) (I hope I'll draw this week's winning ~!) 7. a box ~ (as at a post office) 8. the call ~ (of a book) 9. a serial ~ (of a product; of a soldier) (don't tell them anything but your name, rank, and serial ~!) 10. a fax; telephone ~ (let me give you my fax ~ and my E-mail address) 11. a registration ~ ["quantity"] 12. to decrease, reduce; increase a ~ (to reduce the ~ of traffic accidents) 13. a considerable, goodly, large; enormous, great, untold

~; any ~ (any ~ of people have played this game and a great ~ of them have liked it!) 14. an approximate, average, round; certain; exact, precise; decreasing, falling; growing, increasing; small; total ~ 15. in ~ (few in ~) ["telephone number"] 16. to call; dial a ~ 17. an unlisted ~ (AE; BE has *an ex-directory listing/number*) ["issue"] 18. a back ~ ["single selection in a program of entertainment"] 19. the eleven o'clock ~ (the audience left humming the hit eleven o'clock ~); a (big) production ~ (also fig.) (slang) (to make a big production ~ out of smt.) ("to make a big fuss over smt.") 20. to do, perform a ~ ["misc."] 21. to do a ~ on smb. (slang) ("to bamboozle or hoodwink smb."); to carry a ~ (when adding) USAGE NOTE: Note the difference between "*a* number of people *were* present" and "*the* number of people present *was* high." (see also **numbers**)

number II *v.* 1. (d; refl., tr.) to ~ among (I ~ her among my friends) 2. (D; tr.) to ~ from; to (we ~ed the tickets from one to five hundred) 3. (d; intr., tr.) to ~ in (our books ~ in the thousands) 4. (S) (esp. BE) our books ~ thousands

numbers *n.* ["form of gambling"] (US) 1. to play the ~ ["large group"] 2. in ~ (there is safety in ~) ["misc."] 3. by ~ (BE), by the ~ (AE) ("done according to specific directions and typically in a mechanical way") (it's no good trying to make love by the ~!)

numeral *n.* an Arabic; Roman ~

numerous *adj.* too ~ to mention (the people who have helped me are too ~ to mention)

nuptials *n.* (formal or humorous) to officiate at, perform (the) ~

nurse I *n.* 1. a community-health (AE), public-health (AE) ~ (BE is approximately *health visitor*) 2. a community (BE), district (BE), visiting (AE) ~ 3. a geriatric, gerontological; home-health; industrial-health, occupational-health; maternal-child health; medical-surgical; nursery; obstetric; operating-room (AE), operating-theatre/theatre (BE); pediatric; psychiatric-mental health; school; veterinary ~ 4. a graduate (AE); Licensed Practical (AE), State Enrolled (BE); practical; professional; Registered (AE), State Registered (BE) ~ 5. a general-duty; private-duty ~ 6. a charge (BE); head; supervising ~ 7. (misc.) an advanced practice ~; a ~ practitioner; a nurse-midwife; a male ~

nurse II *v.* 1. (d; tr.) to ~ back to (to ~ smb. back to health) 2. (D; tr.) to ~ through (to ~ a patient through an illness)

nursery *n.* 1. a day ~ 2. at, in a ~

nursing *n.* 1. to practice; study ~ 2. community-health, public-health ~ (AE; BE has *health-visitor service*) 3. geriatric, gerontological; home-health; industrial-health, occupational-health; maternal-child health; medical-surgical; nursery; obstetric; operating-room (AE), operating-theatre/theatre (BE); pediatric; psychiatric-mental health; school; veterinary ~ 4. practical; professional ~ 5. general-

duty; holistic; primary; private-duty ~ 6. (misc.)
advanced practice ~
nut *n.* 1. to crack a ~ 2. to shell ~s 3. (misc.) a
hard/tough ~ to crack ("a difficult problem to deal
with")
nutrients *n.* basic, essential ~
nuts *adj.* (colloq.) ["infatuated"] 1. ~ about (he's ~
about her) ["crazy"] 2. to go ~
nutshell *n.* (colloq.) ["brief form"] in a ~ (to put smt.
in a ~) ("to state smt. very succinctly")

nutty *adj.* (slang) 1. ~ to + inf. (it's ~ to behave like
that! = you must have been ~ to behave like that!)
2. (misc.) as ~ as a fruitcake
nuzzle *v.* (D; intr.) to ~ against (the dog ~d against
her)
nuzzle up *v.* (D; intr.) to ~ against; to (the dog ~d
up against her)
nylon *n.* 1. sheer ~ 2. a pair of ~s ("a pair of nylon
stockings")

O

oaf *n.* a clumsy; stupid ~

oar *n.* to feather; peak; pull on; ship ~s

oath *n.* ["solemn promise; solemn promise to tell the truth"] 1. to administer an ~ to smb. 2. to put smb. under ~ 3. to swear, take an ~ (of office) 4. to break, violate an ~ 5. a sacred, solemn ~ 6. a loyalty ~ 7. an ~ to + inf. (she took an ~ to do her duty) 8. an ~ that + clause (she took an ~ that she would do her duty) 9. on (BE), under ~ (to testify under ~ to tell the truth) 10. (misc.) to take the Hippocratic ~ ["swearword"] 11. to mutter, utter an ~ 12. a mild; strong ~ 13. a string of ~s

oatmeal *n.* ["porridge"] (esp. AE) 1. to cook, make, prepare ~ 2. a bowl of ~

oats *n.* porridge ~ (BE) ("oats used for oatmeal/porridge") (see also **wild oats**) USAGE NOTE: In AE, oatmeal can be eaten raw or cooked. In BE, (porridge) oats can be eaten raw or cooked into porridge.

obedience *n.* 1. to demand, exact ~ from 2. to instill ~ in 3. to pledge, swear ~ to 4. blind, strict, unquestioning ~ 5. ~ to

obedient *adj.* ~ to

obeisance *n.* (formal) ["curtsy"] ["bow"] 1. to make (an) ~ (to) 2. a deep ~

obituary *n.* 1. to send in; write an ~ 2. to print, publish an ~ 3. an ~ for 4. (misc.) to read the ~ries

object I *n.* 1. an immovable; inanimate; material, physical; solid ~ (what happens when an irresistible force meets an immovable ~?) 2. a sex ~ 3. (grammar) a direct; indirect ~ 4. (misc.) an ~ of derision; an unidentified flying ~ (= UFO) (see **UFO**)

object II *v.* 1. to ~ strenuously, strongly, violently 2. (D; intr.) to ~ to (to ~ strongly to new taxes) 3. (L; to) she ~ed (to us) that the new taxes were too high

objection *n.* 1. to have; lodge, make, raise an ~ (we lodged our ~s with the relevant authority; they made their ~s to the relevant authority) 2. to brush aside; deal with, meet an ~ 3. to overrule; sustain an ~ 4. to withdraw an ~ 5. a valid ~ 6. a serious, strenuous, strong, violent, vociferous ~; conscientious ~ (to military service) 7. (legal) ~ overruled!; ~ sustained! 8. an ~ against, to (to raise an ~ to a proposal; we have no ~s to your going) 9. an ~ that + clause (the judge overruled their ~ that illegal evidence had been introduced) 10. over smb.'s ~s (the resolution was adopted over the vociferous ~s of the opposition)

objectionable *adj.* ~ to

objective *n.* 1. to achieve, attain, gain, meet, an ~ 2. to formulate, set, state an ~ 3. (mil.) to take an ~ 4. a major, primary; realistic; worthy ~ 5. an

economic; military; political ~ 6. a long-range; short-range ~ 7. the ultimate ~

objectivity *n.* in all ~

objector *n.* a conscientious ~ (to military service)

obligate *v.* (H) what does the agreement ~ us to do?

obligated *adj.* 1. ~ to (I'm ~ to you) 2. ~ to + inf. (what are we ~ to by the agreement?)

obligation *n.* 1. to assume, take on an ~ 2. to feel an ~ 3. to discharge, fulfill, meet an ~ 4. to default on an ~ 5. a contractual; family; legal; moral; social; solemn ~ 6. a military ~ ("required military service") 7. an ~ to (an ~ to one's parents) 8. an ~ to + inf. (we have an ~ to help them) 9. under (an) ~ (she was under no ~ to help them) 10. without ~ (you can take advantage of our free offer without any further ~!)

obligatory *adj.* 1. ~ for (doing his duty is ~ for a soldier) 2. (formal) ~ on, upon (doing his duty is ~ on a soldier) 3. ~ to + inf. (it's ~ for a soldier to do his duty)

oblige *v.* 1. (d; tr.) to ~ by (would you ~ me by not smoking?) 2. (H) what does the agreement ~ us to do?

obliged *adj.* 1. ~ to (I'm much ~ to you for not smoking!) 2. ~ to + inf. (what are we ~ to (do) by the agreement?)

obliterate *v.* 1. to ~ completely, entirely, totally, utterly 2. (D; tr.) to ~ from

oblivion *n.* 1. to fall, sink into ~ 2. consigned to ~

oblivious *adj.* (cannot stand alone) ~ of, to (~ of one's surroundings; she was ~ to what was going on)

obnoxious *adj.* 1. ~ to 2. ~ to + inf. (it was ~ of them to do that)

oboe *n.* to play the ~

obscene *adj.* 1. ~ to + inf. (it's ~ for the abuse of women to be tolerated in many parts of the world) 2. ~ that + clause (it is ~ that the abuse of women is still/should still be tolerated in many parts of the world)

obscenity *n.* 1. to shout ~ties 2. (misc.) the ~ of tolerating the abuse of women in many parts of the world

obscure *adj.* ~ to (the meaning was ~ to me)

obscurity *n.* 1. to emerge from ~ 2. to sink into ~ and remain in ~

observance *n.* 1. a religious ~ 2. solemn, strict ~ (of the rules) 3. in ~ (of a holiday)

observant *adj.* ~ of (strictly ~ of the rules)

observation *n.* ["comment"] 1. to make an ~ 2. an astute, keen, penetrating, shrewd ~ 3. a personal ~ 4. an ~ about, on 5. an ~ that + clause (she made the astute ~ (to us) that the whole matter had been exaggerated) ["condition of being observed"] 6. to keep; place smb. under ~ 7. close ~ 8. to be under ~ (they were kept under close ~ for any problems that might develop) ["act of observing"] 9. to make ~s 10. (an) empirical; scientific ~ 11. (misc.) powers of ~ (Sherlock Holmes's remarkable powers of ~)

observe v. 1. to ~ attentively, carefully, closely 2. (I) we ~d them enter the building = they were ~d to enter the building 3. (J) we ~d them entering the building 4. (L; to) ("to comment") she astutely ~d (to us) that the whole matter had been exaggerated = "the whole matter has been exaggerated," she astutely ~d (to us) 5. (Q) we ~d how they had entered the building

observer n. 1. a casual; impartial; keen, perceptive; outside; participant; shrewd; skilled ~ 2. a military ~ 3. a team of ~s

obsess v. (D; intr.) (colloq.) to ~ about, over (don't ~ about your appearance)

obsessed adj. ~ by, with (~ by greed; ~ with one's appearance)

obsession n. an ~ about, with (an ~ about/with one's appearance)

obsolescence n. built-in; planned ~

obstacle n. 1. to constitute, pose, present, represent an ~ 2. to place, put an ~ in the way of smb. 3. to come across, confront, encounter an ~ 4. to clear, overcome, surmount an ~ 5. (of a horse) to take an ~ 6. to remove an ~ 7. a formidable, great, huge; insurmountable ~ 8. an artificial; natural ~ 9. an ~ to (an ~ to progress)

obstinate adj. ~ about; in

obstruction n. 1. to remove an ~ 2. an intestinal; respiratory ~ 3. an ~ to

obtrude v. (formal) (d; intr.) ("to intrude") to ~ on, upon

obvious I adj. 1. ~ from; to 2. ~ that + clause (from the vote so far, it is ~ to us all that she will be elected)

obvious II n. to state the ~

occasion I n. ["opportunity"] 1. to have; take an ~ (to do smt.) 2. a propitious, suitable ~ 3. an ~ for 4. an ~ to + inf. (I had no ~ to speak with them; there was no ~ for me to tell her) 5. an ~ arises ["happening"]["event"] 6. to celebrate; mark, observe an ~ 7. a festive, gala; happy, joyful, joyous ~ 8. an auspicious; fitting; special ~ 9. a memorable; momentous; unforgettable ~ 10. an official; state ~ 11. a sober; solemn ~ 12. on an ~ (on this ~; on numerous ~s; on many similar previous ~s) ["challenge"] 13. to rise to the ~ ["reason"] 14. an ~ for (there is no ~ for alarm) ["misc."] 15. on ~ ("sometimes") (see also *a sense of occasion* at **sense I** n.)

occasion II v. (rare) (O; can be used with one object) your actions have ~ed (us) a great deal of expense

Occident n. in the ~

occlusion n. a coronary ~

occupation n. ["profession"] 1. to have an ~ 2. a hazardous; profitable, rewarding ~ 3. by ~ (she is a waitress by ~) ["act of occupying"] 4. a military ~ 5. under ~ 6. (misc.) a zone of ~

occupied adj. 1. deeply; exclusively, solely ~ 2. ~ in; with (they are ~ in dealing with their own concerns; they are ~ with their own concerns)

occupy v. (d; refl., tr.) to ~ with (she ~pied them

with minor chores; they ~pied themselves with their own concerns)

occur v. (d; intr.) ("to come to mind") to ~ to (an idea ~red to her; it never ~red to me to ask; it suddenly ~red to me that we could ask her for help)

occurrence n. a common, daily, everyday, regular, usual; frequent; infrequent; rare, unusual ~

ocean n. 1. to cross the ~ (by ship) 2. across the ~ (to fly across the ~) 3. in the ~ 4. (misc.) a drop in the ~ (BE: AE has "a drop in the bucket")

o'clock adv. at (ten) ~

odd adj. 1. very ~ 2. ~ to + inf. (how ~ of her to have done that!) 3. ~ that + clause (how ~ that she did/should have done that!)

odds n. ["allowance designed to equalize a bettor's chances"] 1. to give, lay ~ (he laid me (~ of) two to one that it would not rain) 2. to accept, take ~ 3. to buck ("oppose") the ~ ["disadvantages"] 4. to beat the ~ 5. considerable, formidable, great, heavy, hopeless, insurmountable, long, overwhelming ~ 6. ~ against (all the ~ were against David and in favor of Goliath) 7. against ~ (to struggle against formidable ~; David succeeded against all (the) ~) ["advantages"] 8. ~ in favor of (all the ~ were in Goliath's favor and against David = all the ~ were in favor of Goliath and against David) ["disagreement"] 9. at ~ about, over; with (we were at ~s with the government about/over taxation) ["possibility"] 10. the ~ that + clause (what were the ~ that David would beat Goliath?) ["misc."] 11. by all ~ ("without question")

ode n. 1. to compose an ~ 2. an ~ to (an ~ to joy)

odious adj. ~ to

odometer n. (AE) to turn back an ~ (BE has *mileometer*)

odor, odour n. ["smell"] 1. to emit, exude, give off, have, produce an ~ 2. to perceive; recognize an ~ 3. a good; pleasant ~ 4. a faint, slight ~ 5. a heavy; persistent; pungent, strong ~ 6. a bad, disagreeable, fetid, foul, rank, unpleasant; musty ~ 7. an ~ emanates from 8. an ~ permeates smt. (an unpleasant ~ permeated the entire room) 9. an ~ of (the unpleasant ~ of rotting flesh) ["repute"] (BE) 10. in bad; good ~ (with)

off adv. ["situated, esp. with respect to money"] 1. badly, poorly; worse ~ 2. better; comfortably; well ~ ["not exact"] 3. far, way ~ 4. ~ in (he's way ~ in his calculations) 5. ~ out (BE) ("where's the wife?" "she's ~ out (somewhere)") ["misc."] 6. to have, take a day ~ ("to have, take a day free from work") USAGE NOTE: Since *off* is also a preposition, one can say: to have, take a day off work.

off-balance adj., adv. caught ~

offend v. 1. to ~ deeply, gravely, terribly 2. (D; intr.) to ~ against (to ~ against common decency/public morals) 3. (R) it ~ed me deeply that you did not come

offender n. a chronic; first; juvenile, young; sex ~

offense, offence n. ["infraction"] 1. to commit an ~

2. a first; minor, petty, trivial ~ 3. a serious ~ 4. a capital; civil; criminal; impeachable; indictable ~ 5. an ~ against (an ~ against common decency/public morals) ["feeling of outrage"] 6. to take ~ at (she takes ~ at every remark) ["insult"] (formal) 7. to cause, give ~ 8. an ~ to

offensive I *adj.* 1. ~ to (his actions were ~ to everyone) 2. ~ to + inf. (it's ~ to read such things in the newspaper)

offensive II *n.* 1. to assume, go on, go over to, start (up), take the ~ 2. to launch, mount an ~ 3. to carry out, conduct, undertake an ~ 4. to break off an ~ 5. an all-out; economic; military; peace ~ 6. (usu. mil.) an air; ground; full-scale ~ (their forces launched a full-scale ground ~) 7. an ~ against (they mounted an economic ~ against the neighboring countries) 8. on the ~ (the candidate went on the ~)

offer I *n.* 1. to make an ~ (she made me an attractive ~ I couldn't refuse) 2. to consider an ~ (I considered ~s of employment from several firms) 3. to accept, agree to an ~ 4. to decline, refuse, reject, spurn, turn down an ~ 5. to withdraw an ~ 6. an attractive, generous; firm; kind; reasonable; tempting ~ (her kind ~ of help was accepted gratefully) 7. a tentative ~ 8. an introductory; job; trial ~ 9. an ~ to + inf. (her kind ~ to help was accepted gratefully) 10. (BE) on ~ ("available")

offer II *v.* 1. (A) she ~ed the job to me; or: she ~ed me the job 2. (D; refl., tr.) to ~ as (the money was ~ed (me/to me) as an inducement) 3. (D; tr.) to ~ for (to ~ a reward for information; we ~ed them one hundred thousand dollars for the house) 4. (E) she kindly ~ed to help

offering *n.* 1. to make an ~ 2. a burnt; peace; sacrificial; votive ~ 3. an ~ to

offer up *v.* 1. (d; tr.) to ~ as (to ~ smt. as a sacrifice = to ~ smt. up as a sacrifice) 2. (D; tr.) to ~ for (they ~ed up the child for adoption = they ~ed the child up for adoption) 3. (D; tr.) to ~ to (to ~ prayers to God = to ~ prayers up to God)

office *n.* ["function"] 1. to assume (an) ~ 2. to seek (public) ~ 3. (pol.) to run for (esp. AE), stand for (BE) ~ 4. to hold; take ~ 5. to resign from (an) ~ 6. (pol.) (an) appointive; elective; high; public ~ 7. (pol.) in; out of ~ (our party is out of ~) 8. a term of ~ 9. (misc.) smb.'s good ~s ("smb.'s services as a mediator") (the deal was arranged through the good ~s of the Minister responsible) ["ministry"] (BE) 10. the Foreign (and Commonwealth); Home ~ ["place where a function is performed"] 11. to open; set up an ~ 12. to lease; rent an ~ 13. to manage, run an ~ 14. a branch; head, home, main ~ 15. a booking; box, ticket ~ 16. a business; dentist's (AE); doctor's (AE); lawyer's ~ 17. a left-luggage (BE); lost-and-found (AE), lost property (BE) ~ 18. a customs; dead-letter; Met (BE), Meteorological (BE); patent; post; registry (BE) ~ 19. at, in an ~ (she works at our ~) USAGE NOTE: In

North America, doctors and dentists have *offices*; in Great Britain, they have *surgeries*. (See also *office-holder* at **holder**)

office hours *n.* 1. to have, keep ~ 2. after; during; (BE) out of, outside ~

officer *n.* ["person holding a certain rank in the armed forces"] 1. to commission an ~ 2. to promote an ~ 3. to break, demote; cashier, dismiss an ~ 4. a commissioned; non-commissioned; petty; warrant ~ 5. a company-grade (AE); field-grade (AE); junior ~ 6. a commanding; flag; general; high-ranking; ranking; senior; superior; top-ranking ~ (which military unit does a general ~ command?) 7. a line; staff ~ 8. an air-force; army; military; naval ~ 9. a duty; executive; gunnery; intelligence; liaison ~ 10. ~ of the day; ~ of the deck ["person holding a position of authority"] 11. a case; correctional (AE); court; juvenile (AE); law-enforcement; peace; probation; truant (AE) ~ (see also **police officer**) 12. a customs; revenue (BE) ~ 13. a health; medical; senior nursing (BE) ~ 14. an executive; personnel; public-relations ~ 15. (misc.) a chief executive ~ (CEO); to install newly elected ~s; (GB) a returning ~ (at an election); an ~ of the law; please don't arrest us, Officer (Krupke)!

official *n.* 1. a high, high-ranking, senior, top-ranking; responsible ~ 2. an appointed; elected ~ 3. a church; public ~ 4. a city; county; federal (US); government; local; state ~ 5. a customs; health; law-enforcement, police; postal; union ~ 6. (misc.) to bribe an ~

officiate *v.* 1. (D; intr.) to ~ as (she ~d as the chairperson) 2. (D; intr.) to ~ at (to ~ at a ceremony)

offing *n.* in the ~ ("forthcoming")

off-putting *adj.* 1. very ~ 2. to find smt. ~ (I find it very ~ to be lied to = I find it very ~ when smb. lies to me)

offspring *n.* to produce ~

ogle *v.* (d; intr.) to ~ at

oik *n.* (BE) (slang) (derog.) a jumped-up ~

oil *n.* ["petroleum"] 1. to drill for; hit, strike ~ 2. to pump ~ 3. to produce; refine ~ 4. crude; refined ~ 5. offshore ~ 6. ~ gushes from a well ["lubricant"] 7. to change; check the ~ 8. household; linseed; lubricating; machine; motor ~ ["fatty liquid"] 9. canola (esp. US); coconut; cooking; corn; cottonseed; olive; palm; peanut; safflower; salad; sesame (-seed); salad; sunflower; vegetable ~ (pour/drizzle a little olive ~ over everything and fry it in ~) 10. castor; cod-liver; mineral; suntan ~ 11. a film of ~ ["misc."] 12. to burn the midnight ~ (colloq.) ("to work or study until very late at night"); ~ and water do not mix (see also **oils**)

oils *n.* to paint in ~

ointment *n.* 1. to apply, put on, rub in, rub on (an) ~ 2. a soothing ~ 3. a skin ~ 4. a tube of ~ 5. (misc.) a fly in the ~ ("smt. that irritates or causes harm")

OK I *adj., adv.* (colloq.) 1. to do; go ~ (the exam went ~ and I think I did ~ on it) 2. ~ by, for; with (is that ~ with you? is that ~ for you?) 3. ~ to + inf. (it is ~ to bring your lunch with you)

OK II *n.* (colloq.) ["approval"] 1. to give one's ~ 2. to get the ~ 3. the ~ to + inf. (we got the ~ to bring our lunch with us)

old *adj.* (misc.) how ~ is she?; she's ten years ~; to grow ~ gracefully; any ~ thing; good ~; poor ~; same ~ (good ~ dad has to put up with poor ~ mom complaining of the same ~ arthritis year after year!); she looks (too) ~ to be his daughter; in fact, she looks ~ enough to be his mother!

old age *n.* 1. to live to, reach a ripe ~ 2. to spend one's ~ (she spent her ~ learning new skills) 3. extreme; ripe ~ 4. in ~ (she took up painting)

old hand *n.* 1. an ~ at (she's an ~ at politics) 2. an ~ of a certain type (he's an old China hand who lived out East for many years)

O-levels *n.* ["ordinary-level secondary school examinations"] (GB) 1. to do, sit, take (one's) ~ 2. in one's ~ (to do well in one's French and German ~) 3. ~ in (to have ~ in French and German) USAGE NOTE: O-levels have been largely replaced by GCSEs.

olive branch *n.* ["symbol of peace"] 1. to extend, hold out, offer the ~ 2. to accept; decline, reject the ~

omelet, omelette *n.* 1. to make an ~ 2. a cheese, cheesy; mushroom; plain; Spanish; Western ~

omen *n.* 1. a bad; good ~ 2. an ~ for (we took the rain as a good ~ for the harvest)

omission *n.* 1. to correct, rectify an ~ 2. a glaring ~ 3. an ~ from (an ~ from a list)

omit *v.* 1. (D; tr.) to ~ from (she ~ted his name from the list) 2. (E) (esp. BE) he ~ted to explain why he had been late

on *prep., adv.* 1. to have smt. ~ smb. ("to have evidence against smb.") 2. the fire went out ~ me ("the fire went out through no fault of mine") 3. we were ~ to what was happening ("we were aware of what was happening") 4. well ~ in years ("rather old") 5. (misc.) (the) drinks are ~ me ("I will pay for the drinks") (see also *drinks are on the house* at **house**)

once *adv.* 1. at ~ 2. ~ again, more 3. (misc.) ~ upon a time

once-over *n.* (colloq.) ["a look"] to give smb./smt. the ~ (lightly)

one *pronoun* 1. ~ by ~ 2. ~ of (~ of them; ~ of the students) USAGE NOTE: CE has "one must do one's best to make people respect one." AE prefers "one must do his best to make people respect him."

online, on line *adv.* ["linked by computer"] 1. to be ~ 2. to get, go ~ 3. to communicate ~

only *adv., adj.* (misc.) not ~ (¬but/but also¬) USAGE NOTE: *Only adv.* has a unique syntactic property that can be seen by considering the following example and its transformations: (1) "With this he did not merely gain control of himself; he gained control over everything." – Philip K. Dick,

"The Electric Ant" (1969) = (2) with this he did not just gain control of himself; he gained control over everything.= (3)? with this he did not only gain control of himself; he gained control over everything. = (4) with this he not only gained control of himself; (¬but/but also¬) he gained control over everything. = (5) with this he not only gained control of himself ¬but/but also¬ gained control over everything. The replacement of "did not X gain" by "not X gained" is possible when X = *only* but not when X = *merely* or *just*. In fact, some people actually consider (3) wrong by contrast with (4) or (5)! However, if an inverted word-order is used this property of *only adv* vanishes and it functions like *merely*: with this he not only/merely/*just did he gain control of himself ... The adverb *just* cannot be used in that way.

onslaught *n.* 1. to face; resist an ~ 2. an enemy; sudden ~

onus *n.* 1. the ~ is on smb. to do smt. (the ~ is on you to get the job done) 2. the ~ lies, rests with smb. (the ~ of proof lies with the police) 3. to put the ~ on smb.

ooze *v.* 1. (d; intr.) to ~ from, out of; into (blood was ~ing from the wound) 2. (d; intr.) to ~ with (to ~ with charm)

open I *adj.* 1. wide ~ (he threw the door wide ~ and strode into the house) 2. ~ about; for (~ about one's awful childhood; ~ for business) 3. (cannot stand alone) ~ to (~ to the public; I'm ~ to suggestions; a system ~ to abuse) 4. (misc.) to lay oneself ~ to criticism; the system lays itself ~ to abuse

open II *n.* 1. in, into the ~ (to bring smt. out into the ~) 2. (misc.) it is all out in the ~ now ("everything has been revealed")

open III *v.* 1. (D; intr., tr.) to ~ by, with (we ~ed our meeting by singing a song; we ~ed our meeting with a song) 2. (D; tr.) to ~ for (to ~ new land for development) 3. (d; intr.) to ~ into, onto, to (the gate ~s into the garden; to ~ onto the terrace; the door ~s to the street; the government has ~ed the files to the public) 4. (D; tr.) to ~ to (they ~ed their meetings to the public) 5. (N; used with an adjective) ~ your mouth wide 6. (misc.) does the door ~ in or out?; ~ your books at/to (AE) page three

opener *n.* ["device that opens"] 1. a bottle; can (AE), tin (BE) ~ 2. a letter ~ (AE; BE has *paper knife*)

open house *n.* to have, hold, keep (an) ~

opening *n.* ["vacancy"] 1. an ~ for (we have an ~ for an engineer) ["putting into operation"] 2. a grand ~ (the grand ~ of a new supermarket)

open up *v.* (D; intr., tr.) to ~ to (the government has ~ed up the files to the public; he finally ~ed up to the press)

opera *n.* 1. to perform, stage an ~ 2. (a) comic; grand; light ~ 3. a soap ~ (now called typically just *a soap*) 4. a horse ~ ("western film") 5. at the ~ (*A Night at the Opera* – the Marx Brothers, 1935)

operate *v.* 1. (d; intr.) to ~ against (the enemy

troops were ~ing against our guerrillas) 2. (med.) (D; intr.) to ~ for; on (the surgeon ~d on her for appendicitis = she was ~d on for appendicitis)
operation *n.* ["surgical procedure"] 1. to perform an ~ 2. to have, undergo an ~ 3. to come through, go through, survive an ~ 4. a delicate; emergency; exploratory; major; minor ~ 5. an ~ for; on (an ~ for the removal of gallstones) ["military or police activity"] 6. to conduct; launch, mount, undertake an ~ 7. covert; guerrilla; joint; large-scale; mine-sweeping; mopping-up ~s ["state of being functional"] 8. to put into ~ (the plant has been put into ~) 9. in ~ (the factory is in ~) ["project"] 10. a cloak-and-dagger, covert, secret; rescue ~ ["misc."] 11. during an ~ (there were no complications during the ~) (see also **operations**)
operations *n.* 1. to conduct ~ 2. combined, joint; drilling; military; mining; mopping-up; naval; offensive; salvage ~ 3. (mil.) a theater of ~ 4. during the ~ (there were no complications during the ~)
operator *n.* 1. a computer; crane; elevator (AE: BE has *liftman*); ham, radio; machine (AE); radar; switchboard; telephone; tour ~ 2. (colloq.) a slick, smooth ~
opine *v.* 1. (D; intr.) to ~ about, on (he'll ~ for hours on just about anything!) 2. (L; to) he ~d (to us) that things were better in the old days
opinion *n.* 1. to air, express, give, offer, pass, state, venture, voice an ~ 2. to form an ~ about (I still have not formed an ~ about the candidates) 3. to mold (public) ~ 4. to entertain, have, hold an ~ 5. (legal) (AE) to hand down an ~ (the court handed down an ~ on the case) 6. to ask for, seek smb.'s ~ 7. a candid, frank, honest ~ 8. a considered; informed; objective; strong ~ (she has strong ~s about everything) 9. a personal; prevailing, prevalent ~ 10. a negative; positive ~ 11. a contrary, dissenting; opposing ~ 12. a high; low ~ of (he has a high ~ of himself) 13. (an) expert; lay; legal; medical ~ 14. political; popular ~ (see also **public opinion**) 15. a second ~ (as given by a doctor) (to ask for and get a second ~ from a specialist before making a decision) 16. shades of ~ 17. an ~ about, on 18. the ~ that + clause (she expressed her ~ that a compromise would be reached) 19. in smb.'s ~ (in my humble ~) 20. of an ~ (she is of the ~ that nothing will help) 21. (misc.) a clash of ~s; a difference of ~; a matter of ~ is a matter of ~ whether the drug is effective); ~s differ ¬about/as to¬ whether the drug is effective
opponent *n.* 1. a formidable, strong; weak ~ 2. (ironic) my worthy ~
opportunity *n.* 1. to grab, seize, take an ~ 2. to afford, give, offer an ~ 3. to find; have an ~ 4. to lose, miss; pass up an ~ 5. a fleeting; lost, missed ~ 6. a golden, once-in-a-lifetime; great ~ 7. ample ~ 8. (an) equal ~ ("government policy of giving all citizens an equal chance") 9. (an) ~ arises 10. an ~ for (they had a once-in-a-lifetime ~ for a visit

to Europe) 11. an ~ to + inf. (they had a once-in-a-lifetime ~ to visit Europe) 12. at the first available ~; at smb.'s earliest ~ 13. (misc.) ~ knocks ("appears"); a window of ~ USAGE NOTE: The US has *equal-opportunity employers*. The UK has *equal-opportunities employers*.
oppose *v.* 1. to ~ adamantly, bitterly, implacably, resolutely, strongly, vehemently, vigorously 2. (G) they ~d dropping out of college 3. (K) they ~d his dropping out of college
opposed *adj.* 1. adamantly, implacably; diametrically; ideologically; strongly, vehemently ~ 2. ~ to (they are adamantly ~ to his dropping out of college)
opposite I *adj.* (BE) ~ to USAGE NOTE: When *opposite* means 'facing,' it can be an adjective in BE – her house is opposite to ours. More typically, *opposite* is used as a preposition in both BE and AE – her house is opposite ours. When *opposite* means "diametrically opposed", it is used only in BE as an adjective – her opinions are opposite to ours.
opposite II *n.* 1. a direct, exact, polar ~ 2. an ~ of, to (her opinions are the exact ~ of ours = her opinions are exactly the ~ of ours) 3. (misc.) ~s attract
opposition *n.* 1. to arouse, give rise to, stir up ~ 2. to offer, put up ~ 3. to crush, overcome, overpower, smash, wear down ~ 4. to come across, encounter, face, meet, meet with, run into, run up against ~ 5. to brook no ~ 6. (ling.) to neutralize an ~ 7. bitter, determined, fierce, stiff, strong, stubborn, unbending, unyielding, vehement ~ 8. growing, mounting; sporadic; token ~ 9. ~ hardens, stiffens; crumbles; wanes, weakens 10. ~ to (~ to new taxes) 11. against, despite, in spite of, over (the) ~ (we adopted the resolution over the ~ of the other party) 12. in ~ to
oppression *n.* under ~ (to live/suffer under (the yoke of) ~)
opt *v.* 1. (d; intr.) to ~ for (they decided to ~ for the company pension plan) 2. (d; intr.) to ~ out of (to ~ out of the conflict; they decided to ~ out of the company pension plan) 3. (d; intr.) to ~ into (esp. BE) (they decided to ~ into the company pension scheme) 4. (E) they ~ed to decline the invitation
optimism *n.* 1. to display, radiate, show; express ~ 2. cautious, guarded; eternal, incurable, inveterate, unflagging ~ 3. ~ about, at, over (we expressed ~ about the eventual results)
optimist *n.* an eternal, incurable, inveterate ~
optimistic *adj.* 1. cautiously, guardedly; incurably ~ 2. ~ about, at, over (we are ~ about the eventual results) 3. ~ that + clause (we are ~ that the results will be favorable)
option *n.* 1. to exercise an ~ 2. to give; take an ~ on (they gave me the ~ of joining them or not joining them) 3. an exclusive; feasible, viable; first ~ (CE: BE also has *first refusal*) 4. (AE) a local ~ (of a political subdivision) 5. a share; stock ~ 6. an ~ on

(they took an ~ on the shares) 7. an ~ to + inf. (they had an ~ to buy the shares) 8. (misc.) to have no ~ but to...; to keep one's ~s open
oracle *n.* ["authority"] to consult an ~
orange *n.* 1. to peel; squeeze an ~ 2. a mandarin; navel ~ 3. a segment of an ~ = an ~ segment (see also *orange juice* at **juice**; *orange peel* at **peel**)
oration *n.* 1. to deliver an ~ 2. a funeral ~
oratory *n.* 1. eloquent, persuasive, powerful ~ 2. inflammatory; rabble-rousing ~ 3. campaign ~
orbit *n.* 1. to make an ~ around, of, round (the spaceship made five ~s of the moon) 2. to be in; go into ~ 3. a geostationary ~ 4. in; into ~ (to put a satellite into ~)
orchard *n.* an apple; cherry; peach ~ (compare **grove**)
orchestra *n.* 1. to conduct, direct (esp. AE), lead (esp. AE) an ~ 2. a chamber; dance; philharmonic, symphony; pops; string ~ 3. an ~ performs, plays; tunes up 4. an ~ under (the Berlin Philharmonic Orchestra under (the baton of) Wilhelm Furtwängler) USAGE NOTE: The chief of the first violins in an orchestra is called the *concertmaster* in AE and the *leader* in BE. In AE, *leader* sometimes means 'conductor.'
ordain *v.* 1. (D; tr.) he was ~ed as a priest 2. (D; tr.) he was ~ed to the priesthood 3. (L; subj.) (formal) the emperor ~ed that all foreigners be/should be expelled 4. (N; used with a noun) he was ~ed (a) priest
ordeal *n.* 1. to go through, undergo; survive an ~ 2. a dreadful, terrible, terrifying, trying ~ 3. (an) ~ by fire; water 4. (misc.) fortunately I was spared the ~ of having to listen to any more boring speeches!
order I *n.* ["request for goods or services"] 1. to give, place, put in an ~ 2. to make out, write out an ~ 3. to fill; receive, take an ~ (has the waiter taken your ~?) 4. to cancel an ~ 5. a back; mail; prepublication; rush; shipping; standing ~ 6. a side (in a restaurant) ~ (a hamburger with a side ~ of fries) 7. (new) ~s are falling off; are picking up 8. on ~ (the merchandise is on ~) 9. to ~ (made to ~) 10. (misc.) a tall ~ to fill ("a difficult task to carry out") ["command"] 11. to give, hand down (AE), issue an ~ 12. to carry out, execute; obey, take an ~ 13. to cancel, countermand, rescind, revoke; violate an ~ 14. a direct; executive; preservation (BE); specific ~ (see also *slap a preservation order on* at **slap II** *v.*) 15. doctor's; marching; sealed; standing; verbal; written ~s 16. an ~ to + inf. (we received an ~ to attack) 17. an ~ that + clause; subj. (headquarters issued an ~ that the attack be/should be resumed) 18. at, by, on smb.'s ~ (by whose ~ was this done?; these premises have been closed by ~ (of some authority)) 19. under ~s (we were under ~s to remain indoors) ["court decree"] 20. to issue an ~ 21. an affiliation (BE); cease-and-desist; court; deportation; gag; maintenance (BE), support (AE); restraining ~ ["association, group"] 22. a cloistered; Masonic; mendicant; monastic;

religious; secret ~ ["system"] 23. an economic; pecking; social ~ (he's at the bottom of the pecking ~) ["proper procedure"] 24. (a) point of ~ 25. in ~; out of ~ (the senator was out of ~) 26. to call a meeting to ~ ("to begin a meeting"; "to reestablish proper procedure at a meeting") ["state of peace"] 27. to establish; keep, maintain; restore ~ 28. good; public ~ (see also **law and order**) ["state in which everything is in its proper place or condition"] 29. to put smt. in/into ~ 30. apple-pie, good, shipshape ~ 31. in; out of ~ (everything is in good ~; this machine is out of ~ again) ["condition"] 32. working ~ (in working ~) ["sequence"] 33. alphabetical; chronological; correct; logical; numerical ~ (see also **word order**) 34. ascending; descending ~ 35. in; out of ~ (in ~ of importance; in alphabetical ~; these entries are out of ~; that rude remark was completely out of ~!) ["military formation"] 36. close; extended; open ~ ["instructions to pay"] 37. a money (esp. AE), postal (BE) ~ (he made out and sent a money ~, which I received and cashed) ["misc."] 38. a new ~; a new world ~; an old ~; of the ~ of (BE)/on the ~ of (AE) ("approximately"); research of the highest ~ (see also **holy orders**; **law and order**; **marching orders**)
order II *v.* 1. (C) ~ a copy for me; or: ~ me a copy 2. (D; tr.) to ~ from (~ me a copy from the publisher = ~ a copy for me from the publisher = ~ a copy from the publisher for me) 3. (d; tr.) to ~ from, out of (she ~ed him out of the house) 4. (d; tr.) to ~ off (the referee ~ed the player off the field) 5. (H) the referee ~ed the player to go off the field 6. (L; subj.) the referee ~ed that the player go/should go off the field 7. (M) the referee ~ed the player to be sent off the field 8. (esp. AE) (N; used with a past participle) the referee ~ed the player sent off the field 9. (misc.) the doctor ~ed her to bed
orders *n.* ["ordination"] see **holy orders**
ordinance *n.* ["local law"] 1. to adopt, enact, pass; draft, draw up an ~ 2. to issue an ~ 3. to apply, enforce an ~ 4. to amend, change; approve; repeal, rescind, revoke an ~ 5. to obey, observe an ~ 6. to violate an ~ 7. a city, municipal; local; township (esp. AE) ~ 8. an ~ that + clause; subj. (the town issued an ~ (to the effect) that all dogs be/should be muzzled)
ordinary *n.* out of the ~
ordnance *n.* naval ~
ore *n.* 1. copper; iron ~ 2. a vein of ~
organ *n.* ["part of the body"] 1. body; genital, reproductive, sexual; internal; major; sense, sensory; speech; vital; vocal ~s (see also **sex organs**) ["large wind instrument"] 2. to play the ~ 3. a barrel; electronic; pipe; reed ~ (see also **hand organ**; **mouth organ**) ["publication"] 4. a government; house (esp. BE); official; party ~
organism *n.* 1. a dead; healthy; living ~ 2. a deadly; harmful; infectious ~ 3. microorganisms; minute ~s

organization *n.* 1. to establish, form an ~ 2. to run an ~ 3. to disband, dissolve an ~ 4. a charitable, philanthropic; relief ~ 5. a civic, community; non-governmental (NGO); nonprofit, not-for-profit (esp. AE); professional; religious; voluntary ~ 6. a student; women's; youth ~ 7. an international; local; national; state; UN ~ 8. a central; umbrella ~ 9. a government; official ~ 10. a health-maintenance (HMO) (AE) ~ 11. a profit-making, proprietary (AE) ~ 12. a front ~ for (accused of having belonged to a Communist front ~; an ~ that was a front for organized crime)

orgasm *n.* 1. to achieve, reach; have an ~ 2. to fake an ~ 3. a simultaneous ~

orgy *n.* 1. to engage in, stage an ~ 2. a drunken ~

orient, orientate *v.* (D; refl., tr.) to ~ to (to ~ oneself to one's surroundings)

Orient *n.* in the ~

orientated, oriented *adj.* ~ towards (~ towards the needs of young consumers; ~ to one's surroundings)

orientation *n.* ["introduction"] 1. to give, offer smb. (an) ~ to 2. to get, go through, receive (an) ~

origin *n.* 1. to have an ~ in (the problem has its ~s in the nineteenth century) 2. in ~ (the documents were Norse in ~) 3. of ~ (she is of Norwegian ~; the fire was of undetermined ~)

original *n.* in the ~ (to read a text in the ~ (language))

originality *n.* 1. to display, show ~ 2. ~ in

originate *v.* (d; intr.) to ~ from; in; with (the idea ~d with her; the problem ~d in the nineteenth century)

orphan *n.* 1. to be left an ~ 2. a war ~

orthodoxy *n.* (a) rigid, strict ~

Oscar (T) *n.* 1. to get, receive, win; have an ~ 2. (misc.) to be nominated for an ~; to be an Oscar-winner

oscillate *v.* (D; intr.) to ~ between

osmosis *n.* by ~ (to absorb by ~)

ossify *v.* (D; intr.) to ~ into (their ideas ~fied into a rigid orthodoxy)

other *adj.* ["second"] 1. every ~ (I go jogging every ~ day) ["misc."] 2. each ~ (we ought to help each ~)

ought *v.* (E) we ~ to help each other, oughtn't we?; we don't always do what we ~ (to)

oust *v.* (D; tr.) to ~ from

out *adj., adv.* ["unconscious"] 1. ~ cold ("completely unconscious") ["intent on"] 2. ~ for (she is ~ for revenge) 3. ~ to + inf. (she is ~ to get revenge) ["gone"] 4. ~ to (~ to lunch) ["misc."] 5. over and ~ (used at the end of a radio message); to turn smt. inside ~; down and ~ ("destitute"); they are ~ for a walk; he is ~ for your money ("he is attempting to get your money") (see also *off out* at **off**)

outbreak *n.* sporadic ~s

outburst *n.* an angry; furious; spontaneous; sudden; violent ~

outcome *n.* 1. to decide the (final) ~ of 2. a favorable,

successful; probable; unfavorable, unsuccessful ~ 3. to evaluate, measure ~s ("to evaluate results") 4. (misc.) whatever the ~ of the election (may be), we shall abide by it!

outcry *n.* 1. to cause, spark (off); make, raise an ~ 2. an international; public ~ 3. an ~ against; about; for; over; from (the incident sparked off an international ~ about it from many countries)

outdo *v.* 1. (D; tr.) to ~ in (she outdid them in every field) 2. (misc.) not to be outdone

outdoors I out of doors *adv.* to be; go ~

outdoors II *n.* in the great ~

outgrowth *n.* a direct; indirect ~ (of)

outing *n.* to go on an ~ (to)

outlay *n.* ["spending of money"] 1. to make ~s for, on 2. a capital; huge; large; modest; small ~ (you will be able to recoup/recover/get back with interest the modest ~s you make on the project now)

outlet *n.* ["passage"] 1. an ~ to (an ~ to the sea) ["means of expression"] 2. to find an ~ for (to find an ~ for one's emotions) 3. to provide an ~ for ["retail store"] 4. a factory; retail; sales ~ ["socket"] (AE) 5. an electrical ~ (to plug an appliance into an electrical ~)

outline I *n.* 1. to draw up, make; give, provide an ~ 2. a bare; broad, general; dim; rough ~ (can you give us a rough ~ of how the project will proceed?) 3. in ~ (to draw in ~; to present a project in broad ~)

outline II *v.* 1. (B) they ~d the project to us 2. (d; tr.) to ~ against (the ship was ~d against the horizon)

outlook *n.* ["viewpoint"] 1. to have an ~ on (she has a healthy ~ on life) 2. a cheerful, optimistic, positive; healthy ~ 3. a negative, pessimistic ~ 4. in ~ (we are quite similar in (our) ~ = we are people of quite similar ~) ["prospects"] 5. a bright, promising ~ 6. a bleak, dark, dim, dismal, dreary, gloomy, unpromising ~ 7. the long-range, long-term; short-range, short-term ~ 8. an ~ for (the ~ for the future is bright)

outnumber *v.* 1. to ~ heavily; hopelessly (we were heavily ~ed) 2. to ~ by (we were ~ed (by) at least ten to one!)

outpost *n.* a military ~

output *n.* 1. to increase, step up ~ 2. to curtail, cut back, reduce ~ 3. annual; daily; industrial; monthly ~ 4. a level of ~ (falling levels of ~ are causing concern in government circles)

outrage I *n.* ["anger"] 1. to express; feel ~ (we all expressed our ~ at the crime) 2. to provoke, spark (esp. AE), spark off (BE), stir up ~ 3. (misc.) a sense of ~ ["offensive act"] 4. to commit an ~ 5. an ~ against (an ~ against public morality) 6. an ~ to + inf. (it was an ~ to take innocent civilians hostage!) 7. an ~ that + clause (it was an ~ that innocent civilians were/should be taken hostage!)

outrage II *v.* we were ~d (to learn) that she had been arrested = (R) it ~d us (to learn) that she had been arrested

outrageous *adj.* 1. ~ to + inf. (it's ~ to permit such behavior) 2. ~ that + clause (it's positively / absolutely ~ that she has been / should have been arrested !)

outs *n.* (colloq.) (AE) to be on the ~ with smb. ("to be on bad terms with smb.")

outset *n.* at; from the (very) ~

outside *n.* 1. from the ~ 2. on the ~

outsider *n.* a complete, rank ~ (how could a rank ~ in the race win first prize ?)

outskirts *n.* on, through the ~ (of a city)

outsource *v.* (D; tr.) to ~ to (the work was ~d to several sub-contractors)

outspoken *adj.* ~ in (~ in their opposition to new taxes)

outstanding *adj.* 1. to leave ~ (at the end of the meeting we left several matters still ~ and unresolved) 2. ~ in (~ and excellent in scientific achievement)

outward *adv.* ~ bound

outweigh *v.* to far, more than ~ (the benefits of this new treatment more than ~ any possible side-effects involved !)

ovation *n.* 1. to get, receive an ~ 2. to give smb. an ~ (the audience gave them a thunderous ~) 3. a standing; thunderous, tremendous ~ 4. to an ~ (they walked out on the stage to a thunderous ~ from the audience)

oven *n.* 1. to light, turn on an ~ 2. to turn off an ~ 3. an electric; gas; microwave; self-cleaning ~ 4. a hot; pre-heated ~ 5. in an ~ USAGE NOTE: A microwave oven is nowadays called typically a microwave.

over *adj.* ["finished"] 1. ~ between; with (it's all ~ between them) 2. (misc.) ~ and done with; ~ and ~; ~ and out; ~ to (I've done all I can – it's ~ to you now !)

overboard *adv.* 1. to fall ~ 2. (misc.) man ~ ! to go ~ over smt. / smb. ("to show excessive enthusiasm for smt. / smb.") (see also *to be washed overboard* at **wash II** *v.*)

overcharge *v.* 1. (D; tr.) to ~ by (they ~d us (by) twenty percent) 2. (D; tr.) to ~ for (they ~d us for the book; we were ~d for it by twenty percent)

overcome *v.* 1. (D; tr.) to be ~ by (they were overcome by smoke) 2. (D; tr.) to be ~ with (I was overcome with emotion)

overcompensate *v.* (D; intr.) to ~ for (he ~s for his poor performance in class by doing extra assignments for the teacher)

overdose I *n.* 1. to give; take an ~ 2. a fatal, lethal; massive ~ 3. a drug ~ = an ~ of a drug

overdose II *v.* (D; intr.) to ~ on (to ~ on a medication)

overdue *adj.* 1. long; several years ~ 2. ~ for (we are long ~ for change)

overflow I *n.* 1. to catch the ~ 2. the ~ from

overflow II *v.* 1. (D; intr.) to ~ into (the mob ~ed into the street) 2. (d; intr.) to ~ with (the stadium was ~ing with spectators)

overground *n.* ["transportation"] (esp. BE) by ~ (I often travel by ~)

overgrown *adj.* ~ with

overhaul I *n.* ["repairs"] a complete; major; thorough ~ (our car needs a major ~)

overhaul II *v.* to ~ completely; thoroughly

overhear *v.* 1. (I) we overheard him say it = he was overheard to say it 2. (J) we overheard him saying it

overindulge *v.* (D; intr., refl., tr.) to ~ in (we ~d ourselves in the rich pastries)

overindulgence *n.* ~ in (our ~ in the rich pastries)

overjoyed *adj.* 1. ~ about, at (we were ~ at your success) 2. ~ to + inf. (we were ~ to hear that you'd succeeded) 3. ~ that + clause (we were ~ that you'd succeeded) 4. (misc.) we were not exactly ~ at the news that we'd failed !

overlap *v.* (D; intr.) to ~ in; with (our role ~s with theirs in jurisdiction; their territory ~s with ours = their territory and ours ~ with each other)

overload I *n.* circuit; sensory ~

overload II *v.* (D; tr.) to ~ with (the ship was ~ed with cargo)

overpass *n.* (esp. AE) 1. an ~ over (an ~ over a road) 2. in; into; through an ~ (BE has *flyover*)

overqualified *adj.* 1. clearly ~ 2. ~ for (she is clearly ~ for such a lowly job) 3. ~ to + inf. (she is clearly ~ to work at such a lowly job)

overrated *adj.* vastly, very (much) ~

overreact *v.* (D; intr.) to ~ to (they ~ed to the news)

overrun *adj.* ~ with (~ with weeds)

overseas *adv., n.* 1. to go, travel ~ 2. (misc.) to return from ~

oversight *n.* 1. an ~ that + clause (it was through an ~ that her name was omitted) 2. by, through an ~ (her name was omitted through an ~)

overstocked *adj.* ~ with (~ with merchandise)

overtime *n.* ["extra time worked"] 1. to do, put in, work (five hours) ~ ["extra wage"] 2. to earn ~ 3. to pay ~ 4. on ~ (I was on ~ all week) ["extra period"] (sports) (AE; BE has *extra time*) 5. in ~ 6. a sudden-death ~

overtones *n.* 1. to develop, take on; have ~ 2. nasty; political; racial ~ (the dispute took on political ~)

overture *n.* ["musical introduction"] 1. to compose; perform, play an ~ 2. an ~ to (to play the ~ to an opera) ["introductory proposal"] 3. to make an ~; to make ~s to 4. to spurn smb.'s ~s 5. diplomatic; friendly ~s (Flatland spurned Ruritania's diplomatic ~s)

overview *n.* to get; give; have an ~ of

owe *v.* 1. (A) she ~s ten dollars to her sister; or: she ~s her sister ten dollars (the *to* is usu. not used when the indirect object is a pronoun : she owes her ten dollars) 2. (D; tr.) to ~ for, on (we still ~ one hundred dollars for the car) 3. (misc.) we ~ it to our students to grade their papers promptly

owing *adj.* ~ to (her absence was ~ to illness)

owl *n.* ~s hoot

own *determiner, pronoun* 1. to hold one's ~ ("to continue to survive") 2. to come into one's ~ ("to receive recognition") 3. on one's ~ ("independently") 4. of one's ~ (for reasons of one's ~) ("for one's own reasons")

owner *n.* 1. a part ~ 2. the lawful, rightful; lucky, proud ~ (congratulations! you are now the lucky ~ of a lovely puppy!)

ownership *n.* 1. collective; communal; joint; part; private; public; state ~ 2. under ~ (the restaurant has improved now that it's under new ~)

own up *v.* (colloq.) (D; intr.) ("to confess") to ~ to (she ~ed up to stealing the watch)

ox *n.* 1. oxen bellow 2. a pair; team; yoke of oxen 3. (misc.) as strong as an ~

oxygen *n.* 1. to administer ~; to give smb. ~ 2. to get, receive ~ 3. liquid ~

P

pace I *n.* ["rate of movement"] 1. to set the ~ 2. to keep ~ with 3. to change ~; to slacken the ~ 4. an even, steady ~ 5. a blistering, brisk, cracking, fast, rapid; dizzy, frantic, hectic; grueling, killing ~ 6. a faltering, slack, slow, slowing, sluggish; snail's ("extremely slow"); walking ~ 7. a ~ picks up, quickens; slows, slows down 8. at a certain ~ (at a fast ~) 9. (misc.) at one's own ~ (don't hurry – do the work at your own ~!); a change of ~ (also fig.) ["step"] (esp. mil.) 10. to take a ~ (to take three ~s forward) ["misc."] 11. to put smb. through their ~s ("to subject smb. to a test of skill")

pace II *v.* (P; intr.) she was ~ing back and forth, up and down

pacemaker *n.* (med.) 1. to fit smb. with a ~ 2. to insert, put in a ~

pacifier *n.* (AE) to suck on a ~ (BE has *dummy*)

pack I *n.* ["deck of playing cards"] 1. to cut; shuffle a ~ (of cards) ["load, bundle"] 2. a backpack; full field (mil.); parachute ~ ["mass"] 3. an ice ~ ["misc."] (AE: BE prefers *packet* here) 4. a ~ of cigarettes

pack II *v.* 1. (C) ~ a sandwich for me; or: ~ me a sandwich 2. (d; intr.) to ~ into (they all ~ed into the auditorium) 3. (D; tr.) to ~ into (I ~ed everything into one suitcase; the organizers ~ed everyone into the auditorium) 4. (N; used with an adjective) ~ everything tight

package *n.* 1. to deliver a ~ 2. to address; insure; mail (esp. AE), post (BE); send a ~ 3. to get, receive a ~ 4. to open, unwrap; seal; wrap a ~ 5. a bulky; neat ~ 6. (computers) a software ~ (see also *package deal* at **deal I** n.)

packaging *n.* tamper-proof; tamper-resistant ~

packed *adj.* 1. densely, tightly ~ 2. loosely ~ 3. vacuum ~ 4. ~ with (streets ~ with people)

packet *n.* 1. a pay ~ (BE; AE has *pay envelope*) ["a large amount of money"] 2. (slang) (BE) to cost; make a ~ ["misc."] (BE: AE prefers *pack* here) 3. a ~ of cigarettes; a ~ of crisps

packing *n.* ["act of packing"] 1. to do the ~ 2. (misc.) postage and ~

pack off *v.* (D; tr.) to ~ to (to ~ the children off to camp = to ~ the children to camp)

pact *n.* 1. to agree to, have; make; sign a ~ 2. to abrogate, denounce a ~ 3. a formal; informal; official ~ 4. a mutual-assistance; nonaggression; suicide; trade ~ (see also **defense pact**) 5. a ~ between 6. a ~ to + inf. (we had a ~ not to reveal the facts of the case; the two governments signed a ~ to defend their borders jointly) 7. a ~ that + clause (the two governments signed a ~ that they would jointly defend their borders)

pad *n.* ["cushion"] 1. a heating; heel; knee; shoulder ~ ["piece of material"] 2. a gauze; quilted; scouring ~; a sanitary ~ (CE; AE has *sanitary napkin*; BE has *sanitary towel*) (see also **tampon**) ["connected sheets of paper"] 3. a note; scratch (esp. AE); writing ~ (to write smt. in/on a note ~) ["airstrip"] 4. a helicopter; launch, launching ~ ["smb's residence"] (slang) 5. at smb.'s ~

paddle I *n.* a ping-pong, table-tennis ~

paddle II *v.* (P; intr., tr.) I ~d the canoe across the lake; we ~d down the river

paean *n.* (lit.) ["hymn of praise"] 1. to sing a ~ (of praise) 2. a ~ to (to sing a ~ to smb.'s glory)

page I *n.* ["leaf of a book, journal, newspaper"] 1. to turn a ~ 2. to turn down a ~ 3. to turn to a certain ~ 4. to cite a (volume and) ~ 5. to set a ~ (in type) 6. a title ~ (in a book) 7. the amusement; back; editorial; front; society; sports ~ (in a newspaper) 8. on ~ one; turn to ~ five; open your books at (BE)/ to (AE) ~ five 9. (misc.) you will not find a dull ~ in the whole book; a glorious ~ in our history; it reads like a ~ from real life ["one side of a sheet of paper"] 10. a blank; a facing; the opposite ~ (see also **home page**)

page II *n.* ["youth who serves"] 1. (BE) a hotel ~ (AE has *bellboy, bellhop*) 2. (US) a congressional ~

page III *v.* to ~ smb. on, over a loudspeaker or a pager

pageant *n.* 1. to put on, stage a ~ 2. a beauty; colorful ~

paid *adj.* badly, poorly; highly, well ~ USAGE NOTE: It is correct to talk of "high-paid workers," "highly paid workers," or "low-paid workers." It is incorrect, though common, to talk of "*lowly paid workers."

pail *n.* (esp. AE or old-fashioned BE) 1. a garbage (AE); ice; lunch; milk ~ 2. a metal; wooden ~ 3. an empty; full ~ (see also Usage Note at **bucket**)

pain I *n.* ["sensation of suffering"] 1. to cause ~ 2. to inflict ~ (on) 3. to exacerbate the ~ 4. to bear, endure, stand, take ~ (she cannot stand ~) 5. to experience, feel, have, suffer ~ (she experienced constant ~) 6. to allay, alleviate, control, deaden, dull, ease, kill, manage, relieve, soothe ~ 7. (an) acute, agonizing, excruciating, great, intense, severe, sharp, unbearable ~ 8. (a) burning, searing; piercing; shooting; stabbing; throbbing ~ 9. a dull; slight ~ 10. (a) chronic, constant, gnawing, intractable, lingering, nagging, persistent, steady ~ 11. (a) recurrent; referred; sudden ~ 12. (an) abdominal, stomach; back; chest; phantom limb; physical ~ (he felt sharp chest ~s and went to see the doctor) 13. ~ appears; disappears, wears off; intensifies 14. a spasm; stab; twinge of ~ 15. a ~ in (she has severe ~s in her back) 16. in ~ (to be in chronic ~) 17. (misc.) the ~ shot through her arm; a high (or low) threshold of ~ = a high (or low) ~ threshold ["penalty"] 18. on, under, upon ~ of (mass meetings were forbidden on ~ of death) ["bother"] 19. (colloq.) a ~ to + inf. (it's a ~ to get up so early in the morning = it's a ~ getting up so early in the morning) 20. (misc.) he's a ~ in the neck ("he's a bothersome person"); what a ~!

pain II v. 1. to ~ badly, deeply 2. (R) it ~ed me to watch them quarrel; it ~ed me that I had to watch them quarrel 3. (misc.) it ~ed me when I had to watch them quarrel

pained adj. (cannot stand alone) ~ to + inf. (I was ~ to watch them quarrel)

painful adj. 1. ~ for (watching them quarrel was very ~ for me) 2. ~ to (watching them quarrel was very ~ to me) 3. ~ to + inf. (it's ~ to watch them quarrel; it's ~ to cough = it's ~ coughing) 4. (misc.) it's ~ when I watch them quarrel; it's ~ when I cough

pains n. ["trouble"] 1. to go to, spare no, take ~ to + inf. (she took great ~ to get her message across; the Prime Minister went to great ~ to deny the charges) ["physical suffering"] 2. (med.) aches and ~; chest; labor ~ 3. (usu. fig.) growing ~ ["misc."] 4. (esp. BE) at ~ to + inf. (the Prime Minister was at ~ to deny the charges)

paint I n. 1. to apply, spread ~ (to apply ~ to a surface; to spread ~ evenly) 2. to spray ~ (to spray ~ on a wall; to spray a wall with ~) 3. to daub ~ (to daub ~ on a wall; to daub a wall with ~) 4. to dilute, thin ~ 5. to mix ~s 6. to remove; scrape ~ 7. exterior; flat; floor; gloss; house; latex; lead-based; metallic; oil-based; wall ~ 8. grease; war ~ 9. wet ~! 10. ~ chips; dries; peels; smears 11. a blob, dab, daub, lick, speck, spot; splash of ~ 12. a coat of ~ (to apply a second coat of ~) 13. a set of (oil) ~s

paint II v. 1. (usu. D; tr.; C occurs occ.) to ~ for (she ~ed a beautiful portrait for us) 2. (D; tr.) to ~ from (to ~ a scene from life) 3. (d; intr. tr.) to ~ in (to ~ in oils) 4. (J) the artist ~ed them strolling through their garden 5. (N: used with an adjective) to ~ a house white 6. (misc.) to ~ the town red ("to go on a binge or spree")

painter n. 1. a house; sign ~ 2. a landscape; portrait ~ 3. (misc.) (BE) a ~ and decorator

painting n. 1. to do; restore a ~ 2. to exhibit ~s 3. to authenticate a ~ 4. (a) finger; oil; water-color ~ 5. (an) abstract, non-representational; representational ~ 6. an original ~ 7. a ~ depicts, portrays, shows (smt.)

pair n. (ling.) see **minimal pair**

pair off, pair up v. (D; intr., tr.) to ~ with

pajamas, pyjamas n. a pair of ~

pal n. a pen ~ (BE also has *pen friend*)

palace n. 1. a bishop's (BE); imperial; presidential (not US); royal ~ 2. at; in a ~ (a ceremony at the ~; to live in a ~)

pal around v. (AE) (d; intr.) to ~ with

palatable adj. ~ to

palate n. 1. a cleft; perforated ~ 2. the hard; soft ~ 3. (misc.) to tickle the ~ ("to be very tasty") (food to tickle even the most sophisticated or jaded ~s!)

pale I adj. ["devoid of color"] 1. deathly; very ~ 2. to

go, turn ~ 3. ~ with (rage) 4. (misc.) as ~ as a ghost; ~ and drawn; ~ and wan ("Why so ~ and wan, fond lover?" – Sir John Suckling, 1609–42)

pale II v. 1. (d; intr.) ("to become devoid of color") to ~ at ("to ~ at the sight of blood") 2. (d; intr.) ("to become less important") to ~ before, beside (everything ~d before the possibility of war) 3. (d; intr.) ("to fade") to ~ into (to ~ into insignificance)

pale III n. ["prescribed area"] beyond, outside the ~

pall I n. ["blanket of gloom"] to cast a ~ over

pall II v. (D; intr.) ("to become less attractive") to ~ on, upon (her constant preaching began to ~ on everyone)

palm I n. ["part of the hand"] 1. to read smb.'s ~ ("to tell smb.'s fortune") 2. (misc.) to have an itchy ~ ("to have a great desire for money, bribes"); to grease smb.'s ~ ("to bribe smb."); to have in the ~ of one's hand ("to seem able to control completely")

palm II n. a potted; royal ~

palm off v. 1. (D; tr.) to ~ as (he ~ed off the copy as an original = he ~ed the copy off as an original) 2. (D; tr.) to ~ on (to ~ inferior merchandise on customers = to ~ inferior merchandise off on customers)

palpable adj. ~ to

palsy n. cerebral ~

pal up v. (d; intr.) to ~ with

pan I n. 1. to grease a ~ 2. (AE) a baking; cake ~ (BE has *baking tin; cake tin*) 3. a chip ~ (BE) (for deep-frying potatoes) 4. a frying, fry (AE) ~ 5. (misc.) to scour (the) pots and ~s

pan II v. (d; intr.) to ~ for (to ~ for gold)

panacea n. 1. to find a ~ 2. a universal ~ 3. a ~ for

panache n. (with) great ~

pancake n. 1. to make a ~ 2. (misc.) as flat as a ~

pandemic n. see **epidemic**

pandemonium n. 1. to cause, create, stir up ~ 2. sheer ~ 3. ~ breaks out; reigns; subsides

pander v. (d; intr.) to ~ to (to ~ to the worst elements in society)

panegyric n. 1. to deliver a ~ 2. a ~ on

panel n. ["board"] 1. a control, instrument ~ ["group that discusses or investigates a topic"] 2. to select a ~ 3. to be, serve on a ~ 4. an impartial ~ 5. an advisory; blue-ribbon (esp. AE), expert; consumer; fact-finding; government ~ 6. a member of a ~ 7. a ~ on (a ~ on drug addiction) 8. (misc.) to convene a ~ of judges

paneling, panelling n. wood ~

pangs n. ~ of conscience; hunger; jealousy (she felt (the) ~ of conscience) (see also **birth pangs**)

panic I n. 1. to cause, create ~ 2. to spread ~ 3. to feel ~ at (they felt ~ at the thought of leaving their family) 4. to avert, prevent ~ 5. sheer, total, utter ~ 6. ~ spreads; subsides 7. in a ~ over (they were / got in a ~ over the news) 8. in ~ (they fled the city in ~) 9. (misc.) a state of ~

panic II v. 1. (D; intr.) to ~ about, at, over (they

panicked ~ over the news) 2. (d; tr.) to ~ into (the bad news panicked many people into fleeing the city)

panicky *adj.* to get (very) ~ over (they got (very) ~ over the news)

pant *v.* (D; intr.) to ~ for (to ~ for breath)

pants *n.* 1. (esp. AE) see **trousers** 2. ski; sweat ~ 3. a pair of ~

pantyhose *n.* (AE; BE has *tights*) she got a run in her ~

paper I *n.* ["lecture, treatise; manuscript for publication"] 1. to deliver, give, offer, present, read a ~ 2. to publish; write a ~ 3. a discussion; invited; working ~ 4. a ~ about, on ["essay; written assignment"] 5. (in a school, at a university) to do, write; grade, mark; hand in, submit a ~ (the pupils did a ~ on the problem of air pollution; the students were required to hand in their ~s by the end of the semester) 6. an exam, examination, test; term; written ~ (the course requires an oral exam as well as a written ~ prepared/set (BE) by Prof. Smith) 7. a ~ about, on 8. a ~ for (I had to do a ~ for my history course) ["document"] 9. a green (BE) ~ (see also **white paper**) 10. a position ~ ["negotiable instruments"] 11. commercial; negotiable ~ ["material made from wood pulp"] 12. to recycle (scrap) ~ 13. blank; graph; lined; unlined ~ 14. bog (BE, slang), lavatory (BE), loo (BE, colloq.), toilet; cigarette; filter; litmus; wrapping ~ 15. crepe; glossy; manila; tar; tissue; wax, waxed ~ 16. bond; carbon; scrap; scratch (esp. AE); tracing; typing ~ (see also **writing paper**) 17. a quire; ream; roll of ~ ["sheet of writing material"] 18. to line ~ 19. a piece, sheet; scrap; slip; side of ~ 20. on ~ ("in written form") (we got it down on ~ when we finally managed to put pen to ~) ["newspaper"] 21. to get a ~ out, publish a ~ 22. a daily; school; Sunday; trade ~ (see also **newspaper**; **papers**)

paper II *v.* 1. (D; tr.) to ~ with (she ~ed the walls with wallpaper) 2. (N) she ~ed the ceiling white

paperback *n.* in ~ (the book came out in ~)

papers *n.* ["documents"] 1. to draw up ~ 2. to show one's ~ 3. (US) to take out first ~ ("to begin the process of becoming a naturalized citizen") 4. first (US); naturalization; second (US); ship's; working ~ 5. forged ~ ["schoolwork"] 6. to correct, grade (esp. AE), mark ~ ["articles sent by mail"] 7. printed ~ (BE; CE has *printed matter*)

par *n.* ["nominal value"] 1. at ~ ["common level"] 2. on a ~ with ["average"] 3. above, over; below, under ~ (the golfer was feeling a bit below ~ and so he finished the round of golf five over ~) 4. up to ~ (to feel up to ~)

parachute I *n.* 1. to pack a ~ 2. a ~ opens; fails to open

parachute II *v.* 1. (B) we ~d supplies to the stranded climbers 2. (P; intr., tr.) they ~d behind enemy lines; we ~d to safety

parade I *n.* 1. to have, hold, stage a ~ 2. to review

a ~ 3. a church (BE); identification (BE), identity (BE; AE has *police lineup*); inaugural; military; sick (BE; AE has *sick call*); ticker-tape; torchlight ~ (she picked out the criminal in the identification ~) 4. a ~ takes place 5. at a ~ (we met them at the ~) 6. on ~ (the regiment was on ~) 7. (misc.) to rain on smb.'s ~ (colloq.) ("to spoil smb.'s triumph") (I don't want to rain on your ~ – but you're under arrest!)

parade II *v.* (P; intr., tr.) to ~ in front of an audience; to ~ around the room

paradise *n.* 1. an earthly ~ = a ~ on earth 2. sheer ~ 3. ~ to + inf. (it is sheer ~ to relax in the sun)

paradox *n.* 1. to resolve a ~ 2. a ~ that + clause (it's a ~ that such good friends cannot work together)

paradoxical *adj.* ~ that + clause (it's ~ that such good friends cannot work together)

paragraph *n.* 1. to indent; write a ~ (to ~ each new paragraph several spaces) 2. to divide smt. into ~s 3. a ~ about, on (she wrote a few short ~s on that subject) 4. in a ~ (she drew some conclusions in the final ~)

parallel I *adj.* ~ to, with

parallel II *n.* 1. to draw a ~ between; with 2. to find ~s among, between 3. a striking ~ 4. (misc.) without ~ (in history); their accomplishment has no ~ (in history); (esp. BE) her career developed in ~ with his

paralysis *n.* 1. to cause, induce ~ 2. to contract, develop, get; have ~ 3. to prevent ~ 4. complete; creeping; partial; temporary; total ~ 5. infantile ~

paramount *adj.* ~ over

paranoid *adj.* ~ about (don't get/go all ~ about them!)

paraphernalia *n.* drug ~

paratroops *n.* to commit, deploy; drop ~

parcel *n.* 1. to deliver a ~ 2. to address; insure; mail (esp. AE), post (BE); send a ~ 3. to get, receive a ~ 4. to open, unwrap; seal; wrap a ~ 5. a bulky; neat ~

parcel out *v.* 1. (B) she ~ed out the work to us = she ~ed the work out to us 2. (D; tr.) to ~ among (she ~ed out the assignments among us = she ~ed the assignments out among us)

pardon I *n.* 1. to grant a ~ 2. to ask, beg smb.'s ~ 3. a full; royal ~

pardon II *v.* (D; tr.) to ~ smb. for

pare down *v.* (D; tr.) to ~ to (to ~ expenses to the minimum = to ~ expenses down to the minimum)

parent *n.* 1. to obey one's ~s 2. a loving; permissive; strict; unfit ~ 3. an adoptive; biological, natural; foster; grandparent; lone (BE), single ~; stepparent

parentheses *n.* (esp. AE; BE prefers *brackets*) 1. to put smt. in, into ~ 2. between, in ~

parenthood *n.* planned ~

parity *n.* ["equality"] 1. to achieve, attain, establish ~ 2. ~ among, between; with ["equivalence in value"] 3. at ~

park I *n.* 1. to lay out a ~ 2. an amusement; safari (BE); theme ~ 3. a city; national; public; state ~ 4. a caravan (BE), trailer (AE) ~ 5. a car ~ (BE; AE has *parking lot*); a multi-storey car ~ (BE; AE has *parking garage*) 6. (BE) a coach; lorry ~ 7. an industrial ~ (AE; BE has *industrial estate*); a science ~ (BE) 8. at, in a ~

park II *v.* (colloq.) ("to deposit with") (d; tr.) to ~ on (AE), with (they ~ed their children on us and went to the theater)

parking *n.* 1. to allow; ban, restrict ~ 2. illegal; legal ~ 3. long-term; short-term ~ 4. (misc.) no ~!

parlance *n.* common; legal ~ (in common ~)

parlay *v.* (esp. AE) (d; tr.) ("to convert") to ~ into (to ~ a small investment into a fortune)

parley I *n.* to hold a ~ with

parley II *v.* (D; intr.) to ~ with

parliament *n.* 1. to convene (a) ~ 2. to adjourn; disband, dismiss, dissolve (a) ~ 3. a bicameral; national; provincial; unicameral ~ 4. the British, UK; European; Scottish ~ 5. a hung; rump ~ 6. a ~ adjourns; convenes, meets; disbands 7. a house of ~ 8. in ~ (to sit in ~) 9. (misc.) an act of ~; to stand for (BE) ~; a member of ~ (in GB abbreviated as MP) USAGE NOTE: In Great Britain, the Queen or King *opens* (a *session* of) Parliament. After the *State Opening*, Parliament is *in session*. Parliament *sits* until the session is over and then it *rises*.

parlor, parlour *n.* 1. a beauty; funeral (AE); ice-cream (AE); massage ~ 2. a sun ~ (AE; BE has *sun lounge*) USAGE NOTE: The services offered by a *massage parlor* are often sexual rather than therapeutic.

parody *n.* 1. to compose, write a ~ 2. a ~ of, on

parole I *n.* ["conditional release from prison"] 1. to grant a ~ 2. to violate (one's) ~ 3. early ~ 4. on ~ (to release smb. on ~)

parole II *v.* (D; tr.) to ~ from (to ~ smb. from prison)

part I *n.* ["share"] 1. to do one's ~ ["viewpoint, position"] 2. for, on one's ~ (for my ~, I will say no more; it was sheer madness on his ~ to risk everything!) ["participation"] 3. to take ~ (in) (to take ~ in an activity) 4. an active ~ ["role"] 5. to play a ~ (to play the ~ of Hamlet) 6. to act; dress; look the ~ 7. to learn, memorize, study one's ~; to understudy a ~ 8. a bit; cameo; leading, major; minor; speaking; walk-on ~ (she had a bit ~ in the play) ["element, portion"] 9. to spend a ~ of (they spent the major ~ of their life in England) 10. an essential, intrinsic; important, significant, vital; large, major ~ 11. an equal; insignificant, minor, small ~ 12. the (a) better ("greater"); good ("large") ~ (the better ~ of an hour) 13. a component, constituent, integral ~ 14. for the most ~ ("mostly") 15. in ~ ("partly") (in great ~) ["component of a machine"] 16. a defective; spare ~ 17. a moving ~ 18. automobile (AE), (motor)car (BE); spare ~s ["division"] 19. in ~s (a story in five ~s) 20. the best; difficult, hard; early; easy;

first; last; latter; tricky; worst ~ (in the latter ~ of the 19th Century; the worst ~ (of it) is having to get up so early!) ["side"] 21. to take smb.'s ~ (in a dispute) 22. (legal) of a ~ (the party of the first ~) ["dividing line in hair"] (AE; BE has *parting*) 23. to have; make a ~ (in one's hair) ["component of body"] 24. body ~s ["sexual organs"] 25. the private ~s ["area"] 26. a remote ~ (in a remote ~ of the country)

part II *v.* 1. (D; intr.) to ~ as (to ~ as friends) 2. (d; intr., tr.) to ~ from (the children were ~ed from their parents) 3. (d; intr.) to ~ with (she hates to ~ with her money)

partake *v.* (d; intr.) to ~ of (to ~ of food and drink)

partial *adj.* ["fond of"] (colloq.) (cannot stand alone) ~ to (she's ~ to expensive clothes)

partiality *n.* ["bias"] 1. to show ~ in ["liking"] 2. a ~ for (she shows a ~ for expensive clothes)

participant *n.* 1. an active; reluctant, unwilling; willing ~ 2. a ~ in (a ~ in an activity)

participate *v.* 1. to ~ actively; fully; reluctantly, unwillingly; willingly 2. (D; intr.) to ~ in (to ~ in an activity)

participation *n.* 1. active ~ 2. reluctant, unwilling; willing ~ 3. audience ~ 4. ~ in (~ in an activity)

participle *n.* (grammar) an active; dangling (esp. AE), misrelated (BE); passive; past; perfect; present ~

particle *n.* 1. a dust; minute ~ 2. (physics) an alpha; elementary; subatomic ~

particular I *adj.* 1. ~ about (~ about one's appearance) ["misc."] 2. in ~ ("especially")

particular II *n.* ["detail"] in every ~; in all ~s –

parting *n.* (BE) see **part I**, *n.* 23

partition I *n.* 1. to build, erect, put up a ~ 2. to dismantle, take down a ~ 3. a movable ~ 4. a ~ between; into (the ~ of the area between the two countries that bordered on it; the ~ of the area into two countries)

partition II *v.* (D; tr.) to ~ between; into (the area was ~ed between the two countries that bordered on it; the area was ~ed into two countries)

partner *n.* 1. an active; full; junior; senior ~ (after several years she was made a (full) ~ in her law firm) 2. a business; trading ~ (some of Britain's principal trading ~s are in the EU) 3. a silent (AE), sleeping (BE) ~ 4. (boxing) a sparring ~ 5. (misc.) a ~ in (~s in crime) USAGE NOTE: Nowadays *partner* is perhaps the most popular name for the person you live with: John and Mary got divorced and now have new ~s.

partnership *n.* 1. to form; go into a ~ 2. to break up, dissolve a ~ 3. a ~ between 4. a ~ in 5. in ~ (with)

partner up *v.* (BE) (D; tr.) to ~ with

partridge *n.* a covey of ~s

party I *adj.* ["participating"] ~ to (don't blame me! I wasn't ~ to the arrangement/ agreement!)

party II *n.* ["social gathering"] 1. to arrange, give, have, throw; host a ~ (for) 2. to attend, go to; crash a ~ 3. to liven up a ~ 4. a birthday; Christmas; New

Year's Eve ~ 5. a cocktail; dinner; garden, lawn (AE); tea ~ 6. a coming-out; farewell; housewarming; going-away ~ 7. a pajama, slumber; surprise ~ 8. a lavish; wild ~ 9. a hen; singles; stag ~ 10. a ~ breaks up (the ~ broke up at midnight) 11. at a ~ (we had a good time at the ~) ["political organization"] 12. to establish, form a ~ 13. to break up, disband, dissolve a ~ 14. a centrist; conservative; fascist; liberal; populist; progressive; radical; reactionary ~ 15. a communist; labor; social-democratic; socialist ~ 16. a left-wing; right-wing ~ 17. a majority; minority; opposition; political; ruling; splinter ~ 18. (misc.) the ~ in power; the ~ in opposition; the parliamentary ~ (BE); a constituency ~ (BE) (the parliamentary ~ required a local constituency ~ to de-select a militant candidate) ["litigant"] (legal) 19. an aggrieved; disinterested; guilty; innocent; third ~ 20. the interested ~ties 21. a ~ to (a lawsuit) 22. (misc.) the ~ of the first, second part ["group sent on a mission"] 23. a boarding; landing; raiding; rescue; scouting; stretcher; surveying ~ (see also **search party**) ["participant"] 24. a ~ to (don't blame me! I wasn't a ~ to the arrangement/agreement!)

party line n. 1. to follow, hew to (AE) the ~ 2. to deviate from, veer from the ~

pass I n. ["permission; permit"] ["leave of absence"] 1. to issue a ~ 2. to cancel, revoke; show a ~ 3. a boarding; bus (BE); Freedom (BE); rail (BE); safe-conduct ~ 4. a ~ to (we got a ~ to town) 5. on (a) ~ (they are in the city on ~) ["flight"] 6. to make a ~ (over a target) ["sexual approach"] 7. to make a ~ (at smb.) ["transfer of a ball, puck"] 8. to complete; throw a ~ (to) 9. to block; intercept a ~ (from) 10. (Am. football) a forward; Hail-Mary ("desperate"); incomplete; lateral; touchdown ~ ["ticket"] 11. a free ~ 12. a ~ to (we got free ~es to the concert) ["passing grade"] (BE) 13. to get a ~ (at; in) (she managed to get a ~ in French at A-level) ["misc."] 14. things came to a pretty ~ ("the situation became very complicated") (see also **pass III** n.)

pass II v. 1. (A) ("to hand"); ("to throw") ~ the sugar to me; or: ~ me the sugar; my teammate ~ed the ball to me; or: my teammate ~ed me the ball; ~ the message to the others; or: ~ the others the message 2. (D; intr., tr.) to ~ as, for; by ("to be accepted") (she can ~ as/for a Russian; the bill (was) ~ed by a large majority) 3. (d; intr.) to ~ between ("to be exchanged") (a significant look ~ed between them) 4. (D; intr.) ("to go past") to ~ by (they ~ed by my house) 5. (d; intr.) ("to shift") to ~ from; to (to ~ from one subject to another) 6. (d; intr.) to ~ on, upon ("to judge") (to ~ on the merits of a case) 7. (D; tr.) ("to deliver") to ~ on, upon (the judge ~ed sentence on the accused; to ~ judgment on smb.) 8. (d; intr.) ("to go"); ("to fly") to ~ over (several planes ~ed over our house; to ~ over a bridge) 9. (d; intr.) to ~ over ("to disregard") (they ~ed over her for promotion when promotions were handed out) (see also **pass over**) 10. (d; intr.)

("to go") to ~ through (she was just ~ing through town) 11. (d; tr.) ("to insert") to ~ through (he ~ed the cable through the loop; to ~ meat through a grinder) 12. (d; intr.) to ~ to ("to be handed down to") the estate ~ed to the daughter 13. (P; intr.) ("to move") to ~ into history; rumors ~ed around town 14. (s) to ~ unnoticed 15. (misc.) (BE) to be ~ed fit for (service) (see also *come to pass* at **come**)

pass III n. ["passage"] 1. to clear; cross a ~ 2. to block a ~ 3. a mountain ~ 4. a ~ between; over; through (a ~ through the mountains)

passage n. ["transit"] 1. to book ~ (on a ship) 2. free ~ ["section"] 3. an obscure; purple ("ornate, flowery") ~ (in a text or piece of music) ["way, channel"] 4. to clear; force a ~ 5. a secret ~ ["channel in the body"] 6. nasal ~s (blocked, congested nasal ~s) 7. (BE) the back ~ ("the rectum") ["transition"] 8. a ~ from; through; to 9. (misc.) a rite of ~ (getting a driver's license can be a rite of passage ~ from childhood to adulthood); the ~ of time (with the ~ of time everything is bound to look different) ["trip"] 10. an outward ~

passageway n. a ~ between

pass along v. (B) ~ the message along to the others = ~ the message to the others

pass around v. (B) ~ the chocolate around to the children

pass down v. 1. (d; intr., tr.) to ~ from; to (to ~ a tradition to the next generation = to ~ a tradition down to the next generation; to ~ old clothes from one child to the next = to ~ old clothes down from one child to the next) 2. (misc.) she ~ed it down to me from the shelf

passenger n. 1. to carry ~s (trains carry many ~s every day) 2. to pick up, take on ~s 3. to drop (off), let off ~s 4. a business-class; economy-class; first-class; second-class; standard-class (BE); steerage; tourist-class; transit ~ 5. a ~ for (~s for the next flight should go to the last gate) USAGE NOTE: Passengers are increasingly being called customers.

passing n. ["death"] 1. to commemorate, mark; mourn smb.'s ~ ["misc."] 2. in ~ ("incidentally")

passion n. 1. to arouse, excite, inflame, stir up ~ 2. to gratify, satisfy one's ~ 3. to control, curb, restrain one's ~ 4. (an) all-consuming; burning, deep, smoldering; animal, frenzied, wild ~ 5. ~s run high 6. a burst, surge of ~ 7. a ~ for (a ~ for gambling) 8. (misc.) to fly into a ~; his eyes blazed with ~ (see also *a crime of passion* at **crime**)

pass off v. (d; refl., tr.) to ~ as (he ~ed himself off as a doctor; she can ~ herself off as a Russian)

pass on v. 1. (B) they ~ed the information on to us 2. (d; intr.) to ~ to (let's ~ to another topic)

pass out v. (B) they ~ed the food out to all who came = they ~ed out the food to all who came

pass over v. (D; tr.) to ~ for (they ~ed her over for promotion when promotions were handed out) (see also *pass over* at **pass II** v.)

passport *n.* 1. to issue; renew a ~ 2. to have, hold a ~ 3. to apply for a ~ 4. to falsify, forge a ~ 5. to stamp, validate a ~ 6. to revoke a ~ 7. a diplomatic; Nansen ~ 8. a false; valid ~ 9. a ~ expires, runs out 10. (fig.) a ~ to (a ~ to happiness) 11. in a ~ (what's stamped in your ~?) 12. on a ~ (to travel on a U.S. ~)

pass round (BE) see **pass around**

password *n.* 1. to give the ~ 2. (computers) to enter, key in the ~

past *n.* ["past time"] 1. to glorify; recall, recapture the ~ 2. to forget the ~ 3. the distant ~ 4. a colorful, glorious ~ 5. (to have) a checkered (AE), chequered (BE); dark, lurid, murky ~ 6. in the ~ ["past tense of a verb"] 7. in the ~

paste I *n.* to make, mix a ~

paste II *v.* (D; tr.) to ~ on, to (to ~ a piece of paper on/to the wall) (see also *cut and paste* at **cut II**)

pastiche *n.* 1. to compose, write a ~ 2. a ~ of

pastime *n.* 1. a popular; the national ~ (in America the national ~ is baseball) 2. a ~ among; for (is fishing a ~ popular among all classes of the population?)

pastry *n.* 1. to bake, make ~ 2. light; puff (BE) ~ 3. (a) Danish ~

pasture *n.* 1. to put smb. out to ~ (fig.) 2. (misc.) to leave for greener ~s

pasty *n.* (BE) a Cornish ~

pat I *adj., adv.* (colloq.) (esp. AE) to stand ~ ("to refuse to change")

pat II *n.* to give smb. a ~ (on the back)

pat III *v.* (D; tr.) to ~ on (to ~ smb. on the back)

patch *n.* ["piece of material used to cover a hole"] 1. to have; sew on a ~ (to have a ~ on one's shirt) ["insignia"] 2. a shoulder ~ ["area"] 3. a brier; cabbage; fog; potato ~ ["period"] 1. to go through, have a ~ 2. a bad; purple ~

patch through *v.* (D; tr.) ("to connect") to ~ to (she ~ed me through to headquarters)

patent *n.* 1. to grant, issue a ~ 2. to apply for; obtain, take out a ~ 3. to hold a ~ 4. to infringe a ~ 5. ~ applied for; pending 6. a ~ expires, runs out 7. a ~ for, on (she took out a ~ on her invention)

paternity *n.* 1. to establish ~ 2. to acknowledge (one's) ~

path *n.* 1. to beat, blaze, clear, make a ~ (to clear a ~ through a jungle) 2. to cross smb.'s ~ 3. to follow a ~ (to follow a ~ along a river) 4. a beaten, well-worn ~ 5. a bridle ~; a towpath 6. a ~ goes, leads somewhere 7. a ~ from; to (on the ~ to success) 8. (misc.) to lead smb. up the garden ~ ("to deceive smb."); to lead smb. down the primrose ~ ("to lead smb. in an ill-advised search for pleasure"); off the beaten ~ ("in an unfamiliar or unusual place") ("off the beaten track"); he found many obstacles in his ~

pathetic *adj.* 1. ~ to + inf. (it was ~ to watch her condition deteriorate day by day) 2. ~ that + clause (it's ~ that her condition is deteriorating day by day)

pathway *n.* a ~ to (on the ~ to success)

patience *n.* ["quality of being patient"] 1. to display, show ~ 2. to tax, test, try smb.'s ~ (these delays are enough to try the ~ of a saint!) 3. to lose one's ~ 4. to run out of ~ 5. endless, inexhaustible, infinite ~ 6. smb.'s ~ runs out; wears thin 7. ~ for; with (she has endless ~ with the children that he has lost ~ with) 8. the ~ to + inf. (do you have the ~ to do this job?) 9. out of ~ with ["card game"] (BE) 10. to play ~ (AE has *solitaire*)

patient I *adj.* ~ about; in; with (up to now I've been very ~ about all these delays; she is endlessly ~ with the children that he has lost patience with)

patient II *n.* 1. to cure; handle; treat a ~ 2. to admit a ~ (to a hospital) 3. to discharge a ~ (from a hospital) 4. an ambulatory; hospital ~; inpatient; outpatient; private ~ 5. a cardiac; comatose; mental ~ 6. a ~ admits himself; discharges himself; responds to treatment

patio *n.* on a ~ (let's have a drink on the ~)

patriot *n.* an ardent, fervent, staunch; sincere ~

patriotism *n.* 1. to display, show ~ 2. (an) ardent, fervent, staunch, strong; sincere ~

patrol *n.* 1. a border; highway (AE), motorway (BE); military; police; reconnaissance ~ 2. (naval) (a) shore ~ 3. on ~ (they are out on ~)

patron *n.* 1. a regular, steady ~ 2. (misc.) a ~ of the arts

patronage *n.* 1. political ~ 2. under smb.'s ~

patronizing *adj.* ~ to, towards (~ towards people with poor taste)

patter *v.* (d; intr.) to ~ against, on (the rain was ~ing on the windows)

pattern I *n.* 1. to establish, set a ~ 2. to follow a ~ 3. an intricate; overall; set; strange; underlying ~ 4. a holding; traffic ~ (our plane was in a holding ~) 5. (ling.) an intonation; speech ~ 6. a behavior; personality ~ 7. a sewing ~ 8. a floral ~

pattern II *v.* (d; tr.) to ~ after, on (the academy was ~ed after a British public school)

patty *n.* (esp. AE) a beef; lamb; meat ~

pause *n.* ["temporary stop"] 1. an awkward; long, prolonged; pregnant; short ~ 2. a ~ after; before; between; for; in ["reason or cause for hesitating"] 3. to give smb. ~

pavement *n.* ["paved surface"] 1. to tear up the ~ (in order to lay pipes) 2. the ~ buckles 3. (misc.) to pound the ~ ("to walk about aimlessly or with determination") USAGE NOTE: In BE, *pavement* also means "sidewalk".

pawn *n.* a helpless ~ (in someone else's game)

pay I *n.* 1. to boost, raise smb.'s ~ 2. to cut; dock; withhold smb.'s ~ 3. to draw, receive ~ 4. back; disability; equal; full; half; incentive; mustering-out (mil.); overtime; severance (AE; BE has *redundancy payment*); retroactive; sick; strike; take-home ~ 5. annual, yearly; daily; hourly; monthly; weekly ~ 6. a level, rate of ~ (high rates of ~ for the bosses; low rates of ~ for the workers;

equal rates of ~ for equal work) 7. ~ for (equal ~ for equal work) 8. in smb.'s ~ (he was in the ~ of the enemy) 9. on; with; without ~ (he's been on sick ~ since the accident; to take time off without ~)

pay II *v.* 1. to ~ dearly; handsomely, highly, well 2. (A) she paid the money to me; or: she paid me the money 3. (D; intr.) to ~ by, in (to ~ by check; to ~ in cash; to ~ by the hour) 4. (D; intr., tr.) to ~ for (have you paid for the book?; I paid ten dollars for this shirt; he paid us for watching his house) 5. (D; intr., tr.) to ~ into (we have been ~ing into a pension fund; the money was paid into her account) 6. (d; intr., tr.) to ~ out of (she paid out of her own pocket) 7. (E) it doesn't ~ to economize on essentials 8. (H) he paid us to watch his house

payable *adj.* 1. ~ to (make the check ~ to me) 2. (misc.) ~ at sight; ~ in advance; ~ on (is any tax ~ on this investment?); ~ on demand

pay back *v.* 1. (A) we must pay the money back to her for the tickets = we must ~ the money to her for the tickets; or we must pay her back the money for the tickets 2. (D; tr.) to ~ for (we must ~ her back for the tickets)

paycheck, pay envelope, pay packet *n.* a monthly; weekly ~

pay dirt *n.* (colloq.) (AE) ["success"] to hit, strike ~

payment *n.* 1. to accept, receive ~ (for) 2. to make (a) ~ (to) 3. to stop ~ (of, on a check) 4. to suspend ~s 5. a cash; redundancy (BE; AE has *severance pay*); mortgage; token; transfer ~ (to fail to keep up one's mortgage ~s and lose one's home) (see also **down payment**) 6. (an) advance; part, partial; prompt ~ 7. (a) ~ from; for, on 8. in full ~ (of a bill) 9. (misc.) the balance of ~s

payoff *n.* 1. to make a ~ 2. to get, receive a ~ 3. a political ~ 4. a ~ for

pay out *v.* (B) the benefits have been paid out to the workers = they paid out the benefits to the workers = they paid the benefits out to the workers

payroll *n.* 1. to meet (esp. AE) a ~ 2. a monthly; weekly ~ 3. on the ~ (how many workers are on the ~?)

peace *n.* 1. to achieve, bring about; promote ~ 2. to make ~ (with) 3. to negotiate (a) ~ with 4. to sue for ~ (with) 5. to impose (a) ~ on 6. to keep, maintain the ~ 7. to break, disturb, shatter, undermine the ~ 8. a durable, lasting, permanent ~ 9. a fragile, uneasy ~ 10. ~ reigns (between us and our neighbors) 11. at ~ (with) (we were at ~ with our neighbors) 12. in ~ (to live in ~ with our neighbors) 13. (misc.) a breach of the ~; ~ and quiet; ~ of mind (see also *peace march* at **march I** *n.*)

peacetime *n.* during, in ~

peacock *n.* 1. a ~ struts 2. (misc.) as proud as a ~

peak *n.* 1. to reach a ~ 2. to scale the ~ (of a mountain) 3. mountain; snow-capped; towering ~s 4. at the ~ (at the ~ of her career)

pearls *n.* 1. to string ~ 2. cultured; imitation; natural ~ 3. a string of ~

peas *n.* 1. to shell, shuck (AE) ~ 2. split ~ 3. (misc.) as alike as two ~ in a pod

peck I *n.* (colloq.) ["kiss"] to give smb. a ~ on the cheek

peck II *v.* (d; intr.) to ~ at (to ~ at one's food)

pecker *n.* ["spirits"] ["courage"] (colloq.) (BE) to keep one's ~ up

peculiar *adj.* 1. very ~ 2. ~ to (habits ~ to the very rich) 3. ~ to + inf. (how ~ of her to have done that!) 4. ~ that + clause (how ~ that she did/ should have done that!)

pedal I *n.* 1. to depress, put one's foot on, step on a ~ 2. to ease up on, let up on; take one's foot off a ~ 3. an accelerator (BE); brake; clutch ~

pedal II *v.* (P; intr., tr.) she ~ed the bicycle down the hill; they ~ed their way across the state; we were ~ing through town

peddler, pedlar *n.* a drug; influence; itinerant; smut ~

pedestal *n.* 1. to put smb./smt. on a ~ ("to hold smb./smt. in high esteem") 2. on a ~ ("held in high esteem")

pedigree *n.* of (a) certain ~ (of unknown ~)

pee *n.* (colloq.) to have, take; need a ~

peek I *n.* to have, take a ~ (at; through)

peek II *v.* 1. (D; intr.) to ~ at (to ~ at smb. in the next room) 2. (d; intr.) to ~ into (to ~ into smb.'s dossier) 3. (d; intr.) to ~ under (to ~ under the bed) 4. (P; intr.) to ~ over the bushes; to ~ through the window

peek in *v.* 1. (D; intr.) to ~ at (we ~ed in at the dress rehearsal) 2. (misc.) she ~ed in from behind the bushes

peek out *v.* 1. (D; intr.) to ~ at (we ~ed out at the dress rehearsal) 2. (D; intr.) to ~ from behind (she ~ed out from behind the bushes) 3. (D; intr.) to ~ from under (to ~ from under the bed)

peel I *n.* (an) apple; banana (esp. AE; CE prefers *a banana skin*); lemon; orange; potato ~ (see the Usage Note for **rind**)

peel II *v.* 1. (C) ~ a banana for me; or: ~ me a banana 2. (D; intr., tr.) to ~ from, off, off of (AE) (he ~ed the bark from the tree; the paper was ~ing from the wall)

peep I *n.* ["sound"] 1. to let out a ~ 2. a ~ out of (we didn't hear a ~ out of her; we haven't had a ~ out of them all day)

peep II *n.* ["look"] to have, take a ~ (at; through)

peep III *v.* ("to look") 1. (D; intr.) to ~ at (to ~ at smb. in the next room) 2. (d; intr.) to ~ into (to ~ into smb.'s dossier) 3. (d; intr.) to ~ under (to ~ under the bed) 4. (P; intr.) to ~ over the bushes; to ~ through the window

peep in *v.* 1. (D; intr.) to ~ at (we ~ed in at the dress rehearsal) 2. (misc.) she ~ed in from behind the bushes

peep out *v.* 1. (D; intr.) to ~ at (we ~ed out at the dress rehearsal) 2. (D; intr.) to ~ from behind (she ~ed out from behind the bushes) 3. (D; intr.) to ~ from under (to ~ from under the bed)

peer I n. (GB) 1. to create, make smb. a ~ 2. a hereditary; life ~ 3. a ~ of the realm (see also *peer group* at **group I** n.; *peer pressure* at **pressure I** n.)

peer II v. 1. (d; intr.) to ~ at; through (to ~ at smb. through a window) 2. (d; intr.) to ~ into (to ~ into smb.'s eyes)

peerage n. (GB) 1. to elevate, raise smb. to the ~ 2. to bestow, confer a ~ on (a ~ was conferred on John Buchan) 3. to accept; refuse; renounce a ~ (John Buchan accepted a ~; Sir Winston Churchill refused and Tony Benn renounced a ~ so that they could continue to sit in the House of Commons) 4. a hereditary; life ~

peer out v. 1. (D; intr.) to ~ at (to ~ at smb. through a window) 2. (D; intr.) to ~ from behind (she ~ed out from behind the bushes) 3. (D; intr.) to ~ from under (to ~ from under the bed)

peeve n. smb.'s pet ~

peevish adj. ["irritable"] ~ about

peg n. ["degree, step"] (fig.) 1. to come down a ~ 2. to bring, take smb. down a ~ ["misc."] (BE) 3. (to buy clothing) off the ~ ("ready-made")

peg away v. (BE) (D; intr.) ("to work hard") to ~ at (to ~ at one's job)

pelt v. (d; tr.) to ~ with (to ~ smb. with rocks)

pelt down v. (D; intr.) to ~ against, on (the rain was ~ing down on the roof)

pen I n. ["enclosure"] 1. a pig; sheep ~ ["dock"] 2. a submarine ~

pen II n. ["device for writing"] 1. a ballpoint; felt-tip (AE), fibre-tip (BE); fountain ~ 2. (misc.) with a stroke of the ~, the new law was enacted; ~ and ink (to write in pencil rather than in/with ~ and ink)

penalize v. (D; tr.) to ~ by; for; with (he ~d me for coming late by imposing a fine = he ~d me with a fine for coming late)

penalty n. 1. to impose a ~ (he ~d a penalty on me for coming late) 2. to pay a ~ (to pay the full ~ for one's mistakes) 3. to rescind a ~ 4. a heavy, severe, stiff, strict; light, mild; maximum; minimum ~ 5. the death ~ (see also **death penalty**) 6. a ~ for 7. on, under ~ (of death)

penance n. to do, perform ~ for

penchant n. a ~ for

pencil n. 1. to sharpen a ~ 2. a colored; graphite, lead; indelible; mechanical (AE), propelling (BE) ~ 3. a cosmetic, eyebrow ~ 4. a styptic ~ 5. in ~ (to write in ~ rather than in/with pen and ink)

pendulum n. 1. to swing a ~ 2. a ~ swings 3. a swing of the ~

penetrate v. 1. to ~ deeply 2. (D; intr.) to ~ behind; into (enemy troops ~d deeply behind our lines)

penetration n. 1. (a) deep ~ 2. (mil.) (a) ~ in depth

penicillin n. 1. oral ~ 2. an injection, jab (BE; colloq.), shot of ~ 3. (misc.) a course of ~

penitence n. 1. to show ~ (for) 2. true ~ (for)

penitent adj. ~ for

pennant n. ["baseball championship"] (AE) to lose; win the ~

penny n. 1. to pinch ~nies ("to be frugal") 2. (misc.) a new (BE; old-fashioned); pretty ~ ("a large sum of money"); (BE; colloq.) the ~ drops ("somebody finally understands"); (BE; colloq.) to spend a ~ ("to use a toilet") USAGE NOTE: Seven US *pennies* are worth seven *cents*. Seven UK *pennies* are worth seven *pence*.

pension n. 1. to award, grant a ~ 2. to draw, receive a ~ 3. to revoke a ~ 4. a disability; index-linked; old-age; survivor's ~ 5. on a ~ (to live on a ~; to retire on a ~) (see also *pension plan* at **plan I** n.)

people n. 1. common, little, ordinary, plain ~ 2. business; city; country; local; professional; working ~ 3. old; young ~ 4. the chosen ~ 5. the right; wrong ~ 6. boat ~ ("refugees escaping in boats") 7. (misc.) of all ~! (I was just walking along when who should I see but John of all ~!) (see also Usage Note at **tribe**)

peopled adj. ~ by, with (an imaginary landscape ~ with unforgettable characters)

pepper I n. ["spice"] 1. ground ~ (season with salt and freshly ground ~) 2. black; hot; red; white ~ 3. a dash of ~ 4. (misc.) salt and ~ ["vegetable"] 5. (a) green; red; sweet; yellow ~ 6. stuffed ~s

pepper II v. (d; tr.) ("to shower") to ~ with (she was ~ed with questions)

pep up v. (D; tr.) to ~ with (to ~ a dish with unusual spices = to ~ a dish up with unusual spices)

perceive v. 1. (d; tr.) to ~ as (we ~d the situation as critical) 2. (L) we ~d that the situation was critical 3. (M) we ~d the situation to be critical 4. (Q) they could not ~ how critical the situation was USAGE NOTE: *Perceive* can mean 'realize, understand': they finally perceived that the government was lying to them. But *perceive* can also mean 'believe (perhaps incorrectly)': the government is worried that it is perceived to be lying.

percentage n. ["profit"]["advantage"] (colloq.) (a) ~ in (there is no ~ in investing more money) (see also *percentage point* at **point I** n.)

perceptible adj. 1. barely ~ 2. ~ to (not ~ to the touch)

perception n. 1. to gain; have a ~ 2. (a) clear; keen; widespread ~ 3. color; depth; extrasensory ~ (ESP) 4. a ~ of (events confirmed our ~ of the situation as critical) 5. the ~ that + clause (events confirmed our ~ that the situation was critical) USAGE NOTE: *Perception* can refer to a correct realization or understanding: finally, events confirmed the widespread perception that the government was lying. But *perception* can also refer to a belief that may be incorrect: the government is worried about the widespread perception that it is lying.

perceptive adj. 1. ~ of (that observation was very ~ of her) 2. ~ to + inf. (it was ~ of her to make that observation)

perceptiveness *n.* the ~ to + inf. (she had the ~ to make that observation)

perch I *n.* 1. a high ~ 2. from one's ~ 3. (misc.) (colloq.; BE) to fall off one's ~ ("to die")

perch II *v.* (P; intr.) the birds ~ed on the wire

percolate *v.* (P; intr.) ("to pass slowly") the news ~d down to the troops; the water ~d through the sand; ideas that ~ throughout society

per diem *n.* ["daily allowance for expenses"] 1. to pay (a) ~ 2. to get, receive a ~

perennial *n.* ["flower"] a hardy ~

perfect I *adj.* ~ for (she would be ~ for the job)

perfect II *n.* (grammar) the future; past; present ~

perfection *n.* 1. to achieve, attain, reach ~ 2. sheer ~ 3. the acme, point of ~ 4. to ~ (cooked to ~)

perfidy *n.* (formal) an act of ~

perform *v.* 1. to ~ in concert; live 2. (D; intr.) to ~ in (to ~ in a play) 3. (D; intr., tr.) to ~ for (to ~ for a live audience; to ~ a concerto for a live audience) 4. (D; intr., tr.) to ~ on (to ~ on the piano; to ~ a concerto on the piano before a live audience)

performance *n.* ["act of performing"] 1. to deliver, give, put on a ~ 2. to arrange, schedule a ~ 3. to cancel; postpone; reschedule a ~ 4. a breathtaking, brilliant, electrifying, inspired, outstanding, remarkable, spellbinding, superb, wonderful ~ 5. a listless, mediocre, run-of-the-mill; uneven ~ 6. a benefit; cameo; command; farewell; gala; live; premier; public; repeat; request; solo ~ 7. a ~ as, in; before, for (her ~ as the mother was inspired; her ~ in the play was inspired; her ~ of the concerto before a live audience was inspired; her ~ on the piano before a live audience was inspired) 8. on smb.'s ~ (on (the basis of) her past ~, we can expect something memorable tonight) ["functioning of a machine"] 9. (high) engine ~

performer *n.* a polished; star ~

perfume *n.* 1. to dab on, daub on, put on, spray on ~ 2. to apply, use, wear ~ 3. to reek of (derog.); smell of ~ 4. (a) heady, strong ~ 5. a bottle of ~ 6. a whiff of ~

perfumed *adj.* ~ with (the air was ~d with the scent of honeysuckle)

peril *n.* 1. to confront, face a ~ 2. to avert a ~ 3. at one's ~ 4. in ~ (our lives were in ~ from wild animals)

perimeter *n.* ["boundary"] 1. (mil.) to guard, protect a ~ 2. beyond, outside; inside; on a ~

period *n.* ["portion of time"] 1. a cooling-off; honeymoon (fig.); rest; set; trial; waiting ~ 2. an off-peak; peak; study; transition, transitional; trial ~ 3. an incubation ~ 4. a question-and-answer ~ 5. (sports) an extra ~ 6. a ~ begins; comprises, includes; covers; ends 7. a ~ from; to 8. for a ~ 9. in; throughout; within a certain ~ (in that ~ of history) ["menstruation"] 10. to have a ~ 11. a monthly ~ ["punctuation mark"] (esp. AE; BE prefers *full stop*) 12. to place, put a ~ (at the end of a sentence)

periodical *n.* 1. to publish, put out a ~ 2. to subscribe to, take (BE) a ~ 3. a current ~ (where does the library keep current ~s?) 4. bound ~s 5. a copy; issue of a ~

peripheral *adj.* ~ to

periphery *n.* on the ~ (of)

periscope *n.* 1. to lower; raise a ~ 2. (as commands) ~ down! ~ up!

perish *v.* (formal) 1. (D; intr.) to ~ by (to ~ by the sword) 2. (D; intr.) to ~ from, of (to ~ from disease) 3. (D; intr.) to ~ in (to ~ in a disaster) 4. (misc.) ~ the thought!

perjury *n.* to commit ~

perm *n.* ["permanent wave"] 1. to give smb. a ~ 2. to get a ~

permeated *adj.* (cannot stand alone) ~ with (~ with idealism)

permissible *adj.* ~ to + inf. (it is not ~ to smoke in the library)

permission *n.* 1. to give, grant ~ 2. to deny, refuse ~ 3. to apply for, ask, ask for, request, seek ~ 4. to get; have ~ 5. planning ~ (BE; AE has *building permit*) 6. official; oral, verbal; written ~ 7. ~ for (we applied for and got planning ~ for a new garage) 8. with; without ~ (I can't go out without my father's ~) 9. ~ to + inf. (we applied for and got planning ~ to erect a new garage)

permit I *n.* 1. to give, grant a ~ 2. to cancel, rescind, revoke a ~ 3. to apply for, request, seek a ~ 4. to get; have a ~ 5. a building (AE; BE has *planning permission*); work ~ 6. an export; import; travel ~ 7. a ~ for (we applied for and got a building ~ for a new garage; have you got a ~ for your gun?) 8. a ~ to + inf. (we applied for and got a building ~ to erect a new garage; have you got a ~ to carry a gun?)

permit II *v.* 1. (A; usu. without the preposition *to*) she did not ~ herself time for relaxation 2. (formal) (d; intr.) to ~ of (our financial situation ~s of no unnecessary expenditures) 3. (H) we ~ted the children to go to the park 4. (O; can be used with one inanimate object) the doctors ~ two meals a day; the doctors ~ him two meals a day; she ~ted herself one glass of wine (see also *weather permitting* at **weather**)

pernickety (esp. BE) see **persnickety**

perpendicular *adj.* ~ to

perpetuity *n.* in ~ ("forever")

perplex *v.* (R) it ~ed me to learn that they had refused the offer; it ~ed me that they had refused the offer

perplexed *adj.* 1. ~ about, at, by, over (I was ~ at their refusal of the offer) 2. ~ to + inf. (I was ~ to learn that they had refused the offer) 3. ~ that + clause (I was ~ that they had refused the offer)

perplexing *adj.* 1. ~ to + inf. (it was ~ to learn that they had refused the offer) 2. ~ that + clause (it was ~ that they had refused the offer)

persecute *v.* 1. to ~ relentlessly; ruthlessly 2. (D;

tr.) to ~ for (they were ~d relentlessly for their religious beliefs)

persecution *n.* 1. to suffer ~ 2. relentless; ruthless ~ 3. political; racial; religious ~ 4. ~ for (they suffered relentless ~ for their religious beliefs)

perseverance *n.* 1. to display, show ~ 2. dogged; sheer ~ 3. ~ at, in (~ in doing smt.) 4. the ~ to + inf. (she displayed enough sheer ~ to finish)

persevere *v.* (D; intr.) to ~ at, in (to ~ in doing smt.)

persist *v.* (D; intr.) to ~ in, with (to ~ in doing smt.)

persistence *n.* 1. to display, show ~ 2. dogged, sheer ~ 3. ~ in (~ in doing smt.) 4. the ~ to + inf. (she displayed enough sheer ~ to finish)

persistent *adj.* 1. doggedly ~ 2. ~ in (doggedly ~ in doing smt.)

persnickety *adj.* (colloq.) (esp. AE) ["fussy"] ~ about

person *n.* 1. a juridical; private; real ~ 2. a displaced; missing ~ 3. (legal) a ~ aggrieved; concerned 4. (grammar) the first; second; third ~ 5. as a ~ (she is warm as an actress but cold as a ~) 6. in ~ (to appear in ~) 7. on one's ~ (can you be arrested for having a gun on your ~?)

personality *n.* ["famous person"] ["celebrity"] 1. a celebrated; media; TV ~ ["behavioral characteristics"] 2. a charismatic, charming, dynamic, forceful, magnetic, striking ~ 3. a domineering; strong ~ (her strong ~ was expressed in the way she spoke) 4. a dual, split; multiple ~ ["misc."] 5. to indulge in ~ties ("to make impolite remarks about people") (see also *personality cult = cult of personality* at **cult**)

personnel *n.* enlisted (AE; BE has *other ranks*); government; indigenous; military; qualified, skilled; support ~ (our highly qualified ~ are available to help you)

perspective *n.* 1. to put smt. in/into ~ 2. to put a new ~ on smt. 3. a distorted ~ 4. the proper, right, true; wrong ~ 5. from a ~ (to view a situation from a new ~) 6. in ~ (to look at, see smt. in ~)

perspicacity *n.* (formal) the ~ to + inf. (she had enough ~ to see through their schemes)

perspiration *n.* 1. excessive, profuse ~ 2. beads, drops of ~ (ran down my face) 3. (misc.) to be dripping with ~

perspire *v.* to ~ freely, profusely

persuade *v.* 1. (D; tr.) to ~ of (he ~d me of his sincerity) 2. (H) we ~ed her to stay home 3. (L; must have an object) we ~d her that she should stay home

persuaded *adj.* 1. not entirely ~ (I'm still not entirely ~ of his sincerity) 2. ~ that + clause (we are ~ that our project will succeed)

persuasion *n.* 1. political ~ 2. religious ~ (what is their religious ~?) (sometimes humorous) (your friend seems to be of the vegetarian ~) 3. powers of ~ (her powers of ~ are (good) enough to convince anyone)

persuasiveness *n.* the ~ to + inf. (she has enough ~ to convince anyone)

pertain *v.* (d; intr.) to ~ to (these facts ~ to the case)

pertaining *adj.* (cannot stand alone) ~ to (facts ~ to the case)

pertinent *adj.* 1. ~ to (the evidence is not ~ to the case) 2. ~ to + inf. (it's not ~ to cite such outdated evidence) 3. ~ that + clause (it's not ~ that she was out of town) 4. (misc.) is it ~ whether she was present at the scene of the crime?

perturb *v.* (R) it ~ed me (to learn) that she was late again

perturbed *adj.* 1. ~ about, at, by, over (I was ~ over her repeated lateness) 2. ~ to + inf. (I was ~ to learn that she was late again) 3. ~ that + clause (I was ~ that she was late again)

perturbing *adj.* 1. ~ to + inf. (it was ~ to learn that she was late again) 2. ~ that + clause (it was ~ that she was late again)

perusal *n.* 1. a casual, quick; detailed ~ (of smt.) 2. to do; give a ~ (I gave the document a casual ~ and filed it away again until I had the time to give it a detailed ~) (see also Usage Note at **peruse**)

peruse *v.* to ~ carefully; casually; quickly (I ~d the document casually and filed it away again until I had the time to ~ it more carefully) USAGE NOTE: *Peruse* can nowadays mean both 'read hastily and perhaps not completely' and 'read thoroughly from beginning to end.'

pervaded *adj.* (cannot stand alone) ~ with (~ with cynicism)

perverse *adj.* ~ to + inf. (it was ~ to behave like that)

perversion *n.* sexual ~

pessimism *n.* 1. to display, show; express ~ 2. incurable, inveterate ~ 3. to overcome ~ 4. ~ about, at, over (we expressed ~ about the eventual results)

pessimist *n.* an inveterate ~

pessimistic *adj.* ~ about, at, over (we are ~ about the eventual results)

pest *n.* 1. a garden ~ 2. (misc.) he can be a real ~

pester *v.* 1. (D; tr.) to ~ about, for (she kept ~ing me for a new car) 2. (D; tr.) to ~ into (she ~ed me into buying a new car) 3. (H) she kept ~ing me to buy a new car

pet *n.* 1. to have, keep a ~ 2. a household ~ 3. a teacher's ~ (see also *pet animal* at **animal**)

petition I *n.* 1. to circulate, get up a ~ 2. to file, present, submit a ~ 3. to sign a ~ 4. to grant a ~ 5. to withdraw a ~ 6. to deny, reject a ~ 7. a ~ about; against; for; to (they submitted a ~ to the city council for more teachers to be provided = they submitted a ~ for more teachers) 8. a ~ to + inf. (they submitted a ~ to the city council) to provide more teachers) 9. a ~ that + clause; subj. (they submitted a ~ (to the city council) that more teachers be/should be provided)

petition II *v.* 1. (D; intr., tr.) to ~ about; against; for (they ~ed for more teachers = they ~ed the city council for more teachers to be provided) 2. (E) they ~ed to have more teachers provided 3. (H) they ~ed the city council to provide more teachers 4. (formal) (L; subj.) they ~ed the city council that more teachers be/should be provided

petrol (BE) see **gasoline**

petty *adj.* ~ to + inf. (it was ~ of him to do that = it was a ~ thing for him to do)

phalanx *n.* ["formation"] to form a (solid) ~

pharmacy *n.* 1. a hospital ~ 2. at, in a ~ (she works down at the ~)

phase *n.* 1. to begin, enter; reach a ~ 2. to go through a ~ (it's just a passing ~ he's going through) 3. a closing, final, last ~ 4. a critical, crucial ~ 5. an early; first, initial, new, opening; passing ~ (the war was entering its final ~) 6. during, in a ~

pheasant *n.* 1. a brace of ~s 2. a male ~ is a cock 3. a female ~ is a hen 4. a young ~ is a chick

phenomenon *n.* 1. an isolated, rare ~ 2. a natural ~ 3. a common ~ 4. a new ~ 5. a ~ occurs

philosophical *adj.* ~ about

philosophize *v.* (D; intr.) to ~ about

philosophy *n.* ["belief"] 1. to espouse, have a ~ 2. a homespun; moral; political ~ 3. a ~ underpins smt. (the ~ underpinning his actions) 4. the ~ behind; of (the ~ behind his actions; the ~ of science) 5. ~ that + clause (it was her ~ that people should help each other) 6. (misc.) smb.'s ~ of life

phlegm *n.* to cough up ~

phobia *n.* to have a ~ (about)

phone I *n.* 1. to answer, pick up the ~ 2. to hang up; put down; slam down the ~ 3. a cell, cellular, mobile (esp. BE); cordless ~ 4. a new ~ rings; is busy, is engaged (BE); the ~ died on me 5. (misc.) to be wanted on the ~; to call smb. on the ~; to call smb. to the ~ (see also **telephone I**)

phone II *v.* see **telephone II**

phone book *n.* see **telephone directory**

phoneme *n.* (ling.) an independent, separate ~

photo see **photograph I**

photocopy *n.* to make a ~

photofinish *n.* (to end) in a ~

photograph I *n.* 1. to snap, take a ~ 2. to develop; touch up a ~ 3. to blow up, enlarge a ~ 4. to crop a ~ 5. to mount a ~ 6. an aerial; black-and-white; color; family; group; still ~ 7. (misc.) to pose for a ~

photograph II *v.* 1. (J) I ~ed him posing for me 2. (P; intr.) he ~s well

photographer *n.* an amateur; court; fashion; press; professional ~

photography *n.* color; still; trick ~

phrase *n.* 1. to coin; turn a ~ (a good writer knows how to turn a ~ neatly) 2. a choice; well-turned ~ 3. a colloquial; illustrative ~ 4. an empty; glib; hackneyed, stock, trite ~ 5. (grammar) an adjectival, adjective; adverbial, adverb; nominal, noun; participial; prepositional; verb ~ 6. (misc.) a turn of ~ (a good writer with a neat turn of ~)

physical, physical examination *n.* 1. to do, give a ~

2. to get, have a ~ 3. to fail; pass a ~ 4. a complete, thorough ~ (the doctor did a thorough physical ~ of/on the patient, which revealed no signs of disease)

physician *n.* (esp. AE) 1. an attending; family; house; personal; practicing ~ 2. an allopathic; homeopathic; osteopathic ~ (CE has *doctor*)

physics *n.* 1. applied; classical, Newtonian; high-energy, particle; nuclear; quantum; solid-state; theoretical ~ 2. a law of ~ (do all miracles violate the laws of ~?)

physique *n.* 1. a burly, magnificent, muscular, powerful; slim; stocky; sturdy ~ 2. the ~ of (he has the ~ of a champion) 3. the (right; wrong) ~ to + inf. (he has the (right) ~ to become a champion)

pianist *n.* a concert; jazz ~

piano *n.* 1. to play the ~ 2. to tune a ~ 3. a baby grand; (concert) grand; modern; prepared; upright ~ 4. at the, on (the); from the ~ (a concerto with Alfred Brendel at the ~; a jazz number with Thelonius Monk on ~; a Mozart concerto with András Schiff conducting from the ~) 5. (misc.) to sit at the ~; a ~ is in tune or out of tune

piazza *n.* ["open square"] in, on a ~

pick I *n.* ["tool for breaking"] an ice ~

pick II *n.* (colloq.) ["selection, choice"] 1. to take one's ~ 2. to have one's ~ (of)

pick III *v.* 1. (C) ("to select") ~ a nice melon for me; or: ~ me a nice melon 2. (D; tr.) ("to select") to ~ as (they ~ed me as secretary) 3. (d; intr.) to ~ at ("to eat sparingly") (to ~ at one's food) 4. (d; tr.) ("to scratch") to ~ at (to ~ at a scab) 5. (D; tr.) ("to select") to ~ for (she was ~ed for the team) 6. (D; tr.) ("to select") to ~ from, out of (she ~ed this album from our record library) 7. (colloq.) (d; intr.) to ~ on ("to find fault with") (she's always ~ing on me!) 8. (H) ("to select") they ~ed me to serve as secretary 9. (M) ("to select") they ~ed me to secretary 10. (N; used with an adjective) the animals ~ed the carcass clean

picketing *n.* 1. informational; mass ~ 2. to organize ~ (the union organized mass ~ around the factory)

picket line *n.* 1. to form, organize a ~ 2. (esp. AE) to join, walk a ~ 3. to honor a ~ 4. to cross a ~ 5. in, on (AE) a ~

pickings *n.* (colloq.) ["choice"] easy; lean (AE), slim ~

pickle *n.* 1. a dill; sour; sweet ~ 2. (BE) mustard ~; ~s and chutney 3. (misc.) in a ~ ("in trouble") USAGE NOTE: In the United States, a pickle is a pickled cucumber. In Great Britain, the typical pickle is a thick sauce of pickled vegetables.

pick out *v.* 1. (C) ~ a nice melon for me, ~ a nice melon out for me; or: ~ me out a nice melon 2. (D; tr.) to ~ as (they ~ed me out as secretary) 3. (D; tr.) ("to select") to ~ for (she was ~ed out for the team) 4. (D; tr.) ("to select") to ~ from (she ~ed out this album from our record library = she ~ed this album out from our record library) 5. (H) they ~ed me out to serve as secretary 6. (M) they ~ed me out to be secretary

pick up v. 1. (C) ~ a nice melon for me at the supermarket, ~ a nice melon up for me at the supermarket; or: ~ me up a nice melon at the supermarket 2. (d; intr.) to ~ after ("to clean up for") (I was always ~ing up after them) 3. (D; tr.) to ~ by (I ~ed the knife up by the handle = I ~ed up the knife by the handle) 4. (slang) (d; intr.) to ~ on ("to continue"); ("to become aware of")

picnic n. ["outing with a meal"] 1. to go on, have a ~ ["picnic meal"] (BE) 2. to make; pack a ~ ["pleasure"] ["easy task, piece of cake"] (colloq.) 3. a ~ to + inf. (it's no ~ to work there = it's no ~ working there)

picture I n. ["photograph"] 1. to enlarge; pose for; snap, take a ~ 2. in, on a ~ ["drawing, image, painting"] 3. to draw; paint; retouch a ~ 4. to frame; hang; mount a ~ 5. (BE) an Identikit (T) ~ 6. in a ~ (did you see the animals in the ~?) 7. (misc.) to pose, sit for a ~; as pretty as a ~ ["film"] 8. a motion (AE), moving (esp. AE) ~ 9. in a ~ (who played in that ~?) 10. (esp. BE) to go to the ~s ["description"] 11. to draw, paint a ~ 12. a clear; detailed; gloomy, grim; realistic; rosy; vivid ~ 13. a mental ~ 14. (misc.) (colloq.) to get the ~ ("to comprehend the situation"); to get the big ~ ("to comprehend the essence of smt. by contrast with its details"); to keep/put smb. in the ~ ("to keep smb. informed"); the big, larger ~ ("the overall view")

picture II v. 1. (d; tr.) to ~ as (can you ~ him as an actor?) 2. (J) can you ~him becoming an actor? 3. (Q) can you ~ (to yourself) how thrilled he must have been to become an actor?!

pie n. 1. to bake, make a ~ 2. an apple; blueberry; cherry; deep-dish; lemon-meringue; mince; pecan; pumpkin ~ 3. (AE) ~ a la mode 4. a cottage, shepherd's (BE); gala (BE); meat; pork; steak-and-kidney ~ 5. a piece, slice, wedge of ~ 6. (misc.) as easy as ~

piece n. ["(in a game)"] 1. chess ~s ["coin"] 2. a fifty-pence, fifty-penny, fifty-p; gold; ten-pence, ten-penny, ten-p ~ ["an artistic work"] 3. a collector's ~ (BE; CE has *collector's item*) 4. a conversation ~ 5. a ~ of music ["unit"] 6. by the ~ ["fragment"] 7. to cut, slice smt. into ~s 8. to slice off a ~ of smt. 9. to break into ~s (the vase fell and broke into small ~s; she broke the dish into ~s and it lay in ~s on the ground) 10. ~ by ~ ["misc."] 11. to go to ~s ("to fall apart"); a solid ~ of work ("high-quality work"); to give smb. a ~ of one's mind ("to tell smb. brusquely what one thinks"); to speak one's ~ ("to state one's opinion frankly"); a ~ of news; (BE; colloq.) a nasty ~ of work ("a nasty person"); to pick a theory to ~s ("to disprove a theory"); bits and ~s; my party ~ is to recite lots of Shakespeare from memory

piecemeal adv. to do smt. ~

piecework n. to do ~

pier n. 1. a loading ~ 2. at, on a ~ (to meet smb. at the ~)

pig n. ["hog, swine"] 1. a sucking (BE), suckling (AE) ~ 2. ~s grunt, oink, squeal 3. a young ~ is a piglet, shoat (AE) 4. a female ~ is a sow 5. a male ~ is a boar ["glutton"] (colloq.) 6. to make a ~ of oneself ["misc."] 7. as fat as a ~; to buy a ~ in a poke ("to buy, accept smt. with no previous inspection") (see also **guinea pig**)

pigeon n. 1. a carrier, homing ~ 2. a clay ~ 3. ~s coo; strut 4. a flight, flock of ~s

piggyback adv. to carry smb. ~ ("to carry smb. on one's shoulders")

pigheaded adj. 1. ~ of (that was ~ of him) 2. ~ to + inf. (it was ~ of him to do that = he was ~ to have done that)

pig out v. (slang) (D; intr.) to ~ on (to ~ on ice cream)

pile I n. ["concrete post"] to sink a ~

pile II n. ["soft raised surface on a rug"] (a) shaggy; smooth; soft; thick ~

pile III n. ["fortune"] (colloq.) 1. to make a ~ ["reactor"] 2. an atomic ~ ["building"] (BE) 3. a stately ~ ["stack"] 4. to put things in/into a ~ ["mass"] 5. a ~ of rubble/rubbish

pile IV v. 1. (P; intr.) ("to crowd") the children ~d into the car 2. (P; tr.) ("to stack") to ~ wood on the fire 3. (misc.) to ~ books in a stack 4. (misc.) to ~ high (the shelves were ~d high with books)

pileup n. (colloq.) a traffic ~ (AE)

pilfer v. (D; intr., tr.) to ~ from

pilgrimage n. 1. to go on, make a ~ 2. a ~ to (they went on a ~ to Jerusalem) 3. on a ~

pill n. ["tablet of medicine"] 1. to prescribe a ~ 2. to swallow, take a ~ 3. (colloq.) to pop ~s 4. a headache; sleeping ~ ["oral contraceptive"] 5. to take the ~ 6. the morning-after ~ 7. to be on the; to come off the ~ ["misc."] 8. it was a bitter ~ to swallow ("it was very difficult to experience failure")

pillar n. from ~ to post

pillbox n. to storm; take a ~

pillow n. to fluff up, plump up a ~ (see also *pillow case* at **case I** n.; *pillow slip* at **slip I** n.; *pillow talk* at **talk I** n.)

pilot I n. ["person who flies aircraft"] 1. an air-force; airline, commercial; bomber; fighter; glider; helicopter; kamikaze; licensed; test ~ ["person who guides ships into and out of a port"] 2. to drop; take on the ~ 3. a harbor ~ (see also **automatic pilot**)

pilot II v. (P; tr.) ("to guide") the bill was skillfully ~ed through the Senate; they ~ed the refugees to safety

pin I n. ["metal fastener"] 1. to stick a ~ into smt. 2. a safety; straight ~ 3. a bobby ~ (AE; BE has *hair grip*) 4. a drawing ~ (BE; AE has *thumbtack*) 5. a ~ pricks (see also *pin-prick* at **prick I** n.) 6. (misc.) the head of a ~ ["tube-shaped implement"] 7. a rolling ~ ["target in bowling"] 8. to spot ("place") ~s ["support"] 9. to insert, put in a ~ (as in hip surgery) ["misc."] 10. a sensation of ~s and needles; on ~s and needles ("extremely anxious"); it was so quiet you could have heard a ~ drop

pin II *v.* 1. (D; tr.) ("to trap") to ~ against (~ned against the wall) 2. (D; tr.) ("to trap") to ~ beneath, underneath (he was ~ned beneath the car) 3. (d; tr.) ("to place") to ~ on (we ~ned our hopes on her; to ~ the blame on smb.) 4. (d; tr.) ("to secure") to ~ to (her arms were ~ned to her sides; to ~ a notice to the wall)

pincers *n.* a pair of ~

pinch I *n.* ["painful squeeze"] 1. to give smb. a ~ ["emergency"] 2. at (BE), in (esp. AE) a ~ ["arrest"] (colloq.) 3. to make a ~ ["suffering"] 4. to feel the ~ ["misc."] 5. to take smt. with a ~ of salt ("to regard smt. with skepticism")

pinch II *v.* 1. (colloq.) (D; tr.) ("to arrest") to ~ for (~ed for speeding) 2. (D; tr.) ("to squeeze") to ~ in (she ~ed her finger in the door) 3. (D; tr.) ("to squeeze") to ~ in; on (she ~ed my finger in the door; he ~ed me on the cheek)

pinch-hit *v.* (AE) (from baseball) (D; intr.) to ~ for ("to replace")

pin down *v.* (D; tr.) to ~ to (to ~ smb. down to a specific time)

pine *v.* 1. (d; intr.) to ~ after, for (to ~ for home) 2. (E) they were ~ing to return home

pink I *adj.* tickled ~

pink II *n.* (colloq.) ["good health"] in the ~ (of condition)

pinnacle *n.* 1. to reach a ~ (to reach the ~ of one's power) 2. at a ~ (at the ~ of one's power)

pint *n.* 1. an imperial ~ 2. by the ~ (to sell milk by the ~)

pintable (BE) see **machine** 11

pip *v.* (see *pip smb. at the post* at **post V** *n.*)

pipe I *n.* ["device for smoking"] 1. to light a ~ 2. to puff on, smoke a ~ 3. to fill one's ~ 4. a peace ~ ["long tube"] 5. to install, lay ~s 6. a drain; exhaust; gas; overflow; sewage; steam; water ~ 7. a length, piece of ~ 8. a ~ bursts; gets blocked; leaks

pipe II *v.* 1. (D; tr.) to ~ from; into, to (to ~ water from a stream to a house) 2. (misc.) to ~ all hands on deck; to ~ an admiral aboard/on board

pipeline *n.* 1. a gas; oil ~ 2. in a ~ (also fig.) (there are several projects in the ~)

pipe up *v.* (colloq.) (D; intr.) to ~ with (she ~d up with the correct answer)

piping *n.* 1. copper; lead; plastic ~ 2. a length, piece of ~

pique *n.* (in) a fit of ~

piracy *n.* 1. to commit ~ 2. air; literary ~; ~ on the high seas 3. an act of ~

pistol *n.* 1. to cock a ~ 2. to aim, point; level a ~ at 3. to fire a ~ (at) 4. to load; unload a ~ 5. to draw, whip out a ~ 6. an air; automatic; dueling; starting; toy; water ~ 7. the ~ fired, went off; jammed; misfired

pit I *n.* 1. to dig a ~ 2. a bottomless ~ 3. a gravel ~

4. a sandpit (for children to play in) (BE; AE has *sandbox*) 5. (misc.) an orchestra ~

pit II *v.* (d; tr.) to ~ against (we were ~ted against a formidable opponent)

pitch I *n.* ["high-pressure sales talk"] (colloq.) 1. to deliver a ~ 2. a sales ~ (see also *queer smb.'s pitch* at **queer II** *v.*) ["blade angle"] 3. a propeller ~ 4. reverse ~ ["intensity"] 5. a fever; high; low ~ (to reach (a) fever ~) 6. at a certain ~ (during the last weeks of the campaign, activity was at a high ~) ["throw of a baseball or softball"] 7. to throw a ~ 8. an underhand ~ 9. a wild ~ (to uncork a wild ~) ["playing field"] (BE) 10. the ~; football ~ (fans invaded/rushed onto the ~) 11. off; on the ~ ["musical tone"] 12. to give the ~ 13. a high; low; musical ~ 14. absolute, perfect ~ (she has perfect ~)

pitch II *v.* 1. (A) ("to throw") ~ the ball to me; or: ~ me the ball 2. (d; intr.) to ~ into ("to begin to work together enthusiastically") (let's all ~ into this job)

pitch in *v.* (D; intr.) ("to contribute") to ~ by; with (they ~ed in by contributing a hundred dollars each; they ~ed in with a hundred dollars each)

pitfall *n.* 1. to avoid a ~ 2. a hidden ~ 3. a ~ waits for smb., awaits smb. (try to avoid the hidden ~s awaiting first-time house-buyers)

pitiful *adj.* ~ to + inf. (it's ~ to see what has happened)

pittance *n.* a mere ~

pity *n.* 1. to arouse ~ (in) 2. to feel; show ~ 3. to have, take ~ on smb. 4. ~ about; for 5. a ~ to + inf. (it's a real ~ to see what has happened) 6. a ~ that + clause (it's a real ~ that smt. so bad has happened = what a ~ that smt. so bad has happened!) 7. out of ~ (he agreed out of ~ for her children) 8. (misc.) for ~'s sake; a sense of ~; a beautiful spot – (what a) ~ about the weather, though!

pivot *v.* (d; intr.) to ~ on (the dancer ~ed on the ball of her foot; the future ~s on what we decide now)

placard *n.* to carry a ~ (as in a demonstration)

place I *n.* ["space occupied at a table"] 1. to lay (BE), set (esp. AE) a ~ for smb. ["position"] 2. to take smb.'s ~ 3. to change, swap, switch, trade ~s (with) 4. to keep, save smb.'s ~ 5. to give up, relinquish one's ~ (as to smb. else) 6. to lose one's ~ 7. to fall into ~ 8. (misc.) to know one's ~ (in life); to give up one's ~ in line/in a queue (to smb. else); to occupy a prominent ~ in world literature; to put people in their ~ (he thought he was as good as me – but I soon put him in his ~!); please let me show you to your ~ ["point in space"] 9. a meeting ~ 10. at, in a ~ (at the same old ~) ["dwelling"] 11. at smb.'s ~ (let's meet at your ~) ["appropriate position"] 12. in; out of ~ (everything was in ~) ["seat"] 13. to take one's ~ (they took their ~s) ["standing in a competition"] 14. to take a ~ (she took second ~ in the competition) (see also **second place**) 15. a ~ goes to (first ~ went to Smith) ["duty, function"] 16. smb.'s ~ to + inf. (it's not my ~ to criticize them) ["stage"]["step"] 17. in a ~ (in the first ~) ["as at an institution or in a team"] 18. to apply

for, try for; get; have; turn down; turn smb. down
for a ~ (she got a ~ at the university of her choice
and turned down a ~ at another one) ["misc."] 19. to
take ~ ("to happen – used typically of a planned
occurrence"); to go ~s ("to be successful"); all over
the ~ ("everywhere"); in ~ of ("instead of") (see
also *birthplace* = *place of birth* at **birth**; *place of
worship* at **worship I** *n.* ; **workplace**)
place II *v.* 1. (d; tr.) ("to put") to ~ above (to ~ one's
family above all other concerns) 2. (d; tr.) ("to
put") to ~ at (she ~d her car at our disposal) 3. (d;
tr.) ("to present") to ~ before (to ~ evidence before
a grand jury; to ~ a proposal before a committee)
4. (d; tr.) ("to put") to ~ in (to ~ one's confidence
in smb.) 5. (D; tr.) to ~ with ("to find a home for")
(to ~ a child with a family) 6. (P; tr.) ("to put") to ~
books on a table 7. (s) she ~d first in the race
placebo *n.* 1. to administer, give a ~ 2. (misc.) a ~
effect
placed *adj.* highly ~
plagiarism *n.* to be guilty of ~
plagiarize *v.* (D; tr.) to ~ from (she ~d the paragraph
from a book)
plague I *n.* 1. bubonic ~ 2. a ~ spreads 3. an outbreak
of (the) ~ 4. (misc.) to avoid smb. like the ~ ; a ~ on
(a ~ on you both! you're as bad as each other!)
plague II *v.* (D; tr.) ("to bother") to ~ with (to ~
smb. with repeated requests)
plain I *adj.* 1. ~ to (the truth is ~ to everybody) 2.
~ to + inf. (the facts are ~ to see; it's ~ to see that
she will never return) 3. ~ that + clause (it's ~ to
everyone that she will never return) 4. (misc.) as ~
as day; or: as ~ as the nose on your face; to make
smt. ~ (see also *plain vanilla* at **vanilla**)
plain II *n.* 1. a broad, vast; coastal ~ 2. on a ~
plaintiff *n.* to find for the ~
plait I *n.* ["braid"] in a ~ (they wore their hair in ~s)
plait II *v.* (D; tr.) to ~ into (to ~ one's hair into
pigtails)
plan I *n.* 1. to come up with, conceive, concoct,
devise, lay, make a ~ 2. to cobble together, draw
up, formulate, map out, work out a ~ 3. to outline,
sketch out a ~ 4. to announce, unveil a ~ 5. to present, propose a ~ 6. to accept, approve a ~ 7. to carry
out, execute, go ahead with, implement a ~ 8. to
put a ~ into effect/operation 9. to abandon, drop,
scrub; shelve a ~ 10. to reject, turn down a ~ 11. to
foil, frustrate, thwart a ~ 12. a brilliant, ingenious;
well-thought-out ~ 13. a feasible; realistic ~ 14.
a complicated, elaborate; detailed; grandiose,
sweeping ~ 15. an impracticable; impractical;
unrealistic ~ 16. a contingency; master; tentative ~
17. a secret; security ~ 18. a five-year; long-term;
short-term ~ 19. (see **installment plan**) 20. a flight
~ 21. a floor, seating ~ 22. a health ~ ("health
insurance"); a pension, retirement ~ 23. an easy-
payment ~ 24. retirement; travel; wedding ~s (they
have announced their wedding ~s) 25. a ~ calls for
(smt.) 26. ~s materialize; succeed, work; go ahead

27. ~s fail 28. a ~ for (the mayor had a ~ for reducing traffic congestion) 29. a ~ to + inf. (the mayor
had a ~ to reduce traffic congestion) 30. (misc.) to
go according to ~ (things didn't quite go according
to ~); to make ~s (for a wedding; for early retirement); the best-laid ~s (don't always succeed); a
backup ~ ; ~ A and ~ B (if Plan A doesn't work we
can always go to Plan B, our backup ~) (see also
keep a plan under wraps at **wraps**)
plan II *v.* 1. (d; intr.) to ~ for (to ~ for one's old
age; to ~ for early retirement) 2. (d; intr.) to ~ on
(to ~ on early retirement; we ~ned on spending a
month in Europe) 3. (E) we ~ to take early retirement; we ~ned to spend a month in Europe 4. (Q)
we ~ned very carefully how we would budget for
early retirement 5. (misc.) as ~ned (things didn't
quite go as ~ned)
plan ahead *v.* (D; intr.) to ~ for (to ~ for one's old
age; for retirement)
plane I *n.* ["airplane"] 1. to board, get on, hop, take;
get off a ~ 2. to charter a ~ 3. to go by, travel by ~ 4.
to catch; miss a ~ 5. to change ~s (we changed ~s
in Chicago) 6. to clear a ~ (for landing or takeoff)
7. a cargo; fighter ~ (see also entry for **airplane**)
plane II *n.* ["level surface"] 1. an inclined ~ 2. on a
lofty ~
plane III *v.* (N; used with an adjective) to ~ a board
smooth
plank *n.* ["board extending from a ship"] to walk the
~ ("to go to one's death") (see the Usage Note for
platform)
planning *n.* 1. advance; careful; grandiose; long-
range, long-term; short-range, short-term ~ 2.
central; city; discharge; estate; family; financial;
language; town (BE) ~ (see also *family planning* at
family) 3. ~ for (~ for early retirement) 4. ~ to +
inf. (~ to retire early)
plant I *n.* ["shrub, bush"] 1. to grow ~s 2. to water a ~ 3.
an annual; biennial; climbing; decorative; exotic;
perennial; pot; tropical ~ (see also *plant life* at **life**)
4. a ~ dies; grows ["factory"]["utility"] 5. to manage,
operate, run a ~ 6. to open a ~ 7. to close, shut down
a ~ 8. a nuclear; power; waste-disposal ~ 9. at, in a
~ (she works at/in a waste-disposal ~) ["buildings"]
["equipment"] 10. (the) physical ~ (of an institution)
plant II *v.* 1. (D; tr.) ("to place secretly") to ~on (the
police ~ed evidence on her) 2. ("to sow") (D; tr.) to
~ in; with (to ~ a field with rye= to ~ rye in a field)
3. (misc.) to ~ an idea in smb.'s head; to ~ a kiss
on smb.'s cheek
plantation *n.* a coffee; cotton; rubber; sugar; tea ~
planter *n.* a coffee; cotton; rubber; sugar; tea ~
plaque *n.* ["filmy deposit on teeth"] 1. to remove ~
(from teeth) 2. dental ~ 3. ~ accumulates, builds up,
forms ["tablet"] 4. to put up; unveil a ~ (in smb.'s
honor) 5. a commemorative, memorial ~
plaster I *n.* ["pasty composition"] 1. to apply ~ (to
apply ~ to a wall) 2. to daub ~ (to daub ~ on a wall
= to daub a wall with ~) 3. crumbling, falling ~ 4.

~ comes off, falls off, peels; sets ["pastelike mixture used for healing purposes"] 5. a mustard ~ ["tape"] 6. (BE) (a) sticking ~

plaster II *v.* 1. (d; tr.) ("to cover") to ~ with (they ~ed the walls with notices) 2. (P; tr.) ("to put up") to ~ notices all over the walls; they ~ed notices on every bulletin board

plastic *n.* laminated ~

plate *n.* ["dish"] 1. a cake; dinner; paper; salad; soup ~ 2. on a ~ (they ate all the rice on their ~s) ["plateful"] 3. a ~ of (they ate several ~s of rice) ["denture"] 4. a dental; lower; partial; upper ~ ["tag"] 5. a license (esp. AE), number (BE) ~ ["thin layer"] 6. armor; silver ~ ["container passed around for donations of money"] 7. to pass the ~ 8. a collection ~ ["geological feature"] 9. a tectonic ~ ["goal"] (esp. AE) 10. (baseball) home ~ USAGE NOTE: British black taxis bear both a licence plate (as a taxi) and a number plate (as a vehicle).

plateau *n.* 1. a high ~ 2. (misc.) to reach a ~ ("to cease making progress")

platform *n.* ["raised stage"] 1. to get up on, mount ("ascend"); stand on a ~ 2. from; on a ~ (to speak from a ~) 3. a launching ~ ["flat surface"] 4. from a ~ (trains leave from that ~) ["statement of policies"] 5. AE; BE prefers *manifesto*) 5. to draft, draw up a ~ 6. to adopt a ~ 7. a party; political ~ USAGE NOTES: (1) A political platform consists of various statements that are called planks. (2) In BE, the train for Birmingham leaves from platform 29. In AE, the train for Birmingham leaves from track 29.

platitude *n.* 1. to mouth, utter a ~ (he's always mouthing ~s) 2. a well-worn ~ 3. (misc.) in ~s (to speak in well-worn ~s)

platoon *n.* 1. to form a ~ 2. to deploy a ~ 3. to command a ~ (a lieutenant commands a ~)

plaudits *n.* to earn, receive, win ~ (for) (to get (a lot of) ~ for reducing taxes)

plausible *adj.* 1. ~ to + inf. (it is ~ to assume that they will not accept our invitation) 2. ~ that + clause (it's ~ that they will not accept our invitation)

play I *n.* ["stage presentation"] 1. to direct; do, present, produce, put on, stage; revive; write a ~ 2. to perform; rehearse a ~ 3. to see a ~ 4. to criticize, pan (colloq.); review a ~ 5. an historical; miracle; morality; mystery; nativity; one-act; passion; radio; TV ~; screenplay 6. a ~ closes; flops; opens; runs (the ~ ran for two years on Broadway) 7. (misc.) the ~ about the War got rave reviews; the ~ was a (smash) hit ["action, activity"] 8. to bring into ~ (to bring various forces into ~) 9. to come into ~ ["competition, playing"] 10. fair; rough; team ~ (see also **foul play**) 11. at; in; into; out of ~ (to put the ball into ~; the children were at ~) ["attempt to attract"] (colloq.) 12. to make a ~ for (he made a ~ for her) ["misc."] 13. a ~ on words ("a pun"); rain stopped ~ (esp. BE); England were in the lead at close of ~ (see also **child's play**)

play II *v.* 1. ("to compete") to ~ fair; foul; rough 2.

(C) ("to perform") ~ a nice song for me; or: ~ me a nice song 3. (d; intr.) ("to compete") to ~ against (to ~ against a strong opponent = to ~ with a strong opponent = to ~ a strong opponent; they ~ed (against) each other in the final) 4. (D; intr.) ("to amuse oneself") to ~ at (she ~s at being a writer) 5. (d; intr.) ("to gamble") to ~ for (to ~ for money) 6. (d; intr.) ("to perform") to ~ for (she ~s for our team) 7. (d; intr.) to ~ for ("to attempt to obtain") (to ~ for time) 8. (d; intr.) to ~ on, upon ("to exploit") (to ~ on smb.'s fears) 9. (d; intr.) to ~ on ("to pun") (to ~ on words) 10. (D; tr.) ("to do, make") to ~ on (they ~ed a joke on us; she ~ed a trick on me) 11. (d; intr.) ("to perform") to ~ to (to ~ to a full house) 12. (esp. tennis) (d; intr.) ("to direct one's strokes") to ~ to (to ~ to an opponent's forehand) 13. (D; intr., tr.) ("to amuse oneself (with)") to ~ with (to ~ with the children; to ~ a game with the children) 14. (L) (esp. in children's language) ("to pretend") let's ~ that I'm the teacher and you're the pupil 15. (O; can be used with one object) ("to oppose in") I'll ~ you a game of cards = I'll ~ a game of cards with you 16. (s) ("to feign") they ~ed dead 17. (misc.) to ~ smb. for a fool ("to ridicule smb."); to ~ (it) by ear ("to improvise"); to ~ into smb.'s hands ("to come under smb.'s control")

play about (BE) see **play around**

play along *v.* (D; intr.) to ~ with (we had to ~ with their various proposals)

play around *v.* (D; intr.) to ~ with

play back *v.* (B) she ~ed the tape back to us = she ~ed back the tape to us

player *n.* ["athlete"] 1. a clean; dirty ~ 2. a key ~ ["electronic instrument"] 3. a cassette; compact disc; record ~ ["participant"] 4. a key; major ~ (a major ~ in the international futures market) (see also ¬*football player / footballer*¬ at **football**; *tennis player* at **tennis**)

playground *n.* 1. (BE) an adventure ~ ("children's playground designed for spontaneous play") 2. a city, municipal, public; school ~ 3. in, on a ~

playing *n.* clean; dirty ~

play off *v.* (d; tr.) to ~ against ("to set against") (she ~ed one side off against the other = she ~ed off one side against the other)

playoffs *n.* to get/go through to the; get into, get to, reach the ~

play up *v.* (d; intr.) to ~ to ("to flatter") (to ~ to the boss)

plea *n.* 1. to enter, make, put forward a ~ 2. to answer, respond to a ~ 3. to deny, reject a ~ 4. (slang) (esp. AE) to cop a ~ ("to plead guilty to a lesser charge") 5. an ardent, emotional, fervent, impassioned, moving, passionate, tearful; urgent ~ 6. (to enter) a guilty ~; (to enter) a ~ of not guilty; more usu. is: to plead guilty; to plead not guilty 7. a ~ of insanity 8. a ~ for (a ~ for mercy) (see also *plea bargaining* at **bargaining**)

plead *v.* 1. to ~ fervently 2. (D; intr.) to ~ for; with (to ~ with the judge for mercy; she ~ed with the judge to show mercy for her crime) 3. (E) she ~ed to be shown mercy for her crime 4. (legal) (s) to ~ guilty (to a charge) 5. (legal) (s) to ~ not guilty (to a charge)

pleasant adj. 1. ~ to (she is ~ to everyone) 2. ~ to + inf. (it's ~ to lie in the sun = it's ~ lying in the sun; she is ~ to work with = it is ~ to work with her = it is ~ working with her = she is a ~ person to work with)

pleasantry n. to exchange ~tries

please v. 1. to ~ greatly, highly, very much 2. (R) it ~d us greatly to learn that you could accept our invitation; it ~d us greatly that you could accept our invitation 3. (misc.) ~ be seated

pleased adj. 1. greatly, highly, very ~ 2. ~ about, at, by, with (we were very ~ by your acceptance of our invitation) 3. ~ to + inf. (we were very ~ to learn of your acceptance of our invitation; we are ~ to be here; (I'm) ~ to meet you) 4. ~ that + clause (we were very ~ that you could accept our invitation) 5. (misc.) as ~ as Punch ("very pleased")

pleasing adj. ~ to

pleasure n. 1. to afford, give, provide ~ (it gives me great ~ to present the next speaker) 2. to feel; find, have, take ~ in 3. to derive, get ~ from 4. to forgo a ~ 5. (a) genuine, great, real; rare ~ 6. a dubious; perverse; vicarious ~ 7. a ~ for (working here is a ~ for me) 8. a ~ to + inf. (it's a ~ to work with them = it's a ~ working with them = they are a ~ to work with; it is a ~ to teach these children = it is a ~ teaching these children = these children are a ~ to teach; it was a ~ for me to teach these children) 9. at smb.'s ~ (to serve at the president's ~) 10. for ~ (she reads history for ~) 11. with ~ (I accept with ~) 12. (misc.) may I have the ~ of your company a little while longer?

plebiscite n. 1. to conduct, have, hold a ~ on (to hold a ~ on the status of a territory) 2. a ~ to + inf. (to hold a ~ to determine the status of a territory) 3. (misc.) to decide (the status of a territory) by ~

pledge I n. 1. to make, take a ~ 2. to give smb. a/ one's ~ 3. to fulfill, honor, redeem one's ~ 4. to break, renege on, repudiate, violate a ~ 5. a broken ~ 6. a firm; sacred, solemn ~ 7. a campaign, election ~ (politicians sometimes break their campaign ~s) 8. a ~ to + inf. (she made a solemn ~ not to drink again) 9. a ~ that + clause (she made a solemn ~ that she would not drink again) 10. (misc.) to take the ~ ("to vow to stop drinking")

pledge II v. 1. (A) she ~d her support to us; or: she ~d us her support 2. (d; tr.) to ~ as (they ~d their assets as collateral/security for the loan) 3. (D; tr.) to ~ to (she was ~d to secrecy) 4. (E) she ~ed not to drink again 5. (H; refl.) she ~ed herself not to drink again 6. (L; to) she ~d (to them) that she would not drink again

plenty determiner, n., pronoun 1. ~ of (~ of money) 2. ~ to + inf. (she gave us ~ to do) 3. (formal) in ~

(to live in ~) 4. (formal) of ~ (a time of ~) (see also plenty more at **more II**)

pliers n. a pair of ~

plod v. 1. (d; intr.) to ~ through ("to go through laboriously") (to ~ through a long reading list) 2. (P; intr.) ("to move") they ~ded slowly along the road

plod away v. (D; intr.) to ~ at (to ~ at one's job)

plot I n. ["conspiracy"] 1. to devise, hatch; weave a ~ 2. to foil, thwart a ~ 3. to expose, uncover a ~ 4. a cunning, diabolic(al); sinister ~ 5. a ~ against (to expose a ~ against the government) 6. a ~ to + inf. (to expose a ~ to overthrow the government) ["story"] 7. to build, construct the ~ (of a novel) 8. a contrived; intricate ~ 9. a simple ~ 10. the ~ develops; thickens 11. (misc.) a twist, wrinkle in the ~ (there was an unexpected wrinkle in the ~) (see also plot line at **line I** n.) ["piece of ground"] 12. a burial, cemetery; garden ~; a ~ of land

plot II v. 1. (D; intr.) to ~ against, with (to ~ against the government with other conspirators) 2. (E) they ~ted to overthrow the government 3. (Q) they were ~ting how to overthrow the government

plow, plough I n. to pull a ~

plow, plough II v. 1. (d; intr.) to ~ into ("to strike") (the racing car skidded and ~ed into the crowd) 2. (d; intr.) to ~ through ("to go through laboriously") (to ~ through a long reading list; to ~ through a crowd; to ~ through deep snow)

plow back, plough back v. (d; tr.) to ~ into (to ~ all profits into the firm)

ploy n. 1. to resort to, use a ~ 2. a clever, ingenious; cynical ~ 3. a ~ fails; works 4. a ~ for (it was a clever ~ for getting money) 5. a ~ to + inf. (it was a clever ~ to get money)

pluck I n. ["courage"] 1. to display, show ~ 2. to require, take ~ (standing up to the boss took a lot of ~) 3. the ~ to + inf. (he had enough ~ to stand up to the boss)

pluck II v. 1. (C) ("to pull") ~ a nice flower for me; or: ~ me a nice flower 2. (d; intr.) ("to tug") to ~ at 3. (D; tr.) ("to pull") to ~ from, off (to ~ a flower from a bush; to ~ feathers from a chicken = to ~ a chicken)

plug I n. ["electrical fitting"] 1. to insert, put a ~ into a socket 2. a ~ fits into a socket ["device carrying an electric current"] 3. a spark, sparking (BE) ~ ["word of praise"] (colloq.) 4. to put in a ~ for ["misc."] (colloq.) 5. to pull the ~ ("to cut off a life-support system"); to pull the ~ on smb. ("to put an end to smt.") (see also plug hole at **hole**)

plug II v. (d; intr., tr.) to ~ into (the lamp ~s into this socket so ~ it into the socket now!; to ~ into a computer network; (also fig.) how can young people ~ into the world of work?)

plug away v. (D; intr.) to ~ at ("to work at laboriously") (to ~ at a job)

plumber n. 1. to call (in) a ~ 2. a master ~

plumbing n. 1. to install, put in ~ 2. indoor ~ 3. ~ can leak

plummet v. (d; intr.) to ~ to; towards (to ~ to earth)

plump I adj. pleasingly ~

plump II v. (colloq.) (D; intr.) to ~ for ("to support")

plump down v. (colloq.) (D; refl., intr., tr.) to ~ in, into, on (she ~ed herself down into the chair)

plunge I n. ["risk"] (colloq.) 1. to take the ~ ["act of plunging"] 2. to take a ~ 3. a ~ into (to take a ~ into the water)

plunge II v. 1. (d; intr.) ("to throw oneself") to ~ from, off; to (to ~ to one's death from a cliff) 2. (d; intr.) ("to dive"); ("to rush") to ~ into (to ~ into the water; to ~ into war) 3. (d; tr.) ("to throw"); ("to thrust") to ~ into (the room was ~ed into darkness; to ~ a dagger into smb.'s heart) 4. (d; intr., tr.) ("to throw oneself"; "to thrust") to ~ through (she ~d through the ice; he ~d the spear through the barrier)

plural n. in the ~

plurality n. by a ~ (AE: to win the election by a ~)

plus n. 1. a big ~ (it was a big ~ in her favor) 2. (misc.) to weigh the ~es and the minuses

ply v. 1. (d; intr.) ("to travel") to ~ between (these ships ~ between the two cities) 2. (d; tr.) ("to provide") to ~ with (they plied him with liquor)

pneumonia n. 1. to come down with, contract, develop, get, go down with (BE); have ~ 2. bronchial; viral ~

poach v. (D; intr., tr.) ("to hunt illegally on smb.'s property") to ~ on, upon (to ~ on smb.'s land)

pocket n. 1. to empty; fill one's ~s 2. to turn out one's ~s 3. to pick smb.'s ~ 4. a back; breast; coat; hip; inside; jacket; pants (AE), trouser; shirt; side; vest (AE), waistcoat; watch ~ 5. an air ~ 6. (misc.) (BE) in ~ ("with a profit"); out of ~ ("with a loss") USAGE NOTE: In AE, *vest-pocket* can be used of something small and compact: *a vest-pocket dictionary*.

pocketbook n. ["handbag"] (AE) to carry a ~

podium n. 1. to get up on, mount a ~ 2. to stand at / on a ~ 3. from; on a ~

poem n. 1. to compose, write a ~ 2. to memorize; read; recite; scan a ~ 3. a dramatic; epic, heroic; lyric; narrative; prose ~ 4. an anthology; collection of ~s

poet n. 1. the ~ laureate (how many ~s laureate have there been? = how many ~ laureates have there been?) 2. a poet-in-residence (how many poets-in-residence have there been at this university?) 3. a published ~

poetry n. 1. to compose, write ~ 2. to memorize; read; recite; scan ~ 3. dramatic; epic, heroic; lyric; narrative; romantic ~ 4. an anthology; collection of ~

pogrom n. to carry out; instigate; organize a ~

point I n. ["location, position, place, spot"] 1. to arrive at, reach a ~ 2. an assembly; rallying ~ 3. a central; focal; salient; vantage ~ 4. an entry; crisis; flash; jumping-off; starting; turning ~ 5. a cutoff; fixed ~ 6. an acupuncture; pressure ~ 7. a vanishing ~ 8. the ~ of no return 9. at a ~ (at that ~ in history; at this ~ in time (considered a cliché)) 10. for a ~ (for all ~s east) 11. from; to a ~ (from this ~ to that ~) ["level"]["degree"] 12. to arrive at, reach a ~ 13. a high; low ~ (she has reached the high ~ in / of her career) 14. the boiling; freezing; melting ~ (see also **boiling-point**; **freezing-point**; **melting-point**; **turning point**) 15. the breaking; saturation ~ 16. up to a ~, to a ~ (AE) (to a certain ~ they are right) ["step, stage"] 17. at, on the ~ (they were on the ~ of leaving; the commissioners were at a delicate ~ in the negotiations) ["argument"]["topic"] 18. to bring up, make, raise a ~ 19. to argue, debate; cover, discuss; emphasize, stress, underscore; explain; illustrate; keep to; prove, win; review a ~ 20. to belabor, labor; strain, stretch a ~ 21. to drive, hammer, press a ~ home = press home a ~; to make one's ~; to get a ~ across 22. to concede, yield a ~ 23. a controversial; crucial; debating; fine; major; minor; moot; (unique) selling; sore; sticking; subtle; talking; telling ~ 24. a ~ comes up (the same ~ has come up several times) 25. the ~ that + clause (she made the ~ that further resistance was useless) 26. beside the ~ (her remarks were beside the ~) 27. on a ~ (on that ~ we disagree) 28. to the ~ (to speak to the ~; she was brief and to the ~) 29. (misc.) to come to the ~; ~ by ~; a good ("convincing") ~; to have a ~ ("to have a convincing argument") ["core, essence"] 30. to get, see the ~ (she never did see the ~ of the joke) 31. to come to, to get to the ~ 32. to miss the ~ (we missed the ~ of the story) ["emphasis"] 33. to make a ~ of (he made a ~ of repeating her name several times = he made it a ~ to repeat her name several times) ["distinguishing feature"] 34. smb.'s bad, weak; good, strong ~s ["punctuation mark"] 35. a decimal; exclamation (AE) ~ ["scoring unit"] 36. to score a ~ (also fig.); to rack up ~s 37. to shave ~s ("to manipulate the results of a contest for illegal purposes") 38. (esp. tennis) a game; match; set ~ 39. by ~s (to lead by five ~s) 40. (boxing) on ~s (to win on ~s) ["regard"] 41. in ~ of (in ~ of law; in ~ of fact) ["aim, object, purpose, reason"] 42. to get, see the ~ 43. to have a ~ 44. a ~ in (there is no ~ in complaining = there is no ~ complaining) 45. a ~ to (there is no ~ to your complaining) 46. (misc.) "what's the ~?" "the (whole) ~ is that our party cannot win the election" ["tapered end"] 47. a sharp ~ (this pencil has a sharp ~) ["socket"] (BE) 48. a cooker; mains; power ~ ["misc."] 49. at the ~ of a gun = at gunpoint; a Brownie ~ (colloq.) ("ingratiation in the eyes of a superior") (to get / make Brownie ~s); a case in ~ ("a pertinent case"); a ~ of order; the cardinal ~s of the compass; the speaker kept wandering off the ~; stocks have risen (by) several (percentage) ~s (see also **point of view**; **standpoint**; **vantage point**; **viewpoint**)

point II *v.* 1. (D; intr.) to ~ at, to, towards ("to draw attention to") (she ~ed at me) 2. (d; tr.) ("to aim") to ~ at (to ~ a gun at smb.) 3. (D; intr.) to ~ to ("to cite") (they ~ed to poverty as a major problem; the evidence ~s to him as the criminal) 4. (P; intr., tr.) ("to aim, direct") the needle ~s north; to ~ a boat downstream; she ~ed the muzzle towards the door (see also *point the way to smt.* at **way**)
pointers *n.* ["advice"] 1. to give smb. ~ on 2. to ask for; get ~ on
pointless *adj.* ~ to + inf. (it's ~ (for you) to complain = it's ~ (your) complaining)
point of view *n.* 1. to have, hold a ~ 2. a fresh; optimistic, positive ~ 3. a negative, pessimistic ~ 4. a ~ that + clause (he explained his ~ that taxes should be increased) 5. from smb.'s ~ (from his ~, taxes should be increased) (see also *view* I *n.*; **viewpoint**)
point out *v.* 1. (B) she ~ed out the sights to us = she ~ed the sights out to us 2. (L; to) they were at pains to ~ out (to us) that such investments would be risky 3. (Q; to) I ~ed out to them where I work
poise I *n.* 1. to keep, maintain one's ~ 2. to lose; recover, regain one's ~ 3. the ~ to + inf. (do you have enough ~ to speak without notes?)
poise II *v.* (D; refl.) ("to brace oneself") to ~ for (she ~d herself for the ordeal)
poised *adj.* ["ready"] 1. ~ for; on the brink of (~ for action; ~ on the brink of action/acting) 2. ~ to + inf. (they were ~ to act) (see also *poised to spring* at **spring** II *v.*)
poison I *n.* 1. to administer, give (a) ~ 2. to swallow, take ~ 3. (a) deadly, lethal; slow; strong ~ 4. rat ~ (to spread rat ~)
poison II *v.* to ~ smb.'s mind against smb.
poison gas *n.* to use ~ against
poisoning *n.* blood; food; lead; ptomaine ~
poke I *n.* ["punch"] (colloq.) to give smb. a ~ (in the eye)
poke II *v.* 1. (d; intr.) to ~ at ("to jab") (he kept ~ing at me) 2. (D; tr.) ("to jab") to ~ in (to ~ smb. in the ribs) 3. (d; intr., tr.) ("to make by poking") to ~ in (to ~ a hole in a wall) 4. (d; tr.) ("to extend") to ~ out of (to ~ one's head out of the window) 5. (d; intr., tr.) ("to make by poking") to ~ through (to ~ a hole through a wall) 6. (P; tr.) ("to thrust") to ~ one's head through a window 7. (misc.) to ~ fun at smb.
poke about see **poke around**
poke around *v.* (colloq.) (D; intr.) to ~ in ("to look through") (stop ~ing around in my desk)
poker *n.* to play ~
polarization *n.* ~ between (there is increasing ~ of the two ethnic communities into opposing camps)
polarize *v.* (D; intr., tr.) to ~ into (the two ethnic communities have increasingly been ~d into opposing camps)
pole I *n.* ["long slender shaft"] 1. to put up a ~ 2. a breakaway; fishing; ski; tent; totem ~ 3. a flagpole; telegraph; telephone (AE); utility (AE) ~

pole II *n.* ["end of the earth's axis"] 1. the North; South Pole (a camp was set up at the North Pole) 2. a celestial; magnetic ~ ["terminal of a battery"] 3. a negative; positive ~ ["misc."] 4. ~s apart; or: at opposite ~s ("diametrically opposed"); from ~ to ~ ("Out of the night that covers me, Black as the Pit from ~ to ~" – W.E. Henley (1849–1930), "Invictus")
police *n.* 1. to call the ~ 2. border; campus (US); city, municipal; local; military; mounted; riot; secret; security; state ~ 3. (misc.) the ~ are investigating the crime, have detained and are questioning several suspects, have made no arrests, but are appealing for witnesses; however, a man is helping ~ with their enquiries (BE) (see also *police brutality* at **brutality**; *police chief* at **chief**; *police department* at **department**; *police presence* at **presence**)
policeman *n.* 1. a military ~ (abbreviated as *MP*) 2. see **police officer**
police officer *n.* an off-duty; plainclothes; uniformed ~
policewoman see **police officer**
policy I *n.* ["plan"] ["principle"] 1. to adopt, establish, formulate; pursue a ~ 2. to adhere to, follow, pursue a ~ 3. to carry out, implement a ~ 4. to develop, form, frame, make, shape (a) ~ (see also *policymaker* at **maker**) 5. to change, modify, revise (a) ~ 6. to violate (a) ~ 7. a clear, clear-cut; prudent; sound, wise ~ 8. a friendly; open-door ~ 9. a conciliatory; flexible ~ 10. a cautious; deliberate; established, firm, set ~ 11. a controversial; divisive; foolish; ill-conceived; rigid; wait-and-see ~ 12. a scorched-earth ~ 13. a long-range, long-term; short-range, short-term ~ 14. an official; standard ~ 15. an established; written ~ 16. (a) company; personnel ~ 17. (a) domestic; economic; educational; financial, fiscal, monetary; foreign; government, public; military; national; population; social; tax ~ 18. a ~ on, towards 19. a ~ to + inf. (it is our established ~ to treat everyone fairly) 20. a ~ that + clause; subj. (it is our established ~ that everyone be/should be/is (BE) treated fairly)
policy II *n.* ["contract for insurance"] 1. to take out a ~ 2. to issue, write up a ~ 3. to reinstate a ~ 4. to cancel a ~ 5. an endowment; homeowner's; insurance; lifetime; straight life; term ~ 6. a ~ matures (see also *policy-holder* at **holder**) ["contract"] 7. a service ~ (we have a service ~ for all of our major appliances)
polio, poliomyelitis *n.* ["infantile paralysis"] 1. to contract, develop, get; have ~ 2. to prevent ~
polish *n.* ["gloss"] 1. to apply ~ 2. floor; French (BE); furniture; shoe; silver ~ 3. nail ~ (BE also has *nail varnish*)
polite *adj.* 1. ~ to (interrupting people who are speaking is not ~ to them) 2. ~ to + inf. (it is not ~ to interrupt someone who is speaking; it was not ~ of them not to respond)
politeness *n.* 1. studied ~ 2. ~ to 3. out of ~ (he did it out of ~ to her)

politic *adj.* ["expedient"] ~ to + inf. (it would not be ~ to get involved in their affairs)

political fences *n.* ["political standing"] to mend one's ~

politician *n.* an astute, shrewd; crafty, crooked, cunning, scheming, wily; glib; great; hack; honest; prominent; senior ~

politics *n.* 1. to go into ~ 2. to play ~ 3. to talk ~ 4. consensus; electoral; identity; local, parish-pump (BE); national; partisan, party; pork-barrel; power; practical; sexual ~

poll *n.* 1. to carry out, conduct, take a ~ 2. an exit ~ (taken of voters leaving the voting booths) 3. a straw ("unofficial") ~ 4. a public-opinion ~ 5. a national, nationwide ~ 6. a ~ among, of (to conduct a ~ among students) 7. in a ~ (their strong feelings came out in several ~s; he's leading in all the ~s) (see also **polls**; *poll rating* at **rating**)

pollination *n.* cross ~

polls *n.* 1. to go to the ~ (in order to vote) 2. the ~ close; open (at a certain time) 3. at the ~ (to be defeated at the ~) (see also **poll**)

pollution *n.* 1. to cause; control ~ 2. air; environmental; light; noise, sound; water ~

polo *n.* 1. to play ~ 2. water ~

polyandry *n.* to practice ~

polygamy *n.* to practice ~

polygraph test *n.* 1. to administer, give a ~ 2. to subject smb. to a ~ 3. to take, undergo a ~ 4. to fail; pass a ~

polyp *n.* 1. to remove a ~ 2. a benign; malignant ~

pomp *n.* 1. ceremonial ~ 2. ~ and circumstance

pond *n.* 1. to drain a ~ 2. a deep; shallow; stagnant ~ 3. a duck; fish ~

ponder *v.* 1. (d; intr.) to ~ on, over, upon (to ~ over a problem) 2. (Q) I ~ed how we could finish on time

pontificate *v.* (D; intr.) to ~ about, on (he'll ~ for hours on just about anything!)

pony *n.* 1. to ride a ~ 2. a pit; polo; Shetland; wild ~ (see also **horse**)

pool I *n.* ["joint enterprise"] 1. to form a ~ 2. a car; stenographic (AE), typing ~ ["group of vehicles"] 3. a motor ~ ["total of money bet by gamblers"] 4. a football ~ (BE has *the pools*) ["billiards"] 5. to play, shoot ~ ["stock, supply"] 6. a gene ~

pool II *n.* ["basin"] 1. an indoor; outdoor; paddling (BE), wading (AE); swimming ~ ["small body of water"] 2. a deep; empty; shallow; stagnant ~ (see also *in a pool of blood* at **blood**)

pools see pool I *n.*

poor *adj.* 1. ~ at (the country is ~ at exploiting its natural resources) 2. ~ in (the country is ~ in natural resources) 3. (misc.) rich and ~ (alike)

pop I *adv.* (colloq.) to go ~ ("to make a short explosive sound")

pop II *v.* (P; intr., tr.) we have to ~ into the store for a minute; ~ your head out of the window and see if it's raining; to ~ (a)round the corner; could

you ~ this thermometer in your mouth for me, please?

popular *adj.* 1. ~ as (she was ~ as a nightclub singer) 2. ~ among, with (she was ~ with teenagers) 3. ~ for (she was ~ for her singing)

popularity *n.* 1. to acquire, gain, win ~ 2. to enjoy ~ 3. to lose ~ 4. declining; great; growing, increasing ~ 5. ~ declines, slips; grows, increases 6. ~ among, with; as; for (she enjoyed great ~ with teenagers as a singer)

populated *adj.* 1. densely, heavily; sparsely, thinly ~ 2. by, with (an area densely ~ with both people and wildlife)

population *n.* 1. a decreasing, shrinking; dense; excess, overflow; expanding, growing, increasing, rising; sparse; stable; transient ~ 2. an aging; civilian; foreign-born; indigenous; local; native-born; rural; urban ~ (see also *population control* at **control**; *a population explosion* at **explosion**; *population level(s)* at **level**)

porch *n.* 1. (AE) a back; front ~ (BE uses *veranda*) 2. (AE) a sun ~ (BE has *sun lounge*) 3. (AE) a screened, screened-in ~ (BE uses *veranda*) 4. (BE) a church ~ 5. in, on a ~

pore *v.* (d; intr.) to ~ over ("to examine") (to ~ over a document)

pores *n.* blocked, clogged, closed; open ~

pork *n.* 1. to roast ~ 2. roast ~ 3. a loin; piece, slice of ~

pornography, porn *n.* 1. to peddle ~ 2. explicit, hard-core; soft, soft-core ~

porpoise *n.* 1. a school of ~s 2. a young ~ is a calf 3. a female ~ is a cow 4. a male ~ is a bull

porridge *n.* (esp. BE) 1. to cook, make, prepare ~ 2. a bowl of ~ 3. (misc.) (BE; slang) to do ~ ("to spend time in prison")

port I *n.* ["harbor"] 1. to clear, leave ~ 2. to come into, make, reach ~ ("to arrive at a port") 3. to call at a ~ 4. a fishing; free; home ~ 5. in; into ~ (to put into ~) 6. (misc.) a ~ of call; a ~ of entry; any ~ in a storm! ("(take) whatever help is available in an emergency")

port II *n.* ["type of wine"] ruby; tawny; vintage ~

portfolio *n.* ["a set of shares"] 1. an investment ~ ["area of responsibility of a government minister"] 2. a minister without ~

portion *n.* 1. a generous; individual; small ~ (of) 2. equal ~s (of)

portion out *v.* (B) they ~ed the food out to the needy = they ~ed out the food to the needy

portrait *n.* 1. to do; draw; paint; retouch a ~ 2. to commission a ~ 3. to frame; hang; mount a ~ 4. a composite; family; full-length; group; idealized; realistic, warts-and-all ~ 5. (misc.) to pose for, sit for one's ~

portray *v.* 1. (d; tr.) to ~ as (to ~ smb. as a hero) 2. (J) the artist ~ed them looking out at the sea

pose I *n.* to assume, strike; hold a ~

pose II *v.* 1. (d; intr.) to ~ as ("to pretend to be")

(to ~ as an expert) 2. (D; intr.) to ~ for ("to serve as a model for") (to ~ for an artist) (see also *to ~ a threat to smb.*/*smt.* at **threat**)

posit *v.* (formal) (L) her book ~s that the soul and the spirit are distinct

position I *n.* ["posture"] 1. to assume, take; change a ~ 2. an awkward, uncomfortable; comfortable ~ (standing in an uncomfortable ~) 3. a kneeling; lotus; lying; prone; reclining; sitting; squatting; standing; straddle, straddling; supine; upright ~ 4. the fetal, foetal ~ ["attitude"] 5. to adopt, assume, take a ~ 6. a controversial; extreme, extremist; firm; flexible; hostile; middle-of-the-road, moderate; radical; strong; uncompromising; untenable; weak ~ 7. an official; unofficial ~ 8. a ~ on (to take a ~ on foreign aid) 9. a ~ that + clause (they took the ~ that further aid would be useless) ["site"] ["military site"] 10. to attack, overrun, storm a ~ 11. to consolidate; hold, maintain; occupy, take up; regain a ~ 12. to give up, lose, relinquish, surrender, yield a ~ 13. a defensive; dominant; enemy; favorable; fortified; impregnable; key; powerful, strong; unfortified; untenable, vulnerable, weak ~ ["place"] ["situation"] 14. to occupy, take a ~ 15. to jockey for, maneuver for ~ 16. an embarrassing; ludicrous; unenviable ~ 17. a dominant; enviable; high, leading, pre-eminent; prominent; monopoly; responsible; unique ~ (to occupy a prominent ~) 18. a legal; political; social ~ 19. a ~ to + inf. (we may be in a ~ to help you) 20. from a certain ~ (they negotiated from a ~ of strength) 21. in a ~ (she is in a ~ to know) 22. (misc.) a ~ of power; a ~ of strength; a ~ of weakness ["proper place"] 23. in ~ (the players were in ~) 24. out of ~ ["job"] 25. to create a (new) ~ 26. to apply for, look for, seek a ~ 27. to find, get, land, take; have a ~ 28. to fill a ~ 29. to hold, hold down a ~ 30. to give up, quit; resign from a ~ 31. to lose a ~ 32. a demanding ~ 33. a permanent; temporary ~ 34. a teaching; tenured; tenure-track ~ 35. a government; official ~ 36. a managerial; senior ~ 37. a ~ as; in; with (she holds a responsible ~ as an executive secretary in/with a law firm) ["misc."] 38. "which ~ does he play?" "shortstop"; (as in chess) a drawn; losing; winning ~ (see also *position paper* at **paper**)

position II *v.* 1. (H) they ~ed the bomb to go off when the first car reached the gate 2. (P; refl., tr.) I ~ed myself near the entrance; observers were ~ed along the ridges

positive *adj.* 1. ~ about, of (they were ~ of the outcome) 2. ~ that + clause (they were ~ that their party would win) (see also *test positive* at **test II** *v.*)

possess *v.* (H) what ever ~ed you to do it?

possession *n.* 1. to gain, get, take ~ of (to take ~ of many priceless antiques) 2. to come into ~ of many priceless antiques 3. in ~ of (they are in ~ of many priceless antiques) 4. in smb.'s ~ (they have in their ~ many priceless antiques)

possessions *n.* 1. smb.'s earthly; material; personal ~ 2. smb.'s cherished; priceless; valuable ~ 3. a country's overseas/colonial ~

possibility *n.* 1. to consider, entertain; face; raise a ~ 2. to discount, dismiss, eliminate, exclude, rule out a ~ 3. a distinct, good, real, strong ~ 4. a remote, slim ~ 5. little; no ~ 6. a ~ of (there is a strong ~ of snow but no ~ of sunshine) 7. a ~ that + clause (there's a strong ~ that it will snow) 8. (misc.) within the realm of ~; to reject a ~ out of hand

possible *adj.* 1. easily, perfectly, very; humanly ~ 2. ~ for (anything is ~ for them) 3. ~ to + inf. (it is not ~ for them to predict the future; it is not ~ to control that child) 4. ~ that + clause (it is ~ that we will be able to attend)

possum *n.* (colloq.) to play ~ ("to pretend to be asleep")

post I *n.* ["mail"] 1. (BE) see **mail I** 2. (UK) first-class; free; second-class ~ 3. (CE) parcel ~ 4. (BE) by return of ~ (AE has *by return mail*)

post II *v.* (BE) 1. (A) she ~ed the book to me; or: she ~ed me the book 2. (D; tr.) to ~ from; to (the letter was ~ed from London to Edinburgh) (AE has **mail II**)

post III *n.* ["station"] 1. a command; listening; observation; trading ~ ["place of duty"] ["job, position"] 2. to leave; quit; take (up) a ~ (he left his ~ as CEO of a multinational to take up one with an NGO) 3. at one's ~ (he remained at his ~ until the end; to be asleep at one's ~)

post IV *v.* 1. (esp. BE) (d; tr.) ("to assign") to ~ to (she was ~ed to Berlin) 2. (P; tr.) ("to place, position") they ~ed him at the gate; I was ~ed near the door

post V *n.* ["pole"] 1. a starting ~ (at a horse race) 2. (misc.) from pillar to ~ ("from one situation to another without letup"); (BE) to pip at the ~ ("to overtake and defeat at the very end") (see also **last post**)

postage *n.* 1. to pay the ~ 2. the return ~ 3. ~ due; ~ for; ~ paid 4. (misc.) ~ and packing

postcard *n.* 1. to send a ~ 2. to drop smb. a ~ 3. a picture ~ 4. on a ~

posted *adj.* to keep smb. ~

poster *n.* 1. to mount, put up a ~ 2. to take down a ~ 3. a campaign ~ 4. on a ~

posterior *adj.* (formal) ["after, later"] ~ to

posterity *n.* preserved for ~

postgraduate work *n.* to do ~

posting *n.* (esp. BE) 1. to accept, get; refuse, turn down; take up a ~ 2. a ~ to (she managed to get a ~ to Berlin)

postmaster *n.* the ~ general

postmortem *n.* to do, hold, perform a ~ (on) (to perform a ~ on the murder victim) (also fig.) (to do a ~ on the failed project)

postpone *v.* 1. to ~ indefinitely 2. (D; tr.) to ~ to, until (the concert has been ~d (from Monday) to

Wednesday) 3. (G) they ~d holding the concert because of the weather 4. (misc.) the concert has been ~d (for) two days because of the weather

postscript *n.* 1. to add a ~ 2. a ~ to

postulate I *n.* (formal) a ~ that + clause (their ~ that the collision had been caused by fog proved to be true)

postulate II *v.* (formal) (L) they ~d that the collision had been caused by fog

posture I *n.* 1. to adopt, assume; maintain a ~ 2. a bad; erect, upright; good; slouching ~ 3. a defense; political ~

posture II *v.* (D; intr.) ("to pretend") to ~ as

pot I *n.* 1. (fig.) a melting ~ 2. a pepper ~ (BE; AE has *pepper shaker*) 3. a chamber ~ 4. a coffeepot; teapot (is there any more coffee in the coffeepot?) 5. (misc.) to scour (the) ~s and pans; to go to ~ ("to be ruined")

pot II *n.* (colloq.) ["marijuana"] to smoke ~

potato *n.* 1. to bake; boil; fry; mash; peel; roast; sauté ~es 2. a baked, jacket (esp. BE) ~ 3. a baking; sweet ~ 4. chipped (BE), French-fried (AE); scalloped ~es 5. mashed ~es, mashed ~ (esp. BE) 6. (misc.) a couch ~ (who sits around all the time watching TV)

potential *n.* 1. to develop; realize, reach one's (full) ~ 2. to have (great) ~ 3. a ~ as; for (to reach one's full ~ as a musician; to have the ~ for true greatness) 4. ~ to + inf. (to have the ~ to achieve true greatness)

potion *n.* a love; magic; sleeping ~

potluck *n.* ["whatever is offered (esp. to eat)"] to take ~

potshot *n.* (colloq.) ["critical remark"] to take a ~ at

potter *v.* (BE; AE has *putter*) 1. (d; intr.) to ~ about (to ~ about the house) 2. (misc.) he loves ~ing about in his garden

pottery *n.* to glaze ~

potty *adj.* (colloq.) (esp. BE) ["crazy"] ~ about

pouch *n.* 1. an ammunition; tobacco ~ 2. (a) diplomatic ~ (the top-secret letter was sent by diplomatic ~) (AE; BE has *diplomatic bag*)

poultice *n.* to apply a ~ (to)

pounce *v.* (d; intr.) to ~ on, upon (the cat ~d on the mouse)

pound I *n.* ["enclosure"] a dog ~

pound II *v.* 1. (d; intr.) to ~ against, at (to ~ at the door; the enemy's artillery was ~ing (away) at our positions) 2. (d; tr.) to ~ into (I've been trying to ~ some facts into their heads) 3. (d; intr.) to ~ on (to ~ on a table)

pound III *n.* 1. a ~ sterling 2. a falling; rising; strong; weak ~ (the international markets experienced difficulties with the falling ~) 3. (misc.) the dollar was strong against the ~ (see also *pound sign* at **sign I** *n.*)

pour *v.* 1. (C) she ~ed (out) a cool drink for me; or: she ~ed me (out) a cool drink 2. (d; intr.) to ~ down (tears ~ed down her cheeks) 3. (d; intr., tr.) to ~ from (blood ~ed (out) from the gaping wound; she

~ed (out) the solution from the large flask into the even larger one = she ~ed the solution (out) from the large flask into the even larger one) 4. (d; intr., tr.) to ~ into (water ~ed (out) into the pit) 5. (d; intr., tr.) to ~ out of (blood ~ed out of the gaping wound; the water ~ed out of the tank into the street; the spectators ~ed out of the stadium onto the parking lot) 6. (d; tr.) to ~ over (to ~ gravy over meat) (see also *pour out one's heart to smb.* at **heart**)

pout *v.* (D; intr.) to ~ about, at

poverty *n.* 1. to breed ~ (illiteracy breeds ~) 2. to alleviate; eliminate, eradicate, wipe out ~ 3. abject, dire, extreme, grinding, severe ~ 4. ~ of (his work exhibits a certain ~ of invention) 5. in ~ (to live in grinding ~)

poverty line *n.* above; below the ~ (many people live below the ~)

powder *n.* 1. to put on ~ 2. baby; dusting; face; talcum ~ 3. baking; curry; garlic ~ 4. bleaching; scouring ~ 5. tooth ~ 6. gunpowder; smokeless ~ 7. (misc.) (slang) to take a ~ ("to run off unexpectedly"); (colloq.) to keep one's ~ dry ("to remain calm")

power *n.* ["authority"] 1. to assume, gain, take; concentrate, consolidate; exercise, have, hold, wield; share ~ 2. to abuse; seize usurp ~ 3. to delegate; give up, relinquish; lose; transfer ~ 4. emergency; executive; political ~ 5. discretionary ~s 6. ~ over (they seized ~ over several provinces) 7. the ~ to + inf. (the prime minister has the ~ to dissolve parliament) 8. in; into; out of ~ (the government in ~; to come into ~ and go out of ~ again) 9. (misc.) the ~ behind the throne; the corridors of ~ (where the real decisions are made); does ~ really rest with/reside in the people? ["dominance"] 10. the balance of ~ (see also **balance of power**) 11. to have smb. in one's ~ 12. absolute ~ 13. ~ corrupts ("Power tends to corrupt and absolute ~ corrupts absolutely." – Lord Acton, 1834–1902) ["nation"] 14. the great, world ~s; a superpower 15. (the) warring ~s 16. a colonial; foreign; industrial; occupying ~ ["capability"] 17. to develop one's ~s (of observation) 18. bargaining; earning; purchasing ~ 19. curative, healing; recuperative ~s 20. psychic; supernatural ~s 21. in, within smb.'s ~ (I tried to do everything in my ~ for her but unfortunately it was not within my ~ to help) (see also **staying power**) ["military force, police force"] 22. air; military; naval, sea; police ~ 23. fire ~ ["source of energy"] 24. to provide ~ for; turn on the ~ 25. to cut off, turn off the ~ 26. to consume; lose; waste ~ 27. to conserve ~ 28. to harness ~ (to harness solar ~) 29. atomic, nuclear; electric; geothermal; hydroelectric; kinetic; renewable; solar; steam; water; wind ~ 30. sources of ~ 31. (misc.) (AE) a ~ outage ("failure") ["motive force"] 32. under one's own ~ ["exponent"] (math.) 33. to raise to a ~ (to raise five to the third ~ and get 125) (see also *power dressing* at **dressing**; *power walking* at **walking**)

powerless *adj.* ~ to + inf. (I tried to do everything in my power for her but unfortunately I was ~ to help)

power of attorney *n.* 1. to give, grant a ~ 2. to notarize a ~ 3. to hold a ~ 4. a ~ to + inf. (we had a ~ to conduct her business)

powwow *n.* (colloq.) ["conference"] to hold a ~ (with)

pox *n.* ["plague"] a ~ on

practicable *adj.* ["feasible"] ~ to + inf. (it was not ~ to put up a new building there)

practical *adj.* ["realistic"] 1. ~ about; in ["sensible"] 2. ~ to + inf. (it is not ~ to live in one city and work in another)

practice I practise *n.* ["habit"] 1. to make a ~ of smt. 2. a common, normal, standard, usual ~ 3. a local; universal, widespread ~ 4. a ~ to + inf. (it was her ~ to drink a glass of wine every evening) ["exercise"] 5. to get; have; need ~ (we have ~ today at four o'clock) 6. target ~ 7. ~ at, in (~ at tying knots) 8. the ~ to + inf. (I've had enough ~ to pass the test) 9. in; out of; with ~ (since they closed the gym, I've been out of ~ but I hope to improve with more ~) ["professional activity"] 10. to have one's own; join; leave, resign from; start a ~ 11. (a) law, legal; medical; nursing; professional ~ (she joined their legal ~ and became a partner before leaving that ~ to start one of her own) 12. (of doctors) (a) family, general ~ 13. (of doctors) (a) group; private ~ (they went into private ~) 14. a lucrative ~ ["application"] 15. in; into ~ (to put a theory into ~; in theory and in ~) ["method of conducting business"] 16. best ~ (adopt/generalize best ~ throughout the whole industry) 17. sharp, unethical, unfair, unscrupulous ~s 18. (esp. AE) fair-trade ~s USAGE NOTE: In Great Britain, *private practice* refers to a practice that is not under the National Health Service.

practice II practise *v.* 1. (d; intr.) ("to work") to ~ as (to ~ as a lawyer) 2. (D; intr.) ("to train") to ~ at; for (to ~ at batting the ball for the major-league try-outs) 3. (D; intr.) to ~ on (you can ~ mouth-to-mouth resuscitation on me) 4. (G) the boy ~d batting the ball

practitioner *n.* a family, general; nurse; private ~

prairie *n.* 1. a rolling; treeless; windswept ~ 2. across; on the ~

praise I *n.* 1. to earn, merit; get, receive, win ~ 2. to bestow, heap, lavish ~ on smb. 3. to give ~ to smb. 4. to sing smb.'s ~s 5. faint; fulsome, unctuous; glowing, high, lavish, strong, unrestrained, unstinting; universal ~ 6. ~ as; from; for (she got ~ for her work from everyone; she got ~ from everyone as an outstanding worker) 7. beyond ~ (are Shakespeare's plays so good as to be beyond ~?) 8. in ~ of 9. (misc.) a chorus; paean of ~

praise II *v.* 1. to ~ highly, strongly, to the skies 2. (D; tr.) to ~ as; for (everyone ~ed her for her work; everyone ~ed her work as outstanding; everyone ~d her as an outstanding worker)

praiseworthy *adj.* (formal) ~ to + inf. (it is ~ to do volunteer work)

pram *n.* (BE) 1. to push, wheel a ~ (AE has *baby carriage, carriage*) 2. in a ~

prance *v.* (P; intr.) to ~ around the room

prank *n.* 1. to play a ~ on smb. 2. a childish; cruel, mean, wanton; foolish; harmless; innocent; mischievous ~

prate see **prattle**

pratfall *n.* ["an embarrassing failure"] to take a ~

prattle *v.* 1. to ~ endlessly 2. (D; intr.) to ~ (on) about (he ~d on endlessly about his operation)

pray *v.* 1. to ~ aloud; devoutly, fervently; silently 2. (D; intr.) to ~ for; to (she ~ to God for pardon for her transgressions) 3. (E) she ~ed (to God) to be pardoned for her transgressions 4. (H) she ~ed God to be pardoned for her transgressions 5. (L; to) she ~ed (to God) that she would be pardoned for her transgressions 6. (L; may have an object) she ~ed (God) that she would be pardoned for her transgressions 7. (misc.) we hope and ~ that she will be forgiven (see also *pray tell* at **tell II** *v.*)

prayer *n.* 1. to chant; offer; say; utter a ~ 2. to answer; hear a ~ 3. a devout, fervent, solemn ~ 4. a silent ~ 5. (a) communal; daily; evening; morning ~ 6. a ~ for, of (she offered a ~ to God) for pardon for her transgressions; a ~ of repentance) 7. a ~ that + clause; subj. (she offered a prayer (to God) that she be/would be pardoned for her transgressions) 8. in ~ (the group was deep in ~ when we entered) 9. (misc.) the answer to all our ~s (see also *prayer meeting* at **meeting**)

preach *v.* 1. (D; intr.) to ~ about (he's always ~ing (to us) about one thing or another) 2. (D; intr.) to ~ against (to ~ against sin) 3. (colloq.) (D; intr.) to ~ at (stop ~ing at me!) 4. (D; intr.) to ~ to (to ~ to one's congregation) 5. (L; to) to ~ (to us) that the end of the world is near 6. (misc.) to ~ to the converted

preacher *n.* an itinerant; lay ~

preamble *n.* a ~ to

precaution *n.* 1. to take ~s 2. elaborate ~s 3. a wise ~ (you should take the wise ~ of consulting a lawyer) 4. health; safety; security ~s 5. a ~ against 6. a ~ to + inf. (it would be a wise ~ (for you) to consult a lawyer) 7. as a ~ (it would be wise (for you) to consult a lawyer just as a precaution)

precedence *n.* 1. to have, take ~ over 2. to give ~ to

precedent *n.* 1. to create, establish, set a ~ 2. to cite a ~ 3. to break (a) ~ 4. a dangerous ~ 5. a ~ for 6. without ~

precept *n.* a ~ that + clause (we adhere to the ~ that all criminals can be rehabilitated)

preceptor *n.* a ~ to

precinct *n.* a pedestrian (BE); police (AE); shopping (BE); voting ~

precious *adj.* ~ to

precipitate *v.* (d; tr.) to ~ into (to ~ a country into war)

precipitation *n.* heavy; light ~
precise *adj.* ~ about; in
precision *n.* 1. great, utmost; military; surgical; unerring, unfailing ~ 2. ~ in (unfailing ~ in handling the instruments is required for this task) 3. with ~ (it must be done with the utmost ~)
preclude *v.* (formal) 1. (d; tr.) to ~ from (that will ~ us from having to do it again) 2. (K) that will ~ our having to do it again
precondition *n.* to set ~s (for)
precursor *n.* a ~ of, to
predecessor *n.* smb.'s immediate ~
predestine *v.* 1. (d; tr.) to ~ for (fate ~d her for greatness) 2. (H) fate ~d her to go far in life
predestined *adj.* (cannot stand alone) 1. ~ for, to (~ for greatness; ~ to glory) 2. ~ to + inf. (she was ~ to go far in life) 3. ~ that + clause (it was ~ that she was to go far in life)
predicament *n.* 1. an awkward; dire ~ (to get into an awkward ~) 2. in a ~
predicate *v.* (d; tr.) ("to base") to ~ on, upon (to ~ a theory on certain facts)
predict *v.* 1. (K) nobody could have ~ed his running away 2. (L) nobody could have ~ed that he would run away 3. (Q) who can ~ from the available evidence how the elections will turn out?
predictable *adj.* ~ that + clause (it was ~ that their party would win the election)
prediction *n.* 1. to make a ~ 2. a dire, gloomy, unfavorable ~ 3. a favorable ~ 4. a ~ that + clause (she made a ~ that their party would win the election) 5. a ~ comes true
predilection *n.* a ~ for
predispose *v.* (formal) 1. (d; tr.) to ~ to (what ~d them to violent behavior?) 2. (H) what ~d them to behave violently?
predisposed *adj.* (cannot stand alone) 1. ~ to (~ to violent behavior) 2. ~ to + inf. (~ to behave violently)
predisposition *n.* 1. a ~ to, towards (a ~ to violent behavior) 2. a ~ to + inf. (a ~ to behave violently)
predominance *n.* 1. ~ in 2. ~ over (their ~ over everyone else in the arts and sciences)
predominant *adj.* 1. ~ in 2. ~ over (they're ~ over everyone else in the arts and sciences)
predominate I *adj.* ~ over
predominate II *v.* 1. (D; intr.) ~ in 2. (D; intr.) ~ over (they ~ over everyone else in the arts and sciences)
preeminence *n.* 1. to achieve, win ~ 2. ~as (she achieved ~ as a painter) 3. ~ in (their ~ in the arts and sciences)
preeminent *adj.* 1. ~ as (she was ~ as a painter) 2. ~ in (they're ~ in the arts and sciences)
preen *v.* (formal) (d; refl.) to ~ oneself on ("to pride oneself on") (she ~ed herself on her preeminence as a painter)
preface I *n.* a ~ to (a ~ to a book)
preface II *v.* (d; tr.) to ~ by; with (she ~d her

remarks with a personal anecdote = she ~d her remarks by telling a personal anecdote)
prefer *v.* 1. (D; tr.) ("to bring") to ~ against (to ~ charges against smb.) 2. (D; tr.) to ~ to (she ~s fish to meat) 3. (E) we ~ to remain at home 4. (G) we ~ remaining at home 5. (H; no passive) I'd ~ you to remain at home (esp. BE); I'd ~ for you to remain at home (AE) = what I'd ~ is for you to remain at home = I'd ~ it if you remained at home 6. (K) I would ~ your remaining at home 7. (L; subj.) I ~ that you not go out/should not go out/don't go out (esp. BE) 8. (M) I ~ my coffee to be hot 9. (N) I ~ my coffee hot 10. (misc.) we (very) much ~ remaining at home and not going out; remaining at home is (very) much to be ~red to/over going out USAGE NOTE: This verb can be used in several ways to express preference – I prefer walking to riding; I prefer to walk rather than (to) ride; I prefer not to ride.
preferable *adj.* 1. ~ to (remaining at home is ~ to going out) 2. ~ to + inf. (it is ~ to remain at home) 3. ~ that + clause; subj. (it is ~ that you not go out/should not go out/don't go out (esp. BE)) 4. (misc.) remaining at home is far ~ to going out USAGE NOTE: This adjective can be used in several ways – walking is preferable to riding; it's preferable to walk rather than (to) ride; it's preferable not to ride.
preference *n.* 1. to give ~ to (they gave ~ to veterans over non-veterans) 2. to demonstrate, display, show; express; have a ~ 3. a decided; individual, personal; marked; strong ~ 4. (US) (a) veterans' ~ 5. a ~ for (she showed a decided ~ for classical music over pop music) 6. in ~ to (she listened to classical music in ~ to pop music)
prefix *v.* (d; tr.) to ~ to (to ~ a title to a name)
pregnancy *n.* 1. to terminate a ~ 2. an ectopic; false; full-term; normal; teenage ~ 3. all through, throughout; during, in a ~
pregnant *a.* 1. to become, fall (BE), get ~ 2. heavily, very 3. ~ by (she got ~ by her husband before he was sent to the front) 4. ~ with (at that time she was six months ~ with her first child)
prejudice I *n.* ["bias"] 1. to arouse, stir up ~ (against, towards) (to stir up ~ among poor people against immigrants) 2. to have, hold (a) ~ 3. to display, show ~ (towards) 4. to break down, eliminate; confirm; strengthen ~ 5. (a) blind, deep, deep-rooted, deep-seated, ingrained, strong; vulgar ~ 6. race, racial; religious ~ 7. ~ against, towards; among ["harm"] 8. without ~ (to) (without ~ to our claims)
prejudice II *v.* 1. to ~ strongly 2. (D; tr.) to ~ against (to be strongly ~d against immigrants) 3. (misc.) her reputation for honesty ~d me strongly in her favor
prejudicial *adj.* ~ to
preliminary I *adj.* ~ to
preliminary II *n.* a ~ to
prelude *n.* a ~ to

premature adj. 1. ~ in (they were ~ in their celebrations) 2. ~ to + inf. (it was ~ (for them) to celebrate)

premiere, première n. 1. to give, have, hold, perform, stage a ~ 2. to attend a ~ 3. a film; lavish; UK; world ~

premise n. ["proposition"] (logic) 1. the major; minor ~ ["assumption"] 2. the ~ that + clause (their ~ that unemployment would rise proved to be true)

premised adj. ~ on, upon (their fiscal policy was ~ on the assumption of rising unemployment)

premises n. ["property"] on the ~ (to be consumed on the ~)

premiss n. (BE) (see **premise** 1)

premium n. ["high value"] 1. to place, put a (high) ~ on (she puts a high ~ on punctuality) ["additional sum or value"] 2. to pay a ~ (of) 3. at a ~ (to sell at a ~) ["fee paid to an insurance company"] 4. an insurance ~ 5. a ~ on a policy (I pay the ~ on my policy every six months whether the ~ rises or falls)

premonition n. 1. to have a ~ 2. a ~ that + clause (she had a ~ that an accident would happen)

preoccupation n. a ~ with

preoccupied adj. ~ with

preordained adj. 1. ~ to + inf. (they were ~ to meet) 2. ~ that + clause; subj. (it was ~ that they meet/should meet/would meet)

preparation n. in ~ for (we are resting in ~ for the strenuous journey)

preparations n. 1. to make ~ 2. careful, elaborate, thorough ~ 3. ~ for

preparatory adj. ~ to

prepare v. 1. to ~ carefully, thoroughly 2. (C) I'll ~ a nice supper for you; or: I'll ~ you a nice supper 3. (D; intr., refl., tr.) to ~ for (she was ~ing for the examination; they ~d themselves for unpleasant news; she is ~ing a paper for presentation at the national meeting; "if you want peace, ~ for war" – proverb) 4. (E) they were ~ing to leave 5. (H) parents should ~ children to cope with life

prepared adj. 1. ~ for (they were ~ for their departure; I am not ~ for such a responsibility) 2. ~ to + inf. (they were ~ to leave; I am not ~ to take on such a responsibility) USAGE NOTE: The sentence "I am not prepared to take on such a responsibility" is ambiguous. It can mean 'I am not ready to take on such a responsibility = I am unprepared for such a responsibility' or 'I am not willing to take on such a responsibility = I am unwilling to take on such a responsibility.'

preparedness n. 1. military ~ 2. ~ for 3. (misc.) a state of ~ (for)

preposition n. 1. a compound; simple ~ 2. (misc.) a preposition-noun-preposition combination such as "in readiness for."

preposterous adj. 1. ~ to + inf. (it's ~ to have to show our pass each time we come here!) 2. ~ that + clause (it's ~ that we have to show our pass each time we come here!)

prequel n. (colloq.) a ~ to (Henry IV, Part 1 is the ~ to Henry IV, Part 2)

prerequisite I adj. (usu. does not stand alone) ~ to

prerequisite II n. a ~ for, to (Sociology 101 is a ~ for Sociology 102)

prerogative n. 1. to exercise one's ~ 2. the exclusive; royal ~ 3. smb.'s ~ to + inf. (it's our ~ to order an investigation)

prescribe v. 1. (D; tr.) to ~ for (to ~ a remedy for the common cold) 2. (formal) (L; subj.) regulations ~ that a lawyer draw up/should draw up/draws up (esp. BE) the papers 3. (Q) the court ~d how the papers should be drawn up

prescription n. 1. to fill (AE), make up a ~ 2. a free; NHS ~ (are you entitled to a free NHS ~?) 3. a ~ for (a ~ for a remedy for the common cold) 4. by ~; on (a) ~ (to obtain a drug on (a) doctor's ~; by ~ only)

presence n. 1. to make one's ~ felt, known ("to make others notice one's presence") 2. a commanding ~ 3. a police ~ (there was a strong police ~ at the demonstration) 4. in smb.'s ~ (don't do that in the ~ of royalty)

presence of mind n. 1. to display; show (great) ~ 2. the ~ to + inf. (she had the ~ to call the police)

present I n. ["present time"] 1. at ~ 2. for the ~ ["present tense of a verb"] 3. in the ~

present II n. ["gift"] 1. to give smb. a ~ 2. to unwrap; wrap a ~ 3. to make smb. a ~ of smt. 4. an anniversary; birthday; Christmas; graduation; wedding ~ 5. a ~ for

present III v. 1. (B) ("to give") they ~ed an award to her 2. (d; tr.) ("to introduce") to ~ as (she was ~ed as a computer expert) 3. (D; tr.) ("to introduce") to ~ to (the new employees were ~ed to the rest of the staff) 4. (d; tr.) to ~ with ("to give a gift to") (they ~ed her with an award) 5. (d; tr.) to ~ with (med.) (the patient ~ed with ("complained of") severe pains)

presentable adj. to make oneself ~

presentation n. ["position of a fetus"] (med.) 1. a breech; face ~ ["act of presenting"] 2. to deliver, make a ~ (who will make the ~ at the awards ceremony?) ["report"] 3. to give a ~ 4. an oral; written ~ 5. a ~ of, on (she gave an oral ~ of/on her current research)

presenter n. (BE) a chat-show; game-show ~

presentiment n. (formal) ["foreboding"] 1. to have a ~ 2. a ~ that + clause (she had a ~ that an accident would happen)

preservative n. 1. a food ~ 2. an artificial ~

preserve I n. 1. a forest; game, wild-life ~ 2. (BE) see **preserves**

preserve II v. 1. (D; tr.) to ~ against, from (to ~ the environment from the ravages of pollution) 2. (D; tr.) to ~ for (we wish to ~ this tradition for our grandchildren)

preserver n. a life ~ USAGE NOTE: Especially in AE, *life preserver* means "life belt", "life jacket"; in BE, it means "club used for self-defence".

preserves *n.* ["fruit preserved by cooking with sugar"] 1. to spread ~ (on bread) = to spread (bread) with ~ 2. apricot; blackberry, blueberry; cherry; gooseberry; grape; peach; plum; quince; (red) raspberry; strawberry ~

preside *v.* (D; intr.) to ~ at; over

presidency *n.* 1. to gain the ~ 2. to assume the ~ 3. a rotating ~ 4. during, under a ~ (under Britain's ~ of the EU)

president *n.* 1. to elect; inaugurate a ~ 2. a vice ~ 3. a college (esp AE); former, past; incoming; incumbent; outgoing ~ 4. an ex-president 5. a ~ elect 6. (misc.) what do you think of that, Mister / Madam President?

press I *n.* ["instrument for crushing, shaping, squeezing"] 1. a cider; cookie (AE); hydraulic; wine ~ ["publishing house"] 2. a university; vanity ~ ["device for printing"] 3. a printing ~ 4. the ~es roll 5. (misc.) to go to ~; hot off the ~; stop the ~es! 6. in ~ (our book is now in ~) ["newspapers, magazines"] ["reporters"] 7. to censor; control; muzzle the ~ 8. a free ~ 9. the foreign; gutter, yellow; local; popular; tabloid ~ (see also *press clipping* at **clipping**; *press cutting* at **cutting**; *press release* at **release I** *n.*) ["publicity"] 10. a bad; good ~ (we got a bad ~) ["smoothness of a fabric"] 11. (a) permanent ~ ["aggressive defense used in basketball"] 12. a full-court ~ ["type of lift used by weight lifters"] 13. to do a ~ 14. a bench; military ~

press II *v.* 1. to ~ hard (see also **hard-pressed**) 2. (d; intr., tr.) ("to push") to ~ against (to ~ against a door) 3. (d; intr., tr.) to ~ for ("to urge") (to ~ for tax reform; to ~ the authorities for information) 4. (D; tr.) ("to shape") to ~ into (to ~ clay into various forms) 5. (d; tr.) ("to place") to ~ into (to ~ all equipment into service) 6. (D; intr.) ("to squeeze") to ~ on (to ~ on a button) 7. (H) ("to urge") to ~ the authorities to give them information; they were ~ing me to agree to the compromise 8. (P; intr.) ("to push") the crowd ~ed around the candidate; the fans ~ed into the stadium

press on *v.* 1. to ~ regardless; relentlessly 2. (D; intr.) to ~ to (the troops ~ed on to the next town) 3. (D; intr.) to ~ with (the police ~ed on with the investigation)

press-up *n.* (BE) to do ~s (see also **push-up**)

pressure I *n.* 1. to exert, place, put ~ on smb. 2. to bring ~ to bear on smb. 3. to keep up, maintain the ~ on 4. to build up, increase (the) ~ 5. to feel (the) ~ 6. to bear up under, withstand (the) ~ 7. to ease, relieve (the) ~ 8. to face; resist (the) ~ (to resist ~ from extremist groups) 9. enormous, great, heavy, inexorable, intense, maximum, relentless, severe, strong, unrelieved ~ 10. firm; light ~ 11. financial; outside; parental; peer; population; public ~ (to resist public ~) 12. air; oil; water ~ (see also **blood pressure**) 13. (esp. meteorology) atmospheric; barometric ~ 14. high; low ~ 15. ~ builds up, increases, rises 16. ~ eases, falls 17. ~ for (~ for tax reform) 18. ~ from (to face inexorable ~ from the media) 19. ~ on (there is ~ on the authorities for tax reform) 20. ~ to + inf. (they are putting ~ on the authorities to reform taxation) 21. under ~ (the authorities are under relentless ~ for tax reform / to reform taxation)

pressure II *v.* (AE) 1. (D; tr.) to ~ into (the authorities were ~d into tax reform) 2. (H) the authorities were ~d to reform taxation

pressurize *v.* (BE) see **pressure II**

prestige *n.* 1. to enjoy, have ~ 2. to gain ~ 3. to damage smb.'s ~ 4. great, high; little, low ~ 5. the ~ to + inf. (does she have enough ~ to get the party nomination?) 6. of ~ (of little ~)

presume *v.* 1. (d; intr.) to ~ on, upon (to ~ upon smb.'s good nature) 2. (E) I will not ~ to give you advice 3. (L) we must ~ that she is innocent 4. (M) we must ~ her to be innocent 5. (N; used with an adjective) we must ~ her innocent; she must be ~d innocent until proven guilty

presumption *n.* 1. a ~ of (our decision was based on the ~ of her innocence until she is proven guilty) 2. a ~ that + clause (our decision was based on the ~ that she is innocent until proven guilty)

presumptuous *adj.* ~ to + inf. (it's ~ of / for me to give you advice)

presuppose *v.* (L) we ~ that she is innocent until proven guilty

presupposition *n.* a ~ that + clause (our decision was based on the ~ that she is innocent until proven guilty)

pretence see **pretense**

pretend *v.* 1. (d; intr.) ("to claim") to ~ to (to ~ to expert knowledge in a field) 2. (E) ("to feign"); ("to make believe") she ~ed not to notice; I ~ed to be busy; the children ~ed to be cowboys 3. (L; to) ("to feign"); ("to make believe") she ~ed she hadn't noticed; I ~ed I was busy; the children ~ed (to their parents) that they were cowboys

pretender *n.* a ~ to (a ~ to a throne)

pretense, pretence *n.* ["simulation"] ["false show"] 1. to make a ~ (he made no ~ of being objective) 2. to see through smb.'s ~ 3. under a ~ (under the ~ of patriotism; under false ~s) 4. without ~ (a person totally without ~) ["unsupported claim"] 5. to see through smb.'s ~ 6. a ~ that + clause (he saw through the ~ that lower taxes would cause unemployment) ["appearance"] 7. to keep up, maintain a ~ (to maintain some ~ of legality) ["attempt"] 8. a ~ at; of (without any ~ of being objective)

pretentious *adj.* ~ to + inf. (it was ~ of / for them to put on a tuxedo even when they were dining alone)

pretext *n.* 1. to find a ~ for 2. a flimsy; mere ~ 3. a ~ to + inf. (it was a ~ to occupy more territory) 4. a ~ that + clause (she refused to attend on the ~ that she would be out of town) 5. at, on, under a ~ (he would call for help at / on the slightest ~; under what ~ did she refuse to attend?) 6. (misc.) they start quarreling at the slightest ~

pretty *adj.* 1. to be sitting ~ ("to be well off or in a good position") 2. (misc.) as ~ as a picture

prevail *v.* 1. (D; intr.) to ~ against, over (to ~ against overwhelming odds) 2. (d; intr.) to ~ on, upon smb. to do smt. (they ~ed on me to buy a new television set)

prevent *v.* 1. (D; tr.) to ~ from (nothing can ~ this disease from spreading; you cannot ~ Romeo and Juliet from getting married) 2. (J) (BE) nothing can ~ this disease spreading; you cannot ~ Romeo and Juliet getting married 3. (K) you cannot ~ their getting married

prevention *n.* 1. (health care) primary; secondary ~ 2. accident; crime; disease; fire ~ 3. (misc.) "~ is better than cure = an ounce of ~ is worth a pound of cure" – *proverb*

preview *n.* 1. to give a ~ 2. a sneak ~ (of a film)

prey I *n.* 1. to stalk one's ~ 2. to fall ~ to (they fell ~ to a swindler) 3. easy ~ 4. ~ for; to (they were easy ~ for a swindler) (see also *bird of prey* at **bird**)

prey II *v.* (d; intr.) to ~ on (to ~ on small game; swindlers ~ on gullible people)

price I *n.* 1. to fix, set a ~ 2. to place, put a ~ on 3. to quote a ~ 4. (BE) to agree a ~ 5. to drive up; hike (AE; colloq.), increase, mark up, raise ~s 6. to curb, hold down, keep down; freeze; maintain, stabilize ~s 7. to bring down, drive down ~s (the latest news brought down oil ~s) 8. to cut, lower, mark down, reduce, roll back, slash ~s 9. to undercut (smb.'s) ~s 10. to bring, command, fetch, get a ~ (icons bring a high ~) 11. an attractive, fair, moderate, popular, reasonable ~ 12. a bargain, low, reduced ~ 13. an exorbitant, high, inflated, outrageous, prohibitive, steep, stiff ~ 14. an asking; buying, purchase; cost; discount; going; list; market; reduced, knock-down; regular; resale; retail; sale; selling; unit; wholesale ~ (to sell smt. at or below (the) list ~) 15. an admission ~ = the ~ of admission 16. (at an auction) a reserve (esp. BE), upset (esp. AE) ~ 17. ~s drop, fall, go down, plummet, slump 18. ~s go up, rise, shoot up, skyrocket, soar; range, vary 19. a ~ for (to pay an exorbitant ~ for smt.) 20. a ~ on 21. at a ~ (to sell merchandise at reduced ~s; you can have anything you want – at a ~!) 22. (misc.) what ~ an economic recovery now? (BE) ("what are the chances of an economic recovery now?"); what ~ glory if you die in the trenches? (BE) ("what is the good of glory if you die in the trenches?"); to put a ~ on smb.'s head ("to post a reward for apprehending or killing smb."); they paid a heavy ~ for their freedom; "eternal vigilance is the ~ of liberty" – *proverb*; eternal vigilance is a small ~ to pay for liberty!

price II *v.* 1. (D; tr.) to ~ at (they ~d it at five hundred dollars) 2. (D; refl., tr.) to ~ out of (they ~d themselves out of the market) 3. (N) they ~d it too high 4. (misc.) attractively, competitively ~d

prick I *n.* a pin-prick

prick II *v.* (D; refl., tr.) to ~ on (to ~ one's finger on a thorn)

pride I *n.* 1. to take ~ in (he takes ~ in his children) 2. to hurt smb.'s ~ 3. civic; community; ethnic; fierce, great, strong; hurt, injured, wounded; justified, proper ~ (she took great but proper ~ in her preeminence as a painter) 4. the ~ to + inf. (do they have enough ~ to defend their principles?) 5. out of ~ (he refused out of ~) 6. (misc.) to appeal to smb.'s ~; to burst with ~; to dent smb.'s ~; to pocket, swallow one's ~; to swell with ~; a feeling/glow/sense of ~; a blow to smb.'s ~

pride II *v.* (d; refl.) to ~ on (she ~ed herself on her preeminence as a painter)

priest *n.* 1. to ordain a ~ 2. to defrock, unfrock a ~ 3. an Anglican; Catholic; Episcopalian; Hindu; Mormon; Orthodox ~ 4. a high; local, parish (abbreviated PP by Roman Catholics) ~

priesthood *n.* to enter; leave the ~

primacy *n.* ~ over

primary *n.* ["intra-party election"] (esp. US) 1. to hold a ~ 2. a closed; direct; open; preferential; presidential; runoff ~

prime *n.* 1. to come into, reach one's ~ 2. to pass one's ~ 3. in one's ~ 4. (misc.) past one's ~; to be cut down in one's ~

primed *adj.* 1. ~ for (~ for the big game) 2. ~ to + inf. (we are ~ to play the big game)

prince *n.* 1. a crown ~ 2. (misc.) a ~ consort; regent USAGE NOTES: (1) The British Crown Prince is the Prince of Wales. (2) In Britain the title Prince Consort is in the gift of Parliament. It was bestowed on HRH the Prince Albert, husband to Queen Victoria; but it has not yet been bestowed on HRH the Prince Philip, husband to the present Queen.

princess *n.* 1. a crown ~ 2. a ~ royal USAGE NOTE: In Britain the title Princess Royal is in the gift of the Sovereign. It has been bestowed on HRH the Princess Anne, the eldest (and only) daughter of the present Queen.

principal *n.* ["an official"] 1. a school ~ ["money invested"] 2. to repay the ~ as well as the interest

principle *n.* 1. to establish, formulate, lay down a ~ 2. to apply a ~ 3. to adhere to, stick to (a) ~ 4. to betray, compromise one's ~s 5. an abstract; basic, fundamental; general; guiding; moral; sound; strict; underlying ~ 6. high ~s 7. a ~ applies; underlies (which ~s apply here?) 8. the ~ behind (the underlying ~ behind our decision is that everyone should be treated fairly) 9. the ~ that + clause (we adhere to the underlying ~ that everyone should be treated fairly) 10. against smb.'s ~s 11. in ~ (to agree in ~) 12. on ~ (to disagree on ~; on ~, I am opposed to the decision) 13. (misc.) a matter, question; person of ~; we make it a ~ to treat everyone fairly

print I *n.* ["photograph"] 1. to develop; make a ~ ["printed state"] 2. in ~; out of ~ (I have not seen the story in ~; the book is out of ~) (see also *print media* at **media**) ["text as of a contract"] 3. the fine, small ~ (people should always read the fine ~) ["printed letters"] 4. clear; fine; large; small ~ ["impression made by type"] 5. dark; light ~ (see also **fingerprints; footprints**)

print II *v.* to ~ smt. in block capitals (BE); in block letter(s) (BE); (in) boldface; in italics; in Roman

printer *n.* ["device for printing computer data"] a daisy-wheel; dot-matrix; laser; letter-quality; serial; thermal ~

printing *n.* 1. to put out a ~ (of a book) 2. offset ~ 3. (misc.) the book went through three ~s

print out *v.* (C) she ~ed me out a copy; or: she ~ed out a copy for me; or: she ~ed a copy out for me

prior *adj.* (cannot stand alone) ~ to (it happened subsequent to World War I but ~ to World War II)

priority *n.* 1. to establish, set a ~ 2. to have, take ~ over 3. to give ~ to 4. high; low ~ 5. (a) first, number-one, top ~ 6. (misc.) to re-examine, re-think; reorder, sort out one's (order of) ~ties

prise, prize (BE) see **pry** 2, 3

prise off, prize off (BE) see **pry off**

prison *n.* 1. to go, be sent, be sentenced to ~ 2. to keep smb. in ~ 3. to serve/spend time in ~ 4. to release smb. from ~ 5. to be released from ~ 6. to break out of, escape from ~ 7. a maximum-security, minimum-security; open (BE) ~

prisoner *n.* 1. to take smb. ~; to take a ~ (we took many ~s and took them all ~) 2. to hold, keep smb. ~ (we held them all ~) 3. to free, release a ~ 4. a political ~ 5. a ~ escapes 6. (misc.) a ~ of conscience

prisoner of war *n.* 1. to hold prisoners of war 2. to interrogate prisoners of war 3. to exchange, free, liberate, repatriate prisoners of war

privacy *n.* 1. to disturb, invade, violate smb.'s ~ 2. an invasion of smb.'s, an intrusion on smb.'s ~ 3. in ~ (to do smt. in the ~ of one's (own) home)

private I *n.* in ~ (to do smt. in ~)

private II *n.* ["common soldier"] 1. a buck ~ (AE) 2. (US) a ~ first-class (the British Army has *lance corporal*) 3. to have, hold the rank of ~ 4. (misc.) what's your opinion, Private (Smith)?

privilege *n.* 1. to award, give, grant a ~ 2. to enjoy, exercise; have a ~ (to enjoy guest ~s) 3. to abuse a ~ 4. to revoke, withdraw; suspend a ~ 5. a class; exclusive; special ~ 6. full; franking; guest; kitchen ~s 7. executive ~ 8. a ~ to + inf. (it was a ~ to work with them = it was a ~ working with them)

privileged *adj.* 1. very ~ 2. (usu. does not stand alone) ~ to + inf. (we were ~ to be able to work with them)

privy *adj.* ["having access"] 1. ~ to (they are ~ to secret documents) ["aware"] 2. ~ to (don't blame me! I wasn't ~ to the arrangement!)

prize I *n.* 1. to award, give, present a ~ 2. to distribute ~s 3. to accept; receive, win a ~ (for) (he won a ~ for the largest carrot) 4. to take a ~ (who took first ~?) 5. a booby; consolation; door; first;

second; third ~ 6. a ~ goes to (second ~ went to my sister) 7. (misc.) the glittering ~s (of life in the fast lane) ("The world continues to offer glittering ~s to those who have stout hearts and sharp swords." – Lord Birkenhead, 1923)

prize II (BE) see **pry** 2, 3

prized *adj.* ["valued"] 1. highly ~ 2. ~ among 3. ~ as (this wine is highly ~ among connoisseurs as the best of its kind) 4. ~ for (this wine is highly ~ for its bouquet)

pro see **professional**

probability *n.* 1. (a) real, strong ~ 2. little ~ 3. a ~ of (there is a strong ~ of her coming) 4. a ~ that + clause (there is a strong ~ that she'll come) 5. in all ~ (in all ~ she'll come)

probable *adj.* 1. hardly ~ (it's hardly ~ that she will show up after she was insulted last time!) 2. equally; highly, very ~ 3. ~ that + clause (it's ~ that she will not show up; more usu. is: she'll probably not show up)

probate *n.* 1. to grant ~ 2. to prove a will at ~

probation *n.* 1. to place, put smb. on ~ 2. to release smb. on ~ 3. to violate (the terms of one's) ~ 4. on ~ (he's out on ~ for a year)

probe I *n.* 1. to conduct; launch a ~ 2. an exhaustive, thorough ~ 3. an interplanetary; space ~ 4. a police ~ 5. a ~ into, of (a police ~ into racketeering)

probe II *v.* 1. to ~ deeply, thoroughly 2. (d; tr.) to ~ about, on (to ~ smb. on a matter) 3. (D; intr.) to ~ for (to ~ for weak spots) 4. (D; intr.) to ~ into (to ~ into the facts)

problem *n.* ["unsettled question"] ["source of difficulty"] 1. to cause, create, pose, present a ~ 2. to have a ~ (about/with); to have ~s about/with (colloq.) (we're having meat for dinner – do you have a ~ about/with that?) 3. to be, constitute a ~ 4. to address; bring up, raise; confront, face; discuss, explore a ~ 5. to attack, come to grips with, deal with, get to grips with (BE), grapple with, tackle a ~ 6. to lick, resolve, settle, solve a ~ 7. to avoid, sidestep a ~ 8. an acute, daunting, difficult, grave, major, pressing, serious; insoluble, insurmountable ~; the real, underlying ~ 9. a complex, complicated, involved, knotty, perplexing, thorny ~ 10. a delicate, ticklish ~ 11. a minor, petty ~ 12. an environmental; moral; political; social ~ 13. a global; local; national ~ (there are a number of important ~s about climate change that have arisen in our discussions) 14. an attitude; drink (BE), drinking (AE); emotional; physical; psychological; social; weight ~ 15. a perennial ~ 16. a ~ arises, comes up 17. a ~ to + inf. (it's a real ~ to make ends meet = it's a real ~ making ends meet) 18. (misc.) the crux of a ~; to get to the heart of a ~ ["mathematical statement requiring a solution"] 19. to do, solve a ~ 20. a complicated; difficult; easy; simple ~ USAGE NOTE: The question "what's your/his problem?" is ambiguous. It can function like "what's wrong?" ("what's your problem? whatever it is, we can help!") or like "what's wrong with you?" ("you're rude to everybody! what's your problem?")

procedure *n.* 1. to establish a ~ (you can't do that under the established ~) 2. to adopt; follow a ~ 3. (a) correct, proper; normal, regular, standard ~ (for) (to follow regular ~s for dealing with a problem) 4. a complex, complicated; delicate ~ 5. a simple ~ 6. a scientific; surgical ~ 7. (surgery) a major; minor ~ 8. bureaucratic; parliamentary; safety ~s 9. (misc.) a point of ~

proceed *v.* 1. to ~ apace; smoothly 1. (d; intr.) to ~ against (to ~ against smb. in court) 2. (d; intr.) to ~ from; to (to ~ from New York to Philadelphia) 3. (d; intr.) to ~ with (to ~ apace with one's research) 4. (E) she ~ed to tell us every detail 5. (P) ~ left about a hundred yards, then ~ along the road till you see a turning

proceedings *n.* (often legal) 1. to bring, initiate, institute; conduct ~ against (to initiate legal ~ against a competitor) 2. judicial, legal ~ 3. bankruptcy; criminal; divorce; impeachment ~ (to institute divorce ~) 4. (misc.) Proceedings of the Royal Society (title of magazine)

proceeds *n.* ["profit"] 1. net ~ 2. the ~ amount to; go to 3. ~ from, of (the ~ from the sale of our surplus property will go to paying our creditors) 4. on, with the ~ (our creditors got rich on the proceeds of the sale of our surplus property)

process *n.* 1. a creative ~ 2. a democratic; electoral; manufacturing ~ (a waste product of the manufacturing ~) 3. the aging; transformation ~ = the ~ of aging; transformation 4. the judicial, legal ~ 5. mental ~es 6. a stage, step in a ~ (see also **due process**)

processing *n.* 1. data; food ~ 2. (computers) batch ~

procession *n.* 1. to head, lead a ~ 2. a ceremonial; funeral; religious; torchlight; triumphal; wedding ~ 3. a ~ moves, wends its way 4. in (a) ~ (to march in a ~)

processor *n.* a food ~ (see also **word processor**)

proclaim *v.* (formal) 1. (L; to) the president ~ed (to the nation) that the entire state was a disaster area 2. (N; used with a noun) the entire state was ~ed a disaster area

proclamation *n.* 1. to issue, make a ~ 2. a ~ that + clause (the president issued a ~ (to the nation) that the entire state was a disaster area)

proclivity *n.* (formal) 1. a ~ for; to, towards (we noted her ~ for (forming) strong attachments) 2. a ~ to + inf. (we noted her ~ to form strong attachments)

procure *v.* 1. (C) (BE) she was unable to ~ a ticket for us; or: she was unable to ~ us a ticket 2. (D; tr.) to ~ for (she was unable to ~ us a ticket even for £50!) 3. (D; tr.) to ~ from (she was unable to ~ us a ticket from the box office even for £50!)

prod *v.* 1. (D; tr.) to ~ into (they ~ded me into buying a new car) 2. (H) they kept ~ding me to buy a new car 3. (misc.) to ~ smb. in the ribs

prodigy *n.* a child; infant ~

produce I *n.* ["fruits and vegetables"] 1. farm ~ 2. fresh; perishable ~

produce II *v.* 1. (d; tr.) to ~ as (she ~d several letters as evidence) 2. (D; tr.) to ~ for (to ~ food for export; she ~d several letters for me from her pocket) 3. (D; tr.) to ~ from (she ~d several letters from her pocket; to ~ gas from coal)

producer *n.* 1. an executive; film, movie; radio; stage, theater; steel; television, TV ~ 2. a ~ of (a ~ of films)

product *n.* 1. to market, promote a (new) ~ 2. a by-product; an end, finished; manufactured ~ 3. a waste ~ (a waste ~ of the manufacturing process) 4. the gross domestic ~ (= GDP); the gross national ~ (= GNP) 5. a wide range of ~s 6. (misc.) to endorse a ~

production *n.* ["work presented on the stage, radio, TV, etc."] 1. to put on, stage a ~ 2. a Hollywood; stage, theatrical; TV ~ ["process of producing"] 3. to go into; start up ~ 4. to beef up, boost, increase, speed up, step up ~ 5. to halt, stop ~ 6. to cut back (on), decrease, roll back ~ 7. industrial; mass ~ 8. coal; oil; steel ~ 9. (misc.) the means of ~ ["misc."] 10. (slang) (esp. AE) to make a big ~ out of smt. ("to make a big fuss over smt.")

productive *adj.* ~ of

productivity *n.* 1. to decrease, lower; increase, raise ~ 2. high; low ~ 3. a level of ~

products *n.* agricultural; dairy ~

profess *v.* (formal) 1. (E) he ~ed to know nothing about the matter 2. (L) he ~ed that he knew nothing about the matter 3. (M; refl.) he ~ed himself to be ignorant of the matter 4. (N; refl.) he ~ed himself ignorant of the matter

profession *n.* 1. to practice a ~ 2. the legal; medical; nursing; teaching ~ 3. by ~ (she's a lawyer by ~)

professional, pro *adj., n.* 1. (usu. sports) to turn ~ (he turned ~ at the age of twenty) 2. a real, true ~ (she is a real ~) ("she does her work seriously and well") USAGE NOTE: A *professional tennis player* and a *professional golfer* compete for money. A *tennis professional* and a *golf pro* coach for money, typically at clubs.

professor *n.* 1. (AE) an adjunct; assistant; associate; full ~ 2. (GB) a Regius ~ (appointed by the Crown) 3. a research; visiting ~ 4. a ~ emerita, emeritus = an emerita, emeritus ~ 5. a college (esp. US); university ~ 6. (misc.) an absent-minded ~ USAGE NOTE: We speak of a professor *of* mathematics, but of a lecturer or reader *in* mathematics.

professorship *n.* 1. to endow; establish a ~ 2. to be appointed to, get, receive a ~ (she was appointed to an endowed ~) 3. to have, hold, occupy a ~ (to hold a ~ in biology = to hold the ~ of biology) 4. to give up, relinquish a ~ 5. a personal (BE); university ~

proficiency *n.* 1. to demonstrate, display ~ 2. to achieve ~ 3. language ~ 4. a level of ~ 5. ~ at, in (she has achieved a high level of ~ in English)

proficient *adj.* ~ at, in (she has become highly ~ in English)

profile *n.* ["public exposure"] 1. to have a high; low ~ 2. to keep, maintain a high; low ~ ["side view"] 3. in ~

profit I *n.* 1. to clear, earn, make, realize, reap, show, turn a ~ 2. to bring (in), yield; to maximize a ~ (maximize your ~s and minimize your losses) 3. a fat, handsome, juicy, large, tidy; marginal, small; quick ~ 4. an excess, exorbitant, windfall ~ 5. a clear; net; gross ~ 6. ~s decline, fall; increase, rise 7. a ~ on (to make a ~ on a deal) 8. at a ~ (to operate at a ~) 9. (misc.) to share (in) the ~s; ~s were up (by) ten percent

profit II *v.* (D; intr.) to ~ by, from (will the rich ~ by/from the new tax laws? (= will the new tax laws ~ the rich?))

profitable *adj.* ~ to + inf. (is it ~ to work this mine?)

profiteer *n.* a black-market; war ~

profuse *adj.* ~ in (~ in one's apologies)

profusion *n.* in ~ (~ in one's apologies; apologies in ~)

prognosis *n.* 1. to make a ~ 2. to confirm a ~ (further tests confirmed the initial ~) 3. a favorable; gloomy, unfavorable ~ 4. a ~ that + clause (further tests confirmed the initial ~ that she had not much longer to live)

program I *n.* ["plan"] 1. to chart, draw up; organize a ~ 2. to carry out, implement; evaluate; introduce; launch; phase out, terminate a ~ 3. a crash; long-range; pilot; short-range ~ 4. a building; development; political ~ 5. a ~ to + inf.; a ~ that + clause (to launch a ~ (whose purpose is) to reduce crime = to launch a ~ that is intended to reduce crime) ["schedule"] 6. on smb.'s ~ (what's on your ~ (for) today?) ["entertainment"] 7. to make; produce; put on a ~ ["broadcast, telecast"] 8. a call-in (AE), phone-in (BE); radio; television, TV ~ 9. a ~ airs; comes on; goes off (a TV ~ about drugs will air today) ["coded instructions for a computer"] 10. to boot up; debug; download; execute; load; reboot; run; write a ~ 11. a user-friendly ~ 12. a computer; software; word processing ~ ["academic course of study"] 13. a graduate, postgraduate (esp. BE); honors; training; undergraduate ~ 14. a ~ in (a ~ in linguistics) ["organized activities"] 15. an orientation; outreach; recreation; work-study (AE) ~ (our outreach ~ includes visits to local schools = there are visits to local schools in our outreach ~) ["misc."] 16. a reading ~ (for a dictionary) USAGE NOTE: The BE spelling is *programme*, except for the computer uses (10–12).

program II *v.* (H) to ~ a computer to store certain information USAGE NOTE: Except when referring to the computer, the BE spelling is *programme* – to programme an alarm system.

programme see Usage Notes for **program I, II**

programmer *n.* a computer ~

programming *n.* computer ~

progress I *n.* 1. to make ~ 2. to facilitate ~ 3. to block, hinder, impede, obstruct ~ 4. amazing, considerable, good, great; material, significant; rapid; smooth; steady ~ 5. little; slow; spotty ~ 6. economic; scientific; technological ~ 7. ~ in (to make little ~ in solving the problems of air pollution) 8. ~ towards (to make little ~ towards solving the problems of air pollution) 9. in ~ (negotiations are in ~) (see also *progress report* at **report I** *n.*)

progress II *v.* (D; intr.) to ~ from; to (to ~ from the basics to advanced concepts)

progression *n.* 1. an arithmetic; geometric; harmonic ~ 2. ~ from; to 3. ~ through

prohibit *v.* 1. (D; tr.) to ~ from (she has ~ed him from smoking in her presence) 2. (rare) (K) she has ~ed his smoking in her presence

prohibition *n.* 1. to impose; abolish, lift, repeal ~ 2. a ~ against, on (her prohibition against his smoking in her presence)

project I *n.* ["organized undertaking"] 1. to conceive; draw up a ~ 2. to launch a ~ 3. to carry out a ~ 4. to do a ~ (on) (the children did a (class) ~ on dinosaurs) 5. to shelve a ~ 6. an irrigation; land-reclamation; pilot ("experimental"); public-works; research; water-conservation ~ 7. a ~ to + inf.; a ~ that + clause (to launch a ~ (whose purpose is) to reduce crime = to launch a ~ that is intended to reduce crime) ["publicly financed housing"] (AE) 8. a housing ~ (BE has *council estate, housing estate*)

project II *v.* 1. (D; tr.) to ~ into (to ~ a missile into space) 2. (D; tr.) to ~ onto (to ~ slides onto a screen)

projected *adj.* ~ to + inf. (production is ~ to increase by five percent)

projectile *n.* to fire; launch a ~

projection *n.* ["estimate"] 1. to make; revise a ~ 2. a computer ~ 3. according to, on certain ~s (according to our latest ~s, production will increase by five percent) ["system of presenting a map"] 4. an isometric; Mercator ~

projector *n.* 1. to operate, run, work a ~ 2. a cine-projector (BE); film, motion-picture (AE); opaque; overhead; slide ~

proliferation *n.* nuclear ~

prologue *n.* a ~ to (Chaucer's Prologue to *The Canterbury Tales*)

prom *n.* ["formal school dance"] (AE) 1. the junior; senior ~ 2. at the ~ 3. (misc.) to go to the ~; to take smb. to the ~ USAGE NOTE: In BE, *prom* means "a promenade concert".

prominence *n.* 1. to achieve, acquire, come into, come to, gain ~ (he gained ~ as an athlete) 2. to give ~ to (to give ~ to a story)

prominent *adj.* 1. socially ~ 2. to become ~ (he became ~ as an athlete)

promiscuity *n.* sexual ~

promise I *n.* ["vow"] 1. to make a ~ 2. to give smb. a/one's ~ 3. to elicit, extract; fulfill, keep a ~ (we managed to extract a ~ from him that we hope he'll keep) 4. to break, renege on, repudiate a ~ 5. a broken; empty, false, hollow; rash; vague ~ 6. a sacred, solemn ~ 7. a campaign, election ~ (politicians sometimes break their campaign ~s) 8. a ~ to + inf. (she made a solemn ~ to contribute fifty pounds) 9. a ~ that + clause (she made a solemn ~ that she would contribute fifty pounds) 10. (misc.) to hold smb. to a ~ ["basis for hope"] 11. to show ~ (the young boxer showed real ~) 12. great, real; little ~ 13. ~ as (he showed great ~ as a boxer) 14. of ~ (a young boxer of ~ = a promising young boxer)

promise II v. 1. to ~ solemnly 2. (A) he ~d the book to me; or: he ~d me the book 3. (E) she ~d solemnly to contribute fifty pounds; it ~s to be an exciting year 4. (H; often used in neg. constructions) he ~d me never to show up late again 5. (L; may have an object) he ~d (me) that he would never show up late again 6. (misc.) (BE) I ~ you ("I assure you") (I *did* see a whale in the river, I ~ you!) USAGE NOTE: In pattern H, *promise* is unique. "He promised me never to show up late again. = He promised me that HE would never show up late again." Compare *tell*, which is typical of verbs in pattern H. "He told me never to show up late again. = He told me that I should never show up late again."

promote v. 1. (D; tr.) to ~ as (we ~d our dictionary as the best of its kind) 2. (D; tr.) to ~ from; to (she was ~d from captain to major) 3. (old-fashioned) (BE) (N; used with a noun) she was ~d major

promotion n. ["advancement in rank"] 1. to put smb. in for (a) ~ 2. to recommend smb. for (a) ~ 3. to approve smb. for (a) ~ 4. to approve a ~ 5. to put in for, try for (a) ~ (she put in for ~ to floor supervisor last month; he never tried for a ~) 6. to get, make (AE), win (a) ~ (she finally made her ~ to major; she got a ~ very quickly) 7. a ~ from; to (a ~ from captain to major; a ~ to the rank of professor) ["furtherance, fostering"] 8. health ~ ["advertising"] 9. prepublication ~ 10. sales ~ 11. in ~ (she is in ~)

prompt I adj. 1. ~ at, in (~ in fulfilling one's obligations) 2. ~ to + inf. (~ to fulfill one's obligations)

prompt II v. (H) what ~ed you to say that?

promptness n. ~ at, in (~ in fulfilling one's obligations)

prone adj. ["likely, liable"] (cannot stand alone) 1. ~ to (she is ~ to coughs and sneezes; ~ to exaggeration) 2. ~ to + inf. (she is ~ to exaggerate) (see also *accident-prone* at **accident**)

pronoun n. a demonstrative; indefinite; interrogative; personal; possessive; reflexive; relative ~

pronounce v. 1. (D; intr., tr.) to ~ on, upon (he is willing to ~ upon subjects he knows nothing about!) 2. (formal) (M) the physician ~d him to be healthy 3. (N; used with an adjective, noun) the physician ~d him healthy; she was officially ~d dead; they were ~d husband and wife; the priest said, "I now ~ you man and wife" 4. (P) ~ it after me; ~ it as I do = ~ it like me; ~ it like this = ~ it this way; the "c" in "cow" is ~d like "k"

pronouncement n. 1. to issue, make a ~ 2. a ~ about, on (the government issued a ~ about lowering taxes) 3. a ~ that + clause (the government issued a ~ that taxes would be lowered)

pronunciamento n. (derog.) 1. to issue, make a ~ 2. a ~ that + clause (they issued a ~ that only their theories would be acceptable)

pronunciation n. 1. to acquire; have a (good) ~ 2. to correct smb.'s ~ 3. a native ~ (of a language) 4. (a) spelling ~ 5. (a) nonstandard; standard ~ 6. BBC, Received (RP); General American ~

proof n. ["conclusive evidence"] 1. to furnish, give, offer, present, produce, provide, show ~ 2. to have ~ 3. ample, clear, conclusive, concrete, convincing, definite, incontestable, incontrovertible, indisputable, irrefutable, living, positive, tangible, undeniable, unquestionable ~ 4. documentary; mathematical; scientific ~ 5. ~ that + clause (the prosecutor furnished convincing ~ that the accused could have been at the scene of the crime, which did not of course constitute incontrovertible ~ of his guilt!) 6. (misc.) the burden, onus of ~ (the burden of ~ lies/rests with the police) ["composed type"] 7. to correct, read ~ (s) 8. galley; page; reproduction; uncorrected ~s

proofreading n. to do (the) ~

prop v. 1. (d; tr.) to ~ against (she ~ped the chair against the door) 2. (N; used with an adjective) she ~ped the window open

propaganda n. 1. to engage in, spread ~ 2. to counteract, neutralize ~ 3. enemy; ideological; political; vicious ~ 4. ~ about; against

propeller n. 1. a ~ spins, turns 2. (misc.) the blade of a ~

propensity n. (formal) 1. a ~ for (she has a ~ for exaggerating) 2. a ~ to + inf. (she has a ~ to exaggerate)

proper adj. 1. ~ for (their attire is not ~ for this occasion) 2. ~ to + inf. (it is not ~ to enter that restaurant without a jacket; it is ~ for her not to state her own opinion) 3. ~ that + clause; subj. (it is ~ that she not state/should not state/doesn't state (BE) her own opinion; "It is altogether fitting and ~ that we should do this." – Abraham Lincoln, The Gettysburg Address (Nov. 19, 1863))

property n. ["smt. owned"] 1. to attach; confiscate, seize ~ 2. to buy; develop; inherit; lease; let (esp. BE), rent; sell; transfer ~ 3. to reclaim; recover (stolen) ~ 4. (an) abandoned; beachfront; commercial ~ 5. common; communal; government; individual; joint; movable; personal; private; public; real ~ 6. intellectual ~ 7. community ~ ("property held jointly by two spouses") 8. a piece of ~ 9. (misc.) a man/woman of ~ ["quality"] 10. (to have) medicinal ~ties

prophecy n. 1. to make a ~ 2. to fulfill a ~ 3. a

gloomy; self-fulfilling ~ 4. a ~ comes true; proves
to be true 5. a ~ about; of (she made a ~ of gloom
about their future) 6. a ~ that + clause (her ~ that
you would become governor came true)
prophesy v. 1. (K) no one but her could have ~sied
your becoming governor! 2. (L; to) she ~sied that
you would become governor
prophet n. 1. a false ~ 2. (rel.) a major; minor ~
propinquity n. (formal) ~ to
propitious adj. ~ for, to
proportion n. 1. (a) direct; inverse ~ 2. in ~ (to)
(is the number of people with lung cancer in direct
~ to the number of people who smoke?) 3. out of
(all) ~ to (the punishment was out of (all) ~ to the
crime) 4. (misc.) (to have/keep) a sense of ~; does
the ~ of people with lung cancer vary directly with
the ~ of people who smoke?; does the ~ of people
with lung cancer fall as smoking falls?
proportional adj. 1. directly; inversely; roughly ~
2. ~ to
proportionate adj. ~ to (the punishment was not ~
to the crime)
proportions n. ["extent"] 1. to assume, take on ~ 2.
astronomical, huge; epic; epidemic; menacing ~
(the outbreak assumed epidemic ~) 3. of certain ~
(of astronomical ~)
proposal n. 1. to draw up, make, present, put forth,
put forward, submit a ~ 2. to back, support a ~ 3. to
accept, adopt a ~ 4. to consider, entertain; receive
a ~ 5. to block, kill (colloq.), reject, turn down a
~ 6. to withdraw a ~ 7. a concrete ~ 8. a ~ falls
through (the ~ to reduce taxes fell through) 9. a
~ for (the committee rejected the ~ for reducing
taxes) 10. a ~ to + inf. (the committee rejected the
~ to reduce taxes) 11. a ~ that + clause; subj. (the
committee considered a ~ that taxes ¬be/should
be¬ reduced)
propose v. 1. (B) she ~d a new plan to us 2. (D; tr.)
to ~ as; for (to ~ smb. for membership in a club;
to ~ smb. as a member of a club) 3. (D; intr.) to ~
to ("to offer marriage to") (he ~ to her by saying,
"will you marry me?") 4. (E) I ~ to leave very early
5. (G) she ~d leaving very early 6. (K) she ~d his
going in my place = what she ~d was his going
in my place = what she ~d was for him to go in
my place 7. (L; subj.; to) we ~d (to them) that she
¬be/should be/was (BE)¬ appointed 8. (misc.) are
you really/seriously -sing to leave so soon after we
got here?!
proposition n. ["unethical, immoral proposal"] (colloq.) 1. to make (smb.) a ~ ["subject, question to be
discussed"] 2. a group, series, set of ~s 3. the ~ that
+ clause (the committee considered the ~ that taxes
should be reduced) ["business proposal"] 4. an attractive; business; paying ~
proprieties n. ["accepted behavior"] to observe the ~
propriety n. ["conformity with accepted standards
of behavior"] 1. to doubt, query, question the ~ of
smt. (we doubted the ~ of passing off smb. else's

work as one's own) 2. doubtful; due ~ 3. with ~ (to
behave with due ~)
propulsion n. jet; nuclear; rocket ~
prop up v. 1. (D; tr.) to ~ against (she ~ped up
the chair against the door = she ~ped the chair up
against the door) 2. (D; refl., tr.) to ~ with (she
~ped herself up with pillows) 3. (misc.) (colloq.)
to ~ up the bar ("to stand at the bar having drink
after drink")
pros and cons n. 1. to consider, weigh the ~ 2. to
debate the ~
prose n. 1. to write (in) ~ 2. descriptive; flowery,
purple; limpid; poetic ~ 3. a passage, piece of ~
prosecute v. 1. to ~ vigorously 2. (D; tr.) to ~ for (to
~ smb. for murder)
prosecution n. 1. to conduct a ~ 2. to face ~ 3. a
vigorous ~ 4. criminal ~ 5. ~ for 6. (legal) the ~
rests its case, the ~ rests (AE) 7. (misc.) subject to
(criminal) ~
prosecutor n. a public ~ (esp. BE; AE has *district
attorney*)
proseminar n. 1. to conduct, give, hold a ~ 2. to
attend a ~ 3. a ~ on
prospect I n. ["anticipated outcome"] 1. a bright,
rosy; inviting ~ 2. a bleak, grim; daunting; dim ~
3. ~ that + clause (is there any ~ that the situation
will improve in the long term?) 4. in ~ (is there any
improvement in ~ in the long term?) 5. (misc.) is
there any ~ of improvement in the long term?
prospect II v. (D; intr.) to ~ for (to ~ for gold)
prospects n. ["chances"] 1. to have ~ for (to have ~
for the future?) 2. job; long-term ~ 3. ~ that + clause
(are there any ~ that the situation will improve
in the long term?) 4. (misc.) are there any ~ of
improvement in the long term? ["financial expectations"] 5. with; without ~
prospectus n. (BE) a college, university; school ~
(AE uses *catalog*)
prosperity n. 1. to create ~ 2. to enjoy ~ 3. durable,
lasting, long-term; economic; sustainable ~ 4. a
period, time of ~
prostitution n. 1. to engage in ~ 2. to decriminalize,
legalize ~ 3. to ban, criminalize, outlaw ~
prostrate I adj. ~ with (~ with grief)
prostrate II v. (D; refl.) to ~ oneself before
prostration n. heat; nervous ~
protect v. 1. (D; refl., tr.) to ~ against, from 2. (D;
refl., tr.) to ~ by; with (~ yourself against loss by
taking out insurance! = ~ yourself against loss with
insurance!)
protection n. 1. to afford, give, offer, provide; get
~ 2. government; police ~ 3. consumer; environmental ~ 4. a degree, measure of ~ 5. ~ against,
from 6. ~ by; with (get ~ against loss by taking out
insurance! = get ~ against loss with insurance!) 7.
under smb.'s ~ (she was placed under our ~)
protective adj. 1. overly, too; very ~ 2. ~ of,
towards
protector n. a chest; surge ~

protein n. 1. (for food) to furnish, provide ~ 2. (a) complete; incomplete; simple; total ~ 3. poor in; rich in ~(s)

protest I n. ["complaint"] ["dissent"] 1. to enter, file, lodge, register a ~ 2. to express, make, voice a ~ (we made a strong ~ to their government) 3. to cause, draw, spark (AE), spark off (BE), trigger a ~ 4. to dismiss, reject a ~ 5. a strong, vehement, vigorous; violent (we lodged a strong ~ with their government) 6. a mild; weak ~ 7. a ~ against, at, over 8. a ~ that + clause (the court rejected their ~ that due process had not been observed) 9. in ~ (to resign in ~ against/at/over the war) 10. under ~ (they complied with the order under ~) ["public demonstration of disapproval"] 11. to organize, stage a ~ 12. to put down, quell a ~ 13. an anti-nuclear; anti-war; mass; noisy; political; public ~ 14. a ~ against 15. (misc.) a storm of ~

protest II v. 1. to ~ bitterly, strongly, vehemently, vigorously 2. (D; intr.) to ~ about, against, at, over (to ~ against a war; AE also has: to ~ a war) 3. (K) (AE) we ~ed his being released 4. (L; to) we ~ed (to the mayor) that due process had not been observed USAGE NOTE: BE distinguishes between "she protested ["asserted"] her innocence = she protested that she was innocent" and "she protested against/at ["opposed"] her parking fine." AE can make that distinction, too – but is more likely nowadays to have both "she protested her innocence" and "she protested her parking fine."

protestation n. 1. a ~ against 2. a ~ of (we believe her ~s of innocence) 3. a ~ that + clause (we believe her ~s that she is innocent)

protocol n. ["minutes"] ["statement"] 1. to draw up a ~ ["official code of conduct"] 2. to observe; violate ~ 3. court, palace, royal; diplomatic; military ~ 4. the rules of ~ 5. ~ demands/requires that + clause (~ demands that he ¬visit/should visit/visits (BE)¬ the embassy) 6. (misc.) according to ~; a breach of ~

protrude v. (D; intr.) to ~ from

proud adj. 1. justly ~ 2. ~ of (~ of one's children) 3. ~ to + inf. (will they be ~ enough to defend their principles?) 4. ~ that + clause (they are ~ that they defended their principles) 5. (misc.) to do smb. ~; as ~ as a peacock

prove v. 1. to ~ conclusively 2. (B) she was able to ~ innocence to us 3. (E) she ~d to be a good worker; the rumor ~d to be true 4. (H) she ~d herself to be a good worker 5. (L; to) she was able to ~ (to us) that she was innocent 6. (M) history ~d her to have been right and ~d her detractors to have been wrong 7. (N; used with an adjective, past participle, noun) history ~d her right and ~d her detractors wrong; she ~d herself a good worker 8. (Q; to) she ~d (to us) how it had been done 9. (S) she ~d a good worker; the rumor ~d true 10. (misc.) "why are you behaving like that? what are you trying to ~?"

proverb n. 1. a common, old, popular, wise ~ 2. a ~ goes, runs 3. a ~ that (there is an old ~ (to the effect) that haste makes waste)

provide v. 1. (d; intr.) to ~ for (to ~ for one's family; to ~ for every contingency) 2. (D; tr.) to ~ for, to (to ~ blankets for the refugees; to ~ services to the needy) 3. (d; tr.) to ~ with (they were ~d with the proper equipment; we ~d the refugees with blankets; the phone call ~d her with an excuse to leave) 4. (L; subj.) this bill ~s that money ¬be/should be¬ allocated for flood control 5. (O) (colloq.) (esp. AE) the phone call ~d her an excuse to leave 6. (misc.) tonight's buffet supper has been ~d courtesy of the mayor's office

provided, providing adj. ~ that (she will join us ~ that you are also there)

providence n. divine ~

providential adj. (formal) ~ that + clause (it was ~ that we ¬arrived/should have arrived¬ at exactly the same time!)

province n. 1. an autonomous ~ 2. (esp. in Canada) an inland; maritime ~; the Province of Alberta, Ontario, etc. 3. the capital of a ~ (the capital of the Province of Alberta is Edmonton) 4. (misc.) (BE) are there as many opportunities in the ~s as there are in London?; can smb. from the ~s be as successful as smb. from London?

proving ground n. a ~ for

provision n. ["preparations"] 1. to make ~ for (what ~ have you made for your old age?) 2. private; public, state ~ (of) (is private ~ of health care adequate for your needs?) 3. financial ~s ["clause in a legal document"] 4. to violate a ~ (of a contract) 5. according to a ~ (that is impermissible according to Provision 25 of the contract) 6. under a ~ (that is impermissible under Provision 25 of the contract) 7. (esp. AE) with a ~ that + clause (she will join us with the ~ that you are also there)

proviso n. 1. to add a ~ 2. with a ~ that + clause; subj. (she will join us with the ~ that you ¬also be/are also (esp. BE)¬ there)

provocation n. 1. deliberate; extreme, gross, severe ~ 2. ~ for (there was no ~ for such behavior) 3. at a ~ (he loses his temper at the slightest ~) 4. under ~ (he did use strong language, but only under extreme ~) 5. without ~ (he used strong language without the slightest ~!)

provocative adj. highly, very ~

provoke v. 1. (D; tr.) to ~ into, to (to ~ smb. into getting angry = to ~ smb. to anger) 2. (H) what ~d you to get angry?

prowess n. 1. to demonstrate, display ~ 2. athletic; military ~ 3. ~ as, at, in (he demonstrated his ~ as an athlete, at being an athlete, at throwing the javelin, in athletics) 4. ~ with (he demonstrated his ~ with the javelin)

prowl I n. on the ~ (for) (journalists on the ~ for juicy stories)

prowl II v. (P; intr.) to ~ around the neighborhood; they ~ed through the forest

proximate *adj.* (cannot stand alone) ~ to

proximity *n.* 1. close ~ 2. ~ to 3. in ~ to 4. in the ~ of (a new hotel will be built in the ~ of the airport)

proxy *n.* 1. to appoint, name, nominate a ~ 2. to get, have, hold smb.'s ~ 3. a ~ to + inf. (I named him my ~ to vote for me = he had my ~ to vote for me) 4. by ~ (to vote by ~)

prudent *adj.* ~ to + inf. (it was not ~ of you to sell that property so soon = you were not ~ to sell that property so soon)

prudish *adj.* ~ about

pry *v.* 1. (D; intr.) to ~ into (to ~ into smb.'s affairs) 2. (D; tr.) to ~ out of (to ~ information out of smb.) 3. (N; used with an adjective) they pried the door open USAGE NOTE: For senses two and three, BE uses *prise* or *prize*.

pry off *v.* (AE) (D; tr.) to ~ with (they pried off the door with a crowbar = they pried the door off with a crowbar) (BE has *prise off, prize off*)

P.S. *n.* to add a ~ (to)

psalm *n.* to recite a ~

p's and q's *n.* ["manners"] to mind one's ~

pseudonym *n.* 1. to adopt, take; use a ~ (Samuel L. Clemens adopted the ~ (of) Mark Twain) 2. under a ~ (Samuel L. Clemens wrote under the ~ (of) Mark Twain)

psychology *n.* ["science of the mind"] 1. abnormal; applied; behavioral; child; clinical; cognitive; developmental; educational; experimental; general; Gestalt; social ~ ["attitudes"] 2. group; mob ~ ["knowledge of a person's habits, reactions"] (colloq.) 3. to use ~

psych up *v.* (colloq.) (H; refl.) they ~ed themselves up to do well on the exam

pub *n.* 1. to manage, operate, run a ~ 2. to work at/in a ~ 3. to go down (to) the ~, stop at a ~ (on the way home); to drink at/in a ~; to drop into a ~ (see also *pub grub* at **grub I** *n.*)

pub-crawl *n.* (esp. BE) to go on a ~

puberty *n.* 1. to reach (the age/onset of) ~ 2. at ~

public *n.* 1. to educate, enlighten the ~ 2. to fool, mislead the ~ 3. the general; Great British (BE; humorous); listening; reading; theatergoing; traveling; viewing ~ 4. a member of the ~ 5. in ~

publication *n.* ["act of publishing"] 1. to begin, start ~ 2. to cease, stop; suspend ~ 3. to ban ~ (the government banned ~ of the newspaper) ["printed work"] 4. a government; official ~ 5. a copy; issue of a ~

publicity *n.* 1. to give, provide ~ 2. to gain, get, receive ~ 3. to seek ~ 4. to avoid, shun ~ 5. advance; enormous, extensive, wide ~ 6. adverse, bad; unwelcome ~ 7. favorable, good ~ 8. ~ surrounds (the blaze of ~ surrounding their trip to Europe) 9. ~ for 10. (misc.) a blaze of ~ (they left for Europe in a blaze of ~)

publicized *adj.* highly, widely ~

public opinion *n.* 1. to arouse, stir up ~ 2. to form, mold ~ 3. to affect, influence, sway, swing;

manipulate ~ 4. to express ~ 5. to canvass, poll, probe, sound out ~

publishing *n.* desk-top ~

puff I *n.* a powder ~

puff II *n.* to have, take a ~ (at/on a cigarette)

puff III *v.* 1. (d; intr.) to ~ at, on (to ~ on a pipe; he sat ~ing away at his pipe) 2. (misc.) to ~ smoke into smb.'s face

pull I *n.* ["force"] 1. to give a ~ (at/on) (she gave a ~ on the rope = she gave the rope a ~) 2. gravitational ~ ["influence"] (colloq.) 3. to use one's ~ (she used her ~ to avoid paying the fine) 4. the ~ to + inf. (she had enough ~ to avoid paying the fine)

pull II *n.* 1. to ~ hard 2. (d; intr.) ("to tug") to ~ at (the little boy was ~ing at his father's coat; she ~ed at the door but it wouldn't open) 3. (AE; colloq.) (d; intr.) to ~ for ("to support") (we were ~ing for the home team; they were ~ing for our team to win) 4. (d; intr.) ("to move") to ~ into (the train ~ed into the station) 5. (d; intr.) to ~ off ("to turn off") (to ~ off the road) 6. (D; tr.) ("to tug") to ~ off (she ~ed the sheets off the bed) (see also **pull off**) 7. (D; intr.) ("to tug") to ~ on (to ~ on a rope till it is tight) (see also **pull on**) 8. (d; intr.) ("to move") to ~ out of (the train ~ed out of the station; to ~ out of a dive) 9. (d; tr.) ("to lift") to ~ out of (they ~ed her out of the water; the pilot ~ed the plane out of the dive) 10. (d; tr.) ("to tug") to ~ over (she ~ed her sweater over her head) (see also **pull over**) 11. (N) ("to tug") she ~ed the rope tight; she ~ed the child free 12. (P; tr.) ("to tug") they ~ed the cart across the field 13. (misc.) to ~ a gun/knife on smb.; (esp. BE) to ~ a door to; she ~ed the child towards her (see also *to pull a fast one (on)* at **fast one**; *to pull oneself to one's feet* at **foot**)

pull ahead *v.* (D; intr.) to ~ of (to ~ of the other runners; the faster car ~ed ahead of the slower one)

pull alongside *v.* (D; intr.) to ~ of (esp. AE) (to ~ of the other car)

pull away *v.* (D; intr., tr.) to ~ from (to ~ from the curb; she ~ed the child away from the fire; the faster car ~ed away from the slower one)

pull back *v.* (D; intr., tr.) to ~ from; to (to ~ from the others; to ~ to our original position; they ~ed back from the brink of war; she ~ed the child back from the fire)

pull down *v.* (D; tr.) to ~ over (she ~ed her sweater down over her head)

pulley *n.* a fixed; movable ~

pull off *v.* (D; tr.) to ~ over (she ~ed her sweater off over her head) (see also *pull off* at **pull II** *v.*)

pull on *v.* (D; tr.) to ~ over (she ~ed her sweater on over her head) (see also *pull on* at **pull II** *v.*)

pull over *v.* (D; intr., tr.) to ~ from; to (she ~ed her car over to the curb when the policeman ordered her to ~ to the curb) (see also *pull over* at **pull II** *v.*)

pull up *v.* 1. (D; tr.) to ~ over (she ~ed her sweater up over her head) 2. (D; intr., tr.) to ~ to (she ~ed her car up to the curb when the policeman ordered her to ~ to the curb)

pulp *n.* 1. wood ~ 2. to beat smb. to a ~

pulpit *n.* 1. to ascend, mount the ~ 2. a bully ~ (AE) ("a place or a chance to promulgate one's views") (her media exposure gives her a bully ~ for influencing public opinion) 3. from; on the ~ (to denounce wrongdoing from the ~)

pulse *n.* 1. to feel; take ("measure") smb.'s ~ 2. to quicken smb.'s ~ (the excitement quickened his ~) 3. an erratic, irregular, unsteady; normal; rapid; regular, steady; strong; weak ~ 4. a ~ races; slackens, slows

pump I *n.* 1. to prime; work a ~ 2. a bicycle; gasoline (AE), petrol (BE) ~ 3. a centrifugal; heat; stomach; suction; sump ~

pump II *v.* 1. (D; tr.) ("to interrogate") to ~ for (they ~ed her for information) 2. (d; tr.) to ~ into (to ~ investments into a company; to ~ water into a tank) 3. (D; tr.) to ~ out of (to ~ water out of a tank) 4. (N; used with an adjective) they ~ed the tank dry, empty; full

pun *n.* to make a ~

punch I *n.* ["blow"] 1. to deliver, give, land, throw a ~ 2. to pull ("soften") one's ~es (also fig.) 3. to roll with a ~ 4. a hard; knockout; one-two; rabbit; solid; sucker; Sunday ~ 5. a ~ in, on, to (a ~ in the face; a ~ on the nose) ["misc."] 6. to pack a ~ ("to be powerful") (also fig.) (this cocktail packs quite a ~!); to beat smb. to the ~

punch II *v.* (D; tr.) to ~ in, on (I ~ed him in/on the nose)

punch III *n.* ["mixed drink typically consisting of fruit juice, liquor, etc."] 1. to make ~ 2. to spike ("add alcohol to") the ~ 3. to water down the ~ 4. fruit ~

Punch *n.* as pleased as ~ ("very pleased")

punctilious *adj.* ~ about

punctual *adj.* ~ about, in (~ in paying one's rent)

punctuality *n.* ~ in

punctuate *v.* (d; tr.) to ~ with (to ~ one's comments with quotations from the Bible)

punctuation mark *n.* to place, put a ~ somewhere

puncture *n.* (esp. BE) 1. to get; have a ~ 2. to fix, mend, patch, repair a ~ 3. a slow ~ (see also **lumbar puncture**)

pundit *n.* a political ~

punish *v.* 1. to ~ cruelly; harshly, severely; lightly, mildly; summarily 2. (D; tr.) to ~ as (they were ~ed harshly as dangerous criminals) 3. (D; tr.) to ~ by; with 4. (D; tr.) to ~ for (they were ~ed harshly for their crime ¬by being executed/with execution¬)

punishable *adj.* ~ by (~ by death)

punishment *n.* 1. to administer, mete out ~ to 2. to impose, inflict ~ on 3. to escape ~ 4. to suffer, take ~ 5. cruel, cruel and unusual; harsh, severe, unjust ~ 6. fitting, just; light, mild ~ 7. corporal; summary ~ (see also **capital punishment**) 8. (mil.) company ~ 9. ~ for (their ~ for that crime was execution)

10. as, in ~ (for) (they were executed in ~ for their crime)

pupil I *n.* ["opening in the iris of the eye"] constricted; dilated ~s

pupil II see the Usage Note for **student**

puppet *n.* 1. to manipulate, move, pull the strings of a ~ 2. a glove (BE), hand (esp. AE) ~

purchase I *n.* ["act of buying"] to make a ~

purchase II *v.* 1. (D; tr.) to ~ for 2. (D; tr.) to ~ from (we ~d a book (for her) (for twenty dollars) from a local bookshop) 3. (misc.) to ~ as is ("to purchase with no guarantee of quality"); to ~ retail; to ~ wholesale; to ~ at a reasonable price; to ~ compulsorily (esp. BE) (the government ~ed the land compulsorily to build housing on it)

pure *adj.* as ~ as the driven snow

purge I *n.* 1. to carry out, conduct a ~ 2. a radical, sweeping ~ (the party conducted a sweeping ~ of all dissidents)

purge II *v.* 1. (D; tr.) ("to remove") to ~ from (all dissidents were ~d from the party) 2. (D; tr.) ("to cleanse") to ~ of (the party was ~d of all dissidents)

purify *v.* (D; tr.) to ~ of (the party was ~fied of all dissidents)

purity *n.* 1. to maintain ~ 2. great; moral ~

purple I *adj.* ["livid"] ~ with (~ with rage)

purple II *n.* 1. dark; deep; light ~ 2. a shade of ~ 3. a patch of ~ 4. in ~ (dressed in ~)

purple III *n.* (BE) born to the ~ ("born into a royal or aristocratic family")

purport *v.* (formal) (E) ("to claim") they ~ to be rich

purported *adj.* (cannot stand alone) ~ to + inf. (they are ~ to be rich = they are ~ly rich)

purpose *n.* 1. to accomplish, achieve, fulfill a ~ 2. to serve a ~ 3. to put smt. to a good ~ 4. a lofty, worthy; stated; useful ~ 5. smb.'s ~ in (what was your ~ in criticizing the authorities?) 6. for a ~ (it was done for a good ~; we arranged the meeting for the ~ of preventing a strike) 7. (misc.) at cross ~s; for all practical ~s ("in reality"); the herb can be used for medicinal ~s; the money is considered income for tax ~s; for the ~s of this discussion, let's assume an annual growth rate of 3%; on ~ ("purposely") ("did it happen by accident or on ~?" "it happened accidentally on ~ – if you know what I mean!"); with the express ~ of (we arranged the meeting with the express ~ of preventing a strike); to no ~ (we did what we could to prevent a strike but unfortunately it was all to no ~)

purse strings *n.* ["finances"] to control, hold the ~

pursuance *n.* (formal) in ~ of (in ~ of one's aims)

pursuant *adv.* (formal) (cannot stand alone) ~ to (~ to one's aims)

pursue *v.* to ~ aggressively; doggedly, patiently, relentlessly

pursuit *n.* ["chase"] 1. dogged, relentless; hot ~ 2. in ~ of (in hot ~ of the terrorists) 3. (misc.) "Life, Liberty and the ~ of Happiness" – U.S. Declaration of Independence, July 4, 1776 ["hobby"] 4. smb.'s favorite ~

purview *n.* to fall outside; under; within the ~ of smt. (this question falls outside the ~ of this investigation)

pus *n.* 1. to discharge ~ 2. ~ forms

push I *n.* ["act of pushing"] 1. to give smb./smt. a ~ (our car was stuck and they gave us a ~) 2. a hard ~ ["advance"] 3. to launch a ~ (the army launched a ~ to reach the sea) 4. a big ~ 5. a ~ to; towards (the army launched a ~ to the sea) 6. at a ~ (all your household chores can now be done at the ~ of a button!)

push II *v.* 1. ("to shove") to ~ hard 2. (D; intr.) ("to shove") to ~ against (she ~ed against the door but it wouldn't open) 3. (d; intr., tr.) to ~ for ("to urge") (to ~ for reform; to ~ the government for reform) 4. (d; intr.) to ~ into ("to force one's way") (to ~ (one's way) into a crowded bus) 5. (D; tr.) ("to force to move") to ~ into (we ~ed the stalled car into the garage) 6. (d; intr.) ("to press") to ~ on (to ~ on a handle) 7. (d; intr.) to ~ through ("to force one's way through") (to ~ (one's way) through a crowd) 8. (d; intr.) ("to move") to ~ to, towards (our troops ~ed towards the next village) 9. (H) ("to urge") to ~ smb. to do smt. 10. (N; used with an adjective) ~ the chair closer; ~ the door open/closed/shut 11. (P; tr.) ("to shove") she ~ed the book under the bed; I was ~ed out of the way 12. (misc.) the army was ~ed to the breaking point; to ~ at (she ~ed at the door but it wouldn't open); I ~ed past the other people to get on the bus (see also *pushed for time* at **time I** *n.*)

push ahead *v.* (D; intr.) to ~ with, on (they ~ed ahead with their plans and then ~ed ahead on/with their project)

push-chair *n.* (BE) to push, wheel a ~ (BE also has *(baby) buggy*; AE has *stroller*)

push down *v.* (D; intr.) to ~ on (to ~ on a handle)

push on *v.* (D; intr.) ("to continue") to ~ to, towards (our troops ~ed on towards the next village)

pushover *n.* ["easy target"] a ~ for

push-up *n.* (esp. AE) to do ~s (see also **press-up**)

push up *v.* (D; intr.) to ~ on (to ~ on a handle)

put I *adj.* (colloq.) ["in one place"] to stay ~

put II *v.* 1. (B) ("to pose") to ~ a question to smb. 2. (d; tr.) ("to place") to ~ before (to ~ evidence before a grand jury; to ~ a proposal before a committee; to ~ one's family before all other concerns) 3. (d; tr.) ("to place") to ~ in; into (to ~ milk in/into the refrigerator; to ~ new equipment into service; to ~ a criminal in prison; to ~ money in/into circulation; to ~ a plan into operation; to ~ one's affairs in order; to ~ a theory into practice; to ~ wood into a stove; to ~ sugar in/into tea; to ~ a car into a garage; to ~ words into smb.'s mouth; to ~ one's confidence/faith in smb.; ~ yourself in my place; to ~ smb. in a bad mood) 4. (d; intr.) ("to move") to ~ into (the ship put into port) 5. (d;

tr.) ("to express") to ~ into (to ~ one's feelings into words) 6. (d; tr.) ("to place") to ~ on (to ~ books on a table; to ~ a stamp on a letter; to ~ smb.'s name on a list; the doctor put the patient on a diet) 7. (d; tr.) ("to bet") to ~ on (to ~ money on a horse) 8. (d; tr.) ("to place") to ~ out of (the enemy has put all our tanks out of action) 9. (d; tr.) ("to assign") to ~ to (we put them all to work) 10. (d; tr.) ("to place") to ~ to (she put her fingers to her lips) 11. (d; tr.) ("to set") to ~ to (to ~ words to music) 12. (P; tr.) ("to place") to ~ one's family above all other concerns; she put her car at our disposal; ~ your shoes near the door; ~ the skis next to the fire; ~ the children to bed; ~ your things under the bed; to ~ troops across a river; she put her hand over her mouth; he put his arm around my shoulder 13. (misc.) to ~ a question to a/the vote; to ~ smb. to shame; to ~ smb. to death; to ~ smb. under arrest; to ~ smb. to great expense; to put smt./smb. through a long process of investigation; I put it ("suggested") to them that the plan should be revised; to ~ it crudely – you've lied to me!; let me ~ it another way – I don't think you're telling the truth; after hours of waiting I was – to ~ it mildly – a little upset (see also *to put smb. through their paces* at **pace I** *n.*)

put ahead *v.* (D; tr.) to ~ by (we put the clocks ahead (by) one hour)

put aside *v.* (D; tr.) to ~ for (we put aside some money for our future needs)

put back *v.* 1. (D; tr.) to ~ (by) (we put the clocks back by one hour) 2. (P) I put the book back ¬on the shelf/where it belonged¬ after I'd finished reading it

put down *v.* 1. (d; tr.) ("to consider") to ~ as (we put this trip down as a business expense = we put down this trip as a business expense) 2. (d; tr.) to ~ for ("to enter a pledge for") (I'll ~ you down for five tickets) 3. (BE) (d; tr.) ("to enter") to ~ for (he put down his son for Eton = he put his son down for Eton) 4. (D; tr.) to ~ on (she put the books down on the table) 5. (d; tr.) ("to attribute") to ~ to (she put the blunder down to inexperience = she put down the blunder to inexperience)

put forward *v.* (D; tr.) to ~ by (we put the clocks forward (by) one hour)

put in *v.* (D; tr.) to ~ for ("to submit") (the victim put in a claim for damages = the victim put a claim in for damages); I'll put in a good word for you with the authorities)

put off *v.* ("to postpone") 1. (D; tr.) to ~ until (she put the trip off because of the snow) 2. (G) we put off leaving because of the snow

put out *v.* 1. (D; refl.) ("to disturb") to ~ oneself out for (don't ~ yourself out for us) 2. (misc.) (for a vessel) to ~ to sea; to ~ to stud (see also *put out to grass* at **grass**; *put out to pasture* at **pasture**)

put over *v.* (D; tr.) ("to fob off") to ~ smt. over on smb. (he put his scheme over on the unsuspecting investors)

putter *v.* (AE: BE has *potter*) 1. (d; intr.) to ~ around (to ~ around the house) 2. (misc.) he loves ~ing around in his garden
put through *v.* (D; tr.) ("to connect") to ~ to (she was finally put through to her number)
put up *v.* 1. (B) ("to propose") I'll put the idea up to the whole committee 2. (d; tr.) ("to propose") to ~ as (we put her up as a candidate) 3. (old-fashioned) (BE) (d; intr.) ("to stay") to ~ at; with (to ~ at a hotel; to ~ with friends in/at Exeter) 4. (d; tr.) ("to offer") ("to propose") to ~ for (to ~ smt. up for sale; to ~ smb. up for an award) 5. (d; tr.) ("to provide") to ~ for (she put up the money for the flowers = she put the money up for the flowers) 6. (D; tr.) ("to give shelter to") to ~ for (my friends in Exeter put me up for a/the night) 7. (d; intr.) to ~ with ("to tolerate") (we will not ~ with such behavior) 8. (H) ("to place") to ~ water up to boil; he put the meal up to cook 9. (misc.) I put her up to it ("I persuaded her to do it")
puzzle I *n.* 1. to do, solve a ~ 2. a crossword ~ (see also **jigsaw**; **jigsaw puzzle**) 3. a ~ to (those matters were a ~ to the police until they realized what the key to the whole ~ was) 4. to put the pieces of a ~ together

puzzle II *v.* 1. (d; intr.) to ~ over (to ~ over a problem) 2. (R) it ~d me that they never answered the telephone 3. (misc.) it ~d me why they never answered the telephone
puzzled *adj.* 1. ~ about; at, by (I was ~ at her decision) 2. ~ to + inf. (I was ~ to learn of her decision) 3. ~ that + clause (I was ~ that they never answered the telephone) 4. (misc.) I was ~ ¬about/as to¬ why they never answered the telephone
puzzlement *n.* in ~ (they looked at us in great ~)
puzzle out *v.* (Q) I finally ~d out why they never answered the telephone
puzzling *adj.* 1. ~ to (her decision was ~ to everybody = it was a ~ decision for everybody) 2. ~ to + inf. (it was very ~ learn of her decision) 3. ~ that + clause (it was very ~ (to me) that they never answered the telephone) 4. (misc.) it was very ~ (to me) why they never answered the telephone
pyjamas *n.* (BE: AE has *pajamas*) a pair of ~
pyramid *n.* the food ~ ("the hierarchy of living beings in which each one feeds on the one below; the top of the food chain") (are we human beings really at the top of the food ~?)
pyre *n.* a funeral ~

Q

quagmire *n.* 1. to get bogged down in a ~ 2. in a ~ of

quail I *n.* a bevy, covey of ~

quail II *v.* (d; intr.) ["to lose courage"] to ~ at, before (we ~ed at the thought of getting lost in the forest; the servant ~ed before his master)

quake *v.* 1. (D; intr.) to ~ at (to ~ at the sight of the apparition) 2. (D; intr.) to ~ with (to ~ with fear) 3. (misc.) we were ~king in our boots; we ~d to see the apparition = we ~d when we saw the apparition

qualification *n.* ["limitation"] 1. with; without ~ 2. a ~ that + clause (we agreed to the proposed settlement with the ~ that there should be adequate compensation)

qualifications *n.* ["qualities, attributes"] 1. excellent, fine, outstanding, strong ~ 2. the necessary, right ~ 3. academic; educational; physical; professional ~ 4. the ~ for (she has the right ~ for the job) 5. the ~ to + inf. (she has the right ~ to do the job)

qualified *adj.* 1. eminently, fully, highly, suitably ~; well-qualified 2. poorly ~ 3. ~ as (she is ~ as an engineer) 4. ~ by (~ by education and experience for the position) 5. ~ for (she is highly ~ for the job) 6. ~ to + inf. (she is highly ~ to do the job)

qualify *v.* 1. (D; intr.) to ~ as (she ~fied as an engineer) 2. (D; intr., tr.) to ~ for (goods ~ for a discount if bought in large quantities; she ~fied for the job; what ~fied her for the job?) 3. (E) she ~fied to work as an engineer 4. (H) what ~fied her to do the job? 5. (misc.) a two-week course hardly ~fies her to do such a demanding job!

quality *n.* ["feature"] 1. admirable; endearing; innate; moral; personal; redeeming ~ties (he has no redeeming ~ties) 2. (misc.) there was a rhapsodic ~ about her playing ["degree of excellence"] 3. excellent, sterling, superb, superior; fine, good, high ~ 4. inferior, low, poor ~ 5. of a certain ~ (of good ~) 6. (misc.) (the) ~ of life

qualms *n.* 1. to feel, have ~ 2. ~ about (I have no ~ about borrowing money) 3. without (any) ~ (he's willing to ask for money without any ~!)

quandary *n.* 1. a hopeless ~ 2. in a ~ (we were in a hopeless ~) 3. a ~ about, over (they are in a hopeless ~ about their finances)

quantity *n.* ["amount"] 1. a considerable, huge, large, vast ~ 2. a sufficient ~ 3. a negligible, small ~ 4. in ~ (goods qualify for a discount if bought in ~) 5. in (large) ~ties ~ (goods qualify for a discount if bought in large ~ties) ["factor"] ["person"] 6. an unknown ~

quarantine *n.* 1. to impose, institute a ~ 2. to put smb. in ~ 3. to lift a ~ 4. strict ~ 5. a period of/in ~ 6. in, under ~ (to place under ~)

quarrel I *n.* 1. to cause, lead to a ~ (their political differences led to a bitter ~) 2. to have, pick, provoke, start a ~ (she picked a ~ with her neighbor) 3. to patch up, settle a ~ 4. a bitter, furious, violent; long-standing; never-ending ~ 5. a domestic, family ~ 6. a ~ breaks out, ensues 7. a ~ about, over; between; with (a bitter ~ broke out between them over the use of the telephone; she had a ~ with her neighbor about the money that he had borrowed)

quarrel II *v.* 1. to ~ bitterly, furiously, violently 2. (D; intr.) to ~ about, over; with (she ~ed with her neighbor about the money that he had borrowed)

quarry I *n.* ["prey"] 1. to stalk one's ~ 2. to bring one's ~ to bay 3. hunted ~

quarry II *n.* ["open excavation"] 1. to work a ~ 2. an abandoned ~ 3. a marble; stone ~

quarter I *n.* ["mercy"] 1. to give, show ~ (the invaders showed no ~) 2. to ask for; receive ~ ["one fourth"] 3. (in telling time) (a) ~ of (AE), to (the hour) (it was a ~ to five) 4. (a) ~ after (AE), past (the hour) (it is a ~ past five) 5. (misc.) to divide into ~s

quarter II *v.* (esp. mil.) (D; tr.) ("to assign to a lodging place") to ~ among; on, upon (to ~ troops on the local population; "~ing large bodies of armed troops among us" – U.S. Declaration of Independence, July 4, 1776)

quarters *n.* ["housing"] 1. to find ~ 2. bachelor; living; officers'; servants' ~ 3. cramped ~ 4. ("misc.") confined to ~ ["assigned stations on a ship"] 5. battle, ~ (see also **general quarters**) ["sources"] 6. from certain ~ (from the highest ~) ["misc."] 7. at close ~ ("close together")

quartet *n.* 1. to play, perform a ~ 2. a ~ performs, plays 3. a piano; string; woodwind ~ 4. a barbershop ~

quay *n.* at, on a ~

queasy *adj.* ["uneasy"] ~ about (to feel ~ about smt.)

queen *n.* 1. to crown a ~ 2. to crown; proclaim smb. ~ 3. to depose, dethrone a ~ 4. a despotic; popular; strong; weak ~ 5. a ~ ascends, mounts, succeeds to the throne 6. a ~ reigns; rules 7. a ~ abdicates 8. a ~ consort; mother 9. (misc.) to toast the ~; how was life under the old ~?; a beauty ~; a drag ~ (colloq. and derog.) ("a male transvestite"); a drama ~ (who over-dramatizes things)

queen's evidence *n.* (BE) to turn ~ (see also **king's evidence, state's evidence**)

queer I *adj.* 1. ~ about (there is smt. ~ about them) 2. ~ to + inf. (it's ~ to be speaking of the heat in January) 3. ~ that + clause (it's ~ that January has been so hot)

queer II *v.* (colloq.) 1. (d; refl.) ("to put oneself in a bad light") to ~ with (he ~ed himself with all his professors) 2. (misc.) ~ smb.'s pitch (that mistake of his really ~ed his pitch with all his professors!)

query *n.* 1. to put a ~ to 2. to reply, respond to a ~ 3. a ~ about

quest *n.* 1. to set out on a ~ (for) 2. a ~ for (she set out on a ~ for perfection) 3. in ~ of (she set out in ~ of perfection)

question I *n.* ["query"] 1. to ask (smb.) a ~ ; to ask a ~ of smb. ; to have a ~ for smb. 2. to address, pose, put a ~ to smb. 3. to bring up, raise a ~ 4. to fire, shoot a ~ at 5. to answer, field, reply to, respond to ; take a ~ (the senator fielded all ~s expertly) 6. to avoid ; beg ("evade") the ~ 7. to parry, sidestep smb.'s ~s 8. a civil ("polite") ; relevant ; straight-forward ~ 9. an academic, hypothetical, rhetorical ; debatable, moot ~ 10. a complex ; complicated ; puzzling ~ 11. a blunt, direct ; pointed ; probing ~ 12. an awkward, embarrassing, sticky, ticklish ; irrelevant ; leading ; loaded, tricky ; thorny ; trick ; trivial ~ 13. (on an examination) an essay ; mul-tiple-choice ; true-false ~ 14. an exam(ination), test ; quiz ~ 15. a ~ about, as to, concerning (the senator fielded expertly all ~s from the press about his activities but he did take a few ~s from the floor / audience) ["matter being discussed"] 16. to consider, debate, discuss ; look into ; raise a ~ 17. to put the ~ ("to vote on the matter being discussed") 18. a burning ; controversial ; crucial ; explosive ; open ; vexed (esp. BE) ~ 19. (misc.) (colloq.) to pop the ~ (to) ("to propose marriage") ["doubt"]["dispute"] 20. to clear up, resolve a ~ 21. a ~ about, as to, of (there is no ~ about her sincerity) 22. beyond (all) ~ 23. in, into ~ (to come into ~ ; to call smt. into ~) 24. open to ~ 25. without ~ ["inter-rogational form"] (ling.) 26. a tag ; wh- ; yes-no ~ (a tag ~ has a ~ tag, hasn't it ?) ["misc."] 27. out of the ~ ("impossible") ; the ~ of / as to / whether he'll go ; there's some ~ (¬about / as to¬) whether he'll go USAGE NOTE : The sentence *there's no question that he'll go* is ambiguous. It could mean "there's no question of him / his going – he'll stay". Or, it could mean "there's no question but that he'll go – he'll go".

question II *v.* 1. to closely ; intensively ; repeatedly 2. (D ; tr.) to ~ about (the police ~ed her closely about where the money had gone) 3. (Q) they ~ed where the money had gone

questionable *adj.* 1. highly, very ~ 2. (misc.) it's ~ whether she was actually there

questioning *n.* 1. close ("intensive") ~ 2. under ~ (under close ~ by the district attorney)

question mark *n.* 1. a big, huge ~ 2. a ~ hangs over (after those revelations, there's a huge ~ (hanging) over the senator's fitness to continue in office) (see also *question mark* at **mark I** *n.*)

questionnaire *n.* 1. to draw up, formulate a ~ 2. to circulate, distribute, hand out, send out a ~ 3. to answer, complete, fill in, fill out (esp. AE), fill up (BE ; old-fashioned) ; hand in, return a ~

queue I *n.* (esp. BE) 1. to form a ~ (to form a ~ for fresh fruit) 2. to join ; jump the ~ (AE has *buck the line*) 3. in a ~ (to stand / wait in a ~ for fresh fruit)

queue II *v.* (esp. BE) (D ; intr.) to ~ for (they had to ~ for fresh fruit)

queue up *v.* (esp. BE) (D ; intr.) to ~ for (they had to ~ for fresh fruit)

quibble I *n.* a minor ~

quibble II *v.* (D ; intr.) to ~ about, over ; with (to ~ with smb. about trifles)

quick I *adj.* 1. ~ about (be ~ about it) 2. ~ at (~ at picking up a new language) 3. ~ with (~ with one's hands) 4. (cannot stand alone) ~ to + inf. (she is ~ to pick up new languages ; he is ~ to take offense) 5. (misc.) ~ on (~ on one's feet ; ~ on the uptake) ; as ~ as a flash

quick II *n.* 1. to cut smb. to the ~ ("to offend smb. gravely") 2. (misc.) the ~ and the dead

quicksand *n.* a bed of ~

quiet I *adj.* 1. to be ; keep ~ 2. (misc.) as ~ as a mouse

quiet II *n.* 1. to shatter the (peace and) ~ 2. (misc.) peace and ~

quilt *n.* a crazy ; down ; patchwork ~

quintet *n.* 1. to play, perform a ~ 2. a ~ performs, plays 3. a piano ; string ; woodwind ~

quip I *n.* 1. to make a ~ about 2. a ready ~

quip II *v.* 1. (D ; intr.) to ~ about ; at 2. (L) she ~ped that a woman needs a man like a fish needs a bi-cycle = "a woman needs a man like a fish needs a bicycle," she ~pped (to me)

quirk *n.* 1. a strange ~ 2. by a ~ of fate

quit *v.* 1. (D ; intr., tr.) to ~as ; because of, over (he quit his job as a civil servant because of the bribe) 2. (colloq.) (esp. AE) (D ; intr.) ("to stop") to ~ on (the engine quit on us) 3. (G) she quit smoking

quits *n.* (colloq.) to call it ~ ("to cease doing smt.")

quiver I *n.* to feel a ~ (of excitement)

quiver II *v.* (D ; intr.) to ~ with (to ~ with excitement)

quiz I *n.* ["short test"] 1. to draw up, make up, prepare a 2. to give a ~ 3. to take a ~ 4. to fail ; pass a ~ 5. a daily ; general-knowledge ; pop (AE) ; pub ; weekly ~ 6. an oral ; unannounced ; written ~ (see also *quiz question* at **question I** *n.*)

quiz II *v.* (D ; tr.) to ~ about, on (the police ~zed the neighbors about the incident)

quoits *n.* 1. to pitch, play ~ 2. a game of ~

quorum *n.* 1. to constitute, make (up) a ~ 2. to have ; lack a ~

quota *n.* 1. to assign, establish, fix, set a ~ 2. to fill, fulfill, meet a ~ 3. to exceed one's ~ 4. an import ; production ; racial ~ 5. a ~ for ; on (congratula-tions ! you've exceeded your ~ for the week ! = you've exceeded your weekly ~ !)

quotation *n.* ["citation"] 1. to give ; take a ~ from 2. a direct ~ 3. a ~ comes from 4. a dictionary of ~s (from ; about, on ; for) (a dictionary of ~s from famous authors on just about every subject and for just about every occasion !) ["estimate of cost"] 5. to give, put in, send in, submit a ~ (for) 6. to invite ~s (for / from) 7. the highest ; lowest ~ (see also *quotation mark* at **mark I** *n.*)

quote I *n.* 1. scare ~s 2. in ~s 3. (misc.) ~ ¬unquote/ end of quote¬ (the President said – ~ "the only thing we have to fear is – fear itself!" – ¬unquote/ end of quote¬) see **quotation** (see also *quote mark* at **mark I** *n.*)
quote II *v.* 1. to ~ directly; in full 2. (A) she ~d several verses to us; or: she ~d us several verses 3. (d; intr.) to ~ from (she loves to ~ from Shakespeare) 4. (D; tr.) to ~ from (she loves to ~ verses from Shakespeare) 5. (misc.) to ~ about, on (she loves to ~ Shakespeare on just about any subject!); to ~ as (Hamlet's "To be or not to be" is frequently/ widely ~d as an example of Shakespeare at his best); I think she's going to resign – but don't ~ me on that!; the article ~d above = the above-quoted article; the President said – and I ~ – "the only thing we have to fear is – fear itself!" = the President said – ~ ~ "the only thing we have to fear is – fear itself!"

quotient *n.* an intelligence ~ (IQ)

R

r *n.* 1. to roll, trill an ~ 2. a retroflex; rolled, trilled; uvular ~

rabbi *n.* a chief; Conservative; Liberal (BE), Progressive (BE); Orthodox; Reform ~ USAGE NOTE: See the entry for **Judaism**

rabbit *n.* 1. ~s breed quickly; burrow; hop (see also *rabbit warren* at **warren**)

rabbit on *v.* (colloq.) (BE) (D; intr.) ("to chatter") to ~ about

rabid *adj.* ["fanatical"] ~ about, on (~ on a certain subject)

rabies *n.* 1. to catch, get; have ~ (can humans get rabies from mad dogs?) 2. to transmit ~ (can mad dogs transmit ~ to humans?)

race I *n.* ["group distinguished by certain physical traits"] 1. the Caucasoid; Mongoloid; Negroid ~ 2. the human ~ 3. the (so-called) master ~ 4. between ~s (have relations between ~s ever been better ~?) 5. of a ~ (have relations ever been better between people of different ~s?) 6. (misc.) a person of mixed ~ (see also *all races and creeds* at **creed** 4)

race II *n.* ["contest of speed"] ["competition"] 1. to have, hold, organize, stage a ~ 2. to drive; row; run a ~ 3. to enter; lose; take part in; win a ~ 4. to fix (the results of) a ~ 5. a close, even, hotly contested, tight; grueling; one-sided, uneven ~ 6. an automobile (AE), motor (esp. BE); boat; cross-country; cycle; dog; drag ("acceleration") ~; footrace; horse; long-distance; relay ~ 7. (pol.) a congressional; governor's, gubernatorial; political; presidential; senatorial ~ 8. a ~ against, with; between; for (the ~ for the presidency was run between well-qualified candidates; it was a ~ against time to get the patient to the hospital) 9. a ~ to + inf. (the ~ to conquer space) ["misc."] 10. a rat ~ ("very hectic activity"); since both parties have fielded strong candidates, the election is now very much a two-horse ~ (see also **arms race**)

race III *v.* 1. (D; intr.) to ~ against, with (to ~ against time) 2. (D; intr.) to ~ for (to ~ for a prize) 3. (D; intr., tr.) to ~ to (let's ~ to school; I'll ~ you to the car; we ~d the child to the emergency room) 4. (E) we ~d to get there in time 5. (P; intr., tr.) to ~ through the park; they ~d around the corner; we ~d them down the hill; they ~d down the hill to the bottom; they ~d up the hill from the bottom

race down *v.* (D; intr.) to ~ from; to (they ~d down from the top of the hill to the bottom)

race up *v.* (D; intr.) to ~ from; to (they ~d up from the bottom to the top of the hill)

racialism (BE) see **racism**

racing *n.* auto (AE), motor (esp. BE); cycle; drag ("acceleration"); flat; harness; horse; stockcar ~

racism *n.* 1. to stamp out ~ 2. blatant, out-and-out; endemic; institutionalized; rampant; vicious, virulent ~

rack I *n.* ["framework, stand"] 1. a bicycle; bomb; clothes; hat; luggage (AE), roof (BE); magazine; rifle; toast; spice; towel; wine ~ 2. a dish (esp. AE), plate (BE) ~ 3. in a ~ ["instrument of torture"] 4. on the ~

rack II *n.* ["destruction"] to go to ~ and ruin

racked *adj.* 1. ~ by (~ by doubt) 2. ~ with (~ with pain)

racket I *n.* ["noise"] 1. to make a ~ 2. an awful, terrible ~ 3. over the ~ (I can't hear anything over this terrible ~!) ["dishonest practice"] 4. to operate, run a ~ 5. a numbers; protection ~ 6. in a ~ (also humorous) ("what ~ are you in, then?" "I'm a gynecologist, actually.")

racket II racquet *n.* ["bat used to play tennis, etc."] 1. to swing a ~ 2. to restring; string a ~ 3. a badminton; squash; tennis ~

racketeer *n.* a big-time, notorious; petty ~

radar *n.* 1. to track by ~ 2. off, under the ~ (also fig., colloq.) (he got in under my ~ and I fell for him before I knew what he was really like; a major player in the international futures market who fell off the ~ after losing a lot of money)

radiant *adj.* ~ with (she was ~ with joy) USAGE NOTE: In this sense, *radiant* is used of women rather than of men.

radiate *v.* (D; intr.) to ~ (out) from; to (joy ~d (out) from her to everyone else at the party)

radiation *n.* 1. to emit, give off ~ 2. nuclear ~ 3. background; harmful ~ 4. a dose; level of ~ (even high doses of ~ may not cure certain cancers; low levels of background ~ have been reported here)

radical I *adj.* 1. politically; very ~ 2. ~ in (~ in one's views)

radical II *n.* a diehard; political ~

radio I *n.* ["radio receiving set"] 1. to plug in; put on, switch on, turn on a ~ 2. to switch off, turn off; unplug a ~ 3. to turn down; turn up a ~ 4. to listen to the ~ 5. an AM, medium-wave (esp. BE); (CB) Citizens' Band; clock; digital; FM, VHF (esp. BE); long-wave (esp. UK); portable; shortwave; transistor ~ 6. on, over the ~ (I heard the bad news over the ~) ["radio broadcasting industry"] 7. commercial; local; national; public (esp. AE) ~ 8. (to be/work) in ~

radio II *v.* 1. (A) we ~ed the message to them; or: we ~ed them the message 2. (d; intr., tr.) to ~ for (they ~ed (to) us for help) 3. (H) they ~ed (to) us to help them 4. (L; to) they ~ed (to) us that they needed our help

radioactivity *n.* 1. to emit, generate, give off, produce ~ 2. (a) dangerous (level of) ~

radishes *n.* a bunch of ~

radius *n.* 1. a cruising ~ 2. in, within a ~ of (within a ~ of fifty miles)

raffle I *n.* 1. to hold a ~ 2. to win a ~ 3. a ~ raises/

makes money 4. a ~ for (a ~ that made lots of money for our local church) 5. in a ~ (I won this in a ~)

raffle II v. 1. (D; tr.) to ~ (off) for (we ~d (off) lots of things for our local church) 2. (misc.) (we ~d (off) lots of things (in order) to raise money for our local church)

raft n. 1. to launch a ~ 2. a life ~ 3. on a ~ (to float on a ~)

rafting n. white-water ~

rag I n. to chew the ~ (colloq.) ("to chat") (see also **rags**)

rag II v. (slang) (D; tr.) to ~ about (they ~ged him about his beard)

rage I n. ["anger"] 1. to arouse, provoke, stir up smb.'s ~ 2. to express; feel ~ 3. to fly into a ~ 4. to face; placate ~ (to face the ~ of one's victims and try to placate it) 5. (a) blind, towering, ungovernable, violent; jealous; sudden ~ 6. ~ builds up; bursts out; subsides 7. an explosion, fit, outburst of ~ 8. a ~ against 9. in a ~ 10. (misc.) to be beside oneself with ~; quiver with; seethe with ~ ["fashion, vogue"] (colloq.) 11. the latest ~ 12. a ~ for (the latest ~ is for short skirts) ["misc."] 13. road ~ (an accident caused by a fit of road ~); it's all the ~ (are short skirts all the ~ right now?)

rage II v. 1. (D; intr.) to ~ against, at ("Rage, ~ against the dying of the light" – Dylan Thomas, "Do Not Go Gentle Into That Good Night," 1951) 2. (misc.) to ~ out of control (the fire ~d out of control); the epidemic ~d through the city

ragged adj. to run smb. ~

rags n. 1. a bundle of ~ 2. (dressed) in ~ (and tatters) 3. (misc.) from ~ to riches ("from poverty to prosperity")

raid n. 1. to carry out, conduct, make a ~ 2. a bombing; border; dawn; guerrilla; police; retaliatory; suicide ~ 3. a ~ into (the enemy carried out a ~ into our territory) 4. a ~ on, upon (a ~ on an illegal gambling casino) (see also **air raid**)

rail I n. ["barrier, handrail"] 1. at the ~ (to stand at the ~) 2. (to jump) over the ~ 3. (misc.) a towel ~; to hold on to a ~ (see also **rails**)

rail II v. (d; intr.) ("to complain") to ~ about, against, at

railroad I n. (esp. AE) 1. to manage, operate, run a ~ 2. a double-track; elevated; single-track ~ 3. a transcontinental ~ 4. a ~ from; to 5. on a ~ ("I've been working on the ~ All the live-long day" – American folk-song)

railroad II v. (colloq.) ("to force") 1. (d; tr.) to ~ into (they ~ed us into signing the contract) 2. (d; tr.) to ~ through (to ~ a bill through a legislature and then ~ another one through)

rails n. 1. to go off, jump the ~ (the train ¬went off / jumped¬ the ~s and there was a serious accident) (also. fig.) (he went off the ~s and got into serious trouble) 2. to ride the ~ (see **rod** 5)

railway n. 1. (esp. BE) see **railroad I** 2. a scenic ~

(BE) 3. a cable; cog; light; miniature; rack ~ 4. a broad-gauge; narrow-gauge; normal-gauge ~

rain I n. 1. to make, produce ~ 2. to keep the ~ out 3. (a) drenching, driving, heavy, pouring, soaking, torrential; freezing; intermittent; light; steady ~ 4. acid ~ 5. ~ falls; freezes; lets up; pours; starts; stops 6. ~ beats, patters (against the windows) 7. (misc.) the ~ came down in buckets; to get caught in the ~; (BE) it's pouring with ~

rain II v. 1. to ~ buckets, cats and dogs, hard 2. (D; intr., tr.) to ~ on (it was ~ing on us; they ~ed blows / gifts on us) 3. (misc.) tears ~ed down her cheeks (see also *to rain on smb.'s parade* at **parade I** n.)

rainbow n. a ~ appears, comes out

rain check n. (colloq.) (esp. AE) ["a deferred offer"] 1. to give, offer a ~ on 2. to take a ~ on ("how about dinner tonight?" "I'll have to take a ~ on that: I've got a previous engagement")

rain down v. (D; intr.) to ~ on (confetti ~ed down on the spectators; it was ~ing down on us)

raindrops n. ~ fall

rainfall n. 1. to measure ~ 2. annual, yearly; average; heavy; light, low; measurable; normal ~

rain in v. (D; intr.) to ~ on (it was ~ing in on us)

rainwater n. to catch, collect ~ (in a barrel)

raise I n. (AE) 1. to give smb. a ~ (in salary) 2. to deserve; get a ~ 3. a pay ~ 4. an across-the-board; annual ~ (BE has *rise*)

raise II v. 1. (D; tr.) ["to lift"] to ~ above (~ your hand above your head) 2. (D; tr.) ("to increase") to ~ by (they ~d their offer by one thousand dollars) 3. (D; tr.) ("to lift") to ~ from; to (to ~ a sunken ship from the bottom of the sea to the surface) 4. (d; tr.) ("to elevate") to ~ to (to ~ smb. to the peerage) 5. (D; tr.) to ~ as (our parents ~d us as atheists) 6. (H) ("to bring up") our parents ~d us to be atheists but also to respect others

raising n. consciousness-raising

raisins n. seeded; seedless ~

rake v. 1. (D; tr.) to ~ into (to ~ hay into piles) 2. (d; intr.) to ~ through (they ~d through piles of rubbish to find the lost items and then they ~d through them again = they ~d through piles of rubbish to find the lost items and then they ~d them through again) (see also *to rake smb. over the coals* at **coal**)

rally I n. ["mass meeting"] 1. to go in, join, take part in; mount, organize, stage a ~ 2. to ban; break up, quell; call off a ~ 3. an antinuclear; antiwar, peace; civil-rights; political ~ 4. a disorderly, violent; non-violent, orderly, peaceful ~ 5. a mass; organized; peace; pep (AE); political; protest ~ 6. a ~ calls for, demands; takes place 7. a ~ against 8. a ~ for, in favor of, in support of 9. at, in a ~ (we met at a student ~ against the wars) ["competition, race between cars"] 10. to have, hold, organize, stage a ~

rally II v. 1. (d; intr., tr.) to ~ around, round (to ~ around a leader; "Oh we'll ~ round the flag, boys" – George F. Root, "The Battle Cry of Freedom,"

1862) 2. (d; intr., tr.) to ~ for (the commanders ~ied their troops for a counterattack) 3. (d; intr., tr.) to ~ to (they ~ied to the support of their country) 4. (H) (the commanders ~ied their troops to counterattack)

ram I *n.* a battering ~

ram II *v.* 1. (d; tr.) to ~ into (to ~ piles into a river bed) 2. (misc.) to ~ smt. down smb.'s throat ("to force smb. to accept smt.")

ramble *n.* 1. to go for, go on; organize a ~ 2. a ~ across; through (to go for a ~ through glorious countryside) 3. on a ~

ramble on *v.* (D; intr.) ("to talk in a disorganized manner") to ~ about (she ~d on about her childhood)

ramp *n.* 1. a steep ~ 2. (misc.) to go down a ~; to go up a ~

rampage I *n.* to go on a ~

rampage II *v.* (P; intr.) to ~ through the streets; they ~d around the city hall

rampant *adj.* to run ~ (inflation was running ~)

ramparts *n.* to storm the ~

ranch *n.* 1. a cattle; dude ~ 2. at, on a ~ (he works at the ~; to live on a ~)

rancher *n.* a cattle; sheep ~

rancor, rancour *n.* 1. to stir up ~ 2. to express; feel; show ~ 3. deep-seated ~ 4. ~ against, towards (to feel ~ towards smb.) 5. with; without ~

random *n.* at ~ (to choose at ~)

range I *n.* ["series of connecting mountains"] 1. a mountain ~ ["distance that a gun fires, can fire"] 2. close, short; long; point-blank ~ 3. artillery; rifle ~ 4. at; from a certain ~ (at close ~) 5. in, within ~ 6. out of ~ ["place where shooting is practiced"] 7. an artillery; firing; rifle; rocket ~ 8. at, on a ~ ["extent, scope"] 9. a narrow; whole; wide; an age; price ~ (we stock the/a whole ~ of organic health-foods; a club with a wide age ~) 10. within a ~ (within a narrow price ~) 11. (misc.) top-of-the-range (a state-of-the-art top-of-the-range product) ["cooking stove"] 12. an electric ~ (see also **gas range**) ["open region on which livestock graze"] 13. to ride the ~ 14. on the ~ ["misc."] 15. a driving ~ (where one practices driving golf balls); the short-range outlook is bleak but the long-range outlook gives grounds for hope

range II *v.* 1. (d; tr.) ("to align") to ~ against (they were all ~d against us) 2. (d; intr.) ("to extend") to ~ from; to (prices ~ from ten dollars to thirty dollars) 3. (P; intr.) our discussion ~d over a wide variety of subjects = we had a wide-ranging discussion; the troops ~d through the fields 4. (misc.) prices ~ between ten and thirty dollars

ranger *n.* a forest ~

rank I *n.* ["row"] (esp. mil.) 1. to form a ~ 2. to break ~s (also fig.) ("to differ from the rest") (she broke ~s and voted against the war) 3. (misc.) to come up, rise from the ~s ["position, grade"] 4. to attain; have, hold a ~ (to hold the ~ of captain) 5. to pull

(colloq.), use one's ~ 6. to strip smb. of a ~ 7. high; junior; low; senior ~ 8. (mil.) permanent (AE), substantive (BE) ~ 9. (mil.) other ~s (BE; AE has *enlisted personnel*) 10. cabinet, ministerial (BE) ~ 11. above; below; by, in ~ (officers above the ~ of captain; to be seated by ~) 12. of ~ (of cabinet ~; of high ~) ["misc."] 13. to close ~s ("to unite") (her colleagues closed ~s behind the government); a taxi ~ (BE; CE has *taxi stand*); the ~ and file ("everyone"); to swell the ~s ("to increase the numbers of")

rank II *v.* 1. to ~ high, highly; low (we ~ the service very high indeed!; a high-ranking service = a highly ~ed service) 2. (d; intr., tr.) ("to be rated; to rate") to ~ above (nobody ~s above Shakespeare = we do not ~ anybody above Shakespeare) 3. (d; intr.) to ~ among (she ~s among our best instructors) 4. (d; intr., tr.) to ~ as (to ~ as an outstanding chess player; we ~ her as our very best instructor; she ~s as ¬Number 1/First¬ in the world!) 5. (d; intr., tr.) to ~ alongside, with (Pushkin ~s (right up there) with Tolstoy) 6. (N) we ~ her Number 1 in the world! = we ~ her First in the world! 7. (S) she ~s Number 1 in the world = she ~s First in the world! 8. (misc.) on a scale of one to five we ~ the service four

rankle *v.* (R) it ~d me that they ¬got/should have gotten¬ all the credit

ransom I *n.* 1. to pay (a) ~ for 2. to demand; exact a ~ from 3. to hold smb. for ~ 4. (usu. fig.) to hold smb. to ~ (I refuse to be held to ~ for the misdeeds of my colleagues!) 5. (misc.) the enemy exacted a king's ~ from us for the return of their hostages!

ransom II *v.* (D; tr.) to ~ for; from (she was ~ed from her captors for two million dollars)

rant *v.* 1. (D; intr.) to ~ about; at 2. (misc.) to ~ and rave

rap I *n.* (colloq.) ["blame"] 1. to take the ~ for (I refuse to take the ~ for my colleagues!) 2. (AE) a bad, bum ~ (she got a bum ~) ("she was punished for smb. else's misdeeds") ["charge"] (esp. AE) 3. to beat the ~ 4. on a ~ (he was sent to prison on a murder ~)

rap II *v.* 1. (d; intr.) ("to strike") to ~ at, on; with (to ~ on the window with a stick) 2. (d; tr.) ("to strike") to ~ over (she ~ped him over the knuckles with her ferrule) (see also **knuckle**)

rap III *v.* (slang) (D; intr.) ("to converse") to ~ about; with

rape *n.* 1. to commit ~ 2. attempted ~ 3. acquaintance, date; gang; marital; statutory ~ 4. a brutal ~ (see also *rape victim* at **victim**)

rapidity *n.* (with) great, lightning; ever-increasing ~

rapids *n.* 1. to ride, shoot ("pass through") (the) ~ 2. a stretch of ~

rapport *n.* 1. to develop, establish; feel; have ~ 2. close, good ~ 3. a ~ between; with 4. in ~ with (they worked in close ~ with us)

rapprochement *n.* to bring about a ~ between; with

rapture *n.* 1. complete, total, utter ~ 2. ~ about, at, over 3. in ~(s) over 4. (misc.) to go into ~s over

rare *adj.* 1. extremely, very ~ 2. ~ to + inf. (it's ~ to see snow here in September = it's ~ for there to be snow here in September) 3. ~ that + clause (it is ~ that there is snow here in September)

raring *adj.* (colloq.) ["eager"] (cannot stand alone) ~ to + inf. (we are ~ to go)

rash I *adj.* ~ to + inf. (it was ~ of her to try that = she was ~ to try that)

rash II *n.* 1. a diaper (AE), nappy (BE); heat; skin ~ (the baby has heat ~) 2. nettle ~ 3. a ~ breaks out 4. (misc.) to break out in a ~

raspberry *n.* (colloq.) ["contemptuous noise"] 1. to give, let out a ~ 2. to give smb. the ~

rat I *n.* 1. to catch ~s 2. a black; brown; water ~ 3. ~s bite, gnaw; scamper; squeak 4. (misc.) to smell a ~ ("to suspect that the truth is not being told"); a dirty ~ ("a contemptible person")

rat II *v.* (colloq.) 1. (D; intr.) ("to inform") to ~ on (the criminal ~ted on his accomplices (to the police)) 2. (d; intr.) to ~ to (the criminal ~ted (on his accomplices) to the police)

rate I *n.* ["amount in relation to something else"] 1. to fix, set; increase, raise; lower, reduce a ~ 2. a fast; flat; high; low; moderate; slow; steady ~ 3. bargain; reasonable; reduced; regular ~s 4. an accident; birth; crime; cure; death; detection; divorce; dropout; fertility; growth; marriage; morbidity; mortality; survival ~ 5. a base; discount; exchange; group; inflation; interest; mortgage; primary; prime; tax ~ (a drop/rise in mortgage ~s) (see also *rate of exchange* at **exchange**; **exchange rate**) 6. a metabolic; pulse; respiration ~ 7. an annual; hourly; monthly; seasonal; weekly ~ 8. a ~ falls; rises 9. at a certain ~ (at a steady ~; she borrowed money at a high interest ~) ["misc."] 10. at any ~ ("in any case"); first ~ ("top quality")

rate II *v.* 1. to ~ high, highly; low (we ~ the service very high indeed!; a highly ~d service) 2. (d; intr., tr.) ("to be ranked; to rank") to ~ among (that player is ~d among the very best) 3. (d; intr., tr.) ("to be ranked; to rank") to ~ as (this wine ~s as excellent; we ~ her as our very best instructor; she is ~d as one of the best tennis players in the country) 4. (d; intr., refl., tr.) ("to compare") to ~ alongside, with (this wine ~s with the very best; Pushkin is ~d (right up there) with Tolstoy) 5. (colloq.) (AE) (D; intr.) ("to enjoy a favored status") to ~ with (she really ~s with them) 6. (P; intr., tr.) ("to rank") this restaurant is ~d very highly = this restaurant ~s very highly 7. (GB) (P; tr.) ("to assess for tax purposes") their flat is ~d at eight hundred pounds this year 8. (s) I ~ this restaurant very high = this restaurant ~s very high 9. (misc.) on a scale of one to five we ~ the service four

rather *adv.* 1. ~ + inf. + than (she would ~ play

tennis than watch TV) 2. ~ + clause + than (I would ~ you stayed home than go/went out in this blizzard; she would ~ you did your homework than watched/watch TV) 3. ~ + inf. (she would ~ not watch TV) 4. ~ + clause (she would ~ you didn't watch TV = she would ~ you not watch TV) 5. (misc.) I prefer to walk ~ than (to) ride = I prefer walking to riding

rating *n.* ["classification"] ["limit"] 1. a high; low ~ 2. an approval; credit; efficiency; octane; poll; power ~ 3. a ~ for, on (she got a high poll ~ for decisiveness) ["ordinary seaman"] (BE) 4. a naval ~

ratio *n.* 1. a compression ~ 2. a direct; inverse ~ 3. a ~ between (is there a direct ~ between the proportion of people with lung cancer and the proportion of people who smoke?) 4. at a ~ of; to (at a ~ of three to one)

ration I *n.* ["fixed allowance"] 1. a daily; monthly; weekly ~ (our daily food ~) 2. a food; gasoline (AE), petrol (BE) ~ (our daily food ~) (see also *ration book* at **book I** *n.*; *ration card* at **card I** *n.*) 3. a ~ of (our daily ~ of food) (see also **rations**)

ration II *v.* 1. to ~ strictly 2. (D; tr.) to ~ to (we were ~ed to ten gallons of gasoline/petrol a month)

rational *adj.* ~ to + inf. (it was not ~ to expect miracles)

rationalization *n.* ["excuse"] 1. a mere ~ 2. a ~ for (a ~ for refusing to contribute) 3. a ~ to + inf. (it was a ~ to argue that increased spending would harm the economy) 4. a ~ that + clause (their ~ for refusing to contribute, that increased spending is bad, has been disproved)

rationing *n.* 1. to introduce ~ 2. to end, terminate ~ 3. food; gasoline (AE), petrol (BE) ~ 4. emergency; wartime ~

ration out *v.* (D; tr.) to ~ among, to

rations *n.* 1. to issue ~ 2. army; emergency; short ~ 3. on ~ (we were on short ~)

rattle I *n.* ["noise in the throat caused by air passing through mucus"] 1. the death ~ ["device producing a rattling sound"] 2. a baby's ~

rattle II *v.* (colloq.) (R) it ~d me to realize how close we had been to a real catastrophe

rattled *adj.* badly, very ~ (she was badly ~ at the news)

rattlesnake *n.* a ~ bites, strikes

ravages *n.* ["destruction"] to repair the ~ (wrought by war)

rave *v.* (D; intr.) 1. to ~ about, over; to (she was ~ving to us about her grandchild) 2. (D; intr.) to ~ against/at (she was ~ving at the new taxes) 3. (L; to) she kept ~ving to everyone that the new taxes were wrong

ravine *n.* a deep ~

raw *n.* ["natural state"] in the ~

ray *n.* 1. to emit, send forth, send out ~s 2. a cathode; cosmic; death; gamma; infrared; ultraviolet; X ~ 3. dying, last; heat; light ~s (we said farewell in the dying ~s of the sun) 4. a ~ of hope (the court's temporary reprieve provided a ~ of hope to the condemned man)

raze *v.* (D; tr.) to ~ to the ground (to ~ a building to the ground)

razor *n.* 1. to hone, set, sharpen a ~ 2. a dull; keen, sharp ~ 3. a double-edged; electric; safety; single-edged; straight (AE), cut-throat (esp. BE) ~

reach I *n.* 1. arm's, easy ~ 2. beyond, out of ~ 3. in, within ~ (to bring smt. within (arm's) ~; within easy ~) 4. (misc.) a boardinghouse ("very long"), long ~ (see also **reaches**)

reach II *v.* 1. (A; used without *to*) ("to pass") ~ me the salt 2. (d; intr., tr.) ("to extend") to ~ across, around (she could easily ~ her hand across the table) 3. (d; intr.) ("to extend one's hand") to ~ for (she ~ed for a cigarette) (also fig.) (to ~ for the moon) 4. (d; intr.) ("to extend one's hand") to ~ into (she ~ed into her pocket for her keys) 5. (D; intr.) ("to extend") to ~ to (the rope doesn't ~ to the ground)

reaches *n.* ["area"] 1. the lower; upper ~ (the upper ~ of the river) 2. vast ~ (the vast ~es of the western plains)

reach out *v.* 1. (d; intr.) to ~ for ("to attempt to obtain") (to ~ for mutual understanding) 2. (D; tr.) ("to extend") to ~ for (she ~ed out her hand for the change = she ~ed her hand out for the change) 3. (d; intr.) to ~ into, to ("to attempt to help") (to ~ to the local community) (see also *outreach program* at **program I** *n.*) 4. (D; tr.) ("to extend") to ~ to (she ~ed her hand out to us in friendship = she ~ed out her hand to us in friendship)

react *v.* 1. to ~ calmly; strongly 2. (D; intr.) to ~ against (to ~ against unfair treatment) 3. (D; intr.) to ~ to (to ~ to a stimulus; to ~ to a provocation) 4. (d; intr.) to ~ with (this medication ~s with aspirin) 5. (d; intr.) to ~ by, with (he ~ed to my provocation by punching me on the nose = he ~ed to my provocation with a punch on the nose)

reaction *n.* 1. to cause, provoke, spark, trigger a ~ 2. to encounter, meet with a ~ 3. to have a ~ 4. an enthusiastic; favorable, positive ~ 5. an immediate, instantaneous, quick, spontaneous; instinctive, knee-jerk (usu. fig.); natural, normal ~ 6. an adverse, negative; angry, hostile ~ 7. (a) delayed ~ 8. a strong; weak ~ 9. an allergic; chain; chemical; nuclear; physiological ~ 10. a ~ against, to (a natural ~ to provocation; an allergic ~ to nuts) 11. in ~ to (in ~ to provocation) (see also *reaction time* at **time I** *n.*)

reactionary I *adj.* 1. deeply; politically ~ 2. ~ in (~ in one's views)

reactionary II *n.* a diehard, dyed-in-the wool, political ~

reactor *n.* an atomic, nuclear; breeder; fission ~

read I *n.* 1. to have a ~ (I like to have a quiet ~ of the paper when I get home after work) 2. to be, make a ~ 3. a good, interesting ~ (her latest novel makes a very good ~)

read II *v.* 1. (A) she read a nice story to the children; or: she read the children a nice story 2. (D; intr.) to ~ about, of (I read about/of the accident in the paper; to ~ about a subject) 3. (d; tr.) ("to interpret") to ~ as (this story should be read as a satire) 4. (d; intr., tr.) to ~ for (she used to ~ for the patients in the nursing home; could you ~ that material for me?) 5. (esp. BE) (d; intr.) ("to study") to ~ for (to ~ for a degree; to ~ for the bar) 6. (d; intr.) ("to audition") to ~ for (she will ~ for the role of the ingenue in the new play) 7. (D; intr., tr.) to ~ from; to (she read from page ten to page thirty; she read to the children from *Peter Rabbit*) 8. (d; tr.) to ~ into ("to attribute") (don't try to ~ anything else into her letter) 9. (d; tr.) ("to enter") to ~ into (to ~ data into a computer) 10. (AE) (d; tr.) to ~ out of ("to exclude") (he was read out of the party) 11. (d; intr.) to ~ through (she read through the book at one sitting and he read through it , too = she read the book through at one sitting and he read through it , too) 12. (d; intr.) to ~ to (she loves to ~ to the children; she read to the children from *Peter Rabbit*; my daughter is old enough to ~ to herself) 13. (L) we read (in the papers) that prices would be going up 14. (misc.) they can ~ and write; to ~ by candlelight; to ~ a language fluently; to ~ between the lines; to ~ aloud, to ~ out loud (she read a nice story aloud to the children); to ~ silently (my daughter is old enough to ~ silently to herself); the letter ~s like an accusation; the play ~s well; the cablegram ~s as follows...; to ~ a child to sleep; to ~ oneself to sleep; to ~ smb. like a book ("to comprehend smb.'s motives very clearly"); a widely read column; she's widely read in the classics ("she has extensive knowledge of the classics")

read back *v.* (B) she read the sentence back to me = she read back the sentence to me

reader *n.* ["one who reads"] 1. an avid, omnivorous, voracious ~ 2. a regular ~ (of a newspaper) 3. a copy ~ (AE; AE also has *copy editor*; BE has *subeditor*) 4. (rel.) a lay ~ ["university teacher below the rank of professor"] (BE) 5. a ~ in (a ~ in physics) ["practice book for reading"] 6. a basic ~ ["assessor of a dissertation, thesis"] 7. a first; second ~ ["misc."] 8. a publisher's ~ 9. a mind ~ (see the Usage Note for **professor**)

readiness *n.* 1. combat; tactical ~ 2. ~ for 3. ~ to + inf. (her ~ to help was appreciated) 4. (to hold oneself) in ~ (for) 5. (misc.) a state of ~ (for); she indicated clearly her ~ to help

reading *n.* ["act of reading"] 1. extensive; good, interesting; heavy; light; remedial; responsive; serious; solid ~ (her latest novel makes very good ~) 2. a dramatic; poetry; staged ~ (they gave/ presented a staged ~ of *Paradise Lost*) 3. assigned; background; required; suggested ~(s) (have you done the assigned ~ for the course?) 4. at, on a ~ (at the first ~) 5. in a ~ (you will not be able to absorb the material in one ~) ["interpretation"] 6. a new ~ of

(Shakespeare); a pianist who gave a compelling ~ of a Beethoven sonata

readjust *v.* 1. to ~ downward; upward (our original estimate had to be ~ed upward (to allow) for inflation) 2. (D; intr., refl., tr.) to ~for; to (he had to ~ to the new climate; we ~ed our watches to (show) local time)

readjustment *n.* 1. to make a ~ 2. a price; rate ~ 3. a ~ for; in, of (an ~ in/of his salary (to allow) for inflation; a ~ of the brakes) 4. a ~ to (a ~ to a new environment)

read out *v.* (A) she read out a nice story to the children = she read a nice story out to the children; or: she read the children out a nice story

read up *v.* (d; intr.) to ~ on (to ~ on a subject)

ready I *adj.* 1. ~ for (~ for any emergency; we are ~ for you to start) 2. ~ with (she is always ~ with an answer) 3. ~ to + inf. (we are ~ to start) 4. (misc.) to get (smb.) ~ for; we made ~ to repel the attack; we stand ~ to do whatever we must; Ready, Aim, Fire!; ~ or not, here I come!; ~ when you are!; I'm ~, willing, and able to do it! USAGE NOTE: At the start of a race, the set phrases *Ready, set, go!* or *Get ready, get set, go!* or *On your mark* (AE) = *marks* (BE), *get set, go!* are used to competitors; the BE phrase *Ready, steady, go!* is fig.

ready II *n.* at the ~

ready III *v.* 1. (D; refl., tr.) to ~ for (she readied herself for the confrontation with her accusers) 2. (H) she readied herself to confront her accusers

reaffirm *v.* (L; to) the ministry ~ed (to us) that the visit had been postponed

reaffirmation *n.* ~ that + clause (I believed the ministry's ~ (to us) that the visit had been postponed)

realism *n.* 1. down-to-earth, gritty, hard-headed, kitchen-sink, no-nonsense ~; socialist 2. to lend ~ 3. a degree of ~ (the sound effects lend a degree of ~ to the scene)

realist *n.* a down-to-earth, hardheaded, kitchen-sink ~; socialist

realistic *adj.* 1. ~ about (let's be ~ about our chances of winning) 2. ~ to + inf. (is it ~ to expect us to win?)

reality *n.* 1. to become a ~ 2. (the) grim, harsh, sober ~ (the harsh ~ of life) 3. (computers) virtual ~ 4. in ~ 5. (misc.) to accept ~; to deny ~; to face (up to) ~

realization *n.* 1. to come to the ~ 2. a full; growing; sudden ~ 3. the ~ that + clause (they finally came to the ~ that a catastrophe could occur at any time)

realize *v.* 1. to ~ finally; fully 2. (L) they finally ~d that a catastrophe could occur at any time 3. (Q) they finally ~d how close they were to a catastrophe

realm *n.* in a ~ (in the ~ of science)

reaper *n.* the grim ~ ("death")

reapply *v.* ("to apply again") 1. (D; intr.) to ~ for; to (we ~lied to the authorities for assistance; the captain ~lied to headquarters for a transfer; she ~lied

for a fellowship) 2. (D; intr.) to ~ to (she ~lied to the three universities that had rejected her) 3. (D; refl.) to ~ to (she ~lied herself to her old duties with renewed energy) 4. (D; tr.) to ~ to (to ~ paint to the same surface; to ~ ointment to the same rash) 5. (E) ("to request") he ~lied (to the same university) to be admitted (to it)

reappoint *v.* ("to appoint again") 1. (D; tr.) to ~ as (we ~ed the same person as treasurer) 2. (D; tr.) to ~ to (we ~ed the same person to the committee) 3. (H) we ~ed the same person to serve as treasurer 4. (M and N; used with a noun) we ~ed the same person (to be) treasurer

reappraisal *n.* 1. to carry out, do, make a ~ of 2. an agonizing; careful; fair, objective, realistic; thorough, thoroughgoing ~

rear I *n.* 1. to bring up the ~ 2. at, from, in, to the ~ (the column was attacked from the ~)

rear II *v.* 1. (D; tr.) to ~ as (our children were ~ed as atheists) 2. (H) we ~ed our children to be atheists but also to respect others

reason I *n.* ["cause, justification"] 1. to cite, give a ~ 2. a cogent, compelling, convincing, good, important, plausible, solid, sound, strong, urgent ~ 3. a logical; personal; prime; real; underlying; valid ~ 4. every ~; (a) sufficient ~ 5. a ~ against; behind; for (the real ~ behind their decision was never made public; to have a ~ for not going; did he give any ~ for not going?) 6. a ~ to + inf. (we had every ~ to complain; there is sufficient ~ to be concerned; have they any ~ to believe that the earth is really flat?) 7. a ~ that + clause (the ~ that/why she did it is a mystery; did he give any ~ why he didn't go?) 8. by ~ of 9. for a ~ (he quit for personal ~s; for no apparent ~; I'm against it for the simple ~ that any new project is bound to fail; for some strange and unknown ~ he hasn't answered my letter) 10. with ~ (I fear him – and with good ~) ["logic"] 11. to listen to; see ~ 12. to stand to ~ ("to be logical") (it stands to ~ that the majority party will be reelected) 13. (misc.) an appeal to ~ ["reasonable limits"] 14. within ~ (I'll do anything for you within ~) ["sanity"] 15. to lose one's ~

reason II *v.* 1. (D; intr.) to ~ with ("to attempt to persuade") (you can't ~ with him) 2. (L) ("to argue") they ~ed that any new project would fail

reasonable *adj.* 1. ~ about (let's be ~ about this) 2. ~ of (that was not very ~ of you) 3. ~ to + inf. (it is not ~ (of/for you) to demand that employees work without a break)

reasoning *n.* 1. cogent, logical, plausible, solid, sound; objective; subjective ~ 2. faulty; shrewd; specious ~ 3. deductive; inductive ~ 4. ~ that + clause (their ~ that any new project would fail proved to be specious)

reassign *v.* ("to assign again") (D; tr.) to ~ to (headquarters ~ed the soldiers to the same unit; an experienced detective was ~ed to a more difficult case; to ~ a painting to a later century)

reassure v. ("to assure again") 1. (d; tr.) to ~ about, of (the contractor ~d us of the work's completion on time) 2. (L; must have an object) the contractor ~d us that the work would be completed on time 3. (misc.) let me ~ you (despite all rumors to the contrary, let me ~ you that he's not dead)

reassuring adj. 1. ~ to + inf. (it is ~ to note that airport security has been improved) 2. ~ that + clause (it is ~ that airport security has been improved)

rebate n. 1. to give a ~ 2. to get, receive a ~

rebel I n. a ~ against (a ~ against tyranny)

rebel II v. (D; intr.) to ~ against, at (to ~ against tyranny; they ~led at the thought of getting up before dawn)

rebellion n. 1. to foment, stir up; to spark (esp. AE), spark off a ~ 2. to crush, put down, quash, quell, smash, stifle a ~ 3. open ~ 4. an armed ~ 5. a ~ breaks out, takes place 6. a ~ against 7. in ~ (in open ~ against tyranny)

rebound I n. 1. (basketball) to grab a ~ 2. (misc.) on the ~ (right after her divorce she married smb. on the ~) 3. a ~ from (a ~ from a setback)

rebound II v. (D; intr.) to ~ from (to ~ from a setback)

rebuff I n. 1. to get, meet with, receive; risk a ~ 2. a brusque, curt; polite; sharp ~ 3. a ~ from; to

rebuff II v. 1. to ~ brusquely, curtly; politely; sharply

rebuke I n. 1. to administer, deliver, give a ~ 2. to draw, get, receive a ~ 3. a mild; polite; scathing, sharp, stern, stinging ~ 4. a ~ from; to

rebuke II v. 1. to ~ mildly; sharply, sternly 2. (D; tr.) to ~ for (to ~ smb. for sloppy work)

rebuttal n. 1. to make, offer a ~ 2. a ~ to 3. in ~ (to)

recall I n. ["remembrance"] 1. beyond ~ ["memory"] 2. complete, total ~

recall II v. 1. ("to remember") to ~ distinctly, vividly; fondly 2. (d; tr.) ("to remember") to ~ as (I ~ him as a very bashful child) 3. (D; tr.) ("to call back") to ~ from; to (to ~ smb. from retirement to active duty) 4. (G) ("to remember") she ~ed having seen him somewhere 5. (J) I ~ them visiting us 6. (K) ("to remember") I ~ed their having visited us 7. (L) ("to remember") she ~ed that she had seen him somewhere 8. (Q) ("to remember") she could not ~ exactly where she had seen him 9. (misc.) (the reader will) ~ that this subject has been discussed earlier

recede v. 1. (D; intr.) to ~ from 2. (misc.) to ~ into the background; to ~ into the distance

receipt n. ["receiving"] 1. to acknowledge ~ of 2. in ~ of (we are in ~ of your letter) 3. on ~ of ["written acknowledgment of something received"] 4. to give, make out, write out a ~ 5. to get a ~ 6. (esp. US) a return ~ (for registered mail) 7. a ~ for (you'll get a ~ for your purchase, which you must produce/show if you want a refund) 8. (misc.) box office ~s for the show have risen by 25% since opening night

receive v. 1. to ~ badly, coldly, coolly; favorably; warmly, well (the book was well ~d by the critics) 2. (d; tr.) to ~ as (the astronauts were ~d as conquering heroes) 3. (D; tr.) to ~ from (he ~d a letter from her) 4. (d; tr.) to ~ into (to ~ smb. into a church)

receive back v. to ~ into the fold (after many years of wandering, they were ~d back into the fold)

receiver n. ["part of a telephone"] 1. to pick up the ~ 2. to hang up, put down, replace a ~ 3. a telephone ~ ["radio"] 4. a shortwave ~ ["one who catches a forward pass"] (Am. football) 5. to hit; spot a ~ (to spot a ~ down the field) ["misc."] (comm.) 6. the official ~ (the bankrupt firm is now in the hands of the official ~)

receivership n. 1. to put a firm into ~ 2. in ~ (the bankrupt firm is now in ~)

reception n. ["social gathering"] 1. to give, hold; host a ~ 2. a diplomatic; formal; informal; official; wedding ~ 3. a ~ for (a ~ for graduating students) 4. at a ~ (we met at the ~) ["reaction, response"] ["greeting"] 5. to get, meet with a ~ 6. to accord, give (smb.) a ~ 7. a cordial, friendly, warm; emotional; enthusiastic; favorable; jubilant; lavish; rousing ~ (they gave us a warm ~; the book received a favorable ~ from the critics) 8. a chilly, cold, cool; hostile; lukewarm; mixed; unfavorable; unfriendly ~ (their proposal got a mixed ~) ["registration desk in a hotel"] (BE) 9. at ~ (leave your key at ~) ["receiving of broadcasts"] 10. good, strong; poor, weak ~ 11. radio; television ~

receptive adj. ~ to (~ to any reasonable offer)

recess n. 1. to take a ~ 2. to declare a ~ 3. a spring; summer; winter ~ 4. in ~ (parliament was in ~)

recession n. 1. a business, economic ~ 2. a major ~ 3. in (a) ~ 4. (misc.) to cause; come out of a ~; go into a ~ (the country has gone into a major ~)

recipe n. 1. to follow a ~ 2. the ~ calls for, requires; makes; serves (the ~ calls for enough eggs to make a large cake that will serve at least six people) 3. a ~ for

recipient n. an intended; worthy ~

reciprocate v. (D; intr.) to ~ by; for; with

reciprocity n. 1. ~ between 2. (misc.) on a basis of ~

recital n. 1. to attend, go to; give, hold, stage a ~ 2. to cancel a ~ 3. an organ; piano; poetry; song; violin ~ (to attend a wonderful piano ~) 4. a ~ by (to attend a ~ by a wonderful pianist) 5. a ~ of (a ~ of Schubert songs) 6. at a ~ (we met at a ~ to raise money for charity)

recite v. (B) she ~d her poetry to the audience from memory

reckless adj. ~ to + inf. (it was ~ of them to go out alone at night)

reckon v. 1. (BE) (D; tr.) to ~ among, as (I ~ them ¬(to be) among my friends/as my friends¬) 2. (colloq. in AE) (d; intr.) ("to depend") to ~ on (you can always ~ on my support; we ~ed on reaching our destination before nightfall) 3. (colloq. in AE) (d;

intr.) ("to deal") to ~ with (we'll have to ~ with him later) 4. (BE) (E) we ~ed to reach our destination before nightfall 5. (colloq.) (L) I ~ we'll reach our destination before nightfall 6. (BE) (M) I ~ them to be my best friends 7. (misc.) I ~ their chances highly; I ~ so; I ~ not

reckoning n. ["navigation"] 1. dead ~ ["calculations"] 2. by smb.'s ~ (by my ~) 3. (misc.) the day of ~

reclaim v. (D; tr.) to ~ from

reclamation n. land; water ~

recluse n. an aging, elderly; virtual ~

recognition n. 1. to give, grant ~ 2. to achieve, gain, get, receive, win ~ 3. belated; dawning; general, universal; growing; international, worldwide; national; official; public; tacit; wide ~ (to receive universal ~) 4. (diplomatic) de facto; de jure ~ 5. ~ for; from (to receive ~ for one's accomplishments from one's colleagues) 6. beyond ~ (burned beyond ~; my home town has changed beyond ~!) 7. in ~ of 8. out of all ~ (my home town has changed out of all ~!) 9. (misc.) she gave/showed no sign(s) of ~ except the briefest flicker of ~ when I entered the room – but eventually the ~ dawned on her that it really was me!; new techniques for voice ~

recognizance n. (legal) on one's own ~ (she was released on her own ~)

recognize v. 1. to ~ belatedly; generally, universally; increasingly; internationally, worldwide; nationally; officially; publicly; tacitly; widely ~ (to be ~d universally) 2. (D; tr.) to ~ as (she is universally ~d as an authority on the subject = she is a universally ~d authority on the subject) 3. (L) we ~d that she was an authority on the subject 4. (M) she is universally ~d to be an authority on the subject

recoil v. 1. (D; intr.) to ~ at, from 2. (misc.) to ~ in horror (she ~ed in horror from the awful sight)

recollect v. 1. to ~ dimly, hazily, vaguely; vividly 2. (G) she vaguely ~ed having seen him somewhere 3. (K) I vividly ~ed their having visited us 4. (L) I ~ that the weather was cold; she ~ed that she had seen him somewhere 5. (Q) she could not ~ exactly where she had seen him

recollection n. 1. to have a ~ of (I have a hazy ~ of the weather being cold) 2. a dim, hazy, vague; painful; vivid ~ 3. a ~ that + clause (I have a hazy ~ that the weather was cold)

recommend v. 1. to ~ enthusiastically, highly, strongly 2. (BE) (A) she ~ed a good dictionary to me; or: she ~ed me a good dictionary 3. (AE) (B) she ~ed a good dictionary to me 4. (D; tr.) to ~ as (she was ~ed as a suitable candidate for the job) 5. (D; tr.) to ~ for (she was/came highly ~ed for the job) 6. (G) she ~ed buying this dictionary 7. (BE) (H) she ~ed me to buy this dictionary = I was ~ed to buy this dictionary 8. (K) she ~ed my buying this dictionary 9. (L; subj.; to) she ~ed (to me) that I ¬buy/should buy¬ this dictionary

recommendation n. 1. to give smb. a ~ 2. to provide, write a ~ for smb. 3. to make a ~ 4. to act on, carry

out, implement; consider a ~ 5. a glowing, warm; lukewarm; negative; positive; strong; weak ~ 6. a ~ for 7. a ~ to (her ~ to us was to postpone the trip) 8. a ~ to + inf. (we ignored her ~ to postpone the trip) 9. a ~ that + clause; subj. (we ignored her ~ that our trip ¬be/should be¬ postponed) 10. at, on smb.'s ~ (we postponed our trip on her ~)

recommit v. (D; tr.) ("to confine again") to ~ to (to ~ smb. to a mental hospital after another breakdown; ~ted to prison for another crime)

recompense I n. (formal) 1. as (a) ~ (for) 2. in ~ (for) (she received a prize from the government in ~ for her charity work)

recompense II v. (formal) (D; tr.) to ~ for

reconcile v. 1. (D; refl., tr.) to ~ to (he had to ~ himself to his fate) 2. (d; tr.) to ~ with (we tried to ~ her with her sister = we tried to ~ her and her sister (with each other); to ~ a checkbook with a bank statement)

reconciliation n. 1. to bring about, effect a ~ 2. a ~ between; with (we tried to bring about a ~ between her and her sister) 3. (misc.) in a spirit of ~

reconnaissance n. 1. to carry out, conduct ~ 2. aerial ~ 3. (a) ~ in force

reconstruct v. (D; tr.) to ~ from (to ~ a crime from the evidence)

record I n. ["best performance"] 1. to establish, set a (new) ~ 2. to equal, tie a ~ 3. to beat, better, break, surpass a ~ 4. to hold a ~ 5. an unbroken ~ 6. an attendance; speed ~ 7. an all-time; national; Olympic; world ~ 8. ~ fall; stand (her ~ stood unbroken for many years until it was finally bettered) ["account of events"]["file"] (see also **records**) 9. to keep; make a ~ (to keep a ~ of events; there is nothing about that in the ~s we've been keeping) 10. to close; open up a ~ 11. an accurate; detailed; official; sketchy; verbatim; written ~ 12. a daily; monthly; weekly ~ 13. an archeological; fossil; historical ~ (how far back do the historical ~s go?; how old do the fossil ~s suggest Earth is?) 14. (a) public ~ (a matter of public ~) 15. dental; medical; school ~s (the patient's medical ~s show clearly the sort of treatment he requires) 16. of; on ~ (the coldest day on ~) 17. (misc.) to set the ~ straight ("to correct a misunderstanding") ["past performance"] 18. to have a ~ 19. a clean impeccable, spotless, unblemished ~ (when she came to the firm, she had a spotless ~) 20. a brilliant, distinguished, outstanding; excellent; good ~ (she has an excellent academic ~) 21. a mediocre, spotty ~ 22. an academic; employment; safety; service; track ~ (this airline's safety ~ is impeccable: it has a proven track ~ of many years with no accidents, so its track ~ for safety is wonderful!) ["recorded crimes"] 23. to have a ~ (he's been in jail and has a ~) 24. a criminal, police; prison ~ ["publication"] ["public disclosure"] 25. to go on ~ (by; with) 26. for the ~ (was her statement for the ~?) 27. off; on the ~ (what she told the reporters was off the

~) ["grooved disc"] 28. to cut, make; release a ~ 29. to play a ~ 30. a gramophone (BE), phonograph (AE); long-playing ~

record II *v.* 1. to ~ live; openly; secretly 2. (D; tr.) to ~ as (the investigators ~ed the case as closed) 3. (D; tr.) to ~ from, off; on (we ~ed the program from the radio on our new tape recorder) 4. (L) ("to report") the investigators ~ed that the crime syndicate had been protected by corrupt officials 5. (Q) ("to report") the investigators ~ed how the crime syndicate had been protected by corrupt officials

recorder *n.* a flight; video, video-cassette; voice ~ (see also **tape recorder**; **VCR**)

recording *n.* 1. to make; release a ~ 2. to play, play back a ~ 3. a tape; video ~

records *n.* ["recorded information"] 1. to file; keep ~ 2. to dig up ~ 3. to destroy; falsify ~ 4. accurate; inaccurate ~

recount I *n.* 1. to do, make a ~ (of votes) 2. to ask for, demand a ~

recount II *v.* 1. (B) to ~ a story to smb. 2. (Q; to) she ~ed (to us) how it happened

recourse *n.* 1. to have ~ to 2. by ~ to; without ~ to (she coped with her pain by ~ to meditation and without ~ to drugs)

recover *v.* (D; intr., tr.) to ~ from (to ~ from an illness; the police ~ed the missing items from the bottom of the river)

recovery *n.* 1. to make a ~ 2. a complete; gradual; partial; quick, rapid, speedy; remarkable; slow ~ 3. an economic ~ 4. a ~ from (the patient made a quick and complete ~ from her illness) 5. (misc.) on the road to ~ (the patient is well on the road to ~ from her illness); to wish smb. a speedy ~

recreation *n.* for ~ (what do you do for ~?)

recriminations *n.* 1. bitter; mutual ~ 2. without ~

recruit I *n.* a fresh, green, raw ~

recruit II *v.* 1. (D; tr.) to ~ for (to ~ mercenaries for the army) 2. (D; tr.) to ~ from; to (to ~ mercenaries for the army from various countries; to ~ members to a political party) 3. (H) to ~ mercenaries to serve in the army

recruiter *n.* 1. an air-force; army; marine; navy ~ 2. a ~ for (a ~ for the army)

rectitude *n.* moral ~

recuperate *v.* (D; intr.) to ~ from (to ~ from the flu)

recuperation *n.* 1. ~ from (smb.'s ~ from the flu) 2. (misc.) smb.'s powers of ~

recur *v.* 1. (D; intr.) ("to come again to mind") to ~ to 2. (D; intr.) to ~ throughout (that thought kept ~ring to me throughout the evening)

recuse *v.* (esp. US) (D; refl.) to ~ from (the judge ~d herself from the case)

red I *adj.* 1. (of a traffic light) to go, turn ~ 2. bright; dark; light ~ 3. (misc.) to blush, go, turn ~ (in the face) with embarrassment; as ~ as a beet (AE), beetroot (BE)

red II *n.* ["color"] 1. to dress in, wear ~ 2. (a) bright; dark; light ~ 3. a shade of ~ ["something red"] 4. a patch of ~ 5. dressed in ~ ["red light"] 6. on ~ (no turn on ~) ["debt"] 7. in; out of the ~ (to operate in the ~) ["misc."] 8. to see ~ ("to become furious")

rededicate *v.* (d; refl., tr.) to ~ to (we must ~ ourselves to our cause with renewed vigor)

rededication *n.* ~ to (our ~ to our cause)

redeem *v.* (D; tr.) to ~ from

redemption *n.* 1. ~ from 2. beyond, past ~

redeploy *v.* (D; tr.) to ~ from; to (troops were being ~ed from Europe to Asia)

redeployment *n.* 1. large-scale ~ (the large-scale ~ of troops) 2. ~ from; to

redevelopment *n.* urban ~

red-faced *adj.* ~ with (~ with shame)

red light *n.* 1. to go through, jump (BE), run (AE) a ~ (she ran a ~ and was fined) 2. at a ~ (to stop at a ~) 3. on a ~ (he went right through the intersection on a ~)

redolent *adj.* (formal) (cannot stand alone) ~ of, with (~ of honeysuckle)

redound *v.* (formal) (d; intr.) to ~ to ("to affect") (her success ~s to the credit of her teachers)

redress *n.* 1. to seek ~ 2. legal ~

red tape *n.* 1. to get caught up in, get involved in ~ 2. to cut, eliminate (the) ~ 3. bureaucratic; government ~

reduce *v.* 1. (D; tr.) to ~ by (production was ~d (by) ten percent) 2. (D; tr.) to ~ from; to (the physician ~d the dosage from four to one) 3. (d; tr.) to ~ in (he was ~d in rank) 4. (d; tr.) to ~ to (she was ~d to poverty; the corporal was ~d to the rank of private)

reduction *n.* 1. to take a ~ (in salary) 2. to make a (price) ~ 3. a considerable, dramatic, large, sharp, significant, sizable, substantial; gradual; moderate; slight, small; steady ~ 4. risk; stress; weight ~ 5. a ~ in (a ~ in salary) 6. a ~ from; to (a ~ in dosage from four to one; a ~ in rank from corporal to private) 7. at a ~ (to sell merchandise at a substantial ~)

redundancy *n.* (comm.) (BE) 1. to announce; make ~cies 2. to face; take ~ 3. compulsory; voluntary ~ (the company announced several hundred compulsory ~cies and the workers who faced ~ had to decide whether to take ~ or strike)

redundant *adj.* (comm.) (BE) to be made ~

reef *n.* 1. to strike a ~ (the ship struck a ~) 2. a barrier; coral ~

reek *v.* 1. (d; intr.) to ~ of (to ~ of alcohol) 2. (d; intr.) to ~ with (to ~ with sweat)

reel *v.* 1. (D; intr.) ("to stagger") to ~ under (to ~ under blows) 2. (misc.) it made my head ~ (to look down from such a great height)

re-elect *v.* 1. to ~ unanimously 2. (D; tr.) to ~ as (she was ~ed as vice-president for a second term) 3. (D; tr.) to ~ to (she was ~ed to the vice-presidency for a second term) 4. (H) she was ~ed to represent us for a second term 5. (M) the nation ~ed her to be vice-president for a second term 6. (N; used with a noun) the nation ~ed her vice-president for a second term

re-election n. 1. to run for (esp. AE), seek, stand for (BE); win ~ 2. smb.'s ~ to (we welcomed her ~ to the vice-presidency for a second term) 3. for ~ (she was defeated for ~)

reeling adj. to send smb. ~

re-entry n. 1. to allow, grant; refuse ~ (they refused us ~ into the country that we'd left) 2. a ~ into (a spacecraft's ~ into the atmosphere)

refer v. (d; intr., tr.) to ~ to (in her autobiography she never ~red to her parents; the problem was ~red to a committee; they ~red me to the manager; my GP ~red me to a specialist; he ~red to his opponent in his speech; he ~red to his opponent as a liar)

refer back v. (d; tr.) to ~ to (the report was ~red back to the committee)

reference n. ["mention, allusion"] 1. to make (a) ~ (she made no ~ to the incident; there is an index of ~s at the back of the book) 2. to contain a ~ (the statement contains several ~s to the incident) 3. a cross-reference; direct; indirect, oblique; literary; passing; vague, (thinly) veiled ~ 4. (a) ~ to (without ~ to age) ["regard, relation"] 5. in, with; without ~ to (in ~ to your request, no decision has been made) 6. a frame, term of ~ (this question falls outside the limited terms of ~ of this investigation) ["recommendation"] ["statement"] 7. to give, provide a ~ 8. a glowing, good, positive, satisfactory; negative ~ 9. a character ~ (her employer gave her a good character ~) ["consultation"] ["source of information"] 10. easy; further; future; quick ~ 11. for ~ (to file for future ~; arranged for easy ~ = arranged for ease of ~)

referendum n. 1. to conduct, have, hold a ~ on (to hold a ~ on the status of a territory) 2. a ~ to + inf. (to hold a ~ to determine the status of a territory) 3. (misc.) to decide (the status of a territory) by ~

referral n. 1. to give; make a ~ 2. a ~ from; to (my GP gave me a ~ to a specialist)

refill n. 1. to give smb. a ~ 2. a ~ for (a ~ for a ball-point pen)

refine v. (d; intr.) (esp. BE) to ~ on, upon ("to improve on") (to ~ on previous methods)

refinement n. a ~ on ("an improvement on") (a ~ on previous methods)

refinery n. an oil; sugar ~

reflect v. 1. ("to think about") to ~ closely; seriously 2. (D; intr.) to ~ on, upon ("to think about") (to ~ on one's past mistakes) 3. (d; intr.) to ~ on ("to discredit") (her unfounded accusations ~ed on her credibility) 4. (d; intr.) to ~ on ("to show") (her actions ~ badly/well on her upbringing) 5. (d; tr.) to ~ on ("to bring to") (the team's victory ~ed credit on the coach) 6. (L) ("to think, consider") he ~ed that he should answer as truthfully as possible 7. (Q) does this answer ~ how you feel?

reflection, reflexion n. ["criticism"] 1. a ~ on (this is no ~ on your qualifications) ["meditation, thought"]

2. quiet; serious; sober ~ 3. ~ on (~s on the war) 4. after, on ~ (on further ~ she saw her mistake) 5. a ~ that + clause (he changed his story because of his ~ that he should answer as truthfully as possible) 6. (misc.) time for ~ (I'll need more time for ~ before I can give you my answer)

reflex n. 1. to test smb.'s ~es 2. a conditioned ~ 3. abnormal; diminished; hyperactive; lightning-fast; normal ~es 4. (misc.) to trigger a ~ (a light tap to the right place can trigger a ~ in susceptible people)

reform n. 1. to carry out, effect a ~ 2. a far-reaching; radical; sweeping, wholesale ~ 3. (an) agrarian, land; economic; educational; fiscal; labor; penal, prison; political; social; tax; welfare ~ (to carry out a tax ~ = to carry out a ~ in/of taxation) 4. (an) orthographic, spelling ~ 5. (misc.) piecemeal ~s; the need for ~ is great but the pace of ~ should not be hurried

reformatory n. (now AE; obsol.) at, in a ~ (he spent time at/in a ~)

reformer n. an economic; political; social ~

refraction n. ["eye examination"] (AE) to do a ~ (the oculist did a ~)

refrain I n. to repeat; sing a ~

refrain II v. (D; intr.) to ~ from (to ~ from smoking)

refresh v. (d; refl., tr.) to ~ by; with (they ~ed themselves with a dip in the pool = they ~ed themselves by having a dip in the pool)

refreshing adj. ~ to + inf. (it was ~ to have a dip in the pool; it was ~ to find such honesty; how ~ly honest!)

refreshments n. 1. to offer, provide, serve ~ 2. light; liquid ~

refrigeration n. under ~ (to keep food under ~)

refrigerator n. 1. to defrost a ~ 2. a frostfree ~ 3. an electric; gas ~ 4. (misc.) to raid the ~ ("to consume large quantities of food from the refrigerator, esp. at night")

refueling, refuelling n. inflight, midair ~

refuge n. 1. to give, provide ~ 2. to find, take; seek ~ 3. a wildlife ~ 4. a place of ~ 5. ~ from (to take ~ from the storm)

refugee n. 1. a bogus; political; stateless ~ 2. a ~ from 3. among ~s (among the ~s (fleeing) from tyranny there may be a few bogus ones)

refund I n. 1. to give, pay a ~ 2. to get, receive a ~ 3. a full; partial; tax ~ (they gave us a full ~ of the money)

refund II v. 1. (A) (BE) they ~ed the money to us; or: they ~ed us the money 2. (B) (AE) they ~ed the money to us 3. (misc.) they ~ed the money (to us) in full

refusal n. 1. an adamant, brusque, categorical, curt, flat, out-and-out, outright, point-blank, unyielding ~ 2. a polite ~ 3. a straightforward ~ 4. (a) first ~ (BE; CE has *first option*) 5. a ~ to + inf. (I could not comprehend her ~ to help) 6. (misc.) to meet with a ~

refuse I *n.* (BE) to collect the ~ (see also **garbage, rubbish, trash**)

refuse II *v.* 1. to ~ brusquely, categorically, completely, curtly, flatly, outright, point-blank 2. (E) she ~d to see him 3. (O; can be used with one object) he ~d them nothing

refute *v.* to ~ completely (he denied the charge but he couldn't ~ it completely)

regain *v.* (D; tr.) to ~ from

regale *v.* (d; tr.) to ~ by; with (to ~ one's guests with funny stories = to ~ one's guests by telling funny stories)

regalia *n.* in full ~

regard I *n.* ["consideration"] 1. to have; show ~ 2. ~ for (she shows no ~ for the feelings of others; you must have ~ for our safety) 3. little, scant ~ ["esteem"] 4. high; low ~ (to hold smb. in high ~ = to have a high ~ for smb.) (see also **regards**) ["aspect, relation"] 5. in a ~ (in this ~) 6. in, with ~ to (in ~ to your request, no decision has been made)

regard II *v.* 1. to ~ highly (highly ~ed in the scientific community) 2. (d; tr.) to ~ as (to ~ smb. as a friend that others might consider an enemy) 3. (d; tr.) to ~ with (to ~ smb. with contempt) 4. (misc.) as ~s, ~ing (as ~s/~ing your request, no decision has been made)

regardless *adj.* ~ of

regards *n.* ["greetings"] 1. to convey smb.'s ~; to send one's ~ 2. to give smb. one's ~ 3. best, cordial, friendly, kind, kindest, sincere, warm, warmest; personal ~ (with best personal ~) 4. ~ from; to (best ~ to your family from all of us) USAGE NOTE: Such formulas as "With best regards to your family from us all" are used typically in the complimentary close of letters.

regatta *n.* an annual ~

regime *n.* (pol.) (typically derog.) 1. to establish a ~ 2. to bring down, overthrow a ~ 3. an authoritarian, dictatorial, totalitarian; puppet; repressive ~ 4. under a ~ (we all suffered under the repressive regime)

regimen *n.* 1. to put smb. on a ~ 2. to follow a ~ 3. a daily; strict ~

regiment *n.* 1. a Guards (GB); infantry ~ 2. a colonel commands a ~

region *n.* 1. a border; mountainous; outlying, remote; polar; tropical; unpopulated ~ 2. an autonomous ~ 3. (misc.) some features are found throughout the entire/whole ~; in the ~ of the lungs; to earn (something/somewhere) in the ~ of $50,000 a year

register I *n.* ["record, record book"] 1. to keep; sign a ~ 2. a case; hotel ~ ["roster"] 3. (BE) an electoral ~ 4. the Medical Register; the Social Register (she's (entered/listed) in Who's Who even though her family is not (listed) in the Social Register) ["machine that registers the amount of each sale"] 5. a cash ~

register II *v.* 1. (D; intr., tr.) to ~ as (she ~ed as a Republican and is therefore a ~ed Republican; he

was not ~ed as a voter) 2. (D; intr., tr.) to ~ for (she ~ed for two courses; our department(al) secretary has ~ed ten students for the seminar) 3. (D; intr., tr.) to ~ in (how many ~ed/are ~ed in the course?) 4. (D; intr., tr.) to ~ with (he had to ~ with the authorities; to ~ a pistol with the police) (also fig.) I'd like to ~ a strong protest with the authorities; although the news was important, it failed to ~ with them and hardly ~ed at all with me! 5. (E) have you ~ed to vote? 6. (misc.) the earthquake ~ed six on the Richter scale

registration *n.* 1. to conduct ~ 2. gun; voter ~ 3. ~ as (~ as a Republican) 4. ~ for (~ for this course has been completed) 5. ~ with (~ with the police) 6. ~ to + inf. (~ to vote)

regress *v.* (D; intr.) to ~ to (to ~ to one's childhood)

regret I *n.* 1. to express; have ~(s) 2. to feel; show ~ 3. bitter; deep, great, keen, sincere ~ 4. a token of (one's); twinge of ~ 5. ~ at, over; for (to express ~ at not being able to accept an invitation; ~ for one's mistake) 6. to smb.'s ~ ((much/greatly) to my ~, she retired last year) 7. with ~ (with sincere ~ we announce that he passed away last night) (see also **regrets**)

regret II *v.* 1. to ~ deeply, really, very much 2. (formal) (E) we ~ to inform you that your position has been eliminated 3. (G) we ~ having to inform you that your position has been eliminated 4. (K) we ~ your having to be dismissed 5. (L) we really ~ that we cannot accept your invitation; we ~ that your position has been eliminated

regrets *n.* ["expression of regret at declining an invitation"] 1. to send (one's) ~ 2. (esp. AE) ~ only (appears on invitations instructing recipients to respond only if they are unable to accept)

regrettable *adj.* ~ that + clause (it was ~ that we couldn't accept your invitation; it was ~ that your position had been eliminated)

regular *adj.* (misc.) as ~ as clockwork

regulation *n.* 1. to adopt, enact a ~ 2. to apply, enforce a ~ 3. to comply with, obey, observe a ~ 4. to contravene, violate; ignore a ~ 5. rigid, strict ~s 6. army; government; health; police; safety, security; traffic ~s 7. against ~s (it's against ~s to park cars there) 8. a ~ that + clause; subj. (we obeyed the ~ that no cars ¬be/should be/can be¬ parked there)

rehab *n.* (colloq.) in; into; out of ~ (she went into ~ a drunk, stayed in ~ for a while, and came out of ~ sober)

rehabilitation *n.* physical ~

rehearsal *n.* 1. to attend; conduct, have, hold; schedule a ~ 2. a dress, final ~ 3. a ~ for; of 4. at; during a ~ (I'll see you at the dress ~ of *Hamlet*) 5. in ~ (the play is in ~)

rehearse *v.* (D; intr., tr.) to ~ for (to ~ for *Hamlet*)

reign I *n.* during smb.'s ~

reign II *v.* 1. (D; intr., tr.) to ~ as (she ~ed as queen for many years) 2. (D; intr.) to ~ over (see also *to reign supreme* at **supreme**)

reimburse *v.* 1. to ~ amply, fully = in full, generously 2. (rare) (B) all expenses will be ~d to you 3. (D; tr.) to ~ for (you will be ~d for all expenses)

reimbursement *n.* ~ for (you will receive full ~ for/ of all expenses)

rein I *n.* ["control"] 1. to keep a ~ on 2. to give free, full ~ to ("to remove restraints on") (he finally gave free ~ to the emotions he had previously reined in) 3. a tight ~ (to keep a tight ~ on smb./smt.) (he finally gave free ~ to the emotions he had previously kept a tight ~ on) (see also **reins**)

rein II *v.* (D; tr.) to ~ to (to ~ a horse to the left)

reinforcements *n.* to bring up; commit; send ~

reins *n.* ["straps used to control an animal"] 1. to draw in, tighten the ~ 2. to pull, tug on the ~ ["control"] 3. to hold; seize, take over, take up the ~ (of government)

reinstate *v.* 1. (D; tr.) to ~ as (she was ~d as treasurer) 2. (D; tr.) to ~ in (to ~ people in their former positions)

reissue *v.* (B) the school ~d the same old textbooks to the pupils

reiterate *v.* 1. (B) she ~d her story to the police 2. (L) he ~d (to us) that he would resign

reject *v.* 1. to ~ completely, flatly, outright, totally 2. (D; tr.) to ~ as (he ~ed our argument as flawed)

rejection *n.* 1. complete, flat, outright, total ~ 2. ~ of; as (we bridled at his ~ of our argument as flawed)

rejoice *v.* 1. (D; intr.) to ~ at, in, over (we ~d at the good news that the war was over) 2. (E) (rare) we ~d to learn that the war was over 3. (L) we ~d that the war was over

rejoinder *n.* 1. a sharp; telling ~ 2. a ~ to

relapse I *n.* (esp. medical) 1. to experience, have, suffer; trigger a ~ 2. a complete, total ~ 3. a ~ occurs (what triggered the ~ that occurred after the patient's last remission?) 4. a ~ into (the patient suffered a ~ into a coma again; a ~ into previous bad habits) 5. in ~ (sometimes the patient is in ~; sometimes, in remission)

relapse II *v.* (D; intr.) to ~ into (to ~ into a coma again; to ~ into previous bad habits)

relate *v.* 1. (B) she ~d her version of the incident to the police 2. (d; intr.) to ~ to (this law does not ~ to your case; how do they ~ to each other?) 3. (L; to) she ~d to the police that the attack was unprovoked 4. (Q; to) she ~d to the police how the attack had been planned 5. (misc.) "you had an unhappy childhood? I can ~ to that: my childhood was unhappy, too!"; she had an unhappy childhood and, sad to ~, his childhood was unhappy, too

related *adj.* 1. closely; distantly ~ 2. directly; indirectly ~ 3. ~ by; to (I am ~ to him by marriage; are poverty and crime directly ~ (to each other)?)

relation *n.* 1. to bear; have a ~ to (X bears no ~ to Y) 2. a close; distant ~ 3. a direct; indirect ~ 4.

a ~ between (is there a direct ~ between poverty and crime?) 5. in ~ to (in ~ to crime, I think we've made some progress in reducing it) 6. (misc.) "what ~ was Queen Elizabeth I to Mary Queen of Scots?" "I believe they were cousins." (see also **relations**)

relations *n.* 1. to establish; have, maintain; normalize; renew ~ 2. to cement, improve, promote, strengthen ~ 3. to break off, sever; strain ~ (to break off diplomatic ~ with a country) 4. close, intimate; cordial, friendly, harmonious; strained, troubled ~ 5. business, commercial, economic, trade; diplomatic; foreign; industrial, labor; international ~ 6. human; public; race ~ 7. extramarital; marital; premarital; sexual ~ (to have sexual ~ with smb.) 8. ~ among, between; with 9. (misc.) friends and ~ ("friends and relatives")

relationship *n.* 1. to build; cement; enter into, establish, strike up a ~ (to establish a ~ with smb.) 2. to have a ~ with smb. 3. to bear, have a ~ (to bear a ~ to smt.) 4. to break off a ~ (to break off a ~ with smb.) 5. a casual; close, intimate; direct; indirect; meaningful; sexual; solid; stormy, tempestuous; symbiotic; tenuous; warm ~ 6. a doctor-patient ~ 7. an adulterous; extramarital; incestuous ~; interpersonal; spatial ~s 8. a direct; inverse ~ 9. a ~ between; to, towards; with (is there a direct ~ between poverty and crime?) 10. in a ~ (she is in an extramarital ~ with her husband's best mate; there should be some give-and-take in any ~ (between people))

relative I *adj.* ~ to

relative II *n.* a blood; close; distant ~; smb.'s closest, nearest ~s; friends and ~s ("is he a blood ~ or a ~ by marriage?" "he's not my son: he's my son-in-law")

relax *v.* 1. (D; intr.) to ~ by (they ~ by watching TV) 2. (G) they ~ watching TV

relaxant *n.* a muscle ~

relaxation *n.* 1. for ~ (what do you do for ~?) 2. (misc.) a ~ of the rules/restrictions

relaxing *adj.* ~ to + inf. (it is ~ to spend a few days on the beach)

relay I *n.* 1. to run a ~ 2. (misc.) to work in ~s

relay II *v.* (B) she ~ed the information to us

release I *n.* ["liberation"] 1. to bring about, effect, secure smb.'s ~ 2. a ~ from (a ~ from prison) ["surrender of a claim or right"] (legal) 3. to agree to; sign a ~ ["handing over"] 4. ~ to (the ~ of information to the press) 5. a news, press ~ ["recording"] 6. a new ~; the latest ~s ["misc."] 7. on general ~ (BE) (the film will go/be on general ~ from next week and you'll be able to see it at your local cinema)

release II *v.* 1. (D; tr.) to ~ from (he has been ~d from prison) 2. (D; tr.) to ~ into; to (the judge ~d the youthful culprit to his parents; the film has been ~d to various movie theaters; the information was ~d to the press; some offenders were ~d into the community)

relegate *v.* 1. (d; tr.) to ~ to (to ~ smb. to second-

class status) 2. (misc.) (GB) to ~ a team to the second division
relevance *n.* 1. to have ~ to (the evidence has no ~ to the case) 2. of ~ to (the evidence is of no ~ to the case)
relevant *adj.* 1. ~ to (the evidence is not ~ to the case) 2. ~ to + inf. (it's not ~ to cite such outdated evidence) 3. ~ that + clause (it's not ~ that she was out of town) 4. (misc.) is it ~ whether she was present at the scene of the crime?
reliance *n.* ~ on (I'd place no ~ on such evidence)
reliant *adj.* (cannot stand alone) ~ on (the prosecution is heavily ~ on questionable evidence)
relics *n.* ancient; holy ~; ~ of the past
relief *n.* ["easing of pain, of a burden"] 1. to bring; give ~ 2. to seek ~ 3. to find; receive ~ (they found ~ in looking at their late son's photographs) 4. to express; feel ~ 5. blessèd; great, immense; instant; pain; permanent; temporary; welcome ~ (a pain-relief clinic) 6. (esp. BE) (eligible for) tax ~ 7. ~ from (the rain brought instant ~ from the heat) 8. ~ to (the news came as a great ~ to us) 9. a ~ to + inf. (it was a ~ to get home) 10. ~ that + clause (they expressed ~ that they'd finally gotten home) 11. in, with ~ (to sigh in ~) 12. to smb.'s ~ ((much) to my ~ they got home safely) ["welfare, government aid"] (esp. AE; obsol.) 13. on ~ (in the l930s they were on ~) ["comic scenes"] 14. comic; light; mock (AE) ~ ["differences in height"] 15. bold; high; low ~ 16. in ~ (to show terrain in ~) ["sharpness of outline"] 17. in bold / sharp ~ against (a light background) (Count Dracula's castle stood out in sharp ~ against the snow-capped hills) ["material help"] 18. to provide, send ~ 19. disaster; emergency; famine; flood; humanitarian ~
relieve *v.* 1. (D; tr.) to ~ of (the general was ~d of her command) 2. (R) it ~d us to learn that they had arrived safely
relieved *adj.* 1. ~ at (we were ~ at the news that they had arrived safely) 2. ~ to + inf. (we were ~ to learn that they had arrived safely) 3. ~ that + clause (we were ~ that they had arrived safely)
religion *n.* ["formal belief in a divine power"] 1. to adhere to; embrace; have; practice a ~ (the hospital receptionist asked me if I had a ~ at all) 2. to abjure, recant, renounce a ~ 3. a fundamentalist; monotheistic; polytheistic ~ 4. (an) established, organized ~ 5. a personal; state ~ 6. a ~ teaches (our ~ teaches us to be kind to animals) 7. the teachings, tenets of a ~ 8. by ~ (he's Jewish by ~) ["study of systems of worship"] 9. comparative ~(s)
religious *adj.* deeply, devoutly, profoundly, very ~
relinquish *v.* (B) ("to yield") he ~ed his business interests to his children
relish I *n.* ["enjoyment"] 1. to show ~ for 2. with ~ (we listened to their story with great ~)
relish II *v.* 1. (G) we really ~ed listening to their story; I don't exactly ~ confronting him 2. (K) no one ~es his coming here

relocate *v.* 1. (P; tr.) ("to locate again") we ~d our firm in / to Florida 2. (P; intr.) ("to locate again") our firm is going to ~ in / to Florida
reluctance *n.* 1. to display, show ~ 2. extreme, great ~ 3. ~ to + inf. (her ~ to get involved was understandable) 4. with ~ (she got involved only with the greatest ~)
reluctant *adj.* (usu. does not stand alone) ~ to + inf. (she was understandably ~ to get involved in smt. so dangerous)
rely *v.* 1. to ~ heavily 2. (d; intr.) to ~ on, upon (the prosecution relied heavily ~ on questionable evidence for support) 3. to ~ on, upon; to + inf. (the prosecution relied heavily ~ on questionable evidence to support their case)
remain *v.* 1. (D; intr.) to ~ of (did anything ~ of the wreckage?) 2. (E) that ~s to be seen 3. (S) she ~ed a widow for the rest of her life; to ~ silent; (obsol.) "I ~ Your most humble and obedient servant, Martin Chuzzlewit" (used formerly in the complimentary close of letters)
remains *n.* 1. to exhume ~ 2. animal; human; mortal ~
remand I *n.* on ~ ("in prison awaiting trial") (to be held) on ~)
remand II *v.* 1. (d; tr.) ("to send") to ~ to (the judge ~ed the accused to the county jail) 2. (misc.) ~ed in custody ("sent back to prison")
remark I *n.* 1. to drop, make; address a ~ (please address your ~s to the chair, not to the last speaker) 2. to pass a ~ (they passed several sarcastic ~s about the food) 3. a complimentary; flattering; friendly; kind; reassuring; timely ~ 4. a droll; facetious; tongue-in-cheek; witty ~ 5. a pertinent; pithy; pointed ~ 6. a casual, throwaway; innocent; innocuous; off-the-cuff; passing ~ 7. a controversial; cryptic, puzzling; provocative; suggestive ~ 8. an inane; indiscreet; tasteless; trite; trivial ~ 9. a biting, catty, caustic, cutting, nasty, sarcastic, scathing, snide; cruel, unkind; cynical; derogatory; disparaging, insulting, offensive, rude; impertinent; slanderous ~ (I decided to take no notice of his snide ~s about me) 10. smb.'s closing, concluding; introductory, opening ~s 11. a ~ about (she made a ~ (to us) about how boring being interviewed was) 12. a ~ that + clause (she made the ~ (to us) that being interviewed was boring)
remark II *v.* 1. (d; intr.) to ~ on, upon (the visitors were heard to ~ on the excellent condition of the streets) 2. (L; to) she ~ed (to us) that being interviewed was boring
remarkable *adj.* 1. ~ for (the city is ~ for its clean streets) 2. ~ to + inf. (it's ~ to see such clean streets) 3. ~ that + clause (it's ~ that the streets are so clean after the parade) 4. (misc.) (it's ~ how clean the streets are after the parade)
remedy *n.* 1. to resort to, use a ~ 2. to prescribe a ~ 3. to provide a ~ (for) 4. (legal) to pursue a (legal) ~ 5. (legal) to exhaust all (legal) ~ies 6. a certain,

reliable, sure; effective, efficacious ~ 7. a cold; cough ~ 8. a folk; herbal; home; homeopathic ~ 9. a ~ works 10. a ~ for (my granny's home ~ for coughs certainly worked on me!)

remember v. 1. to ~ clearly, distinctly; dimly, vaguely; to ~ aright, correctly, rightly, well (we met in 1966, if I ~ aright) 2. (B; colloq. the direct object is always a personal pronoun) please ~ me to your family ("please give my regards to your family") 3. (D; tr.) to ~ about ("do you ~ anything about the incident?" "no, I'm afraid I can't ~ anything about it") 4. (D; tr.) to ~ as; for (I well ~ her as a young girl; Laurence Olivier will always be ~ed for his Shakespeare performances) 5. (D; tr.) to ~ of (what do you ~ of them?) 6. (E) she ~ed to buy a newspaper 7. (G) she ~ed buying the newspaper 8. (J) I ~ him being very generous 9. (K) I ~ his being very generous 10. (L) she ~ed that she had bought a newspaper 11. (Q) she couldn't ~ where or when she'd bought the newspaper USAGE NOTE: The sentence *she didn't remember to buy a newspaper* means "she forgot to buy a newspaper". The sentence *she didn't remember buying a newspaper* means "she had no memory of buying a newspaper", whether she bought one or not.

remembrance n. in ~ of

remind v. 1. (d; tr.) ("to cause to remember") to ~ about, of (he ~ed me of my promise; we ~ed them of why the meeting had been postponed) 2. (d; tr.) ("to call to mind") to ~ of (she ~s me of my cousin) 3. (H) she ~ed me to buy a newspaper 4. (L; must have an object) we ~ed them that the meeting had been postponed 5. (Q; must have an object) we ~ed them why the meeting had been postponed 6. (misc.) the merest hint served to ~ me of my promise; I think I need hardly ~ you that your rent is now due!

reminder n. 1. to serve as a ~ (of) (the merest hint served as a ~ (to me) of my promise to pay the rent) 2. a bitter; eloquent; final; gentle; grim ~ 3. a ~ to + inf. (we received a final ~ to pay the rent) 4. a ~ that a + clause (we received a final ~ that the rent was due)

reminisce v. (D; intr.) to ~ about

reminiscences n. 1. personal ~ 2. ~ about

reminiscent adj. (cannot stand alone) ~ of (that melody is very ~ of the music we listened to in the old days)

remiss adj. (formal) 1. ~ about, in (~ in (performing) one's duties; I was very ~ in not writing to you) 2. ~ to + inf. (it was ~ of me not to write to you)

remission n. ["lessening of the effects of a disease"] (esp. med.) 1. to experience, have a ~ 2. a complete, total; partial ~ 3. a ~ occurs (what triggered the relapse after the patient's last ~ had occurred?) 4. in ~ (sometimes the patient is in relapse; sometimes, in ~)

remit I n. (BE) ["assignment, area of responsibility"] 1.

a limited; wide ~ 2. a ~ to + inf. (they have a ~ to investigate the company's affairs) 3. (misc.) to fall outside; under; within the ~ of smt. (this question falls outside the limited ~ of this investigation)

remit II v. 1. (BE) (A) they ~ted the money to us; or: they ~ted us the money 2. (AE) (B) they ~ted the money to us

remittance n. 1. to enclose; send a ~ 2. (obsol.) (BE) a ~ man ("one living abroad on money emitted from home") 3. on ~ of (you will receive the book on ~ of the balance)

remonstrate v. (formal) (D; intr.) to ~ about, against; with (they ~d with the neighbors about the noise)

remorse n. 1. to display, exhibit, show ~ 2. to express; feel ~ 3. bitter, deep, profound, sincere ~ 4. a feeling; pang; stab; twinge of ~ 5. ~ for, over (he displayed no ~ for his crimes) 6. with ~ (he confessed his crimes with sincere ~)

remote adj. ~ from

removal n. 1. snow ~ 2. (BE) furniture ~ (see also *removal van* at **van**) 3. ~ from; to

remove v. (D; tr.) to ~ from; to (to ~ a dressing from a wound)

removed adj. 1. easily ~ 2. once; twice ~ (a first cousin once ~) 3. far ~ from

remover n. (a) nail-polish, nail-varnish (BE); paint; rust; spot ~

remunerate v. (formal) (D; tr.) to ~ for

remuneration n. 1. to offer ~ 2. to accept ~ 3. ~ for

rename v. (N) the file that had been named "urgent" has now been ~d "miscellaneous"

rend v. (D; tr.) ("to tear") to ~ into (to ~ one's clothes into shreds)

render v. 1. (A) she ~ed a valuable service to me; or: she ~ed me a valuable service 2. (formal) (D; tr.) to ~ into (to ~ a text into English) 3. (D; tr.) to ~ to (to ~ suspected terrorists to other countries for interrogation) 4. (N; used with an adjective) her remark ~ed me speechless

rendezvous n. 1. to have; make a ~ with 2. a secret ~

rendition n. 1. to give a ~ 2. a letter-perfect (AE), word-perfect (BE) ~ 3. ~ to (the ~ of suspected terrorists to other countries for interrogation)

renege v. (D; intr.) to ~ on (to ~ on a commitment)

renewal n. urban ~

renounce v. (D; tr.) to ~ for (to ~ wealth for happiness)

renovations n. 1. to make; undergo ~ 2. in; to (to make ~s in/to an old building)

renown n. 1. to achieve, attain, win ~ 2. great, wide ~ (to achieve great ~ as a pianist for one's performances of Beethoven) 3. international, worldwide; national ~ 4. of ~ (an artist of great ~)

renowned adj. 1. internationally; nationally; widely ~ 2. ~ as; for (~ as a pianist; ~ for one's inventions)

rent I n. 1. to pay ~ for 2. to raise the ~ 3. (AE) for

~ (the house is for ~) (BE has *the house is to let*) 4. (misc.) to pay five hundred dollars (in) ~ (see also *rent control* at **control**)

rent II *v.* 1. (A) to ~ a room to a student; or: to ~ a student a room 2. (D; tr.) to ~ from (to ~ a house from smb.) 3. (esp. AE) (d; intr.) to ~ to (she ~s to students) 4. (esp. AE) (d; intr., tr.) to ~ at, for (the room ~ed at five hundred dollars a month)

rental *n.* 1. car; film; office ~ 2. ~ to

rent out *v.* (B) to ~ rooms to students = to ~ rooms out to students (see also **let out**)

reorganization *n.* to undergo ~

repair I *n.* ["process of restoring to working order"] 1. to carry out, do, make a ~ (we have done the necessary ~s) 2. extensive, major; minor; necessary ~s 3. ~s to (the ~s to our roof cost one hundred dollars) 4. under ~ (the road is under ~) ["condition"] 5. in ~ (to keep a car in good ~; in poor ~)

repair II *v.* (formal or humorous) (d; intr.) ("to go") to ~ to (to ~ to the drawing room)

reparations *n.* 1. to pay ~ 2. war ~ 3. ~ for

repartee *n.* witty ~

repast *n.* (formal or humorous) a light, meager ~

repatriate *v.* (D; tr.) to ~ from; to

repatriation *n.* 1. forced ~ 2. ~ from; to

repay *v.* 1. (A) we must ~ the money to her for the tickets; or: we must ~ her the money for the tickets 2. (D; tr.) to ~ by; with (the firm repaid me with a promotion for my hard work = the firm repaid me for my hard work by promoting me) 3. (D; tr.) to ~ for (we must ~ her for the tickets) 4. (D; tr.) to ~ to (to ~ a loan to a bank)

repeat *v.* 1. (B) she ~ed her story to us 2. (D; intr.) ("to cause an unpleasant aftertaste") to ~ on (this type of food ~s on me) 3. (L; to) he ~ed (to me) that he would buy some stamps 4. (misc.) ~ after me; to ~ verbatim = to ~ word for word

repellent I *adj.* 1. ~ to 2. (misc.) a water-repellent fabric

repellent II *n.* an insect; mosquito ~

repent *v.* 1. to ~ sincerely 2. (D; intr.) to ~ for, of (to ~ of one's sins) 3. (rare) (G) he ~ed having stolen the car

repentance *n.* 1. to show ~ for 2. genuine, sincere ~ (to show genuine ~ for one's sins)

repercussions *n.* 1. to have ~ for; on 2. far-reaching; serious; unexpected ~

repertoire *n.* 1. the standard ~ 2. in a ~ (our company has several new plays in its ~)

repertory *n.* in ~ (to play in ~)

replace *v.* 1. (D; tr.) to ~ as (when my sister fell ill, they asked me to ~ her as secretary; when Jones couldn't play, the coach ~d him as quarterback) 2. (D; tr.) to ~ with (when Jones couldn't play, the coach ~d Jones with Smith: Smith has now ~d Jones) 3. (P) I ~d the book ¬on the shelf / where it belonged¬ after I'd finished reading it (see also **substitute II** *v.*)

replacement *n.* 1. to make a ~ 2. to be; get, receive a

~ for (Smith is now the ~ for Jones as quarterback) (see also **substitute I** *n.*) 3. (misc.) the ~ of smt. by smt. else (the coach's ~ of Jones by Smith as quarterback) (see also **substitution**)

replay *n.* (an) action (BE), instant (AE) ~

replenish *v.* (D; tr.) to ~ with

replete *adj.* ~ with

reply I *n.* 1. to give a ~ 2. to send a ~ 3. to get, have, receive a ~ 4. to draw, elicit a ~ 5. a favorable; witty ~ 6. a straightforward; succinct ~ 7. an immediate, prompt ~ 8. a brusque, curt, gruff; stinging; sullen; terse ~ 9. a ~ to 10. in ~ (to nod in ~) 11. in ~ to (in ~ to your letter)

reply II *v.* 1. ("to respond") to ~ brusquely, curtly; clearly, unequivocally; immediately, promptly; vaguely 2. (D; intr.) to ~ to (she did not ~ to my letter) 3. (D; intr.) to ~ with (she replied to my letter with one of her own) 4. (L; to) she replied (to us) that she would be happy to accept our invitation

report I *n.* 1. to file, give, make, present, submit a ~ 2. to do, draw up, issue, make, make out, prepare, produce, write, write out, write up a ~ 3. to confirm a ~ 4. an accurate; balanced; confirmed; detailed, exhaustive, full; favorable, positive; impartial, objective ~ 5. a biased, slanted; negative, unfavorable; sketchy; unconfirmed ~ 6. an annual; daily; monthly; morning; weekly ~ 7. a final; interim; preliminary; progress; status ~ 8. an oral; written ~ 9. an eyewitness; firsthand ~ 10. an accident; incident ~ 11. a live; news; newspaper; press; radio; traffic; TV; weather ~ 12. a classified; committee; confidential; intelligence; official; restricted; secret; special; top-secret ~ 13. a majority; minority ~ 14. a school ~ (BE; AE has *report card*) 15. a ~ about, on; from; to; with (she filed a ~ about the incident with the authorities; the annual ~ from the company to stockholders) 16. a ~ that + clause (we have heard ~s that the road is closed)

report II *v.* 1. (B) ("to relate") she ~ed the incident to the authorities 2. (D; intr.) to ~ about, on ("to describe") (the correspondent ~ed on the situation at the front) 3. (d; tr.) ("to describe") to ~ as (the fire was ~ed as burning out of control; the stolen car was ~ed by several people as having been seen = several people ~ed the stolen car as having been seen; he was ~ed as missing in action) 4. (D; intr.) ("to present oneself") to ~ for; to (to ~ to headquarters for duty) 5. (D; tr.) ("to inform on") to ~ for; to (to ~ smb. to the police for violating an ordinance) 6. (d; intr.) ("to send information") to ~ from (during the war, she ~ed from London) 7. (pol.) (D; tr.) to ~ out of ("to return smt. for further action") (to ~ a bill out of committee) 8. (d; intr.) to ~ to ("to answer to") (she ~s directly to the dean) 9. (D; intr.) ("to give information") to ~ to (I'll be ~ing to you soon) 10. (G) ("to make known") several people ~ed having seen the stolen car 11. (H) the stolen car was ~ed to have been seen in several places 12. (K) ("to make known") smb. ~ed their leaving early 13. (L; to) ("to relate") she ~ed (to us) that they had left early and that he was missing in action 14. (M) ("to describe") the fire was ~ed to be burning out of control; he was ~ed to be missing in action 15. (N; used with an adjective, past participle) ("to describe") the patrol ~ed the entire area clear/cleared; he was ~ed missing in action 16. (Q; to) ("to describe") she ~ed to the authorities how the incident had taken place; several people ~ed to the authorities where the stolen car had been seen 17. (esp. BE) (s) to ~ sick

report back v. 1. (D; intr.) to ~ to (you will ~ to the chairperson of the committee) 2. (L; to) they ~ed back to the committee that all goals had been reached

reported adj. (cannot stand alone) 1. ~ to + inf. (they were ~ to be safe; the stolen car was ~ to have been seen in several places) 2. ~ that + clause (it was ~ed that they were safe; it was ~ (to the authorities) that the stolen car had been seen in several places) 3. (misc.) they were ~ safe

reporter n. 1. a court; cub; financial; free-lance; investigative; news; police; radio; roving; science; society; sports; TV ~ 2. a ~ for, on, with (a ~ for/on/with *The Times* = a *Times* reporter)

report in v. (AE) (s) to ~ sick

reporting n. 1. balanced; impartial, objective ~ 2. biased, slanted ~ 3. investigative ~

repose n. in (a state of) ~

represent v. 1. ("to depict") to ~ graphically 2. (B) ("to be the equivalent of, to symbolize") this room ~ed home to them 3. (esp. BE) (B) ("to convey") to ~ one's grievances to the authorities 4. (d; refl., tr.) ("to depict") to ~ as (she was ~ed as an heroic pioneer) 5. (S; used with nouns) ("to be") this ~s a serious problem

representation n. ["statement"]["protest"] 1. to make ~s to (our ambassador made ~s to their government) ["act of representing"] 2. legal ~ (they insisted on having legal ~) 3. proportional; virtual ~ 4. ~ as (her ~ as an heroic pioneer)

representative I adj. 1. ~ of 2. as ~ (a sample selected as ~ of the whole)

representative II n. 1. a sales ~ (BE also had *commercial traveller*) 2. an elected ~ 3. as a ~ (of) (Mrs. Smith has been selected as a ~ of American homemakers)

repression n. 1. political; sexual ~ 2. (to live) under ~

repressive adj. ~ of

reprieve n. 1. to give, grant a ~ 2. to get, receive a ~ 3. a last-minute ~ 4. a ~ from

reprimand I n. 1. to administer, give, issue a ~ (the judge issued a ~ from the bench) 2. to get, receive a ~ (an employee who got a ~ for being late) 3. a mild; severe, sharp, stern ~ 4. an oral, verbal; written ~ 5. a public ~

reprimand II v. 1. to ~ mildly; severely, sharply, sternly 2. to ~ orally, verbally; in writing 3. to

~ publicly 4. (D; tr.) to ~ for (to ~ an employee publicly for being late)

reprint n. to issue a ~ (of a book)

reprisal n. 1. to carry out ~s 2. a harsh ~ 3. a ~ against, on 4. in ~ (for) 5. (misc.) as a ~; by way of ~

reproach I n. 1. a bitter ~ 2. a term of ~ 3. above, beyond ~ (his behavior is above/beyond ~ = his behavior is irreproachable)

reproach II v. 1. to ~ bitterly 2. (D; refl., tr.) to ~ for (to ~ an employee bitterly for being late)

reproduce v. (D; tr.) to ~ from (to ~ a photograph from an old negative)

reproduction n. ["copy"] 1. (a) high-fidelity; stereophonic ~ 2. a ~ (a ~ of a photograph from an old negative) ["biological process of reproducing"] 3. animal; human; plant ~ 4. asexual; sexual ~

reprove v. (formal) 1. to ~ harshly 2. (D; tr.) to ~ for (to ~ an employee harshly for being late)

reptile n. ~s crawl, creep, slither

republic n. 1. to establish a ~ 2. an autonomous; banana (obsol. derog.); democratic; people's ~

Republican n. (US) a registered ~

repugnance n. 1. to feel ~ 2. with ~ 3. (a) deep, profound ~ (she regards smoking with deep ~)

repugnant adj. 1. to find smt. ~ (she finds smoking deeply ~) 2. ~ to (smoking is deeply ~ to her)

repulsive adj. ~ to

reputation n. 1. to acquire, earn, establish, gain, get a ~ 2. to enjoy, have a ~ (he had the ~ of being a heavy drinker) 3. to guard, protect one's ~ 4. to compromise, blacken, blemish, damage, destroy, ruin, smear, tarnish smb.'s ~ 5. an enviable, excellent, fine, good, impeccable, spotless, unblemished, unsullied, untainted, untarnished ~ 6. a tainted, tarnished, unenviable ~ 7. an international, worldwide; local; national ~ 8. a ~ suffers 9. a ~ as, for (that judge has a ~ for being fair) 10. by ~ (to know smb. by ~) 11. (misc.) to live up to one's ~; to stake one's ~ on smt.

repute n. 1. high ~ (to be held in high ~) 2. ill, low ~ (a place of ill ~; to be held in low ~) 3. by ~ (to know smb. by ~)

reputed adj. (cannot stand alone) 1. generally, widely ~ 2. ~ to + inf. (she is widely ~ to be very generous)

request I n. 1. to file, make, submit a ~ (to file a ~ with the appropriate authorities; she has a ~ to make of us; to submit a ~ to the mayor's office) 2. to act on, agree to; grant, honor a ~ (I agreed to her ~ that I ¬be/should be/was (esp. BE)¬ there) 3. to deny, refuse, reject, turn down a ~ 4. a moderate, modest; polite; reasonable ~ 5. a desperate, urgent; unreasonable ~ 6. a formal; official; written ~ 7. an informal; oral; unofficial ~ 8. a ~ for (to make a ~ for more money) 9. a ~ to + inf. (she made a ~ for me to be there; a ~ to be allowed to leave) 10. a ~ that + clause; subj. (she made a ~ that I ¬be/should be/was (esp. BE)¬ there) 11. at smb.'s ~ (I was there at her ~) 12. by, on, upon ~ (brochures are mailed out on ~) 13. (misc.) this radio station takes and plays ~s if you phone them in

request II v. 1. (D; tr.) to ~ from; of (to ~ a favor of smb.) 2. (H) to ~ smb. to do smt. (she ~ed me to be there) 3. (L; subj.) she ~ed that I ¬be/should be/ was (esp. BE)¬ there

require v. 1. (D; tr.) to ~ from, of (she ~s attendance at meetings from everyone) 2. (E) one is not ~d to be a specialist = (esp. BE) "one does not ~ to be a specialist" – Elizabeth Bowen, 1899–1973 3. (G) the house ~s painting 4. (H) she ~d everyone to attend the meeting 5. (K) this position ~s everyone's attending all our meetings 6. (L; subj.) she ~d that everyone ¬attend/should attend/attended (esp. BE)¬ the meeting

requirement n. 1. to establish, set ~s 2. to fill, fulfill, meet, satisfy a ~ 3. to waive a ~ 4. admission, entrance; distributional (AE); legal; minimum; physical ~s 5. a ~ to + inf. (she has made it a ~ for everyone to attend all meetings) 6. a ~ that + clause; subj. (she has made it a ~ that everyone ¬attend/ should attend/attends (esp. BE)¬ all meetings) 7. (misc.) Sociology 101 is a ~ for Sociology 102

requisite n. a ~ for

requisition I n. 1. to make out, write out a ~ 2. to send in, submit a ~ 3. to fill a ~ 4. a ~ for 5. on ~ (that item is on ~)

requisition II v. (D; tr.) to ~ for

rerun n. to show a ~ (that channel keeps showing ~s of old TV programs)

rescue I n. 1. to attempt; effect, make, mount a ~ 2. to come/go to smb.'s ~ 3. a daring, heroic ~ 4. a ~ from (see also *rescue attempt* at **attempt I** n.; *rescue bid* at **bid I** n.)

rescue II v. (D; tr.) to ~ from

research I n. 1. to carry out, conduct, do, pursue ~ 2. to publish one's ~ (see also *research findings* at **finding**; *research project* at **project I** n.) 3. detailed, diligent, laborious, painstaking, solid, thorough ~ 4. independent; original ~ 5. empirical; further; qualitative; quantitative ~ (further ~ is necessary) 6. animal; biological; historical; medical; scientific ~ 7. market; operations; space ~ 8. ~ shows (has ~ shown that smoking is bad for health?) 9. an area of ~ 10. ~ in, into, on (~ on the development of an electric engine)

research II v. (BE) (D; intr.) to ~ into (to ~ into the development of an electric engine)

researcher n. an independent ~

resemblance n. 1. to bear, have a ~ to 2. a close, strong; faint, remote, slight; passing; striking; superficial; uncanny ~ 3. a family ~ 4. a ~ between; to

resemble v. to ~ closely, strongly; remotely, slightly

resent v. 1. to ~ bitterly, deeply, greatly, strongly 2. (G) she bitterly ~s not being the center of attention 3. (J) she bitterly ~s him being the center of

attention 4. (K) she bitterly ~s his being the center of attention

resentful adj. 1. bitterly, very ~ 2. ~ about, at, of (she's bitterly ~ at not being the center of attention)

resentment n. 1. to arouse, cause, stir up ~ 2. to bear, feel, harbor ~ 3. to express, voice ~ 4. bitter, deep, profound, smoldering, sullen ~ 5. unspoken; widespread ~ 6. ~ about, over; against; at, towards (she feels bitter ~ at not being the center of attention) 7. ~ that + clause (she feels bitter ~ that she isn't the center of attention)

reservation n. ["booking"] 1. to make a ~ (we made a ~ at a very good restaurant) 2. to confirm a ~ 3. to have a ~ (we have a ~ at the restaurant) 4. to cancel a ~ 5. an advance ~ 6. an airline; concert; hotel, motel, room; restaurant; theater ~ 7. a ~ for (I'd like to make a ~ for two people for 8 o'clock, please) ["qualification"] 8. a mental ~ 9. without ~ (see also **reservations**) ["tract of land"] 10. an Indian (Canadian English has *(Indian) reserve*); military ~ 11. on a ~ ["strip of land"] (BE) 12. a central ~ (on a road)

reservations n. ["doubts"] 1. to have ~ 2. to express ~ (they expressed strong ~ about the plan) 3. deep, strong; initial ~ 4. ~ about (do you have any ~ about the agreement?) 5. without ~ (to accept a proposal without ~ = to accept a proposal unreservedly)

reserve I n. ["restraint, coolness"] 1. to display, show ~ 2. to break down smb.'s ~ ["limitation, restriction"] 3. without ~ (to accept a proposal without ~) ["ability"] 4. dwindling ~s 5. in ~ (to hold/keep smt. in ~) ["tract of land"] 6. an Indian (in Canada: AE has *(Indian) reservation*); nature; wild-life ~ ["military force kept available for future use"] 7. the active; inactive ~ ["store"] 8. to build up; deplete a ~ (see also **reserves**)

reserve II v. 1. (esp. AE: BE also has *to book*) (C) ("to order in advance") she ~d a seat for me; or: she ~d me a seat 2. (esp. AE: BE also has *to book*) (D; tr.) to ~ for (I'd like to ~ a table for two people for 8 o'clock, please) 3. (D; tr.) ("to set aside") to ~ for (these seats are ~d for the handicapped)

reserved adj. ["restrained, reticent"] 1. very ~ 2. ~ about 3. ~ towards, with

reserves n. ["forces kept available for future use"] (usu. mil. and sports) 1. to call out, call up the ~ 2. to commit one's ~ 3. limited; unlimited ["stores"] 4. to build up ~ 5. to deplete, exhaust the ~ 6. coal; currency; gas; oil ~ 7. abundant; dwindling; limited, meager; limitless, unlimited; untapped ~

reservoir n. 1. an artificial; natural ~ 2. (misc.) an untapped ~ of talent that we need to tap (into)

reside v. (P; intr.) they ~ in London

residence n. ["home, abode"] 1. to establish, take up ~ 2. to change one's (place of) ~ 3. one's legal; permanent ~ ["state of being officially present"] 4. in ~ (a poet in ~; the Queen is in ~ at Balmoral: how long will she remain in ~ there?)

resign *v.* 1. (D; intr.) to ~ from (she ~ed (from) her job) 2. (d; refl.) to ~ to (he ~ed himself to his fate and to losing his job)

resignation *n.* ["act of resigning"] 1. to hand in, offer, submit, tender one's ~ 2. to withdraw one's ~ 3. to accept; reject smb.'s ~ 4. a ~ as (he offered his ~ as party leader) 5. a ~ from (he offered his ~ from the party leadership)

resigned *adj.* ["submissive"] ~ to (~ to one's fate)

resist *v.* 1. to ~ strenuously, stubbornly, vigorously 2. (G) they couldn't ~ making fun of him

resistance *n.* 1. to offer, put up ~ 2. to break down, crush, overcome, overpower, put down, smash, wear down ~ 3. to arouse, come up against, give rise to, stir up; encounter, face, meet, meet with, run into ~ 4. bitter, determined, fierce, stiff, strong, stubborn, unyielding, valiant ~ 5. armed; nonviolent, passive; sporadic; spotty; token; weak ~ 6. ~ hardens, stiffens 7. ~ crumbles; wanes, weakens 8. ~ to (~ to a disease; ~ to new taxes) 9. against, despite, in spite of (the) ~ (we adopted the resolution despite the ~ of the other party) 10. (misc.) a pocket of (isolated) ~; the line/path (AE) of least ~; her ~ was low and she came down with a severe cold

resistant *adj.* ~ to (~ to change)

resolute *adj.* ~ in (~ in one's decision to do smt.)

resolution *n.* ["decision"] 1. to draft; propose a ~ 2. to adopt, pass a ~ 3. to reject a ~ 4. a joint ~ (of Congress) 5. a ~ to + inf. (they adopted a ~ to increase membership dues) 6. a ~ that + clause; subj. (they adopted a ~ that membership dues ¬be/should be¬ increased) ["vow"] 7. to make a (New Year's) ~ ["resolve"] 8. (a) firm ~ ["fine detail"] (optics) 9. sharp ~

resolve I *n.* 1. to display, show ~ 2. to strengthen one's/smb.'s ~ 3. to shake, weaken smb.'s ~ 4. (a) firm ~ 5. a ~ to + inf. (nothing shook her ~ to become an engineer) 6. a ~ that + clause (nothing shook her ~ that she would become an engineer)

resolve II *v.* 1. (BE) (d; intr.) ("to decide") to ~ against (they ~d against going out on strike) 2. (D; tr.) to ~ into (to ~ a problem into its simpler components) 3. (BE) (d; intr.) ("to decide") to ~ on (they ~d on not striking) 4. (E) they ~d not to go out on strike 5. (L) they ~d that they would not go out on strike; "we here highly ~ that the dead shall not have died in vain" – Abraham Lincoln, "The Gettysburg Address," 1863 USAGE NOTE: The collocation "resolve highly" is a literary equivalent of "resolve firmly."

resolved *adj.* (usu. does not stand alone) 1. firmly ~ 2. ~ to + inf. (she is ~ to become an engineer) 3. (formal) ~ that + clause; subj. (be it hereby ~ that membership dues ¬be/should be¬ increased)

resort I *n.* ["recourse"] 1. (formal) to have ~ to 2. a last ~ (as a last ~) ["recreational center"] 3. a beach; fashionable; health; holiday, vacation (esp. AE); popular; ski; summer; winter ~ 4. at, in a ~

resort II *v.* (d; intr.) to ~ to (to ~ to trickery)

resound *v.* (P; intr.) applause ~ed in/throughout the hall = the hall ~ed with applause; the shouts of the hunters ~ed through the forest = the forest ~ed with the shouts of the hunters

resourceful *adj.* ~ to + inf. (it was ~ of them to find the solution so quickly)

resources *n.* 1. to develop; exploit, tap; mobilize ~ 2. to conserve, husband; marshall; pool, share one's ~ 3. to deplete, exhaust, squander, use up, waste ~ 4. abundant; dwindling; limited, meager; limitless, unlimited; untapped ~ 5. economic; natural ~ (to exploit natural ~) 6. human; inner ~ 7. the ~ to + inf. (we have the ~ to do the job) 8. (misc.) left to one's own ~s ("left on one's own; unaided; left to one's own devices")

respect I *n.* ["esteem"] 1. to accord, pay, show; have ~ (to have ~ for smb.; to show ~ for/to smb.; to pay a lot of respect to smb.) 2. to command, inspire ~ (she commands ~ from everyone = she commands everyone's ~) 3. to earn, gain, get, win ~ 4. to lose smb.'s ~ (if I do that will I lose your ~?) 5. deep, great, profound, sincere, utmost; due; grudging; mutual ~ 6. a mark, sign, token of ~ (we observed a minute's silence as a mark of ~ for the fallen) 7. ~ for (~ for the law; if I do that will you lose ~ for me?) 8. out of ~ (we observed a minute's silence out of ~ for the fallen) 9. in ~ (to hold smb. in ~) 10. with ~ (with (all due) ~, I disagree) ["regard"] 11. in a ~ (in this/that ~; in all ~s) 12. in, with ~ to; (esp. BE) in ~ of (see also **respects**)

respect II *v.* 1. to ~ deeply, very much; widely 2. (D; tr.) to ~ as (to ~ smb. as a scholar) 3. (D; tr.) to ~ for (I ~ them for their scholarship)

respected *adj.* 1. highly; universally, widely ~ 2. ~ as (highly ~ as scholars) 3. ~ for (highly ~ for their scholarship)

respectful *adj.* 1. very ~ 2. ~ of; to (very ~ of one's elders)

respects *n.* to pay; send one's ~ (to pay one's last ~ after smb.'s death)

respiration *n.* artificial; labored; normal ~ (to give smb. artificial ~)

respite *n.* 1. to allow, give ~ (the cold allowed us no ~) 2. to get, have a ~ (we finally got a brief ~ from the cold) 3. a brief, temporary; welcome ~ 4. a ~ from (there was no ~ for us from the cold!) 5. without ~

resplendent *adj.* ~ in; with (~ in their academic gowns)

respond *v.* 1. ("to respond") to ~ affirmatively, positively; brusquely, curtly; clearly, unequivocally; enthusiastically; favorably; immediately, promptly; negatively; vaguely, wittily 2. (D; intr.) ("to react") to ~ by (they ~ed by walking out) 3. (D; intr.) to ~ to ("to answer") (to ~ to a letter) 4. (D; intr.) ("to react") to ~ to (to ~ well to kind treatment) 5. (D; intr.) ("to react") to ~ with (they ~ed to our demands with an immediate walkout) 6. (L; to) she ~ed (to us) that she would be happy to accept our invitation = "¬I'd be/I'm¬ happy to accept your invitation!" she ~ed (to us)

response n. 1. to call forth, draw (forth), elicit, evoke a ~ 2. to give, make a ~ 3. to get, have, receive a ~ 4. a brusque, curt; clear, unequivocal; enthusiastic; favorable; vague; witty ~ 5. a glib; lukewarm; sullen ~ 6. a delayed; immediate ~ 7. an affirmative, positive; negative ~ 8. a ~ to (there was no lack of enthusiastic ~s to our offer!) 9. in ~ to

responsibility n. ["accountability"] ["obligation"] 1. to accept, assume, bear, have, shoulder, take, take on (a) ~ 2. to exercise 3. to discharge a ~ 4. to abandon, abdicate, disclaim, dodge, evade, give up, shirk (a) ~ 5. to delegate; share; shift (a) ~ 6. an awesome, grave, great, heavy, terrible (colloq.); clear ~ 7. (a) collective; joint; moral; personal ~ 8. the ultimate ~ 9. (a) ~ falls on; lies, rests with smb. 10. (a) ~ for (the ultimate ~ for the decision rests/lies with the president = the president bears the ultimate ~ for the decision; the president said he would take personal ~ for the consequences of his decision) 11. a ~ to (have you no ~ to your country?!) 12. the ~ to + inf. (everyone has a/the ~ to pay taxes) 13. ~ that + clause; subj. (it was her ~ that all members ¬be/should be/were (esp. BE)¬ notified) 14. on one's ~ (she did it on her own ~) ["blame"] 15. to lay the ~ (fairly and squarely) at smb.'s door 16. to admit, claim; bear ~ (a shadowy group claimed ~ for the hijacking; the president must bear the ultimate ~ for the decision) 17. to disclaim (all) ~ 18. ~ for USAGE NOTE: In reporting smt. bad, it has been recommended that those responsible should be said to "admit" responsibility rather than to "claim" responsibility. That is probably because of the collocations "admit guilt" (for smt. bad) and "claim credit" (for smt. good).

responsible adj. 1. directly; personally 2. ~ for; to (politicians are ~ to the voters; people are ~ for their actions) 3. (misc.) to hold smb. ~ for smt. (you'll be held personally ~ for the consequences of your decision!; you'll be held personally ~ if anything goes wrong!)

responsive adj. ~ to (~ to flattery)

responsiveness n. ~ to

rest I n. ["repose"] 1. to have, take a ~ 2. to get some ~ 3. a well-earned ~ 4. bed; complete ~ 5. ~ from 6. at ~ (at last he is at ~ from his labors!) 7. (misc.) to come to ~ ("to stop"); to go to one's eternal ~ ("to die"); laid to ~ ("buried"); at parade ~ (mil.) (the platoon was at parade ~); to set one's mind at ~ 8. (misc.) to find ~ (may your troubled spirit find ~!) ["support"] 9. an armrest; chin ~

rest II v. 1. (d; tr.) ("to support") to ~ on (~ your head on my shoulder) 2. (d; intr.) ("to stand") to ~ on (the statue ~s on a pedestal) 3. (d; intr.) ("to depend") to ~ with (the decision ~s with the court; it ~s with the court to make the decision) 4. (misc.) to ~ in peace ("to lie buried") (may she ~ in peace!) (see also *rest easy* at **easy**)

restaurant n. 1. to manage, operate, run; go to a ~ 2. an elegant, first-class ~ 3. a dairy; fast-food; fish, seafood; kosher; vegetarian ~ 4. (BE) a licensed ~ (that may sell alcoholic drinks) 5. at, in a ~

restful adj. ~ to + inf. (it's ~ just to sit and read = it's ~ just sitting and reading)

restitution n. 1. to make; offer ~ 2. full ~ 3. ~ for 4. ~ to

restock v. (D; tr.) to ~ with (they ~ed their store with more merchandise; to ~ a pond with more fish)

restore v. (d; tr.) to ~ to (to ~ people to their former positions)

restrain v. (D; refl., tr.) to ~ from (to ~ smb. from committing violence)

restraint n. ["control"] ["act of restraining"] 1. to display, exercise, show; impose ~ 2. to cast off, fling off, shake off (all); lift ~ 3. (legal) prior ~ 4. ~ in; on (they showed ~ in responding to the provocation; the government has sought to impose ~s on violence) 5. in ~ of (in ~ of trade) ["device for restraining"] 6. to apply, put on ~s

restrict v. (D; refl., tr.) to ~ to (the chair ~ed discussion to items on the official agenda; she ~ed herself to two meals a day)

restriction n. 1. to impose, place, put ~s on 2. to lift a ~ 3. ~s on

result I n. 1. to achieve, get, produce, show ~s 2. to announce; evaluate, measure; tabulate ~s 3. to negate, nullify, undo a ~ 4. an end, final; direct; interim, preliminary; lasting; logical; negative; net; positive; striking; surprising; tangible ~ 5. overall; surefire ~s USAGE NOTE: In BE, "get a result" can refer to getting a clear-cut definite victory or defeat by contrast with a draw or other such outcome.

result II v. 1. (d; intr.) to ~ from (her death ~ed from an overdose of pills) 2. (d; intr.) to ~ in (an overdose of pills ~ed in her death)

resume v. (G) she ~d working

resurrect v. (D; tr.) to ~ from (to ~ smb. from the dead)

resurrection n. ~ from (smb.'s ~ from the dead)

resuscitation n. 1. to give ~ (the victim was given mouth-to-mouth ~) 2. cardiopulmonary (= CPR); mouth-to-mouth ~

retail I adv. to buy; sell ~

retail II v. (D; intr.) to ~ at, for (it ~s for fifty dollars)

retainer n. ["advance fee"] to pay, put down a ~

retaliate v. 1. (D; intr.) to ~ against; for (the enemy ~ed against us for shelling civilian targets) 2. (D; intr.) to ~ by, with (the enemy ~d by bombarding our positions = they ~d with a bombardment of our positions)

retaliation n. 1. massive ~ 2. military ~ 3. ~ against; for 4. an act of ~ 5. in ~ (for)

retardant n. a fire; rust ~

retardation n. mental ~

retarded adj. mentally ~

retell v. (usu. B; occ. A) she has retold the story to us many times

reticence n. 1. to display, show ~ 2. ~ about

reticent adj. ~ about

retina n. a detached ~

retire v. 1. (D; intr.) ("to end one's working career") to ~ from (to ~ from one's job) 2. (D; intr.) ("to withdraw") to ~ to (the troops ~d to safer positions; let's ~ to the drawing room)

retirement n. 1. to go into ~ 2. to come out of ~ 3. compulsory, forced; early ~; semi-retirement; voluntary ~ 4. in ~ (to live in ~) 5. (misc.) to take early ~

retool v. 1. (D; intr., tr.) to ~ for (to ~ for wartime production) 2. (H) to ~ a plant to build prefabricated houses

retort I n. 1. to make a ~ 2. a quick; angry; curt, sharp, stinging; witty ~ 3. a ~ to

retort II v. 1. to ~ angrily, heatedly; curtly; wittily 2. (L) she ~ed heatedly that she needed no favors = "I don't need any favors!" she ~ed heatedly

retraction n. to issue, publish a ~ (they issued a quick and unqualified ~)

retreat I n. ["withdrawal"] 1. to beat, carry out, make a ~ (they made good their ~; the regiment carried out its ~ in good order) 2. a disorderly, hasty, ignominious, precipitate; orderly ~ 3. full ~ (in full ~) 4. a strategic; tactical ~ 5. a ~ from ["signal for withdrawal"] 6. to sound ~ ["music for a flag-lowering ceremony"] (mil.) 7. to play, sound ~ ["secluded gathering"] 8. to go on (a) ~ 9. a meditation; religious; weekend ~ ["secluded spot"] 10. a country ~

retreat II v. (D; intr.) to ~ before, in the face of; from; into; to (our troops ~ed from the border to safer positions; our government has ~ed from its hard-line position in the face of much public criticism; when challenged, he ~ed into silence)

retribution n. 1. to exact ~ from; to visit ~ on 2. divine; swift ~ 3. ~ against (~ against the invaders was swift) 4. in ~ for (he was punished in ~ for sins)

retrieval n. data, information ~

retrieve v. (D; tr.) to ~ from (to ~ data from a computer)

retroactive adj. ~ to

retrorocket n. to activate, fire a ~

retrospect n. in ~

retrospection n. in ~

return I n. ["official statement"] 1. to file a (census; tax) ~ 2. a joint ~ (see also **tax return**) ["going back, coming back"] 3. a safe ~ (home) 4. a ~ from; to (his ~ to civilian life) 5. on smb.'s ~ (on their ~ from a trip abroad) 6. the point of no ~ ["profit"] 7. to bring in, produce, yield a ~ (this investment will yield a ~ of ten percent) 8. a ~ from, on ["compensation"] 9. in ~ (to give smt. in ~) 10. in ~ for ["next post"] (BE; AE has by return mail) 11. by ~ (of post) (send us an answer by ~) (see also **returns**)

return II v. 1. (BE) (A) she ~ed my book to me; or:

she ~ed me my book 2. (AE) (B) she ~ed my book to me 3. (D; intr., tr.) to ~ from; to (to ~ from a holiday/vacation; she ~ed to her home; to ~ books to the library)

returns n. ["election results"] 1. early; election; final; late ~ ["misc."] 2. many happy ~ (of the day) ("happy birthday"); the law of diminishing ~ USAGE NOTE: The formula "Many happy returns" is used in wishing people a happy birthday because it expresses the hope that they will have many more happy birthdays.

reunion n. 1. to hold a ~ 2. a touching ~ 3. an annual; class; family ~

reunite v. (D; tr.) to ~ with (to ~ people with their families = to ~ people and their families (with each other))

reveal v. 1. (B) she ~ed the secret of her illness to us 2. (L; to) she ~ed (to us) that she had been ill for years 3. (M) the document ~ed her to have been a conscientious employee 4. (Q; to) she ~ed (to us) how long she had been ill

reveille n. (mil.) 1. to play, sound ~ 2. to fall out for ~

revel v. (D; intr.) to ~ in

revelation n. 1. to make a ~ 2. an amazing, astonishing, astounding, startling, stunning, surprising ~ 3. (a) divine ~ 4. a ~ comes (the ~ came when we least expected it) 5. a ~ about 6. a ~ to (the story ¬was/ came as¬ a ~ to us) 7. a ~ that + clause (the ~ that she had been in prison surprised everybody)

revenge I n. 1. to exact, get, have, take ~ on 2. to plot, seek; vow ~ 3. sweet ~ 4. an act of ~ 5. ~ for; on (to take ~ on smb. for smt.) 6. in ~ for (she did it in ~ for her father's murder)

revenge II v. (esp. BE) (d; refl.) to ~ on, upon (she avenged her father's murder by ~ging herself on his murderer)

revenue n. ["income"] 1. to generate, produce, raise, yield ~ 2. to collect ~ 3. government; tax ~ 4. smb.'s annual, yearly; monthly; weekly ~ 5. oil ~s 6. falling; rising ~s USAGE NOTE: The UK Inland Revenue (now incorporated into HM Revenue & Customs) corresponds to the US Internal Revenue Service.

reverberate v. (P; intr.) the cheers ~d through the arena = the arena ~d with cheers; the news ~d around the world

revere v. 1. (D; tr.) to ~ as (to ~ smb. as a saint) 2. (D; tr.) to ~ for (to ~ smb. for their saintliness)

reverence n. 1. to feel ~ 2. to show ~ 3. deep, profound ~ 4. ~ for (to feel ~ for smb.) 5. in ~ (to hold smb. in ~)

reverie n. 1. to indulge in ~s 2. to be lost, sunk in ~ 3. (misc.) to fall into a ~; to wake from a ~

reversal n. 1. to experience; suffer a ~ 2. a complete; minor ~ 3. a role ~ 4. a ~ in, of, on (a ~ of/in roles) 5. (misc.) a ~ of fortune (AE) = a ~ of ~s (BE)

reverse n. ["setback"] 1. to suffer, sustain a ~ 2. a serious; slight; tactical ~ 3. financial ~s ["reverse gear"]

4. to put a transmission/car into ~ 5. to change into, go into, shift (AE) into, throw into ~ 6. in ~ ["reversing mechanism"] 7. a/an (automatic) ribbon ~ (on a typewriter)

reversion *n.* ~ to (to undergo (a) ~ to an earlier state) (see also *reversion to type* at **type I** *n.*)

revert *v.* (d; intr.) to ~ to (her property ~ed to the state; to ~ to enlisted status; he reformed for a while but eventually ~ed to type)

review I *n.* ["renewed study"] 1. to do a ~ 2. a comprehensive ~ ["military ceremony"] 3. to hold a ~ (of troops) 4. to pass in ~ ["critical evaluation"] 5. to do, write a ~ (as of a book/play/concert) 6. to conduct a ~ 7. to get, receive; have a ~ 8. a complimentary, favorable, glowing, positive, rave; critical; negative, unfavorable ~ (the play got/had rave ~s from the critics = the critics gave the play rave ~s) 9. a book ~ 10. (legal) judicial ~ 11. (an) independent; peer ~ 12. a ~ concludes; shows (a comprehensive ~ of the system showed the need for its reform) 13. under ~ (the entire matter is under ~; we're keeping the matter under (constant) ~)

review II *v.* (AE) (D; intr., tr.) ("to study again") to ~ for (to ~ for an exam)

revise 1. (BE) see **review II** 2. (D; tr.) to ~ from; to 3. (misc.) to ~ downward; upward

revision *n.* ["renewed study"] (BE) 1. to do ~ (he had to do some ~ for the examination; he had some ~ to do for the examination) ["revised version"] 2. to do a ~ (we had to do a complete/major ~ of the manuscript) ["change"] 3. to make a ~ 4. to need, require; undergo (a) ~ 5. a ~ in, to (they made several ~s in/to their plans, which may still have to undergo further extensive ~(s))

revival *n.* a ~ in; of (there are signs of a ~ in/of faith healing)

revolt I *n.* 1. to foment, incite, stir up; cause, lead to, produce a ~ 2. to organize a ~ 3. to carry out a ~ 4. to crush, defeat, quash, quell, put down, stifle a ~ 5. an armed; open; peasant ~ 6. a ~ breaks out, erupts; fails; spreads; succeeds 7. a ~ against 8. in ~ (to rise in open ~ against intolerable conditions)

revolt II *v.* (D; intr.) to ~ against, at (to ~ against intolerable conditions)

revolting *adj.* 1. ~ to (such obscene language is ~ to us) 2. ~ to + inf. (it's ~ to hear them use such obscene language) 3. ~ that + clause (it's ~ that they use such obscene language)

revolution *n.* ["complete change"] 1. to foment, incite, stir up a ~ 2. to organize a ~ 3. to carry out, conduct, fight a ~ 4. to crush, defeat, put down a ~ 5. a cultural; industrial; palace; political; sexual; social ~ 6. a ~ breaks out, erupts; fails; spreads; succeeds 7. a ~ against 8. in ~ (to rise in ~ against intolerable conditions) 9. a ~ in (a ~ in hair styles) ["complete orbital turn (as of the Earth around the Sun)"] 10. to make a ~ 11. a ~ about, around, round (the Moon's rotation ~ around the Earth and the Earth's ~ around the Sun)

revolve *v.* (D; intr.) to ~ about, around, round (the Moon rotates ~s around the Earth and the Earth ~s around the Sun)

revolver *n.* see **pistol** 1–5, 7

revue *n.* to produce, put on, stage a ~

revulsion *n.* 1. to express; feel ~ 2. deep, utmost, utter ~ 3. a feeling of ~ 4. ~ against, at, towards 5. in ~ (we drew back in ~ at hearing them use such obscene language)

reward I *n.* 1. to offer, post; pay a ~ 2. to claim; deserve; get, receive; reap; a ~ 3. an ample, handsome; just; tangible; well-deserved ~ 4. a ~ for 5. as a ~ (she got a bonus as a ~ for her outstanding work) 6. (misc.) virtue is its own ~ (proverb)

reward II *v.* 1. to ~ amply, handsomely 2. (D; tr.) to ~ by; for; with (she was ~ed with a bonus for her outstanding work)

rewarding *adj.* 1. financially; very ~ 2. ~ to + inf. (I find it very ~ to work with deprived children = I find it very ~ working with underprivileged children)

rhapsodize *v.* (d; intr.) to ~ over

rhapsody *n.* to compose; play a ~

rhetoric *n.* 1. to resort to, spout ~ 2. eloquent; impassioned, passionate; soothing ~ 3. ~ about (for all the ~ he spouts about helping underprivileged children, nothing actually gets done!)

rheumatism *n.* 1. to develop ~ 2. to suffer from ~ 3. chronic ~

rhubarb *n.* ["argument"] (slang) (AE) 1. to get into a ~ 2. a ~ about

rhyme I *n.* 1. to compose, write a ~ 2. a nursery, Mother Goose (AE) ~ 3. (poetry) a feminine; masculine ~ 4. an eye; internal ~ 5. a ~ about (a nursery ~ about three mice) 6. a ~ for (what is a ~ for *sing*?) 7. in ~ (poetry in ~) 8. (misc.) without ~ or reason ("with no apparent reason") (see also *rhyme scheme* at **scheme I** *n.*)

rhyme II *v.* (D; intr., tr.) to ~ with (this word ~s with that word = this word and that word ~ (with each other); to ~ one word with another)

rhythm *n.* 1. to beat (out) a ~ 2. (a) dance; frenzied; pulsating; steady; undulating ~ 3. to a ~ (to dance to the ~ of drums) 4. a sense of ~ (see also *rhythm section* at **section**)

rib I *n.* 1. to nudge; poke smb. in the ~s (see also *a nudge in the ribs* at **nudge I** *n.*) 2. a broken, fractured; false; floating ~ 3. (misc.) to break, fracture a ~

rib II *v.* (colloq.) (D; tr.) to ~ about; for (they ~bed me about my new hair color)

ribbing *n.* ["teasing"] to get, take a ~

ribbon *n.* ["(of a typewriter)"] 1. to change a ~ 2. a typewriter ~ 3. the ~ reverses (automatically) ["misc."] 4. a blue ~ ("a first prize"); to cut to ~s ("to destroy completely")

rice *n.* 1. to mill, winnow ~ 2. brown; enriched; polished; quick-cooking; wild ~ 3. a bowl; grain of ~

rich *adj.* 1. (colloq.) filthy, stinking ~ 2. very ~ 3. ~ in (~ in coal deposits) 4. (misc.) the idle ~ ; to strike it ~ ; ~ and poor (alike) ; ~ beyond the dreams of avarice ; gossip about the ~ and famous

riches *n.* 1. to accumulate, acquire, amass ~ 2. great, untold, vast ~

ricksha, rickshaw *n.* 1. to pedal ; pull a ~ 2. to ride in a ~

ricochet *v.* (D ; intr.) to ~ off

rid I *adj.* to be ; get ~ of (the town has gotten ~ of its rats and is now ~ of rats = now that the rats have been gotten ~ of, the town is ~ of rats)

rid II *v.* (d ; refl., tr.) to ~ of (to ~ the town of rats)

riddance *n.* ["act of getting rid of smt."] good ~ ! (good ~ to bad rubbish ! ; they're gone – and good ~ , if you ask me !)

riddle I *n.* 1. to pose a ~ 2. to solve a ~ 3. a ~ to (the whole business was a ~ to me) 4. (misc.) to speak in ~s ; "a ~ wrapped in a mystery inside an enigma" – Winston Churchill, 1939

riddle II *v.* (d ; tr.) to ~ with (the plane was ~d with anti-aircraft fire)

ride I *n.* ["short trip by vehicle, on horseback"] 1. to catch, get a ~ 2. to go for, go on, have (esp. BE), take a ~ 3. (colloq.) to bum (AE, colloq.), cadge (esp. BE, colloq.), hitch, thumb a ~ (as a hitch-hiker) 4. to give (smb.) a ~ 5. to take (smb.) for a ~ 6. a bicycle ; boat ; bus ; horse, horseback ; joy ; train ~ (to go on a joy ~ in a stolen car) 7. a bumpy, rough ; smooth ~ 8. a ~ on (a ~ on a camel/horse) 9. a ~ into, to (a ~ into/to town) ["attraction"] (in an amusement park) 10. to go on the ~s ["misc."] 11. to take smb. for a ~ ("to victimize or cheat smb.")

ride II *v.* 1. (d ; intr.) to ~ by, in, on (to ~ ¬in a car/on a bus¬) 2. (d ; intr.) to ~ from ; to (we ~ to work by bus) 3. (d ; intr.) to be riding on ("to be wagered on") (a lot of money was ~ing on one horse) 4. (P ; intr.) to ~ across town ; to ~ through a forest ; to ~ around the neighborhood 5. (misc.) to ~ bareback ; to ~ sidesaddle ; to go riding (esp. on horseback) ; the ship was ~ing at anchor (see also *ride rough-shod over smb.* at **roughshod**)

ride back *v.* (d ; intr.) to ~ from (he rode back from the procession)

ride out *v.* (d ; intr.) to ~ to (he rode out to the procession)

rider *n.* ["amendment, addition"] to attach a ~ to (a bill)

ridicule *n.* 1. draw, incur ~ 2. to heap, pour ~ on 3. public ~ 4. an object of ~ (he became an object of ~ after his speech had drawn so much ~) 5. (misc.) to hold smb./smt. up to ~

ridiculous *adj.* 1. absolutely, completely, downright, obviously, patently, perfectly, simply, totally, truly, utterly ~ 2. ~ to + inf. (it's ~ for them to keep applying for visas !) 3. ~ that + clause (it's ~ that they keep applying for visas !) 4. (misc.) it's ~ ¬how/the way¬ they keep applying for visas !

rife *adj.* ["abounding"] 1. (cannot stand alone) ~ in ; with (the city was ~ with rumors about them = rumors about them were ~ in the city) ["misc."] 2. to run ~ ("to be out of control") (rumors about them were running ~ in the city)

riffle *v.* (d ; intr.) to ~ through (to ~ through the documents in the drawers)

rifle I *n.* 1. to load ; reload a ~ 2. to aim, point ; level a ~ 3. to fire a ~ 4. to handle, operate a ~ 5. to assemble ; disassemble a ~ 6. an air ; assault ; automatic ; high-powered ; hunting ; recoilless ; semiautomatic ~ 7. a ~ fires, goes off ; jams ; misfires

rifle II *v.* (d ; intr.) to ~ through ("to search") (to ~ through the drawers for documents)

rift *n.* 1. to cause a ~ 2. to heal a ~ 3. an ideological ~ 4. a ~ among, between

rig *n.* ["large vehicle"] (esp. AE, Australian English) 1. to drive a ~ ["equipment"] 2. an oil-drilling ~

right I *adj.* 1. absolutely, completely, dead (colloq.), quite ~ 2. morally ~ 3. ~ about (to be ~ about smt./smb.) 4. ~ in (she was ~ in refusing) 5. ~ to + inf. (it was ~ of her to refuse = she was ~ to refuse) 6. ~ that + clause (it's not ~ that they should be treated in that manner ; it was ~ that she refused) 7. (misc.) that picture is just ~ for this room ; she is the ~ person for the job = she is ~ for the job ; to be in one's ~ mind ("to be sane") ; to put things ~ ("to straighten things out") ; we were worried, but fortunately everything came ~ in the end ; everything went all ~ at the office (see also **all right**)

right II *adv.* 1. to bear, go, turn ~ 2. ~ away ; now 3. to do smt. ~ 4. (misc.) to do ~ by smb. ; to see smb. ~ (I'll see you ~ if you do ~ by me) ; go ~ back ; go ~ home after dinner ; ~ in front of us ; ~ on, man ! (slang) ; ~ the way through/round/along etc. (BE ; CE has : *all the way through/round/around/along* etc.)

right III *n.* ["that which is due"] 1. to assert, claim reserve a ~ (all ~s reserved) 2. to demand one's ~s 3. to achieve, gain, get a ~ (to achieve full civil ~s) 4. to enjoy, exercise, have a ~ 5. to forfeit, lose ; give up, relinquish, renounce, sign away, waive a ~ 6. to defend, protect, safeguard, uphold smb.'s ~s 7. to give, grant a ~ (to) 8. to deny (smb.) a ~ 9. to violate smb.'s ~s 10. a divine ; exclusive, sole ; inalienable ; inherent ; legal ; natural ~ 11. animal ; civil ; constitutional ; political ; reproductive ; states' ; voting ~s 12. children's ; consumers' ; gay ; human ; individual ; patients' ; squatters' ; veterans' ; women's ~s 13. film ; grazing ; mineral ; property ; publishing ; translation ~s 14. conjugal ; visiting, visitation ~s 15. the ~ of assembly ; asylum ; free speech 16. a ~ to (the ~ to privacy ; the ~ to a free press ; everyone has the ~ to a fair trial ; the ~ to life) 17. the ~ to + inf. (the ~ to choose ; the ~ to vote ; the ~ to protest ; you have the ~ to remain silent ; we reserve the ~ to exercise our option within 90 days) 18. within one's ~s (she was within her ~s to remain silent) 19. (misc.) a bill of ~s; to read the accused her/his ~s ["right side"] 20. to keep to the ~ 21. on the ~; to the ~ ["conservative group"] 22. the extreme, far, radical ~; right-leaning ~ (a right-leaning think tank) 23. the religious ~ ["punch delivered with the right hand"] 24. to deliver, throw a ~ 25. a hard, stiff ~ 26. a ~ to (a ~ to the jaw) ["turn to the right"] 27. (colloq.) to hang (slang), make, take a ~ 28. to make a sharp ~ ["misc."] 29. in the ~ ("in accordance with the truth, accepted standards") (she was in the ~ when she refused = she was in the ~ to refuse); she has a promising career in her own ~; as of (BE), by ~ ("properly"); by ~ of conquest; ~ and wrong; by ~s ("ideally"); two wrongs do not make a ~; to know ~ from wrong; the ~s and wrongs (I'm not interested in the ~s and wrongs of the case: let's forget the whole thing!); you have every ~ to feel hard done by

right-of-way n. 1. to have the ~ 2. to give (esp. AE), yield the ~ 3. the ~ over (ambulances have the ~ over other vehicles)

right-winger n. an extreme ~

rigid adj. ~ about, in, on (~ on points of procedure; they are ~ in their views)

rigor mortis n. ~ sets in

rig out, rig up v. 1. (D; tr.) to ~ as (to ~ smb. out as a clown) 2. (D; tr.) to ~ in (to ~ smb. out in a clown costume)

rile v. (R) it ~d me that they were paying no taxes

riled adj. (colloq.) ["annoyed"] 1. ~ at (I was ~ at them for paying no taxes) 2. ~ that + clause (I was ~ (up) that they were paying no taxes)

rim n. along; on; up to a ~ (on the ~ of a crater)

rind n. 1. to scrape the ~ 2. lemon; melon ~ USAGE NOTE: One usu. speaks of the *rind* of a melon, the *peel* or the *rind* of a lemon, the *peel* of an orange, and the *skin* or the *peel* of a banana.

ring I n. ["circular band"] 1. a diamond; gold; platinum; sapphire ~ 2. an earring; engagement; signet; wedding ~ 3. a key; napkin; teething ~ 4. a piston ~ 5. smoke ~s (to blow smoke ~s) 6. (misc.) to have, wear a ~ on one's finger ["group"] 7. a drug; smuggling; spy; vice ~ ["enclosed square area"] 8. a boxing; wrestling; prize ~ 9. to climb into, step into the ~ ["telephone call"] 10. to give smb. a ~ ["misc."] 11. to run ~s (a)round smb. ("to far outperform smb.")

ring II n. ["sound"] 1. a false, hollow; familiar ~ (there was a false ~ to his words) 2. (misc.) it has a nice ~ to it; her story had a ~ of truth (to it)

ring III v. 1. (D; tr.) to ~ for ("to call by ringing") (to ~ for the maid) 2. (s) to ~ false; hollow; true (her story rang false)

ringer n. (colloq.) to be a dead ~ for smb. ("to resemble smb. very closely")

ringside n. at ~ (the)

ring up v. (D; tr.) ("to record") to ~ on (she rang up a bill on a cash register = she rang a bill up on a cash register)

rink n. 1. an ice-hockey; ice-skating; roller-skating ~ 2. at a ~

rinse I n. to give smt. a ~ (I gave my hair a good ~ in the water)

rinse II v. (D; tr.) to ~ from, out of; in; with (~ the soap out of your hair; I ~d my hair in the water)

riot n. 1. to cause, foment, incite, instigate, spark (AE), spark off (BE), stir up, touch off a ~ 2. to crush, put down, quell a ~ 3. a communal; food; race ~ 4. a ~ breaks out, erupts, flares up 5. ~s swept the country 6. a ~ subsides 7. (misc.) to run ~ ("to act wildly")

riot act n. ["stern warning"] to read the ~ to smb. = to read smb. the riot act

rioting n. 1. to crack down on, put down, quell ~ 2. communal ~ 3. sporadic; widespread ~ 4. ~ breaks out, erupts, flares up; spreads 5. ~ ceases; dies down, subsides 6. a flare-up, outbreak of ~

rip v. 1. (d; intr.) to ~ into ("to attack") (colloq.) (the politician ~ped into her opponent) 2. (misc.) an explosion ~ped through the laboratory; she ~ped her skirt on a nail = her skirt ~ped on a nail; to ~ smt. ¬to pieces/apart¬ (also fig.) (the politician ~ped her opponent apart)

ripcord n. to pull the ~

ripe adj. ~ for (~ for the picking; the time is ~ ¬for action/to act¬)

ripen v. (d; intr.) to ~ into (their friendship ~ed into love)

ripple v. (P; intr.) applause ~d through the auditorium

rise I n. ["origin"] 1. to give ~ to ["angry reaction"] 2. to get a ~ out of smb. ["pay increase"] (BE) 3. an across-the-board pay, wage ~ 4. a ~ in (wages) (AE has *raise*) ["increase"] 5. a sharp, steep; sudden ~ 6. a ~ in (a sudden sharp ~ in prices) 7. on the ~ (prices are on the ~) ["success"] 8. a meteoric ~ ["move upwards"] 9. a dramatic, sharp; steady; sudden ~ 10. a ~ during, throughout; from; to (a steady ~ from the bottom to the top; during Napoleon's ~ to power) 11. (misc.) *The Rise of the Dutch Republic* – J.L. Motley, 1855/6

rise II v. 1. ("to ascend") to ~ sharply, steeply; suddenly 2. (D; intr.) ("to ascend") to ~ above (to ~ above last year's level) 3. (D; intr.) ("to ascend") to ~ by (prices rose (by) ten percent) 4. (D; intr.) ("to revolt") to ~ against (they rose ~ against tyranny) 5. (D; intr.) ("to ascend") to ~ from, out of (smoke rose from the chimney; after many years he rose out of poverty) 6. (d; intr.) ("to be resurrected") to ~ from (to ~ from the dead; to ~ from the ashes) 7. (D; intr.) ("to ascend") to ~ into (the smoke rose into the air) 8. (D; intr.) ("to ascend") to ~ off (to ~ off the ground) 9. (D; intr.) ("to ascend") to ~ over (the sun rose over the city) 10. (D; intr.) ("to ascend") to ~ through (to ~ through the ranks) 11. (d; intr.) ("to ascend") to ~ to (to ~ to the surface; to ~ to one's feet) 12. (d; intr.) ("to be equal") to ~ to (to ~ to the challenge; can you ~

to the occasion?) 13. (E) he rose (out of poverty) to become a member of the House of Lords 14. (misc.) he rose (in order) to greet me

riser *n.* an early; late ~

rise up *v.* (D; intr.) to ~ against (they rose up against tyranny)

risk I *n.* 1. to assume, incur, run, take a ~ (to run the ~ of being outvoted) 2. to face a ~ 3. to entail, involve a ~ 4. to outweigh a ~ (the advantages outweigh the ~s) 5. to minimize; reduce a ~ 6. a grave, great, high ~ 7. a low, slight, small ~ 8. a calculated ~ (to take a calculated ~) 9. a bad, poor; credit; good; health; safety; security ~ (she is a security ~ and is therefore considered a bad/poor credit ~ by her bank) 10. a degree; element of ~ (there's a degree of ~ in any money-making venture) 11. a ~ of; to (a ~ to safety; there was a ~ of fire breaking out) 12. a ~ to + inf. (it was a ~ to enter that area) 13. a ~ that + clause (there was a ~ that a fire might break out) 14. at (a) ~ (at one's own ~; at the ~ of being ridiculed; lives were at ~; esp. BE: children at ~) 15. (misc.) we diversified our investments in order to spread the ~ (see also *risk assessment* at **assessment**; *risk factor* at **factor**)

risk II *v.* 1. (G) she ~ed losing everything 2. (K) he ~ed their turning against him 3. (misc.) it was a good deal and she decided to ~ it but he decided he couldn't ~ it

risky *adj.* ~ to + inf. (it's ~ to play with fire = it's ~ playing with fire) (see also *a risky business* at **business**)

rite *n.* 1. to administer, perform a ~ 2. a pagan; religious; solemn ~ 3. funeral; initiation; marriage ~s 4. fertility ~s (see also **last rites**; *rite of passage* at **passage**) 5. a ~ takes place (the ~s take place in the spring)

ritual *n.* 1. to go through; perform a ~ 2. to make a ~ of smt. 3. a pagan; religious; solemn ~ 4. a ~ takes place (the ~s take place in the spring) 5. during, throughout; in a ~ (silence is required throughout the ~)

rival I *n.* 1. an arch, bitter, keen ~ 2. a political ~ 3. a ~ for; in

rival II *v.* (D; tr.) to ~ in (to ~ smb. in skill)

rivalry *n.* 1. to stir up ~ 2. (a) bitter, deep, fierce, intense, keen, strong ~ 3. (a) friendly ~ 4. sexual; sibling ~ 5. intercollegiate; internecine; interservice ~ 6. ~ among, between; for; in; with (there was keen ~ between them for the award) 7. ~ to + inf. (there was keen ~ between them to win the award)

river *n.* 1. to cross; ford a ~ 2. to dam; drag; dredge a ~ 3. a broad, wide; deep ~ 4. a ~ floods; flows (into the sea); meanders, winds; narrows; overflows (its banks); rises; widens 5. the bank; course; mouth; source of a ~ 6. down ~; up ~ 7. (misc.); to send up the ~ (AE; slang) ("to send to prison") (see also *to sell smb. down the river* at **sell II**)

rivet *n.* to drive a ~ (into metal)

riveted *adj.* (cannot stand alone) ~ on, to (all eyes were ~ on the door/speaker; she stood ~ to the spot)

road *n.* 1. to pave; resurface; surface a ~ 2. to widen a ~ 3. to block, cordon off a ~ 4. to cross a ~ 5. a macadam; metalled (BE); paved, surfaced; smooth (also fig.); straight; wide ~ 6. a connecting; main, trunk (BE); ring (BE); toll ~ 7. a service; slip (BE) ~ 8. a back, country; busy; congested; deserted, lonely; good; long; minor; mountain; narrow; secondary; side; through; whizzy (BE; colloq.); winding ~ (the sign said "No Through Road") 9. a bumpy; dirt (AE), gravel, unpaved; icy; impassable; rocky (also fig.); rough (also fig.); unmetalled (BE) ~ 10. intersecting; merging ~s 11. the right; wrong ~ (they took the wrong ~; we were on the right ~) 12. a ~ goes, leads, runs (in a certain direction) 13. a ~ curves, winds; forks; zigzags 14. a ~ from; to (the ~ to town) 15. across; along; over a ~ 16. down; up a ~ 17. in, on; off a ~ (there were a lot of cars on the ~) 18. (also fig.) on the ~ (on the ~ to recovery) 19. (misc.) the bottom/end/middle/top of the ~ (also fig.) (is it the end of the ~ for heavy industry?; a party with moderate middle-of-the-road policies); to take a ~ (they took the wrong ~); one for the ~ ("a final drink"); follow this ~ for two miles; the car holds the ~ well; a stretch of (the) ~; the ~ is clear (also fig.); some drivers hog the ~ (see also **high road**) USAGE NOTE: Between towns there are typically roads or highways rather than streets. Within towns there are both roads and streets, and both *Road* and *Street* are used in names: in London, Caversham *Road* runs parallel to Islip *Street*; to live in (BE)/on Constantine *Road*. Both *road* and *street* can include the pedestrian walkways beside them or refer to only the part for vehicles: don't ride your bicycle on the sidewalk: ride it in the ~!; walk along/up/down the ~ until you come to the corner; a paved/gravel ~. When either *road* or *street* is possible in CE, AE may prefer *street*; BE, *road*: go across the *street* (esp. AE)/*road* (esp. BE) and you'll see it.

road block *n.* 1. to establish, put up, set up a ~ 2. to remove a ~ 3. to break through, crash through, run a ~ 4. a police ~ 5. at; through a ~ (we stopped at the police ~ but the other car drove right through it!)

roadhouse *n.* at a ~ (to stop at a ~ for a drink)

roadside *n.* by, on the ~

roadster *n.* (obsol.) to drive a ~

roadwork *n.* ["running"] to do ~ (the boxer did ~ every day) (see also *road works* at **works**)

roam *v.* (P; intr.) to ~ around town

roar I *n.* 1. to give, let out a ~ 2. a deep, thunderous ~ 3. a ~ from; of (there was a deep ~ of anger from the lion; the crowd gave a thunderous ~ of approval)

roar II *v.* 1. (D; intr.) to ~ at 2. (D; intr.) to ~ with (to ~ with laughter)

roast *n.* 1. to cook, do, make a ~ 2. to have a ~ (we had a ~ for dinner) 3. a chuck; eye (AE); lamb; pork; pot; rib; veal ~
rob *v.* 1. (D; tr.) to ~ of (the bandits ~bed the passengers of their money) 2. (misc.) to ~ smb. blind
robbery *n.* 1. to commit (a) ~ 2. armed; bank; daylight (BE), highway ~ (fig.) ("overcharging") (it's highway ~ to charge that much!) 3. a ~ takes place (the police got an anonymous tip-off that the ~ would take place at night)
robed *adj.* ~ in (the judges were ~ in red = they were red-robed judges)
robot *n.* an industrial ~
rock I *n.* ["stone"] 1. to throw a ~ at (see Usage Note) 2. jagged; rugged ~s 3. falling ~s 4. solid ~ 5. (misc.) as hard/solid as a ~ USAGE NOTE: In BE, a *rock* is typically too big to be thrown. Thus, *to throw a rock at smb.* is esp. AE (CE has *to throw a stone at smb.*). However, the figurative expression *to throw rocks at smb.* ("to criticize smb.") is CE.
rock II *n.* ["type of music"] hard; punk ~; rock-and-roll, rock-'n'-roll
rock III *v.* (D; tr.) ("to lull") to ~ to (to ~ a baby to sleep)
rocket I *n.* ["device propelled by a rocket engine or explosives"] 1. to fire; launch a ~ 2. a booster; liquid-fuel; long-range; multistage; solid-fuel; space ~ 3. a ~ blasts off; goes into orbit (see also *rocket science* at **science**; *rocket ship* at **ship I** *n.*) ["reprimand"] (colloq.) (BE) 4. to give smb. a ~ 5. to get a ~ (from)
rocket II *v.* (d; intr.) to ~ to (she ~ed to stardom)
rocks *n.* 1. on the ~ ("with ice") (scotch on the ~) 2. on the ~ ("ruined")
rod *n.* ["bar, shaft"] 1. a connecting; divining; lightning; piston ~; ramrod ["pistol"] (slang) (AE) 2. to pack ("carry") a ~ ["metal track"] 3. a curtain; traverse ~ ["pole"] 4. a fishing ~ ["misc."] 5. to ride the ~s (AE) ("to ride illegally in the framework below a railroad car")
rodent *n.* ~s gnaw
rodeo *n.* to hold, stage a ~
roe *n.* 1. to spawn ~ 2. hard; soft ~
role *n.* 1. to assume, find, get, have, take (on) a ~ ("Great Britain has lost an empire and has not yet found a ~" – Dean Acheson, 1893–1971) 2. to assign, hand out ~s 3. to do, perform, play; interpret; learn, memorize, study; understudy a ~ 4. a decisive; important; key; leading; prominent, vital ~ 5. a cameo; starring; supporting; title ~ 6. an active; passive ~ 7. a main, major; minor ~ 8. a primary; secondary ~ 9. a ~ as, of (fathers have more than just a ~ as disciplinarians = a father has more than just the ~ of disciplinarian) 10. a ~ for (is there still a ~ for fathers in the modern family?) 11. a ~ in (they played a key ~ in the uprising) 12. (misc.) to cast in the ~ of (see also *role model* at **model**)
roll I *n.* ["list of names"] 1. to call, take the ~ 2. an

electoral ~; honor ~ (AE; BE has *roll of honour*) ["small cake or bread"] 3. to bake ~s 4. a bread (BE); hamburger; jelly (AE), Swiss (BE); kaiser (esp. US); poppyseed; sweet ~ 5. on a ~ (ham on a ~) 6. (misc.) ~s and butter; coffee and ~s ["act of rolling"] 7. on a ~ (from success to success) (colloq.) (with three Oscars in succession, Kylie Sweetheart seems to be on something of a ~!)
roll II *v.* 1. (A) ~ the ball to me; or: ~ me the ball 2. (C) ~ a cigarette for me; or: ~ me a cigarette 3. (d; intr., tr.) to ~ down (the children ~ed down the hill; we ~ed the barrels down the incline) 4. (d; intr.) to ~ in (to ~ in the mud) 5. (d; intr.) to ~ off (the football ~ed off the field; new cars ~ed off the assembly line) 6. (d; intr.) to ~ with ("to lessen the impact by moving in the same direction") (he ~ed with the punch) 7. (P; intr., tr.) the ball ~ed across the field, through the tunnel, and out the other side; you can't expect me to just ~ over and play dead!
rollaway, rollaway bed *n.* (AE) to fold up; open up a ~
roll up *v.* 1. (d; tr.) to ~ in (he ~ed smt. up in a blanket = he ~ed up smt. in a blanket) 2. (D; intr., tr.) to ~ into (he ~ed up smt. into a ball = he ~ed smt. up into a ball) 3. (D; intr., tr.) to ~ to (the ball ~ed up to me) 4. to ~ tightly
romance *n.* 1. to find ~ (are we ever too old to find love and ~?) 2. a blossoming; shipboard; wartime; whirlwind ~
romanticize *v.* (D; intr.) to ~ about
romp *v.* 1. (d; intr.) ("to deal with easily") to ~ through (she ~ed through the test) 2. (D; intr.) ("to play") to ~ with (to ~ with the children) 3. (misc.) our team ~ed home first ("our team won easily")
romp around, romp about *v.* (D; intr.) ("to play") to ~ with the children
roof *n.* 1. to install a ~ 2. a corrugated (iron); gabled; shingled; slate; thatched; tiled; tin ~ 3. a ~ leaks 4. on a ~ (*Fiddler on the Roof* – musical by Bock, Harnick, and Stein, 1964) 5. (misc.) to raise the ~ ("to complain vociferously"); to hit the ~ (colloq.) ("to lose one's temper") (mom will really hit the ~ if we get back late!); to have a ~ over one's head ("to have shelter")
room I *n.* ["(of a building)"] 1. to rent a ~ from 2. to let (BE), let out (BE), rent, rent out a ~ to 3. to book (BE), reserve a ~ 4. a back ~; bathroom; bedroom; boxroom (BE); dining; drawing, front (BE), reception (BE), sitting; family (AE); game, recreation; guest; rumpus (AE); spare; utility ~; workroom (see also *fitting room* at **fitting II**; **living room**) 5. a banquet; board; common (BE); reading ~; showroom; waiting ~ 6. a baggage (AE); lumber (BE), storage ~ 7. an adjoining ~, the next ~ 8. a changing (BE), dressing; locker ~ 9. a double; single ~ 10. (in a hospital) a delivery; emergency (AE); hospital; operating (esp. AE; BE prefers ¬*operating theatre/theatre*¬); private; recovery; semiprivate ~ 11. a ladies'

(esp. AE), powder; men's (esp. AE); rest (AE) ~; (BE; euphemism) the smallest ~ ("the room with the toilet") 12. a furnished; rented ~; (a) ~ to let (BE) 13. (misc.) a smoke-filled ~ (fig.) (the committee met in a smoke-filled ~ and decided everything secretly) ["space"] 14. to leave, make ~ for 15. to occupy, take up ~ 16. elbow ~; headroom; legroom 17. (in a theater) standing ~ only 18. ~ for (there is ~ for another bed) 19. ~ to + inf. (the children have ~ to play) ["possibility"] 20. ~ for (there is no ~ for doubt) USAGE NOTE: In the US, a *bathroom* usu. contains a toilet, sink, and bathtub or shower. In GB, it must contain a bath or shower and may have a toilet and washbasin. In CE, a *cloakroom* is a place in a public building where coats, umbrellas, etc. may be left temporarily. In GB, it can also denote a small room on the ground floor of a house near the front door; this room often contains a toilet and a place for hanging coats. *Ladies' room* and *men's room* are esp. AE. BE has *ladies'* and *gents'*.

room II v. (d; intr.) ("to reside") to ~ at; with

roomer n. (AE) ["lodger"] to have, keep, take in ~s

room service n. to call, call for, get ~

rooster n. (esp. AE) a ~ cock-a-doodle-doos, crows, goes cock-a-doodle-doo (BE has *cock* or *cockerel*)

root I n. 1. to strike, take ~ (see also **cube root**; **square root**) 2. to get at, to the ~ of smt. ("to tackle smt. at the source"); (BE) ~ and branch ("wholly"); the ~ of all evil (see also **roots**)

root II v. (D; intr.) to ~ for ("to support") (AE) (to ~ for a team)

root about, root around v. (D; intr.) to ~ for ("to search for") (to ~ in a stack of papers for a specific document)

rooted adj. 1. deeply ~ 2. ~ in (~ in poverty) 3. ~ to (~ to the spot)

rooter n. (AE) an ardent ~

roots n. 1. to put down ~ 2. to go back to one's ~ 3. to search for one's ~ 4. deep ~ 5. ethnic ~ 6. by the ~ (to pull smt. up by the ~) 7. (misc.) her ~ are in Canada

rope I n. 1. to pull; tie a ~ 2. to jump (esp. AE), skip ~ 3. to ease up on; tighten a ~ 4. a loose, slack; tight ~ 5. a coil; length; piece of ~ 6. by a ~ (to lower smt. by a ~) 7. (misc.) (boxing and fig.) on the ~s ("in a weak, vulnerable position"); at the end of one's ~ (esp. AE) ("in a desperate situation, at the end of one's tether"); to know the ~s ("to be well informed")

rope II v. 1. (colloq.) (d; tr.) to ~ into ("to induce") (to ~ smb. into doing smt.) 2. (D; tr.) to ~ to (the horse was ~d to a tree; the two horses were ~d to each other ("roped together")

rosary n. to pray, recite, say the ~

rose n. 1. a long-stemmed; rambling; wild ~ 2. a bouquet of ~s 3. (misc.) a bed of ~s ("an ideal situation") (see also *rose garden* at **garden**)

roster n. 1. to make up a ~ 2. a duty; personnel ~

rostrum n. 1. to get up on, mount the ~ 2. to stand on a ~ 3. from; on a ~

rot n. 1. black; creeping; dry; wet ~ 2. (misc.) to talk ~ ("to talk nonsense, rubbish")

rotate v. 1. (D; intr.) to ~ around (to ~ around an axle) 2. (D; intr.) to ~ on (the earth ~s on its axis)

rotation n. 1. to make a ~ 2. crop ~ 3. a ~ around (a wheel's ~ around an axle) 4. a ~ on (the earth's ~ on its axis) 5. in ~ (the leaders serve in strict ~)

rote n. ["repetition"] by ~ (to learn by ~)

rotten adj. 1. (colloq.) to feel ~ about smt. 2. (colloq.) ~ to + inf. (it was ~ of him to have done that) 3. (misc.) ~ to the core

rouge n. 1. to apply, put on; use ~ 2. to remove ~

rough adj. (colloq.) ["not gentle"] 1. ~ on, with (you've been pretty ~ on the children) ["difficult"] 2. ~ to + inf. (it's ~ to work at night = it's ~ working at night) 3. (misc.) it was ~ on her, losing her job like that (see also *sleep rough* at **sleep II** v.)

roughshod adv. to ride, run ~ over smb. ("to treat smb. in an inconsiderate manner")

roulette n. 1. to play ~ 2. Russian ~

round I adv., prep. ~ about (~ about midnight)

round II n. ["unit of ammunition"] 1. to fire a ~; to get a ~ off 2. a blank; incoming; live ~ (of gunfire) 3. the ~ jammed ["drinks served to everyone in a group"] 4. to buy; order a ~ (of drinks) (it's my ~ now: let me buy this ~!) ["complete game"] 5. to play, shoot a ~ (of golf) ["song sung in unison in which each part is repeated"] 6. to sing a ~ ["part of a boxing match"] 7. in a ~ (the challenger was knocked out in the seventh ~) (see also **rounds**; **ward round**)

roundabout n. 1. to ride (on) a ~ 2. to get on a ~ 3. get off a ~ (BE; CE has *merry-go-round*)

roundhouse n. ["type of blow"] to throw a ~

rounds n. 1. to do, go on, make one's ~ (the doctor was making her ~) 2. on one's ~ (the doctor was on ~ (AE) = the doctor was on her ~ (BE)) 3. (misc.) "And Priests in black gowns, were walking their ~" – William Blake, *Songs of Experience*, 1794

roundup n. a police ~ (of all suspects)

rouse v. 1. (D; tr.) to ~ from, out of (to ~ smb. out of bed) 2. (D; tr.) to ~ to (to ~ smb. to action)

rouser n. a rabble ~

roust v. (esp. AE) to ~ smb. out of bed

rout I n. 1. a complete, total, utter ~ 2. (misc.) to put the enemy to ~; the retreat turned into a total ~

rout II v. 1. to ~ completely, utterly 2. ~ smb. out of bed

route I n. 1. to map out, plan a ~ 2. to follow, take a ~ 3. to introduce a ~ 4. to discontinue a ~ 5. an alternate (AE), alternative; circuitous; direct; devious; indirect; roundabout ~ 6. an escape ~ 7. a scenic ~ (to take the scenic ~) 8. a bus; newspaper; streetcar (AE), tram (BE); truck (esp. AE) ~ 9. an air; overland; sea; trade ~ 10. a ~ between; from; to 11. along a ~ (along the sea ~ from Venice to Constantinople) 12. a ~ through (a sea ~ through the Bosphorus) (see also **en route**)

route II v. (P; tr.) they ~d the shipment around the war zone; to ~ a memorandum to the appropriate people

routine n. 1. to change; vary; establish; get stuck in, settle into a ~ 2. (a) daily, ordinary; domestic; dull ~ 3. a dance ~

rove v. (P; intr.) they ~d around the lobby; we ~d through the mall (see also *roving reporter* at **reporter**)

row I /rou/ n. ["arrangement in a straight line"] 1. an even, straight ~ 2. a back; front ~ 3. in a ~ 4. (misc.) the third year in a ~ ; ~s and ~s (there were ~s and ~s of corn in the field) = ~ on/upon ~ (there was ~ upon ~ of corn in the field; "In Flanders fields the poppies blow Between the crosses, ~ on ~" – John McRae, "In Flanders Fields," 1915) ["misc."] 5. death ~ ("cell block where prisoners await execution") (on death ~); skid ~ (AE) ("area in a city where destitute people congregate") (on skid ~); her hair was (arranged) in cornrows

row II n. 1. to go for a ~, have a ~ 2. a ~ across (let's go for a ~ across the lake) 3. a ~ on (let's go for a ~ on the lake)

row III v. 1. (P; intr., tr.) we ~ed across the lake; we ~ed on the lake 2. (misc.) to go ~ing (let's go ~ing on the lake)

row IV /rau/ n. 1. to kick up, make, raise a ~ 2. to have a ~ 3. an awful ~ 4. a ~ about, over; with (to have a ~ with smb. about a trifle)

row V v. (D; intr.) to ~ about, over; with

rowboat n. (AE) to row a ~

row down v. (d; intr., tr.) (they ~ed us down to the bridge)

rowing n. 1. to go ~ 2. to go in for ~

rowing-boat (BE) see **rowboat**

row out v. (d; intr., tr.) to ~ to (they ~ed us out to an island)

royalty n. ["percentage of revenue"] 1. to pay a ~/ ~ties on (the publisher paid them ~ties on their dictionaries) 2. to bring in, earn ~ties (the book brings in handsome ~ties) 3. to earn, get, receive ~ties (the author received ~ties on her book) 4. author's ~ties 5. from ~ties 6. in ~ties (the author earned a lot in ~ties from her book)

rub v. 1. (D; intr., tr.) to ~ against; with (one part was ~bing against the other; ~ your hand against this surface; ~ wet dishes with a dishcloth) 2. (d; tr.) to ~ into, on (to ~ lotion into one's skin) 3. (N; used with an adjective) ~ wet dishes dry with a dishcloth

rubber n. 1. crude; foam; sponge; synthetic ~ 2. ~ stretches (see the Usage Note for **eraser**)

rubbers n. (AE) ["rubber overshoes"] 1. to put on; wear ~ 2. a pair of ~

rubbish n. 1. (esp. BE) to collect; put out the ~ 2. (esp. BE) household ~ (AE usu. has *garbage*, *trash*) 3. an accumulation, heap, pile of ~ 4. (misc.) (CE) to talk (utter) ~ (about)

rubble n. 1. a heap, pile of ~ 2. (misc.) to reduce smt. to ~

rubdown n. to give smb. a ~

Rubicon n. to cross the ~ ("to commit oneself irrevocably")

rub off v. 1. (D; intr.) to ~ on, onto (the paint ~bed off on my shirt) 2. (colloq.) (D; intr.) to ~ on, onto ("to affect") (we hoped that some of these cultural activities would ~ on our children)

rub up v. 1. (d; intr.) to ~ against ("to touch") (don't let the wire ~ against the pipe) 2. (colloq.) (d; intr.) to ~ against ("to have contact with") (she used to ~ against many famous movie stars) 3. (misc.) to ~ the wrong way (they never got on because they kept ~bing each other up the wrong way) (BE; esp. AE is *to rub the wrong way*)

ruck n. (esp. BE) ["mass of undistinguished people"] 1. the common ~ 2. above; out of the ~

ruckus n. (esp. AE) to cause, create, kick up, make, raise, stir up a ~

ructions n. (BE) to cause, create ~

rude adj. 1. ~ about 2. ~ of (that was ~ of him) 3. ~ to 4. ~ to + inf. (it was ~ of him to talk during the concert = he was ~ to talk during the concert)

rudeness n. 1. to display, show ~ 2. ~ to

rug n. 1. to braid; weave a ~ 2. to clean; shampoo; vacuum a ~ 3. a scatter, throw (AE) ~ 4. a hooked; oriental; Persian; rag ~ 5. a prayer ~ (see also *to sweep under the rug* at **sweep**)

rugby n. 1. to play ~ 2. the game of ~ 3. (misc.) a ~ ball; field (AE), pitch (BE); game, match; international; player

ruin I n. 1. to cause, spell ~ 2. to face; fall into ~ 3. complete, utter ~ 4. financial ~ (to face financial ~) 5. (misc.) on the brink of ~; on the road to ~; the credit crunch threatened the economic system with complete financial ~; alcohol proved (to be) his ~ (see also **ruins**)

ruin II v. to ~ completely, utterly (the credit crunch threatened to ~ the financial system completely)

ruins n. 1. ancient; charred, smoking ~ 2. a heap, pile of ~ 3. (misc.) to sift through the ~; to lie in ~ (to sift through the smoking ~ of the bombed building)

rule I n. ["regulation"] ["principle"] 1. to establish, lay down, make (the) ~s 2. to formulate, set down a ~ 3. to adopt a ~ 4. to apply, enforce a ~ 5. to bend, relax, stretch; waive a ~ 6. to rescind, revoke a ~ 7. to abide by, comply with, obey, observe a ~ 8. to break, violate a ~ 9. a binding; cardinal; firm, hard-and-fast, inflexible, ironclad, strict ~ 10. an unwritten ~ 11. a general; ground ~ 12. an exclusionary (AE); gag; parliamentary ~ 13. (ling.) a deletion; grammatical; rewrite; substitution ~ 14. a ~ against (a ~ against smoking at staff conferences) 15. a ~ for (is there one ~ for the rich and another ~ for the poor?) 16. a ~ to + inf. (it's their ~ not to smoke at staff conferences) 17. a ~ that + clause (they established a ~ that no one was to smoke at staff conferences) 18. (to be) against, in violation of the ~s 19. (misc.) a set of ~s that permit some things and forbid others; the golden ~; a ~ of thumb; as a (general) ~ ("generally"); the ~ of law (see also **ground rules**) ["government, reign"] 20. to establish; extend one's ~ 21. to overthrow smb.'s ~ 22. authoritarian; benevolent; despotic; harsh ~ 23. civilian; military; mob; popular ~ (to re-establish civilian rule after a military dictatorship) 24. majority; minority ~ 25. colonial; foreign; home ~ 26. ~ over 27. under smb.'s ~ (under foreign ~) (see also **slide rule**)

rule II v. 1. (d; intr.) to ~ against (the judge ~d against the plaintiff) 2. (D; intr.) to ~ in favor of (the judge ~d in favor of the defendant) 3. (D; intr.) to ~ on (to ~ on a question) 4. (D; intr.) to ~ over (to ~ over a country) 5. (L; can be subj.) the court ~d that the witness ¬be/should be¬ disqualified; they ~d that he was incompetent to stand trial 6. (M) the judge ~d him to be incompetent to stand trial 7. (N; used with an adjective) the judge ~d him incompetent to stand trial 8. (misc.) the judge ~d him out of order

rule out v. (D; tr.) to ~ as (the police can't ~ her out completely as a suspect in the case)

ruler n. ["person who rules"] 1. to put a ~ into power 2. to overthrow, unseat a ~ 3. an absolute, authoritarian, despotic, dictatorial, tyrannical; strong; weak ~ 4. a colonial; military ~ 5. (misc.) a tyrannical ~ who came to power but was unseated by those who had put him into power

ruling n. 1. to give, hand down (AE), make a ~ (the court handed down a ~) 2. a fair, just ~ 3. an unfair, unjust ~ 4. a court; official ~ 5. a ~ about, on (the court handed down a ~ on the company's violation of the law) 6. a ~ that + clause (the court handed down a ~ that the company had violated the law)

rumblings n. ["rumors"] ~ about; of (~ of discontent were heard)

ruminate v. (D; intr.) ("to reflect") to ~ about, on, over

rummage v. 1. (D; intr.) to ~ for (he was ~ging in his pockets for change) 2. (D; intr.) to ~ through (to ~ through old clothes/crowded drawers; he was ~ging through his pockets for change)

rumor, rumour n. 1. to circulate, spread a ~ 2. to confirm; trace, track down a ~ 3. to deny; dispel, put paid to (BE), quash, scotch, silence, spike, squash a ~ 4. a malicious; persistent; vicious; widespread; wild ~ 5. a baseless, unconfirmed, unfounded; idle, vague ~ 6. ~s circulate, fly, go around, spread 7. a ~ that + clause (have you heard the ~ that he intends to resign?) 8. a ~ about (have you heard the ~(s) about his intention to resign?) 9. amid ~s (he resigned amid ~s that he was guilty) 10. (misc.) ~ has it/~s are rife that he intends to resign

rumored adj. (cannot stand alone) 1. ~ to + inf. (he is ~ to be intending to resign) 2. ~ that + clause (it is ~ that he intends to resign)

rumpus n. (colloq.) to cause, create, kick up, make, raise, stir up a ~

run I n. ["course"] 1. a ski ~ ["freedom of movement"] 2. to have the ~ of the house ["race"] 3. a cross-country ~; a fun ~; a sponsored ~; the mile ~ ["series of demands"] 4. a ~ on a bank; a ~ on the dollar ["running away"] 5. on the ~ (escaped criminals on the ~ from the police) 6. (misc.) to make a ~ for it ("to flee") ["trial, experiment"] 7. a dry, dummy (BE), trial ~ (to do/have a trial ~ = to give smt. a trial ~) ["flight"] 8. to make a ~ (over a target) 9. a bombing ~ ["point scored"] (baseball, cricket) 10. to score a ~ 11. (baseball) a home ~ ["unraveled stitches in a stocking"] (AE also has *runner*; BE often has *ladder*) 12. to get, have a ~ (in a stocking) ["duration"] 13. in the long; short ~ (see also **long run**; **short run**) ["period of activity"] 14. to have a ~ (we've had a ~ of bad luck recently) 15. a brief, short; long; record ~ (the play had a record ~ on Broadway) ["act of running"] 16. to go for, have a ~ (let's go for a short run in the park) 17. to go on, take part in (let's go on a sponsored ~ for charity) 18. to break into a ~ (when I saw they were following me I broke into a ~ to escape them) ["misc."] 19. an event quite different from the general ~ of things

run II v. 1. (C) ("to fill") ~ a bath for me; or ~ me a bath 2. (d; intr.) to ~ across ("to meet by chance") (to ~ across an old friend) 3. (d; intr.) to ~ after ("to chase") (to ~ after a bus) (also fig.) (she ran after him but he refused to date her) 4. (d; intr.) to ~ against ("to oppose") (I would not like to ~ against her in the senatorial race; popular feeling was ~ning against the president; in 2008 Obama and McCain ran against each other for President of the USA) 5. (d; intr.) ("to ply") ~ between (this train ~s regularly between New York and Philadelphia) 6. (d; intr.) to ~ down ("to descend quickly"); ("to pour") (to ~ down the stairs; tears ran down her face) 7. (esp. AE) (D; intr., tr.) ("to be or make a candidate") to ~ for (to ~ for office; to ~ for Congress; to ~ a candidate for Congress/office) (BE has *stand* intr.) 8. (d; intr.) ("to extend") ("to ply") to ~ from; to (the sale will ~ from the first of the month to the tenth; the fence ~s from the house to the road; this train ~s regularly from New York to Philadelphia and back (again)) 9. (d; intr.) to ~ in ("to be present") (ability in languages ~s in their blood; talent ~s in the family) 10. (d; intr.) to ~ into ("to meet") (to ~ into an old friend; to ~ into trouble) 11. (d; intr.) to ~ into ("to hit") (¬he/the car¬ ran into a pole) 12. (d; intr.) to ~ into ("to enter quickly") (to ~ into the house) 13. (d; intr.) to ~ into ("to amount to") (the expenses will ~ into thousands of dollars) 14. (d; intr.) ("to move quickly") to ~ off (the car ran off the road) 15. (d; tr.) ("to force") to ~ off (she ran the other car off the road) 16. (d; intr., tr.) to ~ on ("to operate") (the engine ~s on diesel oil; they ran the business on borrowed money) 17. (d; intr.) to ~ out of ("to use up") (she ran out of money) 18. (d; intr.) to ~ out of ("to leave quickly") (to ~ out of the room) 19. (d; intr.) to ~ over ("to crush") (the car ran over an animal, then backed up and ran over it again = the car ran over an animal, then backed up and ran it over again) 20. (d; intr.) ("to pass") to ~ through (a blue thread ~s through the cloth; a strange thought ran through her mind) 21. (d; intr.) to ~ through ("to examine") (~ through the material again) 22. (d; tr.) to ~ through ("to process") (~ the data through the computer again) 23. (d; intr.) ("to go quickly") to ~ to (she ran to the doctor) 24. (d; intr.) to ~ to ("to seek help from") (he keeps ~ning to his mother (over every little thing); don't ~ to the police (with unfounded suspicions)) 25. (d; intr.) to ~ to ("to amount") (the dictionary ~s to a thousand pages; the expenses will ~ to thousands of dollars) 26. (d; tr.) ("to drive") to ~ to (I'll ~ you to the station) 27. (d; intr.) to ~ up ("to ascend quickly") (to ~ up the stairs) 28. (P; intr., tr.) ("to go") ("to move") ("to move quickly") the road ~s south; to ~ across the street; to ~ for the doctor; the children ran through the park; the smugglers are ~ning guns across the border 29. (s) supplies are ~ning low; the differences ~ deep 30. (misc.) Romeo ran through Tybalt with his sword = Romeo ran Tybalt through with his sword; the wastrel ran through the family fortune quickly and was left destitute; the trains are ~ning behind schedule; the trains are running late; do the trains ever ~ on time?; she ran her hand through her hair; we are ~ning short of coffee and may soon ~ out (of it) completely; things are ~ning smoothly; to ~ against the clock (esp. AE) ("to time one's performance"); a fast runner ~s fast; to ~ fast ("to be ahead of schedule"); to ~ slow ("to be behind schedule"); to ~ smb. out of town ("to expel smb. from a town"); to ~ rampant/riot ("to run wild"); (colloq.) ~ that by me again ("repeat that for me"); to go ~nning (let's go ~nning in the park)

run afoul v. (AE) (d; intr.) to ~ of (to ~ of the law)
run aground v. (D; intr.) to ~ on (the boat ran aground on a sandbank)
runaround n. (colloq.) ["delaying action"] to give smb. the ~
run around v. (D; intr.) to ~ with (he ~s around with a fast crowd)
run away v. 1. (D; intr.) to ~ from (to ~ from home) 2. (D; intr.) to ~ to (she ran away to California) 3. (D; intr.) to ~ with (he ran away with his firm's money and with his boss's wife)
run back v. (D; intr.) to ~ to (she ran back to her room)
run counter v. (d; intr.) to ~ to (their actions ~ to their promises)
rundown n. ["summary"] 1. to give smb. a ~ 2. to get a ~ 3. a ~ on
run down v. 1. (d; intr.) ("to go") to ~ to (to ~ to the grocery store) 2. (D; intr.) ("to descend quickly")

to ~ to (to ~ to the bottom of the hill; she ran down to her basement room) 3. (misc.) she ran down from her attic room
run foul v. see **run afoul**
rung n. on the bottom, lowest; highest, top ~ (of a ladder)
run-in n. ["clash"] to have a ~ with smb.
run low v. (D; intr.) to ~ on (to ~ on fuel)
runner n. ["one who runs"] 1. a distance, long-distance; fast ~ (a fast ~ runs fast) ["unraveled stitches in a stocking"] (AE) 2. see **run I** n. 12
runner-up n. a ~ to
running n. ["competition"] 1. in the ~ 2. out of the ~ ["racing"] 3. cross-country ~
run off v. 1. (D; intr.) to ~ to (she ran off to California) 2. (D; intr.) to ~ with (he ran off with his firm's money and with his boss's wife)
run out v. 1. (D; intr.) to ~ into (to ~ into the street) 2. (D; intr.) to ~ on ("to abandon") (he ran out on his family)
run over v. (d; intr.) to ~ to (she ran over to her friend's place; I'll ~ you over to the station)
run short v. (d; intr.) to ~ of (they never ~ of money)
run-up n. (BE) ["preparatory period"] a ~ to (during/in the ~ to the election)
run up v. 1. (d; intr.) to ~ against ("to encounter") (to ~ against strong competition; to ~ against difficulties) 2. (D; intr.) to ~ to ("to approach quickly") (she ran up to me) 3. (D; intr.) ("to ascend quickly") (she ran up to her attic room)
runway n. 1. to clear a ~ (for an emergency landing) 2. to overshoot a ~ 3. on a ~ (the plane was still on the ~)
ruse n. 1. a clever, successful; subtle; unsuccessful ~ 2. a ~ fails; succeeds 3. a ~ to + inf. (it was a ~ to get their money)
rush I n. 1. to make a ~ (to make a ~ for the door) (see also **bum's rush**) 2. to beat the ~ (let's leave early and beat the ~) 3. a gold ~ 4. a headlong; mad; sudden ~ 5. a ~ for (there was a sudden ~ for tickets to the concert) 6. a ~ to + inf. (there was a sudden ~ to buy tickets for the concert) 7. in a ~ (everyone was in a ~ to buy tickets for the concert) 8. (misc.) I felt a ~ of dizziness after I drank the punch; a ~ to judgment
rush II v. 1. to ~ headlong, pell-mell 2. (d; intr.) to ~ at ("to attack") 3. (D; intr.) to ~ into (to ~ headlong into a business deal) 4. (d; intr., tr.) to ~ to (to ~ to the office; to ~ to smb.'s assistance; to ~ smb. to the hospital) 5. (P; intr., tr.) they were ~ing across the street; they ~ed over to the other side of the street; I had to ~ home; she ~ed down/up to her room 6. (misc.) she ~ed (in order) to catch the train
rush around v. (P; intr.) they are always ~ing around from one place to another
rush away v. (D; intr.) to ~ from (we had to ~ (home) from the party)

rush off *v.* 1. (D; intr.) to ~ to (they ~ed off to the theater; she ~ed off to her room) 2. (E) she ~ed off (in order) to catch the train

rut *n.* ["groove, furrow"] 1. a deep ~ (in a road) ["dreary routine"] 2. to get into a ~ 3. in a ~ 4. out of a ~ (she got into a ~ at work, felt she had been in a ~ long enough, and got out of her ~ by changing jobs)

ruthless *adj.* ~ in (he is ~ in his methods)

rye *n.* 1. winter ~ 2. a sheaf of ~ 3. (misc.) a ham sandwich on ~ (bread)

S

sabbath *n.* 1. to keep, observe the ~ 2. to break, desecrate, violate the ~ 3. on the ~

sabbatical *n.* 1. to give, grant a ~ 2. to get; have; take a ~ 3. (to be, go) on (a) ~ (she was on (a) ~)

saber, sabre *n.* 1. to draw one's ~ 2. to brandish a ~ 3. (misc.) saber-rattling ("threatening to wage war")

sabotage *n.* 1. to commit ~ 2. an act of ~

sack *n.* ["bag"] 1. a mail ~ 2. a ~ bursts; contains, holds ["sackful"] 3. a ~ of (bought a ~ of potatoes) ["bed"] (colloq.) (AE) 4. to hit the ~ ("to go to bed") ["dismissal"] (colloq.) 5. to get the ~ 6. to give smb. the ~

sackcloth *n.* in ~ and ashes ("in deep repentance")

sacrament *n.* 1. to administer a ~ 2. to receive a ~

sacred *adj.* ~ to (the shrines were ~ to them)

sacrifice I *n.* 1. to make; offer a ~ 2. to entail a ~ 3. a great; heroic; personal ~ 4. a human ~ 5. the supreme, ultimate ~ ("death") 6. a ~ for (our heroic soldiers who made the supreme ~ for their country) 7. the ~ of (we offered the ~ of a goat to our God) 8. a ~ to 9. as a ~ (we offered a goat as a ~ to our God) 10. at (a) ~ (they achieved success at great personal ~)

sacrifice II *v.* 1. (D; refl., tr.) to ~ for (to ~ oneself for a just cause) 2. (D; intr., refl., tr.) to ~ to (to ~ a goat to our God)

sacrilege *n.* 1. to commit (a) ~ 2. (a) ~ to + inf. (it was ~ to speak like that)

sacrilegious *adj.* ~ to + inf. (it's ~ to speak like that)

sad *adj.* 1. very ~ 2. ~ about, at (we felt ~ about being alone) 3. ~ to + inf. (we felt ~ to be alone; she'll be ~ to leave here) 4. ~ that + clause (we felt ~ that we were alone) (see also *sad to relate* at **relate**; **sad sack**; *sad to say* at **say**)

sadden *v.* (R) it ~ed us to be alone; it ~ed us that we were alone

saddened *adj.* 1. ~ to + inf. (we were ~ to be alone) 2. ~ that + clause (we were ~ that we were alone)

saddle I *n.* 1. to put a ~ on (an animal such as a horse) 2. an English; stock, western ~ 3. in the ~ (also fig.) (after a few nervous moments, the President is back in the ~ again!) (see also **saddle sore**)

saddle II *v.* 1. (D; tr.) to ~ for (they ~d (up) a gentle pony for the child) 2. (d; tr.) to ~ with (to ~ smb. with an unpleasant task)

saddle sore *n.* to develop ~s

sadism *n.* to display ~

sadness *n.* 1. to experience, feel; express ~ 2. deep, profound ~ 3. a feeling; pang, touch of ~ (we felt a pang of ~ at being alone = we experienced a feeling of ~ at being alone) 4. ~ about, at, over; of (we felt

deep ~ at being alone; we felt the deep ~ of being alone) 5. ~ that + clause (we felt deep ~ that we were alone)

sad sack *n.* (slang) (AE) ["inept person"] a hopeless ~

safari *n.* 1. to organize a ~ 2. to go on (a) ~ 3. a ~ to

safe I *adj.* 1. absolutely, completely, very ~ 2. ~ for (it is ~ for children) 3. ~ from (~ from attack) 4. ~ to + inf. (it is not ~ to drive without putting on seat belts; it's ~ to say that their party will win) 5. (misc.) better ~ than sorry ("prevention is better than cure"); ~ and sound

safe II *n.* 1. to open; unlock a ~ 2. to close; lock a ~ 3. to break open, crack a ~ 4. a wall ~

safe-conduct *n.* to issue a ~

safeguard I *n.* 1. an adequate; built-in ~ 2. a ~ against (here's our latest built-in ~ against theft)

safeguard II *v.* (D; refl., tr.) to ~ against, from (to ~ one's property from theft)

safe-keeping *n.* in ~

safety *n.* ["security"] 1. to assure, ensure, guarantee smb.'s ~ 2. to jeopardize smb.'s ~ 3. air; industrial; public ~ 4. for ~ (fasten your seat belt for your own ~) 5. in ~ (to live in ~) 6. (misc.) a margin of ~; there is ~ in numbers; ~ first!; for safety's sake (for safety's sake, fasten your seat belt) ["device that prevents accidental discharge of a firearm"] 7. to set the ~ 8. to release the ~ (see also *safety catch* at **catch I** *n.*)

safety factor *n.* a built-in ~

sag *v.* 1. (D; intr.) to ~ to (to ~ to one side) 2. (D; intr.) to ~ against; under (the fat man ~ged against the door and the floor ~ged under the weight of him)

saga *n.* a ~ about, of

sagacity *n.* the ~ to + inf. (she had the ~ to diversify her investments)

said *adj.* 1. ~ to + inf. (she is ~ to be very wise) 2. ~ that + clause (it is ~ that she is very wise) (see also **say**)

sail I *n.* 1. to hoist, raise the ~s 2. to let out the ~s 3. to furl, take in a ~; to reduce; slacken ~ 4. to trim ("adjust") the ~s 5. to lower, strike the ~s 6. (misc.) to set ~ for; from ("to leave for by ship, boat"); to go for a ~

sail II *v.* 1. (d; intr.) to ~ along (to ~ along the coast) 2. (d; intr.) to ~ around, round (to ~ around the world) 3. (d; intr.) to ~ down (to ~ down a river) 4. (d; intr.) to ~ for (to ~ for Europe) 5. (d; intr.) to ~ from; to (to ~ from New York to Liverpool) 6. (d; intr.) to ~ into (the ship ~ed into port) 7. (colloq.) (d; intr.) to ~ into ("to attack") (the opposing candidates ~ed into each other) 8. (d; intr.) to ~ through (to ~ through the straits) 9. (colloq.) (d; intr.) to ~ through ("to cope with easily") (she just ~ed through her finals!) 10. (d; intr.) to ~ up (to ~ up a river) 11. (P; intr.) to ~ across the ocean; to ~ towards the coast; to ~ east 12. (misc.) to go ~ing

sailing *n.* plain, plane, smooth ~ ("unimpeded progress")

saint *n.* a patron ~ (see also *the patience of a saint* at **patience**)

sake *n.* 1. for smb.'s ~ (do it for my ~) 2. for old times' ~ 3. for the ~ of (for the ~ of argument) 4. for pity's ~ 5. for argument's ~ 6. (misc.) it's worth doing for its own ~; for God's/Christ's/goodness'/heaven's/Pete's/pity's ~ (used as expressions of exasperation or urgency) (for heaven's ~, could/will you hurry up?!) (see also **sakes**)

sakes *n.* (AE) (colloq.) ["sake"] for God/Christ/goodness/heaven ~ ("for God's/Christ's/Pete's/goodness'/heaven's/pity's sake") (for heaven ~, could/will you hurry up?!)

salad *n.* 1. to make, prepare; toss a ~ 2. to garnish; season a ~ 3. a chicken; egg; fruit; green; ham; mixed; pasta; potato; salmon; seafood; tuna(fish); tomato; tossed ~ (an egg-salad sandwich) 4. a side ~ (the main course comes with vegetables and a side ~) 5. a bowl; helping, serving of ~ (see also *salad bar* at **bar I** *n.*)

salary *n.* 1. to pay a ~ 2. to command, draw, get, receive; earn a ~ 3. (colloq.) to pull down (AE), pull in (BE) a ~ 4. to boost, increase, raise ~ries 5. to cut, reduce, slash ~ries; to freeze ~s 6. to attach, garnishee smb.'s ~ 7. to withhold smb.'s ~ 8. an annual, yearly; monthly; weekly ~ 9. a fixed; full ~ 10. a big, handsome, high; decent, good; final; low, meager, poor; small; modest; starting ~ 11. at a ~ (she was employed at a starting ~ of £50 a week) 12. on a ~ (can anyone survive on a ~ of £25 a week?) 13. (misc.) the union successfully negotiated (for) a higher ~; a four-figure ~ ("in the thousands"); a five-figure ~ ("in the tens of thousands")

sale *n.* ["selling"] 1. to make a ~ 2. a cash ~ 3. for, on ~ ("being sold") (house for ~; the book will be on ~ next month) 4. to put smt. up for ~ 5. a ~ falls through; goes ahead, goes through (we had high hopes that the ~ would go ahead but our hopes were dashed when it fell through at the last moment) ["sale at reduced prices"] 6. to conduct, have, hold, run (colloq.) a ~ 7. an annual; boot, car-boot (BE); clearance; closeout; fire; garage (AE), yard (AE); going-out-of-business; jumble (BE), rummage (AE); storewide; warehouse ~ 8. on ~ (AE) = at, in a ~ (BE) ("being sold at a reduced price") (see also **sales**)

sales *n.* 1. to boost ~ 2. brisk ~ 3. gross; high-street (BE); net; retail ~ 4. ~ drop off, slump; level off; peak; pick up 5. a decline, dip, fall; increase, rise in ~ 6. the level; volume of ~ (there's been a decline in the volume of high-street ~; they hope they'll pick up later in the year) 7. (misc.) all ~ are final

salesman, salesperson, saleswoman *n.* 1. a door-to-door ~ 2. a traveling ~ (BE also has *commercial traveller*)

salesmanship *n.* aggressive, high-pressure ~

salient *n.* (mil.) 1. to form a ~ 2. a ~ juts out (into enemy lines)

saliva *n.* 1. to dribble, drool ~ 2. ~ dribbles, drools 3. a dribble, drool of ~

sally *n.* ["sortie"] 1. to make a ~ against ["trip"] 2. a ~ into (a ~ into strange territory)

salmon *n.* 1. canned (AE), tinned (BE); fresh; pink; red; smoked; wild ~ 2. ~ spawn 3. a can (AE), tin (BE) of ~

salon *n.* a beauty; hair; literary ~

salt *n.* 1. to pour ~ (pour the ~ into the saltshaker; pour some ~ on the icy driveway) 2. to put, sprinkle ~ in, on (sprinkle some ~ on the meat; put some ~ in the soup) 3. common, table; fine; garlic; mineral; onion; rock; sea ~ 4. a dash, pinch; grain of ~ 5. a spoonful of ~ 6. (misc.) ~ and pepper; to take smt. with a grain/pinch of ~ ("to regard smt. with skepticism"); the ~ of the earth ("the very best"); to be worth one's ~ ("to be worthy of respect") (see also *saltcellar* at **cellar**; *saltshaker* at **shaker**; **salts**)

salts *n.* bath; smelling ~

salute I *n.* 1. to fire; give a ~ (the president was given a 21-gun ~) 2. to return; take a ~ 3. a smart, snappy ~ 4. a military; naval; 19-gun; rifle; royal; 21-gun ~ 5. a ~ to 6. in ~ (to) (in ~ to our fighting forces we will play a march)

salute II *v.* 1. to ~ smartly (the soldier ~d smartly) 2. (D; tr.) to ~ for, on (I ~ you for your magnificent achievement)

salvage *v.* (D; tr.) to ~ from (to ~ records from a fire)

salvation *n.* 1. to bring; preach ~ 2. to attain, find; seek ~ 3. ~ from 4. ~ by, through (preaching ~ from sin through faith)

salve *n.* 1. to apply, rub in, rub on (a) ~ 2. a ~ for; to (it was a ~ to my wounded feelings)

salvo *n.* 1. to fire a ~ 2. an opening ~

Samaritan *n.* a good ~ ("a person who helps those in need")

same *pron., adj., adv.* it's all the ~ to me ("it makes no difference to me"); go or stay: it's all the ~ to me! = it's all the ~ to me whether you go or stay!; we tried our best but we failed all/just the ~ ("but we failed nevertheless"); a puma and a cougar are one and the ~ animal = a puma and a cougar are exactly the ~ animal = a puma and a cougar are the exact ~ animal (colloq.) = a puma is the ~ animal as a cougar; that puma is the ~ one (that) I saw yesterday – at least it looks the ~ as the one (that) I saw yesterday!; that puma is the ~ in size as the one I saw yesterday = that puma is the ~ size as the one I saw yesterday = that's the same-size puma (that/as) I saw yesterday – at least it looks exactly the ~ size as the one I saw yesterday!

sample *n.* ["representative item"] 1. to distribute, hand out (free) ~s 2. (med.) to give, leave, provide a ~ 3. (med.) to analyze; collect, take a ~ 4. (med.) a blood; urine ~ (we'd like to take a blood ~ from

you that we'll analyze later) 5. a floor; free ~ ["selected segment"] (statistics) 6. to select, take a ~ 7. a
random; representative ~
sampler n. ["needlework"] to work a ~
sampling n. (a) random ~
sanction I n. ["approval"] 1. to give ~ to (no one gave
~ to his smoking marijuana) 2. to receive ~ 3. legal
~ (see also **sanctions**)
sanction II v. 1. to ~ officially; tacitly 2. (K) no one
~ed his smoking marijuana
sanctions n. ["coercive measures"] 1. to apply, impose
~ 2. to clamp ~ on 3. to lift ~ 4. economic, trade;
military ~ 5. ~ against, on; for (the U.N. imposed
economic ~ against/on the dictatorship for violating human rights)
sanctuary n. 1. to give, grant, offer, provide (a) ~ 2.
to ask for, request, seek; find, receive ~ 3. to deny,
refuse smb. ~ 4. a bird; wildlife ~ 5. (a) ~ for 6.
(a) ~ from (they sought a ~ from persecution for
themselves and their children)
sanctum n. an inner ~
sand n. 1. to scatter, spread, sprinkle, strew ~ 2.
coarse; fine ~ 3. a grain of ~ 4. a pile of ~ (see also
sandbox at **box I** n.; *sand dune* at **dune**; *sandpit*
at **pit I** n.)
sandals n. 1. beach ~ 2. a pair of ~
sandwich I n. 1. to fix (esp. AE), make, prepare a ~
from, of, out of, with (to make a ~ out of leftovers
with a lot in it) 2. to make smt. into a ~ (to make
leftovers into a ~) 3. to eat, grab, have a ~ (there's
just time to grab a quick ~ before the meeting) 4.
a cheese; club (AE); corned-beef; doorstep (BE);
double-decker; grilled-cheese (AE), toasted-cheese
(BE); ham; open, open-face; tomato-and-lettuce,
lettuce-and-tomato; tuna ~
sandwich II v. (d; tr.) to ~ (in) between (to ~ (in) a
meeting between a staff conference and lunch)
sanitation n. environmental ~
sanity n. 1. to keep, maintain, preserve, retain one's
~ 2. to lose one's ~
sarcasm n. 1. biting, devastating, keen, piercing,
scathing, withering; mild; (thinly) veiled ~ 2. an
edge, hint of ~ (there was a hint of ~ in her remarks) 3. ~ about 4. (misc.) dripping with ~ (her
remarks were dripping with ~)
sardines n. 1. canned (AE), tinned (BE); fresh ~ 2. a
can (AE), tin (BE) of ~ 3. (misc.) to pack in like ~
sashay v. (colloq.) (AE) 1. (P; intr.) ("to stroll")
she ~ed down to the beach and then ~ed along it
2. (misc.) to come; go ~ing (she went ~ing along
the beach)
satellite n. 1. to launch; orbit a ~ 2. an artificial
(earth); communications; orbiting; spy; weather ~
3. by ~ (an event telecast by ~) 4. from a ~ (pictures
sent to earth from an orbiting ~)
satire n. 1. (a) biting, scathing ~ 2. political ~ 3. a
~ on
satisfaction n. ["act of satisfying"] ["state of being satisfied"] 1. to afford, give ~ to 2. to express; feel ~

3. to find, take ~ in 4. deep, great, profound ~ 5.
quiet ~ 6. ~ that + clause (they felt ~ that a fair
compromise had been reached) 7. ~ about, at, over,
with (they felt ~ with the compromise that had
been reached) 8. to smb.'s ~ (the work was done
to my (complete) ~) ["compensation for a wrong or
injury"] 9. to demand; seek ~ 10. to get, receive;
have ~ 11. ~ for (to receive ~ for an insult)
satisfactory adj. 1. completely; highly, very ~ 2. ~
for (her qualifications are not ~ for our needs) 3. ~
in (they were not ~ in their job performance) 4. ~
to (not ~ to anyone concerned)
satisfied adj. 1. completely, fully, perfectly, thoroughly ~ 2. ~ with (we are ~ with the good results)
3. ~ to + inf. (she is not ~ to spend her days doing nothing) 4. ~ that + clause (we are ~ that all
requirements have been met)
satisfy v. 1. to ~ completely, thoroughly 2. (D; tr.)
to ~ on (can you ~ me on just one more point?) 3.
(L; refl.) we ~fied ourselves that all requirements
had been met
satisfying adj. 1. completely, deeply, totally, very ~
2. emotionally; intellectually ~ 3. ~ to + inf. (she
does not find it ~ to spend her days doing nothing) 4. ~ that + clause (we find it ~ that at last all
requirements have been met)
SATS n. ["Scholastic Aptitude Tests"] (US) 1. (for admission to US universities) to take the ~ ["Standard
Assessment Tasks"] (GB) 2. (given to school children
since 1991 as part of the national curriculum) to
do the ~
saturate v. (D; tr.) to ~ in; with
sauce n. in; with (a) rich; savory, spicy; sweet;
thick ~
saunter v. 1. (P; intr.) she ~ed down to the beach
and then ~ed along it 2. (misc.) to come; go ~ing
(she went ~ing along the beach)
sausage n. 1. liver ~ (CE; AE has *liverwurst*) 2.
beef; garlic; pork ~ 3. a link; piece, slice of ~
savagery n. 1. to demonstrate, display, exhibit,
show ~ 2. extreme; great; sheer; unprovoked 3.
an act; degree, level; outburst of ~ 4. ~ to, towards
5. with ~ (the police behaved with great ~ towards
the demonstrators) 6. ~ to + inf. (it was sheer ~
¬for/on the part of ¬ the police to behave like that
towards the demonstrators!)
save I n. ["action that prevents an opponent from scoring"] 1. to make a ~ 2. a brilliant, spectacular ~
save II v. 1. (C) ~ a place for me; or: ~ me a place
2. (D; intr., tr.) to ~ for (they are ~ing for a new
car; to ~ money for a new car; to ~ for a rainy
day) 3. (D; tr.) to ~ from (to ~ valuable records
from destruction; the knight ~d the maiden from a
dragon; it will ~ you from having to make a second
trip) 4. (D; intr., tr.) to ~ on (during the mild winter
we ~d (lots of money) on fuel) 5. (J) (esp. BE) it
will ~ you having to make a second trip 6. (O) it
will ~ you the trouble of making a second trip; the
computer will ~ (us) a lot of time; buying it here

will ~ (you) a lot of money 7. (misc.) to ~ money towards a new car; to scrimp and ~

save up *v.* (D; intr.) to ~ for (they are ~ing up for a new car; to ~ up money for a new car; to ~ up for a rainy day)

saving *n.* to make a ~ (on) (during the mild winter we made a huge ~ on fuel bills) (see also **savings**)

savings *n.* 1. to make ~ (on) (during the mild winter we made huge ~ on fuel bills) 2. to set aside ~ 3. to deposit; invest one's ~ 4. to withdraw one's ~ (from a bank) 5. to dip into; squander one's ~

savings bond *n.* (AE) 1. to issue a ~ 2. to cash (in), redeem a ~ 3. to roll over a ~

savings certificate *n.* 1. to issue a ~ 2. to cash (in), redeem a ~ 3. (AE) to roll over a ~

savor, savour *v.* (lit.) (d; intr.) to ~ of ("to suggest") (to ~ of arrogance)

savvy *n.* ["knowledge"] (colloq.) 1. to demonstrate ~ 2. political ~ (to demonstrate considerable political ~)

saw I *n.* 1. to set ("put an edge on") a ~ 2. a band; buzz (AE); circular (BE), carpenter's; chain; coping; hand; musical; power; two-handed ~

saw II *v.* 1. (d; intr.) to ~ through (they ~ed through the cable and then they ~ed through it again = they ~ed through the cable and then they ~ed it through again) 2. (misc.) to ~ smt. up into little pieces

saw III *n.* ("saying") 1. a common, old, popular, wise ~ 2. a ~ goes, runs 3. a ~ that (there is an old ~ (to the effect) that haste makes waste)

say I *n.* ["decision"] 1. to have the final ~ ["opportunity to speak"] 2. to have one's ~ ["role"] 3. to have a ~ in

say II *v.* 1. (B) ("to utter") she said a few words to us 2. (d; tr.) ("to state") to ~ about, of (what did they ~ about our offer?) 3. (d; tr.) to ~ for ("to say in justification of") (what do you have to ~ for yourself?) 4. (d; tr.) to ~ to ("to respond to") (what do you ~ to the charges?) 5. (colloq.) (E) ("to state") the instructions ~ to take one tablet every morning 6. (L; to) ("to state") they said (to us) that they would be late; the instructions ~ that I should take one tablet every morning; people ~ that she is very wise 7. (Q; to) ("to state") she did not ~ (to us) when our next meeting would be; the instructions ~ how many tablets to take and when to take them 8. (misc.) "Hello!" she said (to me) = she said "Hello!" (to me); to ~ smt. in jest; to ~ smt. under one's breath; ~ no more; that ~s it all; needless to ~ (after that she got very angry and – needless to ~ – I didn't see her again); would it be fair/true to ~ that her anger ended your friendship?; what a thing to ~?!; it goes without ~ing that we will help (see also **saying**) USAGE NOTE: It is correct to use "You're wrong, I regret to say" or "You're wrong, I'm sorry to say" or "You're wrong, I'm afraid." But it's incorrect to use "?? You're wrong, I'm afraid to say," even though "?? I'm afraid to say," an incorrect blend of "I'm afraid" with "I'm sorry to say," is very common nowadays and is found even in writing.

saying *n.* 1. a common, old, popular, wise ~ 2. a ~ goes, runs 3. a ~ that (there is an old ~ (to the effect) that haste makes waste)

say-so *n.* (colloq.) ["statement"] on smb.'s ~ (I believed it was true on her ~)

scab *n.* a ~ falls off; forms

scabies *n.* to catch, get ~

scaffolding *n.* 1. to erect, put up ~ 2. to remove, take down ~ 3. ~ comes down; goes up; stays up 4. on the ~ (is there anyone working on the ~ you put up yesterday?)

scald *v.* (D; tr.) to ~ with (he was ~ed with boiling water)

scale I *n.* ["series of notes arranged in a certain sequence"] (mus.) 1. to play; sing a ~ 2. a chromatic; diatonic; major; minor; natural ~ ["system of classifying in a series of steps"] 3. a sliding; social ~ 4. a pay, salary, wage; union ~ ["relative size"] 5. an enormous, grand, large; full; moderate; monumental; small ~ 6. on a certain ~ (everything was planned on a monumental ~; on a ~ of one to ten; on a ~ of one inch to ten miles) 7. (misc.) drawn to ~; a small-scale problem = a problem that is small in ~ = a problem on a small ~

scale II *n.* ["weighing machine"] (AE) 1. a bathroom; kitchen; spring; table ~ 2. on a ~ (to weigh smt. on a ~) (see also **scales**)

scale down *v.* (D; tr.) to ~ to (they ~d down production to decreased demand = they ~d production down to decreased demand)

scales *n.* ["weighing machine"] 1. bathroom; kitchen; spring; table ~ 2. a pair, set of ~ 3. on ~ (to weigh smt. on ~) 4. (misc.) to tip the ~ at 150 pounds ["decisive influence"] 5. to tip the ~ ("to have a decisive influence") (the event tipped the ~ in their favor)

scallions *n.* (esp. AE; BE often prefers *spring onions* or *salad onions*) a bunch of ~

scalp *n.* a dry; itchy; oily ~

scamper *v.* (P; intr.) to ~ across the field

scan *n.* ["radiographic image"] 1. to do, take, perform; interpret, read a ~ (of) 2. to get, have, undergo a ~ (of) 3. to go for a ~ 4. (in, on) a bone; brain; CAT, CT; heart; liver; lung; MRI; PET; ultrasound ~ 5. a ~ indicates, reveals, shows

scandal *n.* 1. to cause, create a ~ 2. to cover up, hush up; expose, uncover a ~ 3. a juicy, sensational ~ 4. an open; political; public ~ 5. a ~ breaks, erupts; brews; dies down (a juicy ~ is brewing) 6. a breath, hint, suggestion of ~; series of ~s 7. a ~ about, over (we were shocked at the ~ about the mayor taking bribes) 8. a ~ that + clause (it's a ~ that the mayor has taken bribes)

scandalize *v.* (R) it ~d us that the mayor had taken bribes; we were ~d to hear that the mayor had taken bribes

scandalized *adj.* 1. ~ at (we were ~ at the news that the mayor had taken bribes) 2. ~ to + inf. (we were ~d to hear that the mayor had taken bribes)

scandalous *adj.* 1. ~ to + inf. (it is ~ for the mayor to have taken bribes) 2. ~ that + clause (it is ~ that the mayor has taken bribes)

scanner *n.* a CAT, CT; code; heart; liver; lung; MRI; PET; text; ultrasound ~

scapegoat *n.* 1. to make a ~ of smb. 2. a convenient; obvious ~ 3. a ~ for (I turned out to be a convenient ~ for their incompetence) 4. (misc.) to make smb. a ~ (they made me a ~ for their incompetence)

scar *n.* 1. to leave a ~ 2. to bear, carry, have a ~ 3. an emotional, psychological; hideous, ugly; identifying; noticeable, prominent; permanent ~ (she had to bear the emotional ~s left by her unhappy childhood) 4. a ~ on (she has a ~ on her arm) 5. a ~ forms; grows fainter

scarcity *n.* 1. to cause, lead to a ~ 2. a severe ~ (the drought has led to a severe ~ of grain) (see also *scarcity value* at **value**)

scare I *n.* (colloq.) 1. to give smb. a ~; to put, throw a ~ into smb. 2. to get, have a ~ 3. a nasty; sudden ~ 4. a bomb ~ (see also *scare story* at **story I** *n.*; *scare tactics* at **tactics**)

scare II *v.* (colloq.) 1. (D; tr.) to ~ into (to ~ smb. into doing smt.) 2. (D; tr.) to ~ out of (she ~d me out of doing it; she ~d me out of my wits) 3. (N; used with an adjective) to ~ smb. stiff 4. (R) it ~d us that no one answered the doorbell 5. (misc.) to ~ smb. (half) to death = to ~ the life out of smb.

scared *adj.* (colloq.) 1. ~ stiff, (half) to death, out of one's wits 2. ~ at, by, of (~ at the very thought; ~ of the dark; they are ~ed of saying anything) 3. ~ to + inf. (they are ~ to say anything) 4. ~ that + clause (we were ~ that the roof would collapse)

scare up *v.* (colloq.) (AE) to ~ for; from (to ~ a meal from leftovers)

scarf *n.* 1. to knit a ~ 2. to wear a ~ (around one's neck) 3. to tie, wrap a ~ (around smb.'s/one's head) 4. a knitted; silk; woolen ~

scarlet fever *n.* to develop, get; have ~

scar tissue *n.* ~ forms

scatter *v.* (P; intr., tr.) they ~ed through the woods; the pamphlets were ~ed around the neighborhood; the wind ~ed leaves on the ground = the ground was ~ed with leaves by the wind; the groups are ~ed throughout the various states; the rioters ~ed in all directions

scavenge *v.* 1. (D; intr.) to ~ for (they were ~ging for spare parts from wrecked cars) 2. (d; tr.) to ~ from (they were ~ging spare parts from wrecked cars)

scenario *n.* ["film outline"] 1. to write a ~ 2. a film ~ ["potential situation"] 3. a doomsday; likely ~ 4. a worst-case ~ (in the worst-case ~ we lose all our money)

scene *n.* ["division of a play"] 1. to play; rehearse a ~ 2. to steal ("dominate") a ~ 3. the ~ shifts 4. (in) a love ~ 5. a change of ~ ["display of anger, feelings"] 6. to make a ~ 7. an awkward, painful, ugly ~ (ugly ~s between parents and children) ["location"] 8. to arrive/come on the ~ ("to appear"); to leave, vanish from the ~ ("to disappear") 9. at, on a ~;

amid, among ~s (she was at the ~ of the crime; she interviewed the victims amid ~s of carnage) 10. on the national ~ ["spectacle, picture"] 11. to depict a ~ 12. a beautiful; idyllic; touching ~ 13. a funny; ridiculous ~ 14. an ever-changing; familiar ~ 15. a disgraceful, shameful; distressing; gruesome; revolting; tragic ~ ["misc."] 16. behind the ~s ("in secret"); a change of ~ (usu. fig.); to set the ~ ("to describe a situation") ("to prepare for the occurrence of smt.")

scenery *n.* ["stage props"] 1. to set up ~ 2. to move, shift ~ 3. to dismantle ~ 4. stage ~ ["landscape"] 5. beautiful, glorious, majestic, picturesque; wild ~ 6. amid; through ~ (we picnicked amid glorious mountain ~) 7. (misc.) (usu. fig.) a change of ~

scent *n.* ["track, trail"] 1. to have; follow; pick up a (the) ~ (the dogs picked up the ~) 2. to leave a ~ 3. a cold; false; hot ~ 4. (misc.) to throw smb. off the ~ ["intuition"] 5. a ~ for (a ~ for news) ["odor"] 6. to perceive; recognize an ~ 7. a delicate; faint; lingering; pungent, strong ~ 8. a ~ permeates smt. 9. a ~ of (the delicate ~ of lavender permeated the entire room) ["sense of smell"] 10. a keen ~ ["perfume"] (see **perfume**)

sceptical see **skeptical**

scepticism see **skepticism**

schedule I *n.* 1. to draw up, make out, make up, plan, prepare, set up, work out a ~ 2. to follow, stick to a ~ 3. to issue a ~ 4. a fixed; flexible; full; heavy; rigid; rotating ~ 5. (esp. AE) an airline; bus; train ~ (CE has *timetable*) 6. a production ~ 7. a ~ for 8. according to, on; ahead of; behind ~ (our work is coming along according to/on ~; the trains are running behind ~) 9. in a ~ (is there anything left to do in your ~?) 10. to be on smb.'s ~ (what's on your ~ ¬tomorrow/for tomorrow¬?)

schedule II *v.* 1. (D; tr.) to ~ for (we will ~ her for surgery next week) 2. (H) we're ~d to arrive at one o'clock; can you ~ her to speak in the afternoon?; we will ~ her to have surgery next week

scheme I *n.* 1. to come up with, conceive, concoct, cook up, devise, think up a ~ 2. to cobble together, work out a ~ 3. to outline, sketch out a ~ 4. to announce, unveil a ~ 5. to present, propose a ~ 6. to accept, approve a ~ 7. to carry out, go ahead with, implement a ~ 8. to put a ~ into effect/operation 9. to abandon, drop, scrub; shelve a ~ 10. to reject, turn down a ~ 11. to foil, thwart a ~ 12. a clever; complicated, elaborate; detailed; grandiose ~ 13. a diabolical; fantastic; get-rich-quick; grandiose; harebrained; ill-conceived; impracticable; impractical; unrealistic; nefarious; preposterous, wild-eyed ~ 14. a ~ calls for (smt.) (the ~ called for massive investment) 15. ~s materialize; succeed, work; go ahead 16. ~s fail 17. a ~ for (she concocted a harebrained ~ for getting publicity) 18. a ~ to + inf. (she concocted a harebrained ~ to get publicity) 19. (misc.) in the overall ~ of things; what rhyme ~ does the poet use? USAGE NOTE:

scheme II   score I

In CE, a *scheme* can be dishonest or crafty; this connotation is probably encountered more frequently in AE than in BE, where *scheme* can be similar in connotation to *plan*. So in AE a *scheme* is more likely to be *harebrained* than *clever*; but in BE it can be either.

scheme II *v.* (derog.) 1. (D; intr.) to ~ against; for 2. (E) they are ~ing to take over the government

schism *n.* 1. to cause, create a ~ 2. a ~ between

scholar *n.* 1. an eminent; productive ~ 2. a ~ in residence 3. (colloq.) a ~ of (a ~ of early French literature)

scholarship *n.* ["systematized knowledge, research"] 1. to foster, promote ~ 2. productive; scientific; solid, sound, thorough ~ ["aid to a student, researcher, writer"] 3. to establish, found a ~ 4. to award, grant a ~ 5. to apply for a ~ 6. to get, receive, win a ~ (she won a ~ to a leading university) 7. to have, hold a ~ 8. a ~ for (to receive a ~ for language study) 9. a ~ to (she won a ~ to Oxford) 10. a ~ to + inf. (she won a ~ to study at Oxford) 11. on a ~ (she went to Oxford on a ~)

school I *n.* ["educational institution"] ["education given by a school"] 1. to direct; operate, run a ~ 2. to accredit a ~ 3. to attend, go to (a) ~ (they go to a good ~) 4. to start ~ 5. to enter (a) ~ 6. to finish, graduate from (AE), leave (BE) ~ (she left ~ and went to university) 7. to drop out of, leave, quit (esp. AE) ~ 8. (by level) an elementary, grade (AE), grammar (AE), primary; first (BE); infant (BE); junior (BE); nursery ~ 9. (by level) a junior high (AE); middle; prep (BE) ~ 10. (by level) a comprehensive (BE), high (esp. AE), secondary; grammar (BE); prep (AE), public (BE) ("private secondary"); secondary modern (BE; now rare) ~ 11. (by level) a graduate, postgraduate (esp. BE); undergraduate ~ 12. (by subject) an art; ballet; beauty; business; dancing; divinity; drama, theater; driving; fencing; military; naval; riding; secretarial; technical; trade, vocational ~ 13. (by type) a boarding; church; consolidated; correspondence; progressive; public (AE), state (BE); day; evening; finishing; magnet; night; parochial; preparatory; private; reform (AE; now rare); religious; special; summer; Sunday ~ 14. (at a university; see also **faculty** 1) a business; dental; divinity; engineering; law; medical; nursing (US; CE has *school of nursing*); professional ~ 15. at, in (a) ~ (she works at/in a ~; their son is still at ~; AE also has: their son is still in ~) 16. a ~ for (a ~ for gifted children) 17. (misc.) to be kept after ~; late for ~; (AE) ~ lets out (at three o'clock); (BE) ~ breaks up for the holidays ["group of people holding similar views"] 18. an avant-garde ~ of artists; a radical ~ of economists 19. a ~ of opinion, thought 20. (misc.) of the old ~ ("adhering to established traditions") ["misc."] 21. the ~ of hard knocks ("life with all its difficulties") USAGE NOTES: (1) One says *to attend school* and *to go to school*, but with a modifier an article must be included – *to attend a good school, to go to a good school, they go to the school of their choice*. Note that one can say *they go to school in California, where they go to a very good school indeed!* (see the Usage Notes for **college**; **university**) (2) In England the phrase *high school* is used chiefly in the names of state secondary schools that are or have been selective (i.e. grammar schools): *she went to Slough High School for Girls*. Elsewhere, *high school* is typically more or less synonymous with *secondary school*: *she went to high school before she went to college*.

school II *v.* 1. to ~ thoroughly 2. (D; tr.) to ~ in (to ~ smb. in the martial arts) 3. (H) they were ~ed to obey instantaneously

schooled *adj.* ~ in (well ~ in the martial arts)

schooling *n.* 1. to receive one's ~ 2. formal ~ 3. ~ in (receive ~ in the martial arts)

schoolwork *n.* to do one's ~

science *n.* 1. to advance, foster, promote ~ 2. an exact; hard; inexact; pure; soft ~ 3. applied; basic; popular ~ 4. computer, information; library; linguistic ~ 5. agricultural; medical; nursing; veterinary ~ 6. military; naval; space ~ 7. behavioral; natural; physical; political; social ~ 8. the life ~s 9. (misc.) rocket ~ ("very complicated ideas") (colloq.); the history/philosophy of ~

scientist *n.* 1. a nuclear; political; rocket (colloq.); social ~ 2. a ~ discovers (smt.) 3. a group, team of ~s (a team of nuclear ~s have discovered a new subatomic particle)

scissors *n.* 1. to use ~ 2. to grind, sharpen ~ 3. bandage (AE); left-handed; manicure; nail ~ 4. a pair of ~ USAGE NOTE: Some speakers of AE can use "a scissors" to mean 'a pair of scissors.'

scoff *v.* (D; intr.) to ~ at

scold *v.* 1. to ~ severely 2. (D; tr.) to ~ about, for (they ~ed me for being late)

scolding *n.* 1. to give smb. a (good) ~ 2. to get, receive a ~

scoop I *n.* ["utensil for scooping"] 1. a coal; flour; grain; ice-cream ~ ["hot news item"] (colloq.) 2. to get the latest ~

scoop II *v.* (d; tr.) to ~ from, off, out of (she ~ed the ice cream from the plate)

scoop up *v.* (D; tr.) to ~ from, off (she ~ed up the ice cream from the plate = she ~ed the ice cream up from/off the plate)

scoot *v.* (P; intr.) the boys ~ed out of the room

scooter *n.* to ride a ~ (see also **motor scooter**)

scope *n.* 1. to broaden, widen the ~ of smt. 2. a broad; narrow ~ 3. beyond, outside the ~ of smt. 4. within the ~ of smt. 5. (misc.) this project will give your talent full ~ to express itself

score I *n.* ["tally"] (usu. sports) 1. to keep ~ 2. a close; even; lopsided ~ 3. (AE) (usu. baseball) a box ~ 4. a ~ stands (the ~ stood five to three (AE) = the ~ stood five – three (AE) = the ~ stood at five to three; how does the ~ stand?) 5. by a ~ (we won by a lopsided ~) ["points"] (sports, tests) 6. (esp. AE) to run up a ~ 7. a lopsided ~ (our team ran up a lopsided ~) 8. a high; low; perfect ~ (the judges gave her a perfect ~; the test ~s ranged from very low to very high) ["grievance"]["matter"] 9. to pay off, settle a ~ 10. an old ~ (they had some old ~s to settle) 11. a ~ between (there are some old ~s between them) ["musical composition"] 12. to play; write a ~ ["copy of a musical composition"] 13. a film; full; orchestra; piano; vocal ~ ["matter"] 14. on a certain ~ (we are even on that ~) ["facts of a situation"] (colloq.) 15. to know the ~

score II v. 1. (D; intr., tr.) ("to make a score") to ~ against (to ~ against a team; they ~d five points against the visiting team) 2. (D; intr., tr.) ("to make a score") to ~ for (she ~d ten points for her team; who ~d for their team?) 3. (d; intr., tr.) ("to write music") to ~ for (to ~ for full orchestra) 4. (colloq.) (BE) (d; intr.) to ~ off ("to beat in an argument") (it's difficult to ~ off him in an argument) 5. (colloq.) (D; intr.) ("to achieve success") to ~ with (I really ~d with the boss; I ~d with a pretty girl at the party last night) 6. (P) ("to get a certain score") in/on the proficiency tests they ~d badly/low/20%/high/well/80%/in the top 10/among the top 10

scoreboard n. an electronic ~

scorer n. (sports) a high; low; top ~ (who was the game's highest/top ~?)

scorn I n. 1. to express; feel ~ 2. to heap, pour ~ on 3. bitter, withering ~ 4. ~ for (to feel ~ for smb.) 5. with ~

scorn II v. (formal) 1. (D; tr.) to ~ as (he was ~ed as a traitor) 2. (BE) (E) she ~s to compromise 3. (G) she ~s compromising

scornful adj. ~ of (they are ~ of him as a traitor; she is ~ of compromises)

scorpion n. ~s sting

scot-free adj. to get off, go (AE) ~

scourge n. a ~ of; to (the ~ of war is a ~ to the human race)

scout I n. 1. a boy ~ (esp. AE; BE usu. has *Scout*) 2. a girl ~ (AE; BE had *girl guide* but now has *Guide*) 3. a talent ~ USAGE NOTE: In CE, *boy scout* can also be fig., meaning 'a clean-living well-intentioned but naïve young man.'

scout II v. (D; intr., tr.) to ~ for (to ~ the city for building sites; to ~ for new talent)

scout out, scout around v. (D; intr.) to ~ for (to ~ for new talent)

scowl I n. 1. to wear a ~ 2. to have a ~ on one's face 3. a permanent, perpetual ~

scowl II v. (D; intr.) to ~ at

Scrabble n. (T) ["game"] to play ~

scramble I n. 1. a mad, wild ~ 2. a ~ for (a wild ~ for tickets) 3. a ~ to + inf. (there was a wild ~ to buy tickets) 4. during, in a ~ (people bumped each other in the ~ to buy tickets)

scramble II v. 1. (C) ~ a couple of eggs for me; or: ~ me a couple of eggs (see also *scrambled egg(s)*)

at **egg**) 2. (d; intr.) to ~ for, over (AE) (to ~ for government subsidies) 3. (P; intr.) the hikers were ~ling down the mountain; the children ~d through the forest; the passengers ~d aboard

scrap I n. ["waste metal"] to sell (smt.) for ~ (see also *scrap metal* at **metal**)

scrap II n. (colloq.) ["fight"] to put up a (good) ~

scrap III v. (colloq.) (D; intr.) ("to fight") to ~ over

scrapbook n. to keep a ~

scrape I n. ["awkward predicament"]["fight"] to get into a ~

scrape II v. 1. (D; intr., tr.) to ~ against (she ~d against the wall; I ~d the chair against the table) 2. (D; intr.) to ~ at (she ~d at the furniture; she ~d at the paint on the furniture) 3. (D; tr.) to ~ from, off (to ~ paint off furniture) 4. (D; intr.) to ~ through ("to manage to get through") (to ~ through a crisis to triumph) 5. (N; used with an adjective) (she ~d the dishes clean; she ~d the furniture clean of paint) 6. (misc.) to bow and ~ ("to be obsequious") (see also *to scrape acquaintance with* at **acquaintance**)

scrape along v. (D; intr.) to ~ on; with (to ~ on a small salary)

scrape through v. (D; intr.) to ~ to (we somehow ~d through to triumph)

scratch I n. ["injury produced by scratching"] 1. (to come through a fight) without a ~ 2. a deep; slight; superficial ~ (she had only a slight ~ on her arm) ["beginning"] 3. from ~ ["prescribed level"] 4. up to ~

scratch II v. 1. (d; intr.) to ~ at (the cat was ~ing at the door with its claws) 2. (d; tr.) to ~ off (he ~d the paint off the wall) 3. (D; tr.) to ~ on (I ~ed my hand on a nail)

scrawl n. ["bad handwriting"] 1. to decipher a ~ 2. an illegible; incomprehensible ~ (to write in an illegible ~)

scream I n. 1. to give, let out a ~ 2. a bloodcurdling; ear-piercing, loud; high-pitched, shrill ~ (he let out a loud ~ of terror)

scream II v. 1. to ~ hysterically; to ~ in agony 2. (B) she ~ed a few words to the children 3. (D; intr.) to ~ at; for (she ~ed at the children for making noise) 4. (d; intr.) to ~ for (to ~ for help) 5. (D; intr.) to ~ with (to ~ with pain) 6. (E) she ~ed at/for/to the children to stop making noise 7. (L; to) she ~ed (at/to us) that the house was on fire; "Stop making noise!" she ~ed (at/to the children) 8. (N; used with a reflexive pronoun and an adjective) (she ~ed herself hoarse) (see also *scream at the top of one's lungs* at **lung**)

screech I n. 1. to give, let out a ~ (to let out a ~ of delight) 2. a bloodcurdling; ear-piercing, loud; high-pitched, shrill ~ (he let out a loud ~ of terror)

screech II v. 1. (D; intr.) to ~ with (to ~ with delight) 2. (misc.) to ~ to a halt/stop = to come ~ing to a halt/stop

screen I n. 1. to erect, put up a ~ (what is ¬behind/on the other side of¬ the ~ they put up?) 2. a computer; radar; television, TV ~ 3. a smoke ~ (often fig.) (to ¬lay down/put up/throw up/use¬ a smoke ~ of obfuscation to conceal the truth) 4. the big, silver ~ (in the movies) 5. the small ~ (TV) 6. a blank ~ 7. a ~ between 8. on a ~ (there was no picture on the TV ~) 9. (misc.) to clear a ~ (as on a computer); actors who are on-screen enemies but off-screen friends

screen II *v.* 1. (D; intr., tr.) to ~ for (to ~ for cancer) 2. (d; tr.) to ~ from (they ~ed the bed from the rest of the ward)

screening *n.* 1. to do a ~ 2. (a) mass ~ 3. a ~ for

screen off *v.* (D; tr.) to ~ from (they ~ed off the bed from the rest of the ward = they ~ed the bed off from the rest of the ward)

screen test *n.* 1. to get, have a ~ 2. to give smb. a ~ 3. to do a ~ (they did a ~ on her)

screw I *n.* 1. to loosen; tighten; turn a ~ 2. a loose ~

screw II *v.* 1. to ~ securely; tightly; together (to ~ two things together securely = to ~ one thing and another together securely) 2. (d; tr.) to ~ into (to ~ a bracket into a wall; to ~ smt. into place) 3. (d; tr.) to ~ onto, to (they ~ed the desk to the floor; to ~ one thing to another) 4. (slang) (D; tr.) to ~ out of ("to cheat out") (they ~ed him out of his bonus) 5. (N; used with an adjective) ~ the cap tight

screw on *v.* (N; used with an adjective) ~ the cap on tight

scribble *v.* 1. (A) she ~d a note to me; or: she ~d me a note 2. (D; intr., tr.) to ~ with (to ~ with a pencil)

scrimp *v.* 1. (D; intr.) ("to be frugal") to ~ on (to ~ on food) 2. (misc.) to ~ and save

script *n.* ['alphabet'] 1. cuneiform; phonetic ~ (transcribed in phonetic ~) ['text'] 2. a film ~ (wrote a film ~ for a major Hollywood studio)

Scriptures *n.* the Holy ~ (to be found in the Holy ~)

scrounge *v.* (colloq.) 1. (D; intr.) ("to scavenge") to ~ for 2. (D; tr.) ("to wheedle") to ~ from, off (he ~d a cigarette from me)

scrounge around *v.* (colloq.) (D; intr.) ("to scavenge") to ~ for

scrub *v.* 1. (D; intr.) to ~ at (we ~bed (away) at the tables until they were clean of dirt) 2. (N; used with an adjective) we ~bed the tables clean of dirt

scruff *n.* (to take smb.) by the ~ of the neck

scruples *n.* 1. to have; overcome ~ 2. moral; religious ~ 3. ~ about (she had moral ~ about referring to her opponent in public)

scrupulous *adj.* ~ in (she was ~ in avoiding references to her opponent in public)

scrutinize *v.* 1. to ~ closely, intently, thoroughly 2. (D; tr.) to ~ for (we've ~d the text thoroughly for errors)

scrutiny *n.* 1. to bear ~ (his record will not bear close ~) 2. to subject smt. to ~ 3. close, intense, strict, thorough; constant; public ~ (we've subjected the

text to thorough ~ for errors) 4. open to ~ 5. under ~ (under constant ~; to come under ~)

scud *v.* (P; intr.) the clouds ~ded across the sky

scuffle I *n.* 1. to get into a ~ (with) 2. to have a ~ (with) 3. an angry; loud ~ 4. a ~ breaks out 5. a ~ about, over 6. a ~ between; with 7. in a ~ (several people were involved in the ~ between the gangs that broke out over smt. insignificant)

scuffle II *v.* (D; intr.) to ~ about, over; with

sculpt *v.* see **sculpture II** *v.*

sculpted *adj.* see **sculptured**

sculpture I *n.* 1. to create, do, produce a ~ 2. to cast a ~ 3. an abstract ~ 4. modern ~ 5. a piece of ~

sculpture II *v.* 1. (d; tr.) to ~ into (I ~d the stone into a figure) 2. (d; tr.) to ~ from, out of (I ~d a figure from/out of the stone)

sculptured *adj.* ~ in; out of (~ in stone; ~ from stone)

scurry *v.* 1. (d; intr.) to ~ for (to ~ for cover) 2. (P; intr.) to ~ along the street 3. (misc.) we ~ied (in order) to find cover

sea *n.* 1. to sail the ~s 2. a calm, smooth; choppy, heavy, high, raging, rough, stormy, turbulent ~ 3. the deep; open ~ 4. at ~ (buried at ~) 5. (esp. BE) by the ~ (a holiday by the ~) 6. (misc.) (at) the bottom of the ~; to drift out to ~; to go to ~ ("to become a sailor"); to put out to ~; (all) at ~ ("bewildered") ['misc.'] 7. I couldn't recognize her in the ~ of faces in the auditorium (see also **seas**)

seaboard *n.* (esp. AE) 1. the eastern ~ (of the U.S.A.) 2. along; down; on; up the (eastern) ~

seal I *n.* ['sea mammal'] 1. ~s bark 2. a colony, pod of ~s 3. a young ~ is a pup (they tried to prevent the culling of ~ pups) 4. a female ~ is a cow 5. a male ~ is a bull

seal II *n.* ['piece of molten wax'] 1. a privy; wax ~ ['closure'] 2. to break a ~ 3. a hermetic ~ ['stamp, symbol'] 4. to affix a ~ 5. an official; royal ~ 6. a ~ of approval (they got/received the official ~ of approval)

seal III *v.* 1. to ~ firmly, tightly; hermetically; together (they ~ed the flaps of the envelope together) 2. (N; used with an adjective) they ~ed the area/envelope shut

sea lion *n.* 1. a colony of ~s 2. a young ~ is a pup 3. a female ~ is a cow 4. a male ~ is a bull

seal off *v.* (D; tr.) to ~ from

seam *n.* 1. to let out; rip open, tear open a ~ 2. (misc.) to be bursting at the ~s (also fig.); to come apart at the ~s (also fig.)

seaman *n.* an able, able-bodied; junior (BE) ordinary; merchant ~

seance *n.* 1. to conduct, hold a ~ 2. at; during a ~

seaport *n.* a bustling, busy ~

search I *n.* 1. to conduct, do, make a ~ 2. to abandon, call off a ~ 3. a careful, exhaustive, painstaking, systematic, thorough ~ 4. a fruitless ~ 5. a body, strip; door-to-door, house-to-house ~ 6. a literature ~ 7. a computer; online ~ (to do a computer ~) 8. a

~ for (the ~ for truth) 9. in ~ of 10. (misc.) (legal) unwarranted ~ and seizure

search II *v.* 1. to ~ carefully, painstakingly, systematically, thoroughly 2. to ~ all over, everywhere, high and low 3. (D; intr.) to ~ for (to ~ for a lost child) 4. (d; intr.) to ~ through (she ~ed through her purse for the keys and then ~ed through it again)

searching *n.* online ~

searchlight *n.* 1. to direct, focus, shine a ~ 2. ~s play on (a wall)

search party *n.* to organize; send out a ~

seared *adj.* ~ in, into (that day is ~ into my memory)

seas *n.* 1. the high ~ (on the high ~) 2. see **sea** 2; calm, smooth; choppy, etc. ~

seashore *n.* at the ~

seasick *adj.* to get; feel ~

seaside *n.* (BE) at, by the ~ (a holiday at the ~ = a ~ holiday) (esp. AE has *seashore, shore*)

season I *n.* 1. to open, usher in the (a) ~ 2. to close, usher out the (a) ~ 3. the dead, low, off, slack ~ 4. the high ~ 5. (sports) the baseball; basketball; fishing; football; hunting; open ~ 6. the dry; hurricane; monsoon; rainy ~ 7. the harvest; planting ~ 8. the Christmas, festive; holiday; tourist ~ 9. the breeding, mating, rutting ~ 10. at a ~ (at that ~ of the year) 11. in ~; out of ~ 12. (misc.) the height of the ~; it's open ~ on members of the opposition – the government has declared open ~ on them! ("members of the opposition are being subjected to attack")

season II *v.* 1. (D; tr.) to ~ with (we will ~ the salad with dill) 2. (misc.) mix the ingredients and ~ to taste

seasoned *adj.* highly; lightly ~

seat *n.* ["place to sit"] 1. to get; have a ~ 2. to take one's ~ 3. to assign ~s 4. to book (esp. BE), reserve a ~ 5. to give up, relinquish one's ~ 6. to keep one's ~ 7. to save a ~ (for smb.) 8. a back; bucket; car; front; jump; passenger ~ (see also **backseat**; *backseat driver* at **driver**) 9. a box; front-row; ringside ~ 10. the driver's (AE), driving (BE) ~ (when the accident happened he was in the driver's ~, she was in the passenger ~, and the children were in the back ~) 11. this ~ is free, vacant; occupied, taken 12. (misc.) please have, take a ~ ("please sit down") ["right to sit"]["public office"] 13. to hold; win a ~ (she held a safe ~ easily whereas he managed to win a marginal ~!) 14. to contest a ~ 15. to lose one's ~ ["administrative center"] 16. a county ~ (AE; BE has *county town*) ["dominant position"] 17. the catbird (AE), driver's (AE), driving (BE) ~

seatbelt *n.* 1. to buckle, do up, fasten; put on a ~ 2. to unbuckle, undo, unfasten; take off a ~ 3. to adjust a ~ 4. to wear a ~

seated *adj.* 1. to be ~ 2. to remain ~ 3. ~ at; in; on (he was ~ at the steering wheel, she was ~ in the passenger seat, and the children were ~ on stools at home)

secateurs *n.* (esp. BE) a pair of ~ (see also **shears**)

secede *v.* (D; intr.) to ~ from (a township cannot ~ from a county; there was a Civil War when the Confederacy tried to ~ from the USA)

secession *n.* ~ from (the Confederacy's attempted ~ from the USA)

seclude *v.* (D; refl., tr.) to ~ from

seclusion *n.* in ~

second I *adj.* ["inferior"] 1. ~ to (~ to none) ["placing after the first"] 2. to come (in), finish, place ~ (in a race) 3. the ~ to + inf. (she was the ~ to arrive and among the last to leave)

second II *n.* ["one who ranks after the first"] 1. a close ~ ["assistant"] 2. a ~ to smb. 3. (misc.) ~s away! (in wrestling); ~s out! (in boxing) ["second gear"] 4. to put (a vehicle) into ~ 5. in ~ (the car's in ~; don't start in ~) ["vote of endorsement"] 6. (do I hear) a ~ to (the motion?) ["undergraduate second-class honours degree at a British university"] 7. to get a ~ 8. a lower (2.2); upper (2.1) ~ 9. a ~ in (to get an upper ~ in English) (see also **seconds**)

second III *n.* ["sixtieth part of a minute"]["short time"] 1. a split ~ 2. for a ~ (I'm stepping out into the corridor for a ~) 3. in a ~ (she'll be here in a ~) 4. (misc.) wait a ~; just a ~; it will take a ~; it all happened in a fraction of a ~!; "If you can fill the unforgiving minute With sixty seconds' worth of distance run…" – Rudyard Kipling (1865–1936), "If –"

second IV /si'kond/ *v.* (BE) (D; tr.) ("to assign temporarily") to ~ from; to (she was ~ed from the British Council to a university)

secondary *adj.* ~ to

second best *adj., adv., n.* 1. to come off ~ 2. to settle for ~

second-class *adv.* to travel ~

second fiddle *n.* ["subordinate role"] to play ~ to

second hand *n.* at ~ ("indirectly")

second place *n.* to take ~ to (her personal life took ~ to her job)

second thought *n.* 1. to have ~s about smt. 2. on ~ (AE)/ on ~s (BE) ("after reconsideration") 3. (misc.) without (giving the matter) a ~

secondment *n.* (BE) on ~ from; to (she was on ~ from the British Council to a university)

seconds *n.* ["second helping of food"] (colloq.) 1. to ask for ~ 2. to offer ~ 3. (misc.) who wants ~? = who's for ~?

secrecy *n.* 1. to ensure ~ 2. strict ~ 3. ~ about 4. ~ in (~ in conducting negotiations) 5. in ~ (to meet in ~; the meetings were held in the strictest ~; cloaked/ shrouded/ veiled in ~) 6. to swear smb. to ~ (we were all sworn to ~ about the project) 7. ~ shrouds, surrounds (the ~ surrounding the project) 8. (misc.) a veil of ~

secret I *adj., n.* 1. strictly ~ 2. most; top ~ 3. to keep smt. ~ (from smb.) 4. in ~ (they got engaged in ~ and kept meeting in ~)

secret II *n.* 1. to make a ~ of smt.; to make no ~ of smt. (they made no ~ of the fact that they were engaged = they made no ~ of their engagement) 2. to guard, keep a ~ (can you keep the project a ~ from everyone else?) 3. to betray, blurt out, divulge, reveal a ~ 4. to ferret out, uncover, unearth a ~ 5. a dark, deep, guilty, ugly ~ 6. a closely guarded; military; open; state; trade ~ 7. a ~ that + clause (it was no ~ that they were engaged = it was an open ~ that they were engaged)

secretary *n.* ["administrative assistant"] 1. a corresponding; executive; personal; press; recording; social ~ 2. a private ~ (AE; BE has *personal assistant*) 3. a ~ of, to ["company officer"] (BE) 4. a company ~ ["cabinet official supervising a government department"] 5. (GB) the Defence; Foreign; Home Secretary (etc.) 6. (US) the Secretary of Labor; Secretary of State ["misc."] 7. the Secretary General (the Secretary General of the U.N.; the Secretary General of the Communist Party)

secretion *n.* 1. an internal ~ 2. a ~ from

secretive *adj.* ~ about (very ~ about one's plans)

sect *n.* 1. a political; religious ~ 2. to join a ~ 3. a member of a ~

section *n.* ["division of a newspaper"] 1. the business; classified; news; sports; travel ~ ["plane figure"] (geometry) 2. a conical; cross; vertical ~ ["group of instruments"] 3. a brass; percussion; rhythm; string; woodwind ~ 4. in a ~ (to play in the woodwind ~) ["group"] (esp. AE) 5. a cheering ~ (in a grandstand) ["surgical cutting"] 6. an abdominal; caesarean/cesarean ~ ["area"] 7. a business; residential ~ 8. a non-smoking; smoking ~ ["department"] 9. the cultural; political ~ (of an embassy) 10. the children's; fiction; non-fiction ~ (of a library or bookstore) ["part"] 11. in ~s (the bookcases come in ~s; the Act is divided into 24 Sections) 12. under a ~ (the case falls under Section 22 of the Act) 13. (misc.) a political program intended to appeal to all ~s of society

sector *n.* 1. the private; public ~ 2. in a ~ (in the private ~)

secure I *adj.* 1. ~ about (to feel ~ about the future) 2. ~ against, from (~ against attack) 3. ~ in (~ in one's beliefs)

secure II *v.* 1. (D; refl., tr.) to ~ against (to ~ borders against attack) 2. (D; tr.) to ~ for; from (I ~d a loan for the project from the bank) 3. (D; tr.) to ~ by; with (to ~ a bundle by using ropes = to ~ a bundle with ropes)

securities *n.* 1. to buy; issue; register; sell ~ 2. corporate; gilt-edged; government; negotiable; tax-exempt ~

security *n.* ["safety"] 1. to ensure, provide ~ 2. to beef up, strengthen, tighten ~ 3. to compromise; undermine ~ 4. collective; financial; internal; job; maximum; national; personal; state; top ~ (to compromise national ~) (see also *security of tenure* at **tenure**) 5. heightened; lax; strict, tight ~ 6. ~ against (~ against attack) 7. (misc.) a feeling, sense of ~; a breakdown in ~; a lack of ~; a lapse in/of

~ (don't let yourself be lulled into a false sense of ~) (see also *to pledge smt. as security for a loan* at **pledge II** *v.*) ["system of social insurance"] 8. (on) social ~ USAGE NOTE: In GB, *social security* refers to the whole system of public welfare provision. In the US, *social security* refers to the federal program that provides old-age, survivors', and disability benefits.

sedation *n.* under ~

sedative *n.* 1. to administer, give; prescribe a ~ 2. to take a ~ 3. a heavy, strong; light, mild ~

sediment *n.* to deposit ~

sedition *n.* 1. to foment, incite, stir up ~ 2. an act of ~

see *v.* 1. (d; intr.) to ~ about, after ("to take care of") (to ~ about an important matter) 2. (d; tr.) to ~ as ("to visualize") ("to consider acceptable") (I can't ~ them as members of our organization; can you ~ him as Hamlet?) 3. (d; tr.) ("to find attractive") to ~ in (what does she ~ in him?) 4. (d; tr.) to ~ of ("to encounter") (we haven't seen much of you recently; you haven't seen the last of them) 5. (d; intr.) to ~ through ("to comprehend what's wrong with") (she saw through their crooked scheme immediately – she saw through it without difficulty!) 6. (d; tr.) to ~ through ("to assist, guide") (my friends saw me through my period of grief; I'm grateful because when I was grieving my friends saw me through!; the supporters of the bill saw it through Congress) 7. (d; tr.) ("to accompany") to ~ to (she saw him to the door) 8. (d; intr.) to ~ to ("to attend to") (I had to ~ to the arrangements; he saw to it that the same mistake was not repeated; ~ to it that you get there on time!) 9. (d; tr.) to ~ (through) to ("to be sufficient for") (this money will have to ~ us through to the end of the month – I hope it will be enough to ~ us through!) 10. (I) we saw him enter the building = he was seen to enter the building 11. (J) we saw him entering the building = he was seen entering the building; somehow I can't quite ~ them becoming members of our organization; can you ~ him playing Hamlet? 12. (L) ("to perceive") they saw that further resistance was hopeless 13. (L) ("to make certain") ~ that you get there on time! 14. (N; used with a past participle) ("to watch") we saw the play performed in New York 15. (Q) ("to perceive") I could not ~ how the trick was done = I could not ~ how to do the trick; "I can't do it!" "I don't ~ why not!" 16. (P; tr.) ("to accompany") I'll ~ you home/out; I'll ~ myself out 17. (P; intr.) ("to look") to ~ over the fence; to ~ into the room; to ~ through the window 18. (misc.) they are ~ing each other regularly ("they are dating each other"); I ~ by/from/in the newspapers that... (see also *go see* at **go II** *v.*; *let's see* at **let's**; *live to see the day* at **live II** *v.*; *wait and see* at **wait II** *v.*; *see one's way (clear)* at **way**)

seed I *n.* 1. to plant, sow, spread ~s 2. ~s germinate; sprout; grow 3. (misc.) to go to ~ ("to be neglected and become useless")

seed II v. 1. (D; tr.) to ~ with (to ~ a field with rye) 2. (D; tr.) to ~ in (to ~ rye in a field) 3. (misc.) (tennis) to be ~ed third; the third-seeded player made it to the final!

seeding n. cloud ~

seek v. 1. (D; tr.) to ~ from (to ~ help from smb.) 2. (E) smb. sought to help her

seeker n. an asylum; status ~

seem v. 1. (d; intr.) to ~ like (she ~s like a reasonable person) 2. (E) she ~s to be well; she ~ to be a fool; they ~ to like me; they ~ not to like him = they don't ~ to like him; the door ~s not to open easily = the door doesn't ~ to open easily; I ~ not to be able to open the door = I don't ~ to be able to open the door = I can't ~ to open the door 3. (L; to) it ~s (to me) that they will not come = it doesn't ~ (to me) that they'll come 4. (S) to ~ foolish; sad; well (she ~s well/foolish); to ~ a fool; it ~ed a waste of time; I don't ~ able to open the door 5. (misc.) it ~s as if they will win, it ~s as though they will win, it ~s like they will win (colloq.); so it ~s, so it would ~; it ~s not

seen adj. ["regarded"] 1. ~ as (a new tax cut was ~ as necessary) 2. to + inf. (a new tax cut was ~ to be necessary)

seep v. (P; intr.) the water ~ed into the basement; the rain ~ed through the ceiling

seesaw v. (d; intr.) ("to alternate") to ~ between (the lead ~ed between the two teams)

seethe v. (D; intr.) to ~ at, with (to ~ with rage at an insult)

segregate v. 1. (D; tr.) to ~ according to, by (the pupils were ~d by age) 2. (D; tr.) to ~ from (to ~ one group from another = to ~ groups (from each other)) 3. (D; tr.) to ~ into (to ~ people into different groups)

segregation n. 1. to maintain, practice ~ 2. racial; religious; social ~ 3. ~ according to, by (~ by age)

seize v. 1. (D; tr.) to ~ by (he ~d me by the arm = he seized my arm) 2. (d; intr.) to ~ on, upon (I ~d upon a chance remark that was also ~d upon by the media) (see also *seize hold of* at **hold I** n.)

seized adj. ~ with (an acute illness)

seizure n. ["convulsion, paroxysm"] 1. to have a ~ 2. a cardiac, heart; epileptic; uncontrollable ~ ["act of seizing"] 3. (legal) unwarranted search and ~

select v. 1. (D; tr.) to ~ as (we ~ed her as our candidate) 2. (D; tr.) to ~ for (who was ~ed for the assignment?) 3. (D; tr.) to ~ from among (we ~ed her from among many candidates) 4. (H) we ~ed her to be our candidate

selection n. ["choice"] 1. to make a ~ 2. natural; sexual ~ (to defend intelligent design against natural ~; natural ~ leading to the survival of the fittest) 3. a wide ~ 4. a ~ as (her ~ as party candidate was not popular) 5. a ~ for (her ~ for the assignment) ["selected piece of music"] 6. to play a ~ 7. a musical ~

self n. 1. smb.'s inmost, inner; real, true ~ 2. one's former, old; usual; whole ~ (she performed like

her old ~) 3. (formal) one's better ~ (her plea recalled me to my better ~ and I repented)

self-assurance see **self-confidence**

self-confidence n. 1. to acquire, gain; display, exude, radiate, show; have ~ 2. to instill ~ 3. to boost, increase; restore smb.'s ~ 4. to shake, undermine smb.'s ~ 5. to lose one's ~ 6. the ~ to + inf. (she doesn't have the ~ to run for public office)

self-conscious adj. ~ about

self-consciousness n. 1. to display ~ (in) 2. ~ about

self-control n. 1. to display, exhibit, show; exercise; maintain; practice ~ 2. to lose one's ~ 3. admirable, commendable, complete, great, total ~ 4. ~ by, in (they showed great ~ in not responding to the provocation)

self-defense, self-defence n. 1. in ~ (to kill smb. in ~) 2. the art of ~ 3. (misc.) the manly art of ~ ("boxing")

self-denial n. to exercise, practice ~

self-determination n. 1. to give, grant ~ 2. to achieve, enjoy ~ 3. national ~

self-discipline n. 1. to display, exhibit; exercise; have ~ 2. admirable; great, tremendous ~ 3. ~ breaks down, gives way 4. the ~ to + inf. (who has the ~ to write a dictionary?)

self-evident adj. 1. ~ from; to 2. ~ that + clause (from the vote so far, it is ~ to us all that she will be elected)

self-examination n. 1. to do a ~ 2. a frank, honest ~

self-flattery n. to indulge in ~

self-fulfillment, self-fulfilment n. to achieve; seek ~ (by; in) (to seek ~ by working = to seek ~ in work)

self-government n. 1. to grant ~ 2. to enjoy ~

self-image n. 1. to bolster, improve; change one's ~ 2. a good, positive; negative, poor ~

self-interest n. 1. enlightened ~ 2. in smb.'s own ~ (it's in your own ~ to sign the contract) 3. ~ dictates (~ alone would dictate that you should sign the contract)

selfish adj. ~ to + inf. (it was ~ of them to do that)

self-management n. workers' ~ (of industry)

self-medication n. to resort to ~

self-pity n. 1. to exhibit; feel ~ 2. to give way to, indulge in; wallow in ~

self-portrait n. to do, paint a ~

self-respect n. 1. to keep, preserve; lose; regain one's ~ 2. a lack; loss of ~

self-restraint n. 1. to display, exercise, maintain, practice, show ~ 2. to cast off, fling off, lose, shake off (all) ~ 3. admirable, commendable, complete, great, total ~ 4. ~ by, in (they showed great ~ in not responding to the provocation)

self-rule n. 1. to grant ~ 2. to enjoy ~

self-sufficiency n. 1. to achieve, attain ~ 2. economic ~ 3. ~ in

self-sufficient adj. ~ in

self-treatment n. to resort to ~

sell I n. (colloq.) ["method of selling"] a hard; soft ~

sell II *v.* 1. to ~ cheap, cheaply; dear; retail; wholesale 2. (A) we sold our old car to him; or: we sold him our old car 3. (d; intr., tr.) to ~ at, for (it normally ~s at twelve pounds but yesterday it sold for ten pounds; we sold the car to them for three thousand dollars) 4. (D; tr.) to ~ into (to ~ smb. into slavery) 5. (colloq.) (d; tr.) to ~ on ("to convince of") (to ~ smb. on an idea) 6. (misc.) to ~ as is ("to sell with no guarantee of quality"); to ~ at a reasonable price; to ~ at/for a profit; to ~ smt. at a loss; to ~ by the dozen; to ~ in bulk; to ~ like hot cakes ("to be sold very quickly in large quantities"); to ~ smb. down the river ("to betray and ruin smb.")

sell back *v.* (D; tr.) to ~ to

seller *n.* a best ~ (this book was a best ~)

selling *n.* panic ~

sell off *v.* 1. (D; tr.) to ~ for 2. (D; tr.) to ~ to (we sold it off for scrap to the highest bidder)

sell out *v.* (D; intr., tr.) to ~ to (she sold out to her partner)

semantics *n.* general; generative ~

semester *n.* (esp. US) the fall; spring; summer ~

semicircle *n.* 1. to form a ~ 2. in a ~

semicolon *n.* to place, put in a ~

seminar *n.* 1. to conduct, give, hold a ~ 2. to attend a ~ 3. a ~ on

seminary *n.* 1. to attend; graduate from a ~ 2. a theological ~

senate *n.* 1. to convene, convoke a ~ 2. to disband, dissolve a ~ 3. a university ~ 4. a ~ meets, is in session 5. a ~ adjourns

senator *n.* (US) a junior; senior ~ (the junior senator from Idaho)

send *v.* 1. (A) we sent the manuscript to her; or: we sent her the manuscript 2. (D; tr.) to ~ as (he was sent as our representative) 3. (D; tr.) to ~ by (to ~ a letter (by) airmail) 4. (d; intr.) to ~ for ("to ask to come") (to ~ for the doctor) 5. (d; tr.) to ~ for ("to send smb. to fetch smt.") (she sent me for some beer) 6. (d; tr.) ("to insert") to ~ into (the coach sent some new players into the game) 7. (d; tr.) to ~ on (to ~ students on a field trip) 8. (d; tr.) to ~ out of (the teacher sent the unruly pupils out of the room) 9. (d; tr.) to ~ to (her parents sent her to camp) 10. (H) she sent me to buy some beer 11. (J) the explosion sent things flying; we sent him packing ("we dismissed him summarily")

send around, send round *v.* 1. (D; tr.) ("to circulate") to ~ to (the director sent a memo around to the staff = the director sent around a memo to the staff) 2. (H) ("to dispatch") I sent a car around to pick you up = I sent around a car to pick you up

send away *v.* (d; intr.) to ~ for; to (the children sent away box tops to the magazine for prizes = the children sent box tops away to the magazine for prizes)

send back *v.* (A) she sent the money back to me, she sent back the money to me; or: she sent me back the money

send down *v.* 1. (BE) (D; tr.) ("to expel") to ~ from (he was sent down from Oxford) 2. (esp. BE) (D; tr.) ("to sentence to prison") to ~ for (he was sent down for five years) 3. (d; intr., tr.) to ~ for (to ~ for pizza; they sent him down for beer)

send in *v.* (D; intr., tr.) to ~ for; to (the children sent in box tops to the magazine for prizes = the children sent box tops in to the magazine for prizes)

send-off *n.* to give smb. a (big) ~ (they gave her quite a ~)

send off *v.* 1. (D; tr.) to ~ to (we sent the children off to Europe) 2. (the children sent off box tops to the magazine for prizes = the children sent box tops off to the magazine for prizes)

send on *v.* (D; tr.) to ~ to (they sent the package on to my new address = they sent on the package to my new address)

send out *v.* 1. (B) they sent out invitations to many people = they sent invitations out to many people 2. (d; tr.) to ~ as (they were sent out as our representatives) 3. (d; intr., tr.) to ~ for (she sent out for some beer; she sent me out for some beer) 4. (d; tr.) to ~ on (the young reporter was sent out on her first assignment) 5. (H) she sent me out to buy some beer

send up *v.* 1. (esp. AE) (D; tr.) ("to sentence to prison") to ~ for (he was sent up for five years) 2. (D; tr.) to ~ to (they sent tea up to my room)

senior I *adj.* 1. ~ in (~ in rank) 2. ~ to (he is ~ to me by three years)

senior II *n.* 1. ~ by (he is my ~ by three years). (AE) a college; graduating; high-school ~

seniority *n.* according to, by ~ (to promote according to ~)

sensation *n.* ["excitement"] 1. to cause, create a ~ 2. a great ~ (her appearance created a great ~) 3. an overnight ~ ["feeling"] 4. to feel; have a ~ 5. to lose ~ (he lost all ~ in his foot) 6. a pleasant ~ 7. a burning; choking; indescribable; numbing; queasy; strange; tingling; unpleasant ~ 8. a ~ in (I had a choking ~ in my throat) 9. a ~ that + clause (I had the sensation that smb. was in the room)

sense I *n.* ["judgment"] 1. to display, have, show ~ 2. common, good, horse (colloq.); innate ~ (see also **common sense**) 3. a grain of ~ 4. the ~ to + inf. (they don't have the ~ to admit defeat) 5. (misc.) to bring people to their ~s; to come to one's ~s; to take leave of one's ~s ["logic"] 6. to make ~ (her choice makes ~; it makes ~ to file an application; can you make any ~ out of this?) 7. to talk ~ 8. to talk ~ into smb. 9. ~ in (there is no ~ (in) losing your temper) 10. (misc.) that makes no ~ (to me) ["reaction to stimuli"] 11. to sharpen the ~s 12. to dull the ~s 13. an acute; intuitive; keen ~ (she has a very acute ~ of smell) 14. the five ~s (of sight, hearing, smell, taste, and touch) 15. a sixth ~ ("intuition") ["feeling"] 16. (to have) a false ~ (of security) (the swindler lulled her into a false ~ of security) 17. a ~ of relief (he felt an immediate indescribable ~ of

relief when he heard the good news) ["meaning"] 18.
a figurative; literal, narrow, strict ~ 19. in a ~ (in
the literal ~ of the word; in every ~ of the word; in
a certain ~, you are right; you're right in the ~ that
the figures do tend to support you) ["appreciation"]
20. a ~ of beauty; a ~ of occasion; a ~ of timing
(see also **sense of humor**)
sense II v. 1. (L) she ~d immediately that smt. was
wrong 2. (Q) I ~d where the problem was
senseless adj. ~ to + inf. (it was (of/for them) ~ to
lie = lying was a ~ thing (for them) to do!)
sense of humor n. 1. to demonstrate, display, have a
~ 2. a subtle; wry ~
sensibility n. 1. to display, show ~ 2. ~ to (to display
~ to pain)
sensible adj. ["reasonable"] 1. ~ about, when it comes
to (she was eminently/very ~ about postponing the
trip = she was eminently/very ~ when it came to
having to postpone the trip) 2. ~ to + inf. (it was
eminently/very ~ of/for her to postpone the trip =
postponing the trip was ¬an eminently/a very¬ ~
thing for her to do) ["aware"] (formal) (BE) 3. ~ of
(they were acutely ~ of the danger that they faced)
sensitive adj. 1. highly, very ~ 2. ~ about (very ~
about charges of corruption); 3. ~ to (~ to charges
of corruption; ~ to criticism; ~ to the feelings of
others)
sensitivity n. 1. to display, show ~ 2. great ~ 3. ~ to
(to display great ~ to criticism)
sensitize v. (D; tr.) to ~ to (to ~ smb. to suffering)
sensor n. to activate, set off, trip a ~
sentence I n. ["judgment of a court"] 1. to give, impose; pass, pronounce (a) ~ (on) 2. to carry out,
execute a ~ 3. to get, receive; serve (out) a ~ 4.
to commute; reduce, remit; suspend; vacate a ~
(her ~ was reduced to five years) 5. a harsh, heavy,
severe, stiff ~ 6. a light ~ 7. a death; custodial, jail,
prison; life ~ (to give smb. a life ~ for murder) 8.
an indefinite, indeterminate; suspended ~ 9. under
~ 10. (misc.) to get off with a light ~ ["independent
group of words"] 11. to form, formulate, make
up; generate a ~ 12. an affirmative; complex;
compound; declarative; elliptical; embedded;
exclamatory; impersonal; interrogative; negative;
simple ~
sentence II v. 1. (D; tr.) to ~ for; to (the judge ~d
her to five years for theft; the convicted murderer
was ~d to death; to ~ smb. to hard labor) 2. (H) the
judge ~d him to do community service
sentiment n. ["feeling"] 1. to echo; express a ~ 2.
to display, show ~ 3. to share a ~ 4. a growing;
lofty; patriotic; public; shocking; strong ~ 5. (a) ~
against; for, in favor of (there is growing ~ in favor
of a tax reduction) 6. (a) ~ that + clause (there was
strong ~ that the government should step down)
7. (misc.) "I think the government should step
down." "(those are) my ~s exactly: I agree with
you 100%!"
sentimental adj. 1. cloyingly, mawkishly ~ 2. to

become, get, wax (formal) ~ 3. ~ about, over (she
waxed mawkishly ~ about the sweet little puppy)
sentimentality n. 1. cloying, maudlin, mawkish ~
2. ~ about (her mawkish ~ about the sweet little
puppy)
sentimentalize v. 1. to ~ cloyingly, mawkishly 2.
(D; intr.) to ~ about, over (she ~d mawkishly about
the sweet little puppy)
sentry n. 1. to post a ~ 2. to relieve a ~
separate I adj. 1. completely ~ 2. ~ from (to keep
~ from)
separate II v. 1. (D; intr., tr.) to ~ from (she was
~d from her family; she and her husband ~d (from
each other) and later got divorced; to be ~d from
the service; the little girl got ~d from her parents)
2. (D; intr., tr.) to ~ by; into (the children were ~d
by age into two groups)
separation n. ~ by; from; into
separatism n. political; racial; religious ~
sequel n. a ~ to (*Henry IV, Part 2* is the ~ to *Henry
IV, Part 1*)
sequence n. 1. an alphabetical; chronological;
natural; random ~ (see also *a sequence of events*
at **event**) 2. in ~
serenade n. 1. to play, sing a ~ 2. a ~ to
sergeant n. 1. a buck (AE); color; drill; first, top;
flight (BE); gunnery; master; platoon; recruiting;
staff; technical ~ 2. a ~ major; (BE) a company
~ major 3. (misc.) here are your orders Sergeant
(Smith)!; to make smb. a ~, to promote smb. to the
rank of ~; to have, hold the rank of ~
series n. ["sequence"] (math.) 1. an alternating; con-
vergent; divergent; geometric; harmonic; infinite
~ ["succession"] 2. an unbroken ~ 3. in a ~ ["cycle
of programs, publications"] 4. a concert; lecture ~;
a miniseries; TV ~ ["misc."] (baseball) 5. the World
Series
serious adj. 1. deadly, very; potentially ~ (this is
potentially a very ~ situation!) 2. ~ about (she is
very ~ about her work)
seriousness n. 1. in all ~ (in all ~, we are facing a
real crisis!) 2. with great ~ 3. ~ about (she spoke
with great ~ about the crisis)
sermon n. 1. to deliver, give, preach a ~ 2. a lay
~ 3. during, in a ~ 4. a ~ against; on (a ~ against
drinking; a ~ on business ethics)
servant n. 1. a civil, public; domestic; personal ~ 2.
a faithful, loyal, trusted ~ 3. a ~ of, to (formal)
serve I n. (tennis) 1. to break; return smb.'s ~ 2. to
hold; lose one's ~ 3. the ~ was good, in 4. the ~ was
long; out; wide 5. a ~ to (a ~ to the backhand)
serve II v. 1. (A) ("to bring") she ~d dinner to us; or:
she ~d us dinner; they ~d the meat to us cold; or:
they ~d us the meat cold 2. (d; intr., tr.) to ~ as ("to
fulfill the functions of") (his illness ~d (him) as an
excuse; to ~ (the town) as mayor) 3. (D; intr.) to ~
on ("to be a member of") (to ~ on a jury) 4. (D; tr.)
to ~ on ("to deliver to") (to ~ a summons on smb.)
5. (tennis) (D; intr.) ("to put the ball in play") to ~

to (I hate to ~ to her – she always returns the ball to my backhand; and what's more, she ~s to my backhand, too!) 6. (D; intr.) ("to be in service") to ~ under (he ~d directly under a general) 7. (d; tr.) ("to be in service") to ~ with (I ~d with Monty at El Alamein) 8. (d; tr.) to ~ with ("to deliver to") (to ~ smb. with a summons; they ~ed the meat with vegetables and a salad) 9. (E) ("to have an effect") it ~d to calm everyone's nerves 10. (N; used with an adjective) they ~d the meat cold 11. (misc.) it ~s him right ("he got what he deserved")

server *n.* an online ~

service *n.* ["work done for others"] 1. to do, offer, perform, provide, render a ~ 2. custom (AE); meritorious; outstanding; public; yeoman ("loyal") ~ 3. professional; social (BE) ~s (a fee for professional ~s) 4. ~ to (she received an award for meritorious ~ to the community) 5. (misc.) to press smb. into ~; goods and ~s ["facility that satisfies a need"] 6. to introduce; maintain; offer, provide; restore (a) ~ 7. to cut, suspend; terminate (a) ~ 8. an ambulance; counseling; emergency; (national) health (UK), (public) health; health-care; health-visitor (BE), visiting-nurse (AE); social ~ 9. an answering; clipping (AE); press-cutting (BE); news, wire; online ~ 10. (a) bus; ferry; limousine; rail (BE), train (AE); shuttle ~ 11. a dating; employment (esp. AE); placement ~ 12. (a) diaper (AE); janitorial (AE); laundry; repair ~ 13. (a) delivery; door-to-door; towing ~ 14. customer; maid ~ (see also **room service**) 15. express; postal; telephone ~ ["operation, use"] 16. to go into ~ 17. to see ~ (this equipment has seen plenty of ~) 18. in; out of ~ (the bus was not in ~) 19. (misc.) to put smt. into ~; to take smt. out of ~ ["disposal"] 20. to be at smb.'s ~ ["help, benefit"] 21. to be of ~ (to) ["solemn ceremony"] 22. to attend a ~; hold a ~; to hold ~s; officiate at a ~ 23. a burial, funeral; marriage; memorial ~ (to hold a funeral ~ for smb.) 24. a church; synagogue; ecumenical; graveside; prayer; religious ~ 25. an evening; mid-day, noontime (esp. AE); morning; sunrise ~ (they hold sunrise ~s once a week) ["set of utensils"] 26. a coffee; dinner; tea ~ 27. a ~ for ["administrative division of government; government service"] 28. the civil; consular; diplomatic; foreign; intelligence, secret ~ (to enter, join; leave; resign from the civil ~) 29. human ~s ("social services") ["game during which one serves"] (tennis) 30. to hold; lose one's ~ 31. to break; return smb.'s ~ ["duty in the armed services"] 32. to see ~ (she saw ~ during the Second World War) 33. national (BE), selective (AE) ~ (see also **military service**) 34. active; inactive ~ 35. in the ~ (s) ["position as a servant"] (esp. BE) 36. domestic ~ 37. to be in ~ 38. to go into ~ 39. ~ as (to go into ~ as a housekeeper; he recalled his years in ~ as a valet) ["scheduled routes, flights"] 40. to introduce; offer, provide ~ 41. to suspend ~ 42. (a) daily; regular ~ 43. ~ between; from; to (regular ~ between two

cities; that airline provides daily ~ from New York to London) ["manner of dealing with customers"] 44. fast; fine; slow ~ (see also **lip service**)

serviette *n.* (BE) 1. to fold a ~ 2. to tuck a ~ (under one's chin) 3. a cocktail; dinner; paper ~

serving *n.* ["portion"] a generous, large, liberal; second; small ~ (of)

servitude *n.* 1. involuntary; penal ~ 2. in ~ to

session *n.* 1. to hold a ~ 2. a briefing; debriefing ~ 3. a bull (AE; colloq.), rap (colloq.); jam ~ 4. a counseling; emergency; joint; legislative; plenary; psychotherapy, therapy; secret; special ~ (when will the plenary ~ take place?) 5. a practice; working ~ 6. a summer; winter ~ 7. a ~ on (to hold a special ~ on problems of air pollution) 8. in ~ (in secret ~; the court was in ~)

set I *adj.* ["opposed"] 1. (cannot stand alone) ~ against (her parents were dead ~ against the marriage) ["ready"] 2. ~ for (we are ~ for the big celebration) 3. ~ to + inf. (we are ~ to begin) ["in favor of"] 4. ~ on (they were ~ on going) 5. (misc.) to get ~ for; (before a race): get ready, get ~, go! (BE fig. has *ready, steady, go!*; AE also has *on your marks, get ~, go!*)

set II *n.* ["collection of things used together"] 1. to complete, make up a ~ 2. to break, break up a ~ 3. a carving; chemistry; chess; tea ~ (how many pieces does a chess ~ comprise/contain? = how many pieces make up/constitute a chess ~? = how many pieces are there in a chess ~?) 4. a complete; incomplete ~ ["group of six or more games"] (tennis) 5. to play a ~ 6. to lose; win a ~ (he won the first ~ and went on to take the match in straight ~s: 6–4, 6–3, 6–0) ["apparatus"] 7. a radio; television, TV ~ ["clique"] 8. the fast (old-fashioned); international; jet; smart (old-fashioned) ~ (to belong to the jet ~) ["stage, film scenery"] 9. to dismantle, strike a ~ (the whole cast gathered on the ~ before it was dismantled) ["misc."] 10. to make a dead ~ at smb. ("to attack smb."); ("to attempt to win smb.'s favor")

set III *v.* 1. (BE) (C) ("to assign") the teacher set several problems for the pupils; or: the teacher set the pupils several problems 2. (d; tr.) ("to place") to ~ against (to ~ a ladder against a wall) 3. (d; tr.) ("to pit") to ~ against (to ~ brother against brother) 4. (D; tr.) ("to arrange") to ~ for (to ~ the stage for smt.; to ~ a trap for smb.; to ~ a date for a wedding) 5. (d; tr.) ("to incite") to ~ on (to ~ dogs on a trespasser) 6. (D; tr.) ("to put") to ~ on (to ~ a price on an article) 7. (d; tr.) ("to adapt") to ~ to (to ~ a poem to music) 8. (d; intr.) to ~ upon ("to attack") (the wolves set upon the sheep) 9. (BE) (H) ("to assign as a task") she set them to write reports; I set myself to study these problems 10. (J) ("to compel") that set me thinking 11. (N; used with an adjective) to ~ smb. free 12. (P; tr.) ("to place") she set the lamp on the table 13. (misc.) that set me to thinking; to ~ smt. apart (certain traits ~ them apart); to ~ store by smb./smt. ("to rely on smb./

smt."); to set smt. in train ("to set smt. in motion"); to ~ one's sights on ("to aspire to") (see also *set an example for* at **example**; *set fire to* at **fire I** *n.*; *set a match to* at **match I** *n.*; *set one's mind to* at **mind I** *n.*; *set smt. in motion* at **motion I** *n.*; *set sail for/from* at **sail I** *n.*)

set about *v.* 1. (E) ("to begin") he set about to undo the damage that he had caused 2. (G) ("to begin") he set about undoing the damage that he had caused

set apart *v.* (D; tr.) to ~ from (certain traits ~ them apart from the others)

set aside *v.* (D; tr.) to ~ for (to ~ money for one's old age)

setback *n.* 1. to experience, have, receive, suffer a ~ 2. a serious; severe; temporary; unexpected ~ 3. a business; diplomatic; financial; military; personal; political; professional ~ 4. a ~ to (it was a ~ to her hopes)

set down *v.* (BE) (L) ("to establish") it was set down that taxes are due in March; where is that set down on paper?

set forth *v.* see **set out** 2

set off *v.* 1. (D; intr.) ("to start") to ~ for, on (to ~ for home; to ~ on a trip) 2. (misc.) to ~ in search of smt. = to ~ (in order) to find smt.

set out *v.* 1. (D; intr.) ("to leave") to ~ for; from (to ~ for town) 2. (d; intr.) to ~ on ("to begin") (to ~ on a new career) 3. (E) ("to resolve") he has set out to get revenge 4. (misc.) to ~ in search of smt. = to ~ (in order) to find smt.

settee I *n.* to lie; sit on a ~

setting *n.* ["set of tableware"] 1. a place ~ (for) ["frame in which a gem is set"] 2. to fashion a ~ for ["surroundings"] 3. a natural; perfect; unlikely ~ (Central Park provided an unlikely ~ for the play) ["arrangement of stage props"] 4. a stage ~ ["point at which a measuring device is set"] 5. to adjust, change, switch the ~ (of a thermostat) 6. to lower; raise the ~

settle *v.* 1. to ~ peacefully (to ~ a dispute peacefully) 2. (d; intr.) to ~ for ("to be content with") (they had to ~ for a very modest house with no garage) 3. (d; intr.) ("to decide") to ~ on (have you ~d on a place for your vacation?) 4. (D; intr., tr.) ("to adjust accounts; to adjust") to ~ with (to ~ with one's creditors; we have ~d our accounts with our creditors) 5. (misc.) to ~ (a case) out of court; to ~ oneself (comfortably) in an armchair; to ~ on the land; to ~ into a routine; she ~d a large portion of her holdings on her children

settle back *v.* (D; intr., refl.) to ~ in, into (she ~d (herself) back comfortably into her armchair = she ~d comfortably back into her armchair)

settled *adj.* to get ~

settle down *v.* 1. (D; intr.) to ~ into, to (to ~ into a routine; to ~ to family life) 2. (D; intr.) to ~ with (she ~d down for the evening with a good book) 3. (E) to ~ to study 4. (misc.) to ~ for the night

settlement *n.* 1. to agree (BE), agree on, agree to,

come to, hammer out, make, negotiate, reach a ~ (on) 2. to mediate a ~ 3. a fair, reasonable; tentative ~ 4. a divorce; lump-sum; marriage; out-of-court; wage ~ 5. in ~ of (the payment was accepted in full ~ of all her debts)

set up *v.* 1. (d; refl., tr.) ("to establish") to ~ as (she set herself up as a real-estate agent) 2. (BE) (d; refl.) ("to claim to be") to ~ as (she ~s herself up as an expert on Chinese art) 3. (D; intr., refl., tr.) ("to establish") to ~ in (to set (oneself) up in business and then set smb. else up in business, too)

several *determiner, pronoun* 1. ~ of (~ of them) 2. (misc.) ~ more (~ more students; ~ more of the students whom we had discussed earlier) USAGE NOTE: The use of the preposition *of* is necessary when a pronoun follows. When a noun follows, the use of *of the* limits the meaning – we saw several students; we saw several of the students whom we had discussed earlier.

sew *v.* 1. to ~ tightly; together (to ~ two edges together tightly) 2. (C) she ~ed a dress for me; or: she ~ed me a dress 3. (P) to ~ a button on/onto a shirt with a needle and thread

sewage *n.* 1. to treat ~ 2. raw, untreated ~

sewer *n.* a sanitary; storm ~

sex *n.* ["sexual relations"] 1. to have ~ (with smb.) 2. good, great ~ 3. casual; consensual ~ 4. extramarital; marital; premarital ~ 5. safe; unsafe ~ (to practice safe ~) 6. illicit; kinky (slang), perverse ~ 7. anal; oral ~ 8. explicit ~ (pictures of explicit ~ were cut from the film) ["division of organisms into male and female"] 9. the female; male ~ 10. a member of the opposite ~ 11. between the ~es (equality between the ~es) 12. (misc.) the equality of the ~es; are women really ¬the fair/the weaker¬ ~?

sex organs *n.* female; male ~

sexuality *n.* female; human; male ~

shack *n.* a dilapidated, run-down; jerry-built ~

shackle *v.* 1. (D; tr.) to ~ to (the prisoner was ~d to the bars; the prisoner was ~d to another prisoner = the prisoners were ~d to each other) 2. (misc.) the prisoners were ~d together

shackles *n.* to cast off, throw off one's ~

shack up *v.* (slang.) (D; intr.) to ~ with (he ~ed up with his girlfriend)

shade I *n.* ["gradation of color, hue"] 1. a delicate, pale, pastel, soft ~ 2. a dark; light ~ (see also **shades**) ["window cover"] (AE; BE has *blinds*) 3. to draw; pull down; raise the ~s (see also **window shade**) ["shaded place"] 4. in the ~ ["misc."] 5. a lampshade; people of all ~s of opinion USAGE NOTE: Remember that to draw the shades is either to open them or to close them!

shade II *v.* 1. (D; tr.) to ~ by, with; from (I must ~ my head from the sun by wearing a hat) 2. (d; intr.) to ~ into (the colors ~ into each other)

shades *n.* in ~ (this fabric comes in several ~)

shadow *n.* 1. to cast, produce, throw a ~ (the setting sun cast long ~s) 2. ~s deepen, fall 3. (misc.)

a (mere) ~ of one's former self; to walk in smb.'s ~ ("to be subservient to smb."); into the ~s; out of the ~s (a strange figure stepped out of the ~s and then stepped back into them again); under a ~ ("under suspicion"); to be afraid of one's (own) ~ ("to fear everything"); beyond a (CE)/the (AE) ~ of a doubt, beyond a ~ of doubt (BE) (see also **eye shadow**)

shaft n. 1. to bore, sink a ~ 2. a cardan (BE), drive (AE) ~ 3. an air; elevator (AE), lift (BE); mine ~

shake I n. ["act of shaking"] 1. to give smb. or smt. a ~ (she gave the rug a good ~) ["opportunity"] (colloq.) (AE) 2. a fair ~ (she got a fair ~)

shake II v. 1. to ~ hard, vigorously; violently 2. (D; tr.) to ~ at; in (he shook his fist at me; he shook his head at my foolishness; he shook his head in disbelief) 3. (d; tr.) to ~ from, out of (to ~ apples from a tree) 4. (D; intr.) to ~ with (to ~ with fear) 5. (N; used with an adjective) the dog shook itself dry 6. (misc.) ~ well before using; let's ~ (hands) on it (to show that we agree); he shook me by the hand = he shook my hand = he shook hands with me

shake down v. (D; tr.) to ~ from, out of (to ~ apples down from a tree)

shaken adj. badly, deeply; easily; visibly ~

shaker n. 1. a cocktail ~ 2. a pepper ~ (AE; BE has *pepper pot*); saltshaker (esp. AE; CE has *saltcellar*)

shake-up n. 1. a personnel ~ 2. during; in a ~ (many jobs were lost in the ~ and there was a lot of uncertainty during it)

shall v. 1. (F) we ~ see, shan't we ?! 2. (misc.) "shall we dance?" "yes, let's!"; "let's go to the movies, shall we?" "yes, let's!; no, let's not."

shamble v. (P; intr.) to ~ across the field; to ~ through the streets

shambles n. 1. to make a ~ of; to turn smt. into a ~ 2. in (a) ~ (their economy is in ~)

shame I n. 1. to bring ~ on, to, upon 2. to feel ~ at (they felt ~ at accepting bribes) 3. (colloq.) an awful, crying, dirty ~ 4. a ~ to + inf. (it's a ~ to waste so much time = it's a ~ wasting so much time) 5. a ~ that + clause (it was a ~ that they'd wasted so much time) 6. in ~ (to hang one's head in ~) 7. to smb.'s ~ (to my ~, I never did help them) 8. with ~ (his cheeks burned with ~) 9. (misc.) to have no (sense of) ~; to put smb. to ~; a damn/damned ~; ~ on you!, for ~! (old-fashioned); a beautiful spot – (what a) ~ about the weather, though!

shame II v. 1. (d; tr.) to ~ into (to ~ smb. into doing smt.) 2. (d; tr.) to ~ out of 3. (R) it ~s me to admit it 4. (misc.) the government wants to name and ~ young offenders publicly

shameful adj. 1. ~ to + inf. (it was ~ of/for them to surrender) 2. ~ that + clause (it was ~ that they surrendered)

shameless adj. ~ to + inf. (it was ~ of/for them to do that)

shampoo n. ["washing of the hair"] 1. to give smb. a ~

2. to get, have a ~ ["shampoo liquid"] 3. to apply ~ 4. an anti-dandruff ~

shape I n. ["form"] 1. to give ~ to 2. to assume a ~; to take ~; to take the ~ of (our plans are beginning to take ~; to take the ~ of a human being) ["good physical condition"] 3. to get (oneself) into ~ 4. to keep (oneself) in ~ 5. in ~ 6. out of ~ ["stated physical or analogous condition"] 7. excellent, fine, superb, tip-top; good ~ 8. bad poor ~ 9. in (certain) ~ (to be in bad ~; she was in superb ~ today – she ran a mile and didn't get out of breath!; our house is in good ~; the roads are in terrible ~; the economy is in worse ~ than ever) 10. (misc.) she is in no ~ to drive

shape II v. 1. (D; tr.) to ~ into (to ~ clay into a jug) 2. (D; tr.) to ~ from, out of (to ~ a jug out of clay)

shape up v. 1. (d; intr.) to ~ as (the election ~d up as a major event) 2. (E) the election is ~ping up to be a major event

share I n. 1. to do one's ~ 2. an equal; fair; full; large, major; minor ~ 3. the lion's ~ 4. a ~ in, of (to have a ~ in/of the profits and get the lion's ~ of the kudos) (see also **shares**)

share II v. 1. to ~ equally; fairly 2. (D; tr.) to ~ among (the thieves ~d the loot among themselves) 3. (D; intr.) to ~ in (to ~ in the profits) 4. (D; tr.) to ~ with (we ~d our food with them)

share out v. 1. to ~ equally; fairly 2. (D; tr.) to ~ among (the thieves ~d out the loot equally among themselves = the thieves ~d the loot out equally among themselves)

shares n. ["units of capital stock"] 1. to buy; sell ~ (on the stock market) 2. ordinary ~ (BE; AE has *common stock*) 3. preference ~ (BE; AE has *preferred stock*) 4. ~ close strong; weak 5. ~ open strong; weak 6. ~ are active; sluggish 7. ~ are firm, steady; rising; up 8. ~ go up, rise; rally 9. ~ are depressed; down; falling 10. ~ collapse, crash; fall, go down; plummet; slump

sharing n. 1. profit ~ 2. revenue ~ (by the states)

shark n. 1. a man-eating ~ 2. (fig.) a loan ~

sharp adj. 1. razor ~ (she has a razor-sharp mind that's as ~ as a razor!) ["severe"] 2. ~ with (the boss was rather ~ with the workers)

sharpener n. a knife; pencil ~

shatter v. (D; intr., tr.) to ~ into (the glass ~ed into many small pieces)

shave I n. 1. to give smb. a ~ 2. to get, have a ~ 3. a close ~ 4. (misc.) a close ~ ("a narrow escape")

shave II v. 1. (d; tr.) to ~ from, off (the carpenter ~d an inch off the door; the runner ~d ten seconds off the record) 2. (N; used with an adjective) she ~d me close; he ~d his head bald

shavings n. wood ~

shears n. 1. garden; pinking; pruning (AE) ~ 2. a pair of ~ (see also **secateurs**)

shed n. 1. a bicycle; garden, potting (BE); tool ~ 2. in a ~ (put the tools back in the tool ~)

sheen n. ["brightness"] 1. to give smt.; produce a ~ 2. a high ~

sheep *n.* 1. to raise, rear (BE) ~ 2. to shear ~ 3. ~ baa, bleat, go baa 4. ~ graze 5. a flock, herd of ~ 6. the meat of the ~ is mutton 7. a young ~ is a lamb; its meat is lamb 8. a female ~ is a ewe 9. a male ~ is a ram 10. (misc.) ~ are tended by a shepherd; to round up stray ~

sheet *n.* ["piece of bed linen"] 1. a bed; cotton; flannel; percale; silk ~ 2. a double; king-sized; queen-sized; single; twin ~ 3. a fitted; flat ~ 4. (misc.) to change the ~s = to put on clean/fresh ~s (I put on fresh ~s and snuggled down between them) ["financial statement"]["record"] 5. a balance ~ 6. (BE) a wages ~ ["diagram"] 7. a flow ~ ["piece of paper"] 8. a blank ~ ["newspaper"] (colloq.) (now esp. AE) 9. a scandal ~ ["statement"] 10. a charge ~ ("a statement of charges brought against an accused person") ["pan"] (now esp. AE) 11. a cookie ~ (BE has *biscuit tin*)

shelf *n.* 1. to put up a ~ 2. adjustable; built-in shelves 3. a continental ~ 4. (misc.) on the ~ ("no longer in demand") (also fig.) she's still unmarried at 28 and beginning to feel she's on the ~; to stock shelves with supplies

shell *n.* ["projectile"] 1. to fire a ~ at 2. to fuse a ~ 3. to lob a ~ (the enemy's artillery was lobbing ~s into our positions) 4. an armor-piercing; high-explosive; hollow-charge; incendiary; mortar; smoke ~ 5. ~s burst, explode ["outer cover"] 6. to come out of, emerge from one's ~ 7. to go into, withdraw into one's ~ (also fig.); talk to him or he'll just go into his ~ again

shellacking *n.* ["beating"] (colloq.) (AE) 1. to give smb. a ~ 2. to get, take a ~

shelling *n.* constant, round-the-clock; heavy; light ~

shell out *v.* (colloq.) ("to pay") 1. (B) they had to ~ money to their creditors 2. (D; intr., tr.) to ~ for (to ~ a lot for a new car) 3. (D; intr., tr.) to ~ on (to ~ a lot on household expenses) 4. (misc.) we had to ~ a lot of money (in order) to take this vacation!

shelter I *n.* 1. to afford, give, offer, provide ~ 2. to seek; take ~ from 3. an air-raid, bomb, underground; fallout; homeless ~ (see also **tax shelter**) 4. in; under a ~ (we thought we were safe in the air-raid ~)

shelter II *v.* (D; intr., tr.) to ~ from

shelving *n.* 1. to put up ~ 2. adjustable; built-in ~

shepherd *v.* (P; tr.) to ~ children around the museum

sheriff *n.* a deputy ~

sherry *n.* 1. cooking; cream; dry; sweet ~ 2. a bottle; glass of ~

shield I *n.* a heat ~ (of a spacecraft)

shield II *v.* (D; tr.) to ~ against, from

shift I *n.* ["change"] 1. to bring about, produce; represent a ~ in 2. (ling.) a consonant; functional; vowel ~ 3. a gradual; dramatic; sudden ~ 4. a ~ away from; in; to, towards (there was a gradual ~ in public opinion away from democracy to

dictatorship) ["work period"] 5. a day; eight-hour; night; split; swing ~ (she works the night ~; to work an eight-hour ~) ["transmission"] (AE) 6. an automatic; standard, stick ~ (CE has *transmission*) (my car has a stick ~ and I know how to work/operate it)

shift II *v.* 1. to ~ gradually; dramatically; suddenly ~ 2. (D; intr., tr.) to ~ from; onto, to (to ~ responsibility to smb. else; public opinion is ~ing gradually away from democracy to dictatorship); (AE) (to ~ from first to second gear) (CE has *to change from first to second gear*) 3. (misc.) to ~ for oneself ("to manage on one's own"); to ~ into neutral (AE; CE has *to change into neutral*)

shin *n.* 1. to bark ("scrape") one's ~s 2. on smb.'s ~ (he got a bad scrape on his ~)

shine I *n.* ["liking"] (colloq.) 1. to take a ~ to ["shining of shoes"] 2. to give smb. a ~, to give smb.'s shoes a ~ ("to shine smb.'s shoes")

shine II *v.* 1. to ~ brightly 2. (D; intr.) ("to give light") to ~ on (the hot sun was ~ing directly on our heads) 3. (P) ("to direct") to ~ on (~ the lights on this part of the field and esp. along the hedges and under the trees)

shiner *n.* ["black eye"] (colloq.) (old-fashioned) 1. to give smb. a ~ 2. to sport a ~

shingle *n.* ["small sign designating a professional office"] (colloq.) (AE) to hang out one's ~

shingles I *n.* ["building material on a roof"] to lay ~

shingles II *n.* ["herpes zoster"] (med.) to come down with, develop, get; have ~

ship I *n.* 1. to build; refit a ~ to christen; commission; launch a ~ 3. to board, get on, get on board; take (a) ~ 4. to disembark from, get off a ~ 5. to berth, dock; command; navigate; pilot, sail, steer a ~ 6. to scuttle; sink; torpedo a ~ 7. to abandon ~ (when it is sinking) 8. to jump ~ ("to desert from a ship's crew") 9. to raise a sunken ~ 10. to load; unload a ~ 11. a battleship; capital; naval; supply; troop ~; warship 12. a cargo; cruise; hospital; merchant; passenger ~ 13. an oceangoing; sailing ~; steamship 14. an airship; rocket ~; spaceship; starship 15. a ~ heaves; leaks; pitches; rolls; sinks 16. a ~ comes into harbor; docks; goes, sails 17. a ~ for; from; to (we took a ~ from New York to Southampton) 18. by ~ (to travel by ~ from New York to Southampton) 19. in; on a ~ (to cross the ocean in a ~ and sleep on the ~) 20. the bow; stern of a ~ 21. (misc.) to run a tight ~ ("to operate efficiently") USAGE NOTE: The terms *rocket ship* and *spaceship* are now used chiefly in science fiction. The terms *spacecraft* and *space vehicle* are now used for the real thing. However, the term *spaceship* is sometimes used for "space shuttle". The term *starship* is used in science fiction for a spaceship capable of interstellar travel; in particular, the Starship Enterprise in the television program *Star Trek*.

ship II *v.* 1. (A) they have ~ped the merchandise

to us; or: they have ~ped us the merchandise 2. (P; tr.) to ~ cargo through the Panama Canal; to ~ goods to South America from New York

shipboard *n.* on ~

ship off *v.* (D; tr.) to ~ to (they ~ped their children off to their favorite summer camp = they ~ped off their children to their favorite summer camp)

ship out *v.* (D; intr., tr.) to ~ from; to (they ~ped the goods out from New York to London = they ~ped out the goods from New York to London = they ~ped the goods from New York out to London; we ~ped out from Philadelphia)

shipping *n.* merchant ~

shipwreck *n.* 1. to experience, suffer (a) ~ 2. to survive a ~

shipyard *n.* a naval ~

shirk *v.* (G) no one should ~ doing their duty

shirt *n.* 1. to put on; take off; wear a ~ 2. to button; unbutton a ~ 3. to tuck in one's ~ 4. a cotton; silk ~ 5. a body; dress; hair; polo (AE); sport (AE), sports (CE) ~; sweatshirt; tee ~, T-shirt; undershirt 6. a long-sleeve (AE), long-sleeved (CE); short-sleeve (AE), short-sleeved (CE) ~ 7. a drip-dry, wash-and-wear ~ 8. (misc.) to lose one's ~ ("to lose everything") (they lost their ~ in the recession) (see also *shirtsleeves* at **sleeve**)

shiver I *n.* 1. to feel a ~ 2. (misc.) a ~ of excitement went up and down my spine at the performance – it was the same ~ that passed through the whole audience (see also **shivers**)

shiver II *v.* 1. (D; intr.) to ~ at (she ~ed at the thought of getting up) 2. (D; intr.) to ~ from, with (to ~ from the cold) 3. (E) she ~ed to think she'd have to get up soon

shivers *n.* (colloq.) 1. to get; have the ~ 2. (misc.) it gave her the ~ to think she'd have to get up soon

shock I *n.* 1. to give smb. a ~ (her arrest gave her quite a ~!) 2. to express; feel a ~ 3. to get; have a ~ 4. to absorb a ~ 5. to get over, recover from a ~ 6. to come as a ~ (to smb.) 7. a mild, slight ~ 8. a first, initial; deep, great, nasty, profound, severe, terrible; rude, sudden ~ (at; of) (the initial ~ of being arrested; her initial ~ at being arrested) 9. (a) culture ~; future ~ 10. (an) electric ~; insulin ~ (she got an electric ~ when she touched the wire) 11. (an) emotional ~ (it came as a deep emotional ~ to her) 12. a ~ to (her arrest was a ~ to everybody) 13. a ~ to + inf. (it was a ~ to learn of her arrest = it was a ~ learning of her arrest) 14. a ~ that + clause (it came as a ~ (to everybody) that she had been arrested) 15. ~ at (everyone expressed ~ at her arrest) 16. in ~ (she seemed to be in ~) 17. (misc.) a bit of a ~ (her arrest was a bit of a ~ to everyone); in a state of ~ (she seemed to be in a state of ~ after the initial ~ of her arrest; ~ and awe) (see also *shock to the system* at **system**)

shock II *v.* 1. to ~ deeply, greatly 2. (D; tr.) to ~ by, with (she ~ed me by her behavior) 3. (D; tr.) to ~ into (to ~ smb. into doing smt.) 4. (R) it

~ed everybody (to learn) that she had been arrested 5. (misc.) their campaign ~ed us out of our complacency

shocked *adj.* 1. deeply, greatly; easily ~ 2. ~ at, by (everybody was ~ at her arrest) 3. ~ to + inf. (everybody was ~ to learn that she had been arrested) 4. ~ that + clause (everyone was ~ that she had been arrested)

shocking *adj.* 1. ~ to + inf. (it was ~ to learn that she had been arrested) 2. ~ that + clause (it was ~ that she ¬had been/should have been¬ arrested)

shoelace *n.* 1. to tie; undo, untie a ~ 2. to knot a ~ (he knotted a ~ that had come undone) 3. a pair of ~s

shoes *n.* 1. to put on; wear ~ 2. to slip off; take off ~ 3. to break in (new) ~ 4. to lace (up); unlace (one's) ~ 5. to brush; polish, shine ~ 6. to fix, mend (esp. BE), repair ~ 7. tight; well-fitting ~ 8. high-heeled; low-heeled ~ 9. ballet; basketball; earth; gym ~; overshoes; running; saddle ~ (esp. AE); snowshoes; sports; tennis; track; walking ~ 10. ~ fit; pinch 11. a pair of ~ 12. (misc.) to fill smb.'s ~ ("to replace smb."); I'd hate to be in your ~s right now! ("in your position")

shoestring *n.* (colloq.) ["limited funds"] on a ~ (to operate a business on a ~)

shoo *v.* (colloq.) (D; tr.) ("to chase") to ~ away from, out of (~ the cat out of the room)

shoot I *n.* ["young plant"] 1. a bamboo ~ ["hunting trip"] 2. (to go on) a tiger ~

shoot II *v.* 1. (D; tr.) ("to execute by shooting") to ~ as; for (he was shot as a deserter = he was shot for desertion) 2. (D; intr.) ("to fire") to ~ at (to ~ at smb. with a gun or perhaps with a bow and arrow) 3. (colloq.) (esp. AE) (d; intr.) ("to aim") to ~ for (to ~ for the top) 4. (D; intr., tr.) ("to fire") to ~ from (to ~ an arrow from a bow) 5. (D; tr.) to ~ in (she shot him in the leg) 6. (D; intr., tr.) ("to fire") to ~ into (to ~ into the air) 7. (N; used with an adjective) ("to hit with gunfire") to ~ smb. dead 8. (P; intr.) ("to move quickly") they shot past us in a sports car 9. (misc.) to ~ on sight; to ~ to kill; to ~ it out with smb.

shoot back *v.* (D; intr.) to ~ at (they shot at us so we shot back at them)

shoot-out *n.* to have a ~ (with)

shoot up *v.* 1. (D; intr.) to ~ into (to ~ into the sky) 2. (D; intr., tr.) to ~ into (he shot up heroin into a vein = he shot heroin up into a vein)

shop I *n.* ["store"] 1. to keep (BE), run; manage, operate a ~ 2. an antique ~; bookshop; butcher (AE), butcher's (BE); chemist's (BE; AE has *drugstore*); duty-free; gift; green-grocer's; high-street (BE); novelty; pastry ~; pawnshop; pet; stationer's (BE; AE has *stationery shop/store*) ~; sweetshop (BE; AE has *candy store*); charity (BE), thrift (AE); toy ~ (see also **workshop**) 3. a draper's ~ (BE; AE has *dry-goods store*) 4. at, in (she works in a ~) ["workshop"] 5. a barbershop (esp. AE), barber's ~ (BE); beauty (esp. AE; CE has *beauty parlor*); body; machine; paint; printing; repair ~ ["place of work"] 6. a closed ~ ("firm that hires only union members") 7. an open ~ ("firm that hires union members and non-union members") 8. a union ~ ("firm that hires only workers who will join the union if they are not already members") ["misc."] 9. to close down (a) ~ ("to stop operations"); to introduce a closed / open / union ~ at work; to set up ~ ("to begin operations"); to talk ~ ("to discuss one's work while not at work"); a coffee ~ (AE; BE has *coffee bar*); a betting ~ (BE; CE has *bookmaker's*) USAGE NOTE: *Shop* and *store* are CE. In BE, *store* tends to be used for a very large retail establishment (*department store*) and *shop* for the others (*bookshop, sweetshop*). In AE, *store* is used for all, regardless of size (*department store, book store, candy store*). However, AE can also use *shop* for a small specialized store or boutique (*bookshop, millinery shop*). In BE *a chemist* (or sometimes *a chemist's*) is more likely than *a chemist's shop*.

shop II v. 1. (D: intr.) to ~ for (to ~ for food) 2. (misc.) to go ~ping (for smt.); let's go window ~ping; to ~ smb. to the police (BE; slang) ("to inform on smb. to the police")

shop around v. (D; intr.) to ~ for (to ~ for bargains)

shopper n. a Christmas; comparison; window ~

shopping n. 1. to do the ~; to go ~ 2. Christmas; comparison; window ~ (to do the Christmas ~; to do comparison ~)

shore n. 1. (AE; BE has *seaside*) at; by the ~ (a vacation at the ~) 2. off ~ (two miles off ~) 3. on a ~ (smb. was standing on the ~ and began walking along it) 4. to reach (a) ~ USAGE NOTE: the bank(s) of a river or canal; the shore of a lake or sea; the coast (of an ocean).

shorefront n. (AE) along, on the ~

short I adj. 1. ~ in (~ in stature) 2. ~ of, on (colloq.) (~ of funds; to go (BE), run (CE) ~ of food; to fall ~ of one's goal; he is a nice fellow, but a bit ~ on common sense) 3. (misc.) she is rather ~ for her age; to be caught ~ ("to find oneself in acute need"); to be caught ~ (BE; colloq.) ("to feel the need to go to the toilet"); the boss was ~ ("impatient") with me; a bit, little ~; Will is ~ for William (see also **stop short**)

short II n. 1. (we called William Will) for ~ 2. in ~ (in ~, it was a disaster)

shortage n. 1. an acute, desperate, severe ~ 2. a food; fuel; housing; labor; teacher; water ~; wartime ~s (facing desperate food ~s) 3. a ~ of (facing desperate ~s of food) 4. no ~ of (there's never any ~ of reasons to be / for being idle!)

shortcut n. 1. to take a ~ (we took a ~ (home)) 2. a ~ from; to (I know a ~ from our house to the station) 3. (misc.) (fig.) a ~ to (a ~ to success)

shorten v. 1. (D; tr.) to ~ by (to ~ trousers (by) two

inches) 2. (D; tr.) to ~ to (to ~ a manuscript to acceptable length)

shortening n. (esp. AE) vegetable ~

shorthand n. 1. to take; transcribe ~ 2. (to take smt. down) in ~

short haul (esp. AE) see **short run** (see also *short-haul flight* at **flight I**)

short-list v. (D; tr.) to ~ for (several applicants were ~ed for the job)

short run n. ["short-range outlook"] in, over the ~

shorts n. 1. Bermuda; boxer ~ 2. a pair of ~

short shrift n. ["short work"] 1. (AE) to make ~ of ("to deal with quickly") 2. to give smb. ~ ("to deal with smb. summarily") 3. to get ~ from smb. ("to be treated summarily by smb.")

shortsighted adj. ~ to + inf. (it was ~ of them not to provide for their old age)

short term see **short run**

short way n. 1. we took the ~ (home) 2. a ~ from; to (it's just a ~ from our house to the station)

shot n. ["act of shooting"] 1. to fire, take a ~ at (she took a ~ at him with a gun or perhaps with a bow and arrow) 2. a random; warning ~ (to send a warning ~ across the bow of a ship) 3. a gunshot; pistol; rifle ~ 4. a ~ from (fire a ~ from a rifle) 5. a ~ in (he got a ~ in the leg) 6. a ~ into (fire a ~ into the air) ["marksman"] 7. a bad; crack, good ~ ["throw, kick of the ball to score points"] 8. (esp. basketball) to make, sink; miss; take a ~ (to take a ~ at the basket) 9. (basketball) a dunk, stuff; foul; jump; lay-up ~ 10. (tennis) a cross-court; drop; passing ~ 11. (ice hockey) a penalty ~ 12. a ~ from (he sank a ~ from the back of the court!) ["metal ball used in the shot put"] 13. to put the ~ ["injection"] 14. to give smb. a ~ 15. to get; have a ~ 16. a booster; flu ~ ["critical remark"] 17. a cheap; parting ~ ["attempt"] (colloq.) 18. to get; have a ~ at (the boxer never got a ~ at the title) ["chance"] (colloq.) (AE) 19. a ~ that + clause (it's a five to one ~ that she'll find out) ["misc."] 20. to call the ~s ("to direct matters"); a ~ in the arm ("a stimulus"); a ~ in the dark ("a wild guess") (see also **potshot**)

shotgun n. a sawed-off (AE), sawn-off (BE) ~ (see also **gun** 1, 2, 4, 5, 6)

should v. (F) she ~ help, shouldn't she?; "~ she?"/ "she ~?"; "yes, she ~"/"no, she shouldn't"

shoulder I n. 1. to shrug one's ~s 2. to square, straighten one's ~s 3. broad, square ~s 4. a dislocated ~ 5. (misc.) ~ to ~ (to work ~ to ~) ("to work closely together"); to put one's ~ to the wheel ("to work very hard"); to rub ~s with ("to associate with"); to tap smb. on the ~; straight from the ~ ("in a direct manner"); we parked our car on the ~ (AE) / hard ~ (BE) of the road; she is head and ~s above any of the other candidates (see also **cold shoulder**)

shoulder II v. (d; intr.) to ~ through (she ~ed her way through the crowd)

shout I n. 1. to give a ~ 2. a jubilant; loud; piercing; triumphant ~ 3. a ~ rang out, went up

shout II v. 1. to ~ jubilantly; loudly; triumphantly 2. (B) she ~ed a few words to me 3. (D; intr.) to ~ at (don't ~ at me) 4. (d; intr.) to ~ for, with (she ~ed for/with joy) 5. (E; at; to) she ~ed at/to us to call the police 6. (L; at; to) she ~ed (at/to us) that we should call the police = "call the police!" she ~ed (at/to us) 7. (misc.) he ~ed himself hoarse

shove I n. to give smb. a ~

shove II v. (P) ~ the suitcases under the bed; she ~d the files into the drawer; she ~d him away; she ~d her way through the crowd and up to the front

shovel I n. a snow; steam ~

shovel II v. (P; tr.) they ~ed the snow to the side; I ~ed the coal into the bin

show I n. ["performance"] ["program"] 1. to direct; do, produce, put on, stage; promote; sponsor a ~ (I saw him in a stage ~) 2. to attend, catch (colloq.), go to, see, take in a ~ 3. a chat (BE), talk; quiz; sketch; TV ~ (to sponsor a TV ~; I saw her on one of the funniest-ever TV sketch ~s) 4. a one-man, one-woman; talent; variety ~ 5. a floor; peep ~ 6. a horse; ice ~ 7. a Punch-and-Judy; puppet; sound-and-light ~ (see also **air show**) ["display, exhibition"] 8. to hold, organize, produce, put on, stage; promote; sponsor a ~ 9. to attend, go to, see, take in a ~ 10. an antique; art; auto (AE), motor (BE); fashion; flower ~ ["misc."] 11. for ~ ("designed to make an impression"); bad ~! ("very bad!"); good ~! ("very good!"); to put on a ~ ("to pretend"); to steal the ~ ("to draw the most attention"); to stop the ~ ("to receive too much applause, attention for the show to continue") (he sang a show-stopping song on stage last night; that song of his was a real show-stopper!); a ~ of strength; who's running the ~? ("who's in charge here?"); to get the ~ on the road (slang) ("to get things going")

show I v. 1. (A) ("to display") ~ the book to me; or: show me the book 2. (d; tr.) ("to guide") to ~ around, over, round (esp. BE), through; in; out; up (she ~ed me through the museum; Lord Fauntleroy asked his butler to ~ me in and to ~ me out afterwards) 3. (d; tr.) to ~ for ("to have as a result of") (what can we ~ for our efforts?) 4. (d; tr.) ("to guide") to ~ to (I ~ed her to her seat; to ~ smb. to the door) (see also *show smb. the door* at **door**) 5. (J) ("to display") the photograph ~ed them conversing 6. (L; may have an object) ("to demonstrate") the research ~ed (¬us/to us¬) that our theory was correct 7. (M) ("to demonstrate") she ~ed herself to be an excellent worker; history ~ed her to have been a prophet 8. (Q; usu. has an object) ("to demonstrate") can you ~ me how to operate the copying machine? 9. (misc.) to ~ to advantage ("to show in the best light"); to ~ oneself in public; don't worry: the stain on your shirt hardly ~s

showdown n. 1. to come to, have; force a ~ (if it comes to a ~, the boss will support her rather than me) 2. a ~ between; over; with (we had a ~ with the boss over the change in plans)

shower I n. ["bath using an overhead spray, showerbath"] 1. to have (BE), take a ~ ["short period of rain"] ["brief downpour"] 2. a heavy; light ~ 3. April; intermittent; passing; scattered ~s 4. a meteor; rain; snow; thunder ~; intermittent; scattered ~s 5. a sun ~ (esp. AE) ("rain that falls while the sun is shining") ["party to which the guests are expected to bring gifts"] (AE) 6. to make a ~ for smb. 7. a baby; bridal ~ ["misc."] 8. a ~ of arrows (rained down on our soldiers)

shower II v. 1. (d; tr.) to ~ on, upon (to ~ gifts on smb.) 2. (d; tr.) to ~ with (to ~ smb. with gifts)

showing n. ["performance"] 1. to make a ~ 2. a disappointing; good; poor ~ (he made a poor ~ in the debate) 3. a private ~ (attend a private ~ of the film at the director's house) 4. on a certain ~ (on its current ~ in the polls, the Conservative Radical Party may defeat the Radical Conservative Party)

show off v. 1. (B) they ~ed off their new car to all the neighbors = they ~ed their new car off to all the neighbors 2. (D; intr.) to ~ to (she was ~ing off to everyone)

show up v. 1. (D; tr.) to ~ as (the incident ~ed him up as a charlatan) 2. (s) he ~ed up drunk

shrapnel n. to catch a piece of ~ (in the leg)

shreds n. 1. to cut, rip, tear smt. to ~ 2. (misc.) her clothing was in ~

shrewd adj. 1. ~ at, in 2. ~ to + inf. (it was ~ of/for her to buy real estate when the market was depressed)

shrewdness n. 1. to display ~ 2. ~ at, in (she showed great/real ~ in buying real estate when the market was depressed) 3. the ~ to + inf. (she had the ~ to buy real estate when the market was depressed)

shriek I n. 1. to give, let out a ~ 2. a loud ~

shriek II v. 1. (D; intr.) to ~ at 2. (D; intr.) to ~ in, with (to ~ with laughter) 3. (H; at) they ~ed at us to stop = "stop!" they ~ed (at us)

shrine n. 1. to consecrate; create, establish a ~ 2. to desecrate a ~ 3. a holy, sacred ~ 4. a ~ to 5. at a ~ (to pray at a ~ to the Virgin)

shrink v. (d; intr.) to ~ from (to ~ from responsibility; "The summer soldier and the sunshine patriot will, in this crisis, ~ from the service of his country" – Thomas Paine, *The American Crisis*, December 19, 1776)

shrouded adj. ~ in (~ in mystery)

shrubbery, shrubs n. 1. to prune; trim ~ 2. ornamental ~

shrug I n. 1. to give a ~ (of the shoulders) 2. with a ~ (of the shoulders)

shrug II v. (D; intr.) 1. to ~ at ("to express indifference to") (she ~ged at the suggestion) 2. (misc.) she ~ged her shoulders at the suggestion

shudder I n. 1. to send a ~ (through the audience) 2. to give a ~ 3. a ~ passed, ran (through the audience) 4. (misc.) the news sent a ~ through our competitors; the shock sent a ~ down my spine (see also **shudders**)

shudder II v. 1. (D; intr.) to ~ at (to ~ at the thought of going back to work) 2. (E) I ~ to think what lies ahead! 3. (misc.) the car ~ed to a stop

shudders n. 1. to give smb. the ~ (her weird appearance gave me the ~) 2. to get the ~ (I get the ~ whenever I think about our narrow escape)

shuffle v. (P; intr.) they ~d idly along the street; they ~d slowly through the park

shufty n. (slang) (BE) ["quick look"] to have a ~ at

shunt v. 1. (d; tr.) to ~ from (the trains were ~ed from the station) 2. (d; tr.) to ~ onto, to (to ~ a train onto a siding)

shut v. 1. (D; tr.) to ~ on (to ~ the door on smb.) (also fig.) (to ~ the door on any change) 2. (D; tr.) to ~ to (they shut their eyes to poverty) 3. (N; used with an adjective) she shut the door tight

shut off v. (D; refl., tr.) to ~ from (they shut themselves off from their neighbors)

shutter n. ["shield in a camera"] 1. to release the ~ ["window cover"] 2. to close; open the ~s

shuttle I n. ["vehicle used on an established route"] 1. to take a ~ 2. a space ~ 3. a ~ between

shuttle II v. 1. (d; intr.) to ~ between (these ships ~ between the two ports) 2. (P; tr.) to ~ tourists to the terminal

shy I adj. ["wary"] ["nervous"] 1. painfully ~ 2. ~ about, of (BE) 3. ~ with (he was very ~ with girls) ["lacking"] (esp. AE) 4. ~ of (we are still a little ~ of our quota)

shy II v. (D; intr.) to ~ at (the horse shied at the noise)

shy away v. (d; intr.) to ~ from (they shied away from contact with their neighbors)

sic v. (D; tr.) ("to urge to attack") to ~ on (to ~ a dog on smb.)

sick adj. 1. ~ at (~ at heart; ~ at the prospect of leaving home) 2. ~ of (we are ~ of the red tape) 3. (misc.) ~ to one's stomach (AE; BE has just sick); worried ~; to be ~ and tired of smt.; to be taken ~; to make smb. ~ ("to disgust smb."); to be off ~ (and not at work) (see also call in sick at **call in**)

sicken v. 1. (BE) (d; intr.) to ~ for; of (they ~ed of the endless parties; she's ~ing for the flu) 2. (R) it ~ed me to watch them bicker constantly

sickening adj. ~ to + inf. (it was ~ to watch them bicker constantly)

sickness n. 1. altitude, mountain; car; decompression; morning; motion, travel; radiation; sea; sleeping ~ 2. in ~ (and in health)

sick parade n. (BE) see sick call at **call I** n.

side I n. ["right or left part"] 1. the left, left-hand; right, right-hand ~ 2. the credit; debit ~ (of a ledger) 3. on a ~ (on the sunny ~ of the street) ["faction, party"] 4. to take smb.'s ~; to take ~s ("to support a faction") 5. the losing; right; winning; wrong ~ 6. on smb.'s ~ (of a dispute) ("Which Side Are You On?" – Florence Reece, labor-union song, 1930s) ["direction"] 7. the opposite ~ 8. from a certain ~ (from the other ~; from all ~s) 9. (to turn) to one ~

["surface"]["part"] 10. a far; near; reverse ~ 11. the east; north; south; west ~ 12. on a ~ (on the other ~; on the north ~ of the town square) ["aspect"] 13. the bright; dark, gloomy; funny, humorous; practical ~ (of things); the seamy ~ of life 14. a ~ to (there are two ~s to every question) 15. (misc.) to study all ~s of a problem ["area near a person"] 16. at, by smb.'s ~ (she sat at my ~) ["shore, bank"] 17. on a ~ (on the other ~ of the river) ["misc."] 18. from ~ to ~; from all ~s; to be on the safe ~; I have a pain in my left ~, which is why I sleep on my right ~; the B ~ ("the less important side or part"); the flip ~ (colloq.) (the car runs well – the flip ~ is that it costs a lot); to tutor smb. on the ~ ("to tutor smb. part-time"); we split our ~s laughing ("we laughed long and hard"); time is on our ~ ("time is working for us"); on smb.'s ~ (of the family); he's a bit on the short ~ (see also bit on the side at **bit I** n.; the Usage Note for **team**)

side II v. (d; intr.) to ~ against; with (to ~ with the union (and) against the bosses)

sideline n. 1. a ~ for; in; of; to (a ~ of doing B&B can develop into a lucrative ~ for people in villages; people in villages can develop a lucrative ~ in (doing) B&B) 2. as a ~ (he's developing B&B as a lucrative ~ to his primary job as a teacher)

sidelines n. on the ~ ("out of action")

sidestroke n. to do, swim the ~

siding n. ["material attached to the outside of a building"] (AE; CE has cladding) 1. to install ~ 2. aluminum ~ ["short stretch of railway track"] 3. a railway ~ 4. on a ~

sidle up v. (d; intr.) to ~ to (she ~d up to me)

siege n. 1. to conduct a ~ of; to lay ~ to 2. to lift, raise a ~ 3. a state of ~ (in a state of ~) 4. at, during a ~ (he was killed at the ~ of Leningrad) 5. under ~ (a city under ~)

siesta n. to have, take a ~

sieve n. to pass smt. through a ~ (see also a memory like a sieve at **memory**)

sift v. 1. to ~ carefully 2. (d; tr.) to ~ from (to ~ fact from fiction) 3. (d; intr.) to ~ through (to ~ through the debris)

sigh I n. 1. to breathe, heave a ~ (of relief) 2. to give, let out a ~ 3. an audible; deep, profound; inaudible ~ 4. a ~ of contentment; a ~ of relief

sigh II v. 1. to ~ audibly; contentedly; deeply; inaudibly 2. to ~ in, with relief

sight n. ["view"] 1. to catch; keep ~ of 2. to lose ~ of 3. at (the) ~ (to faint at the (very/merest) ~ of blood; to fall in love at first ~) 4. by ~ (to know smb. by ~) 5. in, into, within ~ (the ship was no longer in ~; we fired our torpedoes when the ship came into (plain) ~) 6. on ~ (to shoot looters on ~) 7. out of ~ 8. an awe-inspiring; beautiful; interesting; magnificent, marvelous, wonderful; memorable; pleasant; spectacular; thrilling ~ 9. a comical, funny ~ 10. a familiar ~ 11. a miserable; pitiful; sorry ~ 12. a disturbing; horrendous, horrible, horrific; ugly; unpleasant ~ ["device used to aim a gun"] 13. to adjust one's ~s 14. to line up one's ~s (on) 15. a front; panoramic; peep; rear; telescopic ~ 16. (misc.) to have smb./smt. in one's ~s (also fig.) (the government has pollution in its ~s and wants to end it) ["ability to see"] ["sense of sight, eyesight"] 17. deteriorating, failing, poor, weak; keen; perfect ~ 18. to lose; regain one's ~ (see also see also *line of sight* at **line I** *n.* ; **sights**)

sighting *n.* a confirmed; radar; telescopic; unconfirmed; visual ~ (there have been several unconfirmed visual ~s of UFOs)

sights *n.* ["aspirations"] 1. to set one's ~ on (she set her ~ on a career in politics) 2. to lower; raise one's ~ 3. (misc.) to set one's ~ high ["something worth seeing"] 4. to see, take in the ~ (the tourists took in the ~) 5. to show smb. the ~

sign I *n.* ["indication"] 1. to display, give, show a ~ (he showed ~s of advanced emphysema; they showed no ~s of life; the volcano had shown no ~ of erupting) 2. a clear, obvious; sure, telltale, unmistakable ~ 3. an encouraging ~ 4. a danger; warning ~ (see also **stop sign**) 5. vital ~s ("basic indications of life") (to check/take a patient's vital ~s) 6. a ~ that + clause (there had been no ~ that the volcano would erupt) ["mark, symbol"] 7. a minus; plus ~ 8. a dollar; pound ~ 9. a call ~ ("identifying letters of a radio station") ["marker"] ["placard"] 10. to erect; post, put up; set up a ~ 11. a for rent (AE), to let (BE); for sale; no smoking; no trespassing; road, traffic; warning ~ (follow the road ~s; they put up a for-sale ~) 12. a ~ forbids; says; warns (the police put up a warning ~ saying that the road was closed) 13. (esp. AE) a ~ that + clause (the police put up a ~ that the road was closed) ["misc."] 14. to make the ~ of the cross; these new attitudes are a ~ of the times (see also **high sign**)

sign II *v.* 1. (D; intr.) to ~ for (she had to ~ for the letter) 2. (D; intr.) to ~ with (the player ~ed with the team yesterday) 3. (misc.) to ~ on the dotted line 4. (L; to) ("to communicate in sign language") she ~ed (to us) that the road was still closed

signal I *n.* ["sign"] ["message"] 1. to flash, give, send, send out, transmit; put on; use a ~ 2. to get, pick up, receive a ~ 3. to unscramble a ~ 4. a clear, unmistakable ~ 5. a danger, distress; prearranged; warning ~ 6. a smoke ~ (American Indians used to send up smoke ~s) 7. a turn ~ (AE; BE has *indicator*) 8. (AE) a traffic ~ 9. a storm ~ 10. a ~ from; to 11. a ~ to + inf. (the ~ to attack) 12. a ~ that + clause (the troops received the ~ that the attack was to begin) 13. at, on a ~ (the raid began at a given ~) 14. (misc.) she made a ~ for us to leave; (Am. football) to call the ~s (also fig.) ["electrical impulses"] 15. a radar; radio; shortwave ~ 16. a strong; weak ~ ["misc."] 17. to give out the wrong ~s ("to give the wrong impression"); to send mixed ~s ("to be vague about one's intentions")

signal II *v.* 1. to ~ frantically; wildly 2. (B) they

~ed their position to us 3. (d; intr.) to ~ for (to ~ for help) 4. (E; to) she ~ed to us to come closer 5. (H) she ~ed us to come closer 6. (L; to; may have an object) the radio operator ~ed (to us)/~ed (us) that the ship was in distress; she ~ed (to us) that we should come closer 7. (Q; to) she ~ed (to) us how close we should come 8. (misc.) she ~ed for us to come closer

signatory *n.* a ~ to (the ~ries to the treaty)

signature *n.* 1. to affix; scrawl; write one's ~ 2. to put one's ~ on, to 3. to bear a ~ (the treaty bore the president's ~) 4. to notarize; witness a ~ 5. to forge smb.'s ~

significance *n.* 1. to acquire; have ~ for 2. to attach ~ to 3. deep, great; statistical ~ 4. to be of ~ for, to

significant *adj.* 1. ~ for, to 2. ~ to + inf. (it is ~ to note that our ambassador was not invited) 3. ~ that + clause (it is highly/very ~ that our ambassador was not invited)

signify *v.* 1. (L; to) their statements ~ (to us) that no action will be taken 2. (misc.) she ~fied her assent with a nod; all those in favor, ~ by saying "aye"

sign on *v.* 1. (D; intr.) to ~ as (to ~ as a seaman) 2. (D; intr.) (BE) to ~ for (to ~ for the dole)

sign out *v.* (D; tr.) to ~ from (we ~ed out three books from the library = we ~ed three books out from/ of the library)

sign over *v.* (B) she ~ed over the property to her children = she ~ed the property over to her children

sign up *v.* 1. (D; intr.) to ~ as (to ~ as a volunteer) 2. (D; intr., tr.) to ~ for (she ~ed up for an evening course; to sign smb. up for a course) 3. (D; intr., tr.) to ~ with (they ~ed up with the volunteers) 4. (E) they ~ed up to serve as volunteers 5. (H) they ~ed us up to serve as volunteers

silence *n.* 1. to impose ~ 2. to keep, maintain, observe ~ 3. to break (the) ~ 4. (an) absolute, complete, perfect, pindrop (South Asian English), total, utter ~ 5. a deep, pregnant, profound; prolonged; respectful, reverent ~ 6. (an) awkward; pained; shocked; stony; stunned ~ 7. a dead; eerie; hushed; ominous 8. ~ descends; reigns 9. in ~ (we were received in ~) 10. (misc.) radio ~; a conspiracy of ~; a vow of ~; a wall of ~; a deafening ~

silent *adj.* 1. absolutely, completely, totally, utterly ~ 2. to become, fall ~ 3. to keep, remain ~ 4. ~ about

silhouette *n.* in ~ (I saw it only in ~)

silhouetted *adj.* ~ against, on (~ against a light background)

silk *n.* ["fine fabric"] 1. to spin ~ 2. fine ~ 3. artificial, synthetic; natural; pure; raw ~ 4. (misc.) as smooth as ~ ["misc."] (BE) 5. to take ~ ("to become a King's Counsel or Queen's Counsel")

silkworm *n.* 1. to keep (BE), raise (esp. AE), rear (BE) ~s 2. ~s spin cocoons

silly *adj.* 1. ~ about 2. ~ to + inf. (it was ~ of/for her to say that = saying that was a ~ thing for her to do) 3. (misc.) to make smb. look ~

silver *n.* pure, sterling ~

similar *adj.* 1. distinctly, strikingly ~ 2. ~ in (~ in outlook) 3. ~ to (this specimen is ~ to that one)

similarity *n.* 1. to bear, have (a) ~ 2. a distinct, striking ~ 3. a ~ among, between; in; to (~ in outlook)

simmer *v.* (D; intr.) to ~ with (to ~ with excitement)

simple *adj.* ~ to + inf. (it was ~ to do the job = it was ~ doing the job = it was a ~ job to do = the job was ~ to do)

simultaneous *adj.* ~ with

sin I *n.* 1. to commit a ~ 2. to expiate a ~ 3. to absolve smb. of ~ 4. to forgive smb.'s ~ 5. a cardinal; deadly; inexpiable; mortal; unforgivable, unpardonable; venial ~ 6. original ~ 7. a ~ against 8. a ~ to + inf. (it's a ~ to tell a lie) 9. a ~ that + clause (it's a ~ that her talents are being wasted!) 10. (misc.) (obsol.) to live in ~ ("to live together without being married")

sin II *v.* (D; intr.) to ~ against

since *adv., conjunction, prep.* 1. ever ~ 2. long ~

sincere *adj.* 1. ~ about (she was ~ about her promise to retire) 2. ~ in (~ in one's beliefs)

sincerity *n.* 1. to demonstrate, show ~ 2. ~ in (she shows great ~ in her beliefs) 3. (misc.) to doubt smb.'s ~; in all ~

sinful *adj.* 1. ~ to + inf. (it is ~ to lie) 2. ~ that + clause (it's absolutely/positively ~ that her talents are being wasted!)

sing *v.* 1. (C; more rarely A) ~ a song for/to us; or: ~ us a song 2. (D; intr.) to ~ about, of 3. (D; intr.) to ~ to (to ~ to a piano accompaniment) 4. (D; intr.) to ~ with 5. (misc.) she can ~ in tune; to ~ out of tune; to ~ a baby to sleep

sing along *v.* (D; intr.) to ~ with (~ with me)

singer *n.* a blues; folk; jazz; lead; lieder; opera; pop ~

single-minded *adj.* ~ about

single out *v.* 1. (D; tr.) to ~ as (she was ~d out as the leading candidate) 2. (D; tr.) to ~ for (to ~ smb. out for special treatment) 3. (H) to ~ smb. out to get special treatment

singles *n.* (tennis) 1. to play doubles but not ~ 2. ladies' (BE), women's; men's ~ 3. (misc.) to play in the doubles but not in the ~

singular *n.* in the ~

sink I *n.* 1. the bathroom ~ (esp. AE; BE prefers *handbasin, wash-hand basin*) 2. a kitchen ~ 3. a ~ backs up; leaks

sink II *v.* 1. to ~ deep; like a stone 2. (d; intr.) to ~ below (to ~ below the surface) 3. (d; intr., tr.) to ~ into (to ~ into oblivion; to ~ one's teeth into a good steak) 4. (D; intr.) to ~ to (to ~ to the bottom; to ~ to one's knees) (see also *sink without trace* at **trace I** *n.*)

sink back *v.* 1. (D; intr.) to ~ against (she sank back against the cushions) 2. (D; intr.) to ~ into (to ~ into the bed)

sink down *v.* (D; intr.) to ~ into (his head sank down into the soft pillows)

sip *n.* 1. to have, take a ~ 2. (misc.) to drink water in ~s

siphon *v.* (D; tr.) to ~ from, out of (we had to ~ some gasoline/petrol from another car)

siphon off *v.* (D; tr.) to ~ from; onto, to (we had to ~ some gasoline/petrol from another car; the police ~ed off traffic from the main road onto/to a secondary road)

siren *n.* 1. to sound, turn on a ~ 2. an air-raid; ambulance; fire; police ~ 3. a ~ blares, goes off, sounds, wails; dies away

sister *n.* ["relative"] 1. a big, elder, older; kid (colloq.), little, younger; twin ~ 2. a foster; half ~; stepsister 3. a sister-in-law 4. a lay; soul ~ 5. a ~ to (she was like a ~ to us) ["senior nurse"] (BE) 6. a nursing; ward ~

sit *v.* 1. to ~ quietly, still; upright 2. (D; intr.) ("to be seated") to ~ around/round, at (to ~ around a table; to ~ at a desk; to ~ at a piano) 3. (d; intr.) ("to pose") to ~ for (to ~ for ¬a portrait/an artist¬) 4. (d; intr.) to ~ on ("to be a member of") (to ~ on a committee) 5. (d; intr.) to ~ through (we had to ~ through the whole boring speech) 6. (misc.) to ~ astride a horse; to ~ beside a lake; to ~ tight ("to refrain from taking action"); to ~ for an examination (BE) = to ~ an examination (BE) ("to take an examination"); to ~ on the bench ("to be a judge"); to be ~ting pretty ("to be well off and without problems") USAGE NOTE: You *sit on* smt. like a stool or short grass but you *sit in* smt. like an armchair or long grass.

sit down *v.* 1. to ~ hard 2. (d; intr.) to ~ to (to ~ to a meal)

site *n.* 1. to excavate a ~ 2. an archeological; battlefield; building, construction; burial; camping, campsite; caravan (BE), trailer (AE) ~ 3. at, on a certain ~ (the new church will be built on the ~ of the old cathedral) 4. (misc.) protective clothing must be worn on ~ (see also **web site**)

sit-in *n.* to conduct, hold; organize, stage a ~

sit in *v.* 1. (D; intr.) ("to attend") to ~ as (she sat in as our representative) 2. (D; intr.) to ~ for ("to replace") (she sat in for me while I was out of town) 3. (D; intr.) to ~ on ("to attend") (we sat in on a few meetings)

sitter *n.* a baby; house ~

sitting duck *n.* ["easy target"] a ~ duck

situated *adj.* 1. conveniently ~ 2. ~ for (a hotel ~ conveniently for the Lake District)

situation *n.* 1. to comprehend, grasp, size up, take in, understand a ~ 2. to accept; face, face up to a ~ 3. to deal with, handle a ~ 4. a pleasant; stable ~ 5. an awkward; delicate; embarrassing; tense; ticklish, touchy; tricky ~ 6. a complex, complicated; involved ~ 7. a Catch-22, crisis, emergency; critical; desperate; grave, serious; hopeless, no-win (colloq.); life-and-death ~ 8. a fluid, unstable;

explosive; intolerable; unpleasant ~ 9. the current, present ~ 10. the economic; housing; political; social ~ 11. the international, world; local; national ~ 12. a ~ deteriorates; improves 13. in a certain ~ (in the present ~) 14. (misc.) to take stock of the ~ USAGE NOTE: Some people prefer the simple nouns *crisis* and *emergency* to such phrases as *crisis situation* and *emergency situation*. However, *situation* can be useful in such more complex cases as *a Catch-22 situation, a no-win situation, a life-and-death situation, an I-won't-compromise-unless-you-do situation*.

sit-up *n.* ["exercise"] to do ~s

sit up *v.* 1. to ~ straight 2. (D; intr.) to ~ with (to ~ with a sick child) 3. (misc.) to ~ late; to ~ straight 4. to ~ and take notice

sit well *v.* (D; intr.) to ~ with ("to be accepted by") (such behavior doesn't ~ with them)

six-shooter *n.* see **pistol** 1–5, 7

size *n.* 1. (often clothing) to take; wear (a) certain ~ (what ~ do you wear?; I take a large ~; I wear ~ 42) 2. an enormous, tremendous; large; moderate; small ~ 3. (clothing) an extra-large; large; medium; small ~ 4. a standard ~ 5. the right; wrong ~ (they gave me the wrong ~) 6. (clothing) boys'; children's; girls'; junior (esp. AE); men's; misses'; women's ~s 7. life ~ 8. of a certain ~ (of enormous ~) 9. (misc.) what ~ shirt/shoes do you take/wear? to cut to ~

skate I *n.* 1. an ice; roller ~ 2. a pair of ~s

skate II *v.* (P; intr.) we ~d across the lake; the children ~d onto the thin ice; the children ~d on/over the thin ice

skate over *n.* (D; intr.) to ~ to (the children ~d over to us)

skater *n.* a figure; ice; roller; speed ~

skating *n.* figure; ice; roller; speed ~

skeleton *n.* a human ~

skeptical, sceptical *adj.* ~ about, of

skepticism, scepticism *n.* 1. to demonstrate, display ~ 2. to maintain (a) ~ 3. ~ about (to maintain a healthy ~ about smt.) 4. (misc.) an air of ~; to regard/view smt. with ~

sketch *n.* ["drawing"] 1. to do, draw, make a ~ 2. a charcoal; composite; freehand; pencil ~ 3. a rough ~ ["short essay"] 4. a brief, thumbnail ~ 5. a biographical ~ ["radio or television vignette"] 6. a comedy, comic ~ (see also *sketch show* at **show I** *n.*)

ski I *n.* a pair of ~s (see also **skis**)

ski II *v.* 1. (P; intr.) they skied across the valley; I skied down the trail 2. (misc.) to go ~ing

skid *v.* 1. (D; intr.) to ~ on (cars often ~ on ice) 2. (P; intr.) the bus ~ded into the ditch; the car ~ded off the road

skid row see **row I** *n.* 5

skids *n.* (colloq.) 1. to hit the ~s (esp. AE) ("to have difficulties") (her career has hit the ~) 2. on the ~ ("in difficulties") (her career is on the ~)

skiing *n.* cross-country; down-hill; water ~

skill *n.* 1. to acquire, develop, learn, master; hone a ~ 2. to demonstrate, display, show ~ 3. a basic ~ 4. consummate, great ~ 5. diplomatic; entrepreneurial; management, managerial; professional; technical; verbal ~ 6. coping; marketable; survival ~s 7. ~ at, in; with (~ at/in using a computer; ~ with one's hands) 8. the ~ to + inf. (she had the ~ to cope with a difficult job) 9. (misc.) to market one's ~s

skilled *adj.* 1. highly ~ 2. ~ at, in; with (~ at/in using a computer; ~ with one's hands)

skillful, skilful *adj.* 1. very ~ 2. ~ at, in; with (~ at/in using a computer; ~ with one's hands)

skim *v.* 1. (d; tr.) ("to remove") to ~ from (to ~ the fat from the soup) 2. (d; intr.) to ~ through ("to read quickly") (I ~med through the article and then I ~med through it again) 3. (P; intr., tr.) ("to bounce") the boy ~med stones along the surface of the water; the birds ~med across the lake

skimp *v.* (D; intr.) to ~ on (to ~ on food)

skin I *n.* 1. to tan a ~ 2. to cast, shed, slip (esp. AE) one's ~ (the snake shed its ~) 3. clear; delicate; fair; fine; sensitive, tender; smooth; soft ~ 4. chapped; dry; coarse, rough; mottled; oily ~ 5. dark; light ~ 6. (a) banana; human ~ 7. (sunburned) ~ blisters; peels 8. against; beneath, under; on ~ (I like the feel of silk against my ~) 9. (misc.) to save one's ~ ("to save one's life"); a thick ~ ("insensitivity"); a thin ~ ("excessive sensitivity"); to get under smb.'s ~ ("to irritate smb."); to break the ~

skin II *v.* to ~ smb. alive ("to punish smb. severely")

skip *v.* (P; intr.) to ~ from one topic to another; the child ~ped across the playground (see also *skip a grade* at **grade I** *n.*)

skirmish I *n.* 1. a border; brief; minor ~ 2. a ~ between; with (killed in a border skirmish with the enemy)

skirmish II *v.* (D; intr.) to ~ with

skirt I *n.* 1. to have a ~ on, to wear a ~ 2. to put on, slip on a ~ 3. to take off a ~ 4. to hem; lengthen; shorten a ~ 5. a divided; full; gored; long; short ~ 6. a miniskirt; pleated; slit; wraparound ~

skirt II *v.* (d; intr.) to ~ (a)round (they ~ed around the problem)

skis *n.* water ~ (see also **ski**)

skit *n.* 1. to do, perform a ~ on 2. a comedy, comic ~

skunk *n.* (misc.) to smell a ~ (esp. AE; colloq.) ("to sense trouble, to smell a rat")

sky *n.* 1. a blue, clear, cloudless, fair; starry ~ 2. a cloudy; dull, gray, overcast, sullen; (BE) mackerel ~ 3. a ~ clears up; clouds up, clouds over 4. a patch of (blue) ~ 5. the ~ above, over 6. in the ~ (we could see birds in the ~ above us) 7. (misc.) as high as the ~ = skyhigh

skyline *n.* 1. to dominate the ~ (the cathedral spire dominates the ~) 2. an imposing; jagged ~

skyscraper *n.* a huge; tall, towering ~

slab *n.* 1. a concrete; marble; mortuary; stone ~ 2. on a ~ (lying on a mortuary ~)

slack *n.* ["part that hangs loose"] 1. to take up the ~ (of a rope) 2. (misc.) (slang) to cut smb. some ~ ("to give smb. some leeway, to give smb. a break")

slacks *n.* 1. to have ~ on, to wear ~ 2. to put on ~ 3. to take off ~ 4. to button up; unbutton; unzip; zip up one's ~ 5. baggy; long; tight ~ 6. a pair of ~

slam *v.* (P; intr., tr.) she ~med the books down on the table; they ~med right into me; he ~med the door in my face

slander *n.* to spread ~

slang *n.* 1. army; prison; (Cockney) rhyming; student; underworld ~ 2. ~ for ("scram" is ~ for "go away"; what is "shooting gallery" slang for?) 3. in ~ (what does "shooting gallery" mean in ~?)

slanted *adj.* ["biased"] 1. unfairly ~ 2. ~ against; in favor of, towards (the article was ~ against our viewpoint)

slap I *n.* 1. to give smb. a ~ (in the face) 2. (misc.) a ~ in the face ("a direct insult") (the closure of our post office is a ~ in the face to the local community); a ~ on the wrist ("a gentle reprimand")

slap II *v.* 1. (d; intr.) ("to strike") to ~ against (the waves were ~ping against the sides of the boat) 2. (D; tr.) ("to strike") to ~ in (to ~ smb. in the face) 3. (d; tr.) ("to impose") to ~ on (to ~ new restrictions on exporters) 4. (misc.) to ~ smb. on the wrist ("to reprimand smb. gently"); to ~ a preservation order on (BE) (they were going to demolish the old building but the government ~ped a preservation order on it)

slash *v.* 1. (D; intr.) to ~ at (to ~ at smb. with a knife) 2. (D; tr.) to ~ in; on (she ~ed him on the face with her knife)

slate I *n.* ["record of past performance"] 1. a clean ~ (to start off with a clean ~) 2. (misc.) to wipe the ~ clean

slate II *v.* (colloq.) (BE) (D; tr.) ("to criticize severely") to ~ for (the play was ~d for its wooden dialogue)

slated *adj.* (AE) ["scheduled"] (cannot stand alone) 1. ~ for (~ for promotion) 2. ~ to + inf. (she is ~ to be promoted soon)

slaughter *n.* indiscriminate, mass, wanton, wholesale ~

slave I *n.* 1. to free, liberate a ~; to emancipate ~s 2. a fugitive, runaway ~ 3. (fig.) a ~ of; to (a ~ to a habit) 4. (misc.) to buy; sell ~s (see also *slave labor* at **labor I** *n.*)

slave II *v.* (d; intr.) to ~ over (to ~ over a hot stove)

slave away *v.* (D; intr.) to ~ at; over (to ~ over a hot stove)

slavery *n.* 1. to establish, introduce ~ 2. to abolish ~ 3. to free from ~ 4. to sell into ~ 5. white ~ (to sell smb. into white ~) 6. during, under ~ (can anyone remember what conditions were like under ~?)

sledding *n.* (colloq.) (AE) ["progress"] rough, tough ~

sleep I *n.* 1. to induce ~ 2. to get (enough) ~ 3. deep, heavy, profound, sound; fitful; light; restful ~ 4. (misc.) to fall into a deep ~; to go to ~; to walk in one's ~; to put to ~ (also fig. "to kill") (the vet had to put our poor old dog to ~); (also fig. "to make unconscious"); to lose ~ over ("to worry a great deal about"); one's beauty ~; to get/have a good night's ~ (see also *not get a wink of sleep* at **wink I** *n.*)

sleep II *v.* 1. to ~ fitfully; lightly; soundly, well 2. (D; intr.) to ~ on ("to postpone for a day") (to ~ on a decision) 3. (d; intr.) to ~ through (I slept through the lecture) 4. (d; intr.) to ~ with ("to have sexual relations with") 5. (misc.) my foot went to ~; ~ late; to ~ like a baby/log/top ("to sleep very soundly"); to ~ rough (BE) ("to sleep out of doors as through homelessness") (see also *not sleep a wink* at **wink I** *n.*)

sleeper *n.* a heavy, sound; light ~

sleet *n.* 1. to have ~ (we had ~ yesterday) 2. ~ falls; melts 3. in the ~ (to get caught in the ~) 4. through the ~ (to run through the ~)

sleeve *n.* 1. to roll up one's ~s 2. long; short ~s (I always wear ¬short ~s/short-sleeved shirts¬ during the summer) 3. in certain ~s (in the summer I always go around ¬in short ~s/in short-sleeved shirts¬) 4. on a ~ (I got some dirt on my left ~) 5. (misc.) to have smt. up one's ~ ("to have a secret trick"); to roll up one's ~s and get down to work ("to get down to serious work"); to laugh up one's ~ ("to laugh secretly"); in (one's) shirtsleeves (in the summer I take off my jacket and go around in my shirtsleeves)

slice I *n.* 1. to cut off a ~ (of) 2. to cut into ~s 3. a thick; thin ~ 4. (misc.) a ~ of life ("a realistic portrayal of life") (a somber slice-of-life drama that gives audiences a flavor of working-class life during the Great Depression)

slice II *v.* 1. (C) ~ a piece of cake for me; or: ~ me a piece of cake 2. (d; intr., tr.) to ~ into (to ~ into the cake; she ~d the cake into several portions) 3. (d; tr.) to ~ off (she ~d a small piece off the cake (for me)) 4. (d; intr.) to ~ through (the icebreaker ~d through the ice) 5. (N; used with an adjective) she ~d the bread thin

slice up *v.* (D; tr.) ~ into (she ~d up the cake into several portions = she ~d the cake up into several portions)

slick *n.* an oil ~

slide I *n.* a hair ~ (BE; AE has *barrette*) (see also **slides**)

slide II *v.* 1. (d; intr.) to ~ down (to ~ down a hill) 2. (d; intr.) to ~ from, out of (the glass slid from her hand) 3. (d; intr.) to ~ into (the car skidded and slid into a ditch) 4. (AE) (baseball) (D; intr.) to ~ into ("to occupy by sliding") (he slid into second base) 5. (N; used with an adjective) the door slid open but I slid it shut again 6. (P; intr., tr.) to ~ across a frozen pond

slide rule *n.* to operate, use a ~

slides *n.* 1. to project, show ~ 2. to make; mount ~ 3. to look at ~

slight *n.* (lit.) ["slur"] a ~ on, to (a ~ on smb.'s honor)

slime *n.* ~ oozes

sling I *n.* in a ~ (her arm was in a ~)

sling II *v.* 1. (D; tr.) to ~ at (to ~ stones at smb.) 2. (P; tr.) she slung the knapsack over her shoulder 3. (misc.) to ~ mud at smb. ("to slander smb.") (the media have been conducting a mud-slinging campaign against our candidate!)

slink *v.* (P; intr.) to ~ through the bushes

slip I *n.* ["error"] 1. to make a ~ (of the tongue) 2. a Freudian ~ ["escape"] (colloq.) 3. to give smb. the ~ ["small piece of paper"] 4. a credit, deposit, paying-in (BE) ~ (in a bank); a sales ~ (AE) 5. a call ~ ("request for a library book") 6. a pink ~ ("notice of termination of employment") 7. a rejection ~ ("notification that a manuscript has been rejected for publication") (see also *a slip of a girl* at **girl**; *a slip of paper* at **paper I** *n.*) ["cover"] 8. a pillow ~ USAGE NOTE: In AE, a *credit slip* indicates a credit for merchandise returned. BE uses *credit note*

slip II *v.* 1. (A) ("to hand") she ~ped a note to me; or: she ~ped me a note 2. (d; intr.) to ~ by, past ("to get by unnoticed") (they easily ~ped by the roadblock; they ~ped past the sentry) 3. (D; intr.) to ~ from, out of ("to fall from") (the glass ~ped out of her hand) 4. (d; intr.) ("to move quickly") to ~ into (to ~ into a room) 5. (d; intr.) to ~ into ("to change into") (to ~ into smt. more comfortable; to ~ into a dressing gown) 6. (d; tr.) to ~ into ("to insert surreptitiously") (to ~ a clause into a contract; she ~ped a note into his hand) 7. (D; intr.) ("to slide and fall") to ~ on (he ~ped on a banana peel) 8. (d; intr.) ("to move quickly") to ~ out of (to ~ out of a house) 9. (d; intr.) to ~ out of ("to take off") (he ~ped out of his sweat suit) 10. (d; intr., tr.) to ~ through ("to pass through; to cause to pass through") (several scouts ~ped through their lines; we were able to ~ an agent through their security net but we couldn't ~ another one through; the opportunity ~ped through his fingers) 11. (misc.) she let (it) ~ that she was going to retire

slipcovers *n.* 1. to make ~ 2. to put on ~ 3. custommade ~

slip out *v.* 1. (D; intr.) to ~ for (she ~ped out for a walk) 2. (D; intr.) to ~ to (they ~ped out to the bar/pub) 3. (misc.) she ~ped out (in order) to take a walk

slippers *n.* 1. house ~ 2. a pair of ~

slippery *adj.* 1. ~ with (a path ~ with mud) 2. (misc.) as ~ as an eel

slip up *v.* (D; intr.) ("to blunder") to ~ on (she ~ped up on the last question)

slit I *n.* a narrow ~

slit II *v.* (N; used with an adjective) she slit the envelope open

slither *v.* (P; intr.) to ~ along the ground

slobber *v.* (colloq.) to ~ all over smb.

slog I *n.* (esp. BE) a hard, tough ~

slog II *v.* (P; intr.) to ~ through the mud

slogan *n.* 1. to coin, devise a ~ 2. to chant a ~ 3. a catchy ~

slog away *v.* (D; intr.) to ~ at (to keep ~ging away at one's homework)

slope I *n.* 1. a gentle, gradual; steep ~ 2. a slippery ~ (may be fig.) (the first step on the slippery ~ to disaster) 3. a ski ~ 4. down; up a ~

slope II *v.* 1. to ~ gently, gradually 2. (P; intr.) the river bank ~s to the east

slope off *v.* (colloq.) (BE) (P; intr.) ("to slink") to ~ off to a pub; they ~d off home

slosh *v.* (P; intr.) to ~ through the snow

slot *n.* (colloq.) ["position"] to fill; fit into a ~

slouch I *n.* (colloq.) ["incompetent person"] no ~ at (she is no ~ at getting things done)

slouch II *v.* (D; intr.) to ~ over (she was ~ing over the table)

slouch down *v.* (D; intr.) to ~ behind (she ~ed down behind the steering wheel)

slow I *adj.* 1. ~ at, in (she was ~ in reacting) 2. ~ to + inf. (she was ~ to react) 3. (misc.) ~ of speech; ~ on one's feet; ~ on the uptake

slow II *v.* (D; intr., tr.) to ~ to (the influx of immigrants has ~ed to a trickle; she ~ed the car to a stop)

slow burn *n.* (slang) (AE) to do a ~ ("to become angry gradually") (the driver did a slow ~ when the other car got in his way)

slowdown *n.* 1. an economic ~ 2. a ~ in, of

slow motion *n.* ["slow-motion cinematography"] in ~ (they showed the finish in ~)

sludge *n.* activated ~

slug *v.* (colloq.) (esp. AE) 1. (O) (can be used with one animate object) ("to punch") I'll ~ you one 2. (misc.) to ~ it out with smb.

slum *v.* to go ~ming

slumber *n.* deep ~

slump I *n.* 1. a business, economic ~ 2. a ~ in (there is a ~ in the housing market) 3. in a ~ (the housing market is in a ~)

slump II *v.* 1. (D; intr.) to ~ to (the ground) 2. (P; intr.) she was ~ed over her typewriter; profits ~ed from a record high to a new low; profits have already ~ed (by) 10%

slums *n.* 1. to clean up, clear away, tear down ~ (see also *slum clearance* at **clearance**) 2. festering, squalid; inner-city, urban ~

slur I *n.* ["insult"] 1. to cast a ~ 2. an ethnic, racial ~ 3. a ~ on (his remark was a ~ on my character)

slur II *v.* (d; intr.) to ~ over ("to minimize") (esp. AE) (to ~ over a blunder)

sly I *adj.* as ~ as a fox (esp. AE)

sly II *n.* on the ~ (to do smt. on the ~)

smack I *n.* ["heroin"] (slang) to be on ~

smack II *v.* (colloq.) 1. (D; tr.) to ~ on (she ~ed the boy on his behind) 2. (O) (can be used with one animate object) I'll ~ you one

smack III v. (d; intr.) to ~ of ("to suggest") (to ~ of treason)

smallpox n. 1. to contract, develop, get; have ~ 2. to eradicate; immunize against, vaccinate against ~ 3. a case; epidemic; outbreak of ~

small talk n. to make ~ (at the party we made ~ about the weather; at office parties some people prefer to engage in shop talk but others prefer to make small ~)

smart I adj. ["impudent"] (colloq.) (esp. AE) 1. to get ~ with (don't get ~ with me!) ["shrewd"] 2. ~ to + inf. (she was ~ to refuse = it was ~ of for her to refuse = refusing was a ~ thing for her to do)

smart II v. 1. (D; intr.) to ~ at, over (to ~ at an insult) 2. (D; intr.) to ~ from (her eyes were ~ing from the smoke) 3. (D; intr.) to ~ under (to ~ under injustice)

smash v. 1. (d; intr., tr.) to ~ into (she ~ed into another car = she ~ed her car into another car) 2. (d; intr.) to ~ through (to ~ through a fence) 3. (misc.) she ~ed her fist down on the table

smattering n. to acquire, pick up a ~ of (they have picked up a ~ of the language)

smear I n. (med.) 1. to do, take a ~ 2. a Pap ~ (they did a Pap ~ on each patient)

smear II v. 1. (D; tr.) to ~ with (to ~ bread with butter) 2. (P; tr.) to ~ butter ¬on/all over¬ bread; to ~ ointment on one's skin

smell I n. 1. to give off; have a ~ 2. a clean; delicious, good; sweet ~ (the food has a delicious ~) 3. a faint, slight ~ 4. a lingering; persistent; strong ~ 5. an acrid; bad, dirty, disagreeable, foul, putrid, rank; musty; sour ~ (the room has a dirty ~) 6. a smell emanates from 7. a ~ permeates smt. (a delicious ~ permeated the entire room) 8. a ~ of (the ~ of paint) 9. a/the sense of ~

smell II v. 1. (D; intr.) to ~ like; of (that flower ~s like a rose; to ~ of fish) 2. (J) I could ~ smt. burning 3. (L) I could ~ that smt. was burning 4. (Q) I could ~ where the coffee was 5. (s) the food ~s good

smile I n. 1. to crack a ~; flash a ~ (at) 2. to give smb. a ~ 3. to evoke; wear a ~ 4. to hide, repress a ~ 5. a beautiful, lovely, pretty; beguiling, intriguing; cheerful, happy; broad; dazzling; disarming, engaging; friendly; infectious; pleasant; radiant; ready; sunny; sweet ~ 6. a bitter; fixed; forced; sardonic; supercilious ~ 7. a hint, trace of a ~ (the merest hint of a ~ flashed across his handsome features) 8. with a ~ (to answer with a ~ on one's face) 9. (misc.) they are all ~s at the good news

smile II v. 1. to ~ bitterly; broadly; cheerfully; coldly; sardonically; superciliously; sweetly 2. (D; intr.) to ~ at (the teacher ~ed at the well-behaved children) 3. (D; intr.) to ~ on ("to favor") (fortune ~d on us) 4. (misc.) to ~ from ear to ear; to ~ with pleasure/satisfaction; she ~d to herself at the thought of her successful trick

smirk v. (derog.) 1. (D; intr.) to ~ at 2. (D; intr.)

to ~ with (she ~ed with satisfaction at their embarrassment)

smite v. (formal) (N; used with an adjective) God smote the heathen dead (see also **smitten**)

smithereens n. to blow, break, smash smt. into, to ~

smitten adj. ["affected"] (formal) 1. ~ by, with (~ by disease) ["infatuated"] (colloq.) 2. ~ by, with (he was totally ~ with her)

smoke n. ["gaseous products of burning"] 1. to belch, emit, give off ~ (chimneys belch ~) 2. to exhale; inhale ~ 3. heavy, thick; light ~ 4. acrid; black ~ 5. cigar; cigarette ~ 6. (as of cigarettes) active; passive ~ 7. ~ pours, rises from (a chimney) 8. ~ eddies, spirals (upward) 9. a cloud; column; pall; pillar; puff; whiff; wisp of ~ 10. (misc.) to go up in ~ ("to disappear completely") (usu. fig.) (all our plans have gone up in ~!) (see also *a smoke-filled room* at **room**) ["act of smoking"] 11. to have a ~ 12. (to go out) for a ~

smoker n. a chain; habitual, heavy, inveterate; light; occasional; teenage ~

smoking n. 1. to cut down on; give up, stop; start; take up ~ 2. to ban, prohibit ~ 3. chain; habitual, heavy; light; occasional; passive; teenage ~ 4. (misc.) no ~!

smolder, smoulder v. (d; intr.) to ~ with (to ~ with discontent)

smooth adj. 1. ~ to (~ to the touch) 2. (misc.) as ~ as silk/velvet

smother v. (D; tr.) to ~ with (we ~ed the flames with a heavy blanket)

smuggle v. 1. (D; tr.) to ~ across (to ~ goods across a border) 2. (D; tr.) to ~ by, past, through (to ~ goods past customs) 3. (D; tr.) to ~ into (to ~ goods into a country) 4. (D; tr.) to ~ out of (to ~ stolen goods out of a country)

smuggling n. 1. to engage in ~ 2. arms; drug ~

smut n. a ~ peddler

snack I n. 1. to have a ~ 2. to fix, make ("prepare") a ~ 3. a between-meal(s); light; midnight; quick ~ 4. party ~s

snack II v. (D; intr.) to ~ on (to ~ on peanuts)

snag I n. ["obstacle"] (colloq.) 1. to hit a ~ (in) ["jagged tear"] 2. to get; have a ~ (in one's stocking)

snag II v. (D; tr.) to ~ on (I ~ged my stocking on a nail)

snake I n. 1. a poisonous, venomous; non-poisonous ~ 2. ~s bite, strike; coil; crawl; hibernate; hiss; slither 3. ~s molt, shed their skin 4. (misc.) a ~ in the grass ("a treacherous person")

snake II v. (colloq.) he ~d (his way) through the crowd

snap I n. ["spell of weather"] 1. a cold ~ ["something easy"] (colloq.) 2. a ~ to + inf. (it was a ~ to find information about that author = it was a ~ finding information about that author)

snap II v. 1. (D; intr.) to ~ at (the dog ~ped at him; to ~ at the bait) 2. (L; at) she ~ped (at me) that she

was too busy to help me = "I'm too busy to help you !" she ~ped (at me) 3. (misc.) to ~ to attention; to ~ out of a bad mood; the lid ~ped shut
snap back v. (L) when I asked her to help, she ~ped back (at me) that she was too busy
snappy adv. (colloq.) to make it ~ ("to hurry")
snapshot n. to take a ~
snarl v. 1. (B) she ~ed a few words to me 2. (D; intr.) to ~ at (the dog ~ed at him) 3. (L) he ~ed that he would be late = "I'm going to be late !" he ~ed
snatch I n. ["fragment"] to catch, hear; overhear ~es (of conversation)
snatch II v. 1. (d; intr.) to ~ at (she ~ed at the line that the sailors threw to her) 2. (D; tr.) to ~ from, out of (he ~ed the purse from her hand)
sneak v. (P; intr., tr.) they ~ed into the theater; they ~ed their friends into the theater; to ~ around in the bushes (see also *sneak a glance* at **glance I** n.)
sneak away v. see **sneak off**
sneak off v. 1. (D; intr.) to ~ from (she ~ed off from the others) 2. (D; intr.) to ~ to (he ~ed off to the football game) 3. (misc.) they ~ed off (in order) to see the football game
sneak up v. 1. (D; intr.) to ~ behind (he. ~ed up behind them) 2. (D; intr.) to ~ on, to (he ~ed up to them)
sneaky adj. (colloq.) 1. ~ of (that was ~ of him) 2. ~ to + inf. (it was ~ of/for him to do that = that was a ~ thing for him to do)
sneer v. (D; intr.) to ~ at
sneeze v. (colloq.) (d; intr.) to ~ at ("to consider lightly") (their offer is not to be ~d at)
sneezing n. a fit of ~ = a ~ fit
snicker v. (D; intr.) to ~ at
sniff I n. to get, have a ~
sniff II v. (D; intr.) to ~ at (the dog ~ed at her)
sniffles n. to have the ~
snigger v. (esp. BE) (D; intr.) to ~ about, at
snipe v. (D; intr.) to ~ at (the press keeps ~ing at her)
snit n. (colloq.) (AE) ["state of agitation"] in a ~
snitch v. (slang) (AE) (d; tr.) ("to inform against smb.") to ~ on (she ~ed on him to his teacher)
snob n. 1. an intellectual ~ 2. (BE) an inverted ~
snook n. (colloq.) (BE) to cock a ~ at ("to thumb one's nose at")
snore I n. a heavy, loud ~
snore II v. to ~ heavily, loudly
snow I n. 1. to have ~ (we had ~ yesterday) 2. deep; drifting; driving, heavy; falling; powdery; light; wet ~ 3. crisp; new-fallen ~ 4. ~ accumulates; falls; melts; sticks 5. a blanket; coating, dusting of ~ 6. across, through; in the ~ (to play in the ~) 7. (misc.) to clear away, remove, shovel ~; as white as ~ = snow-white; as pure as the driven ~ (see also *fall of snow, snowfall* at **fall I** n.; **snowball**; **snowfall**; *flake of snow, snowflake* at **flake**; *snow flurry* at **flurry**; *snowstorm* at **storm I** n. 3)

snow II v. to ~ hard, heavily; lightly (it began to ~ heavily)
snowball I n. to throw a ~ at
snowball II v. (D; intr.) ("to expand, mushroom") to ~ from; into, to
snowfall n. a heavy; light ~
snowman n. to build, make a ~
snowshoes n. 1. a pair of ~ 2. (to walk) on ~
snowstorm n. see **storm I** 3
snub n. a deliberate; obvious ~
snuff n. 1. to take ~ 2. a pinch of ~ 3. (misc.) not up to ~ ("not up to an acceptable standard")
snuggle v. (d; intr.) to ~ against (the children ~d against each other)
snuggle up v. (d; intr.) to ~ against; to (the children ~d up against each other; the little girl ~d up to her doll)
soak I n. to give; get; have a ~ (to give the laundry a ~ in cold water – and make sure it gets a good long ~ !)
soak v. 1. (D; intr., tr.) to ~ in (to ~ the laundry in cold water; the laundry ~ed in cold water) 2. (d; intr.) to ~ into (the water ~ed into the soil) 3. (d; intr.) to ~ through (the blood ~ed through the bandages)
soaked adj. 1. ~ to the skin 2. ~ through and through 3. thoroughly ~
soaking n. to give; get; have a ~ (to give the laundry a ~ in cold water – and make sure it gets a good long thorough ~ !)
soap n. 1. face; laundry; liquid; powdered; saddle; scented; toilet ~ 2. a bar, cake of ~ (see also *flake of soap, soapflake* at **flake**)
soar v. (d; intr.) to ~ into, to (the temperature ~ed into the eighties; the mercury ~ed to ninety; prices ~ed and then plummeted)
sob I n. 1. to give, let out a ~; be racked with ~s 2. to stifle a ~ 3. a bitter; choking ~ 4. ~s die down, subside
sob II v. 1. to ~ bitterly 2. (B) the child ~bed a few words to the teacher 3. (L; to) she ~bed (to her teacher) that she wanted to go home = "I want to go home !" she ~bed (to her teacher) 4. (misc.) to ~ oneself to sleep
sober adj. 1. cold, stone (AE) ~ 2. as ~ as a judge
soccer n. 1. to play ~ 2. the game of ~ 3. (misc.) a ~ ball; field (AE), pitch (BE); a ~ game (esp. AE), match (BE); player
socialism n. 1. to build; establish ~ 2. democratic; Fabian; Guild; left-wing; libertarian; moderate; scientific; state; utopian ~ 3. under ~ (to live under ~)
socialist n. 1. an avowed, self-styled ~ 2. a democratic; Fabian; Guild; left-wing; libertarian; moderate; scientific ~
socialize v. (D; intr.) to ~ with (she likes to ~ with her neighbors)
society n. ["group, association"] 1. to establish, found, set up; join a ~ 2. to disband, dissolve; leave,

resign from a ~ 3. a burial; historical; honor; humane; learned; literary; medical; musical; secret ~ 4. a friendly (BE), mutual-aid (AE) ~ 5. a building ~ (BE; AE has *building and loan association*) 6. a ~ for; of (she founded a ~ of scientists for peace in which we all were active) ["community"] 7. to polarize; unite a ~ 8. an advanced; affluent; civil; civilized; classless; consumer; primitive ~ 9. a multicultural; pluralistic ~ 10. a closed; open ~ 11. a matriarchal; patriarchal ~ 12. a capitalist; socialist ~ 13. the fabric, foundations, structure of ~ (your ideas threaten the very fabric of ~!) 14. a section of ~ (every section of ~ is against your ideas!) ["class"] 15. high; polite ~ 16. in ~ (such words are not used in polite ~)

sociology *n.* 1. the ~ of (the ~ of knowledge/religion) 2. in ~ (a degree in ~)

sock I *n.* 1. to knit ~s 2. to darn, mend a ~ 3. ankle, ankle-length; athletic; knee; stretch; tube ~s 4. a pair of ~s

sock II *v.* (colloq.) (D; tr.) ("to punch") to ~ in, on (he ~ed me on the jaw)

socket *n.* a wall ~ (to plug an appliance into a wall ~)

soda *n.* ["form of sodium"] 1. baking; caustic; washing ~ ["carbonated beverage"] 2. (a) club; cream; ice-cream ~ ["soda water"] 3. a dash of ~ 4. (misc.) (a) whiskey and ~

sodomy *n.* to commit, practice ~

sofa *n.* to lie; sit on a ~

soft *adj.* ~ on (this judge is not ~ on drunk drivers)

software *n.* 1. to write (the) ~ (for) 2. to download; run ~ 3. computer; proprietary; public-domain ~ 4. a piece of ~

soil I *n.* 1. to cultivate, till, work the ~ 2. to fertilize; irrigate the ~ 3. barren, poor; clayey; fertile; firm; good; packed; porous; rich; sandy; soggy; swampy ~; topsoil 4. in ~ (to plant crops in good ~)

soil II *v.* (D; tr.) to ~ on, with (she would not ~ her hands with such trash)

solace *n.* 1. great ~ 2. to find ~ in (their parents found great solace in the children) 3. to derive, get ~ from (their parents got great solace from the children) 4. a ~ to (the children were a great ~ to their parents) 5. a ~ to + inf. (it was a great ~ to their parents to have the children nearby) 6. a ~ that + clause (it was a great ~ to their parents that the children lived nearby)

solder *n.* to apply; melt ~

soldier *n.* 1. a career; common; fellow; foot; professional; seasoned ~ 2. a ~ enlists; fights; reenlists; serves; trains 3. a ~ defects, deserts; goes AWOL 4. (misc.) the Unknown Soldier; a ~ of fortune ("a mercenary"); a toy ~

sole I *n.* ["bottom part of a shoe"] 1. to put (new) ~s on shoes 2. a half ~

sole II *n.* ["type of fish"] 1. Dover; lemon ~ 2. (a) fillet of ~

solicit *v.* (D; intr., tr.) to ~ for; from (she was ~ing funds for the Red Cross from passers-by)

solicitor *n.* 1. The Solicitor General ("the assistant attorney general") 2. (GB) barristers and ~s

solicitous *adj.* ~ about, of

solicitude *n.* to show ~ for

solid *adj., adv.* 1. in liquid or in ~ form; to be in ~ with smb. (colloq. AE) 2. (misc.) as ~ as a rock

solidarity *n.* 1. to declare, express; feel; show ~ 2. ~ with (to express one's ~ with the protestors)

solitaire *n.* (AE) ["card game"] to play ~ (BE has *patience*)

solitude *n.* 1. complete, utter ~ 2. in ~ (to live in complete ~)

solo I *adv.* to dance; fly; perform; play; sing ~

solo II *n.* to perform a ~

solstice *n.* the summer; winter ~

soluble *adj.* ~ in (water) = water-soluble

solution *n.* ["answer"] ["explanation"] 1. to come up with, find; offer; propose a ~ 2. to apply a ~ 3. a definitive, final; effective; equitable; neat; satisfactory ~ 4. a creative; ideal; ingenious ~ 5. an easy; simple ~ 6. a military; political ~ 7. a permanent; temporary ~ 8. a ~ for, to (a ~ to a problem) ["mixture"] 9. to dilute a ~ 10. a strong; weak ~ 11. an antiseptic; chemical; saline ~ 12. in ~ (salt in ~)

some *pronoun, determiner* 1. ~ to + inf. (we have ~ to sell; we have ~ books to sell) 2. ~ of (~ of them) USAGE NOTE: The use of the preposition *of* is necessary when a pronoun follows. When a noun follows, the use of *of the* limits the meaning – we saw some people; we saw some of the people whom we had discussed earlier. (See also the Usage Note for **something**)

somebody *pronoun* ~ to + inf. (we have ~ to talk to) (see also the Usage Note for **something**)

someone see **somebody**

someplace (AE) see **somewhere**

somersault *n.* to do, execute, turn a ~

something *n., pronoun* 1. a certain, indefinable, indescribable, intangible ~ 2. ~ for (she has ~ for you) 3. ~ to + inf. (we have ~ to say) 4. (misc.) to make ~ of oneself ("to have success in life"); ("slang") I don't know if he wants to make ~ of it ("I don't know if he wants to make an issue of it"); there is ~ unusual about them; she is ~ of a celebrity USAGE NOTE: The form *some* and its compounds are often used in affirmative statements, whereas *any* and its compounds are often used in neg. and interrogative contexts. Compare *we have some books to sell – we don't have any books to sell; we have something to say – do you have anything to say?; we have somebody to talk to – we don't have anybody to talk to; we have somewhere to go – do you have anywhere to go?* However, *some* and its compounds can also be used in neg. and esp. in interrogative contexts (as when an affirmative answer is expected) – *don't you have something to* *say? would you like some brandy? do you have something to say? (Then say it!)*; *if you don't have something/anything relevant to say, then shut up!* Moreover, in the meaning "no matter which/what/who(m)/where...", *any* and its compounds occur in affirmative statements – *we will take any of these; they can say anything they want; we will talk to anyone; we will go anywhere.*

somewhere *adv.* ~ to + inf. (we have ~ to go) (see also the Usage Note for **something**)

son *n.* 1. to adopt a ~ 2. to marry off a ~ 3. an older; only; younger ~ 4. an adopted; foster ~; stepson 5. a son-in-law 6. a ~ to (he was like a ~ to them) 7. (misc.) a favorite ~ (AE; pol.); a prodigal ~ (fig.)

sonar *n.* to track by ~

song *n.* 1. to compose, write a ~ 2. to belt out (colloq.), sing; hum; play; whistle a ~ (the orchestra was playing our ~) 3. a drinking; folk; love, torch; marching; popular; theme; title ~ 4. smb.'s swan ("farewell") ~ 5. a ~ about 6. in a ~ 7. (misc.) the same old ~ ("the same story, complaint"); to burst into ~; for a ~ ("inexpensively") (see also *the lyrics of a song* at **lyrics**; *the words of/to a song* at **words**)

sonnet *n.* 1. to compose, write a ~ 2. an Italian, Petrarchan; Shakespearean; Spenserian ~

soot *n.* (all) covered in, with ~

sop *n.* ["concession"] 1. to throw a ~ to 2. as a ~ to

sophistication *n.* 1. to display, show ~ (she showed great ~ in dealing with their questions) 2. with ~ (she dealt with their questions with great ~) 3. the ~ to + inf. (she had enough ~ to deal with their questions)

sophistry *n.* 1. pure ~ 2. ~ to + inf. (it's pure ~ to extenuate such behavior!)

sophomore *n.* (AE) a college, university; high-school ~

soprano *n.* 1. to sing ~ 2. a coloratura ~

sorcery *n.* to practice ~

sore I *adj.* ["angry"] (colloq.) (esp. AE) 1. to get ~ 2. ~ about, over (~ over smb.'s remark) ~ 3. ~ at (why is she ~ at me?) ["hurt, aching"] 4. to be; get ~ 5. ~ from (she's ~ from riding horseback)

sore II *n.* a bedsore; canker; cold; open, running; saddle ~

soreness *n.* 1. to cause; reduce ~ 2. mild; severe ~ 3. ~ subsides 4. ~ in (to reduce ~ in the legs)

sorority *n.* (US) 1. to pledge a ~ ("to agree to join a sorority") 2. a college ~ (see also **fraternity**)

sorrow *n.* 1. to cause ~ 2. to express; feel; show ~ 3. to alleviate smb.'s ~ 4. deep, great, inexpressible, keen, profound ~ 5. genuine, real; personal ~ 6. ~ at, over (to feel deep ~ at the death of a friend) 7. in, with ~ 8. to smb.'s ~ (to my great ~ I never saw them again) 9. (misc.) an expression; feeling of ~

sorry *adj.* 1. dreadfully, terribly, very ~ 2. genuinely, really ~ 3. to feel ~ 4. ~ about (I'm ~ about your loss) 5. ~ for (she is ~ for him; we are ~ for being late; I feel ~ for you; I'm ~ for your loss

(esp. AE)) 6. ~ to + inf. (I am ~ to (have to) inform you that your application has been rejected) 7. ~ that + clause (we are ~ that we were late)

sort I *n.* 1. a bad; curious; good ~ (a curious ~ of (a) life) 2. of a ~ (of all ~s; of several ~s; a person of that ~ = that ~ of person) 3. (misc.) ~ of thing (always going on about his enemies, his problems – (that) ~ of thing); to like all ~s of music; "was it satisfactory?" "it was nothing of the – – it was awful!"; to be out of ~s ("to be annoyed") (see also **sort of**)

sort II *v.* 1. (D; tr.) to ~ by (to ~ merchandise by size) 2. (D; tr.) to ~ into (to ~ socks into various sizes) 3. (D; intr.) to ~ through (to ~ through old documents)

sortie *n.* 1. to carry out, make a ~ 2. to fly a ~

sort of *adv.* (colloq.) ["more or less, rather"] I ~ expected it (to happen); it was ~ nice, actually

sort out *v.* 1. (D; tr.) to ~ from (to ~ the current receipts from the old ones) 2. (Q) we had to ~ how many votes each one received

SOS *n.* 1. to broadcast, send an ~ 2. to receive an ~

soul *n.* 1. to save smb.'s ~ 2. to bare; search one's ~ 3. an artistic; immortal; kindly; kindred; lost; poor; timid ~ 4. (misc.) body and ~ (I earn hardly enough to make ends meet and keep body and ~ together!); heart and ~ (I'll support you heart and ~!)

sound I *adj.* ["healthy"] 1. ~ in, of (~ in mind and body) 2. (misc.) safe and ~ ["sturdy"] 3. structurally ~

sound II *n.* 1. to emit, make, produce, utter a ~ 2. to transmit (a) ~ 3. to articulate, enunciate, pronounce a ~ 4. to turn down; turn up the ~ (on a radio, TV set) 5. to carry ~ (air carries ~s) 6. a clear; consonant; faint; hollow; inarticulate; loud; muffled; rasping; soft; vowel ~ 7. (a) ~ travels (~ travels much slower than light) 8. a ~ dies away, dies down; rings out 9. at a ~ (at the ~ of the bell, they all assembled) 10. to a ~ (to the ~ of music)

sound III *v.* 1. (D; intr.) to ~ for (the bell ~ed for dinner) 2. (d; intr.) to ~ like (that ~s like a great idea) 3. (BE) (S) that ~s a great idea 4. (s) their excuse ~ed reasonable 5. (misc.) it ~s as if/as though/like (colloq.) they don't know what to do; how does that ~ to you?

sound off *v.* (colloq.) (D; intr.) to ~ about, against ("to criticize") (to ~ against an idea)

sound out *v.* (D; tr.) ("to inquire") to ~ about (I ~ed the experts out about the problem = I ~ed out the experts about the problem)

soup *n.* 1. to eat; make; serve ~ 2. clear; cold; hot; thick; warm ~ 3. cabbage; celery; chicken; mushroom; noodle; onion; pea; tomato; vegetable ~ 4. a bowl; cup; mug; spoonful of ~ USAGE NOTE: We eat soup with a spoon; but we can drink soup from a cup or mug.

sour I *adj.* to go, turn ~ (things went ~; the whole affair turned ~)

sour II *v.* (d; intr.) to ~ on (AE) (they quickly ~ed on the idea)

source *n.* 1. to locate, track down a ~ 2. to tap a ~ 3. to cite; disclose, indicate, reveal one's ~s 4. an impeccable, unimpeachable; informed, well-informed; reliable, reputable, trustworthy ~; one's ~s (according to my ~s, there will be trouble ahead) 5. an unreliable ~ 6. an undisclosed, unnamed ~ 7. an original, primary; secondary ~ 8. an energy; renewable ~ 9. ~s dry up 10. at a ~ (it is best to make inquiries at the original ~) 11. (misc.) ~s close to the government revealed that...; (BE) tax deducted at ~

south I *adj., adv.* 1. directly, due, straight ~ 2. ~ of (~ of the city) 3. down ~ 4. (misc.) to face; to go, head ~; southeast by ~; southwest by ~

south II *n.* 1. from the ~; in the ~; to the ~ 2. (misc.) the Deep South ("certain areas of the southern United States")

southeast I *adj., adv.* 1. ~ of (to be ~ of the city) 2. (misc.) to go, head ~; south by ~

southeast II *n.* from; in; to the ~

South Pole *n.* at the ~

southwest I *adj., adv.* 1. ~ of (to be ~ of the city) 2. (misc.) to go, head ~; south by ~

southwest II *n.* from; in; to the ~

sovereignty *n.* 1. to grant ~ 2. to assert; claim; establish; exercise ~ 3. to violate a country's ~ 4. ~ over

space *n.* 1. to save ~ 2. to clear a ~ 3. to take up ~ 4. to fill (in) the ~s 5. breathing ~ 6. (a) blank, empty ~ 7. a crawl (AE); parking ~ 8. office; storage ~ 9. interplanetary; interstellar; outer ~ (see also **air space**) 10. (a) ~ between 11. (a) ~ for 12. in ~ (to travel in ~) 13. (misc.) the (wide) open ~s; to indent several ~s; to fill every available ~

spacecraft *n.* 1. a manned; unmanned ~ (see the Usage Note for **ship**) 2. a ~ docks

spaceflight *n.* 1. to abort a ~ 2. a manned; unmanned ~ 3. a ~ to (a ~ to the moon)

space vehicle *n.* to launch a ~ (see the Usage Note for **ship**)

spacing *n.* (on a typewriter or word processor) double; single ~

spadework *n.* ["preparations"] to do the ~

span *n.* 1. a brief, short ~ 2. an attention; life; memory ~ 3. a wing ~ 4. in a certain ~ (in the brief ~ of ten years) 5. (misc.) over a ~ of five years = over a five-year ~; records covering the whole ~ of contemporary history

spanking *n.* 1. to give smb. a (good) ~ 2. to get a ~ (he got a good ~ for his misbehavior) 3. (misc.) to deserve a ~

spanner *n.* a box ~ (BE; AE has *lug wrench*)

spar *v.* (D; intr.) ("to fight") to ~ over; with

spare *v.* 1. (C) can you ~ a few minutes for me today? or: can you ~ me a few minutes today?; can you ~ some change for a beggar ~ or: can you ~ a beggar some change? 2. (O; can be used with one animate object) ~ us the gory details!; he wanted to ~ you embarrassment 3. (misc.) we got there

with a few minutes to ~; we got there with time to ~ ("we got there early")

sparing *adj.* (cannot stand alone) ~ of (she's not ~ of herself!)

spark *n.* 1. to emit, produce a ~ 2. ~s fly 3. (misc.) a shower of ~s

sparkle *v.* (D; intr.) to ~ with (to ~ with humor)

sparrow *n.* 1. ~s chirp 2. a flock of ~s

spasm *n.* 1. (a) coughing; muscle ~ 2. to go into ~ (my muscles went into ~) 3. to be in ~ (my muscles are in ~) 4. a ~ passes, subsides (my muscle ~ subsided eventually)

spat I *n.* ["quarrel"] to have a ~ with

spat II *v.* (D; intr.) ("to quarrel") to ~ with

spatter *v.* 1. (D; tr.) to ~ with (the car ~ed me with mud) 2. (D; tr.) to ~ (all) over (the car ~ed mud (all) over me) 3. (P; intr.) the paint ~ed everywhere!

speak *v.* ("to talk") 1. to ~ glibly; loudly; quickly, rapidly; quietly, softly; slowly 2. to ~ clearly, distinctly; coherently; correctly; fluently; politely 3. to ~ bluntly, candidly, frankly, freely; openly; responsibly; truthfully 4. to ~ incorrectly; irresponsibly; rudely 5. (D; intr.) to ~ about, of, on (to ~ about politics) 6. (d; intr.) to ~ against; for, in favor of (to ~ against a bill) 7. (d; intr.) to ~ as (to ~ as the party candidate) 8. (d; intr.) to ~ for, on behalf of ("to be a spokesperson for") (she spoke for all of us; who will ~ for the accused?; "Speak for England, Arthur!" – Leo Amery, M.P., September 2, 1939) 9. (d; intr.) to ~ from (to ~ from the heart; to ~ from experience) 10. (d; intr.) ("to converse") to ~ in (they were ~ing in English; more usu. is: they were ~ing English) 11. (d; intr.) to ~ to ("to address") (she spoke to the crowd; to ~ to the subject; to ~ to the question on the agenda; don't ~ to him) 12. (D; intr.) ("to converse") to ~ to, (esp. AE) with (she spoke to me about several things; (esp. AE) I spoke with them for an hour) 13. (misc.) to ~ well of smb. ("to praise smb."); to ~ ill of smb. ("to criticize smb."); it ~s for itself ("it is self-evident"); roughly ~ing ("approximately"); strictly ~ing ("in exact terms"); generally ~ing

speaker *n.* ["one who speaks"] 1. a native ~ (of a language) 2. an effective, good; eloquent; fluent ~ 3. a poor ~ 4. an after-dinner; guest; public ~ (she is a good public ~) ["device that amplifies sound"] 5. an extension ~; loudspeaker ["misc."] 6. the Speaker of the House (addressed as Mister Speaker or as Madam Speaker)

speaking *n.* public ~

speak out *v.* 1. (D; intr.) to ~ about, concerning, on (to ~ on a subject) 2. (d; intr.) to ~ against ("to oppose") (to ~ against a proposal) 3. (d; intr.) to ~ for, in favor of, on behalf of ("to support") (to ~ for a proposal)

speak up see **speak out**

spear *n.* 1. to hurl, throw a ~ at 2. to thrust a ~ into 3. the point of a ~

spearhead *n.* 1. to send out a ~ 2. an armored ~

special I *adj.* 1. ~ about (there was smt. ~ about her) 2. ~ to 3. extra-special

special II *n.* ["special program"] 1. a TV ~ ["reduced price"] 2. to offer a ~ (on)

specialist *n.* 1. to call in; consult a ~ 2. a ~ in, on (a ~ in plastic surgery; a ~ on Milton)

specialize *v.* (D; intr.) to ~ in

species *n.* 1. an endangered; protected ~ 2. an animal; plant ~ = a ~ of animal; of plant 3. a ~ becomes extinct, dies out; is reintroduced; survives 4. a member of a ~

specific *adj.* 1. ~ about 2. ~ to (these symptoms are ~ to liver disease)

specifications *n.* 1. to adhere to, meet ~ 2. rigid ~

specifics *n.* to get down to ~

specify *v.* 1. (D; tr.) to ~ by (to ~ smb. by name) 2. (L) the contract ~fies that a penalty must be paid if the work is not completed on time 3. (Q) the instructions ~ how the medicine is to be taken

specimen *n.* 1. to get; take a ~ 2. to give, provide a ~ 3. a blood; sputum; stool; urine ~

specs (colloq.) see **specifications**, **spectacles**

spectacle *n.* ["show, exhibition"] 1. to stage a ~ 2. a dramatic ~ ["object of curiosity"] 3. to make a ~ of oneself 4. a curious; magnificent; pitiful; ridiculous ~

spectacles *n.* (now esp. BE) 1. to need; put on; take off; wear ~ 2. to be fitted for ~ 3. horn-rimmed; steel-rimmed ~ 4. a pair of ~

spectators *n.* to seat ~ (the stadium seats sixty thousand ~)

spectrum *n.* 1. a broad, wide ~ 2. (misc.) there was wholehearted endorsement for/of the plan from both ends of the political ~

speculate *v.* 1. (D; intr.) ("to meditate, think") to ~ about, on (to ~ about the election results) 2. (D; intr.) ("to conduct business by taking risks") to ~ in; on (to ~ in oil shares; to ~ in gold; to ~ on the stock market) 3. (L) ("to assume, think") they ~d that the election results would be close

speculation *n.* ["meditation, thinking"] 1. to indulge in ~ 2. idle; pure; widespread; wild ~ 3. ~ is rife 4. a flurry of ~ 5. ~ about, over (~ about the upcoming elections) 6. ~ that + clause (there was ~ that the election results would be close) ["risky business methods"] 7. to engage in ~ 8. property (BE), real-estate (AE); stock-market ~ 9. ~ in (~ in stocks and bonds)

speculator *n.* a property (BE), real-estate (AE); stock-market ~

speculum *n.* a nasal; vaginal ~

speech *n.* ["address, talk"] 1. to deliver, give, make a ~ (to) 2. to ad-lib, improvise a ~ 3. an eloquent; passionate; rousing, stirring ~ 4. a brief, short; impromptu, unrehearsed ~ 5. a boring; long; long-winded; rambling ~ 6. an acceptance; after-dinner; campaign; farewell; inaugural; keynote; maiden; nominating; political; welcoming ~ 7. a ~ about, on; in (to deliver a ~ about climate change in German to a large audience) 8. during; in a ~

(there was a lot of applause during the ~ and there were a lot of good points in it) ["communication in words"] 9. free ~ = freedom of ~ 10. a figure of ~ ["pronunciation"] 11. clipped ~ 12. impaired; slurred ~ ["smb.'s words"] 13. direct; indirect; reported ~

speechless *adj.* 1. to be left ~ 2. ~ with (~ with anger)

speed I *n.* ["swiftness, velocity"] 1. to build up, gain, gather, increase, pick up; maintain (a) ~ 2. to reach a ~ (to reach cruising ~; to reach a ~ of one hundred miles an hour) 3. to decrease, reduce; lose ~ 4. (a) breakneck, breathtaking, high, lightning; cruising; deliberate; full, maximum, top; low; moderate; steady; supersonic ~ 5. a burst of ~ 6. at a certain ~ (at top ~; to travel at a ~ of one hundred miles per hour) 7. with a certain ~ (they finished the work with great ~; with all deliberate ~) 8. (misc.) to adjust the idling ~ on an engine; full ~ ahead!; at ~ (BE) ("at high speed") (the car raced through the village at ~) ["amphetamines"] (slang) 9. to shoot; snort ~ 10. to be on ~

speed *v.* (P; intr., tr.) to ~ south; to ~ smb. to the airport

speed limit *n.* 1. to enforce; establish, impose, set a ~ 2. to keep to, observe a ~ 3. to exceed a ~ 4. at; below, under; over; within the ~

spell I *n.* ["incantation"] 1. to cast a ~ on, over 2. to put smb. under a ~ 3. to break, remove a ~ 4. to fall under smb.'s ~ 5. a magic ~ 6. under a ~

spell II *n.* ["period"] 1. a cold; hot; rainy; sunny; warm ~ 2. a long; short ~ 3. a ~ as (he had a short ~ as a game-show host) ["period of illness"] 4. a coughing; dizzy; fainting ~ (she had been having dizzy ~s)

spellbinding *adj.* ~ to + inf. (it's ~ to read her memoirs = her memoirs are ~ to read)

spell check *n.* to do, run a ~ (she ran a ~ on her computer)

spelling *n.* 1. phonetic ~ 2. (a) correct; incorrect; variant ~ 3. in (phonetic) ~

spell out *v.* 1. (B) they ~ed out their demands to us in considerable detail 2. (Q; to) do I have to ~ (to you) why I did it? 3. (misc.) "why did you do it?" "do I really have to spell it out to/for you? I did it because I had to!"

spend *v.* 1. (D; tr.) to ~ for, on (to ~ a lot of money for/on a new car; to ~ a lot on repairs; during the severe winter we spent lots of money on fuel) 2. (D; tr.) to ~ in (to ~ a great deal of time in studying) 3. (J) to ~ a great deal of time studying; they spent the whole week hiking through the mountains

spender *n.* a big ~

spending *n.* 1. to boost, increase ~ 2. to cap, limit; curtail, cut, cut back (on), decrease ~ 3. deficit; defense; government, public; military; welfare ~

sperm count *n.* a low; normal; high ~

spew *v.* 1. (d; intr.) to ~ from, out of (lava ~ed from the crater) 2. (d; intr.) to ~ into (fumes ~ed into the atmosphere)

spice I *n.* 1. to add ~(s) 2. ground ~(s)

spice II *v.* (d; tr.) to ~ with (to ~ a cake with cinnamon)

spider *n.* 1. ~s crawl 2. ~s spin webs

spike *v.* (D; tr.) to ~ with (to ~ the punch with rum)

spill I *n.* ["accidental pouring"] 1. an oil ~ ["fall"] 2. to take a ~ (from a horse) 3. a nasty ~

spill II *v.* 1. (D; tr.) to ~ all over, on (I ~ed the milk all over her) 2. (d; intr.) ("to pour") to ~ into (the crowd was ~ing into the streets) 3. (d; intr.) ("to flow") to ~ out of (the liquid was ~ing out of the container)

spill over *v.* (D; intr.) to ~ into (the crowd was ~ing over into the adjacent streets)

spin I *n.* ["fast drive"] (colloq.) 1. to go for, take a ~ (let's go for a ~ around town) ["fall"] 2. to go into a ~ (the plane went into a (flat) ~; the market went into a ~) 3. to come out of a ~ ["rotation"] 4. to put a ~ on smt. (to put a ~ on a tennis ball) (see also *spin bowling* at **bowling**) ["interpretation"] 5. to put a ~ on smt. 6. a political; positive ~ (see also *spin doctor* at **doctor**; *spin dryer* at **dryer**)

spin II *v.* 1. (D; tr.) ("to make") to ~ from, out of; into (to ~ wool into yarn = to ~ yarn out of wool) 2. (D; intr.) ("to turn") to ~ on (a wheel ~s on its axle)

spinal tap *n.* to do a ~ (on smb.)

spin-off *n.* a ~ from

spiral I *n.* an inflationary; wage-price ~ (a vicious inflationary ~)

spiral II *v.* (d; intr.) to ~ to (the plane ~ed to earth)

spirit *n.* ["vigor"]["enthusiasm"] 1. to display, show ~ 2. to catch the ~ (of the times) 3. to break smb.'s ~ (her ~ was broken by torture) 4. (a) civic; community; ecumenical; patriotic ~ 5. (a) religious; scientific ~ 6. (a) class; college; school; team ~ 7. (a) competitive; partisan; rebellious ~ 8. a dauntless, hardy ~; (a) fighting; indomitable ~ 9. a guiding; moving ~ 10. with ~ (to work with great ~) 11. (misc.) a ~ of good will pervaded the conversation ["supernatural being, ghost"] 12. to call up, conjure up, invoke a ~ 13. an evil; holy ~ ["soul"] 14. a kindred ~ 15. in ~ (we are with you in ~) ["attitude"] 16. in a ~ (in a ~ of cooperation) 17. (misc.) the letter and the ~ of the law (see also **spirits**)

spirit away *v.* (D; tr.) to ~ from; to (she was ~ed away to the islands for a vacation)

spirit off *v.* (D; tr.) to ~ to (he was ~ed off to prison)

spirits *n.* ["mood, morale"] 1. to boost, lift, raise smb.'s ~; to keep one's ~ up 2. to dampen smb.'s ~ 3. good, high; low ~ 4. ~ droop, flag, sink; rise 5. in ~ (in high ~ = high-spirited) ["alcohol"] 6. to drink ~ 7. a bottle; glass of ~

spit *v.* 1. (D; intr.) to ~ at; on 2. (d; intr.) to ~ in, into (to ~ in smb.'s face) 3. (d; tr.) to ~ out of (to ~ smt. out of one's mouth)

spite *n.* 1. in ~ of (they did it in ~ of my advice = they did it despite my advice) 2. out of ~ (they did it out of (pure) ~)

spiteful *adj.* ~ to + inf. (it was ~ of/for him to say that = that was a ~ thing for him to say)

splash I *n.* (colloq.) ["vivid impression"] to make a (big) ~

splash II *v.* 1. (D; intr., tr.) to ~ against, on, over (the waves ~ed against the rocks; they ~ed water (all) over me) 2. (D; tr.) to ~ with (they ~ed me with water) 3. (misc.) the boys ~ed through the puddle; the children were ~ing around in the water

splashdown *n.* to make a ~ (in)

splatter *v.* 1. (d; tr.) to ~ with (the car ~ed me with mud) 2. (d; tr.) to ~ (all) over (the car ~ed mud (all) over me) 3. (P; intr.) the paint ~ed everywhere!; mud ~ed against the windows of the car

spleen *n.* ["bad temper"] 1. to vent one's ~ on ["ductless organ near the stomach"] 2. a ruptured ~

splendid *adj.* ~ to + inf. (it was ~ of you to make the offer = that was a ~ offer for you to make)

splendor, splendour *n.* 1. regal ~ 2. in ~ (to dine in regal ~)

splice *v.* 1. (D; tr.) to ~ to (to ~ a wire to a cable = to ~ a wire and a cable to each other) 2. (D; tr.) to ~ with (to ~ a wire with tape) 3. (misc.) to ~ a wire and a cable together

splint *n.* 1. to apply a ~ to; to put a ~ on 2. a ~ for (a fractured leg)

splinter *n.* 1. to get; have a ~ (in one's finger) 2. to extract, get out, remove a ~ (she got out of my finger the ~ that had lodged there)

split I *n.* ["breach"] 1. to lead to; produce a ~ 2. a formal; irreparable ~ 3. a ~ between; with (she feared an irreparable ~ with her boyfriend) 4. a ~ in (the party) (the disagreement led to an irreparable ~ in the party between its two wings)

split II *v.* 1. to ~ formally; irreparably 2. (d; tr.) ("to divide") to ~ among, between; with (we split the profits with them rather than ~ting the profits among ourselves) 3. (d; intr., tr.) ("to divide") to ~ into (they split the party into several factions = the party split into several factions; the teacher split the class into two groups) 4. (misc.) the vote (was) split along party lines, with one wing ~ting from the party altogether; we split the profits five ways

split up *v.* 1. (D; intr., tr.) to ~ into (they split the party up into several factions = the party split up into several factions) 2. (colloq.) (D; intr., tr.) to ~ with (she split up with her boyfriend = she and her boyfriend split up with each other; what split her and her boyfriend up with each other?) 3. (misc.) we split the profits up five ways = we split up the profits five ways

splurge *v.* (colloq.) (D; intr.) ("to spend extravagantly") to ~ on (to ~ on a new car)

splutter *v.* (D; intr.) to ~ with (to ~ with rage)

spoil *v.* 1. (d; intr.; usu. in a progressive form) to ~ for ("to seek") (to be ~ing for a fight) 2. (misc.) (BE) to ~ smb. rotten (I love my grand-children but I don't want to ~ them rotten!) (see also *spoilt for choice* at **choice**)

spoils *n.* 1. to divide the ~ (of war) 2. (misc.) a division of the ~ (they argued over the division of the ~)

spoken *adj.* ~ for ("reserved")

spokesman see **spokesperson**

spokesperson *n.* a ~ for (a ~ for the strikers)

spokeswoman see **spokesperson**

sponge I *n.* ["symbol of surrender"] 1. to squeeze a ~ ["spongy substance"] 2. to throw in, toss in the ~

sponge II *v.* (colloq.) 1. (D; tr.) ("to wheedle") to ~ from, off, off of (AE) (he ~d a cigarette from me) 2. (d; intr.) to ~ off (of), on ("to impose on") (to ~ on one's friends)

sponsor I *n.* 1. a radio; television, TV ~ 2. a ~ for, of

sponsor II *v.* 1. (D; tr.) to ~ for (she ~ed me for membership) 2. (H) she ~ed me to become a member

sponsorship *n.* 1. ~ for, of (her ~ of me for membership) 2. under smb.'s ~ (I became a member under her ~)

spoof *n.* ["parody"] a ~ of, on (it was a ~ on the political campaign)

spoon *n.* a coffee; dessert; measuring; soup ~; tablespoon; teaspoon

spoonful *n.* a heaping (AE), heaped (BE); level ~

spoon-fed *v.* 1. (D; tr.) to ~ to (she spoon-fed theory to her students) 2. (D; tr.) to ~ with (she spoon-fed her students with theory)

sport *n.* ["person judged by her/his ability to take a loss or teasing"] 1. a bad, poor; good ~ 2. a ~ about (she was a good ~ about losing the bet) ["mockery"] (old-fashioned) 3. to make ~ of smb. ("to mock smb.") ["type of physical activity"] 4. a contact; spectator; team ~ 5. an exciting; strenuous, vigorous ~ (skiing is an exciting ~) ["physical activity"] (BE) 6. to go in for, play ~ 7. fond of ~; in the world of ~ (AE has *sports*)

sporting *adj.* ~ to + inf. (it was ~ of them to give us a chance = giving us a chance was a ~ thing for them to do)

sports *n.* ["physical activity"] (AE) 1. to go in for, play ~ 2. fond of ~; in the world of ~ (BE has *sport*) ["types of physical activity"] 3. amateur; aquatic, water; competitive; indoor; intercollegiate (AE), inter-university (BE); intramural; outdoor; professional; varsity; winter ~ ["track meet"] (BE) 4. school ~; ~ day

sportsmanship *n.* to display, show (good; poor) ~ (she showed (her) good ~ by congratulating the person who beat her)

spot I *n.* ["mark, stain"] 1. to leave, make a ~ 2. to get out, remove a ~ 3. a grease ~ ["mark on the skin"] 4. a beauty ~ (see also *break out in spots* at **break out**; *come out in spots* at **come out**) ["area, place"] 5. a bald; black; high; isolated, secluded; low ~ 6. the penalty (soccer), the sweet (esp. tennis) ~ 7. at a ~ (let's meet at this same ~ tomorrow) (see also *rooted to the spot* at **rooted**) ["place of entertainment"]

(colloq.) 8. to hit ("visit") all the night ~s ["point, position"] 9. a bright ~; the high; the low ~ (the high ~ of our visit) 10. (misc.) X marks the ~ ["misc."] 11. on the ~ ("immediately"); ("at the center of activity"); ("exposed to the worst danger") to put smb. on the ~ ("to expose smb. to danger"); a blind ~ ("an area that cannot be seen") (also fig.: see also **blind spot**); to have a soft/tender/warm ~ (in one's heart) for ("to have a weakness for"); to be in a tight ~ ("to be in a difficult situation"); a trouble ~ (that reporter has been in many trouble ~s throughout the world); (BE; colloq.) a ~ of bother ("a bit of trouble")

spot II *v.* 1. (d; tr.) ("to identify") to ~ as (the police ~ted him as a known criminal) 2. (J) ("to see") we ~ted them going through the gate 3. (esp. AE) (O) ("to give as a handicap") he ~ted me ten points 4. (misc.) (BE) it is ~ting with rain; "Look! There's a red squirrel!" "Well ~ted!"

spotlight *n.* 1. to direct, focus, shine, turn a ~ on 2. (fig.) in the ~

spouse *n.* a beloved; faithful; unfaithful ~

spout *v.* (d; intr.) ("to spurt") to ~ from

sprawl I *n.* urban ~

sprawl II *v.* (P; intr.) to ~ on the sofa

sprawling *adj.* to send smb. ~

spray I *n.* an aerosol; hair; insect ~

spray II *v.* 1. (D; tr.) to ~ on, onto, over (to ~ paint on the walls) 2. (D; tr.) to ~ with (to ~ the walls with paint)

spread I *n.* ["expansion, transmission"] 1. to arrest, check, halt, stop; prevent the ~ (of a disease) 2. a ~ from; to (we did our best to prevent the ~ of the disease from parents to children) ["food"] 3. a cheese ~ ["misc."] 4. (the) middle-age(d) ~

spread II *v.* 1. to ~ smt. evenly; thickly; thinly (to ~ paint evenly) 2. to ~ quickly; unchecked (the epidemic spread unchecked) 3. (D; tr.) to ~ on (to ~ butter on bread) 4. (D; tr.) to ~ over (to ~ a blanket over a bed; to ~ payments over a year) 5. (D; intr., tr.) to ~ from; to (we did our best to prevent the disease from ~ing from parents to children; the epidemic spread to neighboring countries) 6. to ~ with (to ~ bread with butter) 7. (misc.) to ~ like wildfire; this butter ~s easily (on bread); to ~ papers out on the floor

spree *n.* 1. to go on a ~ 2. a crime; shopping; spending; weekend ~

spring I *n.* ["season"] 1. early; last; late; mid-; next ~ 2. during the, in (the) ~ (we met late in the ~ of 1995 = we met in the late ~ of 1995) 3. (misc.) there is a touch of ~ in the air; a harbinger of ~ (see also *spring equinox* at **equinox**) ["source of water"] 4. a hot, thermal; mineral; subterranean ~ ["bounce, elasticity"] 5. a ~ in, to (there was a ~ to her step) ["device of coiled metal"] 6. a box; watch ~

spring II *v.* 1. (D; intr.) to ~ at (the lion sprang at the hunter) 2. (d; intr.) ("to arise, result") to ~ from 3. (D; tr.) to ~ on ("to present without warning to smb.") (to ~ a surprise on smb.) 4. (d; intr.) ("to jump") to ~ over (to ~ over a wall) 5. (d; intr.) ("to jump") to ~ to (to ~ to smb.'s defense; to ~ to one's feet) 6. (s) the trap sprang shut 7. (misc.) they sprang out of the tank and into action; the tiger was poised to ~

springboard *n.* 1. a ~ for (a ~ for a new campaign) 2. a ~ to (a ~ to success)

spring-clean *n.* (BE) to do, have a ~

spring-cleaning (esp. AE) see **spring-clean**

sprinkle *v.* (D; tr.) to ~ on; with (to ~ water on clothes; to ~ clothes with water)

sprout (D; intr.) to ~ from

spruce up *v.* 1. (D; refl.) to ~ for (they ~d themselves up for the big party) 2. (H) they ~d themselves up to go to the big party

spunk *n.* (colloq.) ["courage"] 1. to show ~ 2. the ~ to + inf. (she had the ~ to defend her rights)

spur I *n.* ["incentive, stimulus"] 1. a ~ to (a ~ to action) 2. a ~ to + inf. (a ~ to act) (see also **spurs**) ["misc."] 3. on the ~ of the moment ("without planning")

spur II *v.* 1. (D; tr.) to ~ to (to ~ smb. to action) 2. (H) what ~red her to act?

spur on *v.* 1. (D; tr.) to ~ to (to ~ smb. on to action) 2. (H) what ~red her on to act?

spurs *n.* ["recognition"] 1. to win one's ~ ["devices worn on a rider's heel"] 2. to dig, drive one's ~ (into the side of a horse) 3. ~ jingle 4. a pair of ~

spurt I *n.* 1. a sudden ~ 2. a growth ~ 3. in a ~ (to work in ~s; the blood came out in a ~)

spurt II *v.* (D; intr.) to ~ from (blood ~ed from the wound)

sputum *n.* to cough up, produce ~

spy I *n.* 1. a foreign ~ 2. a network of spies (see also *spy ring* at **ring I** *n.*)

spy II *v.* 1. (d; intr.) to ~ for (to ~ for a foreign power) 2. (D; intr.) to ~ on, upon 3. (J) we spied them coming through the gate

squabble I *n.* 1. to cause, lead to a ~ 2. to patch up, settle a ~ 3. a domestic, family ~ (their differences led to a family ~) 4. a ~ breaks out, ensues 5. a ~ about, over; between; with (a ~ broke out between them over the use of the telephone; she had a ~ with her neighbor about the money that he had borrowed)

squabble II *v.* (D; intr.) to ~ about, over; with (she ~ed with her neighbor about the money that he had borrowed)

squad *n.* 1. a bomb; demolition; fraud (esp. BE); flying (BE) ~ (see also **firing squad**; *squad car* at **car I** *n.*) 2. a drugs; vice ~ 3. in a ~ (to work in the fraud ~) 4. (misc.) (BE) the awkward ~ (the awkward ~ are causing trouble again)

squalor *n.* 1. in ~ (to live in ~) 2. (misc.) "private affluence and public ~" – attributed to J.K. Galbraith, *The Affluent Society*, 1958

squander *v.* (D; tr.) to ~ on (to ~ a fortune on bad investments)

square I *n.* ["shape"] 1. to draw, make a ~ 2. (misc.) back to ~ one ("back to the beginning") ["place"] 3. the main ~ 4. the public ~ (fig.) (an issue hotly debated in the public ~)

square II *v.* (D; intr., tr.) to ~ with (their story doesn't ~ with the facts; to ~ accounts with smb.)

square root *n.* to calculate, find, extract the ~

squash I *n.* (BE) ["fruit drink"] lemon; orange ~

squash II *n.* (AE) ["marrow-like plant"] summer; winter ~ (BE has *marrow*)

squawk I *n.* to emit, give, let out a ~

squawk II *v.* (colloq.) 1. (D; intr.) ("to complain") to ~ about (she ~ed (to us) about the unfairness of the decision) 2. (L; to) she ~ed (to us) that the decision was unfair = "The decision's unfair!" she ~ed (to us)

squeak *n.* ["shrill cry"] 1. to emit, give, let out a ~ 2. with a ~ (the gate closed with a ~) ["escape"] (colloq.) 3. a close (AE), narrow (BE) ~

squeal I *n.* 1. to emit, give, let out a ~ 2. with a ~ (the car stopped suddenly with a ~ of its brakes; she saw the cake with a ~ of delight)

squeal II *v.* 1. (slang) (d; intr.) ("to inform against smb.") to ~ on (the criminal ~ed on his accomplices (to the police)) 2. (slang) (d; intr.) to ~ to (the criminal ~ed (on his accomplices) to the police) 3. (D; intr.) ("to emit a squeal") to ~ in, with (the car's brakes ~ed as it stopped suddenly; she ~ed with delight when she saw the cake)

squeamish *adj.* ~ about

squeeze I *n.* (colloq.) ["hug"] 1. to give smb. a ~ 2. a gentle; tight ~ ["lover"] (esp. AE) 3. smb.'s main ~ ["misc."] 4. in a tight ~ ("in difficulty"); to put the ~ on smb. ("to put pressure on smb."); a credit ~ (when credit is tight)

squeeze II *v.* 1. (C) ~ some orange juice for me; or: ~ me some orange juice 2. (d; tr.) to ~ from, out of (~ some toothpaste out of the tube) 3. (d; intr., tr.) to ~ into (to ~ into a small room; to ~ juice into a glass) 4. (d; intr., tr.) to ~ through (to ~ through a narrow passage) 5. (N; used with an adjective) ~ the mops dry

squelch *n.* (colloq.) ["crushing rebuke"] a perfect ~

squint *v.* (D; intr.) to ~ at

squirm *v.* (d; intr.) to ~ out of ("to evade") (to ~ out of an obligation)

squirt I *n.* ["instance of squirting"] 1. to give smt. a ~ ["insignificant person"] (colloq.) 2. a little ~

squirt II *v.* 1. (d; intr., tr.) to ~ from, out of (the liquid ~ed out of the bottle; to ~ a liquid out of a bottle) 2. (D; tr.) to ~ on, over (she ~ed water ¬on/over/all over¬ us) 3. (D; tr.) to ~ with (she ~ed us with water)

stab I *n.* ["attempt"] (colloq.) 1. to have, make a ~ at ["sensation"] 2. a sharp; sudden ~ (of pain) ["thrust of a pointed weapon"] 3. a ~ in the back (also fig.) (see also *stab wound* at **wound**)

stab II 1. (D; tr.) to ~ in (to ~ smb. in the leg) 2. (D; tr.) to ~ with (to ~ smb. with a knife) 3. (misc.) to ~

smb. to death; to ~ smb. in the back (usu. fig.); to ~ at smb. – but miss

stability *n.* 1. to lend ~ to 2. economic; emotional; political; social ~ 3. ~ in

stabilization *n.* economic; price ~

stable *n.* a livery; riding (esp. AE) ~

stack I *n.* 1. a bookstack; haystack; smokestack (esp. AE) 2. (misc.) to pile books in a ~; (colloq.) (AE) to blow one's ~ ("to lose one's temper")

stack II *v.* 1. (D; tr.) ("to arrange underhandedly") to ~ against (the cards were ~ed against her) 2. (d; tr.) to ~ with (the floor was ~ed with books) 3. (P; tr.) ~ the books on the floor; ~ the boxes against the door; ~ the merchandise in piles

stacks *n.* (in a library) 1. closed; open ~ 2. in the ~

stack up *v.* (colloq.) (esp. AE) (D; intr.) to ~ against, to ("to compare to") (how do we ~ to the competition?)

stadium *n.* 1. to crowd, fill, jam, pack a ~ 2. to empty a ~ 3. a baseball; football; Olympic ~ 4. a ~ empties; fills 5. a ~ holds, seats (the ~ holds 70,000 people) 6. in, into a ~ (70,000 people can fit into the ~)

staff I *n.* ["personnel"] 1. to dismiss, fire; employ, hire; lay off; recruit ~ 2. an administrative; coaching; editorial; hospital; medical; nursing; office; teaching ~ 3. a skeleton ~ 4. junior; permanent; senior; temporary ~ 5. on the ~ 6. (misc.) to join a ~ (she joined the ~ as an editor); a member of (the) ~ = a ~ member ["group of officers serving a commander"] 7. a general; joint; military; personal; special ~ 8. on a ~ (he was on the general ~) 9. (misc.) to assign smb. to a ~ (she was assigned to the ~ as an intelligence officer); a chief of ~ USAGE NOTE: In AE the teaching staff of an educational institution is typically called its faculty.

staff II *v.* (d; tr.) to ~ by, with (the office was ~ed with part-time workers)

stag *adj., adv.* to go ~ ("unaccompanied by smb. of the opposite sex" = AE, "unaccompanied by smb. of the female sex" = CE)

stage *n.* ["platform on which plays are performed"] 1. a revolving; sinking; sliding ~ 2. off; on (the) ~ (she has appeared many times on ~; to go on ~; she's very different off ~ from on ~) ["scene, setting"] 3. to set the ~ for (the ~ was set for a showdown) (see also **center stage**) ["level, degree, step"] 4. to go through; reach a ~ 5. an advanced; beginning, elementary; closing, final, last; critical, crucial, key; early; intermediate; late; opening ~ 6. flood ~ 7. at a ~ (negotiations were at a crucial ~; the river was at flood ~) 8. in a ~ (in this ~ of one's development) ["portion, part"] 9. easy ~s 10. by, in ~s (to cover a distance by easy ~s; to learn a language in easy ~s)

stagefright *n.* 1. to get; have ~ 2. a (bad) case of ~

stagger *v.* 1. (D; intr.) to ~ from; into (to ~ into a room) 2. (D; intr.) to ~ out of (to ~ out of a building) 3. (D; intr.) to ~ to; toward 4. (R) it ~ed me to

learn of the earthquake 5. (misc.) to ~ to one's feet; to ~ under a heavy burden

staggered *adj.* 1. ~ at, by (~ at the news of the earthquake) 2. ~ to + inf. (I was ~ to learn of the earthquake)

staggering *adj.* ~ to + inf. (it was ~ to learn of the earthquake)

stain I *n.* ["discolored spot"] 1. to leave a ~ 2. to get out, remove a ~ 3. a stubborn ~ 4. a ~ on (there's a ~ on your shirt) (also fig.) (a ~ on smb.'s reputation)

stain II *v.* 1. (D; tr.) to ~ with (he ~ed his shirt with ink) 2. (N; used with an adjective) we ~ed the wood dark brown

staircase *n.* a circular, spiral; winding ~

stairs *n.* 1. to climb, come up, go up, walk up the ~ 2. to come down; go down, walk down the ~ 3. moving ~ 4. service ~ 5. (misc.) a flight of ~; at the bottom, foot/head, top of the ~

stairway see **staircase**

stake I *n.* ["stick"] 1. to drive a ~ (into the ground) 2. to plant a ~ (in the ground) ["post"] 3. (to burn smb.) at the ~ ["share"] 4. to have a ~ in smt. (we want everyone to feel they have a ~ in society!) 5. a personal ~ ["risk"] 6. at ~ (our whole future is at ~); to go to the ~ for/over smt. ("to regard smt. as vitally important") (esp. BE) (he prefers bitter to lager – but he wouldn't go to the ~ for/over it!) (see also **stakes**)

stake II *v.* 1. (d; tr.) to ~ on (to ~ one's hope(s) on an investment) 2. (misc.) to ~ a claim to smt.

stakeholder *n.* a ~ in (we want everyone to feel they are ~s in society!)

stake out *v.* (D; tr.) to ~ on, to (esp. AE) (to ~ a claim to a mine)

stakes *n.* ["wager"]["prize"] 1. to lower; raise the ~s 2. big, high ~ (to play for high ~) ["misc."] (colloq.) 3. to pull up, up ~ ("to move elsewhere") (one day he just upped ~ (and left) without telling anybody!)

stalemate *n.* 1. to end in, reach a ~ 2. to break, end a ~ 3. a continuing ~, a ~ between; in; over (we tried to break the continuing ~ in the negotiations between them over pay)

stalk *v.* (P; intr.) to ~ out of the room

stall I *n.* (BE) 1. a market ~ (see also **stand I** *n.* 9) 2. (misc.) a stallholder

stall II *v.* 1. (D; intr.) to ~ on (they were ~ing on handing over the documents) 2. (misc.) to ~ for time

stamina *n.* the ~ to + inf. (she lacked the ~ to finish the race)

stammer I *n.* (to have, speak with) a nervous ~

stammer II *v.* 1. to ~ nervously 2. (B) she ~ed (out) a few words to us 3. (L; to) she ~ed to us that she was sorry = "I'm sorry," she ~ed (to us)

stamp I *n.* ["postage stamp"] 1. to put, stick a ~ on (an envelope) 2. to lick, moisten a ~ 3. to issue a ~ (the post office has issued a new commemorative ~) 4. to collect ~s 5. to cancel a ~ 6. an airmail; commemorative; postage; revenue; tax ~ 7. a book;

roll; set; sheet of ~s ["coupon"] 8. a food; trading ~ ["device for imprinting"] 9. a rubber ~ (see also *stamp of approval* at **approval**) ["clear sign, mark"] 10. to bear, carry; leave a certain ~ (she bore the ~ of authority from the moment she took over and has certainly left her ~ on the company)

stamp II *v.* 1. (d; tr.) to ~ as ("to mark") (these revelations ~ed him as a cheat) 2. (d; tr.) to ~ in, on ("to affix") (to ~ a date in a passport) 3. (d; intr.) to ~ on ("to crush") (to ~ on an insect) 4. (N; used with an adjective) ("to mark") she ~ed the document *secret* 5. (P; intr.) ("to stomp") she ~ed out of the room

stampede I *n.* 1. to cause, create a ~ 2. a ~ to + inf. (there was a ~ to get to the exit)

stampede II *v.* 1. (D; tr.) to ~ into (they were ~d into selling their homes) 2. (D; intr.) to ~ to, towards (they ~d towards the exit) 3. (E) they ~d to get to the exit

stance *n.* ["attitude, position"] 1. to adopt, take a ~ (the party leaders have adopted an unpopular ~ on the deficit) 2. a controversial; intransigent, uncompromising; middle-of-the-road, moderate; radical; tough ~ 3. a ~ on (the president took a tough ~ on the issue of tax reform)

stand I *n.* ["defense"] 1. to make, put up a ~ 2. a last ~ ["attitude, position"] 3. to take a ~ 4. a controversial; defiant; firm, resolute, strong; intransigent, uncompromising ~ 5. a ~ against; for, in favor of; on (the president took a resolute ~ on the issue of tax reform) ["rack, small table"] 6. a music; umbrella ~ ["place taken by a witness"] 7. to take the ~ 8. a witness ~ (AE; BE has *witness box*) ["small structure used for conducting business"] (BE often prefers *stall*) 9. a fruit; hot-dog ~; newsstand; vegetable ~ ["performance, engagement"] 10. a one-night ~ (also fig.: "a single sexual encounter") ["row"] 11. a taxi ~ (BE prefers *taxi rank*) (see also **stands**)

stand II *v.* 1. ("to hold oneself") to ~ firm; still; straight; tall 2. (BE) (d; intr.) ("to be a candidate") to ~ as (to ~ as a Labour candidate) 3. (d; intr.) ("to hold oneself erect") to ~ at (to ~ at attention; to ~ at ease) 4. (d; intr.) to ~ by ("to support") (her family stood by her throughout the trial) 5. (d; intr.) to ~ for ("to represent") (our party used to ~ for progress) 6. (BE; *run* is esp. AE) (d; intr.) to ~ for ("to be a candidate") (to ~ for Parliament against the incumbent M.P.) 7. (d; intr.) to ~ for ("to tolerate") (we will not ~ for such conduct; I won't ~ for his boasting!) 8. (d; intr.) to ~ on ("to insist on") (to ~ on one's rights; to ~ on ceremony) 9. (d; intr.) to ~ over ("to watch") (he always ~s over me when I work) 10. (d; intr.) ("to be regarded") to ~ with (how do you ~ with your boss?) 11. (E) ("to face") ("to have as a prospect") we stood to gain a great deal 12. (esp. BE) (E; usu. with cannot – can't – couldn't) ("to tolerate") she couldn't ~ to wait any longer 13. (G; usu. with cannot – can't – couldn't) ("to tolerate") she couldn't ~ waiting any longer

14. (K; usu. with cannot – can't – couldn't) ("to tolerate") I can't ~ his boasting 15. (esp. BE) (O) ("to buy") can I ~ you another round of drinks? 16. (P; tr.) ("to place") she stood the bottle on the table; I stood the books in a row; ~ the paintings against the door 17. (s) she stood first in her class; to ~ accused of murder; I ~ corrected 18. (misc.) she couldn't ~ it when she had to wait; I can't ~ it when he boasts; to ~ in smb.'s way; your balance ~s at one thousand dollars; the building ~s five hundred feet high; the inflation rate ~s at sixteen percent; (AE) to ~ by one's guns ("to defend one's viewpoint stubbornly"); to ~ on one's own (two) feet ("to support oneself"); to ~ tall (esp. AE; colloq.) ("to be resolute") (see also *stand pat* at **pat** I *adj.*, *adv.*)

stand apart *v.* (D; intr.) to ~ from (she stood apart from the others)

standard *n.* 1. to establish, set a ~ 2. to apply a ~ 3. to have a ~ (to have high ~s) 4. to adhere to, maintain a ~ 5. to come up to, meet a ~ 6. to lower; raise ¬ ~s/a ¬¬ (to raise the ~ of living; to raise academic ~s) 7. to abandon a ~ (the gold ~ was abandoned) 8. a high; low ~ 9. a double; moral ~ (to apply a double ~) 10. a rigorous, strict ~ 11. the gold ~ (to go off the gold ~) (also fig.) (this dictionary is the gold ~ of excellence against which all other dictionaries must be measured) 12. a living ~, living ~s (see also *standard of living* at **living**; **standard of living**) 13. academic, scholastic; educational; moral; professional ~s 14. below; up to ~; to a certain ~ (the work was not up to ~ so we made sure that it was done again to a very high ~) 15. by a certain ~ (by our ~s the candidate is not satisfactory; in fact, by *any* ~s he's pretty unsatisfactory!) 16. ~s are falling, going down; going up, rising 17. on a ~ (on a gold ~)

standardization *n.* to achieve, bring about ~

standard of living *n.* 1. to raise the ~ 2. a high; low ~ 3. a ~ falls, goes down; goes up, rises

stand back *v.* (D; intr.) to ~ from

standby *n.* ["alert"] to be on ~

stand by *v.* ("to be ready") 1. (D; intr.) to ~ with (they were ~ing by with additional supplies) 2. (E) to ~ to land 3. (misc.) how can you just ~ idly by when millions of children are dying of hunger?!

stand clear *v.* (d; intr.) to ~ of (~ of the closing doors, please!)

stand down *v.* (esp. BE) (D; intr.) ("to withdraw") to ~ in favor of (the other candidate)

stand in *v.* (d; intr.) to ~ for ("to substitute for") (can anyone ~ for her?)

standing *n.* ["duration"] 1. of (long) ~ (a custom of long ~ = a long-standing custom) ["status"] 2. academic; advanced ~ (at a university) 3. ~ among, with (his intransigent stand on tax reform enhanced his ~ among the voters) 4. the ~ to + inf. (who has the ~ to take over the leadership of the party?) 5. (misc.) in good ~; an artist of high ~ ["misc."] 6.

(US; on a traffic sign) ¬No Standing/No Stopping¬ (GB has *No Waiting*)

stand out *v.* 1. (D; intr.) ("to be clearly visible") to ~ against (to ~ against a dark background) 2. (D; intr.) ("to be noticeable") to ~ among, from, in (to ~ among the others; to ~ in a crowd; to ~ from the rest of the group) 3. (D; intr.) ("to be noticeable") to ~ as (she ~s out as the leading candidate) 4. (colloq.) (BE) (d; intr.) to ~ for ("to insist on") (to ~ out for higher wages) 5. (misc.) he stood out for his intransigent stand on tax reform

standpoint *n.* from a ~ (from a practical ~; from our ~) (see also **viewpoint**)

stands *n.* ["(for spectators to stand or sit)"] in the ~ (compare **bleachers**)

standstill *n.* 1. to bring smt. to a ~ 2. to come to, end in, reach a ~ 3. to end a ~ 4. a complete, total ~ 5. a ~ between; in; over (we tried to end the total ~ in the negotiations between them over pay) 6. at a ~ (negotiations were at a complete ~) 7. (misc.) to fight smb. to a ~

stand up *v.* 1. to ~ straight 2. (d; intr.) to ~ for ("to defend") (to ~ for one's rights) 3. (d; intr.) to ~ to ("to resist") (no one dared to ~ to the boss; this jacket will ~ to rough wear) 4. (misc.) the charges will not ~ ("be accepted")

staple *v.* (D; tr.) to ~ to (~ this page to that sheet)

star I *n.* ["heavenly body"] 1. a bright ~ (we walked out under the bright ~s) 2. a falling, shooting ~ 3. a fixed ~ 4. the evening; morning; north ~ 5. a distant ~ 6. ~s come out; shine, twinkle 7. (misc.) a galaxy of ~s ["prominent performer"] 8. a baseball; basketball; box-office; film, movie (AE); football; guest; pop; rising; rock; rugby; soccer; sports; track; TV ~ (we lined up a galaxy of ~s for our all-star show!) ["fortune"] 9. smb.'s ~ rises; sets, wanes (her ~ was rising) 10. under a ~ (she was born under a lucky ~) ["award"] 11. a battle; gold ~ ["shape"] 12. a five-pointed; six-pointed ~ 13. (misc.) the Star of David

star II *v.* 1. (D; intr., tr.) to ~ as (in his last film he ~red as a cowboy) 2. (D; intr., tr.) to ~ in (in his last film he ~red as a cowboy)

starch I *n.* cornstarch (AE; BE has *corn flour*); potato ~

starch II *v.* to ~ stiffly

stardom *n.* to achieve ~ (Vivien Leigh achieved ~ as Scarlet O'Hara in *Gone with the Wind*)

stare I *n.* a blank; cold, icy; fixed; haughty; vacant; wide-eyed ~

stare II *v.* 1. to ~ blankly; coldly, icily; fixedly; haughtily; vacantly; wide-eyed 2. (D; intr.) to ~ at (I ~d at him and he ~d back at me) 3. (D; intr.) to ~ into (to ~ into space) 4. (misc.) the solution was ~ring us in the face ("the solution was obvious")

starlight *n.* 1. by ~ 2. in the ~

start I *n.* 1. to get off to, make a ~ 2. to have a ~ 3. a flying, running ~ (to get off to a flying ~) 4. a head ~ (to have a head ~) 5. a fresh, new ~ (they got off to/

made a fresh ~) 6. an auspicious, promising ~ (the project got off to/had a promising ~) 7. an inauspicious, unpromising; false; shaky ~ (they got off to a shaky ~) 8. a ~ at, on (they made a fresh, new ~ at working out their problems; they got off to a shaky ~ on the project) 9. at the ~ 10. for a ~ (for a ~, let's agree where we should meet) 11. from the (very) ~ 12. (misc.) from ~ to finish ["misc."] 13. by fits and ~ ("in irregular bursts of activity")

start II *v.* 1. to ~ afresh, anew 2. (d; intr., tr.) to ~ as (she ~ed her career as a dancer) 3. (d; intr., tr.) ("to begin") to ~ at (prices ~ at five dollars; they ~ed the bidding at fifty dollars) 4. (D; intr., tr.) to ~ by (they ~ed the proceedings by reviewing the facts of the case) 5. (D; intr.) ("to leave") to ~ for (when did they ~ for the airport?) 6. (d; intr.) ("to leave") to ~ from (we ~ed from Philadelphia) 7. (d; intr.) to ~ on (to ~ on a trip; to ~ on another case) 8. (d; intr., tr.) to ~ with (they ~ed (the proceedings) with a review of the facts of the case; let's ~ with you) 9. (E) they ~ed to cough 10. (G) they ~ed coughing 11. (J) what ~ed them coughing? 12. (misc.) to ~ with, let's consider climate change; to ~ young; she ~ed towards the door; don't ~ anything ("don't cause any trouble")

start back *v.* (P; intr.) let's ~ for home; before it gets dark, we should ~ to the city; while the ferries are still running, we should ~ across the river; we should ~ from this point at dawn

starters *n.* (colloq.) for ~ ("to begin with") (for ~, let's consider climate change)

start in *v.* 1. (D; intr.) to ~ by (they ~ed in by reviewing the facts of the case) 2. (AE) (d; intr.) to ~ on ("to put pressure on") (then they ~ed in on her) 3. (misc.) they ~ed in on me to buy a new car (AE); they're ~ing in again with their critical remarks

startle *v.* (R) it ~d me to see them dressed like that

startled *adj.* 1. ~ at (~ at the news) 2. ~ to + inf. (I was ~ to see them dressed like that)

startling *adj.* ~ to + inf. (it was ~ to see them dressed like that)

start off *v.* 1. see **start II** 1–8 2. (D; intr.) to ~ to (they ~ed off to the airport without saying goodbye) 3. (misc.) to ~ on a new tack; to ~ on the wrong foot 4. (s) to ~ poor and ¬end up/finish up¬ rich; to ~ as you mean to go on

start out *v.* 1. see **start off** 2. (E) they ~ed out to conquer the world of show business but ended up as extras

starve *v.* 1. (D; tr.) to ~ into (to ~ smb. into submission) 2. (misc.) to ~ to death; to ~ oneself to death (see also *starve to death* at **death**)

starved *adj.* ~ for, of (BE) (~ for company)

state I *n.* ["government"] 1. to establish, found, set up a ~ 2. to govern, rule a ~ 3. a city; free; independent; nation; sovereign ~ 4. a buffer; client; puppet ~ 5. a capitalist; communist; socialist; welfare ~ 6. a failed; garrison; one-party; police; totalitarian ~ 7. a secular; theocratic ~ 8. a member

~ (the member ~s of the UN) 9. (misc.) a head of ~; affairs/matters of ~ ["condition"] 10. a good; satisfactory; unspoiled ~ 11. a permanent; temporary; transitional ~ 12. a comatose; moribund; trance; unconscious ~ 13. a bad, poor; sorry; unsatisfactory; weakened ~ 14. a confused; hysterical; nervous ~ 15. an emotional; mental ~ 16. a financial ~ 17. a gaseous; liquid; solid ~ 18. in a ~ (in a good ~ of repair; in a poor ~ of health; in a highly nervous ~) 19. (misc.) the ~ of the art ("the level of development") (is your computer state-of-the-art ("very up-to-date")?) (see also *state of affairs* at **affairs**; *state of mind* at **mind I** *n.*; *state of war* at **war I** *n.*) ["nervous condition"] 20. in a ~ (she was in quite a ~) ["pomp"] 21. to lie in ~ ["any of the states into which a country is divided"] 22. a dry ~ ("a state in which the sale of alcoholic beverages is prohibited") 23. (historical; US) a border; free; slave ~ 24. a fly-over ~ (that one ignores while flying over it between the liberal coastal states of the USA)

state II *v.* 1. to ~ categorically; clearly; emphatically; openly; solemnly; unreservedly 2. (B) we ~d our views to them 3. (L; to) they ~ed (to the reporters) that a summit conference would take place soon = "a summit conference will take place soon," they ~d (to the reporters) 4. (Q) they did not ~ (to the reporters) exactly when the summit conference would take place 5. (misc.) all terms and conditions are as ~d above unless ~d otherwise below

statehood *n.* 1. to achieve ~ 2. to seek, strive for ~ 3. ~ in (the 50 states of the USA have all achieved ~ in the USA)

statement *n.* ["act of stating"]["something stated"] 1. to issue, make a ~ 2. to confirm; sign a ~ 3. to deny; refute; retract, withdraw a ~ 4. a brief, short; preliminary; succinct; terse ~ 5. a clear; definitive ~ 6. a categorical; controversial; fashion; sweeping ~ (to wear big hats today is to make a controversial fashion ~) 7. a prepared; sworn; voluntary ~ 8. a rash; vague ~ 9. an oral; written ~ 10. a false; truthful ~ 11. a ~ that + clause (they issued a ~ (to the reporters) that a summit conference would take place soon) 12. (misc.) to take down smb.'s ~; a ~ to the effect that... (they issued a ~ to the effect that a summit conference would take place soon) ["report"] 13. to issue a ~ 14. a bank; financial; mission; official; policy; political; public ~ (our mission ~ is: give better value for money!) 15. a ~ about, on 16. in a ~ (the government issued a ~ about the strike in which they said they hoped to settle it soon)

state's evidence *n.* (AE) to turn ~ (see also **King's evidence, Queen's evidence**)

statesman *n.* an elder; prominent ~

statesmanship *n.* to practice ~

stateswoman *n.* an elder; prominent ~

static *n.* to produce ~

station I *n.* ["building or place used for a specific purpose"] 1. a broadcasting; radio; television, TV ~

2. a bus; coach (BE); freight (AE); railroad (AE), railway (esp. BE), train; subway (AE), tube (BE), underground (BE) ~; the last; next ~ (I got on at the last ~: please let me off me at the next ~) 3. a fire; police ~ 4. a coast-guard; naval; recruiting ~ 5. a hydroelectric; power ~ 6. a radar; radar-tracking; space; tracking; weather ~ 7. a polling ~ (esp. BE) ["place where motor vehicles are serviced"] 8. a filling, gas (AE), gasoline (AE), petrol (BE), service ~ ["place of duty"] 9. an action; battle ~ (see also **battle station**) ["position"] 10. one's ~ in life 11. above; beneath smb.'s ~ in life ["misc."] 12. to pick up a radio ~

station II *v.* (P; tr.) they were ~ed in Germany; our unit was ~ed near the coast

statistics *n.* 1. to check; collect, gather, take; publish, release, report; record; tabulate ~ 2. to bandy ~ (about); to cite, quote ~ 3. to interpret; manipulate ~ 4. cold, hard ~ 5. vital ~ ("essential data about a population") (also fig.) ("a woman's breast, hip, and waist measurements") 6. crime ~ 7. official ~ 8. reliable; valid ~ 9. ~ indicate, show 10. according to, judging by, to judge by ~ (according to the latest official ~, everything is OK!)

statue *n.* 1. to carve; sculpt, sculpture (esp. AE) a ~ 2. to cast a ~ (in bronze) 3. to erect, put up a ~ (they put up a ~ of/to Winston Churchill) 4. to unveil a ~ (they unveiled a new ~ of Winston Churchill that stands in the park) 5. an equestrian ~

stature *n.* 1. considerable; imposing ~ (a person of imposing ~) 2. the ~ to + inf. (does she have the ~ to run for national office?) 3. in ~ (to grow in ~; small in ~)

status *n.* 1. to achieve ~ 2. to confer, give, grant ~ 3. celebrity ~ 4. most-favored nation ~ 5. legal ~ (to enjoy/have legal ~) 6. smb.'s financial; marital; social ~ 7. equal; high; low ~ 8. smb.'s ~ among; as (this will not affect your ~ as an asylum-seeker, nor will it lower your ~ among your friends) (see also *status symbol* at **symbol**)

status quo *n.* 1. to maintain, preserve; restore the ~ 2. to disrupt threaten; overturn the ~

statute *n.* 1. a penal ~ 2. by ~ (an organization regulated by ~) (see also *on the statute books* at **book I** *n.*)

statute of limitations *n.* 1. the ~ takes effect, goes into effect (or: colloq. and illogically – the ~ expires, runs out) 2. under the ~

stay I *n.* ["delay"] (legal) 1. to grant, issue; vacate a ~ 2. (misc.) a ~ of execution ["time spent"] 3. a long; short ~ 4. during, throughout a ~ 5. (misc.) we had a very pleasant ~ at the hotel, throughout which we enjoyed ourselves thoroughly

stay II *v.* 1. (D; intr.) ("to remain") to ~ for, to (to ~ for, to dinner) 2. (d; intr.) to ~ off ("to keep off") (to ~ off the grass) 3. (d; intr.) to ~ out of ("to avoid") (to ~ out of trouble) 4. (d; intr.) to ~ with smb. ("to be smb.'s guest") (they ~ed with us) 5. (s) to ~ calm; seated 6. (misc.) to ~ from Monday to Wednesday USAGE NOTE: The phrase *from Monday to Wednesday* is ambiguous. Does the stay include Wednesday or not? If it does, you can make that clear by saying *from Monday through Wednesday* (AE) or *from Monday to Wednesday inclusive* (CE). The phrase *from Monday through to Wednesday* is esp. BE and is also somewhat ambiguous: though it is meant typically to include Wednesday it need not do so.

stay abreast *v.* (D; intr.) to ~ of (to ~ of the news; the runners ~ed abreast of each other)

stay ahead *v.* (D; intr.) to ~ of

stay away *v.* (D; intr.) to ~ from (to ~ from smb.)

staying power *n.* the ~ to + inf. (does she have the ~ to finish the race?)

stay on *v.* 1. (D; intr.) to ~ as (she ~ed on as deputy) 2. (D; intr.) to ~ for (to ~ for the evening's entertainment) 3. (misc.) to ~ (in order) to enjoy the evening's entertainment

stay out *v.* 1. to ~ late 2. to ~ on strike

stay up *v.* 1. (D; intr.) to ~ for (they allowed the children to ~ for the evening's entertainment) 2. (D; intr.) to ~ until (we ~ed up until midnight) 3. (misc.) to ~ late; the parents ~ed up with the sick child all night; to ~ (in order) to enjoy the evening's entertainment

stead *n.* to stand smb. in good ~ ("to be useful to smb.")

steady *adj.* 1. (colloq.) (AE) to go ~ with smb. ("to be smb.'s boyfriend or girlfriend") 2. (misc.) to hold smt. ~; (fig. as if before a race) ready, ~, go! (BE; AE has *get ready, get set, go!*)

steak *n.* 1. to broil (AE), grill a ~ 2. a juicy; tender; tough ~ 3. to like one's ~ medium; medium-rare; rare; well-done 4. a beefsteak; club (esp. US); cube (esp. US); flank; minute; Porterhouse; rump; Salisbury (US); salmon; sirloin; Swiss (esp. US); T-bone ~ 5. (BE) braising; stewing ~ (I'd like some stewing ~ for my steak-and-kidney pie, please)

steal *v.* 1. (D; tr.) ("to take or have surreptitiously") to ~ at (to ~ a glance at smb.) 2. (D; intr., tr.) ("to take illegally") to ~ from (to ~ from the rich; he stole money from his employer) 3. (d; intr.) ("to depart silently") to ~ from, out of (she stole out of the room) 4. (P; intr.) ("to move silently") she stole into the house; we stole quietly across the field; the intruder stole through the rooms

stealth *n.* by ~ (to enter a building by ~)

steal up *v.* (D; intr.) ("to sneak up") to ~ behind; on, to (he stole up behind/on me in the dark)

steam I *n.* 1. to emit ~ 2. to get up, produce, work up ~ 3. ~ condenses; forms 4. ~ hisses 5. a cloud; wisp of ~ 6. (misc.) (colloq.) to blow off, let off ~ ("to vent one's feelings"); to run out of ~ ("to use up one's energy"); a head of ~ (fig.) ("energy, momentum") (our indignation helped us to work up/ get up quite a head of ~ even before the campaign got under way!)

steam II *v.* 1. (d; intr.) to ~ into; out of (to ~ into a harbor) 2. (N; used with an adjective) she ~ed the envelope open

steamed up *adj.* (colloq.) ["angry"] ~ about, over (don't get ~ about/over smt. so unimportant!)

steamer *n.* 1. an oceangoing; paddle; tramp ~ 2. by ~ 3. on (board) a ~

steam out *v.* (D; intr.) to ~ to (to ~ to sea)

steamroller *v.* (d; tr.) to ~ through (to ~ a bill through Congress)

steel I *n.* 1. to make, produce ~ 2. to temper ~ 3. solid; stainless ~ 4. a bar; ingot; sheet; slab; strip of ~ 5. (misc.) cold ~ ("bayonet, knife used in close combat")

steel II *v.* 1. (D; refl.) to ~ for (to ~ oneself for the next attack) 2. (H; refl.) to ~ oneself to face an ordeal

steeped *adj.* (cannot stand alone) ~ in (~ in local traditions)

steeple *n.* a church ~

steer I *n.* ["castrated bull or ox"] to rope a ~

steer II *v.* 1. (P; intr., tr.) we ~ed for port; they ~ed into the hotel 2. (misc.) to ~ (well) clear of ("to keep away from") (to ~ clear of danger; ~ clear of him: he's trouble!)

steerage *n.* ["section in a passenger ship"] 1. to travel ~ 2. in ~ (to cross the ocean in ~)

steering *n.* power ~

stem I *n.* (ling.) a consonant; verb ~

stem II *v.* (d; intr.) to ~ from

stench *n.* a dreadful, horrible, unbearable ~

stencil *n.* to cut, make a ~

step I *n.* ["placing the foot"] 1. to make, take a ~ (to take a ~ backward) 2. to retrace one's ~s 3. a giant (usu. fig.); long; mincing; short; small; stutter (AE) ~ ("That's one small ~ for [a] man, one giant leap for mankind." – Neil Armstrong (on the Moon), July 21, 1969) 4. (usu. fig.) ~ by ~ ["sequence of movements"] (dancing) 5. to execute, perform; learn a (dance) ~ ["stride in marching"] (mil.) 6. to keep in ~ 7. to change ~ 8. an even, steady ~ 9. half; route ~ 10. in ~; out of ~ (also fig.: she was out of ~ with everyone else) ["action"] 11. to take a ~ 12. a careful, prudent; positive; precautionary; preventive ~ 13. a bold; critical; decisive; giant; historic ~ (to take a giant ~ forward) 14. a dangerous; drastic; fatal ~ 15. a false; rash, risky ~ 16. (misc.) to keep a/one ~ ahead of everyone; watch your ~! ("be careful!") ["gait"] 17. a heavy; light ~ ["distance"] 18. a ~ from (their place is just a few ~s from the station) (see also **steps**)

step II *v.* 1. (d; intr.) to ~ around (to ~ around a puddle) 2. (d; intr.) to ~ between (the referee ~ped between the two boxers) 3. (d; intr.) to ~ into (to ~ into a room) 4. (d; intr.) to ~ off (to ~ off a train) 5. (d; intr.) to ~ on (she ~ped on my foot; to ~ on the brake) 6. (d; intr.) to ~ out of (to ~ out of a room) 7. (d; intr.) to ~ over (she ~ped over the body) 8. (d; intr.) to ~ to, towards (the pupil ~ped to the blackboard) 9. (misc.) to ~ out of line ("to behave inappropriately"); just ~ this way, madam; ~ lively! ("hurry up!")

step aside v. 1. (D; intr.) to ~ for (she ~ped aside for a younger candidate) 2. (misc.) she ~ped aside in favor of a younger candidate; she ~ped aside (in order) to make way for a younger candidate

step back v. (D; intr.) to ~ from (to ~ from the abyss)

step down v. 1. (D; intr.) to ~ from (to ~ from the presidency) 2. (misc.) she ~ped down in favor of a younger candidate; she ~ped down (in order) to make way for a younger candidate

step out v. 1. (D; intr.) to ~ into (to ~ into the corridor) 2. (D; intr.) to ~ on, onto (she ~ped out on the terrace) 3. (misc.) (esp. AE) he was ~ping out on his wife ("he was betraying his wife")

steppingstone n. a ~ to (a ~ to advancement)

steps n. ["stairs"] 1. to come up, go up the ~ 2. to come down, go down the ~ 3. steep ~ 4. a flight of ~

step up v. (D; intr.) to ~ to (he ~ped (right) up to me and told me who he was)

stereo n. (to broadcast) in ~

stereotype n. 1. to perpetuate; reinforce a ~ 2. to conform to, fit a ~ 3. to challenge; reject a ~ 4. a cultural; ethnic; gender; negative; racial ~

stern adj. ~ towards; with

stew n. 1. to do, make a ~ 2. (a) beef; Irish; lamb; mulligan (esp. US); veal; vegetable ~ 3. (misc.) to be, get in a ~ ("agitated") (about, over)

steward n. a chief; shop ~

stick I n. 1. a hiking; hockey; lacrosse; walking ~ 2. a celery ~ 3. a composing ~ ("device for typesetting") 4. a swagger ~ (carried by a military officer) 5. (misc.) to carry a big ~ ("to threaten to use force to settle a dispute"); to eat fish ~s (AE = BE *fish fingers*); to up ~s (colloq.) (BE) ("to up stakes") ("I think the gene pool of America is made up of the kind of people who just wanted to up ~s and forge something new." – Stephen Fry, *Radio Times*, 11–17 October 2008, p. 18, col. 1) (see also **sticks**)

stick II v. 1. ("to remain fixed") to ~ fast (the car is stuck fast in the mud) 2. (d; intr.) to ~ by ("to be loyal to") (to ~ by one's friends) 3. (d; tr.) ("to thrust") to ~ into (to ~ a needle into a cushion; to ~ one's hands into one's pockets) 4. (d; tr.) ("to fasten, paste") to ~ on, to (to ~ a stamp on an envelope; to ~ one thing to another with glue = to ~ two things ¬to each other/together¬ with glue) 5. (d; tr.) ("to thrust") to ~ through (she stuck her head through the window) 6. (d; intr.) ("to adhere") to ~ to (the stamp didn't ~ to the envelope) 7. (d; intr.) ("to limit oneself") to ~ to (to ~ to the subject) 8. (d; intr.) to ~ to ("to be loyal to") (to ~ to one's principles) 9. (d; intr.) ("to remain") to ~ with (~ with me, and you will not get lost) 10. (P; tr.) ("to put") she stuck it behind the door; she stuck it under the chair 11. (misc.) to ~ it to smb. (slang) (AE) ("to treat smb. badly or unfairly") (the fat cats have

stuck it to us ordinary folks long enough!); it stuck in her mind that she might never see them again; to ~ in smb.'s throat ("to be hard to say"); ("to be a source of irritation"); ("Stick close to your desks and never go to sea, And you all may be Rulers of the Queen's Navee [= Navy]!" – Sir W.S. Gilbert (1836–1911), *H.M.S. Pinafore*)

sticker n. a bumper; price ~

stickler n. ["one who insists on exactness"] a ~ for (a ~ for protocol)

stick out v. 1. (D; intr.) ("to protrude") to ~ from; into (the nail stuck out from the wall; his feet stuck out into the aisle) 2. (D; intr.) (BE) to ~ for ("to hold out for") (they stuck out for better terms) 3. (D; tr.) ("to extend") to ~ to, towards (she stuck out her hand to us) 4. (misc.) to ~ like a sore thumb ("to be very conspicuous")

sticks n. (colloq.) ["rural area"] in the ~ (to live way out in the ~)

stick up v. (d; intr.) to ~ for (colloq.) ("to defend") (to ~ for one's friend)

stiff adj. 1. frozen; scared ~ 2. ~ from; with (~ with mud from being left out too long)

stigma n. 1. to attach a ~ to 2. to bear, carry a ~ 3. a ~ attaches to (no ~ attaches to being poor) 4. a social ~ (does being poor still carry a social ~?) 5. a ~ about, in, to (there is no ~ to being poor)

stigmatize v. (D; tr.) to ~ as (to be ~d as a traitor)

still I adj., adv. 1. deathly; perfectly; quite; stock; very ~ (to stand perfectly ~) 2. to keep; sit; stand ~

still II n. in the ~ of the night

stilts n. 1. (to walk) on ~ 2. a pair of ~

stimulant n. a ~ to (a ~ to the local economy)

stimulate v. 1. (d; tr.) to ~ into (they ~d us into action) 2. (H) they ~d us to act

stimulating adj. 1. intellectually ~ 2. ~ to + inf. (it is intellectually ~ to live in a large city)

stimulation n. 1. to provide ~ 2. erotic, sexual; intellectual ~ (the intellectual ~ provided by living in a large city)

stimulus n. 1. to give, provide a ~ 2. a powerful, strong ~ 3. a ~ to

sting I n. ["skin wound"] 1. a bee; wasp ~ ["con, swindle"] ["trap"] (colloq.) 2. to set up a ~ ["misc."] 3. to take the ~ out of smt. ("to minimize disappointment")

sting II v. 1. (D; intr.) to ~ from (my eyes ~ from the smoke) 2. (D; tr.) to ~ into (her reproaches stung him into acting)

stingy adj. ~ with (~ with one's money)

stink I n. ("outcry") (colloq.) to cause, kick up, make, raise a ~ (about) (they kicked up quite a ~ about the new plan) (see also *stink bomb* at **bomb I** n.)

stink II v. (D; intr.) to ~ of (the place ~s of rotten fish)

stint I n. ["period of service"] 1. to do, serve a ~ (he did his ~ as a soldier) 2. during a ~ (he met his future wife abroad during his ~ as a soldier)

stint II v. (D; intr.) ("to economize") to ~ on (don't ~ on the food)

stipend n. 1. to receive a ~ 2. to pay a ~ 3. a modest ~ (to live on a modest ~)

stipulate v. 1. (L) the contract ~s that the work must be finished by the end of the year 2. (Q) does the contract ~ when the work must be finished?

stipulation n. 1. to make a ~ 2. a ~ that + clause (the contract makes the ~ that the work must be finished by the end of the year)

stir I n. ["disturbance"] 1. to cause, create, make a ~ 2. a big; something of a ~ 3. a ~ among ~ 4. a ~ about, over (they created a big ~ among local people about the new plan)

stir II v. 1. (D; intr., tr.) to ~ from, out of (we could not ~ him from his depression; he could not ~ out of his depression; she would not ~ from her desk) 2. (D; tr.) to ~ into (to ~ one ingredient into another) 3. (D; tr.) to ~ to (the news ~red them to greater efforts) 4. (H) the news ~red them to make greater efforts 5. (misc.) to ~ all the ingredients together

stitch n. 1. to make a ~ 2. to drop; pick up, take up a ~ 3. to cast on ~es 4. (med.) to put ~es in 5. (med.) to remove, take out ~es 6. a cable; chain; cross; knit, plain (BE); purl; running ~ (see also **stitches**)

stitches n. in ~ ("convulsed with laughter")

stock I n. ["inventory, supply"] 1. to take ~ 2. in ~; out of ~ (this item is not in ~) ["share, shares in a corporation"] 3. to buy; issue; sell ~ 4. common ~ (AE; BE has *ordinary shares*) 5. blue-chip; over-the-counter; preferred (AE; BE has *preference shares*) ~ (see also **stocks**) ["equipment"] 6. rolling ~ ("railway vehicles") ["confidence, trust"] 7. to put ~ in smb. ["evaluation"] 8. to take ~ (we must take ~ of the situation) ["stage productions"] (AE) 9. summer ~ ["livestock"] 10. to graze ~ ["lineage"] 11. of good ~ ["misc."] 12. smb.'s ~ in trade ("smb.'s customary practice") (see also *stock cube* at **cube**)

stock II v. 1. (D; tr.) to ~ in (they ~ed new merchandise in their store) 2. (D; tr.) to ~ with (they ~ed their store with new merchandise; to ~ a pond with new fish)

stock exchange see **stock market**

stocking n. 1. mesh; nylon; seamless; silk; surgical ~s 2. a pair of ~s 3. (misc.) she got a ladder (BE)/ run (esp. AE) in her ~

stock market n. 1. to gamble on, play, speculate on the ~ 2. to depress the ~ 3. the ~ closes strong; weak 4. the ~ opens strong; weak 5. the ~ is active; volatile; sluggish 6. the ~ is firm, steady; rising; up 7. the ~ goes up, rises; rallies; slumps 8. the ~ is depressed; down; falling 9. the ~ collapses, crashes; falls, goes down,

stocks n. ["shares on the stock market"] (esp. AE; CE has *shares*) 1. to buy; sell ~ (on the stock market) 2. ~ close strong; weak 3. ~ open strong; weak 4. ~ are active; sluggish 5. ~ are firm, steady; rising; up 6. ~ go up, rise; rally 7. ~ are depressed; down;

falling 8. ~ collapse, crash; fall, go down; plummet; slump

stock up v. (D; intr.) to ~ on, with (to ~ on supplies)

stockyards n. at, in the ~ (to work at/in the ~)

stoical adj. ~ about

stoicism n. 1. to display ~ 2. great ~ 3. with ~ (to meet adversity with great ~) 4. the ~ to + inf. (she had the ~ to meet adversity uncomplainingly)

stole n. a fur; silk; woolen ~

stomach n. ["digestive organ"] 1. to settle; turn, upset smb.'s ~ 2. an empty; full; queasy; sick; sour; strong; upset; weak ~ (see also *sick to one's stomach* at **sick**) 3. smb.'s ~ aches, hurts; growls, rumbles 4. on an empty ~ 5. on one's ~ (to lie on one's ~) 6. (misc.) it turns my ~ ("it disgusts me") (it turns my ~ to see such behavior!) ["inclination"] 7. to have no ~ for smt.

stomachache n. to get; have a ~ (BE also has *to get, have ~*)

stomp v. (P; intr.) she ~ed into my office; they ~ed out of the room; she ~ed on my toe

stone I n. ["piece of rock"] 1. to hurl, throw a ~ 2. a foundation; paving ~ 3. a block, slab of ~ 4. (misc.) to leave no ~ unturned ("to try all methods of achieving an end") ["gem"] 5. to set a (precious) ~ 6. a precious ~ ["stony mass"] 7. a block; piece; slab of ~ (see also *stone quarry* at **quarry II** n.) ["stony mass in the body"] 8. a gallstone; kidney ~

stone II v. to ~ smb. to death

stone's throw n. a ~ away; away from

stool n. 1. get on; get off; perch on; sit on a ~ 2. a bar; ducking ~; footstool; piano; step ~ 3. (misc.) (BE) to fall between two ~s ("to fail to achieve either of two goals")

stoop v. 1. (d; intr.) to ~ to ("to lower oneself to") (she would never ~ to cheating!) 2. (misc.) she ~ed (in order) to pick it up; *She Stoops to Conquer*, Oliver Goldsmith, 1730–74; she would never ~ so low as to cheat!

stop I n. ["halt"]["cessation"] 1. to make a ~ 2. to put a ~ to (the teacher put a ~ to the cheating) 3. to bring to a ~ (the driver brought the bus to a ~) 4. to come to a ~ (the train came to a ~) (see also **stop sign**) 5. an abrupt, sudden; brief; dead; full; smooth ~ 6. a comfort, rest; flag (AE), request (BE); regular, scheduled; unscheduled; whistle (AE) ("very brief") ~ 7. a bus; pit; refueling; streetcar (AE), tram (BE) ~ USAGE NOTE: The phrase *pit stop* means literally a stop made by a racing driver for repairs during a race. But it can also mean figuratively a stop during a trip to eat or to use the toilet. 8. at a ~ (at the bus ~) 9. (misc.) to miss one's ~ ["place for resting"] 10. a truck ~ (esp. AE; BE has *transport café*: see at **café**) ["punctuation mark"] 11. a full ~ (BE; AE has *period*)

stop II v. 1. to ~ dead; short 2. (D; intr.) to ~ at (to ~ at the intersection) 3. (D; intr.) to ~ for (to ~ for lunch; to ~ for a red light; "Because I could not ~

for Death, He kindly ~ped for me" – Emily Dickinson, 1830–86) 4. (D; tr.) to ~ from (you cannot ~ Romeo and Juliet from getting married) 5. (G) they ~ped talking 6. (J) (BE) you cannot ~ Romeo and Juliet getting married 7. (K) you cannot ~ their getting married 8. (misc.) to ~ dead in one's tracks; to ~ at nothing ("to allow no scruples to interfere with one's efforts to achieve an end"); they ~ped (in order) to chat

stop by v. 1. (D; intr.) to ~ at (we'll ~ at your place) 2. (D; intr.) to ~ for (to ~ for tea)

stop in v. 1. (D; intr.) to ~ at (we'll ~ at your place) 2. (D; intr.) to ~ for (to ~ for tea)

stop off v. 1. (D; intr.) to ~ at (we'll ~ at your place on our way home) 2. (D; intr.) to ~ for (to ~ for tea)

stopover n. 1. to make a ~ (for) (we made a ~ at Singapore for refueling en route to Japan) 2. at a ~ (we met at the ~ we made at Singapore)

stop over v. 1. (D; intr.) to ~ at (we'll ~ at your place) 2. (D; intr.) to ~ for (AE) (to ~ for tea)

stoppage n. 1. a work ~ 2. during; throughout a ~ (throughout the work ~ there was no violence)

stopping see the Usage Note for **standing**

stop short v. (d; intr.) to ~ of (they ~ped short of imposing new taxes)

stop sign n. to go through, run (AE) a ~

storage n. ["storing"] 1. to put smt. into ~ 2. to take smt. out of ~ 3. cold ~ 4. in ~ ["memory of a computer"] 5. external; internal; magnetic ~

store n. ["shop, establishment where goods are sold"] (esp. AE; see the Usage Note for **shop**) 1. to manage, operate, run a ~ 2. a bookstore; candy; clothing ~; drugstore; food, grocery; furniture; hardware; jewelry (AE), jewellery (BE); music; shoe; stationery; toy ~ 3. a chain, multiple (BE); company; convenience; department; discount; general; retail; self-service ~ 4. (AE) a dry-goods ~ (BE has *draper's shop*) 5. (AE) a liquor, package ~ (BE has *off licence*) 6. (AE) a five-and-dime, five-and-ten-cent; (AE) a variety ~ (BE has *haberdashery*) 7. at, in a ~ (she works at/in a ~) ["misc."] 8. to set (great; little) ~ by ("to attribute importance to"); to lie/be in ~ ("to be imminent"); to have smt. in ~ for smb. ("to have smt. prepared for smb.")

stores n. ["supplies"] 1. naval ~ 2. a cache of ~

storm I n. ["atmospheric disturbance"] 1. to brave, ride out, weather a ~ (the ship finally rode out the ~) 2. a blinding; fierce, heavy, raging, severe, violent; perfect ~ 3. a dust; electrical ~; firestorm; hailstorm; ice ~; rainstorm; sandstorm; snowstorm; thunderstorm; tropical ~ 4. a ~ batters, hits, strikes; comes up; rages (the ~ struck several cities) 5. a ~ blows itself out, blows over, dies down, subsides 6. a ~ was gathering (also fig.) 7. during a ~; in a ~; (in) the eye of a ~ (also fig.) ["disturbance, commotion"] 8. to cause, raise, stir up a ~ 9. a ~ was brewing, gathering (a ~ was brewing between them over/about the insult) (see also *storm clouds*

at **cloud I** n.; *storm warning* at **warning**) ["assault, attack"] (mil. and fig.) 10. to take by ~ (the new play took Broadway by ~) ["misc."] 11. to talk up a ~ (colloq.) (esp. AE) ("to talk a great deal")

storm II v. (d; intr.) ("to rush angrily") to ~ into; out of (to ~ out of a room)

story I n. ["tale"] 1. to narrate, recount, relate, tell a ~ 2. to concoct, fabricate, invent, make up a ~ 3. to spread a ~ 4. to hear; listen to a ~ 5. to change, revise; embellish, embroider a ~ 6. an amusing, funny, humorous; charming; fascinating; nice, pleasant ~ 7. a coherent; likely, plausible; true ~ USAGE NOTE: The phrase *a likely story* means typically 'an unlikely story': He was abducted by a UFO? A likely ~! (= What an unlikely story!) 8. an unknown; untold ~ 9. a boring; complicated, involved; long ~ 10. a gripping; hard-luck; moving; sad; sob; tragic ~ 11. a horror; ugly; unpleasant ~ 12. a cock-and-bull, farfetched; implausible; improbable; unlikely; unpleasant ~ 13. a dirty, off-color, risqué; juicy ~ 14. an adventure; bedtime, children's, fairy; detective; ghost; hard-luck; life; love ~ 15. conflicting ~ries (they told conflicting ~ries to the police) 16. a shaggy dog ~ ("a long rambling joke with an illogical punch line") 17. a short ~ ("a short prose narrative") 18. the whole ~ (who knows the whole ~ of the incident?) 19. a ~ about, of (she told charming ~ries about her travels; to narrate gripping ~ries of wartime heroism) 20. a ~ that + clause (have you heard the ~ that she intends to resign?) (see also *story line* at **line I** n.) ["newspaper account"] 21. to carry, circulate, print, run a ~ (all the newspapers carried the ~ about the fire) 22. to feature a ~ 23. to edit; rewrite; write a ~ 24. to file a ~ 25. to cover up, hush up, kill, spike, suppress a ~ 26. a breaking ("very new"); cover; exclusive; feature; follow-up; front-page; human-interest; lead; scare; sensational ~ 27. the inside ~ (you can read the inside ~ (of the catastrophe) in tomorrow's edition) 28. a ~ breaks ("becomes known"); circulates ["background information"] 29. to get the (whole) ~ ["misc."] 30. the ~ goes that she intends to resign; I have not heard your side of the ~; to stick to one's ~; the police could not make a coherent ~ out of his ravings; a success ~ ("a successful career")

story II storey n. ["floor level"] 1. a lower; top; upper ~ 2. on a ~ 3. (misc.) a 10-story building (see also *multi-storey car park* at **park I** n.)

stove n. 1. to light a ~ 2. a coal; gas; kerosene (AE), paraffin (BE); kitchen; oil; pot-belly, pot bellied ~ 3. on a ~ (to cook smt. on a ~ (AE) = (BE) to cook smt. on a cooker)

stow away v. to ~ on a ship

straggle v. (P; intr.) to ~ across the border; they ~d into the lecture hall

straight adj. 1. absolutely, dead, perfectly ~ 2. (misc.) to go ~ ("to become law-abiding"); to set smb. (about smt.) ~ ("to disabuse smb.") (let me set you ~ about smt.: I'm not coming back!) 3. to be ~ with smb. about smt. ("to level with smb. about smt.") (let me be absolutely ~ with you: I'm not coming back!) 4. to get smt. ~ (let's get at least one thing ~: I'm not coming back!) (misc.) as ~ as an arrow, as ~ as a die

straightforward adj. 1. ~ about 2. ~ with

strain I n. ["exertion"]["tension"] 1. to impose, place, put a ~ on 2. to feel; stand the ~ 3. to ease, relieve the ~ 4. (a) considerable, great; intolerable; terrible, tremendous ~ 5. (an) emotional, mental; financial; physical ~ 6. back ~; eyestrain 7. a ~ on (the crisis has imposed a nearly intolerable ~ on relations between the two countries) 8. under a ~ 9. (misc.) the stresses and ~s of daily life; "Let the train take the ~!" (originally an advertising slogan promoting trains over private cars)

strain II v. 1. (d; intr.) to ~ at (the dog ~ed at the leash/BE lead) 2. (E) they were ~ing to get the car out of the mud

strain III n. ["variety of microorganism"] a strong, virulent; attenuated, weak ~

straits n. ["difficulties"] 1. desperate, dire; financial ~ 2. in certain ~ (they were left in desperate ~)

stranded adj. to leave smb. ~

strange adj. 1. ~ to 2. ~ to + inf. (it was ~ to work at night = it was ~ working at night) 3. ~ that + clause (it is ~ that she hasn't written for a whole month) 4. (misc.) ~ to say, she hasn't written for a whole month; it was ~ ¬how/the way¬ she kept coming back

stranger n. 1. a complete, perfect, total, utter ~ 2. a mysterious ~ 3. a ~ to (she's no ~ to us; she's no ~ to hardship) 4. (misc.) I don't know the way – I'm a ~ here myself

strangle v. 1. (D; tr.) to ~ with (he ~d her with a scarf) 2. (misc.) to ~ smb. to death

stranglehold n. 1. to get; have a ~ on smb. (a few multinationals have a ~ on their economy) 2. to loosen; release; tighten a ~

strap I n. 1. a bra; chin; shoulder ~; watchstrap (BE; CE has *watchband*) 2. on a ~ (her purse was held on a ~ around her waist)

strap II v. 1. to ~ loosely; securely; tightly; together (to ~ two sticks together securely) 2. (D; tr.) to ~ onto, to (they ~ped the suitcase to the top of the car; to ~ two sticks to each other) 3. (N; used with an adjective) to ~ smt. tight

strapped adj. (colloq.) 1. completely; financially ~ 2. ~ for cash

stratagem n. 1. to resort to, use a ~ 2. a subtle; wily ~

strategist n. an armchair ("amateur") ~

strategy n. 1. to adopt, design, devise, formulate, map out, plan, work out a ~ 2. to apply, implement, pursue a ~ 3. to outline, unveil a ~ 4. a global; grand, long-range, long-term ~ 5. a campaign, political; defense, military; economic, financial ~ 6. a matter; point of ~ 7. a ~ about, for, on (to

work out a ~ for balancing the budget) 8. a ~ to + inf. (they unveiled a ~ to balance the budget) 9. ~ and tactics

straw n. ["drinking tube"] 1. (to drink) through a ~ ["strand of hay"] 2. to decide smt. by drawing ~s to see who gets the short ~ (also fig.); a ~ in the wind ("a hint of smt. to come"); to clutch at (any) ~s ("to try in desperation"); the final/last ~, or: the ~ that broke the camel's back ("a final burden that exceeds smb.'s endurance") ["hay"] 3. in; on ~ (to find a coin in the ~; to spread a blanket on the ~)

stray v. (D; intr.) 1. to ~ from (to ~ from the subject) 2. (d; intr.) to ~ into, onto (to ~ onto smb.'s property)

streak I n. ["tendency, trait"] (usu. derog.) 1. a cruel; jealous; mean, nasty, vindictive; stubborn ~ (people who have a cruel ~ (in them)) 2. a yellow ~ ("cowardice") 3. with a ~ of (people with a ~ of cruelty (in them)) ["series"] 4. a losing; lucky; winning ~ 5. on a ~ (let's keep gambling if we're on a winning ~!)

streak II v. (P; intr.) to ~ across a field

streaked adj. ~ with (~ with gray)

stream I n. 1. to ford a ~ 2. a mountain; running; swollen ~ 3. an endless; steady ~ (a steady ~ of refugees) 4. the jet ~ ("band of high-velocity winds moving high above the earth's surface")

stream II v. 1. (D; tr.) (esp BE) to ~ according to, by (are pupils ~ed by ability?) 2. (P; intr.) people were ~ing towards the town square; the audience came ~ing out of the auditorium

street n. 1. to pave; resurface; surface a ~ 2. to widen a ~ 3. to block, cordon off; cross a ~ 4. to name; number ~s 5. a bustling, busy; congested; crowded ~ 6. a deserted, lonely; quiet ~ 7. a back; high (BE), main (AE) ~ 8. a cross; dead-end; one-way; through ~ 9. a broad, wide; long; narrow; short; sidestreet; winding ~ 10. a ~ curves; goes; runs (in a certain direction) 11. across; along the ~ 12. down; up the ~ 13. in (esp. BE), on (esp. AE); off the ~ (the children were playing in/on the ~ and we told them to get off it) 14. (BE) in the high ~ 15. (AE) on the main ~; on Main Street 16. (misc.) the bottom/end/middle/top of the ~; to take a ~ (they took the wrong ~; we were on/in (esp. BE) the right ~); follow this ~ for two blocks; the ~ is clear; (the) mean ("squalid") ~s; (AE; military) a battery; company ~ (see also **easy street**; Usage Note at **road**)

streetcar n. (AE; BE has *tram*) 1. to drive, operate a ~ 2. (as a passenger) to board, get on; catch a ~; get off a ~; to come; go, travel by ~; to miss a ~; to ride a ~; to ride in/on a ~; to take a ~ 3. a ~ runs; stops; the ~s are not running today but normally run every half hour and pick people up from this ~ stop 4. a ~ for, to; from (is this the ~ from the center of town to the airport?) 5. (misc.) the driver of a ~ is a motorman or an operator

strength n. ["power"] 1. to build up, develop (one's)

~ 2. to find; gain, gather summon (up) (the) ~ 3.
to conserve, husband, save (one's) ~ 4. to recoup,
regain (one's) ~ 5. to overtax, sap, tax; test smb.'s
~ 6. brute, great; inner; physical; tensile ~ 7. ~
grows, increases; declines, ebbs away; fails 8. a
position; show; test of ~ (see also *negotiate from a
position of strength* at **negotiate**) 9. the ~ to + inf.
(she somehow managed to summon up the ~ to lift
the weight!) 10. in ~ ("in large numbers") 11. with
~ (it would take all her ~ to push it so she pushed it
with all her ~) ["number of personnel, units"] 12. full,
maximum ~ (to bring a department up to full ~) 13.
at; below ~ (our police force was at full ~ but it is
now five officers below ~) ["misc."] 14. on the ~ of
smt. ("relying on smt.") (on the ~ of your recommendation, we gave her the job); on the ~ (BE;
colloq.) ("on the full-time permanent staff")
stress I *n.* ["emphasis"] 1. to lay, place, put (the) ~
on 2. to shift the ~ from; to 3. great, particular,
special ~ ["intensity of sound"] (ling.) 4. to place,
put the ~ on (a syllable) 5. to shift the ~ from;
to 6. (a) dynamic; free; fixed; pitch; primary;
qualitative; quantitative; secondary; strong; weak
~ 7. sentence; word ~ ["tension"] 8. to cause, create, generate; increase ~ 9. to alleviate, reduce,
relieve; control; decrease ~ 10. emotional, mental,
psychological; perceived; physical ~ 11. a degree,
level of ~ 12. under ~ (he's been under a lot of
~ lately) ["misc."] 13. with the ~ on (a program of
house-building with the ~ on affordable housing
for key workers) 14. ~es and strains
stress II *v.* (L; to) the police ~ed (to us) that all
regulations would be enforced strictly
stretch I *n.* ["final phase"] (esp. AE) 1. the final ~
2. to fade in the ~ (see also *homestretch* at **home
straight**) ["expanse"] 3. a ~ of 4. on a ~ (the race
took place on a ~ of barren land) ["period of time"] 5.
to do a ~ (in prison) 6. (misc.) for hours at a ~
stretch II *v.* 1. (N; used with an adjective) we ~ed
the rope tight 2. (P; intr.) the prairie ~es for miles;
"The lone and level sands ~ far away" – P. B. Shelley, 1792–1822, "Ozymandias"
stretched *adj.* 1. fully ~ 2. ~ to the limit; ~ tight;
tightly ~
stretch out *v.* (D; tr.) to ~ to (she ~ed her hand out
to us in friendship = she ~ed out her hand to us in
friendship)
stretcher *n.* (to carry smb.) on a ~
strew *v.* 1. (d; tr.) to ~ with (the field was strewn
with bodies) 2. (P; tr.) bodies were strewn all over
the field; their equipment was strewn across the
floor; they ~ed flowers around the auditorium
stricken *adj.* ["afflicted"] 1. ~ by, with 2. (misc.) con-
science-stricken; grief-stricken; panic-stricken;
poverty-stricken
strict *adj.* 1. ~ about, concerning, in 2. ~ towards,
with
strictly *adv.* ~ speaking
stricture *n.* a ~ against, on

stride I *n.* ["normal speed"] 1. to hit one's ~ 2. to
break one's ~ ["progress"] 3. to make great ~s (in) 4.
considerable, giant, great, tremendous ~s ["misc."]
5. to take smt. in (one's) ~ ("to confront a problem
calmly")
stride II *v.* 1. to ~ confidently; purposefully 2. (P;
intr.) she strode confidently into the room; he
strode towards the lectern; they strode angrily out
of the room
strident *adj.* ~ in (they were ~ in their demands)
strife *n.* 1. to cause, create, stir up ~ 2. bitter ~ 3.
civil; communal; domestic; factional; industrial;
internal; internecine; political; sectarian ~ 4. ~
among, between; in (to create ~ between two sisters) 5. during the ~
strike I *n.* ["refusal to work"] 1. to call, go (out) on;
organize a ~ 2. to conduct, stage a ~ 3. to avert;
break (up); mediate; settle a ~ 4. a buyers'; hunger; rent ~ (the prisoners went on a hunger ~) 5.
a general; lightning (BE); nationwide; sit-down;
sympathy; token ~ 6. an official (BE); unofficial
(BE), wildcat ~ 7. a ~ fails; occurs, takes place;
spreads; succeeds 8. an outbreak, series, wave of ~
9. on ~ (some of the workers went (out)/were on ~)
["attack"] 10. to carry out, make a ~ 11. an air; first;
preemptive; retaliatory; second ~ ["disadvantage"]
(from baseball) (AE) 12. they have two ~s against
them ("they are at a decided disadvantage") ["discovery"] 13. an oil ~
strike II *v.* 1. (D; intr.) ("to refuse to work") to ~
against; for (the workers struck against the company for higher pay) 2. (D; intr., tr.) ("to hit") to ~
against, on (she struck her head against the door) 3.
(d; tr.) ("to impress") to ~ as (the idea struck me as
silly) 4. (d; intr.) to ~ at ("to attack") (to ~ at the
root causes of poverty; to ~ at the enemy) 5. (d; tr.)
to ~ from, off (they struck her name off the list) 6.
(N; used with an adjective) ("to make") to ~ smb.
dead 7. (BE) (O: can be used with one object) ("to
give") he struck me a heavy blow 8. (R) it struck
me that the inflation rate has been going down
strike back *v.* (D; intr.) to ~ at (to ~ at the enemy)
strikebreaker *n.* to bring in ~s
strike out *v.* 1. (d; intr.) ("to act") to ~ against, at (to
~ against injustice) 2. (d; intr.) to ~ for ("to set out
for") (to ~ for shore) 3. (misc.) to ~ on one's own
("to begin an independent existence")
string *n.* ["cord"] 1. to tie a ~ 2. to untie a ~ 3. a
ball; length; piece of ~ ["grouping of players according to ability"] (esp. AE) 4. first; second ~ (see also
strings)
string along *v.* (D; intr.) to ~ with
strings *n.* ["strips used for fastening"] 1. apron ~;
shoestrings (see also **purse strings**) ["cords on a
musical instrument"] 2. to pick (esp. AE), pluck ~
["influence"] (colloq.) 3. to pull ~
strip I *n.* ["runway"] 1. an airstrip, landing ~ ["dividing patch"] 2. a centre (BE), median (AE) ~ (on a
road)

strip II *v.* 1. (D; intr.) to ~ for (to ~ for a physical examination) 2. (d; tr.) to ~ of (to ~ smb. of all civil rights) 3. (D; intr., tr.) to ~ to (to ~ to the waist) 4. (N; used with an adjective) to ~ smb. naked; to ~ smt. bare

strip down *v.* (d; intr., tr.) to ~ to (he ~ped down to his underwear)

stripe *n.* ["strip, band"] 1. a horizontal; vertical ~ 2. a sergeant's ~s 3. a service ~ (worn on a soldier's sleeve to indicate length of service) 4. with ~s (a dress with vertical ~s on it) ["sort"] (esp. AE) 5. of a certain ~ (people of that/his ~ are not to be trusted!)

stripping *n.* (BE) (commercial) asset ~ (see also **weather stripping**)

striptease *n.* to do, perform a ~

strive *v.* 1. (d; intr.) to ~ for (to ~ for peace) 2. (formal) (E) we ~ to please

stroke *n.* ["apoplexy"] 1. to have, suffer a ~ 2. a crippling, massive, severe ~ 3. a slight ~ ["movement, series of movements"] 4. (tennis) a backhand; forehand ~ 5. (swimming) to swim a few ~s 6. a backstroke; breast; butterfly ~; sidestroke ["sound of striking"] 7. at, on a ~ (at the ~ of midnight) ["movement of a piston"] 8. an exhaust; exhaust-suction; intake; suction ~ ["action"] 9. a brilliant ~ 10. (misc.) a ~ of genius; to reduce inflation at one/a ~; their hard-won freedoms were abolished with the ~ of a pen ["misc."] 11. a ~ of luck; one golfer led the other by a couple of ~s

stroll I *n.* 1. to go for, have, take a ~ 2. to take smb. for a ~ (she took the children for a ~) 3. a leisurely ~

stroll II *v.* (P; intr.) to ~ through the park

stroller *n.* (esp. AE) 1. to push, wheel a ~ (BE has *(baby) buggy, pushchair*) 2. in a ~

strong *adj.* 1. ~ in (I'm not ~ in mathematics) 2. (colloq.) ~ on, when it comes to (none too ~ on common sense) 3. (misc.) she's still going ~ at 90 years of age!; as ~ as an ox

structure *n.* 1. (ling.) to generate a ~ 2. (ling.) (a) deep; grammatical; intermediate; surface ~ 3. (pol.) a power ~ 4. bone; cellular; molecular ~ 5. a basic; complex; solid ~ 6. a corporate; economic, financial; political; price; tax; wage ~ 7. in ~ (that sonata is quite complex in ~ = that sonata has quite a complex ~)

struggle I *n.* 1. to abandon, give up; carry on, put up, wage; lose; win a ~ 2. a bitter, desperate, fierce, frantic, hard, stubborn, violent; ceaseless, unending, unrelenting, unremitting; last-ditch; uphill ~ (to put up a last-ditch ~; to put up a stubborn ~ against terminal illness) 3. an armed; internecine; life-and-death ~ 4. a power ~ 5. the class ~ 6. a ~ about, over (a ~ over property rights) 7. a ~ against, with (a ~ against poverty; a ~ with one's conscience) 8. a ~ between (a ~ between the two factions) 9. a ~ for (a ~ for justice) 10. a ~ + inf. (it was a ~ to make ends meet = it was a ~

making ends meet; we had quite a ~ to make ends meet = we had quite a ~ making ends meet) 11. in ~ (locked in ~; they were locked in a fierce ~ with the government over pension rights) 12. (misc.) a ~ to the death

struggle II *v.* 1. to ~ bravely, heroically; desperately, hard, stubbornly 2. (D; intr.) to ~ against, with (to ~ against tyranny) 3. (D; intr.) to ~ for (to ~ for freedom) 4. (D; intr.) to ~ about, over (to ~ over property rights) 5. (E) they ~d to remain alive 6. (misc.) to ~ to one's feet

strung out *adj.* (slang) ~ on (~ on heroin)

strut *v.* 1. (d; intr.) to ~ into (to ~ into a room) 2. (d; intr.) to ~ out of (to ~ out of a meeting) 3. (P; intr.) they were ~ting around the auditorium

stub *n.* 1. a cigarette; pencil; ticket ~ 2. a check (AE), cheque (BE) ~

stubborn *adj.* 1. ~ about 2. (misc.) to be as ~ as a mule

stubbornness *n.* 1. sheer ~ 2. ~ about 3. ~ to + inf. (it was sheer ~ not to agree) 4. out of ~ (she refused to compromise out of ~) 5. (misc.) to have the ~ of a mule

stuck *adj.* ["burdened"] (colloq.) 1. ~ with (he always gets ~ with the worst jobs; I am ~ with the chore of breaking the bad news) ["infatuated"] (colloq.) 2. ~ on (he's ~ on her) ["fully involved"] (colloq.) (BE) 3. ~ into (there is no holding him once he gets ~ into smt.) ["fixed"] 4. to get ~ (they got ~ in the mud) 5. ~ fast, firmly 6. ~ on, to (a stamp ~ on an envelope; one thing ~ to another with glue = two things ~ ¬to each other/together¬ with glue)

stud *n.* at ~ ("for breeding") (the retired racehorses are at ~)

student *n.* 1. an excellent, outstanding; good, strong ~ 2. a poor, weak ~ 3. a day; evening; external (BE); foreign, overseas (BE); full-time; part-time; special; transfer; work-study ~ 4. a college, university; degree; doctoral; graduate, postgraduate (esp. BE); high-school (AE); MA; post-doctoral; undergraduate ~ 5. (misc.) a student-teacher USAGE NOTES: (1) A student of law is a law student, a student of geology is a geology student, a student of dentistry is a dentistry student, but a student of medicine is a medical student. (2) To say that a geologist is a student of geology (as some dictionaries still do) is true but misleading. A geologist has been a student of geology long enough to be a professionally qualified expert at it. (3) In GB, *students* usu. refer to those in post-secondary education. Younger ones are usu. called *pupils*. However, secondary-school pupils in Britain have begun to call themselves *students* (or *school students*), too. In the US, the term *students* is used for those at a university and in secondary school – *college students, high-school students*. Children at (BE)/in (esp. AE) primary school are usu. called *pupils* in the US, and almost always in GB. (4) In CE, one can differentiate between a *student of*

Freud ("a student of Freud's ideas") and *Freud's student/a student of Freud's* ("one who was taught personally by Freud").

studies *n.* 1. to begin, take up; complete, finish; pursue one's ~ 2. advanced; further; graduate, postgraduate (esp. BE); undergraduate ~ 3. Black; business; classical; computer; liberal (BE); media; peace, war; social; women's ~ (see also **study I** *n.*)

studio *n.* 1. an art; dance ~ 2. a film, movie; radio; recording; television, TV ~ 3. a soundproof ~ 4. in a ~ (to shoot a film on location rather than in a ~) (see also *studio apartment* at **apartment**; *studio flat* at **flat II** *n.*)

study I *n.* ["investigation"] 1. to conduct, do, make a ~ 2. a careful, detailed, exhaustive, in-depth, intensive, rigorous, thorough ~ 3. a feasibility; follow-up; pilot; statistical ~ 4. a classic, classical; definitive ~ 5. a case; empirical; epidemiological; experimental; research; scientific; time-and-motion ~ 6. a ~ proves; shows; suggests (have research studies shown that smoking is bad for health?) 7. under ~ (the matter is under ~) ["branch of learning, subject"] 8. nature ~ ["learning"] 9. advanced ~ 10. supervised ~ 11. an area of ~ (see also *study period* at **period**; **studies**)

study II *v.* 1. to ~ closely; diligently, hard, seriously 2. (D; intr.) to ~ for (to ~ for a degree) 3. (d; intr.) to ~ under (to ~ under a well-known professor) 4. (Q) to ~ how to survive in the wilderness 5. (misc.) he is ~ing to become a nurse

study up *v.* (colloq.) (AE) (D; intr.) to ~ on (to ~ on a topic)

stuff I *n.* (colloq.) ["subject matter"] 1. to know one's ~ 2. heady ("exciting"); kid ("elementary") ~; the same old ~ ["knowledge, ability"] 3. to show, strut one's ~ 4. (AE) the ~ to + inf. (she has the ~ to succeed) 5. (misc.) (esp. AE) the right ~ (she has the right ~ to succeed) ["duties"] 6. to do one's ~ USAGE NOTE: *Stuff* can be used to replace or refer to a mass or uncountable noun, as *thing* can replace or refer to a countable noun: A container full of liquid fell on the floor: *the thing [= it]* broke and the *stuff* in it poured out.

stuff II *v.* 1. (d; tr.) to ~ in, into (she ~ed all sorts of things into her suitcase) 2. (D; tr.) to ~ with (she ~ed her suitcase with all sorts of things) 3. (N: used with an adjective) she ~ed her suitcase full (of all sorts of things); she ~ed it tight

stumble *v.* 1. (d; intr.) to ~ across, into, on, onto, upon ("to meet by chance") (to ~ across an old manuscript) 2. (D; intr.) to ~ over ("to trip over") (also fig.) (she ~d over every sentence)

stumbling block *n.* 1. an insurmountable ~ 2. a ~ to (their stubbornness constitutes an insurmountable ~ to progress)

stump I *n.* to remove a ~ (of a tree)

stump II *v.* (d; intr.) to ~ for (esp. AE) ("to support by making speeches") (to ~ for a candidate)

stun *v.* (R) it ~ned me to see him drunk

stunned *adj.* 1. ~ at; with (I was ~ with astonishment at his drunkenness) 2. ~ to + inf. (I was ~ to see him drunk)

stunt *n.* 1. to do, perform; pull off a ~ 2. (colloq.) to pull a ~ ("to do smt. unexpected") 3. a publicity ~ 4. a daredevil ~ 5. a ~ backfires; comes off

stupid *adj.* 1. ~ about 2. ~ to + inf. (it was just plain ~ of me to agree = I was just plain ~ to agree)

stupidity *n.* 1. to display ~ 2. sheer ~ 3. the height of ~ 4. ~ to + inf. (it was sheer ~ to agree) 5. ~ that + clause (it was sheer ~ that I decided to agree)

stupor *n.* 1. to fall into a ~ 2. a drunken ~

stutter I *n.* (to have, speak with) a nervous ~

stutter II *v.* 1. to ~ nervously 2. (B) she ~ed (out) a few words to us 3. (L; to) she ~ed to us that she was sorry = "I'm sorry," she ~ed (to us)

style I *n.* ["manner of expression"] 1. to develop; polish, refine one's ~ 2. an affected; classic, classical; elegant; flowery, ornate; formal; informal; pedestrian; plain; poetic; prose; vigorous ~ 3. in a ~ (to write/speak in a flowery ~) ["manner of behaving"] 4. to cramp smb.'s ~ 5. an abrasive; grand ~; smb.'s (characteristic) ~ ("why doesn't he at least apologize?" "that's not his ~. = it's not his ~ to apologize.") 6. in (a) ~ (to live in a/in grand ~) (see also **lifestyle**) ["fashionable elegance"] 7. high ~ 8. in ~ (to live in ~) ["excellence of expression or behavior"] 9. to lack ~ ["fashion"] 10. to keep up with the latest ~s 11. in ~ (running shoes are in ~) 12. out of ~ (dresses like that never go out of ~) (see also **family style**)

style II *v.* (D; tr.) to ~ for (to ~ shoes for comfort)

suasion *n.* ["persuasion"] moral ~

subconscious *n.* in smb.'s ~

subdivide *v.* 1. to ~ equally, evenly 2. (D; tr.) to ~ into

subject I *adj.* (cannot stand alone) ~ to (~ to change)

subject II *n.* ["topic, theme"] 1. to bring up, broach; mention; pursue; tackle a ~ 2. to address, cover, deal with, discuss, take up, treat a ~ 3. to dwell on; exhaust; go into a ~ 4. to avoid; drop a ~ 5. to stick to; change; stray from the ~ 6. an appropriate, suitable; everyday, mundane; favorite; interesting; pleasant ~ 7. a boring, uninteresting; controversial, thorny; delicate, ticklish; inappropriate; taboo; unpleasant ~ 8. a ~ comes up (for discussion) 9. a ~ for (a ~ for discussion) 10. about, on a ~ (we have nothing to say on that ~; and while we're on the ~ of money, when are you going to pay me back?) (see also **subject matter**) ["area, course of study"] 11. to study, tackle, take, take up a ~ 12. to master a ~ 13. an elective (AE), optional (BE); required ~ 14. a major (AE), main (BE); minor (AE), secondary (BE) ~ ["grammar"] 15. a compound; grammatical; impersonal; logical; simple ~ ["citizen of a monarchy"] (esp. BE) 16. a British; loyal; naturalized ~ 17. a ~ of (a loyal ~ of Her Majesty the Queen)

subject III *v.* (d; tr.) to ~ to (to ~ smb. to torture)

subjection *n.* 1. ~ to 2. in ~ (to live in ~ to smb. else)

subject matter *n.* related; unrelated ~

subjugate *v.* (D; tr.) to ~ to

subjugation *n.* 1. ~ to 2. in ~ (to live in ~ to smb. else)

subjunctive *n.* (grammar) in the ~ (the verb was in the ~)

sublease see **sublet**

sublet *v.* 1. (D; tr.) to ~ from (to ~ a house from smb.) 2. (D; tr.) to ~ to (to ~ a house to smb.)

sublimate *v.* (D; tr.) to ~ into

sublime *n.* from the ~ to the ridiculous

submarine *n.* 1. a conventional; midget; nuclear, nuclear-powered ~ 2. ~s dive; hunt in packs; submerge; surface

submerge *v.* (D; refl., tr.) to ~ in (she ~d herself in her work)

submission *n.* ["giving in"] 1. in ~ to (they lived in ~ to the conqueror) ["argument"] (legal) 2. to make a ~ 3. a ~ that + clause (her lawyer made a ~ (to the court) that she had not been informed of her rights)

submissive *adj.* ~ to

submit *v.* 1. (B) ("to present") they ~ted their report to us; they ~ted their case to arbitration 2. (D; intr.) ("to yield") to ~ to (to ~ to superior force) 3. (d; intr.) ("to agree to") to ~ to (to ~ to arbitration) 4. (usu. legal) (L; to) ("to claim") her lawyer ~ted (to the court) that she had not been informed of her rights

subordinate I *adj.* ~ to

subordinate II *v.* (D; refl., tr.) to ~ to (they had to ~ their own needs to the needs of the group)

subordination *n.* ~ to

subpoena I *n.* 1. to issue a ~ 2. to serve a ~ on 3. a ~ to + inf. (she received a ~ to appear in court in two weeks)

subpoena II *v.* 1. (D; tr.) to ~ as (to ~ smb. as a witness) 2. (H) they ~ed her to appear in court in two weeks

subscribe *v.* 1. (D; intr.) to ~ for ("to agree to purchase") (they ~d for a large number of shares) 2. (D; intr.) to ~ to ("to receive regularly") (to ~ to a magazine) 3. (d; intr.) to ~ to ("to agree with") (to ~ to an opinion)

subscriber *n.* a ~ to (a ~ to a magazine)

subscription *n.* ["arrangement for receiving a periodical"] 1. to get, take out; have a ~ to 2. to renew a ~ 3. to cancel a ~ 4. an annual; individual; institutional ~ 5. a ~ comes up for renewal; lapses 6. a ~ to (a ~ to a magazine) ["amount of money pledged"] 7. a public ~

subsequent *adj.* (cannot stand alone) ~ to (it happened ~ to World War I but prior to World War II)

subservience *n.* 1. ~ to 2. in ~ (to live in ~ to smb. else)

subservient *adj.* ~ to

subsidiary *adj.* ~ to

subsidized *adj.* heavily ~

subsidy *n.* 1. to apply for, request a ~ 2. to provide a ~ for 3. to cut, reduce; grant; refuse a ~ to 4. an arts; farm; government, public, state ~ 5. a generous ~ 6. a ~ covers (the ~ does not cover all our expenses) 7. a ~ for; to

subsist *v.* (d; intr.) to ~ on

subsistence *n.* 1. (a) bare, hand-to-mouth ~ 2. a means of ~

substance *n.* ["drug"] 1. (AE) a controlled ~ ("a drug regulated by law") 2. an illegal ~ 3. (misc.) ~ abuse ["meaningful quality"] 4. ~ to (is there any ~ to their claim?) 5. in ~ (their claim is, in ~, that they have been mistreated) 6. (misc.) a matter of ~; a person of ~; a rumor without (any) ~ ["matter"] 7. a chemical; hard; oily; pure; radioactive; toxic ~

substitute I *n.* 1. a poor ~ 2. a ~ for (a ~ for sugar = a sugar ~; Smith is now the ~ for Jones as quarterback)

substitute II *v.* (D; intr., tr.) to ~ for (when Jones couldn't play, the coach ~d Smith for Jones: Smith is now ~ting for Jones)

substitution *n.* 1. to make a ~ 2. a ~ for (the coach's ~ of Smith for Jones as quarterback)

subsume *v.* (formal) (d; tr.) ("to classify") to ~ under (to ~ an item under a more inclusive category)

subterfuge *n.* to resort to, use (a) ~

subtract *v.* (D; tr.) to ~ from (to ~ five from ten and get five)

subtraction *n.* to do ~

suburb *n.* 1. to move from; to a ~ 2. a fashionable; leafy (BE); residential ~ 3. from the ~s (to smb. from the ~s, London is a fabulous place!) 4. in the ~s (to live in the ~s) 5. a dormitory ~ (BE; BE also has *dormitory town*; AE has *bedroom community*)

subvention see **subsidy**

subversion *n.* to engage in ~

subway *n.* ["underground railway"] (esp. US) (GB has *tube, underground*) 1. to take a/the ~ 2. (to go/travel) by, on the ~ (I always travel by ~) 3. (misc.) the driver of a ~ (train) is a motorman (or to be non-sexist) an operator ["system of underground trains and stations"] 4. from; in; to the ~ (crime in the ~; I couldn't find the right entrance to the ~ or the right exit from the ~!) (see also *subway station* at **station I** *n.*; *subway system* at **system**; *subway train* at **train I** *n.*)

succeed *v.* 1. (D; tr.) ("to come after") to ~ as (she ~ed me as treasurer) 2. (D; intr.) to ~ in; with (to ~ in doing smt.; to ~ in business; she ~ed with her plan in the face of serious opposition) 3. (D; intr.) to ~ to ("to inherit") (to ~ to the throne)

success *n.* 1. to achieve, attain (a) ~ 2. to enjoy ~ 3. to score a ~ 4. to make a ~ of smt. 5. a brilliant, dazzling, great, howling (AE), huge, notable, resounding, roaring, rousing, signal, spectacular, thorough, total, tremendous, unequivocal, unqualified ~ 6.

(an) immediate; instant, overnight ~ 7. a modest ~ 8. a box-office; commercial; critical ~ 9. (a) ~ as; in; with (Laurence Olivier scored a notable ~ as Othello in the play of the same name)

successful *adj.* 1. highly, very; moderately ~ 2. ~ as; at, in; with (~ in business; ~ with women)

succession *n.* ["right to succeed to an office, position"] 1. the ~ to (the ~ to the throne) ["misc."] 2. in ~ ("successively, one after the other") (for several years in ~; who is third in ~ to the throne?); in seemingly endless ~; in quick, in rapid ~

successor *n.* 1. smb.'s immediate ~ 2. a worthy ~ 3. a ~ to (the ~ to the throne)

succumb *v.* (D; intr.) to ~ to (to ~ to smb.'s urging; to ~ to a disease)

suck *v.* 1. (d; tr.) to ~ from (to ~ (out) the juice from an orange) 2. (d; tr.) to ~ into (they were ~ed into the family quarrel) 3. (D; intr.) to ~ on (she was ~ing on an orange) 4. (D; tr.) to ~ through (she ~ed the juice through a straw) 5. (N; used with an adjective) she ~ed the lemon dry 6. (misc.) the baby ~ed at its mother's breast

suck away *v.* (D; intr.) to ~ at (to ~ at a lollipop)

sucker *n.* ["easily deceived person"] (colloq.) 1. to make a ~ out of smb. 2. a ~ for (she's a ~ for any hard-luck story) 3. a ~ to + inf. (he's a ~ to have believed her)

sue *v.* 1. (d; intr.) to ~ for ("to request") (to ~ for peace) 2. (D; intr., tr.) ("to seek in court") to ~ for; over (to ~ for damages; she ~d him for a large sum of money; she ~d him over a disputed claim) 3. (E) ("to seek in court") they ~d to get their property back

suffer *v.* 1. (D; intr.) to ~ for (to ~ for one's sins) 2. (D; intr.) to ~ from (to ~ from insomnia) USAGE NOTE: In BE it is now frequent – but wrong! – to have *suffer with insomnia.*

sufferer *n.* 1. a fellow ~ 2. a ~ from (a ~ from insomnia) USAGE NOTE: In BE it is now frequent – but wrong! – to have *a sufferer of insomnia.*

suffering *n.* 1. to inflict ~ on 2. to bear, endure ~ 3. to alleviate, ease, relieve ~ 4. chronic; great, incalculable, intense, untold; mental, psychological; physical ~ 5. the amount, extent, level of ~ (the extent of ~ caused by the war is almost incalculable)

suffice *v.* 1. to barely, hardly, scarcely; just; more than ~ 2. (D; intr., tr.) to ~ for (my salary more than ~s (us) for our basic needs) 3. (E) it should ~ to cite her previous accomplishments; my salary ~s to meet our basic needs 4. (misc.) ~ (it) to say (that) we will do our duty = let it ~ to say that we will do our duty

sufficient *adj.* 1. barely, hardly, scarcely; just; more than ~ 2. ~ for (my salary is more than ~ for our basic needs) 3. ~ unto oneself ("independent") 4. ~ to + inf. (my salary is ~ to meet our basic needs; it would have been ~ to send a brief note)

suffix I *n.* a derivational; diminutive; inflectional ~

suffix II *v.* (d; tr.) to ~ to (to ~ an ending to a word)

suffrage *n.* 1. to extend, grant ~ 2. universal; women's ~

sugar *n.* 1. to produce; refine ~ 2. beet; brown; cane; confectioner's (AE), icing (BE); crude; demerara (BE); granulated; lump; maple; white ~ 3. (med.) blood ~ 4. a lump; spoonful of ~ 5. (misc.) as sweet as ~

suggest *v.* 1. (B) she ~ed a compromise to us 2. (D; refl., tr.) to ~ as (she ~ed a compromise as a possible solution even though no suitable compromise seemed to ~ itself as suitable) 3. (D; tr.) to ~ for (she ~ed a compromise candidate for the position) 4. (G) she ~ed compromising 5. (K) who ~ed his taking part? 6. (L; can be subj.; to) who ~ed that he ¬take/should take/took (BE)¬ part?; she ~ed (to us) that an exception ¬be/should be/was (BE)¬ made; it was ~ed (to us) that an exception had in fact been made; the evidence seemed to ~ strongly that the vicar had been murdered! 7. (Q; to) did she ~ (to us) why the exception had been made?; did she ~ where we should meet? 8. (misc.) may I venture to ~ a possible compromise?

suggestion *n.* ["proposal"] 1. to advance, make, offer, proffer (formal), produce, put forward a ~ 2. to ask for, call for, invite ~s (see also *open to suggestions* at **open I** *adj.*) 3. to act on; adopt; consider; take; welcome a ~ 4. to decline, reject, turn down a ~ 5. an appropriate; constructive; good; helpful; pertinent; tentative ~ 6. an inappropriate; outrageous; preposterous, ridiculous ~ 7. a ~ about, concerning 8. a ~ that + clause; can be subj. (she made the ~ (to us) that an exception ¬be/should be/was (BE)¬ made; she made the ~ (to us) that an exception had in fact been made; there was never any ~ that the vicar had been murdered!) 9. at smb.'s ~ (at her ~, an exception was made) ["hint, overtone"] 10. the merest, slightest ~ (there was just the slightest ~ of menace in his voice; there was just the merest ~ of garlic in the sauce)

suggestive *adj.* 1. strongly, very ~ 2. ~ of

suicide *n.* 1. to commit ~ 2. to attempt; contemplate ~ 3. assisted; mass; political ~ 4. attempted ~ 5. ~ to + inf. (it would be sheer ~ to try to climb that mountain in this weather!) (see also *suicide bomber* at **bomber**; *suicide note* at **note I** *n.*; *suicide pact* at **pact I** *n.*; *suicide threat* at **threat**)

suit I *n.* ["lawsuit"] 1. to bring (a), file (a), institute a ~ against 2. to contest; press; settle a ~ (to settle a ~ out of court) 3. to dismiss; lose; win a ~ 4. a civil; class-action; frivolous; libel; malpractice; pending ~ 5. a ~ against; over (to bring a class-action ~ against the government over civil liberties) ["suit of clothes"] 6. to have a ~ made 7. to have on, wear; put on; take off; try on a ~ (I wore my best ~ to meet her parents; indeed, I wore a ~ and tie for the occasion) 8. a bathing, swimsuit, tank; diving; gym; ski; space; sweat ~ USAGE NOTE: Women wear swimsuits or bathing suits (old-fashioned) or (swimming) costumes (BE). Men wear (swimming) trunks. 9. a bespoke (BE), custom-made, made-to-measure (BE), made-to-order; off-the-peg (BE), ready-made ~ 10. a business (AE), lounge (BE); dress; leisure; sailor ~ 11. a double-breasted; single-breasted; three-piece; two-piece ~ 12. (for women) a pants (AE), trouser (BE) ~ 13. (BE) a boiler ~ ("overalls") 14. a ~ fits (well) 15. (misc.) a ~ of armor; (old-fashioed) a ~ of clothes (for men); (humorous) in one's birthday ~ ("naked") ["set of similar playing cards"] 16. to follow ~ (also fig.) (the government suggested a plan and the opposition followed ~) 17. a major; minor; trump ~ (which ~ is trumps?) ["trait"] 18. smb.'s strong ~

suit II v. 1. to ~ perfectly; very well 2. (R) it ~ed her to keep him guessing 3. (misc.) to ~ smb. down to the ground (BE), to ~ to a T ("to be perfectly appropriate for")

suitability n. ~ for

suitable adj. 1. eminently, very; hardly ~ 2. ~ for, to 3. ~ to + inf. ("would it be ~ to discuss this matter at lunch?" "no: it's hardly a ~ matter for discussion at lunch")

suitcase n. 1. to fill, stuff; pack; unpack a ~ 2. (esp. AE) to check a ~ (through) 3. to label a ~

suite n. ["group of connected rooms"] 1. a bridal; executive; hospitality; hotel; luxury; office; penthouse ~ USAGE NOTE: For en-suite apartment and en-suite bathroom, see **apartment**; **bathroom**. ["set of matched furniture"] 2. a bedroom; living-room; three-piece (BE) ~ (comprising a sofa and two armchairs that all match)

suited adj. 1. ideally, very, well ~ 2. ~ for, to (~ for the job; ~ to each other) 3. ~ to + inf. (is he psychologically ~ to be a police officer?)

sulk v. (D; intr.) to ~ about, over

sum n. 1. to raise a ~ (of money) 2. a considerable, large, not inconsiderable; substantial, tidy; equivalent; flat; lump; nominal; round; trivial ~ 3. (formal) in ~ (in ~, it could not have been worse) 4. (misc.) a three-figure, four-figure … six-figure … ~ (see also sum total at **total I** n.)

summarize v. 1. (D; tr.) to ~ for (she ~d the plot for the class) 2. (misc.) to ~ (then), in Romeo and Juliet, Romeo and Juliet meet, fall in love, and die

summary n. 1. to give; make, prepare a ~ 2. a brief, executive ~ 3. a news ~ 4. in ~ (in ~ (then), in Romeo and Juliet, Romeo and Juliet meet, fall in love, and die)

summer n. 1. Indian; St. Luke's (BE; rare); St. Martin's (BE; rare) ~ 2. early; last; late; mid-; next ~ 3. a (long) hot ~ 4. during, over (esp. AE) the ~ 5. in (the) ~ (we met late in the ~ of 1995 = we met in the late ~ of 1995) (see also summer solstice at **solstice**)

summit n. ["peak"] (also fig.) 1. to reach a ~ 2. at a ~ (to stand at the ~; at the ~ of her career) ["summit conference"] 3. to convene, have, hold a ~ 4. at a ~ (we met at the ~ in Geneva)

summon v. 1. (D; tr.) to ~ as (to ~ smb. as a witness)

2. (D; tr.) to ~ before (to be ~ed before a judge) 3. (D; tr.) to ~ to (we were ~ed to the director's office) 4. (H) to ~ smb. to do smt.

summons I n. 1. to issue a ~ 2. to serve a ~ on smb. = to serve smb. with a ~ 3. a ~ to + inf. (she received a ~ to appear in court)

summons II v. (BE) (H) she was ~ed to appear in court

sums n. to do ~

sun n. 1. to blot out the ~ 2. the blazing; bright; hot; midday, noonday; tropical ~ 3. the ~ is down; up 4. the ~ is in; out 5. the ~ beats down, blazes; climbs (higher in the sky); comes out; comes up, rises; goes down, sets; goes in (behind a cloud); shines 6. an eclipse of the ~ = a solar eclipse 7. the light; rays of the ~ (= sunlight; the sun's rays) 8. on the ~ (changes have been observed on (the surface of) the ~) 9. in, under the ~ (to sit in the ~; "Mad dogs and Englishmen go out in the midday ~" – attributed to or used by Noël Coward, 1931) 10. (misc.) there's nothing new under the ~

sunburn n. 1. to get; have a ~ 2. a painful ~

sundae n. a butterscotch; chocolate; hot-fudge; ice-cream; strawberry ~

sundown n. at ~

sunlight n. 1. bright, brilliant, glaring, strong ~ 2. in the ~ 3. a patch; shaft of ~

sunrise n. at ~

sunscreen n. to apply, put on ~

sunset n. at ~

sunshine n. 1. to bask in; soak up ~ 2. bright, dazzling; warm ~ 3. a ray of ~ (also fig.) (the good news came as a ray of ~ after so much bad news)

sunstroke n. to get; have ~

suntan n. 1. to get; have a ~ 2. a deep ~ (see also suntan lotion at **lotion**; suntan oil at **oil I** n.)

supercilious n. ~ about

superfluous adj. ~ to + inf. (it would be quite ~ to add anything to their remarks)

superhighway n. the Information Superhighway

superimpose v. (D; tr.) to ~ on (to ~ one image on another; to ~ a new way of life on old customs)

superintendent n. a building (AE; AE also has janitor; BE has caretaker); school ~ (US) = ~ of schools (US)

superior I adj. 1. clearly, decidedly, definitely, far, (very) much, vastly ~ 2. ~ in (~ in numbers; ~ in rank) 3. ~ to (~ to all the other competitors) 4. (misc.) a mother ~

superior II n. smb.'s immediate ~

superiority n. 1. to achieve, establish ~ 2. to enjoy, hold ~ 3. clear ~ 4. numerical ~ 5. intellectual; social; (so-called) racial ~ 6. a feeling of ~ 7. ~ in; over, to (a feeling of ~ in skill over/to the other competitors) (See also **air superiority**)

superlative n. (to express oneself) in ~s

supermarket n. at, in a ~ (to shop at/in a ~)

supersensitive adj. 1. ~ about (~ about charges of corruption) 2. ~ to (~ to criticism)

superstition *n.* 1. a common ~ 2. a ~ about (there is a common ~ about the number thirteen) 3. a ~ that + clause (it is a common ~ that thirteen is an unlucky number)

superstitious *adj.* ~ about (a lot of people seem ~ about the number thirteen)

supervision *n.* 1. to exercise ~ of, over 2. to tighten ~ 3. to ease up on, relax ~ 4. close, strict; lax, slack; proper ~ 5. joint ~ 6. under smb.'s ~ 7. with; without ~ (don't let the child out without proper ~!)

supper *n.* 1. to eat (esp. AE), have ~ 2. to cook; make, prepare; serve ~ 3. a cold; hot; light; nutritious, wholesome; substantial ~ 4. at, during; over ~ (what did you discuss at/during/over ~?) 5. for ~ (what was served for ~?) 6. (misc.) to give smb. ~ (esp. BE); to take smb. to ~

supplement I *n.* 1. a color; lifestyle; literary; Sunday ~ (to a newspaper) 2. a dietary; iron; mineral; vitamin ~ (to take a vitamin ~ every day) 3. a ~ to 4. for a ~ (of) (¬for a ~ of $25/for a $25 ~¬ to the standard charge, you can have an en-suite bathroom!)

supplement II *v.* (D; tr.) to ~ by; with (she ~ed her regular income ¬with a part-time job/by doing a part-time job¬)

supplementary *adj.* ~ to

supplicate *v.* (formal) (H) to ~ smb. to do smt.

supply I *n.* 1. to bring up, provide ~lies 2. to lay in, receive; replenish; store ~lies 3. an abundant, liberal, plentiful; inexhaustible ~ (of) 4. a fresh ~ (of) 5. emergency; relief ~lies 6. military; office ~lies 7. the coal; money; water ~ 8. ~lies hold out 9. ~lies run out; run short 10. in short ~ (see also **supply lines**) ["misc."] 11. the law of ~ and demand

supply II *v.* 1. (D; tr.) to ~ to (to ~ power to industry) 2. (D; tr.) to ~ with (to ~ industry with power)

supply lines *n.* 1. to overextend ~ 2. to cut ~

support I *n.* 1. to give, lend, offer, provide ~ 2. to pledge one's ~ 3. to bolster, increase, strengthen; drum up, enlist, line up, mobilize, muster, rally, round up ~ 4. to seek (smb.'s) ~ 5. to gain, get, receive, win (smb.'s) ~ 6. to have; lose the ~ of 7. to derive, draw ~ from 8. to cut off, terminate, withdraw (one's) ~ 9. ardent, complete, enthusiastic, firm, full, fullhearted (esp. BE), overwhelming, solid, strong, unflagging, unqualified, unstinting, unwavering, wholehearted ~ 10. lukewarm, qualified ~ (to give lukewarm ~ to a candidate) 11. active; bipartisan; liberal; loyal; traditional; vocal; wide ~ 12. emotional, psychological; financial; moral ~ 13. government, state; popular, public ~ 14. child ~ (is that mother eligible to claim child ~?) 15. farm; price ~s 16. ~ for; in 17. ~ from 18. in ~ (of) (she came out in ~ of the party) (see also *no visible means of support* at **means**; *support network* at **network**; **life support**)

support II *v.* 1. to ~ completely, enthusiastically, strongly, wholeheartedly 2. (D; tr.) to ~ in (we ~

you in your efforts) 3. (K) we ~ed their seeking office 4. (misc.) we ~ed her financially all through college

supporter *n.* ["fan"] 1. to alienate; attract ~s (the party has alienated many of its traditional ~s in its effort to attract new ones) 2. an ardent, enthusiastic, fervent, firm, loyal, stalwart, staunch, steady, strong; life-long; traditional ~ 3. a lukewarm ~ 4. an active; vocal ~ (see also the Usage Note for **fan II**)

supportive *adj.* 1. very ~ 2. ~ of

suppose *v.* 1. (L) we ~ that the situation will improve 2. (formal) (M) we ~d him to be guilty

supposed *adj.* ~ to + inf. (it was ~ to rain; she was ~ to work today; the situation is ~ to improve – why hasn't it (done so)?)

supposition *n.* 1. to make a ~ 2. (a) mere, pure ~ 3. a ~ that (I reject the ~ that he is guilty) 4. on (a) ~ (of) (to condemn smb. on mere ~ (of guilt))

suppository *n.* 1. to insert; remove a ~ 2. a rectal; vaginal ~

supremacy *n.* 1. to achieve, establish, gain; struggle for ~ (over) 2. to acknowledge smb.'s ~ 3. air; military; naval ~ 4. ~ in; over

supreme *adj.* to reign ~

supremo *n.* (BE) (see **czar**)

surcease *n.* (formal) ~ from, of

surcharge *n.* 1. to add a ~ to 2. to impose a ~ (on); to put a ~ on (the candidates vowed not to impose any ~s after the election; the new government put a ~ on all imported cars) 3. a ~ for, on (there is a ~ on these goods; there is ¬a ~ of $5/a $5 ~¬ for anything extra)

sure *adj.* 1. to make ~ 2. absolutely, quite ~ 3. far from ~ (I am far from ~ that she will pass the exam) 4. for ~ (can you say for ~ where the ceremony will take place?) 5. ~ of (we were ~ of his support) 6. ~ to + inf. (she is ~ to pass the exam) 7. ~ that; wh-word + clause (I am ~ that she will pass the exam; make ~ that all doors are locked; are you ~ that you turned the gas off?; are you ~ where the ceremony will be held?; are you ~ who will officiate at the ceremony?; are you ~ how long the ceremony will take?)

surety *n.* to act as, stand ~ for

surf *n.* to ride the ~

surface *n.* 1. a bumpy, rough, uneven; even, smooth; flat; plane ~ 2. the calm; frozen ~ (of a body of water) 3. below, beneath, under, underneath the ~ (also fig.) 4. above, over; on the ~ (also fig.) (see also *surface area* at **area**; *surface temperature* at **temperature**) 5. (misc.) to scratch, skim (esp. AE) the ~ ("to treat superficially")

surge I *n.* ["military escalation"] 1. a troop ~ ["technical"] 2. a voltage ~ = a ~ in voltage

surge II *v.* (P; intr.) the crowd ~d around the entrance, through the corridor, and into the auditorium

surgeon *n.* 1. a brain; dental; flight; orthopedic

(AE), orthopaedic (BE); plastic; veterinary (BE; BE prefers *vet*; AE has *veterinarian*) ~ 2. a tree ~ 3. a ~ performs operations, operates (on patients) **surgery** *n.* ["branch of medicine"] 1. to perform ~ 2. to undergo ~ 3. corrective, remedial; cosmetic; elective; plastic ~ 4. major; minor ~ 5. brain; by-pass; open-heart; transplant ~ 6. keyhole ~ (BE); laser ~; microsurgery 7. emergency; heroic; radical ~ ["office"] (BE) 8. a dentist's; doctor's ~ (CE has *doctor's office*) ["consultation period"] (BE) 9. to hold a ~ (our MP holds a ~ every week) 10. an MP's ~ ["misc."] 11. tree ~ (see the Usage Note for **office**)

surmise I *n.* (formal) ["conjecture"] a ~ that + clause (she expressed a ~ that the situation would improve)
surmise II *v.* (L) she ~d that the situation would improve
surname *n.* a double-barrelled ~ (esp. BE) (I asked Peregrine Chimp-Gibbon about his double-barrelled ~)
surplus I *adj.* ~ to (BE) (this merchandise is ~ to requirements; workers who are made redundant as ~ to requirements)
surplus II *n.* 1. to accumulate a ~ 2. to run ("have"), show a ~ 3. a budget; trade ~ 4. a ~ in 5. (BE) in ~ (our foreign trade is in ~)
surprise I *n.* 1. to spring a ~ on smb. 2. (mil.) to achieve ~ 3. to express; register ~ 4. to show ~ 5. (a) complete, outright, total ~ (the enemy achieved complete ~) 6. a pleasant; unpleasant ~ (they sprang an unpleasant ~ on us) 7. ~ at (to express ~ at recent events) 8. a ~ to (the results were a complete ~ to everyone) 9. a ~ to + inf. (it was a pleasant ~ to learn of her promotion) 10. a ~ that + clause (it was a ~ that she ¬was/should have been¬ promoted) 11. by ~ (the enemy took our fortress by ~) 12. to smb.'s ~ (to our ~ he was not drunk = to our great ~ he was not drunk = much to our surprise he was not drunk) 13. (misc.) it came as no ~; it will come as no ~ (to anyone) that she has been promoted; the element of ~ (see also *take by surprise* at **take II** *v.*)
surprise II *v.* 1. to ~ greatly, very much 2. (J) I ~d him lurking in the undergrowth 3. (R) it ~d me to see them drunk; it ~d us that their party won the election; it wouldn't ~ me in the least if he won the election 4. (misc.) it ~d me how much they had grown
surprised *adj.* 1. ~ at, by (~ at the news; I was ~ at how much they had grown) 2. ~ to + inf. (I was ~ to see them drunk) 3. ~ that + clause (I was ~ that they were drunk)
surprising *n.* 1. ~ to + inf. (it was ~ to see them drunk) 2. ~ that + clause (it was ~ that they were drunk) 3. (misc.) it is ~ how much they have grown
surrender I *n.* 1. unconditional ~ 2. a ~ to (there will be no ~ to pressure)

surrender II *v.* (D; intr., tr.) to ~ to (to ~ to the enemy; to ~ a fortress to the invader)
surrounded *adj.* ~ by, with
surroundings *n.* 1. comfortable; elegant; luxurious; pleasant; sumptuous ~ 2. austere; unpleasant ~ 3. amid; in ~ (a pleasant cottage (set) amid rural ~)
surtax *n.* to impose, put a ~ (on)
surveillance *n.* 1. to conduct, maintain ~ 2. to keep; place smb. under ~ 3. (a)round-the-clock, constant; close, strict; police ~ 4. electronic ~ 5. under ~ (she was placed under strict police ~)
survey *n.* 1. to carry out, conduct, do, make, undertake a ~ 2. a brief; comprehensive ~ 3. an aerial; geodetic; house-to-house; topographical ~ 4. a ~ reveals, shows 5. the findings, results of a ~ 6. a ~ into, of 7. according to; in a ~
survival *n.* 1. to assure smb.'s ~ 2. ~ against, despite; as; from, since (his ~ against all the odds as dictator since 1973) 3. (misc.) the struggle for ~ resulting in natural selection leading to the ~ of the fittest
survive *v.* 1. (D; intr.) to ~ on (to ~ on bread and cheese; we can barely ~ on our income) 2. (E) she ~d to tell the tale 3. (N) to ~ intact and undamaged 4. (misc.) he has ~d against all the odds as dictator since 1973
survivor *n.* 1. to pick up ~s (at sea) 2. the sole ~ 3. a ~ from; of ("A Survivor from Warsaw" – Arnold Schönberg, 1947)
susceptibility *n.* ~ to (~ to disease)
susceptible *adj.* ~ to
suspect I *n.* 1. to arrest a ~ 2. to interrogate, question a ~ 3. to place a ~ under surveillance 4. to identify a ~ 5. the prime ~ 6. (misc.) "Round up the usual ~s." – *Casablanca* (film), 1942
suspect II *v.* 1. to ~ strongly 2. (D; tr.) to ~ as (to be ~ed as a participant in the robbery) 3. (D; tr.) to ~ of (rightly or wrongly, the police ~ed him of participation in the robbery) 4. (L) we ~ strongly that he participated in the robbery
suspend *v.* 1. (D; tr.) ("to hang") to ~ from (to ~ a hook from the ceiling) 2. (D; tr.) ("to bar temporarily") to ~ from (to ~ smb. from duty)
suspenders *n.* (AE) a pair of ~ (that hold up trousers) (BE has *braces*)
suspense *n.* 1. to break the ~ 2. great; mounting; unbearable ~ 3. in ~ (to keep smb. in ~; to wait in ~) 4. in ~ about, over (everyone was in ~ over the outcome) 5. (misc.) we cannot bear the ~
suspension *n.* independent ~ (on a car)
suspicion *n.* ["suspecting"] ["mistrust"] 1. to arouse, cause, create, evoke, give rise to, sow, stir (a) ~ 2. to entertain, harbor, have a ~ 3. to confirm a ~ 4. to cast ~ on 5. to allay, dispel ~ 6. a groundless, unfounded ~ 7. a deep, profound, strong; lingering, lurking; slight, sneaking; vague; well-founded ~ 8. a ~ about, of (there was some ~ about her motives) 9. (the) ~ falls on smb. 10. a ~ that + clause (these events confirmed my strong ~ that she was

guilty) 11. above ~ ("not suspected") 12. on ~ of (arrested on ~ of murder) 13. under ~ ("suspected") 14. (misc.) a cloud of ~; the finger of ~ points at you; to regard smt. with ~ ["slight trace"] 15. a ~ of (not even the slightest ~ of scandal; a sauce with just a ~ of garlic in it)

suspicious adj. ["suspecting"] 1. ~ about, of (the police were ~ of the butler) ["causing suspicion"] 2. ~ that + clause (it was ~ that no story appeared in the press) (see also *suspicious circumstances* at **circumstances**)

suture n. 1. to put in a ~ 2. to remove, take out a ~

swagger v. (P; intr.) he ~ed into the room; they ~ed down the street

swallow I n. ["act of swallowing"] to have, take a ~

swallow II v. 1. to ~ down; hard 2. (misc.) to ~ smt. whole (also fig.) (they got him to ~ their ridiculous story whole!)

swamp I n. to drain a ~

swamp II v. (d; tr.) to ~ by, with (they were ~ed with work)

swan n. 1. ~s glide; hiss 2. a flock (esp. in flight), herd of ~s 3. a young ~ is a cygnet 4. a male ~ is a cob 5. a female ~ is a pen 6. as graceful as a ~

swap I n. ["exchange"] 1. to make a ~ for; with 2. a straight ~ (she made a straight ~ with me of her bicycle for a hi-fi)

swap II v. 1. (D; tr.) to ~ for (she ~ped her bicycle for a hi-fi) 2. (D; tr.) to ~ with (I ~ped places with my friend = my friend and I ~ped places (with each other)) 3. (O) I'll ~ you my bicycle for your hi-fi

swarm v. 1. (d; intr.) ("to crowd") to ~ around (the autograph seekers ~ed around the actor) 2. (d; intr.) ("to congregate") to ~ in (tourists were ~ing in the streets) 3. (d; intr.) ("to throng") to ~ into (to ~ into an auditorium) 4. (d; intr.) ("to throng") to ~ over, through (to ~ through the streets) 5. (d; intr.) ("to teem") to ~ with (the streets were ~ing with tourists) 6. (P; intr.) the spectators were ~ing across the field

swarming adj. ~ with (the streets were ~ing with tourists)

swath, swathe n. ["path"] to cut a ~ (to cut a wide ~ of destruction through the ranks of the enemy)

swathe v. (d; tr.) ("to wrap") to ~ in (she was ~d in mink)

sway I n. ["dominance"] 1. to hold ~ over 2. under smb.'s ~

sway II v. 1. to ~ gently 2. (D; intr.) to ~ to (to ~ to the music) 3. (misc.) to ~ from side to side; to ~ back and forth; to ~ in the breeze

swayed adj. easily ~ (by an argument)

swear v. 1. to ~ solemnly 2. (B) ("to promise solemnly") they swore allegiance to the government 3. (D; intr.) ("to curse") to ~ at (he swore at them) 4. (d; intr.) ("to rely completely") to ~ by (everyone ~s by her remedy for a cold) 5. (d; intr.) to ~ to ("to confirm solemnly") (to ~ to the truth of a statement) 6. (d; tr.) ("to bind solemnly")

to ~ to (to ~ smb. to secrecy) 7. (E) ("to promise solemnly") she swore to tell the truth; she swore to avenge her father's death 8. (L; to) ("to promise solemnly") she swore (to us) that she would tell the truth 9. (misc.) to ~ on the Bible; to ~ like a trooper ("to use obscene language freely") (see also *swear an oath* at **oath**)

swear in v. (D; tr.) to ~ as (she was sworn in as president)

sweat I n. 1. to break out in a cold ~ 2. beads, drops of ~ (ran down my face) 3. (misc.) to work up a good ~; to be dripping with ~; by the ~ of one's brow ("by working very hard")

sweat II v. to ~ freely, profusely

sweater n. 1. to crochet; knit a ~ 2. to put on; take off a ~ 3. to have on, wear a ~ 4. a light; warm ~ 5. an angora; mohair; turtleneck; woolen ~

sweep I n. ["reconnaissance"] 1. to make a ~ (behind enemy lines) ["winning of a series of contests"] 2. to make a clean ~ (of a series) ["sweeper"] 3. a chimney ~ ["sweeping movement or configuration"] 4. a broad ~ (the broad ~ of the prairie) 5. with a ~ (he dismissed my objections with a ~ of his hand)

sweep II v. 1. (d; tr.) ("to remove") to ~ off (we swept the snow off the car) 2. (d; tr.) ("to remove") to ~ out of (to ~ the debris out of the room) 3. (N; used with an adjective) ("to clean with a broom") to ~ a floor clean 4. (P; intr., tr.) ("to move swiftly and overwhelmingly") the other party swept into office; they were swept into the sea; our troops swept through the village; the enemy column swept across the border 5. (misc.) to ~ smt. under the carpet (BE)/rug (AE) ("to conceal smt.")

sweep away v. (D; tr.) to ~ from (the children swept the snow away from the house)

sweep down v. (d; intr.) to ~ on (the storm swept down on the village)

sweep in v. (D; intr.) to ~ from (the hurricane swept in from the sea)

sweepstakes, sweepstake n. to win the ~

sweet adj. (colloq.) 1. ~ on ("in love with") (he is ~ on her) 2. (used typically by women) ~ to + inf. (it was ~ of you to think of me = you were ~ to think of me) 3. (misc.) as ~ as honey/sugar

swell I n. ["growing wave"] a groundswell (a groundswell of support was building up)

swell II v. (d; intr.) to ~ with (to ~ with pride)

swelling n. 1. to have) a painful ~ 2. (the) ~ goes down, subsides (the ~ went down)

swerve v. 1. (D; intr.) to ~ from; to (to ~ from a course; to ~ to the right) 2. (misc.) the car ~d (¬in order/so as¬) to avoid a rabbit in the road

swift adj. 1. (lit.) ~ of (~ of foot) 2. ~ to + inf. (she was ~ to react)

swig n. (colloq.) ["swallow"] to have, take a ~

swim I n. 1. to have, take a ~ 2. to go for a ~

swim II v. 1. (P; intr.) to ~ for shore; to ~ around the island; to ~ into the wrong lane 2. (misc.) to go ~ming

swindle I *n.* to perpetrate a ~
swindle II *v.* (D; tr.) to ~ out of (to ~ smb. out of money)
swing I *n.* ["attempt to hit"] 1. to take a ~ at 2. a wild ~ ["shift"] 3. a ~ in (there was a ~ in public opinion) 4. a ~ to (in the last elections there was a ~ to the right) 5. (misc.) with that new medication, patients may be subject to frequent mood ~s ["operation"] 6. in full ~ (the work was in full ~)
swing II *v.* 1. (D; intr., tr.) to ~ at (he swung at me; I swung the bat at the ball) 2. (D; intr.) to ~ from; to (to ~ from right to left) 3. (P; intr., tr.) public opinion swung towards the right and away from the left; the cranes swung the cargo onto the ship 4. (misc.) ~ your partner round and round
swings *n.* (children play) on the ~
swipe *n.* (colloq.) ["critical remark"] 1. to have, take a ~ at 2. a side ("indirect, implicit") ~
swirl *v.* (P; intr.) she ~ed (a)round the room
switch I *n.* ["change"] 1. to make a ~ 2. a ~ from; to 3. a ~ in (there was a sudden ~ in official policy) ["device used to open or close an electrical circuit"] 4. to flick on, turn on a ~ 5. to flick off, turn off a ~ 6. to throw a ~ ("to turn off or turn on a switch") 7. a master; power; time; toggle ~ ["movable section of railroad track"] (AE) 8. a railroad ~ (BE has *point*)
switch II *v.* 1. (D; intr., tr.) to ~ from; into; to (to ~ to the metric system; she ~ed her support to the other candidate; to ~ from English into Russian) 2. (D; tr.) to ~ with (I ~ed places with my friend = my friend and I ~ed places (with each other))
switchboard *n.* 1. at, on a ~ (to work at a ~) 2. calls jammed the ~
switch over *v.* (D; intr.) to ~ from; into; to (to ~ from English over to Russian)
switcheroo *n.* (slang) (AE) ["variation"] to pull a ~ (on smb.)
swoon I *n.* (old-fashioned) 1. to fall into a ~ 2. in a ~
swoon II *v.* (now usu. fig.) 1. (d; intr.) to ~ over (to ~ over a new film idol) 2. (d; intr.) to ~ with (to ~ with joy)
swoop *n.* ["stroke"] at one fell ~ ("at one time") (the enemy captured all our positions at one fell ~)
swoop down *v.* (D; intr.) to ~ on (the hawk ~ed down on the sheep)
swop (colloq.) (BE) see **swap I, II**
sword *n.* 1. to draw, unsheathe a ~ 2. to brandish; wield a ~ 3. to cross ~s with smb. (now usu. fig.) 4. to run smb. through with a ~, to run through smb. with a ~; thrust a ~ into 5. to sheathe a ~ 6. (misc.) a double-edged, two-edged ~ ("smt. that can have opposite results to those intended")
syllable *n.* 1. to stress a ~ 2. a closed; open; stressed; unstressed ~
syllabus *n.* 1. to design, draw up, make up a ~ 2. a ~ contains, covers, includes 3. in, on a ~
symbiosis *n.* 1. (a) ~ between 2. in ~ with
symbol *n.* 1. a chemical; phallic; phonetic; potent;

religious; sex; status ~ 2. a ~ for (X is a ~ for an unknown quantity) 3. (misc.) a ~ of authority (the scepter is a ~ of royal authority)
symbolic *adj.* ~ of (the scepter is ~ of royal authority)
symmetrical *adj.* ~ to, with
sympathetic *adj.* 1. very ~ 2. ~ to, with (rare)
sympathize *v.* 1. to ~ deeply, very much 2. (D; intr.) to ~ with
sympathy *n.* 1. to arouse, stir up ~ for 2. to capture; command; gain, get, win ~ 3. to express, extend; feel, have ~ for 4. to display, show ~ for 5. to lavish ~ on 6. to accept smb.'s ~ 7. deep, deepest, great, heartfelt, profound, strong ~ (please accept our deepest ~ on your bereavement) 8. little; no ~ for (to have little ~ for smb.) 9. one's ~ goes out to smb. 10. a token of one's ~ 11. ~ for (to have ~ for the underdog) 12. in ~ with (to be in complete ~ with smb.'s cause) 13. out of ("because of") ~ (we did it out of ~ for your family) 14. out of ("without") ~ (to be completely out of ~ with smb.'s cause) 15. (misc.) an expression of smb.'s ~; a message of ~; our deepest ~ goes out to you at a time like this
symphony *n.* 1. to compose, write a ~ 2. to perform, play a ~ (see also *symphony orchestra* at **orchestra**)
symposium *n.* 1. to conduct, hold a ~ (on) 2. to attend a ~ (on)
symptom *n.* 1. to develop; display, have, manifest, present, present with (med.), show ~s (of) 2. an acute; chronic ~ 3. a classic; specific ~ (the patient presented with all the classic ~s of that disease) 4. a ~ appears, develops; disappears, goes away; persists; recur (seek medical help if ~s persist or recur after treatmen) 5. the onset of ~s 6. withdrawal ~s
symptomatic *adj.* ~ of
synch *n.* (colloq.) ("synchronization") 1. in ~ (with) 2. out of ~ (with) (their ideas are out of ~ with the times)
synchronize *v.* (D; tr.) to ~ with
syndicate *n.* 1. to form a ~ 2. a crime; drug ~
syndrome *n.* 1. the China; Stockholm ~ 2. acquired immune deficiency ~ (AIDS); chronic fatigue ~ (CFS); Down (esp. AE), Down's ~; premenstrual ~ (PMS); sudden infant death ~ (SIDS); toxic shock ~; (post-)traumatic stress ~ USAGE NOTES: PMS is also called PMT (pre-menstrual tension). SIDS is also called cot death (BE) or crib death (AE). Post-traumatic stress syndrome is also called post-traumatic stress disorder and is then abreviated PTSD.
synonymous *adj.* ~ with ("furze" and "gorse" are ~ with each other = "furze" is ~ with "gorse")
synopsis *n.* to give; make, prepare a ~
synthesis *n.* to make a ~
syphilis *n.* 1. to spread, transmit ~ 2. to catch, develop, get; have ~ 3. acquired; congenital; early; late; latent; primary; secondary; tertiary; untreated ~

syringe *n.* a disposable; hypodermic ~

syrup *n.* 1. chocolate; corn; maple ~ 2. cough ~

system *n.* USAGE NOTE: "System" can be preceded by such verbs as bypass, create, develop, replace, overthrow and can be followed by such verbs as break down, fail, permit, succeed, work. ["group of items serving a common purpose"] 1. an air-conditioning; drainage; heating; sprinkler ~ 2. an amplifying; communications; intercom(munication); public-address; stereo ~ 3. a brake; steering ~ 4. a data-processing; filing; software; writing ~ 5. an early-warning; guidance ~ 6. a highway (AE), motorway (BE), road; postal; rail, railroad (AE), railway (esp. BE); sewage; transit (esp. AE), transport (esp. BE), transportation (esp. AE); subway (AE), tube (esp. BE), underground (BE) ~ 7. (misc.) a life-support ~ (to turn off a life-support ~ when a patient's condition becomes hopeless) ["form of organization, principles pertaining to a form of organization"] 8. a belief, philosophical; value ~ 9. an honor; merit; quota; seniority ~ 10. an economic; educational, school; government(al); health-care; judicial; legal; political; social ~ (an educational ~ can also be called a ~ of education; a government(al) ~ can also be called a ~ of government; a judicial ~ can also be called a ~ of justice; an educational ~ can also be called a ~ of education) 11. a capitalist; communist; democratic; socialist ~ 12. an authoritarian; electoral; multiparty; one-party; two-party; totalitarian ~ 13. a banking; monetary ~ 14. a class; hierarchical ~ (see also *caste system* at **caste**) 15. a patronage; spoils ~ 16. (colloq.) (AE) a buddy ~ 17. in, under a ~ (under our political ~; there may be defects in the ~) 18. (misc.) to beat; buck (AE) the ~ ("to challenge established procedures") ["group of items forming a unified whole in nature"] 19. an ecosystem; mountain; river; solar ~ ["functionally related group of bodily elements or structures"] 20. the cardiovascular; central nervous; circulatory; digestive; excretory; genito-urinary; immune; muscular; reproductive; respiratory; skeletal ~ ["classification"] ["type of measurement"] 21. a decimal; metric; monetary; number; taxonomic ~ ["group of substances in or approaching equilibrium"] (chemistry) 22. a binary; ternary ~ ["set of meteorological conditions"] 23. a high-pressure; low-pressure ~ ["procedure"] 24. the touch ~ (of typing) ["elements that allow the operation of a computer"] 25. to boot up; reboot a ~ 26. a disk-operating, operating; retrieval ~ ["misc."] 27. ~s analysis; a ~s analyst; ~s theory; to become/be part of a ~; a ~ for doing smt. = a ~ to do smt. (to devise a ~ for winning at poker = to devise a ~ to win at poker); a shock to the ~ (the current crisis may deliver a much-needed shock to the international economic ~)

T

T *n.* to a ~ ("precisely") (you fit the role to a ~)
tab I *n.* ["tabulator, device for setting a margin"] 1. to set
a ~ ["bill"] (colloq.) (AE) 2. to pick up the ~ for (she
picked up the ~ for everyone) 3. the ~ for (a pretty
high ~ for a mediocre meal!) (see also **tabs**)
tab II *v.* (colloq.) (AE) 1. (d; tr.) ("to identify") to ~
as (she was ~bed as a leading contender) 2. (d; tr.)
("to designate") to ~ for (large sums were ~bed for
school construction)
tabernacle *n.* to build a ~
table *n.* ["piece of furniture"] 1. to lay (esp. BE), set
(esp. AE) a ~ 2. to clear a ~ 3. a bedside; coffee;
corner; dressing; end; night; tray; window; writing ~ 4. a dining-room; dinner; kitchen ~ (set the
dining-room ~ for six) 5. a card; drop-leaf; folding
~ 6. a billiard; ping-pong; pool; snooker ~ 7. the
operating ~ (in a hospital) 8. (AE) a training ~ (for
members of a team) 9. around, round a ~ (to sit
around a ~) 10. ¬at the ~/at ~ (BE)¬ ("while eating") (we never discuss politics at the dinner ~) 11.
across; on; over; under a ~ 12. the foot; head of
a ~ 13. (misc.) to book (BE)/reserve (AE) a ~ in a
restaurant (I see that Sir has reserved the window
~ for tonight) ["table for conducting discussions, negotiations"] ["negotiating session"] 14. a bargaining,
conference, negotiating; round ~ 15. at the ~ (at
the negotiating ~) 16. on the ~ (a new offer was put
on the ~) ["enumeration, list"] 17. to compile, draw
up a ~ 18. a conversion; genealogy; life, mortality;
multiplication; periodic; times ~ (see also *table of
contents* at **contents** 3; **timetable**) 19. logarithmic
~s 20. in a ~ (to give data in ~s) ["level"] 21. a water
~ (the ~ is high; low) ["misc."] 22. to turn the ~s
on smb. ("to reverse the roles in a struggle with
smb."); under the ~ ("illegally")
tablespoon *n.* a heaping (AE), heaped (BE);
level ~
tablet *n.* ["pad"] (AE) 1. a writing ~ ["pill"] 2. to take
a ~ (see also *aspirin tablet* at **aspirin**) 3. a scored ~
["slab"] 4. a bronze; clay; marble; stone ~
taboo *n.* 1. to observe a ~ 2. to break, violate a ~ 3.
a rigid ~ 4. a ~ about, against, on 5. (to place smt.)
under (a) ~ 6. (misc.) the ~s surrounding smt. (See
also *taboo subject* at **subject I** *n.*)
tabs *n.* (colloq.) ["watch, surveillance"] to keep ~ on
tack I *n.* ["short nail"] 1. a carpet; thumb (AE; BE
has *drawing pin*) ~ ["direction of a sailing ship"] 2. the
port; starboard ~ ["course of action"] ["direction"] 3. to
change ~; take a new ~ 4. (misc.) to go off, start off
on the wrong ~ (see also **brass tacks**)
tack II *v.* (d; tr.) ("to attach") to ~ onto, to (an
amendment was ~ed onto the bill)
tackle *n.* fishing ~
tack on *v.* 1. (D; tr.) to ~ as (the clause was ~ed on

as an amendment to the bill) 2. (D; tr.) to ~ to (an
amendment was ~ed on to the bill)
tact *n.* 1. to display, exercise, show, use ~ 2. to have
~ 3. considerable, exemplary, great; subtle ~ 4.
the ~ to + inf. (does she have the ~ to conduct the
negotiations?) 5. (misc.) with ~ and diplomacy (to
resolve a problem with ~ and diplomacy)
tactful *adj.* 1. ~ of 2. ~ to + inf. (it was not ~ of you
to mention that = you were not ~ to mention that)
tactic *n.* 1. a scare ~ (see **tactics**) 2. a ~ boomerangs;
fails; pays off, succeeds
tactics *n.* 1. to adopt; devise; employ; use ~ 2.
aggressive; bullying; delaying; diversionary;
pressure; questionable; roughhouse (AE); scare;
smear; strong-arm; wily ~ (to employ questionable ~) 3. defensive; military; offensive ~ 4. (esp.
AE) Madison Avenue ~ ("reliance on sophisticated
promotion, advertising") 5. salami ~ ("maneuver-
ing by stages") 6. ~ boomerang; fail; pay off, succeed 7. (misc.) strategy and ~
tactless *adj.* 1. ~ of 2. ~ to + inf. (it was ~ of you to
mention that = you were ~ to mention that)
taffy *n.* (esp. AE) 1. to make; pull ~ 2. saltwater ~
tag I *n.* ["children's game"] 1. to play ~ 2. a game of ~
tag II *n.* ["label, marker"] 1. to put a ~ on smt. 2. a
baggage, luggage; name; price ~ 3. (AE) license
~s (on a car) 4. (AE) (mil.) dog (colloq.), identification ~s (BE has *identification disc*) ["short
phrase"] (ling.) 5. a question ~ (a tag question has
a question ~, hasn't it?) (see also *tag question* at
question I *n.*)
tag III *v.* (colloq.) 1. (d; intr.) to ~ after ("to follow") (the child ~ged after the others) 2. (d; tr.)
("to label") to ~ as (they ~ged her as a failure) 3.
(AE) (d; tr.) ("to fine") to ~ for (she was ~ged for
going through a red light) 4. (N; used with a noun)
they ~ged her a failure
tag along *v.* 1. (D; intr.) to ~ after; behind (the child
~ged along after the others) 2. (D; intr.) to ~ with
(the child wanted to ~ with the others)
tag end *n.* (esp. AE) ["very end, tail end"] at the ~ (of
smt.)
tail *n.* ["rear appendage"] 1. to move; swish; wag a ~
(an animal, bird, or fish moves its ~; a dog wags its
~; a horse swishes its ~) 2. to dock ("shorten") a ~
3. a bushy ~ 4. (misc.) to turn ~ ("to flee") ["person
who conducts surveillance"] (colloq.) 5. to put a ~ on
smb. ["misc."] 6. a car was right on my ~ ("a car was
following me very closely"); the traffic was nose
to ~! (BE) ("bumper to bumper")
tail end *n.* ["very end"] at the ~ (of smt.)
tailor I *n.* a bespoke (BE), custom; ladies';
men's ~
tailor II *v.* (d; tr.) to ~ to (to ~ an insurance policy to
the needs of the insured)
tailored *adj.* 1. ~ for (~ed for a young audience) 2.
~ to + inf. (an insurance policy ~ to meet the needs
of the insured)
tailor-made *adj.* ~ for; to (~ for the assignment;

we can offer you an insurance policy ~ to your needs!)

tailspin *n.* to go into a ~

tainted *adj.* ~ by, with (~ by scandal)

take I *n.* (colloq.) ["reaction"] 1. a double ~ ("delayed reaction") (to do a double ~) ["illegal payments"] 2. on the ~ (they were all on the ~) ("they were all accepting bribes") ["view"] (colloq.) 3. to have a ~ on (she has an interesting ~ on the subject)

take II *v.* 1. to ~ badly; hard; lightly; personally; philosophically; seriously; well (she took the bad news well/philosophically) 2. (A) ("to carry") she took a cup of tea to him; or: she took him a cup of tea 3. (d; intr.) to ~ after ("to resemble") (he ~s after his father) 4. (d; tr.) ("to construe") to ~ as (we took her gesture as a sign of friendship; I took his remark as a compliment; I took your silence as disapproval; I ~ it as read ("I assume") that you agree (esp. BE)) 5. (d; tr.) ("to grasp") to ~ by (she took him by the hand) 6. (D; tr.) ("to lead, accompany") to ~ for (she took her daughter for a walk; he took us for a ride) 7. (D; tr.) ("to obtain, secure") to ~ for (I took the book for him) 8. (d; tr.) to ~ for ("to assume to be") (just what do you ~ me for?; do you ~ me for a fool?) 9. (D; tr.) ("to obtain"); ("to remove") to ~ from (she took the empty cup of tea from him; I took the money from the safe) 10. (d; tr.) ("to subtract") to ~ from (~ five from ten and get five) 11. (d; tr.) ("to carry") to ~ into (~ the chairs into the house) 12. (d; tr.) to ~ into ("to bring into") (to ~ smb. into one's confidence; they took the prisoner into custody) 13. (d; tr.) to ~ into ("to include") (to ~ smt. into consideration; we took all the facts into account ("we took account of all the facts")) 14. (d; tr.) ("to remove"); ("to deduct") to ~ off (I took the books off the shelf; they took ten pounds off the bill) 15. (d; tr.) ("to carry") to ~ out of (~ the chairs out of the house) 16. (d; intr.) to ~ to ("to like") (to ~ kindly to an offer; she took to them at once) 17. (d; intr.) to ~ to ("to begin"); ("to engage in") (to ~ to drink; to ~ to drinking in bars; she took to gambling at the casinos; he took to fishing with great gusto) 18. (d; intr.) ("to go"); ("to have recourse") to ~ to (to ~ to one's bed; to ~ to the streets; to ~ to the lifeboats; to ~ to the airwaves) 19. (d; tr.) ("to lead, accompany, transport") to ~ to (to ~ smb. to dinner; she took us to the art museum; we took them to the station) 20. (d; tr.) ("to carry") to ~ to (I took the books to the library; she took the money to the bank) 21. (d; tr.) ("to move, transfer") to ~ to (they took the case to the supreme court) 22. (D; tr.) ("to accept, bear") to ~ with (he took his punishment with a smile; to ~ a remark with a grain of salt) 23. (d; tr.) ("to lead; accompany") to ~ with (they took their daughter with them) 24. (G) ("to tolerate, bear, stand") (used typically after *can, can't, could, couldn't*) he just can't ~ being ignored 25. (H) ("to interpret") I took your silence to mean disapproval 26. (H) ("to

require") it took us two hours to do the job 27. (M) ("to consider"); ("to accept") I took him to be a friend; do you ~ this man to be your lawful wedded husband? 28. (N) ("to seize") we took them prisoner; to ~ smb. hostage 29. (O; can be used with one object of time) ("to require") the job took (us) two hours 30. (P; tr.) her work often ~s her abroad; he threatened to ~ his business elsewhere; the guide took us through the museum; she took them across the street 31. (R) ("to demand, require") it sometimes ~s courage to tell the truth; it took (us) two hours to do the job 32. (s) ("to become") to ~ sick 33. (misc.) she took it on/upon herself to break the news; to ~ five (esp. AE; colloq.) ("to have a five-minute break"); to ~ by surprise ("to surprise") (see also *take smb. to court* at **court**; *take for granted* at **granted**; *take to one's heels* at **heels**; *not take kindly to smt.* at **kindly**; *take the law into one's own hands* at **law**; *take smt. lying down* at **lie down**; *take smt. by storm* at **storm I** *n.*; *take smb. under one's wing* at **wing I** n)

take away *v.* (D; tr.) ("to remove") to ~ from (she took the scissors away from the child = she took away the scissors from the child)

take back *v.* 1. (D; tr.) ("to accept") to ~ from (they took the furniture back from the customer = they took back the furniture from the customer) 2. (D; tr.) ("to return") to ~ into (they took the furniture back into the house) 3. (D; tr.) ("to return") to ~ to (she took the book back to the library; the song took me back to my childhood) 4. (P; tr.) they took the chairs back up to the attic; they took the boxes back down to the basement; they took the visitors back across the river

take down *v.* 1. (D; tr.) ("to remove") to ~ from, off (she took the suitcase down from the attic = she took down the suitcase from the attic; I took the books down off the shelf) 2. (D; tr.) ("to write down") to ~ in (to ~ testimony down in shorthand) 3. (D; tr.) to ~ to ("to move") (she took the suitcase down to the basement)

take in *v.* 1. (D; tr.) ("to accept") to ~ as (we took her in as a partner) 2. (D; tr.) ("to fool") to ~ by (he was taken in by flattery) 3. (D; tr.) ("to lead, accompany") to ~ to (to ~ smb. in to dinner) 4. (misc.) to ~ a car in for service; we took them in out of the cold

taken *adj.* ["impressed"] ["infatuated"] 1. very, very much ~ 2. ~ with (he was very (much) ~ with her)

takeoff *n.* ["parody"] (colloq.) 1. to do a ~ of (esp. BE), on (esp. AE) ["departure of an airplane"] 2. to abort a ~ 3. a smooth ~ 4. on ~

take off *v.* 1. (colloq.) (D; intr.) ("to leave") to ~ for (they took off for town) 2. (D; intr.) ("to begin flight") to ~ from (we took off from a small landing strip) 3. (D; intr.) ("to leave") to ~ with (he took off with their money – and with my wife!)

take on *v.* (D; tr.) ("to accept") to ~ as (we took her on as a partner)

take out v. 1. (D; tr.) ("to remove") to ~ from (I took out ten dollars from my purse) 2. (D; tr.) ("to carry") to ~ into (they took the chairs out into the garden) 3. (d; tr.) ("to vent") to ~ on (don't ~ your anger out on me = don't ~ your anger on me) 4. (D; tr.) ("to accompany") to ~ to (she took them out to a nice restaurant) 5. (misc.) he took her out on a date; to ~ it out on smb. ("to make smb. else suffer for one's own problem")

takeover n. 1. a friendly; hostile ~ (of a firm) 2. a corporate; military ~ (see also *(hostile) takeover bid* at **bid I** n.)

take over v. 1. (D; intr., tr.) to ~ from (the new government has taken over from the outgoing government; we will ~ power from them) 2. (D; tr.) to ~ to (I took some soup over to my neighbor = I took over some soup to my neighbor)

take up v. 1. (D; tr.) ("to carry") to ~ from (she took the suitcase up from the basement = she took up the suitcase from the basement) 2. (D; tr.) ("to remove") to ~ from (they took up the carpeting from the floor) 3. (d; tr.) to ~ on ("to accept, adopt") (he took me up on my offer) 4. (D; tr.) ("to carry") to ~ to (she took the suitcase up to the attic) 5., (d; intr.) to ~ with ("to join") (he took up with a rough crowd) 6. (misc.) I'll ~ ("discuss") the matter with my lawyer = I'll ~ the matter up with my lawyer

taking n. (colloq.) for the ~ (it's there for the ~) ("it can be taken by anyone who wants it")

tale n. 1. to concoct, make up a ~ 2. to narrate, tell a ~ 3. to hear a ~ 4. to listen to a ~ 5. an absorbing, exciting, fascinating, gripping, incredible; fanciful; grisly; hair-raising, harrowing, shocking ~ 6. a fairy; folk; old-wives' ~ 7. a tall ("unbelievable") ~ 8. a cautionary ~ 9. a ~ about 10. (misc.) to tell ~s out of school ("to reveal secrets"); thereby hangs a ~ ("there's a lot to be said about smt.")

talent n. 1. to demonstrate, display, show (a) ~ 2. to cultivate, develop a ~ 3. to have (a) ~ 4. to squander one's ~(s) 5. (a) great; mediocre; outstanding; rare; real ~ 6. (a) natural ~ 7. fresh; local; young ~ 8. the ~ to + inf. (she has the ~ to go far) 9. (a) ~ for (a ~ for painting) 10. of; with ~ (a person of considerable ~ who writes poems with great ~) USAGE NOTE: The phrase *local talent* has besides its literal meaning the sense 'local girls as potential sex objects' (as in "Let's check out the local talent").

talented adj. 1. highly, hugely, very ~ 2. ~ at, in 3. ~ with (~ with one's hands)

talk I n. ["address, lecture"] 1. to deliver, give a ~ 2. a pep; sales ~ (the coach gave the team a pep ~ before the game) 3. a ~ about, on (she gave an interesting ~ on bringing up children) ["conversation"]["chatter"] 4. to have a ~ (with) 5. blunt, plain; idle, loose; pillow ~ (inted); table ~ (see also **small talk**) 6. a long; short ~ (she had a long ~ with him about his work) 7. sweet ~ ("flattery") 8. double, fast ~ ("deception") 9. a heart-to-heart ("frank") ~ 10. straight ("frank") ~ 11. (colloq.) big ~ ("boasting")

12. ~ about, of; with (there is ~ of her resigning) 13. ~ that + clause (there is ~ that she will resign) ["type of speech"] 14. baby ~ ["misc."] 15. it's all ~ but no action; the ~ of the town ("the topic being discussed by everyone"); at office parties some people prefer to engage in shop ~ but others prefer to make small ~ (see also **small talk**; **talks**)

talk II v. 1. to ~ bluntly, candidly, frankly, freely, openly 2. to ~ loud, loudly 3. to ~ quietly, softly 4. (D; intr.) to ~ about, of, on (they were ~ing about the elections; she was ~ing of her trip; to ~ on a topic) 5. (d; tr.) to ~ into ("to persuade") (to ~ smb. into doing smt.) 6. (d; tr.) to ~ out of ("to dissuade") (to ~ smb. out of doing smt.) 7. (d; intr.) ("to speak") to ~ to, with (esp. AE) (I will ~ to them about this problem); (esp. AE – I ~ed with them for an hour) 8. (misc.) to ~ big ("to boast"); to ~ turkey ("to speak frankly"); to ~ oneself hoarse; we have ways of making you ~!

talk back v. (D; intr.) to ~ to (to ~ to one's boss)

talk down v. (d; intr.) to ~ to (to ~ to an audience)

talker n. (colloq.) a fast, glib, smooth ~ ("one who speaks glibly, in a deceptive manner")

talking n. to do the ~ (she did all the ~)

talking-to n. (colloq.) ["scolding"] 1. to give smb. a (good) ~ 2. to get a ~

talk over v. (D; tr.) ("to discuss") to ~ with (we ~ed it over with them)

talks n. ["negotiations"] 1. to conduct, have, hold; open; to resume ~ (about) 2. to break off ~ 3. candid, frank; direct ~ 4. arms-control, arms-limitation; contract; peace ~ 5. exploratory, preliminary; private, secret ~ 6. formal; informal ~ 7. high-level; top-level ~ 8. ~ break down, collapse; are deadlocked 9. ~ about; between; with (~ about smt.; ~ with smb.) 10. ~ to + inf. (we've opened ~ with the rebels to release the hostages) 11. (misc.) the next round of ~ will be held in the summer

tall adj. 1. to stand ~ ("to be resolute") 2. to walk ~ ("to be self-confident") 3. (misc.) she is five feet ~ = she is a five-foot-tall woman; she is rather ~ for her age

tally I n. to keep; make a ~

tally II v. (D; intr.) ("to correspond") to ~ with

tambourine n. to play (on) the ~

tamper v. (d; intr.) to ~ with (to ~ with a lock; one should not ~ with a jury)

tampon n. to insert, put in; remove, take out a ~ (see also *sanitary napkin* at **napkin**; *sanitary pad* at **pad**; *sanitary towel* at **towel**)

tan I n. 1. to get; have a ~ 2. a deep ~

tan II v. (intr.) to ~ easily, readily

tandem n. in ~ (with)

tangent I adj. ~ to (~ to a circle)

tangent II n. ["digression"] to go off at, on (esp. AE) a ~

tangential adj. (formal) ["incidental"] ~ to

tangle I n. 1. to unravel a ~ 2. to get into; get out of a ~ 3. a dense, thick ~ 4. in a ~

tangle II v. (colloq.) (d; intr.) ("to quarrel") to ~ about, over; with (don't ~ with him over money)

tangled adj. ~ in

tango n. 1. to perform, play a ~ 2. to dance, do the ~

tank n. ["armored combat vehicle"] 1. to drive a ~ 2. a heavy; light; medium ~ 3. a column of ~s = a ~ column ["receptacle, container"] 4. a fish; fuel; gas (AE), gasoline (AE), petrol (BE); oil; oxygen; septic; water ~ 5. a ~ holds twenty gallons ["prison"] (slang) (esp. AE) 6. in the ~ ["misc."] 7. a think ~ ("a group of thinkers, planners") (a left-leaning think ~) (compare *brain trust, brains trust* at **trust**)

tanker n. an oil ~; a supertanker

tantamount adj. (cannot stand alone) ~ to

tantrum n. 1. to have, throw a ~ 2. to fly into a ~ 3. a temper ~ (he threw a temper ~)

tap I n. ["faucet"] 1. on ~ ("ready to be drawn") (beer on ~) 2. (fig.) on ~ ("available"); ("imminent") (what's on ~ for tonight?) 3. see **faucet** ["act of tapping"] 4. feel; give a ~ 5. a light ~ 6. a ~ on (I felt a light ~ on my shoulder, turned around, and saw ...!)

tap II v. 1. (d; tr.) ("to ask") to ~ for (to ~ smb. for information) 2. (d; intr.) to ~ into ("to use") (to ~ into reserves) 3. (D; tr.) to ~ on ("to strike lightly") (to ~ smb. on the shoulder)

tape I n. ["narrow strip of material"] 1. adhesive, sticky (BE); friction; insulating; magnetic; masking; measuring; name; ticker ~ (a piece/strip of adhesive ~) ["smt. stretched across the track at the end of a race"] 2. to break, breast, reach the ~ (both runners reached the (finishing) ~ together) ["tape recording"] 3. to make a ~ 4. to fast-forward; play, put on, run; play back a ~ 5. to rewind; wind a ~ 6. to erase a ~ 7. a blank ~ 8. on ~ (I have their testimony on ~) 9. audiotape; videotape (see also **red tape**)

tape II v. 1. (d; tr.) ("to attach") to ~ onto, to (she ~d the announcement to the bulletin board; to ~ X to Y = to ~ X and Y to each other) 2. (misc.) to ~ X and Y together; to have it ~d (colloq.) ("to be familiar with the routine (as by knowing the ropes)")

taper v. (d; intr., tr.) to ~ to (~ed to a point)

tape recorder n. 1. to start; turn on a ~ 2. to operate, play a ~ 3. to stop; turn off a ~ 4. a cassette; reel-to-reel ~

tapestry n. 1. to weave a ~ 2. (misc.) (BE) (it's all part of) life's rich ~

taps n. ["bugle call"] (AE; BE has *the last post*) 1. to play, sound ~ 2. at ~ (lights go out at ~)

tar n. coal ~

tardiness n. ~ in

tardy adj. ~ in

target I n. ["goal, mark"] 1. to aim at; destroy; find, hit; shoot at a ~ 2. to track a ~ 3. to miss; overshoot a ~ 4. to fall short of the ~ 5. a civilian; military; moving; stationary ~ 6. an easy; inviting, soft; sitting ~ 7. off ~, wide of the ~ ("not accurate") 8. on ~ ("accurate") 9. (misc.) to become a ~; use as

a ~ (he became an easy ~ for the opposition) (see also *target audience* at **audience**) ["result, aim"] 10. to achieve, meet, reach; aim at, aim for; exceed; fall short of; set a ~ 11. an achievable, realistic; imposible, unrealistic; long-term; short-term ~ 12. a ~ for (to set unrealistic ~s for short-term growth)

target II v. 1. (d; tr.) to ~ as (she was ~ed as the next victim) 2. (d; tr.) to ~ at (a product ~ed specifically at women) 3. (d; tr.) to ~ for (an old building ~ed for demolition)

tariff n. 1. to impose, levy a ~ 2. to pay a ~ 3. a protective ~ 4. a high; low ~ 5. a ~ on (a stiff ~ was imposed on tobacco products) (see also *tariff barrier* at **barrier**)

tarpaulin n. 1. to spread a ~ 2. a piece, sheet of ~

tarry v. (formal) to ~ long (do not ~ long over dinner)

task n. 1. to carry out, do, fulfill, perform; cope with; take on, take upon oneself; undertake a ~ 2. to assign smb. a ~ 3. an enviable; pleasant; welcome ~ 4. a delicate, ticklish; fruitless, hopeless ~ (she took upon herself the delicate ~ of breaking the news) 5. an arduous; difficult; enormous; formidable; Herculean, monumental; strenuous ~ 6. a dreary; irksome; menial; onerous; thankless; unenviable; unpleasant; unwelcome ~ 7. (misc.) to take smb. to ~ for smt. ("to criticize smb. for smt.")

task force n. 1. to deploy; form, set up a ~ 2. an army; naval, navy ~ 3. a ~ to + inf. (the government has set up a ~ to fight racism)

taskmaster n. a hard, rigid, severe, stern ~

taste I n. ["appreciation"] ["sense of what is proper"] 1. to acquire, cultivate, develop a ~ 2. to demonstrate, display, exercise; show (a) ~; indulge one's ~ 3. to have ~ 4. (an) acquired; artistic; discriminating; elegant, excellent, exquisite, impeccable; good; simple ~ (she has excellent ~ in clothes; contemporary art is very much an acquired ~) 5. bad, poor ~ (it is bad ~ to ignore an invitation to a wedding) 6. a ~ for (to develop a ~ for music and finally be able to indulge it) 7. ~ in (they showed good ~ in planning the decor; excellent/poor ~ in music) 8. in (a certain) ~ (everything was done in ¬good/the best possible¬ ~) 9. for; to smb.'s ~ (these paintings are not to my ~: they are too modern for my ~) 10. (misc.) ~s differ; the sense of ~ (see also *a matter of (personal) taste* at **matter I** n.) ["sensation obtained from tasting, eating; flavor"] (also fig.) 11. to have; leave a ~ (the fruit had a pleasant ~; the whole affair left a bitter ~ in my mouth) 12. to bring out, enhance; disguise; spoil the ~ 13. an acquired; authentic; bad, disagreeable, foul; bitter; delicate; mild; nice, pleasant, sweet; salty; sharp; slight; sour; strong; tart ~ (olives are said to be an acquired ~) 14. a ~ permeates smt. (a garlicky ~ permeated the entire dish) 15. a ~ of (a ~ of garlic permeated the whole dish) 16. (misc.) the/a sense of ~; add salt and pepper to ~ (see also *taste buds* at **bud I** n.) ["small amount tasted or experienced"] 17.

to have, take (esp. AE) a ~ (of) 18. to give smb. a
~ of smt. (often fig.) (they gave him a ~ of his own
medicine; that bit part ¬gave me/was¬ my first
real ~ of show business)
taste II *v.* 1. (d; intr.) to ~ like; of (a nectarine ~s
like a peach; the food ~s of garlic) 2. (s) the food
~s good
tasteless *adj.* ~ to + inf. (it was ~ of them to bring
up that subject)
taster *n.* a wine-taster
tatters *n.* in ~ (the beggars were in (rags and) ~; her
clothing was in ~)
tattle *v.* (colloq.) (D; intr.) ("to inform") to ~ on
taunt I *n.* 1. to hurl a ~ at smb. 2. a cruel ~
taunt II *v.* 1. (D; tr.) to ~ about 2. (d; tr.) to ~ into
(to ~ smb. into doing smt.)
tax I *n.* 1. to impose, levy, put a ~ on 2. to collect a ~
from 3. to pay a ~ (to pay a ~ on a new car; to pay a
large sum in ~es; to pay a ~ to the government) 4.
to avoid (esp. BE); evade a ~ (see also Usage Note
at **avoidance**) 5. to increase, raise ~es 6. to cut,
lower, reduce ~es 7. to rescind, revoke a ~ 8. an
amusement; cigarette; gasoline (AE), petrol (BE);
liquor (esp. AE); road (BE) ~ 9. a direct; indirect ~
10. an excise; nuisance; purchase (BE), sales ~; a
value-added tax (= VAT) (GB) 11. a federal (AE);
local; state (US) ~ 12. a capital-gains; corporate;
excess-profits; windfall-profits ~ 13. an income;
negative income; social-security ~; withholding
~ (esp. AE; BE has *PAYE*) 14. a council ("local
property tax") (GB); personal-property; property;
real-estate; transfer ~ 15. a capital-transfer ~ (BE;
has replaced *death duty*); death (AE), estate, inheritance; gift ~ 16. a flat; graduated, progressive
~ 17. a ~ on (a ~ on cigarettes) 18. after; before
~; net(t) of ~ (esp. BE) (your income before ~ is
of course greater than your income after ~ = your
gross pre-tax income is of course greater than your
income net of ~) 19. (misc.) to exempt from ~
(a tax-exempt purchase); back ~es (to owe back
~es); delinquent ~es (AE); heavy ~es; a ~ haven;
~ relief; a ~ shelter; (BE) these purchases attract
value-added ~ at seventeen per cent (see also *tax
avoidance* & Usage Note at **avoidance**; *tax collector* at **collector**; *tax evasion* at **evasion**; *tax exile*
at **exile I** *n.*; *tax haven* at **haven**; *tax loophole* at
loophole; *for tax purposes* at **purpose**; *tax rate* at
rate I *n.*; **tax return**; **tax shelter**)
tax II *v.* 1. to ~ heavily; lightly 2. (D; tr.) to ~ at
(~ed at 17 percent) 3. (D; tr.) to ~ on (they ~ed
the author on his royalties) 4. (formal) (d; tr.) ("to
accuse") to ~ with (to ~ smb. with negligence)
taxation *n.* 1. to impose; lower; raise ~ 2. direct;
general; indirect ~ (will the new public-works program be paid for out of general ~?) 3. the burden;
level, rate of ~ (does the burden of ~ fall chiefly on
those most able to pay?)
tax return *n.* 1. to complete, fill in, fill out (esp.
AE), make out a ~ 2. to file, send in, submit a ~

tax shelter *n.* a foreign, off-shore; legal ~ (some
investments provide a legal ~ for your money and
produce tax-sheltered income)
taxi I see **cab**
taxi II *v.* (P; intr.) the plane ~ed along the runway;
the jet ~ed to a complete stop
tea *n.* ["plant"] 1. to grow ~ ["beverage"] 2. to brew,
make; steep ~ 3. to drink, have, take ~ (to take ~
with sugar) 4. to have, take (old-fashioned) ~ with
smb. 5. strong; weak ~ 6. hot; iced ~ 7. black; green
~ 8. decaffeinated; herbal; scented ~ 9. camomile;
jasmine; lemon; mint ~ 10. beef ~ (BE; CE has
beef broth) 11. the ~ is brewing 12. a cup; glass;
pot of ~ (a cup of ~ with milk and sugar in it; bring
us two cups of ~; or: bring us two ~s) ["meal"] (GB)
13. to have ~ 14. afternoon; cream; high ~ (see also
tea ceremony at **ceremony**; *tea party* at **party**; *tea
things* at **thing**) USAGE NOTE: In Britain, *tea*
can also mean 'an afternoon or early evening meal
where tea is served.' A *cream tea* features scones,
jam, and thick spreadable cream (such as clotted
cream). *High tea* features more substantial food.
In fact, *high tea* (old-fashioned) and *tea* can mean
'early dinner,' 'dinner,' or 'supper' (we're having
gammon for tea!).
teach *v.* 1. (A) she taught history to us; or: she
taught us history 2. (D; tr.) to ~ about (to ~ children about their heritage) 3. (H) she taught them to
swim 4. (L; typically has a noun or pronoun object)
he taught us that the best policy is to tell the truth
5. (O; can be used with one object) she taught us
history; that is, she taught us and she taught history
6. (Q; must have an object) she taught them how
to swim USAGE NOTES: (1) In pattern L, *teach*
is formal without a noun or pronoun object: The
Buddha teaches that we should be both wise and
compassionate. (2) *Teach* is unusual in that it takes
both pattern A and pattern O.
teacher *n.* 1. to certify; license; train a ~ 2. an
exchange; practice, student ~ 3. (BE) a supply ~
(AE has *substitute*) 4. a ~ of (a ~ of English = an
English ~)
teach-in *n.* to conduct, hold; organize, stage a ~
teaching *n.* 1. practice, student ~ 2. team ~ 3. health
~ 4. (misc.) to go into ~ (see also *teaching load* at
load I *n.*)
teachings *n.* to follow smb.'s ~ (to follow the Buddha's ~ about wisdom and compassion)
teacup *n.* a storm in a ~ (BE) ("much ado about
nothing") (for AE, see **teapot**)
teakettle see **kettle**
team *n.* 1. to field; organize a ~ 2. to coach; manage a ~ 3. to disband, split up a ~ 4. an all-star
(AE); losing; winning ~ 5. a home; opposing,
rival; visiting ~ 6. a baseball; basketball; cricket;
drill; football; hockey; lacrosse; relay; soccer;
track, track-and-field; volleyball ~ 7. (Am. professional football) a wild-card ~ 8. (mil.) a combat
~ 9. a negotiating ~ 10. (misc.) (AE) to make a ~

("to succeed in becoming a member of a team")
USAGE NOTES: (1) AE uses *team* more often
than BE – Chicago has fielded a strong team for
today's game; Chicago is the strongest team in
the league. BE prefers *side* when referring to
a competitive match – Liverpool have fielded a
strong side for today's match. BE often uses *club*
when referring to a team in general – United is /
are the strongest club in the Premier League. In
BE, a player can be *in a side ; in a team*. In AE, a
player cen be *on a side ; on a team*. In CE, a player
can be *in a club*. In references to international
competition, *team* is standard in BE – the England
team in the World Cup. (2) Here, in summary, is
an example of the British English usage of *club,
side,* and *team*. :- Arsenal, one of the Premiership's
most successful *clubs*, fielded a strong *side* for the
F.A. Cup Final, several members of which were
picked for the England *team* in the World Cup.

team up *v.* (D; intr.) to ~ against; with (we ~ed up
with them against our common enemy)

teapot *n.* a tempest in a ~ (AE) ("much ado about
nothing") (for BE, see **teacup**)

tear I /tiy(r)/ *n.* ["teardrop"] 1. to burst into ~s 2. to
shed a ~ 3. to weep (bitter) ~s 4. to choke back,
hold back; dry one's ~s 5. bitter ~s 6. ~s flowed,
ran, rolled, streamed down their cheeks 7. ~s
welled up in my eyes 8. (misc.) crocodile ("false")
~s; to be in ~s over smt.; eyes fill with ~s; bored
to ~s; a flood of ~s; ~s of joy; ~s of gratitude; a
teardrop; a ~ duct; the sad song reduced me to ~s
(see also *brim with tears* at **brim**)

tear II /tey(r)/ *n.* ["rip"] 1. to make a ~ 2. to mend a
~ 3. (misc.) to save wear and ~ (on)

tear III *v.* 1. (d; intr.) to ~ at (she tore at her shackles) 2. (d; tr.) to ~ from, out of (she tore several
pages out of the book) 3. (d; intr.) to ~ into ("to
attack verbally") (he tore into his opponent) 4. (D;
tr.) to ~ into, to (she tore the paper into /to pieces;
to ~ an argument to shreds) 5. (d; tr.) to ~ off (he
tore a button off the coat) 6. (D; tr.) to ~ on (she
tore her blouse on a nail) 7. (N) she tore the envelope open; she tore herself free of her shackles 8.
(s) she tore free of her shackles

tear away *v.* (D; refl., tr.) to ~ from (she couldn't ~
herself away from the book)

tear gas *n.* to use ~ (on)

tease I *n.* ["person who teases"] a terrible ~

tease II *v.* 1. (D; tr.) to ~ about (they ~d her about
her new hairdo) 2. (D; tr.) to ~ by (they ~d her
by joking about her new hairdo) 3. (D; tr.) to ~
into (they ~d her into changing her hairdo) 4. (D;
tr.) to ~with (they ~d her with jokes about her new
hairdo) 5. (misc.) don't take offense: (I was) only
teasing!

teaspoon *n.* a heaping (AE), heaped (BE); level ~

teatime *n.* 1. at ~ 2. past ~

technicality *n.* 1. a legal ~ 2. on a ~ (we lost the
case on a ~)

technician *n.* a dental; lab, laboratory; medical;
radar; television, TV ~

Technicolor *n.* (T) in (glorious) ~

technique *n.* 1. to acquire; develop, devise, work
out; perfect a ~ 2. to apply a ~ 3. an acting; dance
~ 4. a diagnostic ~ 5. relaxation ~s 6. a ~ allows;
encourages (our new relaxation ~s encourage you
to become who you were meant to be!) 7. a ~ for
(they worked out a ~ for analyzing the data) 8. a ~
to + inf. (they worked out a ~ to analyze the data)

technology *n.* 1. to create, develop (a) ~ 2. to apply,
employ, use ~ 3. to export, transfer ~ (to developing countries) 4. computer; information ~ 5. high
~ (also *high tech*) 6. advanced, latest, modern,
state-of-the-art ~ 7. a ~ allows, enables (our new ~
enables you to generate renewable energy!) 8. a ~
for (they developed a ~ for analyzing the data) 9. a
~ to + inf. (they developed a ~ to analyze the data)

teed off *adj.* (colloq.) (AE) ["angry"] ~ about, at

teem *v.* (d; intr.) to ~ in; with (fish were ~ing in the
river = the river was ~ing with fish)

teens *n.* 1. to pass; reach one's ~ 2. early; late; mid-
~ 3. during one's ~ (things that are all right during
your ~ may not seem all right once you have passed
your ~!) 4. in one's ~ (they are still in their ~)

teeter *v.* (d; intr.) to ~ on (to ~ on the edge of a
cliff)

teeth see **tooth**

telegram *n.* 1. to send a ~ 2. to get, receive a ~ 3. a
~ from; to (a ~ from London to Paris)

telegraph I *n.* by ~ (the news was sent by ~)

telegraph II *v.* 1. (A) they ~ed the information to
us; or: they ~ed us the information 2. (D; intr., tr.)
to ~ about (they ~ed (us) about the meeting) 3. (d;
intr.) ("to request by telegraphing") to ~ for (she
~d home for some money) 4. (H; no passive) we
~ed them to return home immediately 5. (L; may
have an object) she ~ed (us) that the manuscript
had been received 6. (Q; may have an object) they
~ed (us) where to meet

telepathy *n.* mental ~

telephone I *n.* 1. to hook up, install a ~ 2. to answer,
pick up; hang up; put down; slam down the ~ 3.
to tap a ~ 4. to disconnect a ~ 5. a car; cellular;
cordless; dial; mobile (esp. BE); pay, public ~ 6. a
~ rings; is busy, is engaged (BE) 7. by ~; on, over
(esp. AE) the ~ (she spoke to him by ~; I enjoyed
our chat on /over the ~; to speak on /over the ~; he
is always on the ~) 8. (BE) on the ~ ("connected to
the telephone system") 9. (misc.) to be wanted on
the ~; to call smb. on the ~; to call smb. to the ~
(see also **phone I**)

telephone II *v.* 1. (B) they ~d the information to us
2. (D; tr.) to ~ about (they ~d me about the meeting) 3. (H; no passive) we ~d them to return home
immediately 4. (L; may have an object) she ~d (us)
that the manuscript had been received 5. (Q; may
have an object) they ~d (us) where to meet

telephone call *n.* see **call I** *n.* 13–22

telephone directory, telephone book *n.* to be in the ~

telephone receiver *n.* see **receiver** 1–2

telescope I *n.* 1. to focus, train a ~ on 2. a reflecting; refracting ~ 3. through a ~ 4. (misc.) the wrong end of a ~ (as weird as seeing smt. through the wrong end of a ~)

telescope II *v.* (D; tr.) to ~ into (to ~ a syllabus into a brief outline)

televised *adj.* 1. nationally ~ 2. ~ live (~ live from Yankee Stadium!)

television *n.* 1. to put on, switch on; turn on the ~ 2. to watch ~ (I watched scenes of violence on ~) 3. to switch off, turn off the ~ 4. to turn down; turn up the ~ 5. black-and-white; color ~ 6. breakfast; cable; closed-circuit; commercial; educational; free-view (esp. BE); local; national; pay; peak-time (BE), peak-viewing-time (BE), prime-time (esp. AE); public (esp. AE); satellite ~ 7. ~ broadcasts, shows (~ broadcasts showed scenes of violence) 8. on ~ (I saw scenes of violence on ~) 9. (misc.) she is, works in ~

television set *n.* 1. to plug in a ~ 2. to put on, switch on, turn on a ~ 3. to switch off, turn off a ~ 4. to unplug a ~ 5. to turn down; turn up a ~ 6. a black-and-white; color ~ 7. a digital ~

tell *v.* 1. (A; usu. without *to*) ("to relate") she told the news to everyone concerned; or: she told everyone the news; he told me his name; she told them a story; ~ me the truth 2. (D; intr.) ("to be certain") to ~ about (you can never ~ about people like that) 3. (d; intr., tr.) ("to inform") to ~ about, of (he didn't want to ~ about the incident; ~ me about the game; she told everyone of her success) 4. (BE; formal) (d; intr.) to ~ against ("to count against") (their past misdemeanors will ~ against them) 5. (d; tr.) ("to ascertain") to ~ from (can you ~ anything from a quick examination?) 6. (d; tr.) to ~ from ("to differentiate") (can you ~ one twin from the other?) 7. (colloq.) (d; intr., tr.) to ~ of (BE), on ("to inform on") (he told on her when the teacher returned; I'm going to ~ my father on you) 8. (D; intr.) to ~ on ("to affect") (the strain was beginning to ~ on her) 9. (H) ("to order") she told me to leave 10. (L; must have an object) ("to inform") she told me that I should leave 11. (Q; must have an object) ("to inform") ~ me how to get there 12. (Q) ("to ascertain") can you ~ from a quick examination where his injuries are?; you can never ~ whether people like that are lying 13. (misc.) I told you so!; pray ~ (old-fashioned or humorous) (and who might you be, pray ~?) (see also tell the difference at **difference**; **telling**; *tell (the) time* at **time**; **told**)

tell apart *v.* (D; tr.) to ~ from (can you ~ one twin apart from the other? = can you ~ the twins apart from each other?)

teller *n.* (AE) a bank ~ (BE has *cashier*)

telling *n.* ["certainty, knowing"] 1. there's no ~ (what they'll do) ["act of narrating"] 2. in the ~ (the story changed in the ~)

temerity *n.* the ~ to + inf. (he had the ~ to file a grievance)

temper I *n.* 1. to control, curb, keep one's ~ 2. to lose one's ~ 3. a bad, explosive, foul, hot, nasty, quick, uncontrollable, ungovernable, violent ~ (he has a very bad ~ = he's very bad-tempered) 4. a calm, even, mild ~ 5. ~s cool down; flare (up); fray 6. a display, fit, outburst of ~ (she said that in a fit of ~) 7. (misc.) she was in quite a (bad) ~ this morning; he flew into a ~

temper II *v.* (D; tr.) to ~ with (to ~ justice with mercy)

temperament *n.* 1. to have a certain ~ (she has a nervous ~) 2. an artistic; poetic ~ 3. a calm, even, mild, quiet ~ 4. an excitable; fiery; nervous ~ 5. by ~ (very excitable by ~)

temperance *n.* ~ in

temperate *adj.* ~ in

temperature *n.* ["degree of heat or cold"] 1. to adjust, control the ~ 2. to take smb.'s ~ (also fig.) (a survey that tried to take the ~ of the American consumer) 3. a high; low; normal ~ 4. (smb.'s) body ~ 5. room ~ (at room ~) 6. the average; surface ~ 7. a ~ drops, falls; goes down 8. a ~ goes up, rises 9. a ~ remains steady 10. at a (certain) ~ (water boils at a certain ~) 11. an increase, rise in ~ 12. a decrease, drop in ~ ["excess over normal body heat, fever"] 13. to develop, have, run a ~ 14. a high; slight ~ 15. a ~ falls; rises; subsides 16. a ~ of (a ~ of 39 degrees)

tempo *n.* 1. to increase, step up the ~ 2. to slow down the ~ 3. a fast; slow ~ 4. the ~ increases, speeds up; slackens, slows down

tempt *v.* 1. (D; tr.) to ~ into (to ~ smb. into doing smt.) 2. (H) to ~ smb. to do smt. (See also *tempt fate* at **fate**)

temptation *n.* 1. to overcome, resist ~ ("I can resist everything except ~" – Oscar Wilde, *Lady Windermere's Fan*, 1891) 2. to be exposed to, face, feel ~ 3. to succumb to ~ 4. to place, put ~ in smb.'s way 5. irresistible, strong ~ 6. a ~ to + inf. (she resisted the ~ to answer back)

tempted *adj.* ~ to + inf. (she was ~ to answer back)

tempting *adj.* ~ to + inf. (she felt it would be ~ to answer back)

tenacity *n.* 1. to demonstrate, display, show ~ 2. to have ~ 3. bulldog; great; sheer ~ (to demonstrate great ~) 4. the ~ to + inf. (she had the ~ to finish the job) 5. by ~ (she finished the job by sheer ~)

tend *v.* 1. (AE) (d; intr.) to ~ to (to ~ to one's own business) (CE has *attend to*) 2. (d; intr.) to ~ towards (she ~s towards exaggeration) 3. (E) she ~s to exaggerate

tendency *n.* 1. to demonstrate, display, show a ~ 2. a growing; marked, pronounced; mounting; natural; strong; universal; worrying ~ 3. artistic; homicidal; suicidal; vicious ~cies (for years he has displayed suicidal ~cies) 4. a ~ among, on the part of (there is a marked ~ towards exaggeration among such people) 5. a ~ towards (she has a ~ towards exaggeration) 6. a ~ to + inf. (she has a ~ to exaggerate)

tender I *adj.* ~ to, towards, with (see also *tender loving care* at **care I** *n.*)

tender II *n.* ["offer, bid"] (esp. BE) 1. to make, put in, send in, submit a ~ 2. to invite ~s; put out to ~ (the government has invited ~s for the construction of the new motorway = the government has put the construction of the new motorway out to ~) 3. to accept; reject, turn down a ~ 4. to lose; win a ~ 5. a sealed ~ 6. the highest; lowest ~ 7. a ~ for 8. a ~ to + inf. (our company won the ~ to construct the new motorway) ["currency"] 9. legal ~

tender III *v.* 1. (B) ("to offer") she ~ed her resignation to the government 2. (BE) (d; intr.) to ~ for ("to bid on") (to ~ for the construction of a new motorway) 3. (BE) (E) to ~ to construct the new motorway

tenderness *n.* ["kindness, care"] 1. to show ~ 2. ~ towards

tendon *n.* 1. to pull a ~ 2. smb.'s/the Achilles ~

tenet *n.* 1. a basic, fundamental ~ 2. a ~ that + clause (our basic ~ is that all people are equal) 3. (misc.) to embrace the ~s of a new philosophy

tennis *n.* 1. to play ~ 2. court (AE), real (BE); lawn; paddle; table ~ 3. (misc.) a ~ match; a ~ player; the game of ~; a game of ~ (let's play a game of ~; she won the first game and went on to win the set and the match) (see also *tennis ball* at **ball I** *n.*; *tennis court* at **court**; *tennis racket* at **racket II** *n.*; *tennis shoes* at **shoes**)

tenor *n.* 1. to sing ~ 2. a high; lyric ~

tenpins *n.* (AE) to play ~

tense I *adj.* 1. ~ about 2. ~ with (~ with anxiety about the future)

tense II *n.* (grammar) 1. the continuous, progressive; future; future perfect; past; past perfect, pluperfect; present ~ 2. in a certain ~ (is that verb phrase in the simple present ~ or in the present continuous ~ ?)

tension *n.* ["strained relations"] ["strain"] 1. to cause, create ~ 2. to exacerbate, heighten, increase ~ 3. to alleviate, ease, lessen, reduce, relieve ~ (to alleviate/ease ~ between the adversaries) 4. acute; growing, mounting ~ 5. arterial; nervous; premenstrual ~ (PMT) (see also *tension headache* at **headache**) 6. international; racial ~ 7. ~ builds up, increases, mounts, rises 8. ~ decreases, eases, subsides 9. ~ between 10. under ~ 11. (misc.) a cause, source of ~ (political differences were a source of ~ between them) ["tautness"] 12. fan-belt ~ ["voltage"] 13. high; low ~

tent *n.* 1. to erect, pitch, put up a ~ 2. to dismantle, take down a ~ 3. a circus; pup; pyramidal; wall ~ 4. a croup; oxygen ~ 5. in a ~ (see also *tent pole* at **pole I** *n.*)

tenterhooks *n.* on ~ ("in suspense")

tenure *n.* ["permanence of employment as a teacher"] 1. to give, grant; deny ~ (a professor who has been granted ~ is a ~d professor) 2. to acquire, get, receive ~ 3. academic ~ 4. (misc.) security of ~ (after several years he was given security of ~ at the university)

term I *n.* ["expression, word"] 1. an abstract; concrete, specific; general ~ 2. a clear; comprehensible ~ 3. an incomprehensible; vague ~ (the lecturer used an incomprehensible; ~ in making her point) 4. a cover-term, generic, umbrella; general; legal; medical; technical ~ (see also **word I** *n.*) ["period of time served"] 5. to serve a ~ (in office) 6. an unexpired ~ 7. a ~ expires, runs out 8. a jail, prison ~ ["division of a school year"] 9. the autumn (BE), fall (AE); school; spring; summer ~ 10. at the end ¬of a/of (BE)¬ ~ ["time at which a normal pregnancy terminates"] 11. to have a baby at ~ after a full-term pregnancy (see also **terms**)

term II *v.* (formal) (rare) (N; used with a noun or adjective) ("to call") they ~ed the compromise acceptable; by what right does he ~ himself an artist ?

terminal *n.* ["point on an electric circuit"] 1. a negative; positive ~ ["device by which information enters or leaves a computer"] 2. a computer ~; Visual Display Terminal = VDT (AE; CE has *Visual Display Unit* = VDU) ["passenger, freight station"] 3. an airline; bus, coach (BE); freight; rail; shipping; trucking ~ 4. at a ~ (let's meet at the bus ~)

terminate *v.* 1. (D; intr.) to ~ in (their efforts ~ed in success) 2. (BE) (P; intr., tr.) this train stops at various stations and ~s here

termination *n.* ["cessation of employment"] 1. voluntary ~ ["abortion"] 2. to have; request; seek a ~

terminology *n.* 1. to codify, create, establish, standardize; use (a) ~ 2. basic; legal; scientific; technical ~ 3. in a certain ~ (a pregnant woman who sought what in medical ~ would be called a termination)

terminus *n.* (esp. BE) 1. a bus, coach; main-line; rail ~ 2. at; in a ~

termites *n.* a colony of ~

terms *n.* ["expressions, words"] 1. absolute; general; relative ~ 2. bold; flattering; glowing ~ (she described him in glowing ~) 3. in ~ (to speak in general ~; in the strongest possible ~; in no uncertain ~; a contradiction in ~) ["conditions, provisions"] 4. to dictate; set; specify, stipulate (the) ~ 5. to state the ~ 6. easy; favorable ~ 7. surrender ~ (to stipulate surrender ~ to an enemy) 8. by the ~ (of an agreement) 9. on certain ~ (on one's own ~; on our ~) 10. under (the) ~ of the agreement ["acceptance"] ["agreement"] 11. to come to ~ with smb. ["relationship"] ["footing"] 12. equal, even; unequal ~ 13. familiar, intimate; speaking ~ 14. friendly, good; unfriendly ~ 15. on certain ~ (with) (to be on speaking ~ with smb.; to be on first-name/Christian-name ~ with smb.; to negotiate with smb. on equal ~; they are not on good ~ with each other) ["aspects"] 16. in certain ~ (in economic ~ [= economically (speaking)], that country is a super-power; in ~ of its foreign trade [= as regards its foreign trade], that country is a serious competitor) 17. (misc.) ~ of reference; this offer is subject to the usual ~ and conditions USAGE NOTE: The phrase *in terms of* is used widely, perhaps too widely, to link constructions in English: (1) This dictionary has done well in terms of sales. Alternatives include: (2) This dictionary has done well in sales terms; (3) this dictionary has done well sales-wise; (4) this dictionary has done well with respect to sales; (5) this dictionary has done well in respect of sales (esp. BE). People who dislike the original example will also dislike the second and esp. the third. Such people will not object to examples four and five, but may well ask: Why not just say "This dictionary has sold well"?

terrace *n.* from; on a ~ (see also *terrace(d) house* at **house**)

terraces *n.* (BE) (as in football stadiums) from; on the ~ (cheers from the ~)

terrain *n.* 1. harsh, rough, rugged; hilly; mountainous; rocky; swampy ~ 2. across ~ (we wondered whether we could get across such rugged ~)

terrible *adj.* 1. really, simply ~ 1. ~ at (she is ~ at bridge) 2. ~ to + inf. (it was really ~ to work there = it was really ~ working there = working there was really ~; it was ~ of them to do that) 3. ~ that + clause (it is ~ that she lost her wallet; I feel ~ that you cannot accept our invitation)

terrified *adj.* 1. ~ at, by, of 2. ~ to + inf. (we are ~ to think that there might be another earthquake) 3. ~ that + clause (we are ~ that there might be another earthquake)

terrify *v.* 1. (D; tr.) to ~ into (she was ~fied into handing over the keys) 2. (R) it ~fied me to contemplate the consequences of your actions; it ~fies us that there might be another earthquake

terrifying *adj.* 1. ~ to + inf. (it was ~ to watch that movie = it was ~ watching that movie = watching that movie was ~; it's ~ to think that there might be another earthquake) 2. ~ that + clause (it's ~ that there might be another earthquake)

territory *n.* 1. to annex; occupy ~ 2. to cede ~ 3. a neutral; trust ~ 4. (an) occupied; unoccupied ~ 5. unexplored ~ 6. (misc.) to reconnoiter enemy ~

terror *n.* 1. to employ, engage in, resort to; unleash ~ 2. to arouse, inspire; sow ~; to strike ~ into (to strike ~ into smb.'s heart) 3. to feel; show ~ 4. to overcome ~ (he finally overcame his ~ of snakes) 5. absolute, blind, mortal, sheer, stark ~ 6. (colloq.) a holy ~ 7. in ~ (to live in ~ of smt.) 8. (misc.) a campaign, reign of ~; a shriek of ~

terrorism *n.* 1. to combat, fight ~ 2. indiscriminate; international; state; urban ~ 3. an act; campaign of ~ 4. see **terror** 1

terrorist *n.* an armed; international; urban ~ (see

also *terrorist attack* at **attack I** *n.*; *terrorist threat* at **threat**)

terrorize *v.* (D; tr.) to ~ into

test I *n.* ["examination, set of questions"] 1. to administer, conduct, give a ~ 2. to draw up, make up, prepare, set (BE) a ~ 3. to sit (for) (BE), take a ~ 4. to fail, flunk (colloq.; esp. AE) a ~ 5. to pass a ~ 6. a demanding, difficult ~ 7. an easy ~ 8. an achievement; aptitude; general-knowledge; intelligence, IQ ~ 9. a placement; proficiency ~ 10. a cloze; completion; essay, essay-type; multiple-choice; objective; oral; true-and-false, true-false; unannounced; written ~ 11. a driving ~ 12. a breath ~ (to have/undergo a breath ~ and fail or pass it) 13. a lie-detector, polygraph ~ (to have/undergo a lie-detector ~ and fail or pass it) (see also **lie-detector test; polygraph test**) 14. a competency; means ~ 15. a ~ in, of, on (a ~ in mathematics; a ~ on new material) ["ordeal, trial"] 16. an acid, demanding, exacting, litmus, rigorous, severe ~ 17. an endurance ~ ["experiment, trial"]["examination"] 18. to carry out, conduct, do, perform, run a ~ 19. to have, undergo a ~ (to undergo a number/series of blood ~s) 20. exhaustive, extensive, thorough ~s 21. a breathing; diagnostic; DNA; drug; PAP; patch; saliva; skin; scratch; tuberculin ~ (see also **blood test**) 22. a personality; psychological ~ 23. a laboratory; nuclear ~ 24. a road ~ 25. a ~ for (to do a skin ~ for tuberculosis) 26. a ~ on (they conducted a series of ~s on me at the health center) 27. (misc.) to stand the ~ of time; the ~ turned out (to be) negative/positive, the ~ was negative/positive; to put smb. to the ~ (see also *test case* at **case I** *n.*; **screen test**) USAGE NOTE: In AE, a *road test* is ambiguous: it can test a vehicle or a driver. In BE, a *road test* tests the vehicle only. In CE, a *test drive* tests the vehicle, and a *driving test* tests the driver.

test II *v.* 1. to ~ carefully, thoroughly 1. (D; intr., tr.) to ~ for (to ~ for excessive air pollution; to ~ the urine for sugar; to ~ a car for defects) 2. (D; tr.) to ~ in, on (we ~ed them ¬in English/on their knowledge of English¬; I was ~ed on irregular verbs) 3. (P; intr.) (esp. AE) some of our students ~ed in the top percentile 4. (esp. AE) (s) some students ~ high, others low; to ~ negative/positive for a disease (see also **tested**)

testament *n.* 1. the New; Old Testament 2. a ~ to (her Nobel Prize is a lasting/fitting ~ to her perseverance) 3. (misc.) smb.'s last will and ~

tested *adj.* 1. sorely ~ 2. (misc.) tried and ~

test flight *n.* to conduct a ~

testicle *n.* an undescended ~

testify *v.* 1. (D; intr.) to ~ about (to ~ about a case) 2. (D; intr.) to ~ against; for, on behalf of (to ~ for the plaintiff) 3. (d; intr.) to ~ to (the results ~ to the quality of their work) 4. (L) she ~fied (to the court) that she had not seen the accident 5. (misc.) to ~ under oath (she ~fied under oath that the driver had been drunk)

testimonial *n.* 1. to give, offer, provide a ~ 2. an eloquent ~ 3. a ~ to (her Nobel Prize provides an eloquent ~ to her perseverance)

testimony *n.* 1. to give, offer ~ (under oath) 2. to cite ~ 3. to recant, repudiate, retract (one's) ~ 4. to contradict; discount; refute (smb.'s) ~ 5. reliable ~ 6. false, perjured; unreliable ~ 7. expert ~ 8. ~ about 9. ~ against (she gave ~ against the defendant) 10. ~ for, on behalf of (she gave ~ for the plaintiff) 11. (a) ~ to (her Nobel Prize is a real ~ to her perseverance) 12. ~ that + clause (nobody could refute her ~, given under oath, that the driver had been drunk)

testing *n.* 1. proficiency ~ 2. drug; mandatory; voluntary ~

tetanus *n.* to develop ~

tether *v.* (D; tr.) to ~ to (the horse was ~ed to the hitching-post; the horses were ~ed to each other [= the horses were ~ed together])

text *n.* 1. to set a ~ (in type); to input a ~ (into a computer); to print a ~; to print out a ~ 2. to edit; copy-edit (esp. AE), sub-edit (esp. BE); proof-read a ~ 3. to annotate a ~ 4. an annotated; complete, full; draft; unexpurgated ~ 5. a machine-readable ~ 6. to stray from the ~ (as of a prepared speech) 7. a piece; section of ~ 8. in a ~

textbook *n.* 1. a basic, introductory; college; school; standard ~ 2. a ~ of, on (a ~ on advanced grammar = an advanced-grammar ~) 3. in a ~

texture *n.* delicate, fine; rough; smooth ~

thank *v.* 1. to ~ profusely; sincerely 2. (D; tr.) to ~ for (she ~ed me profusely for my help) 3. (H; no passive) I'll ~ you to make less noise in the future! 4. (L; must have an object) we can ~ you that we got there on time = we have you to ~ that we got there on time 5. (misc.) ~ you very much! (see also *thank-you letter* at **letter**; Usage Note at **thanks**)

thankful *adj.* 1. ~ for; to (we were ~ to them for still being alive) 2. ~ to + inf. (we were ~ to be still alive) 3. ~ that + clause (we were ~ (to them) that we were still alive)

thanks *n.* 1. to express; give one's ~; to say ~ 2. to accept smb.'s ~ 3. one's heartfelt, sincere, warm ~ 4. ~ for; to (special ~ are due to you for all your help!) 5. (misc.) many ~; ~ ¬a lot/a million¬; "you nearly ruined my work! ~ ¬a lot/a bunch!¬" (sardonic); I finished the whole job on time, no ~ to you; we completed the work on time, ~ to ¬you/your help¬; we owe her a vote of ~ USAGE NOTE: The standard responses to "Thanks" or "Thank you" include "You're welcome," "Don't mention it," "Not at all," "No problem." "You're welcome" is nowadays neutral CE. "No problem" is colloq. CE. "Don't mention it" and "Not at all" are both BE and somewhat old-fashioned.

that *pronoun* 1. at ~ ("in addition") (she was a thief and a clever one at ~) 2. (misc.) take ~! ("I'm going to punch you!")

thaw *n.* 1. the spring ~ 2. a ~ sets in (also fig.) 3. during a ~

theater, theatre *n.* ["building in which plays are performed or (esp. AE) films shown"] 1. to crowd, jam, pack a ~ 2. an art; dinner (esp. AE); movie (AE; BE has *cinema*); open-air; repertory ~ 3. at; in the ~ (we were at the ~ last night; what's on at the ~ tonight?; is there a restaurant at/in the ~?) ["theatrical profession or type of play"] 4. the legitimate ~ (old-fashioned or humorous) 5. musical; physical ~ 6. the ~ of the absurd; the ~ of cruelty; ~ in the round 7. in; into the ~ (she was well thought of in the ~, which she went into after drama school) ["operating room in a hospital"] (BE) 8. an operating ~ 9. in ~ (the patient is still in ~)

theft *n.* 1. to commit (a) ~ 2. petty ~ 3. a ~ from (the daring ~ of a famous painting from a museum)

theme *n.* 1. a basic; central, dominant, main; common; consistent; familiar; underlying ~ 2. a contemporary ~ 3. a recurrent, recurring ~ 4. a ~ for (a ~ for discussion) 5. on a ~ (a seminar on the ~ of poverty) (see also *variation on a theme* at **variation**)

then *adv., n.* 1. just ~ 2. before; by ~ 3. from ~ on 4. since ~ 5. until, up to ~

theorem *n.* 1. to deduce; formulate a ~ 2. to prove; test a ~ 3. to disprove a ~ 4. the binomial ~

theorize *v.* 1. (D; intr.) to ~ about (the police ~d about how the burglar had entered) 2. (L) the police ~d that the burglar had entered through a window

theory *n.* 1. to construct, formulate a ~ 2. to advance, advocate, present, propose, put forth, set forth, suggest a ~ 3. to develop; test a ~ 4. to confirma ~ 5. to debunk, discredit, disprove, explode, refute a ~ 6. to challenge a ~ 7. a pet ~ 8. an economic; political ~ 9. critical; game; information; literary; number; quantum; set; scientific ~ (see also *systems theory* at **system**) 10. the big-bang; steady-state ~ 11. the germ ~ (of disease) 12. a ~ develops, evolves 13. a ~ holds (up) 14. a ~ about (a ~ about the origin of the universe) 15. a ~ that + clause (she has a ~ that drinking milk prevents colds) 16. in ~ (in ~ their plan makes sense but in practice it hasn't worked) 17. on a ~ (they proceeded on the ~ that the supplies would arrive on time) 18. (misc.) the ~ of evolution; the ~ of relativity; to combine ~ and practice

therapist *n.* a family; group; occupational; physical ~ (esp. AE), physiotherapist (esp. BE); psychotherapist; speech ~

therapy *n.* 1. to employ, use ~ (on, with) 2. to get, have; undergo ~ 3. art; dance; music ~ (to employ/use music ~) 4. massage; occupational; recreational; speech ~ (to get speech ~; to employ/use recreational ~); physical ~ (esp. AE), physiotherapy (esp. BE) 5. aversion; electro-convulsive (BE), electro-shock (AE); shock ~ (to get/receive/undergo shock ~; to administer/employ/use electro-shock ~; will the economic crisis be a form of shock ~ to our belief systems ?) 6. behavior(al) ; cognitive ; family ; group ; individual, one-on-one ~ ; psychotherapy 7. chemotherapy ; hormone replacement therapy (HRT) ; inhalation ; radiation, X-ray ~ (to get/have/undergo radiation ~) 8. ~ for 9. in ~ (she was in ~ for emotional problems) (see also *therapy group* at **group I** *n.* ; *therapy session* at **session**)

there *adv.* 1. from, (up) to ~ 2. down ; over ; up ~ 3. from ~ on

thermometer *n.* 1. to read a ~ (to read a clinical ; meat ; oral ; oven ; rectal ~) 2. a ~ reads (I knew I was ill because the ~ read 40 degrees) 3. a ~ shows a temperature (I knew I was ill because the ~ showed a temperature of 40 degrees)

thermostat *n.* 1. to adjust, set ; turn down ; turn up a ~ 2. to calibrate a ~

thesis *n.* ["research paper"] 1. to complete ; submit ; write a ~ (about, on) 2. a doctoral, D.Phil. (GB) ; Ph.D. ; graduate ; master's ~ ["proposition, hypothesis"] 3. to advance, formulate, propose, put forth/forward a ~ 4. to confirm, vindicate ; disconfirm ; support ; test a ~ 5. to challenge ; refute ; reject a ~ 6. smb.'s main, major ~ 7. a ~ about, on (she advanced a ~ about the spread of the disease) 8. a ~ that + clause (she advanced the ~ that the disease was spread by rodents) (see the Usage Note for **dissertation**)

thick I *adj.* 1. (colloq.) (esp. BE) ~ with (they are ~ with each other) 2. (misc.) as ~ as thieves ("very closely allied") ; to lay it on ~ ("to exaggerate")

thick II *n.* ["most intense part"] in the ~ (of the battle)

thick and thin *n.* ["all difficulties"] through ~ (to remain friends through ~)

thief *n.* 1. a car ; jewel ~ 2. a common, petty ; sneak ~ 3. a ~ robs ; steals 4. a band, gang of thieves (a gang of thieves stole a famous painting from a museum)

thing *n.* ["deed"] ["event"] 1. to do a ~ (she did a nice ~ when she offered to help ; to do great ~s ; *Do the Right Thing* – Spike Lee, film, 1989 ; "It is a far, far better ~ that I do, than I have ever done" – Charles Dickens, 1812–70, *A Tale of Two Cities*) 2. a good ; great ; nice ~ ("the tyrant has been overthrown !" "and a good ~, too !") 3. a funny ; strange ~ 4. a bad ; mean ; nasty ; terrible ~ 5. a big ; small ~ 6. a difficult ; easy ~ 7. a sensible ; stupid ~ 8. the decent, right ; wrong ~ 9. a ~ happens ; ~s happen (a strange ~ happened this morning ; *When Bad Things Happen to Good People* – Rabbi Harold S. Kushner, 1981) 10. a ~ to + inf. (it was an easy ~ to do ; it was the wrong ~ to do ; there are still lots of ~s ¬to do/to be done¬) ["object"] 11. to use a ~ for (don't use this ~ for removing paint) ["facts, details"] 12. to discuss ; say ~s (about) 13. to get a ~ out of smb. (I couldn't get a ~ out of her) 14. to know a ~ about (he doesn't know a ~ about music ; don't say a ~ to her about it !) ; to know a ~ or two

("to know quite a bit") 15. (misc.) the way ~s stand (see also 25) ["fact, point"] (colloq.) 16. the ~ is that + clause (the ~ ("problem, difficulty") is that I still have a great deal of work to do ; the other ~ is that I really don't want to go) USAGE NOTE : A phrase like "*The thing *is is* that I still have a great deal of work to do" is heard often but is wrong. It is a blend of "The thing/problem *is* that I still have a great deal of work to do" with "What the thing/problem *is is* that I still have a great deal of work to do." ["article of clothing"] 17. not to have a ~ to wear (I don't have a ~ to wear) 18. to put on ; take off one's ~s ["possessions, effects"] 19. to pack one's ~s ["step"] 20. the first ; last ; next ~ (the next ~ is to submit your application) ["person of a certain type"] 21. a pretty ; poor ~ (a pretty little ~ ; you poor ~ (, you) !) ["thought, idea"] 22. to say the right ~ ["matters"] (used in the plural) 23. to even ~s up 24. to see ~s (as they are) 25. (misc.) all ~s considered ("with everything taken into account") ; ~s don't look good ; ~s are looking up for us ; how do ~s stand ? ; how are ~s ? ; among other ~s ("inter alia") (see also 15) ["utensils"] 26. to clear the (breakfast ; tea) ~s away ["individual"] 27. a living ~ (there wasn't a living ~ in sight) ["fear"] ["obsession"] (colloq.) 28. to ~ about (she has a ~ about flying) ["misc."] 29. let's forget the whole ~ ; to be hearing/seeing ~s ("to be imagining things") ; to do one's (own) ~ ("to do what one feels competent or motivated to do") ; any old ~ ("anything at all") ; a sure ~ ("smt. that is certain to succeed") ; of all ~s ("most surprisingly") ; to tell smb. a ~ or two ("to tell smb. frankly what one thinks") ; to put first ~s first (in their proper order of priority) ; the best/greatest ~ since white bread (AE) = the best/greatest ~ since sliced bread (BE) (see also *let things take their natural course* at **course I** *n.* ; *the shape of things to come* at **come** ; *all other things being equal* at **equal I** *adj.* ; Usage Note at **stuff I** *n.*)

think I *n.* (colloq.) (BE) 1. to have a ~ about 2. a long hard ~

think II *v.* 1. to ~ aloud ; clearly ; fast ; hard ; laterally, outside the box (I thought (long and) hard and finally remembered the name) 2. (D ; intr.) ("to reflect") to ~ about, of (I was ~ing about you ; I thought about you/your working out there in the hot sun ; "kiss my wife ? don't even ~ about it !" ; to ~ of the past) 3. (d ; intr.) ("to be concerned") to ~ about, of (I was only ~ing of your welfare when I declined the offer) 4. (d ; intr.) to ~ of ("to have an opinion of") (to ~ badly, ill ; highly, well of) 5. (d ; intr.) to ~ of ("to consider ; to intend") (she never thought of telephoning ; to ~ of resigning) 6. (E) ("to remember") she never thought to call 7. (L) ("to anticipate") we thought (that) it would rain 8. (L) ("to believe") I ~ it's raining ; I ~ (that) he is ¬a fool/foolish¬ 9. (M ; used typically in the passive) ("to consider") he's generally thought to be a fool ; she is thought to be irreplaceable 10.

(N) ("to consider") many people ~ him ¬a fool/ foolish¬; many people ~ her irreplaceable 11. (Q) I can't ~ where it could be 12. (misc.) to ~ nothing of walking five miles every morning; I thought to myself that it would be nice to have some hot soup; he doesn't ~ of himself as a politician; to ~ better of doing smt. ("to change one's mind about doing smt."); to ~ on one's feet ("to decide or respond quickly"); I dread/hate to ~ that smt. bad will happen but I'm inclined to ~ it might!; I ~ so; I don't ~ so, I ~ not

think ahead v. (D; intr.) ("to direct one's thoughts ahead") to ~ to (to ~ to the future)

think back v. (D; intr.) ("to direct one's thoughts back") to ~ on, to (to ~ to the past)

thinker n. a clear; deep, profound; great; independent; logical; muddled; original ~

thinking n. 1. to do some (serious) ~ 2. clear; good; logical; positive; quick ~ 3. creative; independent; lateral; original ~ 4. critical; deep ~ 5. muddled; wishful ~ 6. a piece of ~ (that was quite a piece of lateral ~ on your part, boss!) 7. the ~ behind (what was the ~ (that lay) behind your decision, boss?) 8. smb.'s ~ on (what is your ~ on this matter, boss?) 9. (misc.) to my way of ~ ("in my opinion")

thinner n. paint ~

third degree n. (colloq.) ["brutal, harsh interrogation"] 1. to give smb. the ~ 2. to get the ~

thirst I n. 1. to experience ~; more usu. is: to be thirsty 2. to quench, slake, satisfy smb.'s ~ 3. unquenchable; unquenched ~ 4. (to have) a ~ for (a ~ for knowledge) 5. of ~ (to die of ~)

thirst II v. 1. (d; intr.) to ~ after (formal), for (to ~ for the truth; "Blessed are they which do hunger and ~ after righteousness" – "The Sermon on the Mount," *The Bible: St. Matthew*) 2. (E) (formal) to ~ to know the truth

thirsty adj. ~ for (~ for the truth)

thorn n. 1. to remove, take out a ~ (from one's finger) 2. (misc.) a ~ in smb.'s side ("a source of irritation")

thorough adj. ~ in

thoroughfare n. ["road"] (formal) 1. a busy, crowded; main ~ ["through road"] 2. No Thoroughfare (BE)

thought n. ["reflection"]["idea"] 1. to entertain, harbor, have a ~ (to harbor ~s of revenge) 2. to relish a ~ 3. to express, present a ~ 4. to collect, compose, gather; sum up one's ~s 5. a consoling, happy; intriguing; refreshing ~ 6. a fleeting, passing ~ (my first ~ was to run away but on second ~ I decided to stay) (see also **second thought**) 7. a disconcerting, upsetting; evil; sobering; ugly ~ 8. the ~ ¬occurred to me/struck me¬ that... 9. a ~ about, on (what are your ~s on this matter?) 10. a ~ that + clause (the ~ that we would soon reach home gave us courage) 11. at a ~ (my mind boggles at the very ~ (of it)) 12. in smb.'s ~s (she was always in my ~s ('my ~s are always with her')) 13. (misc.) the ~ has crossed my mind that...; to read smb.'s ~s; to

spare a ~ for; at a time like this my ~s turn to you; a train of ~; in ~, word, and deed; smb.'s innermost, inmost ~s ["consideration"] 14. to give ~ to; put a lot of ~ into (a lot of ~ has gone into this project but we may well need to put even more ~ into it) 15. to abandon, give up all ~(s) (of doing smt.) 16. (misc.) with no ~ for one's own safety; don't give it a ~; perish the ~! ("one should not even consider the possibility!") ["ideas, principles"] 17. liberal; logical; modern ~ 18. a school of ~ ["opinion"] 19. to express a ~ 20. a ~ about, on 21. a ~ that + clause (she expressed her ~ that the case should be settled without litigation) ["concentration"] 22. (deep) in ~ ["intention"] 23. to have no ~ (of doing smt.)

thoughtful adj. 1. ~ about 2. ~ to + inf. (it was ~ of her to do that)

thoughtless adj. 1. ~ of 2. ~ to + inf. (it was ~ of them to make noise)

thousand n. by the ~s, in the ~s, in their (BE) ~s (the crowd streamed into the stadium by the ~s)

thrall n. (formal) ["slavery"] in ~ to

thrash v. 1. to ~ soundly 2. (D; tr.) to ~ with (to ~ smb. with a cane) 3. (misc.) to ~ from side to side; to ~ about/around in one's sleep; to ~ people within an inch of their lives

thrashing n. 1. to get a ~ 2. to give smb. a ~ 3. a good, sound ~ (he got a good ~ for his misbehavior) 4. (misc.) to deserve a good ~

thread I n. ["fiber, cord"] 1. to make, spin; wind ~ 2. coarse; fine; heavy; thin ~ 3. cotton; lisle; nylon; polyester; rayon; silk ~ 4. a length, piece; reel (BE), spool (AE) of ~ 5. in ~ (there's a tangle in the ~) 6. (misc.) the ~ gets tangled; a loose ~; to hang by a ~ ("to be very uncertain") ["theme"]["train of thought"] 7. to follow; lose the ~ (of an argument) 8. the common ~ (of the stories) 9. a tenuous ~ 10. (misc.) a common ~ runs through all of her stories; to pull all the loose ~s of the story together

thread II v. (C) ~ a needle for me; or: ~ me a needle

threat n. 1. to issue, make, utter; mutter a ~ 2. to carry out, fulfill; withdraw a ~ 3. to be, constitute, pose, represent a ~ 4. to defy; ignore a ~ 5. to give in to a ~ 6. a constant; dire, grave, serious; direct; explicit; imminent ~ 7. a covert; empty, idle; implicit; veiled ~ 8. a death; security; suicide; terrorist ~ (their group poses a security ~; they issued a death ~ against the leader of the rival group; they made terrorist ~s before the rally) (see also **bomb threat**) 9. a ~ against, to (to constitute/pose a ~ to the party leadership) 10. a ~ to + inf. (she carried out her ~ to resign) 11. a ~ that + clause (she carried out her ~ that she would resign) 12. under ~ of (under ~ of reprisals from disaffected elements) 13. (misc.) to take a ~ seriously; a constant ~ hung over them

threaten v. 1. (D; tr.) to ~ with (to ~ smb. with reprisals) (see also *threaten with extinction* at **extinction**) 2. (E) she ~ed to resign

threshold *n.* ["entrance"] 1. (also fig.) to cross a ~ 2. (also fig.) on the ~ (to be on the ~ of a promising career) 3. (med.) a renal ~ ["tolerance"] 4. a boredom; pain ~ 5. a high; low ~ (to have a low pain ~) 6. above; below a ~

thrift *n.* to practice ~

thrifty *adj.* ~ in

thrill I *n.* 1. to give, provide a ~ 2. to experience, feel, get, have a ~ (we got a ~ from riding in your new car) 3. a ~ for smb. (it was a ~ for us to ride in your new car) 4. a ~ to + inf. (it was a ~ to ride in your new car = it was a ~ riding in your new car) 5. (misc.) a cheap ~ ; to gamble for the ~ of it ("to gamble for the sheer excitement of gambling")

thrill II *v.* 1. (d; intr.) to ~ to (she ~ed to the sound of their voices) 2. (R) it ~ed us to ride in your new car

thrilled *adj.* 1. ~ at; with (we were ~ at the thought of riding in your new car; they were ~ with the gift) 2. ~ to + inf. (we were ~ to ride in your new car) 3. ~ that + clause (we were ~ that we could ride in your new car) 4. (misc.) ~ to bits (esp. BE); to pieces (AE); to death

thrilling *adj.* 1. ~ to + inf. (it was ~ to ride in your new car) 2. ~ that + clause (it was ~ that we could ride in your new car)

thrive *v.* 1. (D; intr.) to ~ on (to ~ on hard work) 2. (misc.) to fail to ~ (despite our best efforts, they failed to ~)

throat *n.* 1. to clear one's ~ 2. to gargle one's ~ (AE) 3. to cut, slash, slit smb.'s ~ 4. a clear ~ 5. an inflamed, red, sore; scratchy; strep ~ (to come down with, get; have a sore/strep ~) 6. by the ~ (the mugger grabbed me by the ~) 7. down smb.'s ~ (the cool water went down her ~) 8. (misc.) to cut one's own ~ ("to ruin oneself"); to jump down smb.'s ~ ("to criticize smb."); to ram smt. down smb.'s ~ ("to impose smt. on smb."); the words stuck in her ~ ("she found it difficult to say them"); to be at each other's ~s ("to be constantly quarreling") (see also *bring a lump to smb.'s throat*; *have a lump in one's throat* at **lump**)

throb *v.* (D; intr.) to ~ with (to ~ with excitement)

throes *n.* 1. death ~ 2. in the ~ (in the ~ of a severe economic crisis)

thrombosis *n.* a cerebral; coronary ~

throne *n.* 1. to accede to, ascend, mount, succeed to a ~ 2. to seize, usurp; topple a ~ 3. to occupy, sit on a ~ 4. to abdicate; give up a ~ 5. to lose one's ~ 6. on a ~ (the old Queen remained on the ~ for many years) 7. (misc.) the power behind the ~ (see also *a pretender to the throne* at **pretender**)

throng *v.* (P; intr.) they all ~ed (a)round the speaker

thronged *adj.* ~ with (the beaches are ~ with people; the speaker was ~ with admirers)

throttle I *n.* 1. to open a ~ 2. at full ~ ("at full speed")

throttle II *v.* 1. (D; tr.) to ~ with (he ~d her with a scarf) 2. (misc.) to ~ smb. to death

through *adj., adv., prep.* 1. right, straight ~ (to) (when I dialed, I got right/straight ~; the call went right/straight ~; from spring right/straight ~ to winter) 2. ~ with (after thirty years, he is ~ with teaching – he's had enough!) (see also **come through**; *get through* at **get**; **get through**; *go through* at **go**; **go through**; *look through* at **look II** *v.*; *run through* at **run II** *v.*; *see through* at **see**)

throw I *n.* 1. (basketball) a free ~ (see also **free throw**) 2. (baseball) a wild ~ (see also **stone's throw**)

throw II *v.* 1. to ~ hard; high; straight (she threw the ball hard) 2. (A) she threw the ball to me; or: she threw me the ball 3. (D; tr.) to ~ across, over (to ~ a ball over a fence) 4. (D; tr.) to ~ at (she threw a stone at me) 5. (d; refl., tr.) to ~ into (he threw himself into his work; they threw the ball into the air; the news threw everyone into confusion) 6. (d; refl., tr.) to ~ on (she threw herself on the mercy of the court; she threw the books on(to) the table) (see also *throw light on smt.* at **light II** *n.*) 7. (d; tr.) to ~ out of (they were thrown out of work) 8. (d; refl., tr.) to ~ to (I threw myself to the ground) 9. (P; tr.) she threw the plate against the wall; he threw the tools under the car; he threw himself under a train 10. (misc.) to ~ smb. off balance; he threw himself at her ("he made a maximum effort to win her affections") (see also *throw smt. open* at **open I** *adj.*)

throw away *v.* (D; tr.) ("to squander") to ~ on (he threw away his money on gambling = he threw his money away on gambling)

throwback *n.* ["reversion"] a ~ to (to be a ~ to an earlier state)

throw back *v.* 1. (A) she threw the ball back to me; or: she threw me back the ball 2. see also **throw II** 1–9

throw down *v.* 1. (D; tr.) to ~ on, onto, to (she threw the books down onto the table) 2. see also **throw II** 8, 9

throw up *v.* 1. (B) ("to reproach") (esp. AE) I was late, but she didn't ~ it up to me 2. (D; tr.) ("to toss") to ~ in, into; to (she threw the ball up in the air) (see also **throw II** *v.* 1–5)

thrust I *n.* ["push"] 1. to make a ~ 2. a deep ~ (the enemy made a deep ~ into our lines) 3. a ~ at; into ["main point"] 4. the main, principal ~ (the main ~ of their argument)

thrust II *v.* 1. to ~ deeply 2. (d; tr.) to ~ at (she thrust the money at me) 3. (d; tr.) to ~ into (she thrust the money into my hand) 4. (misc.) to ~ one's way through a crowd

thud *n.* 1. a dull; loud; sickening ~ 2. (misc.) it fell to the ground with a loud ~

thumb I *n.* ["finger"] 1. babies often suck their ~s ["misc."] 2. under smb.'s ~ ("dominated by smb."); to twiddle one's ~s ("to be idle") (see also *stick out like a sore thumb* at **stick out**)

thumb II *v.* (d; intr.) to ~ through (to ~ through a book)

thumbs-down *n.* ["rejection"] (colloq.) to get; give the ~

thumbs-up *n.* ["approval"] (colloq.) to get; give the ~

thunder I *n.* 1. ~ booms, reverberates, roars, rolls, rumbles 2. a clap, crack, crash, peal, roll; rumble of ~ (a deafening clap of ~) 3. (misc.) to steal smb.'s ~ ("to do first what smb. else was going to do")

thunder II *v.* (L; at) he ~ed (at us) that he would never agree = "I shall never agree!" he thundered (at us)

thunderbolt *n.* a ~ struck (a tree)

thunderstruck *adj.* 1. ~ at (~ at the news) 2. ~ to + inf. (they were ~ to learn that the train had already left)

thwart *v.* (D; tr.) to ~ in (we were ~ed in our efforts to help)

tic *n.* a nervous; uncontrollable ~

tick I *n.* (colloq.) (esp. BE) ["credit"] on ~ (to let smb. have smt. on ~)

tick II *n.* (colloq.) (BE) ["moment"] in a ~ (she'll be down in a ~)

tick III *n.* (BE) ["check mark"] to make/put a ~ beside/by the right answer

ticket I *n.* ["document showing that a fare or admission fee has been paid"] 1. to issue a ~ 2. to book, reserve; buy; get a ~ 3. to honor ("accept") a ~ 4. an airplane; bus, coach (BE); platform (BE); rail, train ~ 5. a day-return (BE); one-way (AE), single (BE); return (BE), round-trip (AE) ~ 6. a commutation (AE); season ~ 7. a library (BE; CE has *library card*); meal (AE; BE has *luncheon voucher*) ~ (also fig.) (his rich wife is his meal ~ who gives him everyhting he wants) 8. a pawn ~ 9. a cinema (BE); theater ~ 10. a complimentary, free; valid ~ 11. a ~ for, to (a ~ for a concert; a ~ to a game; a ticket to Birmingham) ["list of candidates"] (pol.) (AE) 12. to split a ~ 13. a dream; split; straight ~ (to vote a split ~) 14. (misc.) who is running on the party ~? ["printed card indicating participation in a game of chance"] 15. a winning ~ (she held the winning ~) 16. a lottery; raffle; sweepstake (BE), sweepstakes (AE) ~ (to buy a whole book of raffle ~s) ["citation for a traffic violation"] 17. to give (smb.); issue, write out a ~ (the police officer wrote out a ~ for illegal parking) 18. to get; pay a ~ 19. a parking; speeding; traffic (AE) ~ 20. a ~ for (she got a ~ for illegal parking) 21. (misc.) to fix a ~ (colloq.) (AE) ("to get a traffic ticket nullified") ["misc."] 22. to write one's own ~ (esp. AE; colloq.) ("to have complete freedom of action")

ticket II *v.* (D; tr.) to ~ for (AE) (she was ~ed for illegal parking)

tickled *adj.* (colloq.) (esp. AE) ["happy"] 1. ~ at (~ at the prospect) 2. ~ to + inf. (they would be ~ to come to the party) 3. ~ that + clause (we're ~ that you'll be at our party) 4. (misc.) ~ pink/silly (AE), ~ to death ("very pleased")

tide *n.* ["rising and falling of the surface of bodies of water"] 1. a daily; ebb; falling; high, spring; flood; low, neap; strong ~ 2. a ~ comes in; ebbs, goes out; is in; is out 3. (misc.) to sail with the ~ ["trend, tendency"] 4. to buck (AE), go/swim against the ~ 5. to go/swim with the ~ 6. to stem; turn the ~ 7. (misc.) the ~ of public opinion is running strongly in our favor

tide over *v.* (D; tr.) to ~ until (this money will ~ us over until next month)

tidings *n.* 1. to bear, bring ~ 2. to receive ~ 3. glad; sad ~

tidy up *v.* (D; intr., tr.) to ~ after smb. (he had to ~ after the children, who wouldn't ~ after themselves)

tie I *n.* ["necktie"] 1. to knot, tie; put on; wear; loosen; tighten a ~ 2. a garish, loud; regimental (GB); school (GB) ~ (see also **bow tie**) ["draw"] (sports) 3. to break a ~ 4. a goalless (esp. BE), scoreless ~ 5. (to end) in a ~ ["match"] (BE) (sports) 6. a cup ~ ["link, bond"] 7. to establish ~s with 8. to cement, strengthen ~s 9. to cut, sever; loosen ~s with 10. close, intimate, strong ~s 11. family ~s 12. ~s between; to, with (~s to other nations) ["support for rails"] (AE) 13. a railroad ~ (BE has *sleeper*) ["misc."] 14. the old school ~ (BE) ("mutual aid of former fellow-students; the old-boy network")

tie II *v.* (d; tr.) ("to fasten") to ~ (a)round (she ~d the cord around the package) 2. (D; tr.) ("to equal the score of") to ~ for (to ~ smb. for the lead) 3. (D; tr.) ("to fasten") to ~ onto, to (they ~d him to a post) 4. (D; intr.) ("to equal the score") to ~ with (our team ~d with them for the lead) 5. (D; tr.) ("to fasten") to ~ with (I ~d the books with a string) 6. (N; used with an adjective) she ~d the rope tight

tied *adj.* ["connected"] ~ to (the raise was ~ to the cost of living)

tie down *v.* (D; tr.) to ~ to (she was ~d down to her job; I tried unsuccessfully to ~ her down to a date for our next meeting)

tied up *adj.* ["busy"] 1. ~ with (I'm ~ with appointments all week) ["connected"] 2. ~ with (they are ~ with several multinational corporations)

tie-in *n.* (colloq.) ["relation"] a ~ between; with

tiers *n.* ["rows"] in ~

tie-up *n.* ["stoppage"] 1. to cause a ~ 2. a traffic ~ ["link"] 3. a ~ to; with

tie up *v.* 1. (D; tr.) to ~ in (they ~d up their money in bonds = they tied their money up in bonds) 2. (D; tr.) to ~ into (she ~d up everything into a bundle = she tied everything up into a bundle) 3. (D; tr.) to ~ to (she tied the horse up to the fence) 4. (D; tr.) to ~ with (I ~d up the package with string = I tied the package up with string)

tiff *n.* ["quarrel"] 1. to have a ~ with 2. a minor ~

tiger *n.* 1. a Bengal; man-eating; saber-toothed; Siberian ~ 2. ~s growl; roar 3. a young ~ is a cub 4. a female ~ is a tigress 5. (misc.) to fight like a ~ ("to fight very fiercely"); a paper ~ ("one who only seems to pose a threat")

tight *adj.* ["stingy"] (colloq.) 1. ~ with (~ with money) ["misc."] 2. to sit ~ ("to maintain one's position")

tighten up *v.* (D; intr.) to ~ on (the police are ~ing up on illegal parking)

tightrope *n.* to walk a ~ (also fig.) (to walk a ~ between fiscal prudence and the increasing demands of the welfare state)

tights *n.* (BE; AE has *pantyhose*) 1. a pair of ~s 2. (misc.) she got a ladder in her ~

tile *n.* ceramic; vinyl ~

till *n.* ["money drawer"] 1. behind, on the ~ (who's (working) on the ~ today?) 2. (misc.) to have one's finger(s) in the ~ ("to steal from a money drawer")

tilt I *n.* ["attack"] (colloq.) (BE) 1. to have, make a ~ at ["inclination"] 2. a ~ to, towards ["misc."] 3. at full ~ ("at full speed")

tilt II *v.* 1. (D; intr.) to ~ to (to ~ to the right) 2. (misc.) to ~ at windmills ("to fight imaginary enemies")

timber *n.* 1. to float, raft ~ (down a river) 2. green, unseasoned; seasoned ~

time I *n.* ["unlimited duration"] ["entire period of existence"] 1. ~ flies; goes by, passes (see also *(the) time flies* at **time I** *n.* 31 below) 2. in ~ (we exist in ~ and space) ["unlimited future or later period"] 3. (only) ~ will tell (~ will tell if we are right; only ~ would tell whether we were right in 1967; "You can fool all the people some of the ~, and some of the people all the ~, but you can not fool all the people all the ~" – attributed to Abraham Lincoln, 1858) 4. in, in the course of, over, with ~ (in/ with ~ everything will be forgotten – just give it ~!; there are bound to be changes over ~) (see also *with the passage of time* at **passage**) ["moment"] ["fixed moment"] ["appropriate moment"] 5. to fix, set, specify a ~ for (to fix a ~ for a meeting) 6. to bide ("wait patiently for") one's ~ 7. arrival; bedtime; check-in; check-out; curtain ~; departure; dinner; lunchtime; mealtime; starting; summertime; supper; wintertime ~ (What is the estimated arrival ~? = What is the estimated ~ of arrival (ETA)?) (see also **peacetime**; **wartime**) 8. the appointed; present; right; wrong ~; an appropriate, suitable ~ 9. a closing; opening ~ 10. (a) ~ for (it's ~ for lunch) 11. ~ to + inf. (it's (high) ~ for us to leave) 12. ~ that + clause (it's (high) ~ that we ¬left/were leaving¬) 13. at a certain ~ (at a bad ~; at the present ~; at that ~; at any old ~; he ¬ran up/took¬ the stairs two at a ~) 14. by a certain ~ (by that ~ she had left) 15. (misc.) in good ~; in plenty of ~; there's a ~ and place for everything; smb.'s ~ has come; when the ~ comes, the ~ will come (the ~ will come when you'll look back on it all and laugh; when the ~ comes ¬to act/for action¬ we'll be ready!) ["duration"] ["period"] ["interval"] 16. to pass, spend ~ (she spends her ~ reading) 17. to gain, save ~ 18. to find ~ (she somehow finds (the) ~ to go jogging every day) 19. to take ~ (it takes quite a bit of time to get there; how much ~ will this job take?) 20. to lose;

waste ~; to fritter away, idle away, while away one's ~ 21. a long; short ~ 22. ancient; Biblical; former; geological; modern; olden; prehistoric; recent ~s (in ancient ~s) 23. (AE) compensatory ~ ("free time given to an employee for previously worked overtime") (BE has *time off in lieu*) 24. equal ~ (for political candidates on TV and radio) 25. peak-time (BE), peak-viewing ~ (BE), prime ~ (what's on TV tonight during prime ~? = what's on prime-time TV tonight?) 26. (a) fast; record ~ (she ran the distance in record ~) 27. released ~ ("time given for extracurricular activities") 28. travel ~ ("time spent in traveling to and from work") 29. (the) running ~ (of a film) 30. (the) ~ drags; is up; runs out (the ~ is up and the class is over) 31. (the) ~ flies (see also *time flies* at **time I** *n.* 1 above) 32. ~ for (will you have ~ for an interview?) 33. (misc.) to kill ~ ("to make time pass"); to play for ~ ("to seek delay"); to take one's ~ (about); ("to act slowly"); for a ~; for the ~ being ("for now"); ~ hangs heavy on our hands; reaction ~ (a quick temper and a fast reaction ~) ["conditions during a period"] 34. to keep up with the ~s = to keep abreast of the ~s 35. bad, difficult, hard, rough ~s (during/ in hard ~s) ["available period"] 36. to find; get; have; take (the) ~ (she doesn't find/get/have/take the ~ to relax; he never finds ~ for his family) 37. to budget; plan one's ~ 38. to run out of ~ 39. to devote ~ to; to put ~ into; to save ~; to waste ~ (don't waste ~ gambling!) 40. free, leisure, spare ~ (what do you do in your leisure ~?) 41. ~ to + inf. (there is no ~ to lose; will you have ~ to give an interview?) 42. ~ for (~ for relaxation; I have no ~ for my family) ["period worked"] 43. double; full ~; overtime; part ~; time-and-a-half (I work part ~) 44. lost ~ (to make up lost ~; to make up for lost ~) ["period of serving, service"] 45. to do, serve ~ (to do/serve ~ in prison) ["tempo, rhythm"] 46. to beat; keep ~ (to music, to a song) 47. (mus.) common; waltz ~ 48. (usu mil.) double; quick ~ (quick ~, march!) 49. in ~ to (the music) ["system of measuring duration"] 50. to gain; keep; lose ~ (my watch gains ~; your watch keeps good ~; her watch loses ~) 51. to show the ~ (that clock shows the ~) 52. to tell ~ (esp. AE)/ the ~ (esp. BE) (a clock tells ~/the ~; the child is learning how to tell ¬ ~/the ~¬) 53. central (US); daylight-saving (AE), summer (BE); eastern (US); Greenwich (mean); local; mountain (US); Pacific (US); solar; standard (AE) ~ 54. (misc.) what ~ is it? = what is the ~?; where were you (at) this ~ last year? ["schedule"] 55. ahead of ~ 56. behind ~ 57. in (good, plenty of) ~ for (we arrived in ~ for the concert) (see also *(just) in the nick of time* at **nick**; *with time to spare* at **spare** *v.*) 58. on ~ (they got there on ~) ["experience"] 59. to have a (good) ~ 60. a delightful, good, great, lovely, pleasant, wonderful; fun (colloq.) ~ (we had a great ~ on our trip) 61. a bad, miserable, rough, tough, unpleasant ~ (see also **hard time**) ["timeout"] (sports) 62. to call

~ ["occasion"] 63. the first; last; next ~; that; this ~ ["end of pregnancy"] 64. her ~ is near ["misc."] 65. at the same ~ ("however"); at ~s ("occasionally"); for the ~ being ("at present"); behind the ~s ("not abreast of recent events"); the bartender called ~ and everybody had to leave; from/since ~ immemorial ("from the earliest period"); (all) in good ~ ("when appropriate"); in the fullness of ~ (all in good ~, my boy: everything will be all right in the fullness of ~!); in no ~ (at all) ("very soon"); to have the ~ of one's life ("to enjoy oneself thoroughly"); it's about ~! ("we must act now"); it's (about) ~ that we ¬left/were leaving¬; to keep up with the ~s ("to keep abreast of the latest developments"); to make good ~ ("to travel quickly"); to make ~ with smb. (esp. AE; colloq.) ("to be successful in attracting smb."); to mark ~ ("to be inactive"); ~ and ~ again; or: ~ after ~ ("frequently"); to live on borrowed ~ ("to live beyond the expected time of death"); pressed/pushed for ~ ("in a hurry"); to work against ~ ("to work to meet a deadline") (see also *battle against time* at **battle**; *race against time* at **race I** *n.*); he died before his ~ ("he died prematurely"); those events were before my ~; at last I've won the Nobel Prize – and not before ~! ("I've deserved it for a long time"); (sports) extra ~ (BE), overtime (AE); once upon a ~ (used to begin a fairy tale); of all ~ (who's the greatest tennis-player of all ~?) (see also *the time is ripe* at **ripe**; *a sign of the times* at **sign I** *n.*) USAGE NOTES: 1. The phrase *in time* can mean "eventually" – in time everything will be forgotten. 2. The phrase *in time* can also mean "with some time to spare" – we arrived in time for the concert. 3. The phrase *on time* means "neither early nor late" – they got there on time. 4. The phrase **of all times* is sometimes heard in BE but is wrong for *of all time*: who's the greatest tennis-player of all time? (see also **big time**)

time II *v.* 1. to ~ smt. badly; well 2. (D; tr.) to ~ at (her performance was ~d at 57 seconds) 3. (H) her performance was ~d to last no longer than one minute 4. (misc.) to ~ smt. (down) to the last second

time bomb *n.* 1. to set off a ~ 2. a ~ ticks away 3. (misc.) they are sitting on a ~ ("disaster is imminent")

time out *n.* 1. to take (a) ~ for (they took ~ for a rest) 2. (misc.) a ~ to + inf. (they took a ~ (in order) to rest) USAGE NOTE: Note the different spellings in: They took time out to rest; they took a time-out to rest.

timer *n.* ["timing device"] to set a ~

timetable *n.* 1. to draw up, make out, make up, prepare, work out a ~ 2. to issue a ~ 3. to follow, stick to a ~ 4. to upset a ~ 5. (esp. BE) an airline; bus; railway, train ~ (AE prefers *schedule*) 6. a ~ for (we have worked out a ~ for our trip) 7. according to, in a ~ (according to the ~ for our trip, we ought to have started out an hour ago!)

timid *adj.* ~ about; with

timing *n.* bad; flawless, perfect; good ~ (the secret of a good comedian is (perfect) ~)

tin *n.* (BE) a baking; biscuit; cake ~ (AE has *baking pan; cookie sheet; cake pan*)

tinged *adj.* (cannot stand alone) ~ with (~ with regret)

tingle *v.* (D; intr.) to ~ with (my ears ~d with the cold)

tinker *v.* (colloq.) (D; intr.) to ~ with

tint *v.* (N; used with an adjective) the windshield is ~ed blue

tip I *n.* ["gratuity"] 1. to give, leave a ~ 2. a big, generous, handsome ~ (I left a five-dollar ~ for the waitress = I left the waitress a five-dollar ~)

tip II *v.* 1. to ~ generously, handsomely, liberally 2. (O) I ~ped the waitress (five dollars)

tip III *n.* ["information"] 1. give smb. a ~ 2. to get, receive a ~ 3. to take a ~ 4. an anonymous; hot; useful ~ 5. a ~ about, on 6. a ~ for (useful ~s for poets about how to get published)

tip IV *n.* ["pointed end"] 1. a filter ~ ["end"] 2. at the ~ (at the northern ~ of the island) 3. on the ~ of smb.'s tongue (the word was on the ~ of my tongue); it was on the ~ of my tongue to say something) (see also **fingertips**)

tip V *v.* (d; tr.) ("to cover") to ~ with (they ~ped their arrows with poison)

tip VI *v.* (BE) see **tipped**

tip-off *n.* 1. an anonymous ~ 2. to get a ~ 3. a ~ about (the police got an anonymous ~ about when the robbery would take place) 4. a ~ that + clause (the police got an anonymous ~ that the robbery would take place at night)

tip off *v.* 1. to ~ anonymously 2. (D; tr.) to ~ about (the police were tipped off anonymously about when the robbery would take place) 3. (L; must have an object + that-clause) (the police were tipped off anonymously that the robbery would take place at night)

tipped *adj.* ["considered likely"] (BE) 1. widely ~ 2. ~ as (~ as the next Prime Minister) 3. ~ for (widely ~ for the job of Prime Minister) 4. ~ to + inf. (she is ~ to become the next Prime Minister)

tiptoe I *n.* (to go, stand, walk) on ~ (they went up the stairs on ~)

tiptoe II *v.* (P; intr.) she ~d into the room and through it; they ~d up the stairs

tirade *n.* 1. to deliver; launch into a ~ 2. a blistering, lengthy ~ 3. a ~ against

tire I tyre *n.* 1. to deflate; inflate, pump up a ~ 2. to mount, put on a ~ 3. to change; patch, repair; recap; retread a ~ 4. to crisscross, rotate ~s (to reduce wear) 5. to slash a ~ 6. a flat ~ (we had a flat ~ during our trip) 7. a bald; worn ~ 8. a balloon; radial; rubber; snow; spare; steel-belted; studded; tubeless ~ 9. whitewall ~s 10. a ~ blows (out), gets/has a puncture; goes flat 11. a set of ~s USAGE NOTE: AE has "change a tire"; BE, "change a wheel". CE has "spare tire/tyre"; BE, "spare wheel". CE has "spare tire/tyre" 'roll of fat around the waist'.

tire II v. (d; intr.) to ~ of (to ~ of watching television)

tired adj. 1. to get ~ 2. dead ~ 3. ~ of (I'm ~ of waiting; "when a man is ~ of London, he is ~ of life" – Samuel Johnson, September 20th, 1777)

tiresome adj. ~ to + inf. (it's ~ to do the same thing every day = it's ~ doing the same thing every day = it's ~ if/when you do the same thing every day)

tissue n. ["structural material"] 1. cellular; conjunctival; connective; fatty; granulation; muscular ~ (see also **scar tissue**) ["soft paper"] 2. absorbent; cleansing; toilet ~ 3. a wad of ~s ["misc."] 4. a ~ of lies

title I n. ["appellation"] 1. to bestow, confer a ~ on (the ~ (of) Baron Tweedsmuir was conferred on John Buchan) 2. to accept; refuse; renounce a ~ (John Buchan accepted the ~ (of) Baron Tweedsmuir; Sir Winston Churchill refused a ~ and Tony Benn renounced the ~ (of) Viscount Stansgate so that they could continue to sit in the House of Commons) 3. an official ~ ["exclusive possession"] 4. to give, grant smb. ~ to smt. 5. to hold ~ to smt. 6. clear ~ 7. ~ to (they hold clear ~ to the property) 8. (misc.) there is a cloud on the ~ ["championship"] 9. to fight for; win a ~ 10. to hold a ~ 11. to clinch a ~ 12. to defend a ~ 13. to give up; lose a ~

title II v. ("to call, name, entitle") (esp. AE) (N) they ~d their dictionary *The BBI*

titter v. (D; intr.) 1. to ~ nervously 2. to ~ at

toady (CE), **toady up** (esp. AE) v. (d; intr.) to ~ to (he ~died to the boss = he ~died up to the boss)

toast I n. ["browned bread"] 1. to make ~ 2. buttered; cinnamon; dry; French; melba ~ 3. a piece, round (BE; old-fashioned), slice of ~ 4. on ~ (butter/cheese/beans on ~)

toast II v. (C) ~ two slices for me; or: ~ me two slices

toast III n. ["act of drinking to honor smb."] 1. to drink; propose a ~ 2. a ~ to (we drank a ~ to her) 3. (misc.) to join smb. in a ~ ["highly admired person"] 4. the ~ of (the ~ of the town; the ~ of high society)

tobacco n. 1. to grow, raise ~ 2. to cure ~ 3. to chew; smoke ~ 4. mild; strong ~ 5. chewing; pipe ~ 6. a plug of (chewing) ~

toddy n. a hot ~ (as for a cold)

to-do n. ["fuss"] to make a (big) ~ over

toe n. 1. to stub one's ~ (on) 2. to curl one's ~s 3. the big; little ~ 4. (misc.) to keep/stay on one's ~s ("to be alert"); to step on smb.'s ~; to tread on smb.'s ~s ("to offend smb."); from head to ~

toehold n. ["footing, foothold"] 1. to gain, get a ~ 2. a precarious ~

toenail n. 1. to cut, trim; file; manicure a ~ 2. an ingrowing (BE), ingrown (AE) ~

together – adv. 1. to go ~ ("to match") (do carrots and peas really go ~?) 2. ~ with (do carrots really go ~

with peas?) 3. all ~ (there were about 50 of them all ~ = all ~, there were about 50 ot them)

toil I n. ["hard work"] 1. arduous, backbreaking, unremitting ~ 2. physical ~ 3. (misc.) "I have nothing to offer but blood, ~, tears and sweat" – Winston Churchill, May 13th, 1940

toil II v. ("to work hard") 1. (D; intr.) to ~ over (to ~ over a hot stove; to ~ over a difficult project) 2. (misc.) to ~ (in order/so as) to finish a difficult project

toilet n. 1. to go to, need, use the ~ 2. to flush a ~ 3. a flush; gents' (esp. BE), men's; ladies', women's; pay; public ~ 4. down the ~ (to flush smt. down the ~)

token n. ["symbol, sign"] 1. to be, constitute a ~ 2. to give, provide a ~ of 3. a tangible ~ 4. (misc.) as a ~ of (here is smt. for you as a ~ of my esteem); by the same ~ ("for a similar reason") (we should always be ready and by the same ~ we should never relax our vigilance); in ~ of ("as evidence of") (here is smt. for you in ~ of my esteem) ["metal or plastic disc used as a substitute for money"] 5. to drop in, insert, put in a ~ (to insert a ~ into a slot) 6. to accept, take a ~ (will this machine take ~s?) 7. a bus; subway (AE) ~ ["coupon, voucher"] (BE) 8. a book; gift; record ~

told adj. all ~ ("altogether") (there were about 50 of them all ~ = all ~, there were about 50 ot them)

tolerance n. 1. to display, show ~ 2. to have (a) ~ 3. ~ for, of, towards 4. a level of ~ (the government showed a quite high level of ~ for/of dissidence) 5. (misc.) zero ~ (as of crime)

tolerant adj. 1. ~ of (~ of criticism) 2. ~ towards

tolerate v. 1. (G) I will not ~ smoking! 2. (K) I will not ~ his smoking!

toleration n. 1. to display, show ~ 2. to have ~ 3. ~ for, of, towards 4. a level of ~ (the government showed a quite high level of ~ of dissidence)

toll I n. ["amount levied"] 1. to charge, impose a ~ 2. to collect ~s (on a bridge, road) 3. to pay a ~ 4. a bridge; tunnel; turnpike (AE) ~ 5. (misc.) ~ free (a toll-free telephone number that you can call ~ free) ["damage"] 6. to take a ~ (on) (the storm took a heavy ~; the earthquake took a heavy ~ on several villages) 7. a heavy; mounting, rising ~ ["casualties"] 8. the death ~ (the mounting death ~ from the epidemic)

toll II v. (D; intr.) to ~ for (the bell ~ed for those who had made the supreme sacrifice; "never send to know for whom the bell ~s; It ~s for thee" – John Donne, 1572–1631, *Devotions*)

tomato n. 1. to grow ~es 2. to can ~es 3. ripe; sundried ~es 4. a can (esp. AE), tin (BE) of ~es 5. a rotten ~ (also fig. in AE) (see also *tomato soup* at **soup**)

tome n. ["volume"] a scholarly; weighty ~

tom-tom n. 1. to beat a ~ 2. the beat of the ~

ton n. 1. a gross; long; metric; short ~ 2. (misc.) (BE; slang) to do the ~ ("to go one hundred miles per hour") USAGE NOTE: The ton in GB is the *long ton* (two thousand two hundred forty pounds). In the US, the ton is the *short ton* (two thousand pounds). The *metric ton* is one thousand kilograms and is officially spelled *tonne* in GB.

tone *n.* ["style, trend"] 1. to set the ~ ["sound"] 2. dulcet, sweet; harsh; strident ~(s) ["manner of speaking that reveals the speaker's feelings"] 3. to adopt, take a certain ~ 4. a conversational; friendly; normal 5. a businesslike; decisive; emphatic; firm ~ 6. an apologetic; subdued ~ 7. a flippant; ironic ~ 8. a serious; solemn ~ 9. a condescending, patronizing; unctuous ~ 10. an arrogant; imperious ~ 11. an abusive; angry, querulous; strident; threatening ~ 12. in a ~ (in angry ~s; she spoke in a normal ~ of voice) 13. (misc.) don't take that ~ with me! smb.'s ~ of voice ["signal"] 14. a dial (AE), dialling (BE); engaged (BE; AE has *busy signal*); ringing ~ ["pitch"] (ling.) 15. a falling; high; low; rising ~ (for music, see **note I** *n.* 11–14)

tongs *n.* 1. coal; curling; ice; sugar ~ 2. a pair of ~

tongue *n.* ["language"] 1. smb.'s mother, native ~ 2. a foreign ~ (to speak in a foreign ~) ["organ of speech"]["speech"] 3. to hold one's ~ ("to be silent") 4. to find one's ~ ("to begin to speak") 5. to stick out one's ~ (the child stuck out its ~ at me) 6. to click one's ~ 7. a coated ~ 8. (misc.) a ~ depressor; on everyone's ~ ("discussed by everyone"); on the tip of smb.'s ~ ("not quite recalled"); ~s were wagging ("people were gossiping"); to speak with a forked ~ ("to be deceitful"); the brandy loosened her ~ ("after drinking she became very talkative") (see also *(with) tongue in cheek* at **cheek** 4) ["manner of speaking"] 9. a caustic, foul, nasty, sharp, vile; civil; glib; loose ~ (he has a nasty ~; I'll thank you to keep a civil ~ in your head!)

tongue-lashing *n.* 1. to give smb. a (good) ~ 2. to get, receive a ~

tonic *n.* 1. to take a ~ 2. a ~ for 3. (misc.) a gin and ~ ("type of mixed drink")

tonnage *n.* dead-weight; displacement; gross; net, registered ~

tonsillectomy *n.* 1. to do, perform a ~ (on) 2. to have a ~

tonsils *n.* 1. enlarged; inflamed ~ 2. (misc.) to have one's ~ out/removed/taken out

tool *n.* 1. to use a ~ 2. a garden; machine; power ~ 3. burglar's; farm ~s 4. a set of ~s 5. (misc.) the ~s of smb.'s/the trade; (BE) to down ~s ("to go out on strike") (see also *tool kit* at **kit**)

toot *n.* (colloq.) to give a ~ (on a horn)

tooth *n.* 1. to cut, get teeth (babies are often fretful when they are cutting teeth) 2. to lose a ~ 3. to brush (esp. AE), clean one's teeth 4. to cap = crown; drill; extract, pull, take out; fill a ~ 5. to pick one's teeth 6. to bare; clench, gnash, grind, grit one's teeth 7. a false; baby (AE), milk; back; front; gold; lower; missing; permanent; upper; wisdom ~ 8. an abscessed; decayed; loose ~ 9. teeth ache; chatter;

decay, rot; erupt ("appear"); fall out; get discolored (see also *tooth decay* at **decay**) 10. a (full) set of teeth 11. between one's teeth (a pipe clamped firmly between his teeth) (see also *to take the bit between one's teeth* at **bit II** *n.*) 12. in one's teeth (to hold smt. in one's teeth) 13. (misc.) to have a sweet ~ ("to love sweets"); to sink one's teeth into smt. ("to become completely engrossed in smt."); to show one's teeth ("to show hostile intentions"); ~ and nail ("with all one's strength") (we fought ~ and nail to save our local post-office!); to cut one's teeth on smt. ("to gain one's first experience with smt.")

toothache *n.* to get, have a ~ (AE)/get, have (a) ~ (BE)

toothbrush *n.* to use a ~

toothpaste *n.* a tube of ~

top I *n.* ["device that spins"] 1. to spin a ~ ["misc."] 2. to sleep like a ~ ("to sleep very soundly")

top II *n.* ["highest point"] 1. to reach, rise to the ~ 2. a mountain ~; rooftop 3. from; to (the) ~ (from ~ to bottom; we climbed to the ~; to fill smt. to the ~) 4. at, on; over the ~ (the liquid spilled over the ~ of the bottle) ["cover, cap"] 5. to put on, screw on a ~ 6. to screw off, take off, unscrew a ~ 7. a bottle; box; screw ~ ["misc."] 8. to blow one's ~ ("to explode in anger"); to go over the ~ ("to begin a mil. charge by going over a parapet"); (fig.) ("to exceed a limit") (the actor's performance was a little over the ~ ("extreme") (abbreviated to OTT in BE)); to be on ~ of a situation ("to be in control of a situation")

top III *v.* (d; tr.) to ~ with (the cake was ~ped with whipped cream)

topic *n.* 1. to bring up, broach, consider, deal with; discuss; explore, go into a ~ 2. an appropriate, suitable; controversial; current; everyday; favorite; interesting; special ~ 3. a boring, uninteresting; inappropriate; taboo; unpleasant ~ 4. a ~ comes up (for discussion) 5. about, on a ~ (which ~ are you going to talk about tonight?) 6. (misc.) a ~ of conversation; a ~ of interest; a ~ for discussion

top off *v.* (d; tr.) to ~ with (we ~ped off our lunch with a nice dessert = we ~ped our lunch off with a nice dessert)

topple *v.* (D; intr., tr.) to ~ from (he was ~d from the throne)

topsy-turvy *adj.* to turn (smt.) ~

torch *n.* ["portable electric light"] (BE; AE has *flashlight*) 1. to turn on a ~ 2. to flash, shine; train a ~ on 3. to turn off a ~ 4. an electric ~ (we could see the light of our electric ~) ["burning stick"] 5. to light a ~ (see also *torchlight* at **light II** *n.*; *torchlight parade* at **parade**) 6. to bear, carry, hold a ~ 7. a flaming ~ ["device used to produce a very hot flame"] 8. a blowtorch (CE; BE typically prefers *blowlamp*); welding ~ ["misc."] 9. to put smt. to the ~ ("to set fire to smt."); to carry a ~ for smb. (colloq.) ("to remain in love with smb. who does not return that love") (see also *torch song* at **song**)

torment *n.* 1. to endure, experience, feel, go through ~(s) 2. to prolong the ~ 3. acute, great, indescribable; unbearable ~ 4. in ~ (in great ~) 5. (misc.) (all) the ~s ¬of hell/of the damned¬
torment II *v.* 1. (D; tr.) to ~ into (to ~ smb. into doing smt.) 2. (D; tr.) to ~ with (they ~ed him with threats to his family)
torn *adj.* ["divided"] (cannot stand alone) ~ between (she was ~ between her family and her job)
tornado *n.* 1. a ~ hits, strikes; rages (the ~ struck several cities) 2. a ~ blows itself out, blows over, dies down, subsides
torpedo *n.* 1. to fire, launch a ~ 2. an acoustic; aerial; bangalore; magnetic ~ 3. a ~ explodes 4. a ~ hits; misses its target (see also *torpedo boat* at **boat**)
torrent *n.* 1. an angry, raging ~ 2. a mountain ~ 3. (misc.) the rain came down in ~s; a ~ of abuse (she vented her feelings in a ~ of abuse)
tort *n.* (legal) to commit a ~
torture I *n.* 1. to employ, inflict, practice, resort to, use ~ 2. to subject smb. to ~ 3. to suffer, undergo ~ 4. cruel; plain, sheer; sadistic; severe ~ 5. the water ~ 6. an act of ~ 7. ~ to + inf. (it was sheer ~ to listen to her sing = it was sheer ~ listening to her sing) 8. under ~ (he confessed under ~)
torture II *v.* 1. to ~ cruelly; sadistically; severely ~ 2. (D; tr.) to ~ into (he was ~d into confessing) 3. (misc.) to ~ smb. to death
toss I *n.* ["flipping of a coin to decide an issue"] to lose; win the ~ (who won the ~ to go first?)
toss II *v.* 1. ("to turn and twist") to ~ (and turn) restlessly (as in one's sleep) 2. (A) ("to throw") ~ the ball to me; or: ~ me the ball 3. (D; intr., tr.) to ~ for ("to decide by flipping a coin") (let's ~ for it) 4. (P; tr.) to ~ a ball into the air; the children ~ed stones over the fence; to ~ a salad in dressing to make a ~ed salad
toss-up *n.* 1. a ~ between (it was a ~ between the two leading candidates) 2. (misc.) it was a ~ who would win; it was a ~ whether to go or stay
total I *n.* 1. to add up, calculate, tally up a ~ 2. a combined; grand; sum ~ 3. (misc.) to add up to; come to a ~ (it comes to a grand ~ of € 3 000)
total II *v.* (S) it ~s € 3 000
touch I *n.* ["social contact"] 1. to be; get in ~ 2. to keep, stay in ~ 3. to lose ~ (with) 4. close ~ 5. in ~ with smb. (keep in close ~ with me) 6. out of ~ with (I am out of ~ with the present situation) ["feel, the sense of touch"] 7. to the ~ (smooth to the ~) ["physical contact"] 8. a deft; delicate; gentle, light, soft, soothing; heavy ~ (the door opened at a light ~ of her hand) ["sensitivity"] 9. to have; lose the common ~ ("to have; lose the ability to appeal to the common people") ("walk with Kings – nor lose the common ~" – Rudyard Kipling (1865–1936), "If –") 10. the human ~ ("the ability to relate with compassion to others") ["ability"] 11. to lose one's ~ ["manner"] 12. a bold; distinctive; magic; man's; personal; woman's ~ ["detail, stroke"] 13. the final;

finishing ~es (to add the final ~es to a painting with a few distinctive ~es of his brush; to put the finishing ~es on/to smt.) ["misc."] 14. a soft ~ ("an overly generous person")
touch II *v.* 1. (d; intr.) ("to stop briefly") to ~ at (the ship will ~ at three ports) 2. (colloq.) (d; tr.) to ~ for ("to ask for") (to ~ smb. for a loan) 3. (d; intr.) to ~ on ("to treat briefly") (to ~ on a topic) 4. (D; tr.) to ~ on ("to make contact by touch with") (she ~ed me lightly on the arm)
touchdown *n.* (esp. Am. football) to score a ~
touched *adj.* 1. deeply, very ~ 2. ~ to + inf. (she was ~ to have been invited) 3. ~ that + clause (she was ~ that she ¬had been/should have been¬ invited)
touching *adj.* 1. ~ to + inf. (it was touching for her to learn that she had been invited) 2. ~ that + clause (it was ~ that they ¬had/should have¬ invited her)
touchy *adj.* (colloq.) ~ about (he's ~ ¬about/when it comes to¬ his appearance)
tough *adj.* (colloq.) ["strict"] 1. to be, get ~ (on) 2. ~ on, with (they are ~ on drunk drivers and are getting ~er with them all the time; "Tough on crime, ~ on the causes of crime" – Tony Blair, 1992, though also attributed to Gordon Brown) ["difficult"] 3. (cannot stand alone) ~ to + inf. (he is ~ to work with = it is ~ to work with him = it is ~ working with him = he is a ~ person to work with; it's ~ on workers when they lose their jobs = it's ~ for workers to lose their jobs) ["unfortunate"] 4. ~ that + clause (it's ~ that you can't be with your family) ["misc."] 5. to hang ~ (esp. AE; slang) ("to be very firm"); to talk ~ ("to take a very firm bargaining position"); as ~ as nails
tour *n.* 1. to conduct, operate a ~ (see also *tour operator* at **operator**) 2. to organize a ~ 3. to do, go on, make a ~ of 4. a barnstorming (AE); campaign; goodwill; lightning, whirlwind ~ 5. a bus; city; walking ~ 6. a concert; lecture, speaking; study ~ 7. a conducted, guided; organized; package ~ (see also *tour guide* at **guide I** *n.*) 8. a city; sightseeing ~ 9. on (a) ~ (to be on ~) 10. (misc.) a grand ~ (did the Grand Tour of Europe before settling down)
tourist *n.* 1. ~s flocked to the ~ sites 2. a flock; party of ~s
tour of duty *n.* 1. to do a ~ 2. on a ~ (they were on a ~ in the Far East)
tournament *n.* 1. to conduct, hold a ~ 2. to enter; win a ~ 3. a bridge; chess; invitational (AE); rapid-transit (for chess) (AE); tennis ~ 4. a ~ takes place 5. in; out of a ~ (he stayed in the ~ until the last round, when he was knocked out of the ~ by the eventual winner)
tourniquet *n.* 1. to apply, put on a ~ 2. to loosen; tighten a ~
tout I *n.* (BE) a ticket ~ (AE has *scalper*)
tout II *v.* (colloq.) ("to praise") ("to tip") 1. (d; tr.) to ~ as (he was ~ed as the next middleweight champion) 2. (misc.) highly ~ed; (BE) to ~ for ("to solicit")

tow I *n.* 1. to give a ~ (to) 2. a ski ~ 3. to have, take in ~ 4. under ~ (she had her little sister in ~; they took the ship in ~ and it's still under ~)
tow II *v.* 1. (D; tr.) to ~ into (to ~ a barge into a port) 2. (D; tr.) to ~ out of (to ~ a boat out of a harbor) 3. (D; tr.) to ~ to (to ~ a car to a garage) 4. (P; tr.) they ~ed the bus across town
towel *n.* ["cloth, paper for drying"] 1. a bath; dish (AE), tea (esp. BE); face; guest; hand; linen; paper; roller; Turkish ~ 2. a sanitary ~ (BE; AE has *sanitary napkin*; CE has *sanitary pad*) 3. a disposable ~ (see also *towel rack* at **rack**; *towel rail* at **rail**) ["symbol of surrender"] 4. to throw in, toss in the ~
tower I *n.* 1. a bell; clock; computer; conning; control; fire; TV; watch; water ~ 2. a signal ~ (AE; BE has *signal box*) 3. a ~ stands (one hundred feet high) 4. (misc.) an ivory ~ ("a sheltered place where life's realities may be avoided"); twin ~s (as of the World Trade Center)
tower II *v.* 1. (d; intr.) to ~ above, over (as a thinker, she ~s over her colleagues) 2. (misc.) to ~ high (the skyscraper ~ed (hundreds of feet) high above the city)
town *n.* 1. a boom; border; country; college (AE), university; ghost ("deserted"); jerkwater (AE; colloq.), one-horse, provincial, sleepy, small; market (BE); seaside (BE); shanty ~ (they live in a sleepy little ~) 2. a company ~ 3. (BE) a dormitory ~ (AE has *bedroom community*) 4. smb.'s hometown 5. a county ~ (BE; AE has *county seat*) 6. in ~; out of ~ (they were out of ~ for six weeks; they are back in ~) 7. (misc.) to come to ~; to go to ~ (colloq.; fig.) ("to go all out"); to leave ~; to blow/skip ~ (esp. AE; colloq.) ("to leave town suddenly"); (out) on the ~ ("enjoying city nightlife") USAGE NOTE: In GB, many places are called *towns* that would be called *cities* in the US. In the US, many places are called *towns* or *small towns* that are *villages* in GB. AE rarely uses *village* for places in the US.
tow out *v.* (d; tr.) to ~ into, to (the boat was ~ed out into the channel; they ~ed the barge out to the freighter)
toy I *n.* 1. to make a ~ 2. to wind, wind up a ~ 3. an educational; executive (BE); mechanical; musical; soft ~ (to wind a mechanical ~) 4. (misc.) to play with ~s; a ~ car/plane/train
toy II *v.* (d; intr.) to ~ with (to ~ with smb.'s affections; cats ~ with mice)
trace I *n.* 1. to leave a ~ 2. to show a ~ of (to show no ~ of remorse) 3. to lose (all) ~ of 4. a slight ~ (he didn't show the slightest ~ of intoxication) 5. without (a) ~ (they disappeared without a ~; they sank/vanished without ~)
trace II *v.* (D; tr.) to ~ to (the letter was ~d to its sender)
traceable *adj.* ~ to
trace back *v.* (d; tr.) to ~ to (the letter was ~d back to its sender; she ~d her origins back to the twelfth century)

tracer *n.* ["inquiry"] (esp. AE) 1. to put out, send out a ~ on ["tracer bullet"] 2. to fire a ~ ["substance used to trace a reaction in the body"] (med.) 3. to inject, introduce a ~ (into the body) 4. to scan (for) a ~ 5. a radioactive ~
traces *n.* to kick over the ~ ("to free oneself")
tracing *n.* to do, make a ~
track I *n.* ["awareness"] 1. to keep ~ of (to keep ~ of expenses) 2. to lose ~ of 3. close ~ (to keep close ~ of smt.) ["course for racing"] 4. a fast; muddy; slow ~ 5. a cinder; indoor ~; racetrack; running ~ ["path, road"] 6. a cart ~ (BE; AE has *dirt road*) 7. off ~ ("straying from one's goals") 8. on ~ ("proceeding towards one's goals") (back on ~ for success = back on ~ to succeed); on the ~ of (hard on the ~ of a scientific discovery) 9. (misc.) on the right ~ ("proceeding correctly"); on the wrong ~ ("proceeding incorrectly"); off the beaten ~ ("isolated") ("off the beaten path"); the ~ goes/leads/runs/winds through the forest ["rail"] 10. to lay ~s 11. a double; main; railroad (AE), railway (BE); single ~ 12. (misc.) on the wrong side of the ~s (esp. AE; colloq.) ("in the poor section of a city") ["recording"] 13. a sound; favorite ~ (what's your favorite ~ on/from their latest album?) ["misc."] 14. the fast ~ ("the quickest route to success"); the inside ~ ("an advantageous position") (see also **tracks**) USAGE NOTES: (1) For footraces, *track* is CE. For horseracing, AE uses *track* and *racetrack*; BE prefers *course* and *racecourse*. (2) In BE, the train for Birmingham leaves from platform 29. In AE, the train for Birmingham leaves from track 29.
track II *v.* (D; tr.) to ~ to (the hunters ~ed the animal (back) to its lair)
track-and-field *n.* (AE) to go in for ~ (BE has *athletics*) (see also *track-and-field events* at **event**)
tracks *n.* ["trail"] 1. to leave ~ 2. to make ~ for ("to go directly to") 3. to cover one's ~ ["misc."] 4. they are hard on the ~ of a scientific discovery; to stop (dead) in one's ~ ("to stop instantaneously"); tire ~
tract *n.* ["system of organs"] the digestive; gastrointestinal; genitourinary; intestinal; respiratory ~ (see also *tract house* at **house**)
traction *n.* 1. to apply ~ 2. in ~ (her broken leg is in ~)
tractor *n.* to drive, operate a ~
trade I *n.* ["commerce, business"] 1. to carry on, conduct, engage in ~ 2. to build up, develop, drum up, promote; lose ~ 3. to stimulate ~ 4. to restrain, restrict ~ 5. (a) brisk, lively, thriving ~ (they built up a lively ~ in organic produce) 6. fair ~ 7. the arms; tourist ~ 8. domestic; export; foreign, international, overseas; free; illicit; maritime; retail; wholesale ~ (to promote international ~) 9. (the) slave; white-slave ("prostitution") ~ 10. the carriage ~ ("business with wealthy people") 11. ~ is booming, thriving; dropping off, falling off; picking up, reviving 12. ~ among, between; with (to

conduct ~ with many countries) 13. ~ in 14. (misc.)
in the ~ (quality obvious to anyone in the ~); (in)
restraint of ~; balance of ~ ["exchange"] 15. to make
a ~ with smb. for smt. (she made a ~ of a knife with
me for a spoon) 16. a fair ~ ["occupation"] 17. to ply
one's, practice a ~ 18. to learn a ~ 19. by ~ (she is a
bookbinder by ~) 20. (misc.) a jack-of-all-trades
trade II *v.* 1. (D; tr.) to ~ for (she ~d a knife for
a spoon) 2. (D; intr.) to ~ in (to ~ in furs) 3. (D;
intr., tr.) to ~ with (to ~ with various countries; to
~ places with smb.) 4. (O) she ~d me a knife for
a spoon
trade in *v.* (D; tr.) to ~ for (she ~d in her old car for
a newer one)
trademark *n.* 1. to issue a ~ 2. to receive, register a
~ 3. to bear; display a ~ 4. to infringe a ~
trade-off *n.* a ~ between (a ~ between advantages
and disadvantages)
trade off *v.* (D; tr.) to ~ against (to ~ the advantages
against the disadvantages)
trade up *v.* (colloq.) (D; intr.) to ~ from; to (to ~ to
a larger car from a smaller one)
trader *n.* 1. a fur ~ 2. a ~ in (a ~ in fur(s))
trading *n.* 1. brisk; heavy; slow, sluggish ~ (slow ~
on the stock market) 2. insider ~ (as on the stock
market) 3. ~ in (~ in fur(s) = fur-trading)
tradition *n.* 1. to hand down, pass down a ~ 2. to establish, start a ~ (we started a new ~) 3. to cherish;
have; keep up, maintain, preserve, uphold a ~ 4. to
break with, depart from; defy (a) ~ 5. an ancient,
old; deep-rooted, deep-seated, established; long ~
(they have a long ~ of spending summers in the
country) 6. a cherished; great; hallowed; popular
~ 7. a family; oral; religious ~ 8. according to, by
~ (according to ancient ~; by popular ~) 9. in a
~ (in our ~; a new release in the great/best ~ of
Hollywood musicals)
traditional *adj.* ~ to + inf. (it's ~ around here to fly
the flag on holidays)
traffic I *n.* ["movement of vehicles, aircraft"] 1. to direct
~ (the police officer was directing ~) 2. to control,
regulate ~ (traffic lights control/regulate ~) 3. to
block, hold up, obstruct, tie up ~ 4. to divert ~ 5.
bumper-to-bumper, heavy; light; rush-hour; slow-
moving ~ 6. air; highway (AE), motorway (BE);
pedestrian; vehicular ~ 7. inbound; outbound ~ 8.
local; long-distance ~ 9. merging; through, thru
(AE) ~ 10. one-way; two-way ~ 11. ~ backs up;
builds up; thins out 12. (misc.) the flow of ~; the
volume of ~; a lane of ~; an update on ~ conditions; a ~ report ["commerce, trade esp. illegal"] 13.
brisk, lively ~ 14. illegal, illicit ~ 15. ~ in (illicit ~
in drugs) ["misc."] 16. (colloq.) to charge what the ~
will bear ("to charge as much as people are willing
to pay")
traffic II *v.* (d; intr.) to ~ in (to ~ in drugs)
traffic light, traffic lights *n.* see **light II** *n.* 16–19
USAGE NOTE: *Traffic lights* is CE; *traffic light*
is esp AE.

traffic ticket (AE) see **ticket I** *n.* 17–21
tragedy *n.* 1. to avert a ~ 2. a great; personal; terrible ~ 3. (a) ~ strikes (~ struck their family) 4.
a ~ for 5. a ~ that + clause (it was a ~ (for their
families) that there were no survivors) 6. (misc.)
a Greek ~; to end in ~ (the story of Romeo and
Juliet ended in ~)
tragic *adj.* ~ that + clause (it was ~ that they all
perished)
trail I *n.* 1. to blaze, make; lay out a ~ 2. to leave
a ~ (the wounded animal left a ~ of blood) 3. to
follow a ~ 4. to cover up a ~ 5. a steep; winding
~ 6. a hiking; nature; ski; vapor ~ (to lay out a
ski ~) 7. a campaign; comeback ~ (she was on the
campaign ~ for months; to hit the comeback ~) 8.
on smb.'s ~, on the ~ of (the police were on his ~;
hard on the ~ of a scientific discovery) 9. (misc.)
the ~ goes/leads/runs/winds through the forest; to
leave a paper ~ ("to leave a record of one's activities behind")
trail II *v.* 1. (D; intr.) to ~ after, behind (to ~ behind
the leaders (by a few points)) 2. (D; intr., tr.) to ~
by (they're still ~ing (the leaders) by a few points)
3. (D; tr.) to ~ to (the police ~ed them to their
hideout)
trailer *n.* 1. a house ~ (AE; BE has *caravan*) 2. a
flatbed ~ 3. a semitrailer (AE), tractor-trailer (AE;
AE also has *semi, trailer truck*; BE has *articulated
lorry*) 4. the ~ jackknifed
trail off *v.* (D; int.) to ~ to a whisper
train I *n.* ["row of connected railroad cars"] 1. to drive a
~ 2. to shunt ~s (onto different tracks) 3. to board,
get on; catch; get off; miss; take a ~ (we took a ~
to the city) 4. to change ~s (we'll have to change ~s
in/at Chicago) 5. to flag down; hold; stop a ~ (to
stop a ~ by pulling the communication/emergency
cord) 6. a boat; commuter; express, fast (esp. BE);
intercity (BE); local (AE), stopping (BE); long-
distance; shuttle; suburban; through ~ 7. a down
(BE) ("from a city"); up (BE) ("to a city") ~ 8.
an inbound; outbound ~ 9. a freight (AE), goods
(BE); hospital; passenger; troop ~ 10. an electric;
elevated; subway (AE); tube (esp. BE), underground (BE) ~ 11. a ~ arrives, pulls in; leaves,
pulls out; runs late; runs on time; stops 12. a ~
for, to; from (the ~ from Exeter to London) 13. by
~ (to travel by ~) 14. aboard, on a ~ (we met on the
~) ["column"] 15. a mule; supply; wagon ~ ["mechanism for transmitting power"] 16. a power ~ (see also
set smt. in train at **set II** *v.*) USAGE NOTE: In
BE, a *train, tram,* or *underground/tube (train)* is
driven by an "engine/train driver". In AE, a *train*
is driven or operated by an "engineer"; a *subway*
or *streetcar* is driven or operated by a "motorman"
(or, to avoid sexist language, an "operator.")
train II *v.* 1. (D; intr., tr.) to ~ as (she ~ed as a ballet
dancer) 2. (D; intr., tr.) to ~ for (to ~ for the ballet) 3. (D; tr.) to ~ in (to ~ smb. in ballet dancing)
4. (d; tr.) ("to aim") to ~ on (he ~ed his gun on

the intruder) 5. (d; intr.) to ~ with (she ~ed with a champion) 6. (E) to ~ to be a dancer 7. (H) they ~ed her to be a dancer; they were ~ed to react instantaneously to an attack; they ~ed the workers to be precise

trained *adj.* 1. poorly; well ~ 2. ~ to + inf. (she is ~ to be a dancer; the dogs are ~ to attack) 3. (misc.) house-trained (esp. BE; AE prefers *house-broken*) (also fig.) (I'm afraid my husband still isn't housetrained: he doesn't even do the washing-up!); potty-trained (BE), toilet-trained

trainer *n.* an animal ~

training *n.* 1. to demand, require; give, provide ~ 2. to do, get, receive, undergo ~ 3. intense; thorough ~ 4. basic; specialized ~ (see also **basic training**) 5. hands-on; in-service, on-the-job (AE); professional; vocational ~ 6. assertiveness; manual; military; physical; sensitivity; toilet; voice; weight ~ 7. ~ in (hands-on ~ in the use of computers) 8. the ~ to + inf. (the soldiers did not have the necessary ~ to carry out the mission) 9. by ~ (she's an engineer by ~) 10. in ~ (he was in ~ for the big fight; she was in ~ with a champion; she was in ~ to be a dancer) (see also *transfer of training* at **transfer I** *n.*)

traipse *v.* (colloq.) (P; intr.) they were ~sing along the road USAGE NOTE: In AE, the verb *traipse* has the connotation of "saunter"; in BE, it typically has the connotation of "trudge" or "tramp heavily".

trait *n.* 1. to display, show; have a ~ 2. an acquired; character; genetic, hereditary; negative; personality; positive ~

traitor *n.* 1. a ~ to (a ~ to one's country) 2. (misc.) to turn ~

tram (BE) see **streetcar**

tramp *v.* (P; intr.) to ~ through the woods

trample *v.* 1. (d; intr.) to ~ on, upon (to ~ on smb.'s rights) 2. (misc.) to ~ underfoot; to ~ smb. to death

trance *n.* 1. to fall, go into a ~ 2. to come out of a ~ 3. a deep; hypnotic; light ~ 4. (to be) in a ~ (see also *trance state* at **state I** *n.*)

tranquillity, tranquility *n.* 1. to disturb; shatter smb.'s ~ 2. domestic; inner ~ ("We the People of the United States, in Order to ... insure domestic Tranquility..." – the Constitution of the USA, 1787) 3. (misc.) an air of ~

tranquillizer, tranquilizer *n.* 1. to take a ~ 2. to prescribe a ~ (for) 3. (to be) on ~s 4. to come off ~s

transaction *n.* 1. to carry out; conduct ~s 2. a delicate ~ 3. business, financial ~s 4. ~s between (the ~s between us went well)

transcribe *v.* 1. (D; tr.) to ~ from; into (to ~ testimony from a tape; to ~ a text into Cyrillic) 2. (D; intr., tr.) to ~ in (to ~ speech in phonetic script)

transcript *n.* 1. a complete, full; official; verbatim ~ 2. (AE) a grade ~ ("a student's record")

transcription *n.* 1. to make a ~ 2. (ling.) a broad; narrow; phonemic; phonetic ~

transfer I *n.* ["act of transferring"] 1. to make a ~ 2. an electronic; technology ~ 3. a ~ from; to 4. (misc.) a peaceful ~ of power; ~ of training (see also *transfer payment* at **payment**) ["ticket allowing a passenger to change from one vehicle to another on public transportation"] (esp. AE) 5. a bus; streetcar; subway ~

transfer II *v.* (D; intr., tr.) to ~ from; to (she was ~red from New York to Toronto)

transfixed *adj.* ~ with (~ with horror)

transform *v.* 1. to ~ ¬beyond/out of¬ all recognition; to ~ completely, drastically, greatly, radically; suddenly; totally; overnight 2. (D; tr.) to ~ from; into; to (to ~ current from one voltage to another)

transformation *n.* ["radical change"] 1. to effect; undergo a ~ 2. a complete, radical, total; sudden, overnight ~ 3. a ~ from; into; to (his ~ from a brute to a good citizen took place almost overnight!) (see also *the transformation process* at **process**) ["transformational rule"] (ling.) 4. to formulate a ~ 5. to apply a ~ 6. to order ~s 7. a dative-movement, indirect-object; imperative; insertion; negative; particle-movement; passive; question ~ 8. a ~ applies

transformer *n.* a step-down; step-up ~

transfuse *v.* (D; tr.) to ~ into, to

transfusion *n.* 1. to administer, do, give a ~ 2. to get, have, receive a ~ 3. a – plasma ~ (see also **blood transfusion**)

transgress *v.* (formal) (D; intr.) to ~ against

transgression *n.* to commit a ~ against

transistor *n.* a solid-state ~

transit *n.* 1. (esp. AE) mass, rapid ~ 2. in ~ (damaged in ~) (see also *transit camp* at **camp**)

transition *n.* 1. to make; undergo a ~ 2. a gradual; peaceful; rapid ~ 3. a ~ from; to 4. a ~ between (the country is in a state of ~ between socialism and capitalism) 5. during; in ~ (at present, our economy is in ~, so please bear with us during the ~) 6. (misc.) in a state of ~

transitional *adj.* ~ between

translate *v.* 1. to ~ freely; literally, verbatim, word-for-word; simultaneously 2. (D; tr.) to ~ as (to ~ *chien* as *dog*) 3. (D; tr.) to ~ from; into (to ~ a book from Russian into Spanish) 4. (misc.) to ~ at sight

translation *n.* 1. to do, make a ~ 2. (a) close, literal, verbatim, word-for-word; free, loose, rough; on-sight ~ 3. an authorized ~ 4. (a) loan ~ 5. (a) machine; running; simultaneous ~ 6. a ~ from; into (a ~ from Russian into Spanish) 7. in ~ (to read a novel in ~; the poem is very effective even ¬in free/in a free¬ ~; some poetry loses a lot in ~)

transliterate *v.* 1. (D; tr.) to ~ as (to ~ a Russian letter as *ch*) 2. (D; tr.) to ~ from; into (to ~ a text from Cyrillic into Roman letters)

transliteration *n.* to do a ~

transmission *n.* ["gearbox"] 1. an automatic; standard; synchromesh ~ ["act of transmitting"] 2. to arrest, check, halt, stop; prevent the ~ (of a disease) 3. a ~ from; to (we did our best to prevent the ~ of the disease from parents to children)

transmit v. 1. (D; tr.) to ~ from; to (the results were ~ted to all local stations from the network; we did our best to prevent the disease from being ~ted from parents to children) 2. (D; tr.) to ~ through (the infection was ~ted through contaminated food) 3. (misc.) to ~ by satellite; to ~ live

transmitted adj. sexually ~ (sexually ~ diseases (= STDs))

transmitter n. 1. a longwave; radar; radio; shortwave ~ 2. a television, TV ~

transmute v. (formal) (D; tr.) to ~ from; into (to ~ base metal into gold)

transpire v. 1. (L) ("to become apparent, evident, known") it ~d that he had gone out of town before the crime occurred 2. (misc.) as it ~d, he had gone out of town before the crime occurred

transplant I n. 1. to carry out, do, perform a ~ (to perform a bone-marrow ~ on a patient) 2. to reject a ~ (her body rejected the ~) 3. a bone-marrow; corneal; gene; heart; kidney; organ; skin ~ 4. a ~ takes; is rejected

transplant II v. (D; tr.) to ~ from; to

transport I n. 1. (esp. BE) see **transportation** 2. a supersonic ~ (also SST) 3. a troop ~

transport II v. 1. to ~ bodily 2. (d; tr.) to ~ from; to

transportation n. (esp. AE; BE usu. has transport) 1. to provide; use ~ 2. air; bus; ground, surface; mass, public ~ 3. a form, mode of ~ (trains are among my favorite forms of ~) 4. ~ from; to (to provide ~ from the city to the airport) 5. in the absence of, without ~ (without public ~, may I stay the night with you?)

transpose v. (D; tr.) to ~ from; into, to (to ~ a song into a different key)

transposition n. a ~ from; into, to (the ~ of a song into a different key)

transship v. (D; tr.) to ~ from; to

transshipment n. ~ from; to

trap n. ["device for catching animals or people"] ["stratagem for tricking unsuspecting people"] 1. to bait; lay, set (up) a ~ (for) 2. to spring a ~ on 3. to fall into a ~ 4. to lure smb. into a ~ 5. a booby; death ~; mousetrap; radar, speed ~; a sand ~ (in golf) (see also **booby trap**) ["mouth"] (slang) 6. to shut one's ~

trapeze n. 1. on a ~ 2. (misc.) to hang from and perform on a ~

trapper n. an animal; fur ~

trash n. (esp. AE; CE has refuse, rubbish) 1. to accumulate ~ 2. to collect, pick up ~ 3. to dispose of, dump ~ (BE prefers to tip refuse) 4. to put out the ~ 5. ~ accumulates, piles up 6. (misc.) (derog.) trailer ~ ("members of the underclass"); white ~ ("poor white people in the southern US") (see also **garbage**)

trauma n. 1. to cause (a) ~ 2. to go through, suffer

(a) ~ 3. (an) emotional; physical; psychological ~ (to go through the psychological ~ of being abandoned as a child)

travel I n. 1. air; rail; sea; space; time ~ 2. business-class; deluxe; first-class; second-class; tourist-class ~ 3. extensive; foreign, international, overseas ~ 4. ~ across; in; through (~ in Canada; ~ through the Rockies) 5. ~ by (~ by air) 6. ~ from; to (~ from London to Tokyo) (see also **travels**)

travel II v. 1. to ~ extensively, widely; far; far and wide; overseas 2. to ~ business-class; deluxe; economy; first-class; second-class; tourist-class 3. to ~ incognito; light 4. (D; intr.) to ~ across; in; through (to ~ in Canada; to ~ through the Rockies) 5. (D; intr.) to ~ by (to ~ by air) 6. (D; intr., tr.) to ~ from; to (to ~ from London to Tokyo) 7. (d; intr.) to ~ with (to be ~ing with a group of students) 8. (misc.) to ~ on business; to ~ downstream; to ~ upstream; to ~ the world

traveler, traveller n. 1. an experienced, seasoned ~ 2. an air ~ 3. a commercial ~ (old-fashioned; BE; CE has traveling salesman) 4. (misc.) a fellow ~ ("a Communist sympathizer")

travels n. on one's ~ (on our ~ we saw many interesting places)

travesty n. 1. to make a ~ of 2. a mere; shocking ~ 3. a ~ of, on (to make a shocking ~ of justice)

tray n. 1. a serving ~ 2. on a ~

treachery n. 1. an act of ~ 2. ~ to + inf. (it is ~ to sell military information to a foreign power)

tread I n. ["step"] 1. a firm; heavy; light ~ (to walk with a heavy ~) ["mark"] 2. tire ~s (as left on mud) ["pattern of ridges"] 3. a worn ~ 4. a tire ~

tread II v. 1. (can be fig.) (d; intr.) to ~ on, upon (to ~ on smb.'s toes) 2. (P; intr.) to ~ softly ("Tread softly because you ~ on my dreams." - W.B. Yeats, "He Wishes for the Cloths of Heaven," 1899)

treadle n. to work a ~

treadmill n. on a ~ (often fig.)

treason n. 1. to commit; plot ~ 2. high ~ 3. an act of ~ (against one's own country) 4. ~ to + inf. (it is ~ to sell military information to a foreign power)

treasonable see **treasonous**

treasonous adj. ~ to + inf. (it is ~ to sell military information to a foreign power)

treasure n. 1. an art ~ 2. a national; priceless; real ~ (also fig.) (my dear, your cleaning lady is a real ~!) 3. (a) buried; sunken ~ (to find ¬buried/a buried¬ ~; to raise sunken ~ from the bottom of the sea) 4. a ~ trove

treat I n. ["source of joy"] 1. to provide a ~ 2. a ~ for (their visit was/provided a real ~ for us) 3. as a ~ (they planned their visit as a ~ for us) 4. a ~ to + inf. (it was a ~ to watch them dance = it was a ~ watching them dance) (see also trick or treat! at **trick I** n.) ["paying for the food or entertainment of others"] 5. to stand ~ (esp. AE) 6. (misc.) it's my ~

treat II v. 1. ("to describe") to ~ (a subject) exhaustively, painstakingly, thoroughly 2. ("to deal with") to ~ badly; cruelly; fairly; harshly; kindly; leniently; successfully; unfairly; unsuccessfully; well 3. (d; tr.) to ~ as ("to deal with") (they ~ed us as honored guests; she ~s me as if I was/were dirt) 4. (D; tr.) ("to try to cure") to ~ for; with (to ~ smb. for a cold with a new drug; to ~ walls for dry rot with chemicals) 5. (d; tr.) ("to deal with") to ~ like (they ~ed us like honored guests; he ~ed him like his own brother; she ~s me like dirt) 6. (formal) (d; intr.) to ~ of ("to deal with") (her books ~ of economic problems) 7. (D; refl., tr.) to ~ to ("to provide with at one's own expense") (to ~ smb. to a decent meal) 8. (d; tr.) ("to deal with") to ~ with (to ~ smb. with kindness)

treatise *n.* (formal) 1. to write a ~ 2. a learnèd; scientific; theoretical ~ 3. a ~ on, upon (she's written several learnèd ~s on economic problems)

treatment *n.* [″care″] [″cure″] 1. to administer, give, provide ~ 2. to get, have, receive, undergo ~ 3. to respond to ~ 4. inpatient; medical; outpatient; radiation; shock ~ 5. the ~ was effective, successful; ineffective, unsuccessful 6. ~ for (to undergo (a course of) ~ for alcoholism; to have ~ for dry rot) 7. in, under ~ (in ~ for alcoholism) 8. (misc.) a beauty ~ [″method of dealing with″] 9. gentle; humane; kid-glove; kind ~ 10. equal, equitable; fair ~ 11. preferential; red-carpet; special ~ (to receive preferential ~) 12. inequitable; shabby; uneven; unfair ~ 13. atrocious, barbarous, barbaric, brutal, cruel, harsh, inhumane ~ (brutal ~ of prisoners) 14. (colloq.) the full; VIP ("special") ~ (they got the full/VIP ~) 15. the silent ~ (to give smb. the silent ~) [″description, study″] 16. a definitive; exhaustive, lengthy ~ 17. a cursory; superficial ~

treaty *n.* 1. to conclude, sign; negotiate, work out a ~ 2. to confirm, ratify; throw out a ~ (the Senate must confirm all ~ties) 3. to honor a ~ 4. to break, violate a ~ 5. to abrogate, denounce, repudiate a ~ 6. a draft ~ 7. a bilateral, bipartite; multilateral ~ 8. a commercial, trade; extradition ~ 9. a nonaggression; peace ~ 10. a nonproliferation; test-ban ~ 11. a ~ between; with (a ~ between former foes) 12. a ~ to + inf. (they signed a ~ to settle all border disputes by arbitration) 13. (misc.) the articles; provisions; terms of a ~ (under the terms of the ~, we have to give up our nuclear weapons); the parties to a ~ = the signatories of a ~; the ~ obliges all its signatories to give up their nuclear weapons

tree *n.* [″woody plant with a trunk″] 1. to grow; plant a ~ 2. to prune, trim a ~ 3. to chop down, cut down, fell a ~ 4. to uproot a ~ (the gale uprooted several ~s) 5. a shade ~ (see also **Christmas tree**) 6. a deciduous; evergreen ~ 7. a tall ~ 8. a ~ grows 9. an avenue, line; clump, cluster; grove; stand of ~s 10. in; on a ~ (monkeys live in ~s; fruit grows on ~s) 11. (misc.) to climb a ~; (colloq.) up a ~ (AE), up a gum ~ (BE) ("stymied"); to be barking up the wrong ~ ("to be mistaken") [″something resembling a tree″] 12. a family, genealogical ~ 13.

a clothes; shoe ~ [″misc.″] 14. they cannot see the forest (AE)/wood (BE) for the ~s ("they see all of the details, but they do not recognize the essence of the problem")

trek I *n.* [″long trip″] to go on, make a ~ from; to

trek II *v.* (P; intr.) to ~ across the fields; "None will break ranks, though nations ~ from progress." – Wilfred Owen, 1893–1918, "Strange Meeting"

tremble *v.* 1. (d; intr.) to ~ at (to ~ at the thought of going back to the front line) 2. (D; intr.) to ~ from, with (to ~ from the cold; to ~ with fear) 3. (E) I ~ to think of going back to the front line!

tremor *n.* 1. a nervous ~ 2. a perceptible; slight ~ 3. uncontrollable; violent ~s (uncontrollable ~s of nervousness) 4. an earth ~

trench *n.* 1. to dig a ~ 2. a slit ~ 3. (misc.) in the ~es (during World War I) (see also *trench warfare* at **warfare**)

trend *n.* 1. to create, set, start a ~ 2. to buck (colloq.) (AE); reverse a ~ 3. a discernible, noticeable; general; marked ~ 4. a growing; recent ~ 5. a downward; upward ~ 6. an unwelcome; welcome ~ 7. an economic; political ~ 8. a ~ away from; towards 9. a ~ in (is there a trend in fashion away from long skirts and towards shorter ones?)

trepidation *n.* fear and ~ (the very idea of work fills him with ~ and trepidation)

trespass I *n.* criminal ~

trespass II *v.* 1. (obsol.) (D; intr.) to ~ against ("And forgive us our trespasses, As we forgive them that ~ against us." – The Lord's Prayer" : *The* (Anglican) *Book of Common Prayer,* 1662) 2. (D; intr.) to ~ on, upon (to ~ on a neighbor's property)

trespassing *n.* No Trespassing!

trial *n.* [″legal proceedings″] 1. to conduct, hold a ~ 2. to bring smb. to ~; to put smb. on ~ 3. to await ~ 4. to face; stand ~ for (he stood ~ for embezzlement) 5. to come, go to ~ (the case went to ~) 6. to waive a (jury) ~ (the accused waived a jury ~) 7. a fair; speedy ~ (to get a fair ~) 8. a closed; open, public; show ~ 9. a court; jury (or: a ~ by jury); summary ~ 10. a murder; war-crimes ~ 11. at a ~ (she testified at his ~) 12. on ~ (for) (he was on ~ for murder) [″test, experiment″] 13. to carry out, conduct a ~ 14. to undergo ~s 15. a clinical; controlled; field ~ 16. a ~ shows; suggests (the clinical ~s suggest that the new drug may not be effective or safe) 17. (misc.) by ~ and error (see also *trial period* at **period**) [″source of worry″] 18. a ~ to (they are a ~ to their parents) 19. (misc.) ~s and tribulations

triangle *n.* 1. to draw, make a ~ 2. an acute; congruent; equilateral; isosceles; obtuse; right (AE), right-angled (BE); scalene ~ 3. the apex of a ~ 4. (fig.) the eternal ~; a love ~

tribe *n.* 1. to lead a ~ 2. a native; nomadic, wandering; primitive ~ 3. (misc.) to belong to a ~; a member of a ~ USAGE NOTE: Because of such collocations as "primitive tribe," *tribe* is nowadays often replaced by *people*, so that "a nomadic tribe" becomes "a nomadic people" and "the Cherokee tribe" becomes "the Cherokee people." In North America, the word *nation* is also used, esp. in connection with political or territorial rights, so that in such contexts "the Cherokee people" becomes "the Cherokee nation."

tribulation *n.* 1. to bear, endure a ~ 2. (misc.) trials and ~s

tribunal *n.* 1. to go to; set up a ~ 2. a military; war-crimes ~ 3. (GB) an industrial ~ 4. at, before a ~ (to appear before a military ~)

tribute *n.* ["money paid under duress"] 1. to exact ~ from 2. to pay ~ to ["testimonial"] 3. to pay (a) ~ to 4. a fitting; glowing; moving, touching ~ 5. a floral ~ ("a bunch of flowers") 6. a ~ to 7. in ~ to (see also *tribute band* at **band I** *n.*)

trick I *n.* ["dexterous feat, as of sleight of hand"] 1. to do, perform a ~ 2. a card; hat; magic; party ~ (performed the hat ~ of hitting three homers in one game) ["prank"]["deceitful act"] 3. to play a ~ on smb.; to fall for a ~ 4. a clever ~ 5. a cheap, contemptible, dirty, low, mean, nasty, shabby, sneaky ~ (our clever ~ ¬worked/came off¬ but their sneaky ~ failed) 6. a con, confidence ~ (BE; AE has *confidence game*) ["scoring unit in a card game"] 7. to lose; take, win a ~ ["misc."] 8. to do the ~ ("to be exactly what is needed"); smb.'s bag of ~s ("smb.'s expertise"); ~ or treat! (at Halloween); she doesn't miss a ~ ("she notices everything"); the ~ is to know when you're beaten and give up quickly (see also *trick question* at **question I** *n.*; **tricks**)

trick II *v.* 1. (D; tr.) to ~ into (to ~ smb. into doing smt.) 2. (D; tr.) to ~ out of (she was ~ed out of her money)

trickle I *n.* 1. a mere ~ 2. (misc.) to dwindle/slow to a ~ and then increase to a flood

trickle II *v.* (P; intr.) stragglers kept ~ling into camp; blood ~d from the cut

trickle down *v.* (D; intr.) to ~ to (to ~ to the general population from the elite)

tricks *n.* 1. (often pol.) dirty ~ 2. (misc.) they are up to their old ~ again

trifle I *n.* a mere ~

trifle II *v.* (d; intr.) to ~ with (to ~ with smb.'s affections; they are not to be ~d with)

trigger *n.* ["device for releasing the hammer of a fire-arm"] 1. to press, pull, release, squeeze a/the ~ 2. a hair ("delicate") ~ 3. (misc.) quick on the ~ (also fig.: "quick to take offense and get hot under the collar") (see also *trigger finger* at **finger I** *n.*) ["device that fires an explosive"] 4. a ~ for (also fig.) (the ~ for their rebellion was an insult to their chief)

trim I *n.* ["good condition"]["condition"] 1. fighting ~ (in fighting ~) 2. in ~ (to be in ~) ["ornamental metalwork on a car"] 3. chrome ~ (he scratched my chrome ~!)

trim II *v.* 1. to ~ neatly (a neatly ~med beard) 2. (d; tr.) to ~ away; from, off (to ~ the fat from the budget)

trimmings *n.* ["garnishings"]["extras"] with all the ~ (roast turkey with all the ~; they got the full treatment with all the ~)

trip I *n.* 1. to go on, make, set off on, take a ~ (she went on a ~; I've made this ~ many times; we would like to take a ~) 2. to arrange, organize, plan a ~ 3. to cancel; postpone a ~ 4. an extended, long; short ~ 5. a boat; business; camping; day; field; overseas; pleasure; return; round; round-the-world; wedding ~ (we are planning a round-the-world ~) 6. a ~ along; around 7. a ~ from; to (they went on a ~ to Canada; to take a ~ from England to Australia) 8. a ~ through (a ~ through the west) 9. on a ~ (she was away on a ~) 10. (misc.) a ~ abroad; a bad ~ (on drugs); an ego ~ ("behavior that satisfies one's ego") (see also **guilt trip**)

trip II *v.* (D; intr.) ("to stumble") to ~ on, over (to ~ on a rock and fall; she was ~ping over every word)

triplets *n.* 1. to have, give birth to ~ 2. a set of ~

triplicate *n.* in ~ (to prepare all documents in ~)

tripod *n.* 1. to set up a ~ 2. on a ~ (the camera rested on a ~)

triumph I *n.* 1. to achieve; score a ~ 2. a glorious, signal, splendid, stunning; hard-won; short-lived ~ 3. a ~ against (a ~ against overwhelming odds) 4. a ~ for (the result was a personal ~ for her) 5. a ~ over (a ~ over evil/adversity) 6. in ~ (to return home in ~)

triumph II *v.* (D; intr.) to ~ over

triumphant *adj.* ~ in; over

trolley *n.* ["small wheeled conveyance"] (BE) 1. to load; push; unload a ~ 2. a (shopping) ~ (in a supermarket) (AE has *shopping cart*) 3. a tea ~ (AE has *tea wagon*) 4. a sweet ~ (in a restaurant) ["streetcar, tram"] (AE) 5. see **streetcar** USAGE NOTE: Wheeled conveyances that are called *trolleys* in BE are often called *carts* in AE. In a library, for example, books are moved on a *trolley* (BE) or on a *cart* (AE).

trombone *n.* to play the ~

troop I *n.* 1. a cavalry ~ 2. a (Boy) Scout; Girl Scout (AE); Guide ~

troop II *v.* (P; intr.) the children ~ed into school

trooper *n.* 1. (US) a state ~ 2. (misc.) to swear like a ~ ("to use vile language")

troops *n.* 1. to commit; deploy; dispatch; lead; rally ~ 2. to review ~ 3. to station ~ (in a country); to withdraw ~ (from a country) 4. green; seasoned ~ 5. victorious ~ 6. defeated; demoralized ~ 7. airborne; armored; ground; motorized; mounted; ski ~ 8. elite; irregular; regular; shock ~ 9. ~ fight; serve; withdraw

trophy *n.* 1. to award, give, present a ~ 2. to get, lift (BE) (colloq.), receive, win a ~ 3. to display a ~ 4. a sports; war ~ 5. a ~ for (they proudly displayed the ~ they'd received for winning the tournament)

tropic *n.* the Tropic of Cancer; Capricorn (see also **tropics**)

tropics *n.* in the ~ (to live in the ~)

trot I *n.* 1. at a ~ 2. (misc.) (BE; colloq.) on the ~ all day ("busy all day"); that driver has won four races on the ~ ("that driver has won four races in succession")

trot II *v.* (P; intr.) the horses ~ted (a)round the track

troth *n.* (old-fashioned) to pledge, plight one's ~ ("to make a promise of marriage, to get engaged to smb.")

trouble I *n.* 1. to cause, foment, make, start, stir up ~ 2. to give smb. ~ (they gave their parents a lot of ~ = they were a lot of ~ to their parents) 3. to be asking for, inviting, looking for ~ (if you go on like that you're just asking for ~!) 4. to go through, have, run into ~ (she had a lot of ~ with her back) 5. to go to ~ (they went to a great deal of/considerable/enormous ~ to arrange the interview) 6. to get (smb.) into ~ (we got into ~ during our trip; she got herself into serious ~ with the police; they got me into ~ at school; to get a girl into ~ (old-fashioned) ("to get a girl pregnant")) 7. to take the ~ to do smt. (I took the ~ to check on her story) 8. to get (smb.) out of ~ (I got out of ~; she got herself out of ~; they got him out of ~) 9. to avoid, steer clear of ~ 10. to prevent ~ 11. deep, real, serious ~ 12. back; engine; heart ~ (to develop engine ~) 13. ~ is brewing 14. ~ blows over 15. ~ about, over; between; with (we had ~ with our neighbors over the noise that they were making – but there's been ~ between us and the neighbors for some time) 16. a bit of ~ 17. no ~ to + inf. (it's no ~ to call them) 18. in ~ (with) (they were in ~; he was in ~ with the police) 19. out of ~ (to keep out of ~) 20. (misc.) there may be ~ ahead!; those events spell/mean ~ for us all!; to put smb. to a lot of ~; smt. isn't worth the ~ = smt. is more ~ than it's worth; sending a telegram will save you the ~ of making a second trip; she has ~ going up steps; he had no ~ memorizing the material for the test (see also *trouble spot* at **spot I** *n.*; *more trouble than it's worth* at **worth I** *adj.*, *prep.*)

trouble II *v.* 1. (d; refl., tr.) to ~ about (don't ~ yourself about the arrangements) 2. (d; tr.) to ~ for (could I ~ you for the salt?) 3. (colloq.) (E; in neg. sentences) she didn't even ~ to lock the door! 4. (colloq.) (H; in interrogative sentences; no passive) could I ~ you to pass the salt ? 5. (R) it ~d me (to read) that no negotiations were scheduled

troubled *adj.* 1. deeply ~ 2. ~ by, with (she is ~ with arthritis) 3. ~ to + inf. (I was ~ to read that no negotiations were scheduled) 4. ~ that + clause (I was ~ that no negotiations were scheduled)

troublesome *adj.* ~ to + inf. (it's ~ to be without electricity = it's ~ being without electricity)

trousers *n.* 1. to have ~ on, to wear ~ 2. to put on ~ 3. to take off ~ 4. to button up; unbutton; unzip; zip up one's ~ 5. baggy; long; short; tight ~ 6. a pair of ~ 7. in ~ 8. (misc.) a trouser leg

trowel *n.* a bricklayer's; gardener's; plasterer's ~

truant *n.* to play ~ (see also *truant officer* at **officer**)

truce *n.* 1. to agree (BE), agree on, agree to, arrange, call, work out a ~ 2. to announce, declare a ~ 3. to violate a ~ 4. to denounce a ~ 5. an armed; uneasy ~ 6. a ~ between 7. during a ~

truck I *n.* ["vehicle"] 1. (esp. AE; BE often has *lorry*, *van*) to drive, operate; steer a ~ 2. to load; unload a ~ 3. (AE) a delivery, panel ~ (BE has *delivery van*) 4. a dump (esp. AE), dumper (BE), tipper (BE) ~ 5. (AE) a garbage, trash ~ (BE has *dustbin lorry, dustcart*) 6. (AE) a pickup; trailer ~ (BE has *articulated lorry*) 7. a breakdown (BE), tow (AE) ~ (BE also has *breakdown lorry, breakdown van*) 8. a railway ~ (BE; AE has *flatcar*) 9. a sound ~ 10. a ~ jackknifes

truck II *n.* ["dealings"] to have no ~ with

trudge *v.* (P; intr.) to ~ through the mud

true *adj.* 1. historically ~ 2. ~ to (~ to one's principles; ~ to form; ~ to life) 3. ~ to + inf. (it's simply not ~ to assume that all politicians are corrupt!) 4. ~ that + clause (it's just not ~ that all politicians are corrupt!) 5. (misc.) to come ~; to ring ~; to hold ~ ("to be valid")

truism *n.* 1. to mouth, utter a ~ (he's always mouthing ~s) 2. a well-worn ~ 3. (misc.) in ~s (to speak in well-worn ~s)

truly *adv.* (as in the complimentary close of a letter) (esp. AE) yours ~; yours very ~; very ~ yours (see **yours**)

trump *n.* ["winning card"] to play a ~

trump card *n.* ["final resource, ace in the hole"] to play one's ~

trumpet *n.* 1. to blow, play a ~ 2. a ~ blares, sounds (see also **horn** *n.* 6)

trumps *n.* to lead ~ (when playing cards)

trunk *n.* ["main stem"] 1. a tree ~ ["large piece of luggage"] 2. to pack; unpack one's ~ 3. to ship a ~ 4. a steamer; wardrobe ~ (see also **trunks**) USAGE NOTE: On cars, *trunk* is AE; *boot* is BE.

trunks *n.* 1. swimming ~ 2. a pair of ~

trust I *n.* ["reliance"] 1. to place, put one's ~ in 2. to earn, gain, win; have smb.'s ~ 3. to abuse, betray, violate smb.'s ~ 4. absolute; blind, unquestioning; universal ~ 5. public ~ ("A public office is a public ~" – attributed to US President Grover Cleveland, 1837-1908) 6. on ~ (to sell on ~) 7. a breach of ~ ["cartel"] 8. to break up a ~ ["fund"] 9. to set up a ~ (for a child) (see also *trust fund* at **fund**) 10. a unit ~ (BE; AE has *mutual fund*) 11. a blind; perpetual ~ (to place one's holdings in a blind ~ during one's term of office) 12. in ~ for (the money is held in ~ for a child)

trust II *v.* 1. to ~ blindly, implicitly 2. (d; intr.) ("to believe") to ~ in (to ~ in God; "In God We Trust." – motto on U.S. money) 3. (d; intr.) to ~ to ("to rely on") (to ~ to one's memory) 4. (d; tr.) ("to entrust") to ~ with (to ~ smb. with one's savings)

5. (H) ("to entrust") I ~ed her to deposit the funds 6. (L) ("to believe") we ~ that you will keep your word 7. (misc.) (ironic) ~ them to do smt. silly!

truth n. 1. to ascertain, elicit, establish, find; face, face up to; get at; search for, seek the ~ 2. to admit; expose, reveal; speak, tell the ~ 3. to distort, pervert, stretch the ~ 4. the absolute, basic, fundamental, Gospel, naked, plain, unvarnished, whole ~ ("I swear by Almighty God that the evidence I shall give shall be the ~, the whole ~ and nothing but the ~." – formula used by court witnesses in England and Wales) 5. the awful; bitter; ultimate ~ 6. (the) historical ~ 7. an element, grain, kernel of ~ 8. (there is) not an iota, shred of ~ (in that) 9. the ~ about (I finally discovered the ~ about their origins) 10. ~ in (there is some ~ in their allegations; is there any ~ in that?) 11. in ~ 12. (misc.) where does the ~ lie?; it had a ring of ~ about it; the ~ is that she actually did serve in the army!; the ~ will out!

truthful adj. ~ about; in

try I n. 1. to have, make a ~ at 2. (colloq.) to give smt. a ~ 3. (rugby) to convert, score a ~ (against) 4. a valiant ~ 5. a ~ at, for 6. a ~ to + inf. (they made another ~ to have the decision reversed) 7. (misc.) to give it the old college ~ (AE; colloq.) ("to make a determined effort"); it's worth a ~

try II v. 1. to ~ hard; to ~ one's best 2. (D; intr.) ("to attempt") to ~ for (to ~ for a prize) 3. (D; tr.) ("to subject to trial") to ~ for (they tried her for murder) 4. (E) ("to attempt") she tried to jog but couldn't 5. (G) ("to attempt") she tried jogging, but her ankles would hurt USAGE NOTES: 1. The phrase *try and do smt.* is a colloq. variant of *try to do smt.*, but has no past tense. 2. The sentence *she tried to jog* usu. means that she never was able to jog; *she tried jogging* means that she was able to jog, but gave it up after a while.

try on v. (misc.) he tried the hat on for size = he tried on the hat for size

tryout n. to hold a ~ for (to hold a ~ for the team) (see also **tryouts**)

try out v. 1. (D; intr., tr.) to ~ for (esp. AE) (to ~ for a major part in a play) 2. (D; tr.) to ~ on (they tried out the new drug on animals = they tried the new drug out on animals)

tryouts n. (esp. AE) to hold ~ for (to hold ~ for the team)

tryst n. (formal) 1. to make, keep a ~ 2. a ~ with ("Long years ago we made a ~ with destiny" – Jawaharlal Nehru, August 14th, 1947)

tsar (BE) see **czar**

tsunami n. 1. a ~ hits, strikes (the ~ struck the coastal areas of several cities) 2. (misc.) the ~ has already claimed many lives

tub n. ["bathtub"] (esp. AE; BE prefers *bath*) 1. to fill the ~ (for a bath) 2. to empty the ~ (after a bath) 3. to clean out; scrub (out) a ~

tube n. ["channel within the body"] 1. bronchial;

Eustachian; Fallopian ~s ["rubber casing"] 2. an inner ~ ["hollow cylinder"] 3. an electron; picture, television; test ~ 4. a vacuum ~ (AE; BE has *valve*) 5. (slang) the boob ~ ("television") ["container"] 6. to squeeze a ~ (of toothpaste) ["underground"] (esp. BE) 7. to take the/a ~ 8. by ~ (to go/travel) by ~ 9. on the ~ (to travel to work on the ~) (AE has *subway*) (see also Usage Note at **train I** n.) ["system of tube trains and stations"] 10. from; in; to the ~ (I couldn't find the right entrance to the ~, the right platform in the ~, or the right exit from the ~!) (see also *tube station* at **station I** n.; *tube system* at **system**; *tube train* at **train I** n.) ["misc."] 11. along; down; up a ~

tuberculosis n. to contract, develop, get; have ~

tubing n. 1. copper; glass; flexible; plastic; rubber ~ 2. a length, piece of ~

tuck v. 1. (d; tr.) to ~ inside; into (to ~ a child into bed; he ~ed his shirt inside, into his trousers) 2. (d; tr.) to ~ behind; under (she ~ed her cigarette behind her ear; she ~ed the napkin under her chin)

tug I n. ["pull"] 1. to give a ~ at; on ["tugboat"] 2. a seagoing ~

tug II v. 1. (D; intr.) to ~ at; on (to ~ at a rope) 2. (P; tr.) they ~ged the ship out of the harbor

tuition n. ["instruction"] (BE) 1. to give ~ 2. to get, have, receive ~ 3. private ~ (in) 4. ~ from 5. ~ for 6. ~ in (she's getting ~ in Italian from Signor Da Ponte for the exam) ["payment for instruction"] (esp. AE) 7. to pay ~ for 8. free; full; half ~ (to pay full ~; to get/have/receive free ~)

tumble I n. (colloq.) ["fall"] 1. to have, take a ~ 2. a bad, nasty ~ (she took a nasty ~; shares have taken quite a ~ recently) 3. a sharp, steep; sudden ~ 4. a ~ from ["sign of recognition"] (AE) 5. to give smb. a ~ (they wouldn't give us a ~) (see also *tumble dryer* at **dryer**)

tumble II v. 1. (d; intr.) to ~ into (to ~ into bed) 2. (d; intr.) to ~ out of (to ~ out of a chair) 3. (colloq.) (esp. AE) (d; intr.) to ~ to ("to catch on to, comprehend") (they didn't ~ to the meaning of the clues) 4. (P; intr.) ("to fall") to ~ down the stairs

tummy n. ["stomach"] 1. to upset smb.'s ~ 2. an empty; full; upset ~ 3. smb.'s ~ aches, hurts; growls, rumbles 4. on one's ~ (to lie on one's ~) USAGE NOTE: In AE, *tummy* is used typically by or to children. In BE it is also used frequently by or to adults as a kind of euphemism for *stomach*.

tumor, tumour n. 1. to excise, remove, take out a ~ 2. a benign; inoperable; malignant ~ 3. a brain ~ 4. a ~ in; on

tumult n. ["violent, noisy agitation"] 1. to cause ~ 2. in ~ over 3. (misc.) "The ~ and the shouting dies; The Captains and the Kings depart" – Rudyard Kipling (1865-1936), "Recessional"

tune I n. ["melody"] 1. to compose, write a ~ 2. to hum; play; sing; whistle a ~ (to play a ~ on the piano) 3. to carry ("sing the notes of") a ~ 4. a ~ of, to (the ~ to a song) 5. a catchy; haunting; lilting ~

6. in ~; out of ~ (to sing in ~; she was playing out of ~) 7. to a ~ (to dance to a ~) 8. (misc.) (BE) a signature ~ ("theme song of a program") ["agreement"] 9. in ~ with (in ~ with the times) 10. out of ~ with ["attitude"] (colloq.) 11. to change one's ~ ["misc."] (colloq.) 12. to call the ~ ("to be in command"); to sing a different ~ ("to begin to act differently"); to the ~ of (we danced to the ~ of a lively old song) (also fig.) ("to about the extent of") (colloq.) (I'm in hock to a loan shark to the ~ of $30,000!)

tune II v. (d; tr.) to ~ to (we ~d our sets to the local station to hear the local news; stay ~d to this station for the latest news)

tune in v. (D; intr.) to ~ on (esp. AE), to (to ~ to a station)

tuner n. a piano ~

tune-up n. 1. to do a ~ (of an engine); to give (an engine) a ~ 2. an engine ~

tuning n. fine ~ (also fig.) (the fine ~ of the economy to meet current needs)

tunnel I n. 1. to bore, build, construct, dig a ~ 2. a Channel; pedestrian; railroad (AE), railway (BE); wind ~ 3. a ~ caves in; extends, goes, leads, runs 4. through a ~ (to drive through a ~) 5. (misc.) (fig.) the light at the end of the ~

tunnel II v. (P; intr.) to ~ under the Channel; termites ~ through wood; the prisoners ~ed their way under the fence and escaped

turbulence n. clear-air ~

turkey n. 1. to breed, raise ~s 2. to carve; roast; stuff a ~ 3. a wild ~ 4. ~s gobble, go "gobble gobble" 5. a female ~ is a hen 6. a male ~ is a cock, gobbler, tom, or turkeycock (see also **cold turkey**)

turmoil n. 1. complete ~ 2. in (a) ~ (the country was in ~) 3. (misc.) the country was plunged/thrown into ~

turn I n. ["change of direction"] ["direction"] 1. to make, negotiate; give smt. a ~ (to negotiate a difficult ~; to give the handle another ~) 2. to take a ~ (the conversation took an interesting ~) 3. a left; right; sharp ~; about-turn, 180-degree turn, U-turn (to do/make a U-turn) 4. a ~ to (a ~ to the right; take the first ~ on the right) ["proper order, opportunity"] 5. to have, take one's/a ~; to give smb. a ~ ("will you please give me a ~ now? everyone else has had one!") 6. to take ~s at; with (we took ~s with them standing/at standing guard = (BE) we took it in ~s with them to stand guard) 7. to wait one's ~ 8. to miss one's ~ 9. smb.'s ~ comes (my ~ came) 10. smb.'s ~ to + inf. (it's my ~ to drive) 11. by ~s 12. in ~ ("in sequence") (everyone criticized him in ~); ("in consequence") (everyone criticized him and he in ~ criticized everyone); out of ~ ["change"] 13. to take a ~ (the situation took a ~ for the better) 14. a dramatic; favorable; unexpected; unfavorable ~ (events took a dramatic ~ for the worse) 15. (usu. of business conditions) a downward; upward ~ (the market took an upward ~) 16. at the ~ (of the century) ["short walk"] 17. to take a ~ (let's take a ~

around/round the park) ["shock"] 18. to give smb. a ~ (the revelation gave me quite a ~) ["misc."] 19. at every ~ ("on every occasion"); every twist and ~ in/of the road; on the ~ (BE) ("about to change") (the political situation is definitely on the ~); to do smb. a good ~ ("to do smb. a favor") (see also *turn of phrase* at **phrase**)

turn II v. 1. ("to change direction") to ~ abruptly, sharply 2. (d; intr., tr.) to ~ against ("to become antagonistic towards"); ("to make antagonistic towards") (to ~ against one's friends; what ~ed him against us?) 3. (d; intr.) to ~ for; to ("to resort to") (she ~ed to her family in her time of need; they had to ~ somewhere for help) 4. (d; intr.) ("to shift") to ~ from; to (let's ~ from this topic to a more pleasant one; to ~ to a new field) 5. (D; intr.) ("to change direction") to ~ into; onto (to ~ into a side street) 6. (d; intr., tr.) to ~ from; into, to ("to be converted, transformed into"); ("to convert, transform into") (caterpillars ~ into butterflies; freezing water ~s (in)to ice; his love ~ed to hate; they ~ed the meeting into a brawl; the incident ~ed her into a better person; he's ~ed from a boy into a man!; the good news ~ed her tears to smiles; ~ your junk into cash by selling it to us!) 7. (D; intr.) to ~ off; onto ("to leave") (to ~ off the main road and onto the first side road) 8. (d; intr.) to ~ on ("to attack") (to ~ on smb. in anger; the speaker finally ~ed on the hecklers) 9. (d; intr.) to ~ on, upon ("to depend, hinge on") (everything ~s on the judge's interpretation of the law) 10. (D; intr.) ("to change direction") to ~ to (to ~ to the right) 11. (d; intr.) ("to direct one's attention, efforts") to ~ to (to ~ to a new subject; she ~ed to the study of art; she ~ed to shouting (in order) to get attention) 12. (d; tr.) ("to direct") to ~ to, towards (to ~ one's attention to a new problem; ~ your face towards the mirror; you should not ~ your back to the audience) 13. (D; intr.) to ~ towards ("to face") (~ towards me) 14. (E) he ~ed to go; he ~ed to face the audience ("he turned and faced the audience") 15. (N; used with an adjective) ("to cause to become") we ~ed the dog loose; worry ~ed her hair gray 16. (S) to ~ traitor; she ~ ed pale; the light has ~ed green 17. (misc.) to ~ anticlockwise (BE)/counterclockwise (AE); to ~ left/right; to ~ smt. inside out; to ~ smt. upside down ("to ~ sixteen ("to reach one's sixteenth birthday"); the road twists and ~s (see *turn one's back on smb.; turn one's back to smb.* at **back II** n.; the Usage Note for **grow**)

turnabout n. ["reversal"] to do a ~

turn away v. (D; intr.) to ~ from

turn back v. (D; intr.) to ~ from; to

turn down v. 1. (D; tr.) to ~ to (please ~ the heater down to a lower setting) 2. (N) to ~ the radio down low; to ~ (smt./smb.) down cold (AE)/flat ("to reject outright")

turn in v. 1. (B) ("to hand over") they ~ed him in to the police; she ~ed the assignment in to the

teacher; he refused to ~ himself in to the authorities 2. (D; tr.) ("to trade in") (esp. AE) to ~ for (she ~ed her old car in for a new one) 3. (s) to ~ early ("to go to sleep early")
turning *n.* (esp. BE) to take a ~ (take the first ~ on the right)
turning point *n.* 1. to be, constitute, mark, represent a ~ (in history) 2. to reach a ~ 3. a ~ for (for us the ~ came when we realized what to do) 4. a ~ in 5. at a ~ (we are at a ~ in history)
turn-off *n.* 1. to take a ~ 2. a ~ for (take the next ~ for the side road) 3. a ~ from; into, onto (take the next ~ from the main road into a side road)
turn off *v.* 1. (D; intr.) to ~ from; into (we ~ed off from the main road into a side road) 2. (misc.) they ~ed off at the last corner/minute
turn on *v.* (slang) 1. (D; intr.) to ~ to ("to become excited about") (to ~ to Beethoven) 2. (D; tr.) to ~ to ("to excite about") (to ~ smb. on to Beethoven) 3. (R) it really ~s me on to hear Beethoven 4. (Q) (BE) ("hinge on") (the outcome of the election will ~ which candidate the voters trust more)
turnout *n.* ["attendance"] ["participation"] 1. to attract a (large) ~ 2. an above-average; big, enormous, heavy, huge, large; good; record, unprecedented ~ 3. a disappointing; light, poor, small ~ 4. (a) voter ~ (the election has attracted an unprecedented voter ~)
turn out *v.* 1. (D; intr.) ("to appear") to ~ for (a large crowd ~ed out for her first concert) 2. (E) ("to prove") a large crowd ~ed out to attend her first concert; the test ~ed out to be positive; they ~ed out to have been away on a trip at the time = they had been away on a trip at the time, as it ~ed out; Samuel L. Clemens ~ed out to have written the works of Mark Twain. = the works of Mark Twain ~ed out to have been written by Samuel L. Clemens 3. (L) it ~ed out that they had been away on a trip at the time 4. (s) the test ~ed out positive
turnover *n.* ["movement of goods or personnel"] 1. to have; record a ~ 2. a brisk, quick, rapid ~ 3. a high; low; record ~ 4. (a) staff ~ ["filled pastry"] 5. an apple ~
turn over *v.* (B) ("to hand over") to ~ a thief over to the police
turnpike *n.* ["toll expressway"] (AE) 1. (to travel) by ~ 2. (to drive) on a ~
turnstile *n.* 1. to go through, pass through a ~ 2. a subway (AE), underground (BE) ~
turn up *v.* ("to appear") 1. (D; intr.) to ~ as (she ~ed up as the new principal of the school) 2. (D; intr.) to ~ for (they did not ~ for the ceremony) 3. (D; intr.) to ~ in (she finally ~ed up in London) 4. (D; tr.) to ~ to (please ~ the heater up to a higher setting) 5. (D; intr.) to ~ with (she ~ed up with the missing money) 6. (E) things were looking bad but he was sure smt. or smb. would ~ to/and save him 7. (s) he ~ed up drunk at/for work 8. (misc.) they ~ed up unexpectedly; they ~ed ¬the radio/the

volume/the sound¬ up high ("they turned the radio on very loud")
turpitude *n.* moral ~
turtle *n.* 1. a fresh-water; land (AE); mud; sea; snapping ~ 2. (misc.) to turn ~ ("to capsize") USAGE NOTE: Although CE has both *turtle* and *tortoise*, the two are distinguished much more clearly in BE than in AE. In BE, turtles are aquatic; tortoises, terrestrial. In AE, the word *turtle* often serves as a generic term covering tortoises as well as turtles.
tusk *n.* an elephant; walrus; wild-boar ~
tussle I *n.* (colloq.) 1. to get into, have a ~ 2. a ~ about, over; between; for; with (there was quite a ~ between them for control of the company) 3. a ~ to + inf. (there was quite a ~ between them to control the company)
tussle II *v.* (colloq.) (D; intr.) to ~ about, over; for; with (they ~d with each other for control of the company)
tutelage *n.* under smb.'s ~
tutor I *n.* 1. a course (BE); private ~ 2. a ~ of, to (old-fashioned or formal)
tutor II *v.* (D; intr., tr.) to ~ in (to ~ smb. in physics)
tutorial *n.* ["course"] 1. to give smb. a ~ 2. to have a ~ with 3. a ~ about, on
TV see **television; television set**
TV set see **television set**
twang *n.* (typically somewhat derog.) 1. (to have) a nasal ~ 2. (misc.) to speak with a ~ (they speak with a nasal ~)
tweed *n.* 1. Harris; herringbone ~ 2. in ~s (dressed in ~s)
tweezers *n.* a pair of ~
twilight *n.* 1. at ~ 2. in the ~ (in the ~ of smb.'s career) (see also *twilight zone* at **zone I** *n.*)
twin *v.* (D; tr.) to ~ with (which town is your town ~ned with ?) (see also **twins**)
twine I *n.* a ball of ~
twine II *v.* (d; intr., refl.) to ~ around, round (the vines ~d (themselves) around the tree)
twinkle I *n.* 1. a ~ in smb.'s eyes (there was a ~ of amusement in her eyes) 2. with a ~ in one's eyes
twinkle II *v.* (D; intr.) to ~ with (her eyes ~d with amusement)
twins *n.* 1. to have, give birth to ~ 2. conjoined, Siamese; fraternal; identical ~ 3. a pair, set of ~ USAGE NOTE: The misleading phrase *Siamese twins* is increasingly being replaced by the more accurate phrase *conjoined twins*.
twirl *v.* (D; intr., tr.) to ~ around (she ~ed the baton around her finger)
twist I *n.* ["type of dance"] 1. to dance, do the ~ ["twisting or being twisted"] 2. to give smt. a ~ 3. to have a ~ (the rope has a ~ in it) ["unexpected turn"] 4. to take a ~ 5. a bizarre, strange, unusual; ironic ~ (the matter took a bizarre ~) ["interpretation"] 6. to give a (new) ~ (to the news) ["approach, method"] 7. a new ~ (to) ["misc."] 8. every ~ and turn in/of the road

twist II v. 1. (D; tr.) to ~ (a)round (she ~ed the thread around her finger) 2. (D; tr.) to ~ into (to ~ smt. into a certain shape) 3. (D; tr.) to ~ off (he ~ed the cap off the bottle) 4. (D; tr.) to ~ out of (to ~ smt. out of shape) 5. (D; tr.) to ~ to (~ the knob to the right) 6. (N; refl.) the prisoner ~ed himself free of his captors 7. (s) the prisoner ~ed free of his captors 8. (misc.) to ~ smb.'s arm ("to coerce smb."); to ~ smb. around one's little finger ("to manipulate smb."); the road ~s and turns

twitch I n. a nervous; uncontrollable ~

twitch II v. 1. to ~ nervously; uncontrollably 2. (D; intr.) to ~ in; with (to ~ in/with pain)

two n. to put ~ and ~ together ("to comprehend the significance of smt.")

two cents' worth n. (slang) (AE) ["opinion"] to add, get in, put in one's ~

twopenn'orth n. (colloq.) (BE) ["opinion"] to add, get in, put in one's ~

tycoon n. a business ~

type I n. ["metal blocks used in printing"] 1. to set ~ (to set ~ by hand) 2. bold, boldface, boldfaced; elite; italic; pica; regular; roman ~ 3. a font (esp. AE)/fount (BE) of ~ 4. in ~ (to set a book in ~) ["sort, category"] 5. a blood ~ 6. of a certain ~ (of all ~s; of several ~s; a person of that ~ = that ~ of person) 7. (misc.) ~ of thing (always going on about his enemies, his problems – that ~ of thing); to like all ~s of music; true to ~; a reversion to ~

type II v. (D; tr.) ("to typewrite") to ~ for (~ this letter for me)

typecast v. (D; tr.) to ~ as; in (to be typecast in a certain role; that actor has been typecast as a villain)

typewriter n. 1. to operate, use; pound (colloq.) a ~ 2. an electric; electronic; manual; portable ~ 3. a ~ skips 4. on a ~ (I did the letter on my electric ~)

typhoid n. to contract, develop, get; have ~

typhoon n. 1. a ~ hits, strikes; rages (the ~ struck several cities) 2. a ~ blows itself out, blows over, dies down, subsides

typhus n. to contract, develop, get; have ~

typical adj. 1. ~ of 2. ~ to + inf. (it was ~ of her to say such things) 3. (misc.) how very ~ (it was) of her to say such things!

typing n. 1. to do (the) ~ 2. hunt-and-peck ~ (colloq.) 3. touch ~

typist n. 1. a copy; shorthand ~ (BE; AE has stenographer) 2. a clerk-typist; a hunt-and-peck ~ (colloq.); a touch-typist

tyranny n. 1. to impose ~ on 2. to overthrow (a) ~ 3. cruel, merciless; ruthless ~ 4. petty ~ 5. an act of ~ 6. ~ over ("I have sworn upon the altar of God ... eternal hostility against every form of ~ over the mind of man." – Thomas Jefferson, 1800) 7. under (a) ~

tyrant n. 1. to overthrow a ~ 2. a cruel, merciless; ruthless ~ 3. a petty ~ 4. a ~ oppresses 5. the rule of a ~ 6. under a ~

tyre (BE) see **tire I** n.

U

UFO *n.* ["unidentified flying object, flying saucer"] 1. to sight a ~ 2. (misc.) a ~ abduction; sighting

ukase *n.* ["edict"] 1. to issue a ~ 2. a ~ that + clause; subj. (the tyrant issued a ~ that all prisoners ¬be/ should be¬ beheaded)

ulcer *n.* 1. to have an ~ 2. a bleeding; duodenal; gastric, stomach; mouth; peptic; perforated ~

ultimate *n.* ["acme, the nth degree"] 1. the ~ in (the ~ in comfort) 2. (carried) to the ~

ultimatum *n.* 1. to deliver, give, issue, present an ~ 2. to get, receive an ~ 3. to accept an ~ 4. to defy; ignore; reject an ~ 5. to rescind, withdraw an ~ 6. an ~ demands, insists 7. an ~ that + clause; subj. (their government issued an ~ to our government demanding that all our troops ¬be/should be¬ disarmed at once.)

umbilical cord *n.* 1. to tie (off) an ~ 2. to cut the ~ (also fig.)

umbrage *n.* ["offense"] 1. to give ~ 2. to take ~ at

umbrella *n.* 1. to open an ~ 2. to fold (up) an ~ 3. a beach ~ 4. under an ~ (also fig.) (need Europe still shelter under the American nuclear ~?) (see also *umbrella organization* at **organization**; *umbrella term* at **term I** *n.*)

unable *adj.* (typically cannot stand alone) ~ to + inf. (she was ~ to reach him today, she tried to reach him but she was ~ to) USAGE NOTE: In passive constructions, *unable to* is replaced by *cannot* – X is sometimes unable to replace Y = Y can't always be replaced by X.

unacceptable *adj.* 1. completely, totally, wholly; socially ~ 2. ~ to (the conditions proved/were completely ~ to all concerned) 3. ~ to + inf. (it's wholly ~ to behave like that) USAGE NOTE: Perhaps under the influence of cultural relativism, the word *unacceptable* is used increasingly where people of an older generation would use *wrong*. Malcolm Bradbury's novel *Eating People is Wrong* (1959) might if published today be called *Eating People Is Unacceptable*.

unaccounted *adj.* ~ for (several items are still ~ for)

unaccustomed *adj.* (cannot stand alone) ~ to (~ to public speaking) USAGE NOTE: It was a cliché attributed to inexperienced public speakers that they would begin their speeches by saying: Unaccusomed as I am to public speaking, ...

unaffected *adj.* 1. ~ by 2. to remain ~

unafraid *adj.* 1. ~ of 2. ~ to + inf. (she was ~ to dive off the high board)

unaided *adj.* ~ by; in

unamenable *adj.* (formal) ~ to

unanimity *n.* 1. to reach ~ 2. virtual ~ 3. ~ in

unanimous *adj.* 1. almost, virtually, well-nigh ~ 2. ~ in

unanswerable *adj.* ~ for; to (bureaucrats who think they are above the law and ~ for their actions to anybody)

unanswered *adj.* to go, remain ~ (that question remained ~)

unappreciative *adj.* ~ of (he was ~ of our help)

unasked *adj.* ~ for

unattended *adj.* to leave ~

unaware *adj.* (cannot stand alone) 1. blissfully; completely, totally ~ 2. ~ of (they were completely ~ of the harmfulness of smoking) 3. ~ that + clause (they were totally ~ that smoking is harmful)

unawares *adv.* ["unexpectedly"] 1. to catch, take smb. ~ 2. completely, totally ~

unbalanced *adj.* mentally ~

unbeatable *adj.* ~ at, in (~ at chess)

unbecoming *adj.* ~ of; to (conduct ~ to an officer = conduct ~ an officer)

unbeknown *adj.* (cannot stand alone) ~ to (~ to us, they had already left)

unbeknownst *adj.* (formal) (cannot stand alone) ~ to (~ to us, they had already left)

unbelievable *adj.* 1. absolutely ~ 2. ~ to 3. ~ that + clause (it was absolutely ~ to me that nobody ¬paid/should have paid¬ attention to the new invention = I find it absolutely ~ that nobody ¬paid/ should have paid¬ attention to the new invention)

unbending *adj.* ~ in (~ in one's manner)

unbiased *adj.* 1. completely, totally ~ 2. ~ towards (they were completely ~ towards foreigners)

unburden *v.* 1. (B; refl.) he finally ~ed himself to his family 2. (D; refl.) to ~ of (he finally ~ed himself of his secret)

uncalled *adj.* (cannot stand alone) ~ for (that remark was completely ~ for! = that was a completely uncalled-for remark!)

uncanny *adj.* 1. positively ~ 2. ~ to + inf. (it's ~ to see how closely the twins resemble each other) 3. ~ that + clause (it's positively ~ that the twins resemble each other so closely) 4. (misc.) it's ~ how much the twins resemble each other

uncared *adj.* (cannot stand alone) ~ for (the children were ~ for)

uncensured *adj.* to go ~

uncertain *adj.* 1. ~ about, as to, of (~ about the outcome; we were ~ of his support) 2. (misc.) it is ~ whether (or not) they will sign the contract; I am still ~ (as to) when they are coming

uncertainty *n.* 1. to express ~ 2. grave, great ~ 3. ~ surrounds 4. a degree, element of ~ (there is still an element of ~ surrounding their time of arrival) 5. ~ about, as to, over (there was no ~ about the matter; there is still some degree of ~ as to when they are coming)

unchallenged *adj.* to go, pass ~ (Mr. Chairman, I cannot let the last speaker's scurrilous remark go ~!)

unchanged *adj.* to remain ~

uncharacteristic *adj.* 1. ~ of 2. ~ to + inf. (it was

completely / very ~ of them not to answer their correspondence promptly)

uncharitable adj. 1. ~ of 2. ~ towards 3. ~ to + inf. (it was ~ of her to say that)

unchecked adj. to go, remain ~

unclaimed adj. to go, remain ~

uncle n. 1. a great ~ 2. (misc.) (colloq.) (AE) to say ~ ("to admit defeat")

unclear adj. 1. ~ about (are you still ~ about the situation?) 2. ~ from (the answer is still ~ from these facts) 3. ~ to (the answer was still ~ to us) 4. ~ how; whether; why (it was still ~ to us why she quit her job; it was ~ whether (or not) they would attend)

uncomfortable adj. 1. to feel ~ 2. to make smb. ~ 3. ~ about; with (I felt ~ about discussing this matter in public) 4. ~ to + inf. (it is ~ to sit here in the blazing sunshine = it is ~ sitting here in the blazing sunshine)

uncommitted adj. ~ to (~ to any principles)

uncommon adj. ~ to + inf. (it is not ~ to find people here who know several languages)

uncommunicative adj. ~ about, regarding

uncompromising adj. ~ in; on; towards (~ in one's attitude; ~ towards their proposal)

unconcerned adj. ~ about, over; with (see Usage Note for **concerned**)

unconscious I adj. 1. to become; remain ~ 2. ~ of 3. to beat smb. ~

unconscious II n. in smb.'s ~

unconsciousness n. to lapse into ~

unconstitutional adj. ~ to + inf. (it is ~ to censor the press)

unconventional adj. 1. ~ in (~ in one's tastes) 2. ~ to + inf. (it is ~ to go to work in shorts)

unconvinced adj. 1. to remain ~ 2. ~ of (they're still ~ of the feasibility of our project) 3. ~ that + clause (they remain ~ that our project will succeed)

uncooperative adj. 1. ~ about; in; towards (~ in working out a compromise) 2. ~ to the point of (the witness was ~ to the point of refusing to testify)

uncorrected adj. to go, remain ~ (see also *uncorrected proofs* at **proof**)

uncouple v. (D; tr.) ("to separate") to ~ from (to ~ a trailer from a tractor)

uncritical adj. ~ of (he was ~ of my work)

unction n. (rel.) 1. to give ~ 2. to receive ~ 3. Extreme Unction USAGE NOTE: The term *the Anointing of the Sick* is now preferred to *Extreme Unction.*

undaunted adj. ~ by; in (~ in one's resolve)

undecided adj. 1. to remain ~ 2. ~ about, as to (we are ~ as to whether we will attend) 3. ~ whether (we are ~ whether we will attend) 4. ~ whether + inf. (we are ~ whether to attend)

undemonstrative adj. ~ towards

undeniable adj. ~ that + clause (it's ~ that she is the best candidate)

underbrush n. (AE) in the ~ (see **undergrowth**)

undercharge v. 1. (D; tr.) to ~ by (they ~d us (by) twenty percent) 2. (D; tr.) to ~ for (they ~d us for the book; we were ~d for it by twenty percent)

undercoating n. (AE) (on a car) to apply ~ (BE has *underseal*)

undercover adv. ["acting in secret"] 1. to work ~ 2. to go ~

undergraduate n. 1. a college (esp. AE), university ~ 2. a first-year; second-year; etc. ~

underground I adv. 1. to go ~ (during the war they went ~) 2. buried ~

underground II n. ["transportation"] (BE; AE has *subway*) 1. to take the ~ 2. by ~ (I always travel by ~) 3. on the ~ (we went there on the ~) (see also Usage Note at **train I** n.) ["system of underground trains and stations"] 4. from; in; to the ~ (I couldn't find the right entrance to the ~, the right platform in the ~, or the right exit from the ~!) (see also *underground station* at **station I** n.; *underground system* at **system**; *underground train* at **train I** n.)

undergrowth n. 1. to chop away, clear, remove the ~ 2. dense, heavy; tangled; thick ~ 3. from; in; into; through; out of the ~ (we cleared a path through the tangled ~)

underpass n. 1. a pedestrian ~ 2. an ~ under (an ~ under a road) 3. in; into; through an ~

underseal (BE) see **undercoating**

understand v. 1. to ~ clearly, fully, perfectly 2. (D; intr., tr.) to ~ about (they do not ~ (anything) about computers) 3. (d; tr.) to ~ by (what do you ~ by this term?) 4. (G) I can ~ lying to save your life but I can't ~ lying when you don't have to 5. (H) I understood her to say that she would attend the meeting 6. (K) I just cannot ~ her not attending the meeting! 7. (L) I understood (from what she said) that she would attend the meeting and I thought it was understood that she would! 8. (Q) I fail to ~ why she didn't ~ the meeting! 9. (misc.) she gave me to ~ that she would attend the meeting = I was given to understand (by her) that she would attend the meeting (see also **understood**)

understandable adj. 1. barely; perfectly, quite (esp. BE) ~ 2. ~ to (we want this dictionary to be ~ to its users) 3. ~ that + clause (it was perfectly ~ that they would refuse) 4. (misc.) it was perfectly ~ why they refused

understanding I adj. ~ about, of

understanding II n. ["agreement"] 1. to arrive at, come to, reach an ~ 2. to have an ~ 3. a clear; complete, full; secret; tacit; verbal; written ~ 4. an ~ about; with (we have a tacit ~ with them about the matter) 5. an ~ to + inf. (we reached an ~ to keep the dispute out of the newspapers) 6. an ~ that + clause (it was my ~ that we would share the expenses) 7. on an ~ (we bought the supplies on the ~ that we would be reimbursed) ["harmony"] ["comprehension"] 8. to bring about, create, develop, promote ~ 9. to display, evidence, evince, show ~ (for, of) 10. deeper; genuine; mutual ~ 11. a lack;

degree, level of ~ 12. ~ between (to promote deeper ~ between nations; to develop mutual ~)

understatement n. 1. to make an ~ 2. to go in for ~ 3. a massive ~ (to say I was pleased would be a massive ~ – I was absolutely ecstatic!) 4. (misc.) a masterpiece of ~; the ~ of the year (to say I was pleased would be the ~ of the year – I was absolutely ecstatic!)

understood adj. 1. generally, usually ~ 2. ~ by (what is generally ~ by this term?) 3. ~ that + clause (it was ~ that everyone would help; I understood (from what she said) that she would attend the meeting and I thought it was ~ that she would!)

undertake v. (E) she undertook to complete the project in six months

undertaking n. ["promise"] (esp. BE) 1. to give smb. an ~; to honor an ~ 2. an ~ to + inf. (she gave us an ~ to complete the project in six months – and she intends to honor it!) 3. an ~ that + clause (she gave us an ~ that she would complete the project in six months – which she intends to honor!) ["task, enterprise"] 4. a joint; large-scale ~

undertones n. 1. to take on; have ~ 2. nasty; political; racial ~ (the dispute took on nasty political ~)

underwear n. 1. long; thermal ~ 2. children's; men's; women's ~ 3. a change of ~ 4. an item of ~ 5. in one's ~

underworld n. 1. the criminal ~ 2. in the ~

underwriter n. an insurance ~

undeserving adj. ~ of (~ of any help)

undesirable adj. 1. highly, very ~ 2. ~ to + inf. (it is ~ (for you) to be there after two o'clock) 3. ~ that + clause; subj. (it is ~ that you ¬be/should be/(BE) are¬ there after two o'clock)

undeterred adj. ~ by (~ by our advice)

undignified adj. ~ to + inf. (it was ~ to behave like that)

undiminished adj. ~ by; in (~ in stature)

undiplomatic adj. ~ to + inf. (it was ~ to make such demands)

undisturbed adj. ~ by (~ by the commotion)

undoing n. ["ruin"] to prove (to be) smb.'s ~ (alcohol proved (to be) his ~ = alcohol proved (to be) the ~ of him)

undone adj. to come ~ (her necklace came ~)

undreamed, undreamt adj. ~ of (undreamt-of riches)

undressed adj. to get ~

unease n. 1. to cause ~ 2. to conceal ~ 3. to allay smb.'s 4. ~ about, at (we can't conceal our ~ at the prospect of a recession)

uneasiness n. 1. to cause ~ 2. to allay smb.'s ~ 3. ~ about

uneasy adj. ~ about

unemployed n. ["unemployed people"] 1. the hard-core; long-term ~ 2. (misc.) to join/swell the ranks of the ~

unemployment n. 1. to cause, create ~ 2. to eliminate; reduce ~ 3. falling; high; low; mass; mounting,

rising; seasonal; widespread ~ 4. ~ bottoms out; falls; hits, reaches; peaks; rises (~ has already hit 2,000,000) 5. a level of ~ (rising levels of ~ led to government policies aimed at reducing ~) 6. (misc.) ~ is down; up (~ is way up over last year)

unemployment compensation n. (esp. AE) 1. to pay ~ 2. to draw, get, receive ~ 3. to be on ~ 4. to go on ~ 5. to apply for ~

unemployment insurance (esp. AE) see **unemployment compensation** 1, 2, 5

unequal adj. 1. ~ in (they are ~ in every way) 2. ~ to (she felt ~ to the task)

unequaled, unequalled adj. 1. ~ as (she was ~ as a dancer) 2. ~ at, in; by; for

unerring adj. (often does not stand alone) ~ in (she was ~ in her judgment = her judgment was ~ = she had ~ judgment)

unessential adj. 1. ~ for; to 2. ~ to + inf. (it is ~ for all students to be present) 3. ~ that + clause; subj. (it is ~ that all students ¬be/should be/are (BE)¬ present)

unethical adj. ~ to + inf. (it was ~ of them to plagiarize)

unexcelled adj. ~ at, in (~ at sports)

unfair adj. 1. grossly, very ~ 2. ~ to (~ to certain groups) 3. ~ to + inf. (it was ~ to take advantage of the situation) 4. ~ that + clause (it's ~ that she has to work so hard)

unfaithful adj. ~ in; to

unfaithfulness n. ~ in; to

unfaltering adj. ~ in (they were ~ in their efforts to reduce crime)

unfamiliar adj. ~ to; with (the area was ~ to me = I was ~ with the area)

unfamiliarity n. ~ to; with (my ~ with the area = the area's ~ to me)

unfashionable adj. 1. among, with (has recycling ever been ~ among the young?) 2. ~ to + inf. (it is ~ to wear boots to a formal reception)

unfasten v. 1. (D; tr.) to ~ from 2. (misc.) to come ~ed

unfavorable, unfavourable adj. ~ for, to

unfed adj. to go ~

unfeeling adj. 1. ~ towards 2. ~ to + inf. (it was ~ of them to turn down her request)

unfit adj. 1. mentally, psychologically; physically ~ 2. ~ for (~ for military service; ~ for human consumption; ~ for purpose (BE)) 3. ~ to + inf. (he is ~ to work)

unfortunate adj. 1. ~ for 2. ~ in (we consider ourselves ~ in not having a nice house) 3. ~ to + inf. (we consider ourselves ~ not to have a nice house) 4. ~ that + clause (it is ~ (for us) that we don't have a nice house)

unfriendliness n. 1. to show ~ 2. ~ to, towards, with

unfriendly adj. 1. ~ of (that was ~ of you) 2. ~ to, towards, with 3. ~ to + inf. (it was ~ of you to refuse to help) 4. (misc.) user-unfriendly

ungrateful *adj.* ~ for; to (he was ~ to us for our help)

unhappy *adj.* 1. bitterly, very ~ 2. ~ about, at, over; in; with (she was ~ about/at/over the bad news; we felt ~ about being alone; he was ~ in his boring work; they were ~ with the poor results) 3. ~ to + inf. (we felt ~ to be alone; she'll be ~ to leave here) 4. ~ that + clause (we felt ~ that we were alone) 5. (misc.) she'll be ~ working there

unharmed *adj.* 1. to go, remain ~ 2. ~ by 3. (misc.) to escape ~

unhealthy *adj.* 1. ~ for (smoking is ~ for you) 2. ~ to + inf. (it's ~ (for you) to smoke)

unheard-of *adj.* ~ to + inf. (it's ~ to come to a reception without an invitation)

unheeded *adj.* 1. to go ~ (her advice went ~) 2. ~ by

unheedful *adj.* (cannot stand alone) ~ of (~ of advice/danger/threats)

unification *n.* 1. to achieve, bring about (the) ~ (to achieve the ~ – or re-unification – of Germany) 2. ~ with (to achieve the ~ – or re-unification – of East Germany with/and West Germany)

uniform I *adj.* ~ in; with

uniform II *n.* 1. to don, put on a ~ 2. to have on, wear a ~ 3. to take off a ~ 4. a dress, full-dress; fatigue; military; naval; nurse's; parade; police; regulation; school ~ 5. in ~; out of ~ (he was out of ~ when he was picked up by the military police)

uniformity *n.* ~ in

unify *v.* 1. (D; tr.) to ~ into (East Germany and West Germany were ~fied – or re-unified – into one nation) 2. (D; tr.) to ~ with (East Germany was ~fied – or re-unified – with West Germany = East Germany and West Germany were ~fied – or re-unified (with each other))

unimportant *adj.* 1. ~ for; to 2. ~ to + inf. (it is ~ for everyone to attend the meeting provided they make their views known to the chairman) 3. (misc.) it is ~ whether or not anyone attends the meeting

uninformed *adj.* ~ about, of

uninhibited *adj.* ~ about, from, in (after a few drinks, he felt ~ about/in talking to women)

unintelligible *adj.* 1. mutually ~ (are Old English and Modern English mutually ~?) 2. ~ to (is Old English ~ to speakers of Modern English?)

uninterested *adj.* ~ in (we are ~ in politics)

uninvited *adj.* to appear, show up, turn up ~

union *n.* 1. to form a ~ 2. to break up, dissolve a ~ 3. a company; craft; credit; currency, monetary; customs; industrial; labor (AE), trade (BE); postal; student ~ 4. a ~ forms; breaks up, dissolves 5. a ~ between; with (the ~ between East Germany and West Germany = the ~ of East Germany with West Germany = the ~ of East Germany and West Germany (with each other)) 6. (misc.) to recognize a labor/trade ~; a civil ~ (as between partners of the same sex) (the registrar performed a civil ~ between Adam and Steve)

unique *adj.* 1. ~ in 2. ~ to (~ to a certain area) USAGE NOTE: *More unique* and *most unique* are used: "She's the most ~ person I ever met." – Arthur Miller (1915–2005). Nevertheless, some people would apparently prefer, even here, some such phrase as "the *most remarkable* person." Likewise, such people would prefer "very remarkable" to "very unique."

unison *n.* in ~ (with)

unit *n.* ["single constituent of a whole"] 1. a basic, primary; discrete; individual ~; the intensive care ~ of/in a hospital ["united whole such as a military formation"] 2. to activate; form; weld into a ~ 3. to commit; manage a ~ (to commit a ~ to combat) 4. to deactivate; disband a ~ 5. an advance, advanced; airborne; armored; coherent, cohesive; combat; crack, elite; efficient, productive; mechanized, motorized; naval; tactical ~ (advance armored ~s have reached the river; the CEO welded the team he managed into a cohesive and productive ~) ["standard"] 6. a message ~ (used for telephone calls) 7. a currency; monetary ~ (the Euro is the monetary ~ of most of the EU; a pound can be a ~ of money or a ~ of weight) ["single residence"] 8. a rental ~ ["computer terminal"] 9. a Visual Display Unit = VDU (CE; AE also has *Video Display Terminal* = VDT)

unite *v.* 1. (D; intr., tr.) to ~ against (to ~ against aggression; to ~ one's allies against the common foe) 2. (D; intr., tr.) to ~ for (we must ~ for the common good; the nation was ~d for the struggle against terrorism) 3. (D; intr., tr.) to ~ in (we must ~ in our struggle against terrorism; to ~ a nation in the fight against inflation) 4. (D; intr., tr.) to ~ into (we had to ~ the competing factions into a cohesive whole) 5. (D; intr.) to ~ with (our countries must ~ with each other against the common enemy; East Germany and West Germany (were) ~d – or re-united – (with each other) into one country) 6. (misc.) to ~ (¬in order/so as¬) to succeed

united *adj.* ~ in (a nation ~ in the fight against inflation)

United States *n.* 1. the contiguous ~ (without Alaska and Hawaii) 2. the ~ of (the ~ of America; the ~ of Brazil; the ~ of Mexico)

unity *n.* 1. to achieve, bring about ~ 2. to destroy, shatter ~ 3. national; party ~ (to achieve national ~) 4. ~ among; between; with (who brought about such ~ between the factions?) 5. in ~ (in ~ there is strength) 6. (misc.) the USA's motto "E Pluribus Unum" expresses its commitment to ~ in diversity

universe *n.* 1. the entire, whole; known ~ 2. in; throughout the ~

university *n.* 1. to establish, found a ~ 2. ¬to go to a ~/to go to ~ (BE)¬ (she goes to a good ~) 3. a free, open; people's ~ 4. an ancient (BE); Ivy-League (US); redbrick (GB); state (US) ~ 5. at; in a ~ (to teach at a ~; there is a spirit of cooperation at/in our ~; BE: what did you read at ~? = AE: what did you major in at college?) USAGE NOTE: In

CE "a university" is a building or an institution (*there's a big prestigious university in another town but she goes to a university near her home*). In BE "university" is the educational activity that goes on in a university (*university takes up a lot of her time; she goes to university near her home; we lost touch with each other after university*). In AE, the examples above would have to be re-phrased (e.g. *university work takes up a lot of her time; she attends a university near her home; we lost touch with each other after we got our university degrees*). A very likely alternative in AE would be to use "college" (*college takes up a lot of her time; she goes to college near her home; we lost touch with each other after college*). See also the Usage Notes for **college, school**.

unjust *adj.* 1. ~ of 2. ~ to, towards 3. ~ to + inf. (it was ~ of him to accuse me without proof) 4. ~ that + clause (it's ~ that he ¬accused/should have accused¬ me without proof)

unjustified *adj.* 1. completely, totally ~ 2. ~ in (she was ~ in complaining)

unkind *adj.* 1. ~ of (that insult was very ~ of you) 2. ~ to (~ to animals) 3. ~ to + inf. (it was ~ of you to insult him)

unknown *adj.* ~ to (the facts were ~ to us)

unlawful *adj.* 1. ~ for (smoking is ~ for minors) 2. ~ to + inf. (it's ~ for minors to smoke)

unleash *v.* (D; tr.) to ~ against; on (to ~ a new arms race on the world)

unlike *prep.* ~ to + inf. (it was very ~ them to be late)

unlikely *adj.* 1. equally; highly, very ~ 2. ~ to + inf. (she is ~ to show up; it is ~ to snow) 3. ~ that + clause (it is ~ that she will show up; it is ~ that it will snow)

unload *v.* 1. (D; tr.) to ~ from (to ~ cargo from a ship) 2. (D; tr.) (fig.) to ~ on (they were ~ing defective merchandise on unsuspecting customers)

unlucky *adj.* 1. ~ at, in; for; with (~ at cards; ~ in love; ~ for some people; they were ~ with their old car) 2. ~ to + inf. (some people feel that it is ~ to walk under a ladder) 3. ~ that + clause (it was ~ that we got there late = we were ~ to have gotten there late)

unmarked *adj.* ~ by

unmarred *adj.* ~ by (the ceremony was ~ by any untoward incidents)

unmatched *adj.* 1. ~ as (she was ~ as a dancer) 2. ~ at, in; by; for

unmerciful *adj.* ~ to, towards

unmindful *adj.* (cannot stand alone) ~ of (~ of danger; ~ of one's responsibilities)

unmoved *adj.* ~ by (they were left ~ by her tears)

unnamed *adj.* to remain ~ (I was told so by a certain person who shall remain ~)

unnatural *adj.* 1. ~ to + inf. (it's ~ of parents to reject their own children) 2. ~ that + clause (it's ~ that parents should reject their own children)

unnecessary *adj.* 1. ~ for 2. ~ to + inf. (it's ~ for you to get involved) 3. ~ that + clause (it's ~ that you should get involved)

unnoticed *adj.* to go, pass ~ (the incident went/passed ~)

unobserved *adj.* to go, pass ~ (the incident went/passed ~)

unopposed *adj.* ~ to

unorthodox *adj.* ~ to + inf. (it is ~ to bypass the channels of command in the army)

unparalleled *adj.* ~ in (~ in ferocity)

unperturbed *adj.* ~ by (she was ~ by the loud noise)

unpleasant *adj.* 1. ~ to (he is ~ to everyone) 2. ~ to + inf. (it's ~ to talk to him = it's ~ talking to him = he's ~ to talk to = he's an ~ person to talk to)

unpopular *adj.* 1. ~ as (she became ~ as a night-club singer) 2. ~ among, with (she became ~ with teenagers)

unprepared *adj.* 1. ~ for (I am ~ for such a responsibility) 2. ~ to + inf. (I am ~ to take on such a responsibility)

unprofessional *adj.* 1. ~ in (she was ~ in not investigating the matter) 2. ~ to + inf. (it was ~ of her not to investigate the matter = she was ~ not to have investigated the matter) 3. (misc.) (she was ~ in that she didn't investigate the matter)

unprofitable *adj.* ~ to + inf. (is it ~ to work this mine?)

unpunished *adj.* 1. to go, remain ~ (the criminals went ~) 2. ~ for

unqualified *adj.* 1. clearly; grossly ~ 2. ~ for 3. ~ to + inf. (she is ~ to work as a teacher)

unquote *n.* see quote I *n.*

unrealistic *adj.* 1. ~ about 2. ~ to + inf. (it is ~ to hope for an improvement so soon = you are being ~ to hope for an improvement so soon)

unreasonable *adj.* 1. ~ about (let's not be ~ about this) 2. ~ of (that was ~ of you) 3. ~ to + inf. (it is ~ (of/for you) to demand that employees work without a break)

unrecognized *adj.* 1. to go, pass, remain ~ 2. ~ by

unreported *adj.* to go, remain ~ (the story went ~)

unresponsive *adj.* ~ to (~ to flattery)

unrest *n.* 1. to foment, stir up ~ 2. to crush, quell ~ 3. industrial; labor; political; social ~ (see also **civil unrest**) 4. violent ~ 5. a wave of ~ (a wave of ~ swept through the whole country) 6. during; throughout the ~

unrivaled, unrivalled *adj.* 1. ~ as (she was ~ as a dancer) 2. ~ at, in; by; for

unsafe *adj.* 1. ~ for (it is ~ for children) 2. ~ to + inf. (it's ~ to drive without putting on seat belts)

unsaid *adj.* to leave smt. ~

unsanctioned *adj.* ~ by (~ by custom)

unsatisfactory *adj.* 1. highly, very ~ 2. ~ for (her qualifications are ~ for our needs) 3. ~ in (they were ~ in their job performance) 4. ~ to (~ to all concerned) 5. ~ to + inf. (she finds it ~ to spend her days doing nothing) 6. ~ that + clause (we find it ~ that all the requirements have still not been met)

unsatisfying *adj.* 1. completely, very ~ 2. emotionally; intellectually ~ 3. ~ to + inf. (she finds it ~ to spend her days doing nothing) 4. ~ that + clause (we find it ~ that all the requirements have still not been met)

unscathed *adj.* 1. ~ by 2. to emerge ~ 3. to go ~

unschooled *adj.* ~ in (completely ~ in the martial arts)

unscrupulous *adj.* 1. ~ in (~ in his business dealings) 2. ~ to + inf. (it was ~ of their lawyer to withhold evidence)

unseemly *adj.* (formal) ~ to + inf. (it was ~ of them to show up at the reception without an invitation)

unseen *adj.* 1. to remain ~ 2. (misc.) to buy smt. sight ~

unselfish *adj.* ~ to + inf. (it was ~ of her to make the offer)

unsettle *v.* (R) it ~d me to see them quarrel; it ~d me that they were quarreling

unsettling *adj.* 1. profoundly, very ~ 2. ~ to + inf. (it was ~ to see them quarrel) 3. ~ that + clause (it was ~ that they were quarreling)

unshakable *adj.* ~ in (~ in one's faith)

unshaken *adj.* ~ in (~ in one's faith)

unshaven *adj.* to go ~ (he went ~ for a week)

unsightly *adj.* ["not pleasing to the sight"] it was ~ to behold such a thing

unskilled *adj.* ~ at, in; with (~ at/in using a computer; ~ with one's hands)

unskillful, unskilful *adj.* 1. very ~ 2. ~ at, in; with (~ at/in using a computer; ~ with one's hands)

unsound *adj.* ["healthy"] 1. ~ in, of (~ in mind and body) ["sturdy"] 2. structurally ~

unsparing *adj.* ~ in, of (~ in one's criticism; ~ of praise; ~ of herself)

unspoiled, unspoilt *adj.* ~ by (~ by success)

unstinting *adj.* ~ in (~ in one's praise)

unstuck *adj.* ["ruined"] (colloq.) to come ~ (the whole scheme came ~)

unsuccessful *adj.* ~ as; at, in; with (~ in business; ~ with women)

unsuitable *adj.* 1. highly, very ~ 2. ~ for; to 3. ~ to + inf. ("would it really be so ~ to discuss this matter at lunch?" "yes, it would be: it's a highly ~ matter for discussion at lunch!")

unsuited *adj.* 1. ~ for, to (~ for the job; ~ to each other) 2. ~ to + inf. (he was turned down as psychologically ~ to be a police officer)

unsure *adj.* 1. ~ about 2. ~ of

unsurpassed *adj.* 1. ~ at, in (~ at learning languages) 2. ~ by (~ by any competitor)

unsuspicious *adj.* ~ of

unswerving *adj.* ~ in (~ in one's determination to stamp out corruption)

unsympathetic *adj.* 1. very ~ 2. ~ to

untainted *adj.* ~ by, with (~ by scandal)

untarnished *adj.* ~ by

unthanked *adj.* to go ~

unthinkable *adj.* 1. ~ to + inf. (it would be ~ to build a house so close to the river) 2. ~ that + clause (it is ~ that they would ever build a house so close to the river)

untiring *adj.* (usu. does not stand alone) ~ in (~ in one's efforts)

untold *adj.* to remain ~ (the story remained ~ for years)

untouched *adj.* ~ by

untreated *adj.* to go, remain; leave ~ (the disease went ~ = the disease was left ~)

untroubled *adj.* ~ by

untrue *adj.* 1. historically ~ 2. ~ to (~ to one's principles) 3. ~ to + inf. (it's simply ~ to assume that all politicians are corrupt!) 4. ~ that + clause (it's simply ~ that all politicians are corrupt!)

untruth *n.* 1. to tell an ~ 2. a blatant, deliberate, transparent ~

untruthful *adj.* 1. ~ about, in 2. ~ to + inf. (it would be ~ to deny it)

untutored *adj.* ~ in

untypical *adj.* 1. ~ of 2. ~ to + inf. (it was altogether ~ of them to come without calling first)

unusable *adj.* ~ for

unused *adj.* ["unaccustomed"] (cannot stand alone) ~ to (they are ~ to hard work = they are ~ to working hard)

unusual *adj.* 1. ~ for 2. ~ to + inf. (it's ~ to visit a class without ¬asking/asking for¬ permission first; it's ~ for two world records to be set in/on one day) 3. ~ that + clause (it's ~ that two world records should be set in/on one day)

unversed *adj.* (cannot stand alone) ~ in (~ in the ways of big business)

unwarranted *adj.* ~ by

unwavering *adj.* ~ in (~ in one's support; ~ in one's determination to stamp out corruption)

unwilling *adj.* 1. ~ to + inf. (she is ~ to help: I'd like her to help but she's ~ to) 2. (misc.) we are ~ for them to share in the benefits – although some of us are not ~ for them to

unwillingness *n.* 1. to demonstrate, show ~ 2. to express ~ 3. the ~ to + inf. (we deplored her ~ to work for us)

unwise *adj.* 1. ~ of 2. ~ to + inf. (it was ~ of you not to remain silent = you were ~ not to remain silent)

unworthy *adj.* 1. ~ of (~ of praise; such behavior is ~ of you) 2. ~ to + inf. (~ to be praised)

unyielding *adj.* ~ in (~ in one's demands)

up I *adv.* (cannot stand alone) ["abreast"] 1. ~ on (are you ~ on the news?) ["dependent"] 2. ~ to (the decision is ~ to you; it's ~ to you to decide; it's ~ to you whether we go) ["misc."] 3. inflation is ~ by ten percent; the dollar was ~ against the yen; she is ~ for reelection; that topic was ~ for discussion; my car is ~ for sale

up II *v.* 1. (D; tr.) ("to increase") to ~ by (they ~ped the price (by) ten percent) 2. (misc.) (colloq.) they just ~ped and left! (see also *up stakes* at **stake**; *up sticks* at **stick I** *n.*)

upbraid *v.* (D; tr.) to ~ for (they ~ed him for his sloppy work)

upbringing *n.* 1. a bad; good; strict ~ 2. smb.'s family; religious ~ 3. (misc.) she had a good ~ because she was brought up well

update I *n.* (colloq.) ["bringing up to date"] 1. to give an ~ on (I'll give you an ~ on the situation) 2. an ~ on (here is an ~ on the situation)

update II *v.* (colloq.) (D; tr.) to ~ on (could you ~ me on the situation?)

upgrade *v.* (D; tr.) to ~ to (our legation was ~d to an embassy)

upheaval *n.* 1. to experience, undergo an ~ 2. to cause, provoke, give rise to an ~ 3. a big, great; dramatic; violent ~ 4. an economic; political; social ~ 5. during, throughout an ~ (we stayed calm throughout the whole great economic ~ provoked by the credit crunch)

upholstery *n.* leather; plastic; vinyl ~

upkeep *n.* ["cost of maintenance"] the ~ of, on (esp. AE) (the ~ on this machinery is very costly) (see also **keep up**)

upper hand *n.* ["control"] 1. to gain, get; have the ~ 2. to lose the ~ 3. the ~ in; over (we gained the ~ over them in that contest)

upright *adv.* to sit bolt ~

uprising *n.* 1. to foment, incite, spark (esp. AE), spark (esp. BE) an ~ 2. to crush, put down, quash, quell an ~ 3. an armed; peasant; popular ~ 4. an ~ against 5. during, in, throughout (they were active throughout the ~ they had fomented when they rose up against tyranny)

uproar *n.* 1. to cause, create an ~ 2. an ~ about, over 3. amid, during, in, throughout an ~ (we stayed calm throughout the whole great ~ caused by the credit crunch)

uproot *v.* (D; tr.) to ~ from (they were ~ed from their homes)

upset I *adj.* 1. to be, feel; get ~ about, over 2. ~ with (she was ~ with me about my expenses) 3. ~ to + inf. (she was ~ to learn that they could not attend) 4. ~ that + clause (she was ~ that they could not attend)

upset II *n.* ["unexpected victory"] 1. (sports) to score an ~ over (see also *upset victory* at **victory**) ["malaise"] 2. a stomach ~

upset III *v.* 1. (R) it upset me to learn of their attitude = it upset me that they ¬had had/should have had¬ that kind of attitude 2. (misc.) it ~s me when they behave like that

upsetting *adj.* 1. ~ to (recent events have been very ~ to us) 2. ~ to + inf. (it was ~ to learn of their attitude) 3. (misc.) it was ~ to me that they had that kind of attitude

upside down *adv.* to turn smt. ~

upstairs *adv.* to come; go; run; walk ~

upstanding *adj.* 1. a fine ~ pillar of the community

2. be ~ ("stand up") (esp. BE) (be ~ for the judge; be ~ for a toast)

upsurge *n.* an ~ in (there was an ~ in violence)

uptake *n.* ["comprehension"] (colloq.) (quick/slow) on the ~

uptight *adj.* (colloq.) 1. ~ about 2. (misc.) just don't get all ~ about it!

upturn *n.* 1. a modest, slight ~ 2. a sharp ~ 3. an ~ in (there was a sharp ~ in the economy = there was a sharp economic ~) 4. (misc.) the economy took a slight ~

upwards *adv.* ~ of (~ of an hour) ("somewhat more than an hour")

uranium *n.* depleted; enriched ~

urchin *n.* a street ~

urge I *n.* 1. to feel; get; have an ~ 2. to satisfy an ~ 3. to control; resist; overcome; stifle an ~ 4. an irrepressible, irresistible, uncontrollable; natural; sudden ~ 5. an ~ to + inf. (she felt an irresistible ~ to respond)

urge II *v.* 1. to ~ forcefully, strongly 2. (H) we ~d her not to respond 3. (L; subj.) we ~d that she ¬not/should not¬ respond

urgency *n.* 1. great, utmost ~ 2. ~ about, in (there is no ~ about this matter) 3. with ~ (she spoke with great ~) 4. (misc.) a matter of great ~ (it is a matter of great ~ that they all ¬be/should be/are (BE)¬ present); a note of ~ (their repeated warnings lent a note of ~ to our appeals); a sense of ~

urgent *adj.* 1. ~ in (she was ~ in her demands) 2. ~ that + clause; subj. (it is ~ that they all ¬be/should be/are (BE)¬ present)

urging *n.* at smb.'s ~ (at our ~ they accepted the invitation)

urge on *v.* 1. (D; tr.) to ~ to (they ~d me on to greater efforts) 2. (H) they ~d me on to make greater efforts

urn *n.* a burial; coffee ~

usable, useable *adj.* ~ for

usage *n.* 1. common; constant; correct; incorrect ~ 2. in ~ (this word is not in common ~)

use I /ju:s/ *n.* 1. to make ~ of 2. to put smt. to (good) ~ 3. to find, have a ~ for 4. to have; lose; regain the ~ of (she lost the ~ of one arm) 5. to deny; grant (the) ~ of (the visitors were denied ~ of the library) 6. constant; daily; emergency; official; practical ~ 7. exclusive; extensive; free; full, maximal, maximum; optimal; universal; wide ~ (they made extensive ~ of computers) 8. external; internal ~ (this medicine is for external ~ only!) 9. (legal) fair ~ 10. ~ for (do you have any ~ for this old paper?) 11. ~ (in) (is there any ~ (in) trying again?) 12. ~ of (what's the ~ of ¬worrying/trying again¬?) 13. for ~ (for official ~ only; only for ~ as directed) 14. in ~ (the copying machine is in ~) 15. of ~ to (it was of no earthly ~ to us; can I be of any ~ to you?; computers are of great ~ when (it comes to) compiling statistics) 16. (misc.) she has no ~ for them ("she dislikes them"); to come into ~; to go out of ~; her ~ of a candle as a paperweight; it's no ~ trying to convince her (see also *for (greater) ease of use* at **ease**) USAGE NOTE: The following constructions are variants; the constructions with no prepositions are colloquial – *is there any use in trying again? – is there any use trying again? what's the use of worrying? – (AE) what's the use worrying?*

use II / juːz/ *v.* 1. to ~ widely 2. (D; tr.) to ~ as (she ~d the candlestick as a paperweight) 3. (D; tr.) to ~ for (let's ~ paper plates for the picnic; she ~d the candlestick for holding down the papers) 4. (misc.) she ~d the candlestick (in order) to hold down the papers 5. (E; in positive sentences and negative sentences with *never* this verb is used only in the past tense to denote a former practice or state; in interrogative sentences the infinitive of this verb occurs with *didn't, did not*) she ~d to use candlesticks as paperweights; she ~d to work there; there ~d to be an open field here; she never ~d to work there, did she?; didn't she ~ to work there? USAGE NOTE: In negative sentences with *didn't, did not*, this verb occurs with the infinitive and, in colloquial writing, with the past tense – she didn't use/used to work there. In old-fashioned BE, constructions such as the following may occur – used she (not) to work there?; she used not to work there.

used I /juːzt/ *adj.* (cannot stand alone) ["accustomed"] to be; get ~ to (they are ~ to working hard = they are ~ to hard work; to get ~ to hard work)

used II /juːzd/ *adj.* ["employed"] 1. ~ for (this machine is ~ for making copies) 2. ~ to + inf. (this machine is ~ to make copies)

useful *adj.* 1. highly, very ~ 2. ~ as (a combinatory dictionary is ~ as an aid to learning a language) 3. ~ for, to (a combinatory dictionary is ~ for/to students) 4. ~ for, in, when (it comes to) (computers are ~ when (it comes to) compiling statistics) 5. ~ to + inf. (it's ~ to know several foreign languages when you are traveling abroad = it's ~ knowing several foreign languages when you are traveling abroad)

usefulness *n.* 1. great; limited ~ 2. ~ for; to 3. ~ for, in, when (it comes to) 4. of ~ (computers are of great ~ when (it comes to) compiling statistics)

useless *adj.* 1. absolutely, completely ~ 2. ~ as (I'm absolutely ~ as a carpenter!) 3. ~ at, when it comes to (I'm absolutely ~ at putting up shelves!) 4. ~ to + inf. (it's ~ to try to convince her = it's ~ trying to convince her)

user *n.* 1. a casual ~ (of drugs) = a casual drug-user 2. a wheelchair-user (access is provided for wheelchair-users)

usher *v.* 1. (d; tr.) to ~ into (they ~ed the guests into a large waiting room) 2. (d; tr.) to ~ out of 3. (d; tr.) to ~ through (the guests were quickly ~ed through the crowd) 4. (d; tr.) to ~ to (we were ~ed to our seats)

usual *adj.* 1. ~ for 2. ~ to + inf. (it's ~ to ¬ask/ask for¬ permission before visiting a class) 3. (misc.) as ~, as per ~ (colloq.) (everything will go on as (per) ~) (see also *business as usual* at **business**)

usury *n.* 1. to engage in, practice ~ 2. to condemn; outlaw ~

utensils *n.* cooking, kitchen; household ~

utility *n.* ["company providing a public service"] a public ~ (have public ~ties been privatized in your country?)

utilize *v.* (more formal than *use*) 1. to ~ extensively, widely; fully 2. (D; tr.) to ~ as (she ~d the candlestick as a paperweight) 3. (D; tr.) to ~ for (she ~d the candlestick for holding down the papers) 4. (misc.) she ~d the candlestick (in order) to hold down the papers

utmost *n.* ["maximum effort"] to do one's ~ (we did our ~ to help)

utter *v.* (B) she ~ed a few words to them

utterance *n.* 1. (formal) to give ~ to 2. a prophetic; public ~

U-turn *n.* 1. to do, execute, make, perform a ~ 2. a complete, dramatic; sudden, unexpected 3. a ~ on (the government made a sudden dramatic ~ on foreign policy)

V

vacancy *n.* 1. to create a ~ 2. to have a ~ 3. to fill a ~ 4. a ~ for (we have a ~ in our sales department for a clerk) 5. (misc.) no ~ (the sign reads *no vacancy/ vacancies*)

vacation *n.* ["period of rest"] (esp. AE; CE has *holiday*) 1. to spend; take a ~ 2. to be on; go on ~ 3. an extended, long; paid; short ~ 4. a spring; summer; winter ~ 5. a ~ from 6. during a ~; on ~ (she was away on ~) ["period during which a college or university is closed"] 7. (BE) the long ~ USAGE NOTE: Soldiers and sailors go on *leave* or (esp. AE) on *furlough*; civilians go on *holiday* (BE) or on *vacation* (AE). British students go on *holiday* during the long *vacation/vac.*

vaccinate *v.* (D; tr.) to ~ against, for (to ~ smb. against/for a disease)

vaccination *n.* 1. to carry out, do a (mass) ~ (of the population) 2. (a) compulsory; mass ~ 3. a ~ against, for (to carry out a mass ~ against/for a disease)

vaccine *n.* 1. to administer, give a ~ 2. BCG; influenza; polio; Sabin; Salk; smallpox; tetanus; yellow-fever ~ 3. a ~ against, for (to carry out a mass ~ against/for a disease)

vacillate *v.* (D; intr.) to ~ between; in

vacuum *n.* 1. to create, leave, produce a ~ 2. to break; fill a ~ 3. a partial ~ 4. a power ~ 5. in a ~ (nothing can live in a ~)

vague *adj.* ~ about, as to (she was ~ about her plans and about when she would have decided)

vain *adj.* 1. ~ about, of (formal) (~ about one's appearance) 2. ~ to + inf. (it is ~ to protest) 3. (misc.) in ~ ("without success") (to work/protest in ~); to take the Lord's name in ~ ("to treat the Lord's name in a disrespectful manner")

valedictory *n.* ["farewell speech"] to deliver, give a ~

valid *adj.* 1. ~ for (~ for one year) 2. ~ to + inf. (is it ~ to say that Olympic athletes are amateurs?)

valise *n.* to fill, stuff; pack; unpack a ~

valley *n.* 1. a ~ between (high mountains) 2. in a ~ (they live down in the ~)

valor, valour *n.* 1. to demonstrate, display, show ~ 2. uncommon ~ 3. for ~ (to get a medal for ~) 4. of ~ (a person of great ~) 5. (misc.) (discretion is) the better part of ~

valuable *adj.* 1. very ~ 2. ~ as (knowing languages is very ~ as a way into other cultures) 3. ~ for; to 4. ~ to + inf. (it's ~ to know languages if you work in an export firm)

valuables *n.* to check (esp. AE); deposit one's ~

value I *n.* ["worth"]["monetary, numerical worth"] 1. to attach ~ to 2. to place, put, set a ~ on (it's impossible to put a cash ~ on friendship) 3. to acquire, take on; have, keep, retain (a) ~ 4. to have (a) ~

(of) (their holdings have little ~) 5. (a) great, high; inestimable ~ 6. (a) little; low ~ 7. a book; cash; face; market; nominal; re-sale; trade-in ~ (your car has a cash ~ of five thousand dollars) 8. entertainment; intrinsic; material; nuisance; rarity, scarcity; sentimental; strategic; symbolic, token ~ 9. (math.) an absolute; numerical; relative ~ 10. a fair ~ (the commission set a fair ~ of five million dollars on the property) 11. (economics) surplus ~ 12. (economics) present ~ 13. a (market) ~ falls, goes down; goes up, rises 14. at a certain ~ (at face ~) 15. in ~ (land tends to appreciate in ~ with time) 16. of ~ (to) (a discovery of great ~; it's of great ~ to know languages to anyone who works in an export firm) 17. (misc.) they took her story at face ~; to get ~ for (your) money; the street ~ (as of illegal drugs) ["principles, qualities"] 18. to cherish; foster ~s 19. basic; core; enduring; lasting; traditional ~s (a return to traditional ~s) 20. esthetic; family; human; moral; religious, spiritual; social ~s 21. middle-class; Victorian ~s ["misc."] 22. a set, system of ~es (see also *value system* at **system**)

value II *v.* 1. to ~ greatly, highly, very much 2. (d; tr.) to ~ as (to ~ smb. as a friend) 3. (d; tr.) to ~ at (to ~ a painting at five thousand pounds) 4. (D; tr.) to ~ for (to ~ smt. for sentimental reasons)

valve *n.* ["device that regulates flow"] 1. to close, shut; fit, install; open a ~ 2. to grind ~s 3. a ball; blocked; butterfly; check; exhaust; gate; globe; needle; safety; shunt; suction ~ ["membranous fold that permits body fluids to flow in one direction"] (anat.) 4. a heart ~ (the patient has a defective heart ~)

van I *n.* ["road vehicle"] 1. to drive a ~ 2. (BE) a breakdown ~ (BE also has *breakdown lorry, breakdown truck*; AE has *tow truck*) 3. (BE) a delivery, Transit (T) ~ (AE has *delivery truck, panel truck*) 4. a moving (AE), removal (BE) ~ ["rail vehicle"] 5. a guard's ~ (BE; AE has *caboose*) 6. a luggage ~ (BE; AE has *baggage car*) 7. a minivan (esp. AE)

van II *n.* ["vanguard"] in the ~

vandalism *n.* 1. to commit ~ 2. mindless ~ 3. an act of ~ (to commit an act of mindless ~)

vane *n.* a weather ~

vanguard *n.* in the ~ (of)

vanilla *adj.* plain ~ ("basic, no-frills") (colloq.) (our plain-vanilla plan is the cheapest but offers the fewest advantages)

vanish *v.* 1. to ~ completely 2. (D; intr.) to ~ from (to ~ from sight) 3. (D; intr.) to ~ into (to ~ into thin air) (see also *vanish without trace* at **trace I** *n.*)

vanity *n.* 1. to appeal to, flatter, tickle smb.'s ~ 2. personal; sheer ~

vantage point *n.* from a certain ~

vapor, vapour *n.* 1. to emit (a) ~ 2. water ~ 3. (a) ~ condenses, forms; rises 4. a cloud of ~

vapor trail, vapour trail *n.* to leave a ~ (high-flying aircraft leave ~s)

variable *n.* (math.) a dependent; independent; random ~

variance *n.* ["permission to bypass a regulation"] (legal) (AE; BE has *derogation*, esp. for EU regulations) 1. to grant a ~ 2. to apply for a ~ 3. a zoning ~ ["disagreement"] 4. at ~ with (a theory at ~ with the facts)

variation *n.* ["deviation, change"] 1. (a) considerable, great; slight; wide ~ 2. ~ according to, by; across; between; within 3. ~ from; to (day-to-day price ~ from ten to fifteen dollars) 4. ~ in (there is considerable ~ in price across and even within our range of products according to quality; there is wide ~ in/of opinion throughout our party) ["modified repetition of a theme"] 5. a ~ on a theme (the government's new position is merely a ~ on the same old theme)

varied *adj.* 1. highly, very ~ 2. ~ in (those birds are very ~ in color)

variety *n.* 1. to add, lend ~ to 2. (a) great; wide ~ 3. a limited ~ 4. in a ~ of (in a ~ of roles/colors) 5. (misc.) this is just a common-or-garden variety product (CE) = this is just a common-or-garden product (BE); ~ is the spice of life (proverb)

varnish *n.* 1. to apply ~ 2. nail ~ (BE; CE has *nail polish*) 3. a coat, layer of ~

varsity *n.* ["college or secondary-school team"] (AE) 1. to make ("be selected to join") the ~ 2. the junior ~ 3. on the ~ (we play on the ~)

vary *v.* 1. to ~ considerably, greatly; directly; inversely; slightly (does the proportion of people with lung cancer ~ directly with the proportion of people who smoke?) 2. (D; intr.) to ~ according to, by; across; between; within (prices ~ considerably across and even within our range of products according to quality) 3. (D; intr.) to ~ from; to (prices may ~ from ten to fifteen dollars) 4. (d; intr.) to ~ in (to ~ in size/price; they ~ in their opinions)

VAT *n.* (GB) 1. to attract ~ at seventeen percent 2. (misc.) VAT-registered (does your business have to be VAT-registered?)

vault I *n.* 1. a bank ~ 2. a family ~ (for burial) 3. (misc.) to keep one's valuables in a ~

vault II *v.* 1. (d; intr.) to ~ into (to ~ into prominence) 2. (d; intr.) to ~ over (he ~ed over the bar)

VCR *n.* to program a ~ (to record exactly what you want it to) [VCRs have now largely been replaced by DVD players or DVD recorders.]

veal *n.* 1. to roast ~ 2. roast ~ (see also *veal stew* at **stew**) 3. a leg; piece, slice; shoulder of ~

veer *v.* 1. (D; intr.) to ~ from; to (to ~ from one's course; to ~ to the right) 2. (P; intr.) to ~ across the field

veer away *v.* 1. (D; intr.) to ~ from; to (to ~ from one's course; to ~ to the right) 2. (P; intr.) to ~ across the field

veer off *v.* 1. (D; intr.) to ~ from; to (to ~ from one's course; to ~ to the right) 2. (P; intr.) to ~ across the field

vegetables *n.* 1. to cook; eat, have; grow ~ 2.

canned/tinned (BE); fresh; frozen; organic ~ 3. green; leafy; root ~ 4. garden ~ 5. boiled; cooked; raw; steamed; stir-fried ~

vegetation *n.* dense, lush, rank; sparse; subtropical; tropical ~

vehicle *n.* ["conveyance"] 1. to drive, operate; register a ~ 2. an all-purpose; amphibious; armored; half-track(ed); motor; passenger; recreational (esp. AE); re-entry ~ (see also **space vehicle**) 3. a hired (BE), rented, self-drive (BE) ~ ["means"] 4. a ~ for (a ~ for spreading propaganda; the film was nothing more than a ~ for a top movie star!) USAGE NOTE: Bear in mind also the AE expressions *ATV* ("All-Terrain Vehicle"), *Humvee* (a military "High-Mobility Multipurpose Wheeled Vehicle"), *SUV* ("Sport-Utility Vehicle").

veil *n.* 1. to draw a ~ (over) 2. to lift, raise a ~ 3. a bridal ~ 4. (misc.) under a ~ of mystery/secrecy; to take the ~ ("to become a nun") USAGE NOTE: A veil can cover the head and shoulders (as a nun's veil does) or the face (as a bridal veil does), or perhaps even both.

veiled *adj.* 1. thinly ~ (a thinly ~ reference) 2. (misc.) ~ in secrecy

vein *n.* ["blood vessel"] 1. to open a ~ 2. the jugular ~ 3. varicose ~s 4. a ~ stands out; throbs (a ~ in his forehead stands out and throbs when he's angry) ["mood"] ["manner"] 5. a happy; humorous; light; lighter; merry ~ 6. a gloomy; melancholy; serious ~ 7. a different; the same, a similar ~ 8. in a certain ~ (let's continue our discussion in a lighter ~) 9. (misc.) a rich ~ of humor runs through her works

velocity *n.* 1. to develop; gain, increase; lose ~ 2. to reach a ~ (to reach maximum ~) 3. to decrease, reduce; lose ~ 4. escape; high; low; maximum ~ 5. muzzle ~ 6. at a certain ~ (at the ~ of sound)

velvet *n.* (misc.) as smooth as ~

vendetta *n.* 1. to conduct, lead, pursue, wage a ~ 2. a personal ~ 3. a ~ against

vendor *n.* a fruit; street ~

veneer *n.* ["superficial gloss"] 1. to strip away, strip off a ~ 2. a polished; superficial, thin ~ 3. beneath a ~ of

venerate *v.* 1. (D; tr.) to ~ as (she is now ~d as an elder stateswoman) 2. (D; tr.) to ~ for (she is now ~d for being an elder stateswoman)

veneration *n.* 1. deep, profound ~ 2. ~ for (she is now held in profound ~ for being an elder stateswoman) 3. to hold smb. in ~ (she is now held in deep ~ as an elder stateswoman)

venetian blinds *n.* 1. to close, shut; lower; open; raise ~ 2. to install ~

vengeance *n.* 1. to exact, take, wreak ~ on, upon 2. to vow ~ 3. to seek ~ for 4. an act of ~ 5. ~ for; on (to take ~ on smb. for smt.) 6. (misc.) with a ~ ("to an extreme degree") (it started snowing with a ~)

venom *n.* ["poison"] 1. to neutralize ~ 2. snake ~ ["malice"] 3. to spew, spit, spout ~ 4. unadulterated, pure ~ 5. with ~

vent I *n.* ["opening"] 1. an air ~ 2. through a ~ ["outlet"] 3. to give ~ to (he gave ~ to his pent-up feelings)

vent II *v.* (d; tr.) to ~ on (to ~ one's fury on smt.)

ventriloquism *n.* to practice ~

venture I *n.* 1. to undertake a ~ 2. a business, commercial; collaborative, cooperative, joint ~ 3. (misc.) to join smb. in a ~ (see also *venture capital* at **capital**)

venture II *v.* (formal) 1. (E) I ~ to suggest that your whole idea is unworkable 2. (L; to) (rare) ("to express") she ~d (to us) that our whole idea might be unworkable 3. (P; intr.) to ~ into the unknown; to ~ out of doors

venue *n.* ["site of a trial"] (AE) 1. a change of ~ (her lawyer requested a change of ~) ["site"] (BE) 2. a ~ for (the best ~ for a pop concert) 3. at; in a ~

veracity *n.* (formal) to doubt, question smb.'s ~

veranda 1. see **porch** 1, 3 2. on a ~

verb *n.* 1. to conjugate, inflect; passivize a ~ 2. an auxiliary, helping; compound; copular (esp. BE), copulative, linking; defective; irregular; main; modal; phrasal; prepositional; phrasal-prepositional; regular; strong; weak ~ 3. an active; passive ~ 4. an intransitive; reflexive; transitive ~ 5. an imperfective; perfective ~ 6. ~s agree (with); ~s govern, take a case (a ~ agrees with its/the subject in number) 7. a ~ has aspect; mood; tense; voice 8. ~s have complements; objects USAGE NOTE: In BBI, *hold up* is called a compound verb. Elsewhere, it would be called a phrasal verb and *uphold* might be called a compound verb.

verdict *n.* ["law"] 1. to arrive at, reach a ~ 2. to announce; bring in, deliver, hand down (AE), render, return a ~ 3. to sustain, uphold a ~ (the higher court sustained the ~) 4. to overturn, quash, set aside a ~ 5. to appeal (AE), appeal against a ~ 6. a fair, just; unfair, unjust ~ 7. an adverse, unfavorable; directed; favorable; sealed; unanimous ~ 8. a ~ comes down 9. a ~ of guilty; or: a guilty ~; a ~ of not guilty; a ~ of not proven (Scottish law); an open ~; a ~ for the defendant; a ~ for the plaintiff (the jury brought in a ~ of not guilty) 10. a ~ that + clause (they appealed the court's ~ that fraud had been committed) 11. (misc.) to defy/ignore a ~ ["opinion"] 12. to give a ~ (have the critics given a ~ on the new play yet?) 13. a ~ on (the critics' ~ on the new play was that it was awful)

verge I *n.* ["brink"] 1. on the ~ of (he was on the ~ of a nervous breakdown) 2. (misc.) driven to the ~ of bankruptcy

verge II *v.* (d; intr.) to ~ on, upon (her actions ~d on the ridiculous)

verification *n.* 1. official; written ~ 2. to obtain; seek ~ 3. ~ of (the police obtained official ~ of her alibi but they could not obtain ~ of where the money had been deposited) 4. ~ that + clause (the police obtained official ~ that she had an airtight alibi)

verify *v.* 1. (L) the police ~fied that she had an airtight alibi 2. (Q) they could not ~ where the money had been deposited

vermin *n.* 1. to exterminate ~ 2. (misc.) infested with ~

vernacular *n.* in the ~ (to express oneself in the ~)

versatile *adj.* 1. very ~ 2. ~ at, in; with

versatility *n.* 1. to demonstrate, display, show ~ 2. great, remarkable ~ 3. ~ at, in; with

verse *n.* 1. to compose, write; memorize; recite ~(s) 2. to scan ~ 3. blank; free; heroic; light; macaronic; rhymed, rhyming; unrhymed ~ 4. in ~ (see also *chapter and verse* at **chapter**; *verse form* at **form I** *n.*)

versed *adj.* (cannot stand alone) (well) ~ in

version *n.* 1. to give one's ~ (of a story) 2. to corroborate smb.'s ~ (of an event) 3. an abridged, condensed; expurgated; watered-down ~ 4. an unabridged, uncut; unexpurgated ~ (an uncut ~ of a film) 5. an accepted, authorized, official ~ 6. a conflicting; different, differing ~ (the police heard conflicting ~s of the incident) 7. an unauthorized, unofficial ~ 8. a censored; uncensored (an uncensored ~ of the book was smuggled into the country) 9. an oral; written ~ 10. a film, movie (AE); stage ~ (of a novel) 11. a cover ~ (of a pop song) 12. (misc.) to bring out, produce a ~ (the band is going to bring out a cover ~ of a Beatles hit); a ~ appears, comes out (the unexpurgated ~ appeared only very recently)

vertebra *n.* a cervical; lumbar; sacral; thoracic ~

vessel *n.* ["ship, boat"] 1. to charter a ~ 2. to launch a ~ 3. a cargo; escort; fishing; naval; oceangoing, seagoing ~ (for more combinations, see **boat**; **ship**) ["for liquids"] 4. a drinking ~ (see also **blood vessel**)

vest I *n.* 1. a bulletproof; stab ("stab-proof"); life (AE) (CE has *life jacket*); string (BE) ~ 2. in a ~ USAGE NOTE: In BE, the basic meaning of *vest* is "undershirt"; in AE, it is "waistcoat".

vest II *v.* (formal) 1. (d; tr.) to ~ in (to ~ power in smb.) 2. (d; tr.) to ~ with (to ~ smb. with power)

vested *adj.* (cannot stand alone) 1. ~ in (the power to impose taxes is ~ in Congress; by the power ~ in me) 2. ~ with (Congress is ~ with the power to impose taxes)

vestiges *n.* ["traces"] 1. to lose all (remaining) ~ of 2. the last ~ of

vet *v.* (BE) 1. to ~ thoroughly 2. (D; tr.) to ~ for (all candidates are ~ted thoroughly for loyalty before appointment)

veteran *n.* a disabled; war ~ (to retrain disabled ~s) USAGE NOTE: *Veteran* 'ex-serviceman; ex-servicewoman' is AE when used by itself: a veteran who joined a veterans' organization to campaign for veterans' rights on Veterans' Day. *Veteran* 'ex-serviceman; ex-servicewoman' is now CE with appropriate modification: a war veteran who joined a war-veterans' organization to campaign for the rights of Korean/Korean-war veterans.

veto *n.* 1. to exercise, impose, use a ~ 2. to sustain a

~ 3. to override a ~ (Congress overrode the President's ~) 4. (US) a line-item; pocket; presidential ~ 5. (AE) (legal) a heckler's ~ 6. a ~ of, over 7. (misc.) European Union members have the power of ~ in certain cases; permanent members of the UN Security Council have the right of veto

vex *v.* 1. to ~ deeply, greatly 2. (R) it ~es me greatly to read such things in the newspapers; it ~es me that they are always late 3. (misc.) it ~es me greatly when I read such things in the newspapers; it ~es me when they come late

vexation *n.* 1. in ~ (she shouted in ~) 2. (misc.) my great ~ to read such things in the newspapers

vexed *adj.* (formal) 1. to become, get; grow ~ 2. deeply, greatly, very ~ 3. ~ about, at, with (we were ~ at the mix-up: I'm ~ at how such lies can be printed!; I'm ~ with them for coming late!) 4. ~ to + inf. (I am very ~ to read such things in the newspapers) 5. ~ that + clause (I am greatly ~ that they are always late 6. (misc.) I am very ~ when I read such things in the newspapers; I'm ~ when they come late)

vexing *adj.* 1. deeply, greatly, very ~ 2. ~ to + inf. (it is very ~ to read such things in the newspapers) 3. ~ that + clause (it is ~ that they are always late) 4. (misc.) it is ~ how such lies can be printed!; it's very ~ when they come late!

viability *n.* commercial, financial ~

vibes *n.* (slang) 1. to get (certain) ~ (from) 2. bad; good ~ (to get good ~ from smb.)

vibration *n.* 1. to feel a ~ 2. a slight; strong; weak ~ 3. ~ from; of

vice I *n.* 1. to stamp out ~ 2. legalized ~ 3. (misc.) poverty and ~ (see also *vice squad* at **squad**)

vice II (BE) see **vise**

vicinity *n.* 1. the close, immediate ~ 2. in the ~ (in the immediate ~ of the school)

vicious *adj.* ~ to + inf. (it was ~ of him to make such an accusation)

vicissitude *n.* the ~s of life

victim *n.* 1. to fall ~ to (they fell ~ to a swindler) 2. an innocent; unsuspecting ~ (of) (they were unsuspecting ~s of a swindler) 3. an accident; amnesia; disaster; earthquake; flood; hurricane; murder; rape; storm ~ 4. (misc.) a ~ of circumstance; the tsunami has already claimed many ~s

victorious *adj.* ~ in; over (~ in a long and bloody struggle; ~ over an enemy)

victory *n.* 1. to achieve, chalk up, gain, notch (up) (colloq.), pull off (colloq.), rack up (AE) (colloq.), score, sweep to, win; assure, clinch a ~ 2. a clear, clear-cut, decisive, outright, signal ~ 3. a landslide, lopsided (esp. AE), overwhelming, resounding, stunning, sweeping ~ 4. a famous; glorious; hard-won ~ 5. a bloodless; easy ~ 6. a narrow; upset ~ 7. a cheap; hollow; Pyrrhic ~ 8. a military; moral ~ 9. a ~ against (a ~ against overwhelming odds) 10. a ~ for (the result was a personal ~ for her) 11. a ~ in; over (a ~ in a long and bloody struggle; a ~

over an enemy) 12. (misc.) to snatch, wrest ~ from the jaws of defeat

video *n.* 1. to make, produce, record a ~ (of) 2. to play, run, show a ~ 3. to watch a ~ 4. a blank ~ 5. on ~ (to record on ~; the film came out on ~) (see also *video recorder* & *video-cassette recorder* at **recorder**; *video recording* at **recording**)

videotape *n.* see **video**

vie *v.* 1. (formal) (d; intr.) to ~ for; with (she had to ~ for the prize with formidable competitors) 2. (E) she ~d with formidable competitors to win the prize

view I *n.* ["opinion"]["outlook"] 1. to air, express, make known, present, put forth, put forward, voice a ~ 2. to harbor, hold a ~ 3. to advance, advocate, support; reject a ~ 4. to exchange ~s 5. to have; take a ~ 6. a cheerful, favorable, optimistic, rosy; positive; sound ~ (she expressed very optimistic ~s about the project) 7. a cynical; dim; grave, grim, pessimistic; slanted; unpopular ~ (she took a dim ~ of the matter) 8. a contrary, unfavorable; divergent; diverse; opposing ~ (they hold opposing ~s on various matters) 9. a extreme; strong ~ (they aired strong ~s about the candidates) 10. a conservative; liberal, progressive; moderate; radical; reactionary ~ (she presented moderate ~s at the rally) 11. an ideological; philosophical; political; world ~ (we do not support that political ~) 12. an advanced; modern ~ 13. a conventional, majority, orthodox, popular; prevailing, widespread; minority, unorthodox ~ 14. an old-fashioned; outdated, outmoded ~ 15. a ~ about, of, on, 16. a ~ that + clause (they disputed my ~ that taxes should be raised because they took the ~ that taxes should be reduced) 17. in smb.'s ~ (in my ~ the offer is unacceptable) ["sight"] 18. to get; have a ~ of 19. to block smb.'s; to hide from ~ 20. a beautiful, breathtaking, magnificent, majestic, marvelous, superb, wonderful ~ 21. a clear, unhampered, unimpaired ~ 22. a bird's-eye; close-up; full; full-length; panoramic; sectional ~ 23. in, within; on ~ (in full ~ of the public; the exhibition will be on ~ for a month) 24. (misc.) to come into; disappear, vanish from ~ ["perspective"] 25. an exploded ~ ["what can be seen"] 26. a rear ~ 27. a ~ across; from (the ~ across the lake from the window) 28. (misc.) a room with a (nice) ~ (of the ocean) ["aim"] 29. with a ~ (we entered talks with a ~ to reestablishing diplomatic relations) ["misc."] 30. in ~ of ("in consideration of"); of a ~ (they are of the ~ that taxes should be reduced); your ~ reflects your environment (see also *exchange of views* at **view I** *n.*; **point of view**; **viewpoint**)

view II *v.* ("to consider") 1. to ~ favorably; generally, widely; increasingly; unfavorably 2. (d; tr.) to ~ as (she was increasingly ~ed as a serious threat to the party leadership) 3. (d; tr.) to ~ with (to ~ recent developments with alarm)

viewer *n.* 1. a regular ~ (regular ~s of the channel will note some changes) 2. younger ~s (a TV program unsuitable for younger ~s)

viewpoint *n.* 1. a ~ that + clause (he explained his ~ that taxes should be increased) 2. from smb.'s ~ (from his ~, taxes should be increased) (see also **point of view**; **view I** 1–17)

vigil *n.* 1. to hold a ~; to keep (a) ~ 2. an all-night; bedside; lonely; prayer ~ 3. a ~ over

vigilance *n.* 1. to display, show; exercise ~ 2. constant; eternal ~ ("Eternal ~ is the price of liberty." – attributed to Wendell Phillips, 1852)

vigor, vigour *n.* 1. to regain one's ~ 2. to lose one's ~ 3. to sap smb.'s ~ 4. great ~ (he rejected the accusation with great ~) 5. the ~ to + inf. (does he have enough ~ to get everything done?) 6. (misc.) vim and ~

vile *adj.* (formal) ~ to + inf. (it was ~ of them to issue such a statement)

village *n.* 1. an agricultural, farming; fishing ~ 2. the global ~ (see also *village hall* at **hall**; the Usage Note for **town**)

village green *n.* on the ~

villain *n.* an arch, consummate ~ USAGE NOTE: In AE, *villain* is mostly literary or humorous; in colloq. BE it can still mean "criminal".

vim *n.* ["energy"] with ~ and vigor; full of ~ and vigor

vindictive *adj.* 1. ~ of (that was ~ of him) 2. ~ to + inf. (it was ~ of them to issue such a spiteful statement)

vinegar *n.* 1. balsamic; cider; malt; wine ~ 2. oil and ~ (as a vinaigrette salad dressing)

vintage *n.* ["period"] 1. of a certain ~ (a mansion of prewar ~; a car of ancient ~) (see also *vintage car* at **car**; *vintage port* at **port II** *n.*; *vintage wine* at **wine**)

viola *n.* 1. to play the ~ 2. to string, tune a ~ 3. for; on the ~ (a sonata for unaccompanied ~; a sonata for ~ and piano; to play smt. on the ~)

violation *n.* 1. to commit; constitute a ~ 2. a brazen, flagrant, gross; major ~ 3. a minor ~ 4. a human-rights ~ 5. a moving; parking; traffic ~ (by a motorist) 6. in ~ of (he acted in ~ of the law)

violence *n.* ["devastating force"] 1. to commit, resort to, use ~ 2. excessive ~ 3. domestic; sexual ~ 4. an act of ~ 5. ~ against ["distortion"] ["harm"] 6. to do ~ to (the decision does ~ to our whole judicial tradition) ["rioting"] 7. to incite, stir up ~ 8. to crack down on ~ 9. communal; continuing; ethnic; mob; racial; sporadic; urban; widespread ~ 10. ~ breaks out, erupts, flares up 11. ~ ceases, dies down 12. an eruption, flare-up, outbreak, outburst of ~ 13. a cessation; reduction of ~ 14. the amount, incidence, level of ~ (hoping for a reduction in the level of communal violence)

violin *n.* 1. to play the ~ 2. to string, tune a ~ 3. a first; second ~ 4. for; on the ~ (a sonata for unaccompanied ~; a sonata for ~ and piano; to play smt. on the ~) 5. (misc.) the principal first violinist of an orchestra is called its leader in BE and its concertmaster in AE

virgin *n.* a vestal ~ (historical)

virginity *n.* to keep one's ~; to lose one's ~

virtue *n.* ["admirable feature"] ["moral excellence"] 1. to have a ~ (our budget has the ~ of providing for a small surplus) 2. a cardinal ~ 3. (misc.) a paragon of ~; to extol the ~s of ["misc."] 4. by, in ~ of ("because of"); a woman of easy ~ (old-fashioned) ("a sexually promiscuous woman"); to make a ~ of necessity ("to make the best of smt. bad")

virus *n.* 1. to culture a ~ 2. to isolate a ~ 3. to come down with, get a ~ 4. a (common) cold; flu, influenza; intestinal; HIV/AIDS ~ 5. a computer ~ (a computer ~ is spreading) 6. a ~ is going around, spreading

visa *n.* 1. to apply for a ~ 2. to get, receive a ~ 3. to overstay; violate a ~ 4. to grant, issue a ~ 5. to extend; renew a ~ 6. to deny, refuse smb. a ~ 7. to cancel a ~ 8. an entry; exit; student; tourist; transit ~ 9. a ~ expires, runs out 10. a ~ for (do I need a ~ for that country?) 11. on a ~ (to enter a country on a student ~)

vise, vice *n.* ["tool for holding an object being worked on"] 1. to loosen; tighten a ~ 2. in a ~ USAGE NOTE: The AE form is *vise*; the BE form is *vice*; they have the same pronunciation.

visibility *n.* ["degree of being visible"] 1. clear, good; unlimited ~ 2. limited, poor, reduced; marginal; zero ~ (all planes were grounded because of poor ~) 3. (misc.) ~ is down to fifty yards ["exposure to publicity"] 4. high; increased; low; maximum ~

visible *adj.* 1. barely, hardly, scarcely; clearly, plainly ~ 2. ~ from; to (the house was not ~ from the road; not ~ to the naked eye) 3. (misc.) (fig.) a highly/very ~ public figure

vision *n.* ["sight"] 1. acute; clear; keen; normal; twenty-twenty ~ 2. blurred; deteriorating, failing; dim; double; impaired; tunnel ~ 3. binocular; peripheral ~ 4. to lose; regain one's ~ 5. (misc.) a field of ~ ("a visual field"); a ~ of the future; a ~ of loveliness ["foresight"] 6. the ~ to + inf. (she had the ~ to make wise investments several years ago) 7. of ~ (a person of great ~) 8. (misc.) tunnel ~ ("narrow horizons") ["imaginary picture"] 9. a ~ that + clause (she had a ~ that her country would be liberated) 10. in a ~ (to see smt. as if in a ~)

visit I *n.* 1. to make, pay a ~ (to) 2. to schedule a ~ (to) 3. to have a ~ from 4. to cancel; postpone a ~ 5. to cut short; prolong a ~ 6. a brief, flying, short; extended, lengthy, long ~ 7. a formal; friendly; home ~ (esp. BE; AE prefers *house call*); informal; official; return; state; unscheduled; weekend ~ 8. a ~ lasts (how long did his visit last?) 9. a ~ to (this is my first ~ to your country) 10. during a ~ 11. on a ~ (on a ~ to South America)

visit II *v.* 1. (obsol. or formal) (d; tr.) to ~ on (the Lord's anger was ~ed on the people) 2. (AE) (d; intr.) to ~ with ("to meet up and chat with") (she likes to ~ with the neighbors on the front porch)

visitor *n.* 1. to greet, welcome; introduce a ~ 2. to

get; have, receive a ~ (this town doesn't get many ~s; we had some ~s this weekend) 3. a frequent ~ 4. a weekend ~ 5. (BE) a prison ~ 6. (BE) a health ~ (AE has *public-health nurse*) 7. a ~ from (~s from abroad) 8. a ~ to (~s to our city)

vista *n.* ["view"] 1. to open up new ~s (of the future) 2. a broad, wide ~

visualize *v.* 1. to ~ easily, readily 2. (d; tr.) to ~ as (I cannot ~ him as a famous star) 3. (J) I cannot ~ him becoming a famous star 4. (K) I cannot ~ his becoming a famous star 5. (Q) I could not ~ how he could become a famous star

vital *adj.* 1. ~ for, to (their aid is ~ to/for our success) 2. ~ to + inf. (it is ~ for us to be prepared for any eventuality) 3. ~ that + clause; subj. (it is ~ that we ¬be/should be/are (BE)¬ prepared for any eventuality)

vitamins *n.* 1. to be rich in ~ 2. to contain ~ 3. to take ~ 4. multivitamins (see also *vitamin deficiency* at **deficiency**)

vocabulary *n.* 1. to command a ~ 2. to build, develop, enlarge one's ~ 3. an extensive, huge, large, rich ~ 4. a limited, meager, restricted, small ~ 5. a basic; essential; technical ~ 6. an active; passive ~ 7. a ~ for (he has the ~ essential for his needs) 8. when did the word "surrender" enter your ~? (see also *item of vocabulary = vocabulary item* at **item**)

vocation *n.* 1. to have a ~ 2. a genuine, real ~ 3. (misc.) to have missed one's (true) ~ ("not to have chosen an occupation or vocation at which one is particularly adept"); to have a (genuine) ~ for the priesthood = to have a (genuine) ~ to the priesthood = to have a (genuine) ~ to be a priest = to have a (genuine) ~ as a priest

vogue *n.* ["popularity"]["current fashion"] 1. to be the ~ (home computers are the latest ~) 2. to be in ~; to come into ~ (home computers have come into ~) 3. to enjoy, have (BE) a ~ 4. to go out of ~ 5. the current; latest ~ 6. a ~ for (the latest ~ is for home computers) 7. (misc.) to be all the ~

voice I *n.* ["sound produced by vocal cords"] 1. to raise one's ~ (in anger to to make oneself heard) 2. to drop, lower one's ~ 3. to keep one's ~ down 4. to disguise one's ~ 5. to lose one's ~ 6. a friendly, gentle, good, kind, pleasant, soft; mellifluous, melodious, sweet ~ 7. a clear; firm, steady ~ 8. a deep; mellow; resonant; rich ~ 9. a high; high-pitched; low, low-pitched ~ 10. a booming; loud; stentorian; strident; thundering ~ 11. a quaking, quivering, shaking, shaky, trembling ~ 12. a guttural; hoarse; husky; muffled; nasal; subdued ~ 13. a gruff, harsh, raucous; shrill ~ 14. a ~ bellows; booms out; breaks, cracks; carries; changes; drones away/on; drops, falls; quivers, shakes, trembles; rises 15. in a certain ~ (in a loud ~) 16. (misc.) (to shout) at the top of one's ~; ventriloquists throw their ~; actors must learn to project their ~ (see also *voice mail* at **mail I** *n.*; *voice recognition* at **recognition**; *tone of voice* at

tone) ["expression"] 17. to give ~ to ["verbal form indicating the relation of the verb to its subject"] 18. the active; middle; passive ~ ["influence"] 19. to have a ~ in smt. ["misc."] 20. an inner ~ ("conscience"); a lone dissenting ~; the ~ of reason; the still small ~ (of God) USAGE NOTE: *Hearing voices* may of course be perfectly normal. But the phrase is also used about auditory hallucinations, and is then like *hearing things* and is analogous to *seeing things* for visual hallucinations.

voice II *v.* (B) she ~d her concerns to us

void I *adj.* ["devoid"] 1. (cannot stand alone) ~ of 2. (misc.) null and ~ (to declare smt. null and ~)

void II *n.* 1. to fill a ~ 2. to leave a ~ 3. an aching, painful ~ 4. a ~ in

volatile *adj.* highly, very ~

volcano *n.* 1. an active, live; dead, extinct; dormant, inactive; intermittent ~ 2. a ~ erupts 3. a ~ spews lava 4. (misc.) the mouth of a ~

volition *n.* ["act of choosing"] of, on one's own ~ (they agreed of their own ~; to act on one's own ~)

volley I *n.* ["simultaneous discharge of weapons"] 1. to fire a ~ ["tennis ball in flight"] 2. (to hit/return a ball) on the ~

volley II *v.* (P; tr.) she ~ed the ball across the court

volleyball *n.* to play ~

voltage *n.* 1. to step up (the) ~ 2. high; low ~ (at a very high ~) (see also *a voltage surge = a surge in voltage* at **surge I** *n.*)

volume *n.* ["loudness"] 1. to amplify; increase, turn up the ~ 2. to decrease, turn down the ~ 3. at a certain ~ (at full ~) ["space occupied in three dimensions"] 4. molecular ~ ["book"] 5. a rare; single ~ (Shakespeare's complete works ¬in a single/in one¬ ~, whereas they often run to several ~s!) 6. a companion ~ (this work is a companion ~ to our first dictionary) 7. bound ~s (of a periodical) 8. (misc.) to speak ~s ("to imply a lot") (a single glance can speak ~s)

volunteer I *n.* 1. to recruit ~s 2. a ~ for (I recruited several ~s for the job of tutor)

volunteer II *v.* 1. (D; intr.) to ~ as (she ~ed as a tutor) 2. (D; intr.) to ~ for (she ~ed for the job of tutor) 3. (E) she ~ed to be a tutor

vomiting *n.* 1. to cause, induce ~ 2. projectile ~

voodoo, voodooism *n.* to practice ~

vortex *n.* to draw, suck into a ~

vote I *n.* ["collective opinion as determined by voting"] 1. to have, take a ~ on (a motion) 2. to put a motion to a ~; to bring a motion to a ~ 3. to influence, swing a ~ (recent events swung the ~ in our favor; the press can influence the ~) 4. to count, tabulate, tally; recount the ~ 5. a close; free (as in Parliament); lopsided (esp. AE); majority; No; overwhelming; popular; solid; unanimous; Yes ~ 6. a straw; voice; write-in ~ 7. a ~ on (a ~ on an issue) 8. (esp. BE) a ~ to + inf. (we took a ~ to adjourn) 9. by a ~ (by a unanimous ~) 10. a ~ of censure; confidence; no confidence; thanks 11.

(misc.) to fix, rig a ~; the ~ went ¬in our favor/ against us¬ ["individual expression of opinion, ballot"] 12. to cast a ~ 13. to change, switch one's ~ 14. to get, receive smb.'s ~ (you'll never get my ~) 15. the casting (BE), deciding ~ (to cast the deciding ~; if there's a tie the chairman has the deciding ~) 16. a write-in ~ 17. a ~ against; for; on (to cast a ~ for a proposal) 18. the ~s to + inf. (we have enough ~s to carry the state) ["group of voters"] 19. the bloc; conservative; floating (BE) ("unattached"); independent; labor; liberal; undecided ~ (the bloc ~ of certain groups made their victory certain) ["voters as a group"] 20. to deliver the ~(s); to get out the ~ (the party machine delivered the ~s; a series of interesting debates helped to get out the ~) 21. a heavy; light ~ ["right to vote, franchise, suffrage"] 22. to get, receive; give, grant the ~ (in some countries women got the ~ only after World War I)

vote II *v.* 1. to ~ No; overwhelmingly; solidly; Yes 2. (C; usu. used without *for*) Congress ~d him a pension 3. (D; intr.) to ~ against; for (to ~ against a bill by 12 to three) 4. (d; tr.) to ~ into (to ~ smb. into office) 5. (D; intr.) to ~ on, upon (to ~ on a resolution) 6. (d; tr.) to ~ out of (to ~ smb. out of office) 7. (E) Parliament ~d to approve the report 8. (L; subj.) Parliament ~d that the report ¬be/should be¬ approved 9. (N; used with an adjective/noun) she was ~d most likely to succeed 10. (misc.) to ~ by a show of hands or by a secret ballot (see also *the right to vote* at **right III** *n.*); to ~ smb. onto a committee and smb. else off the committee; most MPs ~d with their party but some rebelled

voter *n.* 1. an absentee; floating (BE), swing ("unattached"); independent; registered; undecided ~ 2. a ~ casts a vote; registers (to vote) (see also *voter registration* at **registration**)

voting *n.* absentee; bloc; tactical ~ (see also *voting irregularities = irregularities in voting* at **irregularity**; *voting machine* at **machine**)

voting lists *n.* to tamper with ~

vouch *v.* 1. (d; intr.) to ~ for (I can ~ for the truth of her statement) 2. (L) I can ~ that her statement is true

voucher *n.* 1. an education; gift (BE); hotel; luncheon (BE; AE has *meal ticket*); travel; tuition (AE) ~ 2. a ~ for

vouchsafe *v.* (formal or ironic; rare) 1. (B) ("to grant") she ~d me a word 2. (E) ("to condescend") she ~d to help

vow I *n.* 1. to make, take a ~ 2. to fulfill, keep one's ~ 3. to break, repudiate, violate a ~ 4. a formal, sacred, solemn ~ 5. clerical; marriage; monastic; religious ~s (priests take religious ~s) 6. a ~ to + inf. (she made a solemn ~ not to drink again) 7. a ~ that + clause (she made a solemn ~ that she would not drink again) 8. (misc.) to exchange; renew marriage ~s; a ~ of silence

vow II *v.* 1. (D; tr.) to ~ to (she was ~d to secrecy) 2. (E) she ~ed not to drink again 3. (L; to) she ~ed (to them) that she would not drink again

vowel *n.* 1. to articulate, pronounce a ~ 2. a back; closed; front; high; lax; long; middle; nasal; open; reduced; rounded; short; stressed; tense; unstressed ~ (see also *vowel sound* at **sound II** *n.*)

voyage *n.* ["journey"] 1. to begin, embark on, go on, set off on, start on a ~ 2. to make, undertake a ~ 3. a long; maiden; ocean, sea; round-the-world; short; space ~ 4. a ~ around (a ~ around the world) 5. a ~ from; to (a ~ to the islands) 6. a ~ through (a ~ through the Panama Canal) 7. during; throughout a ~ 8. on a ~ (they were on a ~ to Europe) 9. (misc.) the ~ out; the ~ back/home; bon ~! (have a) safe journey!

V-sign *n.* 1. to give, make the/a ~ (showing triumph or encouragement) 2. (BE) to give, make a/the ~ (showing vulgar contempt or rage) USAGE NOTE: The favorable V-sign is made with the palm outwards and the hand held steady. The vulgar V-sign is made with the back of the hand outwards and the hand typically moved up and down rapidly.

vulgar *adj.* ~ to + inf. (it's ~ to spit in public)

vulnerable *adj.* 1. very ~ 2. ~ to

vulture *n.* 1. ~s feed on carrion 2. (misc.) ~ are supposed to gather near the dead or dying (also fig.)

vying see **vie**

W

wad *n.* (slang) (AE) ["a large amount, as of money"] to shoot one's ~ ("to spend all of one's money" or "to make a last-ditch effort")

waddle *v.* (P; intr.) to ~ across the road

wade *v.* 1. (d; intr.) to ~ across (to ~ across a stream) 2. (d; intr.) to ~ into (to ~ into a river) 3. (d; intr.) to ~ into ("to attack") (the speaker ~d into the opposing candidate) 4. (d; intr.) to ~ through (to ~ through deep water) 5. (d; intr.) to ~ through ("to read through with difficulty") (to ~ through a long report) (see also *wading pool* at **pool II** *n.*)

wade in *v.* (colloq.) (D; intr.) to ~ with (she ~d in with a few choice comments)

waft *v.* (P; intr.) an aroma ~ed in from the kitchen

wage I *n.* 1. to draw, earn, get, receive a ~ 2. to pay a ~ 3. to boost, increase, raise ~s 4. to cut, reduce, slash ~s 5. to freeze ~s 6. to attach, garnishee ~s 7. to withhold smb.'s ~s 8. a decent, living; minimum; high; low; subsistence ~ (to pay workers a decent ~) 9. an annual, yearly; daily; hourly; monthly; weekly ~ 10. a union ~ 11. (misc.) the union successfully negotiated (for) a higher ~ (see also **wages**)

wage II *v.* (D; tr.) to ~ against (to ~ a campaign/war against smoking)

wager I *n.* 1. to lay, make, place a ~ on 2. a ~ that + clause (she made a ~ that her team would win)

wager II *v.* 1. (D; tr.) to ~ on (he ~ed a month's salary on that horse) 2. (L; may have a personal object) he ~ed (me) that it would rain 3. (O; can be used with one object, two objects, or two objects + *that*-clause) we ~ed ten dollars; we ~ed him ten dollars; we ~ed him ten dollars that it would rain

wages *n.* 1. see **wage I** 2. meager; starvation ~

waggon (BE) see **wagon**

wagon *n.* 1. a station ~ (AE; BE has *estate car*; old-fashioned BE also has *shooting brake*) 2. a tea ~ (AE; BE has *tea trolley*) 3. (esp. AE) a paddy, patrol ~ (for other equivalents, see **car** 17; CE also has *black maria*) 4. (AE) a welcome ~ ("a car sent with gifts from local merchants to a family that has just moved into a neighborhood") 5. a Conestoga; covered ~ 6. a goods ~ (BE; AE has *freight car*) 7. (colloq.) (AE) a chuck ("food") ~ (on a ranch) 8. (misc.) on the ~ ("pledged not to drink alcoholic drinks")

waist *n.* 1. a slender, slim ~ 2. around, round the ~ (she wore a belt around her ~) 3. (misc.) (see also *waist-high* at **high I** *adj.*; *stripped to the waist* at **strip II** *v.*)

wait I *n.* 1. to lie in ~ for 2. to have a (long) ~ for (we had a long ~ for the bus) 3. a long; short ~ 4. quite a ~ (see also *worth the wait* at **worth I** *adj., prep.*)

wait II *v.* 1. (BE) (d; intr.) to ~ at (to ~ at table) (cf.

3) 2. (D; intr.) to ~ for (they ~ed for me; they could hardly ~ for me to leave!) 3. (AE) (d; intr.) to ~ on (to ~ on tables) (cf. 1) 4. (d; intr.) to ~ on, upon ("to attend to") (to ~ on smb. hand and foot) 5. (E) we are ~ing to go; I can't ~ to find out the results! 6. (misc.) to keep smb. ~ing; they ~ed until she returned; ~ and see; ~ a minute/moment/second (see also *a wait-and-see attitude* at **attitude**; *wait with bated breath* at **breath**)

waiter *n.* 1. to call a ~ over 2. to catch a waiter's eye 3. to give a ~ one's order 4. to tip a ~ 5. a head; wine ~ 6. a ~ takes smb.'s order

waiting *n.* (GB; on a traffic sign) No Waiting (US has *No Standing* or *No Stopping*)

waitress *n.* see **waiter** 1–4, 6

wait up *v.* (D; intr.) to ~ for (they ~ed up for her until she returned = they ~ed up for her to return)

waiver *n.* to agree to, sign a ~

wake I *n.* ["vigil over a corpse"] to hold a ~

wake II *n.* ["aftermath"] in the ~ (of) (war brings misery in its ~; security was beefed up in the ~ of the explosion)

wake III *v.* 1. (D; intr.) to ~ from, out of (she woke from a deep sleep) 2. (d; intr., tr.) to ~ to (I woke to bright sunlight; it woke the community to the danger of pollution; "I woke to black flak and the nightmare fighters" – Randall Jarrell, 1914–65, "The Death of the Ball Turret Gunner") 3. (E) they woke to find the house in flames 4. (s) I woke refreshed

wake up *v.* 1. (D; intr., tr.) to ~ from, out of (she woke up from a deep sleep) 2. (d; intr., tr.) to ~ to (the community must ~ to the danger of pollution!) 3. (E) they woke up to find the house in flames; I woke up only to find it had all been a dream! 4. (s) I woke up refreshed 5. (misc.) to ~ with a start (see also *wake-up call* at **call I** *n.*)

walk I *n.* ["journey on foot"] 1. to have (BE), take a ~ 2. to take smb. for a ~ (BE also has: to take smb. a long ~ round the grounds) 3. to go for, go on a ~ 4. a brisk; easy; leisurely; long; nature; short; sponsored (money-raising) ~ (to take a brisk ~) 5. a ~ lasts, takes (the ~ from here to school takes only 5 minutes) 6. a ~ from; to (we took a ~ from our house to the center of town; it's an easy 5-minute ~ from here to school) 7. at a ~ (we set off at a brisk ~) 8. during, on a ~ (see also **walk II** *v.* for more prepositions used also with **walk I** *n.*) ["profession"] ["class"] 9. from ¬every ~/all ~s¬ of life

walk II *v.* 1. to ~ fast; slow 2. (d; intr.) to ~ across (to ~ across the street) 3. (d; intr.) to ~ along (to ~ along a river bank) 4. (d; intr.) to ~ around, round (to ~ around a house) 5. (d; intr.) to ~ by, past (to ~ past the library) 6. (d; intr.) to ~ down; up (to ~ down the street and then back up it again) 7. (D; intr., tr.) to ~ from; to, towards (we ~ed from the park to the station; I ~ed her to the library; I ~ed my bicycle to the garage) 8. (d; intr.) to ~ into (to ~ into a room; to ~ into an ambush; to ~ into a punch) 9. (d; intr.) to ~ on, over (don't ~ on the wet floor!; don't ~ on the grass!) 10. (d; intr.) to ~ out of (to ~ out of a meeting) 11. (d; intr.) to ~ (all) over ("to treat badly") (they ~ed all over us) 12. (d; intr.) to ~ through (to ~ through the park; to ~ through a puddle; she was so good she just ~ed through the exams!) 13. (d; tr.) to ~ smb. through ("to help with smt. complicated") (she ~ed me through the procedure) 14. (misc.) she ~ed her dog in the park; they ~ed off the job in protest against the long hours; they ~ed me home; to ~ up and down/back and forth; they like to go ~ing (see also **walking**)

walkabout *n.* (colloq.) ["a walk through a crowd by an important person"] (BE) 1. to do, go on a ~ (the Queen went on a ~ after the ceremony) ["misc."] 2. the Queen went ~ after the ceremony; my camera seems to have gone ~ ("my camera seems to be missing")

walk away *v.* 1. (D; intr.) to ~ from (he ~ed away from me without saying a word; to ~ from an accident ("to survive an accident unhurt"); you can't just ~ from your responsibilities!) 2. (d; intr.) to ~ with ("to win") (she ~ed away with all the top prizes)

walk down *v.* (d; intr.) to ~ from; to (they ~ed down to the river bank)

walker *n.* a tightrope ~

walk in *v.* 1. (d; intr.) to ~ from (they ~ed in from the street) 2. (d; intr.) to ~ on ("to come across unexpectedly") (I ~ed in on an interesting scene)

walking *n.* 1. heel-and-toe ~ 2. power ~ (see also *at a walking pace* at **pace I** *n.*)

walking papers *n.* (colloq.) (AE) ["notice of dismissal"] to give people their ~ (BE has *marching orders*)

walk off *v.* (d; intr.) to ~ with ("to win") (she ~ed off with first prize)

walkout *n.* 1. to stage a ~ 2. to end a ~ 3. a sympathy ~

walk out *v.* 1. (D; intr.) to ~ on ("to leave") (she ~ed out on her husband) 2. (D; intr.) to ~ onto (they ~ed out onto the veranda)

walk over *v.* (d; intr.) to ~ from; to (he ~ed over to her table; she ~ed over from her house to our house)

walk up *v.* (d; intr.) to ~ to (I ~ed up to them and said a few words)

wall *n.* 1. to build, erect, put up a ~ 2. to demolish, tear down a ~ 3. to climb, scale a ~ 4. to paint; panel; paper; plaster a ~ 5. to line a ~ (to line a ~ with bookshelves) 6. a high; low; solid, thick ~ 7. a brick; fire; inside; load-bearing; outside; retaining ~; seawall; stone; supporting ~ 8. a (Chinese) ~ between (also fig.) (the (Chinese) ~ (of strict separation) between church and state) 9. against the ~ (they were lined up/stood up against the ~ and shot) 10. on a ~ (there were several pictures on the ~) 11. (misc.) we had our backs to the ~ ("we

were in a desperate situation"); (slang) to drive smb. up the ~ ("to frustrate smb. completely")

wallet *n.* 1. a leather ~ 2. (misc.) his ~ was bulging with banknotes

wall off *v.* (D; tr.) to ~ from

wallop *n.* (colloq.) ["force"] 1. to pack a ~ (the winds packed a real ~) ["blow"] 2. to give smb. a ~ (on)

wallow *v.* (d; intr.) to ~ in (to ~ in the mud; to ~ in self-pity)

wallpaper *n.* 1. to hang, put up ~ 2. to scrape (off), take off ~ 3. a roll of ~

waltz I *n.* 1. to perform, play a ~ 2. to dance, do a ~ (see also *waltz time* at **time I** *n.*)

waltz II *v.* 1. (colloq.) (d; intr.) to ~ through ("to complete with ease") (she was so good she just ~ed through the exams!) 2. (P; intr.) they ~ed around the room together

waltz off *v.* 1. (d; intr.) to ~ with (she ~ed off with first prize) 2. (P) "You ... ~ed me off to bed Still clinging to your shirt." – Theodore Roethke, "My Papa's Waltz" (1948)

wan *adj.* pale and ~

wand *n.* 1. to wave a ~ 2. a magic ~

wander *v.* 1. (d; intr.) ("to stray") to ~ from (to ~ from the subject) 2. (P; intr.) we ~ed across the park; they ~ed along the river bank; she ~ed into the village; he ~ed through the town 3. (misc.) his mind is ~ing, poor man!

wander away *v.* (D; intr.) to ~ from (the children ~ed away from their parents)

wanderer *n.* a homeless ~

wane I *n.* ["decrease"] ["period of decrease"] on the ~ (the moon is on the ~; the Roman Empire was on the ~ for several centuries before it fell)

wane II *v.* 1. (D; intr.) to ~ into (to ~ into insignificance) 2. (misc.) to wax and ~

wangle *v.* (colloq.) 1. (C) could you ~ an invitation for me?; or: could you ~ me an invitation? 2. (D; tr.) to ~ from, out of (she ~d an invitation out of them) 3. (misc.) to ~ one's way into a party

want I *n.* ["need"] 1. to fill, meet, satisfy a ~ 2. to minister to smb.'s ~s 3. a long-felt ~ 4. for ~ of (to die for ~ of medical care) 5. in ~ of (in ~ of a job) ["poverty"] 6. in ~ (to live in ~)

want II *v.* 1. to ~ badly, desperately, very much (they ~ed very badly to see us) 2. (d; intr.) to ~ for ("to be in need of") (they will never ~ for anything) 3. (D; tr.) ("to seek") to ~ for (he is ~ed for murder in three states) 4. (D; tr.) ("to desire") to ~ for (we ~ you for our team) 5. (E) ("to desire") I ~ to help 6. (E) ("ought") you ~ to think carefully about what you say to them 7. (BE) (G) ("to be in need of") your shirts ~ mending; the house ~s painting; her hair ~s cutting 8. (H; no passive) ("to desire") they ~ us to finish the job today 9. (J) I ~ them singing in tune! 10. (M) ("to desire") I ~ them to be kept busy at all times 11. (N; used with an adjective, past participle) ("to desire") I ~ them busy at all times; I ~ them kept busy at all times; I ~ them ready in one hour; she ~s the house painted tomorrow 12. (s; used with a past participle) (BE) (nonstandard) your shirts ~ mended 13. (misc.) I ~ them out of the house by tomorrow; (esp. AE) they ~ out of the deal but we ~ in (on it)!; your present is just what I've always ~ed!; all I've ever ~ed is your love! USAGE NOTE: It should be noted that the construction *want + for + to + inf.* can be acceptable in CE as in – *what they want is for us to finish the job today*; *they want very much for us to finish the job today.* In addition, a construction such as *they want very much that we should finish the job today* (Pattern L) is acceptable in CE, but typically only when a modifier such as *very much* appears between *want* and the dependent clause introduced by *that.* Nevertheless, *want* does appear in Pattern L in certain regional varieties of English and sometimes in literature: "How long ago Hector took off his plume, Not wanting that his little son should cry" – Frances Cornford (1886–1960), "Parting in Wartime"

wanted *adj.* ["sought"] 1. ~ by (he is ~ by the police) 2. ~ for (he is ~ed (by the police) for murder in three states)

wanting *adj.* ["deficient, lacking"] 1. ~ in 2. (misc.) to be found ~

wapiti *n.* see **elk**

war I *n.* 1. to conduct, fight, wage ~ against, with 2. to make ~ (Make Love, Not War!) 3. to declare ~ on; to go to ~ over 4. to drift into; plunge into (a) ~ 5. to provoke (a) ~ 6. to escalate, step up a ~ 7. to avert (a) ~ 8. to survive (a) ~ 9. to lose; win a ~ 10. to ban, outlaw ~ 11. to end a ~ 12. an all-out, full-scale, total; global, world ~ 13. a limited, local ~ 14. (a) civil; class; guerrilla; revolutionary ~ 15. a cold; hot, shooting ~ 16. a defensive; offensive ~ 17. a holy, religious ~ 18. a trade ~ 19. an atomic, nuclear, thermonuclear; conventional ~ 20. star ~s 21. a gang; price ~ 22. a ~ of aggression; attrition; extermination; nerves 23. a ~ breaks out; rages; spreads (the ~ spread to the north) 24. an act of ~ 25. a ~ against; between (a ~ against an aggressor; a ~ between former allies) 26. a ~ on (a ~ on drugs/poverty) 27. at ~ (with) (to be at ~ with one's neighbors) 28. during, throughout a ~ 29. in ~ (all's fair in love and ~) 30. (misc.) a theater of ~; a state of ~ (to be in a state of ~ with a country) (see also *the brink of war* at **brink**; *war crime* at **crime**; *war criminal* at **criminal**; *war footing* at **footing**; *war hero* at **hero**; **prisoner of war**)

war II *v.* 1. (d; intr.) to ~ against, with (to ~ with one's neighbors) 2. (d; intr.) to ~ over (to ~ over disputed territory)

ward *n.* ["hospital room"] 1. an emergency; maternity; obstetrics; pediatrics; private (BE) ("not under the National Health Service") ~ 2. in, on a ~ (to work in the emergency ~; who works in/on this ~?) (see also **ward round**; *ward sister* at **sister**)

warden *n.* 1. a prison ~ (AE; BE has *governor*) 2.

(BE) a traffic ~ 3. an air-raid ~ USAGE NOTE: An AE *prison warden* should not be confused with a BE *prison warder*, who in AE is a *prison guard.*

wardrobe *n.* ["clothes"] 1. an autumn (esp. BE), fall (AE); spring; summer; winter ~ 2. (misc.) I bought a whole new ~ for the cruise

ward round *n.* to do, make a ~ (the consultant will be making his ward rounds about now)

ware *n.* earthenware; glassware USAGE NOTE: *Ware* is often used in naming goods of a certain type. See also **wear I** *n.*

warehouse *n.* a bonded ~

wares *n.* to display; hawk, peddle one's ~

warfare *n.* 1. to engage in ~ 2. armored; guerrilla; naval; trench ~ 3. conventional; push-button ~ 4. atomic, nuclear, thermonuclear ~ 5. bacteriological, germ; biological; chemical ~ 6. desert; jungle; tribal ~ 7. all-out; class; global; total ~ 8. economic; psychological; modern ~ 9. ~ against; between (~ against an aggressor; ~ between former allies)

warhead *n.* 1. to fire, launch a ~ 2. a conventional; multiple; nuclear ~

warm *v.* (d; intr.) to ~ to ("to begin to like") (I was just ~ing to the task)

warming *n.* global ~

warmth *n.* 1. body ~ 2. ~ spreads

warm up *v.* 1. (D; intr.) to ~ for (the players were ~ing up for the game) 2. (d; intr.) to ~ to (after a few drinks he ~ed up to the other guests)

warn *v.* 1. (D; intr., tr.) to ~ about, against, of (they ~ed me about his bad temper; I ~ed her against smoking; the police ~ed us of the pickpockets; the newspapers are ~ing of a severe winter) 2. (D; tr.) to ~ off (esp. BE) (the police ~ed us off the landlord's property; I ~ed her off smoking) 3. (H) they ~ed him to be careful; I ~ed her not to smoke 4. (L; typically has a personal object) they warned him that he should be careful; I warned her that she shouldn't smoke; the newspapers are ~ing (their readers) that the winter will be severe

warn away *v.* (D; tr.) to ~ from (the police ~ed us away from the burning building)

warning *n.* 1. to give, issue, send, sound a ~ 2. to shout a ~ 3. to get, receive; have; heed a ~ 4. to disregard, ignore a ~ 5. a cryptic; dire; tacit; timely ~ 6. (an) advance; fair ~ 7. ample, plenty of ~ 8. a storm ~ 9. a ~ comes (your ~ came just in time!) 10. a word of ~ (let me give you a word of ~, young man: don't mess with me!) 11. a ~ about (they gave me a ~ about his bad temper) 12. a ~ against (a ~ against smoking) 13. a ~ to (a ~ to all; let this ¬be/serve as¬ a ~ to you!) 14. a ~ to + inf. (a ~ to her not to smoke) 15. a ~ that + clause (they issued a ~ to her that she shouldn't smoke) 16. without ~ 17. (misc.) (formal) take ~: something awful may happen to you if you don't stop smoking! (see also *warning light* at **light II** *n.*; *warning signal* at **signal I** *n.*)

warpath n. (usu. colloq. and humorous) 1. to go on the ~ 2. to be on the ~ (they are on the ~ again)

warrant I n. 1. to issue a ~ (the court issued a search ~) 2. (AE) to swear out a ~ against smb. 3. to serve a ~ on (a ~ was served on her) 4. a bench; death; search ~ (to sign smb.'s death ~) (also fig.) 5. a ~ for (the court issued a ~ for her arrest) 6. a ~ to + inf. (the police have a ~ to search the house) 7. (misc.) a ~ is out for her arrest (see also **arrest warrant**)

warrant II v. 1. (K) ("to justify") the insult hardly ~ed his behaving like that! 2. (L) ("to guarantee") I cannot ~ that the coins are genuine 3. (formal and rare) (M) I cannot ~ the coins to be genuine

warranty n. 1. to give, offer, provide a ~ 2. an implied; limited; special; written ~ 3. a ~ expires, runs out; lasts 4. a ~ on (a two-year ~ on a new car) 5. under ~ (the new car is still under ~)

warren n. a rabbit ~

wart n. to remove a ~

wartime n. during, in ~

wary adj. ~ of (be ~ of strangers)

wash I n. ["laundry"] 1. to do the ~ 2. to hang out the ~ (to dry) 3. the weekly ~ (see also **laundry** n. 1–3) ["installation for washing"] 4. a car ~

wash II v. 1. (d; intr.) to ~ against (the waves ~ed against the pier) 2. (D; tr.) to ~ for (would you please ~ the dishes for me?) 3. (d; tr.) to ~ off, out of (she ~ed the marks off the wall; I ~ed the mud out of my shirt) 4. (d; intr.) to ~ over (the waves ~ed over the deck) 5. (D; tr.) to ~ with (I ~ed my hands with soap) 6. (misc.) to be ~ed overboard

wash down v. (D; tr.) to ~ with (I like ~ing down a meal with a glass of beer = I like ~ing a meal down with a glass of beer)

washing (esp. BE) see **laundry** n. 1–3; **wash I** n. 1–3

washing machine n. 1. to run, use a ~ 2. to load; empty, unload a ~ 3. an automatic ~

washing-up n. (BE) to do the ~ ("to wash the dishes") (see the Usage Note for **wash up**)

washing-up machine n. (BE colloq.; CE has *dishwasher*) 1. to run, use a ~ 2. to load, stack; empty, unload a ~ 3. an automatic ~

wash up v. (D; intr.) to ~ on (the wreckage ~ed up on shore) USAGE NOTE: In AE, *to wash up* means "to wash one's dirty hands (and perhaps face)"; in BE, it means "to wash the dirty dishes".

wasp n. 1. ~s buzz; sting 2. ~s live in nests

wastage n. (esp. BE) natural ~ (the staff will be reduced by natural ~) (CE has *attrition*)

waste I n. 1. to cause ~ 2. to cut down on ~ 3. hazardous; nuclear; radioactive; solid; toxic ~(s) 4. complete, sheer, total, utter ~ 5. (misc.) to go to ~ ("to be wasted"); to lay ~ to ("to destroy"); a terrible ~ of time, money, and effort (see also *waste disposal* at **disposal**) USAGE NOTE: Note the following equivalence: (1) The fire laid waste to the land. = (2) The fire laid the land waste. However,

(2) is nowadays more formal and less common than (1).

waste II v. 1. (D; tr.) to ~ on (we ~d a lot of time, money, and effort on that project) 2. (misc.) we ~d a lot of time going through the files

wasteful adj. 1. ~ of (~ of natural resources) 2. ~ to + inf. (it's ~ to use so much fuel)

wasteland n. 1. to reclaim ~ 2. (a) barren, desolate; cultural; industrial ~

watch I n. ["timepiece"] 1. to adjust; set; wind (up) a ~ 2. to synchronize ~es 3. to clean; repair a ~ 4. a pocket; self-winding ~; stopwatch; waterproof; wrist ~ 5. an analog; digital ~ (by / according to my digital ~, it's ten thirty) 6. a ~ is fast; right; slow 7. a ~ goes, runs; keeps time, tells the time (BE); tells time (AE); runs; ticks 8. a ~ gains time; loses time; runs down; stops 9. the dial, face; hands of a ~ 10. the crystal (esp. AE) of a ~ (see also *watch band* at **band II** n.; *watch bracelet* at **bracelet**; *watchstrap* at **strap I** n.) 11. (misc.) to put, set, turn a ~ ahead / forward / back (by) one hour ["surveillance"] 12. to keep, maintain a ~ on 13. a close ~ 14. on the ~ (for) (to be on the ~ for bargains) ["sailor's duty"] 15. to stand ~ 16. on ~ (several sailors were on ~) (also fig.) (that would never happen on my ~!) ["volunteers organized to prevent crime"] 17. a crime (esp. AE); neighborhood; town (esp. AE) ~ ["preliminary warning"] (esp. AE) 18. a storm ~

watch II v. 1. to ~ closely; like a hawk 2. (d; intr.) to ~ for (to ~ for the train) 3. (d; intr.) to ~ over (to ~ over one's property) 4. (I; no passive) we ~ed them enter the auditorium 5. (J) we ~ed them entering the auditorium 6. (L; used in the imper.) ~ that they don't take everything! 7. (Q) ~ how it's done 8. (misc.) we could only ~ helplessly as / while they took everything!

watchdog n. a consumer ~ (esp. BE) (profiteers exposed by consumer ~s)

watcher n. ["observer"] a bird; poll ~

watching n. ["observation"] 1. to bear ~ (her activities bear ~) ("her activities should be watched") ["act of watching"] 2. bird; poll ~

watchman n. a night ~

watch out v. 1. (D; intr.) to ~ for 2. (esp. AE) (L; used in the imper.) ~ that they don't take everything! = ~ or they'll take everything!

water I n. 1. to turn on the ~ 2. to turn off the ~ 3. to cut off, disconnect the ~ 4. to draw, run ~ (for a bath) 5. to add ~ 6. to drink; sip ~ 7. to pour; spill ~ 8. to drain (off) ~ (from) 9. to splash; sprinkle; squirt ~ on 10. to boil, sterilize; chlorinate; distill; filter; fluoridate; purify; soften ~ 11. to pollute ~ (see also *water pollution* at **pollution**) 12. drinking; safe ~ 13. carbonated, fizzy (BE); mineral; soda ~ 14. clear; fresh; running ~ 15. distilled; soft ~ (see also **rainwater**) 16. hard ~ 17. salt, sea ~ 18. holy ~ (to sprinkle holy ~ on smb.) 19. heavy ~ 20. boiling; hot ~ 21. cold; cool; ice ~ 22. lukewarm; tepid; warm ~ 23. contaminated, polluted; murky; stagnant ~ 24. ~ boils; evaporates; freezes; vaporizes 25. ~ drains (off) from; flows, pours, runs; leaks; oozes; rises; splashes; spills; sprinkles; squirts 26. a body; drop of ~ 27. by ~ (to travel by ~) 28. under ~ (after the flood our basement was under ~) 29. (misc.) a bottle of ~; a glass of ~; to make/pass ~ ("to urinate"); to hold ~ ("to be valid") (your theory doesn't hold ~); to tread ~ (when swimming); ~ under the bridge ("past events that are done with; bygones"); to pour cold ~ on ("to discourage"); to keep one's head above ~ ("to keep out of difficulty"); toilet ~ ("liquid used as a skin freshener"); hot ~ ("trouble") (to be in hot ~; to get in/into hot ~; he got into hot ~ with his boss for being late); the boat was shipping ~ ("the boat was taking in water") (see also **deep water**; *water cure* at **cure I** *n.*; *water level* at **level II** *n.*; *water power* at **power**; *water pressure* at **pressure I** *n.*; *water shortage* at **shortage**; *water table* at **table**; *water wheel* at **wheel I** *n.*; **waters**)

water II *v.* (misc.) to make smb.'s mouth ~ ("to create a desire or appetite in smb."); her mouth ~s at the sight of popcorn

watercolors, watercolours *n.* to paint in ~

waterfront *n.* along, on the ~

watermark *n.* 1. to reach a ~ 2. a high; low; record ~

waters *n.* 1. flood ~ (the raging rising flood ~ eventually receded/subsided) 2. coastal; international; navigable; territorial; uncharted ~ 3. in ~ (the ship was in international ~) 4. (misc.) to fish in muddy (AE)/troubled ~ ("to attempt to stir up trouble"); to take the ~ ("to take a water cure")

watershed *n.* 1. to be, constitute, mark, represent a ~ (in history) 2. to reach a ~ 3. a ~ for (for us the ~ was when we realized what to do) 4. a ~ in 5. at a ~ (we are at a ~ in history)

waterway *n.* an inland ~

waterworks *n.* 1. a municipal ~ 2. (misc.) to turn on the ~ ("to start to cry") (colloq.)

wave I *n.* ["moving ridge on the surface of water"] 1. a high, tall; mountainous; perfect ~ (looking for a perfect ~ to ride) 2. a tidal ~ 3. ~s break (on the rocks); crest; lap; rise (see also *on the crest of a wave* at **crest**) 4. beneath the ~s ["upsurge"] 5. a crime ~ 6. in ~s ["physical disturbance that is transmitted in the propagation of sound or light"] 7. light; radio; sound; transverse ~s 8. long; medium; short ~s ["brain rhythm"] 9. an alpha; brain; theta ~ ["period of weather"] 10. a cold; heat ~ ["reaction"] 11. a shock ~ (the credit crunch sent massive shock ~s through the country) ["waviness of the hair"] 12. a natural; permanent ~ ["misc."] 13. to attack in ~s; to make ~s ("to have an impact"); (BE) a Mexican ~ ("a wave-like motion made by a crowd at a sporting event") USAGE NOTE: In colloq. BE, a *brain wave* can also mean a "sudden bright idea", which in AE is a *brainstorm*. In colloq. BE, a *brainstorm*

is a "sudden mental aberration". However, the verb *to brainstorm* (as in *a brainstorming session*) is now CE.

wave II *v.* 1. (A) ~ goodbye to them; or: ~ them goodbye 2. (D; intr., tr.) to ~ at, to (we ~d to her and she waved back at/to us; she ~d her arm at me; she ~d to them to come closer; she ~d at us from the airplane) 3. (P) she ~d them ahead/away/ on

wave back *v.* (D; intr.) to ~ at, to (we waved to her and she ~d back at/to us)

wavelength *n.* ["manner of thinking"] (colloq.) to be on the same ~; to operate on different ~s

waver *v.* (D; intr.) to ~ between (to ~ between two possibilities)

wax I *n.* beeswax; sealing ~ (see also **earwax**)

wax II *v.* (formal or humorous) 1. (s) ("to become") to ~ indignant; to ~ eloquent over ("to express one's enthusiasm concerning") 2. (misc.) to ~ and wane

way *n.* ["path, route"] 1. to blaze, clear, cut, open, pave, prepare the ~ for (to pave the ~ for reform) (see also **give way**) 2. to smooth the ~ for 3. to take the easy ~ out (of a difficult situation) 4. to lead; point, show the ~ (to point the ~ to reform) 5. to edge; elbow; fight; force; hack; inch; jostle; make; muscle; push; shoulder; shove; slash; squeeze; thread; tunnel; wedge; work one's ~ through; to (to elbow one's ~ through a crowd; the battalion fought its ~ through enemy lines to the coast; he pushed his ~ through the mob; to shove one's ~ through the revelers; we made our ~ to the door; to tunnel one's ~ to freedom) 6. to twist; weave, wend, wind one's ~ (the river winds its ~ to the sea) 7. to feel; find one's ~ 8. to wangle, worm one's ~ (into smb.'s confidence) 9. to know the ~ (do you know the ~ to the station?) 10. to lose one's ~ 11. to bar, block the ~ 12. (BE) a permanent ~ ("a railroad track") 13. the ~ from; to (he kept chattering all the ~ from our house to the airport) 14. the ~ into, to (the ~ into the park; can you show me the ~ to the station?) 15. the ~ out of (the ~ out of the city; show me the ~ out of this building; there is no easy ~ out of this mess) 16. along; on the ~ (a letter is on the ~; she is on her ~ to the airport; there were lots of problems along the ~) 17. (misc.) to work one's ~ through college; to make one's ~ in life; they went their separate ~s; my gift is winging its ~ to you by airmail; to come to a parting of the ~s; by ~ of ("via") ("Before we go to Paradise by ~ of Kensal Green." – G.K. Chesterton (1874–1936), "The Rolling English Road"); to know one's ~ around ("to be familiar with procedures"); to bluff one's ~ out of a predicament (see also *way of all flesh* at **flesh**; *harm's way* at **harm**) ["room for movement"] 18. to make ~ for (make ~ for the king!) 19. in the ~ (to be/stand in the ~; to get in smb.'s ~) 20. out of the ~ (to get out of the ~) ["progress"] 21. under

~ (an investigation is getting) under ~) ["distance"] 22. to come; go the whole ~; go a long ~; to go all the ~ (also fig.) ["direction"] 23. both ~s; this ~; that ~; the other ~ (she went that ~; please step this ~; they went the other ~) ["aspect, respect"] 24. in a certain ~ (in every ~; in no ~; in more ~s than one) ["manner, method"] 25. to find a ~ (they found a ~ to spend less money on electricity) 26. the proper, right; wrong ~ 27. the easy; hard ~ (to do smt. the hard ~; to learn about life the hard ~ ("through pain and difficulty"); let's do it the easy ~) 28. charming, winsome ~s 29. that; this ~ (do it this ~) 30. the ~ to + inf. (show me the ~ to work this washing machine; that's the ~ to do it; there is no easy ~ to learn a new language) 31. in a certain ~ (in her own ~; in such a ~ that...; in a small ~; they behaved in a statesmanlike ~; in an awkward ~; everything was done in a well-organized ~) 32. (misc.) to mend one's ~s; to fall into evil ~s ["purpose"] 33. by ~ of (by ~ of apology; by ~ of example; by ~ of illustration) ["effective manner"] 34. to have a ~ with (she has a ~ with children/words) ["goal"] 35. to get, have one's (own) ~ (she always gets her ~; you can't always have everything/things your own ~!; OK, have it your own ~, then!) ["misc."] 36. to know the ~s of the world; to know one's ~ around; to make one's ~ in the world; to get under ~ ("to start out"); in a ~ ("to some degree"); to go out of one's ~ ("to make a special effort"); to give ~ ("to collapse") ("to yield"); to pay one's own ~ ("to pay for oneself"); (old-fashioned) to be in the family ~ ("to be pregnant"); by the ~ ("incidentally"); on the ~ out ("becoming obsolescent"); the box says "This Way Up"; there are no two ~s about it ("it is definitely true"); out our ~ (esp. AE), down our ~ (esp. BE) ("where we live"); we are in a fair ~ to get our new library ("it appears as if we will get our new library"); this compromise goes a long ~ towards resolving our differences; can you see your ~ (clear) to accepting their compromise?; the ~ to smb.'s heart; to my ~ of thinking; a ~ of life; no ~ is he going to agree! (see also **long way**; **short way**) USAGE NOTE: Constructions such as *to hack one's way through the jungle* cannot be passivized; and in them the phrase *one's way* can sometimes be omitted: *to hack through the jungle*. Compare *they hacked a path through the jungle – a path was hacked (by them) through the jungle*.

wayside *n*. to fall by the ~

weak *adj*. 1. ~ at, in (he's ~ in mathematics) (see also *weak at the knees* at **knee I** *n*.) 2. ~ on, when it comes to (a bit ~ on common sense = a bit ~ in the common-sense department) 3. ~ from, with (~ with hunger)

weakened *adj*. ~ by (~ by hunger)

weakness *n*. ["quality of being weak"] 1. to reveal, show (a) ~ 2. a basic; fatal; fundamental; glaring; inherent; structural ~ 3. ~ in (his ~ in mathematics; there's a fundamental ~ in your reasoning)

["fondness"] 4. to have a ~ 5. a ~ for (to have a ~ for chocolate)

wealth *n*. ["abundance of material possessions, riches"] 1. to accumulate, acquire, amass, attain ~ 2. to dissipate, squander ~ 3. to flaunt one's ~ 4. enormous, fabulous, great, untold ~ ("malefactors of great ~" – Theodore Roosevelt, 1858–1919) 5. hereditary ~ 6. ~ accumulates ("the land ... Where ~ accumulates and men decay" – Oliver Goldsmith (1728–74), "The Deserted Village") ["abundance of resources"] 7. mineral; natural ~ (the natural ~ of a country) ["abundance, profusion"] 8. a ~ of information

wean *v*. 1. (D; tr.) to ~ a calf from its mother) 2. (d; tr.) to ~ off; on (the children were ~ed on television and had to be ~ed off it) 3. (misc.) to ~ smb. away from bad company

weapon *n*. 1. to load a ~ 2. to fire a ~ 3. to brandish; carry; draw; handle a ~ 4. to calibrate; zero in a ~ 5. to lay down, throw down one's ~s 6. a concealed; deadly, lethal ~ 7. automatic; defensive; heavy; light; offensive; semiautomatic ~s 8. atomic, thermonuclear; biological; chemical; conventional ~s (see also **nuclear weapons**) 9. (misc.) (they entered the building) with drawn ~s/ with ~s drawn; the ultimate ~ ("nuclear bombs or missiles"); to stockpile ~s (see also *weapons of mass destruction (WMD)* at **destruction**)

wear I *n*. ["clothing"] 1. beach; bridal; casual; children's; evening ~; footwear; infants'; ladies', women's; men's; sports; everyday ~ ["wearing out"] 2. to save ~ and tear (on) (to save ~ and tear on one's curtains) 3. from; with ~ (the curtains had become worn from/with constant ~)

wear II *v*. 1. (N; used with an adjective) she ~s her hair short 2. (s) my patience is ~ing thin 3. (misc.) she ~s her hair in a bun/in a bob/in plaits/ in braids; she wore a hole through/in her sock; ladies' ready-to-wear ("ready-made") garments

weary I *adj*. ~ of (they grew ~ of his preaching)

weary II *v*. (d; intr.) to ~ of (they ~ied of his preaching)

weasel *v*. (colloq.) (AE) (d; intr.) to ~ out of ("to evade") (to ~ out of one's obligations)

weather *n*. 1. to forecast, predict the ~ 2. (good) beautiful; clear, fair; dry; fine, good, nice, pleasant; mild; seasonable ~ (we had nice ~ all week) 3. (bad) atrocious, bad, beastly, bleak, dismal, dreary, foul, gloomy, inclement, nasty, stormy; threatening; ugly; unseasonable ~ 4. (rainy) cloudy, overcast; damp; foggy; overcast; rainy; stormy; unsettled; wet ~ 5. (warm) hot; humid, muggy; sultry; sunny; sweltering; tropical; warm ~ 6. (cold) arctic; cold; cool; freezing; windy; wintry ~ 7. the ~ clears up; the ~ turns cold/warm 8. ~ sets in (bad ~ set in) 9. a period, spell of ~ (we're in for another spell of bad ~) 10. in ~ (restaurants lose customers in bad ~) 11. (misc.) we'll go there, ~ permitting; under the ~ ("slightly ill") (see also *weather conditions* at **conditions**)

weather stripping *n.* to install, put on ~

weave I *n.* a coarse; fine; loose; plain; satin; tight; twill ~

weave II *v.* 1. (C) she wove a basket for us; or: she wove us a basket 2. (d; tr.) to ~ around, round (she wove the story around a specific theme) 3. (d; tr.) to ~ from, out of; into (she wants to ~ a scarf from this wool = she wants to ~ this wool into a scarf) 4. (d; tr.) ("to insert") to ~ into (to ~ some humor into a plot) 5. (misc.) to ~ together (she wove several themes together into a coherent plot); to ~ in and out of traffic

web *n.* 1. to spin; weave a ~ 2. an intricate, tangled ~ (a tangled ~ of intrigue) 3. a spider, spider's ~ ["computers"] 4. to browse; cruise; surf the ~ 5. the World Wide Web 6. on the ~ (to find smt. on the ~) USAGE NOTE: Spiders *spin* webs. People *weave* webs: "Oh what a tangled ~ we weave, When first we practise to deceive!" – Sir Walter Scott (1771–1832), *Marmion*

web site *n.* (computers) 1. to access; build, create; design; maintain; visit a ~ 2. on a ~ (see also *website address* at **address I** *n.*)

wedded *adj.* (cannot stand alone) ~ to ((firmly) ~ to tradition) (see also *wedded bliss* at **bliss**)

wedding *n.* ["ceremony"] 1. to have, hold a ~ 2. to officiate at, perform a ~ 3. to attend a ~ (see also *wedding anniversary* at **anniversary**; *wedding bells* at **bell**; *wedding cake* at **cake**; *wedding date* at **date I** *n.*; *wedding day* at **day**; *wedding guest* at **guest**) 4. a big; church; (humorous) shotgun ~ (where the bride is already pregnant); white ~ (where the bride wears white esp. because it's her first marriage) 5. a ~ takes place 6. at a ~ ["anniversary"] (esp. BE) 7. see **anniversary**

wedge I *n.* to drive a ~ between; into

wedge II *v.* 1. to ~ firmly; tightly, tight 2. (d; intr., tr.) to ~ between; into; under 3. (N; used with an adjective) she ~d the door open/shut 4. (misc.) to ~ firmly in place

wedged *adj.* (cannot stand alone) 1. ~ firmly; tightly, tight 2. ~ between; in

wedlock *n.* (formal or old-fashioned) 1. to join in ~ 2. holy ~ 3. out of ~ (born out of ~)

wee *n.* (colloq.) to have, take; need a ~

weed out *v.* (D; tr.) to ~ from (they ~ed out the fit from the unfit = they ~ed the fit out from the unfit)

weeds *n.* 1. to pull ~ 2. to kill ~ (as with weed-killer)

week *n.* 1. to spend a ~ (somewhere) 2. every; last; next; this ~ 3. the coming; current; past ~ 4. future; past; recent ~s 5. a ~ from (Tuesday) 6. by the ~ (she is paid by the ~) 7. by ("before or in") a ~ (by next ~, prices may have risen again) 8. during the ~ 9. for a ~ (they came here for a ~) 10. for ~s (she hasn't been here for ~s; esp. AE is: she hasn't been here in ~s) 11. in a ~ (we can't finish the whole job in just one ~; they will get here in a ~, (esp. BE) they will get here in a ~'s time) 12. (misc.) a ~ ago; once a ~; ~ after ~; ~ by ~; ~ in, ~ out; from ~ to

~; to take a ~ off; all ~ (long); the first time in (esp. AE), for (BE) a ~; she is five ~s old; ¬up to/until¬ last ~; mid-week; the working ~; (AE) freshman ~ USAGE NOTE: In the meaning "a week from Tuesday", BE also has – a week on Tuesday, (on) Tuesday week. Note also the BE expressions – she arrived a week last Tuesday; she will arrive a week next Tuesday.

weekday *n.* on ~s; AE also has: ~s (she works ¬ ~s/on ~s¬)

weekend *n.* 1. to spend a ~ somewhere 2. at (BE), during, over (esp. AE) the ~ 3. (AE) on ~s (she works on ~s) 4. (AE) ~s (she works ~s) 5. (BE) at ~s, at the ~ (she works at ~s) 6. (misc.) a long ~; a holiday ~; a ~ ¬away/off/in the country¬; have a nice ~!

weeknight *n.* on ~s; AE also has: ~s (she works ¬ ~s/on ~s¬)

weep *v.* 1. to ~ bitterly 2. (d; intr.) to ~ about, at, over (to ~ over one's misfortune; she wept at the sight of all the poor people) 3. (d; intr.) to ~ for, with (to ~ for joy at the good news) 4. (E) she wept to see them so poor 5. (misc.) she wept at seeing them so poor

weevil *n.* an alfalfa; boll ~

weigh *v.* 1. to ~ heavily, strongly 2. (d; intr.) ("to count") to ~ against (his testimony will ~ heavily against you) 3. (d; tr.) ("to balance") to ~ against (to ~ one argument against another = to ~ the arguments against each other) 4. (d; intr.) ("to press") to ~ on (legal problems ~ed heavily on her mind) 5. (S) ("to have a certain weight") "¬how much/what¬ does the suitcase ~?" "it ~s quite a lot; in fact, it ~s 10 pounds!" 6. (misc.) my testimony will ~ heavily in your favor

weigh down *v.* 1. (D; tr.) to ~ by, with (we were ~ed down with packages) 2. (esp. AE) (D; intr.) to ~ on (snow ~ed down on the roof)

weigh in *v.* (D; intr.) to ~ at (the boxer ~ed in at 150 pounds)

weight I *n.* ["amount weighed, heaviness"] 1. to carry; gain, put on ~ (see also *weight gain* at **gain I** *n.*) 2. to lose, take off ~ (see also *weight loss* at **loss**) 3. to check; control; watch one's (body) ~ (see also *weight control* at **control I** *n.*) 4. to bear a ~ (the central beam must bear a very heavy ~) 5. (a) dead; gross; minimum; net ~ 6. atomic; avoirdupois; birth; molecular; ideal, optimum ~ 7. under a ~ (the table gave way and collapsed under the sheer ~ of the food) 8. (misc.) excess ~ (as in air travel); ~ can ¬go up/increase¬, ¬go down/decrease¬, or fluctuate (see also *weight problem* at **problem**) ["device used in athletic exercises for its heaviness"] 9. to lift ~s (see also *weight training* at **training**) 10. heavy; light ~s 11. a set of ~s ["importance"] 12. to carry ~ (with) 13. to add; attach, give, lend ~ to; to place considerable ~ on 14. considerable; great ~ 15. (misc.) to throw one's ~ about (BE)/around ("to flaunt one's influence"); to pull one's ~ ("to do one's fair share"); to take a (great) ~ off smb.'s mind ("to ease or relieve smb.'s mind"); it was/ took a (great) ~ off my mind ("I felt relieved"); of ~ (that will be an argument of considerable ~ with the directors)

weight II *v.* 1. to ~ heavily 2. (D; tr.) ("to slant") to ~ against; in favor of (the evidence was ~ed heavily against me and in favor of her)

weighting *n.* (BE) ["salary supplement"] to get (the) London ~

weigh up *v.* 1. (d; tr.) ("to balance") to ~ against (to ~ one argument against another = to ~ the arguments against each other) 2. (BE) (Q) to ~ whether to do smt.

weird *adj.* (colloq.) 1. ~ about (there is smt. ~ about them) 2. ~ to + inf. (it was ~ to see her again = it was ~ seeing her again) 3. ~ that + clause (it's ~ that you never noticed her) 4. (misc.) it was really / very ~ when I saw her again

welcome I *adj.* 1. perfectly, very ~ 2. ~ to (you are ~ to my share; ~ to New York!) 3. ~ to + inf. (you are always ~ to borrow my car at any time) 4. (misc.) to make smb. feel ~; ~ back; ~ home!

welcome II *n.* 1. to bid, extend, give a ~ to 2. to receive, meet with a ~ 3. to outstay, overstay one's ~ 4. a cordial, effusive, enthusiastic, hearty, rousing, royal, warm ~ (we gave them a rousing ~) 5. a chilly, cool; guarded ~ 6. a ~ from; to (we received a warm ~ from the mayor; the government proposal met with a cool ~ from the opposition; the immigrants received a cool ~ to their new country) 7. in ~ (to raise one's voice in ~)

welcome III *v.* 1. to ~ cordially, enthusiastically, warmly 2. to ~ coolly 3. (D; tr.) to ~ from (they ~ inquiries from readers) 4. (D; tr.) to ~ into; to (we ~d the immigrants to our country; we ~d you into our home and you betrayed us!) (see also *welcome with open arms* at **arm I** *n.*)

welcome mat *n.* (colloq.) (esp. AE) to put out the ~ for smb.

weld *v.* 1. (D; tr.) to ~ into (the US Constitution ~ed the states into a nation) 2. (D; tr.) to ~ onto, to (to ~ one thing to another = to ~ two things together)

welfare *n.* ["government financial aid"] 1. public ~ 2. (esp. US) on ~ (to be on ~; to go on ~) (see also *welfare state* at **state I** *n.*) ["well-being"] 3. "promote the general ~" – the U.S. Constitution, 1787 4. the public ~ 5. child; social ~ 6. for smb.'s ~

well I *adv.* 1. to leave ~ enough alone (AE) = to leave ~ alone (BE) ("not to interfere with smt. that is satisfactory") 2. to do ~ (at, in, on) 3. (misc.) are things going ~ for/with you? you did ~ to tell me; to mean ~; to think ~ of; that's all very ~, but ..., that's all ~ and good, but ...

well II *n.* ["hole dug to tap a supply of oil or water"] 1. to bore, dig, drill, sink a ~ 2. an abandoned; deep ~ 3. an artesian; oil ~ 4. a ~ dries up 5. (misc.) a wishing ~ (make a wish and throw a coin into a wishing ~)

well-advised *adj.* ~ to + inf. (you would be ~ to come early)

well-being *n.* 1. to threaten smb.'s ~ 2. material; physical; psychological ~ 3. (misc.) a sense of ~

well-disposed *adj.* (formal) (cannot stand alone) ~ to, towards (they are not ~ towards me)

well-grounded *adj.* ~ in

well-informed *adj.* ~ about, on

well-intentioned *adj.* ~ towards

well on *adv.* 1. ~ in (he's ~ in years) 2. ~ with (he's ~ with his latest novel)

well up I *adv.* 1. (AE) ~ in years 2. ~ on (the latest styles)

well up II *v.* (D; intr.) to ~ in; with (her eyes ~ed up with tears = tears ~ed up in her eyes)

welt *n.* to raise a ~ (on the skin)

wend *v.* (P; intr.) the procession ~ed its way through the town

west I *adj., adv.* 1. directly, due, straight ~ 2. ~ of (~ of the city) 3. (misc.) to face; go, head ~; to go ~ (esp. BE; old-fashioned) ("to die"); northwest by ~; southwest by ~

west II *n.* 1. from the ~; in the ~; to the ~ 2. (AE) out ~ ("in the western part of the US") 3. (misc.) the Wild West (old-fashioned colloq.) ("the western part of the US"); (BE) up ~ (London slang) ("to the West End of London from the East End")

wet *adj.* 1. dripping, soaking, sopping, wringing; very ~ 2. ~ from; with (~ with dew) 3. (misc.) she got her shoes ~; he got ~ through (and through)

whack I *n.* (colloq.) ["blow"] 1. to give smb. a ~ ["attempt"] 2. to have, take a ~ at 3. to have the first ~ at ["share"] (colloq.) (BE) 4. a fair; full ~ (of) ["misc."] 5. out of ~ (esp. AE) (she threw her shoulder out of ~); to have a ~ at smt. (esp. BE) ("to have a try / go at smt.")

whack II *v.* (colloq.) (O) ("to strike") I'll ~ you one

whale *n.* ["sea mammal"] 1. to harpoon a ~ 2. a blue; bowhead; right; sperm; white ~ 3. a pod, school of ~s 4. a young ~ is a calf 5. a female ~ is a cow 6. a male ~ is a bull 7. (misc.) they managed to rescue a beached ~ ["misc."] 8. a ~ of a good time ("a very good time")

whammy *n.* (slang) (esp. AE) ["jinx"] 1. to put a (the) ~ on smb. 2. a double ~

wharf *n.* at; on a ~ (the ship was tied up at a ~)

what *determiner, pronoun* 1. ~ about, of (~ about them?) 2. (used in exclamatory sentences) ~ a (~ a (wonderful) day!) 3. (misc.) ~ (wonderful) days!; she has ~ it takes (colloq.) ("she is very capable"); to know ~'s ~ ("to understand clearly what the situation is"); ~ else is new? (esp. AE); so ~? ~ on earth / ever¬ can she mean?; ~'s new?; ~ else?

wheat *n.* 1. to grow; harvest; plant ~ 2. to grind; thresh ~ (to grind ~ into flour = to grind flour out of ~) 3. summer; winter ~ 4. club; common; durum; hybrid ~ 5. cracked; whole ~ 6. an ear; grain of ~ (see also *a wheat field* = *a field of wheat* at **field**) USAGE NOTE: AE has *whole wheat bread, whole* *wheat flour*; BE has *wholemeal bread, wholemeal flour.*

wheedle *v.* 1. (d; tr.) to ~ from, out of (to ~ information from smb.) 2. (d; tr.) to ~ into (to ~ smb. into doing smt.)

wheel I *n.* ["circular rim or solid disc joined to a hub that turns"] 1. to spin; turn a ~ 2. to align; balance; rotate ~s (on a car) 3. a balance; driving; front; idler; mill; paddle; potter's; ratchet; rear; retractable; roulette; spinning; sprocket; undershot; water ~ 4. a big (BE), Ferris ~ (in an amusement park) 5. a ~ spins; turns 6. (misc.) on ~s (towing a box on ~s); to break on the ~; (humorous) to reinvent the ~ ["device that turns a car"] 7. to take the ~ 8. a steering ~ (to turn the steering ~) 9. (to be) at, behind the ~ (who was at the ~ when the accident occurred?) ["misc."] 10. a big ~ ("an influential person") (AE; CE has *bigwig*) USAGE NOTE: For vehicles, AE has "change a tire"; BE, "change a wheel". CE has "spare tire/tyre"; BE, "spare wheel". CE has "spare tire/tyre" 'roll of fat around the waist'.

wheel II *v.* (P; refl., tr.) she ~ed the chair into the room; she ~ed herself into the room and had tea with the rest of us

wheelbarrow *n.* to maneuver; push, roll a ~

wheelchair *n.* 1. to maneuver; push; use a ~ 2. a motorized ~ 3. by ~ 4. in a ~ (see also *wheelchair access* at **access I** *n.*; *wheelchair-accessible* at **accessible**; *confined to a wheelchair* at **confine**; *wheelchair-user* at **user**)

wherewithal *n.* ["resources"] 1. the ~ for (they didn't have the ~ for a trip abroad) 2. the ~ to + inf. (they didn't have the ~ to take a trip abroad)

which *determiner, pronoun* ~ of (~ of them did you see?; ~ three (of them) did you see?) USAGE NOTE: The use of the preposition *of* is necessary when a pronoun follows. When a noun follows, the use of *which of the* limits the meaning – which student(s) did you see? which of the students whom we had discussed did you see?

whiff *n.* (colloq.) ["smell, odor"] 1. to catch; get; have; take a ~ of (to get a good ~ of tear gas) 2. to give smb. a ~ of smt. 3. at a ~ (she lost consciousness at the first ~ of ether)

while *n.* 1. a good, long; little; short ~ (I had to wait a (good) long ~) 2. after; for; in a ~ (he came back after a ~) (misc.) it was worth our ~ (to do it = doing it) USAGE NOTE: The adverb *awhile* can be used to mean 'for a while': you'll have to wait ¬a while/for a while/awhile¬.

whim *n.* 1. to have, pursue; satisfy a ~ 2. to indulge a ~ 3. an idle; passing; sudden ~ 4. a ~ to + inf. (I had a sudden ~ to go for a walk) 5. at; on a ~ (they went there on a ~) 6. (misc.) smb.'s every ~ (courtiers who indulged the king's every ~)

whine *v.* 1. (B) she ~d a few words to them 2. (D; intr.) to ~ about (she kept ~ing about how she had been cheated) 3. (L; to) she ~d (to them) that she

had been cheated = "I've been cheated!" she ~d (to them)

whinge *v.* (colloq.) (BE) see **whine** 2, 3

whip I *n.* ["lash used for whipping"] 1. to crack, snap a ~ (see also *the crack of a whip* at **crack I** *n.*) ["dessert made by whipping"] 2. a prune ~ ["member of a political party who enforces party discipline"] 3. a government (GB); majority; minority; opposition (GB); party ~ ["official party edict"] (GB) 4. to defy a ~ (against) 5. a three-line ~ ("most insistent") (the rebels who defy a government three-line ~ may have the party ~ withdrawn as a punishment)

whip II *v.* 1. (d; tr.) ("to beat") to ~ into (I ~ped the eggs into a froth) 2. (colloq.) (d; tr.) ("to bring") to ~ into (the sergeant ~ped the recruits into shape) 3. (d; tr.) ("to incite") to ~ into (the speaker ~ped the crowd into a frenzy) 4. (P; intr.) ("to move very quickly") they ~ped into position

whip hand *n.* ["control"] to get; have the ~ over

whipping *n.* ["beating"] 1. to get, receive, take a ~ (from) 2. to give smb. a ~

whip-round *n.* (BE) ["collection"] to have a ~

whip up *v.* 1. (d; tr.) ("to beat") to ~ into (I ~ped up the eggs into a froth = I ~ped the eggs up into a froth) 2. (d; tr.) ("to incite") to ~ into (the speaker ~ped up the crowd into a frenzy = the speaker ~ped the crowd up into a frenzy)

whirl I *n.* (colloq.) ["try"] 1. to give smt. a ~ ["hectic activity"] 2. the social ~ 3. (misc.) my mind is in a (mad) ~

whirl II *v.* (P; intr.) the leaves ~ed through the air

whirlpool *n.* to be drawn into a ~

whisk I *n.* an egg ~ (BE; AE has *eggbeater*)

whisk II *v.* (P; intr., tr.) ("to move quickly") they were ~ed into the hotel; the important visitors were ~ed through customs; "her face dissolved in laughter and she ~ed past him" – Philip K. Dick, *Do Androids Dream of Electric Sheep?* (1968), Chap. 13

whisk away *v.* see **whisk off**

whiskers *n.* ["beard"] 1. to grow ~ 2. to shave off one's ~ 3. rough ~

whiskey, whisky *n.* 1. to age; distill, produce ~ 2. neat (esp. BE), straight (esp. AE) ("undiluted") ~ 3. blended; bonded (US); corn; Irish; malt; rye; Scotch; single-malt ~ 4. ~ ages 5. a shot of ~ USAGE NOTE: The spelling *whiskey* is usu. used in Ireland and the US.

whisk off *v.* (colloq.) (d; tr.) to ~ to (they were ~ed off to prison)

whisper I *n.* 1. a loud, stage ~ 2. in a ~ (to speak in a ~)

whisper II *v.* 1. (B) he ~ed a few words to her 2. (d; intr.) to ~ about (what was he ~ing (to her) about? = what was he ~ing about (to her)?) 3. (d; intr., tr.) to ~ into (he ~ed a few words into her ear) 4. (E) he ~ed to her to be careful 5. (L; to) he ~ed (to her) that she should be careful = "Be careful!" he ~ed (to her) (see also *whisper sweet nothings* at **nothing**)

whistle I *n*. ["instrument that produces a whistling sound"] 1. to blow (on) a ~ (the guard blew a blast on his whistle to attract our attention) 2. a bird; factory; police; referee's ~ 3. a ~ blows, sounds ["act of whistling"] 4. to give a ~ 5. a loud; shrill ~ ["misc."] 6. a wolf ~ (to show sexual interest); as clean as a ~ ("very clean"); to blow the ~ on smb. ("to reveal smb.'s evil intentions, to be a whistle-blower")

whistle II *v*. 1. (A) she ~d a song to me; or, she ~d me a song 2. (D; intr.) to ~ at; to (who ~d at you?) 3. (D; intr.) to ~ with (to ~ with surprise) USAGE NOTE: One whistles *to* people to attract their attention. One whistles *at* people to express one's feelings about them.

white I *adj*. 1. to go, turn ~ 2. lily ~ 3. (misc.) as ~ as a ghost/sheet, as ~ as chalk = chalk-white; as ~ as snow = snow-white; ~ with anger

white II *n*. ["color"] 1. to dress in, wear ~ ["something white"] 2. a patch of ~ 3. in ~ (dressed in ~) ["the albumen of an egg"] 4. an egg ~ (for this recipe, beat two egg ~s until stiff)

white feather *n*. ["symbol of cowardice"] 1. to give smb. the/a ~ ["cowardice"] 2. to show the ~

white paper *n*. ["official government report"] 1. to issue a ~ 2. a ~ on

whittle *v*. 1. (D; intr.) to ~ at (to ~ at a piece of wood) 2. (D; tr.) to ~ into (to ~ a reed into a whistle) 3. (D; tr.) to ~ out of (to ~ a whistle out of a reed)

whittle away *v*. (D; intr.) to ~ at (to ~ at a piece of wood; to ~ at smb.'s alibi)

whiz, whizz I *n*. (colloq.) a ~ at (she is a ~ at languages)

whiz, whizz II *v*. (P; intr.) to ~ through the air

whole *n*. 1. to constitute, form a ~ 2. a complete; integrated; single ~ 3. (a) part of a ~ 4. as a ~ 5. on the ~ (the situation is, on the ~, satisfactory)

whole hog *n*. (colloq.) ["the whole way"] to go ¬ ~ (AE)/the ~¬

wholesale *adv*. to buy; sell ~

whoop *n*. ["loud cry"] to emit, let out a ~

whoopee *n*. (colloq.) ["boisterous fun"] to make ~

whooping cough *n*. to catch (the) ~

whopper *n*. (colloq.) ["a big lie"] to tell a ~

wicked *adj*. 1. ~ of 2. ~ to + inf. (it was (of them) ~ to do that = they were ~ to have done that = it was a ~ thing for them to do)

wide *adj*. ["deviating"] 1. (cannot stand alone) ~ of (you are ~ of the mark) ["misc."] 2. far and ~

widow *n*. 1. a war ~ 2. (humorous) a golf; grass ~

widower *n*. (humorous) a grass ~

width *n*. 1. full ~ 2. in ~ (ten feet in ~)

wife *n*. 1. (old-fashioned) to take a ~ 2. to beat; desert, leave; divorce one's ~ 3. an abused, battered; common-law; estranged ~; ex-wife, former; future; jealous; late; unfaithful ~ 4. (misc.) he had two children by his first ~; husband and ~; I now pronounce you man and ~: you may kiss the bride; smb.'s lady ~ ("smb.'s wife") (BE) (considered

somewhat condescending to women) (and how's your lady ~?) (see also *smb.'s good lady* at **lady**)

wig *n*. 1. to wear a ~ 2. to put on; take off a ~ 3. in a ~ 4. (misc.) a bigwig (CE; AE also has *big wheel*)

wild I *adj*. ["enthusiastic"] (colloq.) 1. to go ~ (the spectators went ~) 2. ~ about, over (the audience went ~ over the new play) ["furious"] 3. ~ with (~ with anger) 4. (misc.) to drive smb. ~ ["out of control"] 5. to run ~

wild II *n*. ["wilderness"] in the ~ (to live in the ~) (see also **wilds**)

wilderness *n*. 1. a desolate; trackless; unexplored ~ 2. in the ~

wildfire *n*. to spread like ~ ("to spread very quickly")

wild oats *n*. ["youthful excesses"] to sow one's ~

wilds *n*. see **wild II**; lost in the ~ of the Yukon

will I *n*. ["desire"] 1. to impose one's ~ (on) 2. to implement the ~ (of the majority) 3. the ~ to + inf. (lacking the ~ to live) 4. (misc.) to lose the ~ to live; a clash of (strong) ~s; against smb.'s ~; with a ~ (to work with the/a ~ to succeed) ["attitude"] 5. to show good ~ (see also **ill will**) ["choice"] 6. at ~ (to fire at ~) (see also **free will**) ["legal document disposing of an estate"] 7. to draw up, make, make out a ~ 8. to change a ~ 9. to administer; execute; read (out) a ~ 10. to probate, validate a ~ 11. to challenge, contest a ~ 12. to break, overturn, set aside a ~ 13. to repudiate a ~ 14. a deathbed ~ 15. a living ~ (an advance directive by smb. requesting no life support in case of terminal illness) 16. the terms of a ~ (under the terms of the deceased's ~, you inherit his estate) 17. (misc.) to be cut out of a ~; to be named in a ~; to be remembered in smb.'s ~; smb.'s last ~ and testament ["spirit"] ["power to make decisions, willpower"] 18. to break smb.'s ~ 19. an indomitable, strong; inflexible, unbending ~; an iron ~ = a ~ of iron 20. an effort of ~

will II *v*. 1. (A) he ~ed his entire estate to her; or: he ~ed her his entire estate 2. (H) the runner ~ed herself to keep going

will III *v*. (auxiliary) 1. (F) she ~ return, won't she? 2. (misc.) do what/whatever you ~: I don't care!; leave if you ~: I don't care

willies *n*. (colloq.) ["jitters"] 1. to get; have the ~ 2. to give smb. the ~ (her behavior gives me the ~)

willing *adj*. 1. ~ to + inf. (she is ~ to help: I asked her to help and she's ~ to) 2. (misc.) we are ~ for them to share in the benefits – although some of us are not ~ for them to

willingness *n*. 1. to demonstrate, show ~ 2. to express ~ 3. the ~ to + inf. (she expressed her ~ to work for us)

willpower *n*. 1. to demonstrate, show ~ 2. great; sheer ~ 3. the ~ to + inf. (do you have the ~ to stick to the diet?) 4. by ~ (the runner managed to finish the race by sheer ~ alone!)

wily *adj*. 1. ~ of (that was ~ of him) 2. (esp. AE) as ~ as a fox

win I *n.* to chalk up, notch up, record, score a ~ (against/over)

win II *v.* 1. to ~ easily, handily, hands down 2. (D; intr., tr.) to ~ against, over; from (to ~ against considerable odds; to ~ against the champions; to ~ a match against the champions; we won over the opposition; she won the trophy from her chief rival) 3. (D; intr.) to ~ at (to ~ at cards) 4. (O) her perseverance won her the award 5. (misc.) to ~ by a mile; to ~ by three points; to ~ (by) 5–2

win back *v.* (D; tr.) to ~ from (she won the trophy back from her chief rival = she won back the trophy from her chief rival)

wince *v.* 1. (D; intr.) to ~ at (to ~ at the thought of going back to work) 2. (misc.) to ~ in/with pain

winch I *n.* to operate, use a ~

winch II *v.* (P; tr.) they ~ed the victims to safety

wind I *n.* /wind/ ["movement, current of air"] 1. a balmy, gentle, light; fair, favorable ~ 2. a brisk, heavy, high, stiff, strong; gale-force; gusty ~ 3. a biting, cold, cutting, icy; raw ~ 4. an adverse; head; tail ~ 5. a trade ~ 6. the prevailing ~s 7. the ~ blows; changes, shifts; picks up 8. the wind dies down, drops, falls, slackens, subsides 9. the ~ howls; whistles 10. a blast, gust; puff of ~ 11. a down; up ~ 12. against the ~ 13. into the ~ 14. out of the ~ 15. with the ~ 16. (misc.) as free as the ~ (see also *wind power* at **power**; *wind tunnel* at **tunnel I** *n.*) ["knowledge"] 17. to get ~ of smt. ["breath"] 18. to catch, get one's second ~ 19. out of ~ ["misc."] 20. to break ~ ("to expel rectal gas"); in the ~ ("imminent"); to take the ~ out of smb.'s sails ("to deflate smb."); to see how the ~ blows ("to see what is likely to happen")

wind II *v.* /waynd/ 1. (d; tr.) to ~ around, round (she wound the string around her finger) 2. (d; tr.) to ~ into (she wound the string into a tight mass) 3. (P; intr.) the procession wound (its way) through the town 4. (misc.) to ~ smb. around one's little finger ("to manipulate smb.")

winded *adj.* ["out of breath"] easily ~

windfall *n.* ["a stroke of good fortune"] 1. to get, have a ~ 2. a sudden, unexpected ~ (see also *windfall profit* at **profit I** *n.*)

windmill *n.* 1. a ~ turns 2. (misc.) to tilt at ~s ("to struggle with imaginary opponents")

window *n.* 1. to open a ~; to roll down a ~ (in a car) 2. to close, shut a ~; to roll up a ~ (in a car) 3. to clean, wash; face a ~ 4. a bay; bow; French (BE; AE has *French door*); lattice; picture; storm ~ 5. a shop, store (esp. AE) ~ 6. a back, rear; front; side ~ (as of a car) 7. a ~ faces smt.; fogs up, sweats; frosts over 8. a ~ on (a ~ on the sea; a good book can be a ~ on the world) 9. at, by a ~ (sit at a ~ and look out) 10. from a ~ (what can you see from your ~?) 11. in a ~ (to see a sign in a shop ~) 12. out (esp. AE), out of a ~ (what can you see out of your ~; don't lean out of the ~!) 13. through a ~ (what can you see through your ~?) ["(computers)"] 14. to close; enlarge; minimize; open a ~

window shade *n.* (AE) 1. to lift, raise a ~ 2. to draw, drop, lower a ~ (BE has *blind*)

wind up *v.* /waynd əp/ ("to end up") 1. (d; intr., tr.) to ~ by (she wound up her affairs by selling all her stock) 2. (d; intr.) to ~ with (I wound up with the estate) 3. (G) I wound up paying for everyone 4. (misc.) to ~ out in the cold; she wound up worse off than when she started; to start off/out poor and ~ rich

wine *n.* 1. to make, produce ~ (a) 2. to decant, pour ~ 3. (a) dry; fortified; sweet ~ 4. (a) cooking; dessert; table; vintage ~ 5. (a) red; rosé; sparkling; white ~ 6. (a) communion; sacramental ~ 7. mulled ~ 8. (a) domestic; imported ~ 9. a house ~ (of a restaurant) 10. ~ ferments 11. a bottle; carafe; decanter; glass of ~ (see also *wine cellar* at **cellar**; *wine list* at **list I** *n.*; *wine rack* at **rack I** *n.*; *wine waiter* at **waiter**) USAGE NOTE: The phrase *domestic wine* seems to be reserved for wine produced in English-speaking countries. English-speakers in France or Italy, for example, usu. do not refer to French or Italian wine as *domestic*.

wing *n.* ["faction of a political party"] 1. a conservative; left; liberal; radical; right ~ ["a bird's appendage used for flying"] 2. a bird beats, flaps, flutters; spreads its ~s (the bird spread its ~s and flew off) 3. (misc.) to clip smb.'s ~s ("to restrict smb.'s freedom"); to grow, sprout ~s (when did dinosaurs sprout ~s and become birds?); to spread one's ~s ("to develop one's full potential"); a pair of ~s ["protection"] 4. to take smb. under one's ~ ["act of flying"] 5. to take ~ (also fig.) 6. on the ~ ["extension, annex of a building"] 7. to add a ~ (to a building) 8. (BE) see **fender** ["misc."] 9. to wait in the ~s ("to await the opportunity to take over a job"); the political ~ ("the political section of an organization")

wink I *n.* 1. to give smb. a ~ 2. a suggestive ~ 3. (misc.) I didn't get a ~ of sleep last night = I didn't sleep a ~ last night; to get, have forty ~s ("to take a brief nap"); (BE) to tip smb. the ~ ("to give smb. secret information")

wink II *v.* (D; intr.) to ~ at (also fig.: the police ~ed at illegal gambling)

winkle *v.* (colloq.) (BE) (d; tr.) ("to obtain") to ~ out of (to ~ the truth out of smb.)

winner *n.* 1. a clear; likely; real; sure ~ 2. the lucky; outright, overall ~ (the rich will be the real ~s under the government's tax policy) 3. (misc.) to be on to a (sure) ~ (at a racetrack)

win out *v.* (d; intr.) to ~ over (we won out over the opposition)

win over *v.* (d; tr.) to ~ to (we won them over to our side)

winter *n.* 1. early; last; late; mid-; next ~ 1. a cold, cruel, hard, harsh, severe, terrible ~ 2. a mild ~ 3. during, in, over (esp. AE) (the) ~ (we met late in the ~ of 1995 = we met in the late ~ of 1995) 4. (misc.) in the dead of ~ (see also *winter solstice* at **solstice**)

wipe *v.* 1. (d; tr.) to ~ off ("to erase from") (to ~ a city off the map; I'll ~ that smile off your face!) 2. (D; tr.) to ~ on; with (she ~d her hands on the towel) 3. (N; used with an adjective) she ~d her hands clean/dry on the towel; he ~d the dishes clean/dry with a cloth

wipers *n.* 1. to turn on the ~ 2. windscreen (BE), windshield (AE) ~

wire I *n.* ["long metal thread"] 1. to string ~ 2. barbed; chicken; copper ~ 3. a high; trip ~ 4. a ~ goes, runs 5. a length, piece, strand of ~ (he got caught on a strand of barbed ~) ["cable conducting electric current"] 6. to cross, jump ~s (in order to start a car) 7. (esp. AE) to tap ~s 8. telegraph; telephone ~s 9. (an) electric; high-tension ~ 10. heavy-duty ~ ["cablegram, telegram"] (esp. AE) 11. to send a ~ ["finish line"] (esp. AE) (also fig.) 12. (right) down to the ~ ("to the very end") 13. (misc.) to get in under the ~ ("to enter barely in time")

wire II *v.* (esp. AE) (CE has *telegraph*) 1. (A) ("to send by wire") we ~d the money to her; or: we ~d her the money 2. (D; intr., tr.) to ~ about (they ~ed (us) about the meeting) 3. (d; intr.) ("to request by sending a wire") to ~ for (she ~d home for some money) 4. (H; no passive) ("to inform by wire") we ~d them to return home immediately 5. (L; may have an object) ("to inform by wire") she ~d (us) that the manuscript had been received 6. (Q; may have an object) we will ~ (you) where to meet

wire III *v.* 1. (D; tr.) ("to provide with wire") to ~ for (the auditorium was ~d for sound) 2. (d; tr.) ("to connect") to ~ to (the explosives were ~d to the door; the two things were ~d to each other = the two things were ~d together)

wire back *v.* (esp. AE) (see **wire II**) 1. (L; to) she ~d back (to us) that the manuscript had been received 2. (Q; to) we ~d back (to you) where to meet = we ~d you back where to meet

wireless *n.* (BE) (now less common than *radio*) see **radio I** 1–4, 6

wiring *n.* 1. defective, faulty ~ 2. electric ~

wisdom *n.* 1. to impart ~ 2. to doubt, question smb.'s ~ (to question the ~ of an action) 3. (the) conventional, (the) received ~ 4. earth, folk, homespun ~ 5. the ~ to + inf. (will they have the ~ to make the correct choice?) 6. of ~ (a person of great ~) 7. (misc.) in their (infinite) ~, the council members voted to cut the police budget in the midst of a crime wave; wit and ~ (see also *with the wisdom of hindsight* (sarcastic) at **hindsight**; *words of wisdom* at **words**)

wise *adj.* ["sagacious"] 1. ~ to + inf. (it was ~ of you to remain silent = you were ~ to remain silent) ["aware of"] (colloq.) 2. ~ to (she was ~ to their scheme; I finally got ~ to his tricks; she put me ~ to his tricks) (see also *wise words* at **words**)

wisecrack I *n.* ["flippant remark"] 1. to make a ~ 2. a ~ about (she made a ~ about a woman needing a man like a fish needs a bicycle)

wisecrack II *v.* (colloq.) 1. (D; intr.) to ~ about (she ~ed about a woman needing a man like a fish needs a bicycle) 2. (L) ("to remark flippantly") she ~ed that a woman needs a man like a fish needs a bicycle = "a woman needs a man like a fish needs a bicycle," she ~ed

wise up *v.* (colloq.) (AE) (D; intr.; tr.) to ~ to (I finally ~d up to his tricks after she had ~d me up to them)

wish I *n.* ["desire"] 1. to make a ~ 2. to fulfill, realize a ~ 3. to get one's ~ 4. to express a ~ 5. to respect smb.'s ~(es) 6. to grant smb.'s ~ 7. a fervent, strong; unfulfilled ~ 8. smb.'s dying ~ (her dying ~ to see her children was granted) 9. a/the death ~ 10. a ~ comes true 11. a ~ for (a ~ for peace) 12. a ~ to + inf. (they expressed a ~ to visit the museum; my only ~ is for you to stay) 13. a ~ that + clause; subj. (the editor respected her ~ that the contribution ¬not be/should not be/was not (BE)¬ announced publicly; my only ~ is that you would stay) 14. against smb.'s ~es (the project was carried out against our ~es) 15. in accordance with smb.'s ~es (see also *wish fulfillment* at **fulfillment**; *wish list* at **list I** *n.*) ["greetings"] 16. to extend, offer, send one's (best) ~es 17. one's best, good, warm, warmest ~es 18. one's ~es for (one's best ~es for the New Year) 19. with best ~es

wish II *v.* 1. (A; usu. without *to*) they ~ed us good luck; we ~ you a Merry Christmas and a Happy New Year! 2. (D; intr.) to ~ for (we were ~ing for cool weather) 3. (formal) (E) I ~ to lodge a complaint 4. (formal) (H; no passive) "do you ~ me to stay?" "yes: what I ~ is for you to stay!/yes: I ~ more than anything else for you to stay!" 5. (L) I ~ only that you would stay 6. (misc.) to ~ smb. well ("to hope that things will go well for smb.")

wit I *n.* 1. to display, show; have ~ 2. (a) coruscating, sparkling; keen, penetrating, sharp; sophisticated ~ 3. (a) dry; quick, ready; sly ~ 4. (an) acerbic, acid, biting, caustic, cutting, mordant, trenchant ~ 5. the ~ to + inf. (he didn't have the ~ to realize what was happening) 6. (misc.) at one's ~'s end; ~ and wisdom (see also **wits**)

wit II to ~ ("namely")

witchcraft *n.* 1. to practice ~ 2. sheer ~ (it was sheer ~ the way she could make us all a slap-up meal at such short notice!)

witch-hunt *n.* to conduct a ~ against

withdraw *v.* 1. (D; intr., tr.) to ~ from; into, to (our troops have withdrawn from the border area; to ~ money from a bank; to ~ to a safer area; to ~ into one's shell 2. (misc.) I'd like to ~ (my candidacy) in favor of my worthy opponent)

withdrawal *n.* ["removal of funds"] 1. to make a ~ 2. mass ~s 3. a ~ from (a (cash) ~ from an account) ["retreat"] (often mil.) 4. to carry out, make a ~ 5. to complete a ~ 6. an orderly; phased; precipitate; strategic; tactical; unilateral ~ 7. a ~ from; into, to (a ~ to a safer area; a ~ into one's shell; a ~ in favor of a worthy opponent) (see also *withdrawal symptoms* at **symptom**)

withhold *v.* (D; tr.) to ~ from (to ~ information from the police)

within *n., prep.* 1. ~ a mile of 2. (misc.) an attempt to reform the system from ~

witness I *n.* ["testimony"] 1. to bear ~ to 2. false ~ (to bear false ~) ["one who testifies"] 3. to produce a ~ (the district attorney finally produced a credible ~) 4. to call, subpoena; swear in a ~; to hear ~es 5. to cross-examine; examine, interrogate, question; interview a ~ 6. to badger; bribe; confuse; discredit; lead; suborn; trap a ~ 7. a defense; expert ~; prosecution ~ (see also **eyewitness**) 8. a competent; credible; reliable ~ 9. a character; hostile ~ 10. a key; material ~ 11. a ~ is sworn in = a ~ takes the oath (see also *witness box* at **box I** *n.*; *witness stand* at **stand I** *n.*) 12. a ~ testifies (under affirmation or oath) 13. a ~ stands down, steps down 14. a ~ against (a ~ against one's former accomplices) 15. a ~ for (a ~ for the prosecution) 16. a ~ to (a ~ to an accident)

witness II *v.* 1. (J) who ~ed him signing the documents? 2. (K) who ~ed his signing the documents?

wits *n.* 1. to collect one's ~ 2. to match ~ with smb. 3. the ~ to + inf. (he didn't have enough ~ to realize what was happening) 4. (misc.) keep your ~ about you! ("stay alert!"); to live by one's ~; at one's wits' end; a battle of ~; to drive people out of their ~; to be frightened out of one's ~

witty *adj.* 1. ~ of (that was ~ of her) 2. ~ to + inf. (it was ~ of her to say that)

wizard *n.* 1. a financial; mathematical ~ 2. a ~ at (a ~ at solving crossword puzzles)

wizardry *n.* sheer ~ (it was sheer ~ the way he could make us all a slap-up meal at such short notice!)

woe *n.* a tale of ~

wolf *n.* 1. wolves howl 2. wolves hunt in packs 3. a pack of wolves 4. a young ~ is a pup 5. (misc.) to keep the ~ from the door ("to provide the necessities"); a ~ in sheep's clothing ("one who disguises hostile intentions"); a lone ~ (see also *to cry wolf* at **cry II**)

woman *n.* 1. to deliver a ~ (of a baby) 2. an attractive, beautiful, pretty; average; desirable; fat; grown; handsome; middle-aged; old; short; tall; thin; ugly; wise; young ~ 3. a divorced; married; single ~ 4. a career; ideas; liberated; organization; professional; right-hand; self-made; stunt; university (BE; AE has *college graduate*); working ~ 5. an anchor ~; businesswoman; newspaperwoman 6. (AE) a cleaning ~ (BE has *charlady, charwoman, char*) 7. (BE) a lollipop ~ (AE has *crossing guard*) 8. (AE) enlisted women (BE has *other ranks*) 9. a battered ~ 10. the other ~ ("a married man's paramour") 11. (misc.) a ~ of letters; a ~ of action; a ~ of the world; the ~ of the year (see *women's lib* at **lib**; *women's liberation* at **liberation**;

women's magazine at **magazine**; *women's movement* at **movement**; *women's rights* at **right III** *n.*) USAGE NOTE: The terms *career woman* and *working woman* are becoming old-fashioned. (See also the Usage Note for **girl**)

womanhood *n.* to reach ~

wonder I *n.* 1. to perform, work ~s 2. to achieve ~s 3. to do ~s for 4. a natural ~ 5. a ~ that + clause (it's a ~ to me that we didn't get lost; small/no ~ they had so much trouble, given their lack of preparation!) 6. in ~ (to look around in ~) 7. (misc.) the seven ~s of the world; a nine-days ("short-lived") ~; the eighth ~ of the world (see also *wonder drug* at **drug**)

wonder II *v.* 1. to ~ really, very much (I really ~ if/whether they'll come) 2. (D; intr.) to ~ about, at (to ~ about a problem) 3. (L) I shouldn't ~ that you are tired after all that work 4. (Q) I ~ why they left

wonderful *adj.* 1. ~ to + inf. (it was ~ to see each other again; it was ~ of them to come) 2. ~ that + clause (it was ~ that we could see each other; it was ~ that they could come)

wonderland *n.* a scenic ~

wonderment *n.* in ~

wont I *adj.* (formal) (rare) ["accustomed"] (cannot stand alone) ~ to + inf. (she is ~ to call at any time; she arrived late, as she is ~ to do)

wont II *n.* (formal) (rare) ["custom"] 1. it is her ~ to arrive late 2. she arrived late, as was/is her ~

wood *n.* 1. to chop, cut ~ 2. to gather ~ 3. firewood; kindling ~ 4. a block; cord; piece; sliver of ~ 5. (misc.) out of the ~ (BE)/~s (CE) ("safe from danger"); in our neck of the ~s ("where we live")

wool *n.* 1. to produce ~ 2. to comb; process; sort ~ 3. lamb's; sheep's; steel, wire (BE) ~ 4. (one hundred percent) pure ~ 5. (CE) cotton ~ (AE has *absorbent cotton*) 6. a ball; skein of ~ 7. (misc.) to pull the ~ over smb.'s eyes ("to deceive smb.")

woozy *adj.* (colloq.) ["dazed, dizzy"] ~ from (~ from lack of sleep)

word I *n.* ["independent meaningful linguistic form"] 1. to coin, make up a ~ 2. to define; enter; look up a ~ (as in a dictionary) 3. to spell; write a ~ 4. to pronounce, say, utter a ~ 5. to mispronounce a ~ 6. an archaic; old-fashioned; obsolete ~ 7. a compound; simple ~ 8. a big, long; monosyllabic; polysyllabic, sesquipedalian; short; vague ~ 9. a borrowed; dialectal, regional; foreign; native; operative ~ 10. a ghost; nonce ~ 11. a four-letter, naughty, obscene; swear; taboo ~ 12. a portmanteau ~ 13. a guide ~ (at the top of a page in a dictionary, reference work) 14. (misc.) (upon) my ~! ("really!"); what's the ~ for "cat" in your language? = what's the ~ that means "cat" in your language = ?; ~ for ~ ("verbatim"); a household ("common") ~; to get a ~ in (edgewise (AE)/edgeways (BE)) ("to manage to say smt., as in a dispute"); to put in a good ~ for smb. ("to plead smb.'s case"); in a ~ ("briefly"); in ~ and deed; begin at the ~ *go*; a buzz ~; a code ~; a cover ~

(see also *a word of advice* at **advice**; *a word of caution* at **caution I** *n.*; *a word game* at **game II** *n.*; *in the accepted meaning of the word* at **meaning**; *by word of mouth* at **mouth**; *in every sense of the word* at **sense I** *n.*; *word of warning* at **warning**; **last word**; **term**; **word order**) ["promise"] 15. to give one's ~ 16. to take smb.'s ~ (I trust you, so I'll take your ~ for it) 17. to take people at their ~ 18. to break; keep one's ~ 19. one's solemn ~; one's ~ of honor 20. one's ~ that + clause. (she gave me her ~ that she would deliver the message) 21. of one's ~ (she's a woman of her ~) ("she keeps her promises") ["command"] 22. to give/say the ~ (just give/say the ~ and I'll do it!) ["information, news"] 23. to bring; send ~ 24. to breathe, say a ~ (don't breathe a ~ about it to anyone) 25. to get/receive ~ (we got/received ~ that the contract would be signed) 26. the latest; last ~ (it's the latest/last ~ in fashion!; she always wants to have the last ~ in an argument!) 27. (esp. AE) advance ~ 28. ~ about, of (there was no ~ of the incident in the newspapers; she would like to say a few ~s about the incident) 29. ~ that + clause (they sent ~ that they would be late) 30. (misc.) there has been no ~ from them; ~ has it that he intends to resign = ~ has got out that he intends to resign; and now a ~ from our sponsor (see also *have a word in smb.'s ear* at **ear**; *put in a good word for smb.* at **put in**) ["conversation"] 31. to have a ~ with smb. about smt. (see also **words**) USAGE NOTE: The construction *I'd like (to have) a word with you* usu. indicates that the conversation will be of a serious nature. Compare *I had words with him* "I had an argument with him".

word II *v.* to ~ smt. carefully; strongly; tactfully (a strongly ~ed statement)

word order *n.* (a) fixed; flexible; normal; reverse ~

wording *n.* the exact ~ (of a text)

word processor *n.* a dedicated ~

words *n.* ["text"] 1. (the) ~ of, to (a song) ["discussion"] 2. to bandy, exchange ~ with smb. ["argument"] 3. to have ~ with smb. 4. (misc.) ~ passed between them ["words that constitute a statement"] 5. to say a few ~ about smt. 6. to weigh ("consider with care") one's ~ (carefully) 7. to distort smb.'s ~ 8. to not mince any ~ ("to speak frankly") 9. (misc.) smb.'s dying/last ~ ["words that express strong feeling"] 10. kind; sincere; warm ~ 11. choice; eloquent; high-sounding ~ 12. angry, cross, sharp; fighting; harsh; hasty; heated, hot; threatening ~ 13. hollow, hypocritical; meaningless; weasel ~ ("polite meaningless ~" – W.B. Yeats, "Easter 1916") ["misc."] 14. to choose one's ~ carefully; in so many ~ ("precisely"); in one's own ~; of few ~ ("not talkative"); to hang on (to) smb.'s ~ ("to listen to smb. very attentively"); at a loss for ~, lost for ~; she took the ~ right out of my mouth ("she said exactly what I wanted to say"); a play on ~ ("a pun"); wise ~ = ~ of wisdom

work I *n.* ["labor"] 1. to do ~ (they never do any ~) 2. to begin, start; quit (AE), stop ~ (they quit ~ at one o'clock) 3. to take on ~ 4. creative; delicate; easy, light; fulfilling ~ 5. meticulous, painstaking, precise; skilled; productive; unskilled ~ 6. backbreaking, hard, heavy; demanding; exhausting, tiring ~ 7. dirty, donkey (esp. BE), scut (AE); intellectual; manual, physical; menial ~ 8. shoddy, slipshod, sloppy ~ 9. clerical, office; engineering; paper ~ (trains will not be running because of planned engineering ~) 10. fieldwork; legwork 11. casual (BE); full-time; part-time; seasonal; steady ~ 12. ~ begins, starts; finishes, stops 13. (misc.) he never does a lick/stitch (AE)/stroke of ~; to make short ~ of ("to dispose of quickly"); to undo smb.'s ~ ("to destroy the results of smb.'s labor") (see also *work-life balance* at **balance I** *n.*; **graduate work**; **guesswork**; **postgraduate work**; **roadwork**) ["employment"] 14. to create, give, provide ~ (a plan to provide ~ for the unemployed) 15. to find; look for, seek ~ (I found ~ as a receptionist in an office) 16. to get to, go to ~ 17. to begin, start ~ 18. to finish, stop ~ 19. to return to ~ 20. to take (time) off from ~ 21. to leave ~ (early) 22. a job; line, type of ~ (there's still a job of ~ to be done!; what line of ~ are you in?) 23. at ~ (they are still at ~) 24. (BE) in ~ ("employed") 25. out of ~ (they have been out of ~ for a week) ["result of research, labor, artistic effort"] 26. to exhibit; hang one's ~s (in a gallery) 27. coursework; written ~ 28. (a) literary; scholarly ~ = a ~ of literature; scholarship (see also *a work of genius* at **genius**) 29. collected; published; selected ~s 30. (misc.) ~ in progress; a ~ of art = an artwork; their life's ~ was writing novels ["service"] 31. social ~ (to do social ~) 32. undercover ~ (to do undercover ~ for the police) 33. volunteer ~ ["treatment"] 34. root-canal ~ (to do root-canal ~ on smb.) ["misc."] 35. to go to ~ on smb. ("to put pressure on smb.") (see also **works**)

work II *v.* 1. ("to labor") to ~ effectively; full-time; hard, like a horse, strenuously; part-time 2. (d; intr.) to ~ against ("to oppose") (to ~ against a proposed law) 3. (D; intr.) ("to labor") to ~ as (to ~ as a teacher) 4. (d; intr.) ("to labor") to ~ at, on (they were ~ing on a new book; you have to ~ at being friendlier with people) 5. (d; intr.) ("to be employed; to labor") to ~ for (she ~s for a large firm; to ~ for a living) 6. (d; intr.) to ~ for ("to support") (to ~ for a good cause; the committee ~ed for a reduction of tension) 7. (d; refl.) ("to excite") to ~ into (she ~ed herself into a rage) 8. (d; tr.) to ~ into ("to insert") (she ~ed a few jokes into her speech) 9. (d; intr.) to ~ through ("to go through") (to ~ through difficult material) 10. (d; intr.) ("to progress") to ~ towards (to ~ towards a common goal) 11. (d; intr.) ("to labor") to ~ under ("to ~ under a noted scientist") 12. (d; intr.) ("to collaborate") to ~ with (to ~ closely with one's colleagues) 13. (misc.) to ~ far/late into the night; to ~ one's way through college; to ~ one's way through a crowd; I slowly ~ed my way through the long report; the committee ~ed to reduce tension; to ~ against the clock; they are ~ing us very hard; indeed, they are ~ing us to death; the screw ~ed (itself) loose; the drug needs time to ~ through the system; to ~ one's fingers to the bone; (BE) to ~ to rule ("to conform to all rules governing work so as to do only the minimum, as in a go-slow (AE)"); to ~ like a charm, to work like magic ("to succeed quickly and completely") (the offer ~ like a charm and satisfied everybody)

worked up adj. (colloq.) ~ about, over (he got himself all ~ about/over a mere trifle)

worker n. 1. to hire, take on a ~ 2. to retrain; train ~s 3. to organize, unionize ~s 4. to dismiss, fire, sack (colloq.) a ~; lay off a ~ (temporarily or permanently), to make a ~ redundant (as by eliminating the worker's job) (BE) 5. an assiduous, diligent, efficient, good, hard, indefatigable; key; meticulous ~; a fast ~ (also fig.: "one who succeeds fast with women") 6. an idle; poor; slow ~ 7. an assembly-line; blue-collar (esp. AE); construction; dock; factory ~ 8. an office; research; white-collar ~ 9. an immigrant; migrant; undocumented (AE) ~ 10. a full-time; part-time ~ 11. a skilled; unskilled ~ 12. (misc.) a social; welfare; youth ~; a sex ~ ("a prostitute"); a gang, group of ~s (see also *miracle-worker* at **miracle**)

workforce n. 1. to cut (down), downsize, reduce; expand the ~ 2. an ageing; growing; productive; shrinking ~ 3. a member of the ~ 4. among, in the ~ (there is great variation in skill among/in the ~) 5. throughout the ~ (there is dissatisfaction throughout the whole ~)

working hours n. flexible; regular; staggered; unsocial (BE) ~ (during regular ~)

workings n. the inner, internal ~

workman n. see **worker**

workmanship n. 1. conscientious, good, meticulous, sound; delicate, exquisite, fine ~ 2. poor, shoddy ~ 3. a standard of ~

workout n. ["exercise"] 1. to do, get, have; give a ~ 2. a daily ~ (she does a daily ~ with weights in a gym)

work out v. 1. (D; intr.) to ~ with (to ~ with weights daily in a gym) 2. (D; intr.) to ~ for (everything ~ed out just fine for us in the end; let's try to work out the answer for ourselves) 3. (L) we ~ed out that she was probably lying 4. (Q) we ~ed out for ourselves how to proceed; we ~ed out why she was lying

workplace n. at, in the ~ (to maintain harmony in the ~)

works n. ["construction projects"] 1. to carry out, do ~ 2. road, public ~ (see also **roadwork**) ["preparation"] (colloq.) 3. in the ~ ["operations"] 4. to gum up, mess up the ~ ["everything available"] (colloq.) 5. to give smb. the ~ ["misc."] 6. ~ of art = artworks (see also **work I** n.)

workshop n. ["working seminar"] 1. to conduct,

hold a ~ 2. to participate in, take part in a ~ 3. a member of, participant in a ~ 4. a series of ~s (he participated in a series of Thomas Hardy ~s held last summer) 5. a ~ on (he participated in a series of ~s on Thomas Hardy held last summer)

workup n. ["series of tests"] (esp. AE) 1. to do a ~ (on) 2. a diagnostic ~

work up v. 1. (d; refl., tr.) ("to excite") to ~ into (he ~ed himself up into a rage) 2. (d; refl., tr.) ("to incite") to ~ to (the orator ~ed the crowd up to a fever pitch) 3. (misc.) she ~ed her way up to the top; she ~ed her way up through the ranks; he finally ~ed up the courage to ask for a promotion; he ~ed himself up about/over a mere trifle (see also **worked up**)

world n. ["earth"] 1. across, all over, through, throughout; around, round the ~ (to travel around the ~) 2. (misc.) to see the ~ ("to travel to many parts of the earth") (see also *world-class* at **class I** n.) 3. ["area, part of the earth"] 3. the English-speaking; Arab; Free; known; New; Old; Third ~ (in the Third ~) ["domain, realm, sphere"] 4. the animal ~ 5. the academic; art; business; financial; literary; scientific ~ (a theory that divided/polarized/split the scientific ~) 6. the civilized; outside; real ~ (out in the real ~) (see also *world champion* at **champion**; *world championship* at **championship**; *the World Cup* at **cup**; *world leader* at **leader**; *world music* at **music**; *world record* at **record I** n.; *the World Series* at **series**; *world view* at **view I** n.) ["period"] 7. the ancient; medieval; modern; post-modern ~ (there are many problems in the modern ~) ["life, being"] 8. to bring a child into the ~ 9. to come into the ~ 10. not long for this ~; the next ~ ("life after death") ["misc."] 11. the entire, whole ~; a closed ~; a different ~; living in a ~ of one's own and not caring about the rest of the ~; dead to the ~; in an ideal ~; it makes a ~ of difference; out of this ~ ("remarkable"); ~s apart ("very far apart"); to live in a dream/fantasy ~ = to live in a ~ of dreams/fantasy; welcome to the Real World!; we meet again: isn't it a small ~!; who in the ~ would do smt. like that?; what in the ~ is that?

worm v. 1. (d; intr.) to ~ into (how did they ~ their way into the meeting?) 2. (d; intr., tr.) to ~ out of (to ~ out of an obligation; to ~ information out of smb.) 3. (misc.) to ~ one's way into smb.'s confidence

worried adj. 1. unduly; very ~ 2. ~ about (we were very ~ about smt. bad happening) 3. ~ to + inf. (we were ~ to think that smt. bad might happen) 4. ~ that + clause (we were ~ sick that smt. bad might happen) 5. (misc.) ~ sick; ~ to death

worry I n. 1. to cause ~ 2. deep, serious; groundless; growing, increasing, mounting ~ (the news came amid mounting ~ries that the pound was weakening against the euro) 3. financial ~ries 4. ~ about, over (our constant ~ about smt. bad happening) 5. a ~ to (some children are a (great) ~ to their parents) 6. a ~ that + clause (our constant ~ that smt. bad might happen) 7. (misc.) to be sick with ~ (we were sick with ~ that smt. bad might happen) (see also *the least of my worries* at **least**)

worry II *v.* 1. (D; intr.) to ~ about, over (they ~ about you; we ~ried about smt. bad happening; to ~ over trifles) 2. (L) we ~ that smt. bad might happen 3. (R) it ~ries me sick (to think) that smt. bad might happen 4. (misc.) not to ~ (not to ~: it's only a trifle!)

worse *adj.* none the ~ (you'll be none the ~ for having spent a couple of years on a farm!) (see also *any worse* at **any I** *adv.*)

worship I *n.* 1. ancestor; hero; idol; nature; public ~ (to practice ancestor ~) 2. (misc.) an act; house, place of ~ (see also *freedom of worship* at **freedom**)

worship II *v.* 1. to ~ reverently 2. (D; tr.) to ~ as (to ~ smb. as a god) 3. (misc.) I ~ the ground she walks on

worst *n.* 1. to do one's ~ (do your ~: see if I care!) 2. to prepare for the ~ 3. to bring out the ~ in smb. 4. to expect; fear the ~ 5. to get the ~ of smt. 6. at one's ~ (I'm at my ~ in the morning) 7. (misc.) if ~ comes to ~ (AE)/if the ~ comes to the ~; at (the) ~, our team may lose five matches; can we avoid the ~ of the crisis?; ~ of all

worth I *adj., prep.* 1. well ~ (the cost/wait) 2. ~ to (how much is it ~ to you (to know what really happened)?) 3. ~ + -*ing* (it's not ~ keeping) 4. (misc.) ~ one's salt ("worthy of respect for one's work"); it's ~ a try; ¬how much/what¬ is it ~ (to you)?; it would be (well) ~ your while to visit the exhibition; don't fret: she's not ~ it!

worth II *n.* 1. intrinsic; self-worth; true ~ 2. net ~ 3. (legal) comparable ~ (the theory of comparable ~) 4. of ~ (books of great ~) 5. (misc.) she bought ten dollars ~ of vegetables; the fire did thousands of dollars ~ of damage

worthwhile *adj.* 1. ~ for (visiting that exhibition would be very ~ for you) 2. ~ to + inf. (it would be very ~ to visit the exhibition = it would be very ~ visiting the exhibition)

worthy *adj.* (usu. does not stand alone) 1. ~ of (~ of praise; such behavior is truly ~ of an officer and a gentleman!) 2. ~ to + inf. (~ to be praised)

would *v.* (F) ~ you do it?; "he denies everything" "well, he ~ say that, wouldn't he!"

wound *n.* 1. to inflict a ~ on/upon smb. 2. to get; receive, sustain a ~ 3. to bandage, dress; cauterize; clean, cleanse; suture; swab a ~ 4. a bad; deep; entry; exit; fatal, mortal; festering; flesh; gaping; head; light, slight; self-inflicted; serious, severe; superficial ~ (she received a slight ~ in the arm) 5. a bullet, gunshot; knife; stab ~ 6. a ~ festers; weeps 7. a ~ heals 8. a ~ in; to (the ~ in her arm was less serious than the ~ to her pride) 9. (misc.) to lick one's ~s ("to recover from a beating or defeat"); to open, re-open old ~s ("to stir up bad memories")

wounded *adj.* 1. badly; fatally, mortally; lightly, slightly; seriously ~ 2. (fig.) deeply ~ (I was deeply ~ by your remarks) 3. ~ in (she was slightly ~ in the arm)

wracked *adj.* ["racked"] 1. ~ by (~ by doubt) 2. ~ with (~ with pain)

wrangle *v.* 1. to ~ constantly, incessantly 2. (D; intr.) to ~ about, over; with

wrangling *n.* 1. constant, incessant ~ 2. ~ about, over; with

wrap I *n.* ["substance"] 1. (esp. AE) (a) freezer; plastic ~ ["sandwich"] 2. a beef; chicken ~

wrap II *v.* 1. (d; refl., tr.) to ~ (a)round (to ~ a blanket around oneself) 2. (d; refl., tr.) to ~ in (to ~ oneself in a blanket)

wrapped up *adj.* ["engaged, busy"] 1. ~ in (they are all ~ in campaigning) ["enclosed"] 2. ~ in (I was warmly/snugly ~ in a blanket)

wrapper *n.* a cellophane; plastic ~

wraps *n.* to keep a plan under ~ (colloq.) ("to keep a plan secret")

wrath *n.* (formal) 1. to arouse, provoke; incur smb.'s ~ 2. to bring down smb.'s ~ (on smb.) 3. to visit one's ~ upon 4. to face; placate ~ (to face the ~ of one's victims and try to placate it) 5. ~ bursts out, explodes; subsides 6. an explosion, fit, outburst of ~

wreak *v.* (see *wreak havoc with* at **havoc**; *wreak vengeance on/upon* at **vengeance**)

wreath *n.* 1. to make, weave a ~ 2. to lay, place a ~ (they laid a ~ at the Tomb of the Unknown Soldier) 3. a bridal; Christmas; funeral; laurel ~ 4. a floral ~ = a ~ of flowers

wreathed *adj.* ~ in (~ in flowers; ~ in smiles)

wreck *n.* ["wrecked vehicle"] 1. to tow a ~ 2. (misc.) the car was a total ~ ["person who has suffered a breakdown"] 3. a nervous ~ 4. (misc.) he was a total ~ after his wife died ["wrecked ship"] 5. to raise a ~ (to the surface)

wreckage *n.* 1. to strew ~ (over a wide area) 2. to clear, remove ~ 3. to raise ~ (as to the surface) 4. twisted ~ 5. a piece of ~ 6. among; in the ~ (a wedding ring was found in the ~ of the bombed house)

wrench I *n.* 1. a monkey ~ (see also **monkey wrench** (fig.)) 2. a lug ~ (BE also has *box spanner*)

wrench II *v.* 1. (d; tr.) to ~ from, off (he ~ed the handbag from the old woman) 2. (misc.) she ~ed her handbag ¬free/away from the mugger¬

wrest *v.* (d; tr.) to ~ from (to ~ power from a dictator)

wrestle *v.* 1. (D; intr.) to ~ with (to ~ with various problems) 2. (misc.) they ~d me to the ground

wrestler *n.* to pin; throw a ~

wrestling *n.* arm; catch-as-catch-can; Greco-Roman, Graeco-Roman (BE); Indian ~

wretch *n.* a homeless; miserable, poor ~

wretched *adj.* 1. to feel ~ 2. ~ about ~ (they felt perfectly ~ about the failure of the experiment) 3. ~ of (that was simply ~ of him!)

wriggle v. 1. (d; intr.) to ~ out of (he ~d out of my grip) 2. (s) to ~ free, loose

wring v. 1. (d; tr.) ("to extract") to ~ from, out of (the police finally succeeded in ~ing a confession from the prisoner) 2. (N; used with an adjective) ("to squeeze") to ~ a towel dry

wrinkle n. ["crease"] 1. to make a ~ 2. to iron out, press out ~s 3. ~s appear (~s around the eyes often appear with advancing age) ["innovation"] (colloq.) 4. the latest, newest ~ in (the latest ~ in marketing home computers)

wrist n. 1. to break, fracture; sprain one's ~ 2. around, round smb.'s ~ (wear smt. around one's ~) 3. by the ~ (prisoners fastened by the ~) 4. (misc.) to slash/slit one's ~s (see also *a slap on the wrist* at **slap I** n.)

writ n. ["legal order"] 1. to apply for; get; issue; serve a ~ (to issue/serve a ~ on smb. = to serve smb. with a writ) 2. to quash a ~ 3. in a ~ (what is specified in the?) 4. (misc.) he can't do that: his ~ doesn't run so far

write v. 1. ("to form letters") to ~ illegibly; legibly 2. (A) ("to compose and send") she wrote a letter to me; or: she wrote me a letter 3. (C) ("to compose") he wrote a recommendation for me; or: he wrote me a recommendation 4. (d; intr.) to ~ about, of, on ("to describe") (to write about/of the war) 5. (D; tr.) to ~ about ("to compose about") (she wrote a book about her experiences) 6. (D; intr.) ("to be a writer") to ~ for (she ~s for popular magazines) 7. (d; intr.) to ~ for ("to request") (she wrote for a recommendation; she wrote to me for a recommendation; AE also has: she wrote me for a recommendation) 8. (d; intr.) to ~ to ("to compose and send a letter to") (he ~s to her every day; AE also has: he ~s her every day) 9. (D; tr.) to ~ to ("to compose for") (to ~ the words to a song) 10. (d; intr.) ("to order, command") to ~ to + inf. (she wrote (to us) to come home) 11. (H; no passive) (AE) ("to order, command") she wrote us to come home 12. (L; to; may have a personal object in AE) ("to inform") (¬wrote to us/wrote us (AE)¬ that we should come home 13. (Q; to; may have an object in AE) ("to inform") she ¬wrote to us/wrote us (AE)¬ when we should come home 14. (misc.) she ~s home every week; she ~s extensively and publishes many books; his part was written out of the script; I ~ with a pen; she ~s poetry in French

write away v. 1. (d; intr.) to ~ for (the children wrote away for a puzzle book) 2. (D; intr.) to ~ to (the children wrote away to the company)

write back v. 1. (A) ("to answer") she wrote a long letter back to me; or: she wrote me back a long letter 2. (D; intr.) to ~ for (she wrote back for more information) 3. (D; intr.) to ~ to ("to answer") she wrote back to me = she wrote me back 4. (L; to) she wrote back (to me) that they would attend the conference = she wrote (me) back that they would attend the conference 5. (misc.) she wrote (me) back (in order) to check the details

write off v. 1. (d; intr.) to ~ for (the children wrote off for a puzzle book) 2. (D; intr.) to ~ to (the children wrote off to the company) 3. (D; tr.) to ~ as (he was written off as a has-been)

write out v. 1. (A) she wrote out a receipt to me; or: she wrote me out a receipt 2. (C) she wrote out a receipt for me; or: she wrote me out a receipt

writer n. 1. a free-lance; screen; sports ~ 2. a hack; professional ~ 3. a prolific ~ 4. a ~ about, on (a ~ about/on the war) 5. a ~ for (she is a ~for popular magazines)

write-up n. (colloq.) ["account, review"] 1. to do a ~ (as of a book/play/concert) 2. to get, receive; have a ~ 3. a complimentary, favorable, glowing, good, positive, rave; critical; negative, unfavorable ~ (the play got/had rave ~s from the critics = the critics gave the play rave ~s)

write up v. (D; tr.) to ~ for (to ~ a story for a newspaper; to ~ smb. up for a decoration)

writhe v. (D; intr.) to ~ in (to ~ in pain)

writing n. 1. to decipher smb.'s ~ 2. cuneiform; cursive; hieroglyphic; picture ~ 3. illegible; legible ~ 4. creative; travel ~ 5. a piece of ~ 6. (misc.) to have smt. in ~; to put smt. in ~; in ~; to see the ~ on the wall (CE; for AE, see **handwriting** n.) ("to foresee impending doom") (we saw the ~ on the wall for the international monetary system = the ~ was on the wall for the international monetary system) (see also **writing paper** at **paper I** n.; **writings**)

writing paper n. personalized ~

writings n. ["written works"] 1. collected; selected ~ 2. scientific ~ (her latest scientific ~ appeared in a recent journal)

wrong I adj. 1. all, completely, dead (colloq.), quite, totally ~ 2. morally ~ 3. ~ about (to be ~ about smt./smb.) 4. ~ in (I was ~ in disregarding your advice) 5. ~ with (what's ~ with her?) 6. ~ to + inf. (it was ~ of them to gossip = they were ~ to gossip; I was ~ to disregard your advice; it is ~ to lie) 7. ~ that + clause (it's ~ that they should be treated so badly) 8. (misc.) everything went (all) ~; she is the ~ person for the job = she is ~ for the job; don't get me ~: I'm really on your side! USAGE NOTE: The expression *what's wrong?* can express sympathy; *what's wrong with you?* is often critical.

wrong II adv. to do smt. ~

wrong III n. 1. to do (smb.) a ~ 2. to forgive; redress, right, undo a ~ 3. a grievous; irreparable ~ 4. in the ~ (she was in the ~ when she accepted = she was in the ~ to accept) 5. (misc.) two ~s do not make a right; to know right from ~ = to know the difference between right and ~; the rights and ~s (I'm not interested in the rights and wrongs of the case: let's forget the whole thing!)

wrought up adj. ["upset, worked up"] (colloq.) ~ about, over (he got himself all ~ about/over a mere trifle)

X ray *n.* 1. to do, make, take an ~ (of) (the physician decided to take an ~ of my back) 2. to interpret, read an ~ (the radiologist will read your ~ before you leave) 3. to get, have an ~ (of) 4. to go for an ~ (of) 5. a chest ~ = an ~ of one's chest 6. an ~ indicates, reveals, shows (see also *X-ray machine* at **machine**)

xylophone *n.* 1. to play the ~ 2. (misc.) ~s are played by hitting their keys with mallets

Y

Y *n.* (= YMCA, YWCA, YMHA, YWHA, which are abbreviations of Young Men's or Women's Christian or Hebrew Association) at the ~ (they are staying at the ~)

yacht *n.* 1. to board, get on, get on board (a) ~ 2. to disembark from, get off a ~ 3. to navigate; sail, steer a ~ 4. a ~ docks; goes, sails 5. the bow; stern of a ~ 6. a ~ from; to 7. by ~ 8. aboard, on a ~ (they spent the summer on their ~) (see also *yacht club* at **club I** *n.*)

yammer *v.* (colloq.) (D; intr.) to ~ about; for

yank I *n.* ["tug"] (colloq.) to give a ~ at; on

yank II *v.* (colloq.) 1. (d; intr.) ("to tug") to ~ at, on (the little girl kept ~ing at her mother's apron) 2. (d; tr.) to ~ out of ("to withdraw") (they ~ed their children out of school)

yap I *n.* ["mouth"] (colloq.) to shut one's ~

yap II *v.* (colloq.) 1. (D; intr.) to ~ about 2. (d; intr.) to ~ at

yard I *n.* ["enclosed area"] a barnyard (esp. AE), farmyard; brickyard; coalyard; dockyard (BE), navy ~ (AE); dooryard (AE); graveyard; junkyard (esp. AE), scrapyard (BE); lumberyard (AE), timberyard (BE); prison; railroad (AE), railway (BE); schoolyard (esp. AE), shipyard ~ ("When Lilacs Last in the Dooryard Bloom'd" – Walt Whitman, 1865 (on Lincoln's death)) USAGE NOTE: In BE, a plot of land adjoining a house is called a *garden* if grassy (a *back garden*, a *front garden*) or a *yard* if paved (a *backyard*, a *front yard*). In AE, such a plot is called a *yard* whether grassy or paved; a large grassy plot can also be called a *garden*.

yard II *n.* ["unit of measurement"] 1. a cubic; square ~ 2. by the ~ (to sell carpeting by the square ~)

yardstick *n.* ["standard"] 1. to adopt a ~ 2. to apply a ~ to 3. a reliable, useful, valid ~ 4. a ~ for (adopt a ~ for measuring academic success) 5. against a ~ (adopt a ~ against which to measure academic success) 6. by a ~ (by which ~ do you propose to measure academic success?)

yarn *n.* ["fiber"] 1. to make, spin; wind ~ 2. to snarl, tangle; unsnarl, untangle a ~ 3. coarse; fine; thick; thin ~ 4. wool(en); worsted ~ 5. a ball; hank; length; piece; skein of ~ 6. in ~ (there's a tangle in the ~) ["tale, story"] (colloq.) 7. to spin, tell a ~ about

yawn I *n.* 1. to give a ~ (she gave a big ~ when she heard our story) 2. to stifle, suppress a ~ 3. a big; loud ~ 4. with a ~ (she greeted our story with a big ~)

yawn II *v.* 1. to ~ loudly 2. to ~ at (she ~ed at our story)

year *n.* 1. to spend a ~ (somewhere) 2. a banner (AE); good; happy; healthy; memorable; peak, record; profitable ~ (our firm had a very profitable ~; their team had a good ~) 3. a bad, lean ~ 4. smb.'s formative; golden ~s 5. every; last; next; this ~ 6. the coming; current; past ~ 7. an academic; school; calendar ~ (see also *gap year* at **gap**) 8. an election; presidential (US) ~ 9. a jubilee; sabbatical ~ 10. a financial (esp. BE), fiscal (esp. AE); tax ~ 11. a common; leap ~ 12. a light; sidereal ~ 13. a lunar; solar ~ 14. early; future; past; recent ~s 15. a ~ from (now/today) 16. by the ~ (to be paid by the ~) 17. by ("before or in") a ~ (by the ~ 2050, the population in many countries will have doubled) 18. during the ~ 19. for a ~ (they went abroad for a ~) 20. for, in (esp. AE) ~s (they have not been here for/in ~s) 21. in a ~, in a ~'s time (BE) (we can finish the job in a ~; they'll be back in a ~) 22. in a (certain) ~ (he died in the ~ of the great flood; in future ~s; in ~s to come; in past ~s) 23. (misc.) ~ after ~; all ~ long; once a ~; ~ in, ~ out; the first time in (esp. AE), for (BE) a ~; she is five ~s old; light ~s away; for ~s to come; ¬up to/until¬ last ~; children of tender ~s; she had three ~s of college; donkey's ~s (BE) ("a long time"); from the ~ dot (BE, colloq.), from the ~ one ("from a time long ago") (see also **New Year**)

yearn *v.* 1. (d; intr.) to ~ for (I ~ed for the return of peace) 2. (E) she ~ed to return home; I ~ed for peace to return

yearning *n.* 1. to express; feel, have a ~ for 2. a secret; strong ~ 3. a ~ for (I had a ~ for peace) 4. a ~ to + inf. (I had a ~ for peace to return; she has a ~ to return home)

yeast *n.* brewer's ~

yell I *n.* 1. to give, let out a ~ (to let out a ~ of delight) 2. a bloodcurdling; ear-piercing, loud; high-pitched, shrill; rebel ~ (he let out a loud ~ of terror)

yell II *v.* 1. to ~ hysterically; loudly; shrilly; to ~ in pain/terror 2. (B) she ~ed a few words to the children 3. (D; intr.) to ~ at; for (she ~ed at the children for making noise) 4. (d; intr.) to ~ for (to ~ for help) 5. (D; intr.) to ~ with (to ~ with pain/terror) 6. (E) she ~ed at/for/to the children to stop making noise 7. (L; to) she ~ed (at/to us) that the house was on fire; "Stop making noise!" she ~ed (at/to the children) 8. (N; refl.; used with an adjective) (she ~ed herself hoarse) 9. (misc.) she was ~ing at the top of her voice

yellow I *adj.* 1. to go, turn ~ 2. bright; pale ~

yellow II *n.* 1. to dress in, wear ~ 2. a shade of ~ ["something yellow"] 3. a patch of ~ 4. in ~ (dressed in ~)

yelp I *n.* 1. to give, let out a ~ (to let out a ~ of pain) 2. a loud; high-pitched, shrill ~ (the dog let out a loud ~ of pain when I stepped on its tail) 3. with a ~ (the dog reacted with a loud ~ of pain when I stepped on its tail)

yelp II *v.* 1. to ~ loudly; shrilly 2. (D; intr.) to ~ at (the dog ~ed at me when I stepped on its tail)

yen I *n.* ["desire"] (colloq.) 1. to have a ~ for (she had a ~ for a hamburger) 2. a ~ to + inf. (she had a ~ to have a hamburger)

yen II *n.* 1. a falling; rising; strong; weak ~ (the international markets experienced difficulties with the falling ~) 2. (misc.) the dollar was strong against the ~

yes *n.* ["positive response"] 1. to answer; say; vote Yes 2. a definite, emphatic, resounding ~ 3. (a) ~ to (a request) 4. (misc.) all I want is a simple Yes or No; to say No but (really) mean Yes (see also *a Yes vote* at **vote I** *n.*)

yield I *n.* ["earnings"] 1. to produce a ~ 2. the current ~ (of an investment) 3. an annual ~ 4. a high; low ~

yield II *v.* 1. (B) I ~ed the right of way to the other driver 2. (D; intr.) to ~ to (they finally ~ed to our demands; to ~ to temptation) (see also *yield the floor* at **floor**)

yoga *n.* to do, practice ~

yoke I *n.* ["harness framework"] 1. to put a ~ on (oxen) (see also *a yoke of oxen* at **ox**) ["servitude, bondage"] 2. to cast off, throw off the ~ (of bondage) 3. a foreign ~ 4. under a (foreign) ~

yoke II *v.* 1. (D; tr.) to ~ to (to ~ oxen to a cart; to ~ one ox to another) 2. (misc.) to ~ oxen together

young I *adj.* 1. ~ at heart 2. ~ in spirit 3. (misc.) she's 80 years ~! (used for special effect); she looks (too) ~ to be his mother; in fact, she looks ~ enough to be his daughter!

young II *n.* ["offspring of an animal"] 1. to bring forth ~ (wild animals bring forth their ~ in the wilderness) 2. with ~ ("being a pregnant animal")

yours *pronoun* 1. (in the complimentary close of a letter) Yours faithfully (esp. BE), Yours sincerely, Yours truly (AE) 2. (colloq.) ~ truly ("I myself, I personally") (I don't know about you guys, but as for ~ truly, I could murder a pizza!) 3. Sincerely ~ (AE) USAGE NOTE: At the end of letters, the following combinations can occur – Yours (esp. BE; informal); Yours ever (BE; friendly); Yours faithfully (esp. BE); Yours sincerely; Sincerely yours (AE); Yours truly (AE); Very truly yours (AE); AE also commonly uses Sincerely. In BE, *Yours faithfully* typically ends a letter beginning *Dear Sir/Madam/Colleague(s)*; *Yours sincerely* typically ends a letter beginning *Dear Mr/Mrs/Ms/Dr/Prof Smith*.

youth *n.* ["young age"] 1. to spend one's ~ (she spent her ~ traveling) 2. early; first; flaming; gilded ~ (she's well past her first ~) 3. during, in; from, since smb.'s ~ (she's traveled from/since her earliest ~; things were very different in my ~!) ["adolescent male, young man"] (now typically derog.) 4. a gang of ~s ["male and female young people collectively, typically as specified"] 5. the ~ of today = today's ~; what future for America's/American ~? (see also *youth club* at **club I** *n.*; *youth culture* at **culture**; *youth worker* at **worker**) USAGE NOTE: When *youth* is used of a young man, the young man in question is nowadays one more likely to give cause for worry than cause for hope: I was mugged by a gang of unruly youths but helped by a group of nice young lads. However, in former times this sense of *youth* could be used freely in neutral or favorable contexts: "When Duty whispers low, *Thou must*, The ~ replies, *I can*." – R.W. Emerson (1803–82), "Voluntaries"

Z

zap *v.* (colloq.) (P; intr., tr.) she ~ped the incident out of her memory (esp. AE); I ~ped through the exam
zeal *n.* 1. to demonstrate, display, show ~ 2. great; excessive ~ 3. evangelical; missionary; religious; righteous ~ 4. ~ for (to show ~ for one's project) 5. the ~ to + inf. (does she have enough ~ to finish the project?) 6. in one's ~ (in her ~ to finish the project, she made many blunders) 7. with ~ (she worked with great ~ to finish the project)
zealot *n.* a religious ~
zealous *adj.* ~ about, in
zebra *n.* a herd of ~(s)
zenith *n.* 1. to attain, reach a ~ 2. at a ~ (at the ~ of their power)
zero *n.* 1. absolute ~ 2. above; below ~ (it was five degrees below ~ Fahrenheit) (see also *zero gravity* at **gravity**; *ground zero*; *zero growth* & *zero population growth* at **growth**; *zero hour* at **hour**; *zero tolerance* at **tolerance**)
zero in *v.* (d; intr.) ("to concentrate, to home in") to ~ on (to ~ on a target; they all ~ed in on me)
zest *n.* 1. to add ~ to 2. boundless; flagging; great;

renewed; youthful ~ 3. (a) ~ for (a ~ for life) 4. with (great) ~
zigzag I *n.* to make a ~
zigzag II *v.* (P; intr.) the road ~s across the county
zip I (BE), **zipper** (AE) *n.* 1. to do up, fasten, zip up a ~ 2. to undo, unfasten, unzip a ~ 3. a ~ gets stuck
zip II *v.* (P; intr.) they ~ped past us
zodiac *n.* the signs of the ~
zone I *n.* 1. to establish, set up a ~ 2. a climatic; frigid; temperate; torrid ~ 3. a buffer; combat; communications; demilitarized; drop; Euro-zone; military; neutral; no-fly; no-go; occupation; residential; war ~ 4. a danger; nuclear-free; safety; security ~ 5. a no-parking; no-passing; school; towaway ~ 6. a postal; time ~ 7. an erogenous ~ (of the body) 8. in a ~; in the ~ (colloq.) (the tennis player felt he was in the ~ and couldn't lose) 9. (misc.) a twilight ("transitional") ~
zone II *v.* 1. (d; tr.) to ~ as (they ~d the area as residential) 2. (d; tr.) to ~ for (this area has been ~d for residential use)
zoning *n.* exclusionary (esp. AE); residential ~
zoo *n.* 1. at, in a ~ (she works at the ~; wild animals are well cared for in our ~) 2. (misc.) a person who manages a ~ is a zookeeper (see also *zoo animal* at **animal**)
zoom in *v.* (d; intr.) to ~ on (the cameras all ~ed in on me)

Aston University

Library & Information Services

Aston Triangle
Birmingham
B4 7ET
England

Tel +44 (0121) 204 4525
Fax +44 (0121) 204 4530
Email library@aston.ac.uk
Website http://www.aston.ac.uk/lis